Fodor's 04

CARIBBEAN

Where to Stay and Eat
for All Budgets

Must-See Sights
and Local Secrets

Ratings You Can Trust

Fodor's Travel Publications   New York, Toronto, London, Sydney, Auckland
www.fodors.com

FODOR'S CARIBBEAN 2004

Editors: Douglas Stallings, Jane Driesen

Editorial Production: Linda K. Schmidt

Editorial Contributors: Isabel Abisláiman, Carol M. Bareuther, John Bigley, Kathy Borsuk, Suzanne Gordon, John and Judy Ingrisano, Lynda Lohr, Elise Meyer, JoAnn Milivojevic, Vernon O'Reilly-Ramesar, Paris Permenter, Eileen Robinson Smith, Jordan Simon, Roberta Sotonoff, Jane E. Zarem

Maps: David Lindroth, *cartographer;* Bob Blake and Rebecca Baer, *map editors*

Design: Fabrizio La Rocca, *creative director;* Guido Caroti, *art director;* Melanie Marin, *senior photo editor*

Production/Manufacturing: Robert B. Shields

Cover Photo (Virgin Gorda, British Virgin Islands): Stephen Frink/Corbis

ISBN 1–4000–1247–3

ISSN 1524–9174

SPECIAL SALES

Fodor's Travel Publications are available at special discounts for bulk purchases for sales promotions or premiums. Special editions, including personalized covers, excerpts of existing guides, and corporate imprints, can be created in large quantities for special needs. For more information, contact your local bookseller or write to Special Markets, Fodor's Travel Publications, 1745 Broadway, New York, NY 10019. Inquiries from Canada should be directed to your local Canadian bookseller or sent to Random House of Canada, Ltd., Marketing Department, 2775 Matheson Boulevard East, Mississauga, Ontario L4W 4P7. Inquiries from the United Kingdom should be sent to Fodor's Travel Publications, 20 Vauxhall Bridge Road, London SW1V 2SA, England.

AN IMPORTANT TIP & AN INVITATION

Although all prices, opening times, and other details in this book are based on information supplied to us at press time, changes occur all the time in the travel world, and Fodor's cannot accept responsibility for facts that become outdated or for inadvertent errors or omissions. So **always confirm information when it matters,** especially if you're making a detour to visit a specific place. Your experiences—positive and negative—matter to us. If we have missed or misstated something, **please write to us.** We follow up on all suggestions. Contact the Caribbean editor at editors@fodors.com or c/o Fodor's at 1745 Broadway, New York, New York 10019.

PRINTED IN THE UNITED STATES OF AMERICA

10 9 8 7 6 5 4 3 2 1

DESTINATION
CARIBBEAN

Feel the soft sand beneath your feet on a perfect slip of a beach and you'll soon encounter all the wonderful Caribbean trappings that you may only dream about the rest of the year: a palm tree, a peak cloaked in rain forest, a fishing boat drifting on a multihued sea, a whiff of romance. Whether you come to explore the underwater richness of a living coral reef, play a round of golf on a windswept seaside course, feast on freshly caught lobster or ripe mangoes recently plucked from a tree, or simply relax under a palapa on a perfectly sandy strand with the gentle waves lapping at your outstretched toes, you'll be able to find the spot that suits your temperament. Dance the night away, stroll under the stars, sleep in a hammock or under soft Egyptian-cotton sheets, stay in a quiet hillside villa or a lavish beach resort. The islands of the Caribbean can give you all this and more. Experience them again and again, and your heart is likely to skip a beat or two each time. Most important, have a fabulous trip.

Karen Cure, Editorial Director

CONTENTS

Maps and Charts

ON THE ROAD WITH FODOR'S

Although there's no substitute for travel advice from a good friend who knows your style, our contributors are the next best thing—the kind of people you would poll for travel advice if you knew them.

Isabel Abisláiman, a writer-photographer who also happens to be a lawyer, put her talents to work covering Puerto Rico. Isabel has contributed to the travel section of San Juan's Spanish-language newspaper, *El Nuevo Día.*

St. Thomas–based writer and dietitian **Carol M. Bareuther** publishes two weekly columns on food, cooking, and nutrition in the *Virgin Islands Daily News* and serves as the USVI stringer for Reuters. She's the author of two books, *Sports Fishing in the Virgin Islands* and *Virgin Islands Cooking.*

Although a native of the Windy City, **Kathy Borsuk** now enjoys the much-warmer trade winds of the Turks and Caicos Islands. She is managing editor of *Times of the Islands* magazine, a quarterly publication covering the Turks and Caicos.

Suzanne Gordon followed her bliss and moved to Nevis, leaving behind a career with the *Philadelphia Inquirer.* She's completing a guide to architecture in the Caribbean and is involved in several historic-preservation projects.

St. Maarten/St. Martin updaters **John and Judy Ingrisano** are freelance writers, small-business consultants, and self-described nomads, who live part of each year on the island, which they love for its beautiful weather, wonderful beaches, and friendly people.

Long-time St. John resident **Lynda Lohr** lives above Coral Bay and writes for numerous publications as well as travel Web sites. On her rare days off, she swims at Great Maho Bay and hikes the island's numerous trails.

Friends of **Elise Meyer,** who updated the St. Barths chapter, often joke that her middle name is "Let's Go." She has contributed articles to myriad newspapers, magazines, and Web sites. She lives in Connecticut with her husband and children.

JoAnn Milivojevic is a writer and photographer living in Chicago. She's produced videos in the Cayman Islands and on St. Kitts and Nevis. Her travel articles have appeared in publications nationwide.

Vernon O'Reilly-Ramesar is a broadcaster and writer who divides his time between Trinidad and Canada. He spends much of his time exploring the miracles of the rain forest. Vernon updated the Trinidad and Tobago, Bonaire, and Curaçao chapters for this edition.

After honeymooning in Jamaica, **Paris Permenter** and **John Bigley** decided to specialize in writing about and photographing the Caribbean. They've authored numerous Caribbean guidebooks, the latest of which is *Lovetripper.com's Guide to Caribbean Destination Weddings.* From their home base in Texas they edit *Lovetripper.com Romantic Travel Magazine.*

In 1995, Hurricane Marilyn blew **Eileen Robinson Smith** out of the Caribbean and back to her lakeside home in Charleston, South Carolina. She's lived in St. John, St. Thomas, St. Croix, and Tortola. She writes often about food and travel.

Jordan Simon began his West Indies love affair as a child when his artist mother took him to Haiti. He has since visited and written about nearly every Caribbean island. He writes regularly for national magazines and newspapers. He has authored several books, including *Fodor's Colorado* and the *Gousha/USA Today Ski Atlas.*

Chicago native **Roberta Sotonoff,** who visited Saba and St. Eustatius for this edition, is a confessed travel junkie who writes to support her habit. Her work has appeared in dozens of domestic and international publications, on-line sites, and guidebooks. The Caribbean is one of her favorite destinations, and she writes about the region frequently. She also contributes to *Fodor's Chicago.*

Jane E. Zarem travels frequently to the Caribbean from her Connecticut home. She has contributed to numerous Fodor's guides, among them *New England, USA, Cape Cod, Bahamas, Healthy Escapes,* and *Great American Sports and Adventure Vacations.*

ABOUT THIS BOOK

There's no doubt that the best source for travel advice is a like-minded friend who's just been where you're headed. But with or without that friend, you'll have a better trip with a Fodor's guide in hand. Once you've learned to find your way around its pages, you'll be in great shape to find your way around your destination.

SELECTION

Our goal is to cover the best properties, sights, and activities in their category, as well as the most interesting communities to visit. We make a point of including local food-lovers' hot spots as well as neighborhood options, and we avoid all that's touristy unless it's really worth your time. You can go on the assumption that everything you read about in this book is recommended wholeheartedly by our writers and editors. Flip to On the Road with Fodor's to learn more about who they are. It goes without saying that no property mentioned in the book has paid to be included.

RATINGS

Orange stars ★ denote sights and properties that our editors and writers consider the very best in the area covered by the entire book. These, the best of the best, are listed in the Fodor's Choice section in the front of the book. Black stars ★ highlight the sights and properties we deem Highly Recommended, the don't-miss sights within any region. Fodor's Choice and Highly Recommended options in each region are usually listed on the title page of the chapter covering that region. Use the index to find complete descriptions. In cities, sights pinpointed with numbered map bullets ❶ in the margins tend to be more important than those without bullets.

SPECIAL SPOTS

Pleasures & Pastimes focuses on types of experiences that reveal the spirit of the destination. Watch for Off the Beaten Path sights. Some are out of the way, some are quirky, and all are worth your while. If the munchies hit while you're exploring, look for Need a Break? suggestions.

BUDGET WELL

Hotel and restaurant price categories from ¢ to $$$$ are defined in the opening pages of each chapter—expect to find a balanced selection for every budget. For attractions, we always give standard adult admission fees; reductions are usually available for children, students, and senior citizens. Look in Discounts & Deals in Smart Travel Tips for information on destination-wide ticket schemes.

BASIC INFO

Smart Travel Tips lists travel essentials for the entire area covered by the book; city- and region-specific basics end each chapter. To find the best way to get around, see the transportation section; see individual modes of travel ("By Car," "By Train") for details. We assume you'll check Web sites or call for particulars.

ON THE MAPS

Maps throughout the book show you what's where and help you find your way around. Black and orange numbered bullets in the text correlate to bullets on maps.

FIND IT FAST

Within the book, chapters are arranged in alphabetical order. Some larger islands are divided by region. Heads at the top of each page help you find what you need within a chapter.

DON'T FORGET

Restaurants are open for lunch and dinner daily unless we state otherwise; we mention dress only when there's a specific requirement and reservations only when they're essential or not accepted—it's always best to book ahead. Hotels have private baths, phone, TVs, and air-conditioning. We always indicate the meal plan upon which the price range is based. We always list facilities but not whether you'll be charged extra to use them, so when pricing accommodations, find out what's included.

SYMBOLS

Many Listings

★ Fodor's Choice
★ Highly recommended
⊠ Physical address
✛ Directions
🕮 Mailing address
☎ Telephone
🖷 Fax
⊕ On the Web
✉ E-mail
✆ Open/closed times
▶ Start of walk/itinerary
Ⓜ Metro stations
⊟ Credit cards

Outdoors

⛳ Golf
⛺ Camping

Hotels & Restaurants

🏨 Hotel
🛏 Number of rooms
♨ Facilities
🍴 Meal plans
✕ Restaurant
☝ Reservations
👗 Dress code
🚭 Smoking
🍷 BYOB
✕🏨 Hotel with restaurant that warrants a visit

Other

👪 Family-friendly
☎ Contact information
⇨ See also
⊠ Branch address
☞ Take note

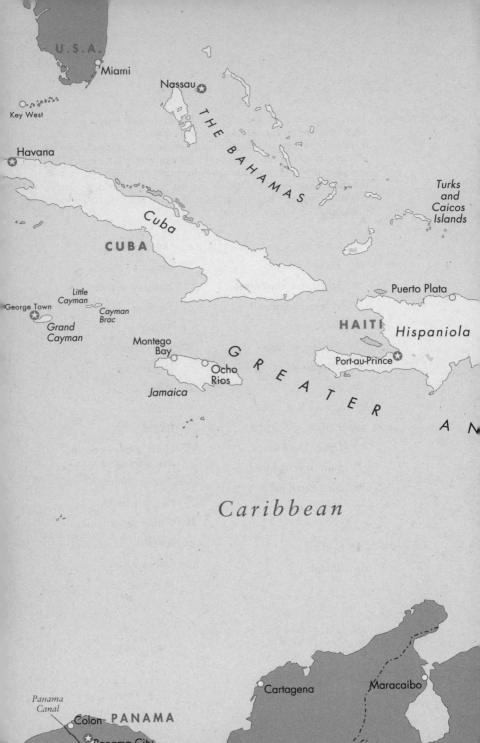

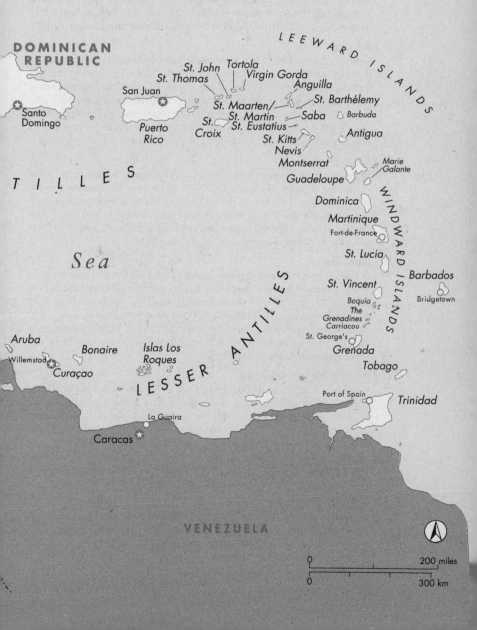

Caribbean

ATLANTIC OCEAN

DOMINICAN REPUBLIC

LEEWARD ISLANDS

Santo Domingo

San Juan

Puerto Rico

Virgin Gorda
St. John
Tortola
St. Thomas
Anguilla
St. Maarten/
St. Barthélemy
St. Martin
Saba
Barbuda
St. Croix
St. Eustatius
Antigua
St. Kitts
Nevis
Montserrat
Marie Galante
Guadeloupe
Dominica
Martinique
Fort-de-France
St. Lucia
Barbados
St. Vincent
Bridgetown
Bequia
The Grenadines
Carriacou
St. George's
Grenada
Tobago

...TILLES

Sea

Aruba
Bonaire
Islas Los Roques
Curaçao
Willemstad

LESSER ANTILLES

La Guaira
Caracas

Port of Spain
Trinidad

VENEZUELA

0   200 miles
0   300 km

WHAT'S WHERE

(1) Anguilla

In tiny Anguilla, where fishermen have been heading out to sea for centuries in handmade boats, the beaches are some of the Caribbean's best and least crowded. Heavy development has not spoiled the island's atmospheric corners, and Johnno's Beach Stop, which pulses on Sunday afternoon, is one of the few gathering places.

(2) Antigua

Paradisiacal beaches—366 of them, all lapped by deep blue water—might make you think that this island has never busied itself with anything more pressing than the pursuit of pleasure. But for much of the 18th and 19th centuries, English Harbour sheltered Britain's Caribbean fleet. These days, pleasure yachts bob where galleons anchored, and once-productive sugar mills litter the interior hills with romantic ruins.

(3) Aruba

Aruba is the island of the trade winds that lured the island's Dutch settlers, whose pastel-colored houses still grace the waterfront in the capital city of Oranjestad. Winds are fierce, even savage, on the north coast. Here, amid a landscape of cacti, rocky desert, and wind-bent divi-divi trees, they churn up the surf and over time create weird formations, such as the Natural Bridge. On the west coast the steady breezes attract windsurfers to the shallow, richly colored waters.

(4) Barbados

In the center of this sunny sliver of land, densely planted sugarcane fields crowd the byways like a jungle. What pulls most vacationers this far south, though, is the warm Bajan hospitality, the British heritage, welcoming hotels like Treasure Beach, and the varied beaches: You'll find warm Caribbean strands with white sand and gentle surf, as well as magnificent, Atlantic-pounded, cliff-edged shoreline.

(5) Bonaire

A market in Kralendijk attracts hagglers who vie for produce brought in by boat from lusher islands. But nature holds sway over human pursuits on this scrubby, cactus-covered landfall. Divers come here from all over the world to swim among some of the most-prized undersea treasures in the Caribbean. Above the water more than 15,000 flamingos—the biggest flock in the Western Hemisphere—wade in Goto Meer and other saltwater lagoons and flats.

(6) British Virgin Islands

Although they fly the Union Jack, these 50-some islands and cays are only a mile or so from the U.S. Virgin Islands at some points, and the local currency is the U.S. dollar. They are laid-back places, so don't come expecting to party 'til dawn, and they're casual, too, so leave the tux at home. Luxury here means getting away from it all rather than getting all the newest state-of-the-art amenities. The sailing here is some of the best in the world, and the islands are rife with yacht harbors, sails dotting the horizon almost anywhere you look.

(7) Cayman Islands

Its more than 500 banks make Grand Cayman the world's largest offshore finance hub, but it's the other offshore activities that put the Caymans on the map. Pristine waters, breathtaking coral formations, and plentiful and exotic marine creatures (their well-being ensured by aggressive conservation efforts) beckon divers from around the world. Windsurfers, golfers, diners, and shoppers join them, drawn by the islands' mellow civility.

8 Curaçao

Willemstad's fancifully hued, strikingly gabled houses glimmering across Santa Anna Bay house shops purveying discounted luxury goods, while vendors at the Floating Market sell tropical fruit from their schooners. Stroll along the waterfront, still crowded with fishing boats, and you can see Curaçao's diversity, its population mixing Latin, European, and African ancestries. Religious tolerance is a hallmark here; the Western Hemisphere's oldest synagogue in use stands in the center of town. All people are welcome in Curaçao, and even tourists feel the warmth.

9 Dominica

Dominica is far removed from the concerns of the rest of the world, where the pleasures are simple rather than sybaritic, made all the more pleasurable by the traditional polite ways of the 70,000 islanders, some of whom are the last remaining Carib Indians. Surrounded by all the mountains, greenery, and waterfalls, you'll find out for yourself why the island's first inhabitants made this their refuge.

10 Dominican Republic

Like the merengue seen on all the dance floors in Santo Domingo, the Dominican Republic is charismatic yet sensuous, pulsing with energy yet elegant. The charm of the people adds a special warmth: a gracious wave of greeting here, a hand-rolled cigar tapped with a flourish there, and the dazzling smiles just about everywhere will quickly beguile you.

11 Grenada

These days the Isle of Spice busies itself cultivating nutmeg, cinnamon, cocoa, cloves, mace, and other spices, and vestiges of its sometimes turbulent past have all but disappeared. The only sounds in the fragrant air are the occasional abrupt call of a cuckoo in the lush rain forests, the crash of surf in the secluded coves, and the slow beat of a big drum dance, which accompanies the launch of a new craft on the boatbuilding islet of Carriacou. Resorts tend to be small and charming, and St. George's, the island's capital, is often called the most beautiful city in the Caribbean.

12 Guadeloupe

A heady blend of French style and tropical delights, butterfly-shaped Guadeloupe is *actuellement* two islands divided by a narrow channel: smaller, flatter, and drier Grand-Terre (Large Land) and wetter and more mountainous Basse-Terre (Low Land). Sheltered by palms, the beaches are beguiling, and the scent of cigarette smoke at beachside cafés makes Guadeloupe sometimes feel oddly like France itself.

13 Jamaica

Chances are you will never fully understand Jamaica in all its delightful complexity, but you will probably have a good time trying. You can party in Negril, shop in Montego Bay, or simply relax at one of the island's many all-inclusive resorts, but you'll also discover a wealth of culture—especially in music and art—and delicious island cuisine.

14 Martinique

La vie en rose is de rigueur in this stylish French enclave, which is often characterized as a Caribbean suburb of Paris. Exotic fruit grows on the volcanoes' forested flanks amid a profusion of wild orchids and hibiscus. The sheer lushness of it all inspired the tropical paintings of one-time resident Paul Gauguin. He would later say that to truly understand him and his art, one had to understand his Martinique period.

15 Puerto Rico

Mother Spain is always a presence here—on a sun-dappled cobblestone street, in the shade of a colonial cathedral or fort. Yet multifaceted Puerto Rico pulses with New World energy. Coquis (frogs) chant vigorously as only Caribbean creatures can. The rhythms of the streets are of Afro-Latin salsa and bomba; the costumes and *vejigantes* (masks) you see in local festivals are bright and colorful. And the U.S. flag flaps in the salty breezes wherever you go.

16 Saba

Mountainous Saba shoots straight out of the sea like one of the volcanoes that formed it, and in its precipitous terrain visitors set their sights on either the highlands or the depths. The Bottom, the island's capital, is actually atop a mountain but nestles in a crater, and from there a trail of 900 rough-hewn steps drops to the sea. Divers and snorkelers take a different plunge and end up eye to eye with denizens of the deep.

17 St. Barthélemy

Chic travelers adore French-speaking St. Barths, and all find time to put aside their cell phones long enough to enjoy the lovely beaches—long, surf-pounded strands; idyllic crescents crowded by cliffs or forests; glass-smooth lagoons perfect for windsurfing. After dark the pace picks up in island restaurants, where talented chefs transform local ingredients into culinary marvels. Nothing on St. Barths comes cheap. But while you're sipping Pouilly-Fumé on a hotel's awning-shaded terrace, St. Barths' civilized ways seem worth every penny.

18 St. Eustatius

Tiny Statia is another quiet Caribbean haven for scuba divers and hikers. When the island was called the Emporium of the Western World, warehouses stretched for a mile along the quays, and 200 boats could anchor at its docks. These days it's the day-trippers from St. Martin who pull up to the shore.

19 St. Kitts & Nevis

A yucca cactus keeps watch over North Friar's Bay on St. Kitts's narrow peninsula as the island trails off to Nevis, its diminutive companion just 2 mi distant. On both islands, brilliant green fields of sugarcane run to the sea, once-magnificent plantation houses are now luxurious inns, and lovely stretches of uncrowded beach, like the snowy-white Pinney's Beach on Nevis and black-sand Dieppe Bay on St. Kitts, stretch out into the deep blue of the Caribbean and the Atlantic.

20 St. Lucia

Explorers, pirates, soldiers, sugar planters, and coal miners have made their mark on this lovely landfall, and the lush tropical peaks known as the Pitons (Gros and Petit) have witnessed them all. Today's visitors come to snorkel and scuba dive in the calm cobalt-blue waters, to sun themselves on the scores of multihued beaches, or to go for a sail off tiny Pigeon Island, which juts off St. Lucia's northwest coast.

21 St. Maarten/St. Martin

St. Martin and St. Maarten, a half-French half-Dutch island, is a place where gastronomy flourishes, where most resorts are large rather than small, where casinos draw gamblers, where sporting opportunities are

plentiful, and where the sunning, as on Cupecoy Beach, is often clothing-optional.

(22) St. Vincent & the Grenadines
There are 32 perfectly endowed Grenadine islands and cays in this
archipelago. When the largest of them, Bequia, gets down to business,
chances are it has to do with boats—whether it's crafting a handsome
scale model or outfitting the real thing at some of the Caribbean's best
anchorages. On land a sense of privilege prevails. Wildlife trusts protect rare species of flora and fauna, and villa walls ensure privacy for
the islands' rich and famous human visitors.

(23) Trinidad & Tobago
The most southerly of the Caribbean islands, Trinidad is also the most
colorful. Cosmopolitan islanders trace their roots to India, China, and
Madeira; they practice Hinduism, Islam, and Christianity; and they
speak English, Spanish, and French Patois. This heady mix comes to a
boil at Carnival ("De Mas," as islanders call it), when calypso and steel
bands play in Port-of-Spain and elsewhere around the island. On much
quieter Tobago the most exciting event is often the palm trees swaying
high above a gentle arc of a beach.

(24) Turks & Caicos Islands
Only 8 of 40 islands are inhabited in this archipelago between the Bahamas and Haiti, with the Atlantic to one side and the Caribbean to the
other. Snorkelers and scuba divers explore one of the world's longest
coral reefs, not to mention the Wall, a subterranean cliff of coral. Sea
creatures far outnumber humans here: the islands' total population is
a mere 25,000. Land-based pursuits don't get much more taxing than
teeing off at Providenciales's Provo Golf Club, or sunset-watching from
the seaside terrace of a laid-back resort.

(25) U.S. Virgin Islands
A perfect combination of the familiar and the exotic, the U.S. Virgin Islands are a little bit of home set in an azure sea. They shelter a remarkable
variety of creatures and hundreds of idyllic coves with splendid beaches.
Chances are that on one of the three islands you'll find your own idea
of an ideal Caribbean vacation spot.

ISLAND FINDER

	Cost of island in high season	Nonstop flights from the U.S.	Cruise-ship port	U.S. dollars accepted	Historic sites	Natural beauty	Lush	Arid	Mountainous	Rain forest	Beautiful beaches	Good roads
Anguilla	$$$			●				●			●	
Antigua & Barbuda	$$$	●	●	●	●			●		●	●	
Aruba	$$	●	●	●		●		●			●	●
Barbados	$$$$	●	●	●	●	●					●	●
Bonaire	$$	●	●	●		●		●				●
British Virgin Islands	$$$		●	●	●	●	●		●	●	●	
Cayman Islands	$$$$	●	●	●					●		●	●
Curaçao	$$	●	●	●	●			●			●	●
Dominica	$		●			●	●	●		●	●	
Dominican Republic	$	●	●	●	●	●	●		●	●	●	●
Grenada	$$$	●	●	●	●	●	●		●	●	●	
The Grenadines	$$$		●	●		●			●		●	
Guadeloupe	$$		●		●	●	●		●	●	●	●
Jamaica	$$$	●	●	●		●	●		●		●	●
Martinique	$$$		●			●	●		●	●	●	●
Nevis	$$$			●	●	●	●		●		●	
Puerto Rico	$$	●	●	●	●	●	●	●	●		●	●
Saba	$		●			●	●		●	●		●
St. Barthélemy	$$$$		●			●			●		●	
St. Eustatius	$			●	●				●	●		
St. Kitts	$$	●	●	●	●	●	●		●	●		●
St. Lucia	$$$	●	●	●	●	●	●		●	●	●	●
St. Maarten/St. Martin	$$$	●	●	●					●		●	●
St. Vincent	$$		●	●	●	●	●		●	●		
Tobago	$$		●	●	●	●	●			●	●	
Trinidad	$	●	●	●			●		●	●		
Turks and Caicos	$$$	●		●	●	●		●			●	
U.S. Virgin Islands:												
St. Croix	$$	●	●	●	●	●	●		●	●		●
St. John	$$		●	●	●	●	●		●		●	●
St. Thomas	$$	●	●	●	●				●		●	●

Public transportation	Fine dining	Local cuisine	Shopping	Music	Casinos	Nightlife	Diving and snorkeling	Sailing	Golf	Hiking	Ecotourism	Villa rentals	All-inclusives	Campgrounds	Luxury resorts	Secluded getaway	Good for families	Romantic hideaway
	O	O	O	O			O	O				O	O		O	O		O
O	O		O	O	O	O	O				O		O	O	O			
O	O	O	O	O	O	O	O	O	O	O	O	O	O		O		O	O
O	O	O	O		O	O		O	O			O	O	O		O		
	O			O		O		O	O	O	O			O	O		O	
O	O	O	O	O		O	O	O		O	O	O	O	O	O	O	O	O
	O	O				O	O	O			O	O			O		O	
O	O	O		O	O	O	O	O	O		O	O		O		O		
O		O		O			O			O	O	O				O	O	O
O	O	O	O	O	O	O	O	O	O	O	O	O	O		O	O	O	O
O	O	O	O	O		O				O	O	O			O	O		O
	O	O					O	O		O	O	O			O	O	O	O
O	O	O	O		O	O	O	O	O	O	O	O	O	O		O	O	
O	O	O	O	O		O	O	O	O	O	O	O	O		O		O	O
O	O	O	O	O	O	O	O	O	O	O	O	O	O	O		O		
	O	O					O	O	O	O					O	O		O
O	O	O	O	O	O	O	O	O		O	O	O	O	O	O	O	O	O
		O					O			O	O	O			O	O	O	O
	O	O	O			O	O	O				O			O	O	O	O
	O						O			O	O				O		O	
	O	O	O		O	O	O	O	O	O	O		O		O	O		O
O	O	O	O	O		O	O	O	O	O	O	O	O	O	O	O	O	O
O	O	O	O		O	O	O	O	O			O	O		O		O	O
O	O	O		O	O	O	O	O		O	O				O	O		
	O	O		O		O		O	O	O	O	O	O		O	O	O	O
O	O	O		O		O	O		O		O				O		O	
		O			O		O	O	O	O	O	O	O		O	O	O	O
O	O	O	O	O	O	O	O	O	O	O	O	O	O		O		O	
O	O	O	O	O		O	O	O		O		O		O	O	O	O	O
O	O	O	O				O	O	O	O			O	O		O		O

WHEN TO GO

°C		°F
100		212
40		105
37		98.6
30		90
25		80
20		70
15		60
10		50
5		40
0		32
-5		20
-10		10
-15		0
-20		

The Caribbean high season is traditionally winter—from December 15 to April 14—when northern weather is at its worst. During this season you're guaranteed the most entertainment at resorts and the most people with whom to enjoy it. It's also the most fashionable, the most expensive, and the most popular time to visit—and most hotels are heavily booked. You must make reservations at least two or three months in advance for the very best places (sometimes a year in advance for the most exclusive spots). Hotel prices drop 20%–50% after April 15; airfares and cruise prices also fall. Saving money isn't the only reason to visit the Caribbean during the off-season. Temperatures are only a few degrees warmer than at other times of the year, and many islands now schedule their carnivals, music festivals, and other events during the off-season. Late August, September, October, and early November are least crowded.

In summer the flamboyant trees are at their peak, as are most of the flowers and shrubs of the West Indies. The water is clearer for snorkeling and smoother for sailing in the Virgin Islands and the Grenadines in May, June, and July. The peak of local excitement on many islands, most notably Trinidad, St. Vincent, Dominica, and the French West Indies, is Carnival—traditionally held in February, the weekend before Ash Wednesday.

Climate
The Caribbean climate is fairly constant. The average year-round temperatures for the region are 78°F–88°F. The temperature extremes are 65°F low, 95°F high; but, as everyone knows, it's the humidity, not the heat, that makes you suffer, especially when the two go hand in hand.

As part of the late-fall rainy season, hurricanes occasionally sweep through the Caribbean. Check the news daily and keep abreast of brewing tropical storms. The southernmost Caribbean islands (from St. Vincent to Trinidad, along with Aruba, Bonaire, and Curaçao) are generally spared the threat of hurricanes. The rainy season consists mostly of brief showers interspersed with sunshine. You can watch the clouds thicken, feel the rain, then have brilliant sunshine dry you off, all while remaining on your lounge chair. A spell of overcast days or heavy rainfall is unusual, as everyone will tell you.

High altitudes can be cool, particularly when winter winds hit Caribbean peaks (late November through January). Since many Caribbean islands are mountainous or at least hilly (notable exceptions are the Cayman Islands, Anguilla, Antigua, Aruba, Bonaire, and Curaçao), the altitude always offers an escape from the latitude. Kingston (Jamaica), Port-of-Spain (Trinidad), and Fort-de-France (Martinique) swelter in summer; climb 1,000 ft or so and everything is cool.

🔛 **Weather Channel Connection** ☎ 900/932-8437, 95¢ per minute from a Touch-Tone phone ⊕ www.weather.com.

VIRGIN ISLANDS

Jan.	86F	25C	May	88F	31C	Sept.	92F	33C
	74	23		75	24		76	24
Feb.	86F	25C	June	88F	31C	Oct.	92F	33C
	74	23		75	24		76	24
Mar.	87F	30C	July	95F	35C	Nov.	86F	25C
	71	22		77	25		72	22
Apr.	87F	30C	Aug.	95F	35C	Dec.	86F	25C
	71	22		77	25		72	22

PLEASURES & PASTIMES

Boating & Sailing Whether you charter a crewed boat or captain the vessel yourself, the waters of the Caribbean are excellent for boating and sailing, and the many secluded bays and inlets provide ideal spots to drop anchor and picnic or explore. The marinas on Tortola in the British Virgin Islands, at Rodney Bay and Marigot in St. Lucia, throughout St. Vincent and the Grenadines, St. Thomas in the U.S. Virgin Islands, and Port la Royale and Oyster Pond in St. Martin are the starting points for some of the Caribbean's finest sailing. Yachtspeople also favor the waters around Antigua and put in regularly at Nelson's Dockyard, which hosts a colorful regatta in late April or early May.

Casinos You can flirt with Lady Luck until the wee hours on several islands. San Juan, Puerto Rico, arguably offers the most elegant, Old World–style casinos, in the suave Bondian tradition, followed by Santo Domingo, Dominican Republic. In the casinos of Aruba and St. Maarten the ambience is distinctly more splashy—and more American. Curaçao, a quieter island in general, has a few more-restrained casinos, while Antigua has perhaps the gaudiest establishment—King's Casino—as well as two other hotel casinos and a few tiny slots saloons. You'll also find casinos on St. Croix, Guadeloupe, Martinique, St. Kitts, St. Vincent, and Providenciales in the Turks & Caicos.

Cuisine Caribbean food is a complex blend of indigenous, African, and colonial influences. The Arawaks, Caribs, and Taíno contributed native tubers (also called "provisions" in the islands) such as *yuca* (also known as cassava) and *tania* (also known as taro), leafy vegetables like callaloo (similar to spinach—though slightly bitter—it also doubles as the name of the soup made from it throughout the Lesser Antilles), and such spices as cilantro and *achiote*. From Africa came plantains, yams, green pigeon peas, and assorted peppers. The Spaniards brought rice, while the British imported such plants as breadfruit from the Pacific.

Don't shy away from such classic dishes as goat water (in Dominica, among others), pepper pot (in Grenada, St. Lucia, and most of the Windwards), and *sancocho* (in the Dominican Republic and Puerto Rico), all thick, sultry stews made with various meats and vegetables. Sample johnnycakes with breakfast, *fungi* at lunch (both made from cornmeal), and local vegetables like christophene (a kind of squash) with dinner. Then try tangy soursop ice cream or passion-fruit sorbet for dessert.

The national dish of Jamaica is salt fish and ackee: salt-cured cod and a plant that, when boiled, tastes remarkably like scrambled eggs. You can still find such exotica as *crapaud* or "mountain chicken" (actually enormous frogs' legs) or agouti (a large rodent delicious when roasted or smoked) on Dominica. And you must try flying fish, the national dish of Barbados. Grenada, the spice island (it produces much of the world's supply of nutmeg and cloves), has an abundance of seafood and an incredible variety of fruits and vegetables. On St. Lucia, where countless banana plantations cover the mountainsides, you'll find many varieties of banana prepared in dozens of ways. The cuisine on Martinique and Guadeloupe is a marvelous marriage of creole cooking and classic French dishes; you'll find much of the same on the other French islands of St. Martin and St. Barths. You'll also find a fine selection of French wines in the French West Indies. Anegada, in the British West Indies, is, arguably, where you'll find the Caribbean's best lobster. And on many islands you'll find *roti* (a pancake stuffed with chicken or pork and rice) and curries, East Indian legacies that have gradually spread north from Trinidad.

Diving

Jacques Cousteau, who invented scuba diving, considered Guadeloupe's Pigeon Island one of the 10 best dive sites in the world. The Wall off Grand Turk in the Turks and Caicos Islands is a sheer drop of 7,000 ft; more than 200 mi (323 km) of reef surround the chain. The eruption of Martinique's Mt. Pelée at 8 AM on May 8, 1902, resulted in the sinking of several ships that are now great sites. St. Eustatius also has an undersea "supermarket" of ships, as well as entire 18th-century warehouses below the surface of Oranjestad Bay. The waters surrounding all three of the Cayman Islands are acclaimed by experts; even novices adore Stingray City on Grand Cayman, where dozens of unusually tame stingrays swim and twist around divers in the shallow waters. Bonaire's 86 spectacular sites, all protected as part of the Bonaire Marine Park, make that island a diving mecca. Tortola is famous in diving circles for the wreck of the RMS *Rhone,* a mail ship sunk by a hurricane in 1867. Tobago has a great array of unspoiled coral reefs, and it's the only place in the Caribbean where divers regularly see huge manta rays. Saba has some of the best advanced diving with its marine park and deep dive sites. Dominica offers dramatic underwater walls and sudden drops, as well as unusual volcanic vents (like diving in warm champagne), off Scott's Head.

Foreign Cultures

Trinidad moves with the rhythm of calypso and is the stomping ground of a flat-out, freewheeling Carnival that rivals the pre-Lenten celebrations in Rio de Janeiro and New Orleans, the legacy of its original Spanish colonizers. But a significant number—almost half the island's inhabitants—are Indian, descended from the indentured servants who were first brought to Trinidad in the mid-19th century by planters seeking a source of cheap labor after slavery had been abolished in 1834.

It was from St. Kitts, known as the Mother Colony of the West Indies, that British colonists were dispatched in the 17th century to settle Antigua, Barbuda, Tortola, and Montserrat. Barbados, with its lovely trade winds, not to mention its cricket and rugby teams, was controlled by the British from 1627 until its independence in 1966. The Cayman Islands and British Virgin Islands are also former parts of the British Empire in the Caribbean.

Saba, St. Eustatius, St. Maarten, Bonaire, and Curaçao all fly the Dutch flag, though the islands themselves have little else in common. Curaçao, whose colorful waterfront shops and restaurants are reminiscent of Amsterdam, has the most Dutch character. Aruba, now independent, was also a Dutch possession, but with its large casino resorts, it has more American-style glitz than Dutch reserve.

Martinique, Guadeloupe, St. Martin, and St. Barthélemy (often called St. Barths or St. Barts) compose the French West Indies. The language, the currency, the culture, and the style are très French. St. Barths is the quietest (and chicest), Martinique the liveliest, St. Martin the friendliest, and Guadeloupe the lushest.

In the Dominican Republic, which occupies the eastern two-thirds of the island of Hispaniola, the language and culture are decidedly Spanish. Santo Domingo is the oldest city in the Western Hemisphere; the restored buildings in its Zona Colonial reflect the 15th-century Columbus period. You also get a sense of the past in Puerto Rico's Old San Juan, with its narrow cobblestone streets and filigreed iron balconies.

Getting Away from It All

With cell phones and satellite television reaching nearly every part of the Caribbean, it's not as easy as it once was to make like Robinson Crusoe. But if you're looking to ease out of the fast lane, there are plenty of places to escape. You can park yourself at a secluded, spartan mountain lodge on Dominica. Or you can do it in higher style at one of the wonderful plantation inns on Nevis or St. Kitts. Tranquil Anguilla, with soft white beaches nudged by incredibly clear water, offers posh resorts as well as small, inexpensive, locally owned lodgings. From the low-key Turks and Caicos Islands, which lie in stunning blue-green waters, you can boat to more than a score of cays so isolated that even the term "low-key" would imply too fast a pace.

On tiny Saba there's little to do but tuck into a small guest house, admire the island's lush beauty, and chat with the friendly Sabans. Nearby St. Eustatius, where adventurers can walk down into a jungle cradled within a crater, is another friendly laid-back island. St. Vincent and the Grenadines offer three tiny, private-island luxury resorts: Young Island, Palm Island, and Petit St. Vincent. Or you can opt for sleepy islands off islands, such as Vieques and Culebra (off Puerto Rico), or Marie Galante, les Iles des Saintes, and la Désirade (off Guadeloupe)—all with practically deserted pristine beaches, true local color, and charming guest houses.

Golf

According to those who have played it, the course at Casa de Campo on the Dominican Republic is one of the best in the Caribbean, as is the seaside course at the Punta Cana Resort & Club. The course at the Four Seasons Resort on Nevis is also challenging (and breathtaking). Golfers on St. Thomas, USVI, play the Mahogany Run. There are superb courses in Puerto Rico, including four shared by the Hyatt Dorado Beach and the Hyatt Regency Cerromar Beach. Among the courses on Jamaica are the top-rated Tryall near Montego Bay, and the Negril Hills Golf Club. Golf is second only to cricket in Barbados; the Royal Westmoreland Golf Club opened its first 18 holes for the 1996 season; another 9 holes are under way. The Cayman Islands and Aruba also have good 18-hole courses.

Music

Calypso was born in Trinidad, its catchy rhythms veiling the barbed working-class satire of many of the lyrics. Jamaica is the home of reggae, the Rastafarian sound that has racial, political, and religious undertones. The wild pulsating merengue, born in the Dominican Republic, is exuberantly danced everywhere on the island. On Puerto Rico you'll find the slightly less frenzied salsa, whose range encompasses unabashed hip-swiveling tunes and wailing ballads lamenting lost love. Both Martinique and Guadeloupe claim to be the cradle of the sinuous beguine, whose lilting rhythm sways like the palm trees. The music that animates Barbados ranges from *soca* (a mix of soul and calypso) and calypso to the hottest jazz. On many islands *zouk* (a syncopated beat, akin to Caribbean house) is now the rage.

Nightlife
Steel drums, limbo dancers, and jump-ups are ubiquitous in the Caribbean. Jump-up? Simple. You hear the music, jump up, and dance. Or just indulge the art of "liming" (we call it "hanging out"), which can mean anything from playing pool or dominoes to engaging in heated political debate to dancing. Bridgetown in Barbados, Jamaica's Montego Bay, and Trinidad's Port-of-Spain are loaded with lively night spots, and in Puerto Rico, San Juan's glittering Vegas-style floor shows are legendary. But each island also takes great pride in its rich heritage. Many major resorts host local floor shows, a riot of song, dance, and color, incorporating such uniquely Caribbean folkloric traditions as *mocko jumbies* (evil spirits) on stilts and re-creations of Carnival costumes and masks. San Juan, Puerto Rico's year-round Le Lai Lo Festival is perhaps the most successful attempt to introduce visitors to local music and dance.

Snorkeling
Snorkeling requires no special skills, and many establishments that rent equipment have a staff member to teach you the basics. As with any water sport, it's never a good idea to snorkel alone. You don't have to be a great swimmer to snorkel, but occasionally currents come up that require stamina. Time seems to slow down underwater, so wear a water-resistant watch and let someone on land know when to expect you back. Remember that taking souvenirs—shells, pieces of coral, interesting rocks—is forbidden. Many reefs are legally protected marine parks, where removal of living shells is prohibited because it upsets the ecology.

Weddings
More and more couples are tying the knot in the sunny Caribbean. Recognizing this trend, many islands have relaxed their marriage requirements with shortened (or no) residency periods and simplified paperwork. In addition, many no longer require blood tests. To marry on most islands, you must submit the necessary paperwork before your stay. Ship your documents by courier or, if acceptable, fax them. Keep copies of all papers, and carry them with you on your trip. If this isn't your first marriage, you'll need to present a certified divorce decree or, if you're widowed, the death certificate of your previous spouse. (If this documentation is not in the island's official language, you may be required to supply a certified translation of it.) You'll also need to provide proof of your identity and citizenship (documentation requirements for this vary slightly). Wedding fees range from about $40 to $200, including a marriage license, but at some resorts, such as Sandals and SuperClubs, weddings are free. Many resorts not only have wedding packages but also coordinators who can help you with all the pre-wedding paperwork as well as with the ceremony itself. As soon as your reservations are confirmed, speak with the hotel's wedding planner.

Windsurfing
Windsurfing is as strenuous as it is exciting, so it may not be the sport to try on your first day out unless you're already in excellent shape. Always windsurf with someone else around who can go for help if necessary. The conditions are excellent in Aruba, Bonaire, St. Barths, St. Lucia, and the Virgin Islands (both British and U.S.). The Dominican Republic's north shore, particularly around Cabarete, is an important center for the sport.

FODOR'S CHOICE

LODGING

$$$$	**Anse Chastanet Hotel**, St. Lucia. Rooms were designed to meld with the mountainside; louvered wooden walls open to stunning Piton and Caribbean vistas or to the deep-green forest.
$$$$	**Caneel Bay Resort**, St. John, U.S. Virgin Islands. With seven beaches spread out over 170 acres, this open-air resort is a sun worshiper's paradise. Numerous tennis courts, myriad water sports, and good restaurants make it hard to stir from this luxury property.
$$$$	**Cap Juluca**, Anguilla. This spectacular 179-acre resort wraps around the edge of Maunday's Bay and almost 2 mi (3 km) of sugary white-sand beach.
$$$$	**Casa de Campo**, Dominican Republic. The island's most luxurious resort draws golfers and sun-worshippers, who dine and shop at Altos de Chavón, from far and wide.
$$$$	**Cobblers Cove**, Barbados. Pretty in pink, this intimate resort on a picturesque cove blends English country-house elegance with casual Caribbean style—the epitome of a perfect Bajan holiday.
$$$$	**Curtain Bluff**, Antigua. The setting, bookended by two exquisite beaches, is breathtaking. The ambience is pure country-club elegance—and a surprisingly good value.
$$$$	**Grand Lido Negril**, Jamaica. This luxury all-inclusive pampers you with fine dining as well as great spa treatments.
$$$$	**Horned Dorset Primavera**, Puerto Rico. The emphasis here is on privacy and relaxation. The pounding of the surf and the squawk of the resident parrot are the only sounds you'll hear as you lounge on the beach.
$$$$	**Hôtel Isle de France**, St. Barthélemy. An intimate resort on a beautiful beach, it's a Caribbean dream come true. If you want to join the lucky few, book your room far, far in advance.
$$$$	**Parrot Cay**, Providenciales, Turks & Caicos Islands. Natural beauty and tranquillity attract jet setters to this resort.
$$$$	**Spice Island Beach Resort**, Grenada. The spacious suites, fabulous bathrooms, and private plunge pools or in-room whirlpools are great, but it's the location on beautiful Grande Anse Beach that steals the show.
$$$$	**Young Island Resort**, Young Island, St. Vincent and the Grenadines. On its own private island a stone's throw from St. Vincent's shore, these luxury cottages fall somewhere between the Swiss Family Robinson's tree house and the Ritz.

$$$–$$$$	**Ottley's Plantation Inn**, St. Kitts. This great house inn with ravishing gardens epitomizes low-key, worldly sophistication and down-home Caribbean hospitality.
$$$–$$$$	**Ritz-Carlton, St. Thomas, U.S. Virgin Islands.** Built like a palatial Italian villa, there's elegance everywhere, from the marbled-floor reception area to a pool that seems to flow right into the sea.
$$$–$$$$	**Sofitel Auberge de la Vielle Tour**, Guadeloupe. Guests love the split-level suites and luxurious amenities at this jewel, which has gotten better over the years. It also has one of the finest restaurants on Guadeloupe.
$$–$$$	**Bucuti Beach Resort, Aruba.** Popular with honeymooners (who receive champagne and other goodies upon arrival), the hacienda-style buildings here house sunny rooms with ocean-view terraces. The resort has an enviable location on the widest, most secluded section of Eagle Beach.
$$–$$$	**Sugar Mill Hotel**, Tortola, British Virgin Islands. With rooms scattered hillside above a sandy beach, this cozy resort exudes tropical ambience.
$–$$$	**Avila Beach Hotel, Curaçao.** Dutch royals and government VIPs have given this 200-year-old mansion the nod for the peace, privacy, and service it offers. Still, you don't need a royal bank account to stay here.
$$	**Horny Toad**, St. Maarten/St. Martin. A marvelous little ocean-front guest house with a funky name offers the island's best value for those who want to keep costs down.
$–$$	**Le Plein Soleil.** This small resort is chic, contemporary creole at its unexpected best. As appealing as the gingerbread guest cottages are, it is the inn's great house that captivates. Très chic, it is a study in white, with classy tropical furnishings, art, and objets d'nature.
$–$$	**Turtle Nest Inn**, Grand Cayman, Cayman Islands. This Spanish-style seaside inn has roomy one-bedroom apartments on a small beach along a strip of vibrant coral reef—a perfect snorkeling spot.

BUDGET LODGING

$	**Auberge Seraphine**, St. Lucia. This small, elegant inn with a great restaurant overlooks Vigie Cove, near Castries.
$	**Barceló Capella Beach Resort**, Dominican Republic. The most elegant of Juan Dolio's all-inclusive resorts is also a great deal.
$	**Carringtons Inn**, St. Croix, U.S. Virgin Islands. A stay at this spacious bed and breakfast harks back to a gentler time, when people spent the winter, rather than a week, in the Caribbean.
$	**Island View Guest House**, St. Thomas, U.S. Virgin Islands. Owners Norman Leader and Barbara Cooper run a homey guesthouse high in the hills overlooking Charlotte Amalie, where breakfast and dinner are served family-style for all who want to join in.

$	**Papillote Wilderness Retreat,** Dominica. The owners and staff have infused this mountain getaway with their charm and warmth—from the lush, sensuous gardens to the homey rooms.
$	**Rockhouse,** Jamaica. Perched on the cliffs of Negril's West End, unique bungalows blend comfort and rustic style.
¢–$	**King's Well Hotel,** St. Eustatius. This charming small hotel overlooking Oranjestad's Lower Town is the island's best.
¢	**Ivan's Stress Free Bar & White Bay Campground,** Jost Van Dyke, British Virgin Islands. Feel like a castaway at this full-service campground with screened cabins, a communal kitchen, and an absolutely gorgeous stretch of beach.

RESTAURANTS

$$$$	**The Cliff,** Barbados. Despite stiff competition for their dining dollars, the well-heeled instinctively head here to enjoy the island's best dining.
$$$$	**Montpelier Plantation Inn Restaurant,** Nevis, St. Kitts & Nevis. Dinner here is a very elegant evening on the inn's covered verandah, with the freshest seafood and herbs from the on-site garden.
$$$–$$$$	**Chez Pascal,** Antigua. Perched on a cliff overlooking the ocean, this restaurant is an authentic piece of sunny, southern France transplanted to the Caribbean. Melt-in-your-mouth seafood specialties particularly shine, as do the silken sauces.
$$$–$$$$	**Hemingway's,** Grand Cayman, Cayman Islands. Enjoy the breezes on Seven Mile Beach while sipping a Seven Mile Meltdown (dark rum, peach schnapps, pineapple juice, and fresh coconut) and savoring grouper stuffed with sweet corn and crab.
$$$–$$$$	**Malliouhana,** Anguilla. Michelin darling Michel Rostang consults on the menu of this sterling, swooningly romantic restaurant overlooking Meads Bay. The remarkable wine list garners international awards.
$$$–$$$$	**Route des Epices,** St. Barthélemy. Enjoy haute cuisine on a buffed mahogany verandah, with stellar service and a marvelous wine list.
$$$–$$$$	**Virgilio's,** St. Thomas, U.S. Virgin Islands. Come here for some of the best northern Italian cuisine in the islands, and don't leave without having a Virgilio's cappuccino, a chocolate-and-coffee drink so rich, it's dessert.
$$–$$$$	**Rijsttafel Indonesia Restaurant,** Curaçao. Walls hung with batik, handwoven baskets, and shadow puppets set the stage for a traditional Indonesian rijsttafel banquet, with as many as 25 dishes served buffet-style.
$$$	**Brandywine Bay,** Tortola, British Virgin Islands. A romantic, candlelit atmosphere coupled with stellar food make this Tortola's best restaurant.

$$$	**Dasheene,** St. Lucia. The exquisite cuisine at the Ladera Resort's restaurant, perched high on a hill between The Pitons, is upstaged only by the view. Whether the panorama is more spectacular at mid-day or at sunset is a toss-up.
$$$	**La Belle Creole,** Grenada. The marriage of Continental and West Indian cuisines is the hallmark of this romantic hillside restaurant.
$$–$$$	**Top Hat,** St. Croix, U.S. Virgin Islands. Both the wonderful Danish menu and the Danish owners are reminders of St. Croix's colonial past. Try the *frikadeller* (meatballs in a tangy sauce) and fried Camembert with lingonberries. $$$
$–$$$	**Basil's Bar,** Mustique, St. Vincent & the Grenadines. The glitterati and the regular folks all come to this thatch-roofed restaurant on Mustique, for simply prepared, fresh seafood and homemade ice cream.
$$	**Turtle Pier,** St. Maarten/St. Martin. A great choice for consistently great seafood also has reasonable prices, especially for lobster and shrimp.
$–$$	**Veni Mangé,** Trinidad, Trinidad & Tobago. Cordon Bleu–trained Allyson Hennessey cooks up the best creole lunches in town.
¢–$$	**'Ti Plage,** Martinique. Just inches from the water, this is one fun beach bar that takes "beach food" and Caribbean cocktails to another level entirely.

BUDGET RESTAURANTS

$	**Skinny Legs Bar and Restaurant,** St. John, U.S. Virgin Islands. Exuding scads of island charm, here is a place where you can gather with the locals for lunch, supper, or just drinks. The owners, Doug and Moe, are characters, as are some of those who frequent the place.
¢–$	**Kite Surf Camp,** Dominican Republic. Set yourself down at one of the long plank tables for perfect barbecue and good conversation.
¢–$	**The Nutmeg,** Grenada. Both locals and visitors come to St. George's for this casual spot serving great, homemade West Indian cuisine featuring the freshest seafood.
¢–$	**Ocho Rios Village Jerk Centre,** Jamaica. You can buy the best jerk on Jamaica at this blue-canopied, open-air eatery in Ocho Rios.
¢–$	**Ric's Place,** St. Maarten/St. Martin. Prices are low but quality is high at this popular café and sports bar on Simpson Bay.

BEACHES

	Bahoruco Beach, Dominican Republic. Eight miles (13 km) from the town of Barahona, on the isolated south coast, this gorgeous stretch of virgin beach goes on for miles in either direction, with rugged cliffs dropping to golden sand and gin-clear water.
	Baie Orientale, St. Maarten/St. Martin. One of the Caribbean's most beautiful beaches has something for everyone, with clean, white sand and clear, blue water, plus an assortment of good bars and restaurants.

The Baths, Virgin Gorda, British Virgin Islands. Giant boulders form grottos filled with seawater that you can swim through and explore.

Grand Anse Beach, Grenada. Gentle surf laps the gleaming sand of this 2-mi (3-km) beach. To the north, you can see the narrow mouth of St. George's Harbour and the pastel houses, with their fish-scale tile rooftops, that climb the surrounding hills.

Grande Saline, St. Barthélemy. This beautiful, secluded beach is just about everyone's favorite place for swimming.

Macaroni Beach, Mustique, St. Vincent & the Grenadines. Surfy swimming, powdery white sand, a few palm huts and picnic tables, and very few people are the draws here.

Magens Bay, St. Thomas, U.S. Virgin Islands. This picture-postcard perfect heart-shaped beach is on many lists of the world's most beautiful.

Negril Beach, Jamaica. Negril's seven-mile-long beach is a microcosm of Jamaica, packed with small restaurants and hotels, beach vendors, watersports, and a laid-back atmosphere.

Seven Mile Beach, Grand Cayman, Cayman Islands. Powder-soft sand stretches for miles, and a gradual drop-off (sans rocks) into a warm sea makes this beach among the Caribbean's best.

Shoal Bay, Anguilla. This 2-mi (3-km), L-shape beach of talcum-powder-soft white sand may get crowded, but that's only because it's one of the prettiest in the Caribbean.

Trunk Bay, St. John, USVI. You'll find sensational snorkeling on this perfect scimitar, one of many such sandy stretches on an island that's 66% protected national park.

DIVING

Anegada, British Virgin Islands. The reefs surrounding this flat coral and limestone atoll are a sailor's nightmare but a scuba diver's dream. Snorkeling, especially in the waters around Loblolly Bay on the north shore, is a transcendent experience.

Bloody Bay Wall, Little Cayman, Cayman Islands. The drop begins at a mere 18 ft (6 m) but plunges to more than 1,000 ft (306 m), with visibility often reaching 150 ft (46 m)—diving doesn't get much better than this.

Bonaire Marine Park, Bonaire. The current is mild, the reefs often begin just offshore, visibility is generally 60 ft–100 ft, and the marine life is magnificent.

Dominica. Serious divers know that the pristine bubbly waters around Dominica's submerged volcanic crater are among the best in the world.

Double Wreck, St. Eustatius. Just offshore are the wrecks of two tall-masted ships from the 1700s, now covered with coral and home to large schools of fish, rays, and eels.

Saba. Within a half-mile of shore, sea walls drop to depths of more than 1,000 ft (300 m) here, and visibility along the living reefs is extraordinary.

Tobago Cays, St. Vincent & the Grenadines. Horsehoe Reef surrounds five uninhabited islets, each with tiny, palm-lined, white-sand beaches. The brilliantly colored water is studded with sponges and coral and populated by countless colorful fish.

GOLF

Casa de Campo, Dominican Republic. The "Teeth of the Dog" course, designed by P.B. Dye, at this world-class golf resort is usually ranked among the top in the world.

Country Club at Sandy Lane, Barbados. Now with three courses, Sandy Lane is becoming an important golf center in the Caribbean.

Four Seasons Nevis, Nevis, St. Kitts & Nevis. The beautiful course, designed by Robert Trent Jones, Jr., has ranked among the best in the Caribbean since opening day in 1991.

Hyatt Dorado Beach Resort & Country Club, Puerto Rico. The two courses here, designed by Robert Trent Jones, draw golfers from around the world.

Mahogany Run Golf Course, St. Thomas, U.S. Virgin Islands. An extensive renovation in 2001 has revived this challenging course, which was designed by George and Tom Fazio.

Punta Cana Resort & Club, Dominican Republic. The Punta Cana Golf Club course has 14 holes with sea views and four on the oceanfront.

Tryall Club, Jamaica. This course, designed by Ralph Plummer and home to several championship events, is the destination for serious golfers visiting the island.

HISTORY

Christiansted, St. Croix, U.S. Virgin Islands. Fort Christiansvaern and other historic sights, which are spread out all over town, let you step back into St. Croix's colonial past.

Fort George, Grenada. Rising above the entrance to St. George's Harbour, the fort has a spectacular view of the capital and the sea.

Fort Oranje, St. Eustatius. The fort itself dates to 1636, but it played an important role in U.S. history, when its cannons were the first to salute the newly declared independent country in 1776.

Nelson's Dockyard, Antigua. An impeccable restoration of Lord Horatio Nelson's 18th-century headquarters has delightful hotels, restaurants, and craft shops.

San Germán, Puerto Rico. Around the town's two main squares are buildings in every conceivable architectural style, including one of the oldest churches in the Americas.

Santo Domingo's Zona Colonial, Dominican Republic. Wandering the narrow cobbled streets, it's easy to imagine what the city was like in the days of Columbus, Cortés, and Ponce de León, especially now that the zone is well-lit by antique lanterns.

NATURE

Asa Wright Nature Centre, Trinidad, Trinidad & Tobago. You might spot blue-backed manakin, yellow oriole, scarlet ibis, or another of the more than 200 varieties of birds at the Asa Wright Nature Centre, one of the top birding destinations in the Caribbean.

Bahía Mosquito, Vieques, Puerto Rico. This bioluminescent bay is best experienced on moonless nights; it's like swimming in a cloud of fireflies.

Boiling Lake, Morne Trois Pitons National Park, Dominica. This bubbly, brackish caulderon is actually a flooded fumerole, but a hike here is an unforgettable trip into an otherworldly place.

Harrison's Cave, Barbados. A limestone cavern, complete with towering stalagmites, subterranean streams, and a 40-ft waterfall, is a rare find in the Caribbean.

Mt. Scenery, Saba. You can climb 1,064 stone steps to the top of Saba's tallest mountain for unparalleled views of the surrounding islands.

The Pitons, St. Lucia. These two incredible mountains rise precipitously from the cobalt blue Caribbean south of Soufrière.

The Quill, St. Eustatius. The crater of Statia's extinct volcano is filled with a primeval rain forest and is a top hiking destination.

Virgin Islands National Park, St. John, U.S. Virgin Islands. Swim, snorkel, and hike at this showpiece of the National Park Service, which occupies a full two-thirds of the island of St. John.

SHOPPING

Curaçao. Stroll the cobblestone streets of Punda in Willemstad for a huge variety of upscale duty-free shops and local boutiques.

Grenada. For nutmeg, cinnamon sticks, cocoa, cloves, and more, visit a historic spice plantation, tour a nutmeg-processing plant, and replenish your spice rack at an outdoor market.

Puerto Rico. From the boutiques of Old San Juan to ateliers of the young designers elsewhere in metro San Juan to galleries scattered all over the island, there's plenty to see and buy.

St. Barthélemy. Without a doubt, the shopping here for luxury goods and fashion is the best in the Caribbean. The variety and quality of goods is astounding.

St. Maarten/St. Martin. Hundreds of duty-free shops make the island the best in the Caribbean for bargain-hunters, especially for quality jewelry and perfumes.

St. Thomas, U.S. Virgin Islands. Main Street in Charlotte Amalie is well known for numerous duty-free shops, selling everything from rum to designer fashions and gems.

SMART TRAVEL TIPS

Finding out about your destination before you leave home means you won't squander time organizing everyday minutiae once you've arrived. You'll be more streetwise when you hit the ground as well, better prepared to explore the aspects of the Caribbean that drew you here in the first place. The organizations listed in this section can provide information to supplement this guide; contact them for up-to-the-minute details, and consult the A to Z sections that end each chapter for facts on the various topics as they relate to the islands. Happy landings!

ADDRESSES

"Whimsical" might best describe some Caribbean addresses. Street names can change for no apparent reason, and most buildings have no numbers. Addresses throughout this guide may include cross streets, landmarks, and other directionals. But to find your destination you might have to ask a local—and be prepared for directions such as, "Go down so, turn at the next gap (road), keep goin' past the church, and you'll see it right down the hill."

AIR TRAVEL

Most regularly scheduled flights to the Caribbean connect through Atlanta (Delta Airlines), Charlotte (US Airways), or Miami or San Juan (American Airlines). There are also some nonstops from the east coast (primarily from New York, Boston, and Philadelphia) and various other cities around the country. Regularly scheduled charter flights also operate, primarily from Canada and the midwestern United States. If you are coming from London, you'll have to transfer, usually in New York, Miami, or San Juan, unless you are on one of the few nonstops or a charter flights from the U.K. If you are coming from Australia or New Zealand, you will probably transfer to a Caribbean-bound flight in Miami.

BOOKING

When you book, **look for nonstop flights and remember that "direct" flights stop at least once.** Try to avoid connecting flights, which require a change of plane. Two airlines may operate a connecting flight jointly, so ask whether your airline operates every segment of the trip; you may find that the carrier you prefer flies you only part of the way. To find more booking tips and to check prices and make online flight reservations, log on to www.fodors.com.

Some destinations are accessed only by small planes operated by local carriers. While international carriers will sometimes book those flights for you as part of your overall travel arrangements, you can confidently **book directly with the local carrier,** using a major credit card, either online or by telephone.

CARRIERS

From the U.S. & Canada Air Canada ☎ 888/247-2262 ⊕ www.aircanada.ca. **Air Jamaica** ☎ 800/523-5585 ⊕ www.airjamaica.com. **American Airlines** ☎ 800/433-7300 ⊕ www.aa.com. **BWIA** ☎ 800/538-2942 ⊕ www.bwee.com. **Continental** ☎ 800/231-0856 ⊕ www.continental.com. **Delta** ☎ 800/241-4141 ⊕ www.delta.com. **Dutch Caribbean Airlines** ☎ 800/327-7230 ⊕ www.flydce.com. **Northwest Airlines** ☎ 800/447-4747 ⊕ www.nwa.com. **United Airlines** ☎ 800/538-2929 ⊕ www.united.com. **US Airways** ☎ 800/428-4322 ⊕ www.usairways.com.

From the U.K. Air Jamaica ☎ 0208/570-7999 ⊕ www.airjamaica.com. **British Airways** ☎ 0845/77-333-77 ⊕ www.britishairways.com. **BWIA** ☎ 0800/169-7745 ⊕ www.bwee.com. **Virgin Atlantic** ☎ 0129/374-7747 ⊕ www.virginatlantic.com.

From Elsewhere in the World Air France ☎ 0/802/802-802 in Paris ⊕ www.airfrance.com. **British Airways** ☎ 1/300-767-177 in Australia; 0/800-274-847 in New Zealand ⊕ www.britishairways.com. **KLM** ☎ 31/20-4-747-747 in Amsterdam ⊕ www.klm.com. **Qantas** ☎ 13-13-13 in Australia; 0800/808-767 in New Zealand ⊕ www.qantas.com.

Caribbean Interisland Carriers Air Caraïbes ☎ 877/772-1005 ⊕ www.aircaraibes.com. **American Eagle** ☎ 800/433-7300 ⊕ www.aa.com. **Air Jamaica Express** ☎ 800/523-5585 ⊕ www.airjamaica.com. **BWee Express** ☎ 800/538-2942 ⊕ www.bwee.com. **Caribbean Star** ☎ 268/461-7827; 800/744-7827 within the Caribbean ⊕ www.flycaribbeanstar.com. **LIAT** ☎ 888/844-5428 ⊕ www.liatairline.com. **SVG Air** ☎ 784/457-5124; 800/744-5777 within the Caribbean ⊕ www.svgair.com. **Trans Island Airways (TIA)** ☎ 246/418-1650 ⊕ www.tia2000.com. **Winair** ☎ 599/545-4237 ⊕ www.fly-winair.com.

CHECK-IN & BOARDING

Always **ask your carrier about its check-in policy.** Plan to arrive at the airport about two hours before your scheduled departure time for domestic flights and 2½ to 3 hours before international flights. You may need to arrive earlier if you're flying from one of the busier airports or during peak air-traffic times. When heading home, **get to the airport at least 1½ hours ahead of time** (2 hours if you plan to squeeze in some duty-free shopping). Checking in, paying departure taxes (which are usually *not* included in your airfare in the Caribbean), clearing security, and boarding can take longer than you expect at some island airports. And from many islands there's often only one flight per day going in the direction you're headed. **Expect security personnel to hand-search all your carry-on items**—sometimes a second time at the gate. To avoid delays at airport-security checkpoints, try not to wear any metal. Jewelry, belt and other buckles, steel-toe shoes, barrettes, and underwire bras are among the objects that can set off detectors.

Assuming that not everyone with a ticket will show up, airlines routinely overbook planes. When everyone does, airlines ask for volunteers to give up their seats. In return, these volunteers usually get a several-hundred-dollar flight voucher, which can be used toward the purchase of another ticket, and are rebooked on the next flight out. If there are not enough volunteers, the airline must choose who will be denied boarding. The first to get bumped are passengers who checked in late and those flying on discounted tickets, so **get to the gate and check in as early as possible,** especially during peak periods.

Always **bring a government-issued photo I.D. to the airport;** even when it's not required, a passport is best.

CUTTING COSTS

The least expensive airfares between the U.S. and the Caribbean must usually be purchased in advance and are nonrefundable and, more often nowadays, nonchangeable unless you pay a substantial fee. It's smart to **call a number of airlines and check the Internet;** when you are quoted a good price, **book it on the spot**—the same fare may not be available the next day, or even the next hour. Always **check different routings** and look into using alternate airports. Also, price off-peak flights, which may be significantly less expensive than others. Travel agents, especially low-fare specialists (⇨ Discounts and Deals), are helpful.

Consolidators are another good source. They buy tickets for scheduled flights at reduced rates from the airlines, then sell them at prices that beat the best fare available directly from the airlines. Sometimes you can even get your money back if you need to return the ticket. Carefully read the fine print detailing penalties for changes and cancellations, purchase the ticket with a credit card, and **confirm your consolidator reservation with the airline.**

Ask about island-hopping passes. Dutch Caribbean Airlines has a 30-day "Visit Caribbean Airpass," for example, that may be used for five destinations, including one gateway such as Miami. Air Jamaica's "Caribbean Hopper" program allows U.S.-originating passengers to visit three or more destinations in its Caribbean and Central American network. American Airlines and American Eagle offer a "Caribbean Explorer" fare to 23 Caribbean destinations out of San Juan. BWIA offers a 30-day "Caribbean Traveller" air pass for travel to its 12 Caribbean and South American destinations. LIAT has three categories of interisland "Explorer" passes for different durations.

🛪 **Consolidators** AirlineConsolidator.com 🖀 888/468-5385 ⊕ www.airlineconsolidator.com; for international tickets. **Best Fares** 🖀 800/576-8255 or 800/576-1600 ⊕ www.bestfares.com; $59.90 annual membership. **Cheap Tickets** 🖀 800/377-1000 or 888/922-8849 ⊕ www.cheaptickets.com. **Expedia** 🖀 800/397-3342 or 404/728-8787 ⊕ www.expedia.com. **Hotwire** 🖀 866/468-9473 or 920/330-9418 ⊕ www.hotwire.com. **Now Voyager Travel** ✉ 45 W. 21st St., 5th floor, New York, NY 10010 🖀 212/459-1616 🖷 212/243-2711 ⊕ www.nowvoyagertravel.com. **Onetravel.com** ⊕ www.onetravel.com. **Orbitz** 🖀 888/656-4546 ⊕ www.orbitz.com. **Priceline.com** ⊕ www.priceline.com. **Travelocity** 🖀 888/709-5983; 877/282-2925 in Canada; 870/876-3876 in the U.K. ⊕ www.travelocity.com.

ENJOYING THE FLIGHT

State your seat preference when purchasing your ticket, and then repeat it when you confirm and when you check in. For more legroom, you can request one of the few emergency-aisle seats at check-in, if you are capable of lifting at least 50 pounds—a Federal Aviation Administration requirement of passengers in these seats. Seats behind a bulkhead also offer more

legroom, but they don't have under-seat storage. Don't sit in the row in front of the emergency aisle or in front of a bulkhead, where seats may not recline.

Ask the airline whether a snack or meal is served on the flight. If you have dietary concerns, **request special meals when booking.** These can be vegetarian, low-cholesterol, or kosher, for example. It's a good idea to pack some healthful snacks and a small (plastic) bottle of water in your carry-on bag. On long flights, try to maintain a normal routine, to help fight jet lag. At night, **get some sleep.** By day, **eat light meals, drink water** (not alcohol), and **move around the cabin** to stretch your legs. For additional jet-lag tips consult *Fodor's FYI: Travel Fit & Healthy* (available at bookstores everywhere). Virtually all airlines forbid smoking on all flights.

FLYING TIMES

The flight from New York to San Juan, Puerto Rico, takes 3½ hours; from Miami to San Juan it's 1½ hours. Flights from New York to Kingston or Montego Bay, Jamaica, take about 4 hours; those from Miami, about an hour. Nonstop flights from London to Antigua and Barbados and from Paris to Guadeloupe, Martinique, and St. Martin are about 7 hours. Once you've arrived in the Caribbean, hops between islands range from 20 minutes to 2 hours.

HOW TO COMPLAIN

If your baggage goes astray or your flight goes awry, complain right away. Most carriers require that you **file a claim immediately.** The Aviation Consumer Protection Division of the Department of Transportation publishes *Fly-Rights,* which discusses airlines and consumer issues and is available on-line.

🛪 **Aviation Consumer Protection Division** ✉ U.S. Department of Transportation, C-75, Room 4107, 400 7th St. NW, Washington, DC 20590 🖀 202/366-2220 ⊕ www.dot.gov/airconsumer. **Federal Aviation Administration Consumer Hotline** ✉ for inquiries: FAA, 800 Independence Ave. SW, Room 810, Washington, DC 20591 🖀 800/322-7873 ⊕ www.faa.gov.

CONFIRMING FLIGHT TIMES

Check the status of your flight before you leave for the airport. You can do this on your carrier's Web site, by linking to a flight-status checker (many Web booking services offer these), or by calling your carrier or travel agent. Always confirm international flights at least 72 hours ahead of the scheduled departure time. Be sure to confirm your flights on interisland carriers, as you may be subject to a small carrier's whims: If no other passengers are booked on your flight, particularly if the carrier operates "scheduled charters," you will be rescheduled onto another flight or at a different departure time (earlier or later than your original reservation) that's more convenient for the airline. Your plane may also make unscheduled stops to pick up more clients or cargo, which also can affect actual departure and arrival times. Don't be concerned. It's all part of the adventure of interisland travel.

AIRPORTS

Airports on most of the islands are modern facilities, with comfortable waiting areas, restaurants, duty-free shops, and other services. The smaller, more remote island destinations, of course, have tiny airfields and few services. However, many airports in the Caribbean are not air-conditioned.

BIKE TRAVEL

Many Caribbean islands are mountainous, and their narrow, steep, winding roads already have difficulty accommodating cars, pedestrians, and occasional livestock. Serious bikers, of course, will take all this in stride. If you're a more laid-back biker, however, good bets include: Antigua, Aruba, Bonaire, Puerto Rico, Grand Turk and Providenciales (Turks and Caicos Islands), St. Croix (USVI), and St. Martin. Most islands have at least one bike-rental company (rates are usually reasonable), and some resorts offer guests the use of bikes at no additional charge.

BOAT & FERRY TRAVEL

Ferry travel is an inexpensive way to island-hop. Ferries ply the waters of the Grenadines, for example, and you can take a day trip or spend a week or more cruising from one lovely island to another. Cargo freighters and mail boats are even less expensive and more adventuresome modes of interisland travel, but you can't be in a hurry. High-speed ferries or catamarans link neighboring islands, such as Grenada with Carriacou and Petite Martinique; Martinique with Dominica, Guadeloupe, and St. Lucia; St. John or St. Croix with St. Thomas; and St. Maarten/St. Martin with Anguilla, St. Barths, and Saba. Reservations aren't usually necessary.

BUS TRAVEL

Some islands, such as Puerto Rico, St. Thomas, the Dominican Republic, Aruba, and Barbados have convenient, inexpensive bus service along regular routes—and with regular schedules. On smaller islands, "bus" service may be provided by privately owned vans that follow regular routes but not necessarily regular schedules—they just keep coming, one after another, all day long. Fares are inexpensive (some buses require exact change in local currency), and this mode of transport is safe for visitors and a good way to absorb the local culture.

BUSINESS HOURS

Though business hours vary from island to island, shops are generally closed Saturday afternoon and all day Sunday. Some shops close for an hour at lunchtime during the week, as well, although this practice is becoming increasingly rare. Farmers markets are often open daily (except Sunday), but Saturday morning is always the most colorful and exciting time to go.

CAMERAS & PHOTOGRAPHY

Frothy waves in a turquoise sea and palm-lined crescents of beach are relatively easy to capture on film or digitally if you **don't let the brightness of the sun on sand and water fool your light meter.** You must compensate or else work early or late in the day when the light isn't as brilliant and contrast isn't such a problem. Try to **capture expansive views** of waterfront, beach, or village scenes; consider shooting down onto the shore from a clearing on a hillside or from a rock on the beach. Or **zoom in on something colorful,** such as a delicate tropical flower or a craftsman at work—but always **ask permission to take pictures of locals or their property. Use a disposable underwater camera** to make your snorkeling and diving adventures more memorable. The *Kodak Guide to Shooting Great*

Travel Pictures (available at bookstores everywhere) is loaded with tips.
Kodak Information Center ☎ 800/242-2424 ⊕ www.kodak.com.

EQUIPMENT PRECAUTIONS

Don't pack film and equipment in checked luggage, where it is much more susceptible to damage. X-ray machines used to view checked luggage are extremely powerful and therefore likely to ruin your film. Try to **ask for hand inspection of film,** which becomes clouded after repeated exposure to airport X-ray machines, and **keep videotapes and computer disks away from metal detectors.** Always **keep film, tape, and computer disks out of the sun.** Carry an extra supply of batteries, and **be prepared to turn on your camera, camcorder, or laptop** to prove to airport security personnel that the device is real.

FILM & DEVELOPING

Film, videotape, batteries, and one-time-use cameras are available in camera stores, souvenir shops, hotel boutiques, and pharmacies—although such items can cost twice as much as at home. In all but the most remote areas, you can find 24-hour film-developing services, as well. Be aware, however, that while most Caribbean countries use the NTSC television and video standard that is used in the United States, the countries in the French West Indies (Guadeloupe, Martinique, St. Barths, and St. Martin) use the SECAM standard used in France; videotapes purchased in those countries will not be usable in your U.S.-purchased video equipment.

CAR RENTAL

Major firms, such as Avis, Hertz, and Budget, have agencies in many islands of the Caribbean. But **don't overlook local firms;** their cars are mechanically sound, and prices are competitive. Cars often have standard transmission, although automatic is usually an option. It's not crucial to reserve a rental car prior to your arrival. Many hotels, especially those far from the airport, include airport transfers, and taxis are always an option. Besides, you may only want a rental car for a day or two of on-your-own sightseeing. For exciting treks into remote areas where roads are hilly or unpaved, **rent a four-wheel-drive vehicle.**
Alamo ☎ 800/522-9696 ⊕ www.alamo.com.
Avis ☎ 800/331-1084; 800/879-2847 in Canada;

0870/606-0100 in the U.K.; 02/9353-9000 in Australia; 09/526-2847 in New Zealand ⊕ www.avis.com. **Budget** ☎ 800/527-0700; 0870/156-5656 in the U.K. ⊕ www.budget.com. **Dollar** ☎ 800/800-6000; 0124/622-0111 in the U.K., where it's affiliated with Sixt; 02/9223-1444 in Australia ⊕ www.dollar.com. **Hertz** ☎ 800/654-3001; 800/263-0600 in Canada; 0870/844-8844 in the U.K.; 02/9669-2444 in Australia; 09/256-8690 in New Zealand ⊕ www.hertz.com. **National Car Rental** ☎ 800/227-7368; 0870/600-6666 in the U.K. ⊕ www.nationalcar.com.

CUTTING COSTS

For a good deal, **book through a travel agent who will shop around.** Also, **price local car-rental companies**—whose prices may be lower still, although their service and maintenance may not be as good as those of major rental agencies—and **research rates on the Internet.** Remember to ask about required deposits, cancellation penalties, and drop-off charges if you're planning to pick up the car in one city and leave it in another. If you're traveling during a holiday period, also make sure that a confirmed reservation guarantees you a car.

INSURANCE

When driving a rented car you are generally responsible for any damage to or loss of the vehicle. You also may be liable for any property damage or personal injury you may cause while driving. Before you rent, see what coverage you already have under the terms of your personal auto-insurance policy and credit cards.

REQUIREMENTS & RESTRICTIONS

Most agencies won't rent to you if you're under the age of 21.

SURCHARGES

Before you pick up a car in one city and leave it in another, **ask about drop-off charges or one-way service fees,** which can be substantial. Note, too, that some rental agencies charge extra if you return the car before the time specified in your contract. To avoid a hefty refueling fee, **fill the tank just before you turn in the car,** but be aware that gas stations near the rental outlet may overcharge. It's almost never a deal to buy the tank of gas that's in the car when you rent it; the understanding is that you'll return it empty, but some fuel usually remains. Surcharges may apply if you're under 25 or if you take the car outside the area approved by the rental agency. You'll pay extra for child seats (about $6 a day), which are compulsory for children under five, and usually for additional drivers (about $10 per day).

CAR TRAVEL

Your driver's license may not be recognized in some Caribbean countries. International driving permits (IDPs) are available from the American and Canadian automobile associations and, in the United Kingdom, from the Automobile Association and Royal Automobile Club. These international permits, valid only in conjunction with your regular driver's license, are universally recognized; having one may save you a problem with local authorities. In some countries a temporary local driving permit, which you can get at rental agencies or local police offices upon presentation of a valid license and a small fee, is often required. Although exploring on your own can give your sightseeing excursions a sense of adventure, tentative drivers should instead consider hiring a taxi for the day. Locals, who are familiar with the roads, often drive fast and take chances. You don't want to get in their way.

EMERGENCY SERVICES

Major-brand gas and service stations, where you can use your credit card, are found throughout the Caribbean but mainly in the larger towns. Before driving off into the countryside, **check your rental car for tire-changing equipment,** including an inflated spare. Roadside assistance may be unavailable.

ROAD CONDITIONS

Island roads, particularly in mountainous regions that experience heavy tropical rains, are often potholed and bumpy—as well as narrow, winding, and hilly. **Drive with extreme caution,** especially if you venture out at night. You won't see guardrails on every hill and curve, although the drops can be frighteningly steep. And pedestrians (including children and the elderly) and livestock often share the roadway with vehicles.

ROAD MAPS

Road maps are available from car-rental agencies and often at your hotel. Small islands have few roads—often one main road around the perimeter and a couple that cross the island. It's hard to get lost.

RULES OF THE ROAD

On islands with a British heritage, **be prepared to drive on the left.** Speed limits are low, because it's often hard to find a road long and straight enough to *safely* get up much speed. And always **wear your seatbelts,** which are required by law. Drivers are generally courteous; for example, if someone flashes car headlights at you at an intersection, it means "after you."

CHILDREN IN THE CARIBBEAN

Kids of all ages love the beach and, therefore, love the Caribbean. Resorts are increasingly sensitive to families' needs, and many now have extensive children's programs and can arrange for a baby-sitter when parents need some time alone. On sightseeing days, try to include some activities that will also interest children. Sights and attractions that children will particularly enjoy are indicated in the Exploring section of each island chapter by a rubber-duckie icon (☺) in the margin. If you are renting a car, don't forget to **arrange for a car seat** when you reserve. For general advice about traveling with children, consult *Fodor's FYI: Travel with Your Baby* (available in bookstores everywhere).

FLYING

If your children are two or older, **ask about children's airfares.** As a general rule, infants under two not occupying a seat fly at greatly reduced fares or even for free. But if you want to guarantee a seat for an infant, you have to pay full fare. Consider flying during off-peak days and times; most airlines will grant an infant a seat without a ticket if there are available seats. When booking, **confirm carry-on allowances** if you're traveling with infants. In general, for babies charged 10% to 50% of the adult fare you are allowed one carry-on bag and a collapsible stroller; if the flight is full, the stroller may have to be checked or you may be limited to less.

Experts agree that it's a good idea to use safety seats aloft for children weighing less than 40 pounds. Airlines set their own policies: If you use a safety seat, U.S. carriers usually require that the child be ticketed, even if he or she is young enough to ride free, because the seats must be strapped into regular seats. And even if you pay the full adult fare for the seat, it may be worth it, especially on longer trips. Do **check your airline's policy about using safety seats during takeoff and landing.** Safety seats are not allowed everywhere in the plane, so get your seat assignments as early as possible.

When reserving, **request children's meals or a freestanding bassinet** (not available at all airlines) if you need them. But note that bulkhead seats, where you must sit to use the bassinet, may lack an overhead bin or storage space on the floor.

FOOD

Even if your youngsters are picky eaters, meals in the Caribbean shouldn't be a problem. Baby food is easy to find (although often pricier than you might find at home, and brands may be limited). Hamburgers and hot dogs are available at many resorts. Chicken legs, fried or baked, are ubiquitous throughout the Caribbean; restaurants offer pasta and vegetarian dishes, pizza, sandwiches, and ice cream—all of which appeal to kids. Supermarkets have cereal, snacks, and other packaged goods that you'll recognize from home. At outdoor markets a few dollars will buy you enough bananas, oranges, and other tropical fruit to last your entire vacation. Just watch out for overly spicy food that may upset children's sensitive stomachs.

LODGING

Children are welcome in most Caribbean resorts; exceptions are couples-only and adults-only establishments and some ultra-exclusive properties in high season. Some places have only limited children's activities and may not welcome kids during peak season. Other properties offer fully supervised kids' programs, in-room baby-sitting, kids' menus, and other family-friendly features. Children under 12 or 16 can often stay free in their parents' room (be sure to **find out the cutoff age for children's discounts** when booking).

Families should also **consider booking a condo or a villa**; a two-bedroom condo (and sometimes even a one-bedroom condo, with a sleeper sofa in the sitting room) is often suitable for two parents and two children traveling together. It may also be cheaper than a larger room or suite in a hotel or resort for a similar time period. Food preparation in the condo's kitchen can save substantially on the cost of meals.

Some condo resorts even have children's programs. On some islands, such as Grand Cayman, condos and villas actually outnumber hotel rooms.

PRECAUTIONS

Don't underestimate the tropical sun. Throughout the day, even away from the beach, lather onto all exposed areas plenty of sunscreen—with a sun protection factor (SPF) of 15 or higher. Small children should also wear a hat. Mosquito bites can become infected when scratched, so **use bug spray** and avoid the problem. To prevent dehydration, **carry plenty of bottled water** to the beach and on sightseeing excursions.

To avoid immigration problems when a child carries a last name that's different from that of an accompanying parent, **bring documentation that clarifies the family relationship** (e.g., a birth certificate identifying the parent or a joint passport). If a child is traveling without both birth parents, a notarized letter should accompany the child from the nonpresent parent(s) granting permission for the child to travel.

SUPPLIES & EQUIPMENT

Suites at many resorts and even small hotels have sofa beds that make it possible for children to share their parents' room. High chairs and cribs are also generally available. Supermarkets sell common brands of disposable diapers, baby food, and other necessities. Bookstores and souvenir shops have activity books and toys that kids will enjoy on vacation and back at home.

COMPUTERS ON THE ROAD

Bring an adapter for your laptop plug. Even if your computer can be used on either a 100v or 220v system, the prongs on your U.S.-standard plug won't fit into Caribbean 220v wall outlets. Adapters are inexpensive and generally available in hardware stores at home and in the Caribbean. Some hotels will lend adapters to guests for use during their stay. In your hotel, stow away and lock up your laptop when you're out of the room. Although thievery isn't a major concern in the Caribbean, don't invite a problem.

CONSUMER PROTECTION

Whether you're shopping for gifts or purchasing travel services, **pay with a major** credit card whenever possible, so you can cancel payment or get reimbursed if there's a problem (and you can provide documentation). If you're doing business with a particular company for the first time, **contact your local Better Business Bureau and the attorney general's offices** in your state and (for U.S. businesses) the company's home state as well. Have any complaints been filed? Finally, if you're buying a package or tour, always **consider travel insurance** that includes default coverage (⇨ Insurance).

🛈 Council of Better Business Bureaus ✉ 4200 Wilson Blvd., Suite 800, Arlington, VA 22203 ☎ 703/276-0100 🖶 703/525-8277 ⊕ www.bbb.org.

CRUISE TRAVEL

Cruising is a relaxing and convenient way to tour this beautiful part of the world. You get all of the amenities of a luxury hotel and enough activities to guarantee fun, even on the occasional rainy day. All your important decisions are made long before you board. Your itinerary is set, and you know the total cost of your vacation beforehand.

Ships usually call at several ports on a single voyage but are at each port for only one day. Thus, although you may be exposed to several islands, you don't get much of a feel for any one of them.

To learn how to plan, choose, and book a cruise-ship voyage, consult *Fodor's FYI: Plan & Enjoy Your Cruise* (available in bookstores everywhere).

🛈 Cruise Lines American Canadian Caribbean Line 🕮 Box 368, Warren, RI 02885 ☎ 401/247-0955 or 800/556-7450 ⊕ www.accl-smallships.com. Carnival Cruise Lines ✉ 3655 N.W. 87th Ave., Miami, FL 33178 ☎ 305/599-2600 or 888/227-6482 ⊕ www.carnival.com. Celebrity Cruises ✉ 1050 Caribbean Way, Miami, FL 33122 ☎ 305/539-6000 or 800/437-1111 ⊕ www.celebritycruises.com. Clipper Cruise Line ✉ 11969 Westline Industrial Dr., St. Louis, MO 63146 ☎ 314/655-6700 or 800/325-0010 ⊕ www.clippercruise.com. Costa Cruise Lines ✉ 200 South Park Rd., Suite 200 Hollywood, FL 33021 ☎ 800/327-2537 ⊕ www.costacruises.com. Crystal Cruises ✉ 2049 Century Park E, Suite 1400, Los Angeles, CA 90067 ☎ 310/785-9300 or 800/446-6620 ⊕ www.crystalcruises.com. Cunard Line ✉ 6100 Blue Lagoon Dr., Suite 400, Miami, FL 33126 ☎ 305/463-3000 or 800/7-CUNARD ⊕ www.cunardline.com. Disney Cruise Line 🕮 Box 10210, Lake Buena Vista, FL 32880 ☎ 407/566-3500 ⊕ www.disneycruise.com. Holland America Line ✉ 300 Elliott Ave. W, Seattle, WA 98119 ☎ 206/

281-3535 or 800/426-6593 ⊕ www.hollandamerica.com. Norwegian Cruise Line ✉ 7665 Corporate Center Dr., Miami, FL 33126 ☎ 305/436-4000 or 800/327-7030 ⊕ www.ncl.com. Princess Cruises ✉ 24303 Town Center Dr. Santa Clarita, CA 91355 ☎ 661/753-0000 or 800/774-6237 ⊕ www.princesscruises.com. Radisson Seven Seas Cruises ✉ 600 Corporate Dr., Suite 410, Fort Lauderdale, FL 33334 ☎ 954/776-6123 or 800/477-7500 ⊕ www.rssc.com. Regal Cruises ✉ 300 Regal Cruises Way, Palmetto, FL 34221 ☎ 941/721-7300 or 800/270-7245 ⊕ www.regalcruises.com. Royal Caribbean International ✉ 1050 Caribbean Way, Miami, FL 33132 ☎ 305/539-6000 or 800/327-6700 ⊕ www.royalcaribbean.com. Seabourn Cruise Line ✉ 6100 Blue Lagoon Dr., Suite 400, Miami, FL 33126 ☎ 305/463-3000 or 800/929-9391 ⊕ www.seabourn.com. Silversea Cruises ✉ 110 E. Broward Blvd., Fort Lauderdale, FL 33301 ☎ 954/522-4477 or 800/774-9996 ⊕ www.silversea.com. Star Clippers ✉ 4101 Salzedo St., Coral Gables, FL 33146 ☎ 305/442-0550 or 800/442-0551 ⊕ www.star-clippers.com. Windjammer Barefoot Cruises ✉ 1759 Bay Rd., Miami Beach, FL 33139 ☎ 305/672-6453 or 800/327-2601 ⊕ www.windjammer.com. Windstar Cruises ✉ 300 Elliott Ave. W, Seattle, WA 98119 ☎ 206/281-3535, 800/258-7245, or 800/544-0443 ⊕ www.windstarcruises.com.

🛈 Organizations Cruise Lines International Association (CLIA) ✉ 500 5th Ave., Suite 1407, New York, NY 10110 ☎ 212/921-0066 ⊕ www.cruising.org.

CUSTOMS & DUTIES

When shopping abroad, **keep receipts** for all purchases. Upon reentering the country, **be ready to show customs officials what you've bought.** Pack purchases together in an easily accessible place. If you think a duty is incorrect, appeal the assessment. If you object to the way your clearance was handled, note the inspector's badge number. In either case, first ask to see a supervisor. If the problem isn't resolved, write to the appropriate authorities, beginning with the port director at your point of entry.

IN AUSTRALIA

Australian residents who are 18 or older may bring home A$400 worth of souvenirs and gifts (including jewelry), 250 cigarettes or 250 grams of cigars or other tobacco products, and 1,125 ml of alcohol (including wine, beer, and spirits). Residents under 18 may bring back A$200 worth of goods. Members of the same family traveling together may pool their allowances. Prohibited items include meat products. Seeds, plants, and fruits need to be declared upon arrival.

Australian Customs Service Regional Director, Box 8, Sydney, NSW 2001 02/9213-2000 or 1300/363263; 02/9364-7222 or 1800/803-006 quarantine-inquiry line 02/9213-4043 www.customs.gov.au.

IN CANADA

Canadian residents who have been out of Canada for at least seven days may bring in C$750 worth of goods duty-free. If you've been away fewer than seven days but more than 48 hours, the duty-free allowance drops to C$200. If your trip lasts 24 to 48 hours, the allowance is C$50. You may not pool allowances with family members. Goods claimed under the C$750 exemption may follow you by mail; those claimed under the lesser exemptions must accompany you. Alcohol and tobacco products may be included in the seven-day and 48-hour exemptions but not in the 24-hour exemption. If you meet the age requirements of the province or territory through which you reenter Canada, you may bring in, duty-free, 1.5 liters of wine or 1.14 liters (40 imperial ounces) of liquor or 24 12-ounce cans or bottles of beer or ale. Also, if you meet the local age requirement for tobacco products, you may bring in, duty-free, 200 cigarettes and 50 cigars. Check ahead of time with the Canada Customs and Revenue Agency or the Department of Agriculture for policies regarding meat products, seeds, plants, and fruits.

You may send an unlimited number of gifts (only one gift per recipient, however) worth up to C$60 each duty-free to Canada. Label the package UNSOLICITED GIFT—VALUE UNDER $60. Alcohol and tobacco are excluded.

Canada Customs and Revenue Agency 2265 St. Laurent Blvd., Ottawa, Ontario K1G 4K3 204/983-3500, 506/636-5064, or 800/461-9999 www.ccra.gc.ca.

IN THE CARIBBEAN

Although customs inspectors in some countries inspect all baggage to allay their concerns about smuggling or drug running, many islands wave those tourists who have no goods to declare through customs inspections with only a cursory question or two. Exceptions include major hubs within the Caribbean, such as Jamaica, Puerto

Rico, and Antigua. If you're yachting through the islands, note that harbor customs are often thorough, as well.

These rules generally apply throughout the Caribbean: you are limited to bringing *in* 2 liters of alcohol, two cartons of cigarettes, and a reasonable amount of duty-free goods for your personal use. More than that, and you'll be asked to pay a hefty import tax.

IN NEW ZEALAND

All homeward-bound residents may bring back NZ$700 worth of souvenirs and gifts; passengers may not pool their allowances, and children can claim only the concession on goods intended for their own use. For those 17 or older, the duty-free allowance also includes 4.5 liters of wine or beer; one 1,125-ml bottle of spirits; and either 200 cigarettes, 250 grams of tobacco, 50 cigars, *or* a combination of the three up to 250 grams. Meat products, seeds, plants, and fruits must be declared upon arrival to the Agricultural Services Department.

New Zealand Customs Head office: The Customhouse, 17-21 Whitmore St., Box 2218, Wellington 09/300-5399 or 0800/428-786 www.customs.govt.nz.

IN THE U.K.

Caribbean nations—even those that are *départements* of France and use the euro as their offical currency—are not part of the European Union (EU) with regard to customs. From countries outside the European Union, including those in the Caribbean, you may bring home, duty-free, 200 cigarettes or 50 cigars; 1 liter of spirits or 2 liters of fortified or sparkling wine or liqueurs; 2 liters of still table wine; 60 ml of perfume; 250 ml of toilet water; plus £145 worth of other goods, including gifts and souvenirs. Prohibited items include meat products, seeds, plants, and fruits.

HM Customs and Excise Portcullis House, 21 Cowbridge Rd. E, Cardiff CF11 9SS 0845/010-9000 or 0208/929-0152; 0208/929-6731 or 0208/910-3602 complaints www.hmce.gov.uk.

IN THE U.S.

U.S. residents who have been out of the country for at least 48 hours may bring home, for personal use, $800 worth of foreign goods duty-free, as long as they haven't used the $800 allowance or any part of it in the past 30 days. In the Caribbean, the $800 exemption applies to Anguilla, the Cayman Islands, Guadeloupe, Martinique, St. Barths, St. Martin (the French side only), and the Turks and Caicos Islands. You may bring back 1 liter of alcohol (for travelers 21 and older), 200 cigarettes, and 100 non-Cuban cigars. Family members from the same household who are traveling together may pool their $800 personal exemptions. For fewer than 48 hours, the duty-free allowance drops to $200, which may include 50 cigarettes, 10 non-Cuban cigars, and 150 ml of alcohol (or 150 ml of perfume containing alcohol). The $200 allowance cannot be combined with other individuals' exemptions, and if you exceed it, the full value of all the goods will be taxed. Antiques, which the U.S. Bureau of Customs and Border Protection defines as objects more than 100 years old, enter duty-free, as do original works of art done entirely by hand, including paintings, drawings, and sculptures. This doesn't apply to folk art or handicrafts, which are in general dutiable.

You may also send packages home duty-free, with a limit of one parcel per addressee per day (except alcohol or tobacco products or perfume worth more than $5). You can mail up to $200 worth of goods for personal use; label the package PERSONAL USE and attach a list of its contents and their retail value. If the package contains your used personal belongings, mark it AMERICAN GOODS RETURNED to avoid paying duties. You may send up to $100 worth of goods as a gift; mark the package UNSOLICITED GIFT. Mailed items do not affect your duty-free allowance on your return.

To avoid paying duty on foreign-made high-ticket items you already own and will take on your trip, register them with Customs before you leave the country. Consider filing a Certificate of Registration for laptops, cameras, watches, and other digital devices identified with serial numbers or other permanent markings; you can keep the certificate for other trips. Otherwise, bring a sales receipt or insurance form to show that you owned the item before you left the United States.

A different exemption, lower than the standard $800 exemption, applies to the 24 countries in the Caribbean Basin Initiative (CBI)—including Antigua and Barbuda, Aruba, Barbados, Bonaire, the British Virgin Islands, Curaçao, Dominica, the Dominican Republic, Grenada, Jamaica, Montserrat, Saba, St. Eustius, St. Kitts and Nevis, St. Lucia, St. Maarten (the Dutch side only), St. Vincent and the Grenadines, and Trinidad and Tobago. U.S. residents who have been out of the country for at least 48 hours may bring home $600 worth of foreign goods duty-free, as long as they have not used the $600 allowance or any part of it in the past 30 days. If you visit a CBI country and a non-CBI country, you may bring in $800 worth of goods duty-free, but no more than $600 may be from a CBI country.

If you're returning from the U.S. Virgin Islands (USVI), a U.S. insular possession, the duty-free allowance is $1,200. If your travel included the USVI and another country—say, the Dominican Republic—the $1,200 allowance still applies, but at least $600 worth of goods has to be from the USVI.

U.S. residents 21 and older may bring back 2 liters of alcohol duty-free, as long as one of the liters was produced in a CBI country. In addition, regardless of your age, you are allowed 200 cigarettes and 100 non-Cuban cigars. If you visit the USVI, you are allowed 1,000 cigarettes (all must be acquired in the USVI); you also are allowed 5 liters of alcohol, but at least 1 liter must be from the USVI. Antiques, which the U.S. Bureau of Customs and Border Protection defines as objects more than 100 years old, enter duty-free, as do original works of art done entirely by hand, including paintings, drawings, and sculptures. This doesn't apply to folk art or handicrafts, which are in general dutiable. You may also send packages home duty-free, with a limit of one parcel per addressee per day (except alcohol or tobacco products or perfume worth more than $5). You can mail up to $200 worth of goods for personal use; label the package PERSONAL USE and attach a list of its contents and their retail value. If the package contains your used personal belongings, mark it AMERICAN GOODS RETURNED to avoid paying duties. You may send up to $100 worth of goods ($200 from the U.S. Virgin Islands) as a gift; mark the package UNSOLICITED GIFT. Mailed items do not affect your duty-free allowance on your return.

🔲 **U.S. Bureau of Customs and Border Protection** ✉ for inquiries and equipment registration, 1300

Pennsylvania Ave. NW, Washington, DC 20229 🌐 www.customs.gov ☎ 202/354-1000 ✉ for complaints, Customer Satisfaction Unit, 1300 Pennsylvania Ave. NW, Room 5.5D, Washington, DC 20229.

DINING

The Caribbean islands offer dining experiences that will delight any palate. You'll find French cuisine with exquisite service, lavish buffets featuring local dishes, fresh seafood served by the waterfront, Italian pasta with a modern twist, Chinese cuisine to eat in or take out, and vegetarian dishes of just-picked produce. Fast-food restaurants usually feature fried chicken, not burgers, but pizza is everywhere. The restaurants we list are the cream of the crop in each price category. Properties indicated by an ✕🏠 are lodging establishments whose restaurant warrants a special trip.

MEALS & SPECIALTIES

Give your taste buds a vacation and try local cuisine, which could be Spanish-style in Puerto Rico and the Dominican Republic, French creole in St. Lucia and Martinique, Indian in Trinidad, Indonesian in Aruba, spicy barbecue in Jamaica, and fresh seafood everywhere. Vegetarians can expect a treat, as the fresh fruit, vegetables, herbs, and spices—both usual and unusual—are plentiful.

Resort breakfasts are frequently lavish buffets that offer tropical fruits and fruit juices, cereal, fresh rolls and pastries, hot dishes (such as codfish, corned-beef hash, and potatoes), and prepared-to-order eggs, pancakes, and French toast. Lunch could be at a beachfront café or a picnic at a secluded cove. But dinner is the highlight, often combining the expertise of internationally trained chefs with local know-how and ingredients.

MEALTIMES

Expect breakfast to be served from 7:30 AM to 10 AM; lunch from noon to 2 PM or so; and dinner from 7 PM to about 10 PM—perhaps later on Spanish-heritage islands. Some restaurants have specific mealtimes; others serve continuously all day long. Unless otherwise noted, the restaurants listed in this guide are open daily for lunch and dinner.

PAYING

Major credit cards (Access, American Express, Barclaycard, Carte Blanche, Diners Club, Discover, EnRoute, Eurocard, MasterCard, and/or Visa) are accepted in most restaurants. Exceptions are noted in the reviews.

RESERVATIONS & DRESS

Reservations are always a good idea; we mention them only when they're essential or not accepted. Book as far ahead as you can, and reconfirm as soon as you arrive. (Large parties should always call ahead to check the reservations policy.) We mention dress only when men are required to wear a jacket or a jacket and tie. Shorts and T-shirts at dinner and beach attire anytime are universally frowned upon in restaurants throughout the Caribbean.

WINE, BEER & SPIRITS

The Caribbean is where "de rum come from," so rum is the base of most cocktails—often fruity, festive ones that really pack a punch. Many islands also have their own breweries, and the local beers are light and refreshing—perfect for hot summer afternoons at the beach.

DISABILITIES & ACCESSIBILITY

Very few attractions and sights in the Caribbean are equipped with ramps, elevators, or wheelchair-accessible toilets. Exceptions include places on Puerto Rico and the USVI, which must abide by the Americans with Disabilities Act—although not all facilities are well equipped.

LODGING

Resorts in hilly or mountainous regions are particularly difficult for travelers with disabilities. Many hotels and resorts have accessible ground-floor guest rooms; others, particularly newer ones, offer some guest rooms with extra-wide doors and bathrooms with grab bars and easily accessible shower stalls. Some hotels may also help arrange rentals of special equipment. Be sure to make your special needs known when reserving your room.

RESERVATIONS

When discussing accessibility with an operator or reservations agent, **ask hard questions.** Are there any stairs, inside *or* out?

Are there grab bars next to the toilet *and* in the shower/tub? How wide is the doorway to the room? To the bathroom? For the most extensive facilities meeting the latest legal specifications, **opt for newer accommodations.** If you reserve through a toll-free number, consider also calling the hotel's local number to confirm the information from the central reservations office. Get confirmation in writing when you can.

TRANSPORTATION

At most Caribbean airports, passengers board and disembark aircraft directly from and onto the tarmac, which requires negotiating a steep staircase. Puerto Rico is one exception, although even there some small planes can't use the connected jetways. It can be a rather long walk to immigration, customs, and the airport exit. Aircraft operated by U.S. carriers must provide accessible lavatories, movable aisle armrests (on planes with 30 or more seats), an onboard wheelchair (on planes with 60 or more seats), and space to store a passenger's own folding wheelchair in the cabin (on planes with 100 or more seats). If you require a special in-flight accommodation (e.g., respirator hook-up), the airline may require up to 48 hours' advance notice. Be sure to **request wheelchairs or escort assistance when booking your flight.**

🔁 Complaints Aviation Consumer Protection Division (⇨ Air Travel) for airline-related problems. **Departmental Office of Civil Rights** ⊠ for general inquiries, U.S. Department of Transportation, S-30, 400 7th St. SW, Room 10215, Washington, DC 20590 ☎ 202/366-4648 ╬ 202/366-9371 ⊕ www.dot. gov/ost/docr/index.htm. **Disability Rights Section** ⊠ NYAV, U.S. Department of Justice, Civil Rights Division, 950 Pennsylvania Ave. NW, Washington, DC 20530 ☎ ADA information line 202/514-0301 or 800/514-0301; 202/514-0383 or 800/514-0383 TTY ⊕ www.ada.gov. **U.S. Department of Transportation Hotline** ☎ for disability-related air-travel problems, 800/778-4838 or 800/455-9880 TTY.

TRAVEL AGENCIES

In the United States, the Americans with Disabilities Act requires that travel firms serve the needs of all travelers. Some agencies specialize in working with people with disabilities.

🔁 Travelers with Mobility Problems Access Adventures ⊠ 206 Chestnut Ridge Rd., Scottsville, NY 14624 ☎ 585/889-9096 ✎ dltravel@prodigy.net, run by a former physical-rehabilitation counselor. **Accessible Vans of America** ⊠ 9 Spielman Rd., Fairfield, NJ 07004 ☎ 877/282-8267; 973/808-9709 reservations ╬ 973/808-9713 ⊕ www. accessiblevans.com. **Flying Wheels Travel** ⊠ 143 W. Bridge St., Box 382, Owatonna, MN 55060 ☎ 507/451-5005 ╬ 507/451-1685 ⊕ www. flyingwheelstravel.com.

🔁 Travelers with Developmental Disabilities New Directions ⊠ 5276 Hollister Ave., Suite 207, Santa Barbara, CA 93111 ☎ 805/967-2841 or 888/967-2841 ╬ 805/964-7344 ⊕ www.newdirectionstravel.com. **Sprout** ⊠ 893 Amsterdam Ave., New York, NY 10025 ☎ 212/222-9575 or 888/222-9575 ╬ 212/222-9768 ⊕ www.gosprout.org.

DISCOUNTS & DEALS

Visit during the off-season, when prices usually plummet at even the glitziest resorts; you'll realize savings of up to 50% between April 15 and December 15. Moreover, you'll usually find fewer tourists, it's easier to rent a car, the sea tends to be calmer and clearer, and you might stumble onto local festivals.

Remember that your budget will go further on some islands (Dominica or Saba, for example) than on others (St. Barths or Anguilla). And more developed islands (St. Thomas, St. Maarten/St. Martin, Aruba, Puerto Rico, Jamaica, Grand Cayman) tend to be more competitive and creative in their package pricing. You'll also find that smaller hotels and guest houses or those that are a short walk from the beach offer very pleasant accommodations that are priced considerably lower than their larger, beachfront neighbors.

Be a smart shopper and **compare all your options** before making decisions. A plane ticket bought with a promotional coupon from travel clubs, coupon books, and direct-mail offers or purchased on the Internet may not be cheaper than the least expensive fare from a discount ticket agency. And always keep in mind that what you get is just as important as what you save.

DISCOUNT RESERVATIONS

To save money, **look into discount reservations services** with Web sites and toll-free numbers, which use their buying power to get a better price on hotels, airline tickets (⇨ Air Travel), even car rentals. When booking a room, always **call the hotel's local toll-free number** (if one is available) rather than the central reservations number—you'll often get a better price. Always ask about special packages or corporate rates.

When shopping for the best deal on hotels and car rentals, **look for guaranteed exchange rates,** which protect you against a falling dollar. With your rate locked in, you won't pay more, even if the price goes up in the local currency.
⚡ Airline Tickets Air 4 Less ☎ 800/247-4537; low-fare specialist.
⚡ Hotel Rooms Accommodations Express ☎ 800/444-7666 or 800/277-1064 ⊕ www.accommodationsexpress.com. **Hotels.com** ☎ 800/246-8357 or 214/369-1246 ⊕ www.hotels.com. **Quikbook** ☎ 800/789-9887 ⊕ www.quikbook.com. **Turbotrip.com** ☎ 800/473-7829 ⊕ www.turbotrip.com.

PACKAGE DEALS

Don't confuse packages and guided tours. When you buy a package, you travel on your own just as though you had planned the trip yourself. Fly/drive packages, which combine airfare and car rental, are often a good deal. In cities, ask the local visitor's bureau about hotel packages that include tickets to major museum exhibits or other special events.

DIVING

The Caribbean offers some of the best scuba diving in the world. The waters around Bonaire's entire coast, for instance, are a protected marine park, with scores of dive sites accessible from the beach. The Cayman Islands, Turks and Caicos, the British Virgin Islands, St. Lucia, Dominica, and St. Vincent and the Grenadines also offer world-class diving experiences. The water throughout the Caribbean is crystal-clear, often with visibility up to 200 ft, and the quantity and variety of marine life is astounding.

Resorts often offer guests introductory scuba instruction in a pool, followed by a shallow dive; some hotels have on-site dive shops. All shops offer instruction and certification according to the standards set by either the National Association of Underwater Instructors (NAUI) or the Professional Association of Diving Instructors (PADI). Dive operators offer day and night dives to wrecks, reefs, and underwater walls.

DIVERS ALERT

Don't fly within 24 hours after scuba diving.
⚡ NAUI Worldwide ⊘ Box 89789, 1232 Tech Blvd., Tampa, FL 33689 ☎ 813/628-6284 or 800/553-6284 ⊕ www.naui.org. **PADI** ✉ 30151 Tomas St., Rancho Santa Margarita, CA 92688 ☎ 800/729-7234 or 949/858-7234 ⊕ www.padi.com ✉ 3771 Jacombs Rd., Bldg. C, #535, Richmond, British Columbia, Canada, V6V 2L9 ☎ 604/273-0277 or 800/565-8130 ✉ Unit 7, St. Philip's Central, Albert Rd., St. Philip's, Bristol, United Kingdom BS2 0PD ☎ 0117/300-7234 ✉ Unit 3, Skyline Pl., French's Forest, Sydney, NSW, Australia 2086 ☎ 2/9451-2300.

ECOTOURISM

Travelers are being lured to the Caribbean as much by the natural beauty of beaches, rain forests, and even desertscapes (on Aruba or Bonaire) as by the fancy resort life. Island governments are becoming increasingly aware of the value of their unique natural resources and are continuing to create national parks, bird sanctuaries, and marine preserves. For example, Bonaire's entire coast is a national marine park, its northern third is a nature preserve, and its southern third a protected salt flat. Two-thirds of St. John, USVI, is national parkland.

Dominica, the Dominican Republic, Grenada, Guadeloupe, Puerto Rico, Saba, St. Vincent, and St. Lucia are other Caribbean leaders in environmental awareness, each with vast forest preserves and hiking trails. Botanical gardens welcome visitors on St. Lucia, St. Vincent, Barbados, and many other islands. Nearly all islands have special programs, hikes, and tours that promote a better understanding of and a deeper appreciation for nature.

ELECTRICITY

On many islands the electric current is 110–120 volts alternating current (AC), and wall outlets take the same two-prong plugs found in the United States. Exceptions include the French islands and those with a British heritage. Check with your hotel about current when making reservations. If the current isn't compatible with your appliances, bring a converter and an adapter. With dual-voltage items (such as many laptop computers), you'll need only an adapter. Some hotels will lend adapter plugs to guests for the duration of their stay. Many establishments also have hair dryers and irons either in their rooms or available for borrowing, so you can leave yours at home. Don't use the 110-volt outlets marked FOR SHAVERS ONLY for high-wattage appliances such as blow-dryers.

FURTHER READING

Caribbean Style (Crown Publishers) is a coffee-table book with magnificent photographs of the interiors and exteriors of homes and buildings in the Caribbean. Short stories—some dark, some full of laughs—about life in the southern Caribbean made *Easy in the Islands,* by Bob Schacochis, a National Book Award winner. Schacochis has an ear for local patois and an eye for the absurd. In *Coming About: A Family Passage at Sea,* author Susan Tyler Hitchcock details her family's adventures sailing for nine months in the Bahamas and the Caribbean; it's an intimate look at the islands and a wonderful meditation on marriage and family. Thinking of running away and starting a business on a sun-drenched island? *A Trip to the Beach* by Robert and Melinda Blanchard is the ultimate inspiration. This funny, adventurous tale of how the Blanchards moved to Anguilla, started a restaurant, and learned innumerable lessons (including how to liberate fresh ingredients from the customs warehouse) will have you fantasizing about your own escape. To familiarize yourself with the sights, smells, and sounds of the West Indies, pick up Jamaica Kincaid's *Annie John,* a richly textured coming-of-age novel about a girl growing up on Antigua. The short stories in *At the Bottom of the River,* also by Kincaid, depict island mysteries and manners.

Omeros is Nobel Prize–winning St. Lucian poet Derek Walcott's imaginative Caribbean retelling of the *Odyssey.* Anthony C. Winkler's novels, *The Great Yacht Race, The Lunatic,* and *The Painted Canoe,* provide scathingly witty glimpses into Jamaica's class structure. *Wide Sargasso Sea,* by Dominica's Jean Rhys, is a provocative novel set in Jamaica and Dominica that recounts the early life of the first wife of Edward Rochester (pre–*Jane Eyre*). James Michener depicted the islands' diversity in his novel *Caribbean.* To probe island cultures more deeply, read Trinidad's V. S. Naipaul, particularly his *Guerrillas, The Loss of El Dorado,* and

The Enigma of Arrival; Eric Williams's *From Columbus to Castro;* and Michael Paiewonsky's *Conquest of Eden.*

Though it was written decades ago, Herman Wouk's hilarious *Don't Stop the Carnival* remains as fresh as ever in its depiction of the trials and tribulations of running a small Caribbean hotel. Mystery lovers should pick up a copy of Agatha Christie's *A Caribbean Mystery.* And kids might enjoy reading the Hardy Boys mystery *The Caribbean Cruise Caper.* If you're keen on specific subjects, such as history, cuisine, folklore, bird-watching, or diving, you'll find wonderful books by local authors on each island.

GAY & LESBIAN TRAVEL

Some Caribbean islands are more welcoming than others as travel destinations for gays and lesbians. Puerto Rico is the most gay-friendly island in the Caribbean—and the only one with extensive gay-oriented nightlife. San Juan has gay and lesbian guest houses, bars, clubs, and two gay-popular beaches. The USVI are also a good choice. St. Thomas has a few gay bars and discos, and the West End of St. Croix has quietly become gay- and lesbian-friendly. St. Maarten has some gay nightlife as well as gay guest houses. Otherwise, the French and Dutch islands are the most tolerant of gay and lesbian travelers. Attitudes are changing, albeit incrementally. The Cayman Islands, which years ago banned a gay-chartered cruise ship, now makes it a point to emphasize that all visitors are welcome if they respect the islands' conservative sensibilities. This is good advice to follow throughout the Caribbean, where nearly every island frowns upon same-sex couples strolling hand in hand down a beach or street, beach attire is welcome only at the beach, and most public displays of affection (either straight or gay) are frowned upon. Upscale resorts for adults, where privacy and discretion are the norm, are often the most welcoming to gay and lesbian travelers, but individually rented villas, many of which have private pools, are another good option. Couples-only resorts throughout the Caribbean, such as the all-inclusive Sandals and Couples resorts, do not, as a rule, welcome same-sex couples.
🔲 **Different Roads Travel** ✉ 8383 Wilshire Blvd., Suite 520, Beverly Hills, CA 90211 ☎ 323/651-5557

or 800/429-8747 (Ext. 14 for both) 🖷 323/651-3678 ✉ lgernert@tzell.com. **Kennedy Travel** ✉ 130 W. 42nd St., Suite 401, New York, NY 10036 ☎ 212/840-8659 or 800/237-7433 🖷 212/730-2269 ⊕ www. kennedytravel.com. **Now, Voyager** ✉ 4406 18th St., San Francisco, CA 94114 ☎ 415/626-1169 or 800/255-6951 🖷 415/626-8626 ⊕ www.nowvoyager. com. **Skylink Travel and Tour** ✉ 1455 N. Dutton Ave., Suite A, Santa Rosa, CA 95401 ☎ 707/546-9888 or 800/225-5759 🖷 707/636-0951; serving lesbian travelers.

GUIDEBOOKS

Plan well and you won't be sorry. Guidebooks are excellent tools—and you can take them with you. You may want to check out the color-photo-illustrated *Fodor's Exploring Caribbean,* thorough on culture and history, and *Fodor's Caribbean Ports of Call,* a primer for cruisers—both available at on-line retailers and bookstores everywhere.

HEALTH

Health-care standards vary from island to island. The staff at your hotel can recommend a doctor, dentist, clinic, or hospital should a need arise. Sometimes, particularly at family resorts, a nurse is on-site during the day and a doctor is on call. Doctor visits, incidentally, can be costly—even on islands where the general cost of living would make you think otherwise. Doctors and hospitals may require cash payment or take a major credit card; Medicare, Medicaid, and many U.S. medical insurance policies are not valid outside the U.S.

DIVERS' ALERT

Do not fly within 24 hours of scuba diving. For more information, *see* Diving.

FOOD & DRINK

Traveler's diarrhea, caused by eating contaminated fruit or vegetables or drinking contaminated water, isn't a big problem in the Caribbean, but it does occur. So **watch what you eat.** Avoid ice, uncooked food, and unpasteurized milk and milk products, and **drink only bottled water** or water that has been boiled for several minutes, even when brushing your teeth. Mild cases may respond to Imodium (known generically as loperamide) or Pepto-Bismol, both of which can be purchased over the counter. Drink plenty of purified water or tea—

chamomile is a good folk remedy. In severe cases, rehydrate yourself with a salt-sugar solution (½ teaspoon salt and 4 tablespoons sugar per quart of water).

MEDICAL PLANS

No one plans to get sick while traveling, but it happens, so **consider signing up with a medical-assistance company.** Members get doctor referrals, emergency evacuation or repatriation, hot lines for medical consultation, cash for emergencies, and other assistance.

🚹 **International SOS Assistance** ⊕ www. internationalsos.com ✉ 8 Neshaminy Interplex, Suite 207, Trevose, PA 19053 ☎ 215/245-4707 or 800/523-6586 🖷 215/244-9617 ✉ Landmark House, Hammersmith Bridge Rd., 6th floor, London, W6 9DP ☎ 20/8762-8008 🖷 20/8748-7744 ✉ 12 Chemin Riantbosson, 1217 Meyrin 1, Geneva, Switzerland ☎ 22/785-6464 🖷 22/785-6424 ✉ 331 N. Bridge Rd., 17-00, Odeon Towers, Singapore 188720 ☎ 6338-7800 🖷 6338-7611.

OVER-THE-COUNTER REMEDIES

Island drug stores and supermarkets are well stocked with familiar over-the-counter medicines and other health products that you might need. If you don't see precisely what you want, ask the pharmacist to recommend an appropriate substitute. If you can only use a specific or an uncommon medicine, be sure to bring a sufficient supply with you.

PESTS & OTHER HAZARDS

The major health risk in the Caribbean is sunburn or sunstroke. Having a long-sleeve shirt, a hat, and long pants or a beach wrap available is essential on a boat, for midday at the beach, and whenever you go out sightseeing. **Use sunscreen** with an SPF of at least 15—especially if your complexion is fair—and apply it liberally on your nose, ears, and other sensitive and exposed areas. **Make sure the sunscreen is waterproof** if you're engaging in water sports, **limit your sun time** for the first few days, and **drink plenty of liquids,** monitoring intake of caffeine and alcohol, which hasten the dehydration process.

Even experienced swimmers should **exercise caution in waters on the windward (Atlantic Ocean) side of the islands.** The unseen currents, powerful waves, strong undertows, and rocky bottoms can be extremely dangerous—and lifeguards are rare. Even in the calmest water, **watch out for black,**

spiny sea urchins; stepping on one is guaranteed to be painful for quite some time.

The small lizards native to the islands are harmless (and actually keep down the bug population), and poisonous snakes are hard to find, although you should exercise caution while bird-watching in Trinidad. **Beware of the manchineel tree,** which grows near the beach and has green applelike fruit that is poisonous and bark and leaves that can burn the skin. The worst insect problem may well be the tiny no-see-ums (sand flies) that appear after a rain, near swampy ground, and around sunset; mosquitoes can also be annoying. **Bring along a good repellent.**

SHOTS & MEDICATIONS

No special shots or vaccinations are required for Caribbean destinations.

🔢 Health Warnings **National Centers for Disease Control and Prevention (CDC)** ⊠ National Center for Infectious Diseases, Division of Quarantine, Travelers' Health, 1600 Clifton Rd. NE, Atlanta, GA 30333 ☎ 877/394-8747 international travelers' health line; 800/311-3435 other inquiries 🖷 888/232-3299 ⊕ www.cdc.gov/travel.

HOLIDAYS

Most islands observe an annual independence or other national day, certain Christian holidays (Easter weekend, various feast days, and Christmas), and New Year's Day. On many islands the biggest holiday of the year is the last day of Carnival (traditionally the Tuesday before Ash Wednesday), a festival that's no longer limited to mid-February. Banks, shops, and offices are closed on holidays.

INSURANCE

The most useful travel-insurance plan is a comprehensive policy that includes coverage for trip cancellation and interruption, default, trip delay, and medical expenses (with a waiver for preexisting conditions).

Without insurance you'll lose all or most of your money if you cancel your trip, regardless of the reason. Default insurance covers you if your tour operator, airline, or cruise line goes out of business. Trip-delay covers expenses that arise because of bad weather or mechanical delays. Study the fine print when comparing policies.

If you're traveling internationally, a key component of travel insurance is coverage for medical bills incurred if you get sick on the road. Such expenses aren't generally covered by Medicare or private policies. U.K. residents can buy a travel-insurance policy valid for most vacations taken during the year in which it's purchased (but check preexisting-condition coverage). British and Australian citizens need extra medical coverage when traveling overseas.

Always **buy travel policies directly from the insurance company;** if you buy them from a cruise line, airline, or tour operator that goes out of business you probably won't be covered for the agency or operator's default, a major risk. Before making any purchase, **review your existing health and home-owner's policies** to find what they cover away from home.

🔢 In the U.S. **Access America** ⊠ 6600 W. Broad St., Richmond, VA 23230 ☎ 800/284-8300 🖷 804/673-1491 or 800/346-9265 ⊕ www.accessamerica. com. **Travel Guard International** ⊠ 1145 Clark St., Stevens Point, WI 54481 ☎ 715/345-0505 or 800/826-1300 🖷 800/955-8785 ⊕ www.travelguard. com.

🔢 In the U.K. **Association of British Insurers** ⊠ 51 Gresham St., London EC2V 7HQ ☎ 020/7600-3333 🖷 020/7696-8999 ⊕ www.abi.org.uk. In Canada: **RBC Insurance** ⊠ 6880 Financial Dr., Mississauga, Ontario L5N 7Y5 ☎ 800/565-3129 🖷 905/813-4704 ⊕ www.rbcinsurance.com. In Australia: **Insurance Council of Australia** ⊠ Insurance Enquiries and Complaints, Level 3, 56 Pitt St., Sydney, NSW 2000 ☎ 1300/363683 or 02/9251-4456 🖷 02/9251-4453 ⊕ www.iecltd.com.au. In New Zealand: **Insurance Council of New Zealand** ⊠ Level 7, 111-115 Customhouse Quay, Box 474, Wellington ☎ 04/472-5230 🖷 04/473-3011 ⊕ www.icnz.org.nz.

LANGUAGE

It becomes obvious that the Caribbean's history is linked with that of European and African countries when you consider all the languages that are spoken on the islands. As for "official" languages, English is well represented (14 island nations), followed by Dutch (6 islands, though English is widely spoken), French (3 islands), and Spanish (3 islands). St. Maarten/St. Martin is split geographically, culturally, and linguistically— Dutch (as well as English) is spoken on one side, and French on the other.

You'll also find a variety of idiomatic expressions, West Indian lilts and patois, and French Creole dialects that transform the official languages. On both St. Lucia and

Dominica, for example, English is the official language, but most locals also speak a patois that's a mix of English, French, and African words; on French-speaking St. Barths, some people use the Norman dialect of their ancestors; and on the Dutch islands, you'll encounter perhaps the most worldly tongue of all, Papiamento—a mixture of African languages and Dutch, English, French, Portuguese, *and* Spanish. There are also places, such as Barbados, where early Irish and Scottish settlers affected the island accent; and in Trinidad, East Indian and Chinese arrivals have contributed to culture, food, and terminology.

LANGUAGES FOR TRAVELERS

A phrase book and language tapes or CDs can help get you started. *Fodor's French for Travelers and Fodor's Spanish for Travelers* (available at bookstores everywhere) are excellent.

LODGING

Decide whether you want a hotel on the leeward side of an island (with calm water, good for snorkeling and swimming) or the windward (with waves, good for surfing, not good for swimming). Decide, too, whether you want to pay the extra price for a room overlooking the ocean. At less expensive properties, location may mean a difference in price of only $10–$20 per room. At luxury resorts on pricey islands, however, it could amount to as much as $100 per room. Also **find out how close the property is to a beach.** At some hotels you can walk barefoot from your room onto the sand; others are across a road or a 10-minute drive away.

If you go to sleep early or are a light sleeper, **ask for a room away from the entertainment area.** Air-conditioning isn't a necessity on all islands, many of which are cooled by trade winds, but it can be a plus if you enjoy an afternoon snooze or are bothered by humidity. Breezes are best in second-floor rooms, particularly corner rooms. If you like to sleep without air-conditioning, make sure that windows can be opened and have screens. If you're staying away from the water, you'll want a ceiling fan. You'll likely notice a candle and box of matches in your room. In even the most luxurious resorts, there are times when things simply *don't* work; it's a fact of Caribbean life. And no matter how diligent the upkeep, humidity and salt air take their toll.

The lodgings we list are the cream of the crop in each price category. We always list the facilities that are available, but we don't specify whether they cost extra. When pricing accommodations, always ask what's included and what costs extra. Properties are assigned price categories based on the range between their least expensive standard double room at high season (excluding holidays) to the most expensive.

Assume that hotels operate on the **European Plan** (EP, with no meals) unless we specify that they use either the **Continental Plan** (CP, with a Continental breakfast), **Breakfast Plan** (BP, with a full breakfast), or the **Modified American Plan** (MAP, with breakfast and dinner) or are **All-inclusive** (including all meals, beverages, and most activities).

APARTMENT & VILLA & HOUSE RENTALS

If you want a home base that's roomy enough for a family and comes with cooking facilities, **consider a furnished rental.** These can save you money, especially if you're traveling with a group. Home-exchange directories sometimes list rentals as well as exchanges. 🇫 **At Home Abroad** ⊠ 405 E. 56th St., Suite 6H, New York, NY 10022 ☏ 212/421-9165 🖷 212/752-1591 ⊕ www.athomeabroadinc.com. **Blue Escapes** 🕿 Box 8376, Richmond, VA 23226 ☏ 804/497-7024 or 800/556-4801 ⊕ www.blueescapes.com. **Hideaways International** ⊠ 767 Islington St., Portsmouth, NH 03802 ☏ 603/430-4433 or 800/843-4433 🖷 603/430-4444 ⊕ www.hideaways.com, membership $129. **Vacation Home Rentals Worldwide** ⊠ 235 Kensington Ave., Norwood, NJ 07648 ☏ 201/767-9393 or 800/633-3284 🖷 201/767-5510 ⊕ www.vhrww.com. **Villanet** ⊠ 1251 N.W. 116th St., Seattle, WA 98177 ☏ 206/417-3444 or 800/964-1891 🖷 206/417-1832 ⊕ www.rentavilla.com. **Villas and Apartments Abroad** ⊠ 370 Lexington Ave., Suite 1401, New York, NY 10017 ☏ 212/897-5045 or 800/433-3020 🖷 212/897-5039 ⊕ www.ideal-villas.com. **Villas International** ⊠ 4340 Redwood Hwy., Suite D309, San Rafael, CA 94903 ☏ 415/499-9490 or 800/221-2260 🖷 415/499-9491 ⊕ www.villasintl.com. **WIMCO Villas & Hotels** 🕿 28 Pelham St., Newport, RI 23226 ☏ 401/849-8012 or 800/449-1553 ⊕ www.wimco.com.

CAMPING

Camping is a big draw on St. John, USVI, and many other islands have facilities if you want to fend for yourself and sleep under the stars. Some islands have no camping facilities at all, and in fact discourage campers.

HOME EXCHANGES

If you would like to exchange your home for someone else's, **join a home-exchange organization**, which will send you its updated listings of available exchanges for a year and will include your own listing in at least one of them. It's up to you to make specific arrangements.
🏠 HomeLink International ⌚ Box 47747, Tampa, FL 33647 ☎ 813/975-9825 or 800/638-3841 🖷 813/910-8144 ⊕ www.homelink.org; $110 yearly for a listing, on-line access, and catalog; $40 without catalog. **Intervac U.S.** ✉ 30 Corte San Fernando, Tiburon, CA 94920 ☎ 800/756-4663 🖷 415/435-7440 ⊕ www.intervacus.com; $105 yearly for a listing, on-line access, and a catalog; $50 without catalog.

HOTELS

All hotels included in this guide have rooms with private baths, unless otherwise noted. Major hotel chains listed below have properties on one or more of the islands.
🏨 Best Western ☎ 800/528-1234 ⊕ www.bestwestern.com. **Choice** ☎ 800/424-6423 ⊕ www.choicehotels.com. **Comfort Inn** ☎ 800/424-6423 ⊕ www.choicehotels.com. **Days Inn** ☎ 800/325-2525 ⊕ www.daysinn.com. **Embassy Suites** ☎ 800/362-2779 ⊕ www.embassysuites.com. **Four Seasons** ☎ 800/332-3442 ⊕ www.fourseasons.com. **Hilton** ☎ 800/445-8667 ⊕ www.hilton.com. **Holiday Inn** ☎ 800/465-4329 ⊕ www.sixcontinentshotels.com. **Hyatt Hotels & Resorts** ☎ 800/233-1234 ⊕ www.hyatt.com. **Inter-Continental** ☎ 800/327-0200 ⊕ www.intercontinental.com. **Marriott** ☎ 800/228-9290 ⊕ www.marriott.com. **Le Méridien** ☎ 800/543-4300 ⊕ www.lemeridien-hotels.com. **Radisson** ☎ 800/333-3333 ⊕ www.radisson.com. **Renaissance Hotels & Resorts** ☎ 800/468-3571 ⊕ www.renaissancehotels.com/. **Ritz-Carlton** ☎ 800/241-3333 ⊕ www.ritzcarlton.com. **Sheraton** ☎ 800/325-3535 ⊕ www.starwood.com/sheraton. **Westin Hotels & Resorts** ☎ 800/228-3000 ⊕ www.starwood.com/westin. **Wyndham Hotels & Resorts** ☎ 800/822-4200 ⊕ www.wyndham.com.

MAIL & SHIPPING

Airmail between Caribbean islands and cities in the United States or Canada takes 7–14 days; surface mail can take 4–6 weeks. Airmail to the United Kingdom takes 2–3 weeks, to Australia and New Zealand, 3–4 weeks.

OVERNIGHT SERVICES

Courier services (such as Airborne, FedEx, UPS, and others) operate throughout the Caribbean, although not every company serves each island. "Overnight" service is more likely to take two or more days, because of the limited number of flights on which packages can be shipped.

MONEY MATTERS

Prices throughout this guide are given for adults. Substantially reduced fees are almost always available for children, students, and senior citizens. For information on taxes, *see* Taxes. For island-specific information on banks, currency, service charges, taxes, and tipping in the Caribbean, *see* the A to Z sections *in* individual island chapters.

ATMS

Debit cards aren't widely used in the islands, although you can use bank cards and major credit cards to withdraw cash (in local currency) at automatic teller machines (ATMs). ATMs can be found on most islands at airports, cruise-ship terminals, bank branches, shopping centers, gas stations, and other convenient locations. Although ATM transaction fees may be higher abroad, the rates are excellent because they're based on wholesale rates offered only by major banks.

CREDIT CARDS

Major credit cards are widely accepted at hotels, restaurants, shops, car-rental agencies, other service providers, and ATM machines throughout the Caribbean. The only places that might not accept them are open-air markets or tiny shops in out-of-the-way villages.

It's smart to write down (and keep separate) the number(s) of the credit card(s) you're carrying and the toll-free number to call in case the card is lost or stolen.

Throughout this guide, the following abbreviations are used: **AE**, American Express; **D**, Discover; **DC**, Diners Club; **MC**, MasterCard; and **V**, Visa.

CURRENCY

The U.S. dollar is the official currency on Puerto Rico and the USVI, as well as the

British Virgin Islands. On Grand Cayman you will usually have a choice of Cayman or U.S. dollars when you take money out of an ATM, and may even be able to get change in U.S. dollars. On most other islands, U.S. paper currency (not coins) is usually accepted. When you pay in dollars, however, you'll almost always get change in local currency; so it's best to carry bills in small denominations. Canadian dollars and British pounds are occasionally accepted, but don't count on this as the norm. If you do need local currency (say, for a trip to one of the French islands), change money at a local bank for the best rate.

Travelers to the Caribbean from countries other than the United States might want to purchase a small amount of local currency (or U.S. dollars) before leaving home to pay for incidentals until you can get to a local bank.

CURRENCY EXCHANGE

For the most favorable rates, **change money through banks.** Although ATM transaction fees may be higher abroad than at home, ATM rates are excellent because they're based on wholesale rates offered only by major banks. You won't do as well at exchange booths in airports or rail and bus stations, in hotels, in restaurants, or in stores. To avoid lines at airport exchange booths, **get a bit of local currency before you leave home.**

⚡ International Currency Express ✉ 427 N. Camden Dr., Suite F, Beverly Hills, CA 90210 ☎ 888/278-6628 orders 📠 310/278-6410 🌐 www.foreignmoney.com. **Thomas Cook Currency Services** ☎ 800/287-7362 orders and retail locations 🌐 www.us.thomascook.com.

TRAVELER'S CHECKS

Do you need traveler's checks? It depends on where you're headed. If you're going to rural areas and small towns, go with cash; traveler's checks are best used in cities. Lost or stolen checks can usually be replaced within 24 hours. To ensure a speedy refund, buy your own traveler's checks—don't let someone else pay for them: irregularities like this can cause delays. The person who bought the checks should make the call to request a refund.

PACKING

Travel light. Dress on the islands is generally casual. Bring loose-fitting clothing

made of natural fabrics to see you through days of heat and humidity. Pack a beach cover-up, both to protect yourself from the sun and as something to wear to and from your hotel room. On all islands, bathing suits and immodest attire off the beach are frowned upon. A sun hat is advisable, but you don't have to pack one—inexpensive straw hats are available everywhere. For shopping and sightseeing, bring walking shorts, jeans, T-shirts, long-sleeve cotton shirts, slacks, and sundresses. Night-time dress can range from really informal to casually elegant, depending on the establishment. A tie is practically never required, but a jacket may be appropriate in the fanciest restaurants and casinos. You may need a light sweater or jacket for evenings and at higher altitudes.

Leave camouflage-pattern clothing at home. It's not permitted for civilians, even children, in some Caribbean countries and may be confiscated if worn.

If you're making one or more airline connections, it's smart to pack some toiletries, a change of clothes, and perhaps a bathing suit in your carry-on bag—just in case your checked luggage doesn't make the connection until a later flight (which may be the next day).

In your carry-on luggage, **pack an extra pair of eyeglasses or contact lenses and enough of any medication** you take to last a few days longer than the entire trip. You may also ask your doctor to write a spare prescription using the drug's generic name, as brand names may vary from country to country. In luggage to be checked, **never pack prescription drugs, valuables, or undeveloped film.** And don't forget to carry with you the addresses of offices that handle refunds of lost traveler's checks. Check *Fodor's How to Pack* (available at on-line retailers and bookstores everywhere) for more tips.

To avoid customs and security delays, carry medications in their original packaging. Don't pack any sharp objects in your carry-on luggage, including knives of any size or material, scissors, and corkscrews, or anything else that might arouse suspicion.

To avoid having your checked luggage chosen for hand inspection, don't cram bags full. The U.S. Transportation Security Administration suggests packing shoes on top and placing personal items you don't want touched in clear plastic bags.

CHECKING LUGGAGE

You're allowed to carry aboard one bag and one personal article, such as a purse or a laptop computer. Make sure what you carry on fits under your seat or in the overhead bin. Get to the gate early, so you can board as soon as possible, before the overhead bins fill up.

Baggage allowances vary by carrier, destination, and ticket class. On international flights you're usually allowed to check two bags weighing up to 70 pounds (32 kilograms) each, although a few airlines allow checked bags of up to 88 pounds (40 kilograms) in first class. Some international carriers don't allow more than 66 pounds (30 kilograms) per bag in business class and 44 pounds (20 kilograms) in economy. On domestic flights the limit may be 50 pounds (23 kilograms) per bag. Most airlines won't accept bags that weigh more than 100 pounds (45 kilograms) on domestic or international flights. Check baggage restrictions with your carrier before you pack.

Airline liability for baggage is limited to $2,500 per person on flights within the United States. On international flights it amounts to $9.07 per pound or $20 per kilogram for checked baggage (roughly $640 per 70-pound bag) and $400 per passenger for unchecked baggage. You can buy additional coverage at check-in for about $10 per $1,000 of coverage, but it often excludes a rather extensive list of items, shown on your airline ticket.

Before departure, **itemize your bags' contents** and their worth, and label the bags with your name, address, and phone number. (If you use your home address, cover it so potential thieves can't see it readily.) Include a label inside each bag and **pack a copy of your itinerary**. At check-in, **make sure each bag is correctly tagged** with the destination airport's three-letter code. Because some checked bags will be opened for hand inspection, the U.S. Transportation Security Administration recommends that you leave luggage unlocked or use the plastic locks offered at check-in. TSA screeners place an inspection notice inside searched bags, which are re-sealed with a special lock.

If your bag has been searched and contents are missing or damaged, file a claim with the TSA Consumer Response Center as soon as possible. If your bags arrive damaged or fail to arrive at all, file a written report with the airline before leaving the airport.

Interisland carriers often use small aircraft with limited space for both carry-on and checked baggage and with weight restrictions. Except for small personal bags that fit in the small overhead compartments or in the limited space under the seats, carry-on bags are often checked on the tarmac as you board and are stowed in the plane's baggage compartment. You retrieve the stowed bags on the tarmac when disembarking the plane. If you take very large or heavy luggage, it may have to follow on another flight, and its delivery can be very erratic.

Complaints U.S. Transportation Security Administration Consumer Response Center ☎ 866/289-9673 ⊕ www.tsa.gov.

PASSPORTS & VISAS

When traveling internationally, **carry your passport** even if you don't need one (it's always the best form of I.D.) and **make two photocopies of the data page** (one for someone at home and another for you, carried separately from your passport). If you lose your passport, promptly call the nearest embassy or consulate and the local police.

U.S. passport applications for children under age 14 require consent from both parents or legal guardians; both parents must appear together to sign the application. If only one parent appears, he or she must submit a written statement from the other parent authorizing passport issuance for the child. A parent with sole authority must present evidence of it when applying. Acceptable documentation includes the child's certified birth certificate listing only the applying parent, a court order specifically permitting this parent's travel with the child, or a death certificate for the non-applying parent. Application forms and instructions are available on the Web site of the U.S. State Department's Bureau of Consular Affairs (⊕ www.travel.state.gov).

ENTERING THE CARIBBEAN

On most Caribbean islands, vacationers who are U.S., Canadian, or British citizens must have either a valid passport or prove citizenship with a birth certificate (with a raised seal) as well as a government-issued photo I.D. Visitors from other countries must present a valid passport. All visitors must have a return or ongoing ticket.

PASSPORT OFFICES

The best time to apply for a passport or to renew is in fall and winter. Before any trip, check your passport's expiration date, and, if necessary, renew it as soon as possible. Current U.S. passport holders may renew by mail; forms are available at local post offices or can be downloaded and printed from the Internet.

7 Australian Citizens **Passports Australia** ☎ 131-232 ⊕ www.passports.gov.au.

7 Canadian Citizens **Passport Office** ✉ to mail in applications: 200 Promenade du Portage, Hull, Québec)8X 4B7 ☎ 819/994-3500 or 800/567-6868 ⊕ www.ppt.gc.ca.

7 New Zealand Citizens **New Zealand Passports Office** ☎ 0800/22-5050 or 04/474-8100 ⊕ www.passports.govt.nz.

7 U.K. Citizens **U.K. Passport Service** ☎ 0870/521-0410 ⊕ www.passport.gov.uk.

7 U.S. Citizens **National Passport Information Center** ☎ 900/225-5674 or 900/225-7778 TTY (calls are 55¢ per minute for automated service or $1.50 per minute for operator service); 888/362-8668 or 888/498-3648 TTY (calls are $5.50 each) ⊕ www.travel.state.gov.

REST ROOMS

Rest rooms in hotels, restaurants, and public buildings are, as a rule, clean and well equipped.

SAFETY

Don't wear a money belt or a waist pack, both of which peg you as a tourist. Distribute your cash and any valuables (including your credit cards and passport) between a deep front pocket, an inside jacket or vest pocket, and a hidden money pouch. Do not reach for the money pouch once you're in public.

Most Caribbean destinations are not particularly unsafe, but street crime is always a possibility where relatively affluent tourists mingle with significantly poorer locals. Crime can be a problem in the Caribbean, especially in large urban areas, but crimes—particularly violent ones—against tourists are still rare. You will avoid most problems by using common sense and simply being as cautious as you would at home, which means not walking alone in unfamiliar places (especially at

night), not going alone to deserted beaches, locking away valuables, and not flaunting expensive jewelry in public places. Additionally, don't swim alone in unfamiliar waters, and don't swim too far offshore; most beaches have no lifeguards.

WOMEN IN THE CARIBBEAN

If you carry a purse, choose one with a zipper and a thick strap that you can drape across your body; adjust the length so that the purse sits in front of you at or above hip level. (Don't wear a money belt or a waist pack.) Store only enough money in the purse to cover casual spending. Distribute the rest of your cash and any valuables between deep front pockets, inside jacket or vest pockets, and a concealed money pouch.

SENIOR-CITIZEN TRAVEL

To qualify for age-related discounts, **mention your senior-citizen status up front** when booking hotel reservations (not when checking out) and before you're seated in restaurants (not when paying the bill). Be sure to have identification on hand. When renting a car, ask about promotional car-rental discounts, which can be cheaper than senior-citizen rates.

7 Educational Programs **Elderhostel** ✉ 11 Ave. de Lafayette, Boston, MA 02111-1746 ☎ 877/426-8056, 978/323-4141 international callers, 877/426-2167 TTY ☐ 877/426-2166 ⊕ www.elderhostel.org. **Interhostel** ✉ University of New Hampshire, 6 Garrison Ave., Durham, NH 03824 ☎ 603/862-1147 or 800/733-9753 ☐ 603/862-1113 ⊕ www.learn.unh.edu.

SHOPPING

Shopping in the Caribbean can mean duty-free bargains on watches and jewelry, perfume, designer clothing, china and crystal, and other luxury goods from around the world. It can also mean buying locally produced straw items, wood carvings, original art, batik beachwear, clay pottery, spices, coffee, cigars, and rum.

Bargaining isn't expected (and is considered insulting) in shops, but at open-air markets and with street vendors it may be acceptable. Keep in mind, however, that selling handicrafts or home-grown produce may be a local person's only livelihood. When bargaining, consider the amount of work or effort involved and the item's value to you. Vendors don't set artificially high prices and then expect to bargain; they bargain so you'll buy from them instead of their neighbor.

KEY DESTINATIONS

On some islands, such as St. Maarten, St. Barths, St. Thomas, and Aruba, all shopping is duty-free. Other islands, like Barbados and St. Lucia, have certain shops or specific areas where you can purchase duty-free goods upon presentation of your passport and/or ongoing ticket; still others, such as Puerto Rico, St. Vincent, and Grenada, have very limited duty-free opportunities—one or two stores or just shops in the airport departure area.

SMART SOUVENIRS

Bring home a pantryful of spices from Grenada, pottery from Barbados, lace from Saba, woven grass mats from St. Vincent, cigars from the Dominican Republic and Puerto Rico, fashions made of hand-printed fabric from St. Lucia, Blue Mountain coffee from Jamaica, Carib straw baskets from Dominica, aloe from Aruba, Angostura bitters from Trinidad—and rum from just about everywhere. St. Maarten and St. Thomas offer the best prices for duty-free shopping on a large scale.

WATCH OUT

U.S. citizens returning home must consume tropical fruits and other produce, smoke those Cuban cigars, and (with rare exceptions) leave the bouquets of flowers behind before heading home.

STUDENTS IN THE CARIBBEAN

Hiking in the rain forest, scuba diving, boating, and other Caribbean activities and adventures seem made-to-order for students—and the cultural enrichment and historical perspective add depth to all that book learning. The Caribbean isn't as far out of a student's budget as you might expect. Summer, when most students have free time, is the least expensive time to travel to the Caribbean. All but the toniest islands, such as St. Barths, have inexpensive guest houses and small no-frills hotels. Tourist boards provide listings of these alternative lodgings on request. You're most likely to meet students from other countries in the French and Dutch West Indies, where many go for vacations or sabbaticals. Puerto Rico, Jamaica, Grenada, and Dominica, among others, have large resi-

dent international student populations at their universities. In many cases, your student I.D. card may provide access to their facilities, from the library to the cafeteria.

An alternative to individual travel is an educational program or expedition. Colleges and universities often sponsor programs that coincide with spring and summer breaks, as do independent—usually non-profit—organizations.
🛫 **STA Travel** ✉ 10 Downing St., New York, NY 10014 ☎ 212/627-3111 or 800/777-0112 📠 212/627-3387 🌐 www.sta.com. **Travel Cuts** ✉ 187 College St., Toronto, Ontario M5T 1P7, Canada ☎ 416/979-2406; 800/592-2887; 866/246-9762 in Canada 📠 416/979-8167 🌐 www.travelcuts.com.

TELEPHONES

Phone and fax service to and from the Caribbean is up to date and efficient. Phone cards are used throughout the islands; you can buy them (in various denominations) at many retail shops and convenience stores. Some must be used in special card phones, which are also widely available.

AREA & COUNTRY CODES

For island area and country codes, *see* the A to Z sections *in* individual island chapters. When calling home, the country code is 1 for the United States and Canada, 61 for Australia, 64 for New Zealand, and 44 for the United Kingdom.

LONG-DISTANCE SERVICES

AT&T, MCI, and Sprint access codes make calling long-distance relatively convenient, but you may find the local access number blocked in many hotel rooms. First ask the hotel operator to connect you. If the hotel operator balks, ask for an international operator, or dial the international operator yourself. One way to improve your odds of getting connected to your long-distance carrier is to travel with more than one company's calling card (a hotel may block Sprint, for example, but not MCI). If all else fails, call from a pay phone. On some islands served by Cable & Wireless, you can use your own cell phone if it is compatible with TDMA digital networks.

TIME

The Caribbean islands fall into two time zones. The Cayman Islands, Cuba, Haiti, Jamaica, and the Turks and Caicos Islands are all in the Eastern Standard Time zone, which is five hours earlier than Greenwich Mean Time (GMT). All other Caribbean islands are in the Atlantic Standard Time zone, which is one hour later than Eastern Standard or four hours earlier than GMT. However, during Daylight Savings Time, between April and October, Atlantic Standard is the same time as Eastern Daylight Time.

TOURS & PACKAGES

Because everything is prearranged on a prepackaged tour or independent vacation, you spend less time planning—and often get it all at a good price.

BOOKING WITH AN AGENT

Travel agents are excellent resources. But it's a good idea to collect brochures from several agencies, as some agents' suggestions may be influenced by relationships with tour and package firms that reward them for volume sales. If you have a special interest, **find an agent with expertise in that area**; the American Society of Travel Agents (ASTA; ⇨ Travel Agencies) has a database of specialists worldwide.

Make sure your travel agent knows the accommodations and other services of the place being recommended. Ask about the hotel's location, room size, beds, and whether it has a pool, room service, or programs for children, if you care about these. Has your agent been there in person or sent others whom you can contact?

Do some homework on your own, too: local tourism boards can provide information about lesser-known and small-niche operators, some of which may sell only direct.

BUYER BEWARE

Each year consumers are stranded or lose their money when tour operators—even large ones with excellent reputations—go out of business. So **check out the operator.** Ask several travel agents about its reputation, and try to **book with a company that has a consumer-protection program.** (Look for information in the company's brochure.) In the United States, members of the National Tour Association and the United States Tour Operators Association are required to set aside funds to cover payments and travel arrangements in the event that the company defaults. It's also a good idea to choose a company that participates in the American Society of Travel Agents' Tour Operator Program; ASTA will act as mediator in any disputes between you and your tour operator.

Remember that the more your package or tour includes, the better you can predict the ultimate cost of your vacation. Make sure you know exactly what is covered, and **beware of hidden costs.** Are taxes, tips, and transfers included? Entertainment and excursions? These can add up.

✈ Tour-Operator Recommendations **American Society of Travel Agents** (⇨ Travel Agencies). **National Tour Association** (NTA) ✉ 546 E. Main St., Lexington, KY 40508 ☎ 859/226-4444 or 800/682-8886 🌐 www.ntaonline.com. **United States Tour Operators Association** (USTOA) ✉ 275 Madison Ave., Suite 2014, New York, NY 10016 ☎ 212/599-6599 or 800/468-7862 🖶 212/599-6744 🌐 www.ustoa.com.

TRAVEL AGENCIES

A good travel agent puts your needs first. Look for an agency that has been in business at least five years, emphasizes customer service, and has someone on staff who specializes in your destination. In addition, **make sure the agency belongs to a professional trade organization.** The American Society of Travel Agents (ASTA)—the largest and most influential in the field with more than 20,000 members in some 140 countries—maintains and enforces a strict code of ethics and will step in to help mediate any agent-client disputes involving ASTA members if necessary. ASTA (whose motto is "Without a travel agent, you're on your own") also maintains a Web site that includes a directory of agents. (If a travel agency is also acting as your tour operator, see Buyer Beware in Tours and Packages.)

✈ Local Agent Referrals **American Society of Travel Agents** (ASTA) ✉ 1101 King St., Suite 200, Alexandria, VA 22314 ☎ 703/739-2782 or 800/965-2782 24-hr hot line 🖶 703/739-3268 🌐 www.astanet.com. **Association of British Travel Agents** ✉ 68-71 Newman St., London W1T 3AH ☎ 020/7637-2444 🖶 020/7637-0713 🌐 www.abtanet.com. **Association of Canadian Travel Agents** ✉ 130 Albert St., Suite 1705, Ottawa, Ontario K1P 5G4 ☎ 613/237-3657 🖶 613/237-7052 🌐 www.acta.ca. **Australian Federation of Travel Agents** ✉ Level 3, 309 Pitt St., Sydney, NSW 2000 ☎ 02/9264-3299 🖶 02/9264-1085 🌐 www.afta.com.au. **Travel Agents' Association of New Zealand** ✉ Level 5, Tourism and Travel House, 79 Boulcott St., Box 1888, Wellington 6001 ☎ 04/499-0104 🖶 04/499-0786 🌐 www.taanz.org.nz.

CONVERSIONS

DISTANCE

KILOMETERS/MILES

To change kilometers (km) to miles (mi), multiply km by .621. To change mi to km, multiply mi by 1.61.

km to mi		mi to km	
1 =	.62	1 =	1.6
2 =	1.2	2 =	3.2
3 =	1.9	3 =	4.8
4 =	2.5	4 =	6.4
5 =	3.1	5 =	8.1
6 =	3.7	6 =	9.7
7 =	4.3	7 =	11.3
8 =	5.0	8 =	12.9

METERS/FEET

To change meters (m) to feet (ft), multiply m by 3.28. To change ft to m, multiply ft by .305.

m to ft		ft to m	
1 =	3.3	1 =	.30
2 =	6.6	2 =	.61
3 =	9.8	3 =	.92
4 =	13.1	4 =	1.2
5 =	16.4	5 =	1.5
6 =	19.7	6 =	1.8
7 =	23.0	7 =	2.1
8 =	26.2	8 =	2.4

TEMPERATURE

METRIC CONVERSIONS

To change centigrade or Celsius (C) to Fahrenheit (F), multiply C by 1.8 and add 32. To change F to C, subtract 32 from F and multiply by .555.

°F	°C
0	-17.8
10	-12.2
20	-6.7
30	-1.1
32	0
40	+4.4
50	10.0
60	15.5
70	21.1
80	26.6
90	32.2
98.6	37.0
100	37.7

WEIGHT

KILOGRAMS/POUNDS

To change kilograms (kg) to pounds (lb), multiply kg by 2.20. To change lb to kg, multiply lb by .455.

kg to lb		lb to kg	
1 =	2.2	1 =	.45
2 =	4.4	2 =	.91
3 =	6.6	3 =	1.4
4 =	8.8	4 =	1.8
5 =	11.0	5 =	2.3
6 =	13.2	6 =	2.7
7 =	15.4	7 =	3.2
8 =	17.6	8 =	3.6

GRAMS/OUNCES

To change grams (g) to ounces (oz), multiply g by .035. To change oz to g, multiply oz by 28.4.

g to oz		oz to g	
1 =	.04	1 =	28
2 =	.07	2 =	57
3 =	.11	3 =	85
4 =	.14	4 =	114
5 =	.18	5 =	142
6 =	.21	6 =	170
7 =	.25	7 =	199
8 =	.28	8 =	227

LIQUID VOLUME

LITERS/U.S. GALLONS

To change liters (L) to U.S. gallons (gal), multiply L by .264. To change U.S. gal to L, multiply gal by 3.79.

L to gal		gal to L	
1 =	.26	1 =	3.8
2 =	.53	2 =	7.6
3 =	.79	3 =	11.4
4 =	1.1	4 =	15.2
5 =	1.3	5 =	19.0
6 =	1.6	6 =	22.7
7 =	1.8	7 =	26.5
8 =	2.1	8 =	30.3

CLOTHING SIZE

WOMEN'S CLOTHING

US	UK	EUR
4	6	34
6	8	36
8	10	38
10	12	40
12	14	42

WOMEN'S SHOES

US	UK	EUR
5	3	36
6	4	37
7	5	38
8	6	39
9	7	40

MEN'S SUITS

US	UK	EUR
34	34	44
36	36	46
38	38	48
40	40	50
42	42	52
44	44	54
46	46	56

MEN'S SHIRTS

US	UK	EUR
14½	14½	37
15	15	38
15½	15½	39
16	16	41
16½	16½	42
17	17	43
17½	17½	44

MEN'S SHOES

US	UK	EUR
7	6	39½
8	7	41
9	8	42
10	9	43
11	10	44½
12	11	46

VISITOR INFORMATION

Many islands have tourist-board offices in Canada, the United Kingdom, and the United States. Such boards can be good sources of general information, up-to-date calendars of events, and listings of hotels, restaurants, sights, and shops. The Caribbean Tourism Organization (CTO) is another resource, especially for information on the islands that have limited representation overseas. Learn more about foreign destinations by checking government-issued travel advisories and country information. For a broader picture, consider information from more than one country.

🔢 Caribbean-wide Tourist Information **CTO** ✉ 80 Broad St., New York, NY 10004 ☎ 212/635-9530 🖶 212/635-9511 ✉ 512 Duplex Ave., Toronto, Ontario M4R 2E3 ☎ 416/485-8724 🖶 416/485-8256 ✉ 42 Westminster Palace Gardens Artillery Row, London SW1P 1RR ☎ 0207/222-4335 🖶 0207/222-4325 ⊕ www.doitcaribbean.com.

🔢 Government Advisories **U.S. Department of State** ✉ Overseas Citizens Services Office, Room 4811, 2201 C St. NW, Washington, DC 20520 ☎ 202/647-5225 interactive hot line or 888/407-4747 ⊕ www.travel.state.gov; enclose a cover letter with your request and a business-size SASE. **Consular Affairs Bureau of Canada** ☎ 800/267-6788 or 613/944-6788 ⊕ www.voyage.gc.ca. **U.K. Foreign and Commonwealth Office** ✉ Travel Advice Unit, Consular Division, Old Admiralty Building, London SW1A 2PA ☎ 020/7008-0232 or 020/7008-0233 ⊕ www.

fco.gov.uk/travel. **Australian Department of Foreign Affairs and Trade** ☎ 02/6261-1299 Consular Travel Advice Faxback Service ⊕ www.dfat.gov.au. **New Zealand Ministry of Foreign Affairs and Trade** ☎ 04/439-8000 ⊕ www.mft.govt.nz.

WEB SITES

Do check out the World Wide Web when planning your trip. You'll find everything from weather forecasts to virtual tours of famous cities. Be sure to visit **Fodors.com** (⊕ www.fodors.com), a complete travel-planning site. You can research prices and book plane tickets, hotel rooms, rental cars, vacation packages, and more. In addition, you can post your pressing questions in the Travel Talk section. Other planning tools include a currency converter and weather reports, and there are loads of links to travel resources. For island-specific sites, *see* Visitor Information *in* the A to Z section at the end of each chapter.

🔢 **Caribbean Aviation Page** ⊕ www.caribbeanaviation.com. **Caribbean Daily News** ⊕ www.caribbeandaily.com **Caribbean Home Page** ⊕ www.caribinfo.com. **Caribbean Hotel Association** ⊕ www.caribbeantravel.com. **Caribbean news** ⊕ www.cananews.com. **Caribbean newspaper links** ⊕ www.caribbeannewspapers.com. **Caribbean Tourism Organization** ⊕ www.doitcaribbean.com. **Cruise Lines International Association** ⊕ www.cruising.org.

ANGUILLA

FODOR'S CHOICE
Cap Juluca, Maundays Bay
Malliouhana restaurant, Meads Bay
Shoal Bay Beach

HIGHLY RECOMMENDED

RESTAURANTS
Blanchard's, Meads Bay
Ferryboat Inn, Blowing Point
Hibernia, Island Harbour
Kemia, Maundays Bay
Old House, George Hill
Pimms, Maundays Bay

HOTELS
Allamanda Beach Club, Upper Shoal Bay Beach
Arawak Beach Inn, Island Harbour
Blue Waters, Shoal Bay West
Covecastles Villa Resort, Shoal Bay West
CuisinArt Resort & Spa, Rendezvous Bay
Malliouhana, Meads Bay
Paradise Cove, The Cove
Rendezvous Bay Hotel, Rendezvous Bay
Temenos, Long Bay

SIGHTS
Island Harbour

Many other great places enliven this area. For other favorites, look for the black stars as you read this chapter.

"But I arranged for lobster in advance," snarled the man at the beachfront table. "That was the whole point of coming here." The waitress tried to soothe him: "I'm sorry; we ran out of lobsters, but it's really no problem—I've talked to the manager." But her gracious assurances and charming West Indian accent had no effect. The man's face reddened until it seemed he would explode. Just then, a handsome, wiry Anguillian man approached from the beach, a bag over his shoulder. "Ah, yes. Here's the manager with fresh lobster now," said the waitress with a smile. "I told you it was no problem."

Updated by
Jordan Simon

Peace, pampering, fine dining, and beaches are among the star attractions on Anguilla (pronounced ang-*gwill*-a). If you're a beach lover, you may become giddy when you first spot the island from the air; its blindingly white sand and lustrous blue and aquamarine waters are intoxicating sights. If you like shopping and late-night action, you won't find a lot to do here. There are no glittering casinos or nightclubs, no duty-free shops stuffed with irresistible buys (although you're only about 30 watery minutes from St. Maarten/St. Martin's bustling resorts and casinos). However, if you like sophisticated cuisine served in stunning open-air settings, this may be your culinary Shangri-La. Despite its small size, Anguilla has nearly 70 restaurants. Some serve up the latest culinary trends in atmospheres that range from casual to chic; others stick to the simple, classic barefoot-friendly, beachfront pub grub.

This dry, limestone isle is the most northerly of the Leeward Islands, lying between the Caribbean Sea and the Atlantic Ocean. It stretches, from northeast to southwest, about 16 mi (26 km) and is only 3 mi (5 km) across at its widest point. The highest spot is 213 ft above sea level, and there are neither streams nor rivers, only saline ponds used for salt production. The island's name, a reflection of its shape, is most likely a derivative of *anguille,* which is French for "eel." (French explorer Pierre Laudonnaire is credited with having given the island this name when he sailed past it in 1556.)

In 1631 the Dutch built a fort here, but no one has been able to locate its site. English settlers from St. Kitts colonized the island in 1650, and except for a brief period of independence with St. Kitts–Nevis in the 1960s, Anguilla has remained a British colony ever since.

From the early 1800s, various island federations were formed and disbanded, with Anguilla all the while simmering over its subordinate status and enforced union with St. Kitts. Anguillians twice petitioned for direct rule from Britain and twice were ignored. In 1967, when St. Kitts, Nevis, and Anguilla became an associated state, the mouse roared; citizens kicked out St. Kitts's policemen, held a self-rule referendum, and for two years conducted their own affairs. A British "peacekeeping force" then parachuted onto the island, squelching Anguilla's designs for autonomy but helping a team of royal engineers stationed there to improve the port and build roads and schools. Today Anguilla elects a House of Assembly and its own leader to handle internal affairs, while a British governor is responsible for public service, the police, the judiciary, and external affairs.

The territory of Anguilla includes a few islets (or cays), such as Scrub Island, Dog Island, Prickly Pear Cays, Sandy Island, and Sombrero Island. The 10,000 or so residents are predominantly of African descent, but there are also many of Irish background, whose ancestors came over from St. Kitts in the 1600s. Historically, because the limestone land was unfit for agriculture, attempts at enslavement never lasted long; consequently, Anguilla doesn't bear the scars of slavery found on so many other Caribbean islands. Instead, Anguillians became experts at making a living from the sea and are known for their boatbuilding and fishing skills. Tourism is the stable economy's growth industry, but the government carefully regulates expansion to protect the island's natural resources and beauty. New hotels are small, select, and definitely casino-free; Anguilla emphasizes its high-quality service, serene surroundings, and friendly people.

WHAT IT COSTS In U.S. dollars

	$$$$	$$$	$$	$	¢
	RESTAURANTS*				
	over $30	$20–$30	$12–$20	$8–$12	under $8
	HOTELS**				
Cost EP/BP/CP	over $350	$250–$350	$150–$250	$80–$150	under $80
Cost AI	over $450	$350–$450	$250–$350	$125–$250	under $125

*Restaurant prices are for a main course at dinner. **EP, BP, and CP prices are per night for a standard double room in high season, excluding taxes, service charges, and meal plans. AI (all-inclusive) prices are per person, per night based on double-occupancy during high season, excluding taxes and service charges.

Where to Stay

Anguilla accommodations range from grand, sumptuous resorts to apartments and villas—deluxe or simple—to small, locally owned inns. Note that many lodgings don't have TV, but some places can provide one on request. Air-conditioning is usually available, but often at an exorbitant surcharge. Because the island has so many beautiful and uncrowded beaches, location isn't really an important part of choosing a resort. When calling to reserve a room, inquire about special packages and meal plans.

Hotels

$$$$ Fodor'sChoice ★ **Cap Juluca.** Chic, sybaritic, and serene, this 179-acre resort wraps around breathtaking Maundays Bay, the glittering sand rivaled only by the sparkling domed, Moorish-style villas, superlative cuisine, and celebrity clientele. Enormous (700 square ft and up) rooms have Moroccan fabrics, Brazilian hardwood furniture, and private patios, balconies, or sun roofs that render sea, sky, and sand part of the decor. Thoughtful extras include complimentary bush teas for "what ails ya" and afternoon sorbet at the beach. In-suite spa treatments are sinfully sensuous; or you can hike on nature trails, use the unique aqua-golf green/driving range, or visit local boatbuilders and artisans. ✉ *Maundays Bay* *Box 240* ☎ *264/497–6666 or 888/858–5822* 🖷 *264/497–6617* 🌐 *www.capjuluca.com* *98 rooms, 18 villas* *3 restaurants, room service, fans, minibars, putting green, driving range, 3 tennis courts, pool, fitness classes, gym, spa, beach, snorkeling, windsurfing, boating, croquet, bar, library, shops, baby-sitting, children's programs (ages 3–14), laundry service, Internet; no room TVs* 💳 *AE, MC, V* *Closed Sept.–Oct.* 🍽 *CP.*

★ $$$$ **CuisinArt Resort & Spa.** This luxurious beachfront resort's design—gleaming white stucco buildings, blue domes and trim—purees Greek island architecture, futurism, and art deco. Huge rooms ("standard" is 900 square feet) are handsomely appointed with wicker and hardwood

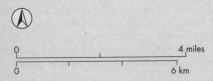

Anguilla

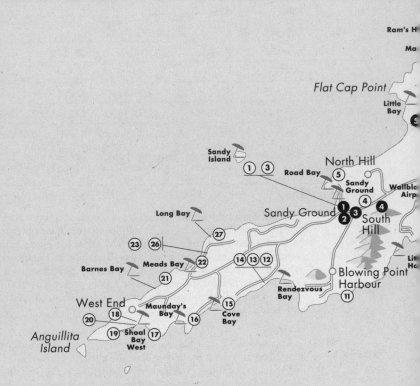

0 ——— 4 miles
0 ——— 6 km

Ram's H

Ma

Flat Cap Point

Little Bay

Sandy Island

1 3 Road Bay

North Hill

5 Sandy Ground

Wallblc Airp

Sandy Ground 1 4 4

2 3 South Hill

Long Bay

27

23 26

22 14 13 12

Barnes Bay Meads Bay

21

Blowing Point Harbour

Rendezvous Bay

11

West End Maunday's Bay

20 18

15 Cove Bay

19 Shoal Bay West 17 16

Anguillita Island

Lit Ho

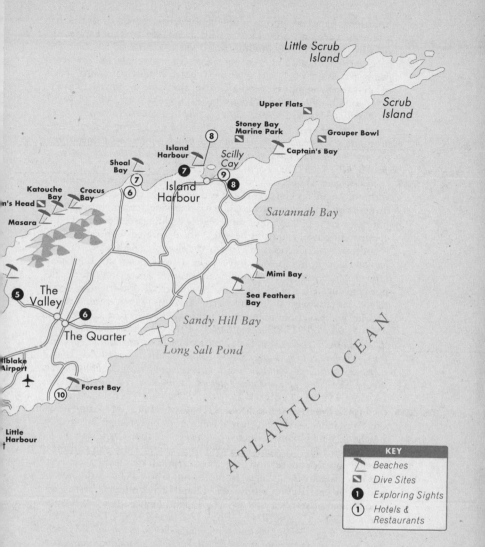

Little Scrub
Island

Scrub
Island

Upper Flats

Stoney Bay
Marine Park

Grouper Bowl

Island
Harbour   8

Captain's Bay

Scilly
Cay

7

9

Shoal
Bay

7   8

Island
Harbour

Savannah Bay

6

Katouche
Bay   Crocus
Bay

n's Head

Masara

Mimi Bay

Sea Feathers
Bay

5

The
Valley

6

Sandy Hill Bay

The Quarter

Long Salt Pond

ATLANTIC OCEAN

lblake
Airport

10   Forest Bay

Little
Harbour

KEY

	Beaches
	Dive Sites
●	Exploring Sights
①	Hotels & Restaurants

furnishings splashed with custom-made Haitian fabrics. A distinctive amenity is a demonstration kitchen with complimentary cooking classes. A hydroponic farm provides ultra-fresh organic produce for the three excellent restaurants and even ingredients for some of the unique treatments in the state-of-the-art spa/fitness center. A museum-quality space exhibits top contemporary Italian artists alongside such masters as Picasso and Chagall. ⊠ *Rendezvous Bay* ⌖ *Box 2000* ☎ *264/498–2000 or 800/943–3210* 🖷 *264/498–2010* ⊕ *www.cuisinartresort.com* ⇖ *93 rooms, 2 penthouses* ⌖ *3 restaurants, in-room safes, refrigerators, 3 tennis courts, pool, health club, hot tub, spa, beach, snorkeling, windsurfing, boating, billiards, 2 bars, shops, baby-sitting, laundry service, Internet* 🖃 *AE, MC, V* ⊗ *Closed Sept.–Oct.* ❑ *EP.*

★ ☾ $$$$ 🏨 **Malliouhana.** The ideal blend of European sophistication and Caribbean warmth, Anguilla's classiest resort is the vision of charming, hands-on owner Leon Roydon, whose passion for fine wine, art, and horticulture informs every aspect. Mediterranean-style buildings, descending a bluff commanding two exquisite beaches, are decorated with one of the world's largest collections of Haitian art, alongside mahogany furnishings and bibelots from Leon's travels. The state-of-the-art spa, supremely refined main restaurant, tranquillity, and near-psychic service lure a high-powered clientele. Yet Malliouhana is wonderfully kid-friendly, down to a water park with slides and pirate ship. It is that rare grand resort offering pomp without pomposity. ⊠ *Meads Bay* ⌖ *Box 173* ☎ *264/497–6111 or 800/835–0796* 🖷 *264/497–6011* ⊕ *www.malliouhana.com* ⇖ *43 rooms, 10 suites, 1 villa* ⌖ *2 restaurants, fans, in-room safes, minibars, 4 tennis courts, 3 pools, hair salon, health club, hot tub, spa, 2 beaches, snorkeling, windsurfing, boating, waterskiing, basketball, bar, library, baby-sitting, playground, Internet, business services, meeting room; no room TVs* 🖃 *AE, MC, V* ⊗ *Closed Sept.–Oct.* ❑ *EP.*

$$$–$$$$ 🏨 **Anguilla Great House Beach Resort.** These white and cotton candy–colored West Indian–style bungalows strung along one of Anguilla's longest beaches (2½ mi [4 km]) seductively whisper old-time Caribbean. From a chaise on your charming verandah, the view of the ocean is framed by vine-covered trellises and gingerbread trim. Rooms feature local artwork, mahogany furnishings, tropical-print fabrics, a huge tile shower, and ceiling fans. Rooms numbered 112 and higher offer the best views. The restaurant serves a mix of West Indian, French, and Continental cuisines. ⊠ *Rendezvous Bay* ⌖ *Box 157* ☎ *264/497–6061 or 800/583–9247* 🖷 *264/497–6019* ⊕ *www.anguillagreathouse.com* ⇖ *27 rooms* ⌖ *Restaurant, fans, pool, gym, beach, boating, snorkeling, windsurfing, business center; no a/c in some rooms, no room TVs* 🖃 *AE, D, DC, MC, V* ❑ *EP.*

$$$–$$$$ 🏨 **Frangipani Beach Club.** Splashy pink, Spanish Mediterranean–style buildings with archways, stone balustrades, wrought-iron railings, and red-tile roofs sit on 1 mi (1½ km) of beach bordered by lavish, colorful landscaping. Interiors are less exciting, ranging from the sterile chain-hotel decor to tasteful rattan furnishings with striped or luscious pastel upholstery. The classiest feature arched windows, French doors opening onto spacious patios or terraces, and exposed beam ceilings; suites offer kitchens and washer/dryers. The restaurant, gaudily dressed in frangipani yellows and reds, overlooks the ocean and has a well-executed French-influenced menu. ⊠ *Meads Bay* ⌖ *Box 1375* ☎ *264/497–6442 or 800/892–4564* 🖷 *264/497–6440* ⊕ *www.frangipani.ai* ⇖ *17 rooms, 8 suites* ⌖ *Restaurant, fans, some kitchens, tennis court, pool, beach, snorkeling, windsurfing, laundry facilities, bar* 🖃 *AE, MC, V* ❑ *EP* ⊗ *Closed Sept.–mid-Oct.*

$$$–$$$$ 🏨 **La Sirena.** Jovial Swiss owners ensure this resort overlooking Meads Bay is well run, hospitable, and lively. The complex's white-stucco-and-

red-tile buildings, amid tropical greenery, feature clean, geometrically interesting angles and circular openings. Interiors mix contemporary touches like halogen lamps with typical Caribbean design: rattan furniture, pastel-print fabrics, potted plants, terra-cotta floors. The second-floor Top of the Palms restaurant is a popular gathering spot. Though it's a four-minute walk from the beach, guests, especially Europeans who appreciate the dependability and fun ambience, return in droves. ⊠ *Meads Bay* ① *Box 200* ☎ *264/497–6827 or 800/223–9815* 📠 *264/497–6829* ⊕ *www.la-sirena.com* ➾ *20 rooms, 4 suites, 6 villas* ⧖ *Restaurant, fans, in-room safes, some kitchenettes, 2 pools, massage, dive shop, bicycles, bar, car rental, Internet; no a/c in some rooms, no room TVs* 🖃 *AE, MC, V* ⑩ *CP.*

$$$–$$$$ ⊡ **Shoal Bay Villas.** The Antillean-style buildings of this small two-story condominium hotel are tucked in a grove of palm trees on 2 mi (3 km) of splendid sand. Units—ranging from studios to 2-bedroom condos—are brightly decorated in nursery pink and blue or vivid abstract linens, with natural wicker and painted rattan furniture. The helpful staff and sublime location attract both families and honeymooners. ⊠ *Shoal Bay* ① *Box 81* ☎ *264/497–2051* 📠 *264/497–3631* ⊕ *www.sbvillas.ai* ➾ *2 studios, 3 2-bedroom condos, 10 1-bedroom condos* ⧖ *Restaurant, fans, kitchens, pool, beach, snorkeling, bar; no a/c in some rooms, no room TVs* 🖃 *AE, D, MC, V* ☉ *Closed Sept.–mid-Oct.* ⑩ *EP.*

$$–$$$$ ⊡ **The Enclave at Cinnamon Reef.** This low-key, luxurious retreat is built in a sort of futuristic Mediterranean style. Lush gardens punctuated with fountains and statuary weave around villas. Split-level interiors define casual chic with Mexican tile, ornate gilt mirrors, antique mahogany cabinets and four-poster beds, glass-top coffee tables, and leather sleeper sofas. All offer stunning views of the Caribbean save for the Garden Suites, which represent excellent value for barely half the price. The intimacy, attention to detail, and gracious staff lure a loyal, quietly well-heeled repeat clientele. ⊠ *Little Harbour* ① *Box 141* ☎ *264/497–2727 or 800/508–1038* 📠 *264/497–3727* ⊕ *www.boutiqueresortsintl.com* ➾ *8 studios, 14 1-bedroom suites* ⧖ *Restaurant, room service, in-room VCRs, 2 tennis courts, pool, hot tub, beach, boating, snorkeling, windsurfing, bar* 🖃 *AE, MC, V* ☉ *Closed Aug.–mid-Dec.* ⑩ *CP*

$$–$$$ ⊡ **Cocoloba Resort.** This casually elegant resort offers a taste of the high life at comparatively low prices. At its western end, the main house perches atop a coral bluff, cleaving the glorious swaths of Barnes and Meads bays. A-frame Euro-Caribbean buildings nestled amid tropical gardens hold accommodations (most with sunken living rooms) whose walls and fabrics favor lemon, cerise, and powder-blue. The worthy Continental-creole restaurant surrounds a leviathan aquarium with seating "islands," but the prime spot is the deck on a moonlit night. ⊠ *Barnes Bay* ① *Box 318* ☎ *264/497–8800 or 800/583–9247* 📠 *264/497–8126* ⊕ *www.cocolobaresort.com* ➾ *110 rooms* ⧖ *Restaurant, in-room safes, fans, refrigerators, tennis court, pool, gym, 2 beaches, boating, snorkeling, windsurfing, bicycles, bar, shops; no room TVs* 🖃 *AE, D, MC, V* ⑩ *EP.*

$$–$$$ ⊡ **Ferryboat Inn.** The spacious one-bedroom apartments at this small, family-run complex are a bargain. Each is simply decorated with white or pastel fabrics and has a full kitchen, dining area, cable TV, and ceiling fans (two have air-conditioning). It's on a small beach and just a short walk from the ferry dock. The two-bedroom beach house is air-conditioned. All rooms and the open-air restaurant look out across the water toward St. Martin. ⊠ *Blowing Point* ① *Box 189* ☎ *264/497–6613* 📠 *264/497–6713* ⊕ *www.aiferryboatinn* ➾ *6 apartments, 1 beach house* ⧖ *Restaurant, fans, kitchens, cable TV, beach, snorkeling, windsurfing, bar; no a/c in some rooms* 🖃 *AE, MC, V* ⑩ *EP.*

★ $–$$$ 🏨 **Rendezvous Bay Hotel.** Opened in 1962, Anguilla's first resort sits amid 60 acres of coconut groves on Rendezvous Bay's fine white sand, patrolled by the owners' parrots and golden retrievers. Funk and elegance co-exist in equal measure. The original guest rooms are 100 yards from the beach and are quite spare. Newer, connected, two-story beachfront villas have spacious one-bedroom suites with cathedral ceilings and a palette of Caribbean blues. The owning Gumbs family are virtual legends, including paterfamilias Jeremiah (a font of anecdotes) and gourmet son Alan, who added the superlative Cedar Grove restaurant, as well as a fine island art gallery. ⊠ *Rendezvous Bay* ⬧ *Box 31* ☎ *264/497–6549, 732/738–0246, or 800/274–4893* 🖶 *264/497–6026* ⊕ *www.rendezvousbay.com* ⇨ *20 rooms, 16 1-bedroom villa suites, 8 studios* ⚙ *2 restaurants, fans, in-room data ports, some kitchens, some refrigerators, 2 tennis courts, windsurfing, lounge, recreation room, bar, shops, laundry service, meeting room, car rental, Internet; no a/c in some rooms* ▤ *AE, D, MC, V* ⊗ *Closed Sept.–Oct.* ⑩ *EP.*

★ $$ 🏨 **Arawak Beach Inn.** This intimate gem sings with island warmth and color. Hexagonal, breezy, two-story villas painted the soft colors of a Caribbean dawn offer spectacular views of the narrow beach and boat-dotted harbor. Deluxe units are far posher, with four-poster rattan beds, mahogany and teak furnishings, and brilliant tropical fabrics. The Arawak Cafe, splashed in hallucinogenic colors, serves chef Maude's lip-smacking Caribbean comfort food. The staff arranges numerous expeditions and the international clientele is cultured (the inn hosts art workshops from pottery to Chinese watercoloring). You pay a hefty surcharge for air-conditioning. ⊠ *Island Harbour* ⬧ *Box 1403* ☎ *264/497–4888* 🖶 *264/497–4889* ⊕ *www.arawakbeach.com* ⇨ *13 rooms, 4 suites* ⚙ *Restaurant, fans, in-room safes, some kitchens, pool, beach, snorkeling, windsurfing, boating, bar, shop; no a/c in some rooms, no TV in some rooms* ▤ *AE, MC, V* ⑩ *EP.*

$ 🏨 **Syd-An's.** These very basic efficiencies are a bargain for those looking to trade luxury for an entertaining location. A terrific beach is across the street, and you're steps from the bustling activity of Road Bay, including island classics Johnno's and Ripples, as well as the Pumphouse nightclub. All units are roomy and fully equipped, but other than the newer villas, desperately need a renovation. ⊠ *Sandy Ground* ☎ *264/497–3180* 🖶 *264/497–5381* ⊕ *www.inns.ai/sydans* ⇨ *10 studios, 2 villas* ⚙ *Fans, kitchenettes, shops* ▤ *AE, MC, V* ⑩ *EP.*

Villas & Condominiums

The tourist office has a complete listing of the plentiful vacation apartment rentals. You can contact the **Anguilla Connection** (⬧ Box 1269, Island Harbour ☎ 264/497–9854 or 800/916–3336 🖶 264/497–9853 ⊕ www.luxuryvillas.com) for condo and villa listings. **Sunshine Villas** (⬧ Box 142, Blowing Point ☎ 264/497–6149 🖶 264/497–6021) offers a wide array of island properties.

$$$$ 🏨 **Altamer.** Architect Myron Goldfinger's geometric symphony of floor-to-ceiling windows, cantilevered walls, and curvaceous floating staircases is fit for any king (or CEO). June Goldfinger's striking interiors fulfill the vision of owners Rebecca and Michael Eggleton, with custom-made and antique pieces: Murano fixtures, Florentine linens, Turkish kilims, Fabergé ornaments, Tsarist silver candelabras. It's also outfitted with the latest gadgetry, from touch-pad stereo systems to wireless Internet. A private staff, including three butlers and a chef, anticipates every whim. Two more villas (each must be rented in its entirety) will open by 2005. ⊠ *Shoal Bay West* ⬧ *Box 3001* ☎ *264/498–4000* 🖶 *264/498–4010* ⊕ *www.altamer.com* ⇨ *3 5-bedroom villas* ⚙ *Dining room, fans, VCRs, tennis court, pool, gym, hot tub, beach, snorkeling, wind-*

surfing, boating, recreation room, laundry service, Internet, business services ☰ *AE, D, DC, MC, V* ⭕ *AI.*

★ **$$$$** ▦ **Covecastles Villa Resort.** Though architect Myron Goldfinger's cold, Frank Lloyd Wrong enclave resembles a series of giant concrete prams from the outside, the interiors bespeak elegance and comfort. Secluded, soaring two- to four-bedroom villas are decorated with custom-made wicker furniture, raw-silk cushions, and hand-embroidered linens in muted, soothing colors. Brazilian walnut louvered doors and windows perfectly frame St. Martin, creating living canvases. Facilities are ultra-contemporary, the restaurant defines French *savoir faire*, the lovely beach beckons, and an unobtrusive staff allows peace and quiet to reign. ✉ *Shoal Bay West* ⭕ *Box 248* ☎ *264/497–6801 or 800/348–4716* 🖷 *264/497–6051* ⊕ *www.covecastles.com* 🗘 *14 apartments* ⅄ *Restaurant, room service, fans, tennis court, beach, boating, snorkeling, bicycles, library, shops* ☰ *AE, MC, V.*

★ **$$$$** ▦ **Temenos.** These incomparably glamorous villas were inspired by the pure, spare architecture of Mykonos and Santorini: sparkling white buildings set off by serene Caribbean blues, justifying the name, Greek for "sanctuary." The three villas—Sea, Sky, and Sand—take their shimmering color schemes from those elements (from ivory and ecru to lapis and azure), but all feature cathedral ceilings, louvered French doors, infinity pools, natural materials, and enormous marble bathrooms with indoor/outdoor showers. They're beautifully textured, with marble, granite, wrought iron, mosaic work, and woven rugs, yet equipped with state-of-the-art equipment. The private staff manages to be friendly yet unobtrusive. What price sanctuary? ✉ *Long Bay* ⭕ *Box 1656* ☎ *264/222–9000* 🖷 *264/498–9050* ⊕ *www.temenosvillas.com* 🗘 *1 5-bedroom villa, 2 4-bedroom villas* ⅄ *Dining rooms, fans, kitchens, in-room VCRs, 3 tennis courts, 3 pools, gym, 3 hot tubs, beach, snorkeling, boating, laundry service, Internet, business services* ☰ *AE, D, MC, V* ⭕ *CP.*

★ **$$$–$$$$** ▦ **Blue Waters.** These Moorish-style buildings sit in a palm grove at one end of a spectacular ½-mi (1-km) beach; excellent restaurants are within walking distance. Sunny, unfussy one- and two-bedroom units have white-tile floors, huge mirrors, hardwood window frames, and patios and balconies often visited by pelicans, bananaquits, and the odd ambling goat. Immaculately kept to the point of Felix Unger obsession, they represent a superb beachfront bargain. ✉ *Shoal Bay West* ⭕ *Box 69* ☎ *264/497–6292* 🖷 *264/497–6982* 🗘 *9 apartments* ⅄ *Fans, kitchens, beach, snorkeling; no a/c* ☰ *AE, MC, V.*

$$$–$$$$ ▦ **Carimar Beach Club.** This horseshoe-shaped, Mediterranean-style complex on beautiful Meads Bay has an upscale Sun Belt condo look. Although only two buildings stand at the water's edge, all have ocean views from balconies or patios. Bright white apartments are fully equipped and carefully maintained. The cordial staff, supreme beachfront location, and several fine restaurants within walking distance make this a winner. Look for aggressive promotions on their Web site, including last-minute on-line auctions. There is a surcharge if you use air-conditioning in the bedrooms. ✉ *Meads Bay* ⭕ *Box 327* ☎ *264/497–6881 or 800/235–8667* 🖷 *264/497–6071* ⊕ *www.carimar.com* 🗘 *24 apartments* ⅄ *Fans, kitchens, 2 tennis courts, beach, snorkeling* ☰ *AE, D, MC, V.*

★ **$$–$$$$** ▦ **Paradise Cove.** This pretty complex of luxury one- and two-bedroom apartments compensates for its nonbeachfront location with two whirlpools, a large pool, and tranquil tropical gardens. Beautiful Cove and Rendezvous bays are just a few minutes' stroll away. Spotless units are attractively appointed with white rattan and natural wicker furniture, gleaming white-tile floors, and soft floral or pastel fabrics from mint to mango. Second-floor units have high beamed ceilings. Maid service and private cooks are available. Families will appreciate such thoughtful touches as cookies-and-cream pool parties and weekend pizza lessons. ⊠ *The Cove* 🕭 *Box 135* 📠 *264/497–6959 or 264/497–6603* 🖨 *264/497–6927* ⊕ *www.paradise.ai* 🛏 *12 studio suites, 17 1- and 2-bedroom apartments* ⟋ *Restaurant, fans, in-room data ports, some kitchens, some kitchenettes, 2 pools, 2 hot tubs, gym, croquet, bar, shops, playground, laundry facilities, laundry service, meeting facilities, Internet* 🖃 *AE, MC, V.*

$$ 🏨 **Easy Corner Villas.** The villas, on a bluff overlooking Road Bay, are a five-minute walk from the beach, with spectacular views of Salt Pond and the ocean beyond. The modest two- and three-bedroom villas, which can be broken down to accommodate couples in one-bedroom units or studios, are cheerfully furnished and well equipped, belying the mousy facade. The price is right, especially the often amazing packages with rental car. ⊠ *South Hill* 🕭 *Box 65* 📠 *264/497–6433, 264/497–6541, or 800/633–7411* 🖨 *264/497–6410* 🛏 *12 villas* ⟋ *Fans, kitchens, kitchenettes, car rental* 🖃 *AE, MC, V.*

★ $–$$ 🏨 **Allamanda Beach Club.** Youthful, active couples from around the globe happily fill this casual, three-story, white-stucco building just off the beach. All units have tile floors and jewel-tone fabrics; ocean views are best from the higher floors. The creative restaurant, Zara's, is a popular draw, as is the boisterous, colorful, inexpensive Gwen's Reggae Grill, giving the resort an upmarket, aging frat party feel on busy days. Dive packages are especially appealing. ⊠ *Upper Shoal Bay Beach* 🕭 *Box 662* 📠 *264/497–5217* 🖨 *264/497–5216* ⊕ *www.allamanda.ai* 🛏 *16 units* ⟋ *Restaurant, grill, fans, kitchens, pool, gym, snorkeling, boating, dive shop* 🖃 *AE, D, MC, V.*

Where to Eat

Anguilla has an extraordinary number of excellent restaurants—from elegant establishments to down-home seaside shacks. Many have breeze-swept terraces, where you can dine under the stars. Call ahead—in winter to make a reservation and in late summer and fall to confirm if the place you've chosen is open. Restaurants not affiliated with a hotel often tack on an additional 5% to the service charge if you pay by credit card. Be forewarned: service even in the best establishments can be spotty, especially during the off-season doldrums and high-season weekends.

What to Wear

During the day, casual clothes are widely accepted: shorts will be fine, but don't wear bathing suits and cover-ups unless you're at a beach bar. In the evening, shorts are okay at the extremely casual eateries. Elsewhere, women should wear sundresses or nice casual slacks; men will be fine in shirtsleeves and casual pants. Some hotel restaurants are more formal and may have a jacket requirement in high season; ask when you make your reservation.

CARIBBEAN
★ $$–$$$ ✕ **Old House.** You'll quickly forget the planes from the nearby airport buzzing this lovely hilltop 1920s cottage eatery, which really takes off with mouth- (and eye-) watering local cuisine. Fresh flowers adorn the tables—even at breakfast—when regulars order the island fruit pancakes (banana takes the cake). For lunch or dinner try the conch creole, barbecue ribs, curried local lamb with pigeon peas and rice, or Anguillian pot fish simmered with limes, garlic, fresh herbs, and tomatoes. The daily happy hour from 5 to 6 is popular. ⊠ *George Hill* 📠 *264/497–2228* 🖃 *MC, V.*

$$ ✕**Flavours.** Kirk Hughes's airy second-floor restaurant overlooking Sandy Ground is devoted to delivering an authentic Caribbean experience, right down to the bright blue napery and cushions. He turns out a classic saltfish and ackee (a Jamaican fruit that tastes like scrambled eggs), pigeon-pea soup, and pot fish with coconut dumplings. But his inventive stylings are equally savory: roasted rack of lamb with stuffed peppers in red-wine sauce or grilled lobster in curried papaya butter. Finish with scrumptious soursop sorbet or sweet-potato pudding with mango sauce and a bracing bush tea. ⊠ *Back St., South Hill* ☎ *264/ 497–0629* ▤ *MC, V* ⊗ *Closed Sun.*

CONTEMPORARY ✕**Altamer.** Austere chic characterizes this formal beachfront restau-
$$$–$$$$ rant—stark white geometric architecture patterned after sails, underlit frosted-glass tables, stainless-steel wine storage units—enlivened by playfully over-the-top table settings and Chef Maurice Leduc's sumptuous inventions. Start with his silken white gazpacho, followed by shelled crayfish over creamed leeks and plantain, or twice-roasted, boned duck in orange-ginger sauce. A special chef's table, to the side of the fashionably open kitchen, is an option; an impressive wine list and multi-course sampler menus are memorable splurges. ⊠ *Shoal Bay West* ☎ *264/498–4040* ⚓ *Reservations essential* ▤ *AE, D, DC, MC, V* ⊗ *Closed Sun. No lunch Wed.*

★ **$$$–$$$$** ✕**Pimms.** Local chef George Reid weaves culinary magic in an equally enchanted setting at Cap Juluca. Coveted tables in the open dining room perch so close to the water that you can actually see fish darting about. Reid's innovative fare is globally-inspired haute Caribbean. Witness scallop and daikon radish ravioli with mango-cucumber relish and pomegranate reduction, pancetta-wrapped grouper with braised leeks and candied carrots in basil sauce, or smashing cumin-scented rack of lamb. A sterling wine list complements the menu, and the perfect end is an aged rum and pre-Castro Cubano from G.M. Eustace "Guish" Guishard's personal selection. ⊠ *Cap Juluca, Maundays Bay* ☎ *264/ 497–6666* ⚓ *Reservations essential* ▤ *AE, MC, V* ⊗ *Closed Sept.–Oct.*

ECLECTIC ✕**Blanchard's.** Bob and Melinda Blanchards' book *A Trip to the Beach*
★ **$$$$** wryly and warmly recounts the experience of opening this quintessential waterfront restaurant. It masterfully combines the ingredients for success: handsome space with son Jesse's multimedia artworks and floor-to-ceiling shutters letting in the breezes, an excellent wine cellar, including a selection of aged spirits, buzz-worthy celebrity sightings, and an exquisitely presented, sensuously textured Asian-Caribbean menu. Standouts include roasted sea bass in saffron-corn sauce, crayfish skewers with lemongrass, toasted sesame seeds, and rum-glazed pineapple, and to finish, lemon-buttermilk pancakes with homemade vanilla-bean ice cream and fresh berries. ⊠ *Meads Bay* ☎ *264/497–6100* ⚓ *Reservations essential* ▤ *AE, MC, V* ⊗ *Closed Sun. and Aug.–Sept. No lunch.*

$$$–$$$$ ✕**Covecastles.** Elegant, intimate dinners are served here in a garden overlooking beautiful Shoal Bay. Each season, Dominique Thevenet devises a new menu, innovatively mating French culinary traditions with Caribbean ingredients. Savory examples might include vermouth-laced crayfish *choucroute* (with sausage and sauerkraut), potato-crusted escargots, or lobster medallions in truffle-cream sauce. Villa guests receive priority for the seven tables, so call for reservations well in advance. ⊠ *Shoal Bay West* ☎ *264/497–6801* ⚓ *Reservations essential* ▤ *AE* ⊗ *Closed Sept.–Nov. No lunch.*

★ **$$$–$$$$** ✕**Hibernia.** Some of the island's most creative dishes are served in this wood-beamed, latticed cottage restaurant overlooking the water.

Unorthodox yet delectable culinary pairings—inspired by chef/owner Raoul Rodriguez's continuing travels from France to the Far East—include crayfish sautéed with shiitakes and ginger sauce, foie-gras paté with tamarind-pumpkin relish, and pigeon breast roasted in honey-soy sauce with purple Lao rice and scallion tempura. The painterly presentation echoes Raoul and wife Mary Pat O'Hanlon's other love, art: their travels also glean marvelous pieces on display in the restaurant and adjacent gallery. Restricted hours during the low season. ⊠ *Island Harbour* ☎ 264/497–4290 ⊟ *AE, MC, V* ⊘ *Closed Mon. and Aug.–Sept. No lunch Sun.*

$$$–$$$$ ✕ **Straw Hat.** Imagine dining above an aquarium: seven picture windows frame seascapes, from floodlit coral reefs to fishing flotillas, in this plain wooden structure built on pilings directly over the water. Aquatic still-lifes, embedded shells, and tables painted in Caribbean colors enhance the theme. The assured food is a feisty fusion of local, Asian, and Mediterranean elements. Start with goat-sausage wonton in lemongrass-sesame broth, or conch chowder perfumed with fennel and saffron, then segue into seared snapper in lime-ginger-saffron sauce, or grilled tuna loin with compote of balsamic-citrus caramelized onions. ⊠ *Forest Bay* ☎ 264/497–8300 ⊟ *AE, MC, V* ⊘ *Closed Sun. No lunch.*

★ **$$–$$$$** ✕ **Ferryboat Inn.** Tables open to the breezes and an almost Impressionist canvas of fishing boats mark John McClean's charming waterside terrace eatery a short walk from the Blowing Point ferry dock. Come evening, the twinkling lights of St. Martin weave a romantic aura. The French onion and black-bean soups, lobster thermidor (the specialty), and entrecôte *du vin au poivre* (steak au poivre with red wine sauce), and veal *Savoyarde* (with a white-wine shallot-cream sauce) are scrumptious, as are such staples as burgers and omelets. ⊠ *Ferryboat Inn, Cul de Sac Rd., Blowing Point* ☎ 264/497–6613 ⊟ *AE, MC, V* ⊘ *No lunch Sun.*

$$–$$$$ ✕ **Zara's.** Chef Shamash presides at this cozy restaurant with beamed ceilings and poolside seating. The kitchen mixes Caribbean, Italian, and Asian preparations with panache. Standouts include the velvety pumpkin soup with coconut milk, crusted garlic snapper with lemon-mojo sauce, or roasted grouper in mango-basil coulis. ⊠ *Allamanda Beach Club, Upper Shoal Bay* ☎ 264/497–3229 ⊟ *AE, MC, V.*

★ **$$–$$$** ✕ **Kemia.** Cap Juluca's seaside "hors d'oeuverie" looks like a posh pasha's oasis transported to the Caribbean: arches, tables and lamps embedded with jewel-like mosaic and colored glass, cushy throw pillows, and billowing tent ceilings. Chef Thomas Bengtsson, who once worked at New York's prestigious Aquavit, prepares a truly global selection of tapas (some of which make a whole meal unto themselves, such as the sublime fish hot pot). He provides a marvelous gastronomic journey, from Indonesian satays to sashimi, shish kebabs to charcuterie, with highlights including coriander-seasoned crayfish with crispy rice cakes and tamarind reduction. Look for special wine dinners and jazz evenings. ⊠ *Cap Juluca, Maundays Bay* ☎ 264/497–6666 ♨ *Reservations essential* ⊟ *AE, MC, V* ⊘ *Closed Sept.–Oct.*

$$–$$$ ✕ **Top of the Palms.** This indoor-outdoor eatery overlooking the pool on the second floor of La Sirena hotel percolates with life, especially when it swings to the rhythms of a steel band on Mondays or the festively costumed Mayoumba Folkloric Theater on Thursdays. Though seafood reigns (catch of the day with tropical-fruit salsa and chunky conch fritters are always reliable), carnivores will appreciate the juicy slabs of steak served with sundried-tomato-basil butter or green-peppercorn sauce. The owners' Swiss roots emerge in the fun Saturday fondue menu, from classic cheese to Caribbean (including lobster). ⊠ *La Sirena, Meads Bay* ☎ 264/497–6827 ⊟ *AE, MC, V.*

$–$$$ ✕ **Ripples.** You'd never guess that this traditional clapboard house a block from the beach holds a long, loud, bustling bar jammed with locals and savvy visitors. The menu takes an international "one from column A" approach (quesadillas to fresh crab wontons), but West Indian's the way to go, with spicy conch creole, or jerk chicken with mango sauce. Ripples is especially hopping and happening late nights (it serves until midnight, unheard of on sleepy Anguilla) and from 5 to 7 Saturday during happy hour (ask for a Bailey's colada). ⊠ *Sandy Ground* ☎ *264/497–3380* ▭ *MC, V.*

FRENCH ✕ **Malliouhana.** Sparkling crystal and fine china, exquisite service, a
$$$–$$$$ wonderful 25,000-bottle wine cellar, and a spectacularly romantic can-
Fodor's Choice dlelit, open-air room complement exceptional haute French cuisine ri-
★ valing any in the French West Indies. Consulting chef Michel Rostang, renowned for his Paris bistros, and chef Alain Laurent revamp the menu seasonally, brilliantly incorporating local ingredients in classic preparations, from fennel-scented conch chowder to grilled sea bass with baby artichoke *barigoule* (an herb-infused vegetable puree). The ultimate in hedonism is sipping champagne as the setting sun triggers a laser show over the bay, before repairing to your table. ⊠ *Meads Bay* ☎ *264/497–6111* ⌣ *Reservations essential* ▭ *AE, MC, V* ☉ *Closed Sept.–Oct.*

ITALIAN ✕ **Trattoria Tramonto & Oasis Beach Bar.** The island's only Italian restau-
$$$–$$$$ rant features a dual (or dueling) serenade of Bocelli on the sound system and gently lapping waves a few feet away. Chef Valter Belli artfully adapts recipes from his home in Emilia-Romagna. Try the gossamer lobster ravioli in truffle-cream sauce, and for dessert don't miss the tiramisu. Although you might wander in here for lunch after a swim, when casual dress is accepted, you'll still be treated to the same impressive menu, and a luscious selection of champagne fruit drinks, a small but fairly priced Italian wine list, and homemade grappas. ⊠ *Shoal Bay West* ☎ *264/497–8819* ⌣ *Reservations essential* ▭ *MC, V* ☉ *Closed Mon. and Sept.–Oct.*

Beaches

Renowned for their beauty, more than 30 dazzling white-sand beaches are the best reason to come to Anguilla. You'll find long, deserted stretches ideal for walking, and beaches lined with bars and restaurants—all accompanied by surf that ranges from wild to glassy-smooth.

NORTHEAST **Captain's Bay.** If you make the grueling four-wheel-drive-only trip along
COAST the inhospitable dirt road that leads to the northeastern end of the island toward Junk's Hole, you will be rewarded with peaceful isolation. The surf here slaps the sands with a vengeance, and the undertow is strong—wading is the safest water sport.

Island Harbour. These mostly calm waters are surrounded by a slender beach. For centuries Anguillians have ventured from these sands in colorful handmade fishing boats. There are several bars and restaurants (Arawak Cafe and Smitty's are best for casual lunches), and this is the departure point for the three-minute boat ride to **Scilly Cay,** where a thatched beach bar serves seafood. Just hail the restaurant's free boat and plan to spend most of the day (the all-inclusive lunch starts at $40 and is worth the price); Wednesdays and Sundays feature live music and calypso line dancing.

NORTHWEST **Barnes Bay.** This is a superb spot for windsurfing and snorkeling. In
COAST high season this beach can get a bit crowded with day-trippers from St. Martin.

Little Bay. Sheer cliffs embroidered with agave and creeping vines rise behind a small gray-sand beach, usually accessible only by water (it's a favored spot for snorkeling and night dives). The hale and hearty can also clamber down the cliffs by rope to explore the caves and surrounding reef.

Road Bay. The clear blue waters of this beach are usually dotted with yachts. Several restaurants, including evergreen classic Johnno's, a watersports center, and lots of windsurfing and waterskiing activity make this area (often called Sandy Ground) a commercial one. The snorkeling isn't very good here, but the sunset vistas are glorious.

Sandy Island. From a distance, nestled in coral reefs about 2 mi (3 km) from Road Bay, it seems no more than a tiny speck of sand and a few spindly palm trees. Still, Sandy Island has the modern-day comforts of a beach boutique, a bar, and a restaurant. Use of snorkeling gear and underwater cameras is free. A ferry heads here every hour from Sandy Ground.

SOUTHEAST **Mimi Bay.** This half-mile-long, remote beach east of Sea Feathers Bay re-
COAST wards snorkelers at low tide with a pyrotechnically hued reef.

Sandy Hill. Not far from Sea Feathers Bay is this base for fishermen. Here you can buy fish and lobster right off the boats and snorkel in the warm waters. Don't plan to sunbathe—the beach is narrow.

Fodor'sChoice **Shoal Bay.** Shoal Bay—not to be confused with Shoal Bay West—is one
★ of the Caribbean's prettiest beaches, anchored by sea-grape and coconut trees. Restaurants like Gwen's Reggae Grill and Madeariman Beach Club offer seafood and tropical drinks, shops sell T-shirts and sunscreen, and the water-sports center arranges diving, sailing, and fishing trips. The quieter east end offers superior snorkeling and The Fountain, a cave filled with millennia-old petroglyphs and tribal artifacts that the Anguilla National Trust is developing as a historic attraction.

SOUTHWEST **Cove Bay.** Lined with coconut palms, this is a quiet spot. There's a lit-
COAST tle bar and a place where you can rent floats, umbrellas, and mats.

Maundays Bay. The dazzling, 1-mi-long (1½-km-long) beach is known for good swimming and snorkeling. You can also rent water-sports gear.

Rendezvous Bay. Here you'll find 1½ mi (2½ km) of pearl-white sand lapped by calm water and with a view of St. Martin. The rockier stretch provides marvelous snorkeling. The open-air bars of the Anguilla Great House Beach Resort and Rendezvous Bay Hotel are handy for snacks and frosty island drinks.

Shoal Bay West. This mile-long sweep of sand is rimmed with mangroves; there are coral reefs not too far from shore. It can be crowded with day-trippers from St. Martin.

Sports & the Outdoors

An 18-hole golf course—Anguilla's first—designed by Greg Norman to accentuate the natural terrain and maximize ocean views, is slated to open in 2004 at a new resort and residential development in Rendezvous Bay West.

BOATING & Anguilla is the perfect place to try all kinds of water sports. The major
SAILING resorts offer complimentary Windsurfers, paddleboats, and water skis to their guests. If your hotel lacks facilities, you can get in gear at **Sandy Island Enterprises** (✉ Sandy Ground ☎ 264/497–6395), which also rents Sunfish and windsurfers and arranges fishing charters. **Island Yacht Charters** (✉ Sandy Ground ☎ 264/497–3743 or 264/235–6555) rents the

35-foot, teak *Pirate* powerboat and the 30-foot Beneteau *Eros* sailboat, and organizes snorkeling, sightseeing, and fishing expeditions.

FISHING Albacore, wahoo, marlin, barracuda, and kingfish are among the fish angled after off Anguilla's shores. **Johnno's Beach Stop** in Sandy Ground (☎ 264/497–2728) has a boat and can help you plan a trip.

HORSEBACK RIDING Scenic nature trails and miles of beaches are the perfect places to ride, even if you're a novice. Ride English- or western-style at **El Rancho Del Blues** (☎ 264/497–6164). Prices start at $35 per hour ($50 for two-hour rides).

SCUBA DIVING Sunken wrecks, a long barrier reef, terrain encompassing walls, canyons, and hulking boulders, varied marine life including greenback turtles and nurse sharks, and exceptionally clear water make for excellent diving. **Stoney Bay Marine Park,** off the northeast end of Anguilla, showcases the late-18th-century *El Buen Consejo,* a 960-ton Spanish galleon that sank here in 1772. Other good dive sites include **Grouper Bowl,** with exceptional hard-coral formations; **Ram's Head,** with caves, chutes, and tunnels; and **Upper Flats,** where you are sure to see stingrays. **Anguillian Divers** (⊠ Meads Bay ☎ 264/497–4750) is a full-service dive operator with a PADI 5-Star training center. At Shoal Bay, contact **Shoal Bay Scuba and Watersports** (☎ 264/497–4371). Single-tank dives start at $45–$50, two-tank dives from $65–$80.

SEA EXCURSIONS **Chocolat** (⊠ Sandy Ground ☎ 264/497–3394) is a 35-ft catamaran available for private charter or scheduled excursions to nearby cays. Captain Rollins is a knowledgeable, affable guide. Rates for day sails start at $50 per person. For an underwater peek without getting wet, catch a ride ($20 per person) on **Junior's Glass Bottom Boat** (⊠ Sandy Ground ☎ 264/497–4456). Snorkel trips and instruction are available, too. Picnic, swimming, and diving excursions to Prickly Pear, Sandy Island, and Scilly Cay are available through **Sandy Island Enterprises** (☎ 264/497–6395).

TENNIS You'll find tennis courts (some lighted) at several resorts. Simply call ahead and make a reservation. Fees average $20 per hour. **Carimar Beach Club** (⊠ Meads Bay ☎ 264/497–6881) has two hard courts. **Rendezvous Bay Hotel** (⊠ Rendezvous Bay ☎ 264/497–6549) has two hard courts. **Ronald Webster Park** (⊠ The Valley ☎ no phone) has one public hard court.

Shopping

The free magazines *Anguilla Life* and *What We Do in Anguilla,* available at the airport and in shops and hotel lobbies, have shopping tips. Outstanding local artists sell their work in galleries, which often arrange studio tours (you can also check with the Antigua Tourist Office). Pyrat rums are golden elixirs blending up to nine aged and flavored spirits, available at the Anguilla Rums distillery and several local shops. For upscale designer sportswear, check out the little shops (some are branches of larger stores in Marigot on St. Martin). For a better selection, catch the ferry to St. Martin and spend a day browsing in chic boutiques that carry the latest European fashions.

CLOTHES ★ **Alberto & Lina/David Yurman Boutique** (⊠ CuisinArt Resort & Spa, Rendezvous Bay ☎ 264/498–2000) carries custom designs by the renowned eponymous jewelers, as well as perfumes from Bulgari to Chanel, Murano glass, La Perla swimwear, Helen Kaminski accessories, and more name merchandise. **Azemmour Boutique** (⊠ Cap Juluca, Maundays Bay ☎ 264/497–6666) specializes in European swimwear and also carries fine jewelry. **Boutique at Malliouhana** (✉ Malliouhana, Meads Bay ☎ 264/497–6111) is the most upscale shop on Anguilla, selling such designer specialties as jewelry by Oro De Sol, Gottex swimwear, and Robert LaRoche sunglasses. **Caribbean Fancy** (✉ George Hill ☎ 264/497–3133) sells Ta-Tee's line of crinkle-cotton resort wear, plus books, spices, and gift items. **Caribbean Silkscreen** (✉ South Hill ☎ 264/497–2272) creates designs and prints them on golf shirts, hats, sweatshirts, and jackets. **Sunshine Shop** (✉ South Hill ☎ 264/497–6964) stocks cotton *pareus* (saronglike beach cover-ups), silkscreen items, cotton resort wear, and hand-painted Haitian wood items. **Irie Lite** (✉ South Hill ☎ 264/497–6526) sells vividly hued beach and resort wear that appeals to the younger set. **Something Special** (✉ The Cove ☎ 264/497–6655) is a duty-free source for stylish resort wear, perfumes, cigars, and jewelry, as well as great java at its espresso bar. **Whispers** (✉ Cap Juluca, Maundays Bay ☎ 264/497–6666) has Caribbean handicrafts and stylish resort wear for men and women.

HANDICRAFTS **Anguilla Arts & Crafts Center** (✉ The Valley ☎ 264/497–2200) carries island crafts, including textiles and ceramics. Look for special exhibits and performances—ranging from puppetry to folk dance—sponsored by the Anguilla National Creative Arts Alliance. **Boopsies** (✉ The Quarter ☎ 264/772–2895), in a Depression-era soda-making factory (antique equipment is displayed throughout), carries everything from bathing suits to local books, woodcarvings to ceramics. **Cheddie's Carving Studios** (✉ The Cove ☎ 264/497–6027) showcases Cheddie Richardson's fanciful creations from marine sculpture to elaborate tables crafted out of mahogany, walnut, and driftwood. **Devonish Art Gallery** (✉ George Hill ☎ 264/497–2949) purveys the wood, stone, and clay creations of Courtney Devonish, an internationally known potter and sculptor, as well as

★ works by other local artists. **Hibernia Restaurant & Gallery** (✉ Island Harbour ☎ 264/497–4290) has striking pieces culled from the owners' travels, from contemporary Eastern European artworks to traditional Indo-Chinese crafts. In the historic Rose Cottage, **Loblolly Gallery** (✉ Coronation St., Lower Valley ☎ 264/497–6006) showcases the work of three expats (Marge Morani, Paula Warden, Georgia Young) working in various media, and also mounts exhibits from Anguilla's artis-

★ tic grande dame, Iris Lewis. **Savannah Gallery** (✉ Coronation St., Lower Valley ☎ 264/497–2263) specializes in Caribbean and Central American art, including watercolors, oil paintings from the renowned Haitian St. Soleil group, Guatemalan textiles, Mexican pottery, and brightly

★ painted metal work. The peripatetic proprietors of **World Arts Gallery** (✉ Old Factory Plaza, The Valley ☎ 264/407–5950 or 264/497–2767 ✉ Cap Juluca, Maundays Bay ☎ 264/497–6666), Nik and Christy Douglas, display a veritable U.N. of antiquities: exquisite Indonesian *ikat* hangings to Thai teak furnishings, Aboriginal didgeridoos to Dogon tribal masks, Yuan Dynasty jade pottery to Uzbeki rugs, Banbara fertility sculptures to 17th-century bronze Buddhas.

Nightlife & the Arts

Nightlife
Most hotels and many restaurants offer live entertainment in high season and on weekends, ranging from pianists and jazz combos to traditional steel and calypso bands. Check the local tourist magazines and newspaper for listings. Fridays and Saturdays, Sandy Ground is the hot spot, while on Wednesdays and Sundays the action shifts to Shoal Bay East.

Corals (⊠ Meads Bay Hideaway, Meads Bay ☎ 264/498–6323) is part of a palapa complex filled with rock gardens and fountains overlooking the Dolphin Encounter attraction and featuring a piano bar, live music, sunset happy hour, lobster bar, and delicious, reasonably priced Middle Eastern *mezes* (small plates). The **Dune Preserve** (⊠ Rendezvous Bay ☎ 264/497–2660) is the home of Bankie Banx, Anguilla's famous Calypso-meets-Dylan recording star, who performs here weekends and during the full moon. Things are lively at **Johnno's Beach Stop** (⊠ Sandy Ground, ☎ 264/497–2728), with live music and alfresco dancing nightly and also on Sunday afternoons, when just about everybody drops by. This is *the* classic Caribbean beach bar, attracting a funky eclectic mix, from locals to movie stars. At the **Pumphouse** (⊠ Sandy Ground ☎ 264/497–5154), in the old rock-salt factory, you'll find live music on weekends, celebrities like Bruce Willis and Charlie Sheen, surprisingly good pub grub, and a mini-museum displaying artifacts and equipment from salt factories of the 19th century. **Rafe's Back Street** (⊠ Sandy Ground ☎ 264/497–3918) is the spot to go for late-night—even all-night on weekends—food, music, and dance. At the **Red Dragon Disco** (⊠ The Valley ☎ 264/497–2687) a DJ plays music Friday, Saturday, and Sunday nights. A faithful clientele gathers in the lively beachfront **Roy's Place** (⊠ Crocus Bay ☎ 264/497–2470) for fabulous sunsets, free Internet access, Roy and Mandy Bosson's British bonhomie, frosty drafts, and the island's best gossip. Friday's 5 to 7 happy hour crams them in for $10–$12 dinner specials. **Uncle Ernie's** (⊠ Shoal Bay ☎ 264/497–3907) often has live music, and a spirited crowd heads here almost every night, as much for the fabulous ribs as the boisterous atmosphere.

Exploring Anguilla

Exploring on Anguilla is mostly about checking out the spectacular beaches and classy resorts. Though the island has only a few roads, some are in bad condition, though the lack of adequate signage is being addressed. Locals are happy to provide directions, but having a good map—and using it—is the best strategy. Get one at the airport, the ferry dock, your hotel, or the tourist office in The Valley.

Numbers in the margin correspond to points of interest on the Anguilla map.

WHAT TO SEE
④ Bethel Methodist Church. Not far from Sandy Ground, this charming little church is an excellent example of skillful island stonework. It also has some colorful stained-glass windows. ⊠ *South Hill* ☎ *no phone.*

❽ Heritage Collection. Anguillian artifacts, old photographs, and records trace the island's history over four millennia, from the days of the Arawaks. The museum is painstakingly curated by Colville Petty, OBE. You can see examples of ancient pottery shards and stone tools along with fascinating photographs of the island in the early 20th century (many depicting the heaping and exporting of salt and the christening of schooners), revealing political campaign displays, and a complete set of beautiful postage stamps issued by Anguilla since 1967. ⊠ *East End, at Pond Ground* ☎ *264/497–4440* ⊕ *www.offshore.com.ai/heritage* ▣ *$5* ⊙ *Mon.–Sat. 9–5.*

★ **❼ Island Harbour.** Anguillians have been fishing for centuries in the brightly painted, simple handcrafted fishing boats that line the shore of the harbor. It's hard to believe, but skillful pilots take these little boats out to sea as far as 50 or 60 mi (80 or 100 km). Late afternoon is the best time to see the day's catch. Hail the boat to **Gorgeous Scilly**

Cay, a classic little restaurant offering sublime lobster and Eudoxie Wallace's knockout rum punches.

❷ **Old Factory.** For many years the cotton grown on Anguilla and exported to England was ginned in this beautiful historic building, now home of the **Anguilla Tourist Office.** Some of the original ginning machinery is intact and on display. ⊠ *The Valley* ☎ *264/497–2759* ☜ *Free* ⊙ *Weekdays 10–noon, 1–4.*

❺ **Old Prison.** The ruins of this historic jail on Anguilla's highest point— 213 ft above sea level—offer outstanding views. ⊠ *Valley Rd., at Crocus Hill.*

❶ **Sandy Ground.** Almost everyone who comes to Anguilla stops by its most developed beach. Little open-air bars and restaurants line the shore, and there are several boutiques, a dive shop, and a small commercial pier. This is where you catch the ferry for tiny **Sandy Island,** just 2 mi (3 km) offshore.

❸ **Wallblake House.** This plantation house with spacious rooms and handsome woodwork was built in 1787 by Will Blake (Wallblake is probably a corruption of his name). The place is associated with many a tale involving murder, high living, and the French invasion in 1796. On the grounds are an ancient vaulted stone cistern and an outbuilding called the Bakery (which wasn't used for making bread at all but for baking turkeys and hams). Call Marjorie McClean at Ferryboat Inn to confirm tour times. ⊠ *Wallblake Rd., The Valley* ☎ *264/497–6613* ☜ *Free* ⊙ *Tours on Tues. and Thurs. at 10 AM.*

❻ **Warden's Place.** This former sugar-plantation great house was built in the 1790s and is a fine example of island stonework. It now houses Koal Keel restaurant (closed indefinitely at this writing) and a sumptuous bakery, Le Petit Patisserie. But for many years it served as the residence of the island's chief administrator, who also doubled as the only medical practitioner. ⊠ *The Valley.*

ANGUILLA A TO Z

To research prices, get advice from other travelers, and book travel arrangements, visit www.fodors.com.

AIR TRAVEL
American Airlines is the major airline, with nonstop flights from the continental United States to its hub in San Juan, from which the airline's American Eagle flies three times daily (twice daily off-season) to Anguilla's Wallblake Airport. Caribbean Star/TransAnguilla offers daily flights from Antigua, St. Thomas, and St. Kitts, and provides air-taxi service on request from neighboring islands. LIAT comes in from Antigua, Nevis, St. Kitts, St. Maarten, St. Thomas, and Tortola. Windward Islands Airways (Winair) wings in daily from St. Thomas and at least three times a day from St. Maarten's Juliana Airport.
🛪 **American Airlines/American Eagle** ☎ 264/497-3131. **Caribbean Star/TransAnguilla** ☎ 264/497-8690. **LIAT** ☎ 264/497-5002. **Windward Islands Airways** ☎ 264/497-2748.

AIRPORTS
Wallblake Airport is the hub on Anguilla. A taxi ride to the Sandy Ground area runs $7–$10; to West End resorts it's $14–$22.
🛪 **Wallblake Airport** ☎ 264/497-2719.

BIKE & MOPED TRAVEL

Scooters run about $25 per day from A & S Scooter, which also rents bicycles—a great way to get around—for $10 per day.

🚲 **A & S Scooter** ✉ The Valley ☎ 264/497-8803.

BOAT & FERRY TRAVEL

FARES & SCHEDULES Ferries run frequently between Anguilla and St. Martin. Boats leave from Blowing Point on Anguilla—approximately every half-hour from 7:30 AM to 6:15 PM—and from Marigot on St. Martin—every half-hour from 8 AM to 7 PM. Check for evening ferries, whose schedule is more erratic. You pay a $3 departure tax before boarding and the $12 one-way fare on board. Don't buy a round-trip ticket, because it restricts you to the boat for which it is purchased. On very windy days the 20-minute trip can be bouncy, so bring medication if you suffer from motion sickness. An information booth outside the customs shed in Blowing Point is usually open daily from 8:30 AM to 5 PM, but sometimes the attendant wanders off. It's also possible to travel directly by ferry from Juliana Airport on St. Maarten to Anguilla (for $5 extra, by reservation only). For schedule information, and info on special boat charters, contact Link Ferries.

🚢 **Link Ferries** ☎ 264/497-2231 ⊕ www.link.ai.

BUSINESS HOURS

BANKS Banks are open Monday–Thursday 8–3 and Friday 8–5.

POST OFFICES The post office is open weekdays 10–noon and 1–4.

SHOPS Most shops are open 10–5 on weekdays, but call first, or adopt the island way of doing things: if it's not open when you stop by, try again.

CAR RENTALS

Your best bet for maximum mobility if you're comfortable driving on the left and don't mind some jostling is to rent a car. To do so, you'll need a temporary local license, which you can obtain for $20 at any of the car-rental agencies; you'll also need your valid driver's license from home.

Apex (Avis), Budget, and Connors (National) rent four-wheel-drive vehicles and sedans. Triple K Car Rental, a local company, is also recommended. Rates are about $45 to $55 per day, plus insurance.

🚗 **Apex/Avis** ✉ Airport Rd. ☎ 264/497-2642. **Budget** ✉ Airport Rd. ☎ 264/497-5871. **Connors/National** ✉ Blowing Point ☎ 264/497-6433. **Triple K Car Rental** ✉ Airport Rd. ☎ 264/497-5934.

CAR TRAVEL

GASOLINE Island gas stations are generally open from 7 AM to 11 PM. Gasoline is expensive; expect to pay EC$7.55 per gallon (about US$2.82).

ROAD CONDITIONS Anguilla's roads are generally paved, but those that are not can be incredibly rutted.

RULES OF THE ROAD Driving is on the left. Observe the 30-mph speed limit and watch out for livestock that amble across the road.

ELECTRICITY

The current is 110 volts, the same as in North America; U.S.-standard two-prong plugs will work just fine.

EMERGENCIES

🚑 **Ambulance & Fire** **Ambulance** ☎ 264/497-2551. **Fire** ☎ 911.
🏥 **Hospitals** **Princess Alexandra Hospital** ✉ Sandy Ground ☎ 264/497-2551.

🔳 Pharmacies **Government Pharmacy** ⊠ Princess Alexandria Hospital, The Valley ☎ 264/497-2551 ⊙ daily 8:30-4. **Paramount Pharmacy** ⊠ Water Swamp ☎ 264/497-2366 ⊙ Mon.-Sat. 8:30-7.
🔳 Police **Police Emergencies** ☎ 911. **Police Nonemergencies** ☎ 264/497-2333.

ETIQUETTE & BEHAVIOR
It's an Anguillian custom to greet people and exchange polite comments about the day or the weather before getting down to business. It's considered quite rude to skip this step, so join in, even if you're in a hurry.

FESTIVALS & SEASONAL EVENTS
In February the Anguilla Cultural Education Festival celebrates island traditions through dance, storytelling, games, and music programs. March brings Moonsplash, a three-day music festival that showcases local talent and begins on the night of the full moon. The Anguilla Culinary Competition is held the last week of May. At the end of July is the International Arts Festival, which hosts artists from around the world. The first two weeks of August is Carnival, which includes parades, street dancing, boat racing, and lots of general merrymaking. BET (Black Entertainment Television) sponsors Tranquility Jazz Festival in November, attracting major musicians.

HOLIDAYS
Public holidays are: New Year's Day, Easter (varies, usually April or May), Easter Monday (the day after Easter), Labour Day (1st Thursday in May), Anguilla Day (last Friday in May), Whit Monday (2nd Monday in May), Queen's Birthday (June 11), August Monday (1st Monday in August), Constitution Day (August 8), Separation Day (December 19), Christmas Day, Boxing Day (December 26).

LANGUAGE
English, with a strong West Indian lilt, is spoken here.

MAIL & SHIPPING
Airmail postcards and letters cost EC$1.50 (for the first ½ ounce) to the United States, Canada, and the United Kingdom, and EC$2.50 to Australia and New Zealand. The only post office is in The Valley; it's open weekdays 8–3:30. When writing to the island, you don't need a postal code; just include the name of the establishment, address (location or post-office box), and "Anguilla, British West Indies."
🔳 **Post Office** ⊠ Wallblake Rd., The Valley ☎ 264/497-2528.

MONEY MATTERS
Prices quoted throughout this chapter are in U.S. dollars unless otherwise indicated.

ATMS The island's five ATMs are often on the blink (Scotia Bank's is the most reliable). Remember, ATMs dispense money in EC dollars only.
🔳 **Scotiabank** ☎ 264/497-3333 ⊕ www.scotiabank.ca.

CREDIT CARDS Credit cards are not always accepted; some resorts will only settle in cash, but a few accept personal checks. Some restaurants add a charge if you pay with a credit card.

CURRENCY Though the legal tender here is the Eastern Caribbean (EC) dollar, U.S. dollars are widely accepted. (You'll often get change in EC dollars, though.) The exchange rate between U.S. and EC dollars is set at EC$2.68 to the U.S. dollar. Be sure to carry lots of small bills; change for a $20 is often difficult to obtain.

PASSPORTS & VISAS

U.S. and Canadian citizens need proof of identity. A passport is preferred (and may be used even if it has expired within the past five years). Also acceptable is a government-issued photo ID, such as a driver's license, *along with* a birth certificate (with raised seal) or naturalization papers. Citizens of the United Kingdom, Australia, and New Zealand must have passports. Everyone must also have a return or ongoing ticket. Visitor's passes are valid for stays of up to three months.

SAFETY

Anguilla is a quiet, relatively safe island, but there's no point in tempting fate by leaving your valuables unattended in your hotel room, on the beach, or in your car.

SIGHTSEEING TOURS

GUIDED TOURS A round-the-island tour by taxi takes about 2½ hours and costs $40 for one or two people, $5 for each additional passenger. Bennie's Tours is one of the island's more reliable tour operators. Malliouhana Travel and Tours create personalized package tours of the island.

🛈 **Bennie's Tours** ⊠ Blowing Point ☎ 264/497-2788. **Malliouhana Travel and Tours** ⊠ The Valley ☎ 264/497-2431.

SPECIAL-INTEREST TOURS Sir Emile Gumbs, former chief minister, runs tours of the Sandy Ground area, highlighting historic and ecological sites Tuesdays at 10 AM for $10 per person (proceeds go to the Anguilla Archaeological Historical Society). The walk includes the 1910 Old Methodist Manse, Anglican graveyards, Amerindian wells, a ruined sugar mill, the Pumphouse (former salt factory), and natural phenomena from lava outcroppings to salt ponds. He also organizes birdwatching expeditions (dozens of species run from frigate birds to turtle doves). The Old Valley Tour conducted by longtime resident Frank Costin ambles the road up Crocus Hill, a treasure trove of Anguilla's best-preserved historic edifices, including Ebenezer's Methodist Church (the island's oldest), the Warden's Place, and typical turn-of-the-century cottages (most housing galleries). The tour is by appointment only and offers a fascinating insight into Anguillian architecture, past and present.

🛈 **Old Valley Tour** ☎ 264/497-2263. **Sir Emile Gumbs** ☎ 264/497-2711.

TAXES

DEPARTURE TAX The departure tax is $20, payable in cash at the airport; $3 if you leave by boat, payable in cash at the ferry dock.

OTHER TAXES A 10% accommodations tax is added to hotel bills.

TAXIS

Taxi rates are regulated by the government, and there are fixed fares from point to point (listed in brochures the drivers should have). Posted rates are for one or two people; each additional passenger adds $3 to the total.

Taxis are always waiting to pick up passengers at the Blowing Point landing docks. It costs $16 to get to Malliouhana, $20 to Cap Juluca, and $22 to most hotels farther afield.

TELEPHONES

Cable & Wireless is open weekdays 8–6, Saturday 9–1, and Sunday 10–2; it sells Caribbean phone cards for use in specially marked phone booths. The cards can be used for local calls, calls to other islands, and calls to the U.S. Inside the departure lounge at the Blowing Point ferry dock and at the airport there's an AT&T USADirect access phone for collect or credit-card calls to the United States.

7 Cable & Wireless ⊠ Wallblake Rd. ☎ 264/497-3100.

COUNTRY & AREA CODES To call Anguilla from the United States, dial 1 plus the area code 264, then the local seven-digit number. From the United Kingdom dial 001 and then the area code and the number. From Australia and New Zealand dial 0011, then 1, then the area code and the number.

INTERNATIONAL CALLS International direct dial is available on the island. To call internationally, dial 1, the area code, and the seven-digit number to reach the United States and Canada; dial 011, 44, and the local number for the U.K.; dial 011, 61, and the local number for Australia; and dial 011, 64, and the local number for New Zealand. Although you can dial direct from your hotel room, it's cheaper to dial the access number for one of the long-distance carriers and charge your call to a major credit card.

7 Cable and Wireless ☎ 800/744-2000 or 800/225-5872.

LOCAL CALLS To make a local call, dial the seven-digit number.

TIPPING

A 10–15% service charge is added to all hotel bills; sometimes it covers all staff members, sometimes not. If you're unsure whether to tip hotel staff, ask the hotel management. Most restaurants include a similar service charge; if not, tip waitstaff as you would at home—15% to 18%. Tip taxi drivers 10% of the fare.

VISITOR INFORMATION

7 Before You Leave Anguilla Tourist Office/River Communications ⊕ www.anguilla-vacation.com ⊙ Oakwood House, Unit 8A, 414–422 Hackney Rd., London 1E2 7SY ☎ 0207/729-8003 ⊟ 0207/729-8829.

7 In Anguilla Anguilla Tourist Office ⊠ Old Factory Plaza, The Valley ☎ 264/497-2759, 800/553-4939 from the U.S. ⊟ 264/497-2710.

ANTIGUA

FODOR'S CHOICE
Chez Pascal restaurant, Five Islands
Curtain Bluff resort, Morris Bay
Historic English Harbour

HIGHLY RECOMMENDED

RESTAURANTS   Alberto's, Willoughby Bay
Coconut Grove, Dickenson Bay
HQ, English Harbour

HOTELS   Admiral's Inn, English Harbour
Catamaran Hotel, Falmouth
Dickenson Bay Cottages, Marble Hill
Erindell Villa Guesthouse, Montserrat
Galley Bay, Five Islands
K Club, Spanish Wells Point
Siboney Beach Club, Dickenson Buy

SIGHTS   Barbuda

Many other great places enliven this area. For other
favorites, look for the black stars as you read this chapter.

It's Antigua Sailing Week, the island's version of the Henley Regatta. Seasoned sea salts claim prized seats on the flagstone terrace of the 18th-century Admiral's Inn in English Harbour. Some boats are docked so close that you can almost eavesdrop from shore. Competitors trade stories (tall and otherwise) of sailing—and drinking—three sheets to the wind, while eyeing the yachts. Blazered bluebloods mingle with lobster-hue tourists; it's Cannes in the Caribbean.

Updated by
Jordan Simon

Antigua (an-*tee*-ga), which at 108 square mi (280 square km) is the largest of the British Leeward Islands, is renowned among sailors for its incomparable air of nautical history. For Anglophiles and history buffs, English Harbour and the surrounding villages and sites are also immensely rewarding. And Antigua seduces landlubbers and sailors alike with its sensuous beaches, 365 in all—one for every day of the year, as locals like to boast. All are public, some are deserted, and others, particularly in the northwest, are lined with resorts that offer dining, nightlife, shopping, sailing, diving, windsurfing, and snorkeling.

The original inhabitants of Antigua were the Ciboney. They lived here 4,000 years ago and disappeared mysteriously, leaving the island unpopulated for about 1,000 years. When Columbus arrived in 1493, the Arawaks had set up housekeeping. The English took up residence in 1632. After 30-odd years of bloody battles involving the Caribs, the Dutch, the French, and the English, the French ceded Antigua to the English in 1667. Antigua remained under English control until achieving full independence on November 1, 1981, along with its sister island, Barbuda, 26 mi (42 km) to the north.

Tourism is the leading industry here, but Antigua maintains a strong sense of national identity to match its rich historic inheritance. Its cricketers, like the legendary Viv Richards (arguably the greatest batsman the game has ever seen), are famous throughout the world. Its people are known for their sharp commercial spirit (a typically revealing—and disarming—sign reads DIANE'S BOUTIQUE AND CAR PARTS); their wit; and unfortunately, at the government level, their corruption.

WHAT IT COSTS In U.S. dollars				
$$$$	**$$$**	**$$**	**$**	**¢**
RESTAURANTS*				
over $30	$20–$30	$12–$20	$8–$12	under $8
HOTELS**				
Cost EP/BP/CP over $350	$250–$350	$150–$250	$80–$150	under $80
Cost AI over $450	$350–$450	$250–$350	$125–$250	under $125

*Restaurant prices are for a main course at dinner. **EP, BP, and CP prices are per night for a standard double room in high season, excluding taxes, service charges, and meal plans. AI (all-inclusive) prices are per person, per night based on double-occupancy during high season, excluding taxes and service charges.

Where to Stay

Scattered along Antigua's beaches and hillsides are exclusive, elegant hideaways; romantic restored inns; go-barefoot-everywhere places; and, increasingly, all-inclusive hot spots for couples. Choose accommodations near St. John's—anywhere between Dickenson Bay and Five Islands Peninsula—if you want to be close to the action. English Harbour, far from St. John's, has the best inns and several excellent restaurants—many closed from August well into October; it's also the yachting crowd's hangout. Elsewhere on the island, resorts cater more to those people who want to stay put or are seeking seclusion. Many smaller establishments have become all-inclusive to survive the fierce competition; some are so remote that trying to arrange an EP rate makes no sense unless you have a car. Another trend: restaurants adding a clutch of charming, affordable cottages.

$$$$ 🏨 **Blue Waters Hotel.** Although its twin beaches are small, the hotel's location—amid 14 acres of tropical gardens—is splendid, luring a soigné British crowd. The colonnaded lobby has sweeping sea views, mosaic tile lamps, peacock wicker chairs, and fountains. Rooms are stark but sparkling in white with teal or floral accents, rattan furnishings, and glazed-tile bathrooms. The four villas and two enormous suites are exquisite, but the ultimate in hedonism is the separate, fully equipped three-bedroom Rock Cottage. Afternoon tea and one sauna per week are included. The casual Palm Restaurant serves Italian cuisine, while Vyvien's has a Continental menu that changes daily. ✉ *Boon Point* ⌂ *Box 256, St. John's* ☎ *268/462–0290 or 800/557–6536* 🖷 *268/462–0293* ⊕ *www. bluewaters.net* ⇆ *73 rooms, 4 villas, 1 2-bedroom cottage* ♿ *2 restaurants, room service, fans, in-room safes, minibars, cable TV, tennis court, 2 pools, gym, hair salon, spa, 2 beaches, snorkeling, windsurfing, boating, 2 bars, shops* ⊟ *AE, D, DC, MC, V* ⍟ *AI.*

$$$$
Fodor'sChoice
★
🏨 **Curtain Bluff.** Howard Hulford continually reinvigorates this beachfront grande dame, which opened in 1962, but it remains devoted to life's (and Howard's) pleasures: lavish gardens, Cubanos, fine food, and finer wines (the resort's 25,000-bottle cellar is legendary). Spacious junior suites are stunning, with marble bathrooms, stylish local artworks, Mexican earthenware, and coffered raw wood ceilings. Ravishing duplex suites zigzag up the bluff. The open-air restaurant provides sterling Continental dining, followed by dancing to live bands. The unparalleled setting, exceptional service, extras (free yoga classes, scuba, and deep-sea fishing), and quietly posh country-club feel make Curtain Bluff that rare world-class resort that's a bargain in its class. ✉ *Morris Bay* ⌂ *Box 288, St. John's* ☎ *268/462–8400, 212/289–8888, 888/ 289–9898 outside NY for reservations* 🖷 *268/462–8409* ⊕ *www. curtainbluff.com* ⇆ *64 rooms, 9 suites* ♿ *2 restaurants, fans, in-room safes, putting green, 4 tennis courts, pool, gym, hair salon, massage, 2 beaches, dive shop, snorkeling, windsurfing, boating, fishing, croquet, squash, bar, shops, library, playground, meeting rooms, Internet; no a/ c, no room TVs* ⊟ *AE* ☉ *Closed mid-May–mid-Oct.* ⍟ *AI.*

★ **$$$$** 🏨 **Galley Bay.** This tony all-inclusive appeals to couples and corporate honchos. A man-made pool grotto, a bleached-wood boardwalk along the champagne-hued beach, a blue lagoon, manicured gardens, and a surrounding bird sanctuary with trails are some of its attractions. African carvings and Caribbean art naïf fill the thatch-roofed public spaces and sinuous stucco walls of the Gauguin Village's slightly claustrophobic wattle-and-daub cottages, whose bathrooms are connected via private walkways. Airy beachfront rooms have terra-cotta tiles, island art, and custom-made rattan and bamboo furnishings; deluxe suites have natural wicker furnishings, huge patios, and Italian marble bathrooms. Afternoon tea and lilting live nightly entertainment are pleasant extras. ✉ *Five Islands* ⌂ *Box 305, St. John's* ☎ *268/462–0302 or 800/345– 0271* 🖷 *268/462–4551* ⊕ *www.eliteislandresorts.com* ⇆ *70 rooms*

Antigua & Barbuda

TO BARBUDA

ANTIGUA

Boon Pt.

Hodges Bay

Prickly Pear Island

Beggar's Pt.

Long Island

No Sou

Cedar Grove

24 25

23

26 – 29

30

21

22

V.C. Bird Int'l. Airport

Dickenson Bay

Runaway Beach

Andes 31

Deepwater Harbour

St. John's

Potters

Parham 10

33 32

1

1 – 3

Five Islands

Hawksbill's Beaches

34

Pares

8

Fullerton Pt.

Parham Rd.

Pearns Pt.

Jennings

2

All Saints

4

Jolly Harbour

5

6

Bolans

Boggy Peak

Fig Tree Drive

3

7

Darkwood Beach

8

Johnson's Pt.

Urlings

Old Road

Falmouth

4

10

English Harbour

Johnson's Point

9

Falmouth Bay

5

16

6

Cades Reef

Carlisle Bay

Rendezvous Bay

Pigeon Point

11 13

14 15

Shirle Heigh

Caribbean Sea

Guadeloupe

0   5 miles

0   5 km

BARBUDA

Goat Pt.
Hog Pt.
Cedar-Tree Pt.
Two Foot Bay
11
Bird Sanctuary
Codrington Lagoon
Low Bay
Codrington
Palmetto Pt.
Martello Tower
Pink Beach
20
Spanish Pt.

5 miles
5 km

Bird Island
North Sound
Guiana Island
Crump Island
ATLANTIC
Long Bay
19 9
Willikies
Nonsuch Bay
7
Green Island
Freetown
OCEAN
Willoughby Bay
Half Moon Bay
18
17
Mamora Bay
Passage

KEY

Beaches
Cruise Ship Terminal
Dive Sites
● Exploring Sights
① Hotels & Restaurants

⚲ *2 restaurants, grill, fans, in-room safes, refrigerators, tennis court, pool, gym, beach, snorkeling, windsurfing, boating, bicycles, croquet, horseshoes, bar, shops; no kids under 16* ▭ *AE, D, DC, MC, V* ⅩⅪ *AI.*

$$$$ ⊡ **Jumby Bay.** New management and nearly $6 million in renovations may return this Long Island resort to ultra-swank status after years of soap-operatic ownership feuds. In "standard" rooms and junior suites, polished teak trimmings and hand-carved mahogany four-poster beds are accented by earth-tone fabrics and local crafts; several have indoor/outdoor bathrooms. Luxe villas have pools and hand-painted tilework. Villa owners—such as Robin Leach and Ken Follett—mingle at the 250-year-old stone-and-mahogany Estate House dining room and its whimsical, jungle-theme lounge. You can turtle-watch in season, bike along nature trails, and luxuriate on secluded beaches anywhere on the island. Airport transfers and ferry service are free. ✉ *Long Island* ⌀ *Box 243, St. John's* ☎ *268/462–6000* ⎙ *268/462–6020* ⊕ *www. jumbybayresort.com* ⇗ *39 rooms, 12 villas* ⚲ *2 restaurants, fans, minibars, putting green, 3 tennis courts, gym, spa, 3 beaches, snorkeling, windsurfing, waterskiing, bicycles, croquet, 2 bars, shops; no room TVs* ▭ *AE, MC, V* ⅩⅪ *AI.*

★ $$$$ ⊡ **K Club.** The *K* is famed Italian designer Krizia, whose dramatic style animates this superdeluxe Barbuda hideaway. Public spaces have gleaming white tiles and columns, natural-wicker furnishings with plush cushions, and cloth-and-bronze sculptures. Beachfront units are equally chic: white wicker and tile, cool, ocean-hued fabrics, wooden chairs whimsically carved with pineapples, bamboo mats, showers submerged in vegetation, wittily provocative paintings (blood-red stilettos sitting on a beach). The kitchen innovatively fuses Tuscan grilling and Caribbean ingredients. Rates—which include a Full American meal plan—are princely, but what price privacy and style if you have the ducats? ✉ *Spanish Wells Point, Barbuda* ⌀ *Box 2288, St. John's* ☎ *268/460–0300* ⎙ *268/ 460–0305* ⊕ *www.lhw.com* ⇗ *35 units* ⚲ *Restaurant, grill, fans, some kitchenettes, 9-hole golf course, 2 tennis courts, pool, hot tub, beach, snorkeling, windsurfing, boating, waterskiing, fishing, bar, recreation room; no room TVs, no kids under 12* ▭ *AE, DC, MC, V* ⅩⅪ *FAP.*

$$$$ ⊡ **St. James's Club.** Spacious accommodations, varied restaurants, a lovely setting (covering 100 acres at Mamora Bay), and extensive facilities make this a popular resort. Unfortunately, it lives off its now faded reputation and tony name. Rooms have fresh, vibrant color schemes, though discolored concrete terraces and often indifferent service undermine the luxe image. A cluster of two-bedroom villas spills down hills toward the main buildings. The oceanfront Beach Club offers the best value: larger, more distinctive rooms at a lower price. Though nonmotorized water sports and afternoon tea are complimentary, most people opt for the all-inclusive package, as the remote location makes dining out difficult. ✉ *Mamora Bay* ⌀ *Box 54, St. John's* ☎ *268/460–5000 or 800/ 345–0271* ⎙ *268/460–3215* ⊕ *www.eliteislandresorts.com* ⇗ *187 rooms, 72 villas* ⚲ *3 restaurants, grill, room service, fans, golf privileges, 7 tennis courts, 4 pools, gym, hair salon, hot tub, spa, 2 beaches, dive shop, dock, snorkeling, windsurfing, boating, croquet, 4 bars, casino, nightclub* ▭ *AE, D, DC, MC, V* ⅩⅪ *AI.*

$$$$ ⊡ **Sandals Antigua Resort and Spa.** This superior resort exclusively for male-female couples percolates with activity, from vigorous volleyball competitions to relaxing karaoke at the swank piano bar. Almost everything—including tennis lessons and scuba diving—is included (spa treatments and weddings are extra). Exceptionally handsome public spaces include the reception area, opening onto a courtyard with painted tile stairways, stained-glass panels, and an unimpeded sea view. The spacious, fresh guest quarters include ocean- or garden-view rooms, beachfront suites, and rondavels, many with four poster beds. Four restaurants prepare superlative Continental, Italian, Japanese, and southwestern fare. There's a three-night minimum. ⊠ *Dickenson Bay* ⌂ *Box 147, St. John's* ☎ *268/462–0267 or 888/726–3257* ⎙ *268/462–4135* ⊕ *www.sandals.com* ⇨ *100 rooms, 77 suites, 16 rondavels* ⌂ *4 restaurants, grill, fans, in-room safes, 2 tennis courts, 5 pools, gym, hair salon, 5 hot tubs, spa, beach, dive shop, snorkeling, windsurfing, boating, waterskiing, 4 bars, nightclub, shops* ▭ *AE, D, DC, MC, V* ⧎ *AI.*

$$$–$$$$ ⊞ **Hawksbill Beach Hotel.** This refined resort straddles 37 lavishly landscaped acres, including five beaches (one clothing-optional). The reception area and main dining room rest on a small bluff with panoramic vistas of the restored sugar mill, the classy three-bedroom West Indian great house, the sea, and Montserrat. The secluded Club rooms have tile floors, light rattan furnishings, hand-painted bathroom tiles, vaulted ceilings, and the most spectacular views (especially numbers 138–142). Gingerbread-trim cottages have smallish deluxe and garden-view rooms (the latter usually have restricted water views and represent better value). Most water sports are free. Hawksbill attracts primarily a mix of mature couples and honeymooners. ⊠ *Five Islands* ⌂ *Box 108, St. John's* ☎ *268/462–0301, 800/223–6510, 416/622–8813 in Canada* ⎙ *268/462–1515* ⊕ *www.hawksbill.com* ⇨ *111 rooms, 1 3-bedroom villa* ⌂ *2 restaurants, fans, refrigerators, tennis court, pool, 5 beaches, snorkeling, windsurfing, boating, 2 bars, shops, Internet, meeting rooms; no a/c in some rooms, no room TVs* ▭ *AE, DC, MC, V* ⧎ *EP.*

$$$–$$$$ ⊞ **Occidental Grand Pineapple Beach.** Buildings at this bustling, beautifully landscaped all-inclusive are ordinary but serviceable; the best cling to the hillside, offering sweeping views of the splendid white-sand crescent below. Public spaces and facilities, including a pool with bridges and waterfall and an elegant plantation-style piano bar, brim with local charm. The buffet-style main restaurant and the intimate Pineapple Grill serve worthy Caribbean and Continental dishes. The latter, a split-level riot of lime, mango, and peach, becomes a late-night disco. The shack-chic hilltop Outhouse Bar is the perfect sunset perch. Despite the resort's remote location, the range of activities entices families and honeymooners alike. ⊠ *Long Bay* ⌂ *Box 2000, St. John's* ☎ *268/463–2006 or 800/345–0271* ⎙ *268/463–2452* ⊕ *www.eliteislandresorts.com* ⇨ *180 rooms* ⌂ *3 restaurants, fans, 4 tennis courts, 2 pools, gym, beach, snorkeling, windsurfing, boating, waterskiing, fishing, croquet, horseshoes, volleyball, 4 bars, nightclub, shops, children's programs (ages 4 to 12)* ▭ *AE, D, DC, MC, V* ⧎ *AI.*

$$$–$$$$ ⊞ **Rex Halcyon Cove Beach Resort.** Tour groups stampede to this lively but somewhat rundown, impersonal hotel on beautiful Dickenson Bay. The institutional concrete buildings, softened by coral or lavender paint jobs, terra-cotta tile walkways, and luxuriant gardens, sit around a courtyard and along the beach. Room sizes, views, and amenities vary widely (poolside rooms with limited sea views are the best buys), but most have white tile, blond-wood furnishings, and rattan beds and mirrors. A water-sports center is on the busy beach. The Warri Pier restaurant, perched dramatically on stilts over the ocean, serves superior seafood and grilled fare. Although other rates are available, all-inclusive is the better bargain. ⊠ *Dickenson Bay* ⌂ *Box 251, St. John's* ☎ *268/462–0256 or 800/255–5859* ⎙ *268/462–0271* ⊕ *www.rexresorts.com* ⇨ *193 rooms, 17 suites* ⌂ *2 restaurants, grill, ice-cream parlor, room service, in-room safes, some refrigerators, 4 tennis courts, pool, hair salon, massage, beach, dive shop, windsurfing, boating, waterskiing, 4 bars, shops, children's programs (ages 3 to 12), business services, car rental* ▭ *AE, D, DC, MC, V* ⧎ *AI.*

$$–$$$$ ⊡ **Inn at English Harbour.** The original hilltop buildings—the bar-dining room and six guest rooms, with majestic views of English Harbour, plus four cramped beachfront rooms and the funky-elegant beach bar—recall this Brit-favored resort's more genteel days. Alas, the three main whitewashed, gray-shingled buildings sit inexplicably in a breezeless area behind the horizon pool far from the beach. The huge, handsome rooms with mahogany four-posters, hand-painted armoires, candelabra sconces, and porphyry bathrooms, are regrettably dark. Opt for top-floor units, with cathedral ceilings, hardwood floors, and better views. The romantic flagstone-terrace dining room serves excellent Continental fare. Water taxis the harbor are free, as are nonmotorized water sports. ⊠ *English Harbour* ⊕ *Box 187, St. John's* ☎ *268/460–1014 or 800/223–6510; 800/424–5500 in Canada* 🖷 *268/460–1603* ⊕ *www. theinn.ag* ⤳ *34 units* ⚥ *Restaurant, grill, fans, some TVs, in-room safes, refrigerators, 2 tennis courts, pool, gym, beach, snorkeling, windsurfing, boating, waterskiing, 2 bars, Internet; no a/c* ▱ *AE, D, DC, MC, V* ☉ *Closed mid-Aug.–Oct.* ⑩ *EP.*

$$–$$$ ⊡ **CocoBay.** A hillside retreat on the west coast, CocoBay aims to "eliminate all potential worries." Creole-style cottages with corrugated iron roofs are staggered amid fragrant tropical gardens. Understated decor stresses natural beauty: bleached wood louvers, stained pine floors, mosquito netting, and sisal rugs. The blue-and-white-tile bathrooms open onto terraces with marvelous bay views (wattle-and-daub walls ensure privacy between adjoining units). A wellness center offers massages, facials, scrubs, and aromatherapy; nature hikes can also be arranged. Complimentary cell phones (you pay for calls) keep the frantic in touch. Only indifferent food and merely average beaches detract somewhat from the restful experience. ⊠ *Valley Church* ⊕ *Box 431, St. John's* ☎ *268/562–2400 or 800/816–7587* 🖷 *268/562–2424* ⊕ *www.cocobayresort.com* ⤳ *42 rooms, 4 2-bedroom houses* ⚥ *Restaurant, fans, in-room safes, refrigerators, pool, gym, spa, 2 beaches, snorkeling, bar, shops, Internet; no a/c, no room TVs* ▱ *AE, MC, V* ⑩ *AI.*

★ **$$–$$$** ⊡ **Dickenson Bay Cottages.** A remarkable buy for families, this small hillside development perches just above Dickenson Bay. Gardens surround the two-story, villa-style buildings; units are attractively appointed with rattan furnishings, blond woods, and vivid abstract and floral fabrics. Larger units have two bedrooms upstairs and large verandahs overlooking the ocean. Resort guests have privileges at Halcyon Cove's active beach, a five-minute walk; you can also use the tennis and water-sports facilities there at a 20% discount. Entertainment and restaurants are available at nearby resorts. This appealing complex is often inexplicably deserted, so ask about last-minute discounts. ⊠ *Marble Hill* ⊕ *Box 1376, St. John's* ☎ *268/462–4940* 🖷 *268/462–4941* ⊕ *www. dickensonbaycottages.com* ⤳ *11 units* ⚥ *Fans, kitchens, kitchenettes, some in-room VCRs, pool* ▱ *AE, DC, MC, V* ⑩ *EP.*

$$–$$$ ⊡ **Jolly Beach Resort.** Colorful splashes and fancy touches like a huge fantasy pool, faux sugar mills, and a charming old-style creole shopping village can't disguise this hotel's gimcrack origins. Its horrid cinderblock structures still have rusting rails and peeling paint, and "supersaver" rooms are the size of monks' cells with bizarre, built-in concrete shelves and tables. Still, the grounds are lovely, the long beach is strewn with inviting palapas, the virtual U.N. of restaurants is good, the service is friendly, the activities and facilities are superior to those of many pricier all-inclusives, and even the smallest quarters have ocean views. It's a remarkable value for budget-minded honeymooners, families, and singles. ⊠ *Jolly Harbour* ⊕ *Box 2009, St. John's* ☎ *268/462–0061 or 866/905–6559* 🖷 *268/562–2117* ⊕ *www.jollybeachresort. com* ⤳ *462 units* ⚥ *4 restaurants, grill, in-room safes, some refriger-*

ators, 4 tennis courts, 2 pools, hot tub, aerobics, gym, beach, dive shop, snorkeling, windsurfing, boating, waterskiing, 7 bars, nightclub, recreation room, shops, children's programs (ages 2–12), Internet, meeting rooms ▤ AE, D, MC, V ⑩ AI.

$$–$$$ ▦ **Rex Blue Heron.** This cozy, welcoming resort sits on a magnificent sweep of sand. Don't be misled by the mousy faux-stucco buildings; each room—save for a few "standard" units—has hardwood or gleaming white-tile floors, powder-blue and tropical-print fabrics, stylish ceramic lamps, and an ocean-view patio or terrace. It's extremely difficult to get a reservation here, because discerning European tour operators keep it booked. The reasonable prices, intimacy, and secluded location lure a young, hip clientele. ⊠ Johnson's Point ⊕ Box 1715, St. John's ☎ 268/ 462–8564 or 800/255–5859 ⊕ 268/462–8005 ⊕ www.rexresorts.com ⇦ 64 rooms ⚹ Restaurant, fans, pool, beach, snorkeling, windsurfing, boating, 2 bars, shops; no a/c in some rooms, no TV in some rooms ▤ AE, D, MC, V ⑩ AI.

$$–$$$ ▦ **Royal Antiguan Resort.** Perfect entry-level Caribbean for singles, honeymooners, groups, and families on a budget, this sterile high-rise has all the amenities and facilities of a moderate American chain. Fortunately, its island flair includes spectacular large murals in the restaurants, plus fountains, hand-painted columns, local pottery, and Carnival costume displays in the lobby. Unusual extras range from dialect classes to palm readings. A lagoon pool with swim-up bar, three restaurants serving Italian to Caribbean cuisine, 150 slot and video-poker machines, a shipwreck reef, and hiking trails and guided nature walks to Ft. Barrington, with its stunning views of St. John's Harbour, are other attractions. ⊠ Deep Bay ⊕ Box 1322, St. John's ☎ 268/462–3733 or 800/345– 0271 ⊕ 268/462–3732 ⊕ www.eliteislandresorts.com ⇦ 266 rooms, 12 suites ⚹ 3 restaurants, room service, refrigerators, some in-room VCRs, golf privileges, 8 tennis courts, pool, gym, hair salon, beach, dive shop, snorkeling, windsurfing, boating, waterskiing, fishing, croquet, horseshoes, 4 bars, shops ▤ AE, D, MC, V ⑩ AI.

★ $$–$$$ ▦ **Siboney Beach Club.** Aussie Tony Johnson arrived in Antigua in the late 1950s on a yacht crew, but ended up building some of the island's finest resorts, eventually opening this small gem on Dickenson Bay. Each suite has a small bedroom, cleverly designed Pullman-style kitchen, living room, and cozy patio or balcony. Rooms vary slightly, but all have bright splashes of color, rattan furnishings, and knickknacks from Tony's travels. Room 9 overlooks the sea, but the soothing sound of the surf permeates even those with partial views. Tony and his staff cordially dispense advice like a de facto tourist board. TVs can be provided on request. ⊠ Dickenson Bay ⊕ Box 222, St. John's ☎ 268/462–0806 or 800/533–0234 ⊕ 268/462–3356 ⊕ www.siboneybeachclub.com ⇦ 12 suites ⚹ Restaurant, fans, in-room safes, kitchenettes, pool, beach, bar; no room TVs ▤ AE, MC, V ⑩ EP, MAP.

$$ ▦ **Jolly Harbour Villas.** Although the main activity area strives to re-create a Mediterranean village with red-tile roofs, faux stucco, and pale mustard arcades, this 350-acre compound lacks style. That said, its fully equipped, two-bedroom villas—cookie-cutter, pastel-hued duplex units that seem straight from the Sunbelt—represent one of Antigua's best values, particularly for families and golfers (unlimited greens fees for $99/ week). Most units feature water views and white and natural rattan or wicker furnishings with floral and jungle fabrics. The complex offers nearly every conceivable facility, including a complimentary shuttle, but you must pay separately for all but swimming pool and Kids Club access. ⊠ Jolly Harbour ⊕ Box 1793, St. John's ☎ 268/462–7771 or 800/345–0356 ⊕ 268/462–7772 ⊕ www.eliteislandresorts.com ⇦ 150 units ⚹ 7 restaurants, fans, in-room safes, kitchens, 3 pools, 4 tennis

courts, squash court, 18-hole golf course, miniature golf, hair salon, 2 beaches, dive shop, snorkeling, windsurfing, boating, marina, waterskiing, 6 bars, shops, casino, nightclub, children's programs (ages 3–11), playground, car rental, helipad; no a/c in some rooms, no TV in some rooms ⊟ AE, D, DC, MC, V ¶⊙| EP.

★ $–$$ ⊞ **Admiral's Inn.** Once the engineers' office and warehouse at what is now Nelson's Dockyard, the lovingly restored, 18th-century "Ads" (as yachtspeople call it) reverberates with history. Its best rooms, upstairs in the main building, have the original timbered ceilings—complete with iron braces—hardwood floors, and brick walls. Straw mats from Dominica, four-poster beds, and sunny harbor views through wispy Australian pines complete the effect. The fully equipped, two-bedroom Loft (once the dockyard's joinery) has a magnificent harbor view from its timbered living room. Avoid the hordes descending on the Dockyard (and the inn's terrace for lunch) by taking advantage of the complimentary shuttle to nearby beaches. ⊠ English Harbour ⑤ Box 713, St. John's ☎ 268/460–1027 or 800/223–5695 ⊟ 268/460–1534 ⊕ www. antiguanice.com/admirals ⤻ 14 rooms, 1 2-bedroom apartment ⚭ Restaurant, fans, pub; no a/c in some rooms, no TV in some rooms ⊟ AE, MC, V ¶⊙| EP.

★ $ ⊞ **Catamaran Hotel.** A wraparound verandah, columns, and hand-carved doors give this shipshape little hostelry a plantation look, accentuated by aqua canopies and peach trim. Cheerful Caribbean-colored fabrics, sailing paintings, faux-Victorian brass sconces, and straw lamps add to the nautical feel; deluxe rooms have four-poster beds. Nonmotorized water sports and instruction are free at the minuscule tawny beach, lined with palm and almond trees and staring straight at mega-yachts bobbing in the marina (locals often race hand-made model boats on Sundays). ⊠ Falmouth ⑤ Box 958, St. John's ☎ 268/460–1036 or 800/223–6510 ⊟ 268/460–1339 ⊕ www.catamaran-antigua.com ⤻ 14 rooms ⚭ Restaurant, in-room safes, some kitchenettes, fans, beach, boating, windsurfing, marina, bar, shops; no TV in some rooms ⊟ AE, D, MC, V ¶⊙|EP.

$ ⊞ **Sunsail Club Colonna.** The British Sunsail outfit is renowned worldwide for its superior, affordable sailing and windsurfing schools, and attentiveness to families. Red-tile and stucco buildings charmingly surround a faux sugar mill. The free-form pool, said to be the largest in the Lesser Antilles, compensates for the smallish man-made beaches. Public areas are a tad dilapidated, but rooms have immaculate tile floors, Italian striped fabrics, and rattan furnishings. Use of the superb state-of-the-art sailing and windsurfing equipment and group instruction are free. Most meals, usually buffet or barbecue, are included. Avid sailors should inquire about weekly discounts and land/sail packages. ⊠ Hodges Bay ⑤ Box 591, St. John's ☎ 268/462–6263 or 800/327–2276 ⊟ 268/462–6430 ⊕ www.sunsail.com ⤻ 102 rooms, 15 villas ⚭ Restaurant, grill, in-room safes, minibars, tennis court, pool, hair salon, massage, spa, 2 beaches, snorkeling, windsurfing, boating, 2 bars, shops, children's programs (ages 3–12) ⊟ AE, D, MC, V ¶⊙| MAP.

¢–$ ⊞ **Ocean Inn.** Scintillating harbor views and a convivial air distinguish this small inn. The main house has six guest rooms; four cottages are on a hillside. Informal parties are thrown by the small, mural-adorned pool, while Thursday steak nights lure local characters, yachties, and eccentric expats to the Tree Trunk Bar. A separate four-bedroom house with kitchen, hot tub, washer-dryer, and private jetty rents for an astounding $600 a night; when not leased by groups, rooms are let individually—and those lucky enough to stay there have the run of the joint. The nearest beach is a five-minute drive. ⊠ English Harbour ⑤ Box 838, St. John's ☎ 268/460–1263 ⊕ www.theoceaninn.com ⤻ 6 rooms, 4 cottages, 1 4-bedroom house ⚭ Grill, fans, pool, bar ⊟ AE, MC, V ¶⊙| CP.

Where to Eat

Antigua's restaurants are almost a dying breed since the advent of all-inclusives. But several worthwhile, lively hotel dining rooms and nightspots remain, especially in the English Harbour and Dickenson Bay areas, in addition to many stalwarts. Virtually every chef incorporates local ingredients and elements of West Indian cuisine.

Most menus list prices in both EC and US dollars, but if not, you should verify in which currency the prices are listed. It's also a good idea to ask if credit cards are accepted and if service is included. Dinner reservations are needed during high season.

What to Wear

Perhaps because of the island's British heritage, Antiguans tend to dress more formally for dinner than dwellers on many other Caribbean islands. Wraps and shorts (no beach attire) are de rigueur for lunch, except at local hangouts.

CARIBBEAN
$$–$$$
✕ **Commissioner Grill.** White-tile floors, powder-blue chairs, floral tablecloths, glass buoys, Antiguan pottery, conch shells, and historic maps give this converted 19th-century tamarind warehouse a timeless island feel. Specials might include whelks in garlic butter, bacon-wrapped plantains in mustard sauce, snapper in lobster sauce, or mahimahi creole. Local seafood is the obvious choice, although beef and poultry are also reliable. Lunch is considerably cheaper and more authentic. ⊠ *Commissioner Alley and Redcliffe St., St. John's* 🕾 *268/462–1883* ⊟ *AE, DC, MC, V.*

$$–$$$
✕ **Sticky Wicket.** With a dining room framed by flagstone columns and an open kitchen—not to mention the creative fare served—this is one of the classiest sports bars imaginable. Cricket is the overriding theme, but whether you are sitting in the posh lounge surrounded by cricket memorabilia or outside on the patio overlooking the equally handsome cricket stadium, you'll enjoy everything from snacks (definitive conch fritters) or local specialties (sterling mahimahi with a passion-fruit, mango, and lime salsa) to knockout house cocktails. It provides a splendid respite while waiting for your flight at the airport across the road. ⊠ *Pavilion Dr., Coolidge* 🕾 *268/481–7000* ⊟ *AE, D, MC, V.*

$–$$$
✕ **Papa Zouk.** Who would have thought that two jovial German gents could create a classic Caribbean hangout? But the madras tablecloths, fish nets festooned with Christmas lights, cartoon Carnival masks, painted bottles of homemade hot sauce and rum punch, dried sea fans, buoys, and lilting rhythms on the sound system justify the name (after Guadeloupe and Martinique's sultry stew of soul and calypso). Seafood is king, from Guyanese butterfish to Bajan flying fish, usually served either deep-fried or steamed with choice of such sauces as guava-pepper teriyaki or tomato-basil-coriander. Tangy Caribbean bouillabaisse and house-smoked tuna are house specialties. ⊠ *Hilda Davis Dr., Gambles Terrace, St. John's* 🕾 *268/562–1284 or 268/464–6044* ⊟ *No credit cards* ⊘ *May–Oct., no lunch Sun.–Tues.*

CONTEMPORARY
★ $$–$$$$
✕ **Coconut Grove.** Coconut palms grow through the roof of this open-air thatched restaurant at the Siboney Beach Club. Flickering candlelight illuminates colorful local murals, waves lap the white sand, and the warm and unpretentious waitstaff provides just the right level of service. Jean-François Bellanger's superbly presented dishes perfectly fuse French culinary preparations with island ingredients. Witness lobster medallions in puff pastry served over calalloo with champagne-saffron sauce, or chicken marinated in fresh herbs and fruit juices, then sautéed

with creole vegetables and finished with kiwi-mango sauce. Cap a memorable meal with an old rum or a Cuban cigar. ⊠ *Siboney Beach Club, Dickenson Bay* 🕾 *268/462–1538* ⊟ *AE, MC, V.*

$$–$$$ ✕ **Bay House.** This romantic hilltop, alfresco eatery (request table 10 for the best views) is in the estimable Tradewinds Hotel above Dickenson Bay. Dishes run the culinary gamut from Thailand to Tuscany, with a healthy dollop of West Indian spice. Excellent starters range from deep-fried pork and prawn *gow gees* (wontons) in sweet-and-sour chile-peanut sauce to seafood boudin on leeks edged with lobster sauce. Main dishes are just as eclectic. After your meal, head to the hip, hopping, happening bar for a cordial and convivial chitchat with the British flight crews who frequent the hotel. ⊠ *Tradewinds Hotel, Dickenson Bay* 🕾 *268/462–1223* ⊟ *AE, MC, V.*

$$–$$$ ✕ **Coco's.** Overlooking the headlands of Five Islands Bay, Coco's could be recommended simply for ravishing sunsets, followed by moonlight spectacularly dappling the bay as if with silver doubloons. But its cheerful aquamarine trim, bougainvillea-draped bleached-wood deck, gingerbread fretwork, and blue-tile tables also handsomely replicate an old chattel house. Although part of the small all-inclusive resort of the same name, the restaurant welcomes outside diners with such skillfully blended Continental and Caribbean dishes as plantain-crusted chicken breast in passion-fruit sauce, or kingfish on a bed of grilled island vegetables with pineapple, grapefruit, and mango salsa. ⊠ *Coco's Resort, Mt. Prospect, Jolly Bay* 🕾 *268/462–9700* ⚱ *Reservations essential* ⊟ *AE, MC, V.*

★ $$–$$$ ✕ **HQ.** At this restaurant occupying part of the Officers' Quarters building in Nelson's Dockyard, adventuresome Aussie chef Darryn Pitman excitingly blends indigenous Caribbean ingredients with preparations—tempura to tandoori—from his Asian postings. Polished hardwood floors, brickwork, and beamed ceilings make an effective contrast to the vivid creole artworks and the contemporary open kitchen, with a vast colonnaded terrace overlooking the water. Impeccably balanced dishes trigger all sets of taste buds, from Thai fishcakes (wahoo seasoned with chili, ginger, and garlic, blended with sweet potato and lime) to white-chocolate and passion-fruit crème brûlée. ⊠ *Nelson's Dockyard, English Harbour* 🕾 *268/562–2563* ⚱ *Reservations essential* ⊟ *AE, MC, V.*

ECLECTIC ✕ **Admiral's Inn.** This English Harbour tavern in the Admiral's Inn hotel
$$–$$$ is a must for Anglophiles and mariners. Soak up the centuries at the inside bar under dark timbers (sailors from Nelson's fleet even carved their names into the bar top). Most diners sit on the terrace under shady Australian gums to enjoy the views of the harbor complex. Specialties include curried conch, fresh snapper with equally fresh limes, and lobster thermidor. The pumpkin soup is not to be missed. ⊠ *Admiral's Inn, Nelson's Dockyard, English Harbour* 🕾 *268/460–1027* ⚱ *Reservations essential* ⊟ *AE, MC, V.*

FRENCH ✕ **Chez Pascal.** Pascal and Florence Milliat built this hilltop charmer, brimming with Gallic brio, themselves. The flagstone terrace overlooks a tinkling fountain and lighted pool (there are also four guest rooms, with whirlpool baths, a pool, and splendid sea views); the tasteful elevated dining room is furnished in dark rattan, with ceramics, local paintings, and copper pots. Pascal's classic Lyonnaise cuisine with tropical touches exhibits his remarkably deft hand with subtle sauces. Witness the gossamer chicken-liver mousse in thyme sauce or sublime steamed grouper in beurre blanc. Finish with a heavenly flourless chocolate cake with strawberry coulis (sauce) or a classic tart Tatin. ⊠ *Galley Bay Hill, Five Islands* 🕾 *268/462–3232* ⚱ *Reservations essential* ⊟ *AE, D, MC, V* ⊘ *Closed Aug.*
$$$–$$$$
FodorsChoice
★

$$$–$$$$ ✕ **Le Bistro.** This Antiguan institution's peach and pistachio accents subtly match the tile work, jade chairs, mint china, and painted lighting fixtures. Trellises cannily divide the large space into intimate sections. Chef Patrick Gaducheau delights in blending regional fare with indigenous ingredients, but the kitchen is surprisingly inconsistent, and the service can be rather stuffy. Opt for daily specials, such as fresh snapper in thyme-perfumed lime-butter sauce or lobster medallions in basil-accented old-rum sauce with roasted red peppers, and almost anything swaddled in puff pastry. ✉ *Hodges Bay* ☎ *268/462–3881* ⌕ *Reservations essential* ▤ *AE, MC, V* ⊘ *Closed Mon. No lunch.*

$–$$ ✕ **Catherine's Café.** This little deck café overlooking English Harbour marina brims with Gallic verve thanks to ebullient hostess Catherine Ricard. The food is simple: ham-and-leek quiche, a proper *salade niçoise*, and crêpes even airier than Catherine herself. Evening delights might include *moules marinières* (marinated mussels) or *gratin de cèpes* (wild mushrooms in a cheese sauce). The fairly priced, extensive wine list offers Catherine's pert comments (for Solaia, she writes, "Just to show we're not narrow-minded Frogs, here is the top from Italy . . ."). This delightful place always percolates with life and good strong espresso. ✉ *English Harbour* ☎ *268/460–5050* ▤ *MC, V* ⊘ *Closed Tues. and Sept.–Oct. No dinner Mon.*

ITALIAN ✕ **Abracadabra.** It's always a party at this busy, bright trattoria. The
$$–$$$ courtyard is strung with lights; R&B and 1980s dance music play in the background; and the cheery rooms are daubed in sea-foam green and full of hand-painted tables and murals of jamming jazz musicians. The food sings with flavor and color. Specialties include an amazing antipasto, bonito marinated in sweet onions and capers, and homemade crab ravioli in pesto. The wine list has some real finds from lesser-known areas of Italy (the owners confide—or rather joke—"We smuggle them in"). ✉ *English Harbour* ☎ *268/460–1732* ▤ *AE, MC, V* ⊘ *Closed July–Sept.*

★ $$–$$$ ✕ **Alberto's.** Vivacious owner Alberto taught his culinary secrets to his English wife, Vanessa; she now bests her mentor with her Italian and French inspirations. Try leek and Parmesan soufflé; melting sushi; veal medallions in mushroom crust; or yummy, traditional linguine with clams. The homemade, lusciously textured sorbets are a must: tangy passion fruit, creamy coconut, lip-smacking lemon. Tables line a trellised balcony open to the breezes and hung with bougainvillea, and painted china graces the walls (check out the octopi and squid on the plates by the bar) of this justly popular trattoria. ✉ *Willoughby Bay* ☎ *268/460–3007* ⌕ *Reservations essential* ▤ *AE, D, MC, V* ⊘ *Closed Mon. and May–Oct. No lunch.*

$–$$ ✕ **Big Banana–Pizzas in Paradise.** This tiny, often crowded spot is tucked into one side of a restored warehouse with broad plank floors, wood beams, and stone archways. Cool Benetton-style photos of locals and jamming musicians adorn the brick walls. It serves some of the island's best pizza (try the lobster or the seafood variety) as well as such tasty specials as conch salad. There's live entertainment some nights, and sports nuts congregate at the bar's huge satellite TV. ✉ *Redcliffe Quay, St. John's* ☎ *268/480–6985* ▤ *AE, MC, V* ⊘ *Closed Sun.*

Beaches

★ Antigua's beaches are public, and many are dotted with resorts that have water-sports outfitters and beach bars. Sunbathing topless or in the buff is strictly illegal except on one of the small beaches at Hawksbill Beach Hotel. Beware that when cruise ships dock in St. John's, buses drop off loads of passengers' on most of the west-coast beaches. Choose such a time to tour the island by car, visit one of the more remote east-end beaches, or take a day trip to Barbuda.

ANTIGUA   **Darkwood Beach.** This delightful taupe ribbon on the southwest coast has views of Montserrat.

Dickenson Bay. Along a lengthy stretch of powder-soft white sand and exceptionally calm water you'll find small and large hotels, water sports, concessions, and beachfront restaurants.

Five Islands Peninsula. Five secluded beige beaches (including one for nude bathing) and coral reefs for snorkeling ring the Hawksbill Beach Hotel, while there's a good surfing beach at Galley Bay.

Half Moon Bay. A ¾-mi (1-km) crescent, it's a prime snorkeling and windsurfing area. On the Atlantic side of the island the water can be quite rough at times. The eastern end is much calmer.

Johnson's Point. This series of connected, deliciously deserted beaches of bleached white sand is on the southwest coast overlooking Montserrat. You can explore a ruined fort at one end; notable beach bars are OJ's (try the snapper) and Turner's.

Long Bay. On the far-eastern coast, you'll find coral reefs in water so shallow that you can actually walk out to them. Along the beach are the Long Bay Hotel and the rambling Occidental Grand Pineapple Beach.

Pigeon Point. Near Falmouth Harbour are these two fine white-sand beaches; the leeward side is calmer, while the windward side is rockier, with sensational views and snorkeling around the point. Several restaurants and bars are nearby.

Runaway Beach. A stretch of glittering sand is still rebuilding after years of hurricane erosion. Both the water and the scene are relatively calm, and beach bars such as Lashings and Amigo's (the surprisingly good Mexican restaurant at Barrymore Beach Hotel) offer cool shade and cold beer.

BARBUDA   **Pink Beach.** On Barbuda you'll find an uncrowded 8-mi (13-km) stretch
★   of white sand that reaches from Coco Point to Palmetto Point. The island, encircled by reefs and shipwrecks, is great for scuba diving.

Sports & the Outdoors

Several all-inclusives offer day passes that permit use of all sporting facilities from tennis courts to water-sports concessions, as well as free drinks and meals. They start around $40 for singles ($170 for couples at Sandals), and generally run from 8 AM to 6 PM, with extensions available until 2 AM.

ADVENTURE   Antigua is developing its ecotourist opportunities, and several memo-
TOURS   rable offshore experiences involve more than just snorkeling. **"Paddles"**
Kayak Eco Adventure (⊠ Seaton's Village ☎ 268/463–1944 ⊕ www.antiguapaddles.com) takes you on a 3½-hour tour of serene mangroves and inlets, while explaining the fragile ecosystem of the swamp and reefs and the rich diversity of flora and fauna, ending with hiking to sunken caves and snorkeling in the North Sound Marine Park. **Adventure Antigua** (☎ 268/727–3261 ⊕ www.adventureantigua.com) is run by Eli Fuller, whose grandfather was American vice consul (and proprietor of the now-defunct Lord Nelson Beach Hotel). Eli is knowledgeable not only about the ecosystem and geography, but Antiguan history and politics. His thorough seven-hour excursion includes stops at Guiana Island for lunch and guided snorkeling (turtles, barracuda, and stingrays

are common sightings), Pelican Island (more snorkeling), Bird Island (hiking to vantage points to admire the soaring ospreys and frigate and tropic birds), and "Hell's Gate" (a striking limestone rock formation where the more intrepid may hike and swim through sunken caves and tidal pools painted with pink and maroon algae). **Stingray City** (✉ Seaton's Village ☎ 268/562–7297) is a carefully reproduced "natural" environment nicknamed by staffers the "retirement home," though the 30-plus stingrays, ranging from infants to seniors, are frisky. You can stroke, feed, even hold the striking gliders, as well as snorkel in deeper protected waters. The tour guides do a marvelous job of explaining the animals' habits, from feeding to breeding, and their predators (including man).

BICYCLING Bicycling isn't terribly arduous on Antigua, except in the southernmost region, where the roads soar, dip, and corkscrew. Try **Bike Plus** (✉ Camacho's Ave., St. John's ☎ 268/462–2453) for rentals, which run about $35 a day. Everything from racing models to mountain bikes is available.

BOATING Experienced boaters will particularly enjoy Antigua's east coast, which is far more rugged and has several offshore islets; be sure to get a good nautical map, as there are numerous minireefs that can be treacherous. If you're just looking for a couple of hours of wave hopping, stick to the Dickenson Bay/Runaway or Jolly Harbour areas.

Nicholson Yacht Charters (☎ 268/460–1530 or 800/662–6066) are real professionals. A long-established island family, they can charter you anything from a 20-ft ketch to a giant schooner. **Sea Sports** (☎ 268/462–3355) in Dickenson Bay rents Jet Skis and Sunfish and offers parasailing and waterskiing trips. This can be a hectic operation. **Sunsail Club Colonna** (☎ 268/462–6263 or 800/327–2276) has an extensive modern fleet of dinghies and 32-ft day sailers available for $25 half day, $50 full day.

CRICKET Practically the only thing most Americans know about this game is that there's something called a sticky wicket. Here, as in Britain and all the West Indies, the game is a national passion. Youngsters play on makeshift pitches, which are comparable to sandlots, and international matches are usually contested at the impressive Stanford Cricket Field opposite the airport. For information on top matches and their venues, call the **Antigua Cricket Association** (✉ Newgate St., St. John's ☎ 268/462–9089 or 268/460–9966).

FISHING Antigua's waters teem with such game fish as marlin, wahoo, and tuna. Most boats include equipment, lunch, and drinks. Figure at least $400 for a half day, $600 for a full day, for up to six people. The 45-ft Hatteras Sportfisherman *Obsession* (☎ 268/462–2824) has top-of-the-line equipment, including an international standard fighting chair, outriggers, and handcrafted rods. *Overdraft* (☎ 268/464–4954 or 268/462–3112) is a sleek, spacious fiberglass 40-footer operated by a knowledgeable professional fisherman.

GOLF **Cedar Valley Golf Club** (✉ Friar's Hill ☎ 268/462–0161), northeast of St. John's, has a 6,100-yard, 18-hole course. The bland, not terribly well-maintained terrain offers some challenge with tight hilly fairways and numerous doglegs. Greens fees are $35, including cart. **Jolly Harbour Golf Course** (✉ Jolly Harbour ☎ 268/480–6950) is a par-71, 6,001-yard, 18-hole course designed by Karl Litten. The layout is hilly and lushly tropical, with seven lakes adding to the challenge. Greens fees are $65 (including cart).

HORSEBACK RIDING Comparatively dry Antigua is best for beach rides, though you won't find anything wildly romantic and deserted à la *The Black Stallion*. **Spring Hill Riding Club** (⊠ Falmouth ☎ 268/460–7787) really specializes in equestrian lessons in show jumping and dressage, but also offers $40 trail rides on the beach or through the bush; half-hour private lessons are $25.

SAILING & SNORKELING TRIPS Not a sailor yourself? Consider signing up for one of the following boat tours. Each provides a great opportunity to enjoy the seafaring life while someone else captains the ship.

Jolly Roger cruises (☎ 268/462–2064), on a true-to-life replica of a pirate ship, come complete with "pirate" crew, limbo dancing, plank walking, and other pranks. Their Saturday night booze cruises with open bar and live bands are legendary for their frat party feel. They also offer Barbuda day trips on their catamaran *Excellence*. **Kokomo Cats** (☎ 268/462–7245) runs several cruises, including one to deserted beaches and islets, one to English Harbour, and one to sunset-gazing spots. **Miguel's Holiday Adventures** (☎ 268/460–9978; 268/723–7418 mobile phone) leaves every Tuesday, Thursday, and Saturday morning at 10 AM from the Hodges Bay jetty for snorkeling, rum punches, and lunch at Prickley Pear Island. The glass-bottom *Shorty's* (☎ 268/462–6326) offers various snorkeling trips to Bird Island, as well as sunset cruises and lobster picnics. **Wadadli Cats** (☎ 268/462–4792) offers several cruises, including a circumnavigation of the island and snorkeling at Bird Island, on its four sleek catamarans, including the handsome *Spirit of Antigua*.

SCUBA DIVING With all the wrecks and reefs, there are lots of undersea sights to explore, from coral canyons to sea caves. The most accessible wreck is the schooner *Andes*, not far out in Deep Bay, off Five Islands Peninsula. Among the favorite sites are **Green Island, Cades Reef,** and **Bird Island** (a national park).

Big John's Dive Antigua (⊠ Rex Halcyon Cove Beach Resort, Dickenson Bay ☎ 268/462–3483) offers certification courses and day and night dives. **Dockyard Divers** (⊠ Nelson's Dockyard, English Harbour ☎ 268/460–1178), owned by British ex-merchant seaman Captain A. G. Fincham, is one of the island's most established outfits and offers diving and snorkeling trips, PADI courses, and dive packages with accommodations. Another top option is **Octopus Divers** (⊠ English Harbour ☎ 268/460–6286), which provides PADI certification and snorkeling trips.

TENNIS & SQUASH Many of the larger resorts have their own tennis courts. Guests at the various hotels have top priority. There is also one public court on the island. **BBR Sportive Complex** (⊠ Jolly Harbour ☎ 268/462–6260) offers two synthetic grass and two HarTru courts, a squash court, a half-size Olympic pool, and a sports bar. The only hotel that allows nonguests to play on a regular basis is the **Royal Antiguan Resort** (⊠ Deep Bay ☎ 268/462–3733), which has eight lighted courts. **Rex Halcyon Cove Beach Resort** (⊠ Dickenson Bay ☎ 268/462–0256) has four lighted courts, and they are sometimes—but not always—available for nonguests to use. The **Temo Sports Complex** (⊠ Falmouth Bay ☎ 268/463–6376 or 268/460–1781) has four floodlit synthetic grass tennis courts, two glass-backed squash courts, showers, a sports shop, and snack bars, including a wonderful kebab stand. Court time is generally $25 per hour.

WINDSURFING Most major hotels offer windsurfing equipment. The best areas are Nonsuch Bay and the east coast (notably Half Moon and Willoughby bays), which is slightly less protected and has a challenging juxtaposition of sudden calms and gusts. **H20** (☎ 268/562–3933), at Dutchman's

Bay, offers state-of-the-art equipment and instruction, as well as snorkeling, ecotours, and a lively little beach bar. **Sea Sports** (☎ 268/462–3355), at Dickenson Bay, rents top-quality boards for $25 per hour. **Sunsail Club Colonna** (☎ 268/462–6263 or 800/327–2276) allows use of its top-of-the-line equipment for $50 a day and $25 a half day.

Shopping

Antigua's duty-free shops are at Heritage Quay, one reason so many cruise ships call here. Bargains can be found on perfumes, liqueurs and liquor (including, of course, Antiguan rum), jewelry, china, and crystal. As for other local items, look for straw hats, baskets, batik, pottery, and hand-printed cotton clothing.

Areas

Redcliffe Quay, on the waterfront at the south edge of St. John's, is by far the most appealing shopping area. Several restaurants and more than 30 boutiques, many with one-of-a-kind wares, are set around landscaped courtyards shaded by colorful trees. **Heritage Quay,** in St. John's, has 35 shops—including many that are duty-free—that cater to the cruise-ship crowd, which docks almost at its doorstep. Outlets here include Benetton, the Body Shop, Sunglass Hut, Dolce and Gabbana, and Oshkosh B'Gosh. There are also shops along **St. John's, St. Mary's, High,** and **Long streets.** The tangerine-and-lilac-hued four-story **Vendor's Mall** at the intersection of Redcliffe and Thames streets gathers the pushy, pesky vendors that once clogged the narrow streets. It's jammed with stalls; air-conditioned indoor shops sell some higher-priced, if not higher-quality merchandise. On the west coast the Mediterranean-style, arcaded **Jolly Harbour Villa Resort and Marina** holds some interesting galleries and shops.

Specialty Items

ART At **Harmony Hall** (✉ Brown's Bay Mill, Brown's Bay ☎ 268/460–4120), near Freetown, you'll find hand-painted Annabella boxes, books and cards, pottery, carved wooden birds, Jennifer Meranto's incomparable hand-colored black-and-white photos of Caribbean scenes, Heather Doram's exquisite, intricately woven "collage" wall-hangings, and ever-changing exhibits. There's also a marvelous Italian restaurant that's open for lunch and on weekends for dinner. **Island Arts Galleries** (✉ Aiton Pl. at Sandy La., Hodges Bay ☎ 268/461–6324 ✉ Heritage Quay, St. John's ☎ 268/462–2787), run by artist-filmmaker Nick Maley, showcases artists from throughout the Caribbean. Some of the art naïf pieces are stunning, and the genre paintings of local life often have a raw elemental power. Call first to ensure that Nick is around, so he can tell fascinating anecdotes about his helping to create Yoda from *Star Wars* and other famed film characters. **Heavenly Hill Art Gallery** (✉ Johnson's Point ☎ 268/560–1245 ⊕ www.antiguaculture.com) doubles as Terrance Sprague's atelier and an exhibit space for the island's leading artists, including Heather Doram, Lydia Llewellyn (whose iridescent marine still lifes extend onto the frames), and Gilly Gobinet.

BOOKS & MAGAZINES **The Best of Books** (✉ Benjie's Mall, Redcliffe St., St. John's ☎ 268/562–3198) is an excellent source for everything from local cookbooks and nature guides to international newspapers. **Map Shop** (✉ St. Mary's St., St. John's ☎ 268/462–3993) has a "must" buy for those interested in Antiguan life: the paperback *To Shoot Hard Labour: The Life and Times of Samuel Smith, an Antiguan Workingman.* Also check out any of the books of Jamaica Kincaid, whose writing about her native Antigua has won international acclaim. The shop also offers a fine assortment of books on Caribbean cuisine, flora, fauna, and history.

CIGARS, LIQUOR & LIQUEURS La Casa Habana (✉ Heritage Quay, St. John's ☎ 268/462–2677) sells Cuban cigars (just remember that it's illegal to take them into the United States). **Manuel Dias Liquor Store** (✉ Long and Market Sts., St. John's ☎ 268/462–0490) has a wide selection of Caribbean rums and liqueurs. **Quin Farara** (✉ Long St., St. John's ☎ 268/462–0463 ✉ Heritage Quay, St. John's ☎ 268/462–1737 ✉ Jolly Harbour ☎ 268/462–6245) has terrific deals on both hard liquor and wines, as well as cigars.

CLOTHING Exotic Antigua (✉ Redcliffe Quay, St. John's ☎ 268/562–1288) sells everything from antique Indonesian *ikat* throws to crepe de chine caf-
★ tans to Tommy Bahama resort wear. At **Galley Boutique** (✉ Nelson's Dockyard, English Harbour ☎ 268/460–1525), Janey Easton personally seeks out exclusive creations from both international couturiers (Calvin Klein, Adrienne Vittadini) and local Caribbean designers, ranging from swimwear to evening garb. She also sells handicrafts and lovely hammocks. **Jacaranda** (✉ Redcliffe Quay, St. John's ☎ 268/462–1888) sells batik, sarongs, and swimwear, as well as Caribbean food and local artwork. **New Gates** (✉ Redcliffe Quay, St. John's ☎ 268/562–1627) is a duty-free authorized dealer for such name brands as Ralph Lauren, Calvin Klein, and Tommy Hilfiger. **Noreen Phillips** (✉ Redcliffe Quay, St. John's ☎ 268/462–3127) creates glitzy appliquéd and beaded evening wear—inspired by the colors of the sea and sunset—in sensuous fabrics ranging from chiffon and silk to Italian lace and Indian brocade. **Sunseakers**(✉ Heritage Quay, St. John's ☎ 268/462–3618) racks up every conceivable bathing suit and cover-up—from bikini thongs to sarongs—by top designers. **A Thousand Flowers** (✉ Redcliffe Quay, St. John's ☎ 268/462–4264) carries resort wear made of comfortable silks, linens, and batiks from all over the world.

DUTY-FREE GOODS Abbott's (✉ Heritage Quay, St. John's ☎ 268/462–3108) sells pricey items from Baume and Mercier watches to Belleek china to Kosta Boda art glass in a luxurious, air-conditioned showroom. **Lipstick** (✉ Heritage Quay, St. John's ☎ 268/562–1130) imports high-priced scents and cosmetics, from Clarins to Clinique and Givenchy to Guerlain.

HANDICRAFTS Cedars Pottery (✉ Buckleys ☎ 268/460–5293) is the airy studio of
★ Michael and Imogen Hunt. Michael produces a vivid line of domestic ware and Zen-simple teapots, vases, and water fountains featuring rich earth hues and sensuous lines. Imogen fashions ethereal paper-clay fish sculptures and mask-shaped, intricately laced light fixtures and candelabras. **Eureka** (✉ Thames St., St. John's ☎ 268/560–3654) spans the globe, from Azerbaijani hand-blown glass to Zambian weavings and carvings. The **Gazebo** (✉ Redcliffe Quay, St. John's ☎ 268/460–2776) is a vast, bilevel jumble of Mexican pottery and ceramics, Indonesian furnishings, gorgeous blue-glaze plates that rival delftware in both beauty and craftsmanship, hand-painted rocking horses, basketry, hammocks, and more. **Isis** (✉ Redcliffe Quay, St. John's ☎ 268/462–4602) sells island and international bric-a-brac, such as antique jewelry, hand-carved walking sticks, and glazed pottery. **Kate Designs** (✉ Redcliffe Quay, St. John's ☎ 268/460–5971) sells acclaimed artist Kate Spencer's distinctive work—lovely silk-screened scarves and sarongs, vividly colored place mats, paintings, prints, note cards—from neighboring St. Kitts as well as Liza Kirwan's delicate hand-painted silk scarves and former fashion designer Heike Petersen's whimsical "ethnic dolls." **Mimosa** (✉ Heritage Quay, St. John's ☎ 268/462–2923) sells hand-painted wind chimes and porcelain clowns in island dress. The **New Pottery** (✉ Redcliffe Quay, St. John's ☎ 268/562–1264) gallery sells the work of gifted potter Sarah Fuller, whose hand-painted tiles, wind chimes, and plates and cobalt-blue glazes are striking. **Pigeon Point Pottery** (✉ Pigeon Point

☎ 268/460–1614) is the atelier of Nancy Nicholson, who's renowned for her exquisite glazed and matte-finish ceramics, featuring Caribbean-pure shades, as well as her black-and-white yachting photos. The delightfully whimsical **Sofa** (✉ English Harbour ☎ 268/463–0610) carries some of the quirkier creations of island artisans, including hand-painted furniture, mosaic vases, and recycled-paper books—justifying the name (an acronym for Sculpture, Objects, Functional Art). Owner Fiona Jade will happily direct you to the studios of such intriguing Antiguan artists as Gilly Gobinet, Gramma Aki, Freeston Williams, and Yolanda Woodberry. **Things Local** (✉ Nelson's Dockyard, English Harbour ☎ no phone) is the bailiwick of local woodcarver Carl Henry, who recycles dead trees into figurative yet intriguingly gnarled sculpture. He also makes splendid warri boards (an ancient African game played with large pods) and painted gourds.

JEWELRY **Colombian Emeralds** (✉ Heritage Quay, St. John's ☎ 268/462–3462) is the largest retailer of Colombian emeralds in the world, and also car-
★ ries a wide variety of other gems. The **Goldsmitty** (✉ Redcliffe Quay, St. John's ☎ 268/462–4601) is Hans Smit, an expert goldsmith who turns gold, black coral, and precious and semiprecious stones into one-of-a-kind works of art.

Nightlife & the Arts

Most of Antigua's evening entertainment takes place at the resorts, which regularly present calypso singers, steel bands, limbo dancers, and folkloric groups. Check with the tourist office for up-to-date information.

Nightlife

BARS **The Beach** (✉ Dickenson Bay ☎ 268/460–6940) is a sophisticated-funky
★ combination of casual beach bar, lounge, and bistro (with Asian-Euro fusion cuisine), all daubed in sexy reds and hung with striking photographs of local scenes. **Castaways** (✉ Jolly Harbour ☎ 268/562–4445) is a boisterous beach bar/bistro with a Kon Tiki feel (from the thatched roof and torches to the colorful local murals), with an inexpensive tapas-style menu and occasional entertainment (go for Sunday pig roasts, with fire dancers and steel bands). **Colombo's** (✉ Galleon Beach Club, English Harbour ☎ 268/460–1452) is the place to be on Wednesday night for live reggae. It's also a yachty hangout, with pennants of various boats hanging from the rafters. Beware: the once-fine Italian fare is overrated. Brits pack **Dickenson Park Leisure Center** (✉ Dickenson Bay Rd., Dickenson Bay ☎ 268/463–4653), even though it's essentially just an open deck overlooking a swamp-like lagoon. There are also a playground, video arcade, the air-conditioned Outback disco, an Internet café, and a lighted miniature golf course where you can access your inner child between brews. **The Inn at English Harbour Bar** (✉ English Harbour ☎ 268/460–1014), with its green-leather and petit-point chairs, wood beams, fieldstone walls, copper pots and warming pans, wagon wheel chandelier, 19th-century maps, and maritime prints, is uncommonly refined.
★ **Lashings** (✉ Runaway Bay ☎ 268/462–4438) is a funky place that attracts world-renowned cricketers, as well as a jovial crowd for liberal happy hours, dirt-cheap Tex-Mex and pizzas, and dirty dancing on the sand. **Life** (✉ Nelson's Dockyard, English Harbour ☎ 268/562–2353) is a semi-enclosed wooden pier that groans under the weight of yachties and their groupies during the 2-for-1 happy hours and Caribbean party nights with live bands. The **Mad Mongoose** (✉ Falmouth Harbour ☎ 268/463–7900) is a wildly popular yachty (and singles) joint, splashed in vivid Rasta colors, with a game room and satellite TV. The crowd at **Millers**

by the Sea (✉ Fort James Beach ☎ 268/462–9414) spills over onto the beach during the ever-popular happy hour and live nightly entertainment. It's packed with cruise-ship passengers tanning and noshing on barbecue and burgers during the day. You can hike to the 18th-century ruins of Fort James at the other end of the beach for stunning views of

★ St. John's. **Shirley Heights Lookout** (✉ Shirley Heights ☎ 268/460–1785) hosts Sunday-afternoon barbecues that continue into the night with reggae and steel-band music and dancing. On Sunday afternoon and Thursday evening, residents and visitors gather for boisterous fun, the latest

★ gossip, and great sunsets. **Trappa's** (✉ Main Rd., English Harbour ☎ 268/562–3534) is a hipster hangout set in a bamboo-walled courtyard amid a virtual jungle of greenery, with everything from columns to booths in blue hues. It serves delectable, sizable tapas (fried mushrooms, Brie dip, Thai mango chicken curry, seafood pizzetta) into the wee hours for just EC$20. Live music is often on the menu.

CASINOS There are three true casinos on Antigua, as well as several holes-in-the-wall that have mostly one-armed bandits. Hours depend on the season,

★ so it's best to inquire upon your arrival. The latest addition is **Grand Princess Casino** (✉ Jolly Harbour), which occupies slick, three-story digs combining English colonial and Mediterranean revival elements; management plans to add shops, a rooftop spa, dining, and entertainment. You'll find abundant slots and gaming tables at the somewhat dilapidated, unintentionally retro (icicle chandeliers, naugahyde seats, and 1970s soul crooners on the sound system), smoky **King's Casino** (✉ Heritage Quay, St. John's ☎ 268/462–1727). The **St. James's Club** (✉ Mamora Bay ☎ 268/463–1113) has an elegant, almost Bondian casino and looks as if it came straight from the Côte d'Azur.

DANCE CLUBS **18 Karat** (✉ Lower Church St., St. John's ☎ 268/562–1858) attracts a casually swanky over-21 crowd for rollicking island sounds and the latest in techno and house; the courtyard restaurant is a favored meeting place for Antigua's young elite. **Traffic** (✉ Independence Dr., St. John's ☎ 268/562–2949) rocks its exquisite 19th-century townhouse location with everything from live jazz and blues to soca and reggae. The **Web** (✉ Old Parham Rd., St. John's ☎ 268/462–3186) attracts a somewhat rowdy local crowd and spins ethnic sounds such as reggae, soca, and salsa.

Exploring Antigua

Major hotels provide free island maps, but you should get your bearings before heading out on the road. Street names aren't posted, though easy-to-spot signs leading the way to restaurants are posted all over the island. Locals generally give directions in terms of landmarks (turn left at the yellow house, or right at the big tree). Wear a swimsuit under your clothes—one of the sights to strike your fancy might be a secluded beach.

Numbers in the margin correspond to points of interest on the Antigua & Barbuda map.

WHAT TO SEE **Barbuda.** This flat, 62-square-mi (161-square-km) coral atoll—with 17
★ ⓫ mi (27 km) of pinkish white-sand beaches—is 26 mi (42 km) north of Antigua. Most of the island's 1,500 people live in Codrington. Pink Beach lures beachcombers, a bird sanctuary attracts ornithologists, caves and sinkholes filled with rain forest or underground pools attract spelunkers, and offshore wrecks and reefs draw divers and snorkelers. **Carib Aviation** flies to Barbuda daily from Antigua, and air and boat charters are available if you want to make a day trip. The sole historic ruin on Barbuda is the 18th-century, cylindrical, 56-ft-tall **Martello Tower**, which

is believed to have been a lighthouse built by the Spaniards before the English occupied the island. The **Bird Sanctuary**, a wide mangrove-filled lagoon, is home to an estimated 400 species of birds, including frigate birds with 8-ft wingspans. Tours commonly take you here and to a beach for snorkeling. Day-trippers can experience Barbada through D&J Tours (*see* Tours *in the* A to Z section).

8 Betty's Hope. Just outside the village of Pares, a marked dirt road leads to Betty's Hope, Antigua's first sugar plantation, founded in 1650. You can tour the twin windmills, and the visitor center has exhibits on the island's sugar era. The village isn't much now, but the private trust overseeing its restoration has ambitious plans. ⊠ *Pares* ☎ *268/462–1469* ▧ *Free* ☉ *Tues.–Sat. 9–4.*

9 Devil's Bridge. This limestone arch formation, sculpted by the crashing breakers of the Atlantic at Indian Town, is a national park. Blowholes have been carved by the hissing, spitting surf. They may be hard to spot at first, but just wait until a wave bursts through. The park also encompasses some archeological excavations of Carib artifacts.

5 English Harbour. The most famous of Antigua's attractions lies on the
Fodor'sChoice coast, just south of Falmouth. In 1671 the governor of the Leeward Is-
★ lands wrote to the Council for Foreign Plantations in London, pointing out the advantages of this landlocked harbor. By 1704 English Harbour was in regular use as a garrisoned station.

In 1784, 26-year-old Horatio Nelson sailed in on the HMS *Boreas* to serve as captain and second-in-command of the Leeward Island Station. Under him was the captain of the HMS *Pegasus,* Prince William Henry, duke of Clarence, who was to ascend the throne of England as William IV. The prince was Nelson's close friend and acted as best man when Nelson married Fannie Nisbet on Nevis in 1787.

When the Royal Navy abandoned the station at English Harbour in 1889, it fell into a state of decay. The Society of the Friends of English Harbour began restoring it in 1951, and on Dockyard Day, November 14, 1961, **Nelson's Dockyard** was reopened with much fanfare. Today it's reminiscent, albeit on a much smaller scale, of Williamsburg, Virginia. Within the compound are crafts shops, restaurants, and two splendidly restored 18th-century hotels, the Admiral's Inn and The Copper and Lumber Store Hotel, worth peeking into. (The latter, occupying a supply store for Nelson's Caribbean fleet, is a particularly fine example of Georgian architecture, with warm brick, hardwood floors, timber ceilings, sailing prints, nautical maps, burgundy leather armchairs and sofas, and an interior courtyard evoking Old England.) The Dockyard is a hub for oceangoing yachts and serves as headquarters for the annual Sailing Week Regatta. Beach lovers tend to stay elsewhere, but those who love history and the nautical scene often choose one of the nearby hotels. Water taxis will ferry you between points for EC$5. The Dockyard National Park also includes serene nature trails accessing beaches, rock pools, and crumbling plantation ruins and hilltop forts.

The **Admiral's House Museum** displays ship models, a model of English Harbour, silver regatta trophies, maps, prints, and Nelson's very own telescope and tea caddy. ⊠ *Nelson's Dockyard* ☎ *268/463–1053 or 268/463–1379* ▧ *$2, suggested donation* ☉ *Daily 8–6.*

4 Falmouth. This town sits on a lovely bay backed by former sugar plantations and sugar mills. The most important historic site here is St. Paul's Church, which was rebuilt on the site of a church once used by troops during the Nelson period.

Fig Tree Drive. This often muddy, rutted, steep road takes you through the rain forest, which is rich in mangoes, pineapples, and banana trees (*fig* is the Antiguan word for "banana"). The rain-forest area is the hilliest part of the island—Boggy Peak, to the west, is the highest point, at 1,319 ft. You'll also pass through several tranquil villages with charming churches.

③ Ft. George. East of Liberta—one of the first settlements founded by freed slaves—on Monk's Hill, this fort was built from 1689 to 1720. Among the ruins are the sites for 32 cannons, water cisterns, the base of the old flagstaff, and some of the original buildings.

★ ⑦ Harmony Hall. Northeast of Freetown (follow the signs) is this interesting art gallery built on the foundation of a 17th-century sugar-plantation great house. Artists Graham Davis and Peter and Annabella Proudlock, who founded the sister gallery in Jamaica, teamed up with local entrepreneur Geoffrey Pidduck to create this Antiguan establishment, which specializes in high-quality West Indian art. A large exhibit space is used for one-person shows; another space displays watercolors. A small bar in a sugar mill and a superlative Italian restaurant occupying the courtyard are open in season. Both are run by the enterprising Italians who operate the top-notch Abracadabra restaurant. There's also a pool, the beach is a five-minute walk down the hill, and you can arrange boat rides to nearby Green Island. You can spend the night in one of the six comfortable, spacious cottages, which rent for $160 (CP); the owners will graciously deliver dinner to your patio at 6 PM during the week. ⊠ *Brown's Mill Bay, Brown's Mill* ☎ *268/463–8657 or 268/460–4120* ☉ *Daily 10–6.*

② Megaliths of Greencastle Hill. It's an arduous climb to these eerie rock slabs in the south-central part of the island. Some say the megaliths were set up by early inhabitants for their worship of the sun and moon; others believe they're nothing more than unusual geological formations.

⑩ Parham. This tiny village is a splendid, sleepy example of a traditional colonial settlement. St. Peter's Church, built in 1840 by Thomas Weekes, an English architect, is an octagonal Italianate building with unusual ribbed wooden ceiling, whose facade is richly decorated with stucco and keystone work, though it suffered considerable damage during the earthquake of 1843.

① St. John's. Antigua's capital, with some 45,000 inhabitants (approximately half the island's population), lies at sea level at the inland end of a sheltered northwestern bay. Although it has seen better days, a couple of notable historic sights and some good waterfront shopping areas and restaurants make it worth a visit. Signs at the **Museum of Antigua and Barbuda** say PLEASE TOUCH, encouraging you to explore Antigua's past. Try your hand at the educational video games or squeeze a cassava through a *matapi* (a grass sieve). Exhibits interpret the nation's history, from its geological birth to its political independence in 1981. There are fossil and coral remains from some 34 million years ago; models of a sugar plantation and a wattle-and-daub house; an Arawak canoe; and a wildly eclectic assortment of objects from cannonballs to 1920s telephone exchanges. The colonial building that houses the museum is the former courthouse, which dates from 1750. The superlative museum gift shop carries such unusual items as calabash purses, seed earrings, and lignum vitae pipes, as well as historic maps and local books. ⊠ *Church and Market Sts.* ☎ *268/462–1469* 🎫 *$2 suggested donation* ☉ *Weekdays 8:30–4, Sat. 10–1.*

At the south gate of the **Anglican Cathedral of St. John the Divine** are figures of St. John the Baptist and St. John the Divine said to have been taken from one of Napoléon's ships and brought to Antigua. The original church was built in 1681, replaced by a stone building in 1745, and destroyed by an earthquake in 1843. The present building dates from 1845. With an eye to future earthquakes, the parishioners had the interior completely encased in pitch pine, hoping to forestall heavy damage. The church was elevated to the status of a cathedral in 1848. ⊠ *Between Long and Newgate Sts.* ☎ 268/461–0082.

Shopaholics head directly for **Heritage Quay,** a continually expanding multimillion-dollar complex. The two-story buildings contain stores that sell duty-free goods, sportswear, T-shirts, imports from down-island (paintings, T-shirts, straw baskets), and local crafts. There are also several restaurants and a casino. Cruise-ship passengers disembark here from the 500-ft-long (153-m-long) pier. ⊠ *High and Thames Sts.*

Redcliffe Quay, at the water's edge just south of Heritage Quay, is the most appealing part of St. John's. Attractively restored (and superbly re-created) buildings in a riot of cotton-candy colors house shops, restaurants, and boutiques and are linked by courtyards and landscaped walkways. At the far south end of town, where Market Street forks into Valley Road and All Saints Road, a whole lot of haggling goes on every Friday and Saturday, when locals jam the **Public Market** to buy and sell fruits, vegetables, fish, and spices. Be sure to ask before you aim a camera; expect your subject to ask for a tip. This is shopping the old-time Caribbean way, a jambalaya of sights, sounds, and smells.

❻ Shirley Heights. This bluff affords a spectacular view of English Harbour. The heights are named for Sir Thomas Shirley, the governor who fortified the harbor in 1787. At the top is Shirley Heights Lookout, a restaurant built into the remnants of the 18th-century fortifications. Most notable for its boisterous Thursday and Sunday barbecues that often continue well into the night with live music and dancing, it serves dependable burgers, pumpkin soup, grilled meats, and rum punches. Not far from Shirley Heights is the **Dows Hill Interpretation Centre,** where observation platforms provide still more sensational vistas of the whole English Harbour area. There's a multimedia sound-and-light presentation on the island's history and culture, in which illuminated displays, incorporating lifelike figures and colorful tableaux, are presented with running commentary and music—resulting in a cheery, if bland, portrait of Antiguan life from the days of the Amerindians to the present. ☎ 268/460–2777 (National Parks Authority) ⊠ EC$15 ☉ Daily 9–5.

Side Trip to Montserrat

Montserrat was always regarded by aficionados as an idyllic, fairy-tale island. But in 1995, Grimm turned grim when the Soufrière Hills Volcano erupted, literally throwing the island into the fire. The frilly Victorian gingerbreads of the capital, Plymouth, were buried, much of the tourism infrastructure was wiped out, and over half the original 11,000 residents have departed. Though the volcano still belches (plumes of ash are visible from as far as Antigua and the lava dome glows eerily at night), plucky locals joke that new beachfront is being created. The volcano itself is an ecotourism spot drawing travelers curious to see the awesome devastation. The most popular way to see the island is on a day trip by ferry or helicopter from nearby Antigua. For those who want to stay longer and enjoy the island's scuba diving, deep-sea fishing, kayaking, or hiking opportunities, there are several small, simple guest houses, rental villas, and inns, as well as a new hotel and a few casual restaurants.

Although an Exclusion Zone covers half the island, the rest is safe; in fact, if the threat of pyroclastic flows subsides, the Exclusion Zone may even be retracted by late 2003. Visitors expecting mass devastation are in for a surprise; Montserrat ranks among the region's most pristine destinations, its luxuriant vegetation and jagged green hills justifying the moniker "Emerald Isle" (most locals are descended from Irish settlers, whose influence lingers in place and family names, folklore, jigs, even a wispy brogue). The combined Carnival and Christmas festivities go on for nearly a month, when the island explodes with color, from calypso competitions to parades and pageants.

Montserrat is reinventing itself as a prime ecotourist destination—and a serene place to lime (hang out). Other than the volcano, the steamiest activities are the fiercely contested domino games outside rum shops. And the people are among the warmest anywhere: chat them up or attend a church service and don't be surprised to be invited to a family dinner or beach picnic.

Where to Stay & Eat

Currently, the island primarily offers villas (housekeepers and cooks can be arranged) or guest houses, the latter often incorporating meals in the rate (ask if the 10% tax and 10% service charge are included and be sure you make dining reservations). Restaurants serve classic Caribbean fare, including such specialties as goatwater (a thick stew of goat meat, tubers, and vegetables that seems to have been bubbling for days), mountain chicken (giant frogs' legs), saal-fish kiac (codfish fritters), and home-brewed ginger beer. The leading villa rental company in Montserrat is **Tradewinds Real Estate** (⌂ Box 365, Old Towne ☎ 664/491–2004 or 664/491–7499 ⊕ www.tradewindsmontserrat.com); many of its properties feature plunge pools. **J.J's** (✉ Sweeney's ☎ 664/491–9024) is a preferred local hangout and big liming spot weekends. **Tina's** (✉ Brades ☎ 664/491–3538) offers less exotic fare for tour groups, but come evening renders staples from souse (pickled pigs parts) to baked chicken. **Ziggy's** (✉ Mahogany Loop ☎ 664/491–8282) is the fancier alternative on the island that serves only dinner.

★ $ ✕▣ **Erindell Villa Guesthouse.** Lou and Shirley Spycalla's peaceful retreat defines "home away from home." Two cozy rooms (opt for the larger, self-contained poolside "villa") offer all amenities, but the real allure is the location, amid tropical gardens framed by rolling hills with sea views, and the Spycallas' warmth and enthusiasm. Small wonder the little alfresco dining room is an impromptu stop for locals and repeat visitors (the best island gossip is at unofficial happy hours). Character and characters abound (including poolman George Riley, "the island philosopher"). Meals are a family affair, practically barefoot, in Lou and Shirley's kitchen, with international inspirations from barbecued ribs to roti. ✉ Gros Michel Dr., Woodlands ☎ 664/491–3655 ⊕ http://home. switchboard.com/erindell ⤴ 2 rooms ⚴ Restaurant, fans, microwaves, refrigerators, pool, laundry service, Internet; no a/c ▤ No credit cards ⧖ CP.

$ ✕▣ **Grand View Bed & Breakfast.** Grand View is the domain of a magnetic dynamo named Theresa Silcott, who's justifiably reckoned one of the island's best traditional chefs (her hot sauces and preserves are for sale), and the goatwater, mountain chicken, and baked goods sing with flavor. No surprise the restaurant is often booked for functions. She's lavished love and time on her soothing landscaping, a combination minibotanical garden and vegetable/herb patch. Her family even runs a radio station from the basement (ask for a tour). Rooms and suites redefine basic, despite cheery powder-blue and hibiscus-patterned fabrics, but deliver the promised vistas. ✉ *Baker Hill* ☎ *664/491–2284* 🖷 *664/491–6876* 🌐 *www.mygrandview.com* ⤳ *3 rooms, 3 suites* ⚲ *Restaurant, fans, some kitchenettes, some refrigerators, bar, Internet, meeting rooms; no a/c, no TV in some rooms* ▭ *No credit cards* 🍽 *CP.*

$ ✕🖾 **Tropical Mansion Suites.** The name would seem grandiose anywhere but on simple Montserrat. Despite the handsome pastel buildings, a central location, sizable "motel" rooms, and comparatively modern facilities and amenities, a slight soullessness pervades the space. Perhaps its odd choices—from an institutional basement restaurant to balconies facing the tranquil interior courtyard rather than the sweep of verdant hills down to the sea. Though quite comfortable, the hotel lacks the warmth of family-run guest houses. And meals—usually a choice of two or three entrées like fried kingfish creole or baked chicken—are overpriced by Montserrat standards; insist on a patio table. ✉ *Sweeney's* ☎ *664/491–8767* 🌐 *www.tropicalmansion.com* ⤳ *18 suites* ⚲ *Restaurant, fans, some kitchenettes, refrigerators, pool, bar, shops, meeting rooms, car rental; no a/c* ▭ *AE, D, MC, V* 🍽 *CP.*

Sports & the Outdoors

Montserrat is capitalizing on its many ecofriendly options. The tourist office provides lists of hiking trails, from easy to arduous. The most spectacular are in the Centre Hills, which offer stirring lookouts over the volcano's barren flanks, surrounding greenery, and ash-covered villages in the Exclusion Zone. Avian aficionados have long considered Montserrat heaven for its nearly 40 land birds and bountiful sea birds, from red-billed tropic birds to frigates. Mountain biking is making a comeback, with a wide network of trails through the lush Centre Hills and, to the north, Silver Hill and Jack Boy Hill. More than 30 practically pristine dive sites surround Montserrat, especially on the calmer west coast. You can even literally hang out with thousands of (harmless) fruit bats in Rendezvous Bay's partly submerged caves. Deep-sea fishing lures anglers to these waters. **Danny Sweeney** (✉ Olveston ☎ 664/491–5645) has won several regional tournaments, including Montserrat's Open Fishing Competition. Half-day charters (up to four people) are $250. An extra bonus on the open water are the gripping views of the simmering volcano. Ecocentric expats James Traylor and David Lea run **Imagine Peace Bicycles** (✉ Brades ☎ 664/491–5812 or 664/492–1707), which rents state-of-the-art equipment from Cygnal and Mongoose and conducts tours through the countryside. **Scriber Tours** (☎ 664/491–2546 or 664/491–3412) is run by the enthusiastic eponymous gentleman, an employee of the Agricultural Department legendary for his uncanny bird calls. He leads nature/bird-watching hikes through the rain forest for $20, seeking sightings of such rare species as the Montserrat oriole, with its distinctive black-and-orange plumage. Wolf Krebs's **Sea Wolf Diving School** (✉ Woodlands ☎ 268/491–7807) offers PADI certification, shore, kayak, and boat dives, even underwater photography classes.

Shopping

Montserrat offers a variety of local crafts and does a brisk trade in vulcanological mementos (many shops sell not only postcards, but small bottles of gray ash capped by colorful homemade cloth). The work of local artists, including the photographer Donaldson Romeo, can be found in island galleries.

Exploring Montserrat

Though the more fertile—and historic—southern half of Montserrat has been destroyed by the volcano, emerald hills still reward explorers.

Hiking and biking are the best ways to experience this island's un-spoiled rain forest, glistening, black-sand beaches, and lookouts over the devastation. The government is constructing a viewing area on Jack Boy Hill, which provides bird's-eye views of the old airport and eastern villages damaged by pyroclastic flows. If you drive, it's also a superb spot from which to watch the glowing lava dome on clear nights.

The fairly strenuous Centre Hills trail leads to **The Cot,** one of Montserrat's few remaining historic sites—the ruins of the once-influential Sturges family's summer cottage—as well as an oki banana plantation. Its Duck Pond Hill perch overlooks the coastline, Garibaldi Hill, Old Towne, abandoned villages, and Plymouth.

The **Montserrat National Trust Natural History Centre** aims to conserve and enhance the island's natural beauty and cultural heritage. The center has exhibits on Arawak canoe building, colonial sugar and lime production, indigenous marine life, West Indian cricket, and the history of Sir George Martin's Air Studios, which lured top musicians from Sting to Paul Mc-Cartney. The lovingly tended botanical gardens in back make for a pleasant stroll. ⊠ *Main Rd., Olveston* ☎ *664/291–3086* ⊕ *www. montserratnationaltrust.com* ⊙ *Mon.–Sat., 10–4* 🖾 *Free.*

The island's must-see is the **Montserrat Volcano Observatory,** which occupies capacious, striking new quarters with stunning vistas of the Soufrière Hills Volcano—a lunarscape encircled by brilliant green—and Plymouth in the distance. The MVO staff runs half-hour tours that explain monitoring techniques on sophisticated computerized equipment in riveting detail and describe the various pyroclastic surge deposits and artifacts on display. ⊠ *Flemings* ☎ *664/491–5647* ⊕ *www.mvo.ms* ⊙ *Tours Mon.–Sat. at 3:30* 🖾 *Observatory free; tours 4$.*

Rendezvous Bay is the island's sole white-sand beach, its calm waters ideal for swimming and snorkeling. A steep trail runs over the bluff to adjacent Little Bay (you can also negotiate boat rides from the fishermen who congregate there).

Montserrat Essentials

AIR & SEA TRAVEL Although a new airport is being constructed, the only air access to Montserrat is via Antigua. Eight-seater helicopters from Montserrat Aviation Services leave Antigua's V. C. Bird airport at 7:30 AM, 9:30 AM, and 4:30 PM Mon., Tues., Thurs., and Fri.; 7:30 AM and 4:30 PM Sat.; and 7:30 AM, 2:30 PM, and 4:30 PM Sun. Summer departures (roughly May–Nov.) are a half hour later. Return flights generally leave Montserrat 15–30 minutes after landing. The cost of the 15-minute flight is $114 round-trip, and there are baggage limitations—make sure to book ahead. The *Opale Express,* an air-conditioned ferry, leaves Heritage Quay in St. John's, Antigua, at 6:30 AM (9 AM Tues. and Thurs.) and 4:30 PM daily for the hour-long trip to Montserrat. It returns a half hour after arrival. The cost is $76 round-trip, $45 Fri. and Sat. Visitors staying more than 24 hours pay a $17 departure tax.

🚩 **Montserrat Aviation Services** ☎ 268/462–3147 in Antigua; 664/491–2533 in Montserrat. *Opale Express* ☎ 268/480–2980 in Antigua; 664/491–2533 in Montserrat.

CAR RENTAL & TAXIS You can rent a car, hire a taxi, or ask a local tour operator to show you around. Temporary driving licenses are available for $19 at the police headquarters in Brades, which is open 24 hours weekdays. You can rent cars and scooters at Tropical Mansion Suites and jeeps and cars at Travel World International. Driving is on the left, and many roads are twisting and pocked with potholes. You're best off with local guides who know where the best views are—and which parts of the island are off

limits due to volcanic activity. Joe "Fergus" Phillip, who operates Avalon Tours, is one such friendly, knowledgeable, reliable taxi and tour driver.
Avalon Tours ⊠ Brades ☎ 664/491-3432. **Travel World International** ⊠ Davy Hill ☎ 664/491-2713. **Tropical Mansion Suites** ⊠ Sweeney's ☎ 664/491-8767.

TOURS Jenny's Tours arranges day trips to Montserrat—including the ferry ride from Antigua, an island tour, breakfast, and lunch—for $130 per person.
Jenny's Tours ⊠ Woods Centre, St. John's ✆ Box W471 ☎ 268/461-9361

VISITOR The Montserrat Tourist Board lists accommodations, restaurants, activities,
INFORMATION car rental agencies, and tours available on the island. In North America, Bob Heim Communications acts as an unofficial tourist adjunct.
Bob Heim Communications ✆ 164 Tardy Lane S, Wantagh, NY 11793 ☎☎ 516/221-1587. **Montserrat Tourist Board** ⊕ www.visitmontserrat.com ⊠ Salem ☎ 664/491-2230 ⊠ in the United Kingdom: ⊠ Montserrat Government Office, Lauderdale House, 30B Wimpole St., London W1G 8YB ☎ 0207/486-7073

ANTIGUA A TO Z

To research prices, get advice from other travelers, and book travel arrangements, visit www.fodors.com.

AIR TRAVEL
American Airlines has daily direct service from New York and Miami, and several flights from San Juan that connect with flights from more than 100 U.S. cities. Continental Airlines offers nonstop service from Newark and Miami. US Airways offers direct service from Baltimore and Philadelphia. Air Jamaica flies direct daily from New York. Air Canada has nonstop service from Toronto. British Airways has nonstop service from London. Virgin Atlantic also offers nonstop London flights. BWIA has nonstop service from New York, Miami, and Toronto. Carib Aviation flies daily to Barbuda, as well as to neighboring islands. LIAT has daily flights to and from many other Caribbean islands. Antigua-based Caribbean Star promises a "whole new altitude" with daily flights to and from several islands; a sister operation, tentatively titled Caribbean Sun, is expected to start operations out of Miami sometime in 2003.
American Airlines ☎ 268/462-0950. **Air Canada** ☎ 268/462-1147. **Air Jamaica** ☎ 268/562-4152. **British Airways** ☎ 268/462-0876. **BWIA** ☎ 268/480-2925 or 268/480-2942. **Carib Aviation** ☎ 268/462-3147 ⊕ www.candoo.com/carib. **Caribbean Star** ☎ 268/480-2591 ⊕ www.flycaribbeanstar.com. **Continental Airlines** ☎ 268/462-5355. **LIAT** ☎ 268/480-5600. **US Airways** ☎ 268/480-5700. **Virgin Atlantic** ☎ 268/560-2079.

AIRPORTS
Antigua's V. C. Bird International Airport, on the northeast coast, is a major hub for traffic between Caribbean islands and for international flights.

Taxis meet every flight, and drivers will offer to guide you around the island. The taxis are unmetered, but rates are posted at the airport, and drivers must carry a rate card with them. The fixed rate from the airport to St. John's is US$9 (although drivers have been known to *quote* in EC dollars), to Dickenson Bay $13, and to English Harbour $26.
V. C. Bird International Airport ☎ 268/462-4672.

BIKE & MOPED TRAVEL
You can rent Honda or Yamaha motorcycles for $35 per day ($150 per week) at J. T.'s Rent-A-Scoot.
J. T.'s Rent-A-Scoot ⊠ Parham ☎ 268/463-3578.

BUSINESS HOURS

BANKS Banks have varying hours but are generally open Monday–Thursday 8–2 and Friday 8–4.

POST OFFICES Post offices are open Monday–Saturday 9–4.

SHOPS Although some stores still follow the tradition of closing for lunch, most are open Monday–Saturday 9–5, especially in season; if a cruise ship is in port, shops in Heritage and Redcliffe Quays are likely to open Sunday.

CAR RENTALS

To rent a car, you need a valid driver's license and a temporary permit ($20), available through the rental agent. Costs average about $50 per day in season, with unlimited mileage, though you may get a better rate if you rent for several days. Most agencies offer automatic, stick-shift, and right- and left-hand drive. Four-wheel-drive vehicles ($55 per day) will get you more places and are refreshingly open; they are also useful because so many roads are full of potholes.

🚗 **Avis** ☎ 268/462-2840. **Budget** ☎ 268/462-3009. **Dollar** ☎ 268/462-0362. **Hertz** ☎ 268/462-4650 and 268/481-4440. **National** ☎ 268/462-2113. **Thrifty** ☎ 268/462-8803 and 268/462-9532.

CAR TRAVEL

GASOLINE At this writing, gasoline costs approximately $2.65 per gallon.

ROAD CONDITIONS The main roads, by and large, are in good condition, although there are bronco-busting dirt stretches leading to some more remote locations and a few hilly areas that flood easily and become impassable for a day or two.

RULES OF THE ROAD Driving is on the left, although many locals drive in the middle—or think nothing of stopping at the roadside to chat. Don't be flustered by honking: it's the Caribbean version of hello.

ELECTRICITY

Antigua runs on 110 volts, allowing the use of most small North American appliances. Outlets are both two- and three-pronged, so bring an adapter.

EMBASSIES & CONSULATES

🏛 **United Kingdom British High Commission** ✉ 11 Old Parham Rd., St. John's ☎ 268/462-0008 or 268/562-2124 ⊕ www.fco.gov.uk.

🏛 **United States United States Consulate** ✉ Hospital Hill, Pigeon Point, English Harbour ☎ 268/463-6531 🖨 268/460-1569 ⊕ usembassy.state.gov.

EMERGENCIES

🚑 **Ambulance & Fire Ambulance** ☎ 268/462-0251. **Fire** ☎ 268/462-0044.

🏥 **Hospitals Holberton Hospital** ✉ Hospital Rd., St. John's ☎ 268/462-0251.

💊 **Pharmacies City Pharmacy** ✉ St. Mary's St., St. John's ☎ 268/480-3314. **Woods Pharmacy** ✉ Woods Centre, Friar's Hill Rd., St. John's ☎ 268/462-9287.

👮 **Police Police assistance** ☎ 268/462-0125 or 268/460-718789.

ETIQUETTE & BEHAVIOR

Antiguans are extremely proud, and don't take kindly to strangers snapping photos without first asking permission.

FESTIVALS & SEASONAL EVENTS

Antigua Sailing Week, which takes place at the end of April and in early May, draws more than 300 yachts for a series of races in several boat classes. It is like a nautical Kentucky Derby, and the salt air crackles with excitement. Late April sees the Antigua Classic Yacht Regatta, a five-day event including the Parade of Classics and Tall Ships race. Antigua Tennis Week, usually held the second week of May, has exhibitions by such masters as Billie Jean King, Kathy Rinaldi, Fred Stolle, and Bob Lutz, plus a pro-am tournament. Carnival runs from the end of July to early August and is one of the Caribbean's more elaborate, with eye-catching costumes, fiercely competitive bands, and the only Caribbean queen show (a.k.a. the Miss Antigua Contest). Antigua International Hot-Air Balloon Festival attracts dozens of fancifully shaped and colored hot-air balloons in early January.

HOLIDAYS
Public holidays are New Year's Day, Good Friday (usually late March to April), Easter Sunday and Monday (usually late March to April), Labour Day (1st Monday in May), Whit Monday (2nd Monday in June), Independence Day (November 1), Christmas Day, and Boxing Day (December 26).

LANGUAGE
Antigua's official language is English, and it's often spoken with a heavy West Indian lilt.

MAIL & SHIPPING
Airmail letters to North America cost EC$1.50; postcards, EC75¢. Letters to the United Kingdom cost EC$1.80; postcards EC90¢. Letters to Australia and New Zealand are EC$1.80, postcards EC90¢. The main post office is at the foot of High Street in St. John's. Note that there are no postal codes; when addressing letters to the island, you need only indicate the address and "Antigua, West Indies."

MONEY MATTERS
Note: prices quoted throughout this chapter are in U.S. dollars unless otherwise indicated.

ATMS ATMs are available at the island's banks and at the airport.
🏧 Bank of Antigua ✉ High and Thames Sts. ☎ 268/480-5300. Barclays Bank ✉ High St. ☎ 268/480-5000.

CREDIT CARDS Most hotels, restaurants, and duty-free shops take major credit cards; all accept traveler's checks.

CURRENCY Local currency is the Eastern Caribbean dollar (EC$), which is tied to the U.S. dollar and fluctuates only slightly. At hotels the rate is EC$2.60 to US$1; at banks it's EC$2.68. American dollars are readily accepted, although you'll usually receive change in EC dollars.

PASSPORTS & VISAS
U.S. and Canadian citizens need proof of identity. A valid passport is most desirable, but a birth certificate is acceptable provided it has a raised seal and has been issued by a county or state (not a hospital), and provided that you also have some type of photo identification, such as a driver's license. A driver's license by itself is not sufficient, nor is a voter registration card. Citizens of Australia, New Zealand, and the United Kingdom need passports. All visitors must present a return or ongoing ticket.

SAFETY
Throughout the Caribbean, incidents of petty theft are increasing. Leave your valuables in the hotel safe-deposit box; don't leave them unattended in your room, on a beach, or in a rental car. Also, the streets of St. John's are fairly deserted at night, so it's not a good idea to wander about alone.

SIGHTSEEING TOURS

ORIENTATION Virtually all taxi drivers double as guides, and you can arrange an island tour with one for about $25 an hour. Every major hotel has a cabbie on call and may be able to negotiate a discount, particularly off-season. Antours, by far the most professional outfit on Antigua, gives half- and full-day island tours that focus on such highlights as Shirley Heights and English Harbour. Antours is also the island's American Express representative.

🚩 Antours ⊠ Long and Thames Sts., St. John's ☎ 268/462-4788.

SPECIAL-INTEREST Jolly Harbour-based Caribbean Helicopters offers bird's-eye views both of the island and of Montserrat's ruins and still simmering volcano. Trips last anywhere from 15–45 minutes; prices run $75–$190. Day-trippers can experience Barbuda through a tour by D&J Tours, which includes a round-trip flight, beach picnic, and full tour for $160. Estate Safari Adventure operates tours to the interior, where there are few marked trails and roads are rough. The cost (about $60 per person) includes lunch and snorkeling at a secluded beach. Tropikelly's four-wheel-drive off-road adventures enable you to fully appreciate the island's topography and rich history. Hiking is involved, though it's not strenuous. Four-wheel-drive tours with hikes are $65; bike tours cost $35; and hikes through the rain forest run $20.

🚩 Caribbean Helicopters ☎268/460-5900 ⊕www.caribbeanhelicopters.net. D&J Tours ☎ 268/773-9766. Estate Safari Adventure ☎ 268/463-4713. Tropikelly ☎ 268/461-0383.

TAXES & SERVICE CHARGES

DEPARTURE TAX The departure tax is $20, payable in cash only—either U.S. or E.C. currency.

SALES TAX Hotels collect an 8½% government room tax; some restaurants will add a 7% tax.

SERVICE CHARGES Hotels and restaurants usually add a 10% service charge to your bill.

TAXIS

Taxis are unmetered, and although fares mount up quickly, rates are fixed (your driver should have a rate card). Some cabbies may take you from St. John's to English Harbour and wait for a "reasonable" amount of time (about a half hour) while you look around, for about $40. You can always call a cab from the St. John's taxi stand.

🚩 St. John's taxi stand ☎ 268/462-5190; 268/460-5353 for 24-hour service.

TELEPHONES

Few hotels have direct-dial phones, but it's easy enough to make connections through the switchboard. You can use the Caribbean Phone Card (available in $5, $10, and $20 denominations in most hotels and post offices) for local and long-distance calls. Phone-card phones work much better than the regular coin-operated phones.

COUNTRY & AREA CODES To call Antigua from the United States, dial 1, then area code 268, then the local seven-digit number.

INTERNATIONAL CALLS To call the United States and Canada, dial 1, the area code, and the seven-digit number, or use the phone card or one of the "CALL USA" phones, which are available at several locations, including the airport departure lounge, the cruise terminal at St. John's, and the English Harbour Marina. These take credit cards and, supposedly, calling cards (though Cable & Wireless tacks on a fee).

LOCAL CALLS To place a local call, simply dial the local seven-digit number.

TIPPING

In restaurants it's customary to leave 5% beyond the regular service charge added to your bill if you're pleased with the service. Taxi drivers expect a 10% tip, porters and bellmen about $1 per bag. Maids are rarely tipped, but if you think the service exemplary, figure $2–$3 per night. Staff at all-inclusives aren't supposed to be tipped unless they've truly gone out of their way.

TRANSPORTATION AROUND ANTIGUA

You'll see two bus stations in St. John's, one near the Botanical Gardens and one near Central Market, but don't expect to see many buses. Schedules follow island time, which is to say that privately owned vehicles roll when the spirit (infrequently) moves them. Taxis are generally your best bet.

VISITOR INFORMATION

There is a tourist-information desk at the airport, just beyond the immigration checkpoint. The tourist office provides limited information. You may have more success with the Antigua Hotels and Tourist Association.

Before You Leave Antigua and Barbuda Tourist Offices ⊕ www.antigua-barbuda. org or www.antiguanice.com ⊠ 610 5th Ave., Suite 311, New York, NY 10020 ☎ 212/541-4117 or 888/268-4227 ⊠ 25 S.E. 2nd Ave., Suite 300, Miami, FL 33131 ☎ 305/381-6762 ⊠ 60 St. Clair Ave. E, Suite 304, Toronto, Ontario M4T 1N5 ☎ 416/961-3085 ⊠ Antigua House, 15 Thayer St., London W1M 5LD ☎ 0207/486-7073.

In Antigua Antigua and Barbuda Department of Tourism ⊠ Newgate St., St. John's ☎ 268/463-0125 🖷 268/462-2483. **Antigua Hotels and Tourist Association** ⊠ Newgate St., St. John's ☎ 268/462-0374.

ARUBA

FODOR'S CHOICE
Bucuti Beach Resort, Eagle Beach

HIGHLY RECOMMENDED

RESTAURANTS Brisas del Mar, Savaneta
Chez Mathilde, Oranjestad
Gasparito Restaurant & Art Gallery, Noord
Le Dôme, Eagle Beach
Papiamento, Noord

HOTELS Aruba Marriott Resort & Stellaris Casino, Palm Beach
Divi Aruba Beach Resort, Manchebo Beach
Hyatt Regency Aruba Beach Resort & Casino, Palm Beach
Radisson Aruba Resort & Casino, Palm Beach
Renaissance Aruba Beach Resort & Casino, Oranjestad

NIGHTLIFE Alhambra Casino, Oranjestad
Carlos & Charlie's, Oranjestad

OUTDOORS Palm Beach
Windsurfing

The California Lighthouse towers above the entire panorama of Aruba. Looking to the south, you see a lush, green 18-hole golf course in the foreground and the Las Vegas–like strip of Oranjestad gleaming in the distance. To the East a starkly arid lunar landscape stretches as far as the eye can see. On this strange island set in the bluest of seas the works of man and the creations of nature face each other in competition, the outcome of which remains to be seen.

Updated by
Vernon
O'Reilly-
Ramesar

That delicate balance is the key to Aruba's undeniable success. Most of the island gleams with a fierce, extraterrestrial beauty, its battered coast defying development. But balmy sunshine, silky sand, aquamarine waters, and constant trade winds (so strong they've bent Aruba's trademark watapanas—commonly known as divi-divi trees—at a surreal 45-degree angle) have made the calmer southwest coast a tourist mecca. Most of its 28 major hotels sit side by side down a single strip of shore, with restaurants, exotic boutiques, fiery floor shows, and glitzy casinos on the premises. Nearly every night there are theme parties, treasure hunts, beachside barbecues, and fish fries with steel bands and limbo or Carnival dancers. Surround all this with warm blue-green waters whose visibility extends up to 100 ft, and you've got the perfect destination for anyone who wants sun salted with lots of activities.

The *A* in the ABC Islands (the other two being Bonaire and Curaçao), Aruba is small—only 19½ mi (31½ km) long and 6 mi (9½ km) across at its widest point. Once a member of the Netherlands Antilles, it became an independent entity within the Netherlands in 1986, with its own royally appointed governor and a 21-member elected parliament.

Aruba's economy was once based on oil. These days, education, housing, and health care are financed by tourism, and the island's population of 110,000 recognizes visitors as valued guests. The national anthem proclaims, "The greatness of our people is their great cordiality," and this is no exaggeration. Waiters serve you with smiles, English is spoken everywhere, and hotel hospitality directors appear delighted to fulfill your special wishes.

The island's distinctive beauty lies in its countryside—full of rocky deserts, divi-divi trees, cactus jungles alive with the chattering of wild parakeets, secluded coves, and blue vistas with crashing waves. With its low humidity and average temperature of 82°F (28°C), Aruba has the climate of a paradise. Sun, cooling trade winds, friendly and courteous service, efficient amenities, golf and tennis clubs, modern casinos, glorious beaches, duty-free shopping, and remarkably varied cuisine help fill Aruba's more than 7,500 hotel rooms.

WHAT IT COSTS In U.S. dollars					
	$$$$	**$$$**	**$$**	**$**	**¢**
RESTAURANTS*					
	over $30	$20–$30	$12–$20	$8–$12	under $8
HOTELS**					
Cost EP/BP/CP	over $350	$250–$350	$150–$250	$80–$150	under $80
Cost·AI	over $450	$350–$450	$250–$350	$125–$250	under $125

*Restaurant prices are for a main course at dinner. **EP, BP, and CP prices are per night for a standard double room in high season, excluding taxes, service charges, and meal plans. AI (all-inclusive) prices are per person, per night based on double-occupancy during high season, excluding taxes and service charges.

Where to Stay

Most hotels are west of Oranjestad along L. G. Smith and J. E. Irausquin boulevards. These complexes have their own fitness centers, hair salons, casinos, restaurants, delis, drugstores, boutiques, and car-rental and travel desks. Room service, laundry and dry cleaning services, and baby-sitting are standard amenities at all but the smallest properties, and activities like water sports are usually part of the package. Children often get free accommodation in their parents' room; ask about age qualifications. Most hotels, unless specified, don't include meals in their room rates.

Hotels here are fairly expensive. To save money, take advantage of airline and hotel packages, which are plentiful. Rates are cheaper in summer, when rates are discounted by as much as 40%.

★ **$$$$** ⊞ **Aruba Marriott Resort & Stellaris Casino.** You'll hear the sound of water everywhere at this high-rise hotel on Palm Beach, whether it's the beating of the surf below your balcony or the trickling of the waterfalls in the marble lobby and around the tropically landscaped pool. Spacious rooms have a distinctly Caribbean feeling. Most have ocean views, as well as walk-in closets, hair dryers, and irons. The walk to the ocean from the garden-view rooms is longer than that from elsewhere in the complex, but the in-room hot tubs more than compensate for this. Express checkout is available. ⊠ *L. G. Smith Blvd. 101, Palm Beach* ☎ *297/58–69000 or 800/223–6388* 🖷 *297/58–60649* ⊕ *www.marriott. com* ➲ *413 rooms, 20 suites* ⚿ *4 restaurants, café, in-room data ports, in-room safes, minibars, refrigerators, cable TV with movies, in-room VCRs, 2 tennis courts, pool, aerobics, hair salon, health club, saunas, spa, beach, dive shop, windsurfing, boating, jet skiing, volleyball, 4 bars, casino, shops, concierge, Internet, meeting rooms, car rental, no-smoking floor* ⊟ *AE, D, DC, MC, V* ◎ *EP.*

★ ♨ **$$$$** ⊞ **Hyatt Regency Aruba Beach Resort & Casino.** A favorite among honeymooners, this resort looks like a Spanish palace, with art deco–style flourishes and a multilevel pool with waterfalls, a two-story water slide, and a lagoon stocked with tropical fish and black swans. Rooms have slim balconies but lots of extras; those on the Regency Club floor have such amenities as complimentary breakfast and concierge service. Relax on the beach, play tennis, or head out for a horseback ride before an afternoon hydrotherapy treatment and a stop at the juice bar. ⊠ *J. E. Irausquin Blvd. 85, Palm Beach* ☎ *297/58–61234 or 800/554–9288* 🖷 *297/58–61682* ⊕ *www.hyatt.com* ➲ *342 rooms, 18 suites* ⚿ *5 restaurants, snack bar, room service, fans, in-room safes, minibars, cable TV with movies, 2 tennis courts, pool, hair salon, health club, 2 outdoor hot tubs, sauna, spa, steam room, beach, dive shop, dock,* *snorkeling, windsurfing, boating, jet skiing, waterskiing, basketball, horseback riding, volleyball, 5 bars, casino, shops, baby-sitting, children's programs (ages 3–12), playground, concierge, concierge floor, Internet, business services, car rental, travel services, some pets allowed, no-smoking floor* ⊟ *AE, D, DC, MC, V* ⏐◯⏐ *EP.*

★ **$$$$**   ⊡ **Radisson Aruba Resort & Casino.** Exotic birds greet you in the expansive lobby of Aruba's largest resort. Colonial Caribbean–style guest

⚓ rooms (each with a view of the ocean or the garden) have mahogany four-poster beds and such singular accents as hand-beaded lamp shades. The designers thought of everything: blue-accent lighting, wood furniture on the balconies, and plantation shutters. In-room perks include minibars (careful, they're touch-sensored), coffeemakers, and hair dryers. Unwind in the fitness center and spa, and then enjoy a meal at one of the hotel's excellent restaurants. ⊠ *J. E. Irausquin Blvd. 81, Palm Beach* ☎ *297/58–66555* 🖷 *297/68–63260* ⊕ *www.radisson.com* ⇆ *358 rooms, 32 suites* ♿ *4 restaurants, room service, in-room data ports, in-room safes, minibars, cable TV with movies, golf privileges, 2 tennis courts, 2 pools, health club, 2 outdoor hot tubs, spa, beach, dive shop, snorkeling, boating, jet skiing, 3 bars, casino, video game room, shops, baby-sitting, children's programs (ages 3-17), dry cleaning, laundry service, Internet, business services, convention center, meeting rooms, car rental* ⊟ *AE, D, DC, MC, V* ⏐◯⏐ *BP.*

☾ **$$$–$$$$**   ⊡ **Allegro Aruba Resort & Casino.** Most activities take place at the cloverleaf-shaped pool (with its waterfall and whirlpool tubs) at the heart of this resort. A popular place with tour groups, it has a buzzing atmosphere, and you can enjoy everything from beer-drinking contests to bikini shows. The tropical rooms have white-tile bathrooms that are snug and balconies that are little more than narrow step-outs. The Kids' Club, open from 9 to 5 daily, keeps children busy with a wide range of activities. Don't miss the Vegas-style dinner show six days a week. ⊠ *J. E. Irausquin Blvd. 83, Palm Beach* ☎ *297/58–64500 or 800/447–7462* 🖷 *297/58–63191* ⊕ *www.allegroresorts.com* ⇆ *403 rooms, 14 suites* ♿ *3 restaurants, in-room safes, cable TV with movies, 2 tennis courts, pool, gym, 2 outdoor hot tubs, spa, beach, snorkeling, windsurfing, boating, waterskiing, basketball, billiards, Ping-Pong, volleyball, 3 bars, casino, dance club, shops, children's programs (ages 4–12), Internet, meeting rooms* ⊟ *AE, D, DC, MC, V* ⏐◯⏐ *AI.*

★ **$$$**   ⊡ **Divi Aruba Beach Resort Mega All Inclusive.** At this Mediterranean-style resort you have your choice of standard rooms, beachfront lanais, or casitas that overlook courtyards and are often only steps from the beach. The white-tile floors and mint and jade color schemes are soothing. Make your own daiquiri at the poolside Pelican Bar, where you can also enjoy pizza hot from the oven. Since there are so many different activities scheduled, you need to check the listings daily. In addition to the many on-site facilities, you can also use those at the adjacent Tamarijn Aruba. ⊠ *L. G. Smith Blvd. 93, Manchebo Beach* ☎ *297/58–23300 or 800/554–2008* 🖷 *297/58–31940* ⊕ *www.diviaruba.com* ⇆ *203 rooms* ♿ *5 restaurants, fans, refrigerators, cable TV, tennis court, 2 pools, gym, hair salon, outdoor hot tub, beach, dive shop, snorkeling, windsurfing, boating, waterskiing, bicycles, shuffleboard, volleyball, 3 bars, shops, baby-sitting, laundry service, Internet* ⊟ *AE, D, DC, MC, V* ⏐◯⏐ *AI.*

$$$ ⊡ **Tamarijn Aruba All Inclusive Beach Resort.** Low-rise buildings stretch along the shore at this all-inclusive resort catering to couples and families. The spacious oceanfront rooms, filled with light-wood furnishings, have private balconies and were renovated in 2002. The rate covers food, beverages, entertainment, an array of activities, and even tickets to the weekly Bon Bini Festival. A bar at one end of the property serves food and drinks as a convenience for guests more removed from the main

California Pt.

Tierra del Sol
Golf Course

Mt. Altovista

Bushiribana

Malmok
Beach

Antilla
Shipwreck

Malmok Reef

Debbie II

Fisherman's Hut

Pedernalis

Paradera

Palm Beach

Noord

Eagle Beach

Manchebo Beach

Santa Cruz

Druif
Bay

L.G. Smith Blv

Oranjestad

Reina Beatrix
International
Airport

Jane Sea Wreck

KEY

- Beaches
- Cruise Ship Terminal
- Dive Sites
- ❶ Exploring Sights
- ① Hotels & Restaurants

Hotels

Allegro Aruba
Resort & Casino **14**

Amsterdam
Manor Beach
Resort **22**

Aruba Grand Beach
Resort & Casino **16**

Aruba Marriott
Resort & Stellaris
Casino **11**

Best Western
Manchebo
Beach Resort **25**

Bucuti Beach
Resort **24**

Divi Aruba
Beach Resort Mega
All Inclusive **26**

Holiday Inn SunSpree
Aruba Resort
& Casino **12**

Hyatt Regency
Aruba Beach
Resort & Casino **13**

La Cabana All Suite
Beach Resort
& Casino **23**

Mill Resort
& Suites **20**

Radisson Aruba
Resort & Casino **15**

Renaissance Aruba
Beach Resort
& Casino **1**

Tamarijn Aruba
All Inclusive
Beach Resort **27**

Vistalmar **5**

Wyndham Aruba
Beach Resort &
Casino **8**

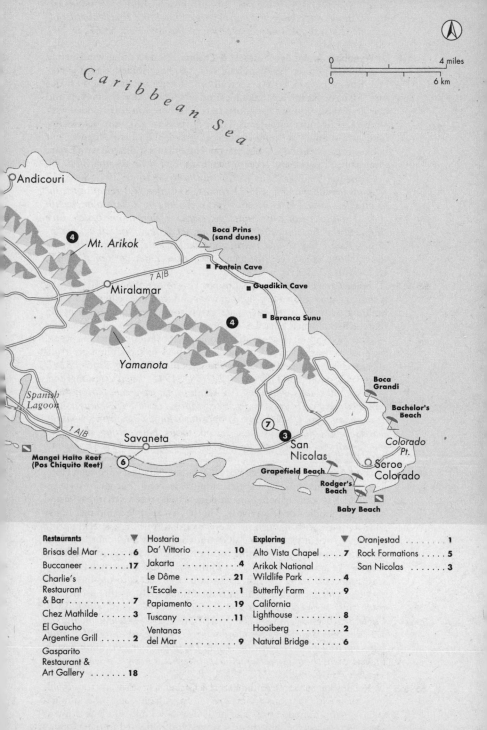

Aruba

Caribbean Sea

Andicouri

4 Mt. Arikok

Boca Prins
(sand dunes)

Miralamar
7 A|B

Fontein Cave

Guadikin Cave

Baranca Sunu

4

Yamanota

Boca
Grandi

Bachelor's
Beach

Spanish
Lagoon

1 A|B
Savaneta

Mangel Halto Reef
(Pos Chiquito Reef)   6

7
3
San
Nicolas

Colorado
Pt.

Seroe
Colorado

Grapefield Beach

Rodger's
Beach

Baby Beach

restaurants. Children under 17 stay free. ✉ *J. E. Irausquin Blvd. 41, Punta Brabo* ☎ *297/58–24150 or 800/554–2008* 🖷 *297/58–31940* ⊕ *www.tamarijnaruba.com* ⌨ *236 rooms ⚿ 3 restaurants, snack bar, fans, cable TV, 2 tennis courts, 2 pools, beach, snorkeling, windsurfing, boating, waterskiing, fishing, bicycles, Ping-Pong, shuffleboard, volleyball, 2 bars, shops, Internet, meeting rooms, car rental* ▭ *AE, D, DC, MC, V* ⑩ *AI.*

$$$ 🏨 **Wyndham Aruba Beach Resort & Casino.** From exciting windsurfing to sizzling nightlife, the Wyndham seems to have something for everyone. Rooms have ocher stucco walls and handsome dark-wood furniture. All have ocean-view balconies and amenities like coffeemakers and hair dryers. Never mind data ports in rooms; here you are provided with your own in-room computer. A day at the pool means more than swimming and sunning; a "pool concierge" makes the rounds, loaning out books, magazines, and CD players; pool attendants spritz you with Evian, offer chilled towels, and serve frozen fruit. ✉ *J. E. Irausquin Blvd. 77, Palm Beach* ☎ *297/58–64466 or 800/996–3426* 🖷 *297/58–68217* ⊕ *www.wyndham.com* ⌨ *481 rooms, 81 suites ⚿ 5 restaurants, in-room safes, cable TV, tennis court, pool, wading pool, hair salon, health club, 2 outdoor hot tubs, massage, sauna, steam room, beach, dive shop, snorkeling, windsurfing, boating, jet skiing, parasailing, waterskiing, Ping-Pong, shuffleboard, volleyball, 6 bars, casino, video game room, shops, concierge, Internet, convention center, car rental* ▭ *AE, D, DC, MC, V* ⑩ *AI.*

$$–$$$ 🏨 **Aruba Grand Beach Resort & Casino.** This resort, though still popular, is showing more than a few signs of wear and tear. The yellow-and-white building, with its distinctive jade green roof, is accompanied by 55 thatched-roof beach huts. Large rooms and suites have such amenities as generous walk-in closets and balconies that overlook either the ocean, the pool, or the garden. Ask about discount packages; discounts are available for children under 12. ✉ *J. E. Irausquin Blvd. 79, Palm Beach* ☎ *297/58–63900 or 800/345–2782* 🖷 *297/58–61941* ⊕ *www.arubagrand.com* ⌨ *130 rooms, 41 suites ⚿ 2 restaurants, ice-cream parlor, snack bar, room service, in-room safes, refrigerators, cable TV, 2 tennis courts, pool, wading pool, beach, dive shop, snorkeling, windsurfing, boating, waterskiing, volleyball, 3 bars, casino, shops, baby-sitting, dry cleaning, laundry service, concierge, Internet, meeting rooms* ▭ *AE, D, DC, MC, V* ⑩ *EP.*

$$–$$$ 🏨 **Bucuti Beach Resort.** Owner Ewald Biemans was named Caribbean Hote-
Fodor'sChoice lier of the Year 2002 for his refreshingly peaceful, European-style re-
★ sort, which is popular with honeymooners (who receive champagne and romantic goodies upon arrival). The hacienda-style buildings house sunny rooms with handsome cherrywood furnishings, sparkling tile floors, and ocean-view terraces. Grounds are lushly landscaped, and the intimate resort has an enviable location on the widest, most secluded section of Eagle Beach. Work out in the open-air exercise pavilion and stay connected using the hotel's 24-hour free access to the Internet, a rare convenience for an Aruban resort. Book early, as this property is often fully booked, even in low season. ✉ *L. G. Smith Blvd. 55-B, Eagle Beach* ☎ *297/58–31100* 🖷 *297/58–25272* ⊕ *www.bucuti.com* ⌨ *58 rooms, 5 suites ⚿ Restaurant, grocery, fans, in-room safes, minibars, microwaves, refrigerators, cable TV, pool, gym, hair salon, beach, bicycles, bar, shop, laundry facilities, Internet, business services, travel services* ▭ *AE, D, DC, MC, V* ⑩ *EP.*

♨ $$–$$$ 🏨 **Holiday Inn SunSpree Aruba Resort & Casino.** Three seven-story buildings filled with spacious rooms are set apart from each other along a sugary, palm-dotted shore. The pool's cascades and sundeck draw as large a crowd as the wide beach, where you're invited to the Monday evening cocktail party. Enjoy live entertainment as you try your luck at the casino, or savor a beachfront meal at the Sea Breeze Grill. Get massaged and wrapped at the Intermezzo Spa. ⊠ *J. E. Irausquin Blvd. 230, Palm Beach* ☎ *297/58–63600* 🖷 *297/58–65165* ⊕ *www.holidayinn-aruba.com* ⤺ *600 rooms, 15 suites* ⌂ *3 restaurants, refrigerators, cable TV with movies, 4 tennis courts, 2 pools, health club, spa, beach, dive shop, dock, snorkeling, windsurfing, boating, waterskiing, basketball, Ping-Pong, volleyball, 3 bars, casino, video game room, shops, children's programs (ages 5–12), concierge, Internet, business services, meeting rooms, car rental, no-smoking rooms* ▤ *AE, D, DC, MC, V* ¶◉¶ *AI.*

$$–$$$ 🏨 **La Cabana All Suite Beach Resort & Casino.** Across the road from Eagle Beach you'll find this huge self-contained resort. The original four-story building facing the beach surrounds two pools, a bar, and a restaurant. About a third of the studios and one-bedroom suites have ocean views. All have kitchenettes, balconies, and even hot tubs. Pricier villas are away from the main building near a parking lot. Las Ramblas, the on-site tapas restaurant, is a fun place to spend an evening. Many guests purchase meal plans or the all-inclusive plan. ⊠ *J. E. Irausquin Blvd. 250, Eagle Beach* ☎ *297/58–79000, 212/251–1710 in NY, 800/835–7193* 🖷 *297/58–70834* ⊕ *www.lacabana.com* ⤺ *803 suites* ⌂ *4 restaurants, grocery, ice-cream parlor, in-room safes, kitchenettes, microwaves, cable TV, 5 tennis courts, 3 pools, aerobics, health club, 3 outdoor hot tubs, sauna, spa, beach, dive shop, dock, basketball, racquetball, shuffleboard, squash, volleyball, 5 bars, video game room, shops, playground, Internet, meeting rooms* ▤ *AE, DC, MC, V* ¶◉¶ *EP.*

★ **$$–$$$** 🏨 **Renaissance Aruba Beach Resort & Casino.** Renaissance is planning a major facelift for this property, which was formerly the Aruba Sonesta Resort. Rooms are airy and comfortable—the garden rooms are an especially good choice. You can board a boat in the lobby for a trip to the resort's 40-acre private island. The gourmet restaurant, L'Escale, is one of Aruba's best. ⊠ *L. G. Smith Blvd. 9, Oranjestad* ☎ *297/58–36000 or 800/766–3782* 🖷 *297/58–25317* ⊕ *www.arubarenaissance.com* ⤺ *300 rooms, 265 suites* ⌂ *4 restaurants, room service, kitchenettes, minibars, some microwaves, cable TV with movies, golf privileges, tennis court, 3 pools, hair salon, 3 health clubs, spa, beach, dive shop, snorkeling, jet skiing, marina, waterskiing, fishing, volleyball, 5 bars, 2 casinos, nightclub, video game room, shops, baby-sitting, children's programs (ages 3-17), playground, laundry facilities, concierge, Internet, convention center, meeting rooms, no-smoking rooms* ▤ *AE, D, DC, MC, V* ¶◉¶ *EP.*

$$ 🏨 **Amsterdam Manor Beach Resort.** This mustard-yellow hotel—all gables and turrets—looks like part of a Dutch colonial village. It's a cozy enclave surrounding a pool with a waterfall. Glorious Eagle Beach is just across the street. Rooms are furnished in either Dutch modern or provincial style and range from small studios—some with private balconies—to two-bedroom suites with peaked ceilings, full kitchens, and whirlpool tubs. Children under 12 stay free with their parents. The hotel can arrange a variety of activities. ⊠ *J. E. Irausquin Blvd. 252, Eagle Beach* ☎ *297/58–71492 or 800/932–6509* 🖷 *297/58–71463* ⊕ *www. amsterdammanor.com* ⤺ *72 units* ⌂ *Restaurant, fans, in-room safes, kitchenettes, microwaves, cable TV, pool, wading pool, hair salon, snorkeling, bar, playground, laundry facilities, Internet, car rental, some pets allowed* ▤ *AE, DC, MC, V* ¶◉¶ *EP.*

$$ 🏨 **Best Western Manchebo Beach Resort.** Set amid 10 acres of gardens, this resort feels away from it all. But it's just five minutes from town and right across from the Alhambra complex of shops, restaurants, and a casino. The international clientele appreciates a bargain, and children under 12 stay free. Rooms are decorated with blond-wood furnishings and bright floral fabrics and equipped with amenities like coffeemakers. Popular with diners from all over the island, the French Steakhouse is renowned for its *churrasco* (Argentine mixed grill) and has a lively piano bar. The chapel, on one of the prettiest stretches of Eagle Beach, is a charming spot for weddings. ⊠ *J. E. Irausquin Blvd. 55, Eagle Beach* ☎ *297/58–23444 or 800/528–1234* 📠 *297/58–33667 or 297/58–32446* ⊕ *www.manchebo.com* 🛏 *72 rooms* ☼ *2 restaurants, snack bar, fans, in-room safes, refrigerators, cable TV, pool, beach, dive shop, snorkeling, 2 bars, shop, Internet, laundry facilities, car rental* ▤ *AE, D, DC, MC, V* ¶⊙¶ *EP.*

$$ ▥ **Mill Resort & Suites.** With clean lines, the geometric architecture of this small resort is striking. The award-winning resort's whitewashed, red-roof buildings surround its open-air common areas. Junior suites have a sitting area and kitchenette. Smaller studios have a full kitchen, a tiny bathroom, and no balcony. The beach is a five-minute walk away; a morning coffee hour and a weekly scuba lesson are among the on-site amenities. At the Garden Café a special menu offers three courses at affordable prices. ⊠ *J. E. Irausquin Blvd. 330, Oranjestad* ☎ *297/58– 67700* 📠 *297/58–67271* ⊕ *www.millresort.com* 🛏 *64 studios, 128 suites* ☼ *Restaurant, grill, grocery, in-room safes, kitchenettes, microwaves, cable TV, 2 tennis courts, 2 pools, wading pool, gym, hair salon, massage, saunas, spa, bar, shops, laundry facilities, Internet, car rental, travel services, some pets allowed* ▤ *AE, D, DC, MC, V* ¶⊙¶ *EP.*

$ ▥ **Vistalmar.** Alby and Katy Yarzagary converted this property across the street from the fishing pier into a homey inn. Their hospitality infuses every part of the place. Simply furnished one-bedroom apartments each have a full kitchen, a living-dining room, and a sunny porch. The Yarzagarys provide snorkel gear and stock the refrigerator with breakfast fixings. There's no beach, but the sea is just across the street. One drawback is the distance from town, but you can ride the bus five times daily or rent a car. ⊠ *Bucutiweg 28, south of Oranjestad* ☎ *297/58–28579* 📠 *297/58–22200* 🛏 *8 rooms* ☼ *Kitchenettes, microwaves, cable TV with movies, hair salon, laundry facilities, car rental* ▤ *No credit cards* ¶⊙¶ *CP.*

Where to Eat

Expect outstanding meals featuring cuisines from around the world. Although most resorts offer better-than-average dining, don't be afraid to try one of the many excellent, reasonably priced independent restaurants. Ask locals about their favorite spots; some of the lesser-known eateries offer food that's definitely worth sampling. Be sure to try such Aruban specialties as *pan bati* (a mildly sweet bread that resembles a pancake) and *keshi yena* (a baked concoction of Gouda cheese, spices, and meat or seafood in a rich brown sauce).

On Sunday you may have a hard time finding a restaurant outside a hotel that's open for lunch, and many restaurants are closed for dinner on Sunday or Monday. Reservations are essential for dinner in high season.

What to Wear
Even the finest restaurants require at most a jacket for men and a sundress for women. If you plan to eat in the open air, remember to bring along insect repellent—the mosquitoes sometimes get unruly.

ARGENTINE ✕ **El Gaucho Argentine Grill.** Faux leather-bound books, tulip-top lamps, **$$$** wooden chairs, and tile floors decorate this Argentine steak house, which has been in business since 1977. Main dishes include a 16-ounce *churrasco* (Argentine steak) smothered in peppers and onions and served with corn on the cob, potatoes, and broccoli, or the catch of the day served with salad, rice, broccoli, and fried plantains. For dessert, go for the *helado argentino* (vanilla ice cream with sweet potato marmalade and caramel) or the *torta de queso,* otherwise known as cheesecake. ⊠ *Wilhelminastraat 80, Oranjestad* ☎ *297/58–23677* ⊟ *AE, D, MC, V* ⊗ *Closed Sun.*

ASIAN ✕ **Jakarta.** The abundant use of flavorful Indonesian spices brings this
$$$ restaurant's cuisine to life. The signature *rijsttafel,* which consists of 20 miniature meat, fish, vegetable, and fruit dishes, jumps off the page of the straw-faced, banana-leaf-covered menu. Vegetarians can order egg rolls, vegetable soup, or meat-free rijsttafel. Sample the java juice (blue Curaçao, vodka, Cointreau, banana liqueur, and orange and pineapple juice) at the bamboo bar on the back patio, which is adorned with wind chimes, big clay pots, and tiki torches. ⊠ *Wilhelminastraat 64, Oranjestad* ☎ *297/58–38737* ⊟ *AE, D, DC, MC, V* ⊗ *Closed Tues.*

CARIBBEAN ✕ **Gasparito Restaurant & Art Gallery.** You'll find this enchanting hide-
★ $$–$$$$ away in a *cunucu* (country house) in Noord, not far from the hotels. The works of local artists are showcased on its softly lit walls. The Aruban specialties—pan bati, keshi yena, fish croquettes, conch stew—are feasts for the eye as well as the palate. The standout dish is the Gasparito chicken; the sauce recipe was passed down from the owner's ancestors and features seven special ingredients, including brandy, white wine, and pineapple juice. (The rest, they say, are secret.). The service is excellent. ⊠ *Gasparito 3, Noord* ☎ *297/58–67044* ⊟ *AE, D, MC, V* ⊗ *Closed Sun. No lunch.*

★ $$–$$$ ✕ **Brisas del Mar.** Eating at this friendly place overlooking the sea (and bus-accessible from hotels) is like dining in a private home. Old family recipes use such indigenous ingredients as the aromatic *yerbiholé* leaf (with a minty basil flavor). Try the conch fritters as an appetizer. The catch of the day cooked Aruban-style (pan-fried and covered with creole sauce, or in garlic butter) has drawn a crowd for more than 20 years. ⊠ *Savaneta 222A, Savaneta* ☎ *297/58–47718* ⊟ *AE, D, MC, V* ⊗ *Closed Mon.*

CONTEMPORARY ✕ **L'Escale.** You're missing out if you don't have at least one meal in this
$$–$$$$ upscale eatery. Sip wine as you gaze over bustling L. G. Smith Boulevard and watch the cruise ships depart. Start with the sautéed baby snails, then move on to Caribbean-style walnut-crusted snapper. For dessert try the rich chocolate soufflé, reinforced with Grand Marnier. The extensive cigar list can turn any night into a celebration. If time is short, opt for the pre-theater menu. ⊠ *Renaissance Aruba Beach Resort, L. G. Smith Blvd. 82, Oranjestad* ☎ *297/58–36000* ⚐ *Reservations essential* ⊟ *AE, D, MC, V* ⊗ *No lunch.*

CONTINENTAL ✕ **Le Dôme.** Belgian Peter Ballière and his partners imported 11,000 bricks
★ $$–$$$$ from Antwerp to authenticate the interior of this fine dining spot. Start with the frogs' legs in lobster sauce and then move on to the delicate and flavorful fillet of lamb. A seven-course set menu is also available. Try one of the eight imported Belgian beers or one of the wine list's 65 varieties. Savor champagne and a cup of coffee with the prix-fixe Sunday brunch. Change for dinner, as shorts are a no-no. ⊠ *J. E. Irausquin Blvd. 224, Eagle Beach* ☎ *297/58–71517* ⚐ *Reservations essential* ⊟ *AE, D, DC, MC, V* ⊗ *Closed Mon. and Sept.*

★ $$$–$$$$ ✕ **Chez Mathilde.** This elegant restaurant occupies one of Aruba's last surviving 19th-century houses. Ask to sit in the greenhouse atrium, which some say has the feel of Paris. The outstanding French-style menu is constantly re-created by the Dutch chef, who has a deft touch with sauces. Feast on baked escargots, roasted breast of duck with tamarind sauce, ostrich fillet, or quail stuffed with calves' sweetbreads in a bell-pepper sauce. Crêpes suzette and chocolate layer cake with *ponche crema* (Venezuelan brandied eggnog) sauce will also win you over. ⊠ *Havenstraat 23, Oranjestad* ☎ *297/58–34968* ♠ *Reservations essential* ⊟ *AE, DC, MC, V* ⊗ *No lunch Sun.*

ECLECTIC
★ $$$–$$$$

✕ **Papiamento.** Longtime restaurateurs Lenie and Eduardo Ellis converted their 130-year-old home into a bistro with an atmosphere that is elegant, intimate, and always romantic. You can feast sumptuously indoors surrounded by antiques or outdoors in a patio garden. The chefs mix Continental and Caribbean cuisines to produce favorites that include seafood and meat dishes. You can't go wrong by sharing the "clay pot" seafood medley for two. ⊠ *Washington 61, Noord* ☎ *297/58–64544* ♠ *Reservations essential* ⊟ *AE, D, MC, V* ⊗ *No lunch. Closed Mon.*

$$$–$$$$

✕ **Ventanas del Mar.** Floor-to-ceiling windows provide an ample view across a golf course and beyond to rolling sand dunes and the sea off the island's western tip. Dining on the intimate terrace in flickering candlelight is especially romantic. Sandwiches, salads, conch fritters, nachos, and quesadillas fill the midday menu; at night the emphasis is on seafood and meat. The herb-marinated sea bass in a saffron sauce is well worth a try. ⊠ *Tierra del Sol Golf Course, Malmokweg* ☎ *297/58–60879* ⊟ *AE, D, DC, MC, V* ⊗ *Closed Mon. Apr.–Nov.*

$$

✕ **Buccaneer.** Imagine you're in a sunken ship where sharks, barracudas, and groupers swim past the portholes. That's what you'll find at Buccaneer, a restaurant with a fantastic 5,000-gallon saltwater aquarium. The chefs prepare surf-and-turf fare with European élan. Head to this old stone building flanked by heavy black chains early (around 5:45 PM) to snag a booth beside the aquarium and order the catch of the day and shrimp with Pernod. ⊠ *Gasparito 11-C, Noord* ☎ *297/58–66172* ⊟ *AE, MC, V* ⊗ *No lunch. Closed Sun.*

¢–$$

✕ **Charlie's Restaurant & Bar.** Charlie's has been a San Nicolas hangout for more than 50 years. The walls and ceiling are *covered* with license plates, hard hats, sombreros, life preservers, baseball pennants, intimate apparel—you name it. The draw here is the nonstop party atmosphere—somewhere between that of a frat house and a beach bar. Decent but somewhat overpriced specialties are tenderloin and "shrimps jumbo and dumbo" (dumb because they were caught). ⊠ *Zeppenfeldstraat 56, San Nicolas* ☎ *297/58–45086* ⊟ *AE, D, MC, V* ⊗ *Closed Sun.*

ITALIAN
$$–$$$$

✕ **Hostaria Da' Vittorio.** Part of the fun at this family-oriented lunch and dinner spot is watching chef Vittorio Muscariello prepare regional specialties in the open kitchen. Try the *branzino al sale* (sea bass baked in a hard salt shell). Exciting presentations and warm service reflect the management's stated desire to honor the essence of Italy: "ancient, but always young." As you leave, pick up some limoncello liqueur or olive oil at the door. A 15% gratuity is automatically added to your bill. ⊠ *L. G. Smith Blvd. 380, Palm Beach* ☎ *297/58–63838* ⊟ *AE, MC, V.*

$$–$$$$

✕ **Tuscany.** When you sample the food, you'll know why the chefs here have won several culinary awards. The *spannochie prima donna con capellini d'angelo* (sautéed shrimp with prosciutto, shallots, wild mushrooms, and artichokes in a light grappa cream sauce on angel-hair pasta) is a delight. The personalized service, excellent wine list, and soft piano music make for a special evening. ⊠ *Aruba Marriott Resort & Stellaris Casino, L. G. Smith Blvd. 101, Palm Beach* ☎ *297/58–69000* ♠ *Reservations essential* ⊟ *AE, DC, MC, V* ⊗ *No lunch.*

Beaches

Beaches in Aruba are legendary: white sand, turquoise waters, and virtually no litter—everyone takes the NO TIRA SUSHI (NO LITTERING) signs very seriously, especially given the $280 fine. The major beaches, which back up to the hotels along the southwestern strip, are public and crowded. You can make the hour-long hike from the Holiday Inn to the Tamarijn without ever leaving sand. Make sure you're well protected from the sun—it scorches fast despite the cooling trade winds. Luckily, there is at least one covered bar (and often an ice-cream stand) at virtually every hotel. If you stroll at night, you can hotel-hop for dinner, dancing, gambling, and late-night entertainment. On the northeastern side, wind makes the waters too choppy for swimming, but the vistas are great, and the terrain is wonderful for exploring.

Baby Beach. On the island's eastern tip, this semicircular beach borders a bay that's as placid and just about as deep as a wading pool—perfect for tots and terrible swimmers. Thatched shaded areas are good for cooling off. Just down the road is the island's rather unusual pet cemetery. You may see some shore divers here. Stop by the nearby snack shop for chicken legs, burgers, hot dogs, beer, and soda.

Boca Grandi. Strong swimming skills are a must near Seagrape Grove and the Aruba Golf Club toward the island's eastern tip.

Boca Prins. You'll need a four-wheel-drive vehicle to make the trek here. Near the Fontein Cave and Blue Lagoon, this beach is about as large as a Brazilian bikini, but with two rocky cliffs and tumultuously crashing waves, it's as romantic as you get in Aruba. Boca Prins is famous for its backdrop of enormous vanilla sand dunes. This isn't a swimming beach, however. Bring a picnic, a beach blanket, and sturdy sneakers, and descend the rocks that form steps to the water's edge.

Eagle Beach. On the southwestern coast, across the highway from what is known as Time-Share Lane, this beach, which is more than a mile long, has been designated one of the 10 best in the world by *Travel & Leisure* magazine.

Fisherman's Hut. Next to the Holiday Inn is a windsurfer's haven. Swimming conditions are good, too. Take a picnic lunch (tables are available) and watch the elegant purple, aqua, and orange sails struggle in the wind.

Grapefield Beach. To the southeast of San Nicolas, a sweep of blinding white sand in the shadow of cliffs and boulders is marked by an anchor monument dedicated to all seamen. Pick sea grapes in high season (January–June). Swim at your own risk; the waves here can be rough.

Malmok Beach. On the northwestern shore, this small, nondescript beach (where some of Aruba's wealthiest families have built tony residences) borders shallow waters that stretch 300 yards from shore. It's the perfect place to learn to windsurf. Right off the coast here is a favorite haunt for divers and snorkelers—the wreck of the German ship *Antilla,* scuttled in 1940.

Manchebo Beach (Punta Brabo). Impressively wide, the shoreline in front of the Manchebo Beach Resort is where officials turn a blind eye to the occasional topless sunbather.

★ **Palm Beach.** The center of Aruban tourism offers the best in swimming, sailing, and other water sports. It runs from the Wyndham Aruba Beach Resort to the Aruba Marriott Resort.

Rodger's Beach. Next to Baby Beach on the island's eastern tip, the beautiful curve of sand is only slightly marred by the view of the oil refinery at the far side of the bay. Swimming conditions are excellent, and there's live entertainment at the water's edge. A snack truck offers good, quick fare.

Sports & the Outdoors

On Aruba you can participate in every conceivable water sport, as well as play tennis and golf or go on a fine hike through Arikok National Park. An up-and-coming sport popular with locals is bouldering. It's similar to mountain climbing and rappelling, only up and down the boulders of the Ayo rock formations or the eastern cliffs, which are more porous and can be dangerous. The Hyatt Regency Aruba Beach Resort & Casino can make arrangements for large groups to be guided—by sergeants of the Royal Dutch Marines, no less.

BIKING Pedal pushing is a great way to get around the island; the climate is perfect, and the trade winds help to keep you cool. **Pablito's Bike Rental** (⊠ L. G. Smith Blvd. 234, Oranjestad ☎ 297/58–78655) rents mountain bikes for about $15 per day.

FISHING With catches including barracuda, kingfish, bonito, and black and yellow tuna, deep-sea fishing is great sport on Aruba. Many charter boats are available for half- or full-day sails. Prices range from $220 to $320 for a half-day charter and from $400 to $600 for a full day.

De Palm Tours (⊠ L. G. Smith Blvd. 142, Oranjestad ☎ 297/58–24400 ⊕ www.depalm.com) runs deep-sea fishing tours seven days a week. **Pelican Tours & Watersports** (⊠ J. E. Irausquin Blvd. 232, Palm Beach ☎ 297/58–72302 ⊕ www.pelican-aruba.com) is not just for the surf and snorkel crowd; the company will help you catch one that didn't get away. **Red Sail Sports** (⊠ J. E. Irausquin Blvd. 83, Oranjestad ☎ 297/58–61603, 877/733–7245 in the U.S. ⊕ www.aruba-redsail.com) will arrange everything for your fishing trip.

GOLF **Aruba Golf & Leisure** (⊠ J. E. Irausquin Blvd. 326, Oranjestad ☎ 297/58–64589) includes a 300-yard driving range, an 18-hole putting green, and a chipping area. Pay $3.50 for a basket of 35 balls and $10 for a half-set of rental clubs. It's open from 7:30 AM to 11 PM daily. **Aruba Golf Club** (⊠ Golfweg 82, near San Nicolas ☎ 297/58–42006) has a 9-hole course with 20 sand traps and five water traps, roaming goats, and lots of cacti. There are 11 greens covered with artificial turf, making 18-hole tournaments a possibility. The clubhouse has a bar and locker rooms. Greens fees are $10 for nine holes, $15 for 18 holes. Golf carts are available. **Tierra del Sol** (⊠ Malmokweg ☎ 297/58–60978) is on the northwest coast near the California Lighthouse. Designed by Robert Trent Jones, Jr., this 18-hole championship course combines Aruba's native beauty—cacti and rock formations—with the lush greens of the world's best courses. The $130 greens fee includes a golf cart equipped with a communications system that allows you to order drinks that will be ready upon your return. Half-day golf clinics, a bargain at $45, include lunch in the clubhouse. The pro shop is one of the Caribbean's most elegant, with an extremely attentive staff.

HIKING Hiking in **Arikok National Wildlife Park** is generally not too strenuous, although you should exercise caution in the strong sun—bring plenty of water and wear sunscreen and a sun hat or visor. Sturdy, cleated shoes are a must to grip the granular, occasionally steep terrain. There are more than 20 mi (34 km) of trails, and it's important to stick to them. Look for different colors on signs to determine the degree of difficulty. The park is crowned by Aruba's second-highest mountain, the 577-ft Mt. Arikok, so climbing is also a possibility.

De Palm Tours (⊠ L. G. Smith Blvd. 142, Oranjestad ☎ 297/58–24400 ⊕ www.depalm.com) offers a guided three-hour trip to sites of unusual natural beauty that are accessible only on foot. The fee is $25 per person, including refreshments and transportation.

HORSEBACK RIDING
Four ranches offer short jaunts along the beach or longer trail rides through countryside dotted with cacti, divi-divi trees, and aloe vera plants. Ask if you can stop off at Conchi, a natural pool that's reputed to have restorative powers. Rides are also possible in the Arikok National Wildlife Park. Rates run from $25 for an hour-long trip to $65 for a 3½-hour tour. Private rides cost slightly more.

Rancho Daimari (⊠ Plantage Daimari ☎ 297/58–60239 ⊕ www.visitaruba.com/ranchodaimari) will lead your horse to water—either at Natural Bridge or Natural Pool—in the morning or afternoon for $55 per person. **Rancho del Campo** (⊠ Sombre 22E, Santa Cruz ☎ 297/58–50290 ⊕ www.ranchodelcampo.com), the first to offer rides to the Natural Pool almost 11 years ago, offers that excursion for $50 per person. **Rancho el Paso** (⊠ Washington 44 Malmokweg ☎ 297/58–73310 or 297/58–67165) has seasoned guides that show you Malmok's beautiful beach and the surrounding countryside. Tours, costing $45 per person, head out daily at 9 AM. **Rancho Notorious** (⊠ Boroncana, Noord ☎ 297/58–60508 ⊕ www.ranchonotorious.com) will take you to the beach to snorkel for $55, on a tour of the countryside for $50, or on a three-hour ride up to the California Lighthouse for $65.

KAYAKING
Kayaking is a popular sport in Aruba's calm waters. Every day except Sunday, **De Palm Tours** (⊠ L. G. Smith Blvd. 142, Oranjestad ☎ 297/58–24400 ⊕ www.depalm.com) offers a four-hour guided kayaking tour that also includes some snorkeling. The cost, including lunch, is $65.

SCUBA DIVING & SNORKELING
With visibility of up to 100 ft, Aruban waters are excellent for snorkeling and diving. Certified divers can go wall or reef diving or explore wrecks sunk during World War II. All sites have several varieties of coral, fish ranging in size from grunts to groupers, sensuously waving sea fans, giant sponge tubes, gliding manta rays, sea turtles, lobsters, octopuses, and green moray eels.

Expect snorkel gear to rent for about $15 per day and trips to cost around $40. Scuba rates are around $50 for a one-tank reef or wreck dive, $65 for a two-tank dive, and $45 for a night dive. Resort courses, which offer an introduction to scuba diving, average $65 to $70. If you want to go all the way, complete open-water certification costs around $300.

Although you can get instruction from **Aruba Pro Dive** (⊠ Ponton 88, Noord ☎ 297/58–25520 ⊕ www.arubaprodive.com), the company's specialty is small-group and private dives for experienced divers. **Dax Divers** (⊠ Kibaima 7, Santa Cruz ☎ 297/58–51270) is the only operator that offers an instructor training course. Some dives are fairly inexpensive, at $35 for 40 minutes with one tank. **De Palm Tours** (⊠ L. G. Smith Blvd. 142, Oranjestad ☎ 297/58–24400) is one of the best options for beginners who don't want to be certified. Don a helmet and walk along the ocean floor near De Palm Island, home of huge blue parrot fish. Have your picture taken at an underwater table loaded with champagne and roses. Try Snuba—like scuba diving but without the heavy air tanks—either from a boat or from an island. Rates are $79 to $99, including meals. **Dive Aruba** (⊠ Williamstraat 8, Oranjestad ☎ 297/58–25216 ⊕ www.divearuba.com) offers resort courses, certification courses, and dives to interesting shipwrecks. **Mermaid Sport Divers** (⊠ Manchebo Beach Resort, J. E. Irausquin Blvd. 55A, Eagle Beach ☎ 297/58–35546 ⊕ www.scubadivers-aruba.com) offers full dive packages with PADI-certified instructors.

Native Divers Aruba (⊠ Koyari 1, Noord ☎ 297/58–64763 ⊕ www.
nativedivers.com) offers all types of dives. Special PADI-specialty courses,
including one to become an underwater naturalist, are taught by PADI-
certified instructors. At **Pelican Tours & Watersports** (⊠ J. E. Irausquin Blvd.
232, Palm Beach ☎ 297/58–72302 ⊕ www.pelican-aruba.com) there
are options for divers of all levels. Novices start with mid-morning
classes and then move to the pool to practice what they've learned; by
afternoon they put their new skills to use at a shipwreck off the coast.
Red Sail Sports (⊠ J. E. Irausquin Blvd. 83, Oranjestad ☎ 297/58–
61603, 877/733–7245 in the U.S. ⊕ www.aruba-redsail.com), with
courses for children and others new to scuba diving, is especially good
for beginners. An introductory class costs about $80. **Unique Sports of
Aruba** (⊠ L. G. Smith Blvd. 79, Oranjestad ☎ 297/58–60096 or 297/
58–63900 ⊕ www.visitaruba.com/uniquesports) lives up to its name,
providing dive master, rescue, and certification courses.

SEA EXCURSIONS Explore an underwater reef teeming with marine life without getting wet.
Atlantis Submarines (⊠ Seaport Village Marina ☎ 297/58–36090 ⊕ www.
atlantisadventures.net) operates a 65-ft air-conditioned sub, *Atlantis VI*,
that takes 48 passengers 95–150 ft below the surface along Barcadera
Reef. Make reservations one day in advance. Another option is the *Seaworld Explorer* (297/58–62416), a semisubmersible that allows you to
sit and view Aruba's marine habitat from 5 ft below the surface.

TENNIS Aruba's winds make tennis a challenge even if you have the best of back-
hands. Although visitors can make arrangements to play at the resorts,
priority goes to guests. Some private tennis clubs can also accommodate you. The **Aruba Racquet Club** (⊠ Rooisanto 21, Palm Beach ☎ 297/
58–60215), host to a variety of international tournaments, has world-
class tennis facilities. The club has eight courts (six lighted), as well as
a swimming pool, an aerobics center, and a restaurant. Fees are $10 per
hour; a lesson with a pro costs $20 for a half hour, $35 for one hour.

WINDSURFING The southwestern coast's tranquil waters make it ideal for both begin-
★ ners and intermediates, as the winds are steady but sudden gusts rare.
Experts will find the Atlantic coast, especially around Grapefield and
Boca Grandi beaches, more challenging; winds are fierce and often shift
course without warning. Most operators also offer complete windsurfing vacation packages.

Fisherman's Huts Windsurf Center (⊠ Aruba Marriott Resort, L. G. Smith
Blvd. 101, Palm Beach ☎ 297/58–69898) is a popular spot among
wannabe and expert windsurfers alike. **Pelican Tours & Watersports** (⊠ J.
E. Irausquin Blvd. 232, Palm Beach ☎ 297/58–72302 ⊕ www.pelican-
aruba.com) usually has boards and sails on hand. **Roger's Windsurf Place**
(⊠ L. G. Smith Blvd. 472, Malmok Beach ☎ 297/58–61918 ⊕ www.
rogerswindsurf.com) has a location where the winds carry fastest over
calmer waters. The day will fly by when you windsurf with **Sailboard
Vacations** (⊠ L. G. Smith Blvd. 462, Malmok Beach ☎ 297/58–61072
⊕ www.sailboardvacations.com). Trade jokes and snap photos with your
fellow windsurfers at **Vela Aruba** (⊠ Palm Beach ☎ 297/58–69000 Ext.
6430 ⊕ www.velawindsurf.com). This is *the* place to make friends on
the water.

Shopping

"Duty-free" *is* a magical term here. Major credit cards are welcome virtually everywhere, U.S. dollars are accepted almost as readily as local
currency, and traveler's checks can be cashed with proof of identity.

Aruba's souvenir and crafts stores are full of Dutch porcelains and figurines, as befits the island's heritage. Dutch cheese is a good buy (you're
allowed to bring up to 10 pounds of hard cheese through U.S. customs),
as are hand-embroidered linens and any products made from the native
aloe vera plant—sunburn cream, face masks, skin refreshers. Local arts
and crafts run toward wood carvings and earthenware emblazoned
with ARUBA: ONE HAPPY ISLAND and the like. Since there's no sales tax,
the price you see on the tag is what you pay. (Note that although large
stores in town and at hotels are duty-free, in tiny shops and studios you
may have to pay the value-added tax of 6.5%.) Don't try to bargain.
Arubans consider it rude to haggle, despite what you may hear to the
contrary.

Areas & Malls

Oranjestad's **Caya G. F. Betico Croes** is Aruba's chief shopping street, lined
with several duty-free boutiques and jewelry stores noted for the ag-
gressiveness of their vendors on cruise-ship days.

For late-night shopping, head to the **Alhambra Casino Shopping Arcade**
(⊠ L. G. Smith Blvd. 47, Oranjestad ☎ 297/58–35000), open 5 PM–11
PM. Souvenir shops, art boutiques, and fast-food outlets fill the arcade,
which is attached to the busy casino. The **Aquarius Mall** (⊠ Elleboogstraat
1, Oranjestad) is a small but relatively upscale shopping center. The **Holland Aruba Mall** (⊠ Havenstraat 6, Oranjestad) houses a collection of
smart shops and eateries.

Port of Call Marketplace (⊠ L. G. Smith Blvd. 17, Oranjestad ☎ 297/58–
36706) sells fine jewelry, perfumes, duty-free liquors, batik, crystal,
leather goods, and fashionable clothing. At **Royal Plaza Mall** (⊠ L. G.
Smith Blvd. 94, Oranjestad), across from the cruise-ship terminal, you'll
find cafés, a post office branch (open Monday–Saturday 7 AM–6:45 PM),
and such stores as Nautica, Benetton, Tommy Hilfiger, and Gandelman
Jewelers. There's also the Internet Café, where you can send e-mail home
and get your caffeine fix all in one stop. **Seaport Village Mall** (⊠ L. G.
Smith Blvd. 82, Oranjestad, across from harbor ☎ 297/58–36000) is
five minutes from the cruise-ship terminal. It includes the Crystal Casino
and more than 120 stores, with merchandise to meet every taste and
budget.

Specialty Items

CLOTHES **Confetti** (⊠ Seaport Village Mall, L. G. Smith Blvd. 82, Oranjestad
☎ 297/58–38614) has the hottest European and American swimsuits,
cover-ups, and other beach essentials. **J. L. Penha & Sons** (⊠ Caya G. F.
Betico Croes 11/13, Oranjestad ☎ 297/58–24160), a venerated name
in Aruba, sells perfumes and cosmetics as well as clothing from such
brands as Boucheron, Swiss Army, Dior, Cartier, and Givenchy. **Wulfsen
& Wulfsen** (⊠ Caya G. F. Betico Croes 52, Oranjestad ☎ 297/58–23823)
has been one of the most highly regarded clothing stores in the Netherlands Antilles for three decades.

DUTY-FREE For perfumes, cosmetics, men's and women's clothing, and leather goods,
GOODS stop in at **Aruba Trading Company** (⊠ Caya G. F. Betico Croes 12, Oranjestad ☎ 297/58–22602), which has been in business since 1930. **Little
Switzerland** (⊠ Caya G. F. Betico Croes 14, Oranjestad ☎ 297/58–21192
⊠ Royal Plaza Mall, L. G. Smith Blvd. 94, Oranjestad ☎ 297/58–34057)
is the place to go for china, crystal, and fine tableware. You'll also find
good buys on Omega and Rado watches, Swarovski and Baccarat crystal, and Lladro figurines. At **Weitnauer** (⊠ Caya G. F. Betico Croes 29, Oranjestad ☎ 297/58–22790) you'll find a wide range of fragrances.

HANDICRAFTS **Art and Tradition Handicrafts** (✉ Caya G. F. Betico Croes 30, Oranjestad ☎ 297/58–36534 ✉ Royal Plaza Mall, L. G. Smith Blvd. 94, Oranjestad ☎ 297/58–27862) sells intriguing items that look hand-painted. Buds from the *mopa mopa* tree are boiled to form a resin colored by vegetable dyes. Artists then stretch the resin by hand and mouth. Tiny pieces are cut and layered to form intricate designs—truly unusual gifts.

The **Artistic Boutique** (✉ Caya G. F. Betico Croes 25, Oranjestad ☎ 297/58–23142 ✉ Wyndham Aruba Beach Resort and Casino, J. E. Irausquin Blvd. 77 ☎ 297/58–64466 Ext. 3508 ✉ Seaport Village Mall, L. G. Smith Blvd. 82, Oranjestad ☎ 297/58–32567 ✉ Holiday Inn Aruba Beach Resort & Casino, J. E. Irausquin Blvd. 230 ☎ 297/58–33383) is known for Giuseppe Armani figurines from Italy, usually sold at a 20% discount; Aruban hand-embroidered linens; gold and silver jewelry; and porcelain and pottery from Spain.

Creative Hands (✉ Socotorolaan 5, Oranjestad ☎ 297/58–35665) sells porcelain and ceramic miniatures of *cunucu* (country) houses and divi-divi trees, but the store's real draw is its exquisite Japanese dolls.

JEWELRY **Boolchand's** (✉ Seaport Village Mall, L. G. Smith Blvd. 82, Oranjestad ☎ 297/58–30147) sells jewelry and watches. It also fills its 6,000-square-ft space with leather goods, cameras, and electronics. If green fire is your passion, **Colombian Emeralds** (✉ Seaport Village Mall, L. G. Smith Blvd. 82, Oranjestad ☎ 297/58–36238) has a dazzling array of emeralds. There's also a fine array of watches by Breitling, Baume & Mercier, Jaeger-Le Coultre, Ebel, Seiko, Citizen, and Tissot. **Gandelman Jewelers** (✉ Royal Plaza Mall, L. G. Smith Blvd. 94, Oranjestad ☎ 297/58–34433) sells Gucci and Rolex watches at reasonable prices, as well as gold bracelets, and a full line of Lladro figurines. **Kenro Jewelers** (✉ Seaport Village Mall, L. G. Smith Blvd. 82, Oranjestad ☎ 297/58–34847 or 297/58–33171) has two stores in the same mall, attesting to the popularity of its stock of bracelets and necklaces from the Ramon Leopard collection; jewelry by Arando, Micheletto, and Blumei; and various brands of watches.

Nightlife & the Arts

Nightlife

Unlike that of many islands, Aruba's nightlife isn't confined to the touristic folkloric shows at hotels. Arubans like to party, and the more the merrier. They usually start celebrating late; the action doesn't pick up until around midnight. One uniquely Aruban institution is a psychedelically painted '57 Chevy bus called the *Kukoo Kunuku* (☎ 297/58–62010). Weeknights you'll find as many as 40 passengers traveling between six bars from sundown to around midnight. The $55 fee per passenger includes dinner, drinks, and picking you up (and pouring you off) at your hotel.

BARS At **Carlos & Charlie's** (✉ Weststraat 3A, Oranjestad ☎ 297/58–20355), ★ you'll find Mexican fare; American music from the 1960s, '70s, and '80s; and a mike-toting emcee. In business since 1948, **Cheta's Bar** (✉ Paradera 119, Paradera ☎ 297/58–23689) is a local joint that holds no more than four customers at a time. There aren't any bar stools, either, which is why most patrons gather out front. **Iguana Joe's** (✉ Royal Plaza Mall, L. G. Smith Blvd. 94, Oranjestad ☎ 297/58–39373) has a creative, reptilian-theme decor and a color scheme featuring such planter's-punch colors as lime and grape. With parrots painted on the ceiling, **Mambo Jambo** (✉ Royal Plaza Mall, 2nd floor, L. G. Smith Blvd. 94, Oranjestad ☎ 297/58–33632) is daubed in sunset colors. Sip one of the special libations sold nowhere else. With front-row seats to view the green flash—that ray of light that flicks through the sky as the sun sinks into the ocean—the **Palms Bar** (⌂ Hyatt Regency Aruba Beach Resort & Casino, J. E. Irausquin Blvd. 85, Palm Beach ☎ 297/58–61234) is the perfect spot to enjoy the sunset.

CASINOS Aruban casinos offer something for both high and low rollers, as well as live, nightly entertainment in their lounges. Diehard gamblers might look for the largest or the most active casinos, but many simply visit the casino closest to their hotel.

★ In the casual **Alhambra Casino** (⌂ L. G. Smith Blvd. 47, Oranjestad ☎ 297/58–35000 Ext. 480/482), a "Moorish slave" named Roger gives every gambler a hearty handshake upon entering (he is apparently in the *Guinness Book of Records* for having shaken the most hands). The smart money is on the **Casablanca Casino** (⌂ Wyndham Aruba Beach Resort & Casino, J. E. Irausquin Blvd. 77, Palm Beach ☎ 297/58–64466). It's quietly elegant and has a Bogart theme. The **Centurion Casino** (⌂ Aruba Grand Beach Resort, J. E. Irausquin Blvd. 79, Palm Beach ☎ 297/58–63900 Ext. 149) is decorated with musical instruments. It opens at 10 AM for slots, 6 PM for all games. The ultramodern **Copacabana Casino** (⌂ Hyatt Regency Aruba Beach Resort & Casino, J. E. Irausquin Blvd. 85, Palm Beach ☎ 297/58–61234) is an enormous complex with a Carnival in Rio theme and live entertainment. The **Crystal Casino** (⌂ Renaissance Aruba Beach Resort, L. G. Smith Blvd. 82, Oranjestad ☎ 297/58–36000) is open 24 hours. The **Excelsior Casino** (⌂ J. E. Irausquin Blvd. 230, Palm Beach ☎ 297/58–67777) has sports betting in addition to the usual slots and table games.

Overhead at the **Radisson Aruba Resort & Casino** (⌂ J. E. Irausquin Blvd. 81, Palm Beach ☎ 297/58–64045), thousands of lights simulate shooting stars that seem destined to carry out your wishes for riches. The slots here open at 10 AM, and table action begins at 4 PM. The **Royal Cabana Casino** (⌂ J. E. Irausquin Blvd. 250, Eagle Beach ☎ 297/58–77000) is the largest in the Caribbean. It has an expansive, sleek interior, 400 slot machines, no-smoking gaming tables and slot room, and the Tropicana nightclub. **Royal Palm Casino** (⌂ Allegro Aruba Resort & Casino, J. E. Irausquin Blvd. 250, Eagle Beach ☎ 297/58–74665) opens daily at noon for slots, 5 PM for all games. Low-key gambling can be found at the waterside **Seaport Casino** (⌂ L. G. Smith Blvd. 9, Oranjestad ☎ 297/58–35027 Ext. 4212). The **Stellaris Casino** (⌂ Aruba Marriott Resort, L. G. Smith Blvd. 101, Palm Beach ☎ 297/58–69000) is one of the island's most popular.

DANCE & MUSIC At **Café Bahia** (⌂ Weststraat 7, Oranjestad ☎ 297/58–89982) an ele-
CLUBS gant spiral staircase leads up to a bar and dance floor backed by a mural of colorful cacti against a cloud-smattered Aruban sky. Locals and tourists drink cocktails and sashay to salsa music provided by island bands. Live bands perform at the **Cellar** (⌂ Klipstraat 2, Oranjestad ☎ 297/58–26490) on weekends. The music might be blues, jazz, funk, reggae, or rock. Bartenders in hard hats serve up drinks at the exotic **E-Zone** (⌂ Bayside Mall, Weststraat 5, Oranjestad ☎ 297/58–87474), where the walls are decorated with hair-dryer tubes and other oddities. The huge stainless-steel dance floor doesn't fill up until after 1 AM.

For jazz and other types of music, try **Garufa Cigar & Cocktail Lounge** (⌂ Wilhelminastraat 63, Oranjestad ☎ 297/58–27205). Stop by for a drink before dining at the nearby El Gaucho Argentine Grill. The laid-back atmosphere may draw you back for an after-dinner cognac. Stop by the cozy **Sirocco Lounge** (⌂ Wyndham Aruba Beach Resort & Casino,

L. G. Smith Blvd. 77, Palm Beach ☎297/58–64466) for jazz performances Thursday through Saturday.

The Arts

ART GALLERIES At **Galeria Eterno** (✉ Emanstraat 92, Oranjestad ☎ 297/58–39607) you'll find local and international artists at work. Be sure to stop by for concerts by classical guitarists, dance performances, visual-arts shows, and plays. **Galeria Harmonia** (✉ Zeppenfeldstraat 10, San Nicolas ☎297/58–42969), the island's largest exhibition space, has a permanent collection of works by local and international artists. **Gasparito Restaurant & Art Gallery** (✉ Gasparito 3, Noord ☎ 297/58–67044) features an permanent exhibition of Aruban artists.

ISLAND CULTURE The **Bon Bini Festival**, a year-round folkloric event, is held every Tuesday from 6:30 PM to 8:30 PM at Fort Zoutman in Oranjestad. Stop by to check out the local arts and crafts, food, drink, music, and dance. The entrance fee is $3. At the **Watapana Food & Art Festival**, listen to live music, enjoy local art, and indulge in authentic Aruban foods and beverages at the festival grounds between the Hyatt Regency Aruba Beach Resort & Casino and the Allegro Aruba Beach Resort & Casino. Held from April to October, the event takes place every Wednesday from 6 PM to 8 PM. Admission is free.

Exploring Aruba

Aruba's wildly sculpted landscape is replete with rocky deserts, cactus clusters, secluded coves, blue vistas, and the trademark divi-divi tree. To see the island's wild, untamed beauty, you can rent a car, take a sightseeing tour, or hire a cab for $30 an hour (for up to four people). The main highways are well paved, but on the windward side (the north- and east-facing side) some roads are still a mixture of compacted dirt and stones. Although a car is fine, a four-wheel-drive vehicle will allow you to explore the unpaved interior.

Traffic is sparse, but signs leading to sights are often small and hand-lettered (this is slowly changing as the government puts up official road signs), so watch closely. Route 1A travels southbound along the western coast, and 1B is simply northbound along the same road. If you lose your way, just follow the divi-divi trees.

Numbers in the margin correspond to points of interest on the Aruba map.

WHAT TO SEE **Alto Vista Chapel.** Alone near the island's northwest corner sits the scenic
❼ little Alto Vista Chapel. The wind whistles through the simple mustard-colored walls, eerie boulders, and looming cacti. Along the side of the road back to civilization are miniature crosses with depictions of the stations of the cross and hand-lettered signs exhorting PRAY FOR US, SINNERS and the like—a simple yet powerful evocation of faith. To get here, follow the rough, winding dirt road that loops around the island's northern tip, or, from the hotel strip take Palm Beach Road through three intersections and watch for the asphalt road to the left just past the Alto Vista Rum Shop.

❹ **Arikok National Wildlife Park.** Nearly 20% of Aruba has been designated part of this national park, which sprawls across the eastern interior and the northeast coast. The park is the keystone of the government's long-term ecotourism plan to preserve resources, and showcases the island's flora and fauna as well as ancient Arawak petroglyphs, the ruins of a gold mining operation at Miralmar, and the remnants of Dutch peasant settlements at Masiduri. At the park's main entrance, Arikok Center houses offices, rest rooms, and food facilities. All visitors must stop here upon entering so that officials can manage the traffic flow and hand out information on park rules and features. Within the confines of the park are Mt. Arikok and the 620-ft Mt. Yamanota, Aruba's highest peak.

Anyone looking for geological exotica should head for the park's caves, found on the northeastern coast. Baranca Sunu, the so-called Tunnel of Love, has a heart-shape entrance and naturally sculpted rocks farther inside that look like the Madonna, Abe Lincoln, and even a jaguar. Guadirikiri Cave and Fontein Cave are marked with ancient drawings (rangers are on hand to offer explanations), as both were used by indigenous people centuries ago. Bats are known to make appearances—don't worry, they won't bother you. Although you don't need a flashlight because the paths are well lighted, it's best to wear sneakers.

❾ Butterfly Farm. Hundreds of butterflies from around the world flutter about this spectacular garden. Guided 20- to 30-minute tours (included in the price of admission) provide an entertaining look into how these insects complete their life cycle: from egg to caterpillar to chrysalis to butterfly. There's a special deal offered here: after your initial visit, you can return as often as you like for free. ✉ *J. E. Irausquin Blvd., Palm Beach* ☎ *297/58–63656* ⊕ *www.thebutterflyfarm.com* 🎫 *$10* ☉ *Daily 9–4:30; last tour at 4.*

❽ California Lighthouse. The lighthouse, built by a French architect in 1910, stands at the island's far northern end. Although you can't go inside, you can ascend the hill to its base for some great views. In this stark landscape you'll feel as though you've just landed on the moon. The lighthouse is surrounded by huge boulders that look like extraterrestrial monsters and sand dunes embroidered with scrub that resemble undulating sea serpents.

❷ Hooiberg. Named for its shape (*hooiberg* means "haystack" in Dutch), this 541-ft peak lies inland just past the airport. If you have the energy, climb the 562 steps to the top for an impressive view of the city.

❻ Natural Bridge. Centuries of raging wind and sea sculpted this coral-rock bridge in the center of the windward coast. To reach it, drive inland along Hospitalstraat and then follow the signs. Just before you reach the geological wonder, you'll pass the massive stone ruins of the Bushiribana Gold Smelter, an intriguing structure that resembles a crumbling fortress, and a section of surf-pounded coastline called Boca Mahos. Near Natural Bridge are a souvenir shop and a café overlooking the water.

❶ Oranjestad. Aruba's charming capital is best explored on foot. The palm-lined thoroughfare in the center of town runs between pastel-painted buildings, old and new, of typical Dutch design. There are many malls with boutiques and shops.

At the **Archaeological Museum of Aruba** you'll find two rooms chockfull of fascinating Indian artifacts, farm and domestic utensils, and skeletons. ✉ *J. Irausquinplein 2A* ☎ *297/58–28979* 🎫 *Free* ☉ *Weekdays 8–noon and 1–4.*

One of the island's oldest edifices, **Fort Zoutman** was built in 1796 and played an important role in skirmishes between British and Curaçaon troops in 1803. The Willem III Tower, named for the Dutch monarch of that time, was added in 1868 to serve as a lighthouse. Over time, the fort has been put to use as a government office building, a police station, and a prison. Now its historical museum displays Aruban artifacts in an 18th-century house. ✉ *Zoutmanstraat* ☎ *297/58–26099* 🎫 *Free* ☉ *Weekdays 8–noon and 1–4.*

The tiny **Numismatic Museum of Aruba,** next to St. Francis Roman Catholic Church, displays coins and currencies—including a few salvaged from shipwrecks in the region. Some of the coins on display circulated during the Roman Empire, the Byzantine Empire, and the ancient Chinese dynasties; a few date as far back as the 5th century BC. The museum had its start as one Aruban's private collection and is now run by a family. ⊠ *Zuidstraat 7* ☎ *297/58–28831* ✑ *Free* ☉ *Weekdays 7:30– noon and 1–4:30.*

⑤ Rock Formations. The massive boulders at Ayo and Casibari are a mystery, as they don't match the island's geological makeup. You can climb to the top for fine views of the arid countryside. On the way you'll doubtless pass Aruba whip-tail lizards—the males are cobalt blue, the females blue with dots. The main path to Casibari has steps and handrails (except on one side), and you must move through tunnels and along narrow steps and ledges to reach the top. At Ayo you'll find ancient pictographs in a small cave (the entrance has iron bars to protect the drawings from vandalism). You may also encounter a boulder climber, one of many who are increasingly drawn to Ayo's smooth surfaces. Access to Casibari is via Tanki Highway 4A to Ayo via Route 6A; watch carefully for the turnoff signs near the center of the island on the way to the windward side.

❸ San Nicolas. During the heyday of the oil refineries, Aruba's oldest village was a bustling port; now it's primary business is tourism. The main promenade is full of interesting kiosks, and the whole district is undergoing a revitalization project that will bring parks, a cultural center, a central market, a public swimming pool, and an arts promenade.

ARUBA A TO Z

To research prices, get advice from other travelers, and book travel arrangements, visit *www.fodors.com.*

AIR TRAVEL

Aruba is 2½ hours from Miami and 4½ hours from New York. Flights leave daily to Aruba's Reina Beatrix International Airport from New York area airports, Miami, and San Juan, with easy connections from most American cities.

Air DCE flies daily from Miami via Curaçao, twice a week nonstop from Atlanta, and twice a week from San Juan, Puerto Rico, through Curaçao. The airline also has connecting flights to Caracas, Bonaire, Curaçao, St. Maarten, and other islands, and it offers the Visit Caribbean Pass for travel between islands.

American Airlines offers daily nonstop service from New York and twice daily service from San Juan. From Toronto and Montréal flights are via San Juan. Continental Airlines has nonstop service daily from Newark. Delta flies nonstop daily from Atlanta and weekly from New York's JFK. KLM offers regular service from Amsterdam. United flies weekly from Chicago and seasonally from Dulles in Washington, D.C. USAirways flies daily from Charlotte and Philadelphia.

🛪 **Air DCE** ☎ 297/58-23546 in Aruba; 800/327-7230 in North America. **American** ☎ 297/ 58-22700. **ATA** ☎ 800/435-9282. **Continental** ☎ 297/58-80044. **Delta** ☎ 297/58-80044. **KLM** ☎ 297/58-34406 in Aruba; 31/20-4-747-747 in Amsterdam. **United Airlines** ☎ 297/58-29592. **USAirways** ☎ 800-1580.

AIRPORT

The island's state-of-the-art Reina Beatrix International Airport is equipped with thorough security, many flight displays, and state-of-the-art baggage handling systems.

Travelers to the U.S. will have to clear U.S. Customs and Immigration before leaving Aruba, so should allow a little extra time. The good news is that when you arrive in the U.S you will be arriving as a domestic passenger.

A taxi from the airport to most hotels takes about 20 minutes. It will cost about $16 to get to the hotels along Eagle Beach, $18 to the high-rise hotels on Palm Beach, and $9 to the hotels downtown.
🚩 **Reina Beatrix International Airport** ☎ 297/58–24800.

BUSINESS HOURS

BANKS Bank hours are weekdays 8:15–5:45; some close from noon to 1. The Caribbean Mercantile Bank at the airport is open Saturday 9–4 and Sunday 9–1.

POST OFFICES The central post office in Oranjestad is across from the San Francisco Church and is open weekdays 7:30–noon and 1–4:30. The post office in the Royal Plaza mall is open Monday–Saturday, 7–6:45.

SHOPS Shops are generally open Monday–Saturday 8:30–6. Some stores stay open through the lunch hour, noon–2, and many open when cruise ships are in port on Sunday and holidays.

BUS TRAVEL

Buses run hourly trips between the beach hotels and Oranjestad. The one-way fare is $1.15 ($2 round-trip), and exact change is preferred (so be sure to keep some U.S. change handy if you plan to pay in U.S. currency). Buses also run down the coast from Oranjestad to San Nicolas for the same fare.

CAR RENTALS

You'll need a valid driver's license to rent a car, and you must meet the minimum age requirements of each rental service (Budget, for example, requires drivers to be over 25; Avis, between the ages of 23 and 70; and Hertz, over 21). A deposit of $500 (or a signed credit-card slip) is required. Rates are between $35 and $65 a day (local agencies generally have lower rates). Insurance is available starting at $10 per day, and all companies offer unlimited mileage. Try to make reservations before arriving, and opt for a four-wheel-drive vehicle if you plan to explore the island's natural sights.
🚩 **Avis** ✉ Kolibristraat 14, Oranjestad ☎ 297/58–28787 ✉ Airport ☎ 297/58–25496. **Budget** ✉ Kolibristraat 1, Oranjestad ☎ 297/58–28600. **Dollar** ✉ Grendeaweg 15, Oranjestad ☎ 297/58–22783 ✉ Airport ☎ 297/58–25651 ✉ Manchebo Beach Resort, J. E. Irausquin Blvd. 55 ☎ 297/58–26696. **Economy** ✉ Kolibristraat 5, Oranjestad ☎ 297/58–25176. **Hedwina Car Rental** ✉ Bubali 93A, Noord ☎ 297/58–76442 ✉ Airport ☎ 297/58–30880. **Hertz** ✉ Sabana Blanco 35, near the airport ☎ 297/58–21845 ✉ Airport ☎ 297/58–29112. **National** ✉ Tanki Leendert 170, Noord ☎ 297/58–71967 ✉ Airport ☎ 297/58–25451. **Thrifty** ✉ Balashi 65, Santa Cruz ☎ 297/58–55300 ✉ Airport ☎ 297/58–35335.

CAR TRAVEL

Most of Aruba's major attractions are fairly easy to find; others you'll happen upon only by sheer luck. Aside from the major highways, the island's winding roads are poorly marked. International traffic signs and Dutch-style traffic signals (with an extra light for a turning lane) can be misleading if you're not used to them; use extreme caution, especially at intersections, until you grasp the rules of the road. Speed limits are rarely posted but are usually 80 kph (50 mph) in the countryside.

Gas prices average $1 a liter (roughly ⅓ gallon), which is reasonable by Caribbean standards.

ELECTRICITY

Aruba runs on a 110-volt cycle, the same as in the United States; outlets are usually the two-prong variety. Total blackouts are rare, and most large hotels have backup generators.

EMERGENCIES

🔹 Ambulance & Fire **Ambulance and Fire emergencies** ☎ 115.
🔹 Hospitals **Dr. Horacio Oduber Hospital** ✉ L. G. Smith Blvd., across from Costa Linda Beach Resort and the Alhambra Bazaar and Casino ☎ 297/58-74300.
🔹 Pharmacies **Botica Eagle** ✉ L. G. Smith Blvd. ☎ 297/58-76103.
🔹 Police **Police emergencies** ☎ 111000.

FESTIVALS & SEASONAL EVENTS

February or March witnesses a spectacular Carnival, a riot of color whirling to the tunes of steel bands and culminating in the Grand Parade, where some of the floats rival the extravagance of those in the Big Easy's Mardi Gras. Held May–October, One Cool Summer is a series of culinary, athletic, musical, cultural, and other events. Check with your hotel for specifics.

HOLIDAYS

Public holidays are New Year's Day, Betico Croes's Birthday (a politician who aided Aruba's transition to semi-independence; January 25), Carnival Monday (Monday before Ash Wednesday), National Anthem and Flag Day (March 18), Good Friday (varies), Easter Monday (varies), Queen's Birthday (April 30), Labor Day (May 1), Ascension Day (May 9), Christmas Day, Boxing Day (December 26).

LANGUAGE

Everyone on the island speaks English, but the official language is Dutch. Most locals, however, speak Papiamento—a fascinating, rapid-fire mix of Spanish, Dutch, English, French, and Portuguese—in normal conversation. Here are a few helpful phrases: *bon dia* (good day), *bon nochi* (good night), *masha danki* (thank you very much).

MAIL & SHIPPING

You can send an airmail letter from Aruba to the United States or Canada (it will take 7–14 days) for AFl2 and a postcard for AFl1.15; a letter to Europe (2–3 weeks) is AFl1.75, a postcard AFl1. Prices to Australia and New Zealand (3–4 weeks) may be slightly higher. When addressing letters to Aruba, don't worry about the lack of formal addresses or postal codes; the island's postal service knows where to go.

MONEY MATTERS

Arubans happily accept U.S. dollars virtually everywhere, so there's no real need to exchange money, except for necessary pocket change (for soda machines or pay phones). The official currency is the Aruban florin (AFl), also called the guilder, which is made up of 100 cents. Silver coins come in denominations of 1, 2½, 5, 10, 25, and 50 (the square one) cents. Paper currency comes in denominations of 5, 10, 25, 50, and 100 florins.

If you need fast cash, you'll find ATMs that accept international cards at banks in Oranjestad, at the major malls, and along the roads leading to the hotel strip.

🏛 **ABN/Amro Bank** ✉ Caya G. F. Betico Croes 89, Oranjestad ☎ 297/58-21515. **Caribbean Mercantile Bank** ✉ Caya G. F. Betico Croes 5, Oranjestad ☎ 297/58-23118.

PASSPORTS & VISAS

U.S. and Canadian citizens need a valid passport or a birth certificate with a raised seal and a government-issued photo I.D. Visitors from the member countries of the European Union must carry their European Union Travel Card as well as a passport. All other nationalities must have a valid passport; a few countries' citizens require a visa.

SAFETY

Arubans are very friendly, so you needn't be afraid to stop and ask anyone for directions. It's a relatively safe island, but commonsense rules still apply. Lock your rental car and leave valuables in your hotel safe. Don't leave bags unattended in the airport, on the beach, or on tour transports.

Mosquitoes and flies can be bothersome during the odd rain shower, so pack some repellent. The strong trade winds are a relief in the subtropical climate, but don't hang your bathing suit on a balcony—it will probably blow away. Help Arubans conserve water and energy: turn off air-conditioning when you leave your room, and don't let water run unnecessarily. Tap water is okay to drink.

SIGHTSEEING TOURS

BOATS If you try a cruise around the island, know that the choppy waters are stirred up by trade winds and that catamarans are much smoother than single-hulled boats. Sucking on a peppermint or lemon candy may help a queasy stomach; avoid boating with an empty or overly full stomach. Moonlight cruises cost about $25 per person. There are also a variety of snorkeling, dinner and dancing, and sunset party cruises to choose from, priced from $25 to $60 per person. Many of the smaller operators work out of their homes; they often offer to pick you up (and drop you off) at your hotel or meet you at particular hotel pier.

🏛 **De Palm Tours** ✉ L. G. Smith Blvd. 142, Oranjestad ☎ 297/58-24400; 800/766-6016 in the U.S. 🌐 www.depalm.com. **Pelican Tours & Watersports** ✉ J. E. Irausquin Blvd. 232, Oranjestad ☎ 297/58-72302 🌐 www.pelican-aruba.com. **Red Sail Sports** ✉ Seaport Village Mall, L. G. Smith Blvd. 82, Oranjestad ☎ 297/58-61603; 877/733-7245 in the U.S. 🌐 www.aruba-redsail.com.

ORIENTATION You can see the main sights in one day, but set aside two days to really meander. Guided tours are your best option if you have only a short time. Aruba's Transfer Tour & Taxi C.A. takes you to the main sights on personalized tours that cost $30 per hour.

De Palm Tours has a near monopoly on Aruban sightseeing; you can make reservations through its general office or at hotel tour-desk branches. The basic 3½-hour tour hits such highlights as the Santa Anna Church, the Casibari Rock Formation, the Natural Bridge, and the Gold Smelter Ruins. Wear tennis or hiking shoes, and bring a lightweight jacket or wrap, as the air-conditioned bus gets cold.

🏛 **Aruba's Transfer Tour & Taxi C.A.** ✉ Pos Abao 41, Oranjestad ☎ 297/58-22116. **De Palm Tours** ✉ L. G. Smith Blvd. 142, Oranjestad ☎ 297/58-24400; 800/766-6016 in the U.S. 🌐 www.depalm.com.

SPECIAL-
INTEREST Romantic horse-drawn carriage rides through the city streets of Oranjestad run $30 for a 30-minute tour; hours of operation are 7 PM–11 PM, and carriages depart from the clock tower at the Royal Plaza Mall.

TAXES

DEPARTURE TAX   The airport departure tax is a whopping $34.50, but the fee is usually included in your ticket price.

SALES TAX   Hotels usually add an 11% service charge to the bill and collect a 6% government tax.

VALUE-ADDED   A 6.5% ABB tax (value-added tax) is included in the price charged in
TAX (V.A.T.)   all nonduty-free shops.

TAXIS

There's a dispatch office at the airport; you can also flag down taxis on the street (look for license plates with a "TX" tag). Rates are fixed (i. e., there are no meters; the rates are set by the government and displayed on a chart), though you and the driver should agree on the fare before your ride begins. Add $1 to the fare after midnight and $1–$3 on Sunday and holidays. An hour-long island tour costs about $30, with up to four people. Rides into town from Eagle Beach run about $5; from Palm Beach, about $8.

🛈 **Airport Taxi Dispatch** ☎ 297/58-22116.

TELEPHONES

When making calls to anywhere in Aruba, simply dial the seven-digit number. AT&T customers can dial 800–8000 from special phones at the cruise dock and in the airport's arrival and departure halls. Otherwise dial 121 to contact the international operator to place a call.

COUNTRY & AREA   To call Aruba direct from the United States, dial 011–297, followed by
CODES   the seven-digit number in Aruba.

LOCAL CALLS   Local calls from pay phones, which accept both local currency and phone cards, cost 25¢.

TIPPING

Restaurants generally include a 10%–15% service charge on the bill; when in doubt, ask. If service isn't included, a 10% tip is standard; if it is included, it's still customary to add something extra, usually small change, at your discretion. Taxi drivers expect a 10%–15% tip, but it isn't mandatory. Porters and bellhops should receive about $2 per bag; chambermaids about $2 a day.

VISITOR INFORMATION

🛈 **Aruba Tourism Authority** ⊕ www.aruba.com ☎ 800/862-7822 ✉ L. G. Smith Blvd. 172, Eagle Beach ☎ 297/58-23777 ✉ 1 Financial Plaza, Suite 136, Fort Lauderdale, FL 33394 ☎ 954/767-6477 ✉ 3455 Peach Tree Rd. NE, Suite 500, Atlanta, GA 30326 ☎ 404/892-7822 ✉ 5901 N. Cicero, Suite 301, Chicago, IL, 60646 ☎ 773/202-5054 ✉ 1000 Harbor Blvd., Ground Level, Weehawken, NJ 07087 ☎ 201/330-0800 ✉ 12707 North Freeway, Suite 138, Houston, TX 77060-1234 ☎ 281/872-7822 ✉ Business Centre 5875, Suite 201, Hwy. 7, Vaughan, Ontario, L4L 8Z7 ☎ 905/264-3434.

BARBADOS

4

FODOR'S CHOICE
Cobblers Cove Hotel, Speightstown
Country Club at Sandy Lane golf courses, Paynes Bay
Harrison's Cave, Welchman Hall
The Cliff, a restaurant in Derricks

HIGHLY RECOMMENDED

RESTAURANTS
Carambola, Derricks
Josef's Restaurant, Dover
La Mer, Speightstown
Orchid Room, Porters

HOTELS
Colony Club Hotel, Porters
Coral Reef Club, Holetown
The Crane, Crane Bay
Sandy Lane Hotel & Golf Club, Paynes Bay
The Savannah, Hastings
Villa Nova, Villa Nova

SIGHTS
Andromeda Gardens, Bathsheba
Gun Hill Signal Station, Gun Hill
Mount Gay Rum Visitors Centre, Brandons
St. Nicholas Abbey, Cherry Tree Hill

SHOPPING
Earthworks Pottery, Edgehill Heights

NIGHTLIFE
Oistins Fish Fry, Oistins

OUTDOORS
Crane Beach, Crane
Mullins Beach, Speightstown

Head wrapped neatly in a kerchief and her skirt sweeping the sand, the doll lady trudges along the beach to the shade of a mahogany tree and settles in for the day. Her bag is full of unfinished poppets and bits of cloth. Today she's making eyes. Using oversize shears with one tip broken off, she deftly cuts white and black snippets that give expression to blank faces. "Doll, lady?" she beckons to passersby. Surrounded by a sea of luxury, the doll lady and her work are cultural anchors.

Updated by
Jane E. Zarem

Barbadians (Bajans) are a warm, friendly, and hospitable people who are genuinely proud of their country and culture. Tourism is the island's number one industry; but with a sophisticated business community and stable government, life here doesn't skip a beat after visitors pack up their sunscreen and return home. Financial services, agriculture (sugar), and light manufacturing (rum, chemicals, and electrical components) are dominant sources of revenue.

About 85% of the 268,000 Bajans live in the urban area around the capital city of Bridgetown, along the west coast north to Speightstown, and along the south coast down to Oistins. Others reside inland, in tiny hamlets scattered throughout the island's 11 parishes.

Barbados stands apart both geographically and geologically from its Caribbean neighbors; it's a full 100 mi (161 km) east of the Lesser Antilles chain that arcs from the Virgin Islands to Trinidad. Although many neighboring islands are the peaks of a volcanic mountain range, Barbados is the top of a single mountain of coral and limestone, sources of building blocks for many a plantation manor. Barbados is 21 mi (34 km) long, 14 mi (22½ km) wide, and relatively flat; the highest point, Mt. Hillaby, is in the north and has an elevation of 1,115 ft. The interior hills and valleys are covered by impenetrable acres of sugarcane, punctuated only by the sugar factories and great houses that the crop has sustained for centuries.

Besides picturesque rolling hills, a perimeter of white-sand beaches, a central flatland, and even deposits of underground oil (providing 60% of the island's petroleum requirements), Barbados's unique geology has created its most popular attraction, Harrison's Cave. This natural phenomenon has bubbling underground streams, cascading waterfalls, and stalactites and stalagmites created through the millennia by the constant drip of calcite-laden water.

Actually, it was during a search for fresh water that Barbados was "discovered" by the Portuguese in 1536. They didn't stay, but did give the island its name: Barbados, or "the bearded ones," after native fig trees with beardlike roots. A century later—and quite by accident—the British landed on the west coast at what is now Holetown. The first British settlement was established two years later, in 1627. In contrast to the turbulent history of most of the Caribbean islands, British rule was uninterrupted until 1966, when Barbados became independent. The island has since had an elected prime minister and membership in the British Commonwealth of Nations.

Facilities here are top-notch. Beaches along the tranquil west coast, facing the Caribbean, are lined with posh resorts and residences that are enveloped in lush foliage and a healthy dose of peace and quiet. This luxurious area, appropriately called the Platinum Coast, is a favorite destination of British vacationers. North Americans tend to prefer the hotels and resorts stretched along the beaches of the trendier south coast, which has good shopping, countless restaurants, and an active nightlife. Bajans, however, spend their holidays along the rugged east coast, where the Atlantic surf pounds the dramatic shoreline with unrelenting force.

Barbados retains a noticeable British feel. Most islanders are members of the Anglican church, afternoon tea is a ritual, polo ("the sport of kings") is played all winter, and cricket is the national passion—Barbados has produced some of the world's top cricketers. The tradition of dressing for dinner is firmly entrenched, yet the island is hardly stuffy. You can dine by candlelight facing the sea, in festive company at a sumptuous Bajan buffet, or casually with a burger at the beach. This is still the Caribbean, after all.

WHAT IT COSTS In U.S. dollars				
$$$$	**$$$**	**$$**	**$**	**¢**
RESTAURANTS*				
over $30	$20–$30	$12–$20	$8–$12	under $8
HOTELS**				
Cost EP/BP/CP over $350	$250–$350	$150–$250	$80–$150	under $80
Cost AI over $450	$350–$450	$250–$350	$125–$250	under $125

*Restaurant prices are for a main course at dinner. **EP, BP, and CP prices are per night for a standard double room in high season, excluding taxes, service charges, and meal plans. AI (all-inclusive) prices are per person, per night based on double-occupancy during high season, excluding taxes and service charges.

Where to Stay

Most people stay on either the fashionable west coast, north of Bridgetown, or the action-packed south coast. The west coast beachfront resorts in the parishes of St. Peter, St. James, and St. Michael are mostly self-contained enclaves. Highway 1, a two-lane road with considerable traffic, runs past these resorts, which makes casual strolling to a nearby bar or restaurant difficult. Along the south coast, in Christ Church Parish, many hotels are clustered near the busy strip known as the St. Lawrence Gap, with its dozens of small restaurants, bars, and nightclubs. On the much more remote east coast, a few small inns offer oceanfront views, cool breezes, and get-away-from-it-all tranquillity. Accommodations range from elegant resorts and private villas to modest but comfortable small hotels and inns. Another popular option is renting a time-share condominium, apartment, or private home. Hotels often operate on the EP, but also offer CP or MAP if you wish; some require MAP in winter, and others offer all-inclusive packages. The hotels below all have air-conditioning, telephones, and TVs in guest rooms unless otherwise noted.

Villas, Apartments & Condominiums

Villas, private homes, and condos are available south of Bridgetown, in the Hastings-Worthing area, and along the west coast in St. James and in St. Peter. Most include maid service, and the owner or manager can arrange for a cook.

A handful of time-share resorts have cropped up along the south and west coasts. Non-owner vacationers can rent the units by the week from the property managers. Two- and three-bedroom condos run $800–$3,800 per week in summer—double that in winter. This can be an economical option for family groups or couples vacationing together.

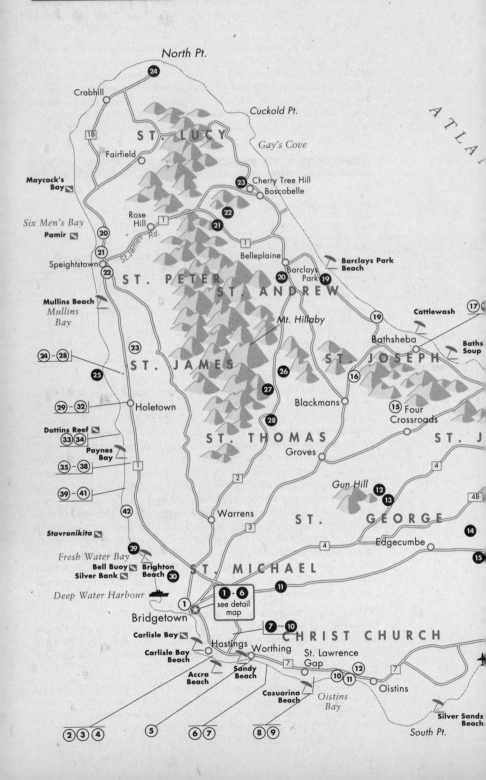

Barbados

North Pt.

Crabhill

Cuckold Pt.

ST. LUCY

Gay's Cove

Fairfield

Maycock's Bay

Cherry Tree Hill
Boscobelle

Rose Hill

Six Men's Bay

Pamir

Belleplaine

Speightstown

Barclays Park

Barclays Park Beach

St. James Rd.

ST. PETER

ST. ANDREW

Mullins Beach
Mullins Bay

Mt. Hillaby

Cattlewash

Bathsheba

Baths Soup

ST. JAMES

ST. JOSEPH

Holetown

Blackmans

Four Crossroads

ST. ST. J

Dottins Reef

Paynes Bay

Groves

ST. THOMAS

Stavronikita

Gun Hill

Fresh Water Bay

Warrens

Bell Buoy
Silver Bank

Edgecumbe

ST. GEORGE

Brighton Beach

ST. MICHAEL

Deep Water Harbour

1 · 6
see detail map

Bridgetown

CHRIST CHURCH

Carlisle Bay

Hastings

Worthing

St. Lawrence Gap

Carlisle Bay Beach

Accra Beach

Sandy Beach

Oistins

Casuarina Beach

Oistins Bay

Silver Sands Beach

South Pt.

A T L A

KEY

- Beaches
- Cruise Ship Terminal
- Dive Sites
- **1** Exploring Sights
- **①** Hotels & Restaurants

ATLANTIC OCEAN

⑰ ⑱ **18**

...thsheba
...up Bowl

Consett
Bay

⑰

Ragged
Pt.

Marley
Vale

JOHN

B

Bottom
Bay

ST. PHILIP

⑭ ⑯

15

The Crane   **Crane Beach**
⑬

Crane
Bay

COBBLER'S REEF

Grantley Adams
International
Airport

Long
Bay

0 ———————————— 3 miles

0 ———————————— 3 km

On the south coast, the seaside villas at **Bougainvillea Beach Resort** (⊠ Maxwell Coast Rd., Maxwell, Christ Church ☎ 246/418–0990 ⊕ www.bougainvillearesort.com) are appropriate for families, couples, or honeymooners. Farther east, but also on the south coast, the upscale private residences at **The Crane** (⊠ Crane Beach, St. Philip ☎ 246/423–6220 ⊕ www.thecrane.com) overlook the ocean at Crane Beach and are perfect for anyone seeking peace, tranquillity, and natural beauty.

On the west coast, **Royal Westmoreland Villas** (⊠ Hwy. 2A, Westmoreland, St. James ☎ 246/422–4653 ⊕ www.royal-westmoreland.com) overlook the Royal Westmoreland Golf Club's championship course and are therefore an ideal base for golfers. Just beyond Speightstown, the luxurious town homes at **Port St. Charles** (⊠ Hwy. 1B, Heywoods, St. Peter ☎ 246/419–1000 ⊕ www.portstcharles.com) are the best choice for boating enthusiasts.

The **Barbados Tourism Authority** (☎ 246/427–2623) on Harbour Road in Bridgetown has a listing of apartments in prime resort areas on both the south and west coasts, complete with facilities offered and the rates. Some apartment complexes are small, with only three or four units; others range up to 30 units or more.

Hotels

EAST COAST
★ $$$$

🏨 **Villa Nova.** Reconstructed on the remnants of a historic great house, this elegant, all-suites hotel is surrounded by 15 acres of gardens and dense woodlands. Exquisitely decorated with antiques and works of art, suites have king-size beds, comfortable sitting areas, and bathrooms with Victorian claw-foot tubs. If you wish, the butler will serve breakfast on your wraparound terrace. Relax in the lounge or on the verandah, swim in the pool, choose a book from the extensive library, picnic at the hotel's beach club at Cattlewash, and enjoy fine dining in the Plantation Room. The pampering begins with limousine service from the airport. ⊠ *Villa Nova, St. John,* ☎ *246/433–1505; 246/433–1524 for reservations* 🖨 *246/433–6363* ⊕ *www.villanovabarbados.com* ⬈ *17 rooms, 11 suites* ⅋ *Restaurant, room service, fans, in-room data ports, in-room safes, golf privileges, 2 tennis courts, pool, gym, spa, billiards, hiking, 3 bars, library, piano, shop, laundry service, concierge, Internet, meeting room, airport shuttle; no kids under 12* ▭ *AE, MC, V* ⅋⊙⅋ *BP.*

$ 🏨 **Atlantis Hotel.** The Atlantis has a spectacular cliffside location overlooking the rocky Atlantic coast, where the sea views are mesmerizing. It's been a modest guest house since the 1880s. Most of the activity happens around midday, when folks touring the east coast stop for a traditional Bajan buffet lunch at the hotel restaurant. Rooms are simply furnished, and some have balconies overlooking that great view. You won't find a TV, and there's no air-conditioning—although the fresh Atlantic breeze that usually wafts through the open windows makes that no problem. Bathsheba Beach—the island's premier surfing spot—is next door. ⊠ *Tent Bay, Bathsheba, St. Joseph* ☎ *246/433–9445* 🖨 *246/433–7180* ⊕ *www.atlantisbarbados.com* ⬈ *10 rooms* ⅋ *Restaurant, beach, bar; no A/C, no room phones, no room TVs* ▭ *AE* ⅋⊙⅋ *MAP.*

$ 🏨 **The Edgewater Inn.** This cliffside hideaway—originally a 1760 beach house—may lack pizzazz, but that is its charm. Oversized, hand-hewn furniture and mahogany woodwork add a rugged quality; beveled-glass windows and parquetry ceilings are truly unusual. Rooms are otherwise basic, but the friendly staff, spectacular ocean views, low prices, and good food easily make up for that. The property backs up to an 85-acre rain forest, providing a serene natural environment—perfect for vacationers who'd rather curl up with a good novel than go clubbing or shopping. Serious surfers love its proximity to the pounding Atlantic surf at

Bathsheba Beach. ⊠ *Bathsheba Beach, Bathsheba, St. Joseph* ☎ *246/ 433–9900* 🖷 *246/433–9902* ⊕ *www.edgewaterinn.com* ⇋ *16 rooms, 4 suites* ♨ *Restaurant, fans, refrigerators, pool, beach, hiking, bar; no A/C in some rooms, no room phones, no room TVs* ⊟ *AE, MC, V* ⫶◯⫶ *CP.*

SOUTH COAST **🏨 Turtle Beach Resort.** Named for the sea turtles that lay their eggs on
$$$$ the beach—which is visible from the three-story open-air lobby—the resort has everything a family could wish for. And it's all here to enjoy—
all the time, all included. Boats and boogie boards are fun at the beach;
golfers get special privileges at the nearby Barbados Golf Club; and the
Kids Club has daily activities for children 3–11. Suites are large and attractively decorated with wicker furniture and tropical colors; many have
have ocean views. With three restaurants (or dining at four sister hotels) and nightly entertainment, you won't want to go home. ⊠ *St.
Lawrence Gap, Dover, Christ Church* ☎ *246/428–7131* 🖷 *246/428–
6089* ⊕ *www.eleganthotels.com* ⇋ *166 suites* ♨ *3 restaurants, snack
bar, room service, fans, in-room safes, refrigerators, golf privileges, 2
tennis courts, 3 pools, aerobics, gym, hair salon, hot tub, beach, snorkeling, windsurfing, boating, waterskiing, 2 bars, sports bar, shops, baby-
sitting, children's programs (ages 3–11), playground, dry cleaning,
laundry service, Internet, business services* ⊟ *AE, DC, MC, V* ⫶◯⫶ *AI.*

$$$ **🏨 Club Rockley Barbados.** On 72 acres near one of the island's most pop-
ular beach areas, this all-inclusive resort offers extensive amenities. The
resort's 9-hole, par-36 golf course is challenging, attractively land-
scaped, and open to the public. Accommodations consist of studios and
one- or two-bedroom apartments. Each room has a balcony or patio;
kettles, toasters, and hair dryers are available. There's free shuttle ser-
vice to the beach, which is five minutes away. ⊠ *Golf Club Rd., Rock-
ley, Christ Church* ☎ *246/435–7880* 🖷 *246/435–8015* ⊕ *www.
clubrockley.com* ⇋ *142 rooms* ♨ *3 restaurants, kitchenettes, 9-hole golf
course, 5 tennis courts, 7 pools, gym, squash, shops, 4 bars, recreation
room, baby-sitting, children's programs (ages 2–11), Internet, meeting
room* ⊟ *AE, DC, MC, V* ⫶◯⫶ *AI.*

$$$ **🏨 Sam Lord's Castle.** About 14 mi (22½ km) east of Bridgetown, this for-
mer pirate's lair is surrounded by 12 acres of grounds, gardens, and a
mile of beach. Seven rooms in the great house have canopy beds; downstairs, the public rooms display furniture by Sheraton, Hepplewhite, and
Chippendale—for admiring, not for sitting. Guest rooms in surrounding cottages have conventional hotel furnishings, and some have kitchenettes. The Wanderer Restaurant offers Continental cuisine, and there
are even a few slot machines. Rates include unlimited daytime tennis,
all meals and beverages, airport transfers, and a Thursday Shipwreck
party. ⊠ *Long Bay, St. Philip* ☎ *246/423–7350* 🖷 *246/423–6361*
⊕ *www.samlordscastle.com* ⇋ *236 rooms, 12 suites* ♨ *4 restaurants,
6 tennis courts, 3 pools, exercise equipment, hair salon, beach, bar, shops,
meeting room* ⊟ *AE, D, DC, MC, V* ⫶◯⫶ *AI.*

★ $$$ **🏨 The Savannah.** The Savannah comprises the completely renovated, his-
toric Sea View Hotel as its main building and two additional wings that
extend to the sea. Waterfalls from the main building spill into a lagoon-
style pool, which separates the two wings. Rooms are beautifully ap-
pointed with antique-style furniture, including carved mahogany
four-poster beds. French doors open to a patio or balcony. All rooms
have state-of-the-art TVs, DVDs, and CD players; duplex suites have
large sitting rooms, bars, fax machines, and printers. The restaurant is
a popular luncheon spot for local businesspeople. ⊠ *Garrison Main Rd.,
Hastings, Christ Church* ☎ *246/228–3800* 🖷 *246/228–4385* ⊕ *www.
gemsbarbados.com/savannah* ⇋ *92 rooms, 8 suites* ♨ *2 restaurants, in-
room data ports, in-room safes, minibars, in-room VCRs, pool, saltwater*

pool, gym, hair salon, spa, beach, 2 bars, shop, Internet, business services, meeting room ≡ *AE, DC, MC, V* ⊙ *EP.*

★ $$–$$$ ▦ **The Crane.** High on a seaside cliff, The Crane's original building (Barbados's first resort hotel) has 18 large suites decorated with antiques; corner suites have walls of windows and broad patios with panoramic ocean views. Two modern buildings, built in corresponding style, house large, luxurious villa suites with hardwood floors, hand-carved four-poster beds, spectacular bathrooms, fully equipped kitchens, central air, entertainment centers, and washer/dryers; many have private plunge pools. A crescent of pink-sand beach, with rolling waves, is 200 steps down the cliff. A testament to the beautiful location, the hotel's signature pool has been the backdrop for numerous photo shoots. ⊠ *Crane, Crane Bay, St. Philip* ☎ *246/423–6220* 🖷 *246/423–5343* ⊕ *www.thecrane.com* ⇨ *4 rooms, 64 suites* ☼ *Restaurant, fans, in-room data ports, in-room safes, kitchenettes, minibars, microwaves, refrigerators, 4 tennis courts, 2 pools, beach, bar, laundry facilities, meeting room; no A/C in some rooms, no TV in some rooms* ≡ *AE, DC, MC, V* ⊙ *EP.*

$$ ▦ **Accra Beach Hotel & Resort.** The beautifully appointed rooms in the four-story resort have balconies facing sandy, white Accra Beach. Six duplex penthouse suites have ocean-view sitting rooms downstairs and spacious bedrooms and huge baths with whirlpools upstairs. All rooms have handcrafted furniture. Between the hotel and its beach are a large cloverleaf-shaped pool, a snack bar, and a poolside bar. In the evening, after sumptuous dining in Wytukai (pronounced Y2K)—the island's first Polynesian restaurant—take a turn on a dance floor that's open to the stars. ⊠ *Hwy. 7, Rockley, Christ Church* 🖅 *Box 73 W* ☎ *246/435–8920* 🖷 *246/435–6794* ⊕ *www.accrabeachhotel.com* ⇨ *125 rooms, 21 suites* ☼ *Restaurant, snack bar, fans, pool, gym, hair salon, beach, squash, 2 bars, shops, meeting rooms* ≡ *AE, MC, V* ⊙ *EP.*

$$ ▦ **Casuarina Beach Club.** Popular with those who prefer self-catering vacations, this is a peaceful place—unique among south coast resorts—but you're within walking distance of restaurants, nightlife, and shopping. The luxury four-story apartment hotel consists of five clusters of Spanish-style buildings in 8 acres of gardens and casuarina pines. The restaurant and a mobile bar are on the beach—1,500 ft of soft, fine sand. All rooms and one- or two-bedroom suites are colorfully decorated; each has a fully equipped kitchenette and a large balcony. ⊠ *St. Lawrence Gap, Dover, Christ Church* ☎ *246/428–3600* 🖷 *246/428–1970* ⊕ *www.casuarina.com* ⇨ *124 rooms, 34 suites* ☼ *Restaurant, fans, kitchenettes, microwaves, 2 tennis courts, pool, wading pool, hair salon, beach, snorkeling, billiards, boccie, shuffleboard, volleyball, 3 bars, piano bar, library, shops, babysitting, children's programs (ages 3–6), playground, laundry facilities, Internet, business services, meeting room* ≡ *AE, D, MC, V* ⊙ *EP.*

$$ ▦ **Divi Southwinds Beach Resort.** The toss-up here is whether to take one of the larger rooms—with a kitchenette and a balcony that overlooks the gardens and pool—or one of the deluxe beach villas just steps from the sandy, white beach. All accommodations are pleasant, and the staff is friendly and eager to be of service. Guests enjoy full use of the watersports facilities, and the resort's 20 lush acres are adjacent to the action-packed St. Lawrence Gap area. ⊠ *St. Lawrence Main Rd., Dover, Christ Church* ☎ *246/428–7181* 🖷 *246/420–2673* ⊕ *www.diviresorts. com* ⇨ *133 rooms* ☼ *3 restaurants, kitchenettes, putting green, 2 tennis courts, 2 pools, hair salon, beach, basketball, volleyball, 2 bars, shops* ≡ *AE, DC, MC, V* ⊙ *EP.*

WEST COAST ▦ **Almond Beach Club & Spa.** A sister property to Almond Beach Village,
$$$$ this convenient all-inclusive resort within strolling distance of Holetown's shops and activities is perfect for couples, honeymooners, or singles. A

horseshoe of rooms and junior suites overlooks the sea or the pool and garden. Lavish breakfast buffets, four-course lunches, afternoon tea, and intimate dinners are served in the main dining room—or enjoy West Indian cuisine for dinner at Enid's, the colorful Bajan restaurant, which also offers free cooking classes. The soundproof piano bar remains open until the last guest leaves. Water sports are included; spa and salon services are extra. ⊠ *Hwy. 1, Vauxhall, St. James* ☎ *246/432–7840* 🖷 *246/432–2115* ⊕ *www.almondresorts.com* 🛏 *133 rooms, 28 junior suites* ♨ *2 restaurants, room service, in-room safes, tennis court, 3 pools, aerobics, hair salon, health club, sauna, spa, beach, snorkeling, windsurfing, boating, waterskiing, 4 bars, nightclub, shop, laundry service, Internet, airport shuttle* ▭ *AE, MC, V* ⑩ *AI.*

$$$$ 🏨 **Almond Beach Village.** A premier family resort on 30 acres, with a 1-mi-long (1½-km-long) beach, the Village has a separate adults-only area—and plenty for all to do. Seven buildings house the guest rooms; the family section has junior and one-bedroom suites, a nursery, a play area, a wading pool, and a supervised Kid's Klub with programs for infants–age 12. A historic sugar mill is a lovely spot for weddings. Restaurants serve Continental, Italian, and Bajan cuisine. Shopping excursions, a Bajan picnic, nightly entertainment, cooking classes, and a dine-around program are included. Need more? Hop the shuttle to Almond Beach Club and enjoy more facilities there. ⊠ *Hwy. 1B, Heywoods, St. Peter* ☎ *246/422–4900* 🖷 *246/422–0617* ⊕ *www.almondresorts.com* 🛏 *289 rooms, 41 suites* ♨ *4 restaurants, room service, in-room safes, 9-hole golf course, 5 tennis courts, 9 pools, wading pool, health club, beach, snorkeling, windsurfing, boating, waterskiing, fishing, billiards, squash, 5 bars, dance club, shops, children's programs (infant–12), playground, Internet, business services, meeting room, airport shuttle* ▭ *AE, MC, V* ⑩ *AI.*

$$$$ 🏨 **Cobblers Cove Hotel.** At this pretty pink resort, flanked by tropical
Fodor'sChoice gardens on one side and the sea on the other, each elegant suite has a
★ comfortable sitting room with a wet bar and a wall of louvered shutters that opens onto a patio or balcony. Only bedrooms are air-conditioned. For all-out luxury, the Colleton and Camelot penthouse suites have richly decorated sitting rooms, king-size four-poster beds, dressing rooms, whirlpool baths, private sundecks, and plunge pools. Enjoy the bar, the lounge-library, and exquisite dining in an intimate, alfresco setting—plus special rates and guaranteed tee times at the Royal Westmoreland Golf Club. ⊠ *Road View, Speightstown, St. Peter* ☎ *246/422–2291* 🖷 *246/422–1460* ⊕ *www.cobblerscove.com* 🛏 *40 suites* ♨ *Restaurant, snack bar, room service, fans, in-room safes, minibars, golf privileges, tennis court, pool, gym, beach, snorkeling, windsurfing, boating, waterskiing, bar, library, shop, baby-sitting, meeting room; no room TVs, no kids Jan.–Mar.* ▭ *AE, MC, V* ☉ *Closed Sept.–mid-Oct.* ⑩ *BP.*

$$$$ 🏨 **Coconut Creek Hotel.** Quiet and secluded, this small, picturesque resort sits on a low bluff, with handsomely landscaped grounds. Steps lead down to two tiny coves and a sandy beach. Rooms have rattan furnishings with tropical accents; some have spectacular ocean views, while others overlook the garden or pool. There is a TV in the lounge. Sunfish, kayaks, and other nonmotorized water-sports equipment are available. Meals are served at the open-air Pavilion Restaurant, with nightly entertainment and dancing at the Cricketers Bar. A free water taxi provides transportation between the four Elegant Hotels on the west coast. ⊠ *Hwy. 1, Derricks, St. James* 🕮 *Box 249, Bridgetown* ☎ *246/432–0803* 🖷 *246/432–0272* ⊕ *www.eleganthotels.com* 🛏 *41 rooms, 12 suites* ♨ *Dining room, in-room safes, refrigerators, golf privileges, pool, beach, snorkeling, windsurfing, boating, waterskiing, bar, baby-sitting, dry cleaning, laundry service; no room TVs* ▭ *AE, DC, MC, V* ⑩ *AI.*

★ **$$$$** ⊞ **Colony Club Hotel.** Once a private gentlemen's club, the hotel offers high style and colonial charm. Rooms are spacious, with whitewashed wood and rattan furniture and neutral fabrics. Twenty rooms have private access to lagoon pools, which flow through the garden. Relax on the beach, soak in one of four pools, and enjoy an exquisite meal in the Orchid Room or a more informal repast at the open-air Laguna Restaurant. Nonmotorized water sports, an in-pool scuba-diving lesson, tennis, and golf privileges at Royal Westmoreland Golf Course are all included. A free water taxi provides transportation between the four Elegant Hotels along the west coast. ⊠ *Hwy. 1, Porters, St. James* ☎ *246/ 422-2335* ⊟ *246/422-0667* ⊕ *www.eleganthotels.com* ➼ *64 rooms, 34 junior suites* ⟋ *2 restaurants, room service, fans, in-room safes, minibars, golf privileges, 2 tennis courts, 4 pools, gym, hair salon, beach, snorkeling, windsurfing, boating, waterskiing, 3 bars, shops, baby-sitting, dry cleaning, laundry service, Internet, meeting room; no kids under 16* ⊟ *AE, D, DC, MC, V* ⟐ *EP.*

★ **$$$$** ⊞ **Coral Reef Club.** Spend your days relaxing on the white-sand beach or around the pool, taking time out for the hotel's superb afternoon tea. Small coral-stone cottages are scattered over 12 flower-filled acres; the public areas ramble along the beach. Each spacious room has a small patio. Junior suites have sitting areas and larger patios or private balconies. Luxury cottages, rebuilt in 2002, have a separate bedroom and living room with sofabed to accommodate families. TV is available by request for an extra charge. ⊠ *Hwy. 1, Holetown, St. James* ☎ *246/ 422-2372* ⊟ *246/422-1776* ⊕ *www.coralreefbarbados.com* ➼ *34 rooms, 30 suites* ⟋ *Restaurant, room service, fans, in-room safes, refrigerators, golf privileges, 3 tennis courts, 2 pools, gym, hair salon, massage, beach, dive shop, snorkeling, windsurfing, boating, waterskiing, billiards, bar, shops, baby-sitting; no room TVs* ⊟ *AE, MC, V* ⟐ *EP.*

$$$$ ⊞ **Crystal Cove Hotel.** White duplex cottages, trimmed in the perky pastels typical of the Caribbean and connected by garden paths, spill down a hillside to the beach. Rooms are bright and spacious, with bleached wood and rattan furniture. During the day, sail on a Hobie Cat, have a scuba lesson, or water-ski, windsurf, or kayak to your heart's content. For a change of scene, a free water taxi serves four west-coast Elegant Hotels properties. Luncheon is generally a beachside buffet; the table d'hôte dinner at Reflections Restaurant is superb, followed by steel pan or other live music. ⊠ *Hwy. 1, Appleby, St. James* ☎ *246/432-2683* ⊟ *246/432-8290* ⊕ *www.eleganthotels.com* ➼ *88 rooms* ⟋ *Restaurant, grill, room service, fans, in-room safes, refrigerators, golf privileges, 2 tennis courts, 3 pools, gym, beach, snorkeling, windsurfing, boating, waterskiing, 2 bars, shop, baby-sitting, children's programs (ages 3–11), laundry service* ⊟ *AE, D, DC, MC, V* ⟐ *AI.*

$$$$ ⊞ **The Fairmont Glitter Bay.** Shipping magnate Sir Edward Cunard built this estate in the 1930s to resemble his palazzo in Venice. Newer buildings have one- and two-bedroom suites and duplex penthouses, all with private balconies or terraces; some have full kitchens. Manicured gardens separate the reception area and lounge from an alfresco dining room (with evening entertainment), pools with a waterfall and footbridge, and ½ mi (1 km) of beach. It's more casual and family-oriented than the Royal Pavilion, its sister property next door; the resorts share facilities, including water sports and dining privileges. Guests also enjoy privileges at Royal Westmoreland Golf Club. ⊠ *Hwy. 1, Porters, St. James* ☎ *246/422-5555* ⊟ *246/422-1367* ⊕ *www.fairmont.com* ➼ *69 suites* ⟋ *Restaurant, room service, fans, in-room safes, minibars, golf privileges, 2 tennis courts, 2 pools, gym, hair salon, massage, beach, snorkeling, windsurfing, boating, waterskiing, shops, baby-sitting, meeting room* ⊟ *AE, D, DC, MC, V* ⟐ *EP.*

$$$$ 🏨 **The Fairmont Royal Pavilion.** Those who want serenity enjoy the ocean-front suites here; only three suites are nestled in a two-story garden villa. Ground-floor rooms allow you to simply step through sliding doors, cross your private patio, and walk onto the sand. Breakfast and lunch are served alfresco at the edge of the beach; afternoon tea and dinner are in the Palm Terrace. Recreational facilities and dining privileges are shared with the adjoining—and less formal—sister hotel, Glitter Bay. ✉ *Hwy. 1, Porters, St. James* 📞 *246/422–4444* 🖨 *246/422–3940* 🌐 *www.fairmont. com* ⏎ *75 suites* ⚬ *2 restaurants, room service, golf privileges, 2 tennis courts, pool, hair salon, beach, snorkeling, windsurfing, boating, waterskiing, 2 bars, shops, laundry service, concierge, meeting room* 🚫 *AE, D, DC, MC, V* ⏐⦿⏐ *EP.*

$$$$ 🏨 **The House at Tamarind Cove.** Privacy, luxury, and service are hallmarks of this boutique hotel. The newest kid on the block is, in fact, an elegant, adults-only enclave where the beautiful people congregate. A 24-hour concierge service attends to every whim—private breakfast service, icy fresh fruits delivered to a beach chair, butler-served canapés before dinner, priority reservations at Daphne's (next door), personal attention whenever and wherever. Rooms are stylishly decorated, with pure white fabrics and minimalist furniture. To see how others vacation, hop aboard the free water taxi and visit sister Elegant Hotels along the west coast. ✉ *Hwy. 1, Paynes Bay, St. James* 📞 *246/432–5525* 🖨 *246/432–5255* 🌐 *www.eleganthotels.com* ⏎ *43 suites* ⚬ *Restaurant, room service, fans, in-room safes, refrigerators, pool, hair salon, hot tub, massage, beach, snorkeling, windsurfing, boating, bar, concierge, airport shuttle; no kids under 12* 🚫 *AE, D, DC, MC, V* ⏐⦿⏐ *BP.*

$$$$ 🏨 **Lone Star Hotel.** For something completely different, this renovated 1940s-era service station is now a four-suite hotel and restaurant. Two suites are at beach level, two are upstairs. The Lincoln Suite is named for the car, as are the Buick, Cord, and Studebaker suites. All are large and beautifully furnished in Bajan mahogany and Italian-designed furniture. Each suite has its own fax line, CD player, walk-in closet, large balcony, and oversize bathroom. The beach is at the door; golf, tennis, fishing, snorkeling, scuba diving, and horseback riding are available nearby. The Lone Star restaurant is extraordinary. ✉ *Hwy. 1, Mount Standfast, St. James* 📞 *246/419–0599* 🖨 *246/419–0597* 🌐 *www. thelonestar.com* ⏎ *4 suites* ⚬ *Restaurant, room service, fans, in-room fax, minibars, beach, bar, Internet* 🚫 *AE, D, DC, MC, V* ⏐⦿⏐ *BP.*

★ **$$$$** 🏨 **Sandy Lane Hotel & Golf Club.** A spectacular coral-stone, Palladian-style mansion overlooking a sweeping stretch of beach shaded by mature trees is the focal point. Its exquisite guest suites, sumptuous in every detail, have remote-controlled lighting, sound, draperies, fans, and temperature; three flat-screen plasma TVs with DVD and Internet access; a Quadriga communication system for e-mail, wake-up calls, and room service; a private bar, luxurious bathrooms, and a personal butler. The 45,000-square-ft spa is a vacation in itself. Elegant dining, 45 holes of championship-level golf, a tennis center, a full complement of water sports, a special lounge for teenagers, and incomparable style complete the extraordinary picture. ✉ *Hwy. 1, Paynes Bay, St. James* 📞 *246/444–2000* 🖨 *246/444–2222* 🌐 *www.sandylane.com* ⏎ *102 rooms, 10 suites* ⚬ *4 restaurants, room service, fans, in-room data ports, in-room fax, in-room safes, minibars, 2 18-hole golf courses, 1 9-hole golf course, 9 tennis courts, pool, hair salon, spa, steam room, beach, snorkeling, windsurfing, boating, 5 bars, shops, children's programs (ages 3–12), dry cleaning, laundry service, concierge, Internet, business services, meeting rooms* 🚫 *AE, DC, MC, V* ⏐⦿⏐ *BP.*

$$$$ 🏨 **Tamarind Cove Hotel.** This large, Mediterranean-style hotel rambles along 750 ft of prime beachfront. Rooms, either close to the action or in cozy privacy, are spacious and attractively decorated with rattan furnishings and subdued colors. Ten luxury ocean-view suites have four-poster beds, marble floors, and coral-stone walls. Four suites have private Jacuzzis. Tangiers serves all meals daily; Sasso and Daphne's Barbados both offer fine dining at dinner. The resort offers a full complement of water sports, as well as golf privileges at the Royal Westmoreland Golf Club. A free water taxi operates between the four Elegant hotels on the west coast. ⊠ *Hwy. 1, Paynes Bay, St. James* ☎ *246/432–1332* 🖳 *246/432–6317* ⊕ *www.eleganthotels.com* 🖗 *58 rooms, 108 suites* ♨ *3 restaurants, snack bar, room service, in-room safes, refrigerators, golf privileges, 2 tennis courts, 4 pools, gym, hair salon, beach, snorkeling, windsurfing, boating, waterskiing, 4 bars, cabaret, shops, baby-sitting, children's programs, dry cleaning, laundry service, concierge, Internet, meeting room* ⊟ *AE, D, DC, MC, V* ⫿⊙⫿ *EP.*

$$$$ 🏨 **Treasure Beach.** Quiet, upscale, and friendly, this resort feels almost residential. Most guests are British, often staying two or three weeks, year after year. Two floors of one-bedroom suites form a horseshoe around a small garden and pool. Most have sea views, but all are just steps from the beach. The super-deluxe Hemingway Suite blends antiques with modern luxury, an enormous terrace, and special amenities. All others have comfortable sitting rooms, with full kitchenettes, a shelf of books, and an open-air fourth wall that can be shuttered at night for privacy. Bedrooms are air-conditioned. The restaurant enjoys a well-deserved reputation for fine dining. ⊠ *Hwy. 1, Paynes Bay, St. James* ☎ *246/432–1346* 🖳 *246/432–1094* ⊕ *www.treasurebeachhotel.com* 🖗 *29 suites* ♨ *Restaurant, room service, fans, in-room data ports, in-room safes, kitchenettes, pool, gym, beach, snorkeling, bar, library, dry cleaning, laundry service, Internet* ⊟ *AE, D, DC, MC, V* ⫿⊙⫿ *EP.*

$$$–$$$$ 🏨 **Mango Bay Hotel & Beach Club.** Within walking distance of Holetown's shops and sights, Mango Bay's whitewashed buildings are on a nice stretch of beach. Each room has a private terrace or balcony and a garden, pool, or ocean view; all are decorated in bright colors and have wicker furniture. The all-inclusive price extends to a dine-around program at two local restaurants for those staying a week or more. Activities include water sports, scuba instruction in the pool, aquacise classes, a catamaran cruise, glass-bottom boat rides, snorkeling trips, walking tours, and a shopping excursion to Bridgetown. Enjoy a nightcap and after-dinner entertainment at the piano bar. ⊠ *2nd St., Holetown, St. James* ☎ *246/432–1384* 🖳 *246/432–5297* ⊕ *www.mangobaybarbados.com* 🖗 *64 rooms* ♨ *Restaurant, in-room safes, 2 pools, beach, snorkeling, windsurfing, boating, waterskiing, bar, piano bar* ⊟ *AE, MC, V* ⫿⊙⫿ *AI.*

Where to Eat

First-class restaurants and hotel dining rooms serve quite sophisticated cuisine—prepared by chefs with international experience—to rival that served in the world's best restaurants. Most menus include seafood: dorado (also known as dolphinfish or mahimahi), kingfish, snapper, and flying fish prepared every way imaginable. Flying fish is so popular a delicacy that it has become a national symbol. Shellfish abounds; on the other hand, so do steak, local black-belly lamb, and fresh fruits and vegetables.

Local specialty dishes include *buljol* (a cold salad of pickled codfish, tomatoes, onions, sweet peppers, and celery) and *conkies* (cornmeal, coconut, pumpkin, raisins, sweet potatoes, and spices, mixed together, wrapped in a banana leaf, and steamed). *Cou-cou,* often served with steamed flying fish, is a mixture of cornmeal and okra topped with a spicy creole sauce made from tomatoes, onions, and sweet peppers. Bajan-style pepper-pot is a hearty stew of oxtail, beef chunks, and "any other meat" in a rich, spicy gravy and simmered overnight.

For lunch, restaurants often offer a traditional Bajan buffet of fried fish, baked chicken, salads, and a selection of local roots and vegetables. Be cautious with the West Indian condiments; like the sun, they're hotter than you think. Typical Bajan drinks, besides Banks beer and Mount Gay rum, are *falernum* (a liqueur concocted of rum, sugar, lime juice, and almond essence) and *mauby* (a nonalcoholic drink made by boiling bitter bark and spices, straining the mixture, and sweetening it). You're sure to enjoy the fresh fruit punch, with or without the rum.

What to Wear

Barbados's dress code is conservative and, on occasion, formal—a jacket and tie for gentlemen and a cocktail dress for ladies in the fanciest restaurants, particularly in winter. Other places are more casual, although jeans and shorts are always frowned upon at dinner. Beach attire should be worn only at the beach.

Bridgetown

CREOLE
$$

✕ **Waterfront Cafe.** This friendly bistro beside the Careenage is the perfect place to enjoy a drink, snack, or meal—and to people-watch. Locals and tourists gather for alfresco all-day dining on sandwiches, salads, fish, pasta, pepper-pot stew, and tasty Bajan snacks such as buljol, fish cakes, or plantation pork (plantains stuffed with spicy minced pork). The panfried flying-fish sandwich is especially popular. In the evening you can gaze through the arched windows while savoring nouvelle creole cuisine, enjoying cool trade winds, and listening to live jazz. There's a special Carib Buffet and steel-pan music on Tuesday night from 7 to 9. ✉ *Bridge House, The Careenage, Bridgetown, St. Michael* ☎ *246/427–0093* ▭ *AE, DC, MC, V* ☉ *Closed Sun.*

East Coast

CARIBBEAN
$$$

✕ **Naniki Restaurant.** Huge picture windows and sliding doors offer exhilarating views of surrounding hills and a pounding Atlantic Ocean, while diners enjoy tasty Caribbean cooking exquisitely prepared. For lunch, seared flying fish fillets, grilled dorado, stewed lambie (conch), curried chicken, and jerk pork are accompanied by cou-cou, peas and rice, or salad. At dinner, grilled snapper, local black-belly lamb, seared shrimp, and pork loin are specialties. On Sundays, lunch is a Caribbean buffet. Vegetarian dishes are always available. Rich wooden beams, stone tiles, clay pottery, straw mats, colorful dinnerware, and fresh flowers from the on-site anthurium farm set the style. ✉ *Suriname, St. Joseph* ☎ *246/433–1300* ▭ *AE, MC, V.*

$$

✕ **Atlantis Hotel.** People have enjoyed lunch with a view at this hotel's restaurant for more than 40 years—especially on Sunday, when an enormous Bajan buffet includes pumpkin fritters, spinach cake, pickled breadfruit, fried flying fish, roast chicken, pepper-pot stew, and fried okra and eggplant. Homemade coconut pie tops the dessert list. The Atlantis is a lunch stop for many organized day tours. ✉ *Atlantis Hotel, Tent Bay, Bathsheba, St. Joseph* ☎ *246/433–9445* ▭ *AE.*

$–$$

✕ **Bonito Beach Bar & Restaurant.** Enid Worrell's wholesome West Indian home cooking has soothed the hunger pangs of many folks who find themselves on the east coast at lunchtime. The view of the Atlantic from the second-floor dining room is striking, and the Bajan buffet lunch includes fried fish and baked chicken accompanied by salads and vegetables fresh from the family garden. If your timing is right, Mrs. Worrell might have homemade cheesecake for dessert. The fresh fruit punch—with or without rum—is great. ✉ *Coast Rd., Bathsheba, St. Joseph* ☎ *246/433–9034* ▭ *AE, D, DC MC, V.*

South Coast

CARIBBEAN
$$$

✕ **David's Place.** Come here for sophisticated Bajan cuisine in a prime waterfront location on St. Lawrence Bay. Waves slap against the pilings of the open-air deck—a rhythmic accompaniment to the soft classical background music. As a starter, the pumpkin soup is divine. Specialties such as flying fish, pepper-pot stew, curried shrimp, and vegetarian dishes come with homemade cheddar-cheese bread. Dessert might be bread pudding, carrot cake with rum sauce, or coconut cream pie. David's has an extensive wine list. ⊠ *St. Lawrence Main Rd., Worthing, Christ Church* 🕾 *246/435–9755* ⌖ *Reservations essential* ▭ *AE, MC, V* ☯ *Closed Mon. No lunch.*

ITALIAN
$$–$$$

✕ **Bellini's Trattoria.** Soft music and waves gently lapping beneath the Mediterranean-style veranda set the stage for informal yet romantic dining. The cuisine at Bellini's is classic northern Italian with a contemporary flair. Toast the evening with a Bellini cocktail (sparkling wine with a splash of fruit nectar), and start your meal with antipasto, an individual pizza, or a tasty homemade pasta dish. Move on to the signature shrimp, veal, steak, or seafood dishes, and top it all off with excellent tiramisu. ⊠ *Little Bay Hotel, St. Lawrence Gap, Dover, Christ Church* 🕾 *246/435–7246* ▭ *AE, DC, MC, V.*

SEAFOOD
★ $$$–$$$$

✕ **Josef's Restaurant.** The signature restaurant of Austrian restaurateur Josef Schwaiger is, perhaps, the most upscale seaside dining spot on the south coast. Fruits of the sea—fillet of dolphinfish with papaya and pineapple salsa or red snapper with sun-dried tomato crust—are prominent on the menu, and the wine list is extensive. Try tuna and salmon tartar with wasabi Dijon dressing as an innovative starter, and free-range chicken teriyaki with stir-fry noodles will tingle your taste buds. Pasta dishes assuage the vegetarian palate. ⊠ *St. Lawrence Gap, Dover, Christ Church* 🕾 *246/435–8245* ⌖ *Reservations essential* ▭ *AE, DC, MC, V* ☯ *No lunch.*

$$–$$$

✕ **The Crane.** Perched on a oceanfront cliff, The Crane in the Crane Beach Hotel is an informal luncheon spot by day. Enjoy seafood chowder—prepared with lobster, shrimp, dolphinfish, local vegetables, and a dash of sherry—or a light salad or sandwich while absorbing the breathtaking view. In the evening, candlelight and a soft guitar enhance fabulous grilled Caribbean lobster seasoned with herbs, lime juice, and garlic butter and served in its shell. Landlubbers can order a perfect filet mignon, too. Sundays are really special, with a Gospel Brunch at 10 AM and a Bajan Buffet at 12:30 PM. ⊠ *Crane Beach Hotel, Crane Bay, St. Philip* 🕾 *246/423–6220* ⌖ *Reservations essential* ▭ *AE, D, DC, MC, V.*

$$–$$$

✕ **Pisces.** Seafood is prepared here in every way—from charbroiled to sautéed. Specialties include conch strips in tempura, rich fish chowder, panfried fillets of flying fish with a toasted almond crust and a light mango-citrus sauce, and seared prawns in a fragrant curry sauce. There are also some chicken, beef, and pasta dishes. Whatever your selection, the herbs that flavor it and the accompanying vegetables will have come from the chef's garden. Save room for the bread pudding, yogurt-lime cheesecake, or homemade rum-raisin ice cream. Twinkling white lights reflect on the water as you dine. ⊠ *St. Lawrence Gap, Dover, Christ Church* 🕾 *246/435–6564* ▭ *AE, DC, MC, V* ☯ *No lunch.*

West Coast

CONTEMPORARY
$$$$
Fodor'sChoice
★

✕ **The Cliff.** The mastery of Chef Paul Owens is the foundation of one of the finest dining establishments in Barbados. Every candlelit table has a sea view. In fact, steep steps hug the cliff to which the restaurant clings and reach down to the sea to accommodate those arriving by yacht. Imaginative art accents the tiered dining terrace. The artistry extends to the innovative menu, which offers excellent cuts of prime meat and fresh fish, creatively presented with nouvelle accents and accompanied by fresh local vegetables. Don't skip dessert, which falls in the sinful category. Service is impeccable, of course. ⊠ *Hwy. 1, Derricks, St. James* ☎ *246/ 432–1922* ⊟ *AE, DC, MC, V* ☉ *No lunch.*

★ $$$$ ✕ **Orchid Room.** Hotel restaurants on Barbados generally offer excellent cuisine, but enjoying a special dinner at the Colony Club's intimate Orchid Room is nothing short of extraordinary. Chef Philippe's haute cuisine appeals to the eye as well as the palate. The à la carte menu changes nightly, but might include chateaubriand for two with sauce bordelaise, veal scallops with mushrooms and escargots, or poached salmon with dill. Dessert is also perfect—perhaps a rich chocolate-mousse cake, passion-fruit brûlée, or banana tartlet with crème anglaise. ⊠ *Colony Club Hotel, Hwy. 1, Porters, St. James* ☎ *246/422–2335* ♙ *Reservations essential* ⊟ *AE, DC, MC, V* ☉ *Closed weekends. No lunch.*

★ $$$–$$$$ ✕ **La Mer.** Chef Hans Schweitzer, who earned a reputation in Barbados for elegant cuisine, works his magic in a more relaxed—but still stylish—way. His restaurant hugs the lagoon at Port St. Charles, an exclusive waterfront community. Fresh fish from Six Men's Bay, just up the road, and tender cuts of meat are seared on either of two grills, wood or lavarock, while vegetarian dishes might be stirred up at the wok station. This is a perfect place for a light meal at the bar, just steps from the dock, or a romantic dinner, with moonlight reflecting on the lagoon. ⊠ *Port St. Charles, Speightstown, St. Peter* ☎ *246/419–2000* ♙ *Reservations essential* ⊟ *AE, DC, MC, V.*

★ $$$–$$$$ ✕ **Carambola.** Dramatic lighting, alfresco dining, and a cliffside location make this one of the island's most romantic restaurants. The menu is a mix of classic French and Caribbean cuisines—with Asian touches for good measure. Start with a spicy crab tart, served with hollandaise sauce on a bed of sweet red peppers. For an entrée, try fillet of mahimahi broiled with Dijon mustard sauce, or sliced duck breast with a wild mushroom fumet served with stuffed tomatoes and *gratin dauphinoise* (potatoes au gratin). For dessert, the *citron gâteau* (lime mousse on a pool of lemon coulis) is a wonderfully light finish. ⊠ *Hwy. 1, Derricks, St. James* ☎ *246/432–0832* ♙ *Reservations essential* ⊟ *AE, MC, V* ☉ *Closed Sun. No lunch.*

ECLECTIC ✕ **The Lone Star.** In the 1940s this was the only garage on the west coast;
$$$–$$$$ today it's the snazzy restaurant in the chic Lone Star Hotel, where top chefs turn the finest raw ingredients into gastronomic delights. In the Oriental Room (upstairs), dishes are influenced by Chinese, Thai, and Vietnamese cuisines. In the main dining room (downstairs) the menu emphasizes Mediterranean, modern European, and Caribbean cuisines. The extensive à la carte choices will please any palate. ⊠ *Lone Star Hotel, Hwy. 1, Mount Standfast, St. James* ☎ *246/419–0599* ⊟ *AE, MC, V.*

$$–$$$$ ✕ **Olives Bar & Bistro.** Chef Scott Ames presides over this intimate restaurant, once a quaint Bajan house in the center of Holetown. Mediterranean and Caribbean flavors enliven inventive pizzas and tasty salads at lunch or dinner; special dishes on the menu might include fresh seafood, such as seared yellowfin tuna with ratatouille, and tasty Swiss-style *rösti* potatoes (shredded and fried like a pancake) with smoked salmon and sour cream. Dine inside or in the courtyard; the popular upstairs bar is a great spot to mingle over coffee, refreshing drinks, or snacks (pizza, pastas, salads). ⊠ *2nd St., Holetown, St. James* ☎ *246/432–2112* ⊟ *AE, MC, V.*

$$–$$$ ✕ **Angry Annie's.** You can't miss this place. Outside and inside, everything's painted in bright Caribbean pinks, blues, greens, and yellows—and it's just steps from the main road. The food is just as lively: great barbecued "jump-up" ribs and chicken, grilled fresh fish or juicy steaks,

"Rasta pasta" for vegetarians, and several spicy curries. Eat inside on gaily colored furniture or outside under the stars—or take it away with you. ⊠ *1st St., Holetown, St. James* ☎ *246/432–2119* ⊟ *AE, DC, MC, V.*

$$–$$$ ✕ **Ragamuffins.** The only restaurant on Barbados in an authentic chattel house, Ragamuffins is tiny, funky, lively, and informal. The menu offers seafood, perfectly broiled T-bone steaks, West Indian curries, and vegetarian dishes such as Bajan stir-fried vegetables with noodles. Dine inside or out. The kitchen is within sight of the bar—which is a popular meeting spot most evenings. ⊠ *1st St., Holetown, St. James* ☎ *246/432–1295* ♧ *Reservations essential* ⊟ *AE, MC, V* ☻ *No lunch.*

$–$$ ✕ **Baku Beach Bar.** Whether you're going to the beach, coming from the beach, or just wanting to be near the beach, this is a great place for lunch or an informal dinner. Tables spill into the courtyard, through tropical gardens, and onto a boardwalk by the sea. Try a Caesar salad, a burger, spareribs, or grilled fish served with the salsa of your choice: fruit, pesto, herb lemon, or ginger soy. On the side, have garlic bread, sautéed onions, rice pilaf, or spicy potato wedges. Got room for crème brûlée, lemon tart, or a brownie with ice cream? Maybe dawdling over cappuccino is enough. ⊠ *Hwy. 1, Holetown, St. James* ☎ *246/432–2258* ⊟ *AE, MC, V.*

ITALIAN ✕ **Daphne's.** The chic and glamorous Caribbean outpost of the famed
$$$$ London eatery is on the property of the Tamarind Cove Hotel. British chef Kelly Jackson whips up contemporary versions of classic Italian dishes. Grilled mahimahi, for example, becomes Italian when combined with Marsala, peperonata, and zucchini. Perfectly prepared pappardelle with braised duck, red wine, and oregano is a sublime pasta choice. Light meals, salads, and half-portions of pasta are available at lunch. The extensive wine lists features both regional Italian and fine French selections. ⊠ *Paynes Bay, St. James* ☎ *234/432–2731* ♧ *Reservations essential* ⊟ *AE, D, DC, MC, V.*

Beaches

Bajan beaches have fine, white sand, and all are open to the public. Most have access from the road, so nonguest bathers don't have to pass through hotel properties.

EAST COAST With long stretches of open beach, crashing ocean surf, rocky cliffs, and verdant hills, the Atlantic (windward) side of Barbados is full of dramatic views. This is also where many Barbadians have second homes and spend their holidays. But be cautioned: swimming at east coast beaches is treacherous, even for strong swimmers, and *not* recommended. Waves are high, the bottom tends to be rocky, the currents are unpredictable, and the undertow is strong.

Barclays Park. Serious swimming is unwise at this beach along the Ermy Bourne Highway, but there are tide pools where you can take a dip, wade, and play—and a lovely shaded picnic area across the road.
Bathsheba Soup Bowl. The rolling surf attracts surfers from around the world to the site of the Independence Classic Surfing Championships each November.
Cattlewash. Just north of Bathsheba is this long stretch of untouched, windswept sand that's great for beachcombing, wading, and expert-only surfing.

SOUTH COAST A young, energetic crowd favors the south coast beaches, which are broad, blessed with white, powdery sand, and dotted with tall palms. The reef-protected waters are crystal-clear and safe for swimming and snorkeling. The surf is medium to high, and the waves get bigger and the winds stronger (windsurfers take note) the farther southeast you go.

Accra Beach. The popular beach in Rockley has gentle surf and a lifeguard. There are plenty of places for a meal or drink and to rent equipment for snorkeling and other water sports. There's also a convenient parking lot.

Bottom Bay. The cove north of Sam Lord's Castle is mesmerizing. Follow the steps down the cliff to a strip of white sand lined by coconut palms and washed by an aquamarine sea. There's even a cave to explore. It's out of the way and not near restaurants, so bring a picnic lunch.

Carlisle Bay Beach. This beach at Needham's Point, not far from Bridgetown, is one of the island's best, and gets crowded with locals on weekends and holidays. The Carlisle Bay Centre has changing rooms and showers to accommodate cruise-ship passengers spending a day at the beach.

Casuarina Beach. At the east end of the St. Lawrence Gap area you'll always get a nice breeze and a fair amount of surf. Public access is from Maxwell Coast Road. Refreshments are available at the Casuarina Beach Hotel.

★ **Crane Beach.** This exquisite crescent of pink sand is protected by steep cliffs. As attractive as this location is now, it was named not for the elegant long-legged wading birds but for the crane used for hauling and loading cargo when this area was a busy port. Protected by a reef, the rolling surf is great for bodysurfing. A lifeguard is on duty. Changing rooms are available at Crane Beach Hotel for a small fee (which you can apply toward drinks or a meal at the restaurant). Beach access is through the hotel and down about 200 steps.

Sandy Beach. In Worthing, next to the Sandy Beach Island Resort, this beach has shallow, calm waters and a picturesque lagoon, making it an ideal location for families. There's parking on the main road, and plenty of places nearby sell food and drink.

Silver Sands/Silver Rock Beach. Close to the southernmost tip of the island, Silver Sands/Silver Rock is a beautiful strand of white sand that always has a stiff breeze, which attracts intermediate and advanced windsurfers.

WEST COAST Gentle Caribbean waves lap the west coast, and the stunning coves and sandy beaches are shaded by leafy mahogany trees. The water is perfect for swimming and water sports. An almost unbroken chain of beaches runs between Bridgetown and Speightstown. Elegant homes and luxury hotels face much of the beachfront property in this area, Barbados's Platinum Coast.

Although west coast beaches are seldom crowded, they aren't isolated. Vendors stroll by, selling handmade baskets, hats, dolls, jewelry—even original watercolors; owners of private boats offer waterskiing, parasailing, and snorkeling excursions. There are no concession stands, but hotels welcome nonguests for terrace lunches (wear a cover-up), and you can buy picnic items at supermarkets in Holetown.

Brighton Beach. Just north of Bridgetown and convenient to the port, Brighton is as calm as a lake. Locals often take quick swims here on hot days.

★ **Mullins Beach.** This picturesque beach just south of Speightstown is a perfect place to spend the day. The water is safe for swimming and snorkeling, there's easy parking on the main road, and Mullins Beach Bar serves snacks, meals, and drinks.

Paynes Bay. South of Holetown, this beach is lined with luxury hotels. It's a very pretty area, with plenty of beach to go around and good snorkeling. Parking areas and public access are available opposite the Coach House. Grab a bite to eat and liquid refreshments at Bomba's Beach Bar.

Sports & the Outdoors

CRICKET   Barbados is mad for cricket. Regional matches are held from January through March, and international test matches are played from March through May. The Sandy Lane Gold Cup match is held in March. Tickets to cricket matches at Kensington Oval, Bridgetown, range from $7.50 to $30. For information about upcoming cricket matches, call the **Barbados Cricket Association** (☎ 246/436–1397).

FISHING   Fishing is great year-round—but ideal from January to April. Half- or full-day charter trips are available for serious deep-sea fishers looking for billfish or for those who prefer angling in calm coastal waters where wahoo, barracuda, and other small fish reside. Charters depart from the Careenage, in Bridgetown. Expect to pay $60–$400 per person, depending on the length of time, size of the boat, and whether it's a shared or private charter.

Billfisher II (☎ 246/431–0741) is a 40-ft Pacemaker that can accommodate up to six people; trips include drinks and transportation to and from the boat. Full-day charters include a full lunch and guaranteed fish (or a 25% refund on a full-day charter). *Blue Jay* (☎ 246/429–2326) is a fully equipped 45-ft Sport Fisherman, with a crew that knows where blue marlin, sailfish, barracuda, and kingfish play. Four to six people can be accommodated—it's the only charter boat on island with four chairs. Drinks, snacks, bait, tackle, and transfers are provided. *Cannon II* (☎ 246/424–6107), a 42-ft Hatteras Convertible, accommodates six fishing passengers; drinks and snacks are complimentary, and lunch is served on full-day charters. *Honey Bea III* (☎ 246/428–5344), a 41-ft Avenger Sport Fisherman (Hatteras design), welcomes both beginners and experienced anglers for a day of fishing. Lunch is provided.

GOLF   Barbadians love golf, and golfers love Barbados. In addition to the courses listed below, Almond Village has a 9-hole, par-3 executive course open to guests only. Learn to play or improve your game at the **Barbados Academy of Golf & Public Driving Range** (✉ ABC Hwy., Balls Complex, Balls, Christ Church ☎ 246/420–7405). It has a chipping and putting green, with sand bunkers and 48 hitting bays. The adjacent 18-hole miniature golf course is fun for the whole family. Both are open daily 8 AM–11 PM, and snacks are available. **Barbados Golf Club** (✉ Hwy. 7, Durants, Christ Church ☎ 246/434–2121), the first public golf course on Barbados, is a par-72, 18-hole championship course designed by Ron Kirby. Greens fees are $119 for 18 holes and $70 for 9 holes, plus a cart fee. Unlimited 3-day and 7-day golf passes are available. Several hotels offer golf privileges, with preferential tee-time reservations and reduced rates. Club and shoe rentals are available. **Club Rockley Barbados** (✉ Golf Club Rd., Rockley, Christ Church ☎ 246/435–7873), on the southeast coast, has a challenging 9-hole course that can be played as 18 from varying tee positions. It's open to the public daily, and club rentals are available. Greens fees in high season are $50 for 18 holes and $37.50 for 9 holes. At the venerable **Country Club at Sandy Lane** (✉ Hwy. 1, Paynes Bay, St. James ☎ 246/432–2829), golfers can play on The Old Nine or on either of two 18-hole championship courses: the Tom Fazio-designed, Country Club Course or the spectacular Green Monkey Course. Greens fees in high season are $40 for 9 holes ($50 for non-guests) or $95 for 18 holes ($140 for non-guests). The **Royal**

FodorsChoice
★

Westmoreland Golf Club (⊠ Westmoreland St. James ☎ 246/422–4653) has a world-class Robert Trent Jones, Jr., par-72, 18-hole championship course that meanders through the former 500-acre Westmoreland Sugar Estate. Greens fees ($190 for visitors in high season; $150 for villa residents) include use of an electric cart; club rental is available.

HIKING Hilly but not mountainous, the northern interior and the east coast are ideal for hiking. The **Arbib Heritage and Nature Trail** (⊠ Speightstown, St. Peter ☎ 246/426–2421), maintained by the Barbados National Trust, is actually two trails—one offers a rigorous hike through gullies and plantations to old ruins and remote north-country areas; the other is a shorter, easier walk through Speightstown's side streets and past an ancient church and chattel houses. Guided hikes take place on Wednesday, Thursday, and Saturday at 9 AM (book by 3 PM the day before) and cost $7.50. The **Barbados National Trust** (⊠ Wildey House, Wildey, St. Michael ☎ 246/426–2421) sponsors free walks, called **Hike Barbados,** year-round on Sunday from 6 AM to about 9 AM and from 3:30 PM to 6 PM, as well as monthly moonlight hikes that begin at 5:30 PM (bring a flashlight). Experienced guides group you with others of similar levels of ability. Stop & Stare hikes go 5–6 mi; Here & There, 8–10 mi; and Grin & Bear, 12–14 mi. Wear loose clothes, sensible shoes, sunscreen, and a hat, and bring your camera and a bottle of water. Hikes start and finish at the same location. Check newspapers or call the trust for the meeting place.

HORSEBACK RIDING A ride through the hilly north country or along the beach is exhilarating, and equestrian tours can accommodate any level of experience. The **Caribbean International Riding Center** (⊠ Cleland Plantation, St. Andrew ☎ 246/422–7433) offers 1½-hour rides through the Scotland District and 2½-hour treks that continue on to Morgan Lewis Beach, on the Atlantic coast. Prices range from $60 to $90; helmets are compulsory and provided.

HORSE RACING Horse racing is administered by the **Barbados Turf Club** (☎ 246/426–3980) and takes place on alternate Saturdays throughout the year at the Garrison Savannah, a six-furlong grass oval in Christ Church, about 3 mi (5 km) south of Bridgetown. The important races are the Sandy Lane Barbados Cup in February and the United Insurance Barbados Derby Day in August. Post time is at 1:30 PM. General admission is $5 for grandstand seats and $12.50 for the Club House. (Prices are double on Gold Cup day.)

PARASAILING Parasailing is available, wind conditions permitting, on the beaches of St. James and Christ Church. The chute is attached to a speedboat with a launching and landing platform; a hydraulic winch system hauls you in simply and safely. You don't even have to get wet! *The Falcon* **Parasail** (☎ 246/419–0579) picks people up all along the beach on either coast, or you can book ahead. Rates are $45 to $60 per person.

POLO Polo matches are inexpensive (about $2.50) and are played at the **Barbados Polo Club** (⊠ Holder's Hill, St. James ☎ 246/427–6022) on Wednesday and Saturday from October through April.

RUGBY The rough-and-tumble game of rugby is played Tuesday and Thursday evenings at the Garrison Savannah, 3 mi (5 km) south of Bridgetown. Touring teams are always welcome to visit the clubhouse and join in the customary social activity. For schedules, call the **Barbados Rugby Football Union** (☎ 246/437–3836).

SCUBA DIVING & SNORKELING More than two dozen dive sites lie along the west coast between Maycocks Bay and Bridgetown and off the south coast as far as the St.

Lawrence Gap. Certified divers can explore flat coral reefs and see sea fans and corals, huge barrel sponges, and more than 50 varieties of fish. Nine sunken wrecks are dived regularly, and at least 10 more are accessible to experts. Underwater visibility is generally 80–90 ft. The calm waters along the west coast are also ideal for snorkeling. The marine reserve, a stretch of protected reef between Sandy Lane and the Colony Club, contains beautiful coral formations accessible from the beach.

On the west coast, **Bell Buoy** is a large dome-shape reef where huge brown coral tree forests and schools of fish delight all categories of divers at depths ranging from 20 to 60 ft. At **Dottins Reef,** off Holetown, you can see schooling fish, barracudas, and turtles at depths of 40–60 ft. **Maycocks Bay,** on the northwest coast, is a particularly enticing site; large coral reefs are separated by corridors of white sand, and visibility is often 100 ft or more. The 165-ft freighter *Pamir* lies in 60 ft of water off Six Men's Bay; it is still intact, and you can peer through its portholes and view dozens of varieties of tropical fish. **Silver Bank** is a healthy coral reef with beautiful fish and sea fans; you may get a glimpse of the *Atlantis* submarine at 60–80 ft. Not to be missed is the *Stavronikita,* a scuttled Greek freighter at about 135 ft; hundreds of butterfly fish hang out around its mast, and the thin rays of sunlight filtering down through the water make fully exploring the huge ship a wonderfully eerie experience.

Farther south, **Carlisle Bay** is a natural harbor and marine park just below Bridgetown. Here you can retrieve empty bottles thrown overboard by generations of sailors and see cannons and cannonballs, anchors, and seven unique shipwrecks (*Berwyn, Fox, CTrek, Eilon,* a barge, *Cornwallis,* and *Bajan Queen*) lying in 25–60 ft of water, all close enough to visit on the same dive. The *Bajan Queen,* a cruise vessel that sank in 2002, is the island's newest wreck.

Dive shops provide a two-hour beginner's "resort" course ($70–$75) or a weeklong certification course (about $350), followed by a shallow dive. Once you're certified, a one-tank dive runs about $50–$55; a two-tank dive is $70–$80. All equipment is supplied, and you can purchase multidive packages. Gear for snorkeling is available (free or for a small rental fee) from most hotels. Snorkelers can usually accompany dive trips for $20 for a one- or two-hour trip.

On the south coast, **Dive Boat Safari** (✉ Grand Barbados Beach Resort, Aquatic Gap, St. Michael ☎ 246/427–4350) offers three dives daily and full instruction. **Dive Shop, Ltd.** (✉ Aquatic Gap, St. Michael ☎ 246/426–9947; 888/898–3483 in the U.S.; 888/575–3483 in Canada), the island's oldest dive shop, offers three dives daily, beginner dives, and certification. Underwater camera rentals are available.

On the west coast, **Dive Barbados** (✉ Mount Standfast, St. James ☎ 246/422–3133) offers all levels of PADI instruction, reef and wreck dives, underwater camera rental, and free transportation. **Hightide Watersports** (✉ Coral Reef Club, Holetown, St. James ☎ 246/432–0931 or 800/513–5763) offers one- and two-tank dives, night reef/wreck/drift dives, PADI instruction, equipment rental, and free transportation.

SEA EXCURSIONS   Minisubmarine voyages are enormously popular with families and those who enjoy watching fish but can't snorkel or dive. Party boats depart from Bridgetown's Deep Water Harbour for lunchtime snorkeling or sunset cruises. Prices are $65 per person and include transportation to and from the dock.

The 48-passenger *Atlantis III* (✉ The Shallow Draught, Bridgetown ☎ 246/436–8929 ⊕ www.atlantisadventures.net) turns the Caribbean into a giant aquarium. The 45-minute trip aboard the 50-ft submarine takes you to wrecks and reefs as deep as 150 ft. Cost for the trip is $80 per person.

A five-hour cruise on the 54-ft catamaran *Cool Runnings* (☎ 246/436–0911) includes stops along the coast for snorkeling on a coral reef, exploring a shallow shipwreck, and visiting sea turtles in a quiet bay; lunch is served on board. The 44-ft CSY sailing yacht *Limbo Lady* (☎ 246/420–5418) sails along the captivating west coast, stopping for a swim, snorkeling, and a Bajan buffet lunch. Sunset cruises are another option. *Secret Love* (☎ 246/432–1972), a 41-ft Morgan sailboat, offers daily lunchtime or evening snorkeling cruises for no more than 14 people. The 53-ft catamaran *Tiami* (☎ 246/430–0900) offers an early-morning breakfast cruise, a luncheon cruise to a secluded bay, or a romantic sunset and moonlight cruise with special catering and live music; all cruises last four hours. Four- and five-hour daytime cruises along the west coast on the 100-ft MV *Harbour Master* (☎ 246/430–0900) stop in Holetown and land at beaches along the way; evening cruises are shorter but add a buffet dinner and entertainment. Day or night you can view the briny deep from the ship's onboard 34-seat semisubmersible. Either cruise runs about $65 per person. The red-sail *Jolly Roger* (☎ 246/430–0900) "pirate" ship runs lunch-and-snorkeling sails along the south or west coasts. Be prepared for a rather raucous time, with rope swinging, plank walking, and other games—and plenty of calypso music. The cruise costs about $65 per person, with complimentary drinks.

SOCCER   The football (soccer) season runs January–June at the National Stadium. For game information contact the **Barbados Football Association** (☎ 246/228–1707).

SURFING   The best surfing is on the east coast, at Bathsheba Soup Bowl, where the Independence Classic Surfing Championship (an international competition) is held every November—when the surf is at its peak. For information, call the **Barbados Surfing Association** (☎ 246/228–5117).

TENNIS &   On the west coast, public tennis courts are available for free on a first-
SQUASH   come, first-served basis at **Folkestone Marine Park & Visitor Centre** (✉ Holetown ☎ 246/422–2314). On the south coast, the **National Tennis Centre** (✉ Sir Garfield Sobers Sports Complex, Wildey, St. Michael ☎ 246/437–6010) charges $12 per hour and requires reservations. At the **Barbados Squash Club** (✉ Marine House, Hastings, Christ Church ☎ 246/427–7913), court fees run $9 for 45 minutes; matches with players of similar ability can be arranged. At **Club Rockley Barbados** (✉ Golf Club Rd., Rockley, Christ Church ☎ 246/435–7880) nonguests can reserve courts for $14 per hour, plus $9 for night (floodlit) play.

WINDSURFING   Barbados is part of the World Cup Windsurfing Circuit and one of the best locations in the world for windsurfing. Winds are strongest November through April at the island's southern tip, at Silver Sands/Silver Rock Beach, which is where the Barbados Windsurfing Championships are held in mid-January. Use of boards and equipment is often among the amenities included at larger hotels; equipment can usually be rented by nonguests.

Club Mistral (✉ Oistins, Christ Church ☎ 246/428–7277) is a great place to learn to windsurf, because the waves here are usually flat. More experienced windsurfers congregate at **Silver Rock Windsurfing Club** (✉ Silver Rock Hotel, Silver Sands/Silver Rock Beach, Christ Church ☎ 246/428–2866), where the surf ranges from 3 to 15 ft and provides an exhilarating windsurfing experience.

Shopping

Areas & Malls

Bridgetown's **Broad Street** is the downtown shopping area. At the **Cruise Ship Terminal** shopping arcade, passengers can buy both duty-free goods and Barbadian-made crafts at more than 30 boutiques and a dozen vendor carts and stalls. **DaCostas Mall**, in the historic Colonnade Building on Broad Street, has more than 25 shops that sell everything from Piaget to postcards. Across the street from the DaCostas Mall, **Mall 34** has 22 shops where you can buy duty-free goods, souvenirs, and snacks.

Holetown and St. Lawrence Gap each have a **Chattel House Village,** a cluster of brightly colored shops selling local products, fashions, beachwear, and souvenirs. **Sunset Crest,** in Holetown, has a branch of the Cave Shepherd department store, a bank, a pharmacy, and several small shops. In Holetown's **West Coast Mall,** you can find duty-free goods, island wear, services, and groceries. The **Quayside Shopping Center,** in Rockley, Christ Church, houses a small group of boutiques.

Department Stores

Cave Shepherd (⊠ Broad St., Bridgetown, St. Michael ☎ 246/431–2121) offers a wide selection of clothing and luxury goods; branch stores are in Holetown, at the airport, and in the Cruise Ship Terminal. **Harrison's** (⊠ Broad St., Bridgetown, St. Michael ☎ 246/431–5500) has 11 locations—including its two large stores on Broad Street and one each at the airport and the Cruise Ship Terminal—offering luxury name-brand goods from the fashion corners of the world.

Specialty Items

ANTIQUES In Barbados you can find British antiques as well as wonderful local pieces—particularly mahogany furniture. Look for planters' chairs and the classic Barbadian rocking chair, as well as old prints and paintings. **Greenwich House Antiques** (⊠ Greenwich Village, Trents Hill, St. James ☎ 246/432–1169) fills an entire plantation house with Barbadian mahogany furniture, crystal, silver, china, books, and pictures; it's open daily 10:30–5:30.

CLOTHES Dresses and resort wear are often handmade of hand-printed fabrics. **Del Sol** (⊠ Galleria Mall, Broad St., Bridgetown, St. Michael ☎ 246/431–0678) has unique shirts, hats, other apparel, and accessories. The designs appear black and white indoors but change to bright colors when exposed to the sun. **Dingolay** (⊠ Bay St., Bridgetown, St. Michael ☎ 246/436–2157 ⊠ Hwy. 1, Holetown, St. James ☎ 246/432–8709) sells tropical clothing designed and made in Barbados for ladies and girls, as well as shoes, handbags, and accessories from around the world. Check out the colorful T-shirts from **Irie Blue** (⊠ DaCostas Mall, Broad St., Bridgetown, St. Michael ☎ 246/431–0017 ⊠ Worthing, Christ Church ☎ 246/435–7699), which are designed and made in Barbados. You can find them in many gift shops as well. **Sandbox & Co.** (⊠ Bell House, Sunbury Plantation, St. Philip ☎ 246/423–0888) offers original designs of swimwear, resort wear, children's clothing, and home furnishings—all made and hand-painted in Barbados.

DUTY-FREE GOODS Duty-free luxury goods—china, crystal, cameras, porcelain, leather items, electronics, jewelry, perfume, and clothing—are found in Bridgetown's Broad Street department stores and their branches, at the Cruise Ship Terminal shops (for passengers only), and in the departure lounge shops at Grantley Adams International Airport. Prices are often 30% to 40% less than at home. To buy goods at duty-free prices, you must produce your outbound travel ticket and passport at the time of purchase—or you can have your purchases delivered free to the airport or harbor for pickup. Duty-free alcohol, tobacco products, and some electronic equipment *must* be delivered to you at the airport or harbor.

Little Switzerland (⊠ DaCostas Mall, Broad St., Bridgetown, St. Michael ☎ 246/431–0030) is the anchor shop at DaCostas Mall and has a branch at the Cruise Ship Terminal. Here you can find perfume, jewelry, cameras, audio equipment, Swarovski and Waterford crystal, and Wedgwood china. The **Royal Shop** (⊠ 32 Broad St., Bridgetown ☎ 246/429–7072) carries fine watches and jewelry fashioned in Italian gold, Caribbean silver, diamonds, and other gems.

HANDICRAFTS Typical crafts include pottery, shell and glass art, hand-printed fabrics, handmade dolls, watercolors, and other artwork (both originals and prints). The **Best of Barbados** (⊠ Worthing, Christ Church ☎ 246/421–6900), which has a total of seven locations, offers high-quality artwork and crafts in both "native" style and modern designs; everything is made or designed on Barbados. **Earthworks Pottery** (⊠ No. 2, Edgehill Heights, St. Thomas ☎ 246/425–0223) is a family-owned and -operated pottery where you can purchase anything from a dish or knickknack to a complete dinner service or one-of-a-kind art piece. The products are sold in gift shops throughout the island, but the biggest selection is at the pottery, where you also can watch the potters work. **Island Crafts** (⊠ 5 Pelican Craft Centre, Bridgetown, St. Michael ☎ 246/426–4391) offers locally made pottery, wood carvings, straw items, glass art, batik, and wire sculptures. Additional shops are at Harrison's Cave, the airport courtyard, and the airport departure lounge. **Pelican Craft Centre** (⊠ Harbour Rd., Bridgetown, St. Michael ☎ 246/427–5350) is a cluster of workshops halfway between the Cruise Ship Terminal and downtown Bridgetown, where craftspeople create and sell "100% Barbadian-made" leather goods, batik, basketry, carvings, jewelry, glass art, paintings, pottery, and other items. It's open weekdays 9–6 and Saturday 9–2, with extended hours during holidays or to accommodate cruiseship arrivals. **Redclay Pottery** (⊠ Fairfield Cross Rd., Fairfield, St. Michael ☎ 246/426–3800) is in an old syrup boiling house 2 mi (3 km) from Bridgetown. Each piece here is handcrafted of local clay and individually painted; call for a tour of the works. Products are for sale on-site and in island gift shops. In the chattel houses at **Tyrol Cot Heritage Village** (⊠ Codrington Hill, St. Michael ☎ 246/424–2074) you can watch local artisans make hand-painted figurines, straw baskets, clothing, paintings, pottery, etc.—and, of course, buy their wares.

Nightlife & the Arts

Nightlife

When the sun goes down, the musicians come out and folks in Barbados "lime" (which can be anything from a "chat-up" to a full-blown "jump-up"). Performances by reggae groups and calypso singers are major events, and tickets can be hard to come by—but give it a try. Most large resorts have nightly entertainment in season, and nightclubs often have live bands for listening and dancing. The busiest bars and dance clubs rage until 3 AM. On Saturday nights, some clubs—especially those with live music—charge a cover of about $10.

★ The **Oistins Fish Fry** is the place to be on weekend evenings, when the south coast fishing village becomes an outdoor street fair. Barbecued chicken and flying fish are served right from the coal pot; servings are huge and inexpensive—about $5. Drinks, music, and dancing add to the fun.

BARS   Barbados supports the rum industry with more than 1,600 "rum shops," simple bars where men (mostly) congregate to discuss the world's ills, and in more sophisticated inns, where you find world-class rum drinks made with the island's renowned Mount Gay and Cockspur brands.

The **Boatyard** (✉ Bay St., Bridgetown, St. Michael ☎ 246/436–2622) is a pub with both a DJ and live bands; from happy hour until the wee hours, the patrons are mostly local and visiting professionals. **Waterfront Cafe** (✉ The Careenage, Bridgetown, St. Michael ☎ 246/427–0093) has live jazz in the evening, with a small dance floor for dancing. The picturesque location alongside the wharf is also a draw.

On the south coast, **Café Sol** (✉ St. Lawrence Gap, Dover, Christ Church ☎ 246/435–9531) has a wraparound terrace with a great view of the St. Lawrence Gap strip. Margaritas (rubbed with sugar not salt) will fortify you for the late-night complimentary Spanish dance lessons. **Champers** (✉ Hwy. 1, Hastings, Christ Church ☎ 246/435–6644) is a waterfront wine bar, where folks gather for good conversation, a great view, snacks, and a selection from the extensive wine list.

On the west coast, **Coach House** (✉ Hwy. 1, Paynes Bay, St. James ☎ 246/432–1163) has live entertainment nightly and live sports via satellite TV. **Upstairs at Olives** (✉ 2nd St., Holetown, St. James ☎ 246/432–2112) is a sophisticated watering hole. Enjoy cocktails and conversation seated amid potted palms and cooled by ceiling fans—either before or after dinner downstairs.

DANCE CLUBS   **After Dark** (✉ St. Lawrence Gap, Dover, Christ Church ☎ 246/435–6547) attracts mostly young people to live appearances of reggae, calypso, and *soca* (an upbeat, sexy variation of calypso) headliners such as Krosfyah and Red Plastic Bag. **Harbour Lights** (✉ Marine Villa, Bay St., Bridgetown, St. Michael ☎ 246/436–7225) claims to be the "home of the party animal" and, most any night, there is dancing under the stars to live reggae and soca music. The **Ship Inn** (✉ St. Lawrence Gap, Dover, Christ Church ☎ 246/435–6961) is a large, friendly pub with local band music every night for dancing.

THEME NIGHTS   On Wednesday and Friday evenings at the **Plantation Restaurant and Garden Theater** (✉ St. Lawrence Rd., Dover, Christ Church ☎ 246/428–5048), the Tropical Spectacular calypso cabaret presents dancing, fire eating, limbo, steel-band music, and the sounds of a top reggae and soca band. The fun begins at 6:30 PM. A Barbadian buffet dinner, unlimited drinks, transportation, and the show cost $75; for the show and drinks only, it's $37.50.

The Arts

THEATER   Every Thursday and Sunday night, 6:30–10, the folkloric show *1627 and All That* (✉ Barbados Museum, Hwy. 7, Garrison, St. Michael ☎ 246/428–1627) traces island culture from colonization through slavery and emancipation to the present time. It's performed by energetic dancers dressed in period costumes and accompanied by lively steel-band music. Unlimited complimentary drinks are included; pay more for a Bajan buffet dinner and transportation. Admission is $27.50 for the show and drinks; $60 for the show, drinks, dinner, and transportation. Major credit cards are accepted.

Exploring Barbados

The terrain changes dramatically from one of the island's 11 parishes to the next, and so does the pace. Bridgetown, the capital, is a rather sophisticated city. West coast resorts and private estates ooze luxury, whereas the small villages and vast sugar plantations found throughout central Barbados retain the island's history. The relentless Atlantic surf designed the cliffs of the dramatic east coast, and the northeast is called Scotland because of its hilly landscape. Along the lively south coast there's a palpable energy day and night.

The **Barbados National Trust** (⊠ Wildey House, Wildey, St. Michael ☎ 246/426–2421) has designed a Heritage Passport to some of Barbados's most popular attractions. When the holder pays full admission to visit some attractions, the passport will be stamped to validate free admission to other sights. Passports are free, and you can pick them up at displays in shops, hotels, and restaurants.

Bridgetown

This bustling capital city is a major duty-free port with a compact shopping area. The principal thoroughfare is Broad Street, which leads west from National Heroes Square. Bridgetown, surprisingly enough, has both rush hours and traffic congestion.

Numbers in the margin correspond to points of interest on the Bridgetown map.

WHAT TO SEE

① **Barbados Synagogue.** Providing for the spiritual needs of one of the oldest Jewish congregations in the Western Hemisphere, this synagogue was formed by Jews who left Brazil in the 1620s and introduced sugarcane to Barbados. The adjoining cemetery has tombstones dating from the 1630s. The original house of worship, built in 1654, was destroyed in an 1831 hurricane. The synagogue was rebuilt in 1833 and restored by the Barbados National Trust in 1992. Services are held, and the building is open to the public. ⊠ *Synagogue La., St. Michael* ☎ *246/426–5792* ☜ *Donation requested* ☉ *Weekdays 9–4.*

② **The Careenage.** Bridgetown's natural harbor and gathering place is where, in the early days, schooners were careened (turned on their sides) to be scraped of barnacles and repainted. Today the Careenage serves as a marina for pleasure yachts and excursion boats. The Chamberlain Bridge and the Charles Duncan O'Neal Bridge cross the Careenage.

③ **National Heroes Square.** Across Broad Street from the Parliament Buildings and bordered by High and Trafalgar streets, this triangular "square" (formerly called Trafalgar Square) marks the center of town. Its monument to Lord Horatio Nelson (although Nelson was in Barbados only briefly in 1777, when he was a 19-year-old navy lieutenant) predates Nelson's Column in London's Trafalgar Square by 36 years. Also here are a war memorial and a fountain that commemorates the advent of running water on Barbados in 1865.

④ **Parliament Buildings.** Overlooking National Heroes Square in the center of town, these Victorian buildings were built around 1870 to house the British Commonwealth's third-oldest parliament. A series of stained-glass windows depicts British monarchs from James I to Victoria. There are twice-daily tours when parliament is not sitting (call ahead to confirm). ⊠ *Broad St., St. Michael* ☎ *246/427–2019* ☜ *Donations welcome* ☉ *Tours weekdays (when parliament isn't in session) at 11 and 2.*

⑥ **Queen's Park.** Northeast of Bridgetown, Queen's Park contains one of the island's largest trees, an immense baobab more than 10 centuries old. Queen's Park Art Gallery, managed by the National Culture Foundation, is the island's largest gallery; exhibits change monthly. Queen's Park House, the historic home of the British troop commander, has been converted into a theater, with an exhibition room on the lower floor and

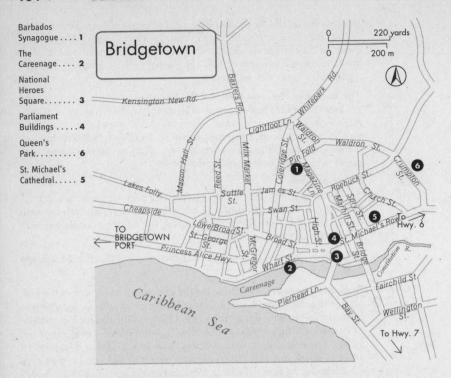

a restaurant. ⊠ *Constitution Rd., St. Michael* ☎ *246/427–2345 for gallery* 🎟 *Free* ☉ *Daily 9–5.*

❺ St. Michael's Cathedral. Although no one has proved it conclusively, George Washington, on his only visit outside the United States, is said to have worshipped here in 1751. The original structure was nearly a century old by then. Destroyed twice by hurricanes, it was rebuilt in 1784 and again in 1831. ⊠ *Spry St., east of National Heroes Sq., St. Michael.*

Southern Barbados

In Christ Church, which is much busier and more developed than the west coast, there are condos, high-rise hotels, beach parks, and St. Lawrence Gap, with its many places to eat, drink, and shop. Moving southeast, the broad, flat terrain comprises acre upon acre of cane fields, interrupted only by an occasional oil rig and a few tiny villages hugging crossroads. Along the byways are colorful chattel houses, the property of tenant farmers. Historically, these typically Barbadian, ever-expandable houses were built to be dismantled and moved as required.

Numbers in the margin correspond to points of interest on the Barbados map.

WHAT TO SEE   The **Barbados Gallery of Art.** The gallery's permanent collection includes
❼   artwork from the Caribbean, South America, and the United States. ⊠ *The Garrison, Garrison Savannah, St. Michael* ☎ *246/228–0149* 🎟 *$2.50 weekdays, $1 Sat.* ☉ *Sun.–Mon.*

💧❽   **Barbados Museum.** This intriguing museum, in the former British Military Prison (1815) in the historic Garrison area, has artifacts from Arawak days (around 400 BC) and galleries that depict 19th-century military history and everyday life. You can see cane-harvesting tools, wedding dresses, ancient (and frightening) dentistry instruments, and slave sale accounts kept in a spidery copperplate handwriting. The museum's

Harewood Gallery showcases the island's flora and fauna; its Cunard Gallery has a permanent collection of 20th-century Barbadian and Caribbean paintings and engravings; and its Connell Gallery features European decorative arts. Along with other galleries, including one for children, the museum also has a gift shop and a café. ⊠ *Hwy. 7, Garrison Savannah, St. Michael* ☎ *246/427–0201 or 246/436–1956* ⊕ *www. barbmuse.org.bb* ☒ *$6* ⊙ *Mon.–Sat. 9–5, Sun. 2–6.*

⑰ Codrington Theological College. An impressive stand of royal palms lines the road leading to the coral-stone buildings and serene grounds of Codrington College, an Anglican seminary opened in 1745 on a cliff overlooking Consett Bay. You're welcome to tour the buildings and walk the nature trails. Keep in mind, though, that beachwear isn't appropriate here. ⊠ *Sargeant St., Consett Bay, St. John* ☎ *246/433–1274* ⊕ *www.codrington.org* ☒ *$2.50* ⊙ *Daily 10–4.*

⑪ Emancipation Statue. This larger-than-life statue of a slave—with raised hands, evoking both contempt and victory, and broken chains hanging from each wrist—is commonly referred to as the Bussa Statue. Bussa was the man who, in 1816, led the first slave rebellion in Barbados. The statue, the work of Barbadian sculptor Karl Brodhagen, was erected in 1985 to commemorate the emancipation of the slaves in 1834. It is all the more poignant in that it overlooks a broad cane field just outside Bridgetown. ⊠ *St. Barnabas Roundabout, intersection of ABC Hwy. and Hwy. 5, Haggatt Hall, St. Michael.*

⑨ Harry Bayley Observatory. Built in 1963, this is the headquarters of the Barbados Astronomical Society. The observatory, equipped with a 14-inch reflector telescope, is the only one in the Eastern Caribbean. ⊠ *Off Hwy. 6, Clapham, St. Michael* ☎ *246/426–1317 or 246/422–2394* ☒ *$4* ⊙ *Fri. 8:30 AM–11:30 PM.*

⑮ Rum Factory and Heritage Park. A long road through acres of cane fields brings you to the first rum distillery to be built in Barbados in the 20th century. Situated on a 350-year-old sugar plantation, the spotless, environmentally friendly, high-tech distillery produces ESA Field white rum and premium Alleyne Arthur varieties. Adjacent is the 7-acre Heritage Park, which showcases Bajan skills and talents in its Art Foundry and Cane Pit Amphitheatre; a row of shops and vendor carts is filled with local products, crafts, and foods. ⊠ *Foursquare Plantation, St. Philip* ☎ *246/420–1977* ☒ *$5* ⊙ *Daily 9–5.*

⑯ Sam Lord's Castle. The Regency house, built in 1820 by the buccaneer Sam Lord, is considered one of the island's finest houses. Now the centerpiece of a resort, the opulent mansion has double verandahs and magnificent plaster ceilings created by Charles Rutter, who also crafted some of the ceilings in England's Windsor Castle. Rooms are filled with fine mahogany furniture and gilt mirrors that Sam Lord is reputed to have pillaged from passing ships. It's said he lured them onto treacherous reefs just offshore by hanging lanterns in palm trees to simulate harbor lights. ⊠ *Long Bay, St. Philip* ☎ *246/423–7350* ⊕ *www. samlordscastle.com* ☒ *$5; hotel guests free* ⊙ *Daily 10–4.*

⑭ Sunbury Plantation House & Museum. Lovingly rebuilt after a 1995 fire destroyed everything but the thick flint-and-stone walls of this 300-year-old plantation house, Sunbury offers an elegant glimpse of the 18th and 19th centuries on a Barbadian sugar estate. Period furniture, old prints, and a collection of horse-drawn carriages have been donated to lend an air of authenticity. Luncheon is served in the back garden. ⊠ *Off Hwy. 5, Six Cross Roads, St. Philip* ☎ *246/423–6270* ⊕ *www. barbadosgreathouse.com* ☒ *$6* ⊙ *Daily 10–5.*

🐾 ⑩ **Tyrol Cot Heritage Village.** This interesting coral-stone cottage just south of Bridgetown was constructed in 1854 and has been preserved as an example of period architecture. In 1929 it became the home of Sir Grantley Adams, the first premier of Barbados. Part of the Barbados National Trust, the cottage is now filled with antiques and memorabilia of the late Sir Grantley and Lady Adams. It's the centerpiece of an outdoor "living" museum of colorful chattel houses, each with a traditional artisan or craftsman at work inside. The crafts are for sale, and refreshments are available at the "rum shop." ⊠ *Rte. 2, Codrington Hill, St. Michael* ☎ *246/424-2074 or 246/436-9033* ☜ *$6* ☉ *Weekdays 9-5.*

Central Barbados

On the west coast, in St. James Parish, Holetown is the center of the Platinum Coast—so called for the vast number of luxurious resorts and mansions that face the sea. Holetown is also where British captain John Powell landed in 1625 to claim the island for King James. On the east coast, the crashing Atlantic surf has eroded the shoreline, forming steep cliffs and rocks that look like giant mushrooms. Bathsheba and Cattlewash are favorite local seacoast destinations on weekends and holidays. In the interior, narrow roads weave through tiny villages and along and between the ridges. The landscape is covered with tropical vegetation and riddled with fascinating caves and gullies.

WHAT TO SEE **Andromeda Gardens.** An intriguing collection of unusual and beautiful
★ ⑱ plant specimens from around the world is cultivated in 6 acres of gardens nestled between streams, ponds, and rocky outcroppings overlooking the sea above the Bathsheba coastline. The gardens were created in 1954 with flowering plants collected by the late horticulturist Iris Bannochie. They're now administered by the Barbados National Trust. The Hibiscus Café serves snacks and drinks. ⊠ *Bathsheba, St. Joseph* ☎ *246/433-9261* ☜ *$6* ☉ *Daily 9-5.*

⑲ **Barclays Park.** Straddling the Ermy Bourne Highway, just north of Bathsheba, this public park was donated by Barclays Bank. Pack a picnic or stop at the popular bar-restaurant and enjoy lunch with a gorgeous ocean view.

⑳ **Chalky Mount.** A handful of potters have workshops in this tiny east coast village, high in the hills that produce the clay that has supplied potters for 300 years. The potteries are open daily to visitors. You can watch as artisans create bowls, vases, candleholders, and decorative objects that they, of course, offer for sale.

㉖ **Flower Forest.** It's a treat to meander among fragrant flowering bushes, canna and ginger lilies, puffball trees, and more than 100 other species of tropical flora in a cool, tranquil forest of flowers and other plants. A ½-mi-long (1-km-long) path winds through the 50 acres of grounds, a former sugar plantation; it takes about 30–45 minutes to follow the path, or you can wander freely for as long as you wish. Seats, where you can pause and reflect, are located throughout the forest. There are also a snack bar, gift shop, and beautiful view of Mt. Hillaby. ⊠ *Hwy. 2, Richmond Plantation, St. Joseph* ☎ *246/433-8152* ☜ *$7* ☉ *Daily 9-5.*

🐾 ㉕ **Folkestone Marine Park & Visitor Centre.** Both on land and offshore, the whole family will enjoy this park just north of Holetown. The museum and aquarium illuminate some of the island's marine life; and for some firsthand viewing, there's an underwater snorkeling trail around Dottin's Reef (glass-bottom boats are available for nonswimmers). A barge sunk in shallow water is home to myriad fish, making it a popular dive site. ⊠ *Church Point, Holetown, St. James* ☎ *246/422-2314* ☜ *Free* ☉ *Weekdays 9-5.*

⑫ **Francia Plantation House.** Built of large coral-stone blocks in 1913, this great house blends French, Brazilian, and Caribbean architectural influences. You can tour the house (descendents of the original owner still live here) and gardens. Most of the antique furniture was made in Barbados of local mahogany; 17th- and 18th-century maps, watercolors, and prints grace the walls. ⌂ *Gun Hill, St. George* ☎ *246/429–0474* ⌨ *$5* ⊙ *Weekdays 10–4.*

★ ⌚ ⑬ **Gun Hill Signal Station.** The 360° view from Gun Hill, 700 ft above sea level, was what made this location of strategic importance to the 18th-century British army. Using lanterns and semaphores, soldiers based here could communicate with their counterparts at The Garrison, on the south coast, and at Grenade Hill in the north. Time moved slowly in 1868, and Captain Henry Wilkinson whiled away his off-duty hours by carving a huge lion from a single rock—which is on the hillside just below the tower. Come for a short history lesson but mainly for the view; it's so gorgeous, military invalids were once sent here to convalesce. ⌂ *Gun Hill, St. George* ☎ *246/429–1358* ⌨ *$5* ⊙ *Weekdays 9–5.*

⌚ ㉘ **Harrison's Cave.** This limestone cavern, complete with stalactites, stalagmites, subterranean streams, and a 40-ft waterfall, is a rare find in the Caribbean—and one of Barbados's most popular attractions. The one-hour tours are on electric trams, which fill up fast; reserve ahead of time. Hard hats are required and provided, but all that may fall on you is a little dripping water. ⌂ *Hwy. 2, Welchman Hall, St. Thomas* ☎ *246/438–6640* ⌨ *$12.50* ⊙ *Daily 9–6; last tour at 4.*

Fodor's Choice
★

㉙ **Malibu Visitor Centre.** Just north of Bridgetown, the fun-loving Malibu Rum people encourage those taking the distillery tour to make a day of it. The beach and water sports are adjacent to the Visitor Centre. Lunch and drinks are served at the beachside grill. ⌂ *Black Rock, Brighton, St. Michael* ☎ *246/425–9393* ⌨ *$7.50; $27.50 with lunch; $37.50 day pass* ⊙ *Weekdays 9–5.*

★ ㉚ **Mount Gay Rum Visitors Centre.** On this popular 45-minute tour you learn the colorful story behind the world's oldest rum—made in Barbados for more than 300 years. Although the distillery is in the north—in St. Lucy Parish—tour guides explain the rum-making procedure. Historic and modern equipment are on display, and rows and rows of barrels are stored in this location. The tour concludes with a tasting and an opportunity to buy bottles of rum and gift items. ⌂ *Spring Garden Hwy., Brandons, St. Michael* ☎ *246/425–8757* ⊕ *www.mountgay.com* ⌨ *$6; $27.50 with lunch* ⊙ *Weekdays 9–4.*

㉗ **Welchman Hall Gully.** This 1-mi-long (2-km-long) natural gully is really a collapsed limestone cavern, once part of the same underground network as Harrison's Cave. The Barbados National Trust protects the peace and quiet here, making it a beautiful place to hike past acres of labeled flowers and stands of trees. You can see and hear some interesting birds and, with luck, a native green monkey. ⌂ *Welchman Hall, St. Thomas* ☎ *246/438–6671* ⌨ *$6* ⊙ *Daily 9–5.*

Northern Barbados

Speightstown, the north's commercial center and once a thriving port city, now relies on quaint local shops and informal restaurants. Many of Speightstown's 19th-century buildings, with typical overhanging balconies, have been or are being restored. The island's northernmost reaches, St. Peter and St. Lucy parishes, are varied and lovely. Between the tiny fishing towns along the northwestern coast and the sweeping views out over the Atlantic to the east are forest and farm, moor and mountain. Most guides include a loop through this area on a daylong island tour—it's a beautiful drive.

WHAT TO SEE **Animal Flower Cave.** Small sea anemones, or sea worms, resemble jewel-like flowers when they open their tiny tentacles. They live in small pools—some large enough to swim in—in this cave at the island's very northern tip. The view of breaking waves from inside the cave is magnificent. ⊠ *North Point, St. Lucy* ☎ *246/439–8797* 🖃 *$2* 🕙 *Daily 9–4.*

Barbados Wildlife Reserve. The reserve is the habitat of herons, innumerable land turtles, screeching peacocks, shy deer, elusive green monkeys, brilliantly colored parrots (in a large walk-in aviary), a snake, and a caiman. The animals run or fly freely, except for the snake and caiman, so step carefully and keep your hands to yourself. Late afternoon is your best chance to catch a glimpse of a green monkey. ⊠ *Farley Hill, St. Peter* ☎ *246/422–8826* 🖃 *$11.50* 🕙 *Daily 10–5.*

Farley Hill. At this national park in northern St. Peter, across the road from the Barbados Wildlife Reserve, the imposing ruins of a plantation great house are surrounded by gardens and lawns, along with an avenue of towering royal palms and gigantic mahogany, whitewood, and casuarina trees. Partially rebuilt for the filming of *Island in the Sun*, the classic 1957 film starring Harry Belafonte and Dorothy Dandridge, the structure was later destroyed by fire. Behind the estate, there's a sweeping view of the region called Scotland for its rugged landscape. ⊠ *Farley Hill, St. Peter* ☎ *246/422–3555* 🖃 *$1.50 per car; walkers free* 🕙 *Daily 8:30–6.*

★ **St. Nicholas Abbey.** There's no religious connection at all. The island's oldest great house (circa 1650) was named after the British owner's hometown, St. Nicholas parish near Bristol, and Bath Abbey nearby. Its stone-and-wood architecture makes it one of only three original Jacobean-style houses still standing in the Western Hemisphere. It has Dutch gables, finials of coral stone, and beautiful grounds. The first floor, fully furnished with period furniture and portraits of family members, is open to the public. Fascinating home movies, shot by the current owner's father, record Bajan life in the 1930s. The Calabash Café, in the rear, serves snacks, lunch, and afternoon tea. ⊠ *Cherry Tree Hill, St. Lucy* ☎ *246/422–8725* 🖃 *$5* 🕙 *Weekdays 10–3:30.*

BARBADOS A TO Z

To research prices, get advice from other travelers, and book travel arrangements, visit www.fodors.com.

AIR TRAVEL

Several international carriers serve Barbados from North America and Europe. Air Canada flies nonstop from Toronto and Montréal. Air Jamaica has nonstop service from New York and from other cities through its Montego Bay hub. American Airlines has nonstop service from New York and Miami and direct service from other U.S. cities, connecting with American Eagle in San Juan. British Airways offers daily service from London, as well as limited Concorde service. BWIA flies nonstop from New York and Miami and from Washington Dulles several times a week; the airline also has weekly flights from Toronto and thrice-weekly flights from the United Kingdom through Trinidad. US Airways has daily nonstop service from Philadelphia. Virgin Atlantic flies nonstop from London Gatwick.

Barbados is also well connected to other Caribbean destinations. BWIA Express flies from Antigua, Grenada, Guyana, Jamaica, St. Lucia, St.

Maarten, St. Vincent, and Trinidad and Tobago. Caribbean Star offers frequent daily service between its Barbados hub and Antigua, St. Maarten, Grenada, St. Vincent, and Dominica. LIAT connects Barbados with Anguilla, Antigua, Dominica, Grenada, Guadeloupe, Guyana, Martinique, Puerto Rico, St. Croix, St. Kitts and Nevis, St. Lucia, St. Maarten, St. Thomas, Trinidad and Tobago, and St. Vincent and the Grenadines. Mustique Airways links Barbados with St. Vincent and the Grenadines (Bequia, Canouan, Carriacou, Mustique, and Union) on scheduled shared-charter flights. SVG Air flies between Barbados and St. Vincent and the Grenadines. Trans Island Air 2000 flies regional shared charters between Barbados and the Grenadines.

✈ **Air Canada** ☎ 246/428-5077. **Air Jamaica** ☎ 246/420-1956 or 800/523-5585. **American Airlines** ☎ 246/428-4170. **British Airways** ☎ 246/436-6413. **BWIA/BWIA Express** ☎ 246/426-2111 or 800/538-2942. **Caribbean Star** ☎ 268/431-0540. **LIAT** ☎ 246/434-5428. **Mustique Airways** ☎ 246/428-1638. **SVG Air** ☎ 784/457-5124. **Trans Island Air 2000** ☎ 246/418-1654. **US Airways** ☎ 800/622-1015. **Virgin Atlantic** ☎ 246/228-4886 or 800/744-7477.

AIRPORTS

Grantley Adams International Airport, a major hub for airlines serving Eastern Caribbean destinations, is situated in Christ Church Parish, on the south coast. It's a large, modern facility; taxis and other ground transportation (such as vans from hotels that provide airport transfers) are available immediately upon exiting the customs area. The airport is about 15 minutes from hotels situated along the south coast, 45 minutes from the west coast, and about 30 minutes from Bridgetown.

Note that airport taxis aren't metered, but fares are regulated (about $28 to Speightstown, $20–$22 to west coast hotels, $10–$13 to south coast ones). Be sure, however, to establish the fare before getting into the cab and confirm whether the price quoted is in U.S. or Barbadian dollars.

✈ **Grantley Adams International Airport** ☎ 246/428-7101.

BOAT & FERRY TRAVEL

Half the annual visitors to Barbados are cruise passengers. Bridgetown's Deep Water Harbour is on the northwest side of Carlisle Bay, and up to eight cruise ships can dock at the Cruise Ship Terminal. Downtown Bridgetown is a ½-mi (1-km) walk from the pier; a taxi costs about $3 each way.

BUSINESS HOURS

BANKS Banks are open Monday–Thursday 8–3, Friday 8–5 (some branches in supermarkets are open Saturday morning 9–noon). At the airport, the Barbados National Bank is open from 8 AM until the last plane leaves or arrives, seven days a week (including holidays).

POST OFFICES The general post office, in Cheapside, Bridgetown, is open weekdays 7:30–5; the Sherbourne Conference Center branch is open weekdays 8:15–4:30 during conferences; and branches in each parish are open weekdays 8–3:15.

SHOPS Most stores in Bridgetown are open weekdays 8:30–5, Saturday 8:30–1. Out-of-town locations may stay open later. Some supermarkets are open daily 8–6 or later.

BUS TRAVEL

Bus service is efficient, inexpensive, and plentiful. Blue buses with a yellow stripe are public, yellow buses with a blue stripe are private, and private "Zed-R" vans (so called for their ZR license plate designation) are white with a maroon stripe. All buses travel frequently along Highway 1 (St. James Road) and Highway 7 (South Coast Main Road), as well as inland routes. The fare is Bds$1.50 (75¢) for any one destination; exact change in either currency is appreciated. Buses pass along main roads about every 20 minutes. Stops are marked by small signs on roadside poles that say TO CITY or OUT OF CITY, meaning the direction relative to Bridgetown. Flag down the bus with your hand, even if you're standing at the stop. Bridgetown terminals are at Fairchild Street for buses to the south and east and at Lower Green for buses to Speightstown via the west coast.

CAR RENTALS

To rent a car in Barbados, you must have a valid driver's license and major credit card. More than 75 agencies rent cars, Jeeps, or minimokes (small, open-air vehicles), and rates are expensive—an average $105 a day (or $400 a week), depending on the vehicle and whether it has airconditioning. Most firms also offer discounted three-day rates. The rental generally includes insurance, pickup and delivery service, maps, 24-hour emergency service, and unlimited mileage. Baby seats are usually available upon request.

🛈 **Coconut Car Rentals** ⊠ Bay St., Bridgetown, St. Michael ☎ 246/437-0297. **Corbins Car Rentals** ⊠ Upper Collymore Rock, Bridgetown, St. Michael ☎ 246/427-9531. **Courtesy Rent-A-Car** ⊠ Grantley Adams International Airport, Christ Church ☎ 246/418-2500. **Drive-a-Matic** ⊠ Lower Carlton, St. James ☎ 246/422-3000. **National Car Rentals** ⊠ Lower Carlton, St. James ☎ 246/426-0603. **Sunny Isle Sixt Car Rentals** ⊠ Worthing, Christ Church ☎ 246/435-7979. **Sunset Crest Car Rental** ⊠ Sunset Crest, Holetown, St. James ☎ 246/432-2222.

CAR TRAVEL

If you are staying in a remote location, such as the east coast, you will find it practical to rent a car for the duration of your stay. Folks staying in more populated areas, where taxis and public transportation are available at the door, might rent a car or minimoke for a day or two of exploring on their own. Bathing suits and beach towels—and a map—are requisite gear for such an adventure; hotels can supply a picnic lunch.

GASOLINE Gas costs about 80¢ per liter (approximately $3 per gallon), and there are stations in Bridgetown, on the main highways along the west and south coasts, and in most inland parishes. Although times vary, you'll find most open daily with hours that extend into the evening; a few are open 24 hours a day.

ROAD CONDITIONS Barbados has nearly 975 mi (1,570 km) of paved roads that follow the coastline and meander through the countryside. A network of main highways facilitates traffic flow into and out of Bridgetown. The Adams-Barrow-Cummins (ABC) Highway bypasses Bridgetown, which saves time getting from coast to coast. Small signs tacked to trees and poles at intersections point the way to most attractions, and local people are helpful if you get lost. Remote roads are in fairly good repair, yet few are well lighted at night—and night falls quickly at about 6 PM year-round. Even in full daylight, the tall sugarcane fields lining both sides of the road in interior sections can make visibility difficult.

RULES OF THE ROAD Drive on the left, British style. Be mindful of pedestrians and occasional livestock walking on country roads. When someone flashes headlights at you at an intersection, it means "after you." Be especially careful negotiating roundabouts (traffic circles). The speed limit, in keeping with the pace of life and the narrow roads, is 30 mph in the country, 20 mph in town. Bridgetown actually has rush hours: 7–9 and 4–6. Park only in approved parking areas; downtown parking costs Bds75¢–Bds$1 per hour.

ELECTRICITY
Electric current on Barbados is 110 volts/50 cycles, U.S. standard. Hotels generally have adapters/transformers for appliances made in countries that operate on 220-volt current.

EMBASSIES
🄵 Australia **Australian High Commission** ⊠ Bishop's Court Hill, Pine Rd., Bridgetown, St. Michael ☎ 246/435-2834.

🄵 Canada **Canadian High Commission** ⊠ Bishop's Court Hill, Pine Rd., Bridgetown, St. Michael ☎ 246/429-3550.

🄵 United Kingdom **British High Commission** ⊠ Lower Collymore Rock, Bridgetown, St. Michael ☎ 246/430-7800.

🄵 United States **Embassy of the United States** ⊠ Broad St., Bridgetown, St. Michael ☎ 246/436-4950.

EMERGENCIES
🄵 Ambulance **Ambulance** ☎ 511.

🄵 Fire **Fire emergencies** ☎ 311.

🄵 Hospitals **Bayview Hospital** ⊠ St. Paul's Ave., Bayville, St. Michael ☎ 246/436-5446. **Queen Elizabeth Hospital** ⊠ Martindales Rd., Bridgetown, St. Michael ☎ 246/436-6450.

🄵 Pharmacies **Collins Ltd.** ⊠ Broad St. Bridgetown, St. Michael ☎ 246/426-4515. **Grant's** ⊠ Fairchild St., Bridgetown St. Michael ☎ 246/436-6120 ⊠ Main Rd., Oistins Christ Church ☎ 246/428-9481. **Knight's** ⊠ Lower Broad St., Bridgetown St. Michael ☎ 246/426-5196 ⊠ Super Centre Shopping Center, Main Rd., Oistins Christ Church ☎ 246/428-6057 ⊠ Suncrest Mall, Hwy. 1, Holetown St. James ☎ 246/432-1290 ⊠ Hwy. 1, Speightstown, St. Peter ☎ 246/422-0048.

🄵 Police **Police** ☎ 211 emergencies; 242/430-7100 nonemergencies.

🄵 Scuba-diving emergencies **Coast Guard Defence Force (24-hour hyperbaric chamber)** ⊠ St. Ann's Fort, Garrison, St. Michael ☎ 246/427-8819 emergencies; 246/436-6185 nonemergencies. **Divers' Alert Network** ☎ 246/684-8111 or 246/684-2948.

ETIQUETTE & BEHAVIOR
The British influence remains strong, in part because Barbados is the favorite island retreat and the retirement choice of many Brits. Most hotels serve afternoon tea, cricket is the national pastime, and patrons at some bars are as likely to order a Pimm's Cup as a rum and Coke. British-style manners combine with a Caribbean friendliness and openness to give Bajans their special charm. Dress appropriately and discreetly, saving swimwear for the beach. Shorts and T-shirts are fine for sightseeing and shopping but frowned upon in restaurants in the evening.

FESTIVALS & SEASONAL EVENTS
In mid-January, the Barbados Jazz Festival is a weekend event jammed with performances by international artists, jazz legends, and local talent. In February the weeklong Holetown Festival is held at the fairgrounds to commemorate the date in 1627 when the first European settlers arrived in Barbados.

Three weeks of opera, concerts, and theatrical performances are presented each March during Holder's Opera Season. The open-air theater at Holder's House, St. James, seats 600, and the program has won acclaim for its productions. Around Easter weekend, Oistins Fish Festival celebrates the rich history of this south coast fishing village. Dubbed the "world's greatest street party," the Congaline Street Festival is a festive celebration of music, dance, and local arts and crafts; held at the end of April.

Gospelfest occurs in May and has performances by gospel headliners from around the world. Dating from the 19th century, the Crop Over

Festival, a monthlong event beginning in July and ending on Kadooment Day (a national holiday), marks the end of the sugarcane harvest.

HEALTH

Insects aren't much of a problem, but if you plan to hike or spend time on secluded beaches in late afternoon, use insect repellent. Tap water on the island is plentiful and pure. It's naturally filtered through 1,000 ft of pervious coral and safe to drink.

HOLIDAYS

Public holidays are: New Year's Day (Jan. 1), Errol Barrow Day (Jan. 21), Good Friday (Fri. before Easter), Easter Monday (day after Easter), National Heroes Day (Apr. 28), Labour Day (May 1), Whit Monday (7th Mon. after Easter), Emancipation Day (Aug. 1), Kadooment Day (first Mon. in Aug.), Independence Day (Nov. 30), Christmas (Dec. 25), and Boxing Day (Dec. 26).

LANGUAGE

English, the official language, is spoken by everyone, everywhere. The Bajan dialect is based on Afro-Caribbean rhythms, but you may notice a distinctly Irish lilt (with a hard "R" sound) that differentiates the Bajan accent from its Caribbean neighbors. As for the African influence, you can see it in names of typical Bajan foods, such as cou-cou and buljol.

MAIL & SHIPPING

An airmail letter from Barbados to the United States or Canada costs Bds$1.15 per half ounce; an airmail postcard, Bds45¢. Letters to the United Kingdom cost Bds$1.40; postcards, Bds75¢. Letters to Australia and New Zealand cost Bds$2.75; postcards, Bds$1.75. When sending mail to Barbados, be sure to include the parish name in the address.

MONEY MATTERS

Prices quoted throughout this chapter are in U.S. dollars unless otherwise noted.

The local Barbados National Bank has a branch at Grantley Adams International Airport that is open every day from 8 AM until the last plane lands or arrives. Barclays Bank is an international bank with several branches in Barbados. The Bank of Nova Scotia, or Scotiabank, is a major Canadian bank that is represented throughout the Caribbean. Caribbean Commercial Bank has convenient Saturday morning hours at its branch at Sunset Crest Mall, in Holetown. CIBC, also a Canadian bank with a network of operations on Caribbean islands, has several branches and ATM machines in Barbados.

🚩 **Barbados National Bank** ✉ Broad St., Bridgetown, St. Michael ☎ 246/431-5800 ✉ Grantley Adams International Airport, Christ Church ☎ 246/428-0921. **First Caribbean International Bank** ✉ Broad St., Bridgetown, St. Michael ☎ 246/431-5151 ✉ Sunset Crest, Holetown, St. James ☎ 246/419-8413 ✉ Speightstown, St. Peter ☎ 246/419-8422 ✉ Oistins, Christ Church ☎ 246/418-8712. **Bank of Nova Scotia** ✉ Broad St., Bridgetown, St. Michael ☎ 246/431-3000 ✉ Holetown, St. James ☎ 246/419-1600 ✉ Worthing, Christ Church ☎ 246/431-3170. **Caribbean Commercial Bank** ✉ Lower Broad St., Bridgetown, St. Michael ☎ 246/431-2500 ✉ Sunset Crest, Holetown, St. James ☎ 246/419-8530 ✉ Hastings Plaza, Christ Church ☎ 246/431-2450.

ATMS Automated teller machines (ATMs) are available 24 hours a day at bank branches, transportation centers, shopping centers, gas stations, and other convenient spots throughout the island.

CREDIT CARDS Major credit cards readily accepted throughout Barbados include American Express, BarclayCard, Carte Blanche, Diners Club, EnRoute, Eurocard, MasterCard, and Visa. You can use major credit cards, if you have a PIN, to obtain cash advances (in Barbadian dollars) from most ATM machines.

CURRENCY The Barbados dollar is tied to the U.S. dollar at the rate of Bds$1.98 to $1. U.S. paper currency, major credit cards, and traveler's checks are all accepted islandwide. Be sure you know which currency is being quoted when making a purchase.

PASSPORTS & VISAS

U.S. and Canadian citizens can enter Barbados for visits of up to three months with proof of citizenship and a return or ongoing ticket. Acceptable proof is a valid passport or a birth certificate with a raised seal and a government-issued photo ID. No other documents, including voter registration cards or baptismal certificates, are acceptable. Nevertheless, it's always best to carry a passport. British subjects and citizens of countries that are members of the British Commonwealth must present a valid passport and ongoing ticket.

SAFETY

Crime isn't a major problem, but take normal precautions. Lock your room, and don't leave valuables in plain sight or unattended on the beach. Lock your rental car, and don't pick up hitchhikers.

SIGHTSEEING TOURS

A half- or full-day bus or taxi tour is a good way to get your bearings and can be arranged by your hotel. The price varies according to the number of attractions included; a full-day tour (five to six hours) costs an average $50–$60 per person and generally includes lunch and admissions. Bajan Helicopters offers an eagle's-eye view of the island for $75 to $125. Family-run Bajan Tours offers eight coach or minivan tours, including cultural, historic, ecological, and general sightseeing routings for $40 to $60 per person. Every Wednesday afternoon from mid-January through mid-April the Barbados National Trust offers a bus tour that stops at historic great houses and private homes. The cost is $18 per person, which includes transportation to and from your hotel. Island Safari will take you to all the popular spots and some that are out-of-the-way and inaccessible by buses or normal vehicles, but you'll be riding in a 4x4 Land Rover. The cost is $40 to $60 per person. L. E. Williams Tour Co. offers island bus tours, which cost $30–$85 per person. Sally Shearn operates VIP Tour Services. Up to four people are picked up in an air-conditioned Mercedes-Benz and charged $40 per hour for a minimum of four hours. Your choice of tours (coastal, inland, cultural, naturalist, architectural, or customized) includes refreshment stops.

🚁 **Bajan Helicopters** ✉ Bridgetown Heliport, Bridgetown, St. Michael ☎ 246/431-0069. **Bajan Tours** ✉ Bishop's Court Hill, St. Michael ☎ 246/437-9389. **Barbados National Trust** ✉ Wildey House, Wildey, St. Michael ☎ 246/426-2421. **Island Safari** ✉ Main Rd., Bush Hall, St. Michael ☎ 246/429-5337 ⊕ www.barbadostraveler.com. **L. E. Williams Tour Co.** ✉ Hastings, Christ Church ☎ 246/427-1043. **VIP Tour Services** ✉ Hillcrest Villa, Upton, St. Michael ☎ 246/429-4617.

TAXES & SERVICE CHARGES

DEPARTURE TAX At the airport, each adult passenger leaving Barbados must pay a departure tax of $12.50 (Bds$25), payable in either Barbadian or U.S. currency; children 12 and under are exempt. While it may be included in cruise packages as a component of port charges, the departure tax is not included in airfare and must be paid by each traveler prior to entering the secure area of the airport.

SALES TAX A 7½% government tax is added to all hotel bills. A 10% service charge is usually added to hotel bills and restaurant checks in lieu of tipping. At your discretion, tip beyond the service charge to recognize extraordinary service.

VALUE ADDED TAX (V.A.T.) A 15% VAT is imposed on restaurant meals, admissions to attractions, and merchandise sales (other than duty-free). Prices are often tax inclusive; if not, the VAT will be added to your bill.

TAXIS
Taxis operate 24 hours a day. They aren't metered but charge according to fixed rates set by the government. They carry up to four passengers, and the fare may be shared. For short trips, the rate per mile (or part thereof) should not exceed $1.50. Drivers are courteous and knowledgeable; most will narrate a tour at an hourly rate of $20 for up to three people. Be sure to settle the price before you start off and agree on whether it's in U.S. or Barbados dollars.

TELEPHONES
COUNTRY & AREA CODES The area code for Barbados is 246.

INTERNATIONAL CALLS Direct-dialing to the United States, Canada, and other countries is efficient and reasonable, but always check with your hotel to see if a surcharge is added. Some toll-free numbers cannot be accessed in Barbados. To charge your overseas call on a major credit card without incurring a surcharge, dial 800/744–2000 from any phone.

LOCAL CALLS Local calls are free from private phones; some hotels charge a small fee. For directory assistance, dial 411. Calls from pay phones cost Bds25¢ for five minutes. Prepaid phone cards, which can be used throughout Barbados and other Caribbean islands, are sold at shops, attractions, transportation centers, and other convenient outlets.

TIPPING
If no service charge is added to your bill, tip waiters 10%–15% and maids $2 per room per day. Tip bellhops and airport porters $1 per bag. Taxi drivers appreciate a 10% tip.

VISITOR INFORMATION
🚩 **Before you leave Barbados Tourism Authority** ⊕ www.barbados.org ✉ 800 2nd Ave., 2nd floor, New York, NY 10017 ☎ 212/986-6516 or 800/221-9831 🖷 212/573-9850 ✉ 150 Alhambra Circle, Suite 1000, Coral Gables, FL 33134 ☎ 305/442-7471 🖷 305/567-2844 ✉ 3440 Wilshire Blvd., Suite 1215, Los Angeles, CA 90010 ☎ 213/380-2198 🖷 213/384-2763 ✉ in Canada: ✉ 105 Adelaide St. W, Suite 1010, Toronto, Ontario M5H 1P9 ☎ 416/214-9880 or 800/268-9122 🖷 416/214-9882 ✉ in the U.K.: ✉ 263 Tottenham Court Rd., London W1T 7LA ☎ 20/7636-9448 🖷 20/7637-1496 ✉ in Australia: ✉ 456 Kent St., 17th floor, Sydney 2000 Australia ☎ 2/9285-6850 🖷 2/9267-4600.
🚩 **In Barbados Barbados Tourism Authority** ✉ Harbour Road, Bridgetown, St. Michael ☎ 246/427-2623 🖷 246/426-4080 ✉ Grantley Adams International Airport, Christ Church ☎ 246/428-5570 ✉ Cruise Ship Terminal, Bridgetown, St. Michael ☎ 246/426-1718. **Barbados Hotel & Tourism Assn.** ✉ 4th Ave., Belleville, St. Michael ☎ 246/426-5041 🖷 246/429-2845 ⊕ www.bhta.org

BONAIRE

FODOR'S CHOICE
Coco Palm Garden, a budget hotel in Belnem
Scuba Diving in Bonaire Marine Park

HIGHLY RECOMMENDED

RESTAURANTS Capriccio, Kralendijk
Rendez-Vous Restaurant, Kralendijk
Richard's Waterfront Dining, Kralendijk

HOTELS Bruce Bowker's Carib Inn, Kralendijk
Captain Don's Habitat, Kralendijk
Harbour Village Beach Club, Kralendijk

NIGHTLIFE Lac Cai's Sunday beach party

It is 6 PM on Sunday and hundreds gather for the weekly party at Lac Bay—a normally peaceful peninsula. "It is not showtime yet ladies and gentlemen," the bandleader says in halting English, "but we want you to have fun so we will play." As waves break a few feet away and spill onto the floor of the outdoor bar the crowd dances and laughs, illuminated by the coral light of another perfect Bonaire sunset.

Updated by
Vernon
O'Reilly-
Ramesar

For years Bonaire was regarded simply as one of the top diving destinations in the Caribbean, with most divers practically oblivious to the equally rich beauty on land. But the government embarked on a program to expand its ecotourism base without succumbing to overdevelopment. Now there are facilities and tours geared toward snorkelers, windsurfers, hikers, bikers, and kayakers, as well as luxury resorts that offer pampering, fine dining, and solitude.

Bonaire, on land, is a stark arid island, perfect for those who are turned off by the overcommercialized high life of the other Antillean islands. While the island does not have a tremendous diversity of flora and fauna, there are still many sights to occupy the ecotourist. You will find it worth your while to rent a vehicle to go flamingo watching or exploring Washington National Park. Bolstering efforts to preserve the region's natural wonders, Bonaire purchased the neighboring deserted island of Klein Bonaire from its private owner, protecting it against development.

Divers still come to Bonaire as pilgrims to a holy land. Here diving is learned and perfected. Even Bonaire license plates tout the island as "Divers' Paradise." But the residents have worked hard to preserve the pristine conditions (any diver with a reckless streak should go elsewhere). Back in 1979 the government made all the waters surrounding Bonaire part of a marine park. These areas are designated a National Park, meaning that anyone who disobeys the area's regulations could face legal action. The entire coastline—from the high-water tidemark to a depth of 200 ft—is protected by strict regulations including mandatory orientation classes, warm-up dives with a local instructor, and bans on spearfishing and coral collecting. But certain hazards can't be avoided, Hurricane Lenny wreaked havoc on some of the island's coastal reefs in 1999. Conditions for divers, who typically descend below 30 ft, have not been significantly affected, but snorkelers who seek out the sea's wonders in the shallow waters will likely notice the damage: while the coral reefs are naturally regenerating (which could take many years), the views in some areas may be disappointing.

Most Bonaireans live on the west coast, an area that's also where you will find the capital city, Kralendijk, as well as many hotels, dive sites, and beaches. In the southeast you'll find mangrove swamps, windsurfing schools, and two small resorts in the Lac Bay area; south of here are a rocky, windswept coast, the magnificent salt ponds, and a flamingo sanctuary. The highest elevation is Brandaris Hill (784 ft [239 m]) in the north. With just over 10,000 inhabitants, this little (116-square-mi [290-square-km]) island has the feeling of a small community with a gentle pace. As the locals say, folks come here to dive, eat, dive, sleep, and dive. But they also come to kayak, windsurf, mountain bike, hike, snorkel, and simply soak in the sunshine and natural beauty.

WHAT IT COSTS In U.S. dollars				
	$$$$	$$$	$$	$	¢
RESTAURANTS*				
	over $30	$20–$30	$12–$20	$8–$12	under $8
HOTELS**				
Cost EP/BP/CP	over $350	$250–$350	$150–$250	$80–$150	under $80
Cost AI	over $450	$350–$450	$250–$350	$125–$250	under $125

*Restaurant prices are for a main course at dinner. **EP, BP, and CP prices are per night for a standard double room in high season, excluding taxes, service charges, and meal plans. AI (all-inclusive) prices are per person, per night based on double-occupancy during high season, excluding taxes and service charges.

Where to Stay

Hotels on Bonaire—with several exceptions—cater primarily to avid divers who spend their days underwater and come up for air only for evening festivities. Hence, facilities tend to be modest, with clean but unadorned rooms, pools, a restaurant, and perhaps a bar. Amenities are often limited to laundry, baby-sitting, car rental, and travel services; unless noted below, room service is usually unavailable. Groomed sandy beaches aren't a requisite for a hotel, but an efficient dive shop is. Many resort rooms have fully equipped kitchens and in-room safes. Although the larger hotels offer meal plans, most are on the EP; and as a rule, hotel restaurants are more expensive than restaurants in town. Some properties offer all-inclusive packages for an extra per-day charge.

Rental Apartments

If you prefer do-it-yourself homestyle comfort over the pampering and services offered by a hotel, rental apartments are also available.

Rental agencies Black Durgon Inn Properties ☎ 599/717–5736; 800/526–2370 in the U.S. ⊕ www.blackdurgon.com is a small, noncommercial community with its own pier on the water, though no beach. **Bonaire Intimate Stays** ☎ 800/388–5951 ⊕ www.bonairestays.com manages 13 small, nonresort-style budget properties (only one is on the water), all with 12 rooms or less. **Sun Rentals** ☎ 599/717–6130 ⊕ www.sunrentals.an offers quite a range of accommodations. You can choose between private ocean view villas in luxurious areas like Sabadeco, furnished oceanfront apartments with a pool in town, or bungalows in Lagoenhill, set inland.

HOTELS ★ $$$–$$$$ 🖫 **Harbour Village Beach Club.** This luxury resort, with lavishly appointed rooms set in ocher-colored villas, is just a short walk from Kralendijk. Furnishings are all rosewood, and every bed is a four-poster. The marble bathrooms are so gorgeous you may never want to leave the shower. You may choose between rooms in the beautiful 4-acre tropical garden or (more expensive) beachfront rooms, which are literally on the beach. Free Internet access in the lobby is a thoughtful touch. The hideaway nature of the hotel and the discreet but highly efficient staff make this a popular home away from home for visiting Hollywood celebrities. ⊠ *Kaya Gobernador N. Debrot, Kralendijk* ☎ *599/717–7500 or 800/424–0004* 🖷 *599/717–7507* ⊕ *www.harbourvillage.com* 🛏 *40 rooms, 10 1-bedroom suites, 10 2-bedroom apartments,* ⚓ *4 restaurants, room service, fans, in-room safes, refrigerators, 4 tennis courts, pool, gym, hair salon, spa, beach, dive shop, snorkeling, boating, marina, 3 bars, shops, laundry service, Internet, meeting rooms* 🖃 *AE, D, DC, MC, V* ⊺⊙⊺ *EP.*

$–$$$ 🖫 **Buddy Dive Resort.** Reasonable rates and cozy, well-equipped accommodations keep divers coming back. The small, raised beach and

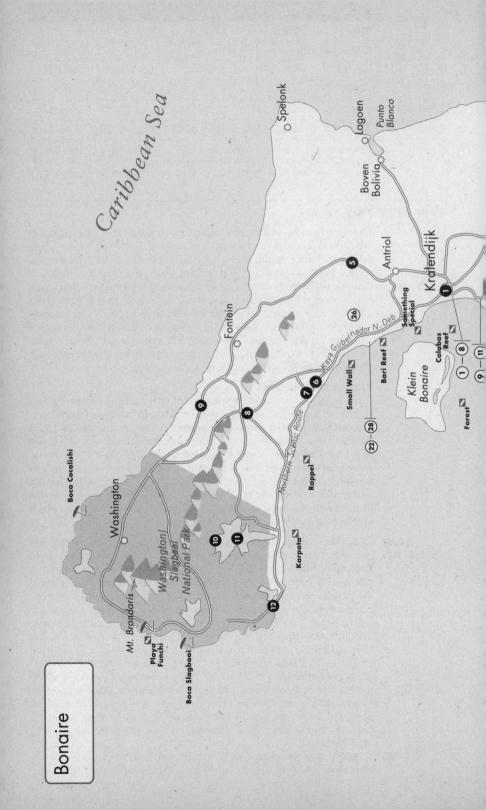

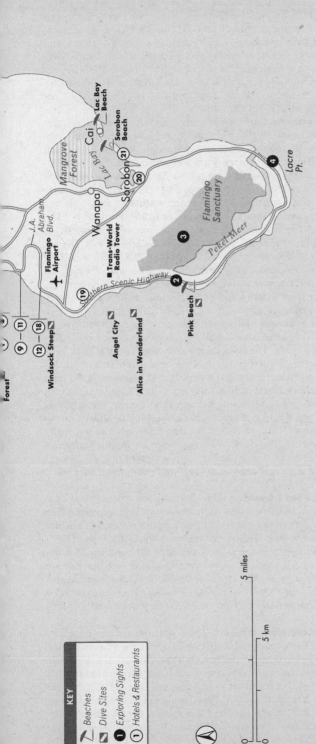

KEY

- ⚘ Beaches
- ◪ Dive Sites
- ➊ Exploring Sights
- ① Hotels & Restaurants

Forest

Windsock Steep

Angel City

Alice in Wonderland

Pink Beach

Mangrove Forest

J.A. Abraham Blvd.

Flamingo Airport

Trans-World Radio Tower

Wanapa

Southern Scenic Highway

Flamingo Sanctuary

Pekel Meer

Lac Baai Cai

Lac Baai Beach

Sorobon Beach

Sorobon

Lacre Pt.

5 miles

5 km

Hotels

Bellafonte–Chateau de la mer	18
Bruce Bowker's Carib Inn	10
Buddy Dive Resort	23
Captain Don's Habitat	26
Carribean Court Bonaire	11
Coco Palm Garden/ Casa Oleander	15
Deep Blue View Bed & Breakfast	27
Divi Flamingo Resort	16
Great Escape	19
Happy Holiday Homes	12
Harbour Village Beach Club	28
Hotel Rochaline	8
Lions Dive Hotel Bonaire	25
Plaza Resort Bonaire	13
Sand Dollar Condominium	14
Sorobon Beach Naturist Resort	21

Restaurants

Capriccio	1
Chez Lucille	17
Coco's Beach	10
Café and Players Bar	2
Croccantino	4
Den Laman Bar & Restaurant	22
It Rains Fishes	5
Kontiki Beach Club	20
Mona Lisa Bar & Restaurant	3
Rendez-Vous Restaurant	6
Richard's Waterfront Dining	9
Zeezicht Bar & Restaurant	7

Exploring

Barcadera Cave	6
Gotomeer	11
Kralendijk	1
Landhuis Karpata	12
1,000 Steps	7
Onima	9
Rincon	8
Salt Flats	3
Seroe Largu	5
Slave Huts	2
Washington/Slagbaai National Park	10
Willemstoren Lighthouse	4

its superb shore snorkeling are a major draw as well. The dive shop has a drive-through air-fill station for Nitrox or compressed air tanks. Each apartment has a phone and a balcony or patio with an ocean or garden view. Rooms in the original building are small, but they're clean and offer the same amenities as newer units. If you are staying for a week, the "Drive and Dive" package, which includes a room, a vehicle, and diving, may be cheaper than simply renting a room. ⊠ *Kaya Gobernador N. Debrot 85, Kralendijk* ☎ *Box 231* ☎ *599/717–5080* ☎ *599/ 717–8647* ⊕ *www.buddydive.com* ⌁ *6 rooms, 40 apartments* ☆ *Restaurant, kitchenettes, 2 pools, beach, dive shop, bar, laundry facilities, car rental* ☰ *AE, D, MC, V* �|◎| *EP.*

★ **$$** ☒ **Captain Don's Habitat.** No longer merely a guest house for divers, this resort offers upscale rooms that are really junior suites, and the spacious Mediterranean-style villas have ocean-view verandahs, kitchens, and stylish appointments. The garden cottages are nicely secluded. This is a laid-back place, where the emphasis is on round-the-clock diving—PADI 5-Star training, SSI referral, Nitrox diving, and more than 20 specialty courses are at your fingertips. Rum Runners restaurant serves all day long, and a pizza oven serves up sizzling slices from 3 PM until 10. The beach is tiny but fine for shore dives or snorkeling, with mesmerizing reef formations just 90 ft from shore. ⊠ *Kaya Gobernador N. Debrot 103, Kralendijk* ☎ *Box 88* ☎ *599/717–8290 or 800/327–6709* ☎ *599/ 717–8240* ⊕ *www.habitatdiveresorts.com* ⌁ *24 suites, 9 villas, 20 cottages* ☆ *Restaurant, fans, in-room safes, some kitchens, refrigerators, pool, beach, dive shop, 2 docks, snorkeling, bicycles, volleyball, bar, business services, meeting room* ☰ *AE, D, DC, MC, V* |◎| *EP.*

$$ ☒ **Caribbean Court Bonaire.** This apartment complex has first-class accommodations in a Netherlands Antilles–style village along a canal dotted with colorful boats. The back of the complex faces a lagoon with access to the ocean; at the front a pool sits in a lovely courtyard. All units have balconies and top-rated amenities. Although most Bonaire hotels cater to divers, here business travelers will feel comfortable, too, as rooms have phones and free Internet access. Of course, divers' needs aren't ignored: you'll find a program that gives those of all levels individualized attention. There is a charming café serving delicious and really inexpensive meals on the dock. ⊠ *J. A. Abraham Blvd., Kralendijk* ☎ *599/717–5353* ☎ *599/717–5363* ⊕ *caribbeancourt.com* ⌁ *26 units* ☆ *Fans, kitchens, 2 pools, dive shop, snorkeling, boating, mountain bikes, Internet* ☰ *MC, V* |◎| *EP.*

$$ ☒ **Deep Blue View Bed & Breakfast.** This charming four-room guest house is in Santa Barbara Heights. Guest rooms have high ceilings, crisp white walls, Italian tile floors, cozy wooden furnishings, fish motifs, and a choice of king- or twin-size beds. Two of the rooms share a bathroom. The 8-inch Meade telescope near the pool is available for guest use. A communal refrigerator is stocked with beverages, and box lunches are available for day trips. ⊠ *Kaya Diamanta 50, Santa Barbara Heights* ☎ *599/717–8073* ☎ *599/717–7826* ⊕ *www.deepblueview.com* ⌁ *4 rooms (2 with shared bath)* ☆ *Fans, pool, laundry service* ☰ *AE, DC, MC, V* |◎| *BP.*

$$ ☒ **Sand Dollar Condominium Resort.** These spacious time-share apartments combine a European design with tropical rattan furnishings, though this varies according to the individual owner's taste. Studios and one-, two-, or three-bedroom units are available. Each has a patio or terrace that looks out to the sea. The minuscule beach disappears at high tide, but this doesn't faze the serious divers and their families. The Sand Dollar Terrace Sports Bar & Restaurant serves three meals a day. A grocery store and bank are next door. ⊠ *Kaya Gobernador N. Debrot 79, Kralendijk (Box 262)* ☎ *599/717–8738 or 800/288–4773* ☎ *599/717–8760* ⊕ *www.*

sanddollarbonaire.com ➲ 85 condos ⚓ Restaurant, grocery, ice cream parlor, kitchens, 2 tennis courts, pool, beach, dive shop, bar, children's programs (ages 3-17) ☰ AE, D, DC, MC, V ⎮⊙⎮ EP.

$$ ▦ **Sorobon Beach Naturist Resort.** At this secluded southeast-shore cluster of chalets, you must bare all at the beach (the beach is open to the public during the day for $15), but you can wear clothing throughout the rest of the premises. Be aware that sunbathers can be seen by windsurfers from the public beach next door. Room furnishings are as minimalist as the dress code, verging on spartan. The shallow water in the crystal-clear bay is perfect for snorkeling. Yoga classes, kayaking, and nude cruises are available, and you can get a manicure and/or pedicure by appointment. ⊠ Sorobon Beach ⌖ Box 14, Kralendijk ☎ 599/ 717–8080 or 800/828–9356 ⎙ 599/717–6080 ⊕ www. sorobonbeachresort.com ➲ 30 1-bedroom chalets ⚓ Restaurant, fans, in-room safes, kitchenettes, hair salon, massage, beach, snorkeling, boating, Ping-Pong, bar, library, laundry service, airport shuttle ☰ AE, MC, V ⎮⊙⎮ EP.

$–$$ ▦ **Bellafonte–Chateau de la mer.** This new Mediterranean-style hotel right on the ocean offers stylishly appointed suites decorated with original artwork. Teak and stainless steel abound, and the oceanfront rooms have magical views. Rooms have kitchenettes, while suites have full kitchens. The stairs up to your room are a bit exhausting, but the attention to detail makes it all worthwhile. A beach is nearby, and the hotel has a sun deck on a pier. The hotel name derives from the fact that singer Harry Bellafonte owned a large tract of land nearby. ⊠ E. E. G. Blvd. 10, Belnem ☎ 599/717–3333 ⎙ 599/717–8581 ⊕ www.belbonaire.com ➲ 6 rooms, 2 1-bedroom suites, 12 2-bedroom suites ⚓ Fans, some kitchens, some kitchenettes, boating, dock, laundry facilities ☰ AE, MC, V ⎮⊙⎮ EP.

$–$$ ▦ **Divi Flamingo Resort.** The brightly colored buildings of this resort are nestled in beautifully landscaped grounds that have especially lush lawns, a rare sight on the island. Rooms are immaculate and have balconies or terraces. If you ask for a ground-floor ocean-view room, the waves will be lapping at your terrace. The bilevel waterfront Chibi Chibi Restaurant offers Caribbean fare. You can munch on your blackened shrimp while watching the dazzling nightly underwater light show. The first-rate dive facility here offers instruction, certification, and excursions to meet your needs. The casino is very popular. ⊠ J. A. Abraham Blvd. 40, Kralendijk ⌖ Box 143 ☎ 599/717–8285 ⎙ 599/717– 8238 ⊕ www.divibonaire.com ➲ 89 rooms ⚓ 2 restaurants, grocery, in-room safes, tennis court, 2 pools, outdoor hot tub, spa, dive shop, dock, snorkeling, volleyball, bar, casino, shops, meeting rooms, car rental ☰ AE, MC, V ⎮⊙⎮ EP.

☾ $–$$ ▦ **Lions Dive Hotel Bonaire.** Pastels, florals, and wicker furnishings set the tone of the rooms in this hotel's two-story, soft-yellow buildings. Second-floor rooms are more private than those on the first floor, which are set around a quadrangle with a small, busy pool and sunbathing area. Studios have kitchenettes, while suites have spacious living rooms with sofa beds, large balconies looking out to sea, and full kitchens. All units are ideal for families. There is a sandy recreational area near the dive shop that is great for socializing. ⊠ Kaya Gobernador N. Debrot 91, Kralendijk ⌖ Box 380 ☎ 599/717–5580 ⎙ 599/717–5680 ⊕ www.lionsdivebonaire. com ➲ 32 rooms ⚓ Restaurant, fans, some kitchens, some kitchenettes, pool, dive shop, dock, snorkeling, bar ☰ AE, MC, V ⎮⊙⎮ CP.

$–$$ ▦ **Plaza Resort Bonaire.** At this flagship property of the Dutch Van der Valk chain, lush landscaped grounds surround a man-made lagoon with bridges. You will also find a gorgeous beach (open to nonguests for $6 per day), loads of amenities, an activities program, and very large guest rooms. Each has terra-cotta tile floors, green rattan furnishings, pastel floral bedspreads, a coffeemaker, big TVs, and an enormous bathroom. One- and two-bedroom villas have full kitchens. Thursday is Bonairean folklore night, with live island music, dancing, and typical local foods. ⊠ *J. A. Abraham Blvd. 80, Kralendijk* ☎ *599/717–2500 or 800/766–6016* 🖶 *599/717–7133* 🛏 *200 rooms, 48 villas* ⚅ *3 restaurants, grocery, room service, fans, in-room safes, some kitchens, refrigerators, 4 tennis courts, 2 pools, aerobics, gym, hair salon, massage, beach, dive shop, dock, windsurfing, boating, bicycles, 4 bars, casino, shops, children's programs (ages 5–15), business services, convention center, meeting rooms* ⊟ *AE, DC, MC, V* ⦿ *EP.*

★ $ 🏨 **Bruce Bowker's Carib Inn.** American diver Bruce Bowker started this small PADI 5-Star diving lodge out of a private home about a mile from the airport. Rooms are clean and cozy, and many have kitchens. Novice divers will enjoy his very small scuba classes, and PADI certification is available. The beach is just a sliver but is fine for shore entries. ⊠ *J. A. Abraham Blvd. 46, Kralendijk* ⅅ *Box 68* ☎ *599/717–8819* 🖶 *599/717–5295* ⊕ *www.caribinn.com* 🛏 *10 units* ⚅ *Fans, some kitchenettes, some microwaves, some refrigerators, pool, beach, dive shop, snorkeling* ⊟ *MC, V* ⦿ *EP.*

$ 🏨 **Coco Palm Garden/Casa Oleander.** Neighbors Marion and Brigitte decided that they would both open small guest houses and manage them together. The result is one of the best-value surprises on the island. Each unit is completely self-sufficient and has its own garden, complete with hammock. A common area has a pool, sunbathing deck, restaurant, and bar. The colorful handiwork you see around you is also done by the owners. Need to send an e-mail? Just ask one of the owners, and they will take care of it for you for free—almost like being home. ⊠ *Kaya van Eps 9, Belnem* ⅅ *Box 216, Kralendijk* ☎ *599/717–2108 or 599/790–9080* 🖶 *599/717–8193* ⊕ *www.cocopalmgarden.org* 🛏 *10 rooms* ⚅ *Kitchens, pool, laundry facilities, shop* ⊟ *MC, V* ⦿ *EP.*

Fodor'sChoice
★

$ 🏨 **Great Escape.** Honeymooners from Venezuela and others in the know come here, a few minutes' walk from Pink Beach, for peace and privacy. The spotless rooms have pastel and beige color schemes and overlook flowers and foliage. Superior rooms have king-size beds and cost only $10 more than standard rooms. The courtyard contains a small waterfall, an open-air bar-and-grill restaurant, a freshwater pool, and a kids' pool with a small playground. ⊠ *E. E. G. Blvd. 97, Belnem* ☎ *599/717–7488* 🖶 *599/717–7412* ✉ *greatescape@bonairelive.com* 🛏 *8 rooms, 2 suites* ⚅ *Restaurant, fans, refrigerators, pool, wading pool, bar, shop, playground* ⊟ *AE, MC, V* ⦿ *BP.*

$ 🏨 **Happy Holiday Homes.** Just south of the airport, this small complex of bungalows is across the street from the ocean in a quiet residential area. The comfortable accommodations are spic-and-span and have wooden ceilings, white-tile floors, fully equipped kitchens, living/dining areas, air-conditioned bedrooms, a selection of books, and cable TV. Each unit also has a barbecue and deck furniture on a sun terrace or garden patio. ⊠ *Punt Vierkant 9, Belnem* ⅅ *Box 216, Kralendijk* ☎ *599/717–8405* 🖶 *599/717–8605* ⊕ *www.happyholidayhomes.com* 🛏 *12 1- and 2-bedroom bungalows* ⚅ *In-room safes, kitchens, laundry facilities, airport shuttle* ⊟ *MC, V* ⦿ *EP.*

$ 🏨 **Hotel Rochaline.** This small hotel in the heart of Kralendijk and above the popular City Café is a good bet for budget travelers who want to be downtown. The clean rooms have single beds, TVs, shower-only baths, and small balconies overlooking the harbor. There is also a super-budget wing, although even these 10 rooms have a shower, television, and air-conditioning. ⊠ *Kaya Grandi 7, Kralendijk* ☎ *599/717–8286* 🖶 *599/717–8258* ⊕ *www.mainstreetbonaire.com* 🛏 *35 rooms* ⚅ *2 restaurants, bar, meeting rooms* ⊟ *AE, MC, V* ⦿ *EP.*

Where to Eat

Dining on Bonaire is far less expensive than on neighboring islands, and you'll find everything from Continental to Mexican to Asian fare. Most restaurants offer seafood fresh from the surrounding waters; in season try the snapper, wahoo, or dorado (a mild white fish). Meat lovers will appreciate the availability of Argentinian beef, and vegetarians will be pleased by the abundance of fresh Venezuelan produce. Many restaurants serve only dinner—only a few establishments not affiliated with hotels are open for breakfast, so check ahead.

What to Wear

Dress on the island is casual but conservative. Most places don't allow beachwear; even casual poolside restaurants prefer a cover-up.

CONTINENTAL × **Rendez-Vous Restaurant.** People (Queen Beatrix among them) come to
★ **$$$** Rendez-Vous for the hearty, consistently well-prepared food: warm French bread with garlic butter, conch chowder, creole-style fresh fish, and seafood, steak, and vegetarian entrées. The dining room showcases works by a local artist. Also marvel at the collection of hundreds of cigarette lighters from around the world on display in the bar area. ⊠ *Kaya L. D. Gerharts 3, Kralendijk* ☎ *599/717–8454* ⊟ *AE, MC, V* ☺ *Closed Sun.*

ECLECTIC × **Zeezicht Bar & Restaurant.** Zeezicht (pronounced *zay-zeekt* and mean-
$$–$$$$ ing "sea view") serves three meals a day. At breakfast and lunch you'll get basic American fare with an Antillean touch, such as a fish omelet; dinner is more Caribbean and mostly seafood, served either on the terrace overlooking the harbor or in the nautically themed homey, rough-hewn main room. Locals are dedicated to this hangout, especially for the ceviche, conch sandwiches, and the Zeezicht special soup with conch, fish, and shrimp. ⊠ *Kaya J. N. E. Craane 12, Kralendijk* ☎ *599/ 717–8434* ⊟ *AE, MC, V.*

$$–$$$ × **Chez Lucille.** You may be hard pressed to choose from the many menu items that span the gamut between French, Thai, and Indian cuisines. A favorite is the classic French onion soup. The restaurant is housed in an early 20th-century building featuring typical Bonairean architecture, but to enjoy the lovely Bonairean weather choose the new outside terrace. ⊠ *Kaya C. E. B. Hellmund 19, Kralendijk* ☎ *599/717–7884* ⊟ *D, MC, V* ☺ *Closed Tues.*

$$–$$$ × **Mona Lisa Bar & Restaurant.** Here you'll find Continental, Caribbean, and Indonesian fare. Popular bar dishes include Wiener schnitzel and fresh fish with curry sauce. The intimate stucco-and-brick dining room, presided over by a copy of the famous painting of the eponymous lady, is decorated with Dutch artwork, lace curtains, and whirring ceiling fans. The colorful bar adorned with baseball-style caps is a great place for late-night schmoozing and noshing on light snacks or the catch of the day, which is served until 10 PM. ⊠ *Kaya Grandi 15, Kralendijk* ☎ *599/ 717–8718* ⊟ *AE, MC, V* ☺ *No lunch. Closed Sun.*

$$ × **Kontiki Beach Club.** The dining room is a harmonious blend of terra-cotta tile floors and rattan furnishings, set around the limestone half-moon bar. There's also a brick terrace for alfresco dining. Dutch chef-owners Miriam and Martin serve dishes such as a delicious creamy curry soup, and Catch Original (pan-fried local fish in red pepper sauce). There are frequent live jazz performances on the outdoor stage. This is the only restaurant on Lac Bay. ⊠ *Kaminda Sorobon 64, Lac Bay* ☎ *599/717–5369* ⊟ *AE, MC, V* ☺ *Closed Mon.*

¢–$$ × **Coco's Beach Café and Players Bar.** This outdoor waterfront eatery with umbrella-shaded tables is a colorful, fun place to grab a bite any time of day. For breakfast, enjoy bagels, croissants, muffins, and pastries. At lunch and dinner you can try your hand at grilling your own selection on the charcoal barbecue. Open until 2 AM, the indoor bar has four pool tables, where any sharks you might encounter are not the underwater kind. ⊠ *Kaya Jan Craane 12, Kralendijk* ☎ *599/717–8434* ▭ *AE, D, MC, V.*

ITALIAN $$–$$$$

✕ **Croccantino.** At this casual restaurant decorated in splashes of purple and green, you can indulge in authentic Italian food on the large outdoor terrace or in the air-conditioned indoor smoking or nonsmoking rooms. For an appetizer try *calamari fritti* with hot marinara sauce, and follow it up with lobster fettuccine. If you are looking for a light and reasonably priced lunch try their US$12 prix-fixe specials. ⊠ *Kaya Grandi 48, Kralendijk* ☎ *599/717–5025* ▭ *MC, V* ☸ *Closed Sun. No lunch Sat.*

★ $–$$$

✕ **Capriccio.** This splendid, family-run Italian eatery has plenty to boast about. The pastas are handmade daily, and fresh mozzarella is imported from Italy once a week. Their wine collection won praise from *Wine Spectator.* You can opt for casual à la carte dining on the terrace or a romantic meal in the tonier air-conditioned dining room. If your appetite is hearty, go for the six-course prix-fixe *Menu del buon appetito.* Otherwise choose from one of the fifty items offered on the menu. ⊠ *Kaya Isla Riba 1, Kralendijk* ☎ *599/717–7230* ▭ *AE, MC, V* ☸ *Closed Tues. No lunch Sun.*

SEAFOOD $$$–$$$$

✕ **It Rains Fishes.** The mood is vivacious at this popular terrace restaurant in a converted mansion overlooking the water. There is an interesting mural of colorful underwater creatures near the bar, each uniquely conceived and hand-painted by a member of the staff or one of the owners. Fish dominate the menu, but tapas and satays are also available. The signature dish is fresh fish in a mustard sauce. ⊠ *Kaya Jan N. E. Craane 24, Kralendijk* ☎ *599/717–8780* ▭ *MC, V.*

$$–$$$

✕ **Den Laman Bar & Restaurant.** A 6,000-gallon aquarium and a nautical theme are the backdrop at this casual restaurant. Eat indoors next to the glass-enclosed "ocean show" (request a table in advance) or outdoors on the noisier patio overlooking the sea. Pick a fresh Caribbean lobster from the tank or order red snapper creole, a hands-down winner. Homemade key lime pie is popular, as is the live entertainment each Saturday night. ⊠ *Kaya Gobernador N. Debrot 77, Kralendijk* ☎ *599/ 717–8955* ▭ *AE, MC, V* ☸ *Closed Tues. No lunch.*

★ $$–$$$

✕ **Richard's Waterfront Dining.** Animated, congenial Richard Beady and his partner Mario own this casually romantic waterfront restaurant, which has become the island's most recommended restaurant—a reputation that's well deserved. The daily menu is listed on large blackboards, and the food is consistently excellent. The fish soup is sure to please, as is the grilled wahoo. ⊠ *J. A. Abraham Blvd. 60, Kralendijk* ☎ *599/717– 5263* ▭ *DC, MC, V* ☸ *Closed Mon. No lunch.*

Beaches

Don't expect long stretches of glorious powdery sand. Bonaire's beaches are small, and though the water is blue (several shades of it, in fact), the sand isn't always white. You have your pick of beaches according to color: pink, black, or white. The best public beach is Pink Beach, and for those who prefer a more complete tan, Sorobon is the island's only nude beach (open to nonguests for $15).

Boca Cocolishi. You'll find hermit crabs along the shore of this blacksand beach in Washington/Slagbaai National Park, on the northeast coast. The term *windswept* has true meaning here: cooling breezes whip the water into a frenzy as the color of the sea changes from midnight blue to aquamarine. The water is too rough for anything more than wading, but the spot is perfect for an intimate picnic *à deux*. To get here, take the Northern Scenic Route to the park; ask for directions at the gate.

Boca Slagbaai. Inside Washington/Slagbaai Park is this beach of coral fossils and rocks with interesting offshore coral gardens that are good for snorkeling. Bring scuba boots or canvas sandals to walk into the water because the beach is rough on bare feet. The gentle surf makes it an ideal place for swimming and picnicking.

Lac Bay Beach. Known for its festive music on Sunday nights, this open bay area with pink-tinted sand is equally dazzling by day. It's a bumpy drive (10–15 minutes on a dirt road) to get here, but you'll be glad when you arrive. It's a good spot for diving, snorkeling, and kayaking (bring your own), and there are public rest rooms and a restaurant for your convenience.

Pink Beach. As the name suggests, the sand here has a pinkish hue that takes on a magical shimmer in the late afternoon sun. The water is suitable for swimming, snorkeling, and scuba diving. Take the Southern Scenic Route on the island's western side; the beach is close to the slave huts. It's a favorite Bonairean hangout on the weekend, but it's almost deserted during the week. Because of the coral that is thrown up on the beach, sandals are recommended.

Playa Funchi. This Washington Park beach is notable for the lagoon on one side, where flamingos nest, and the superb snorkeling on the other, where iridescent green parrot fish swim right up to shore.

Sorobon Beach. Adjacent to the Sorobon Beach Resort's private stretch of sand, this is *the* windsurfing beach. You'll find a restaurant/bar next to the resort and a couple of windsurfing outfitters on the beach. The public beach area has rest rooms and huts for shade.

Windsock Beach. Near the airport, this pretty little spot, also known as Mangrove Beach, looks out toward the north side of the island and has about 200 m of white sand along a rocky shoreline. It's a popular dive site and swimming conditions are good.

Sports & the Outdoors

Cycling

Twenty-one-speed mountain bikes are the perfect way to travel Bonaire's more than 180 mi (290 km) of unpaved routes (as well as the many paved roads). For mountain bike rentals try **Captain Don's Habitat** (⊠ Kaya Gobernador N. Debrot 103, Kralendijk ☎ 599/717–8290 or 599/717–8913). Rates average around $15–$20 per day, and a credit card or cash deposit is usually required. **Cycle Bonaire** (⊠ Kaya L. D. Gerharts 11D, next to Cultimara Supermarket, Kralendijk ☎ 599/717–7558) rents mountain bikes and gear (trail maps, water bottles, helmets, locks, repair and first-aid kits) for $15 a day or $75 a week; half-day and full-day guided excursions start at $40, not including bike rental. **Hot Shot Rentals** (⊠ Kaya Bonaire 4-C, Kralendijk ☎ 599/717–7166) rents regular, hybrid, and Dutch touring bikes for $10 a day.

Fishing

Captain Cornelis of **Big Game Sportfishing** (⊠ Kaya Warawara 3, Kralendijk ☎☎ 599/717–6500) offers deep-sea charters for those in search of wahoo, marlin, tuna, swordfish, and sailfish. His rates—which cover bait, tackle, and refreshments—average $350 for a half-day, $500 for a full day for as many as four people. **Multifish Charters** (☎ 599/717–7033) has day or night reef fishing on a 32-ft Permacraft twin diesel; the cost for six hours is $300 (four-person maximum). A nine-hour day of deep-sea fishing costs $450 (six-person maximum). **Piscatur Charters**

(⊠ Kaya H. J. Pop 4, Kralendijk ☎ 599/717–8774) offers light-tackle angler reef fishing for jacks, barracuda, and snapper from a 15-ft skiff. Rates are $225 for a half-day, $300 for a full day. You can charter the 42-ft Sport Fisherman *Piscatur,* which carries up to six people, for $350 for a half-day, $500 for a full day. Bonefishing runs $200 for a half-day.

Horseback Riding

You can take hour-long trail rides at the 166-acre **Kunuku Warahama Ranch** (⊠ Kaya Guanare 11, east of Kralendijk (off road to Cai ☎ 599/560–7217) for $20. Guides take you through groves of cacti where iguanas, wild goats, donkeys, and flamingos reside. Reserve one of the gentle pintos or palominos a day in advance, and try to go early in the morning, when it's cool. The ranch, open Tuesday–Sunday 10–6, also has an alfresco restaurant, a golf driving range, and two playgrounds.

Kayaking

Divers and snorkelers use the kayak to reach inaccessible dive sites and simply tow the craft along during their dive. Nondivers use kayaks to explore the flora and fauna of the island's rich mangrove forests (apply plenty of insect repellent before touring).

Guided trips and kayak rentals are available from **Bonaire Adventure Diving** (⊠ Kaya Gobernador N. Debrot 79, Kralendijk ☎ 599/717–8738 or 800/288–4773) **Discover Bonaire** (⊡ Box 361 ☎ 599/717–5433 or 599/717–5252) offers kayaking trips (beginning at $45 for a half-day, single-kayak trip), as well as nature tours to explore Bonaire's unique flora and fauna (at $50 per person, led by biologist Jerry Ligon), snorkeling adventures, special children's programs, and mountain biking trips. Guided tours are available. At **Jibe City** (⊠ Sorobon Beach ☎ 599/717–5233; 800/748–8733 in the U.S.), kayaks go for $10 (single) and $15 (double) per hour; $25 and $30, respectively, per half-day (closed in October).

Sailing

Bonaire Boating (⊠ Divi Flamingo Resort, J. A. Abraham Blvd. 40, Kralendijk ☎ 599/790–5353), offers half- or full-day charters aboard a luxury 56-ft sailing yacht ($395 and $695, respectively), a 57-ft motor yacht ($455 for four hours), or the private charter of a 26-ft Bayliner day cruiser for $295 for three hours.

Scuba Diving

FodorsChoice ★ Bonaire has some of the best reef diving this side of Australia's Great Barrier Reef. It takes only 5–25 minutes to reach many sites, the current is usually mild, and although some reefs have sudden, steep drops, most begin just offshore and slope gently downward at a 45° angle. General visibility runs 60–100 ft, except during surges in October and November. You can see several varieties of coral: knobby-brain, giant-brain, elkhorn, staghorn, mountainous star, gorgonian, and black. You'll also encounter schools of parrot fish, surgeonfish, angelfish, eels, snappers, and groupers. Beach diving is excellent just about everywhere on the leeward side, so night diving is popular. There are sites here suitable for every skill level; they're clearly marked by yellow stones on the roadside.

In the well-policed Bonaire Marine Park, which encompasses the entire coastline around Bonaire and Klein Bonaire, divers take the rules seriously. Don't even *think* about (1) spearfishing; (2) dropping anchor; or (3) touching, stepping on, or collecting coral. You must pay an admission of $10 (used to maintain the park), for which you receive a colored plastic tag (to attach to an item of scuba gear) entitling you to one calendar year of unlimited diving. Checkout dives—diving first with a master before going out on your own—are required, and you can arrange them through any dive shop. All dive operations offer classes in free buoyancy control, advanced buoyancy control, and photographic buoyancy control. Tags are available at all scuba facilities and from the **Marine Park Headquarters** (✉ Karpata ☎ 599/717–8444).

DIVE SITES   The *Guide to the Bonaire Marine Park* lists 86 dive sites (including 16 shore-dive-only and 35 boat-dive-only sites). Another fine reference book is the *Diving and Snorkeling Guide to Bonaire,* by Jerry Schnabel and Suzi Swygert. Guides associated with the various dive centers can give you more complete directions. It's difficult to recommend one site over another; to whet your appetite, here are a few of the popular sites.

Angel City. Take the trail down to the shore adjacent to the Trans-World Radio station; dive in and swim south to Angel City, one of the shallowest and most popular sites in a two-reef complex that includes Alice in Wonderland. The boulder-size green-and-tan coral heads are home to black margates, Spanish hogfish, gray snappers, and large purple tube sponges.

Bari Reef. Go to the free slide show on Tuesday at the Sand Dollar Condominium Resort to catch a glimpse of the elkhorn and fire coral, queen angelfish, and other wonders of Bari Reef, just off the resort's pier.

Calabas Reef. Off the coast from the Divi Flamingo Resort, this is the island's busiest dive site. It's replete with Christmas-tree worms, sponges, and fire coral adhering to a ship's hull. Fish life is frenzied, with the occasional octopus putting in an appearance.

Forest. You'll need to catch a boat to reach Forest, a dive site off the southwest coast of Klein Bonaire. Named for the abundant black-coral forests found in it, the site gets a lot of fish action, including a resident spotted eel that lives in a cave.

Rappel. This spectacular site is near the Karpata Ecological Center. The shore is a sheer cliff, and the lush coral growth is the habitat of some unusual varieties of marine life, including occasional orange sea horses, squid, spiny lobsters, and spotted trunkfish.

Small Wall. One of Bonaire's three complete vertical wall dives (and one of its most popular night-diving spots), Small Wall is offshore from the road north of Captain Don's Habitat, near Barcadera Beach. The 60-ft wall is frequented by squid, turtles, tarpon, and barracudas, and has dense hard and soft coral formations; it also allows for excellent snorkeling.

Something Special. South of the marina entrance at Harbour Village Beach Resort, this spot is famous for its garden eels. They wave about from the relatively shallow sand terrace looking like long grass in a breeze.

Windsock Steep. This excellent shore-dive site (from 20 to 80 ft [6 to 24 m]) is in front of the small beach opposite the airport runway. It's a popular place for snorkeling. The current is moderate, the elkhorn coral profuse; you may also see angelfish and rays.

DIVE CENTERS   Many of the dive shops listed below offer PADI and NAUI certification courses and SSI, as well as underwater photography and videography courses. Some shops are also qualified to certify dive instructors. Full certification courses cost approximately $370; open-water refresher courses run about $185; a one tank boat dive with unlimited shore diving costs about $37; a two-tank boat dive with unlimited shore diving is about $55. As for equipment, renting a mask, fin, and snorkel costs about $8.50 all together; for a BC and regulator, expect to pay about $16.

Bonaire Adventure Diving (✉ Sand Dollar Condominium Resort, Kaya Gobernador N. Debrot 79, Kralendijk ☎ 599/717–8738). **Bon Bini Divers** (✉ Lions Dive Hotel Bonaire, Kaya Gobernador N. Debrot 91, Kralendijk ☎ 599/717–5425). **Bonaire Scuba Center** (✉ Black Durgon Inn, Kaya Gobernador N. Debrot 145, Kralendijk ☎ 599/717–5736;

908/566–8866 or 800/526–2370 for reservations in the U.S. ⌂ Box 775, Morgan, NJ 08879). **Bruce Bowker's Carib Inn Dive Center** (✉ J. A. Abraham Blvd. 46, Kralendijk ☎ 599/717–8819). **Buddy Dive Resort** (✉ Kaya Gobernador N. Debrot 85, Kralendijk ☎ 599/717–5080). **Captain Don's Habitat Dive Shop** (✉ Kaya Gobernador N. Debrot 103, Kralendijk ☎ 599/717–8290). **Dee Scarr's "Touch the Sea"** (⌂ Box 369, Kralendijk ☎ 599/717–8529). **Dive Inn** (✉ Kaya C. E. B. Hellmund, Kralendijk, close to South Pier ☎ 599/717–8761). **Photo Tours Divers** (✉ Caribbean Court Bonaire, J. A. Abraham Blvd., Kralendijk ☎ 599/717–5353 Ext. 328). **Toucan Diving** (✉ Plaza Resort Bonaire, J. A. Abraham Blvd. 80, Kralendijk ☎ 599/717–2500).

SNORKELING   Bonaire, in conjunction with *Skin Diver* magazine, developed the **Guided Snorkeling Program.** The highly educational and entertaining program begins with a slide show on important topics, from a beginner's look at reef fish, coral, and sponges to advanced fish identification and night snorkeling. Guided snorkeling for all skill levels can be arranged through most resort dive shops; the cost is $25 (discounts available for more than one session) and includes slide presentations, transportation to the site, and a guided tour. Gear is an additional $9 per 24-hour period. The best snorkeling spots are on the island's leeward side, where you have shore access to the reefs, and along the west side of Klein Bonaire, where the reef is better developed.

In addition to the dive shops, **SeaCow WaterTaxi** (✉ Club Karel's Bar, at the waterfront, Kralendijk ☎ 599/780–7126) has snorkel trips (day and night) and daily excursions to Klein Bonaire.

TENNIS   Tennis isn't a common activity on tiny Bonaire, but you do have a few options to volley about. Court prices generally run about $20 per hour for nonguests (free for guests), but pros aren't available. **Harbour Village Tennis Club** (✉ Kaya Gobernador N. Debrot, Kralendijk ☎ 599/717–7500) has four tennis courts. **Plaza Resort Bonaire** (✉ J. A. Abraham Blvd. 80, Kralendijk ☎ 599/717–2500) has four tennis courts. The **Sand Dollar Condominium Resort** (✉ Kaya Gobernador N. Debrot 79, Kralendijk ☎ 599/717–8738) has two courts.

WINDSURFING   Lac Bay, a protected cove on the east coast, is ideal for windsurfing. Novices will find it especially comforting since there's no way to be blown out to sea. The **Bonaire Windsurf Place** (✉ Lac Bay ☎ 599/717–2288 ⊕ www.bonairewindsurfplace.com), commonly referred to as "the Place," rents the latest Mistral, ProTech, and Naish equipment for $35–$60 per hour. A two-hour group lesson costs $45; private lessons are $75 per hour (these rates do not include equipment, which adds at least $35 to the price). A three-day group-lesson package is a bargain at $190 since it includes a one-hour lesson, 1 hour of practice, and equipment rental; groups are limited to 4 people.

Jibe City (✉ Sorobon Beach ☎ 599/717–5233; 800/748–8733 for a U. S. representative) offers lessons for $45 (includes board and sail for beginners only); board rentals start at $20 an hour, $45 for a half-day. There are pickups at all the hotels at 9 AM and 1 PM; ask your hotel to make arrangements.

Shopping

You can get to know all the shops in Kralendijk in an hour or so. But sometimes there's no better way to enjoy some time out of the sun and sea than to go shopping (particularly if your companion is a dive fanatic and you're not). Almost all the shops are on the Kaya Grandi and adjacent streets and in tiny malls. Harborside Mall is a pleasant, airy, air-conditioned mall with several fine shops. The most distinctive local crafts are fanciful painted pieces of driftwood and hand-painted *kunuku,* or little wilderness houses. One word of caution: buy as many flamingo T-shirts as you want, but don't take home items made of goatskin or tortoiseshell; they aren't allowed into the United States. Remember, too, that it's forbidden to take sea fans, coral, conch shells, and *all* forms of marine life off the island.

Specialty Items

CLOTHING **Benetton** (⊠ Kaya Grandi 49, Kralendijk ☎ 599/717–5107) claims that its prices for men's, women's, and children's clothes are 30% lower than in New York. **Best Buddies** (⊠ Kaya Grandi 32, Kralendijk ☎ 599/717–7570) stocks a selection of Indonesian batik shirts, *pareus* (beach wraps), and T-shirts. Colorful cotton resort wear and T-shirts are available at **Bye-Bye Bonaire** (⊠ Harborside Mall, Kaya Gobernador, Kralendijk ☎ 599/717–7578). At **Island Fashions** (⊠ Kaya Grandi 5, Kralendijk ☎ 599/717–7565) you can buy swimsuits, sunglasses, T-shirts, and costume jewelry.

DUTY-FREE **Flamingo Airport Duty Free** (⊠ Flamingo Airport ☎ 599/717–5563) sells GOODS perfumes and cigarettes. Cigar smokers will find friends at **Littman Gifts** (⊠ Harborside Mall, Kaya Gobernador ☎ 599/717–5670) as they breathe in the smoky splendor of Havanas. Montecristo, H. Upmann, Romeo & Juliet, and Cohiba are all here. Far from being banished to the porch, smokers are welcomed into the acclimatized Cedar Cigar Room. **Perfume Palace** (⊠ Harborside Mall, Kaya Gobernador ☎ 599/717–5288) sells perfumes and makeup from Lancôme, Estée Lauder, Chanel, Ralph Lauren, and Clinique.

HANDICRAFTS **Bon Tiki** (⊠ Kaya C. E. B. Hellmund 3, Kralendijk ☎ 599/717–6877) sells unique works from Bonaire's finest artists. Whatever you do, make a point of visiting **Jenny's Art** (⊠ Kaya Betico Croes #6, Kralendijk, near the post office ☎ 599/717–5004). Roam around her house, which is a replica of a traditional Bonaire town complete with her handmade life-size dolls and the skeletons of all her dead pets. Lots of fun (and sometimes kitschy) souvenirs made out of driftwood, clay, and shells are all handmade by Jenny. **Roselord Souvenir & Gift Shop** (⊠ Kaya Kanari 42, North Nikiboko ☎ 599/717–6765), outside Kralendijk, sells plates and woodwork painted by local artists. **Things Bonaire** (⊠ Kaya Grandi 38C, Kralendijk ☎ 599/717–8423) purveys T-shirts, earrings, batik dresses, souvenirs, and guidebooks.

JEWELRY **Atlantis** (⊠ Kaya Grandi 32B, Kralendijk ☎ 599/717–73030) carries a large range of precious and semi–precious gems. Their tanzanite collection is especially beautiful. You will also find Sector, Raymond Weil and Citizen watches, among others, all at great savings. Their gold jewelry is an especially good buy since they sell by weight. **Littman's** (⊠ Kaya Grandi 33, Kralendijk ☎ 599/717–8160 ⊠ Harborside Mall, Kaya Gobernador, Kralendijk ☎ 599/717–2130) is an upscale jewelry and gift shop where many items are handpicked by owner Steven Littman on his regular trips to Europe. Look for Rolex, Omega, Cartier, and Tag Heuer watches, fine gold jewelry, antique coins, nautical sculptures, resort clothing, and accessories.

Nightlife & the Arts

Nightlife

Most divers are exhausted after they finish their third, fourth, or fifth dive of the day, which may explain why there are so few discos. Indeed, many people's idea of nightlife is looking for the elusive "green flash" just before sunset, a harbinger of luck (some swear it exists, others say that it can only be seen after several daiquiris), or else they go diving, snorkeling, or windsurfing by the light of the moon. Most of the time nightlife consists of sitting on a quiet beach sipping a local Amstel Bright beer. Top island performers, including the Kunuku Band and Foyan Boys, migrate from one resort to another throughout the week. You'll find information in the free magazines (published once a year) *Bonaire Holiday, Bonaire Affair,* and *Bonaire Nights.* The twice-monthly *Bonaire Update Events & Activities* pamphlet is available at most restaurants.

BARS **Amadeus** (✉ Kaya Bonaire 4, Kralendijk ☎ 599/717–2888), a lively outdoor bar across the street from the waterfront, draws throngs of young partiers. The Thursday night happy hour at **Captain Don's Habitat** (✉ Kaya Gobernador N. Debrot 85, Kralendijk ☎ 599/717–8286) is very popular. Downtown, **City Cafe** (✉ Hotel Rochaline, Kaya Grandi 7, Kralendijk ☎ 599/717–8286) is a wacky hangout splashed in magenta, banana, and electric blue. Here you'll find cocktails, snack food, live music on weekends, and karaoke on Wednesday nights. **Karel's** (✉ Kaya J. N. E. Craane 12, Kralendijk ☎ 599/717–8434) sits on stilts above the sea and is *the* place for mingling—especially Friday and Saturday nights, when there's live island and pop music.

CASINOS **Casino Caribe** (✉ Plaza Resort Bonaire, J. A. Abraham Blvd. 80, Kralendijk ☎ 599/717–2500) is the island's newest and most comprehensive casino, offering all the usual thrills until 6 AM. At the **Divi Flamingo Resort** (✉ J. A. Abraham Blvd., Kralendijk ☎ 599/717–8285) you can try your hand at blackjack, roulette, and slot machines until 4 AM.

DANCE CLUBS **City Cafe** (✉ Kaya Grandi 7, Kralendijk ☎ 599/717–8286) is the island's closest thing to a dance club. On weekend nights the restaurant moves the tables aside and it becomes an instant dance floor. On Sunday af-
★ ternoon at **Lac Cai** (✉ Lac Cai) enjoy the festive Sunday Party, where locals celebrate the day with live music, dancing, and food from 3 to 11. Take a taxi, especially if you plan to imbibe a few rum punches.

MOVIES The **Bonaire Twin Cinema** (✉ Kaya Prinses Marie, Kralendijk ☎ 599/717–2400) has four to six daily showings of popular American movies. Tickets are about $6.

The Arts

Nature's artistry earns top billing on Bonaire. Slide shows of underwater and above-water scenes fascinate both divers and nondivers. Dee Scarr, a dive guide, presents the fascinating Touch the Sea show Monday night at 8:45, November–June, at **Captain Don's Habitat** (✉ Kaya Gobernador N. Debrot 85, Kralendijk ☎ 599/717–8290). Flora and fauna of the Caribbean are the focus of the slide show presented by naturalist Jerry Ligon on Thursday night at 8:15 at the **Sand Dollar Condominium Resort** (✉ Kaya Gobernador N. Debrot 79, Kralendijk ☎ 599/717–8738).

Exploring Bonaire

Two routes, north and south from Kralendijk, the island's small capital, are possible on the 24-mi-long (39-km-long) island; either route will take from a few hours to a full day, depending on whether you stop to snorkel, swim, dive, or lounge.

Numbers in the margin correspond to points of interest on the Bonaire map.

Kralendijk

❶ Bonaire's small, tidy capital city (population 3,000) is five minutes from the airport. The main drag, J. A. Abraham Boulevard, turns into **Kaya**

Grandi in the center of town. Along it are most of the island's major stores, boutiques, and restaurants. Across Kaya Grandi, opposite the Littman jewelry store, is Kaya L. D. Gerharts, with several small supermarkets, a handful of snack shops, and some of the better restaurants. Walk down the narrow waterfront avenue called Kaya C. E. B. Hellmund, which leads straight to the **North and South piers.** In the center of town, the Harborside Mall has chic boutiques. Along this route is **Ft. Oranje,** with its cannons. From December through April, cruise ships dock in the harbor once or twice a week. The elegant white structure that looks like a tiny Greek temple is the **fish market;** local fishermen no longer bring their catches here (they sell out of their homes these days), but you'll find plenty of fresh produce. Pick up the brochure *Walking and Shopping in Kralendijk* from the tourist office to get a map and full listing of all the monuments and sights in the town.

South Bonaire

The trail south from Kralendijk is chock-full of icons—both natural and man-made—that tell Bonaire's minisaga. Rent a four-wheel-drive vehicle (a car will do, but during the rainy season of October–November the roads can become muddy) and head out along the Southern Scenic Route. The roads wind through dramatic desert terrain, full of organpipe cacti and spiny-trunk mangroves—huge stumps of saltwater trees that rise from the marshes like witches. Watch for long-haired goats, wild donkeys, and lizards of all sizes.

WHAT TO SEE
3 **Salt Flats.** You can't miss the salt flats—voluptuous white drifts that look something like mountains of snow. Harvested once a year, the "ponds" are owned by Cargill, Inc., which has reactivated the 19th-century salt industry with great success (one reason for that success is that the ocean on this part of the island is higher than the land—which makes irrigation a snap). Keep a lookout for the three 30-ft obelisks—white, blue, and red—that were used to guide the trade boats coming to pick up the salt. Look also in the distance across the pans to the abandoned solar salt works that's now a designated **flamingo sanctuary.** With the naked eye you might be able to make out a pink-orange haze just on the horizon; with binoculars you will see a sea of bobbing pink bodies. The sanctuary is completely protected, and no entrance is allowed (flamingos are extremely sensitive to disturbances of any kind).

2 **Slave Huts.** The salt industry's gritty history is revealed in Rode Pan, the site of two groups of tiny slave huts. The white grouping is on the right side of the road, opposite the salt flats; the second grouping, called the red slave huts (though they appear yellow), stretches across the road toward the island's southern tip. During the 19th century, slaves worked the salt pans by day then crawled into these huts at night. Each Friday afternoon they walked seven hours to Rincon to weekend with their families, returning each Sunday. Only very small people will be able to enter, but walk around and poke your head in for a look.

4 **Willemstoren Lighthouse.** Bonaire's first lighthouse was built in 1837, and is now automated (but closed to visitors). Take some time to explore the beach and notice how the waves, driven by the trade winds, play a crashing symphony against the rocks. Locals stop here to collect pieces of driftwood in spectacular shapes and to build fanciful pyramids from objects that have washed ashore.

North Bonaire

The Northern Scenic Route takes you into the heart of Bonaire's natural wonders—desert gardens of towering cacti (*kadushi,* used to prepare soup, and the thornier *yatu,* used to build cactus fencing), tiny coastal coves, and plenty of fantastic panoramas. The road also weaves between eroded pink-and-black limestone walls and eerie rock formations with fanciful names like the Devil's Mouth and Iguana Head (you'll need a vivid imagination and sharp eye to recognize them). Brazil trees growing along the route were used by Indians to make dye (pressed from a red ring in the trunk). Inscriptions still visible in several island caves were made with this dye.

A snappy excursion with the requisite photo stops will take about 2½ hours, but if you pack your swimsuit and a hefty picnic basket (forget about finding a Burger King), you could spend the entire day exploring this northern sector. Head out from Kralendijk on the Kaya Gobernador N. Debrot until it turns into the Northern Scenic Route. Once you pass the Radio Nederland towers you cannot turn back to Kralendijk. The narrow road becomes one-way until you get to Landhuis Karpata, and you have to follow the cross-island road to Rincon and return via the main road through the center of the island.

WHAT TO SEE

Barcadera Cave. Once used to trap goats, this cave is one of the oldest ⑥ in Bonaire; there's even a tunnel that looks intriguingly spooky. It's the first sight along the northern route; watch closely for a yellow marker on your left before you reach the towering Radio Nederland antennas. Pull off across from the entrance to the Bonaire Caribbean Club, and you'll discover some stone steps that lead down into a cave full of stalactites and vegetation.

⑪ **Gotomeer.** This saltwater lagoon near the island's northern end is a popular flamingo hangout. Bonaire is one of the few places in the world where pink flamingos nest. The shy, spindly legged creatures—affectionately called "pink clouds"—are magnificent birds to observe, and there are about 15,000 of them in Bonaire (the same as the number of permanent island residents). The best time to catch them at home is January to June, when they tend to their gray-plumed young. For the best view take the paved access road alongside the lagoon through the jungle of cacti to the parking and observation area on the rise overlooking the lagoon and Washington/Slagbaai Park beyond.

⑫ **Landhuis Karpata.** This mustard-colored building was the manor house of an aloe plantation more than 100 years ago. The site was named for the *karpata* (castor oil) plants that are abundant in the area—you'll see them along the sides of the road as you approach. Notice the rounded outdoor oven where aloe was boiled down before exporting the juice. Although the government has built a shaded rest stop at Karpata, there's still no drink stand.

⑦ **1,000 Steps.** Directly across the road from the Radio Nederland towers on the main road north, watch closely for a short yellow marker on the opposite side of the road to locate these limestone stairs carved right out of the cliff. If you trek down the stairs, you'll discover a lovely coral beach and protected cove where you can snorkel and scuba dive. Actually, you'll count only 67 steps, but it feels like 1,000 when you walk back up carrying scuba gear.

⑨ **Onima.** Small signposts direct the way to the Indian inscriptions found on a 3-ft limestone ledge that juts out like a partially formed cave entrance. Look up to see the red-stained designs and symbols inscribed on the limestone, said to have been the handiwork of the Arawak Indians when they inhabited the island centuries ago. The pictographs are at least 500 years old, and nobody has a clue what they mean. To reach Onima, pass through Rincon on the road that heads back to Kralendijk, but take the left-hand turn before Fontein.

8 **Rincon.** The island's original Spanish settlement, Rincon is where slaves brought from Africa to work the plantations and salt fields lived. Superstition and voodoo lore still have a powerful impact here, more so than in Kralendijk, where the townspeople work hard at suppressing old ways. Rincon is now a well-kept cluster of pastel cottages and century-old buildings that constitute Bonaire's oldest village. Watch your driving here—goats and dogs often sit right in the middle of the main drag. There are a couple of local eateries, but the real temptation is **Prisca's Ice Cream** (☎ 599/717–6334), to be found at Prisca's house, on Kaya Komkomber (watch for the hand-lettered sign).

5 **Seroe Largu.** Just off the main road, this spot, at 394 ft, is one of the highest on the island. A paved but narrow and twisting road leads to a magnificent daytime view of Kralendijk's rooftops and the island of Klein Bonaire. A large cross and figure of Christ stand guard at the peak, with an inscription reading: *ayera* (past), *awe* (present), and *semper* (future).

10 **Washington/Slagbaai National Park.** Once a plantation producing divi-divi trees (the pods were used for tanning animal skins), aloe (used for medicinal lotions), charcoal, and goats, the park is now a model of conservation. It's easy to tour the 13,500-acre tropical desert terrain on the dirt roads. As befits a wilderness sanctuary, the well-marked, rugged routes force you to drive slowly enough to appreciate the animal life and the terrain. (Think twice about coming here if it rained the day before—the mud you may encounter will be more than inconvenient.) If you're planning to hike, bring a picnic lunch, camera, sunscreen, and plenty of water. There are two routes: the long one (22 mi [35½ km]) is marked by yellow arrows, the short one (15 mi [24 km]) by green arrows. Goats and donkeys may dart across the road, and if you keep your eyes peeled, you may catch sight of large iguanas camouflaged in the shrubbery.

Bird-watchers are really in their element here. Right inside the park's gate, flamingos roost on the salt pad known as **Salina Mathijs,** and exotic parakeets dot the foot of **Mt. Brandaris,** Bonaire's highest peak, at 784 ft. Some 130 species of birds fly in and out of the shrubbery in the park. Keep your eyes open and your binoculars at hand. Swimming, snorkeling, and scuba diving are permitted, but you're requested not to frighten the animals or remove anything from the grounds. Absolutely no hunting, fishing, or camping is allowed. A useful guide to the park is available at the entrance for about $6. To get there, take the secondary road north from the town of Rincon. ☎ 599/717–8444 🖾 $10 ⊙ *Daily 8–5, but you must enter before 3.*

BONAIRE A TO Z

To research prices, get advice from other travelers, and book travel arrangements, visit www.fodors.com.

AIR TRAVEL

BonairExel, the newest airline on the block, is a partner of KLM and serves all of the Dutch Caribbean with frequent daily flights from its base in Bonaire. Air DCA has daily flights via Curaçao from Miami. It also has flights to Aruba; Caracas, Venezuela; St. Maarten; Trinidad; and other Caribbean islands—using Curaçao as its hub. The airline's Visit Caribbean Pass allows easy interisland travel. American Eagle flies daily direct to Bonaire from San Juan. Air Jamaica flies to Bonaire on Wednesday, Saturday, and Sunday from its hub in Montego Bay. Travelers can also connect to the nonstop flight from Montego Bay from the airline's U.S. gateways. KLM flies direct to Bonaire from Amsterdam daily en route to Quito, Ecuador.

✈ **Air DCA** ☎ 599/717-2005. **Air Jamaica** ☎ 599/717-8500 or 800/523-5585. **American Eagle** ☎ 599/717-2005. **KLM/BonairExel** ☎ 599/717-8500; 800/374-7747 in the U.S.; 3120/4-747-747 in the Netherlands.

AIRPORTS

Bonaire's Flamingo Airport is tiny but welcoming (the KLM 747 almost dwarfs the airport when it lands). Rental cars and taxis are available, but try to arrange for pickup through your hotel. A taxi will run between $9 and $12 (for up to four people) to most hotels; $16 to the Lac Bay Resort or Sorobon Beach Resort. Fares are 25% extra from 7 PM to midnight and 50% extra from midnight to 6 AM.
✈ **Flamingo Airport** ☎ 599/717-3800.

BIKE & MOPED TRAVEL

Scooters are a great way to zip around the island. Rates are about $18 per day for a one-seater, and up to $38 for a deluxe two-seater. A valid driver's license and cash deposit or credit card are required.
✈ **Hot Shot Rentals** ✉ Kaya Bonaire 4-C, Kralendijk ☎ 599/717-7166. **Macho! Scooter Rentals** ✉ J. A. Abraham Blvd. 80, Kralendijk ☎ 599/717-2500.

BUSINESS HOURS

BANKS Banks are generally open weekdays 8:30–noon and 1:15–3:30. The bank at the airport has extended hours: weekdays 6:30 AM–11:30 PM and weekends 6 AM–11:30 PM.

POST OFFICES Post offices are open weekdays 7:30–noon and 1:30–4.

SHOPS Stores in the Kralendijk area are generally open Monday–Saturday 8–noon and 2–6.

CAR RENTALS

You'll need a valid U.S., Canadian, or international driver's license to rent a car, and you must meet the minimum and maximum age requirements (usually 21 and 70) of each rental company. There's a government tax of $3.50 per day per car rental; no cash deposit is needed if you pay by credit card.
✈ **Avis** ✉ Kaya Betico Croes 1, Kralendijk ☎ 599/717-5795. **Budget** ✉ Flamingo Airport ☎ 599/717-7424. **Flamingo Car Rental** ✉ Kaya Grandi 86, Kralendijk ☎ 599/717-8888, 599/717-5588 at the airport. **Hertz** ✉ Flamingo Airport ☎ 599/717-7221. **Island Rentals** ✉ Kaya Industria 31, Kralendijk ☎ 599/717-2100. **National** ✉ Kaya Nikiboko Zuid 114, Kralendijk ☎ 599/717-7940 or 599/717-7907.

CAR TRAVEL

GASOLINE Gas costs $3.00–$3.50 per gallon (NAf 1.50 per liter), and you'll find stations in Kralendijk, Rincon, and Antriol.

ROAD CONDITIONS Main roads are very well paved, but remember that there are also many miles of unpaved roads; the roller-coaster hills at the national park require a strong stomach, and during the rainy season (October–November) mud—called Bonairean snow—can be difficult to navigate.

RULES OF THE ROAD All traffic stays to the right, and there's not a single traffic light. Signs or green arrows are usually posted to leading attractions; if you stick to the paved roads and marked turnoffs, you won't get lost.

ELECTRICITY

Bonaire runs on 120 AC/50 cycles. A transformer and occasionally a two-prong adapter are required. Note that some appliances may work slowly (60 cycles are typical in North America), hairdryers may overheat, and sensitive equipment may be damaged.

EMERGENCIES

🔟 Ambulance & Fire Ambulance ☎ 599/717-8900. Fire ☎ 599/717-8000.
🔟 Hospitals St. Franciscus Hospital ✉ Kaya Soeur Bartola 2, Kralendijk ☎ 599/717-8900. Scuba-Diving Emergencies ☎ 599/717-8187.
🔟 Pharmacies Botika Bonaire ✉ Kaya Grandi 27, Kralendijk, by Harborside Mall ☎ 599/717-8905.
🔟 Police Police emergencies ☎ 599/717-8000.

FESTIVALS & SEASONAL EVENTS

Carnival, generally held in February, is the usual nonstop parade of steel bands, floats, and wild costumes, albeit on a much smaller scale than on some other islands. It culminates in the ceremonial burning in effigy of King Momo, representing the spirit of debauchery. April ushers in the festival of Simadan, a celebration of the corn harvest, with special songs paying tribute to the farmers. The week-long Bonaire Dive Festival is held in June, filled with educational and fun activities to raise people's awareness of the importance of the world's coral reefs. Early October sees the well-attended International Sailing Regatta. December marks the beginning of the Bari (Drum) Festival, for which local bands write and play songs about events of the past year.

HOLIDAYS

Public holidays are: New Year's Day, Carnival Monday (the Monday before Ash Wednesday), Good Friday (the Friday before Easter), Rincon Day and Queen's Birthday (Apr. 30), Labor Day (May 1), Bonaire Day (Sept. 6), Antilles Day (Oct. 21), Christmas and the day after (Dec. 25–26).

LANGUAGE

The official language is Dutch, but the everyday language is Papiamento, a mix of Spanish, Portuguese, Dutch, English, and French, as well as African tongues. You'll light up your waiter's eyes if you can say *masha danki* (thank you very much) and *pasa un bon dia* (have a nice day). English is spoken by almost everyone on the island.

MAIL & SHIPPING

Airmail postage to North America and Europe is NAf 2.25 and NAf 1.10 for postcards. The main post office is at the southeast corner of Kaya Grandi and Kaya Libertador S. Bolivar in Kralendijk.

MONEY MATTERS

Prices quoted in this chapter are in U.S. dollars unless otherwise noted.

ATMS You'll find ATMs at the airport, Kralendijk, and Hato branches of MCB, as well as at the Sand Dollar Resort and the Plaza Resort; at the Tourism Corporation of Bonaire; and at Banco di Caribe on Kaya Grandi.
🔟 R.B.T.T Bank ✉ Kaya Corona 15, Kralendijk ☎ 599/717-8417 ✉ Kaya Grandi 22, Kralendijk ☎ 599/717-7595 ✉ Kaya Grandi 49, Kralendijk ☎ 599/717-7660. **Maduro & Curiel's Bank Bonaire N. V. (MCB)** ✉ Flamingo Airport ☎ 599/717-5522 ✉ Kaya L. D. Gerharts, Kralendijk ☎ 599/717-5520 ✉ Rincon ☎ 599/717-6266 ✉ Hato ☎ 599/717-5520.

CURRENCY There's no real need to convert your American dollars into the local currency, the NAf guilder. U.S. currency and traveler's checks are accepted everywhere, and the difference in exchange rates is negligible. Banks accept U.S. dollar banknotes at the official rate of NAf 1.78 to the U.S. dollar, traveler's checks at NAf 1.80. This rate is practically fixed. The rate of exchange at shops and hotels ranges from NAf 1.75 to NAf 1.80. The guilder is divided into 100 cents.

PASSPORTS & VISAS

U.S. and Canadian citizens need proof of identity (a valid passport or an original birth certificate with a raised seal along with a photo ID). All others must carry valid passports, but carrying a passport is a good idea even if you are from the U.S. In addition, everyone must have a return or ongoing ticket and is advised to confirm reservations 48 hours before departure. The maximum stay is 90 days.

SAFETY

Because of strong trade winds pounding against the rocks, the windward (eastern) side of Bonaire is much too rough for diving. The *Guide to the Bonaire Marine Park* (available at dive shops around the island) specifies the level of diving skill required for 44 sites and knows what it's talking about. No matter how beautiful a beach may look, heed all warning signs regarding the rough undertow. Also get an orientation on what stings underwater and what doesn't.

During Bonaire's rainy season (October–November), mosquitoes can be a minor nuisance. Open-air restaurants usually have a can of repellent handy.

Bonaire has a reputation for being friendly and safe, but it's still a good idea to lock car doors, especially in the heart of town. Don't leave your camera in an open car, and keep your money, credit cards, jewelry, and other valuables in your hotel's safety-deposit box.

SIGHTSEEING TOURS

BOAT TOURS & CRUISES — On Bonaire, the myriad choices for getting out and enjoying the deep blue sea seem as limitless as the ocean itself. Among them: snorkeling, picnicking, and sunset cruises (prices range from $25 to $50 per person), and private or group sails (expect to pay about $425 per day for a party of four). The *Sea Witch* is a 56-ft ketch; the *Woodwind* is a 37-ft trimaran; the *Oscarina* is a 42-ft sloop. Glass-bottom boat trips are another highlight: the 1½-hour trip costs $23 per person and leaves twice daily, except Sunday, from the Harbour Village Marina. Achie Tours has several half- and full-day options; Bonaire Sightseeing Tours will chauffeur you around on two-hour tours of either the island's north or south or on a half-day city-and-country tour ($25), which visits sights in both regions. Or simply ask any taxi driver for an island tour (be sure to negotiate the price up front).

🚢 **Day-Sail Contacts** *Sea Witch* ☎ 599/9-560-7449. *Woodwind* ☎ 599/9-560-7055. *Oscarina* ☎ 599/9-560-7674.

🚢 **Glass-Bottom Boat Trips** *Bonaire Dream* ✉ Harbour Village Marina, Kaya Gobernador N. Debrot, Kralendijk ☎ 599/717-8239 or 599/717-4514 ⊕ http://bonairenet.an/bonairedream.

ORIENTATION TOURS — 🚢 **Achie Tours** ✉ Kaya Nikiboko Noord 33, Kralendijk ☎ 599/717-8630. **Bonaire Sightseeing Tours** ✉ Kaya General Manuel Piar, next to the main Air DCA office, Kralendijk ☎ 599/717-8778.

TAXES

DEPARTURE TAX — The departure tax when going to Curaçao is $5.75. For all other destinations it's $20. This tax must be paid in cash at the airport prior to departure. U.S. currency is accepted, but paying in NAf is usually faster.

HOTEL TAXES & SERVICE CHARGES — Hotels charge a room tax of $6.50 per person, per night in addition to the V.A.T. Many hotels add a 10%–15% service charge to your bill.

VALUE ADDED TAX (V.A.T.) — A V.A.T (value-added tax) of 6% is tacked on to dining and lodging costs. V.A.T. may or may not be included in your quoted room rates, so be sure to ask. It is almost always included in restaurant prices.

TAXIS

Taxis are unmetered; they have fixed rates controlled by the government. A trip from the airport to your hotel will cost between $9 and $12 for up to four passengers. A taxi from most hotels into town costs between $5 and $8. Fares increase from 7 PM to midnight by 25% and from midnight to 6 AM by 50%. Drivers are usually knowledgeable enough about the island to conduct half-day tours; they charge about $30 for up to four passengers for half-day northern- or southern-route tours.

🚹 **Taxi Central Dispatch** ☎ 599/717-8100.

TELEPHONES

It's difficult for visitors to Bonaire to get involved in dramatic, heart-wrenching phone conversations or *any* phone discussions requiring a degree of privacy. You can make calls from hotel front desks or from the Telbo central phone company office (next to the tourism office in Kralendijk), which is open 24 hours. Telephone connections have improved, but static is still common. You can rent a cell phone from CellularOne Bonaire. The phone will cost you $1.40 rental a day (plus a deposit), and you can buy prepaid phone cards—cell call costs are about 75% cheaper than a hotel call.

🚹 **CellularOne Bonaire** ✉ Kaya Grandi 26, Kralendijk ☎ 599/717-8787.

COUNTRY &
AREA CODES
The country code for Bonaire is 599; 717 is the exchange for every four-digit telephone number on the island.

INTERNATIONAL
CALLS
Forget about trying to use your own phone cards; it's theoretically possible but utterly maddening trying to get connected to the right operator. You can try AT&T by dialing 001–800/872–2881 from public phones, but there are no guarantees. To call Bonaire from the United States, dial 011–599/717 + the local four-digit number.

LOCAL CALLS
When making interisland calls, dial 717 + the local four-digit number. Local phone calls cost NAf 50¢.

TIPPING

Most restaurants add a 10%–12% service charge. Taxi drivers like a 10% tip, but it isn't mandatory. Bellhops should receive $1 per bag.

VISITOR INFORMATION

🚹 **Before You Leave Bonaire Government Tourist Office** ⊕ www.infobonaire.com ✉ 10 Rockefeller Plaza, Suite 900, New York, NY 10020 ☎ 212/956-5913 or 800/266-2473.
🚹 **In Bonaire Tourism Corporation Bonaire** ✉ Kaya Grandi 2, Kralendijk ☎ 599/717-8322 or 599/717-8649.

BRITISH VIRGIN ISLANDS

FODOR'S CHOICE

The Baths, Virgin Gorda

Brandywine Bay restaurant, Tortola

Ivan's Stress Free Campground, Jost Van Dyke

Scuba Diving the reefs of Anegada

Sugar Mill Hotel, Apple Bay, Tortola

HIGHLY RECOMMENDED

RESTAURANTS   Capriccio di Mare, Road Town, Tortola

The Clubhouse, North Sound, Virgin Gorda

Eclipse, East End, Tortola

Harris' Place, Little Harbour, Jost Van Dyke

Sip and Dip Grill, The Valley, Virgin Gorda

Spaghetti Junction, Road Town, Tortola

HOTELS   Bitter End Yacht Club, North Sound, Virgin Gorda

Olde Yard Inn, The Valley, Virgin Gorda

Sandcastle, White Bay, Jost Van Dyke

NIGHTLIFE   Jost Van Dyke's famous beach bars

SIGHTS   J. R. O'Neal Botanic Gardens, Road Town, Tortola

Sage Mountain National Park, Tortola

Skyworld, Joe's Hill, Tortola

Virgin Gorda Peak National Park, Virgin Gorda

OUTDOORS   Sailing the BVI from Tortola

White Bay Beach, Jost Van Dyke

The eight-seater Cessna took off smoothly and on schedule for the 20-minute flight from St. Thomas. As it flew up the Sir Francis Drake Channel to the Beef Island/Tortola Airport, passengers gazed out at stunning views of island and channel. Suddenly everyone turned from the windows and looked at one another quizzically. They sat in stunned silence as the plane flew past the airport and headed to the little runway on nearby Virgin Gorda. After this unscheduled landing, the pilot turned around nervously and said, "Sorry. I'm late for my wedding. Nelson, my copilot, will fly you back to Tortola."

Updated by Carol M. Bareuther and Lynda Lohr

The British Virgin Islands (BVI) consist of about 50 islands, islets, and cays. Most are remarkably hilly, and all but Anegada are volcanic, having exploded from the depths of the sea some 25 million years ago. The BVI are serene, seductive, spectacularly beautiful, and still remarkably laid-back. At some points they lie only a mile or so from the U.S. Virgin Islands (USVI), but they remain unique and have maintained their quiet, friendly, casual character.

The pleasures here are understated: sailing around the multitude of tiny nearby islands, diving to the wreck of the RMS *Rhone,* sunk off Salt Island in 1867, snorkeling in one of hundreds of wonderful spots, walking empty beaches, taking in spectacular views from the island peaks, and settling in on a breeze-swept terrace to admire the sunset.

Several factors have enabled the BVI to retain the qualities of yesteryear's Caribbean: no building can rise higher than the surrounding palms, and there are no direct flights from the mainland United States, so the tourism tide is held back. Many visitors travel here by water, aboard their own ketches and yawls or on one of the ferries that cross the waters between St. Thomas and Tortola. Such a passage is a fine prelude to a stay in these unhurried havens.

Tortola, about 10 square mi (26 square km), is the largest and most populated of the islands; Virgin Gorda, with 8 square mi (21 square km), ranks second. The islands scattered around them include Jost Van Dyke, Great Camanoe, Norman, Peter, Salt, Cooper, Ginger, Dead Chest, and Anegada. Tortola has the most hotels, restaurants, and shops. Virgin Gorda offers a few restaurants, shops, and resorts (many are self-contained). Jost Van Dyke is a major charter-boat anchorage; little bars line the beach at Great Harbour, but there are few places to stay. The other islands are either uninhabited or have only a single hotel or resort—or even just a restaurant. Many of these, such as Peter Island, offer excellent anchorages, and their bays and harbors are popular with overnighting boaters.

Sailing has always been a popular activity in the BVI. The first arrivals here were a romantic seafaring tribe, the Ciboney Indians. They were followed (circa AD 900) by the Arawaks, who sailed from South America, established settlements, and farmed and fished. Still later came the mighty Caribs.

In 1493 Christopher Columbus was the first European visitor. Impressed by the number of islands dotting the horizon, he named them *Las Once Mil Virgines*—the 11,000 Virgins—in honor of the 11,000 virgin companions of St. Ursula, martyred in the 4th century. In the ensuing years, the Spaniards passed through, fruitlessly seeking gold. Then

British Virgin Islands

ATLANTIC

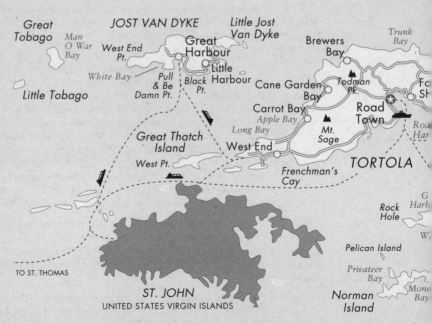

Lo

Guana Islan

Great
Tobago

JOST VAN DYKE

Man
O War
Bay

West End
Pt.

Great
Harbour

White Bay

Pull
& Be
Damn Pt.

Little Tobago

Black
Pt.

Little Jost
Van Dyke

Little
Harbour

Cane Garden
Bay

Brewers
Bay

Trunk
Bay

Todman
Pk.

Carrot Bay

Apple Bay

Road
Town

Fo
Sh

Great Thatch
Island

Long Bay

West End

Mt.
Sage

Roa
Har

West Pt.

TORTOLA

Frenchman's
Cay

G
Harb

Rock
Hole

W.

TO ST. THOMAS

ST. JOHN
UNITED STATES VIRGIN ISLANDS

Pelican Island

Privateer
Bay

Norman
Island

Mon
Bay

Flamingo Pond
Red Pond
West End Pt.
Bones Bight
Loblolly Bay
Table Bay
Pomato Pt.
Saltheap Pt.
The Settlement
Lower Bay
Horse Shoe Reef
ANEGADA
(15 miles north of Necker Is.)
White Bay
Budrock Pond

C OCEAN

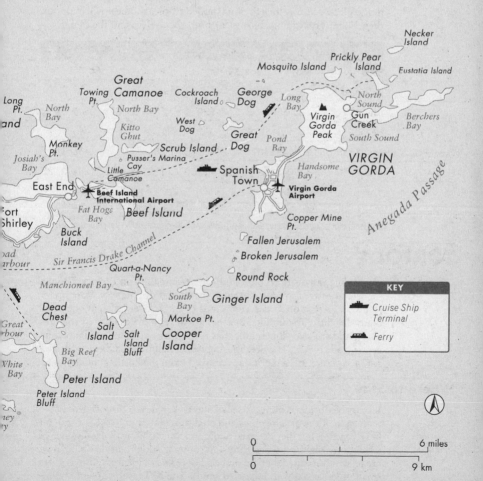

Necker Island

Mosquito Island
Prickly Pear Island
Eustatia Island

Great Camanoe
Towing Pt.
Cockroach Island
George Dog
Long Bay
North Sound
Berchers Bay

Long Pt.
North Bay
North Bay
West Dog
Great Dog
Virgin Gorda Peak
Gun Creek
South Sound

and
Kitto Ghut
Scrub Island
Pond Bay
VIRGIN GORDA

Monkey Pt.
Pusser's Marina Cay
Spanish Town
Handsome Bay

Josiah's Bay
Little Camanoe
Virgin Gorda Airport

East End
Beef Island International Airport
Copper Mine Pt.
Anegada Passage

Fort Shirley
Fat Hogs Bay
Beef Island
Fallen Jerusalem

Buck Island
Broken Jerusalem

ad rbour
Sir Francis Drake Channel
Quart-a-Nancy Pt.
Round Rock

Manchioneel Bay
South Bay
Ginger Island

Great rbour
Dead Chest
Markoe Pt.

Salt Island
Salt Island Bluff
Cooper Island

White Bay
Big Reef Bay
Peter Island

Peter Island Bluff

KEY	
🚢	Cruise Ship Terminal
⛴	Ferry

0 _____ 6 miles
0 _____ 9 km

came pirates and buccaneers, who found the islands' hidden coves and treacherous reefs ideal bases from which to prey on passing galleons crammed with gold, silver, and spices. Among the most notorious of these fellows were Blackbeard Teach, Bluebeard, Captain Kidd, and Sir Francis Drake, who lent his name to the channel that sweeps between the BVI's two main clusters. In the 17th century the colorful cutthroats were replaced by the Dutch, who, in turn, were sent packing by the British. It was the British who established a plantation economy and for the next 150 years developed the sugar industry. When slavery was abolished in 1838, the plantation economy faltered, and the majority of the white population left for Europe.

The islands are still politically tied to Britain. The governor, appointed by the queen of England, has limited powers, and these are concentrated on external affairs and local security. The local legislative council, with representatives from nine districts, administers all other matters. General elections are held every four years, and the political mood is serene.

Although offshore banking is currently the BVI's number one industry, tourism is the second major source of income, and the majority of the islands' jobs are tourism-related. The Beef Island airport's runway was expanded in late 2001 to accommodate larger prop planes and small regional jets, but is still too small for full-size jets, so there's no doubt that BVIers—who so love their unspoiled tropical home—will maintain their islands' easygoing charms for both themselves and their guests.

WHAT IT COSTS In U.S. dollars				
$$$$	**$$$**	**$$**	**$**	**¢**
RESTAURANTS*				
over $30	$20–$30	$12–$20	$8–$12	under $8
HOTELS**				
Cost EP/BP/CP over $350	$250–$350	$150–$250	$80–$150	under $80
Cost AI over $450	$350–$450	$250–$350	$125–$250	under $125

*Restaurant prices are for a main course at dinner. **EP, BP, and CP prices are per night for a standard double room in high season, excluding taxes, service charges, and meal plans. AI (all-inclusive) prices are per person, per night based on double-occupancy during high season, excluding taxes and service charges.

TORTOLA

Unwinding can easily become a full-time occupation on Tortola. Though the island offers a wealth of things to see and do, many visitors prefer just to loll about on its deserted sands or linger over lunch at one of its many delightful restaurants. Beaches are never more than a few minutes away, and the steep green hills that form Tortola's spine are fanned by gentle trade winds. The neighboring islands glimmer like emeralds in a sea of sapphire. It's a world far removed from the hustle of modern life.

Where to Stay

Luxury on Tortola is more a state of mind—serenity, seclusion, gentility—than state-of-the-art amenities and facilities. Hotels in Road Town don't have beaches, but they do have pools and are within walking distance of restaurants, nightspots, and shops. Accommodations outside Road Town are relatively isolated, but are on beaches (some of them exquisite; others small or enhanced with imported sand). The BVI resorts are intimate—

only four have more than 50 rooms. You will likely spend most of your time outside, so the location, size, or price of a hotel are more important than the decor of its rooms. Guests are treated as more than just room numbers, however, and many return year after year. This can make booking a room at popular resorts difficult, even off-season, despite the fact that more than half the island's visitors stay aboard their own or chartered boats.

Throughout the BVI a few hotels lack air-conditioning, relying instead on ceiling fans to capture the almost constant trade winds. Nights are cool and breezy, even in midsummer, and never reach the temperatures or humidity levels that are common in much of the United States during the summer.

Private Homes & Villas

Areana Villas (⌂ Box 263, Road Town ☎ 284/494–5864 🖷 284/494–7626 ⊕ www.areanavillas.com) represents top-of-the-line properties. Homes offer accommodations for 2 to 10 people in one- to five-bedroom villas decorated in soothing pastels. Many have pools, Jacuzzis, and tiled courtyards. On Long Bay, Areana represents Sunset House and Villas, an exquisite hideaway whose first guest was Britain's Princess Alexandra (but you needn't be royalty to receive the royal treatment here). The company also works with Equinox House, also on Long Bay, a handsome three-bedroom estate set amid lavish tumbling gardens. Rates range from expensive ($$$) to very expensive ($$$$) in season. **Lambert Beach Villas** (⌂ Lambert Estate, Box 534, East End ☎ 284/495–2877 🖷 284/495–2876) rents two- and three-bedroom villas on the hills overlooking Elizabeth Beach.

Hotels & Inns

ROAD TOWN
$$–$$$
🔲 **Village Cay Resort and Marina.** Right in town, this pleasant, compact hotel looks out on Road Harbour and several marinas. It's popular with yachters and those who love to shop and dine. Rooms have natural rattan furniture and pastel prints. Some units have cathedral ceilings and harbor views; others are quite small. After shopping in town, you can have a swim in the tiny pool and then head for the bar. ⌂ Wickham's Cay I ⌂ Box 145 ☎ 284/494–2771 🖷 284/494–2773 ⊕ www.villagecay.com ⬎ 19 rooms △ Restaurant, refrigerators, pool, spa, marina, bar, shops ⊟ AE, MC, V ⦿ EP.

$–$$$ 🔲 **Pusser's Fort Burt Hotel.** Originally a Dutch fort, this hillside landmark is at the edge of town and overlooks the harbor. Rooms are painted in pale pastels; cushions and bedspread fabrics are floral prints; and balconies are private. Two suites have private pools. Two-line data port telephones and printer/fax machines in suites and deluxe rooms make it Tortola's only true business hotel. Suites also have kitchenettes. ⌂ Waterfront Dr. ⌂ Box 3380 ☎ 284/494–2587 🖷 284/494–2002 or 888/873–5226 ⊕ www.pussers.com ⬎ 11 rooms, 8 suites △ Restaurant, refrigerators, pool, bar ⊟ AE, MC, V ⦿ EP.

$$ 🔲 **Moorings-Mariner Inn.** This two-story inn is also the headquarters for the Moorings Charter operation. It's popular with both yachting folk and landlubbers who are happy with simple furnishings. It's a laid-back and lively place. The pale peach color scheme is picked up in the floor tiles, and tropical-print fabrics add splashes of contrasting color. All units are on the large side and have balconies. Suites have kitchenettes. ⌂ Waterfront Dr. ⌂ Box 139 ☎ 284/494–2332 or 800/535–7289 🖷 284/494–2226 ⬎ 36 rooms, 4 suites △ Restaurant, refrigerators, pool, dive shop, dock, marina, volleyball, bar, shops ⊟ AE, MC, V ⦿ EP.

$–$$ 🔲 **Maria's Hotel by the Sea.** Perched on the edge of Road Harbour, next to a large government building and the cruise ship dock, this simple hotel

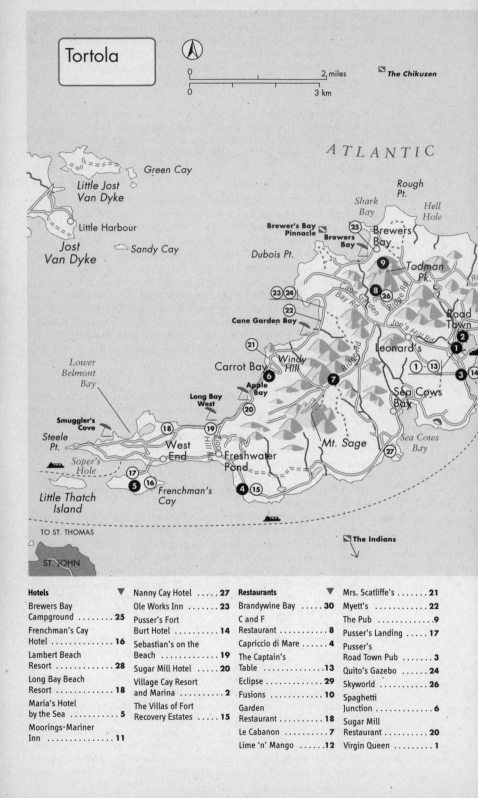

Tortola

0 _____ 2 miles
0 _____ 3 km

The Chikuzen

ATLANTIC

Green Cay

Little Jost
Van Dyke

Little Harbour

Jost
Van Dyke

Sandy Cay

Rough
Pt.

Shark
Bay

Hell
Hole

Brewer's Bay
Pinnacle

25

Brewers
Bay

Brewers
Bay

Dubois Pt.

9

Todman
Pk.

23 24

8

26

Ri

22

Cane Garden Bay

Road
Town

2

Cane Garden
Bay Rd

Ridge Rd

Joe's Hill Rd

1

Leonard's

21

Lower
Belmont
Bay

Carrot Bay

6

Windy
Hill

7

1   13

3   14

Apple
Bay

Sea Cows
Bay

Smuggler's
Cove

Long Bay
West

18

20

19

Steele
Pt.

West
End

Freshwater
Pond

Mt. Sage

Sea Cows
Bay

Soper's
Hole

17

16

5

Frenchman's
Cay

4   15

27

Little Thatch
Island

TO ST. THOMAS

The Indians

ST. JOHN

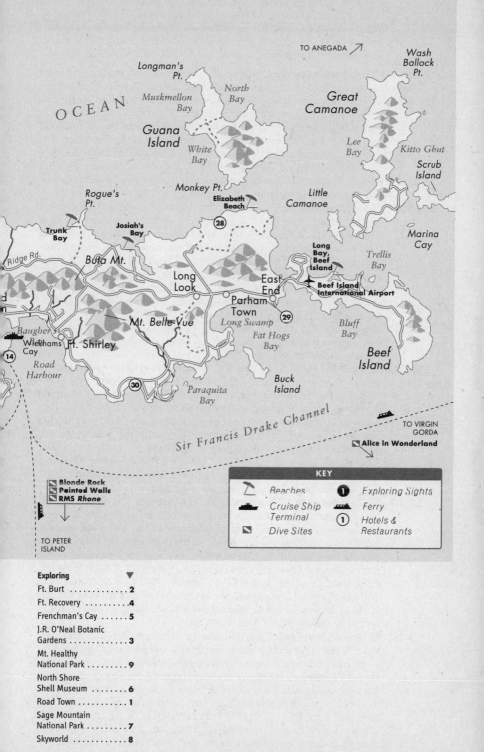

TO ANEGADA ↗

Wash
Ballock
Pt.

Longman's
Pt.

*Muskmellon
Bay*

*North
Bay*

O C E A N

**Great
Camanoe**

*Guana
Island*

*White
Bay*

*Lee
Bay*

Kitto Ghut

*Scrub
Island*

Monkey Pt.

*Little
Camanoe*

**Elizabeth
Beach**

*Marina
Cay*

*Rogue's
Pt.*

28

*Trellis
Bay*

**Trunk
Bay**

**Josiah's
Bay**

**Long
Bay,
Beef
Island**

Butu Mt.

Ridge Rd.

*Long
Look*

East
End

Beef Island
International Airport

Parham
Town

Mt. Belle-Vue

Long Swamp

29

*Bluff
Bay*

Baughers

Wickhams
Cay

Ft. Shirley

*Fat Hogs
Bay*

**Beef
Island**

14

*Road
Harbour*

30

*Paraquita
Bay*

*Buck
Island*

Sir Francis Drake Channel

TO VIRGIN
GORDA

Alice In Wonderland

■ **Blonde Rock**
■ **Painted Walls**
■ **RMS Rhone**

TO PETER
ISLAND

KEY

⚓ Beaches   ❶ Exploring Sights

🚢 Cruise Ship   ⬛ Ferry
   Terminal
             ① Hotels &
◼ Dive Sites   Restaurants

is an easy walk from restaurants in town. The small rooms have a fresh look, with white rattan furniture, floral-print spreads, and murals by local artists. All rooms have balconies, some with harbor views. ⊠ *Waterfront Dr.* ⌂ *Box 206* ☎ *284/494–2595* 📠 *284/494–2420* 📑 *38 rooms* ⚴ *Restaurant, refrigerators, pool, bar* ⊟ *AE, MC, V* ❤❤ *EP.*

OUTSIDE ROAD TOWN

$$$–$$$$

🏨 **Frenchman's Cay Hotel.** This small collection of one- and two-bedroom condos overlooks Sir Francis Drake Channel. Each includes a full kitchen and a dining area. Rooms are done in neutral colors, with cream-colored curtains, bedspreads, and tile floors. Ceiling fans and breezes keep things cool. There's a small pool, a modest-size artificial beach, and good snorkeling. The breeze-swept alfresco bar and dining room offer simple fare. ⊠ *Frenchman's Cay, West End* ⌂ *Box 1054* ☎ *284/495–4844 or 800/235–4077* 📠 *284/495–4056* ⊕ *www.frenchmans.com* 📑 *9 units* ⚴ *Restaurant, fans, kitchenettes, tennis court, pool, beach, snorkeling, bar; no air-conditioning* ⊟ *AE, MC, V* ❤❤ *EP.*

$$$–$$$$

🏨 **Long Bay Beach Resort.** Spectacularly set on a 1-mi-long (1½-km-long) beach, this resort is one of Tortola's best, despite sometimes less than stellar service. Some beachfront hideaways are set on stilts; hillside rooms have dramatic views. In addition, there are spacious one- and two-bedroom hillside villas with kitchenettes. The casual Beach Café offers all-day dining. The Garden Restaurant serves romantic dinners. A full-service spa and fitness center, tennis courts, and a 9-hole, par-3 pitch-and-putt golf course complete the complex. ⊠ *Long Bay* ⌂ *Box 433, Road Town* ☎ *284/495–4252 or 800/729–9599* 📠 *284/495–4677* ⊕ *www.longbay.com* 📑 *78 rooms, 12 suites, 33 villas* ⚴ *2 restaurants, 3 tennis courts, 2 pools, gym, spa, beach, snorkeling, 2 bars, shops, meeting rooms* ⊟ *AE, MC, V* ❤❤ *EP.*

$$–$$$
Fodor'sChoice
★

🏨 **Sugar Mill Hotel.** The owners of this small hotel know what they're doing—they were food and travel writers before they opened the Sugar Mill. The reception area, bar, and restaurant are in the ruins of an old sugar mill. Guest houses are scattered up a hill; rooms are simply decorated in soft pastels. A small pool is set into the hillside, and lunches and dinners (in season) are served on a terrace at the tiny beach. The Sugar Mill Restaurant is well known on the island. ⊠ *Apple Bay* ⌂ *Box 425, Road Town* ☎ *284/495–4355* 📠 *284/495–4696* ⊕ *www.sugarmillhotel.com* 📑 *21 rooms, 2 suites, 1 villa* ⚴ *2 restaurants, pool, beach, snorkeling, 2 bars* ⊟ *AE, MC, V* ❤❤ *EP.*

$$–$$$

🏨 **The Villas of Fort Recovery Estates.** This complex has all the ingredients for a good Caribbean vacation: grounds full of flowers, a remote beachside location including the remnants of a Dutch fort, and friendly, helpful management. All the suites and the four-bedroom villa have excellent views and fully equipped kitchens. The kitchen provides room-service dinners. There are exercise and yoga classes. ⊠ *Waterfront Dr., Pockwood Pond* ⌂ *Box 239* ☎ *284/495–4354 or 800/367–8455* 📠 *284/495–4036* ⊕ *www.fortrecovery.com* 📑 *16 suites, 1 villa* ⚴ *Some kitchens, kitchenettes, pool, exercise equipment, massage, beach, snorkeling, baby-sitting* ⊟ *AE, MC, V* ❤❤ *EP.*

$–$$$

🏨 **Lambert Beach Resort.** On the remote north shore, this Mediterranean-style cottage complex has rooms in eight one-story buildings with red-tile roofs and white stucco exteriors. Two two-bedroom villas on a hillside have full kitchens. Rooms face the beach or look out on tropical gardens. It's a very short walk to the stunning beach or the remarkably large pool. The restaurant offers alfresco breakfasts, lunches, and dinners. ⊠ *Lambert Bay, East End* ⌂ *Box 534* ☎ *284/495–2877* 📠 *284/495–2876* ⊕ *www.lambertbeachresort.com* 📑 *34 rooms, 2 villas* ⚴ *Restaurant, some kitchenettes, refrigerators, tennis court, pool, beach, snorkeling, windsurfing, bar, shop; no room TVs* ⊟ *AE, D, MC, V* ❤❤ *EP.*

$–$$$ 🏠 **Sebastian's on the Beach.** The best accommodations at Sebastian's are the eight small rooms that open onto the beach and the villas that sit just a short walk up the road. They're airy, white, and have terraces or balconies so you can catch the great breezes and views (the ocean lulls you to sleep). The other rooms are very basic, lack views, and can be noisy. The casual restaurant looks out over the water; at lunch you can order fresh salads, grilled vegetables, or soups and sandwiches. The dinner menu includes grilled fish, lobster, and steak. ✉ *Apple Bay ✑ Box 441, Road Town* ☎ *284/495–4212* 🖷 *284/495–4466* ⊕ *www. sebastiansbvi.com* ➘ *26 rooms, 9 villas ♨ Restaurant, snack bar, fans, refrigerators, beach, bar; no TV in some rooms* ⊟ *AE, D, MC* ⦿ *EP.*

$$ 🏠 **Nanny Cay Hotel.** A stay at the Nanny Cay Hotel puts you in the heart of the island's nautical scene, but is close enough to Road Town to make shopping and sightseeing a breeze. The rooms—done in white with bright Caribbean color accents and rattan furniture, overhead ceiling fans, and ceramic-tile floors—have a decidedly tropical feel. Enjoy the trade winds and sea or garden views from your balcony. ✉ *Nanny Cay ✑ Box 281, Road Town* ☎ *284/494–5212 or 866/284–4683* 🖷 *284/ 494–3288* ⊕ *www.nannycay.com* ➘ *38 rooms ♨ 2 restaurants, kitchenettes, tennis court, 2 pools, dive shop, dock, boating, marina, volleyball, shops, meeting rooms* ⊟ *AE, MC, V* ⦿ *EP.*

$–$$ 🏠 **Ole Works Inn.** Tucked against a hill and across the road from a beautiful beach is this rustic inn—owned by local recording star Quito Rhymer. A steeply pitched roof along with wood and stonework adds contemporary flair to what was once an old sugar mill. Rooms are simply decorated with carpeting in most rooms; some have private balconies and kitchenettes. The Honeymoon Suite has an indoor swing for two. You can't beat the Cane Garden Bay location. ✉ *Cane Garden Bay ✑ Box 560, Road Town* ☎ *284/495–4837* 🖷 *284/495–9618* ➘ *15 rooms, 3 suites ♨ Fans, refrigerators* ⊟ *AE, MC, V* ⦿ *EP.*

Campground

¢ 🏕 **Brewers Bay Campground.** The bare sites and rent-a-tents sit cheek by jowl at this beachfront camping spot, with rather ramshackle tarps covering the tent platforms and adjacent cooking areas. That said, you can't beat the beachfront location that has you out of your tent and in the water in a couple of seconds. Showers and bathrooms are down the path, and a small restaurant provides meals. ✉ *Brewers Bay ✑ Box 185, Road Town* ☎ *284/494–3463* ➘ *28 sites ♨ Restaurant, beach, windsurfing, bar, baby-sitting* ⊟ *No credit cards.*

Where to Eat

On Tortola local seafood is plentiful, and although other fresh ingredients are scarce, the island's chefs are a creative lot who apply genius to whatever the weekly supply boat delivers. Contemporary American dishes prepared with a Caribbean influence are very popular. The fancier, more expensive restaurants have dress codes: long pants and collared shirts for men, and elegant, casual resort wear for women.

Road Town

AMERICAN/   ✕ **The Pub.** At this lively waterfront spot tables are arranged along a terrace facing a small marina and the Road Town harbor. Hamburgers, salads, and sandwiches are typical lunch offerings. In the evening you can also choose grilled fish, steak, chicken, sautéed conch, or barbecued ribs. Head here on Thursday night for all-you-can-eat ribs. There's entertainment on weekends, and locals gather here nightly for spirited dart games. ✉ *Waterfront Dr.* ☎ *284/494–2608* ♨ *Reservations not accepted* ⊟ *AE, DC, MC, V* ⊗ *No lunch Sun.*

CASUAL
$–$$$

¢–$$ ✕ **Pusser's Road Town Pub.** Almost everyone who visits Tortola stops here at least once to have a bite to eat and to sample the famous Pusser's Rum Painkiller (fruit juices and rum). The menu includes cheesy pizza, shepherd's pie, fish-and-chips, and hamburgers. Dine inside in air-conditioned comfort or outside on the verandah, which looks out on the harbor. Stop by on Thursdays for nickel beer night. ⊠ *Waterfront Dr.* ☎ *284/494–3897* ▤ *AE, D, MC, V.*

CARIBBEAN ✕ **C and F Restaurant.** Crowds head to this casual spot for the best bar-
$$–$$$$ becue in town (chicken, fish, and ribs), fresh local fish prepared your way, and excellent curries. Sometimes there's a wait for a table, but it's worth it. The restaurant is just outside Road Town, on a side street past the Moorings and Riteway. ⊠ *Purcell Estate* ☎ *284/494–4941* ⌕ *Reservations not accepted* ▤ *AE, MC, V* ⊘ *No lunch.*

CONTEMPORARY ✕ **Fusions.** As its name suggests, Fusions draws from many cuisines to
$$–$$$ create an interesting menu. Tucked upstairs at the Hotel Castle Maria, Fusions conjures up dishes like curried roast pumpkin and ginger bisque or Anegada conch fritters with a spicy cocktail sauce. Segue into a dinner of fettuccini with a roasted garlic, Parmesan, grilled vegetable, and sun-dried tomato sauce or yellowfin tuna with a teriyaki glaze and topped with mango salsa and wasabi. ⊠ *Off Waterfront Drive, follow signs for Hotel Castle Maria* ☎ *284/494–2553* ▤ *D, MC, V.*

ECLECTIC ✕ **Virgin Queen.** The sailing and rugby crowds head here to play darts,
$–$$$ drink beer, and eat Queen's Pizza—a crusty, cheesy pie topped with sausage, onions, green peppers, and mushrooms. Also on the menu is excellent West Indian and English fare: barbecued ribs with beans and rice, bangers and mash, shepherd's pie, chili, and grilled sirloin steak. ⊠ *Fleming St.* ☎ *284/494–2310* ▤ *MC, V* ⊘ *Closed Sun.*

FRENCH ✕ **Le Cabanon.** Birds and bougainvillea brighten the patio of this breezy
$$–$$$ French restaurant and bar, a popular gathering place for locals and visitors alike. Herring salad or the French onion soup are good appetizer choices. Then move on to monkfish in chive butter sauce, veal kidneys, or grilled rib-eye steak with green peppercorn sauce. Save room for such tasty desserts as chocolate mousse, coconut mousse, cherry cheesecake, or a platter of French cheeses. ⊠ *Waterfront Dr.* ☎ *284/494–8660* ▤ *MC, V* ⊘ *Closed Sun.*

ITALIAN ✕ **Spaghetti Junction.** Popular with the boating crowd, this well-known
★ $–$$$ island favorite is right near the cruise-ship dock. Join the crowd outside on the deck overlooking the marina or inside, where it's bustling. The menu includes fresh seafood and many nightly specials, but also house specialties such as penne with a spicy tomato sauce, spinach-mushroom lasagna, *cappellini* (very thin spaghetti) with shellfish, and spicy jambalaya pasta. ⊠ *Wickhams Cay 1* ☎ *284/494–4880* ▤ *AE, MC, V* ⊘ *Closed Sun. No lunch.*

★ ¢–$$ ✕ **Capriccio di Mare.** The owners of the well-known Brandywine Bay restaurant also run this authentic little Italian outdoor café. Stop by for an espresso, fresh pastry, toast Italiano (a grilled ham and Swiss cheese sandwich), a bowl of perfectly cooked linguine, or a crispy tomato and mozzarella pizza. Drink specialties include the Mango Bellini, an adaptation of the famous Bellini cocktail served at Harry's Bar in Venice. ⊠ *Waterfront Dr.* ☎ *284/494–5369* ⌕ *Reservations not accepted* ▤ *MC, V* ⊘ *Closed Sun.*

MEXICAN ✕ **Lime 'n' Mango.** The menu at this popular restaurant includes local spe-
$$–$$$ cialties and authentic Mexican cuisine. Try the conch fritters, salt fish cakes, or Jamaican calamari for an appetizer. The fajitas—chicken, beef, or vegetarian—arrive at your table sizzling in a hot iron frying pan, with a side

of warm tortillas. The coconut shrimp is also popular. Saturday night crowds form here to enjoy the popular West Indian barbecue. ⊠ *Treasure Isle Hotel, Waterfront Dr.* ☎ *284/494–2501* ⊟ *AE, MC, V.*

SEAFOOD
$$–$$$

✕ **The Captain's Table.** Select the lobster you want from the pool here, and be careful not to fall in—it's in the floor right in the middle of the dining room. The menu also includes traditional escargots, fresh local fish, filet mignon with béarnaise sauce, duckling with berry sauce, and creative daily specials. Ceiling fans keep the dining room cool, but there are also tables on a breezy terrace overlooking the harbor. ⊠ *Wickham's Cay I* ☎ *284/494–3885* ⊟ *AE, MC, V* ☉ *No lunch Sat.*

Outside Road Town

AMERICAN/
CASUAL
$–$$$

✕ **Pusser's Landing.** Yachters flock to this waterfront restaurant. Downstairs, from late morning to well into the evening, belly up to the outdoor mahogany bar or choose a waterside table for drinks, sandwiches, rotis, fish-and-chips, and pizzas. At dinnertime head upstairs for a harbor view and a quiet alfresco meal of grilled steak or local fish. ⊠ *Soper's Hole* ☎ *284/495–4554* ⊟ *AE, MC, V.*

CARIBBEAN
$$$–$$$$

✕ **Mrs. Scatliffe's.** The island's best West Indian cooking is served on the upstairs terrace of Mrs. Scatliffe's home. The food is freshly prepared; the baked chicken in coconut is meltingly tender, and the price includes side dishes like stewed okra. If you're lucky, after dinner you'll be treated to a lively *fungi* (bands that make music using household items—washboards, spoons, and the like—as instruments) performance by members of Mrs. Scatliffe's family. ⊠ *Carrot Bay* ☎ *284/495–4556* ⌚ *Reservations essential* ⊟ *No credit cards.*

$$–$$$$

✕ **Myett's.** Right on the beach, this bilevel restaurant-bar is hopping day and night. Chowder made with fresh Anegada lobsters is the specialty, though the menu includes everything from hamburgers to fruit platters and vegetarian dishes to grilled shrimp, steak, and tuna. There's live entertainment on Friday, Sunday, and Monday nights. ⊠ *Cane Garden Bay* ☎ *284/495–9649* ⊟ *MC, V.*

$$–$$$

✕ **Quito's Gazebo.** This rustic beachside bar and restaurant is owned and operated by Quito Rhymer, a multitalented BVI recording star who plays the guitar and sings on Tuesday and Thursday; he performs with his reggae band on Friday and Saturday. The menu is Caribbean with an emphasis on fresh fish. Try the conch fritters or the chicken roti. Wednesday is fish-fry night, an event that brings out locals as well as tourists. ⊠ *Cane Garden Bay* ☎ *284/495–4837* ⊟ *AE, MC, V* ☉ *Closed Mon.*

CONTEMPORARY
$$–$$$$

✕ **Sugar Mill Restaurant.** Candles gleam, and the background music is peaceful in this romantic restaurant that is inside a 360-year-old mill. Well-prepared selections on the à la carte menu, which changes nightly, include pasta and vegetarian entrées. Roasted pumpkin soup or a curried lobster patty are good starters. House favorite entrées include the Jamaican jerk pork roast, the beef curry with *poppadoms* (Indian popovers), pan-seared roast duck, and fresh fish with spicy creole sauce. ⊠ *Apple Bay* ☎ *284/495–4355* ⊟ *AE, MC, V* ☉ *No lunch.*

$$$

✕ **Skyworld.** The top of a mountain is the location for this casually elegant dining room. The filet mignon with a cranberry and tequila sauce is an interesting and tasty combination. Other specialties include chicken with a passion-fruit sauce, grilled local fish, roast duck, rack of lamb with a port sauce, and key lime pie. The very simple lunch menu is mostly hamburgers and sandwiches, though the restaurant can be crowded at this time when a cruise ship docks. ⊠ *Ridge Rd., Joe's Hill* ☎ *284/494–3567* ⊟ *AE, MC, V.*

★ $$–$$$

✕ **Eclipse.** Dine by the waterfront caressed by soft ocean breezes at this popular spot that isn't much more than a terrace filled with tables. The menu is a mixture of fusion and Caribbean cuisine. Spend the evening sampling one dish after another—cracked calamari, chèvre salad, tuna carpaccio—as you order off the two-page grazing menu. Or if you prefer, dig into the spicy curries, fusion chicken, fresh grilled Anegada swordfish, and vegetarian dishes on the regular menu. ⊠ *Fat Hog's Bay, East End* ☎ *284/495–1646* ▭ *MC, V* ☉ *Closed Aug. No lunch.*

$$–$$$ ✕ **Garden Restaurant.** Relax over dinner in this open-air restaurant at Long Bay Beach Resort. Tables are well spaced, offering enough privacy for intimate conversation. The menu changes daily. Appetizers might include garlicky escargots in pastry, Caribbean fish chowder, or shrimp fritters. Entrées run to tuna glazed with soy sauce and served with horseradish yogurt, pan-roasted duck with tamarind glaze, or a filet mignon served with mushrooms. There are always at least five desserts to choose from, such as Belgian chocolate mousse, strawberry cheesecake, and a fluffy lemon and coconut cake. ⊠ *Long Bay Beach Resort, Long Bay* ☎ *284/495–4252* ▭ *AE, MC, V* ☉ *No lunch.*

ITALIAN   ✕ **Brandywine Bay.** Candlelit outdoor tables have sweeping views of neigh-
$$$ boring islands, and owner-chef Davide Pugliese prepares foods the Tus-
Fodor'sChoice can way: grilled with lots of fresh herbs. The remarkable menu can include
★   homemade mozzarella, foie gras, grilled local swordfish, and grilled veal chop with ricotta and sun-dried tomatoes; it always includes duck with a berry sauce. The wine list is excellent, and the lemon tart and the tiramisu are irresistible. ⊠ *Sir Francis Drake Hwy., east of Road Town, Brandywine Bay* ☎ *284/495–2301* ⚠ *Reservations essential* ▭ *AE, MC, V* ☉ *Closed Sun. No lunch.*

Beaches

Beaches in the BVI are less developed than those on St. Thomas or St. Croix. Try to get out on a dive-snorkeling boat or a day-trip sailing vessel at least once. This is often the best way to reach the most virgin Virgin beaches, which are on deserted islands. Tortola's north side has several perfect palm-fringed white-sand beaches that curl around turquoise bays and coves. Nearly all are accessible by car (preferably one with four-wheel-drive), albeit down bumpy roads that corkscrew precipitously. Facilities run the gamut from absolutely none to a number of beachside bars and restaurants as well as places to rent water-sports equipment.

Apple Bay. If you want to surf, the area including Little Apple Bay and Capoon's Bay is the spot—although the beach itself is pretty narrow. Sebastian's, the very casual hotel here, caters to those in search of the perfect wave. Good surf is never a sure thing, but you're more apt to find it in January and February. ⊠ *North Shore Rd.*

Brewers Bay. The water is good for snorkeling, and there are a campground and beach bar here. The beach and its old sugar-mill and rum-distillery ruins are just north of Cane Garden Bay, just past Luck Hill. There's another entrance just east of the Skyworld restaurant. ⊠ *Brewers Bay Rd. W or Brewers Bay Rd. E.*

Cane Garden Bay. This enticing beach has exceptionally calm, crystalline waters and a silky stretch of sand. It's the closest beach to Road Town—one steep uphill and downhill drive—and one of the BVI's best-known anchorages (unfortunately, it can be very crowded when cruise ships are in town). You can rent sailboards and such, stargaze from the bow of a boat, and nosh or sip at several beach-side restaurants, including Quito's Gazebo. ⊠ *Cane Garden Bay Rd.*

Elizabeth Beach. Lined with palm trees, wide, and sandy, the beach is accessible by walking down a private road. However, the undertow can be severe here in winter. ⊠ *Ridge Rd.*

Josiah's Bay. The often deserted Josiah's Bay is a favored place to picnic or to hang ten, although in winter the undertow tends to be strong. ⊠ *Ridge Rd.*

Long Bay, Beef Island. The scenery here draws superlatives: you can catch a glimpse of Little Camanoe and Great Camanoe islands, and if you walk around the bend to the right you can see little Marina Cay and Scrub Island. Long Bay is also a good place to find seashells. ⊠ *Beef Island Rd., Beef Island.*

Long Bay West. Have your camera ready for snapping the breathtaking approach to this stunning 1-mi (1½-km) stretch of white sand. Although Long Bay Resort sprawls along part of it, the entire beach is open to the public. The water isn't as calm here as at Cane Garden or Brewers Bay, but it's still swimmable. ⊠ *Long Bay Rd.*

Smuggler's Cove. After bouncing your way down a pothole-filled dirt road to this beautiful beach, you'll feel as if you've found a hidden piece of the island, although you probably won't be alone on weekends. There's a fine view of Jost Van Dyke Island, and the snorkeling is good. ⊠ *Belmont Rd.*

Trunk Bay. About the only thing you'll find moving is the surf. The beach is directly north of Road Town, midway between Cane Garden Bay and Beef Island, and to reach it you have to hike down a *ghut* (gully) from Ridge Road. ⊠ *Ridge Rd.*

Sports & the Outdoors

CRICKET Fans of this sport are fiercely loyal and exuberant. Matches are held at the New Recreation Grounds, next to the J. R. O'Neal Botanic Gardens, weekends February–April.

FISHING The deep-sea fishing here is so good that tournaments draw competitors from around the world for the largest bluefish, wahoo, swordfish, and shark. You can bring a catch back to your hotel's restaurant, and the staff will prepare it for you for dinner. A half day of deep-sea fishing runs about $425, a full day around $800. If bonefishing is your cup of tea, call **Caribbean Fly Fishing** (⊠ Nanny Cay ☎ 284/499–4797). For a few hours of reel fun, try **Persistence** (⊠ Sopers Hole, West End ☎ 284/495–4122).

HORSEBACK RIDING If you've ever wanted to ride a horse along a deserted beach, now's your chance. Or you can head up to Tortola's ridges for spectacular views. **Shadow Stables** (⊠ Ridge Rd., Todman Peak ☎ 284/494–2262) offers small group rides for $50 per person per hour.

SAILING The BVI are among the world's most popular sailing destinations. ★ They're close together and surrounded by calm waters, so it's fairly easy to sail from one anchorage to the next. If you know how to sail, you can charter a bare boat (perhaps for your entire vacation); if you're unschooled, you can hire a boat with a captain. Prices vary quite broadly depending on the type and size of the boat you wish to charter. In season, a weekly charter runs $1,500–$35,000. If a day sail to some secluded anchorage is more your spot of tea, the BVI has numerous boats of various sizes and styles that leave from numerous points around Tortola. Prices start at around $80 per person for a full-day sail including lunch and snorkeling equipment.

BVI Yacht Charters (⊠ Inner Harbour Marina, Road Town ☎ 284/494–4289 or 888/615–4006) offers 38-ft to 51-ft sailboats for charter—with or without a captain, whichever you prefer. **Catamaran Charters** (⊠ Nanny Cay Marina, Nanny Cay ☎ 284/495–6661 or 800/262–0308) charters catamarans with or without captains. **The Moorings** (⊠ Wickham's Cay

II, Road Town ☎ 284/494–2331 or 800/535–7289), considered one of the best bareboat operations in the world, has a large fleet of well-maintained, mostly Beneteau yachts. Hire a captain or sail the boat yourself. If you prefer a powerboat, call **Regency Yacht Vacations** (✉ Wickhams Cay I, Road Town ☎ 284/495–1970 or 800/524–7676) for both bareboat and captained charters. **Sunsail** (✉ Hodge's Creek Marina, East End ☎ 284/495–4740 or 800/327) offers a full fleet of boats to charter with or without a captain. **Voyages** (✉ Sopers Hole Marina, West End ☎ 284/494–0740) offers the option of booking a cabin instead of a full charter.

Aristocat Charters (✉ West End ☎ 284/495–4087 ⊕ www.aristocatcharters.com) sets sail to the Indians and Peter Island aboard a 48-ft catamaran. **White Squall II** (✉ Village Cay Marina, Road Town ☎ 284/495–2564) takes you to the Baths at Virgin Gorda or The Caves at Norman Island on an 80-ft schooner.

SCUBA DIVING & SNORKELING   Clear waters and numerous reefs afford some wonderful opportunities for underwater exploration. There are several popular dive spots around the islands. **Alice in Wonderland** is a deep dive south of Ginger Island with a wall that slopes gently from 15 ft to 100 ft. It's an area overrun with huge mushroom-shape coral, hence its name. Crabs, lobsters, and shimmering fan corals make their homes in the tunnels, ledges, and overhangs of **Blonde Rock,** a pinnacle that goes from just 15 ft below the surface to 60 ft deep. It's between Dead Chest and Salt Island. When the currents aren't too strong, **Brewer's Bay Pinnacle** (20–90 ft [6–27 m] down) teems with sea life. At **The Indians,** near Pelican Island, colorful corals decorate canyons and grottoes created by four large, jagged pinnacles that rise 50 ft from the ocean floor. The **Painted Walls** is a shallow dive site where corals and sponges create a kaleidoscope of colors on the walls of four long gullies. It's northeast of Dead Chest.

The *Chikuzen,* sunk northwest of Brewer's Bay in 1981, is a 246-ft vessel in 75 ft of water; it's home to thousands of fish, colorful corals, and big rays. In 1867 the RMS *Rhone,* a 310-ft-long royal mail steamer, split in two when it sank in a devastating hurricane. It's so well preserved that it was used in the movie *The Deep.* You can see the crow's nest and bowsprit, the cargo hold in the bow, and the engine and enormous propeller shaft in the stern. Its four parts are at various depths from 30 to 80 ft (9 to 24 m; nearby Rhone Reef is only 20–50 ft [6–15 m] down). Get yourself some snorkeling gear and hop a dive boat to this wreck, off Salt Island (across the channel from Road Town) and part of the BVI National Parks Trust. Every dive outfit in the BVI runs superlative scuba and snorkel tours here. Rates start at around $50 for a one-tank dive and $80 for a two-tank dive.

Baskin' in the Sun (✉ Prospect Reef ☎ 284/494–2858) offers beginner and advanced diving courses and daily trips. Trainers teach open-water, rescue, advanced diving, and resort courses. **Blue Waters Divers** (✉ Nanny Cay ☎ 284/494–2847) teaches resort, open-water, rescue, and advanced diving courses and also makes daily trips. **Underwater Safaris** (✉ The Moorings, Wickham's Cay II, Road Town ☎ 284/494–3235) has resort and advanced diving courses, including rescue and open-water, and schedules day and night dives.

SURFING   Surfing is big on Tortola's north shore, particularly when the winter swells come in to Josiah's and Apple bays. Rent surfboards starting at $25 for a full day.

HIHO (✉ Waterfront Dr., Road Town ☎ 284/494–7694) has a good surfboard selection. The staff will give you advice on the best spots to put in your board.

TENNIS Tortola's tennis options range from simple, untended, concrete courts to professionally maintained facilities that host organized tournaments. The courts listed below are all open to the public; some have restrictions for nonguests.

Frenchman's Cay Hotel (⊠ West End ☎ 284/495–4844) has an unlit artificial-grass court with a pretty view of Sir Francis Drake Channel. Patrons of the hotel or restaurant can use the court free of charge; for others there's an hourly fee of $5. **Long Bay Beach Resort** (⊠ Long Bay ☎ 284/ 495–4252) has three lighted courts and a tennis program run by Peter Burwash International. Private lessons are $55 per hour. Nonguests may rent a court for $10 an hour. Tennis rackets can be rented for $7 an hour.

WINDSURFING The winds are so steady here that some locals use sailboards to get from island to island. Three of the best spots for sailboarding are Nanny Cay, Slaney Point, and Trellis Bay on Beef Island. Rates for sailboards start at about $25 an hour or $75 for a full day.

Boardsailing BVI (⊠ Trellis Bay, Beef Island ☎ 284/495–2447) rents equipment and offers private and group lessons.

Shopping

The BVI aren't really a shopper's delight, but there are many shops showcasing original wares—from jams and spices to resort wear to excellent artwork. Don't be put off by an informal shop entrance; some of the best finds in the BVI lie behind shabby doors.

Areas
Many shops and boutiques are clustered along and just off Road Town's **Main Street.** You can shop in Road Town's **Wickham's Cay I** area adjacent to the marina. There's an ever-growing number of art and clothing stores at **Soper's Hole,** in West End.

Specialty Items
ART **Caribbean Fine Arts Ltd.** (⊠ Main St., Road Town ☎ 284/494–4240) carries Caribbean art, including original watercolors, oils, and acrylics, as well as signed prints, limited-edition serigraphs, and turn-of-the-20th-century sepia photographs. **Sunny Caribbee** (⊠ Main St., Road Town ☎ 284/494–2178) has many paintings, prints, and watercolors by artists from throughout the Caribbean.

CLOTHES & **Arawak** (⊠ On the dock, Nanny Cay ☎ 284/494–5240) carries gifts, batik
TEXTILES sundresses, sportswear, and resort wear for men and women, sandals, accessories, and children's clothing. **Latitude 18°** (⊠ Main St., Road Town ⊠ Soper's Hole Marina, West End ☎ 284/494–7807 for both stores) sells Maui Jim, Smith, Oakley, and Revo sunglasses; Freestyle, Quiksilver, and Roxy watches; and a fine collection of sandals, beach towels, sundresses, and sarongs. **Pusser's Company Store** (⊠ Main St. at Waterfront Rd., Road Town ☎ 284/494–2467 ⊠ Soper's Hole Marina, West End ☎ 284/495–4603) sells nautical memorabilia, ship models, marine paintings, an entire line of clothes (for both men and women), and gift items bearing the Pusser's logo, handsome decorator bottles of Pusser's rum, Caribbean books, Cuban cigars, and luggage. **Sea Urchin** (⊠ Waterfront, Columbus Centre, Road Town ☎ 284/494–2044 ⊠ Mill Mall, Road Town ☎ 284/494–4108 ⊠ Soper's Hole Marina, West End ☎ 284/ 495–4599) is the source for local books, island jewelry, sunglasses, and resort wear—print shirts and shorts, colorful swimsuits, cover-ups, sandals, T-shirts—for the whole family. **Zenaida's of West End** (⊠ Soper's Hole Marina, West End ☎ 284/495–4867) displays the fabric finds of Argentine

Vivian Jenik Helm, who travels through South America, Africa, and India in search of batiks, hand-painted and hand-blocked fabrics, and interesting weaves that can be made into pareus (women's wraps) or wall hangings. The shop also sells unusual bags, belts, sarongs, scarves, and ethnic jewelry.

FOODSTUFFS **Ample Hamper** (⊠ Village Cay Marina, Wickham's Cay I, Road Town ☎ 284/494–2494 ⊠ Soper's Hole Marina, West End ☎ 284/495–4684 ⊠ Hodge's Creek Marina, East End ☎ 284/495–2247) has an outstanding collection of cheeses, wines, fresh fruits, and canned goods from the United Kingdom and the United States. You can have the management here provision your yacht or rental villa.

K-Marks (⊠ Waterfront Dr. at Port Purcell Road Town ☎ 284/494–4649) carries the usual supermarket stuff – albeit a much smaller selection than you might find in your hometown supermarket.

GIFTS **Bamboushay** (⊠ Nanny Cay Marina Nanny Cay ☎ 284/494–0393) sells lovely handcrafted Tortola-made pottery in shades that reflect the sea. **J. R. O'Neal, Ltd.** (⊠ Main St., Road Town ☎ 284/494–3759) stocks the shelves of its somewhat hidden shop with fine crystal, Royal Worcester china, hand-painted Italian dishes, handblown Mexican glassware, Spanish ceramics, and Indian woven rugs and tablecloths. **Sunny Caribbee** (⊠ Main St., Road Town ☎ 284/494–2178), in a brightly painted West Indian house, packages its own herbs, teas, coffees, vinegars, hot sauces, soaps, skin and suntan lotions, and exotic concoctions—Arawak Love Potion and Island Hangover Cure, for example. There are also Caribbean books and art and hand-painted decorative accessories.

JEWELRY **Columbian Emeralds International** (⊠ Wickham's Cay I, Road Town ☎ 284/494–7477), a Caribbean chain catering to the cruise-ship crowd, is the source for duty-free emeralds plus other gems, gold jewelry, crystal, and china. **Samarkand** (⊠ Main St., Road Town ☎ 284/494–6415) crafts charming gold and silver pendants, earrings, bracelets, and pins—many with an island theme: seashells, lizards, pelicans, palm trees. There are also reproduction Spanish pieces of eight (coins—old Spanish pesos worth eight reals—from sunken galleons).

PERFUMES & **Flamboyance** (⊠ Main St., Road Town ☎ 284/494–4099) carries designer
COSMETICS fragrances and upscale cosmetics.

STAMPS The **BVI Post Office** (⊠ Main Street Road Town ☎ 284/494–3701) is a philatelist's dream. It has a worldwide reputation for exquisite stamps in all sorts of designs. The stamps carry U.S. monetary designations, but can be used only in the BVI.

Nightlife & the Arts

Nightlife

Like any good sailing destination, Tortola has watering holes that are popular with salty and not-so-salty dogs. Many offer entertainment; check the weekly *Limin' Times* for schedules. The local beverage is the Painkiller, an innocent-tasting mixture of fruit juices and rums. It goes down smoothly but packs quite a punch, so give yourself a moment before you order another.

Bing's Drop In Bar (⊠ Fat Hog's Bay, East End ☎ 284/495–2627) is a rollicking local hangout that has a DJ nightly in season. By day **Bomba's Surfside Shack** (⊠ Apple Bay ☎ 284/495–4148)—covered with everything from crepe-paper leis to license plates to colorful graffiti—looks like a pile of junk; by night it's one of Tortola's liveliest spots and one of the Caribbean's most famous beach bars. Sunday at 4 there's always some sort of live music, and Wednesday at 8 the locally famous Blue Haze Combo shows up to play everything from reggae to Top 40 tunes. Every full moon, bands play all night long and people flock here from all over. There's a fish fry and a live band every Thursday night at the informal **Ceta's Place** (⊠ Capoon's Bay ☎ no phone). At the **Jolly Roger** (⊠ West End ☎ 284/495–4559) an ever-changing roster of local, U.S., and down-island bands plays everything from rhythm and blues to reggae to country to good old rock and roll Friday and Saturday—and sometimes Sunday—starting at 8. Local bands play at **Myett's** (⊠ Cane Garden Bay ☎ 284/495–9543) on Friday, Sunday, and Monday evenings, and there's usually a lively dance crowd. Thursdays are nickel beer nights at **Pusser's Road Town Pub** (⊠ Waterfront St., Road Town ☎ 284/494–4199), and crowds gather here for courage (John Courage, that is) by the pint. Other nights try Pusser's famous mixed drinks—Painkillers—and snack on the excellent pizza. At **The Pub** (⊠ Waterfront St., Road Town ☎ 284/494–2608) there's an all-day happy hour on Friday, and Ruben Chinnery on the guitar Friday evenings from 6 to 9. BVI recording star Quito Rhymer sings island ballads and love songs, accompanied by the guitar at **Quito's Gazebo** (⊠ Cane Garden Bay ☎ 284/495–4837), a rustic beachside bar-restaurant. Solo shows are on Sunday, Tuesday, Thursday, and Friday nights at 8:30; Saturday night a reggae band performs. There's often live music at **Sebastian's** (⊠ Apple Bay ☎ 284/495–4212) on Sunday evenings, and you can dance under the stars.

The Arts

Musicians from around the world perform in the **Classics in the Atrium** (⊠ The Atrium at the H. Lavity Stoutt Community College, Paraquita Bay ☎ 284/494–4994) series from October to February each year. Past artists have included Britain's premier a cappella group, Black Voices; New Orleans jazz pianist Ellis Marsalis; and Keith Lockhart and the Serenac Quartet (from the Boston Pops Symphony).

Exploring Tortola

Tortola doesn't have many historic sights, but it does have lots of beautiful natural scenery. Although you could explore the island's 10 square mi (26 square km) in a few hours, opting for such a whirlwind tour would be a mistake. Life in the fast lane has no place when you're surrounded by some of the Caribbean's most breathtaking panoramas and beaches. Also the roads are extraordinarily steep and twisting, making driving demanding. The best strategy is to explore a bit of the island at a time. For example, you might try Road Town (the island's main town) one morning and a drive to Cane Garden Bay and West End (a little town on, of course, the island's west end) the next afternoon. Or consider a visit to East End, a *very* tiny town located exactly where its name suggests. The north shore is where all the best beaches are found.

Numbers in the margin correspond to points of interest on the Tortola map.

What to See

❷ Ft. Burt. The most intact historic ruin on Tortola was built by the Dutch in the early 17th century to safeguard Road Harbour. It sits on a hill at the western edge of Road Town and is now the site of a small hotel and restaurant. The foundations and magazine remain, and the structure offers a commanding view of the harbor. ⊠ *Waterfront Dr., Road Town* ☎ *no phone* 🖭 *Free* ☉ *Daily dawn–dusk.*

❹ Ft. Recovery. The unrestored ruins of a 17th-century Dutch fort, 30 ft in diameter, sit amid a profusion of tropical greenery on the Villas of

Fort Recovery Estates grounds. There's not much to see here, and there
are no guided tours, but you're welcome to stop by and poke around.
✉ *Waterfront Dr., Road Town* ☎ *284/485–4467* 🖾 *Free.*

❺ Frenchman's Cay. On this little island connected by a causeway to Tortola's western end, there are a marina and a captivating complex of pastel West Indian–style buildings with shady balconies, shuttered windows,
and gingerbread trim that house art galleries, boutiques, and restaurants.
Pusser's Landing here is a lively place to stop for a cold drink (many
are made with Pusser's famous rum) and a sandwich and watch the boats
in harbor.

★ ❸ J. R. O'Neal Botanic Gardens. Take a walk through this 4-acre showcase
of lush plant life. There are sections devoted to prickly cacti and suc-
culents, hothouses for ferns and orchids, gardens of medicinal herbs,
and plants and trees indigenous to the seashore. From the Tourist Board
office in Road Town, cross Waterfront Drive and walk one block over
to Main Street and turn right. Keep walking until you see the high
school. The gardens are on your left. ✉ *Botanic Station, Road Town*
☎ *no phone* 🖾 *Free* ☉ *Mon.–Sat. 9–4:30.*

❾ Mt. Healthy National Park. The remains of an 18th-century sugar plantation are here. The windmill structure has been restored, and you can
see the ruins of a mill, a factory with boiling houses, storage areas, stables, a hospital, and many dwellings. This is a nice place to picnic. ✉ *Ridge
Rd., Todman Peak* ☎ *no phone* 🖾 *Free* ☉ *Daily dawn–dusk.*

❻ North Shore Shell Museum. On Tortola's north shore, this casual museum
has a very informal exhibit of shells, unusually shaped driftwood, fish
traps, and traditional wooden boats. ✉ *North Shore Rd., Carrot Bay*
☎ *284/495–4714* 🖾 *Free* ☉ *Daily dawn–dusk.*

❶ Road Town. The laid-back capital of the BVI looks out over Road Harbour. It takes only an hour or so to stroll down Main Street and along
the waterfront, checking out the traditional West Indian buildings
painted in pastel colors and with high-pitched, corrugated-tin roofs, bright
shutters, and delicate fretwork trim. For hotel and sightseeing brochures
and the latest information on everything from taxi rates to ferry-boat
schedules, stop in the BVI Tourist Board office. Or just choose a seat
on one of the benches in Sir Olva Georges Square, on Waterfront Drive,
and watch the people come and go from the ferry dock and customs office across the street.

★ ❼ Sage Mountain National Park. At 1,716 ft, Sage Mountain is the highest
peak in the BVI. From the parking area a trail leads you in a loop not
only to the peak itself (and extraordinary views) but also to a small rain
forest, sometimes shrouded in mist. Most of the forest was cut down
over the centuries to clear land for sugarcane, cotton, and other crops;
to create pastureland; or to simply utilize the stands of timber. In 1964
this park was established to preserve what rain forest remained. Up here
you can see mahogany trees, white cedars, mountain guavas, elephant-
ear vines, mamey trees, and giant bullet woods, to say nothing of such
birds as mountain doves and thrushes. Take a taxi from Road Town or
drive up Joe's Hill Road and make a left onto Ridge Road toward Chal-
well and Doty villages. The road dead-ends at the park. ✉ *Ridge Rd.
Sage Mountain* ☎ *no phone* 🖾 *Free* ☉ *Daily, dawn to dusk.*

★ ❽ Skyworld. Drive up here and climb the observation tower for a stunning,
360-degree view of numerous islands and cays. On a clear day you can
even see St. Croix (40 mi [64½ km] away) and Anegada (20 mi [32 km]
away). ✉ *Ridge Rd., Joe's Hill* ☎ *no phone* 🖾 *Free.*

VIRGIN GORDA

Virgin Gorda, or "Fat Virgin," received its name from Christopher Columbus. The explorer envisioned the island as a pregnant women in a languid recline with Gorda Peak being her big belly and the boulders of The Baths her toes. Different in topography from Tortola, with its arid landscape covered with scrub brush and cactus, the pace of life is slower here too. Goats and cattle own the right of way, and the unpretentious friendliness of the people is winning.

Where to Stay

Virgin Gorda's charming hostelries appeal to a select, appreciative clientele; repeat business is extremely high. Those who prefer Sheratons, Marriotts, and the like may feel they get more for their money on other islands, but the peace and pampering offered on Virgin Gorda are priceless to the discriminating traveler.

For approximate costs, *see* the lodging price chart *in* Tortola.

Hotels & Inns

$$$$ ⊞ **Biras Creek Hotel.** This resort is so classy that it's a member of the exclusive Relais & Chateaux family of hotels. Units, decorated in soft Caribbean colors, are in duplex cottages, and each has a separate bedroom and a living room. Although entrances are hidden among the trees, many cottages are feet from the water's edge. Bike paths and trails lead to the beaches and the outstanding Biras Creek restaurant. On a hilltop is the open-air stonework bar-restaurant area. A sailaway package includes two nights on a private yacht. Rates are per couple, per night and include everything but beverages. ⊠ *North Sound* ⌂ *Box 54* ☎ *284/ 494–3555 or 800/223–1108* 🖷 *284/494–3557* ⊕ *www.biras.com* ⇆ *33 suites, 2 villas* ♨ *3 restaurants, 2 tennis courts, pool, beach, snorkeling, windsurfing, boating, bicycles, hiking, bar, shop* ☰ *AE, MC, V* ⍥ *AI.*

★ **$$$$** ⊞ **Bitter End Yacht Club.** This family-oriented, convivial resort-cum-marina is accessible only by boat. Accommodations range from comfortable hillside or beachfront rooms with spacious balconies to live-aboard yachts. Your day can include snorkeling and diving trips to nearby reefs, cruises, windsurfing lessons, excursions to local attractions, and lessons at the well regarded Nick Trotter Sailing School. When the sun goes down, the festivities continue at The Clubhouse, an open-air restaurant-bar overlooking North Sound. ⊠ *North Sound* ⌂ *Box 46* ☎ *284/ 494–2746 or 800/872–2392* 🖷 *284/494–4756* ⊕ *www.beyc.com* ⇆ *95 rooms* ♨ *3 restaurants, pool, beach, dive shop, snorkeling, windsurfing, boating, waterskiing, bar, children's programs (ages 6–18 years); no A/C in some rooms* ☰ *AE, MC, V* ⍥ *AI.*

$$$$ ⊞ **Drake's Anchorage Resort Inn.** Set on the edge of its own 125-acre island, this tiny and secluded getaway provides the utmost in privacy. Dinner attire here means changing from bathing suit to comfortable cottons. Three West Indian–style waterfront bungalows contain four rooms and four suites that are simply furnished. Three villas with full kitchens are also available. The appealing restaurant is an elegant stop for all meals. Hiking trails, water-sports facilities, four delightful beaches, and hammocks here and there make this a place you never want to leave. ⊠ *North Sound* ⌂ *Box 2510* ☎ *284/494–2254 or 800/624–6651* 🖷 *284/494–2254* ⊕ *www.drakesanchorage.com* ⇆ *4 rooms, 4 suites, 3 villas* ♨ *Restaurant, beach, snorkeling, boating, hiking, bar* ☰ *AE, MC, V* ⊙ *Closed July–Sept.* ⍥ *AI.*

$$$$ ⊞ **Little Dix Bay.** Relaxed elegance is the hallmark here. The resort sits along a curving beach. Duplexes with hexagonal units and quadraplex

Virgin Gorda

Cockroach Island

George Dog

Great Dog

West Dog

⑥

Sir Francis Drake Channel

Mountain Pt.

Long Bay ➤

Nail Bay Point ⑫

Mountain Trunk Bay

Mango Bay

Mahoe Bay ⑪

⑩

Pond Bay ⑨

Savannah Bay

Little Dix Bay ⑧

Colison Pt.

⑦

Handsome Bay

TO TORTOLA

St. Thomas Bay

Spanish Town
Fort Pt. ②

① ② Virgin Gorda Airport ③

The Valley

Copper Mine Bay

The Crawl

Spring Bay Beach ④

Devil's Bay ③ ⑤ ⑥ ④

Crook's Bay

Fallen Jerusalem ⑥

Stoney Bay

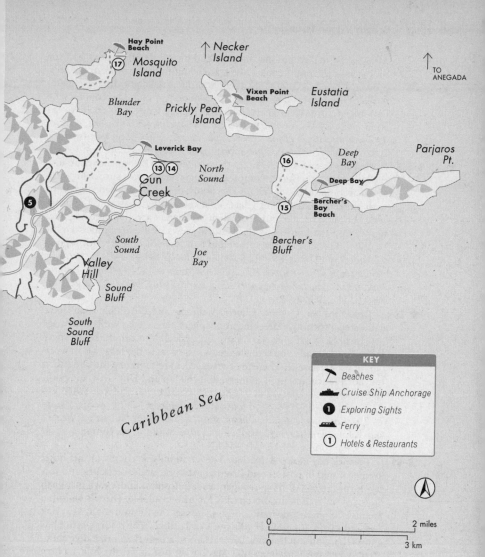

KEY

🏖 Beaches

🚢 Cruise Ship Anchorage

1 Exploring Sights

⛴ Ferry

① Hotels & Restaurants

Caribbean Sea

0   2 miles

0   3 km

cottages are tucked among the trees and on a little hill. About half the rooms are air-conditioned. Lawns are beautifully manicured; the reef-protected beach is long and silken; and the candlelight dining is memorable. This resort is popular with honeymooners and older couples who have been returning for years. ⊠ *Little Dix Bay* ⅅ *Box 70* ☎ *284/495–5555* 🖷 *284/495–5661* ⊕ *www.littledixbay.com* ☞ *94 rooms, 4 suites* ⚫ *3 restaurants, 7 tennis courts, spa, beach, snorkeling, windsurfing, 2 bars, library, children's programs (ages 3–16)* ⊟ *AE, MC, V* ⅪⅪ *EP.*

$–$$$ 🏨 **Nail Bay Resort.** On 147 acres that stretch from three beaches up into the hills, this remarkable complex, though small, has a surprising variety of accommodations. There are rooms, one- and two-bedroom units with kitchens, and elegant villas. Villas are scattered around the property, but most rooms and apartment-style units are clustered together halfway up the hillside, with beautiful views of the Sir Francis Drake Channel. The alfresco restaurant and bar overlooks the free-form pool. ⊠ *Nail Bay* ⅅ *Box 69* ☎ *284/494–8000* 🖷 *284/495–5875* ⊕ *www.nailbay.com* ☞ *16 rooms, 8 1- and 2-bedroom units, 14 villas* ⚫ *Restaurant, tennis court, beach, snorkeling, windsurfing, boccie, croquet, bar* ⊟ *AE, MC, V* ⅪⅪ *EP.*

★ $$ 🏨 **Olde Yard Inn.** Owners Charlie Williams and Carol Kaufman have cultivated a friendly, refreshing atmosphere here. Cedar walls with original Caribbean art give the rooms a cozy feel. You can make arrangements for day sails and scuba excursions, swim in the large pool, work out, or get a massage. There are two excellent restaurants: the Olde Yard Inn, for French-accented dinners, and the Sip and Dip Grill, for poolside lunches. ⊠ *The Valley* ⅅ *Box 26* ☎ *284/495–5544 or 800/653–9273* 🖷 *284/495–5986* ⊕ *www.oldeyardinn.com* ☞ *14 rooms, 1 suite* ⚫ *2 restaurants, 7 tennis courts, pool, health club, hair salon, beach, snorkeling, windsurfing, croquet, bar, library, shops, playground; no A/C in some rooms* ⊟ *AE, MC, V* ⅪⅪ *EP.*

$–$$ 🏨 **Leverick Bay Resort & Marina.** The small hillside rooms at this hotel are decorated in pastels and original artwork, with tile floors and rattan furnishings. All have refrigerators, balconies, and views of North Sound; four two-bedroom condos are also available. Down the hill, a Spanish colonial-style main building houses the Restaurant at Leverick Bay and a store (operated by Pusser's of Tortola). The resort's office has games that you can borrow. Several shops, a beauty salon, a dive shop, a coin-operated laundry, and a market are just down the hill. ⊠ *Leverick Bay* ⅅ *Box 63* ☎ *284/495–7421 or 800/848–7081* 🖷 *284/495–7367* ⊕ *www.leverickbay.com* ☞ *16 rooms, 4 condos* ⚫ *2 restaurants, fans, pool, tennis, beach, bar* ⊟ *AE, D, MC, V* ⅪⅪ *EP.*

Private Homes & Villas

Those craving seclusion would do well at a villa or even a private home. Both offer comfortable lodgings with full kitchens and maid service. **Virgin Gorda Villa Rentals** (ⅅ Box 63, Leverick Bay ☎ 284/495–7421 or 800/848–7081 ⊕ www.virgingordabvi.com) manages over 40 properties that are near Leverick Bay Resort or Mahoe Bay, so it's perfect for those who want to be close to some activity. Many villas—ranging from studios to houses with five or more bedrooms—have private swimming pools and air-conditioning, at least in the bedrooms; all have full kitchens, are well maintained, and have spectacular views. Prices run from $120 to $1,290 per night. Major credit cards are generally accepted.

$$–$$$$ 🏨 **Paradise Beach Resort.** These one-, two-, and three-bedroom beachfront suites and villas have handsome, Caribbean-style furnishings, pastel color schemes, and outdoor showers. Four-wheel-drive vehicles are included in the daily rate. ⊠ *Mahoe Bay* ⅅ *Box 534* ☎ *284/495–*

5871 📠 *284/495–5872* ⊕ *www.paradisebeachresort.com* ⟿ *9 units* ⚴ *Some kitchens, some kitchenettes, beach* ⊟ *No credit cards.*

$$–$$$ 🏠**Guavaberry Spring Bay Vacation Homes.** These hexagonal one- and two-bedroom units are scattered about a hillside from which you can hear chirping birds and feel ocean breezes. It's just a short walk from the cottages down to the tamarind-shaded beach, and not far from the mammoth boulders and cool basins of the famed Baths, which adjoin this property. ⊠ *The Valley* ⌂ *Box 20* 🕾 *284/495–5227* ⊕ *www. guavaberryspringbay.com* ⟿ *12 1-bedroom units, 9 2-bedroom units* ⚴ *Grocery, fans, kitchens, beach* ⊟ *No credit cards.*

$–$$$ 🏠**Mango Bay Resort.** Sparkling-white villas framed by morning glories and frangipanis, handsome contemporary Italian furnishings, and a gorgeous ribbon of golden sand that all but vanishes at high tide make this an idyllic family retreat. Even for Virgin Gorda it's a study in isolation. ⊠ *Mahoe Bay* ⌂ *Box 1062* 🕾 *284/495–5672* 📠 *284/495–5674* ⊕ *www.mangobayresort.com* ⟿ *11 villas* ⚴ *Grocery, kitchens, beach; no A/C, no room phones, no room TVs* ⊟ *V, MC.*

Where to Eat

Restaurants range from simple to elegant. Hotels that are accessible only by boat will arrange transport in advance upon request for nonguests who wish to dine at their restaurants. It's wise to make dinner reservations almost everywhere except really casual spots.

For approximate costs, *see* the dining price chart *in* Tortola.

AMERICAN/
CASUAL
$$–$$$$

✕**Top of The Baths.** At the entrance to The Baths, this popular restaurant starts serving at 8 AM. Tables are outside on a terrace or in an open-air pavilion; all have stunning views of the Sir Francis Drake Channel. Hamburgers, sandwiches, and fish-and-chips are offered at lunch. Conch fritters and pumpkin soup are among the dinner appetizers. Entrées include fillet of yellowtail snapper, shrimp creole, and jerk chicken. For dessert, the mango kiwi tart is excellent. ⊠ *The Valley* 🕾 *284/495–5497* ⊕ *www.thebathsbvi.com* ⊟ *AE, MC, V.*

$$–$$$ ✕**The Flying Iguana.** Local artwork is displayed in this charming restaurant's comfortable lounge. The open-air dining room looks out over Virgin Gorda's tiny airport to the sea. Enjoy classic eggs and bacon for breakfast; for lunch there are sandwiches and juicy hamburgers. The dinner menu includes fresh seafood, grilled chicken, steaks, and a pasta special. ⊠ *Virgin Gorda Airport, The Valley* 🕾 *284/495–5277* ⊟ *MC, V.*

$$–$$$ ✕**The Restaurant at Leverick Bay.** This bilevel restaurant at the Leverick Bay Hotel looks out over North Sound. The upstairs is slightly less casual and more expensive, with a menu that includes prime rib, pork chops, chicken dishes, and fresh fish specials. Below, the bar offers light fare all day—starting with breakfast and moving on to hamburgers, salads, and pizzas until well into the evening. ⊠ *Leverick Bay Resort & Marina, Leverick Bay* 🕾 *284/495–7154* ⊕ *www.therestaurantatleverickbay. com* ⊟ *AE, MC, V.*

★ **$–$$** ✕**Sip and Dip Grill.** Enjoy a pleasant, informal lunch by the pool at the Olde Yard Inn. Come for the grilled fish, pasta salads, spicy chili, chilled soups, and ice cream. Sunday evening there's a barbecue with live entertainment. ⊠ *The Olde Yard Inn, The Valley* 🕾 *284/495–5544* ⊕ *www.oldeyardinn.com* ⊟ *AE, MC, V* ☉ *No dinner Mon.–Sat.*

¢–$$ ✕**The Bath and Turtle.** You can really sit back and relax at this informal patio tavern with a friendly staff—although the TV noise can be a bit much. Burgers, well-stuffed sandwiches, homemade pizzas, pasta dishes, and daily specials like conch gumbo round out the casual menu. Live entertainers perform Saturday nights. ⊠ *Virgin Gorda Yacht Harbour,*

Spanish Town ☎ 284/495–5239 ⊕ *www.islandsonline.com/bathturtle/*
▭ *AE, MC, V.*

¢–$ ✕ **Mad Dog's.** Piña coladas are *the* thing at this breezy bar just outside
the entrance to The Baths. The menu includes great triple-decker sandwiches, hot dogs, and burgers. ⊠ *The Valley* ☎ 284/495–5830 ▭ *No
credit cards* ⊘ *No dinner.*

CAJUN/CREOLE ✕ **Chez Bamboo.** This pleasant little hideaway isn't really that hard to
$$–$$$ find; look for the building with the purple and green latticework. Can-
dles on the dining room tables and the patio help make this a mellow
place where you can enjoy such dishes as conch gumbo, Chez B's bouillabaisse, and steak New Orleans. For dessert, try the chocolate bourbon mint cake. Stop by Friday night for live jazz. ⊠ *Across from and
a little north of Virgin Gorda Yacht Harbour, Spanish Town* ☎ 284/
495–5752 ⊕ *www.islandsonline.com/bathturtle/* ▭ *MC, V* ⊘ *No lunch.*

CONTEMPORARY ✕ **Biras Creek.** This hilltop restaurant at the Biras Creek Hotel has stun-
$$$$ ning views of North Sound. The four-course prix-fixe menu changes daily
and includes several choices per course. Peppered tuna with foie gras
and gnocchi, grilled veal loin with eggplant caviar, and cilantro-en-
crusted beef tenderloin are some of the enticing entrées. Dinner ends with
Biras Creek's signature offering of Stilton and port. ⊠ *Biras Creek
Hotel, North Sound* ☎ 284/494–3555 ⊕ *www.biras.com/menus.htm*
⌖ *Reservations essential* ▭ *AE, MC, V.*

$$$$ ✕ **Drake's Anchorage.** Waves lap almost within reach at the tables of this
waterside, open-air restaurant, where you can watch the twinkling
lights of neighboring resorts. Dinner is an elegant four-course affair. The
meal begins with a soup of the evening. Next comes a salad, then the
entrée you chose, such as filet mignon with black peppercorn and brandy
sauce or jumbo shrimp sautéed with garlic and plum tomatoes. The fourth
course is dessert, naturally. Specialty of the house is chocolate mousse,
though the caramel bananas are delicious, too. Call two days ahead for
reservations. ⊠ *Drake's Anchorage Resort Inn, North Sound* ☎ 284/
494–2254 or 284/494–5871 ⌖ *Reservations essential* ▭ *AE, MC, V*
⊘ *No lunch; Closed July–Sept.*

$$$–$$$$ ✕ **Little Dix Bay Pavilion.** For an elegant evening, you can't do better than
this—the candlelight in the main open-air pavilion is enchanting, the
menu sophisticated, the service attentive. The dinner menu changes
daily, but there's always a fine selection of superbly prepared seafood,
meat, and vegetarian entrées—flaky mahimahi fillet with grilled pineap-
ple–raisin chutney, a risotto-and-cheese encrusted loin of lamb, and
seared red snapper fillet and skewered prawns on a savory black-olive
hash. The breakfast and lunch buffets shine. ⊠ *Little Dix Bay Resort,
Spanish Town* ☎ 284/495–5555 Ext. 174 ⊕ *www.littledixbay.com/
dine.cfm* ▭ *AE, MC, V.*

$$–$$$ ✕ **Olde Yard Inn.** The intimate dining room of The Olde Yard Inn is suf-
fused with gentle, classical melodies and the scent of herbs; a cedar roof
covers the breezy space, which is decorated with old-style Caribbean
charm. The French-accented cuisine includes lamb chops with mango
chutney, chicken breast in a rum cream sauce, grilled fish, steaks, and
lobster. Chocolate mousse, cheesecake, and key lime pie are sweet end-
ings. ⊠ *The Olde Yard Inn, The Valley* ☎ 284/495–5544 ⊕ *www.
oldeyardinn.com* ▭ *AE, MC, V.*

ITALIAN ✕ **Giorgio's Table.** Gaze out at the stars and the lights of Tortola and lis-
$$–$$$$ ten to the water lap against the shore while dining on veal scallopini,
filet mignon with mushrooms, fresh local fish, or penne with garlic and
tomatoes. Lunch fare at this casual establishment includes pizzas and
sandwiches. ⊠ *Mahoe Bay* ☎ 284/495–5684 ▭ *AE, MC, V.*

SEAFOOD
★ $$$–$$$$

✕ **The Clubhouse.** The Bitter End Yacht Club's open-air waterfront restaurant is a favorite rendezvous for the sailing set—busy day and night. At the lavish buffets you get your choice of an entrée for breakfast, lunch, and dinner. Dinner selections include grilled swordfish or tuna, chopped sirloin, scallops, shrimp, and local lobster. ✉ *Bitter End Yacht Club, North Sound* ☎ *284/494–2746* ⊕ *www.beyc.com* ▤ *AE, MC, V.*

Beaches

The best beaches are easily reached by water, although they're also accessible on foot, usually after a moderately strenuous 10- to 15-minute hike. Either way, your persistence is rewarded. Anybody going to Virgin Gorda must experience swimming or snorkeling among its unique boulder formations, which can be visited at several beaches along Lee Road. The most popular of these spots is The Baths, but there are several others nearby that are easily reached.

The Baths. Featuring a stunning maze of huge granite boulders that extend into the sea, this beach is usually crowded mid-day with day-trip visitors. Beach lockers are available to keep belongings safe.

Bercher's Bay Beach. From Biras Creek or Bitter End on the north shore you can walk to Bercher's Bay and along the windswept surf.

The Crawl. Swim or walk north from Spring Bay Beach to reach this small and appealing bounder-strewn beach. It's a super spot for young children and novice snorkelers. Picnic tables are nearby.

Deep Bay. Footpaths from Bitter End and foot and bike paths from Biras Creek lead to the calm, well-protected swimming beach.

Hay Point Beach. Mosquito Island's best beach is a broad band of white sand accessible only by boat or by a path from a little dock on the island's east side.

Leverick Bay. This tiny, busy beach-cum-marina fronts the resort's restaurant and pool. Come here if you want a break from the island's serenity. The view of Prickly Pear Island is a plus, and the dive facility here can arrange to motor you out to beautiful Eustatia Reef, just across North Sound.

Nail Bay. Head to the island's north tip, travel about half an hour after the North Sound Road turnoff on a partial dirt road, and you'll be rewarded with a trio of beaches within the Nail Bay Resort complex that are ideal for snorkeling. Mountain Trunk Bay is perfect for beginners, while Nail Bay and Long Bay beaches boast coral caverns just offshore.

Savannah Bay. For a wonderfully private beach close to Spanish Town, try Savannah Bay. It may not always be completely deserted, but it's a lovely, long stretch of white sand. Bring your mask, fins and snorkel.

Spring Bay Beach. From The Baths you can walk on Lee Road or swim north to this less-populated beach, where the snorkeling is excellent.

Vixen Point Beach. On Prickly Pear Island in North Sound, the calm waters lapping up to this beach are perfect for swimming. There's a beach bar steps away from the sea that offers a variety of liquid refreshments.

Sports & the Outdoors

CRICKET
You can catch a match at the **Recreation Grounds** in Spanish Town February–April. The Virgin Gorda BVI Tourist Board office can give you information on game dates and times.

FISHING
The sportfishing here is so good that anglers come from all over the world. **Virgin Gorda Charter Services** (✉ Leverick Bay, North Sound ☎ 284/495–6666 ⊕ www.fishbvi.com) offers a choice of three boats for trips ranging from full-day marlin hunting to half-day inshore light-tackle angling for species like mackerel and snapper. Plan to spend $250–$1,200.

GOLF The 9-hole professionally-equipped mini golf course at **Golf Virgin Gorda** (⊠ Copper Mine Road, Spanish Town ☎ 284/495–5260 ⊕ www.islandsonline.com/mineshaft) is delightfully nestled between huge granite boulders. Cost for adults is $5, children $3.

SAILING The BVI waters are calm, and terrific places to learn to sail. The **Bitter End Sailing & Windsurfing School** (⊠ Bitter End Yacht Club, North Sound ☎ 284/494–2746 ⊕ www.beyc.com) offers classroom, dockside, and on-the-water lessons for sailors of all levels. Private lessons are $60 per hour. If you just want to sit back, relax, and let the captain take the helm, try **Spice** (⊠ Leverick Bay Marina, North Sound ☎ 284/495–7044 ⊕ www.spicebvi.com), a 51-ft sloop that makes half- and full-day voyages to Anegada, The Baths, and Cooper Island for sunning, swimming and snorkeling.

SCUBA DIVING & There are some terrific snorkel and dive sites off Virgin Gorda, includ-
SNORKELING ing areas around The Baths, North Sound, and The Dogs. The **Bitter End Yacht Club** (⊠ North Sound ☎ 284/494–2746 ⊕ www.beyc.com) offers a number of snorkeling trips day and night. Costs range from $15 per person to $90 per person depending on the length and type of the trip. Contact **Dive BVI** (⊠ Virgin Gorda Yacht Harbour, Spanish Town ☎ 284/495–5513 ⊕ www.divebvi.com) for expert instruction, certification, and day trips. It costs $100 for a resort course, $85 for a two-tank dive, and $65 for a one-tank dive; equipment rental is an additional $15. **Sunchaser Scuba** (⊠ Bitter End Yacht Harbor, North Sound ☎ 284/495–9638 ⊕ www.come.to/bvi), formerly Kilbride's, offers resort, advanced, and rescue courses. The fee for a resort course is $95. One-tank dives run $60, two-tank dives $85. Equipment rental is an additional $15.

WINDSURFING The North Sound is a good place to learn to windsurf: it's protected, so you can't be easily blown out to sea. The **Bitter End Yacht Club** (⊠ North Sound ☎ 284/494–2746 ⊕ www.beyc.com) gives lessons and rents equipment for $30 per hour.

Shopping

Most boutiques are within hotel complexes. Two of the best are at Biras Creek and Little Dix Bay. Other properties—the Bitter End, Leverick Bay, and the Olde Yard Inn—have small but equally select boutiques, and there's a respectable and diverse scattering of shops in the bustling yacht harbor complex in Spanish Town.

CLOTHING **Dive BVI** (⊠ Virgin Gorda Yacht Harbour, Spanish Town ☎ 284/495–5513) sells books about the islands as well as snorkeling equipment, sportswear, sunglasses, and beach bags. **Next Wave** (⊠ Virgin Gorda Yacht Harbour, Spanish Town ☎ 284/495–5623) offers bathing suits, T-shirts, canvas tote bags, and locally made jewelry. **Pavilion Gift Shop** (⊠ Little Dix Bay Hotel, Little Dix Bay ☎ 284/495–5555) has the latest in resort wear for men and women, as well as jewelry, books, housewares, and expensive T-shirts. **Pelican's Pouch Boutique** (⊠ Virgin Gorda Yacht Harbour, Spanish Town ☎ 284/495–5599) carries a large selection of name-brand swimsuits plus cover-ups, T-shirts, and accessories. **Pusser's Company Store** (⊠ Leverick Bay ☎ 284/495–7369) has a trademark line of sportswear, rum products, and gift items.

FOODSTUFFS **Bitter End's Emporium** (⊠ North Sound ☎ 284/494–2745) is the place for such edible treats as local fruits, cheeses, and fresh-baked goods. The **Chef's Pantry** (⊠ The Valley ☎ 284/494–7154) has the fixings for an impromptu party in your villa or boat—fresh seafood, specialty meats, French cheeses, daily baked breads and pastries, and an impressive wine and

spirit selection. The **Commissary and Ship Store** (⊠ The Valley ☎ 284/
495–5555) offers daily specials prepared by Little Dix Resort chefs, as
well as assorted cheeses, canned goods, wines, and fancy foods. The **Wine
Cellar and Bakery** (⊠ Virgin Gorda Yacht Harbour, Spanish Town ☎ 284/
495–5250) sells bread, rolls, muffins, cookies, sandwiches, and sodas
to go.

GIFTS   **The Artistic Gallery** (⊠ Virgin Gorda Yacht Harbour, Spanish Town
☎ 284/495–5104) features Caribbean jewelry, 14-karat-gold nautical
jewelry, maps, collectible coins, and crystal. **Palm Tree Gallery** (⊠ Leverick Bay ☎ 284/495–7479) sells attractive handcrafted jewelry, paintings, and one-of-a-kind gift items, as well as games and books about
the Caribbean. **The Reeftique** (⊠ Bitter End Yacht Harbor, North Sound
☎ 284/494–2745) carries island crafts and jewelry, clothing, and nautical odds and ends with the Bitter End logo. **Scoops** (⊠ Virgin Gorda
Yacht Harbour, Spanish Town ☎ 284/495–5722) has unusual gifts like
photo frames made from Virgin Gorda beach sand and whimsical tiles
hand-painted by a St. Thomas artist.

HANDICRAFTS   **Virgin Gorda Craft Shop** (⊠ Virgin Gorda Yacht Harbour, Spanish Town
☎ 284/495–5137) sells the work of island artisans, and carries West Indian jewelry and crafts styled from straw, shells, and other local materials. It also stocks clothing and paintings by Caribbean artists.

Nightlife

Pick up a free copy of the *Limin' Times,* available at most resorts and
restaurants, for the most current local entertainment schedule.

The Bath and Turtle (⊠ Virgin Gorda Yacht Harbour, Spanish Town
☎ 284/495–5239), one of the liveliest spots on Virgin Gorda, hosts island bands regularly in season from 8 PM until midnight. Local bands
play at **Bitter End Yacht Club** (⊠ North Sound ☎ 284/494–2746) on
weekends during the winter. **Chez Bamboo** (⊠ across from Virgin Gorda
Yacht Harbour, Spanish Town ☎ 284/495–5752) is the place on the island for live jazz. **Little Dix Bay** (⊠ Little Dix Bay ☎ 284/495–5555) presents elegant live entertainment several nights a week in season. **The Mine
Shaft** (⊠ Copper Mine Road ☎ 284/495–5260) has live bands for
Ladies Night on Fridays from 7 PM to 9 PM **The Restaurant at Leverick
Bay** (⊠ Leverick Bay Resort & Marina, Leverick Bay ☎ 284/495–7154)
hosts live bands on Saturday nights in season. The **Rock Café** (⊠ The Valley ☎ 284/495–5672) has live bands Friday, Saturday, and Sunday
nights. The **Sip and Dip Grill** (⊠ Olde Yard Inn, The Valley ☎ 284/495–
5544) hosts a live local band at its Sunday night barbecue.

Exploring Virgin Gorda

One of the most efficient ways to see Virgin Gorda is by sailboat. There
are few roads, and most byways don't follow the scalloped shoreline.
The main route sticks resolutely to the center of the island, linking The
Baths at the tip of the southern extremity with Gun Creek and Leverick Bay at North Sound and providing exhilarating views. The craggy
coast, scissored with grottoes and fringed by palms and boulders, has
a primitive beauty. If you drive, you can hit all the sights in one day.
The best plan is to explore the area near your hotel (either The Valley
or North Sound) first, then take a day to drive to the other end. Stop
to climb Gorda Peak, in the island's center.

*Numbers in the margin correspond to points of interest on the Virgin
Gorda map.*

What to See

❸ The Baths. At Virgin Gorda's most celebrated sight, giant boulders are
Fodor'sChoice scattered about the beach and in the water. Some are almost as large as
★ houses and form remarkable grottoes. Climb between these rocks to swim
in the many pools. Early morning and late afternoon are the best times
to visit if you want to avoid crowds. (If it's privacy you crave, follow
the shore northward to quieter bays—Spring, the Crawl, Little Trunk,
and Valley Trunk—or head south to Devil's Bay.) ⊠ *Lee Rd., The Baths*
🕾 *no phone* 🖾 *Free.*

❻ Coastal Islands. You can easily reach the quaintly named Fallen Jerusalem
Island and the Dog Islands by boat. They're all part of the BVI National
Parks Trust, and their seductive beaches and unparalleled snorkeling dis-
play the BVI at their beachcombing, hedonistic best. 🕾 *No phone*
🖾 *Free.*

❹ Copper Mine Point. Here stand a tall, stone shaft silhouetted against the
sky and a small stone structure that overlooks the sea. These are the ruins
of a copper mine established 400 years ago and worked first by the Spanish, then by the English, until the early 20th century. ⊠ *Copper Mine
Rd.* 🕾 *No phone* 🖾 *Free.*

❷ Little Fort National Park. This 36-acre wildlife sanctuary has the ruins of
an old Spanish fort. Giant boulders like those at The Baths are scattered
throughout the park. ⊠ *Spanish Town Rd.* 🕾 *No phone* 🖾 *Free.*

❶ Spanish Town. Virgin Gorda's peaceful main settlement, on the island's
southern wing, is so tiny that it barely qualifies as a town at all. Also known
as The Valley, Spanish Town has a marina, some shops, and a couple of
car-rental agencies. Just north of town is the ferry slip. At the Virgin Gorda
Yacht Harbour you can stroll along the dock and do a little shopping.

★ ❺ Virgin Gorda Peak National Park. There are two trails at this 265-acre
park, which contains the island's highest point, at 1,359 ft. Small signs
on North Sound Road mark both entrances; sometimes, however, the
signs are missing, so keep your eyes open for a set of stairs that disap-
pears into the trees. It's about a 15-minute hike from either entrance up
to a small clearing, where you can climb a ladder to the platform of a
wooden observation tower and a spectacular 360-degree view. ⊠ *North
Sound Rd., Gorda Peak* 🕾 *No phone* 🖾 *Free.*

JOST VAN DYKE

Named after an early Dutch settler, Jost Van Dyke is a small island northwest of Tortola, and is *truly* a place to get away from it all. Mountainous and lush, the 4-mi-long (6½-km-long) island—with fewer than 200
full-time residents—has one tiny resort, some rental houses, a campground,
a handful of cars, and a single road. This is one of the Caribbean's most
popular anchorages, and there's a disproportionately large number of
informal bars and restaurants, which have helped earn Jost its reputation as the "party island" of the BVI.

Where to Stay

For approximate costs, *see* the lodging price chart *in* Tortola.

$$$ 🏨 **Sandy Ground Estates.** The eight privately owned one- and two-bed-
room houses here are tucked into the foliage along the edge of a beach
at the island's east end. Each house is architecturally distinct, and inte-
riors range from spartan to stylish. The fully equipped kitchens can be
pre-stocked. The Web site has a provisioning list you can download, se-

lect what you'd like, and e-mail back to the provisioner in Road Town along with a credit-card number. There are three very casual restaurants on the other side of the hill—a long walk away. ⊠ *Sandy Ground Estates* ⌂ *Box 594, West End* ☎ *284/494–3391* ⊕ *www.sandyground. com* ⇨ *8 houses* ⚒ *Fans, kitchens, microwaves, beach; no A/C, no room TVs* ⊟ *MC, V* ⍩⎮ *EP.*

★ **$$**   ⌂ **Sandcastle.** This six-cottage hideaway is on a ½-mi (¾-km) stretch of white-sand beach at remote White Bay. There's "nothing" to do here except relax in a hammock, read, walk, swim, and enjoy sophisticated cuisine by candlelight in the Sandcastle restaurant. You can also make arrangements for diving, sailing, and sportfishing trips. ⊠ *White Bay* ☎ *284/495–9888* ⎙ *284/495–9999* ⊕ *www.sandcastle-bvi.com* ⇨ *6 cottages* ⚒ *Restaurant, beach, bar, shops* ⊟ *MC, V* ⍩⎮ *EP.*

¢   ♨ **Ivan's Stress Free Bar & White Bay Campground.** On the east end of
Fodor'sChoice White Bay Beach, this simple campground has bare sites, equipped tent
★   sites (with electricity and a lamp), and screened cabins. There's a communal kitchen stocked with pots and pans, and a small grocery sits just over the hill. The Saturday night barbecue is a winner. Owner Ivan Chinnery will take you on nature walks and can arrange island tours and sailing and diving trips. But Ivan's real celebrity status comes from his musical ability. Don't be surprised to hear impromptu jam sessions featuring Ivan himself, his band buddies, and visiting musicians. ⊠ *White Bay* ☎ *284/495–9312* ⇨ *8 cabins, 5 tents, 15 campsites* ⚒ *Restaurant, beach, bar* ⊟ *No credit cards.*

Where to Eat

Restaurants on Jost Van Dyke are informal (some serve meals family style at long tables) but charming. The island is a favorite charter-boat stop, and you're bound to hear people exchanging stories about the previous night's anchoring adventures. Most restaurants don't take reservations, and in all cases dress is casual.

For approximate costs, *see* the dining price chart *in* Tortola.

ECLECTIC ✗ **Sandcastle.** Candlelit dinners in the tiny beachfront dining room of
$$$$ the Sandcastle cottage complex are four-course, prix-fixe affairs with seating at 7 PM. The menu changes but can include a West Indian pumpkin or curried-apple soup; curried shrimp or three-mustard chicken; and for dessert, rum bananas or key lime pie. Reservations are requested by 4 PM. Sandwiches are served at lunch at the Soggy Dollar Bar, famous as the purported birthplace of the lethal Painkiller drink. ⊠ *White Bay* ☎ *284/495–9888* ⊕ *www.sandcastle-bvi.com/dining.html* ⚒ *Reservations essential* ⊟ *MC, V* ☉ *No dinner Fri. No breakfast or lunch during Sept.*

$$–$$$$ ✗ **Abe's Little Harbour.** Specialties at this informal, popular spot include fresh lobster, conch, and spareribs. During most of the winter season there's a pig roast every Wednesday night. ⊠ *Little Harbour* ☎ *284/ 495–9329* ⊟ *MC, V.*

$$–$$$$ ✗ **Foxy's Tamarind.** One of the true hot spots in the BVI—and a must-stop for yachters from the world over—Foxy's hosts the madcap Wooden Boat Race every May and throws big parties on New Year's Eve, April Fools' Day, and Halloween. This lively place serves local dishes, terrific barbecue dinners on Friday and Saturday nights, and makes a rum punch that's all its own. Famed calypso performer and owner Foxy Callwood plays the guitar and creates calypso ditties about diners. Next door is Foxy's Store, which sells clothing, sundries, souvenirs, and cassettes of Foxy performing. ⊠ *Great Harbour* ☎ *284/495–9258* ⊕ *www. foxysbar.com* ⊟ *AE, MC, V* ☉ *No lunch weekends.*

$$–$$$$ ✕ **Sydney's Peace and Love.** Here you'll find great lobster, barbecue, and a sensational (for the BVI) jukebox. The cognoscenti sail here for dinner, since there's no beach—meaning no irksome sand fleas. ⊠ *Little Harbour* ☎ *284/495–9271* 🖃 *MC, V.*

$$–$$$ ✕ **Club Paradise.** Hamburgers, West Indian conch stew, and curried chicken are all on the lunch menu. At dinner this casual beachfront establishment serves up grilled local fish such as mahimahi, red snapper, and grouper, grilled steaks, and barbecued chicken and ribs. The Bushwacker—a potent frozen drink— is world famous. ⊠ *Great Harbour* ☎ *284/495–9267* 🖃 *MC, V.*

★ $$–$$$ ✕ **Harris' Place.** Owner Harris Jones is famous for his pig-roast buffets and Monday night Lobstermania. Harris' Place is a great spot to rub elbows with locals and the charter-boat crowd. ⊠ *Little Harbour* ☎ *284/495–9302* 🖃 *AE, MC, V.*

$$–$$$ ✕ **Rudy's Mariner's Rendezvous.** Hamburgers, cheeseburgers, and barbecue ribs are the specialties at this beachfront spot at the extreme west of the beach. There's a lobster buffet every Thursday night in season. ⊠ *Great Harbour* ☎ *284/495–9282* 🖃 *D, MC, V.*

Beaches

Sandy Cay. Just offshore, the little islet known as Sandy Cay is a gleaming scimitar of white sand, with marvelous snorkeling.

★ **White Bay.** On the south shore, west of Great Harbour, this long stretch of white sand is especially popular with boaters who come ashore for a libation at the beach bar.

Nightlife

★ Jost Van Dyke is the most happening place to go bar-hopping in the BVI. In fact, yachties will sail over just to have a few drinks. All the spots are easy to find, congregated in two spots: Great Harbour and White Bay (⇨ *see* Where to Eat *above*). On the Great Harbour side you'll find Foxy's, Rudy's, and Club Paradise; on the White Bay side is the Soggy Dollar bar at the Sandcastle restaurant, where legend has it the famous Painkiller was first concocted. If you can't make it to Jost Van Dyke, you can have a Painkiller at almost any bar in the BVI.

ANEGADA

Fodor'sChoice
★ Anegada lies low on the horizon about 14 mi (22½ km) north of Virgin Gorda. Unlike the hilly volcanic islands in the chain, this is a flat coral and limestone atoll. Nine miles (14 km) long and 2 mi (3 km) wide, the island rises no more than 28 ft above sea level. In fact, by the time you're able to see it, you may have run your boat onto a reef. (More than 300 captains unfamiliar with the waters have done so since exploration days; note that bareboat charters don't allow their vessels to head here without a trained skipper.) Although the reefs are a sailor's nightmare, they (and the shipwrecks they've caused) are a scuba diver's dream. Snorkeling, especially in the waters around Loblolly Bay on the north shore, is also a transcendent experience. You can float in shallow, calm, reef-protected water just a few feet from shore and see one coral formation after another, each shimmering with a rainbow of colorful fish. Such watery pleasures are complemented by ever-so-fine, ever-so-white sand (the northern and western shores have long stretches of the stuff) and the occasional beach bar (stop in for burgers, Anegada lobster, or a frosty beer). The island's population of about 150 lives primarily in a small south-side village called The Settlement, which has two grocery

Mega-views: 3,482. Mega-malls: 0.

To be spoiled on our unspoiled islands, visit www.bvitouristboard.com The *last* great undiscovered place. *For further information or to speak to a BVI specialist, call the BVI Tourist Board at* 1-800-835-8530.

THE **BRITISH** VIRGIN ISLANDS
NATURE'S LITTLE SECRETS

Find America *with a Compass*

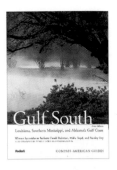

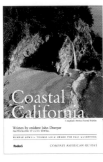

Written by local authors and illustrated throughout
with spectacular color images, Compass American
Guides reveal the character and culture of more than
40 of America's most fascinating destinations. Perfect
for residents who want to explore their own backyards
and for visitors who want an insider's perspective
on the history, heritage, and all there is to see and do.

Fodor's COMPASS AMERICAN GUIDES

At bookstores everywhere.

storcs, a bakery, and a general store. Many local fisherfolk are happy to take visitors out bonefishing.

Where to Stay

For approximate costs, *see* the lodging price chart *in* Tortola.

$$ 🏨 **Anegada Reef Hotel.** If you favor laid-back living, this is the spot for you. Pack a bathing suit and a few warmer garments for the evening, and you're set to go. The hotel's simply furnished rooms are laid out in motel fashion. It has its own narrow strip of beach, but beach lovers will want to spend their days on the deserted strands at the other side of the island. Cool down at the outdoor bar, and be sure to try the island's famous lobster—freshly grilled in the Anegada Reef restaurant. ⊠ *Setting Point* ☎ *284/495–8002* 🖷 *284/495–9362* ⊕ *www.anegadareef. com* ⟿ *16 rooms* ⌂ *Restaurant, beach, bar; no A/C in some rooms* ⊟ *MC, V* ⊺⊙⊺ *AI.*

$ 🏨 **Neptune's Treasure.** This little guest house offers simple double and single rooms that are very basically furnished. However, all have private baths. There's a restaurant, Neptune's Treasure, as well as a little gift shop on the premises. ⊠ *Between Pomato and Saltheap points* ☎ *284/495–9439* ⊕ *www.islandsonline.com/neptunes/index.html* ⟿ *4 rooms* ⌂ *Restaurant, beach* ⊟ *MC, V* ⊺⊙⊺ *EP.*

¢–$ ⛺ **Anegada Beach Campground.** The tents (8×10 ft [2×3 m] or 10×12 ft [3×4 m]), bare sites, and one-bedroom cottages all make use of a marvelously serene setting. There's a small casual restaurant, and grill facilities are available for those who want to cook their own food. The restaurant has lush toilets. ⊠ *The Settlement* ☎ *284/495–9466* ⟿ *10 bare sites, 10 tents, 2 cottages* ⌂ *Restaurant, beach, bar* ⊟ *No credit cards.*

Where to Eat

There are between 6 and 10 restaurants open at any one time, depending on the season and on whim. Check when you're on the island.

For approximate costs, *see* the dining price chart *in* Tortola.

SEAFOOD ✕ **Pomato Point.** This relaxed restaurant-bar is on a narrow beach a short **$$$–$$$$** walk from the Anegada Reef Hotel. Entrées include steak, chicken, lobster, stewed conch, and fresh-caught seafood. Owner Wilfred Creque displays various island artifacts, including shards of Arawak pottery and 17th-century coins, cannonballs, and bottles. ⊠ *Pomato Point* ☎ *284/ 495–8038* ⊕ *www.islandsonline.com/pomato/index.html* ⌂ *Reservations essential* ⊟ *MC, V* ⊙ *Closed Sept.*

$$–$$$$ ✕ **Anegada Reef Hotel.** Seasoned yachters gather nightly at the Anegada Reef Hotel's bar-restaurant to converse and dine with hotel guests. Dinner is by candlelight and always includes famous Anegada lobster, steaks, and chicken—all prepared on the large grill by the little open-air bar. ⊠ *Setting Point* ☎ *284/495–8002* ⌂ *Reservations essential* ⊟ *MC, V.*

$$–$$$$ ✕ **Neptune's Treasure.** The owners catch, cook, and serve the seafood (lobster is a specialty) at this casual bar and restaurant in the Neptune's Treasure guest house. ⊠ *Between Pomato and Saltheap points* ☎ *284/ 495–9439* ⊕ *www.islandsonline.com/neptunes/index.html* ⊟ *AE.*

$–$$$ ✕ **Big Bamboo.** Ice-cold beer, island drinks, burgers, and grilled lobster entice a steady stream of barefoot diners to this beach bar for lunch. Dinner is by request. ⊠ *Loblolly Bay* ☎ *284/495–2019* ⊟ *AE.*

Shopping

Anegada Reef Hotel Boutique (⊠ Setting Point ☎ 284/495–8002) has a bit of everything: resort wear, hand-painted T-shirts, locally made jewelry, books, and one-of-a-kind gifts. **Pat's Pottery** (⊠ Nutmeg Point ☎ 284/495–8031) sells bowls, plates, cups, candlestick holders, and original watercolors.

OTHER BRITISH VIRGIN ISLANDS

Cooper Island

This small, hilly island on the south side of the Sir Francis Drake Channel, about 8 mi (13 km) from Road Town, Tortola, is popular with the charter-boat crowd. There are no roads (which doesn't really matter, because there aren't any cars), but you will find a beach restaurant, a casual little hotel, a few houses (some are available for rent), and great snorkeling at the south end of Manchioneel Bay.

Where to Stay & Eat

For approximate costs, *see* the dining and lodging price charts *in* Tortola.

$$ ✕▣ **Cooper Island Beach Club.** Six West Indian–style cottages—set back from the beach among the palm trees—house 12 no-frills units, each with a living area, a small but complete kitchen, and a balcony. A stay here takes you back to the basics: you use rainwater that has been collected in a cistern, and you can't use any appliances because electricity is so limited. The restaurant serves great ratatouille, grilled fish, chicken and vegetable rotis, penne pasta, and conch creole. For lunch there are hamburgers, conch fritters, sandwiches, and pasta salad. Reservations are essential for the restaurant if you are not a resort guest. ⊠ *Manchioneel Bay* ✆ *Box 859, Road Town, Tortola* ☎ *413/659–2602, 800/ 542–4624 hotel, 284/494–3111 restaurant* ⊕ *www.cooper-island.com* ⇄ *12 rooms* ♢ *Restaurant, fans, kitchens, beach, dive shop, bar; no A/C, no room phones, no room TVs* ⊟ *AE, MC, V* ⦿| *EP.*

Marina Cay

Beautiful little Marina Cay is in Trellis Bay, not far from Beef Island. Sometimes you can see it and its large J-shape coral reefs—a most dramatic sight—from the air soon after takeoff from the airport on Beef Island. With only 6 acres, this islet is considered small even by BVI standards. On it there's a restaurant, Pusser's Store, and a six-unit hotel. Ferry service is free from the dock on Beef Island.

Where to Stay & Eat

For approximate costs, *see* the lodging price chart *in* Tortola.

$$ ▣ **Pusser's Marina Cay Hotel and Restaurant.** The tiny island's only hotel has four rooms and two villas, all with lovely views of the water and neighboring islands. Each has its own porch. The restaurant's menu ranges from fish and lobster to steak, chicken, and barbecued ribs. Pusser's Painkiller Punch is the house specialty. There's free ferry service from the Beef Island dock for anyone visiting the island (call for ferry times, which vary with the season). ⊠ *West side of Marina Cay* ✆ *Box 76, Road Town, Tortola* ☎ *284/494–2174* 🖷 *284/494–4775* ⊕ *www. pussers.com* ⇄ *4 rooms, 2 villas* ♢ *2 restaurants, beach, bar; no A/C, no room TVs* ⊟ *AE, MC, V* ⦿| *EP.*

Exclusive Island Resorts

When the rich and famous want to get away from it all and let their hair down, they head to private island resorts that are true jewels of pampering and luxury. These are all $$$$ places, where you can expect outstanding service but still a fairly laid-back atmosphere.

Guana Island (✉ Hilltop ℗ Box 32, Road Town, Tortola ☎ 284/494–2354 or 914/967–6050 ☎ 284/495–2900 ⊕ www.guana.com) has 15 comfy rooms in seven houses set on a hilltop with a commanding view of Virgin Gorda to the east. The walk to the beach takes about 10 minutes. Guests mingle during cocktail hour and often dine together at several large tables in the main house. Daily rates of $850 to $1,500 per couple include three meals, afternoon tea, and house wine with lunch and dinner. For $15,000 per day, in season, you can rent the entire island.

Necker Island (✉ North Sound ℗ Box 1091, The Valley, Virgin Gorda ☎ 284/494–2757 ☎ 284/494–4396 ⊕ www.virgin.com/necker/), owned by UK entrepreneur Richard Branson, is an opulent 10-room villa and two Balinese cottage complex that can accommodate up to 25 guests. There are five beaches, tennis courts, and beautiful walkways through the lush foliage. A chef prepares meals for you in the state-of-the-art kitchen; a full staff takes care of everything else. From $14,000 to $24,000 per day gets you a stay at this piece of paradise.

Peter Island (✉ Sprat Bay ℗ Box 211, Road Town, Tortola ☎ 284/495–2000 or 800/346–4451 ☎ 284/495–2500 ⊕ www.peterisland.com) floats in a lap of luxury 5 mi (8 km) directly south across the Sir Francis Drake Channel from Road Town, Tortola. There are only 52 sumptuous guest accommodations and two villas on this 1,800-acre island. There's lots to do here: facilities include a Peter Burwash tennis program, a water-sports center, a fitness trail, and a 5-Star PADI dive facility. The air-conditioned Tradewinds Restaurant overlooks the Sir Francis Drake Channel. The à la carte menu offers mostly Continental selections with subtle Caribbean touches. There's a $950 daily double occupancy rate in season, which includes all meals. For $7,250 per day, you and up to 8 fellow guests can vacation like kings and queens in the Crow's Nest villa.

BRITISH VIRGIN ISLANDS A TO Z

To research prices, get advice from other travelers, and book travel arrangements, visit www.fodors.com.

AIR TRAVEL

Beef Island/Tortola, Virgin Gorda, and Anegada airports are classic Caribbean—almost always sleepy. However, the Beef Island terminal can get crowded when several departures are scheduled close together, and lines at service desks move slowly when this happens; give yourself at least an hour. There's no nonstop service from the continental United States to the BVI; connections are usually made through San Juan, Puerto Rico, or St. Thomas, USVI. American Eagle, Cape Air, and Air Sunshine fly from San Juan to Tortola, with Air Sunshine making the flight from San Juan to Virgin Gorda. From St. Thomas, take Cape Air, LIAT, or Air Sunshine to Tortola. Clair Aero flies from St. Thomas on Monday, Wednesdays, and Fridays to Tortola, the flights continuing on to Virgin Gorda and Anegada. Air Sunshine and Air St. Thomas make the St. Thomas to Virgin Gorda run. The charter airline Fly BVI also provides service to wherever you want to go.

▛ Air St. Thomas ☎ 284/495-5935. Air Sunshine ☎ 284/495-8900 ⊕ www.
airsunshine.com. American Eagle ☎ 284/495-2559. Cape Air ☎ 284/495-2100
⊕ www.flycapeair.com. Clair Aero Services ☎ 284/495-2271. Fly BVI ☎ 284/495-1747
⊕ www.fly-bvi.com. LIAT ☎ 284/495-2577.

AIRPORTS

At the Beef Island/Tortola Airport, taxis hover at the exit from customs.
Fares are officially set; they're not negotiable and are lower per person
when there are several passengers. Figure about $15 for up to three peo-
ple and $5 for each additional passenger for the 20-minute ride to Road
Town, and about $20–$30 for the 45-minute ride to West End. Expect
to share your taxi, and be patient if your driver searches for people to
fill his cab—only a few flights land each day, and this could be your driver's
only run. You can also call the BVI Taxi Association.

On Virgin Gorda, call Mahogany Rentals and Taxi Service. If you're
staying on North Sound, a taxi will take you from the airport to the
dock, where your hotel launch will meet you, but be sure to make
launch arrangements with your hotel before your arrival. If your destination is Leverick Bay, your land taxi will take you there directly. Note
that if your destination is Virgin Gorda, you can also fly to Beef Island/
Tortola and catch the nearby North Sound Express, which will take you
to Spanish Town or North Sound.

On Anegada, your hotel will organize your transportation.
▛ BVI Taxi Association ☎ 284/495-1982. Mahogany Rentals and Taxi Service
✉ The Valley ☎ 284/495-5469.

BOAT & FERRY TRAVEL

FARES &
SCHEDULES

Ferries connect the airport gateway of St. Thomas, USVI, with Tortola
and Virgin Gorda. They leave from both Charlotte Amalie and Red Hook.
Ferries also link St. John, USVI, with Tortola, Jost Van Dyke and The Valley, Virgin Gorda, as well as Tortola with Jost Van Dyke, Peter Island and
The Valley, Virgin Gorda. Tortola has two ferry terminals—one at West
End and one in Road Town—so make sure you hop a ferry that disem-
barks closest to where you want to go. There's huge competition among
the Tortola-based ferry companies on the St. Thomas-to-Tortola runs, with
boats leaving close together. As you enter the ferry terminal to buy your
ticket, crews may try to convince you to take their ferry. All ferries from
the BVI to St. Thomas stop in St. John to clear U.S. customs. Ferry schedules vary by day, and not all companies make daily trips.

If you're heading to Tortola from Charlotte Amalie and Red Hook, St.
Thomas, take boats run by Native Son or Smith's Ferry. The boats stop
at West End and Road Town. *Nubian Princess* sails between Red Hook
and West End. Inter-Island Boat Service runs between St. John and West
End. For trips to Road Town and The Valley, Virgin Gorda, from Charlotte Amalie, St. Thomas, take Speedy's Ferries. From St. John to The
Valley, Virgin Gorda, take Inter-Island Boat Services.

To Jost Van Dyke, take Inter-Island Boat Services from St. John and Jost
Van Dyke Ferry Service or New Horizon Ferry Service from West End,
Tortola. To Spanish Town and Bitter End in Virgin Gorda from Beef Is-
land, Tortola, take North Sound Express. To Peter Island, take the Peter
Island Ferry from Road Town.
▛ Inter-Island Boat Services ☎ 284/495-4166. Jost Van Dyke Ferry Service ☎ 284/
494-2997. Native Son ☎ 284/495-4617. New Horizon Ferry Service ☎ 284/495-9278.
North Sound Express ☎ 284/495-2138. *Nubian Princess* ☎ 284/495-4999. Peter Is-
land Ferry ☎ 284/495-2000. Smith's Ferry ☎ 284/495-4495. Speedy's Ferries
☎ 284/495-5240.

BUSINESS HOURS

BANKS Banking hours are usually Monday–Thursday 9–2:30 and Friday 9–2:30 and 4:30–6.

POST OFFICES Post offices are open weekdays 9–5 and Saturday 9–noon.

SHOPS Stores are generally open Monday–Saturday 9–5. Some may be open on Sunday.

CAR RENTALS Both Tortola and Virgin Gorda have a number of car-rental agencies. Although taxi service is good on these two islands, many people who want to explore the islands and try a different beach every day opt for renting a vehicle. On Anegada it's possible to rent a car, but most people rely on taxis for transportation. Jost Van Dyke has a single road, and visitors travel on foot or by local taxi. On the other islands there are no roads.

You'll need a temporary BVI license, available at the rental-car company for $10 with a valid license from another country. Most agencies offer both four-wheel-drive vehicles and cars (often compacts).

On Tortola, try Avis, Hertz, or Itgo Car Rental. On Virgin Gorda, contact Mahogany Rentals and Taxi Service or L&S Jeep Rental. On Anegada, D. W. Jeep Rentals will provide you with wheels.
🚗 **Avis** ⊠ opposite Police Station, Road Town, Tortola ☎ 284/494-3322. **D. W. Jeep Rentals** ⊠ The Settlement, Anegada ☎ 284/495-9677. **Hertz** ⊠ West End, Tortola ☎ 284/495-4405. **Itgo Car Rental** ⊠ Wickham's Cay I, Road Town, Tortola ☎ 284/494-2639. **L&S Jeep Rental** ⊠ South Valley, Virgin Gorda ☎ 284/495-5297. **Mahogany Rentals and Taxi Service** ⊠ Spanish Town, Virgin Gorda ☎ 284/495-5469.

CAR TRAVEL

GASOLINE Gas costs about $2.50 a gallon.

ROAD CONDITIONS Tortola's main roads are well paved, for the most part, but there are exceptionally steep hills and sharp curves; driving demands your complete attention. A main road circles the island and several roads cross it, almost always through mountainous terrain. Virgin Gorda has a smaller road system and a single, very steep road links the north and south ends of the island. Anegada's few roads are little more than sandy lanes.

RULES OF THE ROAD Driving in the BVI is on the left side of the road, British style—but your car will have left-hand drive like those used in the U.S. Speed limits (rarely enforced) are 20 mph in town and 35 mph outside town.

ELECTRICITY
Electricity is 110 volts, the same as in North America, so European appliances will require adaptors. The electricity is quite reliable.

EMERGENCIES
🚑 Ambulance & Fire **General emergencies** ☎ 999.
🏥 Hospitals & Clinics **Anegada Government Health Clinic** ☎ 284/494-8049. **Jost Van Dyke Government Health Clinic** ☎ 284/495-9239. **Peebles Hospital** ⊠ Road Town, Tortola ☎ 284/494-3497. **Virgin Gorda Government Health Clinic** ⊠ The Valley ☎ 284/495-5337.
💊 Pharmacies **Cay Pharmacy** ⊠ Road Town, Tortola ☎ 284/494-8128. **Island Drug Centre** ⊠ Spanish Town, Virgin Gorda ☎ 284/495-5449. **J. R. O'Neal Drug Store** ⊠ Road Town, Tortola ☎ 284/494-2292. **Medicure Health Center** ⊠ Spanish Town, Virgin Gorda ☎ 284/495-5479.
🚓 Police **General emergencies** ☎ 999.

ETIQUETTE & BEHAVIOR
Islanders are religious, and churches fill up on Sunday. You're welcome to attend services, but be sure to dress up. If you encounter any rude-

ness, you probably didn't begin the conversation properly: only after courteous exchanges ("Hello, how are you today?" and "Not too bad, and how are you?") should you get down to the business of buying groceries, ordering lunch, or hiring a taxi.

FESTIVALS & SEASONAL EVENTS

In March, catch the breathtaking displays of local foliage at the Horticultural Society Show at the botanical gardens in Tortola; also in March, gather together with locals and yachties at Foxy's annual St. Patrick's Day celebration on Jost Van Dyke. In April, join the fun at the Virgin Gorda Festival, which culminates with a parade on Easter Sunday; also in April, glimpse the colorful spinnakers as sailing enthusiasts gather for the internationally known BVI Spring Regatta. May is the time for partying at Foxy's Wooden Boat Regatta, on Jost Van Dyke. In August, try your hand at sportfishing, as anglers compete to land the largest catch at the BVI Sportfishing Tournament; August sees two weeks of joyful revelry during Tortola's BVI Emancipation Festival celebrations. To compete in sailing races and games, drop in on Virgin Gorda's North Sound during the last six weeks of the year for the Bitter End Yacht Club's Competition Series, including the Invitational Regatta. For the best in local *fungi* bands (bands that make music using household items as instruments), stop by the Scratch/Fungi Band Fiesta in December.

HOLIDAYS

The following public holidays are celebrated in the BVI: New Year's Day, Commonwealth Day (Mar. 14), Good Friday (the Fri. before Easter), Easter Sunday (usually March or April), Easter Monday (day after Easter), Whit Monday (the first Mon. in May), Sovereign's Birthday (June 16), Territory Day (July 1), BVI August Festival Days (usually the first two weeks in Aug.), St. Ursula's Day (Oct. 21), Christmas, and Boxing Day (day after Christmas).

LANGUAGE

English is the official language, and it's often spoken with a West Indian accent and with a few unusual idiomatic expressions. If someone says he's just limin', it means he's hanging out. If you ask for an item in a store and the shopkeeper replies, "It's finished," then the shop has temporarily run out.

MAIL & SHIPPING

There are post offices in Road Town on Tortola and in Spanish Town on Virgin Gorda (note that postal service in the BVI isn't very efficient). Postage for a first-class letter to the United States, Canada, Australia, New Zealand, or the United Kingdom is 55¢; for a postcard, 35¢. For a small fee, Rush It, in Road Town and in Spanish Town, offers most U.S. mail and UPS services (via St. Thomas the next day). If you wish to write to an establishment in the BVI, be sure to include the specific island in the address; there are no postal codes.

🚹 **Rush It** ⊠ Road Town, Tortola ☎ 284/494–4421 ⊠ Spanish Town, Virgin Gorda ☎ 284/495–5821.

MONEY MATTERS

BANKS & ATMS   On Tortola there's a Barclays Bank near the waterfront in Road Town; First Bank is also near Road Town's waterfront and has an ATM machine. On Virgin Gorda, Barclays Bank isn't far from the ferry dock in Spanish Town.

🚹 **Barclays Bank** ⊠ Wickham's Cay I, Road Town, Tortola ☎ 284/494–2171 ⊠ Virgin Gorda Yacht Harbour, Spanish Town, Virgin Gorda ☎ 284/495–5271 **First Bank** ⊠ Wickham's Cay I, Road Town, Tortola ☎ 284/494–2662.

CREDIT CARDS Most hotels and restaurants in the BVI accept MasterCard and Visa, and some also accept American Express, Diners Club, and Discover. Beware that a few accept only cash or traveler's checks.

CURRENCY The currency is the U.S. dollar. Any other currency must be exchanged at a bank.

PASSPORTS & VISAS

U.S. and Canadian citizens, as well as citizens of all other countries, need a valid passport. While the government says U.S. and Canadian citizens may use a birth certificate and a photo ID, in practice some immigration agents can be a bit sticky if you don't have a passport. If you're wearing dreadlocks, BVI law does not allow you into the territory.

SAFETY

Although crime is rare, use common sense: don't leave your camera on the beach while you take a dip or your wallet on a hotel dresser when you go for a walk.

SIGHTSEEING TOURS

Travel Plan Tours can arrange island tours, boat tours, and yacht charters from its Tortola and Virgin Gorda bases. Or you can just rent a taxi (minimum of three people) on either Tortola or Virgin Gorda.
ii Travel Plan Tours ☎ 284/494-4000.

TAXES & SERVICE CHARGES

DEPARTURE TAX The departure tax is $5 per person by boat and $10 per person by plane. There's a separate booth at the airport to collect this tax, which must be paid in cash. The departure fee is included in your ferry fare.

SERVICE CHARGES Most hotels add a service charge ranging from 5% to 18% to the bill. A few restaurants and some shops tack on an additional 10% charge if you use a credit card.

TAXES There's no sales tax in the BVI. However, there's a 7% government tax on hotel rooms.

TAXIS

Your hotel staff will be happy to summon a taxi for you. Rates aren't published, so you should negotiate the fare with your driver before you start your trip. It's cheaper to travel in groups, because there's a minimum fare to each destination, which is the same whether you're one, two, or three passengers. The taxi number is also the license plate number. On Tortola, the BVI Taxi Association has stands in Road Town near the ferry dock and at Wickham's Cay I. The Beef Island Taxi Association operates at the Beef Island/Tortola airport. You can also usually find a West End Taxi Association ferry at the West End ferry dock.

Andy's Taxi and Jeep Rental offers service from one end of Virgin Gorda to the other. Mahogany Rentals and Taxi Service provides taxi service all over Virgin Gorda.
ii Andy's Taxi and Jeep Rental ✉ The Valley, Virgin Gorda ☎ 284/495-5511. **Beef Island Taxi Association** ✉ Beef Island Airport, Tortola ☎ 284/495-1982. **BVI Taxi Association** ✉ Near the ferry dock, Road Town, Tortola ☎ 284/494-7519 ✉ Wickham's Cay I, Road Town, Tortola ☎ 284/494-2322. **Mahogany Rentals and Taxi Service** ✉ The Valley, Virgin Gorda ☎ 284/495-5469. **West End Taxi Association** ✉ West End ferry terminal, Tortola ☎ 284/495-4934.

TELEPHONES

COUNTRY & AREA CODES The area code for the BVI is 284; when you make calls from North America, you need only dial the area code and the number. From the United

Kingdom you must dial 001 and then the area code and the number. From Australia and New Zealand you must dial 0011 followed by 1, the area code, and the number.

INTERNATIONAL CALLS For credit-card or collect long-distance calls to the United States, use a phone-card telephone or look for special USADirect phones, which are linked directly to an AT&T operator. For access, dial 800/872–2881, or dial 111 from a pay phone and charge the call to your MasterCard or Visa. USADirect and pay phones can be found at most hotels and in towns.

LOCAL CALLS To call anywhere in the BVI once you've arrived, dial all seven digits. A local call from a pay phone costs 25¢, but such phones are sometimes on the blink. An alternative is a Caribbean phone card, available in $5, $10, and $20 denominations. They're sold at most major hotels and many stores and can be used to call within the BVI, as well as all over the Caribbean, and to access USADirect from special phone-card phones.

TIPPING

Tip porters and bellhops $1 per bag. Sometimes a service charge (10%) is included on restaurant bills; it's customary to leave another 5% if you liked the service. If no charge is added, 15% is the norm. Cabbies normally aren't tipped because most own their cabs; add 10%–15% if they exceed their duties.

VISITOR INFORMATION

🛈 Before You Leave BVI Tourist Board (U.S.) ⊕ www.bvitouristboard.com ✉ 370 Lexington Ave., Suite 1605, New York, NY 10017 ☎ 212/696–0400 or 800/835–8530 ✉ 3450 Wilshire Blvd., Suite 1202 Los Angeles, CA 90010 ☎ 213/736–8931 ✉ 3390 Peachtree Rd. NE, Suite 1735, Atlanta, GA 30326 ☎ 404/467–4741. BVI Tourist Board (U.K.) ✉ 55 Newman St., London W1P 3PG, U.K. ☎ 44-20/7947-8200.

🛈 In the British Virgin Islands BVI Tourist Board ✉ Ferry Terminal, Road Town, Tortola ☎ 284/494-3134. Virgin Gorda BVI Tourist Board ✉ Virgin Gorda Yacht Harbor, Spanish Town, Virgin Gorda ☎ 284/495-5181.

CAYMAN ISLANDS

FODOR'S CHOICE

Hemingway's restaurant, Seven Mile Beach, Grand Cayman

Scuba Diving and Snorkeling on the reefs of Little Cayman

Seven Mile Beach, Grand Cayman

Turtle Nest Inn, Bodden Town, Grand Cayman

HIGHLY RECOMMENDED

RESTAURANTS Cassanova, George Town, Grand Cayman

Champion House II, George Town, Grand Cayman

Ottmar's, Seven Mile Beach, Grand Cayman

Smuggler's Cove, George Town, Grand Cayman

HOTELS Brac Caribbean and Carib Sands, Stake Bay, Cayman Brac

Brac Reef Beach Resort, Brac Reef Beach, Cayman Brac

Holiday Inn, West Bay, Grand Cayman

Hyatt Regency Grand Cayman, Seven Mile Beach, Grand Cayman

Pirates Point Resort, Preston Bay, Little Cayman

Southern Cross Club, South Hole Sound, Little Cayman

Sunshine Suites by Wyndham, George Town, Grand Cayman

The Reef Resort, East End, Grand Cayman

SHOPPING Cathy Church's, George Town, Grand Cayman

Pure Art, George Town, Grand Cayman

NIGHTLIFE Royal Palms, George Town, Grand Cayman

OUTDOORS Bird-watching at Governor Gore Bird Sanctuary, Little Cayman

Owen Island Beach, Little Cayman

Smith's Cove Beach, Grand Cayman

The signpost just past the airport/post office/fire station reads
IGUANAS HAVE THE RIGHT OF WAY. Many of these prehistoric-look-
ing lizards lurk about Little Cayman, the smallest of the three Cayman Islands. According to Gladys, of Pirates Point, iguanas love
grapes. She keeps extras on hand just so her guests can feed
them to the beasts. That kind of hospitality is the norm on an island where the repeat guest list is high and the island's police
officer has yet to use his siren. Each of the Cayman Islands has
its own pace; from Grand Cayman to the Brac to Little Cayman,
it's slow, slower, slowest.

Updated by
JoAnn
Milivojevic

This British colony, which consists of Grand Cayman, smaller Cayman
Brac, and Little Cayman, is one of the Caribbean's most popular destinations. Columbus is said to have sighted the islands in 1503, but he
didn't stop off to explore. He did note that the surrounding sea was alive
with turtles, so the islands were named Las Tortugas. The name was later
changed to Cayman, referring to the caiman crocodiles that once roamed
the islands. The Cayman Islands remained largely uninhabited until the
late 1600s, when England took them and Jamaica from Spain under the
Treaty of Madrid. Emigrants from England, Holland, Spain, and France
then arrived, as did refugees from the Spanish Inquisition and deserters
from Oliver Cromwell's army in Jamaica; many brought slaves with them
as well. The Caymans' caves and coves were also perfect hideouts for
the likes of Blackbeard, Sir Henry Morgan, and other pirates out to plun-
der Spanish galleons. Many ships fell afoul of the reefs surrounding the
islands, often with the help of Caymanians who lured vessels to shore
with beacon fires.

The legend of one wreck in particular—the Wreck of the Ten Sails—
has remained popular with Caymanians through the years. In 1794 a
convoy of 10 Jamaican ships bound for England foundered on the reefs.
The islanders saved everyone, including, it was said, a few members of
royalty. The tale has it that a grateful King George III decreed that Caymanians would forever be exempt from conscription and would never
have to pay taxes. However, though Caymanians don't pay taxes, this
tale has been proven pure fiction.

As for current politics, this British colony has a governor, who appoints
three official members to the Legislative Assembly. He must also accept
the advice of the Executive Council in all matters except foreign affairs,
defense, internal security, and civil-service appointments. Though the
governor is appointed from England, locally elected Caymanians greatly
influence how their islands are run.

Today's Caymans may be seasoned with suburban prosperity, particularly Grand Cayman (residents joke that the national flower is the satellite dish), and stuffed with crowds (the hotels that line the famed Seven
Mile Beach are often full, even in the slow summer season), but the 31,000
Cayman Islanders—most of whom live on Grand Cayman—add considerable flavor with their renowned courtesy and civility. The cost of
living may be about 20% higher here than in the United States (one U.
S. dollar is worth only about 80 Cayman cents), but you won't be hassled by panhandlers or feel afraid to walk around on a dark evening (the
crime rate is very low). Add political and economic stability to the mix,
and you have a fine island recipe indeed.

	WHAT IT COSTS In U.S. dollars				
	$$$$	$$$	$$	$	¢
	RESTAURANTS*				
	over $30	$20–$30	$12–$20	$8–$12	under $8
	HOTELS**				
Cost EP/BP/CP	over $350	$250–$350	$150–$250	$80–$150	under $80
Cost AI	over $450	$350–$450	$250–$350	$125–$250	under $125

*Restaurant prices are for a main course at dinner. **EP, BP, and CP prices are per night for a standard double room in high season, excluding taxes, service charges, and meal plans. AI (all-inclusive) prices are per person, per night based on double-occupancy during high season, excluding taxes and service charges.

GRAND CAYMAN

Grand Cayman is world-renowned for two offshore activities: banking and scuba diving. The former pays dividends in the manicured capital of George Town, which bulges with some 554 banks. The latter offers its rewards in translucent waters that are full of colorful and varied life—much of it protected by a marine parks system. Although about a third of Grand Cayman's visitors come for the diving, a growing number are young honeymooners. The island offers many additional pleasures, from shopping for jewelry to fine dining to simply strolling hand-in-hand on a powder-soft beach.

Where to Stay

In the off-season (summer) it's easy to find lodgings, even on short notice, but for peak-season and holiday accommodations book well in advance. Note that most hotels require a 7- or 14-day minimum stay at Christmas time, though condominiums will let you book on a day-to-day basis for stays of any length.

Brace yourself for resort prices—there are few accommodations in the lower price ranges. Most of the larger hotels along Seven Mile Beach don't offer meal plans. Smaller properties that are farther from restaurants usually offer MAP or FAP (to estimate rates for hotels offering MAP or FAP, add about $40 per person, per day to the average EP price ranges below). You can sometimes find deals on Web sites or by calling properties directly; always ask about reduced or package rates.

Hotels

★ $$$$ **Hyatt Regency Grand Cayman.** Enjoy a glorious sunset from your private balcony perched right over the trendy section of Seven Mile Beach. These plush—albeit pricey—ocean-view one-bedroom suites can sleep up to four. Rooms have teak furnishings, marble baths, and formal entryways. The main resort, adjacent to Britannia Golf Course, has gorgeously landscaped grounds. Moderate-size standard rooms have marble entryways, oversized bathtubs, French doors, and verandahs; 44 Regency Club rooms include concierge services and complimentary Continental breakfast, early-evening hors d'oeuvres, and cocktails. Some balconies are small "step-outs," while others have a table and chairs—inquire carefully, as there's no price difference. ✉ *West Bay Rd., Seven Mile Beach* *Box 1698* ☎ *345/949–1234 or 800/233–1234* 🖷 *345/949–8528* 🌐 *grandcayman.hyatt.com* *112 rooms, 63 suites, 70 villas* *3 restaurants, minibars, 9-hole golf course, 4 tennis courts, 7 pools, gym, hair salon, hot tub, outdoor hot tub, spa, beach, dive shop, snorkeling,*

Grand Cayman

KEY

↗ Beaches
◨ Dive Sites
① Exploring Sights
① Hotels & Restaurants

Caribbean Sea

TO CAYMAN BRAC
85 miles

TO LITTLE CAYMAN
80 miles

GRAND CAYMAN

North Sound

Little Sound

Booby Cay

Rum Point

Cayman Wall

Cayman Kai

Water Cay

Stingray Sandbar

Sting Ray City

Barkers

Head of Barkers

Pleasant Mount

Batabano

Upper Land

Welsh Pt.

Old Stores

Hell

North West Pt.

West Bay

Trinity Caves

Orange Canyon

Seven Mile Beach

George Town

Smith's Cove

South West Pt.

Red Bay

South Sound

Prospect

Omega Gardens

Newlands

Lower Valley

North Sound Estates

Bodden Town

Savannah

Pease Bay

Bodden Bay

IRONSHORE

Breakers

Frank Sound

IRONSHORE

Malportas Pond

North Side

Hutland

Old Man Bay

IRONSHORE

Tortuga

Royal Reef

Colliers

Colliers Pt.

East End

Sand Bluff

East End

Gun Bay

Blakes

Owen Roberts Airport

③ ㉑ ㉒ ⑳ ② ④ ⑲ ⑤ ④ ① ⑪ ⑥ ⑫ ⑱ ㉓ ㉖ ⑰ ① ㉗ ⑤ ⑥ ㉙ ㉚ ⑦ ⑧ ⑨ ⑩ ㉛ ㉘

4 miles

6 km

Cayman Brac & Little Cayman

Caribbean Sea

LITTLE CAYMAN

Crawl Bay
East Pt.
Sandy Point
Lower Spot Bay
Charles Bight
Jacksons Pt.
Gov. Gore Bird Sanctuary
South Hole Sound
Owen Island
South Town
Edward Bodden Airfield
Anchorage Bay
West End Pt.
Bloody Bay Wall

CAYMAN BRAC

Booby Pt. Spot North East Pt.
North East Bay
Tibbetts Turn
Pollard Bay
Cat Head Bay
Stake Bay Pt.
Deadman's Pt.
Tom Jennett's Bay
Sea Feather Bay
Frenchman's Fort
West End
Cedar Pt.
Tiara Beach
Brac Reef Beach
M.V. Capt. Keith Tibbetts
Gerrard-Smith Airport
West End Pt.

KEY

⚑	Beaches
◢	Dive Sites
①	Hotels and Restaurants

0 ___ 2 miles
0 ___ 3 km

Hotels

Adam's Guest House	27
The Beachcomber	14
Brac Caribbean and Carib Sands	39
Brac Reef	38
Conch Club	37
Discovery Point Club	20
Eldemire's Guest House	25
Grape Tree/Cocoplum	9
Holiday Inn	15
Hyatt Regency	12
Indies Suites	19
La Esperanza	41
Little Cayman	35
Marriott	8
Paradise Villas	34
Pirates Point	33
Reef Resort	31
Retreat at Rum Point	28
Sam McCoy's	32
Seaview Hotel	19
Southern Cross Club	36
Spanish Bay Reef	22
Sunset House	25
Sunshine Suites	34
Treasure Island	33
Turtle Nest Inn	29
Walton's Mango Manor	38
Westin Casuarina	16

Restaurants

Breadfruit Tree	1
Cassanova	4
Champion House II	5
The Coffee Grinder	11
Cracked Conch by the Sea	21
Crow's Nest	26
Grand Old House	24
Hemingway's	12
Lighthouse at Breakers	30
Lobster Pot	3
Ottmar's	13
Rackam's Pub	2
The Reef Grill	18
Ristorante Pappagallo	22
Smuggler's Cove	6
Thai Orchid	7
The Wharf	10

Exploring

Blow Holes	9
Bodden Town	6
Cayman Island Turtle Farm	18
George Town	1
Hell	4
Mastic Trail	7
Old Homestead	2
Pedro St. James Castle	5
Queen Elizabeth II Botanic Park	8
Queen's View	10

windsurfing, boating, parasailing, waterskiing, croquet, 4 bars, shops, children's programs (ages 3–12), concierge, car rental ▤ *AE, D, DC, MC, V* ⍾ *EP.*

$$$$ ▦ **Marriott Beach Resort.** It's too bad that storms in 2001 and 2002 erased the beachfront here; the elegant balcony patio now abuts the sea, where steps descend into the water. A short walk west, however, leads to beach front that extends for several walkable miles. This five-story luxury property is designed in colonial style with arched doorways and an airy marble lobby that opens onto a plant-filled courtyard. Large adjoining rooms are ideal for families, and all have balconies. Prices vary according to the view. There's a nearby reef with good snorkeling, and a beach bar is near the pool. The Marriott is popular for conventions. ⊠ *West Bay Rd., Seven Mile Beach (Box 30371)* ☎ *345/949–0088 or 800/ 228–9290* 🖷 *345/949–0288* ⊕ *www.marriott.com* ⇗ *309 rooms, 4 suites* ⚘ *Restaurant, snack bar, pool, hair salon, hot tub, spa, beach, dive shop, snorkeling, windsurfing, bar, shops, dry cleaning, laundry service, meeting rooms, car rental* ▤ *AE, DC, MC, V* ⍾ *EP.*

$$$–$$$$ ▦ **Indies Suites.** For a more peaceful and affordable stay, this property is across the road from and on the quieter north end of Seven Mile Beach. One- and two-bedroom suites, with contemporary wood furniture, have a dining-living room (with a sleeper sofa), a terrace, and a storeroom for dive gear. Continental buffet breakfast, maid service, and a free sunset cruise once a week are nice extras. ⊠ *West Bay Rd., Seven Mile Beach* ⌂ *Box 2070 GT* ☎ *345/945–5025 or 800/654–3130* 🖷 *345/945– 5024* ⇗ *38 suites* ⚘ *Grocery, snack bar, kitchens, pool, hair salon, hot tub, dive shop, snorkeling, bar, laundry facilities* ▤ *AE, MC, V* ⍾ *CP.*

$$$–$$$$ ▦ **Westin Casuarina Resort.** Though the surroundings are elegant, be sure to ask for rooms that have at least partial ocean views (standard rooms have an "island" view, which translates into the parking lot and main drag). The lobby spills out onto the waterfront, where tall royal palms shade the elegant walkway. Rooms have bleached-wood furniture and stucco ceilings. The suites aren't much different from regular rooms, so they're hardly worth the extra money. Havana, the Westin's high-end restaurant, deserves praise for its excellent Cuban/Caribbean fare. The luxurious Hibiscus Spa offers many tempting body treatments. ⊠ *West Bay Rd., Seven Mile Beach* ⌂ *Box 30620* ☎ *345/945–3800 or 800/ 228–3000* 🖷 *345/949–5825* ⊕ *www.westin.com* ⇗ *339 rooms, 2 suites* ⚘ *2 restaurants, grill, 2 tennis courts, pool, gym, hair salon, 2 hot tubs, beach, dive shop, 3 bars, shops, meeting rooms* ▤ *AE, MC, V* ⍾ *EP.*

★ $$–$$$$ ▦ **Holiday Inn.** Across the road from Seven Mile Beach, this property is a real value, offering decent standard-size hotel rooms with green carpeting and tropical decor; hair dryers and coffeemakers are in all rooms. The large swimming pool is surrounded by lush palm trees and tropical blooming shrubs. Beachside amenities include towel service, lounge chairs, and a bar/restaurant. Two kids under 18 can stay free in their parent's room. Ask for an upgrade to an ocean-view room upon arrival; it's free pending availability. ⊠ *West Bay Rd., West Bay* ☎ *345/946– 4433 or 800/465–4329* 🖷 *345/946–4434* ⊕ *www.basshotels.com* ⇗ *231 rooms, 1 2-bedroom suite* ⚘ *2 restaurants, minibars, beach, dive shop, pool, gym, bar, dry cleaning, laundry facilities, laundry service, concierge, Internet, business services, meeting rooms, car rental* ▤ *AE, MC, V* ⍾ *EP.*

★ $$–$$$ ▦ **Sunshine Suites by Wyndham.** This pretty lemon-yellow all-suites hotel is comfortable, convenient, and a money saver. It's across the street from a pristine stretch of Seven Mile Beach and the pricey Westin Resort, with shops, world-class golf, and restaurants within walking distance. Each suite has full-size appliances in the kitchen and an eating area. Room sizes vary from studios to one-bedroom suites. There are no balconies or patios, but there is a swimming pool, and lockers are provided for scuba gear. Scuba and golf packages are available. Breakfast is served poolside. ⊠ *West Bay Rd., George Town* ☎ *345/949–3000 or 877-786–1110* 🖷 *345/949–1200* ⊕ *www.sunshinesuites.com* ⌦ *130 suites* ⟡ *Restaurant, fans, in-room data ports, kitchens, cable TV with movies, pool, laundry facilities, business services, meeting room* ⊟ *AE, MC, V* ⦿⧚ *CP.*

$$–$$$ 🖼 **Treasure Island Resort.** There's plenty of room to roam at this sprawling complex, which has a huge pool with adjacent bar and encompasses a small section of Seven Mile Beach for sunbathing and lounging. Rooms here are functional, with tile floors, stucco walls, rattan furniture, and watercolor prints. ⊠ *West Bay Rd., Seven Mile Beach* ⛭ *Box 1817* ☎ *345/949–7777 or 800/203–0775* 🖷 *345/949–8672* ⌦ *280 rooms* ⟡ *Restaurant, 2 tennis courts, 2 pools, hair salon, beach, snorkeling, windsurfing, bar, laundry facilities* ⊟ *AE, DC, MC, V* ⦿⧚ *EP.*

$$ 🖼 **Sunset House.** Low-key and laid-back describe this motel-style resort on the ironshore. A congenial staff, a happening bar, and a seafood restaurant are pluses, but the diving is the star attraction here. Full dive services include free waterside lockers, two- and three-tank dives at the better reefs around the island, and Cathy Church's U/W Photo Centre. Packages include a made-to-order full breakfast. The latest dive attraction is a newly sunk 9-ft bronze mermaid sculpture dubbed Aphrodite. It's a five-minute walk to a sandy beach. ⊠ *S. Church St., George Town* ⛭ *Box 479* ☎ *345/949–7111 or 800/854–4767* 🖷 *345/949–7101* ⊕ *www.sunsethouse.com* ⌦ *58 rooms, 2 suites* ⟡ *Restaurant, in-room data ports, some kitchens, pool, hot tub, dive shop, bar* ⊟ *AE, MC, V* ⦿⧚ *EP.*

$–$$ 🖼 **Spanish Bay Reef.** Secluded on the northwest tip of the island near 27 spectacular North Wall dive sites and a patch of sandy beach are the attractions of this pretty, pale pink, two-story stucco resort surrounded by flowering trees and shrubs. Boardwalks connect simple, comfortable guest rooms. The outdoor bar-dining area surrounds the pool and has views of the ocean; the indoor bar-dining area is spacious and made of coral stone. Spanish Bay Reef is a deep drop-off, which means superior diving and snorkeling. Rates include taxes and gratuities, meals, shore diving, boat dives, and use of bicycles (not in mint condition). ⊠ *167 Conch Point Rd., West Bay* ⛭ *Box 903* ☎ *345/949–3765* 🖷 *345/949–1842* ⌦ *67 rooms* ⟡ *Restaurant, pool, hot tub, beach, dive shop, snorkeling, bar* ⊟ *AE, MC, V* ⦿⧚ *AI.*

$–$$ 🖼 **Turtle Nest Inn.** This affordable, Spanish-style seaside inn has roomy
FodorsChoice one-bedroom apartments on a small beach along a strip of vibrant coral
★ reef—a perfect snorkeling spot. Rooms have island, partial, or full sea views from a patio or balcony, and rates vary according to the view. Preparing your own meals in the full-size kitchen really saves in this pricey paradise. One of the owners is a chef, however, and most evenings she prepares dinner, which she serves on the terrace. Bodden Town is the island's original capital; it's a small district about 10 miles east of downtown George Town and Seven Mile Beach. The location is remote, so you will want a car. ⊠ *Red Bay Rd., Bodden Town* ☎ *345/947–8665* 🖷 *345/947–6379* ⊕ *www.turtlenestinn.com* ⌦ *8 apartments* ⟡ *Restaurant, beach, pool, laundry facilities* ⊟ *AE, MC, V* ⦿⧚ *EP.*

$ 🖼 **Seaview Hotel & Dive Center.** South of George Town, this perfectly pleasant and affordable hotel is good if you are on a tight budget. The staff is friendly, and the amenities are quite adequate. It's a perfect place to go if you're planning a diving vacation. It's on the water, so the best rooms have ocean views; most are decorated with tropical-pattern bedspreads and pale blue walls. However, the closest beach is at Smith Cove, about a mile away. ⊠ *S. Church St., George Town* ⛭ *Box. 260* ☎ *345/*

945–0558 or 945–0577 🖶 *345/945–0559* ⊕ *www.seaviewdivers.com*
🏊 *15 rooms* ♿ *Restaurant, pool, snorkeling, bar* 🖃 *AE, MC, V.*

Guest Houses

They may be some distance from the beach and short on style and facilities, but these lodgings offer rock-bottom prices (all fall below the $
category), a friendly atmosphere, and your best shot at getting to know
the locals. Rooms are clean and simple, often with cooking facilities,
and most have private bathrooms. These establishments do not accept
personal checks but do take reservations and usually some credit cards.

$–$$ 🏨 **Eldemire's Guest House.** It's a 15-minute drive to Seven Mile Beach
from here, but less than 1 mi (1½ km) south of pretty Smith Cove Bay.
Continental breakfast comes only with the rooms. The owner has a boat
and includes free Sting Ray City snorkel trips, a nice extra. ⊠ *S. Church
St.* ✆ *Box 482* 🕾 *345/949–5387* 🖶 *345/949–6987* ⊕ *www.eldemire.
com* 🏊 *7 rooms, 2 studios, 3 1-bedroom apartments, 1 1-bedroom apartment* ♿ *Fans, some kitchens, some kitchenettes; no room phones* 🖃 *MC,
V* 🍽 *EP.*

$ 🏨 **Adam's Guest House.** This economical choice near the Seaview Hotel
is 1 mi (1½ km) south of downtown George Town and 4 mi (6½ km)
from the beach. ⊠ *Melnac Ave., George Town* ✆ *Box 312* 🕾 *345/949–
2512* 🖶 *345/949–0919* ⊕ *www.adamsguesthouse.com.ky* 🏊 *6 rooms*
♿ *Fans, some kitchenettes, bicycles, laundry facilities, Internet; no
room phones* 🖃 *MC, V* 🍽 *EP.*

Villas & Condominiums

Rates are higher in winter, and there may be a three- or seven-night minimum. These complexes are all similar, with telephones, satellite TV, air-
conditioning, living and dining areas, and patios. Differences have to
do with amenities and proximity to town. The **Cayman Islands Department of Tourism** (⊕ www.caymanislands.ky) provides a list of condominiums and small rental apartments.

$$$$ 🏨 **The Beachcomber.** Each of the simply furnished two-bedroom apartments in this older condo community has a view of the ocean from a
private screened patio. When the sun gets too warm, you can retreat to
the shade of the palapas on Seven Mile Beach or go snorkeling in the
reef offshore. A grocery store is across the street, and there are places
to shop and dine within walking distance, so you don't really need a
car. ⊠ *West Bay Rd., Seven Mile Beach* ✆ *Box 1799* 🕾 *345/945–4470*
🖶 *345/945–5019* ⊕ *www.beachcomber1.com* 🏊 *23 condos* ♿ *Kitchens,
pool, hair salon, beach, laundry facilities* 🖃 *AE, MC, V* 🍽 *EP.*

$$$$ 🏨 **Discovery Point Club.** This complex of all ocean-front suites is at the
far north end of Seven Mile Beach in West Bay, 6 mi (9½ km) from George
Town. It has a lovely beach and great snorkeling in the protected waters
of nearby Cemetery Reef. Tennis courts, a hot tub, a pool, and screened-
in private porches add to the appeal here, and kids 6 and under stay free.
⊠ *West Bay Rd., West Bay* ✆ *Box 439* 🕾 *345/945–4724* 🖶 *345/945–
5051* 🏊 *45 condos* ♿ *Grill, some kitchens, 2 tennis courts, pool, hair
salon, hot tub, beach, laundry facilities* 🖃 *AE, MC, V* 🍽 *EP.*

$$$–$$$$ 🏨 **Grape Tree/Cocoplum.** If you want to be close to town, this is a good
choice. Just a half-mile (¾ km) from George Town on Seven Mile Beach,
these sister condos are adjacent to one another. Grape Tree's units are
carpeted and have traditional wicker furnishings and a beige-and-brown
color scheme. Cocoplum's units are similar, though they're decorated
with Caribbean pastel prints, and the grounds have more plants and trees.
⊠ *West Bay Rd., Seven Mile Beach* ✆ *Box 1802* 🕾 *345/949–5640*
🖶 *345/949–0150* ⊕ *www.worlddive.com* 🏊 *51 units* ♿ *Kitchens, ten-
nis court, 2 pools, beach* 🖃 *AE, MC, V* 🍽 *EP.*

$$$-$$$$ ⊞ **Retreat at Rum Point.** The resort has its own narrow beach with casuarina trees, far from the crowd. Up to six people can rent a two-bedroom villa here, and two or three people will be comfortable in a one-bedroom unit. These privately owned condos are individually decorated, but for the most part you'll find tropical motifs and wicker furniture. All units are spacious and have a washer and dryer and screened-in balconies. Take advantage of superb offshore diving, including the famed North Wall. You'll be stranded without a car, though; it's a 35-minute drive to George Town or the airport. ⊠ *North Side* ⬭ *Box 46* ☎ *345/947-9135* ⬭ *345/947-9058* ⊕ *www.theretreat.com.ky* ⇨ *23 units* ⚬ *Restaurant, kitchens, tennis court, pool, gym, sauna, dive shop, dock, boating, beach, racquetball, bar* ⊟ *AE, MC, V* ⊙ *EP.*

★ **$$-$$$$** ⊞ **The Reef Resort.** This small, well-run timeshare property on the less hectic east end of Grand Cayman offers good value for the price. You will need a car, as it's a 45-minute drive back to George Town. Each of the tile-floored villas has a roomy terrace facing the sea and can be divided into a large one-bedroom and studio for weekly rental throughout the year; the entire unit can sleep up to six. All have satellite TV; the larger ones have separate dining areas and stereos. ⊠ *Queen's Hwy., East End* ⬭ *Box 20865 SMB* ☎ *345/345-3100; 800/221-8090; 954/485-5412 for reservations* ⬭ *345/947-3191* ⊕ *www.royalreef. com* ⇨ *32 villas* ⚬ *Restaurant, grocery, fans, some kitchens, kitchenettes, refrigerators, tennis court, pool, gym, hair salon, outdoor hot tub, spa, beach, dive shop, dock, snorkeling, boating, bicycles, bar, laundry facilities, concierge* ⊟ *AE, MC, V* ⊙ *EP.*

Where to Eat

Grand Cayman's restaurants satisfy every palate. There are extravagant and expensive establishments and moderately priced ethnic eateries. In general, portions tend to be quite large and prices about 20% less than in a major U.S. city. Local hangouts that serve West Indian fare offer both flavor and value. Fish—including grouper, snapper, tuna, wahoo, and marlin—is served either simply baked, broiled, steamed, or Cayman style (with peppers, onions, and tomatoes). Conch, the meat of a large pink mollusk, is ubiquitous in stews and chowders and as fritters or panfried (cracked). Caribbean lobster is available but is often quite expensive, and other shellfish are in short supply in local waters. The only traditional culinary treat of the islands is turtle—served in soup or stew or as a steak—though fewer restaurants offer it these days.

Dining out here can be expensive, so replenish your cash reserves because some places do not accept plastic. Many restaurants add a 10%–15% service charge to the bill, so check before leaving a tip.

Alcohol can really send the bill sky-rocketing. Buy a couple of bottles at a duty free store before you leave your airport (Cayman customs limits you to two bottles per person) and enjoy a cocktail or nightcap from the comfort of your room or balcony.

What to Wear

Smart casual wear (slacks and sundresses) is acceptable for dinner in all but a few places. The nicer resorts and more expensive restaurants may require a jacket, especially in high season; ask when making reservations. Shorts are usually acceptable during the day, but unless you're going to an ultracasual beach bar, beachwear (bathing suits, cover-ups, tank tops, etc.) is a no-no. Most restaurants have an alfresco dining section, and if you plan to dine under the stars you may need a spritz of bug spray (mosquitoes can be pesky, especially at sunset), which most places provide.

ASIAN **✕ Thai Orchid.** It looks like a typical Thai restaurant, but the food more
$$–$$$ than makes up for the ordinary decor. Try the delicious *pad thai, ped phad khing* (crispy duck stir-fried with ginger and vegetables), or Thai spring rolls with marinated pork. Many vegetarian dishes are offered as well. The main difference between the lunch and dinner menus is the price. ✉ *Queens Court Shopping Plaza, West Bay Rd., George Town* ☎ 345/949–7955 ☐ *AE, MC, V* ☯ *No lunch Sun.*

CAFÉS **✕ The Coffee Grinder.** For a breakfast or lunch that's tasty and light on
¢–$ your wallet, this bakery and deli serves wraps with ingredients like black beans, seasoned rice, and cheese; sandwich choices include Italian subs, Reubens, and roast turkey Waldorf on a sourdough walnut roll. For breakfast it's bagels, rolls, sweet pastries, and excellent coffees. Dine indoors or out on the sidewalk. ✉ *Seven Mile Shops, West Bay Rd., George Town* ☎ 345/949–6294 ☐ *AE, MC, V* ☯ *No dinner.*

CARIBBEAN **✕ Hemingway's.** Sea views and breezes attract diners to this elegant
$$$–$$$$ open-air restaurant in the Hyatt Regency Grand Cayman. Nouvelle
Fodor'sChoice Caribbean and seafood dishes include lemongrass-crusted grouper with
★ *udon* noodles and baby Portobello mushrooms in a coconut sauce, and sugarcane-skewered tempura lobster with basil mashed potatoes and *ponzu* butter. Portions are large, and service is superb. ✉ *Hyatt Regency Grand Cayman, West Bay Rd., Seven Mile Beach* ☎ 345/945–5700 ☐ *AE, D, DC, MC, V.*

$$ **✕ Breadfruit Tree Garden Cafe.** Favored by locals, the jerk chicken rivals any on the island. Also on the menu are curry chicken and stewed pork, oxtail, rice and beans, and homemade soups. Drinks include breadfruit, mango, passion-fruit, and carrot juices. The interior is kitschy, with silk roses, white porch swings, straw hats, empty birdcages, and fake ivy crawling along the ceiling. It's open until the wee hours, which makes it a good midnight munchie stop. ✉ *58 Eastern Ave., George Town* ☎ 345/ 945–2124 ☐ *No credit cards.*

$$ **✕ Crow's Nest.** This local favorite serves island dishes such as conch burgers, Jamaican curry chicken, turtle steak, and Cayman-style fish. The fiery deep-fried coconut is among the best on the island, as is the Caesar salad with marinated conch. The key lime mousse pie is a must. Dine on the screened patio overlooking the sea. ✉ *South Sound Rd., George Town* ☎ 345/949–9366 ☐ *AE, MC, V.*

★ ¢–$$ **✕ Champion House II.** Tucked back behind the original Champion House restaurant is this eatery serving tasty traditional island dishes, including marinated conch, curried goat, turtle stew, ackee, and codfish—all served with rice and beans, plantains, and veggies. Try one of the fruit juices like tamarind, Irish moss, or soursop, or a spicy, homemade ginger beer. The entrées are large, but half portions are available. The breakfast and lunch buffets are quite popular and reasonably priced. ✉ *43 Eastern Ave., George Town* ☎ 345/949–7882 ☐ *AE, MC, V.*

CONTINENTAL **✕ Grand Old House.** The menu here consists of Continental entrées and
$$$–$$$$ a few local specialties. Among the spicier appetizers is fried coconut shrimp with mustard-apricot sauce. On the milder side are lobster served "the chef's way" (dipped in egg batter and sautéed with shallots, mushrooms, and white wine), and duck with fresh pear chutney. The oceanside gazebos are surrounded by palms and cooled by ceiling fans; service is stellar. ✉ *S. Church St., George Town* ☎ 345/949–9333 ⌨ *Reservations essential* ☐ *DC, MC, V* ☯ *Closed Sun. May–Nov. No lunch weekends.*

★ $$$–$$$$ **✕ Ottmar's.** This quietly elegant restaurant is styled after a West Indian great house: jade carpeting, peach walls, mahogany furniture, glass chandeliers, and a trickling fountain. Service is excellent. Favorites on the international menu include bouillabaisse, the Indonesian rijsttafel, and French pepper steak (flamed in cognac and doused with green peppercorn sauce and crème fraîche). ⊠ *Grand Pavillion Commercial Centre, West Bay Rd., Seven Mile Beach* ☎ *345/945–5879 or 345/945–5882* ⌕ *Reservations essential* ⊟ *AE, MC, V.*

ECLECTIC ✕ **Rackam's Pub.** North of George Town, jutting out onto a jetty, is this
$$–$$$$ low-key bar and grill popular for drinks and terrific sunset views. The young, friendly staff serves good jerk burgers (basted with Jamaican jerk sauce), grouper fish-and-chips, and tasty chiles rellenos. ⊠ *N. Church St., George Town* ☎ *345/945–3860* ⊟ *AE, MC, V.*

ITALIAN ✕ **Lighthouse at Breakers.** About 25 minutes from Seven Mile Beach and
$$–$$$$ worth the drive, this restaurant offers seaside dining with excellent food, a well-chosen wine list (with an especially good selection of wines by the glass), and stellar desserts. Start with the salad of green asparagus points and baby field greens or flash-fried calamari; pastas are all a good bet, as are yellowfin tuna with a brandy-peppercorn sauce or the char-grilled veal chop. Save room for dessert, especially the hot chocolate soufflé or some of the homemade ice creams. The Sunday brunch is especially popular. ⊠ *Breakers* ☎ *345/947–2047* ⌕ *Reservations essential* ⊟ *AE, MC, V.*

★ $$–$$$ ✕ **Cassanova.** This lively seaside restaurant in downtown George Town buzzes with its mostly Italian waitstaff, local crowd, and outstanding authentic dishes such as *gnoccetti alla Genovese* (potato dumplings with pesto) or homemade ravioli with meat sauce, pesto, and a touch of cream. You can dine alfresco or in the mural-decorated interior. ⊠ *S. Church St. George Town* ☎ *345/949–7633* ⌕ *Reservations essential* ⊟ *AE, MC, V.*

$$–$$$ ✕ **Ristorante Papagallo.** If you're not taking a cab, be sure to pack a map for the journey down twisted, unmarked roads to this oversize Polynesian hut at the northernmost tip of the island. Try the arugula salad with mango vinaigrette, followed by the blackened yellowtail or the snapper fillet with pineapple salsa. Caymanians and tourists alike say it's worth the trip for the island's best Italian-Caribbean fusion cuisine. ⊠ *Conch Point Rd., West Bay* ☎ *345/949–1119* ☎ *345/949–1114* ⌕ *Reservations essential* ⊟ *AE, MC, V* ☺ *No lunch.*

SEAFOOD ✕ **Lobster Pot.** The second-floor terrace of this cozy restaurant overlooks
$$$–$$$$ the bay downtown, offering a perfect sunset view. The menu includes Continental dishes and such Caribbean specialties as conch chowder, seafood curry, shrimp Diane, and, of course, lobster. This place is popular, and the constant turnover makes it feel a little frenzied at times. If you can't make it for dinner, drop by the pub and have a frozen banana daiquiri. ⊠ *N. Church St., George Town* ☎ *345/949–2736* ⊟ *AE, D, MC, V.*

$$$ $$$$ ✕ **The Reef Grill at Royal Palms.** The impeccable service by the knowledgeable waitstaff is only surpassed by the divine food served in an elegant dining room or on the more casual garden patio. Try the signature honey-soy-glazed sea bass in a mild Thai curry sauce; it's tender, succulent, and served with coconut rice and a spicy sautéed red cabbage. Other creative dishes include pepper-crusted yellowfin tuna and plank-roasted barbecued salmon. Desserts include fresh sorbets, crème brûlée, and chocolate-almond mousse. The adjoining beach bar is a popular nightspot with live bands most evenings. ⊠ *West Bay Rd., Seven Mile Beach* ☎ *345/945–6358* ⌕ *Reservations essential* ⊟ *AE, D, MC, V* ☺ *No lunch.*

★ $$$–$$$$ ✕ **Smuggler's Cove.** The comfortable, candlelit dining room and lovely deck overlooking the ocean are perfect spots to bring someone for a special or romantic dinner. Excellent appetizers include tuna carpaccio marinated in basil and dill, and jerk duck seasoned with pimiento and scotch bonnet peppers. The best entrées are those with Caribbean lobster—particularly the Smuggler's Fillet (a lobster-stuffed beef tenderloin seared in rosemary butter and glazed with port). ⊠ *N. Church St., George Town* ☎ *345/949–6003* ⚞ *Reservations essential* ▤ *AE, D, MC, V* ⊘ *No lunch weekends.*

$$$–$$$$ ✕ **The Wharf.** Managed by Austrians, this tidy blue-and-white restaurant overlooks the sea. On the surf-and-turf menu are conch fritters, home-smoked salmon, turtle steak, broiled lobster, and steak fillet béarnaise; anything on the fresh daily menu is also recommended. A harpist entertains after a lively happy hour band. The Ports of Call bar is a perfect spot from which to watch the sun set, and tarpon feeding off the deck is a nightly (9 PM) spectacle here. ⊠ *West Bay Rd., George Town* ☎ *345/949–2231* ▤ *AE, MC, V.*

$$$ ✕ **Cracked Conch by the Sea.** Nautical memorabilia and artifacts are scattered throughout the dining room and bar, much of them from famed scuba professional Bob Soto, co-owner of the establishment. The restaurant is next door to the Turtle Farm, and turtle steak is a signature dish. It's tender, succulent, and served with sautéed onions and mushrooms in a coconut-rum sauce. Heavenly. Entrée portions are huge. Bring a hearty appetite or spilt an entrée and a few appetizers. The conch fritters and conch salad are quite good, the lobster bisque outstanding. The Friday happy hour, served on the pier below, is especially popular with locals. ⊠ *N. West Point Rd., West Bay* ☎ *345/945–5217* ▤ *AE, MC, V.*

Beaches

Cayman Kai. This favored hideaway is on the north side of the island.

East End. The best windsurfing is just off the beaches of Grand Cayman's East End, at Colliers, by Morritt's Tortuga Club.

Rum Point. This North Sound beach is convenient for snorkeling and has a bar and grill especially popular on Sundays.

Fodor'sChoice **Seven Mile Beach.** Although Grand Cayman has several smaller beaches,
★ its west coast, the most developed area of the entire island, is where you'll find the famous Seven Mile Beach—5½ mi (9 km) long—and its expanses of powdery white sand. Storms in 2001 and 2002 destroyed about a mile of beachfront at southernmost end, however, near the Marriott Resort. The beach in this area, if there is any at all, is narrow, with rocks and shells in sections, but it starts to widen into its normal silky softness north of the Royal Palms bar and restaurant. The beach is litter-free and sans peddlers, so you can relax in an unspoiled and almost hassle-free (if somewhat crowded) environment. Most of the island's accommodations, restaurants, and shopping centers are on this strip. You'll also find the headquarters for the island's aquatic activities here.

★ **Smith's Cove.** Off South Church Street and south of the Grand Old House, this is a popular local bathing spot on weekends.

Water Cay. If you seek a little more privacy than you can find on Seven Mile Beach, head to this more isolated, unspoiled beach.

Sports & the Outdoors

FISHING If you enjoy action fishing, Cayman waters have plenty to offer. Some 25 boats are available for charter, offering fishing options that include deep-sea, reef, bone, tarpon, light-tackle, and fly-fishing. **Bayside Watersports** (☎ 345/949–3200) offers half-day snorkeling trips, North Sound Beach lunch excursions, and full-day deep-sea fishing and dinner cruises. **Burton's Tourist Information & Activity Services** (☎ 345/949–6598) can hook you up with a number of different charters and tours.

Captain Alphonso Ebanks (☎ 345/949–1012) specializes in fishing and snorkeling tours to Stingray City and has half- and full-day tours. **Island Girl** (☎ 345/947–3029) offers customized private fishing and snorkeling charters; deep-sea fishing excursions include trolling, live bait, and drift fishing for yellowfin tuna and marlin; night fishing trips are also available.

GOLF The **Grand Cayman–Britannia** (✉ West Bay Rd., Seven Mile Beach ☎ 345/949–8020) golf course, next to the Hyatt Regency, was designed by Jack Nicklaus. The course is really three in one—a 9-hole, par-70 regulation course, an 18-hole, par-57 executive course, and a Cayman course (played with a Cayman ball that goes about half the distance of a regulation ball). Greens fees run $60–$90, mandatory golf carts are included in the fees. Windier, and therefore more challenging than most courses, is the **Links at Safe Haven** (✉ off West Bay Rd., Seven Mile Beach ☎ 345/949–5988), Cayman's first 18-hole championship golf course, which is a botanical garden of indigenous trees, plants, and flowering shrubs. The Roy Case–designed, par-71, 6,605-yard course also has an aqua driving range (the distance markers and balls float), a clubhouse, pro shop, and restaurant. Greens fees run $60–$100. Golf carts ($15–$20 per person) are mandatory.

HIKING Guided nature walks are available at the National Trust's **Mastic Trail** (✉ Off Frank Sound Rd., Breakers ☎ 345/945–6588), a rugged 2-mi (3-km) slash through pristine woodlands, mangrove swamps, and ancient rock formations. There is no entry fee; guided hikes are $45 and run daily 9–5 by appointment only.

HORSEBACK **Nicki's Beach Rides** (☎ 345/945–5839) offers 1½-hour leisurely family
RIDING horseback rides along one of the many white-sand beaches; the guides provide bits of island history and lore as you ride. **Pampered Ponies** (☎ 345/945–2262 or 345/916–2540) has horses trained to walk, trot, and canter along the beaches and beach trails. Private rides, early mornings, sunsets, and evenings in the moonlight available.

SCUBA DIVING & Pristine water (visibility often exceeding 100 ft [30 m]), breathtaking
SNORKELING coral formations, and plentiful and exotic marine life mark the **Great Wall**—a world-renowned dive site just off the north side of Grand Cayman. A must-see for adventurous souls is **Stingray City** in the North Sound, noted as the best 12-ft dive in the world, where dozens of stingrays congregate, tame enough to suction squid from your outstretched palm. Nondivers gravitate to **Stingray Sandbar,** a shallower part of the North Sound, which has become a popular snorkeling spot; it is also a popular spot for the stingrays. **Trinity Caves** in West Bay is a deep dive with numerous canyons starting at about 60 ft. **Orange Canyon** starts at the edge of a wall at about 40 ft and is an easy shallow dive. The best shore-entry snorkeling spots are off the ironshore south of George Town, at **Eden Rock**; north of town, at the reef off the West Bay Cemetery on Grand Cayman's **west coast**; and in the reef-protected shallows of the island's **north and south coasts**, where coral and fish life are much more varied and abundant.

Since Grand Cayman is one of the Caribbean's top diving destinations, you will find many top-notch dive operations offering instruction and equipment. Divers are required to be certified and possess a "C" card. Otherwise, you can take a full certification course, which costs $350–$400, lasts four to six days, and includes classroom, pool, boat sessions, and checkout dives. A short resort course lasts a day, costs about $80–$100, and introduces novices to the sport and teaches the rudimentary skills needed to make a shallow, instructor-monitored dive. A

single-tank dive averages $50; a two-tank dive about $75. Snorkel-equip-
ment rental runs $5–$15 a day. Most operations rent gear and underwater photography equipment.

There are many dive operators in Grand Cayman. Call the **Cayman Islands Watersports Operators Association** (☎ 345/949–8522) for details on
local providers. **Bob Soto's Reef Divers** (☎ 345/949–2020 or 800/262–
7686) was the first dive operation in Cayman and now has several island locations; it has film-processing facilities and underwater photo
courses. One-week live-aboard dive cruises are available on the 110-ft
Cayman Aggressor III (☎ 800/348–2628), which cruises around all three
of the Cayman Islands. **Dive Tech** (☎ 345/949–1700) offers Nitrox dives
and certification; it is next to the Turtle Farm, where there are some excellent shore dives. **Don Foster's** (☎ 345/949–5679 or 800/833–4837) is
headquartered in George Town and offers both film processing and underwater photo courses. **Eden Rock** (☎ 345/949–7243) provides easy access to excellent George Town shore diving at Eden Rock and Devil's
Grotto; both reefs are a short swim from shore. **Fish Eye Divers** (☎ 345/
945–4209) is known for its exceptional photo and video courses and
offers a variety of dive packages. **Red Sail Sports** (☎ 345/949–8745 or
800/255–6425) offers daily trips to Stingray City and has branches at
many Grand Cayman hotels along Seven Mile Beach. **Sunset Divers**
(☎ 345/949–7111 or 800/854–4767) has six dive boats, great shore diving, Nitrox tanks, and rebreathers.

KAYAKING **Cayman Kayak Adventures** (☎ 345/926–1234) tours you through Grand
Cayman's mangroves, explaining the flora and fauna of this delicate and
vital wetlands ecosystem. All ages welcome, no experience necessary, single and double kayaks available.

TENNIS & The **South Sound Squash Club** (✉ S. Sound Rd., George Town ☎ 345/
SQUASH 949–9469) has courts available to the general public. Call the resident
pro, John McCrury, for a court or game.

WINDSURFING **Cayman Windsurf** (☎ 345/947–7492) offers lessons and rentals on the
east end of the island at Morritt's Tortuga Beach Club and on North
Sound by Safe Haven.

Shopping

On Grand Cayman the good news is that there's no sales tax *and* there's
plenty of duty-free merchandise. The bad news is that prices on imported
merchandise—English china, Swiss watches, French perfumes, and Japanese cameras and electronic goods—are not always lower than elsewhere. Locally made items to watch for include woven mats, baskets,
jewelry made of a marblelike stone called caymanite (from the cliffs of
Cayman Brac), and authentic sunken treasure. Cigar lovers take note:
some shops carry famed Cubans such as Romeo and Juliet, Cohiba, and
Partagas brands (but enjoy them on the island, as bringing them back
to the United States is illegal).

Although you'll find black coral products in Grand Cayman, they're controversial. Most of the coral used to make items sold here comes from
Belize and Honduras, because Cayman Islands marine law prohibits the
removal of live coral from its own sea. Black coral grows at a very slow
rate (3 inches every 10 years), it is often designated as an endangered
species, and reefs are not always harvested carefully. Environmental groups
generally discourage people from purchasing coral products.

Areas & Malls

The main shopping areas are **Harbour Place,** the latest addition to the shopping mecca just south of the cruise-ship docks on Harbor Drive, with shops featuring upscale beachwear, art, and home accessories, and the chic **Kirk Freeport Plaza,** known for its fine jewelry, plus duty-free china, crystal, Gucci goods, perfumes, and fine cosmetics. The **Queen's Court Shopping Centre,** on Seven Mile Beach close to town, has shops that sell souvenirs, crafts, and gifts. At the **West Shore Shopping Centre** or the **Galleria Shopping Plaza,** both on Seven Mile Beach, you'll find good-quality island art, beachwear, and more.

Specialty Items

ART The waterfront gallery **Artifacts** (⊠ Harbour Dr., George Town ☎ 345/949–2442) sells Spanish pieces of eight, doubloons, and Halcyon Days enamels, which are handpainted collectible pillboxes made in England. ★ **Cathy Church's Underwater Photo Centre and Gallery** (⊠ S. Church St., George Town ☎ 345/949–7415) has a collection of spectacular underwater photos by the famed photographer Cathy Church. You'll find original prints, paintings, and sculpture with a tropical theme at **Island Art Gallery** (⊠ Anchorage Shopping Centre, George Town ☎ 345/949–9861). The **Kennedy Gallery** (⊠ West Shore Centre, West Bay Rd., George Town ☎ 345/949–8077) sells lithographs and prints depicting the Cayman Islands by local artists. At **Kensington Lott Art Gallery** (⊠ Harbour Dr., George Town ☎ 345/969–9696) you'll find fine-art paintings from Caymanian and Caribbean artists. Debbie van der Bol runs the ★ arts-and-crafts shop **Pure Art** (⊠ S. Church St., George Town ☎ 345/949–9133 ⊠ Hyatt Regency, West Bay Rd., Seven Mile Beach ☎ 345/945–5633), which sells watercolors, wood carvings, and lacework by local artists, as well as her own sketches and cards.

CLOTHES **Calico Jack's** (⊠ West Bay Rd., George Town ☎ 345/949–4373) is a good source for T-shirts, casual resort wear, and dive gear. **St. Michael** (⊠ Galleria Plaza, off West Bay Rd., George Town ☎ 345/945–5165) sells clothes and other goods.

FOODSTUFFS For groceries and pharmaceutical needs, try **Foster's Food Fair** (⊠ Strand Shopping Center, George Town ☎ 345/945–4748 store; 345/945–7759 pharmacy), a huge modern supermarket just off Seven Mile Beach. The **Tortuga Rum Company** (⊠ N. Sound Rd., George Town ☎ 345/949–7701 or 345/949–7867) has scrumptious rum cake (sealed fresh) that's sweet and moist and makes a great souvenir.

HANDICRAFTS The coral creations of **Bernard Passman** (⊠ Fort St., George Town ☎ 345/949–0123) have won the approval of the British royal family, and even the pope owns a piece of Passman's work. The **Heritage Crafts Shop** (⊠ George Town ☎ 345/945–6041), near the harbor, sells local crafts and gifts. **Joe Tourist** (⊠ South Church St. George Town ☎ 345/946–5638), carries locally made products, T-shirts, leather bags, and refreshing smoothies. You'll find beautiful coral pieces at **Richard's Fine Jewelry** (⊠ Harbour Dr., George Town ☎ 345/949–7156), where designers Richard and Rafaela Barile attract celebrities.

Nightlife

Look at the free *What's Hot* or check the Friday edition of the *Caymanian Compass* for listings of music, movies, theater, and other entertainment.

On Friday nights the locals head to **Bed** (⊠ Harquail Bypass, George Town ☎ 345/949–7199), a popular bar and restaurant with a comfortable lounge and servers in pajamas. The **Cracked Conch** (⊠ West Bay Rd., West Bay, near the Turtle Farm ☎ 345/945–5217) is where islanders congregate on Thursday night for karaoke, classic dive films, and happy hour. On Tuesdays and Wednesdays locals go to **Legendz** (⊠ West Bay Rd., George Town ☎ 345/945–1950) for the live bands and comedy night, respectively. **Royal Palms** (⊠ West Bay Rd., George Town ☎ 345/945–6358) is where local bands play Wednesday through Saturday nights; it's an outdoor beach bar with plenty of room for dancing under the stars. If you are dying to see a film, **Cinema 1 & 2** (⊠ Harquail Bypass, George Town ☎ 345/949–4011 for show times) is across from Bed.

Exploring Grand Cayman

The historic capital of George Town, which is at one end of Seven Mile Beach, is easy to explore on foot. If you're a shopper, you can spend days here; otherwise, you can tour downtown in an hour. To see the rest of the island, rent a car or scooter or take a guided tour. The portion of the island called West Bay is noted for its jumble of affluent colonial neighborhoods and rather tawdry tourist attractions. A drive along West Bay Road will take you past the dense Seven Mile Beach area and into a less congested scene. It's about a half hour to West Bay from George Town. The less developed East End has natural attractions, from blow-holes to botanical gardens, as well as the remains of the original settlements. Plan on at least 45 minutes for the drive out from George Town. You need a day to circle and explore the entire island—including a stop at a beach for a picnic or swim.

Numbers in the margin correspond to points of interest on the Grand Cayman map.

What to See

❾ Blow Holes. These make the ultimate photo opportunity as crashing waves force water into caverns and send geysers shooting up through the ironshore. ⊠ *Frank Sound Rd., near East End.*

❻ Bodden Town. In the island's original south-shore capital you'll find an old cemetery on the shore side of the road. Graves with A-frame structures are said to contain the remains of pirates. There are also the ruins of a fort and a wall erected by slaves in the 19th century. A curio shop serves as the entrance to what's called the Pirate's Caves, partially underground natural formations that are more hokey (decked out with fake treasure chests and mannequins in pirate garb) than spooky.

☝ ❸ Cayman Island Turtle Farm. The farm has reopened after a hurricane seriously damaged it in 2001, though thousands of turtles are in holding tanks across the street from the original location. You can see turtles in various stages of growth, and some can be picked up from the tanks—a real treat for children and adults. The rebuilding of tanks and replenishment of lost turtles continues. The impressive gift shop has been rebuilt and is filled with educational and fun turtle- and ocean-themed merchandise. ⊠ *West Bay Rd.* ☎ *345/949–3893* ⊕ *www.turtle.ky* ᠌ *$6* ☉ *Mon.–Sat. 8:30–5.*

❶ George Town. Begin exploring the capital by strolling along the waterfront, Harbour Drive. The circular gazebo is where passengers from cruise ships disembark. Diagonally across the street from the cruise-ship dock is the **Elmslie Memorial United Church,** named after Scotsman James Elmslie, the first Presbyterian missionary to serve in the Caymans. The church was the first concrete-block building built in the Cayman Islands.

Its vaulted ceiling, wooden arches, and sedate nave reflect the quietly religious nature of island residents. Along your rambles in George Town you'll easily come across **Fort Street,** a main shopping street where you'll also notice the small clock tower dedicated to Britain's King George V and the huge fig tree manicured into an umbrella shape. Here, too, is a statue of national hero James Bodden, the father of Cayman tourism. Across the street is the Cayman Islands Legislative Assembly Building, next door to the 1919 Peace Memorial Building. That the Caymanians built a memorial to peace rather than war speaks of their character.

On **Edward Street** you'll find the charming library, built in 1939; it has English novels, current newspapers from the United States, and a small reference section. It's worth a visit just for its old-fashioned charms and a look at the shields with insignias of Britain's prominent institutions of learning; they decorate the ceiling beams. Across the street is the courthouse. Down the next block is the financial district, where banks from all over the world have offices.

Down from the financial district is the **General Post Office,** also built in 1939, with its strands of decorative colored lights and some 2,000 private mailboxes on the outside (mail is not delivered on the island). Behind the post office is **Elizabethan Square,** a shopping and office complex on Shedden Road with food, clothing, and souvenir establishments. The courtyard has benches placed around a garden and a fountain; it's a pleasant place to rest your feet.

Built in 1833, the home of the **Cayman Islands National Museum** has had several different incarnations over the years, including that of courthouse, jail (now the gift shop), post office, and dance hall. It's small but fascinating, with excellent displays and videos that illustrate local geology, flora, and fauna, and island history. Pick up a walking-tour map of George Town at the museum gift shop before leaving. ⊠ *Harbour Dr., George Town* ☎ *345/949–8368* ✉ *$5* ⊙ *Weekdays 9–5, Sat. 10–2.*

4 **Hell.** This tiny village is little more than a patch of incredibly jagged rock formations called ironshore. The big attraction here are the small post office and a nearby gift shop, where you can get cards and letters postmarked from Hell (a postcard of bikini-clad beauties emblazoned with WHEN HELL FREEZES OVER gives you a picture of what this place is like).

7 **Mastic Trail.** In the 1800s this woodland trail was often used as a shortcut to and from the North Side. The low-lying area was full of hardwood trees, including mahogany, West Indian cedar, and the mastic that early settlers used in building their homes. Along the trail you'll see an abundance of trees, birds, and plants unique to this old-growth forest. Walk it on your own (about two hours round-trip) or call the National Trust to book a guide. ⊠ *Frank Sound Rd., entrance by the fire station and across from the Botanic Park* ☎ *345/949–0121 for guide reservations.*

2 **Old Homestead.** Formerly known as the West Bay Pink House, this is probably the most photographed home in Grand Cayman. The pink-and-white Caymanian cottage was built in 1912 of wattle and daub around an ironwood frame. Cheery Mac Bothwell, who grew up in the house, takes you on tours that present a nostalgic and touching look at life in Grand Cayman before the tourism and banking booms. ⊠ *West Bay Rd., West Bay* ☎ *345/949–7639* ✉ *$5* ⊙ *Mon.–Sat. 8–5.*

5 **Pedro St. James Castle.** Built in 1780, the great house is Cayman's oldest stone structure and the only remaining late-18th-century residence on the island. The buildings are surrounded by 8 acres of natural parks

and woodlands. You can stroll through landscaping of native Caymanian flora and experience one of the most spectacular views on the island from atop the dramatic Great Pedro Bluff. Don't miss the impressive
multimedia theater show complete with smoking pots, misting rains, and
two film screens where the story of Pedro's Castle is presented. The show
plays on the hour; see it before you tour the site. On Sundays there is
an extra-special brunch serving all local cuisine. ⊠ *S. Sound Rd., Savannah* ☎ *345/947–3329* ✉ *$8.*

8 **Queen Elizabeth II Botanic Park.** This 65-acre wilderness preserve showcases a wide range of indigenous and nonindigenous tropical vegetation.
Interpretive signs identify the flora along the walking trail. Rare blue
iguanas are bred and released in the gardens; there's usually one named
Charlie hanging around the entrance gate. You can also see native orchids and, if you're lucky, the brilliant green Cayman parrot. ⊠ *Frank
Sound Rd., Frank Sound* ☎ *345/947–9462; 345/947–3558 (info line)*
✉ *$3* ☉ *Daily 9–6:30 (last admission at 5:30).*

10 **Queen's View.** This functions as an eastern lookout point and has a monument that commemorates the legendary Wreck of the Ten Sails, which
took place just offshore. ⊠ *Queens Hwy., East End.*

CAYMAN BRAC

Brac, the Gaelic word for "bluff," aptly identifies this island's most distinctive feature, a rugged limestone cliff that runs down the center of
the 12-mi (19-km) island and soars to 140 ft at its eastern end. Lying
89 mi (143 km) northeast of Grand Cayman, Brac is accessible via Cayman Airways and Island Air. Only 1,200 people live on the island, in
communities such as Watering Place and Spot Bay. Residents are very
friendly, so it's easy to strike up a conversation; in fact, you'll often have
to be the one to end the chat if you expect to do anything else that day.

Where to Stay

Hotels here are usually a better value than their prices indicate at first
glance. Rates often include meals, if not drinks and diving. In addition,
lodgings are much cozier and more intimate than their Grand Cayman
counterparts, and hoteliers often treat their guests like family. Most hotels give you the option of including all meals in your stay, but there are
a few restaurants on the island. To reach them, however, you'll need a
taxi or a bike (most hotels have these for guest use). Most restaurants
serve island fare (stewed fish, conch fritters, curries), and portions are
generally large, some will provide free transport to and from their
restaurant.

For approximate costs, *see* the lodging price chart *in* Grand Cayman.

★ **$$** 🏨 **Brac Caribbean and Carib Sands.** These side-by-side condo complexes
offers all the comforts of home in one- to four-bedroom units. Each unit
has white-tile floors, light peach stucco walls, and a private balcony over-
looking the sea. ⊠ *Stake Bay* 📪 *Box 4* ☎ *345/948–2265 or 800/791–
7911* 🖷 *345/948–2206* 🌐 *www.866thebrac.com* ⮑ *42 condos* ♻ *Restau-
rant, pool, hot tub, beach, dive shop, fishing, bicycles, bar* ☰ *AE, MC,
V* ⦿ *CP.*

★ **$$** 🏨 **Brac Reef Beach Resort.** Popular with divers, this well-run resort sits
on a large stretch of beach with plenty of shade trees and hammocks
strung about. The large dock is illuminated nightly and attracts everything from stingrays to squid to tarpon, a great place to hang out after
dinner. The modest all-inclusive package rates include three buffet meals

daily, all drinks, airport transfers, and taxes and service charges for two persons; dive packages cost a little more. ⊠ *Brac Reef Beach* ⊕ *Box 56* ☎ *345/948-1323; 800/327-3835; 727/323-8727 in FL* 🖷 *727/323-8827* ⊕ *www.bracreef.com* ⤸ *40 rooms* ⚭ *Restaurant, tennis court, pool, gym, hot tub, massage, spa, beach, dive shop, dock, snorkeling, bicycles, bar, meeting rooms* ▤ *AE, D, MC, V* ¶❙ *FAP.*

$–$$ ⊞ **Walton's Mango Manor.** This tranquil, two-story traditional West Indian home has five rooms (with bath). Beautiful antique furnishings and architectural details abound. The nearby ironshore beach is the perfect place for a sunrise walk. The proprietors love to relate Brac history and help you make arrangements for game-fishing trips, scuba-diving excursions, and other activities. As only breakfast is included, you'll need a car so you can get out for other meals and exploring the island. The pretty pastel seaside cottage is spacious and private. ⊠ *Stake Bay* ⊕ *Box 56* 🖷🖷 *345/948-0518* ⊕ *www.waltonsmangomanor.com* ⤸ *5 rooms, 1 cottage* ⚭ *Fans* ▤ *AE, MC, V* ¶❙ *CP.*

¢–$ ⊞ **La Esperanza.** This modest, family-run property on the north side of the island offers four two-bedroom apartments with fully equipped kitchens and two three-bedroom houses with two baths. Guest quarters have white-tile floors and simple furnishings. The seaside restaurant terrace offers breathtaking Cayman Brac sunsets—and the owner's famous jerk chicken, which he prepares by the side of the road every Friday and Saturday night. ⊠ *Stake Bay* ⊕ *Box 28* ☎ *345/948-0531 or 345/948-0591* 🖷 *345/948-0525* ⊕ *www.laesperanza.net* ⤸ *11 rooms* ⚭ *Restaurant, kitchens, dive shop, snorkeling, fishing, bar, shop, laundry facilities* ▤ *AE, MC, V* ¶❙ *EP.*

Beaches

Southwest Coast. The accommodations on the southwest coast have fine small beaches, better for sunning than for snorkeling because of the abundance of turtle grass in the water. Everyone is welcome on hotel beaches.

Sports & the Outdoors

HIKING   Nature trails abound on the Brac. Get nature tourism maps at the airport or your hotel. To encourage more hikers, the **Brac Tourism Office** (⊠ Stake Bay [near the airport] ☎ 345/948–1649) offers free guides. It's easy to hike on your own (look for white heritage markers along the way), though some trails could be better maintained.

SCUBA DIVING &   The waters off Cayman Brac are more pristine than those off Grand Cay-
SNORKELING   man, so you'll see more (and larger) critters. The snorkeling is excellent off the **north coast.** Many fish have taken to the Russian warship that was scuttled offshore from the now-defunct Buccaneer's Inn. (Look for the beautiful queen angelfish that makes its home between two of the guns.) All the ship's doors have been removed, so you can swim through it—not for the faint of heart as it's pitch black in some spaces.

Brac Reef Divers (☎ 345/948–1642) offers scuba and snorkeling gear and courses, with two-tank dives priced around $60–$70, night dives are $50.

SPELUNKING   If you plan to explore any of Cayman Brac's caves, wear sneakers, as some of the paths are steep and rocky. **Peter's Cave** is a great place from which to view the south-side bluffs. **Great Cave** is near the old lighthouse and has numerous stalagmites and stalactites. **Bat Cave** is well lighted, and you'll most likely see bats hanging from the ceiling. **Rebecca's Cave** has a grave site where a Cayman Brac family buried baby Rebeka, who lost her life during a hurricane in 1932.

Exploring Cayman Brac

Cayman Brac Museum. In addition to displaying implements used in the daily lives of Bracers in the 1920s and '30s, this two-room museum exhibits a few oddities, such as a 4,000-year-old axe. Examples of Brac flora on the property include unusual orchids, mangoes, papaya, agave, and cacti. ⊠ *Old Government Administration Bldg., Stake Bay* ☎ *345/ 948–2622* ☒ *Free* ☉ *Mon.–Sat. 9–noon and 1–4.*

Parrot Preserve. The easiest place to spot the endangered Cayman Brac parrot is in this preserve on Major Donald Drive (also known as Lighthouse Road). This 6-mi (9½-km) dirt road also leads to ironshore cliffs that offer the best panoramic view of North East Point and the open ocean; it's the best place from which to view the sunrise.

LITTLE CAYMAN

Only 7 mi (11 km) from Cayman Brac, Little Cayman has a population of about 100 on its 12 square mi (31 square km). This is a true hideaway: few phones, fewer shops, no man-made sights or nightlife to speak of—just spectacular diving, great fishing, fantastic bird-watching, placid beaches, and laid-back camaraderie. The newest attraction is a luxurious nature spa, which offers pampering services such as full-body massages, body wraps, and facials; it's fast becoming a popular indulgence for locals and visitors.

Where to Stay

Accommodations are mostly in small lodges, many of which offer meal and dive packages. The meal packages are a good idea; the chefs in most places are impeccably trained.

For approximate costs, *see* the lodging price chart *in* Grand Cayman.

Hotels

★ **$$$$** ▦ **Pirates Point Resort.** The repeat guest list here is long owing to the first-rate gourmet food, the vivacious owner, comfy seaside cottages, and the supreme diving. The guest-house feel of this informal resort generates instant camaraderie. Owner Gladys Howard's down-home welcome (she's originally from Texas) belies her upscale meals (she trained at Cordon Bleu with Julia Child, James Beard, and Jacques Pepin). The main building and the rooms have tile floors, ceiling fans, and white rattan and wicker furnishings. The guest rooms were updated in 2002 with new mattresses, bedspreads, and window blinds. All-inclusive rates include two dives daily; nondiver rates are lower. ⊠ *Preston Bay* ◌ *Box 43* ☎ *345/948–1010* ⊕ *345/948–1011* ⊕ *http://piratespointresort.com* ⊲ *10 rooms* ⚫ *Restaurant, gym, dive shop, bicycles, bar, airport shuttle; no a/c in some rooms* ⊟ *MC, V* ⭘◌ *AI.*

★ **$$$$** ▦ **Southern Cross Club.** The stunning beach is dotted with brightly colored cottages, all with fabulous sea views. The rooms have beautiful hardwood furniture with rattan accents, while tile floors, swirling fans, and air-conditioning keep you cool. The latest addition is the two-bedroom Blossom Cottage which can sleep up to five people. Service and meals are impeccable, though diving and fishing are the true draws here. Wading through seagrass is the norm on all resort beaches, but secluded Owen Island, which has a lovely sandy beach, is a short kayak trip away. Prices include round-trip airport transfers, service charge, and tax but not beverages; dives are extra. ⊠ *South Hole Sound* ◌ *Box 44* ☎ *345/948– 1099 or 800/899–2582* ⊕ *317/636–9503* ⊕ *www.southerncrossclub.*

com 🛏 *11 rooms, 1 cottage* ⚓ *Restaurant, dive shop, snorkeling, fishing, bicycles, bar, airport shuttle* ☰ *AE, MC, V* ⍥ *FAP.*

$$$ 🏨 **Little Cayman Beach Resort.** The rooms in this two-story property have contemporary furnishings and tropical, jewel-tone color schemes. Some rooms have water views and will be quieter than those facing the bar. The resort offers fishing and diving packages and also caters to birdwatchers and soft-adventure ecotourists. The Nature Spa offers such pampering treatments as marine algae body masks, sea-salt body polishes, and relaxing massages. Packages (for spa goers, divers, and nondivers) give significant savings over the regular rates. ⊠ *Blossom Village* 🛏 *Box 51* ☎ *345/948–3835 or 800/327–3835* 🖷 *345/948–1040* ⊕ *www. littlecayman.com* 🛏 *40 rooms* ⚓ *Restaurant, tennis court, pool, gym, hot tub, spa, dive shop, fishing, bicycles, bar, shops, meeting rooms* ☰ *AE, MC, V* ⍥ *FAP.*

$$$ 🏨 **Sam McCoy's Diving and Fishing Resort.** Stays here are ultracasual. Bedrooms (all with bath) are simple but cheerful and are done in royal- and powder-blue. You eat at beachside barbecues or with Sam, the good-natured owner, and his family. "Relaxing" rates (for nondivers) include three meals a day and airport transfers; all-inclusive rates also include beach and boat diving. Sam is a *very* experienced fishing guide; his bonefishing trips cost around $45 an hour for two (slightly less for one). ⊠ *North Side* 🛏 *Box 12* ☎ *345/948–0026 or 800/626–0496* 🖷 *345/948–0057* ⊕ *mccoyslodge.com.ky* 🛏 *8 rooms* ⚓ *Fans, pool* ☰ *AE, MC, V* ⍥ *AI.*

Villas

$$$$ 🏨 **Conch Club.** These two- to three-bedroom town homes can sleep four to six people, are well-appointed, and have pretty aqua floor tiles, vaulted ceilings, fully-equipped kitchens, decks, and patios overlooking the sea. As a guest here, you can use all the facilities of the Little Cayman Beach Resort less than ¼ mi away. These spacious units are a good option for families and couples traveling together. They also offer a dock and huts for dive gear. ⊠ *Blossom Village* 🛏 *Box 51* ☎ *345/948–1033 or 800/327–3835* ⊕ *www.conchclub.com* 🛏 *15 condos* ⚓ *Kitchens, pool, hot tub, spa, dive shop, bicycles, shop, laundry facilities* ☰ *AE, MC, V* ⍥ *EP.*

$$ 🏨 **Paradise Villas.** The cozy one-bedroom units have terraces that open onto the beach. Your quarters are simply but immaculately appointed with rattan furnishings and muted abstract fabrics. Each cottage has a few hammocks for those lazy days when you don't want to go on a dive. If you get tired of cooking for yourself in the well-equipped kitchen, delicious island-style food (not to mention the island's only bar) is just steps away at the Hungry Iguana restaurant. Dive packages are available. ⊠ *Southern Hole Sound* 🛏 *Box 48* ☎ *345/948–0001* 🖷 *345/948–0002* ⊕ *www.paradisevillas.com* 🛏 *12 villas* ⚓ *Kitchenettes, pool, dive shop, bicycles, shop* ☰ *AE, MC, V* ⍥ *EP.*

Beaches

Sandy Point. This beach, at the eastern tip of Little Cayman, is an isolated patch of powder and worth every effort to reach it by boat, car, or bike.

★ **Owen Island.** Rowboating distance (200 yards [183 m]) from the south coast, this island has a sandy beach. You can pack a picnic lunch and spend the day.

Sports & the Outdoors

BIRD-WATCHING **Governor Gore Bird Sanctuary** is home for 5,000 pairs of red-footed boo-
★ bies (the largest colony in the Western Hemisphere) and 1,000 magnificent frigate birds. You may catch black frigates and snowy egrets
competing for lunch in dramatic dive-bombing battles. The sanctuary
is near the airport.

FISHING Bloody Bay, off the north coast, has spectacular fishing, including angling for tarpon and bonefish. Sam McCoy, of **Sam McCoy's Diving and
Fishing Resort** (☎ 345/948–0026 or 800/626–0496), is among the premier fishermen on the island. The **Southern Cross Club** (☎ 800/899–
2582), a resort near South Hole Sound, also offers deep-sea fishing trips
for nonguests.

SCUBA DIVING & Jacques Cousteau considered **Bloody Bay Wall,** just 15 minutes from Lit-
SNORKELING tle Cayman by boat, one of the world's top dives. The drop begins at a
Fodor'sChoice mere 18 ft and plunges to more than 1,000 ft, with visibility often
★ reaching 150 ft—diving doesn't get much better than this. Expect to pay
$60–$75 for a two-tank boat dive. Most hotels have diving instructors
and equipment.

Kirk Sea Tours (☎ 345/949–6986) runs frequent snorkel and scuba diving excursions. The luxury yacht *Little Cayman Diver II* (☎ 800/458–
2722) offers one-week dive cruises focusing on the pristine dive sites
around Little Cayman. **Paradise Divers** (☎ 345/948–0001) runs a 46-ft
pontoon boat from the North Coast of Little Cayman to Bloody Bay
and Jackson Bay. **Reef Divers** (☎ 345/948–1033) has its own dock and
a full-service photo and video center. **Sam McCoy's Diving and Fishing Resort** (☎ 345/948–0026 or 800/626–0496) is run by a Little Cayman family that will transport you to dive boats and shore locations. The **Southern
Cross Club** (☎ 800/899–2582) limits each of its boats to 12 divers and
has its own dock.

CAYMAN ISLANDS A TO Z

*To research prices, get advice from other travelers, and book travel ar-
rangements, visit www.fodors.com.*

AIR TRAVEL

All jet service is to Grand Cayman; you have to hop over to Cayman
Brac and Little Cayman on a small propeller plane. American Airlines
has daily nonstop flights from Miami and twice-weekly flights from New
York (JFK). Air Canada provides direct twice-weekly service from
Toronto on Sunday and Wednesday. British Airways offers twice-weekly
service from London (Gatwick) with an intermediate stop in Nassau,
Bahamas. Cayman Airways flies nonstop from Miami two or three
times daily, from Tampa four times a week, from Orlando three times
a week, and from Houston and Atlanta three times a week. Continental flies nonstop from Newark, New Jersey, three times a week. Delta
has daily nonstops from Atlanta and New York (JFK). Northwest has
nonstops from Detroit from December through April. USAirways flies
nonstop daily from Charlotte, North Carolina, and Philadelphia.

Air service from Grand Cayman to Cayman Brac and Little Cayman is
offered by two airlines: Cayman Airways has daily morning and evening
service to both Cayman Brac and Little Cayman. Island Air offers morning and afternoon service from Grand Cayman to both Cayman Brac
and Little Cayman.

🇫 Air Canada ☎ 345/949-2311 or 345/949-8200 ext 1908/1909. **American Airlines** ☎ 345/949-0666. **British Airways** ☎ 345/945-3459 or 345/949-6899. **Cayman Airways** ☎ 345/949-2311 or 800/422-9626 ⊕ www.caymanairways.com. **Continental** ☎ 345/916-5545. **Delta** ☎ 800/221-1212. **Island Air** ☎ 345/949-5252 ⊕ www.islandaircayman.com. **Northwest** ☎ 345/949-2955. **US Airways** ☎ 345/949-2955.

AIRPORTS

Flights land at Owen Roberts Airport (Grand Cayman), Gerrard-Smith Airport (Cayman Brac), or Edward Bodden Airstrip (Little Cayman). Some hotels offer free pickup at the airport, particularly on Cayman Brac and Little Cayman. Taxi service and car rentals are also available.
🇫 **Owen Roberts Airport** ☎ 345/949-5252 or 345/949-7811. **Gerrard Smith International Airport** ☎ 345/948-1222. **Edward Bodden Airstrip** ☎ 345/948-0021.

BIKE & MOPED TRAVEL

When renting a motor scooter or bicycle, remember to drive on the left—and wear sunblock. Bicycles ($10–$15 a day) and scooters ($30–$35 a day) can be rented from several outlets on Grand Cayman. Since the island is fairly flat, riding is generally not a problem. On Cayman Brac or Little Cayman your hotel can make arrangements for you. Many resorts also offer bicycles for local sightseeing.
🇫 **Cayman Cycle** ☎ 345/945-4021.

BUSINESS HOURS

BANKS Banks are open Monday–Thursday 9–2:30 and Friday 9–1 and 2:30–4:30.

POST OFFICES Post offices are generally open weekdays from 8:30 to 3:30 and Saturday from 8:30 to 11:30.

SHOPS Shops are open weekdays 9–5, and Saturday in George Town from 10 to 2; in outer shopping plazas they are open from 10 to 5. Shops are usually closed Sunday except in hotels.

CAR RENTALS

To rent a car, bring your current driver's license, and the car-rental firm will issue you a temporary permit ($7.50). Most firms offer everything from compacts to jeeps to minibuses. Rates range from $35 to $65 a day. The major agencies have offices in a plaza across from the airport terminal in Grand Cayman, where you can pick up and drop off vehicles. You can rent a car from Ace Hertz, Budget, Coconut, Economy, Soto's, and Thrifty on Grand Cayman. Ace Hertz also has an office on Cayman Brac. B&S Motor Ventures has the newest fleet on Cayman Brac, including cars, scooters, and jeeps. McLaughlin is the only agency on Little Cayman, though you probably won't need to rent a car there.
🇫 **Ace Hertz** ☎ 345/949-2280 or 800/654-3131. **Budget** ☎ 345/949-5605 or 800/472-3325. **B&S Motor Ventures** ☎ 345/948-2517. **Coconut Car Rentals** ☎ 345/949-4377 or 800/941-4562 ⊕ www.coconutcarrentals.com. **Economy** ☎ 345/949-9550. **McLaughlin Rentals** ☎ 345/948-1000. **Soto's 4x4** ☎ 345/945-2424 or 800/625-6174 ⊕ www.sotos4x4.ky. **Thrifty** ☎ 345/949-6640 or 800/367-2277.

CAR TRAVEL

Traffic on West Bay Road in Grand Cayman can be congested, especially during high season, as it's the only thoroughfare on the Seven Mile Beach strip. Head out of the strip and get beyond George Town, and traffic will be sparse. Exploring Cayman Brac on a scooter is easy and fun. You won't really need a car on Little Cayman, though there are a limited number of jeeps for rent.

GASOLINE Gas prices at this writing were about $3 for an imperial gallon, slightly more than a U.S. gallon.

ROAD CONDITIONS

If you're touring Grand Cayman by car, there's a well-maintained road that circles the island; it's hard to get lost. Grand Cayman is relatively flat and fairly easy to negotiate if you're careful in traffic. Roads are well marked and in decent condition on all three islands.

RULES OF THE ROAD

Remember—driving in the Cayman Islands is on the left, so when pulling out into traffic, look to your right.

ELECTRICITY
Electricity is the same in the Caymans as it is in the United States (110 volts, 60 cycles); it's reliable throughout the islands.

EMBASSIES & CONSULATES
🚩 U.S. Consular Representative ⊠ Mrs. Gail Duquesney at Adventure Travel ☎ 345/945-1511.

EMERGENCIES
George Town Hospital has a 24-hour two-person double-lock hyperbaric chamber.

🚩 Ambulance & Fire Medical and Fire emergencies ☎ 911.

🚩 Dentists David Godfrey ☎ 345/949-7623. David Wolfe ☎ 345/945-4388.

🚩 Hospitals George Town Hospital ⊠ Hospital Rd., George Town ☎ 345/949-4234.

🚩 Pharmacies Island Pharmacy ⊠ West Shore Centre, West Bay Rd., George Town ☎ 345/949-8987.

🚩 Police Police emergencies ☎ 911.

ETIQUETTE
You'll hear first names preceded by "Mr." or "Miss" (e.g., Mr. Sam)—these are terms of respect generally used for Caymanian senior citizens.

FESTIVALS & SEASONAL EVENTS
During April's colorful Batabano Carnival, revelers dress up as dancing flowers and swimming stingrays. If you want to see an utterly British parade spiced with island-style panache, check out the Queen's Birthday bash in June. During Million Dollar Month in June, you'll find fishing tournaments on all three islands (five tournaments in all), each with its own rules, records, and entrance fees; huge cash prizes are awarded, including one for a quarter of a million dollars that's given to the angler who breaks the existing blue marlin record (at this writing 584 pounds). October sees the carnival-like atmosphere of Pirates Week (which really lasts 10 days and includes a mock invasion of Hog Sty Bay by a mock Blackbeard and company). Visitors and locals dress up like pirates and wenches; music, fireworks, and competitions take place island-wide.

HOLIDAYS
Public holidays include New Year's Day, Ash Wednesday (46 days before Easter), Good Friday (Friday before Easter), Easter Sunday (usually April or May), Discovery Day (May 19), Queen's Birthday (June 16), Constitution Day (July 7), Christmas, and Boxing Day (Dec. 26).

LANGUAGE
English is the official language in the Cayman Islands, and it is spoken with a distinctive brogue that reflects Caymanians' Welsh, Scottish, and English heritage. For example, *three* is pronounced "tree"; *pepper* is "pepah"; and *Cayman* is "K-*man*." The number of Jamaican residents in the workforce means the Jamaican patois and heavier accent are also common (other Jamaican influences are tales about the *duppy*—pronounced like "puppy"—a scary night creature that haunts the Caymans).

MAIL & SHIPPING

Beautiful stamps are available at the General Post Office in downtown George Town and at the philatelic office in West Shore Plaza. Sending a postcard to the United States, Canada, the Caribbean, or Central America costs CI20¢. An airmail letter is CI30¢ per half ounce. To Europe and South America, rates are CI25¢ for a postcard and CI40¢ per half ounce for airmail letters. When addressing letters to the Cayman Islands, be sure to include "BWI" (British West Indies) at the bottom of the envelope. Note that the islands don't use postal codes, but don't let this worry you; your letter should arrive perfectly well without one.

MONEY MATTERS

All prices quoted in this book are in U.S. dollars unless otherwise noted.

ATMS   ATMs are readily available, particularly on Grand Cayman; they usually give the option of U.S. or Cayman dollars.

CREDIT CARDS   Major credit cards are widely accepted, except for Discover.

CURRENCY   The Cayman dollar is divided into a hundred cents, with coins of 1¢, 5¢, 10¢, and 25¢ and notes of $1, $5, $10, $25, $50, and $100. There is no $20 bill. Although the American dollar is accepted everywhere, you'll often get your change in Cayman dollars. A Cayman dollar is worth about 20% more than a U.S. dollar, so keep this in mind when looking at menu and other prices.

PASSPORTS & VISAS

It is always best when traveling abroad to carry a valid passport. However, U.S., U.K., and Canadian citizens, as well as citizens of Commonwealth countries, may carry an original birth certificate (with a raised seal) and a valid picture ID. A voter registration card is no longer acceptable identification. Citizens of all other countries need a valid passport, and everyone must have a valid return ticket.

SAFETY

The Cayman Islands are relatively safe. Theft is not widespread, but be smart: lock your room and car and secure valuables as you would at home. Outdoors, marauding blackbirds called ching chings have been known to carry off jewelry if it is left out in the open.

SIGHTSEEING TOURS

Half-day tours average $30–$50 a person and generally include a visit to the Turtle Farm and Hell in West Bay, drives along Seven Mile Beach and through George Town, and time for shopping downtown. In addition to those stops, full-day tours, which average $55–$75 per person and include lunch, also visit Bodden Town to see pirate caves and graves and the East End, where you visit blowholes on the ironshore and the site of the famous Wreck of the Ten Sails. Silver Thatch specializes in natural and historic heritage tours.

A. A. Transportation Services ☎ 345/949-7222, ask for Burton Ebanks. **Majestic Tours** ☎ 345/949-7773. **Silver Thatch** ☎ 345/945-6588. **Tropicana Tours** ☎ 345/949-0944.

BOAT TOURS   The most impressive sights in the Cayman Islands are underwater, and several submarine trips will allow you to see these wonders. On Grand Cayman don't miss a trip on the *Atlantis* submarine, which takes 48 passengers, a driver, and two guides down along the Cayman Wall to depths of up to 100 ft. Through its large windows you can see huge barrel sponges, corals in extraterrestrial-like configurations, strange eels, and schools of beautiful and beastly fish. Costs range around $72–$85 per person for trips lasting 1–1½ hours. The *Nautilus* is a semisubmersible (part of the craft remains above water). You can catch some sun on the deck or venture to the cabin below, where windows allow you to see the reefs and marine life. A one-hour undersea tour is $35. In the semisubmersible *Seaworld Explorer* you sit before windows in the hull of the boat just 5 ft below the surface, observing divers who swim around with food, attracting fish to the craft. The cost of this hour-long trip is $38.

Glass-bottom-boat trips cost around $25 and are available through several companies, including Acqua Delights, the *Cayman Mermaid,* and Kirk Sea Tours.

Sunset sails, dinner cruises, and other theme (dance, booze, pirate, etc.) cruises are available aboard several vessels. Party cruises typically run $20–$50 per person. The *Jolly Roger* is a replica of a 17th-century Spanish galleon offering afternoon, sunset, and dinner cruises. *Blackbeard's Nancy* is a 1912 topsail schooner, offering dinner cruises among others. The *Spirit of Ppalu* is a 65-ft glass-bottom catamaran offering dinner cruises.

Acqua Delights ☎ 345/949–8100. **Atlantis Submarines** ☎ 345/949–7700 or 800/877–8571 ⊕ www.atlantisadventures.net. *Blackbeard's Nancy* ☎ 345/949–8988. *Jolly Roger* ☎ 345/949–8534. **Kirk Sea Tours** ☎ 345/949–6986. *Nautilus* ☎ 345/945–1355 ⊕ www.nautilus.ky. *Seaworld Explorer* ☎ 345/949–8534. *Spirit of Ppalu* ☎ 345/949–1234.

TAXES

A 10% government tax is added at all accommodations. Otherwise, there is no tax on goods or services.

TAXIS

Taxis offer 24-hour island-wide service. Fares are determined by an elaborate rate structure set by the government, and although cabs are pricey for a short ride (the fare from Seven Mile Beach for four people to the airport is $15 to $25), cabbies rarely try to rip off tourists. Ask to see the chart if you want to double-check the quoted fare.

A. A. Transportation Services ☎ 345/949–7222. **Cayman Cab Team** ☎ 345/945–1173.

TELEPHONES

COUNTRY & AREA CODES For international dialing to the Cayman Islands, the area code is 345.

INTERNATIONAL CALLS To call outside the Caymans, dial 0 + 1 + area code and number. You can call anywhere, anytime through the cable and wireless system and local operators. To place credit-card calls, dial 110; credit-card and calling-card calls can be made from any public phone and most hotels. Beware though, that most hotels add huge surcharges to all calls local and international, even to toll-free access numbers for prepaid phone cards.

AT&T USADirect ☎ 800/872–2881. **MCI Direct** ☎ 800/888–8000. **Sprint Direct** ☎ 800/366–4663.

LOCAL CALLS To make local calls (on or between any of the three islands), dial the seven-digit number.

TIPPING

At large hotels a service charge is generally included and can be anywhere from 6% to 10%; smaller establishments and some villas and condos leave tipping up to you. Although tipping is customary at restaurants, note that some automatically include 15% on the bill—so check the tab carefully. Taxi drivers expect a 10%–15% tip.

TRANSPORTATION AROUND THE CAYMAN ISLANDS

If your accommodations are along Grand Cayman's Seven Mile Beach, you can walk or bike to the shopping centers, restaurants, and entertainment spots along West Bay Road. George Town is small enough to see on foot. If you want to see Grand Cayman, renting a car for a day is an option. You can also take a taxi, though the cost might be substantial. On Cayman Brac and Little Cayman, renting a car, bike, or moped is a must if you want to see more of the islands. There is no ferry service between any of the islands; you must fly.

VISITOR INFORMATION

🛈 Before You Leave Cayman Islands Department of Tourism ⊕ www.caymanislands. ky ⊠ 6100 Blue Lagoon Dr., Suite 150, Miami, FL 33126-2085 ☎ 305/266-2300 ⊠ 2 Memorial City Plaza, 820 Gessner, Suite 170, Houston, TX 77024 ☎ 713/461-1317 ⊠ 420 Lexington Ave., Suite 2733, New York, NY 10170 ☎ 212/682-5582 ⊠ 9525 W. Bryn Mawr Ave., Suite 160, Rosemont, IL 60018 ☎ 847/678-6446 ⊠ 3440 Wilshire Blvd., Suite 1202, Los Angeles, CA 90010 ☎ 213/738-1968 ⊠ 234 Eglinton Ave. E, Suite 306, Toronto, Ontario M4P 1K5 ☎ 416/485-1550 ⊠ Trevor House, 100 Brompton Rd., Knightsbridge, London SW3 1EX ☎ 0171/491-7771.

🛈 In the Cayman Islands Department of Tourism ⊠ Cricket Sq. and Elgin Ave., George Town ☎ 345/949-0623 ⊠ Grand Cayman Airport ☎ 345/949-2635 ⊠ George Town Craft Market, Cardinal Ave., George Town ☎ 345/949-8342 ⊙ open when cruise ships are in port ⊠ kiosk at the cruise-ship dock, George Town ☎ no phone. Islands-wide tourist hot line ☎ 345/949-8989. Burton's Tourist Information & Activity Services ☎ 345/949-6598 🖶 345/945-6222.

CURAÇAO

FODOR'S CHOICE
Avila Beach Hotel, Willemstad
Rijsttafel Indonesia Restaurant, Willemstad
Shopping in the Punda, Willemstad

HIGHLY RECOMMENDED

RESTAURANTS Astrolab Observatory, Willemstad
Bistro Le Clochard, Willemstad
Fort Nassau Restaurant, Willemstad
Small World International Cuisine, Willemstad
The Wine Cellar, Willemstad

HOTELS Curaçao Marriott Beach Resort & Emerald Casino, Piscadera Bay
Hilton Curaçao Resort, Piscadera Bay

SIGHTS Christoffel National Park, Savonet
Curaçao Seaquarium, Bapor Kibra
Kurá Hulanda Museum, Willemstad
Maritime Museum, Scharloo

Noontime pedestrians go about their business as the jewel-colored buildings of Punda blaze in the Caribbean sun. People make their way home for lunch across the Queen Emma Bridge, which connects the two sides of the city. Suddenly the blare of a ship's horn pierces the air. Within seconds the bridge separates itself from the Punda side and swings away. The crowd crossing the bridge is unconcerned as their pathway moves under their feet. Moments later a giant tanker sails into the city—within feet of a sidewalk café. The bridge leisurely swings back into its original position. Just another magic moment in Willemstad.

Updated by
Vernon
O'Reilly-
Ramesar

Curaçao—the largest island of the Netherlands Antilles (38 mi [61 km] long and 2–7½ mi [3–12 km] wide)—is also the most staunchly Dutch in its culture and its architecture. Although Dutch is the official language, Papiamento is the tongue common to all the Netherlands Antilles and spoken most often by locals. Curaçao's charming capital of Willemstad, its underwater park, and its dozens of little cove beaches make it ideal for exploring. Willemstad's historic city center and the island's natural harbor (Schottegat) are included on UNESCO's World Heritage List, a coveted distinction reserved for the likes of the Palace of Versailles and the Taj Mahal.

Thirty-five miles (56 km) north of Venezuela and 42 mi (68 km) east of Aruba, Curaçao sits below the so-called hurricane belt. The sun smiles down on the island, but it's never stiflingly hot, thanks to the gentle trade winds. Water sports—including outstanding reef diving—attract enthusiasts from all over the world. Curaçao claims 38 beaches, though only a handful are long strips of silky sand; most are stretches of washed-up coral that have broken down into white or pink sand, to varying degrees of smoothness. The island is dominated by arid countryside, rocky coves, and a sprawling capital built around a natural harbor. The economy is based primarily on oil refining and offshore banking; however, tourism is becoming increasingly important, and over the years the government has invested millions of dollars to restore colonial buildings to their original stature.

In Willemstad, Curaçao's "face" is a surprise—spiffy rows of brightly colored town houses that look transplanted from Holland. Although the gabled roofs and red tiles show a Dutch influence, the gay colors of the facades are peculiar to Curaçao. It is said that at one time a large percentage of the population was suffering from migraines. The governor at the time suggested that the preponderance of white buildings was the cause and that changing colors might solve the problem. After his death, it was discovered that he was the owner of the only paint supplier on the island. True or not, this little story is indicative of the Curaçaoan sense of humor. In the countryside, the dollhouse look of the plantation houses, or *landhuizen* (literally, "land houses"), makes a cheerful contrast to the stark cacti and the austere shrubbery.

Curaçao was discovered by Alonzo de Ojeda (one of Columbus's lieutenants) in 1499. The first Spanish settlers arrived in 1527. In 1634 the Dutch came via the Netherlands West Indies Company. They promptly shipped off the Spaniards and the few remaining Indians—survivors of the battles for ownership of the island—to Venezuela. Eight years later Peter Stuyvesant began his rule as governor, which lasted until he left for New York around 1645. Twelve Jewish families arrived from Amsterdam in 1651, and by 1732 there was a synagogue; the present structure is the oldest synagogue still in use in the Western Hemisphere. Over the years the city built fortresses to defend against French and British invasions—many of those ramparts now house restaurants and hotels. The Dutch claim to Curaçao was recognized in 1815 by the Treaty of Paris. In 1954 Curaçao became an autonomous part of the Kingdom of the Netherlands, with a governor appointed by the queen, an elected parliament, and an island council.

Today Curaçao's population is derived from more than 50 nationalities with an exuberant mix of Latin, European, and African roots and with a Babel of tongues, resulting in superb restaurants and an active cultural scene. The island, like its Dutch settlers, is known for its religious tolerance, and tourists are warmly welcomed.

WHAT IT COSTS In U.S. dollars				
$$$$	$$$	$$	$	¢
RESTAURANTS*				
over $30	$20–$30	$12–$20	$8–$12	under $8
HOTELS**				
Cost EP/BP/CP over $350	$250–$350	$150–$250	$80–$150	under $80
Cost AI over $450	$350–$450	$250–$350	$125–$250	under $125

*Restaurant prices are for a main course at dinner. **EP, BP, and CP prices are per night for a standard double room in high season, excluding taxes, service charges, and meal plans. AI (all-inclusive) prices are per person, per night based on double-occupancy during high season, excluding taxes and service charges.

Where to Stay

Beach hotels on the island's southwestern end tend to be small, secluded, and peaceful, but they are a 30- to 45-minute drive from town. Those east and west of Willemstad proper tend to be large-scale luxury resorts. In town you can find places that cater to budget and business travelers. Most hotels provide beach or shopping shuttles. The larger ones provide kids' programs and allow children to stay in their parents' room for free or at a discounted rate. These hotels also include a Continental breakfast or a large buffet breakfast. Full American Plans aren't popular because of the abundance of good restaurants.

The Curaçao Apartments and Small Hotels Association, in conjunction with the CTDB, publishes a brochure on quality accommodations. Rentals are popular with European visitors. Contact the **Curaçao Tourism Development Bureau** (⊠ Pietermaai 19, Willemstad ☎ 5999/461–6000 Ext. 117 or 112) at least two months in advance for a list of available properties.

$$$–$$$$ ⊞ **Hotel Kurá Hulanda.** This is more than a mere hotel; it's an 18th-century village within Willemstad centered around the former courtyard where slaves were bought and sold. Lovingly restored by Dutch millionaire and philanthropist Jacob Dekker and his partner John Padget, this complex includes a boutique hotel, an amazing museum of African history, and a business center. Rooms are large, with high ceilings; each one is individually decorated with Indian and Indonesian furnishings. The Indian Bridal Suite is a work of art by itself, with marble floors and furniture covered with hammered sterling silver. The pools and gardens are exquisite, especially at night. ⊠ Langestraat 8, Willemstad ☎ 5999/434–

7700 ⌨ *5999/434–7701* ⊕ *www.kurahulanda.com* ⮐ *100 rooms, 12 suites* ⌕ *4 restaurants, coffee shop, room service, fans, in-room safe, golf privileges, 2 pools, health club, spa, 2 bars, shops, business services, meeting room* 🖃 *AE, MC, V* ❍❙ *EP.*

★ **$$$** 🖫 **Curaçao Marriott Beach Resort & Emerald Casino.** The Marriott sits on landscaped grounds brimming with oleander, hibiscus, and palms. Its beach is beautiful; facilities include a lively pool with a swim-up bar, tennis courts, a fitness center, an alluring albeit small casino, and a ballroom. Rooms are well equipped, with hair dryers, irons and ironing boards, and balconies or patios. The Curaçao World Trade Center is a stone's throw away, and the hotel's conference service staff will help you coordinate business engagements. ⊠ *Piscadera Bay* ⌂ *Box 6003* ☎ *5999/736–8800* ⌨ *5999/462–7502* ⊕ *www.marriott.com* ⮐ *237 rooms, 10 suites* ⌕ *4 restaurants, room service, minibars, golf privileges, 2 tennis courts, pool, hair salon, health club, hot tub, 2 outdoor hot tubs, sauna, steam room, beach, dive shop, dock, snorkeling, windsurfing, 3 bars, business services, convention center, meeting rooms, car rental, no-smoking rooms* 🖃 *AE, D, DC, MC, V* ❍❙ *EP.*

$$$ 🖫 **Floris Suite Hotel.** Dutch architect Jan des Bouvrie designed this wonderfully minimalist boutique hotel near the Curaçao World Trade Center. Here the rich glow of mahogany is juxtaposed with the cool starkness of stainless steel. Spacious suites equipped with full kitchens have made this a popular choice for visiting business travelers. Start your morning sipping a cappuccino at the coffee bar in the airy lobby before heading out to face the world. A lush tropical garden surrounds the pool and restaurant, and the beach is just across the street. ⊠ *J. F. Kennedy Blvd., Piscadera Bay* ⌂ *Box 6246* ☎ *5999/462–6111* ⌨ *5999/462–6211* ⊕ *www.florissuitehotel.com* ⮐ *72 suites* ⌕ *Restaurant, in-room data ports, golf privileges, tennis court, pool, beach, dive shop, business services, meeting room* 🖃 *AE, MC, V* ❍❙ *EP.*

$$–$$$ 🖫 **Breezes Curaçao.** This all–inclusive family resort has a large private beach, lushly landscaped grounds, and spacious rooms. Basically everything imaginable—other than the resort's casino—is included in the room rate. The activities included are quite astonishing and range from windsurfing to trapeze lessons. There is always some crowd-pleasing activity near the pool day and night. ⊠ *Martin Luther King Blvd. 8, Willemstad* ☎ *5999/736–7888 or 800/467–8737* ⌨ *5999/461–4131* ⊕ *www.breezes.com* ⮐ *285 rooms, 54 suites* ⌕ *4 restaurants, snack bar, in-room safes, refrigerators, 2 tennis courts, 2 pools, health club, spa, beach, dive shop, dock, snorkeling, volleyball, bar, casino, dance club, shops, baby-sitting, children's programs (ages 2–16), dry cleaning, laundry service, business services, meeting rooms, car rental, travel services, no-smoking rooms* 🖃 *AE, DC, MC, V* ❍❙ *AI.*

$–$$$
Fodor'sChoice
★ 🖫 **Avila Beach Hotel.** Dignitaries and celebrities often choose to stay at this 200-year-old mansion overlooking the ocean. The lobby, with gilt mirrors, Asian rugs, porcelain figurines, and gas lamps, evokes a more genteel era. Rooms range from the budget-priced and basic to the luxurious (with whirlpool tubs) in the Blues Wing. The Belle Terrace restaurant, shaded by an enormous tree, serves imaginative international dishes. At the Blues Seafood Restaurant and Cocktail Bar, live jazz takes center stage Thursday and Saturday evenings, and there's a terrific tapas buffet on Friday night. ⊠ *Penstraat 130, Willemstad* ⌂ *Box 791* ☎ *5999/461–4377* ⌨ *5999/461–1493* ⊕ *www.avilahotel.com* ⮐ *100 rooms, 8 suites* ⌕ *3 restaurants, in-room data ports, in-room safes, kitchenettes, refrigerators, tennis court, beach, 2 bars, business services, convention center, meeting rooms* 🖃 *AE, DC, MC, V* ❍❙ *EP.*

$$ 🖫 **Habitat Curaçao.** The sprawling, beachfront Habitat is a diver's dream, with top-notch facilities and 24-hour diving. Clusters of canary-yellow

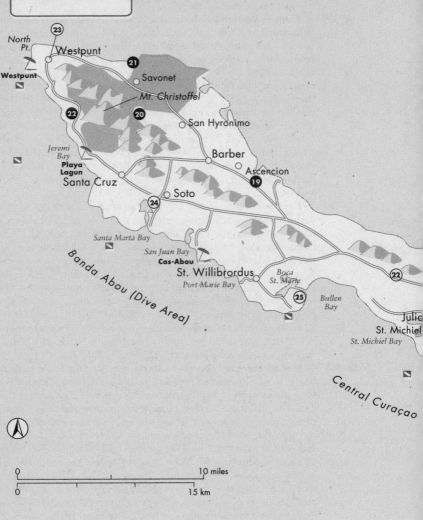

Curaçao

North Pt.
Westpunt
Westpunt
Savonet
Mt. Christoffel
San Hyronimo
Jeremi Bay
Playa Lagun
Santa Cruz
Barber
Ascencion
Soto
Santa Marta Bay
San Juan Bay
Cas-Abou
St. Willibrordus
Port Marie Bay
Boca St. Marie
Bullen Bay
Banda Abou (Dive Area)
Julie
St. Michiel
St. Michiel Bay
Central Curaçao

0   10 miles
0   15 km

Hotels ▼	Holiday Beach Hotel and Casino 4	Plaza Hotel Curaçao 6	Restaurants ▼
Avila Beach Hotel 7	Hotel Kurá Hulanda 18	Sheraton Curaçao Resort 1	Astrolab Observatory 18
Breezes Curaçao 15	Landhuis Daniel 22	Sunset Waters Beach Resort 24	Bistro Le Clochard 8
Chogogo Resort 5	Lions Dive Hotel Curaçao 19		Fisherman's Wharf 12
Curaçao Marriott Beach Resort & Emerald Casino 3	Otrobanda Hotel & Casino 9		Fort Nassau Restaurant 20
Floris Suite Hotel 2			
Habitat Curaçao 25			

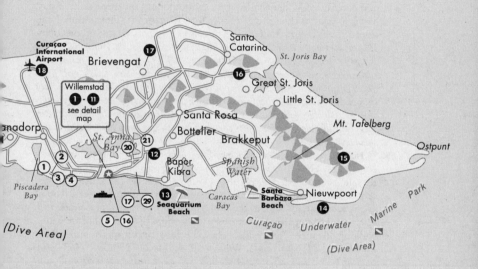

KEY

⚓ Beaches
🚢 Cruise Ship Terminal
◥ Dive Sites
❶ Exploring Sights
① Hotels & Restaurants

Caribbean Sea

Curaçao International Airport
18

Brievengat
17

Santa Catarina
St. Joris Bay

16

Great St. Joris
Little St. Joris

Willemstad
1 - 11
see detail map

anadorp

St. Anna Bay
20
21

Santa Rosa
Bottelier
Brakkeput

Mt. Tafelberg

Ostpunt

2

1
3 4

12

Bapor Kibra

Spanish Water

15

Piscadera Bay

17 - 29
13

Seaquarium Beach

Caracas Bay

Santa Barbara Beach

Nieuwpoort

14

Curaçao Underwater Marine Park

5 - 16

(Dive Area)

Curaçao

Underwater

(Dive Area)

and red buildings are surrounded by tropical foliage and connected by stairways and winding paths. The raised pool affords grand vistas. Rooms are brightly outfitted with marine-life fabrics specially commissioned from local artist Nena Sanchez. Each room has a furnished terrace or balcony and a fully equipped kitchenette. The lanai rooms are excellent for families. Request an ocean view (the price is the same). There is nightly entertainment at poolside. ⊠ *Coral Estates, Rif St. Marie* ☎ *5999/864–8800 or 800/327–6709* 🖷 *5999/864–8464* ⊕ *www. habitatdiveresorts.com* 🛏 *56 suites, 20 2-bedroom cottages* ⚂ *Restaurant, in-room safes, pool, beach, dive shop, dock, bar, shops, meeting rooms* ▭ *AE, DC, MC, V* ⦿⦿ *EP.*

★ **$$** ▦ **Hilton Curaçao Resort.** You may have a hard time choosing between the two fine beaches or the huge, free-form pool, which seems to merge with the ocean. Rooms have many creature comforts; those on the fifth (executive) floor are geared toward business travelers. Staff are polite and knowledgeable. The West Indies Spa offers everything from massage to aromatherapy. The hotel is five minutes from the shops, sights, and eateries of Willemstad; a free shuttle takes you there twice a day. Savor a meal at the hotel's Yellow Bird Restaurant (international cuisine) or La Piazzetta (Italian). There's also a large casino just off the lobby. ⊠ *J. F. Kennedy Blvd., Piscadera Bay* ⅅ *Box 2133* ☎ *5999/462–5000* 🖷 *5999/462–5846* ⊕ *www.hilton.com* 🛏 *197 rooms, 13 suites* ⚂ *3 restaurants, room service, some in-room faxes, in-room safes, golf privileges, miniature golf, 2 tennis courts, 2 pools, health club, outdoor hot tub, spa, beach, dive shop, dock, snorkeling, boating, jet skiing, waterskiing, fishing, volleyball, 3 bars, casino, dance club, shops, baby-sitting, laundry service, business services, meeting rooms, car rental, travel services, free parking, no-smoking rooms* ▭ *AE, DC, MC, V* ⦿⦿ *EP.*

$$ ▦ **Holiday Beach Hotel and Casino.** This older hotel remains popular with Americans. The lobby is spacious, and the island's largest casino, Casino Royale, is attached. There's also a video arcade for the kids. The crescent beach is quite large for Curaçao and dotted with palm trees. Rooms are airy, bright, and clean, but much of the hotel has a dated motel feel. There's a 24-hour Denny's on-site, and the shops of Willemstad are within walking distance. There's also a free shuttle to and from town. ⊠ *Pater Euwensweg 31, Otrobanda, Willemstad* ⅅ *Box 2178* ☎ *5999/462–5400 or 800/444–5244* 🖷 *5999/462–4397* ⊕ *www.hol-beach.com* 🛏 *200 rooms, 1 suite* ⚂ *2 restaurants, in-room safes, refrigerators, 2 tennis courts, dive shop, pool, gym, beach, dive shop, volleyball, 2 bars, casino, video game room, playground, laundry facilities, meeting rooms* ▭ *AE, D, DC, MC, V* ⦿⦿ *EP.*

$$ ▦ **Lions Dive Hotel Curaçao.** This yellow-and-blue caravansary is a hop, skip, and plunge away from the Seaquarium (complimentary admission is given to guests), on ¼ mi (½ km) of private beach. Most guests are dive enthusiasts satisfied by the top-notch scuba center and the young, helpful staff. Rooms are airy, modern, and light-filled, with tile floors, wicker furnishings, and large bathrooms (showers only). French doors open onto a spacious balcony or terrace, and every room has a sea view. The Sunday-night happy hour is especially festive, with a merengue band playing poolside. ⊠ *Bapor Kibra* ☎ *5999/434–8888* 🖷 *5999/434–8889* ⊕ *www.lionsdive.com* 🛏 *72 rooms* ⚂ *Restaurant, fans, in-room safes, pool, health club, massage, beach, dive shop, dock, windsurfing, boating, bar, baby-sitting, laundry service, Internet* ▭ *AE, DC, MC, V* ⦿⦿ *EP.*

$–$$ ▦ **Plaza Hotel Curaçao.** This pink landmark at the entrance to Willemstad's harbor is the only hotel in the world with marine collision insurance, in case arriving ships get too close. The antiques-filled lobby and a winding lagoon and waterfall give the hotel the air of an elegant colonial outpost. Rooms are nicely appointed, and most offer excellent views of either the city or the ocean. You give up beachfront (but you have beach privileges at Seaquarium, and there's a shuttle) for walking access to the city's center. The hotel is popular with business travelers and has a fully equipped business center in the lobby. ⊠ *Plaza Piar, Willemstad* ☎ *5999/ 461–2500* 🖷 *5999/461–6543* ⊕ *www.plazahotelcuracao.com* ↘ *205 rooms, 27 suites* ⚭ *2 restaurants, room service, in-room safes, pool, dive shop, 3 bars, casino, shops, business services, meeting rooms, car rental, no-smoking rooms* ⊟ *AE, MC, V* ⦿ *EP.*

$–$$ 🖻 **Sunset Waters Beach Resort.** This hotel is removed from the bustle of downtown, set in a remote area on a luscious stretch of beach. Rooms are bright and airy, with white-tile floors, a terrace or patio, and sleeping sofas in blue and mauve. All rooms have an ocean or garden view. One area of the beach is designated for nude sunbathing, and some of the rooms afford a full view of this beach, so request a room elsewhere if you'd prefer less exposure. The casino offers slots, blackjack, and roulette. Complimentary shuttles run to and from town. Kids under 12 stay free. An all-inclusive plan is an option. ⊠ *Santa Marta Bay* ☎ *5999/ 864–1233* 🖷 *5999/864–1237* ⊕ *www.sunsetwaters.com* ↘ *70 rooms* ⚭ *2 restaurants, refrigerators, miniature golf, tennis court, pool, health club, outdoor hot tub, beach, dive shop, snorkeling, boating, 3 bars, casino, shop, children's programs (ages 6–16), meeting rooms, car rental, travel services* ⊟ *AE, D, MC, V* ⦿ *EP.*

$ 🖻 **Chogogo Resort.** Vacationers who prefer bungalows over hotel rooms will appreciate Chogogo, on the island's eastern end and a two-minute walk from Jan Thiel Beach. All rooms are spotless and have fully equipped kitchens, TVs, CD players, and balconies or patios. It's a quiet, relaxing place catering mainly to Dutch tourists. There's an excellent outside restaurant near the lovely pool. ⊠ *Jan Thiel Beach* ☎ *5999/747–2844* 🖷 *5999/747–2424* ⊕ *www.chogogo.com* ↘ *26 bungalows, 16 apartments, 18 studios* ⚭ *Restaurant, fans, kitchenettes, pool, beach, laundry service* ⊟ *AE, D, MC, V* ⦿ *EP.*

$ 🖻 **Otrobanda Hotel & Casino.** In the heart of the revitalized Otrobanda neighborhood, this little hotel offers superior value for the money. Standard rooms are cramped but appealing, with terrific harbor views, rattan furnishings, and paintings of country scenes. The most attractive and roomiest are those tucked under the peaked roof. For a good meal and a good view, stop by the Otrobanda Bay Sight Terrace. The hotel's location puts you right in the middle of all the downtown action. ⊠ *Breedestraat, Otrobanda, Willemstad* ☎ *5999/462–7400* 🖷 *5999/ 462–7299* ⊕ *www.otrobandahotel.com* ↘ *42 rooms, 3 suites* ⚭ *Restaurant, pool, bar, casino, shops, baby-sitting* ⊟ *AE, DC, MC, V* ⦿ *BP.*

¢ 🖻 **Landhuis Daniel.** Dating from 1711, this mustard plantation house with white colonnades and red-tile roof has served as an inn since 1997. The property, near the narrow center of the island, has a pool, dive shop, and French-Caribbean restaurant, serving dishes made with organic fruits, vegetables, and herbs grown right on the plantation. The intriguing menu varies according to the seasonal crop yield. Rooms are tiny but clean, with basic furnishings; if possible, choose one of the larger rooms in the main house. Join in the fun at the poolside barbecue on Fridays, Saturdays, and Sundays. ⊠ *Weg Naar, Westpunt* ☎☎ *5999/ 864–8400* ⊕ *www.landhuisdaniel.com* ↘ *8 rooms* ⚭ *Restaurant, fans, pool, dive shop, bar* ⊟ *AE, MC, V* ⦿ *EP.*

Where to Eat

Dine beneath the boughs of magnificent old trees, in the romantic gloom of wine cellars in renovated plantation houses, or on the ramparts of 18th-century forts. Curaçaoans partake of some of the best Indonesian food in the Caribbean; you can also find fine French, Swiss, Dutch, and Swedish fare.

What to Wear

Dress in restaurants is almost always casual (though beachwear isn't acceptable). Some of the resort dining rooms and nicer restaurants require that men wear jackets, especially in high season; ask when you make reservations.

AMERICAN   ✕ **Rodeo House of Ribs.** This family-owned restaurant has been in busi-
$–$$ ness for more than 20 years. The staff (dressed in the requisite cowboy outfits) keeps the place lively all night long. Aside from a couple of fish offerings, everything is strictly red meat. The ribs and steaks are all imported from the United States. Try the charcoal-broiled tenderloin in pepper sauce. ⊠ *Fokkerweg 3, Saliña, Willemstad* ☎ *5999/465–9465* ⊟ *AE, MC, V* ⊘ *Closed Mon.*

ASIAN   ✕ **Rijsttafel Indonesia Restaurant.** An antique rickshaw at the entrance sets
$$–$$$$ the mood. Exotic delicacies make up the traditional Indonesian banquet
Fodor'sChoice   called *rijsttafel*, where some 16 to 25 dishes are set buffet style around
★   you. Smaller appetites should opt for the *nasi rames*, with only eight dishes. A vegetarian rijsttafel is also available. An à la carte menu includes fried noodles and combination meat-and-fish platters. ⊠ *Mercurriusstraat 13–15, Saliña, Willemstad* ☎ *5999/461–2606* ⊟ *AE, DC, MC, V* ⊘ *No lunch Sun.*

CARIBBEAN   ✕ **Jaanchi's Restaurant.** This sheltered, open-air restaurant has lunches
$$–$$$ of mouth-watering Curaçaoan dishes. The specialty is a hefty platter of fresh wahoo with sides of potatoes or *funchi* (a cornmeal dish similar to polenta) and vegetables. Jaanchi's iguana soup is famous on the island. The place usually closes at 6:30 PM, but will stay open later if you call ahead. ⊠ *Westpunt 15, Westpunt* ☎ *5999/864–0126* ⊟ *AE, DC, MC, V.*

CONTINENTAL   ✕ **The Wine Cellar.** Master Dutch chef Nico Cornelisse serves consistently
★ $$$–$$$$ excellent meals in his Victorian-style dining room. The four-course *menu romantique* includes smoked salmon, creamy pumpkin soup, leg of lamb, and banana fritters. The restaurant is wheelchair-accessible. ⊠ *Kaya Zusternan Di Schyndel, Willemstad* ☎ *5999/461–2178* or *5999/767–4909* ⌂ *Reservations essential* ⊟ *AE, DC, MC, V* ⊘ *Closed Sun. No lunch weekends.*

★ $$$ ✕ **Astrolab Observatory.** Choose to eat in the air-conditioned interior or better still on the terrace under the massive ficus tree. Nestled in the middle of the Kurá Hulanda compound, this restaurant is wonderfully intimate and romantic. The starter of oysters in a cilantro batter is melt-in-your-mouth good. The humble-sounding fisherman's stew is a divine combination of poached fish, mussels, and shrimp in a fennel tomato sauce—and fit for a king. ⊠ *Kurá Hulanda, Langestraat 8, Otrobanda, Willemstad* ☎ *5999/434–7700* ⌂ *Reservations essential* ⊟ *AE, DC, MC, V* ⊘ *No lunch.*

★ $$$ ✕ **Bistro Le Clochard.** This romantic gem is built into the 19th-century Riffort—an oasis of arched entryways, exposed brickwork, wood beams, and lace curtains. The waterside terrace has a beautiful view of the floating bridge and harbor. The Swiss chefs prepare exquisite French and Swiss dishes. Their signature dish is La Potence, a swinging, red-hot metal ball covered with bits of sizzling tenderloin and sausage. Leave room for the delicious homemade Swiss Toblerone chocolate mousse. The restaurant is fully wheelchair-accessible. ⊠ *Harbourside Terrace, Riffort, Otrobanda, Willemstad* ☎ *5999/462–5666* ⌂ *Reservations essential* ⊟ *AE, DC, MC, V* ⊘ *No lunch Sat.*

★ **$$$** ✕ **Fort Nassau Restaurant.** On a hill above Willemstad, this restaurant is built into an 18th-century fort with a 360-degree view. Go for a drink in the breezy Battery Terrace bar or dine in air-conditioned comfort beside huge bay windows. Delicious highlights of the diverse menu include Dover sole topped with Calvados and fruit, and oven-baked shrimp in hollandaise sauce. Desserts here are delectable. ✉ *Schottengatweg 82, near Juliana Bridge, Willemstad* ☎ *5999/461–3450 or 5999/461–3086* ⌾ *Reservations essential* ▭ *AE, MC, V* ☉ *No lunch weekends.*

ECLECTIC **$–$$$** ✕ **Otrobanda Bay Sight Terrace.** The best thing about this low-key eatery is the remarkable view of Santa Anna Bay and the colorful town-house façades. As you dine, you're so close to the passing ships it seems you can almost touch them. Meals are reasonably priced. The *keshi yani*, a slice of Gouda cheese stuffed with spicy, shredded chicken is a good choice. ✉ *Otrobanda Hotel & Casino, Breedestraat, Otrobanda, Willemstad* ☎ *5999/462–7400* ▭ *AE, MC, V.*

★ **$–$$$** ✕ **Small World International Cuisine.** For a tasty, pleasant dining experience, try this eclectic eatery, whose outdoor deck juts out over the Caribbean. The menu is broken down into French, Spanish, creole, and Chinese sections. *Gambas al ajillo* (shrimp in garlic sauce, served with flavorful veggies and rice) is a savory choice, as is the salmon fillet papillote (cooked in its own juices and wrapped in a foil pouch with carrots and onions). If you prefer indoor seating, request the nifty glass-top table with the built-in terrarium. ✉ *Waterfort Boogjes 18–19, Willemstad* ☎ *5999/465–5575* ▭ *AE, DC, MC, V.*

$–$$ ✕ **Mambo Beach.** On the west end of Seaquarium Beach, this hip, open-air bar and grill, spread over the sand, serves good food for breakfast, lunch, and dinner. Hearty sandwiches on baguette bread dominate the lunch menu; steaks, fresh seafood, and pasta fill the dinner menu. There is an excellent fish buffet on Fridays. This is a fantastic place to watch the sun set, but don't forget your insect repellent. ✉ *Seaquarium Beach, Bapor Kibra* ☎ *5999/461–8999* ▭ *MC, V.*

¢–$ ✕ **Time Out Café.** Tucked into an alley in the shopping heartland of Punda, this outdoor eatery serves up light bites like tuna sandwiches and *tostis* (toasted cheese), as well as the omnipresent catch-of-the-day option. Drop by for a beer and a game of billiards before venturing out. There are live rock performances on Thursday nights. ✉ *Keukenplein 8, Punda, Willemstad* ☎ *5999/667–2455* ▭ *No credit cards.*

INDIAN **$–$$$** ✕ **Jaipur.** Part of the expansive Kurá Hulanda complex, this upscale Indian eatery serves a superbly varied menu of delights. The lamb samosas make a great starter, and if you can handle it, the tandoori mixed grill is a treat not to be missed. The gentle night breezes, subtle lighting, and sound of the nearby waterfall seem to make the food even more enjoyable. ✉ *Waterfort Archesboog 12, Willemstad* ☎ *5999/461–3482* ▭ *AE, DC, MC, V* ☉ *No lunch Sun.*

ITALIAN **$$–$$$$** ✕ **La Pergola.** Built into the stuccoed walls of the Waterfort Arches, with huge picture windows fronting the rambunctious sea, copper pots hanging everywhere, and a pretty pink-and-white arbor wound with bunches of grapes, La Pergola offers creative variations on Italian standards and has no fewer than 14 pastas and 11 pizza options. ✉ *Langestraat 8, Willemstad* ☎ *5999/461–3482* ▭ *AE, DC, MC, V* ☉ *No lunch.*

SEAFOOD **$$–$$$** ✕ **Fisherman's Wharf.** A terrific outdoor terrace and a comprehensive menu make this restaurant a good choice. Fish lovers will enjoy the barracuda Picasso (barracuda served under flambéed fruit and cashews). The more adventurous meat lovers can have a go at the ostrich loin served on a bed of green peppers and stir-fried shrimp. ✉ *Martin Luther King Blvd. 93, Willemstad* ☎ *5999/465–7558* ▭ *AE, MC, V.*

Beaches

Curaçao has some 38 beaches, many of them quite striking. Those along the southeast coast are often rocky (wear your flip-flops or reef shoes into the water), but in the west you'll find stretches of smooth sand at the shoreline. Rent a jeep, motor scooter, or heavy-treaded car, ask your hotel to pack a picnic basket, and go exploring. You can discover the joy of inlets: tiny bays marked by craggy cliffs, exotic trees, and small pebbly or sandy beaches. There are snack bars and rest rooms on many of the larger beaches.

Among the hotels with the best beaches are the Hilton Curaçao, the Curaçao Marriott Beach Resort, Sunset Waters Beach Resort, and the Lions Dive Hotel Curaçao.

Barbara Beach. To reach this popular family beach on the eastern tip, you can drive through one of Curaçao's toniest neighborhoods, Spanish Water, where gleaming white yachts replace humble fishing fleets. The beach has changing facilities and a snack bar, but charges an admission fee—usually around $2.25 per person, but up to $7 per person on weekends. Around the bend, Caracas Bay is a popular dive site, with a sunken ship so close to the surface that snorkelers can view it clearly.
Cas Abou. This white sand gem has the brightest blue water in Curaçao. Divers and snorkelers will appreciate the on-site dive shop, and sunbathers can make use of the small snack bar. The rest rooms and showers are immaculate.
Playa Lagun. This northwestern cove is caught between gunmetal gray cliffs, which beautifully frame the Caribbean blue. Couples can steal quiet moments here on weekday mornings, but locals flock here on weekends. Canoe trips, dive sessions, and swimming lessons are available through the dive shop on the beach. Cognoscenti know this is one of the best places to snorkel.
Seaquarium Beach. You'll pay a fee ($2.25 per person) to enter here, but the amenities (rest rooms, showers, boutiques, water-sports center, snack bar, restaurants with beach bars, thatched shelters and palm trees for shade, security patrols) on this 1,600-ft man-made sandy beach and the calm waters protected by a carefully placed breakwater are well worth it.
Westpunt. On the northwest tip of the island, Westpunt is shady in the morning. It doesn't have much sand, but you can sit on a shaded rock ledge. The Playa Forti Bar & Restaurant offers refreshing soft drinks and beer and an exquisite fish soup. Take in the view of the boats in the marina and watch the divers jump from the high cliff. Water-sports enthusiasts, take note: the All West Dive Shop is on the beach here.

Sports & the Outdoors

For the full gamut of activities in one spot, nature buffs (especially bird-watchers), families, and adventure-seekers may want to visit **Caracas Bay Island** (☎ 5999/747–0777). Things to do here include hiking, mountain biking, canoeing, kayaking, windsurfing, jet-skiing, and snorkeling. There's a fully equipped dive shop, a restaurant, and a bar on premises. Admission to the scenic area is $3; activities cost extra.

BOATING, **Top Watersports Curaçao** (✉ Seaquarium Beach, Bapor Kibra ☎ 5999/
SAILING & 461–7343) rents smaller craft like Sunfish, as well as canoes, snorkel
WINDSURFING gear, and floating mats. This section of coast tends to be calmer than most, making it ideal for beginners, although the breezes are sufficiently steady to keep experienced windsurfers on their toes.

FISHING　There are surprisingly few charter boats available for deep-sea fishing, but the small 18-ft *Hemingway* (☎ 5999/888–8086) offers Penn International, senator, and spinning reels as well as an experienced guide. It can accommodate no more than two people (one person $45, two $70) but can negotiate fairly deep water where shark, wahoo, tuna, barracuda, sailfish, and marlin are abundant. The captain will pick up at your hotel. For tarpon fishing closer to shore, the **Plaza Hotel Curaçao** (✉ Plaza Piar, Willemstad ☎ 5999/461–2500) offers fishing outings in the 13-ft *Boston Whalers*. If you're in search of marlin, book the 54-ft yacht *War Eagle* (☎ 5999/461–2500).

GOLF　In the mood to hit the green? Try the **Blue Bay Curaçao Golf and Beach Resort** (✉ Landhuis Blauw ☎ 5999/868–1755). This 18-hole, par-72 course beckons experts and novices alike. Facilities include a golf shop, locker rooms, and a snack bar. Greens fees range $65–$105 per person, and you can rent carts, clubs, and shoes. If you'd like to drive your game to a new level, take a lesson from the house pro ($30 for a half hour) or head for the driving range and putting green ($10 per person for unlimited range balls). The 9-hole course at the **Curaçao Golf and Squash Club** (✉ Wilhelmenalaan, Emmastad ☎ 5999/737–3590) is a challenge because of the stiff trade winds and the sand greens. Greens fees are $20 for 18 holes.

SCUBA DIVING &　The **Curaçao Underwater Marine Park** includes almost a third of the is-
SNORKELING　land's southern diving waters. Scuba divers and snorkelers can enjoy more than 12½ mi (20 km) of protected reefs and shores, with normal visibility from 60 to 150 ft. With water temperatures ranging from 75°F to 82°F (24°C to 28°C), wet suits are generally unnecessary. No coral collecting, spearfishing, or littering is allowed. An exciting wreck to explore is the SS *Oranje Nassau*, which ran aground more than 90 years ago. The other two main diving areas are **Banda Abou**, along the southwest coast between West Point and St. Marie, and along **central Curaçao**, which stretches between Bullen Bay to the Breezes Curaçao resort. The north coast is not recommended for diving because of the dangerously rough conditions found there.

Introductory scuba resort courses run about $60–$75. Full certification courses average $200 for three days and $325 for the advanced five-day version. Virtually every operator charges $33–$35 for a single-tank dive and $55–$60 for a two-tank dive. Snorkel gear commonly rents for $12–$15 per day. For detailed information on dive sites and operators, call the **Curaçao Tourism Board** (☎ 5999/461-6000 in Curaçao; 800/328–7222 in the U.S.) and ask for the brochure "Take the Plunge in Curaçao," or pick up the *DIP–Curaçao's Official Dive Guide* at a nominal cost from the CTDB.

Caribbean Sea Sports (✉ Curaçao Marriott Beach Resort, Piscadera Bay ☎ 5999/462–2620) takes divers to popular nearby sites including the *Superior Producer* wreck. **Curaçao Seascape** (✉ John F. Kennedy Blvd., Piscadera Bay ☎ 5999/462–5000) offers shore dives and open-water certification programs. The closest operation to the famous Mushroom Forest dive site, **Easy Divers Curaçao** (✉ Sunset Waters Beach Resort, Santa Marta Bay ☎ 5999/864–2822), will customize dive trips for you, or you can take part in one of the daily two-tank dives from their 38-ft boat. PADI instruction is available. The dive center of **Habitat Curaçao** (✉ Coral Estates, Rif St. Marie ☎ 5999/864–8800) offers everything from a two-day, three-dive introductory course to underwater video and photography courses ($275–$400). **Underwater Curaçao** (✉ Lions Dive Hotel Curaçao, Bapor Kibra ☎ 5999/461–8100) offers shore and boat dives and packages, as well as certified PADI instruction.

TENNIS   If you're not staying at a hotel with a tennis court, try the **Santa Catherina Sports Complex** (⊠ Club Seru Coral, Koraal Partier 10, Santa Barbara ☎ 5999/767–7028). Court time costs $20 an hour.

Shopping

FodorśChoice   Curaçao offers a number of exciting buys, from Dutch classics like embroidered linens, blue Delft china, cheeses, and clogs to local crafts (you ★ can find some marvelous ceramic work). There are also fine local painters, most of whom work in the landscape mode. If you're looking for bargains on Swiss watches, cosmetics, cameras, crystal, perfumes, Nike or Reebok sneakers, or electronic equipment, do some comparison shopping back home and come armed with a list of prices. Willemstad is no longer a free port: there's now a tax, so prices are higher.

Areas

Most shops are concentrated in **Willemstad**'s Punda within about a six-block area. The main shopping streets are Heerenstraat, Breedestraat, and Madurostraat. Heerenstraat and Gomezplein are pedestrian malls, closed to traffic, and their roadbeds have been raised to sidewalk level and covered with pink inlaid tiles. **Otrobanda** can also be a shopping adventure, though it's not as picturesque as Punda. A walk up Breedestraat, starting at the Otrobanda Hotel & Casino on the waterfront, takes you past colorful variety stores and food shops.

Specialty Items

ART   **Gallery Eighty Six** (⊠ Trompstraat, Punda, Willemstad ☎ 5999/461–3417) represents the work of local artists and occasionally that of South Americans and Africans. **Kas di Alma Blou** (⊠ De Rouvilleweg 67, Otrobanda, Willemstad ☎ 5999/462–8896) is in a gorgeous 19th-century indigo town house and presents the top local artists; you can find shimmering landscapes, dazzling photographs, ceramics, even African-inspired Carnival masks. **Open Ateliér** (⊠ F. D. Rooseveltweg 443, Willemstad ☎ 5999/868–6027), just past St. Marie on the way to the airport, is a very special gallery featuring work by children and local artists with disabilities.

CIGARS   The sweet smell of success permeates **Cigar Emporium** (⊠ Gomezplein, Willemstad ☎ 5999/465–3955), where you'll find the largest selection of cigars on the island, including H. Upmann, Romeo & Julietta, and Montecristo. Visit the climate-controlled cedar cigar room. However, remember that Cuban cigars cannot be taken back to the U.S. legally.

CLOTHES   Left your gym shoes at home? Step into **Athlete's Foot** (⊠ Heerenstraat 10, Willemstad ☎ 5999/461–3239) and you'll be up and running in no time. At the Willemstad branch of **Batik Exclusive** (⊠ Handelskade 6, Willemstad ☎ 5999/461–0262), you can outfit yourself in vibrant Caribbean colors. The shop sells batik sarongs for adults and kids ($21), knapsacks, bathing suits, dresses, halter tops, and gift items, including mobiles with aquatic designs and hand puppets. **Benetton** (⊠ Madurostraat 4, Willemstad ☎ 5999/461–4619 ⊠ Curaçao International Airport ☎ 5999/869–6054) has winter stock in July and summer stock in December, all of it 20% off the retail price. At **Big Low Center** (⊠ Heerenstraat 6, Willemstad ☎ 5999/461–1680) there are T-shirts galore. Special deals include three regular tees or two embroidered tees for $15. **Clog Dance** (⊠ De Rouvilleweg 9B, Willemstad ☎ 5999/462–3280) has Dutch clogs and fashions, cheeses, tulips, delftware, and chocolate. **Fendi** (⊠ Breedestraat 9, Willemstad ☎ 5999/461–2618) sells its merchandise for 25% less than in the United States.

FOODSTUFFS **Toko Zuikertuintje** (✉ Zuikertuintjeweg, Willemstad ☎ 5999/737–0188), a supermarket built on the site of the original 17th-century Zuikertuintje Landhuis, is where most of the local elite shop for all sorts of European and Dutch delicacies.

GIFTS **Boolchand's** (✉ Heerenstraat 4B, Willemstad ☎ 5999/461–6233) handles an interesting combination of merchandise behind a facade of red-and-white-checkered tiles. Stock up here on electronics, jewelry, Swarovski crystal, Swiss watches, and cameras. **Julius L. Penha & Sons** (✉ Heerenstraat 1, Willemstad ☎ 5999/461–2266), in front of the Pontoon Bridge, sells French perfumes and cosmetics. At **Little Switzerland** (✉ Breedestraat 44, Willemstad ☎ 5999/461–2111) you can find jewelry, watches, crystal, china, and leather goods at significant savings. The very first gift shop to open on Curaçao more than 60 years ago, **Warenhaus Van Der Ree** (✉ Breedestraat 5, Willemstad ☎ 5999/461–1645) offers quite a selection of novelties. Look for stainless-steel wind chimes, dolls, frames, hammocks, Dutch cheese, and hand-painted whistles.

HANDICRAFTS **Arawak Craft Factory** (✉ Cruise Terminal, Otrobanda, Willemstad ☎ 5999/462–7249) has a factory showroom of locally made crafts. You can purchase tiles, plates, pots, and tiny replicas of land houses. A special walkway allows you to watch the artisans at work and ask questions. **Bamali** (✉ Breedestraat, Punda, Willemstad ☎ 5999/461–2258) sells Indonesian batik clothing, leather bags, and charming handicrafts. **Caribbean Handcraft Inc.** (✉ Kaya Kakina 8, Jan Thiel ☎ 5999/767–1171) offers an elaborate assortment of locally handcrafted souvenirs. It's worth visiting just for the spectacular hilltop view. **Landhuis Groot Santa Martha** (✉ Santa Martha ☎ 5999/864–1559) is where artisans with disabilities fashion handicrafts. An open house is held every last Sunday of the month, when visitors can browse and buy.

JEWELRY **Freeport** (✉ Heerenstraat 13, Willemstad ☎ 5999/461–9500) has a fine selection of duty-free watches and jewelry (lines include David Yurman, Christofle, Movado, and Maurice Lacroix), attracting shoppers who pour in from the cruise ships that dock nearby. **Gandelman** (✉ Breedestraat 35, Willemstad ☎ 5999/461–1854 ✉ Curaçao Marriott Beach Resort, Piscadera Bay ☎ 5999/462–8386) has watches by Cartier and Rolex, leather goods by Prima Classe, and Baccarat and Daum crystal.

LINENS **New Amsterdam** (✉ Gomezplein 14, Willemstad ☎ 5999/461–2437 ✉ Breedestraat 29, Willemstad ☎ 5999/461–3239) is the place to price hand-embroidered tablecloths, napkins, and pillowcases, as well as Italian gold and Hummel figurines.

PERFUMES & **Perfume Palace** (✉ Braastraat 23, Willemstad ☎ 5999/461–7462) carCOSMETICS ries all the major brands of cosmetics and perfume. **The Yellow House** (✉ Breedestraat 23, Willemstad ☎ 5999/461–3222) offers an amazing selection of perfumes at low prices.

Nightlife

Friday is a big night out, with rollicking happy hours—most with live music—at several hotels, most notably the Plaza Hotel Curaçao and the Avila Beach Hotel. And while it might sound surprising, Sunday night revelry into the wee hours is an island tradition. Check with the tourist board for the schedule of events or pick up a copy of the weekly free entertainment listings, *K-Pasa*, available at most restaurants and hotels.

BARS Live jazz electrifies the pier at the **Blues Bar & Restaurant** (✉ Avila Beach Hotel, Penstraat 130, Willemstad ☎ 5999/461–4377) on Thursdays—*the* night to go—and Saturdays. **De Heeren** (✉ Suikertuintjeweg,

Suikertuintjeweg ☎ 5999/736–0491) is a great spot to grab a locally brewed Amstel Bright and meet a happy blend of tourists and transplanted Dutch locals. **Fort Waakzaamheid Tavern & Restaurant** (✉ Seru Domi, Willemstad ☎ 5999/462–3633)—the name means "Fort Alertness"— is a pleasant place for a cocktail day or night, complete with a panoramic view of the island. By day **Hook's Hut** (✉ Next to the Hilton Curaçao Resort, Piscadera Bay ☎ 5999/462–6575) is a local beach hangout. The daily happy hour from 5 to 6 kicks off a lively nighttime scene. The outdoor pool table is in terrible shape, but it's one of the few bar tables around. There's a $3 flat fee per half hour; pay the bartender.

Anchor yourself at a dockside table at the **International Café** (✉ Handelskade 13, Willemstad ☎ 5999/465–1056) and sip frozen cappuccinos as the ships pass by in Santa Anna Bay. Or loosen up with a cocktail—specialties include the Blue Curaçao Margarita and the Pink Panther (Baileys, Amaretto, coconut liqueur, grenadine, Ponche Crema, coconut cream, and pineapple juice). **Keizershof** (✉ Hoogstraat at Rouvilleweg, Otrobanda, Willemstad ☎ 5999/462–3583 for Pianobar Kalimba), a complex of renovated heritage buildings, has two restaurants and a café. You can dance under the stars at Keizershof Terrace or join the sing-alongs at Pianobar Kalimba. Sunday Happy Hours are hot at **Rumors** (✉ Lions Dive Hotel, Bapor Kibra ☎ 5999/461–7555), featuring some of the best rock and reggae bands.

CASINOS Gambling seems almost an afterthought on Curaçao. Although casinos are a staple at most hotels, even the biggest offer only a few card games, and some are limited to slot machines. The following hotels have casinos that are open daily 1 PM–4 AM: the Curaçao Marriott Beach Resort & Emerald Casino, the Hilton Curaçao, the Plaza Hotel Curaçao, Holiday Beach Hotel and Casino, and the Breezes Curaçao. Of these, only the Marriott and Hilton casinos even approach a small Vegas hotel in terms of the number of games and Bond-like elegance.

DANCE & MUSIC CLUBS **Baya Beach** (✉ Caracas Bay Island Park, Caracas Bay Island ☎ 5999/747–0777) is a festive place that lures dancers with its pulsating blend of salsa, merengue, and hip-hop. Saturday nights are the liveliest. **Club Facade** (✉ Lindberghweg 32, Willemstad ☎ 5999/461–4640) seems to be as popular with locals as it is with visitors. A museum by day, **Landhuis Brievengat** (✉ Brievengat ☎ 5999/737–8344) turns into a party house after dark—the night owls flock here Wednesday through Sunday for live music in the outdoor courtyard from 8 PM until dawn. **The Living Room** (✉ Saliña 129, Saliña, Willemstad ☎ 5999/461–4443) is the hippest place to be on weekends. Dance into the wee hours in the chic, burnished-red interior. **Mambo Beach** (✉ Seaquarium Beach, Bapor Kibra ☎ 5999/461–8999), an open-air bar and restaurant, draws a hip, young crowd that flocks here to dance the night away under the stars. Popular with tourists and locals throughout the week, insiders know this as *the* place to be on Sunday night; come in time for happy hour and warm up for the nightlong party with some beach volleyball.

Exploring Curaçao

Willemstad

What does the capital of Curaçao have in common with New York City? Broadway, for one thing. Here it's called Breedestraat, but the origin is the same. Dutch settlers came here in the 1630s, about the same time they sailed through the Verazzano Narrows to Manhattan, bringing with them original red-tile roofs, first used on the trade ships as ballast and later incorporated into the architecture of Willemstad.

The city is cut in two by Santa Anna Bay. On one side is the Punda—crammed with shops, restaurants, monuments, and markets—and on the other is the less touristy Otrobanda (literally, the "other side"), with lots of narrow, winding streets full of private homes notable for their picturesque gables and Dutch-influenced designs. There are three ways to cross the bay: drive or take a taxi over the Juliana Bridge; traverse the Queen Emma Pontoon Bridge on foot; or ride the free ferry, which runs when the Pontoon Bridge is open for passing ships. All the major hotels outside town offer free shuttle service to town once or twice daily. Shuttles coming from the Otrobanda side leave you at Riffort. From here it's a short walk north to the foot of the pontoon bridge. Shuttles coming from the Punda side leave you near the main entrance to Ft. Amsterdam.

Numbers in the margin correspond to points of interest on the Willemstad map.

WHAT TO SEE

⑪ Curaçao Museum. Housed in an 1853 plantation house, this small museum is filled with artifacts, paintings, and antiques that trace the island's history. This is also the venue for art exhibitions that visit the island. ⊠ *V. Leeuwenhoekstraat, Otrobanda* ☎ *5999/462–3873* 💲 *$2.50* ⊙ *Weekdays 9–noon and 2–5, Sun. 10–4.*

⑥ Floating Market. Each morning dozens of Venezuelan schooners laden with tropical fruits and vegetables arrive at this bustling market on the Punda side of the city. Mangoes, papayas, and exotic vegetables vie for space with freshly caught fish and herbs and spices. The buying is best at 6:30 AM—too early for many people on vacation—but there's plenty of action throughout the afternoon. Any produce bought here, however, should be thoroughly washed or peeled before eating. ⊠ *Sha Caprileskade, Punda.*

> **need a break?** For a cooling break from your explorations, **Vienna Ice Café** (⊠ Handelskade 14, Punda, Willemstad ☎ 5999/736–1086) serves up scrumptious homemade ice cream. Indulge your sweet tooth with such flavors as green apple, mango, and rum plum.

② Ft. Amsterdam. Step through the archway and enter another century. The entire structure dates from the 1700s, when it was the center of the city and the island's most important fort. Now it houses the governor's residence, the Fort Church, the Council of Ministers, and government offices. Outside the entrance, a series of majestic gnarled *wayaka* trees are fancifully carved with human forms—the work of local artist Mac Alberto. ⊠ *Foot of Queen Emma Bridge, Punda* ☎ *5999/461–1139* 💲 *$1.75 (to church museum only)* ⊙ *Weekdays 9–noon and 2–5, Sun. service at 10.*

★ ⑩ Kurá Hulanda Museum. This fascinating museum is housed within the confines of a restored 18th-century village in Otrobanda. The museum is built around the square (Kurá Hulanda means "Holland courtyard"), where slaves were sold by the Dutch to be resold throughout the Caribbean. The museum's huge collection is divided into variously themed buildings and covers all aspects of world African history. The most disturbing and profound collection is in the "Black Holocaust" section, which illustrates all aspects of the transatlantic slave trade. It's impossible to enter the replica of a slave ship hold without feeling a shiver. The museum and complex are the brainchild of Dutch millionaire philanthropist Jacob Gelt Dekker. The on-site Kurá Hulanda Conference Center has state-of-the-art facilities for lectures, seminars, and tutorials. The Jacob Gelt Dekker Institute for Advanced Cultural Studies is

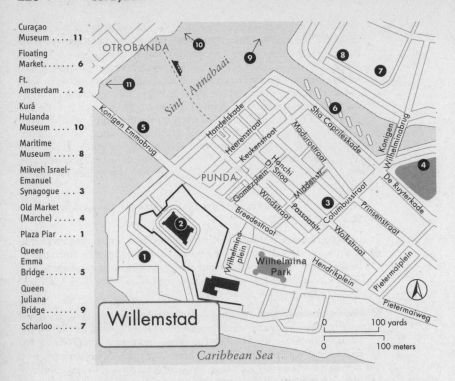

an international think tank and learning exchange center dedicated to the people and ideas of the Atlantic Rim, with an emphasis on African studies and the African diaspora. ⊠ *Klipstraat 9, Otrobanda* ☎ *5999/ 462–1400* ⊕ *www.kurahulanda.com* ✉ *$5* ⊘ *Daily 10–5.*

★ ❽ **Maritime Museum.** The 40-odd chronological exhibits at this museum truly give you a sense of Curaçao's maritime history, using ship models, maps, nautical charts, navigational equipment, and audiovisual displays. Topics explored along the way include the development of Willemstad as a trading city, Curaçao's role as a contraband hub, the explosion of *De Alphen* in 1778, the slave trade, the development of steam navigation, the rise of cruise tourism, and the role of the Dutch navy on the island. The third floor hosts temporary exhibits, and the museum also offers a two-hour guided tour on its "water bus" through Curaçao's harbor—a route familiar to traders, smugglers, and pirates. When you're ready for a break, drop anchor at the Harbor Café or browse through the souvenir shop. ⊠ *Van der Brandhofstraat 7, Scharloo* ☎ *5999/ 465–2327* ✉ *$6 museum only; $12 museum and harbor tour* ⊘ *Tue.– Sat. 10–5.*

❸ **Mikveh Israel-Emanuel Synagogue.** The temple, the oldest still in use in the Western Hemisphere, is one of Curaçao's most important sights and draws 20,000 visitors a year. Brilliant white sand covers the synagogue floor, a remembrance of Moses leading his people through the desert and of the diaspora. The synagogue was dedicated in 1732 by the Jewish community, which originally came from Amsterdam in 1651 to establish a new congregation and to seize freedoms that weren't generally afforded them in Europe at that time. They were later joined by Jews from Portugal and Spain (via Amsterdam) fleeing persecution from the Inquisition. A number of Jews also came from Brazil, after the Portuguese reconquest of Recife—a Dutch trading post—raised fears that the Inquisition would be introduced there, too. By the early 1700s, more than 2,000 Jews resided on Curaçao. The fascinating **Jewish Cultural Museum** (☎ 5999/461–1633), in the back of the synagogue, displays Jewish antiques (including a set of circumcision instruments) and artifacts collected from all over the world. English and Hebrew services are held Friday at 6:30 PM and Saturday at 10 AM. Men who attend should wear a jacket and tie. ⊠ *Hanchi Snoa 29, Punda* ☎ *5999/461–1633* 🖃 *Small donation expected in synagogue; $2 Jewish Cultural Museum* ⊘ *Weekdays 9–11:45 and 2:30–4:45.*

❹ **Old Market (Marche).** Local women prepare hearty Antillean lunches at the Old Market behind the post office. Enjoy such Curaçaoan specialties as funchi (a cornmeal dish), *keshi yena* (a slice of Gouda cheese stuffed with a seasoned chicken mixture), goat stew, fried fish, peas and rice, and fried plantains. Small portions cost $2.50; large plates for $7 are a feast for two. ⊠ *De Ruyterkade.*

❶ **Plaza Piar.** This plaza is dedicated to Manuel Piar, a native Curaçaoan who fought for the independence of Venezuela under the liberator Simón Bolívar. On one side of the plaza is the Waterfort, a bastion dating from 1634. The original cannons are still positioned in the battlements. The foundation, however, now forms the walls of the Plaza Hotel Curaçao.

❺ **Queen Emma Bridge.** This bridge is affectionately called the Swinging Old Lady by the locals. If you're standing on the Otrobanda side, take a few moments to scan Curaçao's multicolored face, on the other side of Santa Anna Bay. If you wait long enough, the bridge will swing open (at least 30 times a day) to let seagoing ships pass through. The original bridge, built in 1888, was the brainchild of the American consul Leonard Burlington Smith, who made a mint off the tolls he charged for using it: 2¢ per person for those wearing shoes, free to those crossing barefoot. Today it's free to everyone.

❾ **Queen Juliana Bridge.** This 1,625-ft-long (497-m-long) bridge was completed in 1974 and stands 200 ft above the water—a great vantage point for photos of the city. It's the bridge you drive over to cross to the other side of the city, and although the route is time-consuming (and more expensive if you're going by taxi), the view is worth it. At every hour of the day, the sun casts a different tint, creating an ever-changing panorama; the nighttime view is breathtaking.

❼ **Scharloo.** The Wilhelmina Drawbridge connects Punda with the once-flourishing district of Scharloo, where the early Jewish merchants first built stately homes. The end of the district closest to Kleine Werf is now a red-light district and is pretty run-down, but the rest of the area is well worth a visit. The architecture along Scharlooweg (much of it from the 17th century) is intriguing, and, happily, many of the structures that had become dilapidated have been meticulously renovated.

The Rest of the Island

The Weg Maar Santa Cruz road through the village of Soto winds to the island's northwest tip through landscape that Georgia O'Keeffe might have painted—towering cacti, flamboyant dried shrubbery, and aluminum-roof houses. Throughout this *kunuku,* or countryside, you can see fishermen hauling nets, women pounding cornmeal, and an occasional donkey blocking traffic. Land houses, large plantation houses from centuries past, dot the countryside, though most are closed to the public. To explore the island's eastern side, take the coastal road— Martin Luther King Boulevard—from Willemstad about 2 mi (3 km) to Bapor Kibra. This is where you'll find the Seaquarium and the Underwater Park.

Numbers in the margin correspond to points of interest on the Curaçao map.

WHAT TO SEE

②① **Boka Tabla.** At Boka Tabla, the sea has carved a magnificent grotto. Safely tucked in the back, you can watch and listen to the waves crashing against the rocks. Several of the surrounding minicaverns serve as nesting places; watch flocks of parakeets emerge in formation, magnificent hawks soar and dip, and gulls dive-bomb for lunch. Steer clear of the many manchineel trees near the cave. ✉ *Westpunt Hwy., just past village center, Soto.*

★ **②⓪** **Christoffel National Park.** This fantastic 4,450-acre garden and wildlife preserve centers on the towering Mt. Christoffel. There are eight hiking trails in the park, which take anywhere from 20 minutes to 2½ hours to complete. You can drive your own car (if it has heavy-treaded tires) or rent a four-wheel-drive vehicle with an accompanying guide (NAf 150 for up to five passengers). Start out early (by 10 AM the park starts to feel like a sauna), and if you're going solo, first study the *Excursion Guide to Christoffel Park,* sold at the front desk of the Savonet Museum. It outlines the various routes and identifies the flora and fauna found here. There's a 20-mi (32-km) network of roads, and no matter what route you take you'll be treated to views of hilly fields full of prickly pear cacti, divi-divi trees, bushy-haired palms, and exotic flowers that bloom unpredictably after November showers. There are also caves—the strong at heart will revel in the rustling of bat wings and the sight of scuttling scorpion spiders (not poisonous)—and ancient Indian drawings. Spectacular bird-watching is abundant, and experts lead the way twice daily.

Watch for goats and small wildlife that might cross your path or dart in front of your car, and consider yourself lucky if you see any of the elusive, protected white-tail deer. The whip snakes and minute silver snakes you may encounter aren't poisonous. White-tail hawks may be seen on the green route, white orchids and crownlike passionflowers on the yellow route. Climbing the 1,239-ft **Mt. Christoffel** on foot is an exhilarating challenge to anyone who hasn't grown up scaling the Alps. The park's guidebook claims the round trip will take an hour, and Curaçaoan adolescent boys do make a sport of racing up and down, but it's really more like two (sweaty) hours from the mountain's base for a reasonably fit person who's not an expert hiker. The view from the peak, however, *is* thrilling—a panorama that includes Santa Marta Bay and the tabletop mountain of St. Hironimus. On a clear day you can even see the mountain ranges of Venezuela, Bonaire, and Aruba.

You might also enjoy one of the park's fascinating tours. Every Friday morning at 10, park rangers lead a 2½-mi (4-km) nature hike, discoursing on the indigenous flora and fauna. The fee ($9) includes an iguana presentation and a soft drink. Jeep tours ($100 for one to five people) go off the beaten track, raising plenty of dust. The 15-minute deer-watching expeditions (with no more than eight people, to prevent startling the skittish creatures) track the herd of 150–200 small white-tail deer in the park for $6 per person (Saturdays and Sundays, beginning at 4:30 PM). ✉ *Savonet* ☎ *5999/864–0363* ▤ *Park and museum $13.50* ⊙ *Mon.–Sat. 8–4, Sun. 6–3; last admission 1 hr before closing.*

①⑨ **Country House Museum.** The thatched-roof cottage is a living museum demonstrating country life as it was in the 19th century. It's filled with antique furniture, farm implements, and clothing typical of colonial life. Out back is a minifarm with a vegetable garden, penned donkeys, and caged parrots, eagles, and iguanas. Look closely at the fence—it's made of living cacti. There's also a snack bar. A festival featuring live music and local crafts takes place here on the first Sunday of each month.

✉ *Dokterstuin 27 (on road to Westpunt from Willemstad), Westpunt* ☎ *5999/864–2742* ✉ *$1.50* ☉ *Tues.–Fri. 9–4, weekends 9–5.*

★ ☙ ⓫ **Curaçao Seaquarium.** The Seaquarium is the best place to see the island's underwater treasures without getting your feet wet. It's the world's only public aquarium where sea creatures are raised and cultivated naturally. Where else can you hand-feed a shark (or watch a diver do it)? The **Animal Encounters** section consists of a broad, 12-ft-deep (4-m-deep) open-water enclosure that brings you face to face with several different species. Snorkelers and divers are welcome to swim freely with stingrays, tarpon, groupers, and such. Diving instruction and equipment are part of the package; it's a thrilling introduction to the sport in a controlled environment, and, in fact, up to 75% of participants have never tried diving before. If shark feeding isn't your cup of tea, there's an underwater observatory. The cost is $55 for divers, $35 for snorkelers, which includes admission to the Seaquarium, training, use of equipment, and food for the fish, turtles, and sharks. Reservations for Animal Encounters must be made 24 hours in advance.

You can spend several hours mesmerized by the 46 freshwater tanks full of more than 400 varieties of fish and vegetation found in the waters around Curaçao. The Maritime Awareness Center offers hands-on discovery of the underworld wonders of coral reefs. In the minitheater, a high-tech, three-dimensional slide show makes you feel as if you're actually in the ocean. There are also glass-bottom boat tours, feeding shows, and a viewing platform overlooking the wreck of the steamship SS *Oranje Nassau,* which sank in 1906. You can stop by the on-site snack bar and restaurant or browse in the souvenir shop. A nearby beach is well suited to novice swimmers and children. ✉ *Bapor Kibra* ☎ *5999/461–6666* ⊕ *www.curacao-sea-aquarium.com* ✉ *$13.25, or $24 for six-week pass* ☉ *Daily 8–5.*

The **Dolphin Academy** is the newest attraction on the island and is attached to The Seaquarium (tell the gate staff at The Seaquarium where you are going, and they will waive the entrance fee). For $13 you can watch a dolphin show and for an additional charge you may choose either to touch them up close or actually swim with them. ✉ *Bapor Kibra* ☎ *5999/465–8900* ⊕ *www.dolphin-academy.com* ✉ *$13* ☉ *Daily 8–5.*

⓮ **Curaçao Underwater Marine Park.** About 12½ mi (20 km) of untouched coral reefs off the southeast shore have been granted the status of a national park. Mooring buoys placed at the most interesting dive sites provide safe anchoring and prevent damage to the reef. Several sunken ships lie quietly in the deep. The park stretches along the south shore from the Breezes Curaçao resort in Willemstad to the island's eastern tip.

⓯ **Den Paradera.** Dazzle your senses at this organic herb garden, where local plants are cataloged according to their traditional use in folk medicine. As part of owner Dinah Veeris's research, she interviewed dozens of older islanders about the plants and their use in treating everything from diabetes to stomach ulcers. A reconstructed settlement at the rear of the property consists of small huts with life-size rag dolls depicting traditional folkloric scenes. Top off your visit with a special refreshing beverage (made of aloe, ginger, and lemon). A shop sells natural perfumes and potpourri. ✉ *Seru Grandi Kavel 105A, Banda Riba* ☎ *5999/767–5608* ✉ *$5.65 with guided tour, $4.25 without guided tour* ☉ *By appointment only.*

⓲ **Hato Caves.** Hour-long guided tours wind down into various chambers to the water pools, a "voodoo" chamber, a wishing well, fruit bats' sleeping quarters, and Curaçao Falls, guarded by a limestone "dragon." Hidden lights illuminate the limestone formations and gravel walkways.

This is one of the better Caribbean caves open to the public, but keep in mind that there are 49 steep steps to reach the entrance, and the cave itself is dank and hot (though they've put electric fans in some areas to provide relief). To reach the caves, head northwest toward airport, take a right onto Gosieweg, follow the loop right onto Schottegatweg, take another right onto Jan Norduynweg, a final right onto Rooseveltweg, and follow signs. ⊠ *Rooseveltweg, Hato* ☎ *5999/868–0379* ✉ *$6.50* ☉ *Daily 10–5.*

⑰ Landhuis Brievengat. This mustard-color plantation house is a fine example of a home from the island's past. You can see the original kitchen still intact, the 18-inch-thick walls, fine antiques, and the watchtowers once used for lovers' trysts. The restaurant, open only on Wednesday and Friday, serves a tasty Indonesian rijsttafel. Friday night a party is held on the wide wraparound terrace, with bands and plenty to drink ($6 cover charge). On the last Sunday of the month (6 PM–7:30 PM), this estate holds an open house with crafts demonstrations and folkloric shows. It's a 15-minute drive northeast of Willemstad, near Centro Deportivo stadium. ⊠ *Brievengat* ☎ *5999/737–8344* ✉ *$1* ☉ *Mon.–Sat. 9:15–12:15 and 3–6.*

㉒ Landhuis Knip. In terms of slave population, this was once the island's largest plantation. It therefore comes as no surprise that the slave revolt took place here in 1795. The renovated plantation house near the island's western tip is filled with period furnishings, clothing, and household objects. ⊠ *Weg Naar Santa Cruz, Knip* ☎ *5999/864–0244* ✉ *$2* ☉ *Weekdays 9–4, weekends 10–4.*

☝ ⑯ Ostrich Farm. If you (and the kids) are ready to stick your neck out for an adventure, visit one of the largest ostrich-breeding farms outside Africa and the only one in the Caribbean. Every hour, guided tours (reservations are essential) show the creatures' complete development from egg to mature bird. At the Restaurant Zambezi you can sample local ostrich specialties and other African dishes (reservations are recommended). Be sure to visit the Art of Africa shop, featuring crafts from Zimbabwe and South Africa including handmade wall hangings, exotic leather products, and wood carvings. ⊠ *Groot St. Joris* ☎ *5999/747–2777* ⊕ *www. ostrichfarm.net* ✉ *$10 (includes tour)* ☉ *Tues.–Sun. 9–4.*

⑫ Senior Curaçao Liqueur Distillery. The charming 17th-century Landhuis Chobolobo (just outside Willemstad) is where the famed Curaçao liqueur, made from the peels of the bitter Iranha orange, is produced. Don't expect a massive factory—it's just a small showroom in an open-air foyer. There are no guides, but delightful old hand-painted posters explain the distillation process, and you'll be graciously offered samples in assorted flavors. If you're interested in buying—the orange-flavored chocolate liqueur is delicious over ice cream—you can choose from a complete selection in equally enticing bottles, including those shaped like Dutch ceramic houses. ⊠ *Landhuis Chobolobo, Saliña Arriba* ☎ *5999/461–3526* ✉ *Free* ☉ *Weekdays 8–noon and 1–5.*

CURAÇAO A TO Z

To research prices, get advice from other travelers, and book travel arrangements, visit www.fodors.com.

AIR TRAVEL

Air DCA offers frequent service from Miami and Atlanta and interisland service to Aruba and Bonaire. For Atlanta departures Air DCA has connecting service to most U.S. gateways with Delta. Aeropostal has nonstop service from Caracas. American Airlines flies direct daily from Miami. E-Liner Airways has interisland service, including sightseeing and beach tours of Aruba and Bonaire. KLM flies direct from Amsterdam (to fly from Australia, New Zealand, or the United Kingdom, consider flying to Amsterdam for this flight to Curaçao). SLM (Suriname Airways) flies direct from Paramaribo, Suriname.

🛈 **Aeropostal** ☎ 5999/888-2818. **Air DCA** ☎ 5999/869-5533. **American Airlines** ☎ 5999/869-5701. **E-Liner Airways** ☎ 5999/465-8099. **KLM** ☎ 5999/465-2747. **SLM** ☎ 5999/868-4360.

AIRPORTS

The airport has car-rental facilities, duty-free shops, and a restaurant. It takes about 20 minutes to get to the hotels in Willemstad by taxi.

🛈 **Curaçao International Airport** ☎ no phone.

BUSINESS HOURS

BANKS Banks are open weekdays 8–3:30 or 8–11:30 and 1:30–4; the airport branch has extended hours: 8–8 Monday–Saturday and 9–4 on Sunday.

POST OFFICES Post office hours are 7:30–noon and 1:30–5 weekdays. The Groot Kwartier branch is open 7–7 on weekdays and 7–3 on Saturday.

SHOPS Some shops remain closed on Monday. Many are open Monday–Saturday 8–noon and 2–6. Some stay open during the lunch hour and on Sunday and holidays when cruise ships are in port.

CAR RENTALS

You can rent a car from any of the major car agencies at the airport or have one delivered free to your hotel. Rates range from about $60 a day for a Toyota Tercel to about $75 for a four-door sedan or four-wheel-drive vehicle; add 6% tax and required $10 daily insurance.

🛈 **Avis** ☎ 5999/461-1255 or 800/228-0668. **Budget** ☎ 5999/868-3466 or 800/472-3325. **Hertz** ☎ 5999/888-0088. **National Car Rental** ☎ 5999/869-4433. **Thrifty** ☎ 5999/461-3089.

CAR TRAVEL

If you're planning to do country driving or rough it through Christoffel Park, a four-wheel-drive vehicle is best. All you need is a valid U.S., Canadian, or British driver's license.

GASOLINE Gas prices in Curaçao at this writing are about NAf 1.56 per liter for unleaded; NAf 1.48 for regular; and NAf 1.50 for diesel. There are many gas stations in the Willemstad area as well as in the suburban areas, including two on the main road as you head to the western tip of the island.

RULES OF THE ROAD Driving in the Netherlands Antilles is the same as in the U.S., on the right-hand side of the road. Right turns on red are prohibited. Local laws require drivers and passengers to wear seat belts and motorcyclists to wear helmets. Children under 4 years of age should be in child safety seats; if older they should ride in the back seat.

ELECTRICITY

The current is 110–130 volts/50 cycles, which is compatible with such small North American appliances as electric razors and blow dryers. Some electrical appliances may overheat, and internal timers in devices such as clock radios and camcorders won't keep the correct time.

EMBASSIES & CONSULATES

🛈 **Canada** **Consulate of Canada** ✉ Plaza Jojo Correa 2–4, Willemstad ☎ 5999/461-3515.
🛈 **United Kingdom** **British Consulate** ✉ Jan Sofat 38, Willemstad ☎ 5999/747-3322.

⚑ United States United States Consulate ⊠ Roosevelthouse, J. B. Gorsira 1, Willemstad ☎ 5999/461-3066.

EMERGENCIES
⚑ Health & Safety Ambulance and fire ☎ 912. On-call dentists ☎ 8888. On-call doctors ☎ 1111.
⚑ Hospitals St. Elisabeth's Hospital ⊠ Breedestraat 193, Willemstad ☎ 5999/462-4900 or 5999/462-5100.
⚑ Pharmacies Botica Popular ⊠ Madurostraat 15, Willemstad ☎ 5999/461-1269.
⚑ Police Police emergencies ☎ 911.
⚑ Scuba-Diving Emergencies St. Elisabeth's Hospital ⊠ Breedestraat 193 ☎ 5999/462-4900 or 5999/462-5100.
⚑ Sea Emergencies Coast Guard ☎ 113.

ETIQUETTE & BEHAVIOR
To guarantee a smile, wish someone *bon dia* (good day) or offer a warm *masha danki* (thank you very much) after someone has performed a service. Dutch culture is stronger on Curaçao than on many Antillean islands, so the island has a European flavor (note that topless sunbathing is tolerated at some hotels).

FESTIVALS & SEASONAL EVENTS
Carnival lasts longer on Curaçao than on many islands: the revelries begin at New Year's and continue until midnight the day before Ash Wednesday. The highlight is the Tumba Festival (dates vary), a four-day musical event featuring fierce competition between local musicians for the honor of having their piece selected as the official road march during parades. Easter Monday's Seú Folklore Parade is made up of groups celebrating the harvest in traditional costumes. May is when the Curaçao International Jazz Festival is held. The Curaçao Salsa Festival is held in June, July, or August and attracts international performers and audiences.

HEALTH
Mosquitoes are a presence on Curaçao, at least during the rainy season. The bad news is that the rainy season falls between October and February, coinciding with the tourist high season. To be safe, keep perfume to a minimum, use insect repellent before dining alfresco, and spray your hotel room at night—especially if you've opened a window.

HOLIDAYS
Public holidays are: New Year's Day, Carnival Monday, Good Friday, Easter Sunday (moveable, usually in April or May), Easter Monday (the day after Easter), the Queen's Birthday (not Beatrix, but rather her mother, Juliana; Apr. 30), Labor Day (May 1), Curaçao Flag Day (July 2), Antilles Day (Oct. 21), and Christmas holiday (Dec. 25 and 26).

LANGUAGE
Dutch is the official language, but the vernacular is Papiamento—a mixture of Dutch, African, French, Portuguese, Spanish, and English. One theory holds that the language developed during the 18th century as a mode of communication between land owners and their slaves. These days English is studied by schoolchildren as well as Spanish and, of course, Dutch. Anyone involved with tourism generally speaks English.

MAIL & SHIPPING
There are post offices in Punda, Otrobanda, and Groot Kwartier on Schottegatweg (Ring Road), as well as small branches at the Curaçao World Trade Center and the airport. Some hotels sell stamps and have letter drops; you can also buy stamps at some bookstores. An airmail letter to the United States, Canada, or Europe costs NAf 2.25, a postcard NAf.90.

MONEY MATTERS

Prices quoted throughout this chapter are in U.S. dollars unless otherwise indicated.

ATMS There are over 50 ATM locations on the island that dispense money in the local currency. The airport has an ATM (it dispenses U.S. dollars) as do many bank branches.

Antilles Banking Corporation ☎ 5999/461-2822. **Maduro & Curiel's Bank** ☎ 5999/466-1100. **RBTT** ☎ 5999/763-8000.

CURRENCY U.S. dollars—in cash or traveler's checks—are accepted nearly everywhere, so there's no need to worry about exchanging money. However, you may need small change for pay phones, cigarettes, or soda machines. The currency in the Netherlands Antilles is the florin (also called the guilder) and is indicated by "fl" or "NAf" on price tags. The florin is very stable against the U.S. dollar; the official rate of exchange at press time was NAf 1.80 to US$1.

PASSPORTS & VISAS

U.S. and Canadian citizens need either a valid passport or a birth certificate with a raised seal along with a government-authorized photo ID. Citizens of Australia, New Zealand, and the United Kingdom must produce a passport. Everyone must show an ongoing or return ticket.

SAFETY

Crime is on the increase (but not rampant) in Curaçao, so commonsense rules apply. Lock rental cars, and don't leave valuables in the car. Use in-room safes or leave valuables at the front desk of your hotel, and never leave bags unattended at the airport, on tours, or on the beach.

SIGHTSEEING TOURS

BOAT TOURS Many sailboats and motorboats offer sunset cruises and daylong snorkel and picnic trips to Klein Curaçao, the "clothes-optional" island between Curaçao and Bonaire. Prices run $50–$65. Or for a unique vantage point, soak up the local marine life from one of Seaworld Explorer/Atlantis Adventures' semi-submersibles. An hour-long tour of the beautiful coral reefs is $40. The *Bounty* is a 90-ft schooner, the *Insulinde* is a 120-ft Dutch sailing ketch, and the *Mermaid* is a 66-ft motor yacht, all of which offer boat tours.

Atlantis Adventures ☎ 5999/462-8833 ⊕ www.atlantisadventures.net. *Bounty* ☎ 5999/560-1887. *Insulinde* ☎ 5999/560-1340. *Mermaid* ☎ 5999/560-1530.

ORIENTATION Does Travel & Kadushi Tours takes you around in an air-conditioned coach with a knowledgeable guide. They can also arrange short hops to Aruba and Bonaire. Peter Trips offers full-day island tours ($37, lunch not included) departing from the hotels Friday, Saturday, and Sunday at 9 AM, with visits to many points of interest, including Scharloo, Slavebridge, Jan Thiel, Fort Nassau, and Knip Bay. Or you can opt for 3½-hour tours of the island's east (Monday at 3 PM, $19) or west side (Tuesday and Thursday at 3 PM, $21). Taber Tours offers a three-hour East Tour ($13) that includes the Curaçao Liqueur Factory at Landhuis Chobolobo, the Curaçao Museum, and the Bloempot shopping center. Day trips to Aruba ($175) and Bonaire ($165) are also available.

Does Travel & Kadushi Tours ✉ Caracasbaaiweg 164 ☎ 5999/461-1626. **Peter Trips** ☎ 5999/561-5368. **Taber Tours** ✉ Dokway ☎ 5999/737-6637.

SPECIAL INTEREST For personalized history and nature tours contact Dornasol Tours; half-day tours run $25, and full-day tours are $40 per person. Dutch Dream Adventures targets the action-seeker with canoe safaris, mountain biking, and jeep tours. The Ostrich Express visits one of the largest ostrich farms outside Africa and gives you a 60-minute guided tour. Kids enjoy the chance to hold an egg, stroke a fluffy day-old chick, and sit atop a fully grown ostrich for an unusual photo op. The price is $8.50 for adults, $5.60 for children 2–14, with pick-up at your hotel. Animal lovers can take an escorted deer-watching tour at Christoffel National Park at a cost of $9 for adults and $5 for children under 15 (reservations required). Wild Curaçao offers expertly guided ecotourism adventures highlighting the island's flora and fauna, with stops at nature preserves, caves, salt lakes, and more. Or keep track of your surroundings as you visit key historic sites aboard the Willemstad Trolley Train ($16 for a 1½-hour tour).

🖪 **Christoffel National Park** ☎ 5999/864-0363. **Dornasol Tours** ☎ 5999/468-2735. **Dutch Dream Adventures** ☎ 5999/461-2500. **Ostrich Express** ☎ 5999/560-1276. **Willemstad Trolley Train** ☎ 5999/462-8833. **Wild Curaçao** ☎ 5999/561-0027.

WALKING TOURS Walking tours of historic Otrobanda, focusing on the unique architecture of this old section of town, are led by architect Anko van der Woude every Thursday (reservations are suggested), leaving from the central clock at Brionplein at 5:15 PM. Jopie Hart offers a walking tour that emphasizes the sociocultural aspects of Otrobanda; it begins at 5:15 PM on Wednesday and departs from the clock at Brionplein. Mention ahead to your tour leader that you speak English.

🖪 **Anko van der Woude/Jenny Smit** ☎ 5999/461-3554. **Jopie Hart** ☎ 5999/767-3798.

TAXES & SERVICE CHARGES

DEPARTURE TAX The airport international departure tax is NAf 35 (or $20), and the interisland departure tax is NAf 17 ($10). This must be paid in cash, either florins or U.S. dollars.

SALES TAX Hotels add a 12% service charge to the bill and collect a 7% government room tax; restaurants add 10%–15%.

VALUE ADDED TAX (V.A.T.) Most goods and services purchased on the island will also have a 5% OB tax (a goods and services tax) added to the purchase price.

TAXIS

Drivers have an official tariff chart, with fares from the airport to Willemstad and the nearby beach hotels running about $10–$15 and those to hotels at the island's western end about $25–$40. Since there are no meters, you should confirm the fare with the driver before setting out. There's an additional 25% surcharge after 11 PM. Taxis are readily available at hotels; in other cases, call Central Dispatch.

🖪 **Central Dispatch** ☎ 5999/869-0752.

TELEPHONES

Phone service through the hotel operators in Curaçao is slow, but direct-dial service, both on-island and to elsewhere in the world, is fast and clear. Hotel operators will put the call through for you, but if you make a collect call, do check to make sure the hotel does not charge you as well.

COUNTRY & AREA CODES To call Curaçao direct from the United States, dial 011–5999 plus the number in Curaçao.

INTERNATIONAL CALLS AT&T Direct service, which connects you with an AT&T International operator, is available, but it's impossible from pay phones, and your hotel will likely add a surcharge.

🖪 **AT&T Direct** ☎ 001-800/872-2881

LOCAL CALLS To place a local call on the island, dial the seven-digit local number. Pay phones charge NAf.50 for a local call—far less than the typical hotel charge.

TIPPING

As service is usually included, tipping at restaurants isn't expected, though if you found the staff exemplary, you can add another 5%–10% to the bill. Taxi drivers normally receive a 10% gratuity, but this is at your discretion. Tip porters and bellmen about $1 a bag, the hotel housekeeping staff $2–$3 per day.

VISITOR INFORMATION

🚩 **Curaçao Tourism Development Bureau** ⊕ www.curacao-tourism.com ✉ Pieter-maai 19, Willemstad ☎ 5999/461-6000 Ext. 117 ✉ Curaçao International Airport ☎ 5999/868-6789.

DOMINICA

FODOR'S CHOICE

Hiking to Boiling Lake, Lake Morne Trois Pitons National Park

Papillote Wilderness Retreat, Trafalgar

Scuba Diving and Snorkeling along Dominica's reefs

HIGHLY RECOMMENDED

RESTAURANTS   La Robe Creole, Roseau

Papillote, Trafalgar

Waterfront Restaurant, Roseau

HOTELS   Castle Comfort Lodge, Castle Comfort

Exotica, Gommier

Fort Young Hotel, Roseau

Picard Beach Cottages, Prince Rupert Bay

Sutton Place Hotel, Roseau

Zandoli Inn, Roche Cassée

OUTDOORS   Champagne Beach, Pointe Michel

Hiking in one of Dominica's national parks

Whale & Dolphin Watching

In the early hours of the morning—after the day's first rainfall has seemingly washed the whole world clean—the sun slides up into the sky over the mountains and under the arch of a faint rainbow. Aroused by the light, birds begin their wildly orchestrated chorus—nature's alarm clock. In breezes heavy with the scents of damp earth and lemongrass and not yet fully warmed by the sun, leaves quiver and sparkle with raindrops and dew and the promise of another beautiful day.

Updated by
Isabel
Abislaimán

"Isle of beauty, isle of splendor," rings the first line of the national anthem of the Commonwealth of Dominica. Indeed, the intensity of the unspoiled beauty and splendor of this isle, dubbed "the nature island of the Caribbean," is truly inspiring, as it turns and twists, towers to mountain crests, then tumbles to falls and valleys. The weather is equally dramatic: torrential rains, dazzling sunshine, and, above all, rainbows are likely to greet you in the course of a day.

Wedged between the two French islands of Guadeloupe to the north and Martinique to the south, Dominica (pronounced dom-in-*ee*-ka) is a wild place. Wild orchids, anthurium lilies, ferns, heliconias, and myriad fruit trees sprout profusely. Much of the interior is still covered by luxuriant rain forest and remains inaccessible by road. Here everything grows more intensely: greener, brighter, and bigger. The ideal environment that gave the early Caribs (the region's original inhabitants) a natural fortress against the European settlers also kept Dominica from being colonized like other Caribbean islands. Today the rugged northeast is reserved as home to the last survivors of the Caribs, along with their traditions and mythology.

Dominica—29 mi (47 km) long and 16 mi (26 km) wide, with a population of just 71,000—is a former British colony; having attained its independence in November 1978, it now has a seat in the United Nations as the central Caribbean's only Natural World Heritage Site. Its capital is Roseau (pronounced rose-*oh*); the official language is English, although most locals communicate with each other in Creole; roads are driven on the left; family and place names are a melange of English, Carib, and French; and the religion is predominantly Catholic. The economy is still heavily dependent on agriculture.

With under 70,000 overnight visitors annually, she is a little-known destination; there are no major hotel chains, but her National Forestry Division has spent the last 50 years preserving and designating more national forests, marine reserves, and parks, per capita, than almost anywhere on earth, Dominica is a popular "alternative" Caribbean experience.

It's an ideal place to go if you want to really get away—hike, bike, trek, spot birds and butterflies in the rain forest, explore waterfalls and discover the world's largest boiling lake; experience a vibrant culture in Dominica's traditions; kayak, dive, snorkel, or sail in marine reserves; or go out in search of the many resident whale and dolphin species. From the Elfin Woodlands and dense rain forest to the therapeutic geothermal springs and world-class dive sites that mirror her terrestrial terrain, to experience Dominica is really to know the earth as it was created.

WHAT IT COSTS In U.S. dollars				
	$$$$	**$$$**	**$$**	**$**	**¢**

	$$$$	$$$	$$	$	¢
RESTAURANTS*					
	over $30	$20–$30	$12–$20	$8–$12	under $8
HOTELS**					
Cost EP/BP/CP	over $350	$250–$350	$150–$250	$80–$150	under $80
Cost AI	over $450	$350–$450	$250–$350	$125–$250	under $125

*Restaurant prices are for a main course at dinner. **EP, BP, and CP prices are per night for a standard double room in high season, excluding taxes, service charges, and meal plans. AI (all-inclusive) prices are per person, per night based on double-occupancy during high season, excluding taxes and service charges.

Where to Stay

Places to stay, amenities offered, and prices asked are as varied as the island's landscapes. Here you'll find intimate city hotels, mountain retreats, secluded bungalows, plantation houses, and seaside cottages. Most properties offer packages with dives, hikes, tours, and/or meal plans included, along with all the usual amenities. Many properties advertise winter rates with a discount for either summer or longer stays.

★ $$ **Castle Comfort Lodge.** Past the lush gardens of this dedicated dive lodge 1 mi south of Roseau, you are greeted by the tranquil Caribbean Sea. The boats anchored just off the pier, the telltale dive log, and the divers in the hot tub with mask imprints on their foreheads give it all away. This lodge offers dive packages with everything included: dives, transfers, meals, accommodation, taxes. The brightly decorated rooms with verandahs are in two buildings, one directly on the sea. Some rooms have balconies. Bountiful meals are served on a large terrace. Nondivers can enjoy the property's pool, kayaking, and a multitude of island adventures. ⊠ *Castle Comfort* ✉ *Box 2253, Roseau* ☎ *767/448–2188 or 888/414–7626* 🖷 *767/448–6088* ⊕ *www.castlecomfortdivelodge.com* 🛏 *15 rooms* ⚒ *Restaurant, fans, cable TV, bar, pool, hot tub, dive shop, boating* ⊙ *Closed Sept.* ⊟ *AE, MC, V* ⦿ *MAP.*

★ $$ **Picard Beach Cottages.** On the grounds of an old coconut plantation and its lushly landscaped gardens sit eighteen cottages, only steps away from Dominica's longest golden-sand beach. A white picket fence with private gates allows you access to the beach. Each cottage accommodates two adults with two children or three adults and has a kitchenette, a living and dining area, and a verandah; most have bathtubs. The casual Le Flambeau Restaurant next door serves creole food, and you are a 15-minute walk from Portsmouth's stores and a 15-minute drive from the areas' key nature attractions. ⊠ *Prince Rupert Bay* ✉ *Box 34, Roseau* ☎ *767/445–5131* 🖷 *767/445–5599* ⊕ *www.avirtualdominica.com/picard.htm* 🛏 *18 cottages* ⚒ *Fans, some in-room data ports, kitchenettes, cable TV, beach, bar* ⊟ *AE, MC, V* ⦿ *EP.*

¢–$$ **Pointe Baptiste.** Set above the windblown Atlantic coast and with two secluded white sand beaches, this weathered plantation house with a large dining and sitting room, four bedrooms, kitchen, and a sprawling veranda with an inspiring view is ideal for families or groups of friends. For a romantic getaway, a separate whitewashed cottage in the garden has a bedroom, kitchenette, and bathroom. The house and the cottage can be rented separately. A cleaner and cook will come daily to the main house, but otherwise you're on your own. Miles from any of the popular nature attractions, you'll need a car, which can be arranged. ⊠ *Cal-*

ibishie ✈ *c/o Annick Giraud, Calibishie* ☎ *767/445–8495 or 767/245–2460* ⊕ *www.pointebaptiste.com* ➫ *1 4-bedroom house, 1 1-bedroom cottage* ⚘ *Fans, kitchens, beach; no a/c* ⊟ *D, MC, V* ⦿ *EP.*

$ 🖵 **Anchorage Hotel.** This is a nesting ground for adventure-seekers of every age who come to use the dive and whale-watching center or to take advantage of the in-house tour company. It's also a comfortable, inexpensive option for those who wish to stay close to Roseau but enjoy being by the ocean. Brightly decorated rooms have all modern conveniences; most have balconies. Twenty oceanfront rooms have two double beds; 12 poolside rooms have twin beds or one double. The Ocean Terrace Restaurant and Bar are open to dramatic sunsets with visiting yachts in the foreground. Both locals and visitors frequent the weekly buffet dinners with live music. ⊠ *Castle Comfort* ✈ *Box 34, Roseau* ☎ *767/448–2638* 🖷 *767/448–5680* ⊕ *www.anchoragehotel.dm* ➫ *32 rooms* ⚘ *Restaurant, some refrigerators, cable TV, pool, dive shop, squash, bar* ⊟ *AE, D, MC, V* ⦿ *BP.*

$ 🖵 **Calibishie Lodges.** Just east of the beautiful seaside village of Calibishie, bright bamboo- and melon-colored buildings emerge from behind the terraced lemongrass. Six one-bedroom, self-contained units offer all the comforts of home, with Scandinavian furnishings throughout. It's a five-minute walk down to the beach in one of Dominica's most picturesque villages. Chef Patrick Borre's feasts utilize all local produce from the earth and the sea with his European flair. A small swimming pool and sun deck lead off from the bar, where bartender Clem is right at home with a passion for potent punches. ⊠ *Calibishie Main Rd., Calibishie* ☎🖷 *767/445–8537* ⊕ *www.calibishie-lodges.com* ➫ *6 apartments* ⚘ *Restaurant, fans, kitchenettes, pool, bar; no a/c* ⊟ *D, MC, V* ⦿ *EP.*

$ 🖵 **Evergreen Hotel.** Just 1 mi (1½ km) south of Roseau on the water's edge, Jenny and her family ensure your stay within these beautiful gardens will be a pleasant one. Spacious rooms in the waterfront annex are decorated with bright floral prints and rattan furniture, and have large showers and balconies. The original stone building houses a meeting room and more guest rooms. Most rooms have balconies with ocean views. Wooden furnishings and needlepoint hangings give these a quaint feel. The Honeymoon Hut is set off in a charming, foliage-filled nook. The Crystal Terrace restaurant, just off the pool, has a creative creole menu. ⊠ *Castle Comfort* ✈ *Box 309, Roseau* ☎ *767/448–3288* 🖷 *767/448–6800* ⊕ *www.avirtualdominica.com/evergreen.htm* ➫ *16 rooms, 1 cottage* ⚘ *Restaurant, some refrigerators, cable TV, pool, bar, Internet, meeting rooms* ⊟ *AE, MC, V* ⦿ *EP.*

★ **$** 🖵 **Exotica.** After winding your way up the mountain through lush vegetation, you arrive at this sanctuary at 1,600 ft. Wooden bungalows have red roofs with solar panels; rooms with bright interiors furnished with rattan and floral fabrics, a bedroom with two (extra-long) double beds, and a large living room with trundle beds. If you don't want to cook, Fae serves delicious creole food at the Sugar Apple Café, including produce from her organic garden; it's a great place to bird-watch. The view of the distant ocean from your bungalow is stunning. You may need to rent a jeep to get around. ⊠ *Gommier* ✈ *Box 109, Roseau* ☎ *767/448–8839* 🖷 *767/448–8829* ⊕ *www.exotica-cottages.com* ➫ *8 bungalows* ⚘ *Restaurant, fans, kitchens* ⊟ *AE, D, MC, V* ⦿ *EP.*

★ **$** 🖵 **Fort Young Hotel.** The ample and breezy terraces at the edge of the tranquil Caribbean belie the structure's military history and vicinity to the city center. Constantly updating its facilities, Fort Young offers a wide range of activities and comforts to both business and adventure travelers. Feel like whale-watching after a business meeting? Let the activities desk make the arrangements for you. Enjoy the shops or take a walk in the Botanical Gardens across the street. Guest rooms have balconies

Dominica

ATLANTIC OCEAN

Petit Soufrière Bay

Roseli

Castle Bruce

5

Londonderry Bay

18

Marigot

6

6

Woodford Hill Bay

L'Anse Tortue

6

Callibishie

Melville Hall Airport

4

Hodges

19 20

Macoucherie River

River

Hampstead

6

Bense

Layou

Indian R.

Indian Rd.

7

Vieille Case

Morne Aux Diables

11

Mero

Castaways

Salisbury

Dominica Passage

Capucin Pt.

Toucari Beach and Reef

Douglas Bay

Purple Beach

10

Portsmouth

9 8

Picard R.

Syndicate R.

Salisbury Falls

22

Cabrits Drop-off

Prince Rupert Bay

Picard Beach

21

Pt. Ronde

Dublanc

Colihaut

Nose Reef

Brain Coral Garden

C a

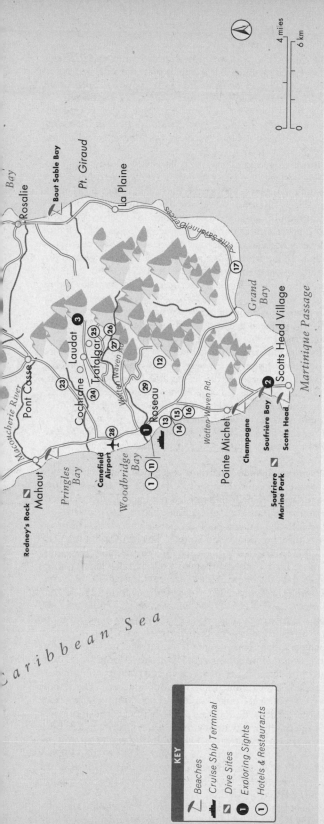

KEY

- Beaches
- Cruise Ship Terminal
- Dive Sites
- Exploring Sights
- Hotels & Restaurants

Hotels

Anchorage Hotel	...13
Calibishie Lodges	...20
Castle Comfort Lodge	...15
Cocoa Cottage	...26
D'Auchamps Cottages	...27
Evergreen Hotel	...16
Exotica	...12
Fort Young Hotel	...5
Garraway Hotel	...3
Hummingbird Inn	...28
Itassi Cottages	...29
Papillote Wilderness Retreat	...25
Picard Beach Cottage	...21
Pointe Baptiste	...19
Roxy's Mountain Lodge	...24
Sunset Bay Club	...22
Sutton Place Hotel	...8
Zandoli Inn	...17

Restaurants

Back-a-Yard	...11
Callaloo Restaurant	...4
Cornerhouse Café	...6
Crystal Terrace Restaurant and Bar	...16
Floral Gardens	...18
Guiyave	...7
La Robe Creole	...9
Miranda's Corner	...23
Papillote	...28
Pearl's Cuisine	...2
Port of Call Restaurant and Bar	...1
Taiwanese Delicacies	...14
Ti Caz Café	...10
Waterfront Restaurant	...5

Exploring

Cabrits National Park	...10
Carib Indian Territory	...5
Emerald Pool	...4
Indian River	...8
Morne Aux Diables	...11
Morne Diablotin National Park	...7
Morne Trois Pitons National Park	...3
Northeast Coast	...6
Portsmouth	...9
Roseau	...1
Soufrière	...2

and spectacular views. The Waterfront Restaurant offers excellent cuisine and ambience, and the Balas Bar is a great place for a drink. ⊠ *Victoria St., Roseau* ☐ *Box 519* ☎ *767/448–5000* ☐ *767/448–5006* ⊕ *www.fortyounghotel.com* ⇲ *49 rooms, 4 suites* ⚅ *2 restaurants, in-room data ports, fans, some in-room hot tubs, some kitchens, refrigerators, in-room safes, cable TV, pool, gym, 3 outdoor hot tubs, spa, dive shop, dock, 2 bars, shops, business services, laundry service, meeting rooms* ☐ *AE, MC, V* ⦿ *EP.*

$ ▣ **Garraway Hotel.** Towering plants, fresh flowers, and original paintings adorn public spaces. The guest rooms and suites are decorated in bright fabrics and cool colors. Views from the higher floors of the hotel, on the western edge of Roseau, survey the town's quaint architecture, a nostalgic foreground for the imposing mountains. The second-floor Balizier Restaurant specializes in creole cuisine, with a daily lunch buffet. At the Ole Jetty Bar and its sidewalk café you can share the sunset with the cocktail. ⊠ *Bayfront, Roseau* ☐ *Box 789* ☎ *767/449–8800* ☐ *767/449–8807* ⊕ *www.garrawayhotel.com* ⇲ *20 rooms, 11 suites* ⚅ *Restaurant, fans, some in-room faxes, cable TV, bar, meeting rooms* ☐ *AE, DC, MC, V* ⦿ *EP.*

$ ▣ **Hummingbird Inn.** Hostess Jeane James Finucane, who has a passion for hummingbirds, is queen bee at this lush hillside retreat 2 mi north of Roseau. Rooms have white walls, terra-cotta floors, wooden ceilings, and verandahs with outstanding Caribbean views. Beds are dressed with handmade quilts. Shutters can be left open all night to let in breezes, soothing honeysuckle and other garden scents, and the sound of the ocean. Phones and TVs can be requested. The Honeymoon Suite has a stately mahogany four-poster bed, a kitchen, and a patio. The reception area, lounge, and dining terrace are all in the main house. ⊠ *Morne Daniel* ☐ *Box 1901, Roseau* ☎☎ *767/449–1042* ⊕ *www.thehummingbirdinn. com* ⇲ *9 rooms, 1 suite* ⚅ *Restaurant, fans, some kitchens, bar* ☐ *AE, D, MC, V* ⦿ *EP.*

$ ▣ **Papillote Wilderness Retreat.** Luxuriant vegetation abounds, the river
Fodor'sChoice beckons you to take a dip, and the 200-ft Trafalgar Falls are a short hike
★ from your room. Owner Anne Jean-Baptiste's botanical garden is a mind-boggling collection of rare and indigenous plants and flowers—all planted around secluded mineral pools and stone sculptures. The property has three natural hot pools, and Suite 11 has its own hot tub. The charming rooms are decorated with local handicrafts: quilts, grass rugs, prints, and pottery. The terrace-style Papillote restaurant, which has spectacular mountain and valley views, serves excellent local cuisine. ⊠ *Trafalgar Falls Rd., Trafalgar* ☐ *Box 2287, Roseau* ☎ *767/448–2287* ☐ *767/ 448–2285* ⊕ *www.papillote.dm* ⇲ *3 rooms, 4 suites* ⚅ *Restaurant, fans, some in-room hot tubs, bar, shop; no a/c, no room phones, no room TVs* ⊘ *Closed Sept.–mid-Oct.* ☐ *AE, D, MC, V* ⦿ *EP.*

$ ▣ **Roxy's Mountain Lodge.** This mountain retreat 4 mi north of Roseau is popular with nature enthusiasts as a gateway to the Morne Trois Pitons World Heritage Site. Regular rooms are clean and comfy, with local furnishings. A second, self-contained building offers a suite. The restaurant, which serves traditional Dominican cuisine, opens onto a huge terrace that overlooks the gardens. Bottles containing herbs steeped in rum line the shelves of the tiny bar, a watering hole frequented by hikers fresh from the nearby trails. Laudat can get chilly during winter months, so be sure to pack something warm. ⊠ *Laudat* ☐ *Box 265, Roseau* ☎☎ *767/448–4845* ⊕ *www.avirtualdominica.com/eiroxys.htm* ⇲ *10 rooms, 1 suite* ⚅ *Restaurant, hiking, bar; no a/c, no room phones, no room TVs* ☐ *AE, MC, V* ⦿ *EP.*

$ ▣ **Sunset Bay Club.** Lush gardens filled with scurrying wildlife are crisscrossed by pathways that meander from rooms to garden benches, to the pool, the sauna hut, and back to the beach and restaurant. This is Dominica's only all-inclusive resort, and it's on a stretch of west coast beach. The rooms are all simply furnished but maintain a crisp feeling, with ceiling fans and bright colors throughout. Cable TV is available for an additional charge. The restaurant is renowned for its seafood and wide selection of cocktails. Although most people opt for the all-inclusive plan, a breakfast-only plan is available. ✉ *Batalie Beach, Coulibistrie* ☎ *767/446–6522* 🖷 *767/446–6523* ⊕ *www.sunsetbayclub.com* 🛏 *12 rooms, 1 suite ⚷ Restaurant, fans, in-room safes, pool, sauna, beach, dive shop, bar; no a/c, no room phones* ☰ *AE, MC, V* ¶◯¶ *AI.*

★ **$** ▣ **Sutton Place Hotel.** In the heart of Roseau, large wrought-iron gates lead up from the street into a cool foyer, reception area, and restaurant, which serves scrumptious contemporary creole cuisine. Up a few more hardwood stairs are the five standard rooms, superbly decorated with imported fabrics and fittings. Hotel guests share a lounge and a kitchenette overlooking the courtyard. Three spacious top-floor suites with their own kitchens have restored antiques and replicas, teak-louvered windows, and polished wood floors. The structure's original 18th-century stonework can be seen in the cozy, air-conditioned Cellars Bar, a popular local hangout. ✉ *25 Old St., Roseau* ⏍ *Box 2333* ☎ *767/449–8700* 🖷 *767/448–3045* ⊕ *www.avirtualdominica.com/sutton.htm* 🛏 *5 rooms, 3 suites ⚷ Restaurant, fans, some kitchenettes, cable TV, bar, dry-cleaning, laundry service, business services* ☰ *AE, D, MC, V* ¶◯¶ *CP.*

★ **$** ▣ **Zandoli Inn.** Perched on an 80-ft cliff overlooking the southeast Atlantic coast, this five-room inn has several amazing views. You'll weave through six acres of luscious gardens and trails. Rooms are elegant and comfortable, with white-tile bathrooms, locally made furnishings, and imported fabrics. Downstairs are the dining room and bar, where hotel guests join Linda for scrumptious organic meals and interesting rumlaced concoctions. Farther down the cliff is the plunge pool—under a canopy of orchids; or you can go for a more adventurous swim from huge boulders in the aqua-blue Atlantic. Car rentals and excursions can be arranged. ✉ *Roche Cassée* ⏍ *Box 2099, Roseau* ☎ *767/446–3161* 🖷 *767/446–3344* ⊕ *www.zandoli.com* 🛏 *5 rooms ⚷ Dining room, fans, pool, hiking, bar, laundry service; no a/c, no room phones, no room TVs, no kids under 12* ☰ *AE, MC, V* ¶◯¶ *EP.*

¢–**$** ▣ **Cocoa Cottage.** Reggae musician Bobby Frederick is your host at this creatively hand-constructed wooden lodge, which has utilized many recycled materials. Bed frames are made from recycled spools, lamps from coconut shells, and flower pots from bamboo. All beds have colorful madras covers and mosquito nets. Some rooms have balconies and hammock chairs. Bobby makes sure you start your day with a cup of hot cocoa made straight from the surrounding trees while you enjoy the melodious sounds of birds. Picnic at a nearby stream or take Bobby's nature tours. Events with local artists provide entertainment. This bed and breakfast is all cozy and organic. ✉ *Trafalgar* ⏍ *Box 1641, Roseau* ☎ *767/448–0412 or 767/235–3412* ⊕ *www.avirtualdominica.com/ cocoacottage* 🛏 *6 rooms ⚷ Fans; no a/c, no room TVs, no room phones* ¶◯¶ *BP.*

¢–**$** ▣ **Itassi Cottages.** These three cottages are on beautifully landscaped grounds. The two-bedroom, two-bath cottage can house as many as six people; the one-bedroom, one-bath cottage accommodates up to four; and the studio cottage comfortably sleeps two. Each has a full kitchen and cable TV, and there's a shared laundry facility. They are furnished with a mix of antiques, straw mats, handmade floral bedspreads, and calabash lamps. Spacious porches with hammocks and sweeping views of the west coast make for an ideal hideaway five minutes southeast of the city. ✉ *Morne Bruce* ⏍ *Box 2333, Roseau* ☎ *767/448–7247*

🏠 *767/448–3045* ⊕ *www.avirtualdominica.comitassi* 🛏 *3 cottages*
⚐ *Fans, kitchens, cable TV, laundry facilities; no a/c* ⊟ *AE, MC, V* ¶◎¶ *EP.*

¢ 🏠 **D'Auchamps Cottages.** Just outside Roseau en route to Trafalgar are
these three cottages amid lush gardens. You'll find a cabin with rustic
fixtures, an outdoor bathroom (no hot water), and a garden view; the
two-bedroom and one-bedroom bungalows are closer to the main estate home and are simple but cozy, with modern fixtures, kitchens, and
covered patios. The gardens have marked walkways through exotic anthuriums and ferns. No meals are provided here, but it's not far from
Roseau and Trafalgar, where you can purchase basic supplies at the local
shops. ⊠ *Trafalgar* 🏠 *Box 1889, Roseau* ☎ *767/448–3346* ⊕ *www.*
avirtualdominica.com/dauchamps/index.html 🛏 *3 cottages* ⚐ *Kitchens;*
no a/c ⊟ *D, MC, V* ¶◎¶ *EP.*

Where to Eat

You can expect an abundance of vegetables, fruits, and root crops to
appear on menus around the island, for Dominica's economy, after all,
is based on agriculture. Sweet ripe plantains, *kushkush* yams, breadfruit,
dasheen (a tuber similar to the potato, called "taro" elsewhere), fresh
fish, and chicken prepared in at least a dozen different ways are among
the staples. The locals drink a spiced rum—steeped with herbs such as
anisette (called "nanny") and *pweve* (lemongrass). And be sure that when
you ask for a glass of juice it's going to come directly from the fruit and
not a box.

Dominican cuisine is also famous for its use of local game, such as the
"mountain chicken"—a euphemism for a large frog called *crapaud*—
and for more intrepid diners, the *manicou* (a small opossum) and the
agouti (a large indigenous rodent).

In and around Roseau and all over the island, throughout villages and
hamlets you can find myriad tiny food shops, where the food is local,
plentiful, and highly seasoned. So if what you are looking for is a quick
bite to sample Dominica's local cuisine, make your way in and ask for
the day's special. Otherwise, you could try roadside vendors making breakfasts of bakes and accras (fried bread and salt-cod fritters) for the
passersby.

What to Wear

Most Dominicans dress elegantly but practically when eating out—for
dinner it's shirts and trousers for men and modest dresses for women.
During the day, nice shorts are acceptable at most places; beach attire
is frowned upon, unless of course you're eating on the beach.

CARIBBEAN ✕ **Crystal Terrace Restaurant and Bar.** You'll find classic local food with
$$–$$$ a very elegant twist at this restaurant in the Evergreen Hotel. Dine on
a large, airy terrace perched right over the sea, or relax at the bar while
sipping a tropical cocktail. Dinners are usually prix-fixe, with a choice
of appetizer such as crab back, soup, or salad; entrées of chicken, fish,
or other meats served with local produce; and a dessert of fresh fruit or
homemade cake and ice cream. Breakfast and lunch are also served here,
and reservations are advised. ⊠ *Evergreen Hotel, Castle Comfort*
☎ *767/448–3288* ⊟ *AE, MC, V.*

$$–$$$ ✕ **Guiyave.** This popular lunchtime restaurant in a quaint Caribbean town
house also has a shop downstairs serving a scrumptious selection of sweet
and savory pastries, tarts, and cakes. These can also be ordered upstairs,
along with more elaborate fare such as fish court bouillon or chicken in a
sweet-and-sour sauce. Choose to dine either in the airy dining room or on
the sunny balcony perched above Roseau's colorful streets—the perfect spot

to indulge in one of the fresh-squeezed tropical juices. ⊠ *15 Cork St., Roseau* ☎ *767/448–2930* ⊟ *AE, MC, V* ⊗ *Closed Sun. No dinner.*

★ **$$–$$$** ✕ **La Robe Creole.** A cut-stone building only steps away from the Old Market Plaza houses one of Dominica's best restaurants. In a cozy dining room with wood rafters, ladder-back chairs, and colorful madras tablecloths, you can dine on a meal selected from an eclectic à la carte menu. Callaloo soup is one specialty, lobster crêpes and salads are others. The downstairs takeout annex, Mouse Hole, is an inexpensive and tasty place to snack when you're on the run. The restaurant makes its own delicious mango chutney and plantain chips, which you can buy in local shops. ⊠ *3 Victoria St., Roseau* ☎ *767/448–2896* ⊟ *D, MC, V* ⊗ *Closed Sun.*

★ **$$–$$$** ✕ **Papillote.** Savor a lethal rum punch while lounging in a hot mineral bath in the Papillote Wilderness Retreat gardens. Then try the bracing callaloo soup, dasheen puffs, fish "rain forest" (marinated with papaya and wrapped in banana leaves), or the succulent freshwater shrimp. This handsome Caribbean restaurant has quite possibly one of the best views in the region. Dine at an altitude cool enough to demand a throw and inspire after-dinner conversation. ⊠ *Papillote Wilderness Retreat, Trafalgar Falls Rd., Trafalgar* ☎ *767/448–2287* ⚊ *Reservations essential* ⊟ *AE, D, MC, V.*

$–$$$ ✕ **Pearl's Cuisine.** From her base in a Creole town house in central Roseau, chef Pearl, with her robust and infectious character, prepares some of the island's best local cuisine. She offers everything—including *sousse* (pickled pigs' feet), blood pudding, and rotis—in typical Dominican style. When sitting down to lunch or dinner, ask for a table on the open-air gallery that overlooks Roseau, prepare for an abundant portion, but make sure you leave space for dessert. If you're on the go, enjoy a quick meal from the daily varied menu in the ground-floor snack bar. You're spoiled for choice when it comes to the fresh fruit juices. ⊠ *50 King George V St., Roseau* ☎ *767/448–8707* ⊟ *AE, D, MC, V.*

$$ ✕ **Floral Gardens.** The sound of water falling in the background, rough-hewn timber beams, and vertivert mats help create the rustic setting for this restaurant. Dinner is served in the main building, but there are more tables in a building across the road overlooking the river. The home-style creole fare includes fresh fish and beef stews, fruits and vegetables, and tropical-flavored pies and tarts. ⊠ *Concord* ☎ *767/445–7636* ⊟ *AE, D, MC, V.*

$–$$$ ✕ **Port of Call Restaurant and Bar.** A haunt of middle-aged barristers and laid-back locals is ideally just around the corner from the bayfront in downtown Roseau. This breezy restaurant with a soothing gray-and-white color scheme occupies a traditional stone building. The layout is such that you can have your privacy or just a laid-back meal. Management here is always ready to meet your needs for homestyle local cuisine or a selection of à la carte dishes such as a hamburger with french fries or maybe just an exotic cocktail from the bar. ⊠ *3 Kennedy Ave., Roseau* ☎ *767/448–2910* ⊟ *AE, D, MC, V.*

$–$$ ✕ **Callaloo Restaurant.** On one of the busiest streets in Roseau you can escape the bustle and step into a quaint informal eatery where the effervescent Marge Peters is queen. Taking pride in age-old cooking traditions, she uses only the freshest local produce. Changing lunch and dinner specials might include curried conch, mountain chicken, or callaloo (fragrant with cumin, coconut cream, lime, clove, and garlic). Don't miss the fresh fruit juices, ice creams, and desserts. ⊠ *66 King George V St., Roseau* ☎ *767/448–3386* ⊟ *AE, D, MC, V.*

¢–$$ ✕ **Miranda's Corner.** Just past Springfield on the way to Pont Casse, you'll begin to see hills full of flowers. At a big bend, a sign on a tree reads MIRANDA'S CORNER, referring to a bar, rum shop, and diner all in one.

Here Miranda Alfred is at home, serving everyone from Italian tourists to banana farmers. The specialties are numerous—all prepared with a potion of passion and a fistful of flavor. It's open for breakfast, lunch, and dinner, and if you want something specially prepared, just call ahead and Miranda will help you out. ⊠ *Mount Joy, Springfield* ☎ 767/449–2509 ⚓ *Reservations essential* ▭ *No credit cards.*

¢–$ ✕ **Back–A–Yard.** Talk about down-home cooking. At the back ("in de yard") of a beautifully restored Creole town house is this mouthwatering vegetarian restaurant. Seated on iron garden chairs, you are served vegetable, pasta, and grain dishes. This is a cool, cheap hangout with great people, food, and drinks. ⊠ *19 Castle St., Roseau* ☎ 767/449–9736 ▭ *No credit cards* ☉ *Closed Sun. No dinner.*

CHINESE ✕ **Taiwanese Delicacies.** Keeping up with their industrious reputation, the
¢–$$ Chinese emigrants (from both Taiwan and mainland China) are the newest ethnic group to be added to Dominica's melting-pot culture. Taiwanese Dominicans are opening businesses including, of course, restaurants. This spot in Castle Comfort has drawn the biggest crowds for hot and spicy dishes, crispy vegetable and tofu selections, tender meats, elegant understated dining, and takeaway service. If you enjoy Chinese, you have to try it Dominican (Taiwanese) style. ⊠ *Castle Comfort* ☎ 767/448–3497 ▭ *No credit cards.*

ECLECTIC ✕ **Waterfront Restaurant.** At the southern end of Roseau's bayfront, this
★ $$–$$$$ elegant restaurant overlooks the tranquil Caribbean coastline. You can dine outdoors on the wraparound verandah or indoors in the air-conditioned formal dining room. New executive chef Mark Rickett is "putting all his love" into developing a spa/vegetarian menu alongside the restaurant's traditional international and local à la carte menu choices. Tropical desserts include cheesecake and guava tart. The bar's happy-hour steel band is a pleasant accompaniment. ⊠ *Fort Young Hotel, Victoria St., Roseau* ☎ 767/448–5000 ▭ *AE, MC, V.*

¢–$$ ✕ **Cornerhouse Café.** Just off the Old Market Plaza in a historic three-story stone and wood town house is Dominica's only true Internet café; the sign on the lattice verandah reads DOMINICA'S INFORMATION CAFÉ. Here an eclectic menu of meals and other treats is on offer: bagels with an assortment of toppings, delicious soups, sandwiches, salads, cakes, and coffee. Computers are rented by the half-hour; relax on soft chairs and flip through books and magazines while you wait. Wednesday is quiz night, and every night is game night—but arrive early, as there's always a full house. ⊠ *Corner of Old and King George V Sts., Roseau* ☎ 767/449–9000 ▭ *No credit cards* ☉ *Closed Sun.*

FRENCH ✕ **Ti Caz Café.** It's hard to miss the umbrella-covered chairs and tables
¢–$$ at this Parisian-style café on a prominent bayfront corner in Roseau. Breakfast crêpes, croissants, baguette sandwiches, and piping hot café au lait are available beginning at 8:30. Throughout the day you can relax indoors or out and enjoy any of the extensive menu's selections with the perfect glass of wine. In the cellar downstairs, the Cocorico wine store has a reasonably priced selection from more than eight countries. You can also choose from a wide assortment of pâtés and cheeses, sausages, cigars, French breads, and chocolates. ⊠ *Corner of Bayfront and Kennedy Aves., Roseau* ☎ 767/449–8686 or 767/449–9774 ▭ *MC, V* ☉ *Closed Sun. No dinner.*

Beaches

As a volcanic island, Dominica offers many powder-fine black-sand beaches. Found mostly in the north and east, they are windswept, dramatic, and uncrowded, lending themselves more to relaxation than swimming because many have undercurrents. However, slightly farther north there are beautiful secluded white- or brown-sand beaches and coves. Although northeast coast beaches offer excellent shallow swimming, their wind-tossed beauty can be dangerous; there are sometimes strong currents with the whipped-cream waves. From these beaches you can see the islands of Marie Galante and Les Saintes and parts of Guadeloupe. On the southwest coast, beaches are fewer and mostly made of black sand and rounded volcanic rocks. Swimming off these rocky shores has its pleasures, too: the water is usually as flat as a lake, deep and blue, and is especially good for snorkeling.

★ **Champagne.** On the west coast, just south of the village of Pointe Michel, this stony beach is hailed as one of the best spots for swimming, snorkeling, and diving. It gets its name from volcanic vents that constantly puff steam into the sea, which makes you feel as if you are swimming in warm champagne.

Hampstead Beach. This beach on the northeast coast actually encompasses three bays (one of which is sheltered and calm) and is a bit off the beaten path.

Hodges Beach. If you're looking for a secluded spot, this beach is just a bit farther along the northeast coast past Woodford Hill Beach. There is also a slow-flowing river here for a refreshing rinse after a hot day at the beach. It's easy to miss this one, as it is accessed through an estate road and private lands, so keep on the look-out.

L'Anse Tortue. This beach on the northeast coast is also a favorite for the more adventurous; it sits on a cove just past Woodford Hill, and some days the odd surfer finds just the right wave.

Mero Beach. A silver-grey stretch of beach is on the west coast, just outside of the village of Mero, where the entire community comes to party on Sunday.

Picard Beach. The golden stretch of sand is the longest on the island and a favorite of both locals and visitors. You'll find many restaurants and hotels along this part of the coast.

Purple Beach. Fringed by sea-almond trees and tucked under the bay of the Cabrits, this wide silver-grey stretch of sand is a popular haunt for weekend partiers; during the week you will often have the whole beach to yourself.

Scotts Head. At the southernmost tip of the island, a small landmass is connected to the mainland by a narrow stretch of stony beach separating the Atlantic and the Caribbean. It's a fantastic spot for snorkeling, and you can have lunch at one of the village restaurants.

Soufrière Beach. By the laid-back village of the same name and in the center of the Soufrière/Scotts Head Marine Reserve, this beach is an ideal spot for enjoying the healthy underwater life.

Toucari Beach. On the extreme northwest coast, this little secret is tucked away in one of the island's most picturesque spots. A long stretch of golden grey sand is spotted with colorful fishing boats and the tangle of nets left to dry after a morning out at sea. From here you can enjoy views of neighboring Guadeloupe and Les Saintes.

Woodford Hill Beach. If you are adventuring out on your own, ask locals for directions to hidden spots like this one on the northeast coast, a favorite just past the village of Woodford Hill, though on holidays it can be crowded.

Sports & the Outdoors

BOATING & SAILING   Motorboat and sailing excursions to neighboring islands like Guadeloupe, Martinique, and Les Saintes can be an exciting add-on to a vacation on Dominica. If the channel crossing is not your thing, a morning at a secluded spot on Dominica's west coast with a picnic and rum punch might be more appealing. A couple of companies organize trips either on an hourly or a daily basis, with costs ranging from $80 per hour to $750 for a full day. You can arrange a sailing trip through **Anchorage Dive & Whale Watch Center** (✉ Anchorage Hotel, Castle Comfort ☎ 767/448–2639 or 767/448–2639).

CYCLING Cyclists find Dominica's rugged terrain to be an exhilarating challenge, but there are routes suitable for all levels of bikers. **Nature Island Dive** (✉ Soufrière ☎ 767/449–8181) has a fleet of bikes in good condition. Knowledgeable guides lead tours through specific areas for $30–$65.

FISHING Anglers will delight in the numerous banks and drop-offs, as well as in the year-round fair weather. **Game Fishing Dominica** (✉ Mero ☎☎ 767/449–6638 ☎ 767/235–6638) works off the Castaways dock in Mero. Eight years ago they started the Annual International Sportfishing Tournament in Dominica. Francis Cambran will take you out for between $450 and $700 for five to eight hours, providing all equipment, bait, and refreshments.

HIKING Dominica's majestic mountains, clear rivers, and lush vegetation con-
★ spire to create adventurous hiking trails. The island is crisscrossed by ancient footpaths of the Arawak and Carib Indians and the Nègres Maroons, escaped slaves who established camps in the mountains. Existing trails range from easygoing to arduous. To make the most of your excursion, you'll need sturdy hiking boots, insect repellent, a change of clothes (kept dry), and a guide. Hikes and tours run $25 to $50 per person, depending on destinations and duration. Some of the natural attractions within the island's National Parks require visitors to purchase a site pass. These are sold for varying numbers of visits. A site pass costs $2, a day pass $5, and a week pass $10. Hiking guides can be arranged through the **Dominican Tourist Office** (✉ Valley Rd., Roseau ☎ 767/448–2045). The **Forestry Division** (✉ Dominica Botanical Gardens, between Bath Rd. and Valley Rd., Roseau ☎ 767/448–2401) is responsible for the management of forests and wildlife and has numerous publications on Dominica as well as a wealth of information on reputable guides. Local bird and forestry expert **Betrand Jno Baptiste** (☎ 767/446–6358) leads hikes up Morne Diablotin and along the Syndicate Nature Trail; if he's not available, ask him to recommend another guide.

SCUBA DIVING & Voted one of the top 10 dive destinations in the world by *Skin Diver*
SNORKELING and *Rodale's Scuba Diving* magazines, Dominica's dive sites are truly
Fodor'sChoice awesome. There are numerous highlights all along the west coast of the
★ island, but the best are those in the southwest—within and around **Soufrière/Scotts Head Marine Reserve.** This bay is the site of a submerged volcanic crater; the Dominica Watersports Association has worked along with the Fisheries Division for years establishing this reserve and have set stringent regulations to prevent the degradation of the ecosystem. Within a half mile (¾ km) of the shore, there are vertical drops from 800 ft to more than 1,500 ft, with visibility frequently extending to 100 ft. Shoals of boga fish, Creole wrasse, and blue cromis are common, and you might even see a spotted moray eel or a honeycomb cowfish. Crinoids (rare elsewhere) are also abundant here, as are giant barrel sponges. Other noteworthy dive sites outside this reserve are **Salisbury Falls, Nose Reef, Brain Coral Garden,** and—even farther north—**Cabrits Drop-Off** and **Toucari Reef.** The conditions for underwater photography, particularly macrophotography, are unparalleled. The going rate is between $65 and $75 for a two-tank dive or $100 for a resort course with an open-water dive. All scuba-diving operators also offer snorkeling; equipment rents for $10–$20 a day.

The **Anchorage Dive & Whale Watch Center** (✉ Anchorage Hotel, Castle Comfort ☏ 767/448–2639) has two dive boats that can take you out day or night. They also offer PADI instruction (all skill levels), snorkeling and whale-watching trips, and shore diving. **Dive Dominica** (✉ Castle Comfort Lodge, Castle Comfort ☏ 767/448–2188 ⊕ www.divedominica.com) conducts NAUI, PADI, and SSI courses as well as Nitrox certification. With four boats, they offer diving, snorkeling, and whale-watching trips and packages including accommodation at the Castle Comfort Lodge. **Fort Young Dive Centre** (✉ Fort Young Hotel, Victoria St. Roseau ☏ 767/448–5000 Ext. 333 ⊕ www.divefortyoung.com) conducts snorkeling, diving, and whale-watching trips departing from the hotel's own dock. **Nature Island Dive** (✉ Soufrière ☏ 767/449–8181) is run by an enthusiastic crew. Some of the island's best dive sites are right outside their door, and they offer diving, snorkeling, kayaking, and mountain biking as well as resort and full PADI courses.

SWIMMING Locals boast of having a river for every day of the year. Some are better for swimming than others, but all guarantee a pick-me-up during a hot day. As an extra treat, you can often find hot springs among the boulders; look for the telltale orange sulfur stains. Any tour guide or taxi driver can take you to one, but it's really more fun to go off discovering the perfect river pool on your own.

WHALE & Dominica records the highest species counts of resident cetacea in the
DOLPHIN region, so it's not surprising that tours claim 90% sighting success for
WATCHING their excursions. Humpback whales, false killer whales, minke, and
★ orcas are all occasionally seen, as are several species of dolphin. But the resident sperm whales (they calve in Dominica's 3,000-ft-deep [900-m-deep] waters) are truly the stars of the show. During your 3½-hour expedition you may be asked to assist in recording sightings, data that can be shared with local and international organizations. Although there are resident whales and dolphins and therefore year-round sightings, there are more species to be observed in November through February. The **Anchorage Dive & Whale Watch Center** (✉ Anchorage Hotel, Castle Comfort ☏ 767/448–2638) offers whale-watching trips. **Dive Dominica** (✉ Castle Comfort Lodge, Castle Comfort ☏ 767/448–2188) is a major whale-watching operator.

WINDSURFING Although windsurfing isn't a very widely practiced sport in Dominica, there are quite a few who swear that the conditions are right for an exhilarating experience. You will need to bring your own gear with you and wait out the weather at beaches like Turtle Beach in the northeast or down at Scotts Head, where chances for waves on the Atlantic side can be mixed with the winds within the Soufrière Bay. For windsurfing information contact **Andrew Armour** at the **Anchorage Dive & Whale Watch Center** (✉ Anchorage Hotel, Castle Comfort ☏ 767/448–2638).

Shopping

Dominicans produce distinctive handicrafts, with various communities specializing in their specific products. The crafts of the Carib Indians include traditional baskets made of dyed *larouma* reeds and waterproofed with tightly woven *balizier* leaves. These are sold in the Carib Indian Territory as well as in Roseau's shops. Vertivert straw rugs, screwpine tableware, fwije (the trunk of the forest tree fern), and wood carvings are just some examples. Also notable are local herbs, spices, condiments, and herb teas. Café Dominique, the local equivalent of Jamaican Blue Mountain coffee, is an excellent buy, as are the Dominican rums Macoucherie and Soca. Proof that the old ways live on in Dominica can be found in the number of herbal remedies available. One stimulating memento of your visit is rum steeped with *bois bandé* (scientific name *Richeria grandis*), a tree whose bark is reputed to have aphrodisiacal properties. It is sold at shops, vendor's stalls, and supermarkets all over the island. The charismatic roadside vendors can be found all over the island bearing trays laden with local and imported souvenirs, T-shirts, and trinkets. Duty-free shopping is also available in specific stores around Roseau.

Dominican farmers from all over the island boast their best crops every Saturday from 6 AM to 1 PM at the Roseau Market, at the end of Dame Eugenia Boulevard and Lainge Lane, probably the largest farmer's market in the Caribbean. Vendors are usually out on roadsides when there are French groups in for the day or on weekend excursions or when there are cruise ships in port.

Major Shopping Areas

One of the easiest places to pick up a souvenir is the Old Market Plaza, just behind the Dominica Museum, in Roseau. Slaves were once sold here, but today handcrafted jewelry, T-shirts, spices, souvenirs, and batik are available from a group of vendors in open-air booths set up on the cobblestones. These are usually busiest when there is a cruise ship berthed across the street. On these days you can also find a vast number of vendors along the bayfront.

Specialty Items

ART   Most artists work from their home studios, and it often takes the right contact to find them. Contact the Old Mill Cultural Center or Earl Etienne, a cultural officer and himself Dominica's most sought after painter. He will be able to put you on the right path to find exactly what you are looking for. Works by Dominican artists can be seen at the Old Mill as well as at Earl's home studio. Hilroy Fingol, a young artist specializing in airbrush painting, has his little studio cum gallery in the heart of Roseau called **Balisier** (⊠ 35 Great George St., Roseau ☎ no phone); it's a real treasure.

CLOTHING   There is such a wide selection when it comes to clothing stores in Roseau that it really is best to walk around and explore for yourself. However, for classic Caribbean and international designer clothing, there are several reliable boutiques to try. At **Desiderata** (⊠ 65 King George V St., 1st floor of J. Astaphans & Co. Ltd., Roseau ☎ 767/448–6522), a little boutique that carries clothing and accessories from Caribbean and American designers, many pieces are made specifically for the store. It's really difficult to leave without picking up at least one thing. **Ego Boutique** (⊠ 9 Hillsborough St., Roseau ☎ 767/448–2336) carries an extensive selection of designer clothing and exquisite crafts and home accessories from around the world. **Mango Tango** (⊠ Fort Young Hotel, Victoria St., Roseau ☎ 767/448–0342) is an exquisite store selling international fashions, including fine Indian silks, linens, beaded evening gowns, and a well-chosen selection of shoes. Be prepared to spend, though. A beautiful but limited selection of men's clothing is available as well.

GIFTS &   With tourism development comes increasing commerce; duty-free shops
SOUVENIRS   are cropping up in Roseau. Some name-brand stores carry jewelry, perfumes, crystals, and leather goods; several of these are within Roseau's bayfront. **Ashbury's and Colombian Emeralds** (⊠ Fort Young Hotel, Victoria St., Roseau) carries perfumes, crystals, gold and silver jewelry alone or with emeralds, diamonds, and other gems, liquor, and other gift items. **Baroon International** (⊠ Kennedy Ave., Roseau) sells unusual jewelry from Asia, the United States, and other Caribbean islands; there

are also pieces that are assembled in the store, as well as personal accessories, souvenirs, and special gifts. **Booze & Smoke** (⊠ Cork St., Roseau) has exactly what its name implies: a large selection of duty-free cigarettes, cigars, and alcohol. **Island Stuff** (⊠ 25 Hanover St., Roseau ☎ 767/449–9969), just a couple of blocks east of the ferry terminal, is a tiny shop, where you can find fine art, souvenirs, or the perfect hand-carved piece of furniture among the numerous items on sale. For quality leather goods and other personal accessories, try **Land** (⊠ Castle St., Roseau). **Rare Earth Treasures** (⊠ Fort Lane, Roseau) is where you will find exactly what the name says, uniquely fashioned fine jewelry. Their collection of gemstones and crystals is a treat not to be missed, even when you can't afford to buy.

HANDICRAFTS **The Crazy Banana** (⊠ 17 Castle St., Roseau ☎ 767/449–8091) purveys everything from earthenware to doorstops, as well as other Caribbean-made crafts, rums, cigars, jewelry, and local art. **Dominica Pottery** (⊠ Bayfront St. and Kennedy Ave., Roseau ☎ no phone) is run by a local priest, whose products are fashioned with various local clays and glazes. **Papillote Wilderness Retreat** (⊠ Trafalgar ☎ 767/448–2287) has an intimate gift shop with an excellent selection of local handcrafted goods and particularly outstanding wood carvings by Louis Desire. **Tropicrafts** (⊠ corner of Queen Mary St. and Turkey La., Roseau ☎ 767/448–2747) has a back room where you can watch local ladies weave grass mats. You'll also find arts and crafts from around the Caribbean, local wood carvings, rum, hot sauces, perfumes, and traditional Carib baskets, hats, and woven mats.

Nightlife & the Arts

The friendly, intimate atmosphere and colorful patrons at the numerous bars and hangouts will keep you entertained for hours. If you're looking for jazz, calypso, reggae, steel-band, *soca* (a variation of calypso), cadence/zouk, or jing ping—a type of folk music featuring the accordion, the *quage* (a kind of washboard instrument), drums, and a "boom boom" (a percussion instrument)—you're guaranteed to find it. Wednesday through Saturday nights are really lively, and during Carnival, Independence, and summer celebrations, things can be intense. Indeed, Dominica's Carnival, the pre-Lenten festival, is the most spontaneous in the Caribbean. The annual World Creole Music Festival in late October or early November also packs in the action, with three days and nights of pulsating rhythm and music. Creole Music enthusiasts come from all over the world to listen to the likes of Kassav, Aswad and Tabou Combo. Throughout the year, however, most larger hotels have some form of live evening entertainment.

Nightlife

Once Friday afternoon rolls around you can sense the mood change. Local bars crank up the music, and each village and community has its own particular nightly entertainment. If by this point in your trip you have made friends with some locals, they will be only too happy to take you to the current hot spot.

At **Cellars Bar** (⊠ Sutton Place Hotel, Old St., Roseau ☎ 767/449–8700), Wednesday night is Amateur Bartenders Soca Rum Night. Volunteer to be the bartender; taste tests of the featured cocktails are free. Friday is Kubuli Karaoke Night, with patrons competing for prize drinks; it's a real blast and perfect way to totally kick back. There is a $4 minimum on both nights. **Symes Zee's** (⊠ 34 King George V St., Roseau ☎ 767/448–2494) draws a crowd on Thursday night from 10 until the wee hours of the morning, when there is a jazz/blues/reggae band. There's no cover, and the food, drinks, and cigars are reasonably priced. **Warehouse** (⊠ Canefield ☎ 767/449–1303), outside Roseau just past the airport, is *the* place to dance on Saturday night. DJs are brought in from other islands to ensure there's variety to all the vibrations. The entrance fee is $5.

The Arts

Arawak House of Culture (⊠ Kennedy Ave., near Government Headquarters, Roseau ☎ 767/449–1804), managed by Aileen Burton at the Cultural Division, is Dominica's performing-arts theater. A number of productions are staged here throughout the year, including plays, recitals, and dance performances. **Old Mill Cultural Center** (⊠ Canefield ☎ 767/449–1804) is one of Dominica's historic landmarks. The Old Mill was once the island's first sugarcane processing mill and rum distillery. This is the place to learn about Dominica's traditions. Performances and events take place here throughout the year.

Exploring Dominica

Despite the small size of this almond-shaped island, it can take a couple of hours to travel between the popular destinations. Many sights are isolated and difficult to find; you may be better off taking an organized excursion. If you do go it alone, drive carefully: roads can be narrow and winding. Plan on eight hours to see the highlights; to fully experience the island, set aside a couple of days and work in some hikes.

Numbers in the margin correspond to points of interest on the Dominica map.

WHAT TO SEE **Cabrits National Park.** Along with Brimstone Hill in St. Kitts, Shirley

10 Heights in Antigua, and Ft. Charlotte in St. Vincent, the Cabrits National Park's Fort Shirley ruins are among the most significant historic sites in the Caribbean. Just north of the town of Portsmouth, this 1,300-acre park includes a marine park and herbaceous swamps, which are an important environment for several species of rare birds and plants. At the heart of the park is the Ft. Shirley military complex. Built by the British between 1770 and 1815, it once comprised 50 major structures, including storehouses that were also quarters for 700 men. With the help of the Royal Navy (which sends sailors ashore to work on the site each time a ship is in port) and local volunteers, historian Dr. Lennox Honychurch restored the fort and its surroundings, incorporating a small museum that highlights the natural and historic aspects of the park, and an open canteen-style restaurant.

5 **Carib Indian Territory.** In 1903, after centuries of conflict, the Caribbean's first settlers, the Kalinago, were granted a portion of land (approximately 3,700 acres) on the island's northeast coast, on which to establish a reservation with their own chief. Today it's known as Carib Territory, clinging to the northeasterly corner of Dominica, where a group of just over 3,000 Caribs, who resemble native South Americans, live like most other people in rural Caribbean communities. Many are farmers and fishermen; others are entrepreneurs who have opened restaurants, guest houses, and little shops where you can buy exquisite Carib baskets and other handcrafted items. The craftspeople retain knowledge of basket weaving, wood carving, and canoe building, which has been passed down from one generation to the next.

The Caribs' long, elegant canoes are created from the trunk of a single *gommier* tree. If you're lucky, you may catch canoe builders at work. The reservation's Catholic church in Salybia has a canoe as its unique altar, which was designed by Dr. Lennox Honychurch, a local historian, author, and artist.

L'Escalier Tête Chien (literally "Snake's Staircase," it's the name of a snake whose head resembles that of a dog), a hardened lava formation that runs down into the Atlantic. The ocean here is particularly fierce, and the shore is full of countless coves and inlets. According to Carib legend, at night the nearby Londonderry Islets metamorphose into grand canoes to take the spirits of the dead out to sea.

Though there's not currently much in the territory that demonstrates the Caribs' ancient culture and customs, plans for a museum showing early Carib life are in the works. In addition, the territory's Karifuna Cultural Group travels nationally and internationally, performing traditional dance and wearing traditional costumes—their bodies painted and adorned with feathers and beads.

4 **Emerald Pool.** Quite possibly the most-visited nature attraction on the island, this emerald-green pool fed by a 50-ft waterfall is an easy trip to make. To reach this spot in the Morne Trois Pitons National Park you follow a trail that starts at the side of the road near the reception center (it's an easy 20-minute walk). Along the way you'll pass lookout points with views of the windward (Atlantic) coast and the forested interior. If you don't want a crowd, check whether there are cruise ships in port before going out, as this spot is popular with cruise-ship tour groups.

8 **Indian River.** Indian River, in Portsmouth, was once a Carib Indian settlement. A gentle rowboat ride for wildlife spotting along this river lined with *terra carpus officinalis* trees, whose buttress roots spread up to 20 ft, is not only a relaxing treat but educational and most times entertaining. To arrange such a trip, stop by the Visitor Center at the mouth of the river and ask for one of the "Indian River boys." These young, knowledgeable men are members of the Portsmouth Indian River Tour Guides Association (PIRTGA) and have for years protected and promoted one of Dominica's special areas. Most boat trips take you up as far as Rahjah's Jungle Bar. You can usually do an optional guided walking tour of the swamplands and the remnants of one of Dominica's oldest plantations. Tours last one to three hours and cost $15 to $30 per person.

11 **Morne Aux Diables.** In the far north of Dominica, this peak soars 2,826 ft above sea level and slopes down to Toucari and Douglas bays and long stretches of dark-sand beach. To reach the mountain, take the road along the Caribbean coast. It twists by coconut, cocoa, and banana groves, past fern-festooned embankments, over rivers, and into villages where brightly painted shanties are almost as colorful as all the flora and fauna.

7 **Morne Diablotin National Park.** The park is named after one of the region's highest mountains, Morne Diablotin—at 4,747 ft, Dominica's highest peak. The peak takes its name, in turn, from a bird, known in English as the black-capped petrel, which was prized by hunters in the 18th century. Though the mountain's namesake bird is now extinct on the island, Dominica is still a major birding destination. Of the island's many exotic—and endangered—species, the green-and-purple Sisserou parrot (*Amazona imperialis*) and the Jaco, or red-neck, parrot (*Amazona arausiaca*) are found here in greater numbers than anywhere else in Dominica. Before the national park was established, the Syndicate Nature Trail was protected with the help of some 6,000 schoolchildren, each of whom donated 25¢ to protect the habitat of the flying pride of Dominica, as well as countless other species of birds and other wildlife. The west coast road (at the bend near Dublanc) runs through three types of forest and leads into the park. The trail offers a casual walk; just bring

a sweater and binoculars. The five- to eight-hour hike up Morne Diablotin isn't for everyone. You need a guide, sturdy hiking shoes, warm
clothing, and a backpack with refreshments and a change of clothes (including socks) that are wrapped in plastic to keep them dry. A good guide
for Morne Diablotin is local ornithology expert **Betrand Jno Baptiste**
(☎ 767/446–6358).

❸ **Morne Trois Pitons National Park.** A UNESCO World Heritage Site, this
17,000-acre swath of lush, mountainous land in the south-central interior (covering 9% of Dominica) is the nature island's crown jewel.
Named after one of the highest 4,600-ft mountains on the island, it contains the world's largest boiling lake, majestic waterfalls, and cool
mountain lakes. There are four types of vegetation zones here. Ferns grow
30 ft tall, wild orchids sprout from trees, sunlight leaks through green
canopies, and a gentle mist rises over the jungle floor. A system of trails
has been developed in the park, and the Division of Forestry and Wildlife
works hard to maintain it—with no help from the excessive rainfall and
the profusion of vegetation that seems to grow right before your eyes.
Access to the park is possible from most points of the compass, though
the easiest approaches are via the small mountaintop villages of Laudat (pronounced low-*dah*) and Cochrane.

About 5 mi (8 km) out of Roseau, the Wotton Waven Road branches
off toward Sulphur Springs, where you'll see the belching, sputtering,
and gurgling releases of volcanic hot springs. At the base of Morne Mi-
cotrin you'll find two crater lakes: the first, at 2,500 ft above sea level,
is **Freshwater Lake.** According to a local legend, it's haunted by a vin-
dictive mermaid and a monstrous serpent. Farther on is **Boeri Lake,** fringed
with greenery and with purple hyacinths floating on its surface. The undis-
FodorśChoice   puted highlight of the park is **Boiling Lake.** The world's largest such lake,
★   it is a cauldron of gurgling gray-blue water, 70 yards wide and of un-
known depth, with water temperatures from 180°F to 197°F. Although
generally believed to be a volcanic crater, the lake is actually a flooded
fumarole—a crack through which gases escape from the molten lava
below. The two- to four-hour (one-way) hike up to the lake is challenging
(on a very rainy day, be prepared to slip and slide the whole way up and
back). You'll need attire appropriate for a strenuous hike, and a guide
is a must. Most guided trips start early (no later than 8:30 AM) for this
all-day, 7-mi (11-km) round-trip trek.On your way to Boiling Lake
you'll pass through the **Valley of Desolation,** a sight that definitely lives
up to its name. Harsh sulfuric fumes have destroyed virtually all the vegetation in what must once have been a lush forested area. Small hot and
cold streams with water of various colors—black, purple, red, orange—
web the valley. Stay on the trail to avoid breaking through the crust that
covers the hot lava. During this hike you'll pass rivers where you can
refresh yourself with a dip (a particular treat is a soak in a hot-water
stream on the way back). At the beginning of the Valley of Desolation
trail is the **TiTou Gorge,** where you can swim in the pool or relax in the
hot-water springs along one side. If you're a strong swimmer, you can
head up the gorge to a cave (it's about a five-minute swim) that has a
magnificent waterfall; a crack in the cave about 50 ft above permits a
stream of sunlight to penetrate the cavern.

Also in the national park are some of the island's most spectacular waterfalls. The 45-minute hike to **Sari Sari Falls,** accessible through the east-
coast village of La Plaine, can be hair-raising. But the sight of water
cascading some 150 ft into a large pool is awesome. So large are these
falls that you feel the spray from hundreds of yards away. Just beyond
the village of Trafalgar and up a short hill, there's the reception facil-

ity, where you can purchase passes to the national park and find guides to take you on a rain-forest trek to the twin **Trafalgar Falls.** If you like a little challenge, let your guide take you up the riverbed to the cool pools at the base of the falls (check whether there's a cruise ship in port before setting out; this sight is popular with the tour operators). You need a guide for the arduous 75-minute hike to **Middleham Falls.** The turnoff for the trailhead is just before the village of Laudat. The trail takes you to another spectacular waterfall, where water cascades 100 ft over boulders and vegetation and then into an ice-cold pool (a swim here is absolutely exhilarating). Guides for these hikes are available at the trailheads; still, it's best to arrange a tour before even setting out.

❻ Northeast Coast. Steep cliffs, dramatic reefs, and rivers that swirl down through forests of mangroves and fields of coconut define this section of Dominica. The road along the Atlantic, with its red cliffs, whipped-cream waves, and windswept trees, crosses the Hatton Garden River before entering the village of Marigot. In the northeastern region there are numerous estates—old family holdings planted with fruit trees. Beyond Marigot and the Melville Hall Airport is the beautiful Londonderry Estate. The beach here is inspiring, with driftwood strewn about its velvety black sands, which part halfway—where the Londonderry River spills into the Atlantic (swimming isn't advised because of strong currents, but a river bath here is a memorable treat). Farther along the coast, beyond the village of Wesley (which has a gas station and a shop that sells wonderful bread) and past Eden Estate, there are still more beautiful beaches and coves. The swimming is excellent at Woodford Hill Bay, Hodges Beach, Hampstead Estate, Batibou Bay, and L'Anse Tortue. A stop in the charming community of Calibishie is a must; here you'll find bars and restaurants right on the beach, as well as laid back villas and guest houses. At Bense, a village in the interior just past Calibishie, you can take a connector road to Chaud Dwe (pronounced show-*dweh*), a beautiful bathing spot in a valley; the only crowd you're likely to encounter is a group of young villagers frolicking in the 15-ft-deep (4½-m-deep) pool and diving off the 25-ft-high (7½-m-high) rocks.

❾ Portsmouth. In 1782 Portsmouth was the site of the Battle of Les Saintes, a naval engagement between the French and the English. The English won the battle but lost the much tougher fight against malaria-carrying mosquitoes that bred in the nearby swamps. Once intended to be the capital of Dominica, thanks to its superb harbor on Prince Rupert Bay, it saw as many as 400 ships in port at one time in its heyday, but on account of those swamps, Roseau, not Portsmouth, is the capital today. Maritime traditions are continued here by the yachting set, and a 2-mi (3-km) stretch of sandy beach fringed with coconut trees runs to the Picard Estate area.

❶ Roseau. Although it is one of the smallest capitals in the Caribbean, Roseau has the highest concentration of inhabitants of any town in the eastern Caribbean. Caribbean vernacular architecture and a bustling marketplace transport visitors back in time. Although you can walk the entire town in about an hour, you'll get a much better feel for the place on a leisurely stroll.

For some years now, the Society for Historical Architectural Preservation & Enhancement (SHAPE) has organized programs and projects to preserve the city's architectural heritage. Several interesting buildings have already been restored. **Lilac House** (✉ Kennedy Ave.) has three types of gingerbread fretwork, latticed verandah railings, and heavy hurricane shutters. The **J. W. Edwards Building** (✉ Corner of Old and King George V Sts.) has a stone base and a wooden second-floor gallery, and is the home of the cozy Cornerhouse Cafe. **The old market plaza** is the center of Roseau's historic district, which was laid out by the French on a radial plan rather than a grid, so streets such as Hanover, King George V, and Old radiate from this area. South of the marketplace is the Fort Young Hotel, built as a British fort in the 18th century; the nearby state house, public library, and Anglican cathedral are also worth a visit.

The 40-acre **Botanical Gardens,** founded in 1891 as an annex of London's Kew Gardens, is a great place to relax, stroll, or watch a cricket match. In addition to the extensive collection of tropical plants and trees, there's also a parrot aviary. At the Forestry Division office, which is also on the garden grounds, you'll find numerous publications on the island's flora, fauna, and national parks. The forestry officers are particularly knowledgeable on these subjects and can also recommend good hiking guides. ⊠ *Between Bath Rd. and Valley Rd.* ☎ *767/448–2401 Ext. 3417* ⊘ *Mon. 8–1 and 2–5, Tues.–Fri. 8–1 and 2–4.*

New developments at bayfront on the Dame M. E. Charles Boulevard have brightened up the waterfront. The old post office now houses the **Dominica Museum.** This labor of love by local writer and historian Dr. Lennox Honychurch contains furnishings, documents, prints, and maps that date back hundreds of years; you'll also find an entire Carib hut as well as Carib canoes, baskets, and other artifacts. ⊠ *Dame M. E. Charles Blvd., opposite the cruise ship berth* ☎ *767/448–8923* ⊘ *Weekdays 9–4 and Saturday 9–noon* ⊜ *$2.*

❷ Soufrière. Tourism is quietly mingling with the laid-back lifestyle of the residents of this gently sunbaked village in the southwest, near one of the island's two marine reserves. Although first settled by French lumbermen in the 17th century, it's mainly fishermen you'll find here today. In the village you'll find a historic 18th-century Catholic church built of volcanic stone, one of the island's prettiest churches; the ruins of the L. Rose Lime Oil factory; Sulfur Springs, with its hot mineral baths to the east; and the best diving and snorkeling on the island within the **Soufrière/Scotts Head Marine Reserve.** To the west you'll find Bois Cotlette (a historic plantation house), and to the south the Scotts Head Peninsula—at the island's southern tip—which separates the Caribbean from the Atlantic. So if there isn't enough treasure here to satisfy you, there's always the rain forest waiting to be challenged.

DOMINICA A TO Z

To research prices, get advice from other travelers, and book travel arrangements, visit www.fodors.com.

AIR TRAVEL

American Eagle flies into Melville Hall Airport every afternoon from San Juan—during peak seasons twice a day. LIAT, Air Caraïbes, and Caribbean Star all bring a number of regional airlines together from various hubs, including Martinique, St. Lucia, and Antigua, into Canefield Airport and Melville Hall Airport on scheduled flights throughout the day. These flights also connect out of other countries in the region, including Guyana.

🛪 Air Caraïbes ☎ 767/448-2181. American/American Eagle ☎ 767/448-6680. LIAT ☎ 767/448-2421. Whitchurch Travel (for Caribbean Star Airlines) ☎ 767/448-2181 or 767/445-8841.

AIRPORTS

Canefield Airport, about 3 mi (5 km) north of Roseau, handles only small aircraft and daytime flights; landing here can be a hair-raising experience for those uneasy about flying. Melville Hall Airport is on the northeast coast, 75 minutes from Roseau, and handles larger planes.

Cab fare from Canefield Airport to Roseau is about $15. The 75-minute drive from Melville Hall Airport to Roseau takes you through the island's Central Forest Reserve and is a tour in itself. The trip costs about $55 by private taxi or $20 per person by co-op cab.

🛈 **Canefield Airport** ☎ 767/449-1199. **Melville Hall Airport** ☎ 767/445-7101.

BOAT & FERRY TRAVEL

FARES & SCHEDULES
Express des Isles has scheduled interisland jet catamaran ferry service, which runs according to a printed schedule; during peak seasons additional arrivals and departures are added. Generally, though, the ferry arrives and departs at the Roseau Ferry Terminal on Monday, Wednesday, and Friday–Sunday from Guadeloupe; it continues south to Martinique, as well as St. Lucia, on specific days. The crossing costs $90–$110, takes approximately 90 minutes, and offers superb views of the other islands.

🛈 **Express des Isles** ☎ 767/448-2181.

BUSINESS HOURS

BANKS
Banks are open Monday–Thursday 8–3, Friday 8–5.

POST OFFICES
Post offices are open Monday 8–5, Tuesday–Friday 8–4, and Saturday 8–1.

SHOPS
Businesses are generally open Monday 8–5, Tuesday–Friday 8–4, and Saturday 8–1. Some stores have longer hours, but you should call ahead to confirm them.

CAR RENTALS

Daily car-rental rates begin at $39 (weekly and long-term rates can be negotiated). Expect to add approximately another $7–$17 a day for optional collision damage insurance; otherwise, you will be asked to leave a credit-card number or cash deposit. You'll need to buy a visitor's driving permit (EC$20) at one of the airports or at the Traffic Division office on High Street in Roseau. Most rental-car companies offer airport and hotel pick-up and drop-off.

🛈 **Best Deal Car Rental** ✉ 15 Hanover St., Roseau ☎ 767/449-9204 or 767/235-3325. **Courtesy Car Rentals** ✉ 10 Winston Lane Goodwill ☎ 767/448-7763 or 767/447-3639 🖷 767/448-7733 ⊕ www.avirtualdominica.com/courtesycarrental/index.htmlental. **Island Car Rentals** ✉ Goodwill Rd., Goodwill ☎ 767/448-2886 or 767/445-8789. **Wide Range Car Rentals** ✉ 79 Bath Rd., Roseau ☎ 767/448-2198.

CAR TRAVEL

GASOLINE
Gasoline stations can be found all over the island; at this writing, gas costs approximately $2.70 per gallon.

ROAD CONDITIONS
Roads can be narrow in places, and they meander around the coast and through mountainous terrain.

RULES OF THE ROAD
Driving in Dominica is on the left side, though you can rent vehicles with a steering wheel on either the left or right.

ELECTRICITY

Electric voltage is 220/240 AC, 50 cycles. North American appliances require an adapter and transformer; however, many establishments provide these and often have dual-voltage fittings (110/120 and 220/240 volts).

EMBASSIES

🛈 **United Kingdom Honorary Consul** ☎ 767/448-7655.

EMERGENCIES
🞂 Ambulance & Fire **Ambulance and fire emergencies** ☎ 999.
🞂 Hospitals **Princess Margaret Hospital** ✉ Federation Dr., Goodwill ☎ 767/448-2231 or 767/448-2233.
🞂 Pharmacies **Jolly's Pharmacy** ✉ 12 King George V St., Roseau ☎ 767/448-3388.
🞂 Police **Police emergencies** ☎ 999.

ETIQUETTE & BEHAVIOR
Unlike neighboring Martinique and Guadeloupe, Dominica frowns on topless bathing. In addition, swimsuits should not be worn on the street. Dominicans, on the whole, are laid-back and polite. You will no doubt be greeted with a warm "good morning" or "good night" by anyone you pass on the street. Yet the people here are very private; it's better to ask permission before photographing someone. Note also that bargaining is not generally appreciated in Dominican shops.

FESTIVALS & SEASONAL EVENTS
Dominicans boast that they have the most spontaneous carnival in the region, Mas Domnik. It's great to join a band and get all costumed and painted. Reveling in the streets during Carnival Monday and Tuesday, it's one big family. Celebrations usually heat up the last 10 days or so before Ash Wednesday. The National Cultural Council hosts the Emancipation celebrations in August. September and October see Independence celebrations, culminating on Independence Day on November 3. Another major event is the Annual World Creole Music Festival, held the last weekend in October or first weekend of November. This three-day music and cultural festival draws performers and Creole music enthusiasts from around the globe. Community Day of Service is November 4. In addition to these major festivals there are a number of Village feasts all over the island from month to month.

HOLIDAYS
Public holidays are: New Year's, Merchant's Holiday (Jan. 2), Carnival Jump-Up Days (two days before Ash Wednesday each year), Ash Wednesday, Labour Day (May 1), Whit Monday (May 24), Emancipation Day (Aug. 5), Independence Day (Nov. 3), Community Service Day (Nov. 4), Christmas Day, and Boxing Day (Dec. 26).

LANGUAGE
The official language is English. Most Dominicans also speak Creole, a language based primarily on a French vocabulary with indigenous Carib loan words and traces of West African syntax.

MAIL & SHIPPING
First-class letters to North America cost EC95¢ and those to the United Kingdom cost EC90¢; postcards are EC55¢ to just about anywhere in the world. The general post office is opposite the ferry terminal in Roseau. Dominica is often confused with the Dominican Republic, so when addressing letters to the island, be sure to write: The Commonwealth of Dominica, Eastern Caribbean. Islands in this part of the Caribbean do not use postal codes.

MONEY MATTERS
Prices throughout this chapter are quoted in U.S. dollars, unless indicated otherwise.

ATMS You'll find ATMs in all the banks in Roseau—including Barclays Bank on Old Street, the Royal Bank of Canada near the cruise-ship berth, Banque Française Commerciale on Queen Mary Street, and the Bank of Nova Scotia on Hillsborough Street—as well as some in larger villages such as

Portsmouth. They dispense EC dollars only and accept international bank cards.

CREDIT CARDS   Major credit cards are widely accepted, as are traveler's checks.

CURRENCY   The official currency is the Eastern Caribbean dollar (EC$) but U.S. dollars are readily accepted. The exchange rate will be EC$2.67 to the US$1, but you'll usually get change in EC dollars.

PASSPORTS & VISAS

U.S. and Canadian citizens must have a valid passport or proof of citizenship (an original birth certificate along with a government-issued photo I.D.) Citizens of other countries must have a valid passport. Citizens from Cuba, Haiti, Russia, The People's Republic of China, and Eastern European countries who wish to stay in Dominica for longer than 21 days are required to obtain a visitor's visa. Everyone needs a return or ongoing ticket.

SAFETY

Petty crime can be a problem on Dominica, as with all destinations in the world. It's always wise to secure valuables in the hotel safe and not carry too much money or many valuables around. Remember that if you rent a car to tour the island, you may have to park it in a remote area; don't leave valuables in your vehicle while you're off on a hike or a tour.

SIGHTSEEING TOURS

Since Dominica is such a nature-centered destination, there is no shortage of certified guides. There are also numerous tour and taxi companies. Ask the staff at your hotel for a recommendation. Ken's Hinterland Adventure Tours & Taxi Service, Dominica Tours, and Whitchurch Tours are among the most reputable operators specializing in ornithological, botanical, or more intense adventure tours, and any of the three will be able to arrange an excursion to suit your desires. Generally tours start off in the Roseau area, but most operators will arrange convenient pick-ups. Prices range between $30 and $75 per person depending on the duration, amenities provided, and number of persons on the excursion.

🄵 **Ken's Hinterland Adventure Tours & Taxi Service** ⊠ Fort Young Hotel, Victoria St., Roseau ☎ 767/448-4850 or 767/235-3517 ⊕ www.kenshinterlandtours.com. **Dominica Tours** ⊠ Anchorage Hotel, Castle Comfort ☎ 767/448-2638 or 767/448-0990 ⊕ www.anchoragehotel.dm. **Whitchurch Tours** ⊠ Old St., Roseau ☎ 767/448-2181 ⊕ www.whitchurch.com.

TAXES & SERVICE CHARGES

DEPARTURE TAX   The departure/embarkation tax is US$20 or EC$50, payable in cash only at the airport at the time of departure from the island.

SALES TAX   Hotels collect a 5% government hotel occupancy tax, restaurants a 5% government sales tax.

TAXIS

Taxis and minibuses are available at the airports and in Roseau, as well as at most hotels and guest houses. Rates are fixed by the government, but if you opt for a co-op—sharing a taxi (and the fare) with other passengers going in the same direction—you will be able to negotiate a special price. Drivers also offer their services for tours anywhere on the island beginning at $20 an hour for up to four persons; a 3½-hour island tour will cost approximately $80. It's best to get a recommendation from your hotel. You can recognize a taxi and/or minibus by the HA plates; simply flag them down or make your way to the nearest bus stop. For more information on reputable taxi companies, contact the Dominica Taxi Association or Nature Island Taxi Association.

🖪 **Dominica Taxi Association** ☎ 767/449-8533. **Nature Island Taxi Association** ☎ 767/448-1679.

TELEPHONES

COUNTRY & AREA CODES To call Dominica from the United States, dial the area code (767) and the local access code (44), followed by the five-digit local number.

INTERNATIONAL CALLS The island has a very advanced telecommunication system and accordingly efficient direct-dial international service. All pay phones are equipped for local and overseas dialing, accepting either EC coins, credit cards, or phone cards, which you can buy at many island stores and at the airports.

🖪 **AT&T Direct** ☎ 800/872-2881. **MCI World Phone** ☎ 800/888-8000. **Sprint** ☎ 800/744-2250.

LOCAL CALLS On the island, dial only the seven-digit number that follows the area code.

TIPPING

Most hotels and restaurants add a 10% service charge to your bill. A 5% tip for exceptionally good service on top of the service charge is always welcome; otherwise just tip accordingly.

VISITOR INFORMATION

🖪 **Before You Leave Dominican Tourist Office** ⊕ www.dominica.dm ✉ 800 2nd Ave., Suite 1802, New York, NY 10017 ☎ 212/949-1711 🖶 212/949-1714. **The Dominica Tourist Office-UK** ✉ MKI Ltd., Mitre House, 66 Abbey Rd., Bush Hill Park, Enfield, Middlesex EN1 2QE, U.K. ☎ 44-208/350-1004 🖶 44-208/350-1011. **Office of the Dominica High Commission, London** ✉ 1 Collingham Gardens, London SW5 0HW, U.K. ☎ 44-207/370-5194 🖶 44-207/373-8743.

🖪 In Dominica **Division of Tourism** ✉ Valley Rd., Roseau ☎ 767/448-2045 ✉ Old Post Office, Dame M. E. Charles Blvd., Roseau ☎ 767/448-2045 Ext. 118 ✉ Canefield Airport, Canefield ☎ 767/449-1242 ✉ Melville Hall Airport, Marigot ☎ 767/445-7051

WEB SITES

The most comprehensive Web portal to all things Dominican is "A Virtual Dominica," which has links to hotels, shops, car-rental agencies, and a wealth of information about visiting the island.

🖪 ⊕ www.avirtualdominica.com.

DOMINICAN REPUBLIC

FODOR'S CHOICE

Bahoruco Beach, Barahona

Barceló Capella Beach Resort, Juan Dolio

Casa de Campo, La Romana

Kite Surf Camp, a restaurant in Cabarete

Playing golf at the Casa de Campo Golf Course, La Romana

Playing golf at the Punta Cana Resort's golf course, Punta Cana

Zona Colonial, Santo Domingo

HIGHLY RECOMMENDED

HOTELS   Barceló Bahoruco Beach Resort, Barahona

Guatapanal Hotel & Resort, Las Terrenas

Hotel Sofitel Frances, Santo Domingo

Iberostar Hacienda Dominicus, Bayahibe

Meliá Caribe Tropical, Punta Cana

Meliá Santo Domingo Hotel and Casino, Santo Domingo

Punta Cana Resort & Club, Punta Cana

Villa Serena, Las Galeras

SIGHTS   Altos de Chavón, La Romana

Punta Cana Beach

Many other great places enliven this area. For other favorites, look for the black stars as you read this chapter.

It was one of those Caribbean days that fulfill all your tropical
dreams. The blue skies and aquamarine waters appeared otherworldly through my Maui Jim's. We drove the hour from Cabarete
with the promise that the "orchid beach" was worth it. The first
sighting of the oceanfront elicited a moan. The only equivalent
was California's Monterey peninsula. But here these fragrant,
almond trees dip sensually to the white sand, like the hip gyra-
tions of the merengue. The final coup is the sea cliffs colored
with wild orchids that bloom a lipstick shade of crimson. On the
Richter scale of tropical ocean settings, does it get any higher
than this?

Updated by
Eileen
Robinson Smith

Sprawling over two-thirds of the island of Hispaniola, the Dominican
Republic is a delightful, almost magical place. Its people are friendly and
hospitable by nature; if you return their courtesy, they'll do their best
to ensure that your vacation is memorable. The D.R. also happens to
be one of the Caribbean's least expensive destinations.

The island has had a stormy history replete with revolutions, military
coups, invasions, epidemics, and bankruptcy. Columbus happened upon
this island on December 5, 1492, and on Christmas Eve his ship, the
Santa María, was wrecked on its Atlantic shore. He named it La Isla
Española (the Spanish Island), established a small colony, and sailed back
to Spain on the *Pinta.* His brother Bartholomeo, along with Nicolás de
Ovando, founded Santo Domingo in 1496, making it the oldest continuously inhabited city in this hemisphere. During the 16th century it
became the bustling New World hub of Spanish commerce and culture.

The continued restoration of its Colonial Zone, under the auspices of
the Office of Cultural Patrimony, includes the renovation of the Parque
de Colón and all of the other parks; the construction of underground
parking garages is underway. A security force, trained especially for the
Zone, more frequent garbage pick-ups, and improvements in lighting
have made this a desirable neighborhood once again.

Still, most Dominican towns and cities are generally not quaint, neat,
or particularly pretty, and poverty is still prevalent. However, the ever-
increasing role of tourism in the economy is bringing about changes that
benefit residents and visitors alike, including some long-needed new major
highways, which are currently under construction.

American influence looms large in Dominican life. Many Dominicans
speak at least rudimentary English and have relatives living in the States.
Baseball is a national passion. Still, this is a vibrantly Latin country—
at times cool, collected, and laid-back; at times fiery hot, frenetic, and
chaotic.

The country is large, and diverse enough to draw a wide range of visitors. Sun-worshipers head to one of the many beach resort areas. The
highest peak in the West Indies, Pico Duarte, lures hikers to the central
mountain range. Ancient sunken galleons and coral reefs divert divers
and snorkelers. And everywhere there's the breathtaking scenery, the land
ever turning and twisting and towering into mountains before tumbling
into the sea.

WHAT IT COSTS In U.S. dollars				
$$$$	**$$$**	**$$**	**$**	**¢**
RESTAURANTS*				
over $30	$20–$30	$12–$20	$8–$12	under $8
HOTELS**				
Cost EP/BP/CP over $350	$250–$350	$150–$250	$80–$150	under $80
Cost AI over $450	$350–$450	$250–$350	$125–$250	under $125

*Restaurant prices are for a main course at dinner. **EP, BP, and CP prices are per night for a standard double room in high season, excluding taxes, service charges, and meal plans. AI (all-inclusive) prices are per person, per night based on double-occupancy during high season, excluding taxes and service charges.

Where to Stay

The Dominican Republic has the largest hotel inventory (at this writing 60,000 rooms) in the Caribbean and is starting to draw Americans in larger numbers. That is a far cry from, say, seven years ago, when most Americans had no idea where it was. The island's lodging options range from rustic country inns to posh beach resorts and sophisticated high-rise hotels in Santo Domingo.

Santo Domingo properties generally base their tariffs on the EP plan and maintain the same room rates year-round. Beach resorts have high winter and low summer rates—with prices reduced by as much as 50%. All-inclusives dominate in Punta Cana. Sosúa and Cabarete are strongholds of the small inn, but there are also all-inclusives as well.

Most tourists traveling to the D.R. take advantage of the many charter air-hotel packages available through travel agents and tour operators, particularly in winter. While the neighbors are shoveling snow and defrosting windshields, you can get a direct flight to Punta Cana and pay only $750 for a week's vacation, everything included.

Santo Domingo

The seaside capital of the country is in the middle of the island's south coast. In Santo Domingo, most of the better hotels are on or near the Malecón, with several small, desirable properties in the trendy Colonial Zone.

$$ ⊞ **Barceló Gran Hotel Lina Spa & Casino.** A steadfast city landmark for decades, painted in bold Caribbean colors (from mango to hot pink), this hotel is near the Malecón and the Presidential Palace. Professional and helpful staff keep business travelers and conventions coming back. Both hotel guests and the capital's movers and shakers still frequent the Restaurante Lina, with its classic Continental dishes and piano bar. The rooftop pool area looks lovely, with the white tenting giving it a resort appeal. ⊠ *Av. Máximo Gómez and Av. 27 de Febrero, Gazcue* ⊕ *Box 1915* ☎ *809/563–5000* 🖷 *809/686–5521* ⊕ *www.barcelo-hotels.com* ⊅ *202 rooms, 15 suites* ⬧ *2 restaurants, coffee shop, minibars, 2 pools, health club, hot tub, piano bar, casino, concierge, Internet, business services, meeting rooms* ⊟ *AE, DC, MC, V* ¶Ol *EP.*

$$ ⊞ **Hotel Santo Domingo.** Surrounded by walled gardens and overlooking the sea, this in-town getaway is favored by diplomats (many VIPs check into one of the Excel Club's eight business rooms, with king-size beds and work areas with 4-line speaker phones). A sophisticated after-work crowd gathers at the Marrakesh Café & Bar, with its American music (jazz on Mondays) and Casablanca-style decor that complements

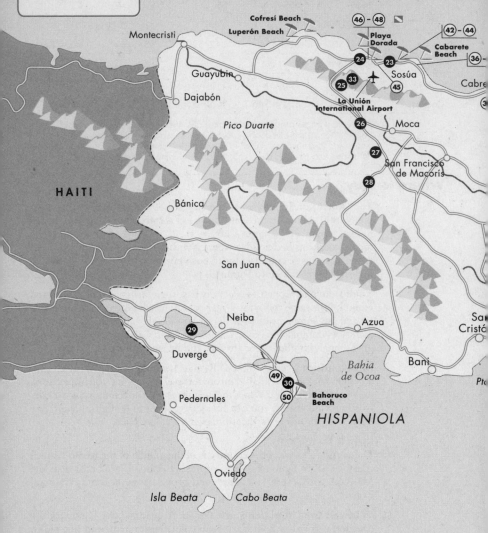

Dominican Republic

HAITI

Montecristi

Cofresí Beach
Luperón Beach

46 – 48

42 – 44

Cabarete
Beach

Playa
Dorada

24   23   Sosúa

36

Cabre

Guayubín

25   33

45

3

Dajabón

La Unión
International Airport

Pico Duarte

26   Moca

27   San Francisco
de Macorís

28

Bánica

San Juan

Neiba

Azua

Sa
Cristó

29

Duvergé

Bahía
de Ocoa

Bani

Pto

49

30

50   Bahoruco
Beach

Pedernales

HISPANIOLA

Oviedo

Isla Beata   Cabo Beata

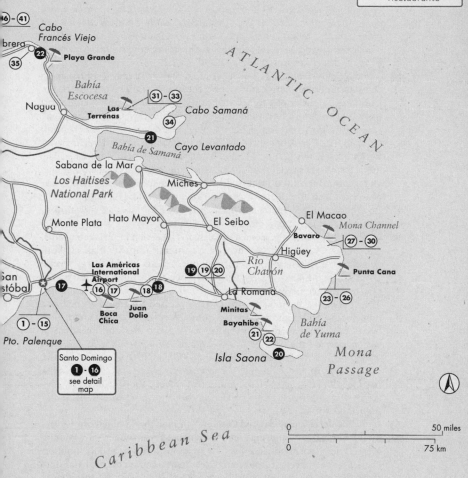

KEY
- Beaches
- Dive Sites
- ❶ Exploring Sights
- ① Hotels & Restaurants

Restaurants ▼

Aqua 5	Restaurant at Natura Cabanas 36
Blue Moon 38	Restaurant Coccoloba 26
El Bohio 33	Scherezade 10
La Briciola 12	Spaghettissimo 6
Café Billini 11	Villa Serena 34
Castle Club 40	
Da Vinci Ristorante 4	
Hemingway's Café 45	
Kite Surf Camp 39	
Meson Bari 7	
Paparazzo 10	
El Pelicano 17	
El Pescador 19	

Exploring ▼

Altos de Chavón 19	Santiago de los Caballeros 26
Barahona 30	Sosúa 23
Isla Saona 20	La Vega Vieja 27
Jarabacoa 28	
Lago Enriquillo 29	
Laguna Gri-Grí ... 22	
Mt. Isabel de Torres 25	
Parque de los Tres Ojos 17	
Puerto Plata 24	
Samaná 21	
San Pedro de Macorís 18	

the lobby's mahogany arches and potted palms. A trellised arcade leads to a large, peaceful pool that's beautifully landscaped. Businesspeople favor this hotel for its professionalism; tourists love the pampering service. ⊠ *Avs. Independencia and Abraham Lincoln, El Malecón* ✆ *Box 2112* ☎ *809/221–1511 or 800/877–3643* 🖷 *809/533–8898* ⊕ *www. hotel.stodgo.com.do* ⇨ *215 rooms* ♨ *3 restaurants, some in-room data ports, some in-room faxes, minibars, cable TV with movies and video games, 3 tennis courts, pool, hair salon, health club, sauna, 2 bars, concierge, concierge floor, business services, meeting rooms, car rental, helipad, travel services* ⊟ *AE, MC, V* ⍥ *EP.*

★ $$ 🏨 **Hotel Sofitel Frances.** The facade of this two-story 16th-century structure has handsome native stonework; the interior is done in pink stucco. Columned arches open to a European-style fountain and a courtyard furnished with teak and shaded by white umbrellas. Classy "antique" rattan furniture and potted plants give second-floor patios a tropical, colonial feel. Euro-style second-floor guest rooms have interesting configurations, with rugs on tiled floors and stylish French bedspreads. The lobby restaurant specializes in French and international cuisine. Personnel at reception are good-humored and English-speaking. ⊠ *Calles Las Mercedes and Arzobispo Merino, Zona Colonial* ☎ *809/685–9331* 🖷 *809/685–1289* ⊕ *www.sofitel.com* ⇨ *19 rooms* ♨ *Restaurant, minibars, cable TV, bar* ⊟ *AE, MC, V* ⍥ *EP.*

★ $$ 🏨 **Meliá Santo Domingo Hotel and Casino.** The lavish lobby, restaurants, and rooms of this Malecón hotel are contemporary yet classic. Wonderful ocean views are found throughout. Guests on the Royal Service Level stay in the lap of luxury, with such special amenities as a full breakfast, complimentary premium liquors, and hors d'oeuvres in the lounge. Your butler will even have your clothes pressed for free. Casabe has a noteworthy buffet and is open 24 hours. A full-service spa and fitness center looks out to the rooftop pool. A piano bar and an adjacent casino provide the fun. ⊠ *Av. George Washington 365, El Malecón* ✆ *Box 8326* ☎ *809/221–6666* 🖷 *809/687–8150* ⊕ *www.solmelia. com* ⇨ *245 rooms, 17 suites* ♨ *2 restaurants, minibars, 2 tennis courts, pool, health club, spa, 2 bars, piano bar, casino, shops, concierge, concierge floor, business services, meeting rooms, travel services, no-smoking rooms* ⊟ *AE, DC, MC, V* ⍥ *EP.*

$$ 🏨 **Occidental El Embajador and Casino.** Although this landmark hotel isn't on the Malecón, its multinational flags wave a welcome from a safe residential neighborhood close by. The spacious lobby is a social hub; orchestras perform near its fountain. Executive rooms on the fifth and sixth floors have extra amenities and comprise the Occidental Club; there's also an upscale concierge level, the Miguel Angel Club. Standard guest rooms are spacious and quiet; bathrooms are exceptional. The appealing pool complex is a popular weekend gathering place. ⊠ *Av. Sarasota 65, Bella Vista* ☎ *809/221–2131* 🖷 *809/532–4494* ⊕ *www. occidental-hoteles.com* ⇨ *286 rooms, 14 suites* ♨ *2 restaurants, cable TV, 4 tennis courts, pool, gym, sauna, 3 bars, casino, shops, concierge floor, business services, meeting rooms* ⊟ *AE, DC, MC, V* ⍥ *CP.*

$–$$ 🏨 **Renaissance Jaragua Hotel and Casino.** Gardens, waterfalls, and fountains surround this luxurious urban oasis. You'll find Champions, a sports bar, serving all-American burgers within the huge casino; local and big-name performers play the 1,000-seat La Fiesta Showroom. Cascade, a glass-enclosed bar, looks out to a waterfall. Rates are based on views of the ocean, garden, or of the huge, free-form pool. The expanded Renaissance Club, the concierge floor, has its lounge and terrace that affords ocean vistas. Suites have Club privileges, data ports, and larger desks. The presidential suite is vast, with its own hot tub. The fitness center is the largest in the city. ⊠ *Av. George Washington 367, El*

Malecón ☎ *809/221–2222* 🖷 *809/686–0528* ⊕ *www.renaissancehotels. com* 🛏 *292 rooms, 8 suites* ♨ *3 restaurants, some in-room data ports, in-room safes, some kitchens, minibars, golf privileges, 4 tennis courts, pool, hot tub, sauna, spa, 5 bars, casino, dance club, concierge, concierge floor, business services* ☰ *AE, MC, V* ¶ *EP.*

$ 🏨 **Hodelpa Caribe Colonial.** This boutique hotel offers yet another option in the burgeoning Colonial Zone. With superior sophistication at a modest price, plus a friendly, accommodating staff, it is wooing business people and tourists away from more established properties. The feel is European, the furnishings art deco, with white gauze canopies draped over king-size beds. Rooms come in standard or superior; suites offer more space and amenities. English is spoken at the front desk, and the staff is especially courteous and accommodating. Go up to the rooftop sundeck or sit out on your balcony and wave to the neighbors. ✉ *Isabel La Católica 59, Zona Colonial* ☎ *809/683–1000 or 888/403– 2603* 🖷 *809/683–2303* ⊕ *www.hodelpa.com* 🛏 *52 rooms, 2 suites* ♨ *Restaurant, room service, minibars, in-room safes, bar, laundry service, concierge, Internet, free parking* ☰ *AE, MC, V* ¶ *EP.*

Boca Chica/Juan Dolio

The Boca Chica/Juan Dolio resort area is the area immediately east of Las Americas airport, where you would fly in.

$ 🏨 **Barceló Capella Beach Resort.** This grand resort's 17 acres are punctuated with benches and manicured shrubbery. It presents an eclectic mix of architectural styles—from Victorian to Moorish. The yellow-stucco exterior is accented by white latticework, columns, and a red-tile roof. The large, quiet rooms have a civilized, almost British-colonial air; some have balconies and sea views; 200 of the newest are on the beach. There's entertainment at the theater or the bar, and a tri-level, palapa disco on the beach near the water-sports club. Barceló, which dominates Juan Dolio, now has six resorts here. ✉ *Juan Dolio* 📦 *Box 4750, Villas Del Mar, Santo Domingo* ☎ *809/526–1080* 🖷 *809/526–1088* ⊕ *www.barcelo-hotels.com* 🛏 *271 rooms, 22 suites* ♨ *3 restaurants, minibars, 2 tennis courts, 2 pools, health club, massage, sauna, beach, snorkeling, windsurfing, boating, 3 bars, dance club, recreation room, theater, shops, children's programs (ages 4–12), concierge, concierge floor, meeting rooms* ☰ *AE, MC, V* ¶ *AI.*

FodorsChoice ★

☾ $ 🏨 **Coral Hamaca Beach Hotel and Casino.** Hamaca has a large fun quotient; its sweet, friendly staffers make you feel a part of the whole. East of Santo Domingo and close to Las Américas Airport, this all-inclusive offers around-the-clock services. Opt for one of the 247 newer rooms. A lovely champagne-color beach has two bars, a juice bar, and an á la carte *palapa* (thatch-roof, open-air) restaurant. Many business people who choose to headquarter here for an overnight or a week pay $25 to upgrade, which includes many perks, including a massage. For fun, head to the casino, amphitheater, or disco. ✉ *Playa Boca Chica* ☎ *809/523– 4611 or 888/942–6725* 🖷 *809/523–6767* ⊕ *www.coralhotels.com* 🛏 *590 rooms* ♨ *5 restaurants, grill, 3 tennis courts, 2 pools, gym, massage, sauna, beach, dive shop, snorkeling, windsurfing, boating, bicycles, 6 bars, casino, dance club, theater, children's programs (ages 4–12), playground, laundry service, Internet, meeting rooms* ☰ *AE, DC, MC, V* ¶ *AI.*

La Romana

La Romana is on the southeast coast of the Dominican Republic, about a two-hour drive from Santo Domingo, southwest of the Punta Cana area. There is an international airport here with direct flights from the U.S. or Canada. La Marina at Casa de Campo with its Mediterranean design and impressive yacht club, is as fine a new facility as can be found anywhere.

☼ **$$$$** 🏨 **Casa de Campo.** Golfers can fly into La Romana and an hour later
FodorsChoice be teeing off on one of three renowned courses. Other sports facilities,
★ from the polo and equestrian center to the shooting complex, are noteworthy, too. Villa rooms in casitas are wonderfully large and commodious—and quiet, each with its own terrace. Service in general is stellar.
A luxurious yacht marina and villa complex adds another whole di-
mension. The sheer number of quality restaurants on the property, in
Chavón, and in the new marina, satisfies high expectations. A spectacular new musical extravaganza, *Kandela,* now plays weekly at the
5,000-seat Altos de Chavón amphitheater. ⊠ *La Romana* 🖂 *Box 140*
🕾 *809/523–3333 or 305/856–7083* 🖷 *809/523–8548* ⊕ *www.
casadcampo.cc* 🛏 *350 rooms, 150 villas* ⅜ *9 restaurants, some kitchens,
3 18-hole golf courses, 13 tennis courts, 16 pools, health club, sauna,
dive shop, snorkeling, windsurfing, fishing, bicycles, horseback riding,
4 bars, theater, shops, children's programs (ages 4–18)* ⊟ *AE, MC, V*
🍽 *AI.*

★ **$$** 🏨 **Iberostar Hacienda Dominicus.** You'll marvel at the sheer beauty of the
grounds and the public spaces here. Elaborate metal chandeliers over-
look replicas of wooden yachts and a fascinating collection of sculptures,
including life-size horses and bulls. The network of lagoons and foun-
tains adds to the tranquillity, as do the gazebos, particularly the wed-
ding chapel in the lagoon, where the flamingos roam. Large rooms have
king-size beds, a living area, and a balcony (request an ocean-view
room, as there is no extra charge). Iberostar's restaurants are among
the best of all the all-inclusives, as are the piña coladas at the swim-up
bar. ⊠ *Playa Bayahibe, Bayahibe* 🕾 *809/688–3600* 🖷 *809/221–0921*
⊕ *www.iberostar.com* 🛏 *460 rooms, 38 junior suites* ⅜ *4 restaurants,
minibars, 2 tennis courts, 4 pools, health club, spa, dive shop, snorkel-
ing, boating, billiards, 7 bars, dance club, showroom, shops, children's
programs (4–12), Internet, business services, meeting room, car rental*
⊟ *AE, MC, V* 🍽 *AI.*

$ 🏨 **Casa del Mar.** With its whimsical gingerbread fretwork awash in
Caribbean colors, this resort is on an exceptional palm-fringed ribbon
of white sand close to Casa de Campo. Most of the guest rooms have
views of the sea, the spectacular pool, or both. In the Bayahibe Restau-
rant, buffets of fresh, tasty dishes are served beneath stunning handcrafted
chandeliers. Asian and Italian restaurants are among the four on-site din-
ing options. The free half-day excursion to pristine Saona Island is a photo
opportunity. ⊠ *Bayahibe Bay, La Romana* 🕾 *809/221–8880* 🖷 *809/
221–8881* ⊕ *www.AMHSAmarina.com* 🛏 *568 rooms* ⅜ *4 restau-
rants, minibars, 4 tennis courts, 2 pools, gym, hot tub, beach, dive
shop, snorkeling, windsurfing, boating, bicycles, archery, horseback
riding, volleyball, 4 bars, dance club, children's programs, meeting
rooms* ⊟ *AE, MC, V* 🍽 *AI.*

Punta Cana

On the easternmost coast, Punta Cana is a 20-mi strand of incredible
beach punctuated by coco palms. The area includes Bávaro Beach. You
will fly into the Punta Cana International Airport. The capital, Santo
Domingo, is about a three-hour trip by car.

☼ **$$$** 🏨 **Paradisus Punta Cana All-Inclusive Exclusive Beach Resort.** Paradisus has
an open-air lobby of lagoons and rock gardens. The path to the elegant
casino is punctuated by sculptures. Bi-level suites have tropical motifs
and brightly painted wooden furnishings. From the simple grilled seafood
and meats at the beach palapa to the sophisticated international fare
(and complimentary cognacs and liqueurs) at the à la carte Romantico
restaurant, the cuisine here is exceptional. You'll find everything from
aqua-aerobics (often followed by cocktails at the swim-up bar) to spa

services, and PADI diving. Honeymoon packages are exceptional, and weddings are blissful. (Love that white, horse-drawn marriage carriage.) ✉ *Playa Bávaro* ☎ *809/687–9923* 📠 *809/687–0752* ✎ *527 suites* ⚭ *8 restaurants, minibars, golf privileges, 4 tennis-courts, pool, health club, spa, beach, dive shop, snorkeling, windsurfing, boating, bicycles, archery, 4 bars, casino, children's programs (ages 4–12)* ═ *AE, DC, MC, V* ¶⊙¶ *AI.*

$$ 🖼 **Barceló Bávaro Palace.** Barceló's Bávaro complex is a mini-city with more restaurants and shops than most towns, tennis and golf complexes, a lakefront church, Vegas-quality reviews, a shuttle train, a dazzling, contemporary, convention center, villas, and four other hotels (Bávaro Golf, Beach, Garden, and Casino) plus the five-star Palace. The Palace is its showplace, where serpentine pools with a swim-up bar border one of the world's best beaches. Gastronomy is a main attraction, noise levels are lower, and the clientele more upscale than at the other resorts; moreover, only those staying at the Palace can use its facilities. ✉ *Playa Bávaro* ☎ *809/686–5797* 📠 *809/788–7723* ⊕ *www.barcelo. com* ✎ *594 rooms* ⚭ *5 restaurants, minibars, 18-hole golf course, 3 tennis courts, 2 pools, health club, beach, snorkeling, boating, volleyball, 5 bars, dance club, theater* ═ *AE, MC, V* ¶⊙¶ *AI.* •

$$ 🖼 **Club Med Punta Cana.** This renovated village is looking fine, with the sleeping rooms particularly attractive. Set on one of the island's best beaches, this is a great resort for families, what with two different kids' clubs (one for toddlers, the other for older kids). Though the resort is American-friendly, there is a lot that happens here in Spanish—and French. Ask about frequent specials, and try for a package that comes with airfare. But mostly have fun. Nonguests can pay for a day pass, which includes lunch with complimentary beer and wine service. For everyone, cocktails and any beverages (even coffee) consumed between meals cost extra. ✉ *Punta Cana* ☎ *809/686–5500* 📠 *809/685–5287* ✎ *522 rooms* ⚭ *3 restaurants, pool, fitness classes, beach, windsurfing, boating, waterskiing, archery, volleyball, 2 bars, nightclub, children's programs (ages 2–13)* ═ *AE, MC, V* ¶⊙¶ *AI.*

☾ $$ 🖼 **Iberostar Bávaro Resort.** This large complex consists of three beautiful resorts (there's also the Punta Cana and Dominicana). The Bávaro, with a dramatic, open-air lobby, has all junior suites and the most dining options. The expansive grounds rarely feel crowded. Tiled rooms have king-size beds and a separate sitting area plus a balcony; marble baths are spacious. The food is exceptional for an all-inclusive, from the buffets to the Mediterranean seafood restaurant. The friendly, energetic, and helpful staff keep you entertained and as active as you wish to be. This stretch of Bávaro Beach is broad and well kept. Americans are a newish but growing presence. ✉ *Playa Bávaro* ☎ *809/221–6500 or 888/923–2722* 📠 *809/ 688–6186* ⊕ *www.iberostarcaribe.com* ✎ *588 jr suites* ⚭ *5 restaurants, ice-cream parlor, snack bar, fans, in-room safes, minibars, cable TV, tennis courts, 3 tennis courts, pool, health club, hair salon, outdoor hot tub, spa, beach, dive shop, snorkeling, windsurfing, boating, volleyball, 3 bars, lounge, casino, dance club, showroom, video game room, shops, children's programs (ages 4 to 12), dry cleaning, laundry service, concierge, Internet, business services, meeting rooms* ═ *AE, MC, V* ¶⊙¶ *AI.*

★ ☾ $$ 🖼 **Meliá Caribe Tropical.** The lobby of this American-friendly resort designed for both couples and families has fountains, lagoons, boardwalks, pillars, and sculptures. The sprawling complex is beautified by waterscapes and mangroves. Hot-pink flamingos aren't plastic, and the pond's white rotunda is the site of many a wedding. Surrounded by palms, the pool has a Jacuzzi at its center and a kids' pool. At the his-and-her spa, with its Grecian-style white columns, you can relax in a whirlpool surrounded by classical sculptures. Gourmet Boulevard lined with specialty restaurants, helps you beat the buffet blues. Golf, all 27 holes, is at the adjacent Cocotal Golf Club. ⊠ *Punta Cana* ☎ *809/221–1290* 🖷 *809/221–4595* ⊕ *www.solmelia.es* ⇨ *1,044 jr suites* ⚅ *15 restaurants, 1 9-hole golf course, 1 18-hole golf course, 8 tennis courts, 2 pools, health club, spa, beach, snorkeling, windsurfing, boating, 6 bars, casino, dance club, showroom, children's programs (ages 4–11), business services, convention center, meeting rooms* 🖃 *AE, DC, MC, V* ⊺◯⫾ *AI.*

★ ⚅ $$ ⊡ **Punta Cana Resort & Club.** A charismatic resort, it continues to reinvent itself. On an incredible 6-mi beach, an injection of $10 million has transformed what was already a handsome property into one destined to be an international star. Opt for the beach wing or the luxurious, beachfront golf villas overlooking a spectacular P. B. Dye golf course. The golf clubhouse, facing the ocean and its own pool, is outstanding. The marina is providing a base for yachtsmen. In Corales, an exclusive, residential development, the oceanfront mansions of investors Oscar de la Renta and Julio Iglesias are flanked by those of other VIPs. ⊠ *Playa Punta Cana* ☎ *809/221–2262 or 888/442–2262* 🖷 *809/687–8745* ⊕ *www.puntacana.com* ⇨ *418 rooms* ⚅ *5 restaurants, minibars, 18-hole golf course, 4 tennis courts, 2 pools, fitness classes, hair salon, health club, beach, dive shop, snorkeling, windsurfing, boating, marina, fishing, horseback riding, 5 bars, dance club, theater, children's programs (ages 5–12), playground, laundry service, business services, meeting rooms* 🖃 *AE, MC, V* ⊺◯⫾ *MAP.*

⚅ $ ⊡ **Catalonia Beach, Golf & Casino Resort.** This handsome resort is punctuated with fountains and sculptures, lagoons, and garden areas. The beach, with no other resort visible on either side, offers a roster of aquatic sports. The tour desk offers a good mix of excursions, many in English. It's big fun at the disco, what with the international music, mystery night, perfect couple night, and the Mr. & Mrs. Catalonia pageant. The Gran Caribe buffet has a theme night cycle—one night is local, Dominican cuisine—and there are Japanese, Brazilian, Italian, and French restaurants. The clientele is equally international. The noise level is acceptable, despite the high occupancy. ⊠ *Cabeza de Toros, Playa Bávaro* ⛬ *Box N8, Higüey* ☎ *809/412–0000* 🖷 *809/412–0001* ⊕ *www.cataloniabavaro.com* ⇨ *704 jr suites, 1 presidential suite* ⚅ *8 restaurants, minibars, 18-hole golf course, 2 tennis courts, 2 pools, gym, hair salon, beach, boating, billiards, 5 bars, casino, dance club, showroom, shops, children's programs (ages 4–12), Internet, convention center* 🖃 *AE, MC, V* ⊺◯⫾ *AI.*

$ ⊡ **Natura Park.** Always environmentally correct, this resort even handcrafted its furniture from the coco palms that were cut down to make room for the gardens, walkways, and man-made lakes. On the grounds are the remains of a coconut plantation as well as a mangrove forest and a natural lake. Guest rooms are in 13 buildings that put stone, wood, and cane to use in an ecosensitive way. The outdoor à la carte restaurant, where meals are made from wholesome, all-natural ingredients, looks onto a spectacular lagoon-style pool and beyond to Bávaro Beach. The luxurious spa is a relaxing place for a physical renewal. ⊠ *Playa Bávaro* ☎ *809/538–3111 or 888/628–8727* 🖷 *809/221–6060* ⇨ *518 rooms, 6 suites* ⚅ *3 restaurants, 3 tennis courts, 2 pools, spa, beach, windsurfing, boating, 4 bars, dance club, children's programs (ages 4–11)* 🖃 *MC, V* ⊺◯⫾ *AI.*

Samaná

Samaná is the name of both the peninsula that curves around the bay of the same name and juts out into the Atlantic and of the largest town. The nearest major international airport is Puerto Plata International Gregorio Luperon.

★ $ ⊞ **Guatapanal Hotel & Resort.** The dirt road from Las Terrenas looks like one less traveled, but it dead ends at a super new hotel on an astounding beach. A waterfall greets guests, as does the helpful, English-speaking staff. To the right is the Club, a swanky, upscale lounge where top-shelf liquors are sold. In front, there is the serpentine pool with its European furniture. It is adjacent to the buffet, which serves up food far above the norm. The yellow-and-white hotel sits amid manicured gardens. Rooms are simple and cheery, done in shades of yellow, blue, and white. Request a sea view, or take one of the beachside bungalows. ⊠ *Bahia de Coson, Las Terrenas* ☎ *809/240–5050* ⎙ *809/240–5536* ⊕ *www.guatapanal.com.do* ⤴ *144 rooms, 42 suites, 10 villas, 12 apartments* ♧ *3 restaurants, cable TV, pool, beach, dive shop, boating, snorkeling, windsurfing, Ping-Pong, 2 bars, dance club, showroom, shop, meeting room, car rental* ⊟ *AE, MC, V* �ⓞ *AI.*

$ ⊞ **Hotel Bahia Las Ballenas.** French-owned, this idyllic cluster of thatched roofed casitas is like something you might find in Mexico or Bali. The bungalows face the ocean blue, the exuberant tropical gardens, or the fabulous pool. The sculpted, alfresco bathrooms have fascinating tile work and decorative water fixtures. There is no air-conditioning or TV, but in-room phones and a nearby Internet office keep those connected who want to be. As for de-stressing, a massage followed by a Jacuzzi works. On-site are a dive shop and a fun restaurant and bar where locals and expats congregate. ⊠ *Playa Bonita, Las Terrenas* ☎ *809/240–6066* ⎙ *809/240–6107* ⊕ *www.las-terrenas-hotels.com* ⤴ *32 rooms* · ♧ *Restaurant, pool, hair salon, hot tub, massage, beach, dive shop, bar, shop* ⊟ *AE, MC, V* ⓞ *CP.*

★ $ ⊞ **Villa Serena.** At the end of the scenic highway from Puerto Plata, this small hotel looks like a century-old gingerbread seaside mansion. It is where honeymooners can happily begin their new life together. With unobstructed views of the pristine Bay of Rincon, rooms are classy, with bamboo canopy beds draped with white fabric. The dining room, where multicourse meals are served, is as romantic as the moonlit waves. Sorry, there is no loud music here, no animated shows, nor any staff blowing whistles—just peace and quiet. Horses can be hired nearby. ⊠ *Las Galeras* ⑉ *Box 51–1* ☎ *809/538–0000* ⎙ *809/538–0009* ⊕ *www. villaserena.com* ⤴ *21 rooms* ♧ *Restaurant, fans, pool, beach, snorkeling, bicycles, bar; no a/c in some rooms* ⊟ *AE, MC, V* ⓞ *BP.*

¢–$ ⊞ **Atlantis Hotel.** The Europeans have the expression *hotel de charme,* and this place fully qualifies for it. Twenty-something years old, it has a fluid, white stucco exterior that merges the guest rooms together like a tiny Mexican village. The ceilings are beamed, the decor artsy and individualistic, the bathrooms marble. Facing the Atlantic, with mature tree cover, this landmark is owned by a Frenchwoman, Veronique. Its restaurant's chef, Gerard Prystasz, was the chef for France's former president, François Mitterrand. The alfresco dining room has vintage European tile work; its sound system is a good one, the international music a real pleasure. The savvy clientele is predominately French and German. ⊠ *Playa Bonita, Las Terrenas* ☎ *809/240–6111* ⎙ *809/240–6205* ⊕ *www.atlantisbeachhotel.com* ⤴ *18 rooms* ♧ *Restaurant, beach, bar; no a/c* ⊟ *MC, V* ⓞ *BP.*

The Amber Coast

Named for the large quantities of amber found in the area, the sands on its 75 mi of beach are also golden. In the northern part of the island, with mountains on one side, the resort area with the major hotels is called Playa Dorada. Plan to fly into Puerto Plata International Gregorio Luperon Airport.

$$$$ ⊞ **Orchid Bay Estates.** There is a place where the oceanfront is so magnificent, where sea-sculpted trees ride low over white sand, and staggered cliffs drop into the aquamarine water. On this mile-plus-long strand of heaven is a boutique collection of fully-staffed, waterfront estates available for a week, a month, or as long as you wish. Homes range from a two-bedroom, honeymoon haven to a real Italian palazzo—a fantasy setting for a fairytale wedding, a corporate retreat, or a Big Chill reunion. The cost, divided by 6 bedrooms, it's affordable, and a stay here is unforgettable. ⊠ *Cabrera* ☎ *809/589–7773* 🖷 *809/589–7447* ⊕ *www.orchidbay.com* 🏄 *5 villas* ⚭ *Kitchens, tennis court, 5 pools, 2 gyms, beach, horseback riding* ▤ *MC, V* ❐ *EP.*

$$$$ ⊞ **Sea Horse Ranch.** Internationally known celebrities frequent this luxury residential resort. Formerly a dairy farm—with more than 250 acres that include preserved ecoareas— it is called a thoroughbred community—and not just because of its horses. All villas—each about 4,000 square ft—have three or four bedrooms, a pool, and sit on sites from half an acre upwards to four acres (the largest has its own private beach). The beach club is nestled in a cove with vistas of rugged cliffs. Prices decrease dramatically when renting by the month. Inquire about special rates for couples and for Miami weekenders. ⊠ *Cabarete* ☎ *809/ 571–3880* 🖷 *809/571–2374* ⊕ *www.sea-horse-ranch.com* 🏄 *75 villas* ⚭ *Dining room, kitchens, 5 tennis courts, beach, snorkeling, horseback riding, bar, baby-sitting* ▤ *AE, MC, V* ❐ *EP.*

$$ ⊞ **Gran Ventana.** This resort is characterized by style and pizzazz. The lobby has a central fountain surrounded by commodious white sofas. The main buffet dining area is within a gazebo. Rooms are in two handsome buildings with canopied entrances, ochre stucco facades, and red-tile roofs. Most rooms have sea views obstructed by only a few palms and a picket fence that keeps the beach private and tranquil. The 141 oversize rooms in the newer building do not face the water, but you'll have a lap pool and peace and quiet. Packages are popular with those renewing vows or getting married. A rooftop bar serves premium liquors. ⊠ *Playa Dorada, Puerto Plata* ⬚ *Box 22* ☎ *809/320–2111* 🖷 *809/ 320–2112* ⊕ *www.victoriahoteles.com.do* 🏄 *504 rooms, 2 suites* ⚭ *5 restaurants, tennis court, 3 pools, gym, hair salon, 2 hot tubs, sauna, beach, snorkeling, windsurfing, boating, bicycles, horseback riding, 6 bars, dance club, recreation room, theater, shops, convention center, meeting rooms, car rental* ▤ *AE, DC, MC, V* ❐ *AI.*

$$ ⊞ **Iberostar Costa Dorada.** You will be dazzled by the sprawling lobby with its hardwood benches and sculptures. The curvaceous pool is known for its central Jacuzzi encircled by Roman pillars, which appears in many wedding photos. The pool action begins with aqua-aerobics, and the animated, sometimes overzealous staff keeps the games and music going. Those seeking quiet head for the delightful stretch of undeveloped beach. Other all-inclusives could learn from the buffet, which includes a surprising variety and quality of international and Dominican dishes. Rodizio, the Brazilian restaurant, is a must-do. You can get a massage outdoors or at the spa. ⊠ *Playa Dorada, Puerto Plata* ☎ *809/ 320–1000* 🖷 *809/320–2023* ⊕ *www.iberostar.com* 🏄 *498 rooms, 16 jr suites* ⚭ *3 restaurants, minibars, pool, health club, spa, snorkeling, boating, billiards, 3 bars, dance club, showroom, shops, Internet, business services, meeting rooms* ▤ *AE, MC, V* ❐ *AI.*

$$ ⊞ **Sosúa Bay Hotel.** This lovely resort and its adjacent sister property, Victorian House, are breathing new life into this long-standing resort town. Both have panoramic views of breathtaking Sosúa Bay. The pool complex is multilevel—a tree "grows" in one—while waterfalls splash and steam rises from the Jacuzzi. Children have their own pool and hot tub plus a darling kids' club. The architecture is Spanish colonial in style, the guest rooms generous in size. An oceanfront conference center and business center are attended by a professional, bilingual staff. The food is far better than you normally find in 24-hour, all-inclusive clubs. ✉ *Calle Dr. Alejo Martinez 1 El Batey, Sosúa* ☎ *809/571–4000* 🖷 *809/571–4545* ⊕ *www.starzresorts.com* ⟳ *193 rooms* ⚘ *4 restaurants, refrigerators, cable TV, tennis court, 2 pools, 2 hot tubs, fitness classes, gym, hair salon, beach, dive shop, snorkeling, windsurfing, boating, jet skiing, water skiing, fishing, mountain bikes, 4 bars, cabaret, children's programs (ages 4–12), laundry facilities, Internet, business services, meeting room,* ☰ *AE, MC, V* ⟨◯⟩ *AI.*

$$ 🖵 **Victorian House.** This boutique hotel is a delightful restoration of a Victorian gingerbread, built around the well-known Italian restaurant Sabatini. (Ask for a table under the turret.) Guests check in at a diminutive, white-pillared cottage with rotating art exhibits. You should consider the suites and penthouses—all very tempting for the price. Built on a cliff that drops into gorgeous Sosúa Bay, this hotel is geared to the individual traveler who enjoys being pampered by a caring, multilingual staff. The numerous facilities at its adjacent sister, the Sosúa Bay Hotel, are shared. Its nightclub is one of the hottest in the area—dance on. ✉ *Calle Dr. Alejo Martinez 1, El Batey, Sosúa* ☎ *809/571–4000* 🖷 *809/571–4545* ⊕ *www.starzresorts.com* ⟳ *32 rooms, 18 suites* ⚘ *Restaurant, room service, some kitchenettes, cable TV, tennis court, 2 pools, 2 hot tubs, fitness classes, gym, hair salon, beach, dive shop, snorkeling, windsurfing, boating, jet skiing, water skiing, fishing, mountain bikes, 4 bars, dance club, children's programs (ages 4–12), laundry facilities, concierge, Internet, meeting room, car rental* ☰ *AE, MC, V* ⟨◯⟩ *CP.*

$ 🖵 **Natura Cabanas.** This spa getaway is paradisiacal. No phones or TVs in the simple, criollo-style, thatched-roof bungalows (sleeping two to six people). The secluded pool is separated by exuberant vegetation from the private beach. The owners' mantra is "peace, quiet, and health." There are yoga lessons, deep massages, mud baths, salt scrubs, facials, and a peaked sauna hut dubbed "The Magic Mushroom." Rates include airport transfers from Puerto Plata. Rent mountain bikes, horses, or four-wheel-drive vehicles. Afterward refresh yourself with fresh juices and head to the alfresco restaurant for a candlelight dinner with a sea view. Day guests are welcome to the spa. ✉ *Playa Perla Marina, Cabarete* ☎ *809/571 1507* 🖷 *809/571 1507* ⊕ *www.naturacabana.com* ⟳ *6 bungalows* ⚘ *Restaurant, kitchenettes, pool, sauna, spa, beach, boating, bar* ☰ *MC, V* ⟨◯⟩ *CP.*

$ 🖵 **Piergiorgio Palace Hotel.** The dream of an Italian fashion designer, this white-clapboard inn has a sweeping verandah and intricate fretwork. It replicates the Victorian splendor for which early Sosúa was known. A gazebo is integrated into the front entrance, and a staircase rises from the marble-tiled lobby. Romantics take to the pink-and-white floral guest rooms. Half have ocean views, the rest overlook the kidney-shaped pool and gardens. Piergiorgio's stretch limo whisks you from the Puerto Plata Airport to the inn, and the moderate rates include breakfast (and for $20 more, dinner) at the cliffside La Puntilla de Piergiorgio Restaurant. ✉ *Calle La Puntilla 1, El Batey, Sosúa* ☎ *809/571–2626* 🖷 *809/571–2786* ⊕ *www.piergiorgiohotel.com* ⟳ *51 rooms* ⚘ *Restaurant, in-room safes, 2 pools, hot tub, 2 bars* ☰ *AE, MC, V* ⟨◯⟩ *CP.*

$ 🖵 **Victoria Resort.** This study in pastels and gingerbread fretwork is adjacent to the Playa Dorada golf course with a view of Isabel de Torres Mountain. The public areas have such touches as marble floors and Carnival masks hung on mint green walls. Deluxe accommodations, set apart for quiet, have plantation-style wicker furniture and terraces. The clubhouse looks onto a lake, a pool, and hot tub. The alfresco café has fine buffets; you can now opt for à la carte service as well. Jardin Victoria offers Continental cuisine, professional service, and strolling musicians. The Victoria Beach Club is just five minutes away. ⊠ *Playa Dorada, Puerto Plata* ✆ *Box 22* ☎ *809/320–1200* 🖶 *809/320–4862* ⊕ *www. victoriahoteles.com.do* ⬦ *190 rooms* ⚒ *4 restaurants, café, pizzeria, minibars, golf privileges, tennis court, 2 pools, gym, outdoor hot tub, dive shop, snorkeling, windsurfing, boating, jet skiing, parasailing, horseback riding, 2 bars, nightclub* ⊟ *AE, MC, V* ⦿ *AI.*

� $ 🏨 **Windsurf Hotel.** Loyal guests at this young and fun, modest hotel are saying, "I knew it when." The Canadian owners continue to improve the offerings. There is a palapa-roofed barbecue area for those who do their own cooking, and a beach club with showers, lockers, towel service, and bar. Windsurf is a great value for the peso, with hotel rooms on a par with the full-service resorts and a kicked-back atmosphere, where American surfers dance with Scandinavian beauties at the welcome mixer. Those staying at the hotel can use CaribBic Center, the watersports school on the beach across the street. ⊠ *Carretera Principal, Cabarete* ☎ *809/571–0718* 🖶 *809/571–0710* ⊕ *www.windsurfcabarete. com* ⬦ *48 rooms, 38 1-bedroom condos, 12 2-bedroom condos, ⚒ Restaurant, picnic area, room service, fans, kitchenettes, refrigerators, pool, windsurfing, boating, boccie, volleyball, 2 bars, shop, playground* ⊟ *MC, V* ⦿ *EP.*

Barahona

The least developed and perhaps most ruggedly beautiful region in the Dominican Republic, Barahona is in the far southwest of the island. Charters occasionally come into the Barahona Airport. Most people fly into Santo Domingo. Buses run here from downtown (but take nearly 5 hours), so many people rent a car for the 3½ hour drive.

★ $ 🏨 **Barceló Bahoruco Beach Resort.** "Maravilloso!" best describes this resort on a gorgeous stretch of virgin beach staggered with rugged cliffs and extending for miles. The trilevel lobby is an artistic mix of West Indian, African-colonial, and contemporary style. Classical music plays, but it's Dominican dance music at the pool complex with its Jacuzzi and swim-up bar, all traversed by wooden bridges. The alfresco buffet restaurant, which is topped by a huge palapa, like the lobby, serves exceptional food. Tasteful guest rooms with balconies face the sea. Ecotours visit national parks and flamingo refuges. Nonguests can buy day passes. ⊠ *Carretera de la Costa, Km 17, Bahoruco, Barahona.* ☎ *809/524– 1111* 🖶 *809/524–6060* ⊕ *www.barcelo-hotels.com* ⬦ *105 rooms* ⚒ *2 restaurants, tennis court, 2 pools, beach, snorkeling, 3 bars, shop, meeting room* ⊟ *AE, MC, V* ⦿ *AI.*

$ 🏨 **Casa Bonita.** In the scenic southwest, this gentrified country inn in the foothills outside Barahona is a charming alternative to high-rise hotels and busy all-inclusives. Julio and Virginia Schiffino expanded their vacation home and added 12 criollo-style cottages with roofs of thatched *cana* palm and rough-hewn walls. Now all have air-conditioning and were redecorated in 2001; all rooms face either the sea or the verdant forest of the Sierra de Bahoruco and two mountain rivers. The openair gallery—adjacent sitting areas—and restaurant overlook the pool area and are tastefully appointed with comfortable sofas and scads of colorful throw pillows. ⊠ *Barahona* ☎ *809/696–0215* 🖶 *809/223–0548* ⬦ *12 cottages* ⚒ *Restaurant, pool, bar* ⊟ *AE, MC, V* ⦿ *MAP.*

Where to Eat

The island's culinary repertoire includes Spanish, Latin American, Italian, Middle Eastern, Indian, Japanese, and Chinese cuisines. The latest trend at the larger, all-inclusive resorts, particularly in Punta Cana, is to offer numerous specialty restaurants, in addition to their buffeteria, to avoid the buffet blues. One megaresort even has a Gourmet Boulevard, with 11 ethnic options, from *haute* French to a Japanese steak house. Another has an authentic Brazilian rodizio, where seven different meats, including sweetbreads, are carved tableside.

The dining scene in Santo Domingo rivals that of any cosmopolitan city, and probably has the largest and finest selection of restaurants anywhere in the Caribbean. *Capitalenos* dress for dinner, and dine late. The crowds pick up after 9 PM, when the Americans are already finishing dessert.

Every year there are more establishments serving contemporary Caribbean dishes as well as places specializing in *nueva cocina Dominicana* (contemporary Dominican cuisine). If seafood is on the menu, it's bound to be fresh.

Among the best Dominican specialties are *sancocho* (a thick stew usually made with five meats and served with rice and avocado slices), *arroz con pollo* (rice with chicken), and *plátanos* (plantains) in all their tasty varieties. Many meals are finished with *majarete*, a cornmeal custard. Shacks and stands that serve cheap eats are an integral part of the culture and landscape. They might offer johnnycakes (fried dough stuffed with everything from chicken to seafood) or pork sandwiches laden with onions, tomatoes, pickles, and seasonings. Presidente is the best local beer; Barceló *anejo* (aged) rum is as smooth as cognac.

What to Wear

In resort areas, shorts and bathing suits under beach wraps are usually (but not always) acceptable at breakfast and lunch. For dinner, long pants, skirts, and collared shirts are the norm. Restaurants tend to be more formal in Santo Domingo, both at lunch and at dinner, with trousers required for men and dresses suggested for women. Ties aren't required anywhere, but jackets are (even at the midday meal) in some of the finer establishments.

Santo Domingo

CARIBBEAN
¢–$

✕ **Meson Bari.** This is what baseball-oriented Dominicans call a "long hitter," since it has been a crowd pleaser for decades. This would be a simple barrio eatery but for the dozen-odd paintings on the wall. Know that this Old World establishment is an artists' hang-out, with writers, poets, and politicians sashaying in for late-night suppers. Go for the yucca empañadas stuffed with minced conch and/or crabmeat. A different twist on eggplant Parmesan is eggplant with red salsa and melted cheese. And you'd be amazed at how good stewed orange peel is. On Saturday nights, the older crowd cuts a rug. ⊠ *Calle Hostos 302 Zona Colonial* ☎ *809/687–4091* ▤ *AE, MC, V.*

ECLECTIC
$–$$$

✕ **Paparazzo.** In the forefront of the restaurant explosion that rocked the culinary boat in Santo Domingo, this restaurant, along with its sister restaurant in Santiago, offers a true example of Dominican fusion food. The chef himself, Perez Breton, a Franco-Mexican-Dominican draws from his multinational repertoire to impress all of your senses. Sushi with land crab wrapped in a thin plantain is one example, Thai sea bass with tamarind sauce another. The classy interior is contemporary, artistic, and romantic, with candles of varying heights and rose petals strewn at the entrance. Music ranges from vintage Johnny Mathis to the latest in Latin. ⊠ *Roberto Pastoriza 313 Naco* ☎ *809/540–5000* ▤ *AE, MC, V.*

ITALIAN
$$$–$$$$

✕ **Da Vinci Restorante.** At the glamorous Meliá Hotel, but with its own entrance, this Italian restaurant is accented with burnished hardwood and is a tribute to the fabled painter. Table settings are elegantly simple. All the traditional classics from carpaccio to risottos and tortellinis are here, but they are given a contemporary twist, as in the veal scallopine with black truffle sauce. Presentation is contemporary, and the plates are artfully painted, particularly for the outstanding desserts. The wine list is admirable, the personalized service totally professional and very caring. Great for a late-night supper, it stays open until 2 AM. ✉ *Meliá Hotel, Av. George Washington 365, El Malecón* ☎ *809/221–6666 Ext. 2510* 🖃 *AE, MC* ☉ *Closed Sun. No lunch.*

$$$–$$$$ ✕ **La Briciola.** This restaurant is the result of an exemplary restoration of the interiors of two adjoining 16th-century colonial buildings. The vaulted-ceiling, stone-and-brick main dining room and the piano bar overlook a courtyard with trees romantically lit at night. Mahogany furnishings and Italian tile work are elegant. Celebrity sightings are frequent. The all-Italian wine list complements excellent homemade pastas, including the velvety gnocchi *fume*. The meat falls away from the bone of the osso buco. A grappa is the perfect accompaniment to the delicious tiramisu. Alas, the Riccobonos have sold their interests to their partners, but one can still expect personalized service. ✉ *Calle Arzobispo Merino 152-A, at Padre Bellini, Zona Colonial* ☎ *809/688–5055* 🍴 *Jacket required* 🍽 *Reservations essential* 🖃 *AE, DC, MC, V* ☉ *Closed Sun.*

$$–$$$ ✕ **Café Billini.** Filled with contemporary Italian furniture (your seat is for sale, as are the books, Venetian vases, grappa in frosted bottles, and Marchessi chocolates), this started out as a place where the ladies come to lunch after they shop 'til they drop at Nuovo Rinascimento. Then an Italian chef came on the scene. Now the same ladies go on the wait list at dinner. Carpaccios are big, from the beef and fresh salmon to illiput, a local fish. You'll find main courses such as veal scaloppini with port, fish, and lobster on the menu, but fresh-made pastas dominate. Take a cappuccino with the mango tiramisu. ✉ *Design Plazoleta Padre Bellini, Zona Colonial* ☎ *809/686–3387* 🖃 *AE, MC, V* ☉ *Closed Sun.*

★ **$$–$$$** ✕ **Spaghettissimo.** This contemporary Italian spot has earned plaudits for its food, wine, and service. Owner Frederic Gollong will charm you with his dry wit and welcoming ways. He gets kudos for the quality and freshness of his cuisine, particularly the imported Angus beef. The carpaccio à la Harry's Bar, finished with an emulsion of mustard and honey, is an example, the seafood cocktail with its shrimp, langostinos, and octopus another. Any of the housemade raviolis, gnocchi, or risottos are guaranteed to be delectable. And there are the creations like red snapper over ravioli filled with radiccio topped by a ginger-cream sauce. ✉ *Paseo de los Locubres 13, Piantini* ☎ *809/565–3708 or 809/547–2650* 🖃 *AE, DC, MC, V.*

JAPANESE ✕ **Aqua.** Sushi aficionados agree that this spot has the best in Santo
★ **$–$$** Domingo. Ask for the famed Aqua roll with avocado, shrimp tempura, and cream cheese or the eggplant rolled and stuffed with ground pork and a sweet-based soy sauce. You must have the fried ice-cream roll for dessert. A study in black and white, this upscale restaurant is crisp and contemporary, with white linen cloths and napkins on black lacquered tables; wooden chopsticks rest on smooth stones. The music is as hip as the two young sisters, Raquel and Mayerlin, who own it. ✉ *Av. Abraham Lincoln, corner of Gustavo Mejía Ricart Plaza Andalucia ll* ☎ *809/541–8781* 🖃 *AE, MC, V.*

MIDDLE EASTERN ✕ **Scherezade.** The exotic decor—Moorish arches, tile work, a terrace
$$$ with orchids—is just one of the reasons why this family-owned restaurant stays busy. The welcome is always warm; the excellent service is provided by waiters who wear embroidered vests and fezzes. Hummus, not butter, comes with the pita bread. A perfect starter is a mixed plate

that includes everything from baba ghanouj to stuffed grape leaves. Main courses run the gamut from shrimp to paella. Desserts include baklava, orange soufflé, and ginger flan. ⊠ *Av. Roberto Pastoriza 226, Naco* ☎ *809/227–2323* ⊟ *AE, DC, MC* ⊗ *Closed Mon.*

Boca Chica/Juan Dolio

SEAFOOD
$$–$$$

✕ **El Pelicano.** Begin with a perfect hazelnut piña colada, then watch the sun drop behind the pier that extends into gin-clear water. The seafood is as fresh as it gets. Professional waiters pamper diners from the arrival of the imaginative soup to the red snapper with an original salsa, to the mango crème brûlée. Although within an all-inclusive resort, the Pelican is open to the public for lunch and dinner. Ten minutes from Las Americas Airport, this is an ideal place to endure a long layover if you are in transit; eat, use the beach and hot tubs, then rinse off with a shower. ⊠ *Coral Hamaca Beach Hotel & Casino, Boca Chica* ☎ *809/523–6506 or 809/523–4611 Ext. 830* ⊟ *AE, MC, V.*

La Romana

★ $$–$$$

✕ **El Pescador.** By day, this is a breezy beach restaurant, as it has always been, overlooking the lagoon smack on Las Minitas Beach. Grilled fish, creative salads, and light fare continue to be on the lunch menu. By night, the crew from the former Casa del Río in Chavón is here. By the light of the moon and with pink and white linen, this becomes a romantic spot with exquisite food. Chef Virginie can prepare a lobster with myriad sauces that you will never have elsewhere. Fresh local fish can be done simply on the grill with three flavored oils or with contemporary French treatments. Call before coming, as the restaurant may close seasonally. ⊠ *Las Minitas Beach, Casa de Campo, La Romana* ☎ *809/959–2262* ⌲ *Reservations essential* ⊟ *AE, MC, V* ⊗ *No dinner Sun.–Wed.*

Samaná

ECLECTIC
¢–$

✕ **El Bohio.** Shrimp fritters, curried chicken with cashews, *lambicitos* (baby conch) in balsamic vinaigrette, and *chillo* (a wonderful local fish) in coconut sauce, are just some of the clever dishes served up by Paco, a long-term island expat and a true Caribbean character. This Frenchman knows his stuff, and lovingly prepares his fave dishes such as shrimp 200; these *camerones* are married with sautéed baby vegetables and spiked with soy sauce, fish sauce, sesame oil, ginger, and cilantro. And then there is the atmosphere, the semicircular bar open to the sea, the French music, the international clientele. The place is cool. ⊠ *Hotel Bahia Las Ballenas Playa Bonita Las Terrenas* ☎ *809/240–6066* ⊟ *AE, MC V.*

SEAFOOD
$$

✕ **Villa Serena.** At the very end of the long road from Puerto Plata, and within the gardens of the Villa Serena Hotel, the restaurant features fresh fish and delicious homemade desserts within prix-fixe menus. Decorated in a romantic, somewhat formal, European style, it is a place to hold hands and look out on the tropical seascape. ⊠ *Las Galeras* ☎ *809/538–0000* ⊟ *MC, V.*

The Amber Coast

AMERICAN
CASUAL
$
Fodor'sChoice
★

✕ **Kite Surf Camp.** This is one of those funky finds that you try to describe to the folks back home. You sit at long tables with a disparate group of strangers from at least three different countries, surrounded by bullrushes poking up from a lagoon. By the light of the moon and torches, you have a good feed for around 10 bucks. Dinner can be perfectly grilled barbecue ribs with a green salad and French fries—plus a shooter of *mamajuana*. In a kind of reverse snobbism, reservations are necessary but there's no phone. You'll have to pass by in the afternoon. ⊠ *Procab Cabarete, Cabarete* ☎ *No phone* ⌲ *Reservations essential* ⊟ *No credit cards.*

CONTINENTAL ✕ **Castle Club.** This couple's home really is their castle, where they stage
$$ wonderful luncheons and dinner parties for visitors, corporations, and
social groups. A huge open-air home with arches and artwork, it over-
looks one of the island's most spectacular valleys. Both Doug and Mar-
guerite Beers are good cooks, and you'll always remember their Caribbean
carrot soup. A coconut sea bass with green rice and a Thai salad fol-
low. The cold lemon soufflé perfectly complements the meal, which is
one of several prix-fixes. The view, the music, the conversation, candles
everywhere, rose petals on antique lace tablecloths, and all for a rea-
sonable price. ✉ *Los Brazos-Cabarete, past Blue Moon Cabarete* ☎ *809/
223–0601* ⌕ *Reservations essential* ▭ *No credit cards.*

ECLECTIC ✕ **Hemingway's Café.** As much a meeting place as a memorial to the late
$–$$ great writer, this café is full of old photos that chronicle his life and serves
dishes whose names bring to mind his work. Everyone, from long-
haired expats to government VIPs, comes to savor For Whom the Bell
Tolls fajitas (in chicken, shrimp, or beef versions) and drink sangria. More
upscale items are also on the menu, from shrimp to Angus beef steaks.
It's a fun place with a young crowd. ✉ *Playa Dorada Plaza, Puerto Plata*
☎ *809/320–2230* ▭ *AE, MC, V.*

INDIAN ✕ **Blue Moon.** This is a happening, 1960s throwback. In the mountains
$$ near Jamoa, Indian fusion cuisine is served family-style on banana leaves
laid out on blue fabric with yellow moons. You sit on pillows in a
thatch-covered hut and eat with your hands. This gets laughable as you
move from the vegetable fritters into the tandoori or curried/coconut
chicken; it's better yet when you go on to the vegetarian dishes like the
eggplant and stewed tomatoes. But you can wash in the pool and then
play the bongos or whatever the rum moves you to do, like spend the
night in one of the artsy bungalows. If you need transportation, reserve
48 hours in advance. ✉ *Cabarete-Los Brazos, Cabarete* ☎ *809/223–
0614* ⌕ *Reservations essential* ▭ *No credit cards.*

SEAFOOD ✕ **Restaurant at Natura Cabanas.** The waves breaking on the coral rock
$$ that frames the virgin beach are reason enough to be here. This alfresco
restaurant has a palapa roof and the unexpected artistry characteristic
of architect/owner Pablo Garimani. It is the seafood for which you
should come: the ceviche, octopus salad with avocado puree, the catch
of the day with pistachio butter, and grilled baby lobster in a Thai sauce
with eggplant. As the sun goes down, riders on horseback pass by, while
Lole, Pablo's wife and the *dueña* of the spa, welcomes patrons in her
charismatic way. ✉ *Natura Cabanas, Perla Marina, Cabarete* ☎ *809/
571–1507* ⌕ *Reservations essential* ▭ *MC, V.*

Punta Cana

CONTEMPORARY ✕ **Restaurant Coccoloba.** This elegant dining room is on the second floor
★ $–$$$ of the newest, most sophisticated club in the country, a golf/beach club
with a gorgeous pool that is steps from the white beach. Oscar de la
Renta, one of the resort's partners, decorated the club, and impressive
details include a huge mirror with metallic grape clusters, a motif that
is carried over to the sconces. The tableware is so chic and colorful—
with plates in different geometric shapes—that it makes the food, al-
ready stellar, taste even better. Take the grilled scallops with raisins, pine
nuts, rosemary, and pineapple mojo—and that's just for starters. ✉ *Punta
Cana Resort & Club, Playa Punta Cana* ☎ *809/221–2262* ⌕ *Reser-
vations essential* ▭ *AE, MC, V* ☉ *No lunch.*

Beaches

The Dominican Republic has more than 1,000 miles (1,600 km) of beaches, including the Caribbean's longest stretch of white sand: Punta Cana/Bávaro. Many beaches are accessible to the public and may tempt you to stop for a swim. That's part of the uninhibited joy of this country. Do be careful, though: some have dangerously strong currents, which may be the reason why they are undeveloped.

Fodor'sChoice ★ **Bahoruco Beach.** Eight miles (13 km) from the town of Barahona, on the isolated south coast, this gorgeous stretch of virgin beach goes on for miles in either direction, with rugged cliffs dropping to golden sand and gin-clear water. It's the ideal wild, undeveloped Caribbean beach.

Boca Chica. The beach closest to Santo Domingo (2 mi [3 km] east of Las Américas Airport, 21 mi [34 km] from the capital) is crowded with city folks on weekends. In the 1900s it was developed by wealthy industrialist Juan Vicini. Entire families moved their households here for the summer. The beach was an immaculate stretch of fine sand, and you could (and still can) walk far out into the gin-clear waters protected by coral reefs. Alas, progress has made its mark; some areas are cluttered with plastic furniture, pizza stands, and cottages. The strip with the mid-rise resorts is well kept but busy. The old Hamaca Hotel was the place to see and be seen; dictator Trujillo kept quarters here, and former President Lionel Fernández stayed (appropriately), in the Presidential Suite.

Cabarete Beach. On the north coast, this beach has ideal wind and surf conditions. It's an integral part of the international windsurfing circuit. Segments of it are strips of golden sand punctuated only by palm trees. In the most commercial area, restaurants and bars are back to back. Moderately priced, the scene is young and fun, with expats and tourists from every imaginable country.

Juan Dolio. A narrow beach of fine white sand, Juan Dolio is a 20-minute drive east of Boca Chica, some 40 minutes from the capital, and has a long row of all-inclusive resorts.

La Romana. This is the site of the 7,000-acre Casa de Campo resort, so you're not likely to find any private place in the sun. The miniature Minitas Beach and lagoon are also here.

Las Terrenas. On the north coast of the Samaná Peninsula, tall palms list toward the sea, the beach is narrow but sandy, and there's plenty of color— vivid blues, greens, and yellows. Two hotels are on the beach at Punta Bonita.

Playa Grande. On the north coast, this long stretch of powdery sand is slated for development. For now the entire northeast coast still seems like one unbroken golden stretch, littered only with kelp, driftwood, and the occasional beer bottle. If you don't mind the lack of facilities, you have your pick of deserted patches.

Puerto Plata. On the north's Amber Coast (so called because of the unusual and abundant appearance of amber here) this is one of the D.R.'s most established resort areas, especially along Playa Dorada. The beaches are of soft beige or white sand, with lots of reefs for snorkeling. The Atlantic waters are great for windsurfing, waterskiing, and fishing. The substantial city of Puerto Plata, with its Victorian vestiges, is a 10-minute cab ride away.

★ **Punta Cana.** The gem of the Caribbean is a 20-mi (32-km) strand of pearl-white sand shaded by swaying coconut palms. It's on the easternmost coast, which includes Bávaro Beach, and it's the home of numerous all-inclusive resorts. There's no major town close to this resort area, however.

Sosúa. Here calm waters gently lap a shore of soft white sand. Unfortunately, the backdrop is a string of tents where hawkers push souvenirs, snacks, and water-sports equipment rentals.

Sports & the Outdoors

Although there's hardly a shortage of activities here, the resorts have virtually cornered the market on sports, including every conceivable water sport. In some cases facilities may be available only to guests of the resorts.

BASEBALL   Baseball is a national passion, and Sammy Sosa is still a legend in his own time. But he is just the most celebrated in a string of Dominican baseball heroes. Triple-A Dominican and Puerto Rican players and some American major leaguers hone their skills in the D.R.'s Professional Winter League, which plays from October through January. Some games are played in the Tetelo Vargas Stadium, in the town of San Pedro de Macorís. As many as 20,000 fans often crowd the **Liga de Béisbol stadium** (☏ 809/567–6371) in Santo Domingo. If your Spanish is good, you can call the stadium or consult local newspaper listings for details on the five teams and game schedules; otherwise, you may want to ask staff at your hotel to arrange for tickets for you.

BOATING   Sailing conditions are ideal, with a constant trade wind. Favorite excursions include day trips to Catalina Island and sunset cruises on the Caribbean. Prices for crewed sailboats of 26 ft and longer with a capacity from 4 to 12 people range from $120 to $700 a day. The **Carib BIC Center** (✉ Cabarete ☏ 809/571–0640) is a renowned windsurfing center that also rents Lasers, 17-ft catamarans, boogie boards, and sea kayaks. Check with **Club Med Punta Cana** (✉ Punta Cana ☏ 809/686–5500) about its boating options. Hobie Cats and pedal boats are available at **Heavens** (✉ Playa Dorada, Puerto Plata ☏ 809/586–5250). **La Marina Casa de Campo** (✉ Calle Barlovento 3 La Romana ☏ 809/523–8646) has much going on, from sailing to motor yachting and socializing at the Casa de Campo Yacht Club. The full-service marina **La Marina Punta Cana** (✉ Punta Cana Resort & Club, Punta Cana ☏ 809/221–2262) rents small boats by the half or full day.

CYCLING   Pedaling is easy on pancake-flat beaches, but there are also some steep hills in the D.R. Several resorts rent bikes. **Dorado Naco** (✉ Playa Dorada Beach, Puerto Plata ☏ 809/320–2019) has bicycle rentals. **Hotel Cofresi** (✉ Puerto Plata ☏ 809/586–2898) rents bikes by the day. **Iguana Mama, Mountain Bike, Hiking & Cultural Vacations** (✉ Cabarete ☏ 800/571–0908) has traditional and mountain bikes and will take you on bike hikes on the flats or test your mettle on the steep grades of the mountain areas. **Jack Tar Village** (✉ Puerto Plata ☏ 809/586–3800) will rent bicycles by the day or week. **Villas Doradas** (✉ Playa Dorada, Puerto Plata ☏ 809/320–3000) has a bike-rental center that is conveniently located within the Playa Dorada strip.

FISHING   Marlin and wahoo are among the fish that folks angle for here (note that fishing is best between January and June). Costs to charter a boat—with a crew, refreshments, bait, and tackle—generally range from $300 to $500 for a half day and from $400 to $700 for a full day. You can arrange fishing trips through **Actividas Acuaticás** (✉ Playa Dorada, Puerto Plata ☏ 809/586–3988). **La Marina Casa de Campo** (✉ Calle Barlovento 3 La Romana ☏ 809/523–8646). At **La Marina Punta Cana** (✉ Punta Cana Resort & Club ☏ 809/221–2262), which is on the southern end of the resort, half-day fishing excursions are available for $75 per person, with a minimum of 2 people.

GOLF   The **Barceló Bávaro Beach Golf and Casino Resort** (⊠ Playa Bávaro ☎ 809/
686–5797) in the Punta Cana area has an 18-hole course, open to its
own guests and those of other hotels. The greens fees for those not staying at Bávaro are $32; golf carts rent for $50. *Golf* magazine has called
FodorśChoice the course at **Casa de Campo** (⊠ La Romana ☎ 809/523–3333) "the finest
★   golf resort in the Caribbean." Greens fees range from $125 to $175; if
you're an avid golfer, though, inquire about the resort's multiday passes
and golf packages. Pete Dye has designed a third 18-hole course close
to Altos de Chavón. It hugs a cliff that overlooks the ocean, as well as
Río Chávon and its palm groves. The **Metro Country Club** (⊠ Juan Dolio
☎ 809/526–3315), east of Santo Domingo on the road to La Romana,
has an 18-hole public course designed by Charles Ankrom. Greens fees
run $35 to $50, and a cart costs $16 to $20. **Playa Dorada** (⊠ Puerto
Plata ☎ 809/320–3344) has an 18-hole Robert Trent Jones–designed
course. Adjacent to the Victoria Resort, it is open to guests of all the
hotels in the complex. Greens fees range from $15 (9 holes) to $27. **Playa
Grande Golf Course** (⊠ Carretera Río San-Juan-Cabrera, Km 9 ☎ 809/
582–0860), between Río San Juan and Cabrera on the north coast, is
described as the "Pebble Beach of the Caribbean," with 10 holes inter-
acting with the Atlantic Ocean. Greens fees to play the 18-hole, par-72
are $57, $32 for nine holes, which includes mandatory carts. Caddies,
also mandatory, are $10 for 18 holes, $5 for nine, and most players dou-
FodorśChoice ble that figure for a tip. **Punta Cana Resort & Club** (⊠ Punta Cana ☎ 809/
★   688–1561 Exts. 101/111) has an 18-hole course by P. B. Dye, with
spectacular views of the Caribbean. Rates (including golf carts) for resort guests are $40 for 9 holes, $65 for 18 holes; for nonguests, 9 holes
are $70, 18 holes $100. The mandatory fees for caddies are $5 for 9
holes, $10 for 18. The resort offers great golf packages. Guests in Santo
Domingo hotels are usually allowed to use the 18-hole course at the **Santo
Domingo Country Club** (⊠ Av. Isabella Guiar, in front of El Club del
Banco Reservo, 40 mins south of Santo Domingo ☎ 809/530–6606) on
weekdays—*after* members have teed off—for $35 (9 or 18 holes).

HIKING   At 10,370 ft, Pico Duarte is the highest peak in the West Indies and a
favorite for serious hikers and mountain climbers. Hire a guide in La
Ciénaga, one hour (8½ mi [14 km]) west of Jarabacoa, if you're prepared and equipped for an arduous 12-mi (19-km) two-day climb; you
can also rent a mule here. The **park service** (☎ 809/472–4204) can assist you in obtaining a guide to lead you up Pico Duarte.

HORSEBACK **Alonzo Horse Ranch** (⊠ Bávaro-Cabeza de Toro ☎ 809/523–3503) has
RIDING   both morning and afternoon rides in the country or on the beach, for
one or two hours, with or without a barbecue. Sunset rides go out daily
(though never on Sundays, the horses' day of rest). On Monday, Wednesday, and Friday, the ride is followed by a barbecue. Prices range from
$20 for an hour, to nearly $45 for two hours with a barbecue. The 250-
acre Equestrian Center at **Casa de Campo** (⊠ La Romana ☎ 809/523–
3333) has something for both western and English riders—a dude ranch,
a rodeo arena, guided trail rides, and jumping and riding lessons. Guided
rides run about $25 an hour; lessons cost $40 an hour. Handsome old-
fashioned carriages are available for hire, too. **The Equestrian Center**
(⊠ Punta Cana Resort & Club, Punta Cana ☎ 809/688–1561 Ext.
7124 or 7124) is across from the main entrance of the resort. The rate
for a 1½-hr trail ride is $24 per person; it winds along the beach, the
golf course, and through tropical forests. A crash course on how to handle your horse precedes the outing. **Rancho Isabella** (⊠ Las Terrenas
☎ 809/847–4849), on the Samaná Peninsula, can give you either a
western or English saddle for one of their 25 mounts. A 1½-hr ride along
the beach is just $10, as is the nocturnal full-moon ride to Boca de la

Diablo. **Sea Horse Ranch** (⊠ Cabarete ☎ 809/571–3880) has an up-scale equestrian center featuring both *paso fino* and dressage instruction for a moderate $25 per hour. Trail riding and endurance riding start at $25 per hour, and reservations are required. The most popular ride is one that includes stretches of beach and a bridle path across a neighboring farm's pasture, replete with wild flowers and butterflies, but tours are custom-designed. And you can feel free to tie your horse to a palm tree and jump into the waves.

HORSE RACING   There are races (flats) year-round at the **Hipódromo V Centenario** (⊠ Av. Las Américas, Santo Domingo ☎ 809/687–6060), daily 8–2:45.

POLO   Casa de Campo is a key place to play or watch the fabled sport of kings. The resort has always prided itself on the polo traditions it has kept alive since its opening some 20 years ago. (For many years a nephew of the Maharajah of Jodhpur, Jaber Singh, was an instructor. One of his pupils was Ramfis Trujillo, son of the former dictator.) Matches are scheduled from October to June, with high-goal players flying in from France and Argentina. Private polo lessons and clinics are available for those who always wanted to give it a shot. There is also a polo field in Santo Domingo.

SCUBA DIVING   Ancient sunken galleons, undersea gardens, and offshore reefs are among the lures here. In the waters off **Sosúa** alone you'll find a dozen dive sites (for all levels of ability) with such catchy names as Three Rocks (a deep, 163-ft [50-m] dive), Airport Wall (98 ft [30 m]), and Pyramids. Some 10 dive schools are represented on Sosúa Beach. Most resorts have dive shops on the premises or can arrange trips for you. In 1979, following a seaquake, three atolls disappeared, providing an opportunity to snorkel forever, according to South African Gerhard Hurst, who, with wife Caron, operates **The Guatapanal Dive Center** (⊠ Guatapanal Hotel, Las Terrenas ☎ 809/240–5050 Ext. 2239). In addition to PADI instruction and certification, they offer a 20-mile sailing trip via catamaran Cabo Cabron, with its turtle population and two-tank, coral wall dive. Another closer dive is Las Ballenas (i.e., "the Whales"), a cluster of four little islands. Popular and inexpensive snorkeling excursions include a half day at El Burro or Playa Jackson with a barbecue or picnic lunch. **Northern Coast Aquasports** (⊠ Sosúa ☎ 809/571–3883) is a five-star PADI instruction center and resort.

TENNIS   There must be a million nets around the island, and most of them can be found at the large resorts. **La Terraza Tennis Club** (⊠ Casa de Campo, La Romana ☎ 809/523–8548) has been called the "Wimbledon of the Caribbean." This 12-acre facility, perched on a hill with sea views, has 13 Har-Tru courts. Nonmembers are welcome (just call in advance); court time costs $20 an hour; lessons are $45 an hour with an assistant pro, $50 with a pro. The **Playa Naco Golf & Tennis Resort** (⊠ Playa Dorada, La Romana ☎ 809/320–6226 Ext. 2568) allows nonguests to play on its four clay courts for $5 an hour—day or night. Lessons from a pro cost $15 an hour. **Punta Cana Resort & Club** (⊠ Playa Punta Cana ☎ 809/ 688–1561 Ext. 7158) has four courts, and tennis clinics Tuesdays and Thursdays. Those who are not resort guests can play for two hours for $26, or $12 an hour for night play; the courts close at 8 PM. **Sea Horse Ranch** (⊠ Cabarete ☎ 809/571–2902) has a tennis center with five clay courts, illuminated for night play, that is open to non-guests. Court time is $7 an hour, with a fee of $4 for night play, $10 to play with the pro, $1.50 for ball boys. Instructions are available in four languages.

WINDSURFING   Between June and October, Cabarete Beach has what many consider to
★   be optimal windsurfing conditions: wind speeds at 20–25 knots and

3- to 15-ft waves. The Professional Boardsurfers Association has included Cabarete in its international windsurfing slalom competition. The novice is also welcome to learn and train on modified boards stabilized by flotation devices. **Carib BIC Center** (✉ Cabarete ☎ 809/571–0640 📠 809/571–0649) offers equipment and instruction. Lessons are generally $30–$35 an hour; boards rent for $20 an hour. A gem of a windsurfing club, this family-owned business has many repeat clients, who made their expansion possible.

For a different take on windsurfing, try kite surfing with **Kitexcite** (✉ Cabarete ☎ 809/571–9509 or 809/838–1225). It's more thrilling and more dangerous than windsurfing because you have a smaller board. Those who are proficient can literally fly through the air. Wake boarding, an alternative to waterskiing—you don't need a boat—is also offered.

Shopping

The hottest items continue to be cigars. Many exquisite hand-wrapped smokes come from the island's rich Ciabo Valley, and Fuente Cigars—handmade in Santiago—are highly prized, but beware of anyone selling cigars on the street. Only reputable cigar shops sell the real thing. You can also buy and enjoy Cuban cigars here, but they can't be brought back to the U.S. legally. Dominican rum and coffee are also good buys. *Mamajuana,* an herbal potion, is the Dominican answer to Viagra. The D.R. is the homeland of designer Oscar de la Renta, and you may want to stop at the chic shops that carry his creations. La Vega is famous for its *diablos cajuelos* (devil masks), which are worn during Carnival. Look also for the delicate, faceless ceramic figurines that symbolize Dominican culture.

Though locally crafted products are often of a high caliber (and often very affordable), expect to pay hundreds of dollars for designer jewelry made of amber and larimar. Larimar—a semiprecious stone the color of the Caribbean Sea—is found on the D.R.'s south coast. Prices vary according to the stone's hue; the rarest and most expensive gems have a milky haze, and the less expensive are solid blue. Amber has been mined extensively between Puerto Plata and Santiago. A fossilization of resin from a prehistoric pine tree, it often encases ancient animal and plant life, from leaves to spiders to tiny lizards. Beware of fakes, which are especially prevalent in street stalls. Visit a reputable dealer or store and ask how to tell the difference between real larimar and amber and imitations.

Bargaining is both a game and a social activity in the D.R., especially with street vendors and at the stalls in El Mercado Modelo. Vendors are disappointed and perplexed if you don't haggle. They're also tenacious, so unless you really plan to buy, don't even stop to look.

Areas & Malls

SANTO DOMINGO The restored buildings of **La Atarazana**, which is across from Alcazar in the Colonial Zone, are filled with shops, art galleries, restaurants, and bars. One of the main shopping streets in the Colonial Zone is **Calle El Conde,** a pedestrian thoroughfare. With the advent of so many restorations and upscale businesses, the dull and dusty stores with dated merchandise are giving way to hip, new shops. Some of the best shops on **Calle Duarte** are north of the Colonial Zone, between Calle Mella and Avenida de Las Américas. **El Mercado Modelo,** a covered market, borders Calle Mella in the Colonial Zone. Vendors here sell a dizzying selection of Dominican crafts. **Plaza Criolla,** on Av. Máximo Gómez, is filled with shops that sell everything from scents to nonsense. **Plaza Central,** between Avs. Winston Churchill and 27 de Febrero, has many top international boutiques. **Unicentro,** on Av. Abraham Lincoln, is a major Santo Domingo mall.

PUERTO PLATA A popular shopping street for costume jewelry and souvenirs is **Calle Beller.** **Playa Dorada Plaza,** on Calle Duarte at Av. 30 de Marzo, is a shopping center in the American tradition. Stores here sell everything from cigars, rum, coffee, and herbal remedies to ceramics, hand-carved wooden ware, and T-shirts; there are Nautica, Guess, and Benetton stores. The seven showrooms of the **Tourist Bazaar,** on Calle Duarte, are in an old mansion with a patio bar.

LA ROMANA **Altos de Chavón** is a re-creation of a Mediterranean village on the grounds of the Casa de Campo resort, where you'll find art galleries, boutiques, and souvenir shops grouped around a cobbled square. Extra special are El Club de Cigaro and the rotating art exhibits at the Museo Arqueológico Regional.

Specialty Items

ART **Arawak Gallery** (⊠ Av. Pasteur 104, Gazcue, Santo Domingo ☎ 809/685–1661) specializes in pre-Columbian artifacts and contemporary pottery and paintings. **Casa Jardin** (⊠ Balacer Gustavo Medjía Ricart 15, Naco, Santo Domingo ☎ 809/565–7978) is the garden studio of abstract painter Ada Balacer. Works by other women artists are also shown; look for pieces by Yolarda Naranjo, known for her modern work that integrates everything from fiberglass, hair, rocks, and wood to baby dresses. **Galería de Arte Mariano Eckert** (⊠ Av. Winston Churchill and Calle Luis F. Tomen, 3rd floor, Evaristo Morales, Santo Domingo ☎ 809/541–7109) focuses on the work of Eckert, an older Dominican artist who's known for his still lifes. **Galería de Arte Nader** (⊠ Rafael Augusto Sanchez 22, between Ensanche Piantini and Plaza Andalucia II, Piantini, Santo Domingo ☎ 809/687–6674 or 809/544–0878) showcases top Dominican artists in various media. The gallery staff is well known in Miami and New York and works with Sotheby's. **Lyle O. Reitzel Art Contemporaneo** (⊠ Plaza Andalucia II, Piantini, Santo Domingo ☎ 809/227–8361) specializes in very contemporary art, such as the very dark paintings of José Garcia Cordero, a Dominican living in Paris. **Mi Pais** (⊠ Calle Villanueva at Antera Mota, Puerto Plata ☎ no phone) is an innovative gallery that showcases paintings and sculptures by such Dominican artists as Orlando Menicucci, Servio Certad, Pedro Terrero, and Celia Vargas Nadel.

CLOTHING **Buongiorno Principini** (⊠ Plaza Andalucia 11, Santo Domingo ☎ 809/549–6322) has darling gifts for your precious little ones. These children's togs are as chic as their brand names—Baby Dior and Cacherel (French), Estupenderia and Mona Lisa (Italian). The tiny purses and shoes have European style, as do the bathing suits and white dresses. There are European maternity clothes, too, all of which are about 25% less than stateside. If luck is with you, you might catch a 50% off sale. **Plaza Central** (⊠ Avs. Winston Churchill and 27 de Febrero, Piantini, Santo Domingo ☎ 809/541–5929) is a major shopping center with a Jenny Polanco shop (an upscale Dominican designer) and other high-end stores.

DUTY-FREE ITEMS **Centro de los Héroes** (⊠ Av. George Washington, El Malecón, Santo Domingo) sells liquor, cameras, and the like.

HANDICRAFTS **Artesanía Lime** (⊠ Autopista Duarte, 1½ mi [2½ km] from Santiago, Santiago ☎ 809/582–3754) is worth a visit for its mahogany carvings and Carnival masks. **Collector's Corner Gallery and Gift Shop** (⊠ Plaza Shopping Center, Calle Duarte at Av. 30 de Marzo, Puerto Plata ☎ no phone) has souvenirs, including many made of amber. **Felipe & Co.** (⊠ El Conde 105, Zona Colonial, Santo Domingo ☎ 809/689–581) has a fascinating assortment of Dominican crafts and artwork, coffee, inexpensive "free spirit" jewelry, and some tropical clothing. **Taimascaros** (✉ Camino Libre 70, Sosúa ☎ 809/571–3138) is a group of artists and Carnival goers organized by artist Jacinto Manuel Beard Gomez to preserve both the event and Dominican culture. They make their own masks and costumes, and Jacinto's striking artwork incorporates Carnival elements.

HOME FURNISHINGS **Nuovo Rinascimento** (✉ Plazoleta Padre Billini, Zona Colonial, Santo Domingo ☎ 809/686–3387) is in the grandiose space formerly occupied by Italian designer Versace. This exquisite emporium, replete with contemporary furniture like leather sofas by Ferrari and antiques such as iron canopy beds, has a room with a treasure full of Venetian linens and towels. Shipping can be arranged. The wooden hacienda doors open to a world of white sculptures and an inner courtyard with a pool dotted with lily pads. It is surrounded by megacandles, for sale at the retail shop within their Café Bellini.

JEWELRY **Ambar Tres** (✉ La Atarazana 3, Zona Colonial, Santo Domingo ☎ 809/688–0474) carries a wide selection of items made with amber, including high-end jewelry. If you tour the in-house museum, you'll have an even deeper appreciation of the gem.

TOBACCO **Cigar King** (✉ Calle Conde 208, Baguero Bldg., Zona Colonial, Santo Domingo, ☎ 809/686–4987) keeps Dominican and Cuban cigars in a temperature-controlled cedar room **Santo Domingo Cigar Club** (✉ Av. George Washington 367, El Malecón, Santo Domingo ☎ 809/221–1483), in the lobby of the Renaissance Jaragua Hotel and Casino, is a great place to find yourself a good smoke.

Nightlife

★ Santo Domingo's nightlife is vast and ever-changing. Check with the concierges and hip *capitalenos*. Get a copy of the *Vacation Guide* and the newspaper *Touring*—both available free at the tourist office and at hotels—to find out what's happening. Look in the *Santo Domingo News* and the *Puerto Plata News* for listings of events.

CAFÉS **Cigarro Café** (✉ Av. Máximo Gómez and Av. 27 de Febrero, Gazcue, Santo Domingo ☎ 809/688–7038) in the Grand Hotel Lina is the place to go for high-quality cigars and coffee, with an appealing assortment of gadgets for the smoker. Cigar brands include the country's best—Aurturo Fuente and Fuente Fuente Opus X—the result of the family's dream to create the world's finest cigar. **Doubles** (✉ Calle Arzobispo Merino 54, Zona Colonial, Santo Domingo ☎ 809/688–3833) looks like a friend's place—that is, if you have a friend who has a hip sense of interior design and would mix rattan furniture, antiques, subdued lighting, and candles in a space that's centuries old. Spanish tiles add interest to this atmospheric piano bar. Don't think of the sandwich when you visit **Monté Cristo** (✉ Av. Jose Armado Soler at Av. Abraham Lincoln, Serralles, Santo Domingo ☎ 809/542–5000), although the crowds can sandwich you in at this pub. The clientele spans the decades, music crosses the Americas, and there is a small dance floor. Both hot and cold tapas and sandwiches are served. Open after work until whenever, usually 4 AM, and there's no cover. It is the only club where there is anything happening on a Tuesday night, which is a wine tasting. Wednesdays is a Boston Ball, Thursday is Yuppy Night. At **Punto Y Corcho** (✉ Av. Abraham Lincoln at Gustavo Mejía Ricart, Piantini, Santo Domingo ☎ 809/683–0533), on Plaza Andalucia, wine (by the glass and bottle) and local and international liquors are the order of the night. This is a great date and late-night spot, and tends to appeal to an older crowd.

CASINOS Well into the wee small hours, casinos keep the action hot. Gambling here is more a sideline than a raison d'être. Most casinos are in the larger hotels of Santo Domingo, a couple in Playa Dorada, and more now in Punta Cana. All offer blackjack, craps, and roulette and are generally open daily 3 PM–4 AM. You must be 18 to enter, and jackets are required.

Barceló Gran Hotel Lina Spa & Casino (⊠ Av. Máximo Gomez and Av. 27 de Febrero, Gazcue, Santo Domingo ☎ 809/563–5000) is a stalwart landmark drawing from its business and convention trade. **Hispaniola** (⊠ Av. Independencia and Av. Abraham Lincoln, Zona Universidad, Santo Domingo ☎ 809/221–7111) attracts a younger crowd, which goes back and forth between the tables and the Neon Disco. **Meliá Santo Domingo Casino** (⊠ Av. George Washington 365 El Malecón Santo Domingo ☎ 809/221–6666) is a hot spot, with exceptional entertainment. The casino at the **Occidental El Embajador** (⊠ Av. Sarasota 65, Bella Vista, Santo Domingo ☎ 809/533–2131) is usually quiet, but can heat up late. The **Renaissance Jaragua Hotel** (⊠ Av. George Washington 367, El Malecón, Santo Domingo ☎ 809/686–2222) has one of the largest and busiest gaming operations, and its live entertainment and restaurants have added to its popularity.

Casino Santana Beach (⊠ Santana Beach, Between La Romana and San Pedro Macoris ☎ 809/412–1104, 412-1051) is surprisingly sophisticated. It's right on the beach; there's a tropical terrace and an aquarium behind the roulette wheel. Drinks are on the house while you play, be it blackjack, Caribbean poker, or the slots. The live music is nice, not crazy.

The casino at the **Occidental Gran Hotel Playa Dorada** (⊠ Playa Dorada, Puerto Plata ☎ 809/320–3988) is *the* most appealing gambling option, with a pleasing mix of CDs and live music that won't damage your eardrums.

DANCE CLUBS Dancing is as much a part of the culture here as eating and drinking. As in other Latin countries, after dinner it's not a question of *whether* people will go dancing but *where* they'll go. Move with the rhythm of the merengue and the pulsing beat of salsa (adopted from neighboring Puerto Rico). Just about every resort in Puerto Plata and Punta Cana has live entertainment, dancing, or both. Many clubs stay open until dawn or until the last couple gives it up.

Bella Bleus (⊠ Av. George Washington El Malecón, Santo Domingo ☎ 809/622–5452) is next to the restaurant Vesuvio. This disco, owned by baseball star Jose Rio, attracts baseball players, business types, and tourists. A study in blue, its walls are adorned with paintings of ballerinas (the bellas). It has an aquarium and a water view, particularly from its open-air terrace. This is one spot that draws an older crowd, not that they don't have some twentysomethings. Closed Mondays. **The Monaco Disco Club** (⊠ Av. John F. Kennedy at Horacio Blanco Fonbona, La Agustina, Santo Domingo ☎ 809/562–6613) is off the tourist path and populated primarily with young, upscale Dominicans. Large, yet still crowded on weekends, it has a sense of humor. For example, on Halloween you could find mummies rising out of their coffins and crypts near the parking lot. Contemporary Latin music dominates. Older couples head to the VIP area. The room is closed on Tuesdays. **Neon Lounge & Discotheque** (⊠ Hotel Hispaniola, Av. Abraham Lincoln at Av. Independencia, Zona Universidad, Santo Domingo ☎ 809/532–0054 or 809/532–0172) has been perennially popular for over 25 years. On Fat Tuesdays (à la New Orleans), live jazz bands play from 7:00 PM. You must be 22 years old to enter, and a strict dress code of no caps, T-shirts, or sneakers is enforced. Closed Mondays.

Andromeda (✉ Playa Dorada, Puerto Plata ☎ 809/586–5250) is a happening dance club cum video bar with frenetic energy and a high-decibel Latin/Afro beat. Dominicans come here from town to "work out" and show the tourists how dancing is done. **Crazy Moon** (✉ Paradise Beach Club and Casino, Playa Dorada, Puerto Plata ☎ 809/320–3663) is a megaspace that's often back-to-back, wall-to-wall. Latin music and hip-hop mixed with Euro sounds are popular. Rest up from time to time at the horseshoe bar, so that you can keep the pace until the wee small hours of the *mañana*.

Exploring the Dominican Republic

Santo Domingo

Parque Independencia separates the old city from the modern Santo Domingo, a sprawling, noisy city with a population of close to 2 million. (Note: hours and admission charges to sights are erratic.)

Numbers in the margin correspond to points of interest on the Santo Domingo map.

WHAT TO SEE
Fodor'sChoice
★

Spanish civilization in the New World began in Santo Domingo's 12-block **Zona Colonial.** Walking its narrow, cobbled streets, it's easy to imagine this old city as it was when the likes of Columbus, Cortés, Ponce de León, and pirates sailed in and out and colonists were settling themselves. Tourist brochures tout that "history comes alive here"—a surprisingly truthful statement.

A quick taxi tour of the old section takes about an hour; if you're interested in history, you'll want to spend a day or two exploring the many old "firsts," and you'll want to do it in the most comfortable shoes you own. Buy a walking tour map in English. Or you can jump on one of the green open-air trolleys that pass the Parque Colón every hour; a 45-minute tour costs about $7, a full-blown two-hour excursion $20. Multilingual guides hit the highlights, and you can hop out to take photos.

④ **Alcazar de Colón.** The castle of Don Diego Colón, built in 1517, has 40-inch-thick coral-limestone walls. The Renaissance-style structure, with its balustrade and double row of arches, has strong Moorish, Gothic, and Isabelline influences. The 22 rooms are furnished in a style to which the viceroy of the island would have been accustomed—right down to the dishes and the viceregal shaving mug. ✉ *Plaza de España, off Calle Emiliano Tejera at ft of Calle Las Damas, Zona Colonial* ☎ *809/687–5361* ✍ *RD$50* ☉ *Mon. and Wed.–Fri. 9–5, Sat. 9–4, Sun. 9–1.*

⑧ **Calle Las Damas.** The Street of the Ladies was named after the elegant ladies of the court who, in the Spanish tradition, promenaded in the evening. Here you'll see a sundial dating from 1753 and the Casa de los Jesuitas, which houses a fine research library for colonial history as well as the Institute for Hispanic Culture; admission is free, and it's open weekdays 8–4:30.

⑨ **Casa de Bastidas.** There's a lovely inner courtyard here with tropical plants and galleries for temporary exhibition. ✉ *Calle Las Damas, off Calle El Conde, Zona Colonial* ☎ *No phone* ✍ *Free* ☉ *Tues.–Sun. 9–5.*

③ **Casa del Cordón.** This structure, built in 1503, is the western hemisphere's oldest surviving stone house. Columbus's son, Diego Colón, viceroy of the colony, and his wife lived here until the Alcazar was finished. It was in this house, too, that Sir Francis Drake was paid a ransom to prevent him from totally destroying the city. ✉ *Corner of Calle Emiliano Tejera and Calle Isabel la Católica (within the Banco Popular), Zona Colonial* ☎ *No phone* ✍ *Free* ☉ *Weekdays 8:30–4:30.*

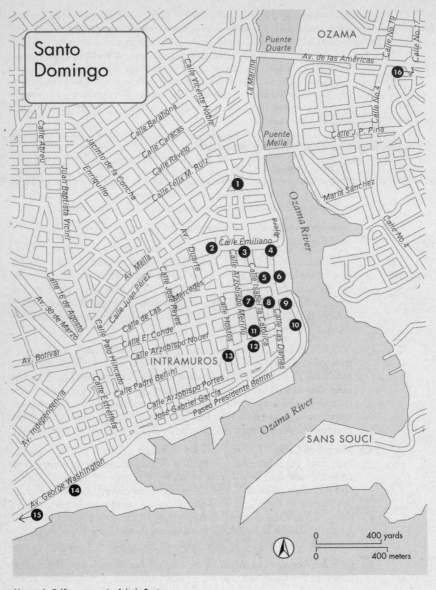

Santo Domingo

OZAMA

Puente Duarte

Av. de las Américas

Puente Mella

Ozama River

María Sánchez

INTRAMUROS

Ozama River

SANS SOUCI

0   400 yards

0   400 meters

⑫ **Casa de Tostado.** The house was built in the early 16th century and was the residence of writer Don Francisco Tostado. Note its unique twin Gothic windows. It now houses the Museo de la Familia Dominicana (Museum of the Dominican Family), which has exhibits on well-heeled 19th-century Dominican society. The house, garden, and antiquities have all been restored. ⊠ *22 Calle Padre Bellini, near Calle Arzobispo Meriño, Zona Colonial* ☎ *809/689–5000* ✍ *RD$50* ◑ *Thurs.–Tues. 9–2.*

⑪ **Catedral Santa María la Menor.** The coral-limestone facade of the first cathedral in the New World towers over the south side of the Parque Colón. Spanish workmen began building the cathedral in 1514, but left to search for gold in Mexico. The church was finally finished in 1540. Its facade is composed of architectural elements from the late Gothic to the lavish plateresque styles. Inside, the high altar is made of hammered silver. A museum is being built for the cathedral's treasures. ⊠ *Calle Arzobispo Meriño, Zona Colonial* ☎ *809/689–1920* ✍ *Free* ◑ *Mon.–Sat. 9–4; Sun. masses begin at 6 AM.*

♨ ⑯ **El Faro a Colón.** This striking, laser-powered lighthouse and monument, dedicated to Christopher Columbus, is shaped like a pyramid cross (although from ground level it looks like a giant concrete casket). Its inauguration coincided with the 500th anniversary (1992) of the great navigator's landing on the island. The complex holds the tomb of Columbus and six museums. ⊠ *Av. España, El Faro* ☎ *809/591–1492* ✍ *RD$50* ◑ *Tues.–Sun. 10–5.*

⑥ **Hostal Palacio Nicolás de Ovando.** This was once the residence of Nicolás de Ovando, one of the principal organizers of the colonial city. It was later transformed into a hotel and is to become a Sofitel, most likely by 2004. Call the Hotel Sofitel Frances for the latest update. ⊠ *Calle Las Mercedes 44, Zona Colonial* ☎ *809/685–9331.*

⑬ **Iglesia y Convento Domínico.** This graceful building with the rose window is the Dominican Church and Convent, founded in 1510. In 1538 Pope Paul III visited here and was so impressed with the lectures on theology that he granted the church and convent the title of university, making it the oldest institution of higher learning in the New World. ⊠ *Calle Padre Bellini and Av. Duarte, Zona Colonial* ☎ *809/682–3780* ✍ *Free* ◑ *Tues.–Sun. 9–6.*

❶ **Iglesia Santa Bárbara.** This combination church and fortress, the only one of its kind in Santo Domingo, was completed in 1562. ⊠ *Av. Mella, between Calle Isabel la Católica and Calle Arzobispo Meriño, Zona Colonial* ☎ *809/682–3307* ✍ *Free* ◑ *Weekdays 8–noon; Sun. masses begin at 6 AM.*

⑭ **El Malecón.** Avenida George Washington, better known as the Malecón, runs along the Caribbean and has tall palms, cafés, hotels, and sea breezes.

❷ **Monasterio de San Francisco.** Constructed between 1512 and 1544, the San Francisco Monastery contained the church, chapel, and convent of the Franciscan order. Sir Francis Drake's demolition squad significantly damaged the building in 1586, and in 1673 an earthquake nearly finished the job, but when it's floodlit at night, the eerie ruins are dramatic indeed. The Spanish government has donated money to turn this into a beautiful culture center; work should be completed by 2004. ⊠ *Calle Hostos at Calle Emiliano, Zona Colonial* ☎ *809/687–4722.*

❺ **Pantheon Nacional.** The National Pantheon (circa 1714) was once a Jesuit monastery and later a theater. ⊠ *Calle Las Damas, near corner of*

Calle de Las Mercedes, Zona Colonial ☎ *No phone* ✉ *Free* ⊙ *Mon.–
Sat. 10–5.*

❼ Parque Colón. The huge statue of Christopher Columbus in the park named
after him dates from 1897 and is the work of French sculptor Gilbert.
Like all the parks in the Zona Colonial, this one is being restored. ⊠ *El
Conde at Arzobispo Meriño, Zona Colonial.*

⓯ Plaza de la Cultura. Landscaped lawns, modern sculptures, and sleek buildings make up the Plaza de la Cultura. There are several museums and
a theater here. The works of 20th-century Dominican and foreign artists
are displayed in the **Museo de Arte Moderno** (Museum of Modern Art;
☎ 809/682–8260). Native sons include Elvis Aviles, an abstract painter
whose works have a lot of texture. His art combines Spanish influences
with Taíno Indian and other Dominican symbols. Tony Capellan is one
of the best-known artists, representing the D.R. in major international
exhibitions. The **Museo de Historia Natural** (Museum of Natural History; ☎ 809/689–0106) examines the flora and fauna of the island. The
Museo del Hombre Dominicano (Museum of Dominican Peoples;
☎ 809/687–3623) traces the migrations of Indians from South America through the Caribbean islands. The **Teatro Nacional** (National Theater; ☎ 809/687–3191) stages performances in Spanish. ✉ *Museums
RD50 each* ⊙ *Tues.–Sat. 10–5.*

❿ Torre del Homenaje. You won't have any trouble spotting the Tower of
Homage in Ft. Ozama. The fort has a brooding crenellated tower that
still guards the Ozama River. ⊠ *Paseo Presidente Bellini, Zona Colonial* ☎ *No phone* ✉ *RD50* ⊙ *Tues.–Sun. 8–7.*

The East Coast

Las Américas Highway (built by the dictator Trujillo so his son could
race his sports cars) runs east along the coast from Santo Domingo to
La Romana—a two-hour drive. Midway are the well-established resort
areas of Juan Dolio and Sammy Sosa's hometown, San Pedro de Macoris. East of La Romana are Punta Cana and Bávaro, glorious beaches
on the sunrise side of the island. Along the way is Higüey, an undistin-
guished collection of ramshackle buildings notable only for its controversial church and shrine (someone had a vision of the Virgin Mary here),
which resembles a pinched, concrete McDonald's arch.

*Numbers in the margin correspond to points of interest on the Dominican
Republic map.*

WHAT TO SEE   **Altos de Chavón.** Cattle and sugarcane used to be the two big mainstays
★ ⓳   around La Romana. That was before Gulf & Western created (and then
sold) the Casa de Campo resort, which is a very big business indeed.
Altos de Chavón, a re-creation of a 16th-century Mediterranean village
and an artists' colony, is on the resort grounds. It sits on a bluff overlooking the Río Chavón, about 3 mi (5 km) east of the main facility of
Casa de Campo. There are cobblestone streets lined with lanterns,
wrought-iron balconies, wooden shutters, and courtyards swathed with
bougainvillea. More than a museum piece, this village is a place where
artists live, work, and play. Dominican and international painters, sculptors, and artisans come here to teach sculpture, pottery, silk-screen
printing, weaving, dance, and music at the art school, which is affiliated with New York's Parsons School of Design. They work in their studios and crafts shops selling their finished wares. The village also has
an archaeological museum, five restaurants, and a 5,000-seat amphitheater where Julio Iglesias has entertained. The focal point of Altos
de Chavón is **Iglesia St. Stanislaus,** which is named after the patron saint
of Poland in tribute to Polish pope John Paul II, who visited the D.R.

in 1979 and left some of the ashes of St. Stanislaus behind. The charming chapel is the romantic setting for many a wedding, with honeymoons at the resort.

㉚ Isla Saona. Off the east coast of Hispaniola lies this island, now a national park inhabited by sea turtles, pigeons, and other wildlife. Caves here were once used by Indians. The beaches are beautiful, and legend has it that Columbus once strayed ashore here. Getting here, on catamarans and other excursion boats, is half the fun.

㉗ Parque de los Tres Ojos. About 1½ mi (2½ km) outside the capital is the Park of the Three Eyes. The "eyes" are cool blue pools peering out of deep limestone caves.

㉘ San Pedro de Macorís. The national sport and the national drink are both well represented in this city, an hour or so east of Santo Domingo. Some of the country's best baseball games are played in Tetelo Vargas Stadium. Many Dominican baseball stars have their roots here, including George Bell, Tony Fernandez, Jose Río, and Sammy Sosa. The Macorís Rum distillery is on the eastern edge of the city. During the 1920s this was a very important town, and mansions from that era are being restored by the Office of Cultural Patrimony, as are some remaining vestiges of 16th-century architecture and the town's cathedral. Outside town is Juan Dolio, a beach and resort area popular with Dominicans and foreign visitors.

The Amber Coast

The Autopista Duarte ultimately leads (a three- to four-hour drive) from Santo Domingo to the Amber Coast, so called because of its large, rich amber deposits. The coastal area around Puerto Plata is a region of splashy resorts and megadevelopments; the north coast has more than 70 mi (110 km) of beaches, with condominiums and villas going up fast. The farther east you go from Puerto Plata and its little sister, Sosúa, the prettier and less spoiled the scenery becomes. The autopista runs past Cabarete, a village that's a popular windsurfing haunt, and Playa Grande. Its white-sand beach is miraculously unspoiled.

WHAT TO SEE

㉒ Laguna Grí-Grí. This swampland looks as if it's smack out of Louisiana bayou country. It also has a cool blue grotto that almost outdoes the Blue Grotto of Capri. Laguna Grí-Grí is only about 90 minutes west of Puerto Plata, in Río San Juan (ask your hotel concierge for directions off the autopista).

㉕ Mt. Isabel de Torres. Southwest of Puerto Plata, this mountain soars 2,600 ft above sea level. On it there are botanical gardens and a huge statue of Christ. Cable cars take you to the top for a spectacular view. Know that they usually wait until the cars are filled to capacity before going up—and that's cozy. ✉ *Off Autopista Duarte, follow the signs* ☎ *No phone* ✇ *Cable car RD$100* ☉ *Cable car: Mon.–Tues. and Thurs.–Sun. 9–5.*

㉔ Puerto Plata. Although now quiet and almost sleepy, this was a dynamic city in its heyday. You can get a feeling for this past in the magnificent Victorian gazebo in the central Parque Independencia. On Puerto Plata's own Malecón, the Fortaleza de San Felipe protected the city from many a pirate attack and was later used as a political prison. Big changes are afoot in this town, which is just realizing what it needs to do to become a tourist destination. The Office of Cultural Patrimony, which has done an admirable job of pulling the Zona Colonial from the darkness to a place to be seen, has set its sights on Puerto Plata. Simultaneously, a group of private business owners and investors has been conferencing to come up with a long-term plan for beautifying this city, which has a wonderful town square and hundreds of classic, wooden gingerbread buildings. Mansions are being restored and opened for tours, as has the lighthouse. Puerto Plata is the home of the **Museo de Ambar Dominicano** (Dominican Amber Museum), which is in a lovely old galleried mansion. The museum displays and sells the D.R.'s national stone. Semiprecious, translucent amber is actually fossilized pine resin that dates from about 50 million years ago, give or take a few millennia. Shops on the museum's first floor sell amber, souvenirs, and ceramics. ⊠ *Calle Duarte 61* ☎ *809/586– 2848* ▣ *RD$15* ☼ *Mon.–Sat. 9–5.*

㉑ Samaná. Back in 1824, a sailing vessel called the *Turtle Dove,* carrying several hundred escaped American slaves from the Freeman sisters' underground railway, was blown ashore in Samaná. The escapees settled and prospered, and today their descendants number several thousand. The churches here are Protestant; the worshippers live in villages called Bethesda, Northeast, and Philadelphia; and the language spoken is an odd 19th-century form of English mixed with Spanish.

Sportfishing at Samaná is considered to be among the best in the world. In addition, about 3,000 humpback whales winter off the coast of Samaná from December to March. Major whale-watching expeditions are being organized and should boost the region's economy without scaring away the world's largest mammals.

Samaná makes a fine base for exploring the area's natural splendors. Most hotels on the peninsula arrange tours to Los Haitises National Park, a remote, unspoiled rain forest with limestone knolls, crystal lakes, mangrove swamps teeming with aquatic birds, and caves stippled with Taíno petroglyphs. Postcard-perfect Las Terrenas is a remote stretch of gorgeous, pristine beaches on the north coast of the Samaná Peninsula, attracting surfers and windsurfers, the young and offbeat. There are modest seafood restaurants, a dusty but burgeoning main street in the town of Las Terrenas, a small airfield, an all-inclusive resort, and several congenial hotels right on the beach. If you're happy just hanging out, drinking rum, and soaking up the sun, this is the place, one that is really catching on. The new highway that will come directly from Las Americas will connect Samaná to Santo Domingo in less than two hours. Slated to be finished by 2004, it's predicted that it will bring major changes. Land has been sold in Samaná, and developers are poised to begin. A new airport should bring yet more progress. It will be built in the Catay area and will serve Sanchez, Nagua, and Samaná.

㉓ Sosúa. This small community was settled during World War II by 600 Austrian and German Jews. After the war many of them returned to Europe or went to the United States, and most who remained married Dominicans. Only a few Jewish families reside in the community today, and there's only the original one-room, wooden synagogue.

Sosúa is called Puerto Plata's little sister, and new hotels and condos are going up at breakneck speed. It actually consists of two communities— El Batey, the modern hotel development, and Los Charamicos, the old quarter—separated by a cove and one of the island's prettiest beaches. The sand is soft and white, the water crystal clear and calm. The walkway above the beach is packed with tents filled with souvenirs, pizzas, and even clothing for sale—a jarring note. Two new fine hotels have opened and condos are springing up. The town fathers are doing their best to prevent this resort area from becoming too garish.

The Cibao Valley

The heavily trafficked four-lane, divided highway north from Santo Domingo, known as the Autopista Duarte, cuts through the lush banana plantations, rice and tobacco fields, and royal poinciana trees of the Cibao Valley. Along the road are stands where for a few pesos you can buy pineapples, mangoes, avocados, *chicharrones* (fried pork rinds), and fresh fruit drinks.

28 Jarabacoa. Nature lovers should consider a trip to Jarabacoa, in the mountainous region known rather wistfully as the Dominican Alps. There's little to do in the town itself but eat and rest up for excursions on foot, horseback, or by motorbike taxi to the surrounding waterfalls and forests—quite incongruous in such a tropical country. Other activities include adventure tours, particularly white-water rafting or canoe trips, jeep safaris, and paragliding. Accommodations in the area are rustic but homey.

27 La Vega Vieja. Founded in 1495 by Columbus, La Vega is the site of one of the oldest settlements in the New World. You may find the tour of the ruins of the original settlement, Old La Vega, rewarding. About 3 mi (5 km) north of La Vega is Santo Cerro (Holy Mount), site of a miraculous apparition of the Virgin and therefore many local pilgrimages. The Convent of La Merced is here, and the views of the Cibao Valley are breathtaking. The town's remarkable Concepción de la Vega Church was constructed in 1992 to commemorate the 500th anniversary of the discovery of America. The unusual modern Gothic style—all curvaceous concrete columns, arches, and buttresses—is striking.

La Vega is also celebrated for its Carnival, featuring haunting devil masks. These papier-mâché creations are intricate, fanciful gargoyles painted in surreal colors; spiked horns and real cow's teeth lend an eerie authenticity. Several artisans work in dark, cramped studios throughout the area; their skills have been passed down for generations. Closest to downtown is the art studio of José Luís Gomez. Ask any local (tip 10–20 pesos) to guide you to his atelier (☎ no phone). José speaks no English but will show you the stages of a mask's development. He sells the masks for $50–$60, a great buy, considering the craftsmanship.

26 Santiago de los Caballeros. The second city of the D.R., where many past presidents were born, sits about 90 mi (145 km) northwest of Santo Domingo. This industrial center has a surprisingly charming, provincial feel. A massive monument honoring the restoration of the republic guards the entrance to the city. Traditional yet progressive, Santiago is still relatively new to the tourist scene, but some fine, contemporary restaurants are thriving, and an extravagant hotel is under construction. It's worth setting aside a day or two to explore this city, which dates from the 1500s. There are colonial-style buildings with wrought-iron details and tiled porticos as well as many homes reflecting a Victorian influence, with the requisite gingerbread latticework and fanciful colors. An original route from centuries past, the highway between Santiago and Puerto Plata is dotted with sugar mills. The Office of Cultural Patrimony will be overseeing their restoration.

Santiago is a center for processing tobacco leaf. The Fuente factory is here, the family-owned cigar company that enjoys an enviable reputation for quality worldwide. Arturo Fuente, the founder, was born in Cuba. His background and knowledge helped Fuente cigars to outdistance Cuba's *Habanos* in popularity. His son, Carlos Fuente, Jr., has brought them to international attention by his contemporary thinking and skill in marketing. Of course, the fact that Dominican stogies can legally be bought or brought into the states, has helped considerably. You can gain an appreciation for the art and skill of Dominican (similar to Cuban) cigar making with a tour of **E. Leon Jiménez Tabacalera** (☎ 809/563–1111 or 809/535–5555).

The Southwest

③⓪ Barahona. Here mountains, carpeted with rain forests and laced with streams, slope down to white stretches of sand and into the Caribbean. You can bathe in the cascades of icy mountain rivers or in hot thermal springs surrounded by dense foliage, *llanai* vines, and fruit trees. Barahona is a tropical Garden of Eden. Be tempted to come while you and yours can still have it to yourself.

②⑨ Lago Enriquillo. The largest lake in the Antilles is near the Haitian border. The salt lake is also the lowest point in the Antilles: 114 ft below sea level. It encircles wild, arid, and thorny islands that serve as sanctuaries for such exotic birds and reptiles as flamingoes, iguanas, and caimans—the indigenous crocodile. The area is targeted by the government for improvements and infrastructure designed for ecotourists, but progress is slow.

DOMINICAN REPUBLIC A TO Z

To research prices, get advice from other travelers, and book travel arrangements, visit www.fodors.com.

AIR TRAVEL

Aeromar flies nonstop from Miami to Santo Domingo daily. Air DCE (formerly Air ALM) connects Santo Domingo to St. Maarten and Curaçao. For U.K. residents, Air France has multiple daily flights from London to Paris which now has direct service into Santo Domingo four times a week and direct flights into Punta Cana three times a week. Air Atlantic has service from Miami and San Juan into Las Américas on Monday, Wednesday, and Friday. Air Caraïbes serves Santo Domingo, connecting it with the French West Indies—Guadeloupe, Les Saintes, Marie-Galante, La Désirade, Martinique, St. Maarten, St. Barths, and St. Lucia. Air Transat serves Santo Domingo from Montréal, Toronto, Vancouver, Victoria, and the maritime provinces; it now has three weekly flights into La Romana/Casa de Campo Airport. American Airlines has the most extensive service to the D.R. It flies nonstop from New York and Miami to Santo Domingo, Puerto Plata, Punta Cana, and La Romana/Casa de Campo Airport and offers connections to both Santo Domingo and Puerto Plata from San Juan, Puerto Rico. From San Juan, American Eagle has six daily flights to Santo Domingo, two daily flights to La Romana/Casa de Campo Airport, two flights daily to Santiago, and several flights weekly to Punta Cana. Continental flies nonstop from Newark to Puerto Plata and Santo Domingo. Queen Air flies from New York to Santo Domingo four times a week. US Airways offers daily service into Santo Domingo directly from Philadelphia; flights from other U.S. cities must connect in Philadelphia. US Airways also has frequent service to San Juan, from Philadelphia, Pittsburgh, and Charlotte, where you can connect for flights to Santo Domingo, Punta Cana, Puerto Plata, and Santiago.

🛪 **Aeromar** ☎ 877/237-6672. **Air Atlantic** ☎ 809/687-4569. **Air Caraïbes** ☎ 011-590-590-21-11-9 [in Guadeloupe]. **Air DCE** ☎ 809/687-4569. **Air France** ☎ 809/686-8432. **Air Transat** ☎ 416/259-1118. **American Airlines/American Eagle** ☎ 809/542-5151. **Continental** ☎ 809/562-6688. **Queen Air** ☎ 809/565-4041. **US Airways** ☎ 809/540-0505.

AIRPORTS

The Dominican Republic has four major airports. The two busiest are Las Américas International Airport, about 20 mi (32 km) outside Santo Domingo, and Puerto Plata International Gregorio Luperon Airport, about

15 mi (24 km) east of Puerto Plata on the north coast, the latter bene-fiting from a much needed, multiphase renovation project. The Punta Cana International Airport is an experience; the terminal building is a thatched-roof structure with cane partitions; it covers several acres and is surrounded by gardens. The La Romana/Casa de Campo International Airport has a creative design that replicates a sugar factory—the area was originally a sugarcane plantation. A fifth, Barahona International Airport on the southwest coast, is served by a limited number of pri-vate charters.

Anticipate long lines and allow 2–3 hours for checking in for an inter-national flight, especially at Las Américas. Due to a $50-million major renovation, this tri-level airport is significantly better than in past years, with many new security measures.Still, it can be daunting for the unini-tiated. Do confirm your flight two days in advance. Keep a sharp eye on your luggage; almost everyone checks black luggage, and between that and the many huge boxes that the Dominicans bring in from the states, the carousels are chaotic. If you fly out of a U.S. airport such as Miami—where a shrink-wrap service is offered—avail yourself of it (plas-tic-wrap your bag like meat in a supermarket, and no one is likely to tamper with it).

Choose wisely in order to fly into the airport closest to where you will be staying. It may also be possible to book an inbound flight into one airport and an outbound flight from another airport, in order to see more of the D.R. This country is larger than most Caribbean islands, and a logistical mistake could place you a four-hour bus ride away (which trans-lates into a $100 taxi), when there is very likely an airport only a 30-minute drive from your hotel.

Taxis are available at the airports, and the 25-minute ride into Santo Domingo from Las Américas averages about $30. Some order has been imposed outside the airport—taxis line up and, for the most part, charge official, established rates. If you've arranged for a hotel transfer (a good idea), a representative should be waiting for you in the immigration hall. Fares from the Puerto Plata airport average $16 to Playa Dorada. Ex-pect to pay about $30 from Punta Cana airport to the hotels, except to the Punta Cana Resort & Club, which is five minutes away and which owns the airport.

🛈 **Barahona International Airport** ✉ Barahona ☎ 809/524-4109. **Las Américas In-ternational Airport** ✉ Santo Domingo ☎ 809/549-0450. **Puerto Plata International Gregorio Luperon Airport** ✉ Puerto Plata ☎ 809/586-0107 or 809/586-0219. **Punta Cana International Airport** ☎ 809/668-4749. **La Romana/Casa de Campo Interna-tional Airport** ☎ 809/556-5565.

BUSINESS HOURS

BANKS   Banks are open weekdays 8:30–4:30.

POST OFFICES   Post offices are open weekdays 7:30–2:30.

SHOPS   Offices and shops are open weekdays 8–noon and 2–6, Saturday 8–noon. About half the stores stay open all day, no longer closing for a midday siesta.

CAR RENTALS

If you are staying at one of the all-inclusive resorts, which are self-con-tained compounds, you will probably not need a car. But if you travel around the D.R. you'll need a valid driver's license from your own coun-try and a major credit card (or cash deposit) to rent a car. Your credit card will be used to secure a deposit of some $200. This should be torn up upon safe return of the vehicle. Make certain that it is. Both international and local companies rent cars in the D.R. Rates average $70 and more per day, and the asking rate is seldom negotiable. To get a lower rate you will usually have to rent a car for a week or more.

Some local agencies give better rates than the "big guys." However, you may feel more confident in going with one of the name brands—there is more recourse, for example, in case of an accident. If you do not receive insurance from your credit card, you will need to buy insurance, which is expensive.

🚗 **Avis** ☎ 809/535-7191. **Budget** ☎ 809/562-6812. **Hertz** ☎ 809/221-5333. **McBeal** ☎ 809/688-6518. **National** ☎ 809/562-1444. **Nelly Rent-a-Car** ☎ 809/544-1800, 800/526-6684 in the U.S.

CAR TRAVEL

GASOLINE Fill up—and keep an eye on—the tank; gas stations are few and far between in rural areas. Gas prices are high by U.S. standards, approximately $2.03–$2.32 a gallon. Make certain that attendants don't reach for the super pump. You don't need to be putting that expensive liquid in a rent-a-car.

ROAD CONDITIONS Many Dominicans drive recklessly, and their cars are often in bad shape (missing headlights, taillights, etc.). It's strongly suggested that you don't drive outside the major cities at night. If you must, use extreme caution, especially on narrow, unlit mountain roads. Watch out for pedestrians, bicycles, motorbikes, and the occasional stray cow, goat, or horse.

Before setting out, consult with your hotel concierge about routes and obtain a good road map. Although some roads are still full of potholes, the route between Santo Domingo and Santiago is now a four-lane divided highway, and the road between Santiago and Puerto Plata is a smooth blacktop. The highway from Casa de Campo to Punta Cana is also a fairly smooth ride—not too long ago it was like a moonscape. Surprisingly, many of the scenic secondary roads, such as the "high road" between Playa Dorada and Santiago, are in good shape.

RULES OF THE ROAD Driving is on the right. The 80-kph (50-mph) speed limit is strictly enforced: there is even radar in areas like Punta Cana. The "old days" of getting stopped for speeding, even if you weren't, and handing the cop the equivalent of $3, are slowly coming to an end. Now you really will get a ticket and have to pay a much higher fine.

ELECTRICITY

The current is 110 volts, 60 cycles—just as in North America. Electrical blackouts occur less frequently than in the past and tend to last only one to two minutes (when they're over, everyone claps). Hotels and most restaurants have generators.

EMBASSIES & CONSULATES

🚩 Canada **Canadian Embassy** ✉ Capitan Eugenia de Marchena 39, La Esperilla, Santo Domingo Box 2054 ☎ 809/685-1136. **Canadian Consulate** ✉ Edificio Isabel de Torres, Suite 311C, Puerto Plata ☎ 809/586-5761.

🚩 United Kingdom **British Embassy** ✉ Edificio Corominas Pepin, Av. 27 de Febrero 233, Naco, Santo Domingo ☎ 809/472-7671 or 809/472-7373.

🚩 United States **United States Embassy** ✉ Leopoldo Navarro esq. Cesar Nicolas Penson, Naco, Santo Domingo ☎ 809/221-5511.

EMERGENCIES

🚩 Ambulance & Fire **Ambulance and fire emergencies** ☎ 911.

🚩 Hospitals **Centro Médico Sosúa** ✉ Av. Martinez, Sosúa ☎ 809/571-3949. **Centro Médico Universidad Central del Este** ✉ Av. Máximo Gómez 68, La Esperilla, Santo

Domingo ☎ 809/221-0171. **Clínica Abreu** ✉ Calle Beller 42, Gazcue, Santo Domingo ☎ 809/688-4411. **Clínica Dr. Brugal** ✉ Calle José del Carmen Ariza 15, Puerto Plata ☎ 809/586-2519. **Clínica Gómez Patino** ✉ Av. Independencia 701, Gazcue, Santo Domingo ☎ 809/685-9131. **Hospiten Hospital Bávaro** ✉ Bávaro ☎ 809/686-1414. **Servimed** ✉ Plaza La Criolla, Sosúa ☎ 809/571-0964.

🚩 Pharmacies Farmacia Deleyte ✉ Av. John F. Kennedy 89, Puerto Plata ☎ 809/586-2583. **San Judas Tadeo** ✉ Av. Independencia 57, Gazcue, Santo Domingo ☎ 809/689-6664.

🚩 Police Police Emergencies ☎ 809/586-2804 in Puerto Plata, 711 in Santo Domingo, 809/571-2233 in Sosúa.

ETIQUETTE & BEHAVIOR

Wearing shorts, miniskirts, and halter tops in churches is considered inappropriate. Men in Santo Domingo never wear shorts.

FESTIVALS & SEASONAL EVENTS

Santo Domingo hosts a day-long Carnival in late February, coinciding with Dominican Independence Day. Pre-Lenten carnivals are held several Sundays prior to Ash Wednesday in Santiago and La Vega, which is renowned for its papier-mâché Carnival masks. The renowned Festival del Merengue is held in late July and early August in Santo Domingo and showcases name entertainers, bands, and orchestras. During the last week in August the island's top restaurants compete in the capital city's Gastronomic Festival. The Jazz Festival is an impressive line-up of international (like Chuck Mangione) and Latino jazz stars (Bobby Sanabria) that runs for three days during the first week of October, with venues in Cabarete, Sosúa, and Puerto Plata. Sea Horse Ranch is a hotbed of activity during the festival and there is music, dance, and art. The Bienal del Caribe occurs every two years in Santo Domingo at the Museum of Modern Art, when four artists are chosen to represent each of 80 Caribbean islands and countries in this major festival; artists' works are exhibited at the museum and some 50 other venues included on walking circuits in the Colonial Zone, in art galleries, and public spaces throughout the city.

HEALTH

Though it's reasonably safe to drink water from the tap (especially in the better resorts), you're better off playing it safe with bottled water. Try to arrive at the very start of a buffet meal, before the food has sat out for a while in the tropical heat.

HOLIDAYS

Public holidays are: New Year's Day, Our Lady of La Altagracia Day (Jan. 21), Duarte's Birthday (Jan. 26), Independence Day (last Mon. in Feb.), Good Friday, Labor Day (1st Mon. in May), Corpus Christi (June 14), Restoration Day (Aug. 16), Our Lady of Las Mercedes Day (Sept. 24), Columbus Day (Oct. 26), Discovery of Hispaniola Day (Dec. 5), and Christmas.

LANGUAGE

Spanish is spoken in the D.R. Staff at major tourist attractions and front-desk personnel in most major hotels speak some English, but you may have difficulty making yourself understood. Outside the popular tourist establishments, restaurant menus are in Spanish, as are traffic signs everywhere. Using smiles and gestures will help, and though you can manage with just English, people are even more courteous if you try to speak their language.

MAIL & SHIPPING

Airmail postage to North America for a letter or postcard is RD$2, to Europe RD$4; letters may take up to three weeks to reach their destination. Or you can pay almost US$1.45 to buy a pale green stamp for "fast mail" in a gift shop (outside Santo Domingo, post offices aren't easy to find). The main branch of the post office in Santo Domingo is on Calle Heroes del Luperon at Rafael Damiron La Ferla.

MONEY MATTERS

Prices quoted in this chapter are in U.S. dollars unless noted otherwise.

ATMS   Banco Popular has many locations throughout the country; many have ATMs that accept international cards.

CREDIT CARDS   Major credit cards are accepted at most hotels, large stores, and restaurants.

CURRENCY   The coin of the realm is the Dominican peso (written RD$). At this writing, RD$22 was equivalent to US$1, which is an excellent rate of exchange for Americans. Sometimes, independent merchants will willingly accept U.S. dollars, but don't count on it, though most of the all-inclusive resorts will. Always make certain you know in which currency any transaction is taking place. Carry a pocket calculator to make conversions easier. You'll find *cambios* (currency exchange offices) at the airports as well as in major shopping areas throughout the island. At times they offer better rates than banks; at others *el banco* is best. Check the posted rates for any given day. In addition, some hotels provide exchange services, but as a general rule hotels and restaurants will not give you as much for your money as cambios and banks.

PASSPORTS & VISAS

U.S. and Canadian citizens must have either a valid passport or proof of citizenship, such as an original birth certificate with a raised seal. Legal U.S. residents must have an alien registration card (green card) and a valid passport from their home country. Citizens of Australia, New Zealand, and the United Kingdom need a valid passport. Additionally, upon arrival all U.S., U.K., Australian, Canadian, and Irish citizens must purchase a tourist card, which costs U.S.$10, in cash unless it is included in your package price. You must return the receipt for this tourist card when you leave or you will be charged an another $10 fee.

SAFETY

In general, the island is very safe—even for women traveling alone—and you rarely hear about violent crime against tourists. Thefts and pickpocketing, however, occur with some frequency. In Santo Domingo, in particular, be conscious of your wallet or pocketbook, especially around the Malecón. At night you may see men in civvies with shoulder rifles standing outside businesses or homes. Don't be unnerved by this. These men are the Dominican equivalents of private security guards. Always lock your car and never leave valuables in it even if it is locked. If you have a safe in your hotel room, use it.

SIGHTSEEING TOURS

Apolo Tours, which is based in Playa Dorada, offers a full-day tour of Playa Grande and tours to Santiago (including a casino excursion) and Sosúa for $40; the company will also arrange transfers between your hotel and the airport, day trips, and custom and small group tours along the north coast, which include stops for swimming and a trip to Samaná ($55). Cabemba Tours, which operates in Playa Dorada, runs various tours of the Cibao Valley and the Amber Coast, including Puerto

Plata, Sosúa, and Río San Juan. Caribbean Jeep Safaris is an English-speaking outfit in Playa Dorada that runs jeep tours in the mountains behind Puerto Plata and Sosúa, ending up at the Cabarete Adventure Park, where you can swim in an underground pool and explore caves with Taíno rock paintings; buffet lunch and drinks are included in the $45 fee. Go Dominican Tours in Playa Dorada has tours to Jarabacoa for $90, which include lunch, drinks, and 3½ hours of river rafting; jumping off cliffs is optional. Jeep safaris trek to flower, fruit, and coffee plantations. Horseback riding in the Puerto Plata area is another option.

Amber Coast Adventures is a terrific new company offering ecoadventures from kitesurfing to cascading and kayaking, deep sea fishing, and dinners at unique, out-of-the-way mountain restaurants, transportation included. Horseback excursions go to caves, beaches, or into the mountains, where riders dismount, let the horses plunge into the river, then float after them in inner tubes.

Iguana Mama, Mountain Bike, Hiking & Cultural Vacations, a company based in Cabarete, offers adventure tours with an ecological conscience: 20% of their profits are donated to local environmental projects and education; a well-established company, it puts a premium on safety.

Playa Colibri, a hotel, acts as a tour operator for excursions in Las Terrenas to such sights as El Limón Cascades and Playa Moron, jeep safaris, and trips to Santi's Restaurant, Casa Berca, accessible only on horseback.

Prieto Tours, which is in Santo Domingo and operates Gray Line of the D.R., has half-day bus tours of Santo Domingo, nightclub tours, beach tours, trips to Cibao Valley and the Amber Coast, and other excursions; prices start at $35. Turinter offers a six-hour trip to Altos de Chavón ($50); a full day of swimming and boating on Saona Island ($80); and specialty trips (museum, shopping, fishing), all from Santo Domingo.
🔏 **Amber Coast Adventures** ✉ Cabarete ☎ 809/254-0281. **Apolo Tours** ☎ 809/586-5329. **Cabemba Tours** ☎ 809/586-2177. **Caribbean Jeep Safaris** ☎ 809/571-1924. **Go Dominican Tours** ☎ 809/586-5969. **Iguana Mama, Mountain Bike, Hiking & Cultural Vacations** ☎ 800/571-0908. **Playa Colibri** ✉ Las Terrenas ☎ 809/240-6434. **Prieto Tours** ☎ 809/685-0102. **Turinter** ☎ 809/685-4020.

TAXES & SERVICE CHARGES

DEPARTURE TAX The D.R. has a $10 departure tax, included in the price of your ticket. This has nothing to do with the cost of the tourist card, which you just purchase in cash upon arrival.

SALES TAX & SERVICE CHARGE A 10% service charge is usually added to restaurant checks and hotel bills, as is a 12% government tax. Don't hesitate to add more *propino* if you enjoyed the service. These people are very appreciative recipients.

TAXIS

Taxis, which are government-regulated, line up outside hotels and restaurants. They're unmetered, and the minimum fare within Santo Domingo is about $4, but you can bargain for less if you order a taxi away from the major hotels. Some taxis aren't allowed to pick up from hotels, so they hang out on the street in front of them. On the average, they're $1 cheaper per ride. Avoid unmarked street taxis, particularly in Santo Domingo—they're a little risky.

Hiring a taxi by the hour—with unlimited stops—is usually $10 per hour with a minimum of two hours. Be sure to establish the time that you start; drivers like to advance the time a little. Always carry small denominations, like 5-, 10-, and 20-peso notes, because drivers rarely seem to have change. Taxis can also drive you to destinations outside the city. Rates are posted in hotels and at the airport. Sample fares from Santo Domingo are $80 to La Romana and $150 to Puerto Plata. If you're negotiating, the going rate is RD$5 per kilometer. Round-trips are considerably less than twice the one-way fare. Two good cab companies are El Conde Taxi and Tecni-Taxi.

Radio taxis are not only convenient but also a wise choice if you don't speak Spanish. The fare is negotiated over the phone when you make the appointment. The most reliable company is Apolo Taxi. The standard charge is about $10 per hour during the day and $11 at night—no minimum, and with as many stops as you like. Call P. Green Taxi for a courteous, English-speaking driver. Another option is to go in high Dominican style and hire a limo, even if it's just for a night. Call the Limousine Connection, whose rates run around $50 per hour.

Apolo Taxi ☎ 809/541-9595. **El Conde Taxi** ☎ 809/563-6131. **Limousine Connection** ☎ 809/540-5304 or 809/567-3435. **P. Green Taxi** ☎ 809/251-0571. **Tecni-Taxi** ☎ 809/567-2010 in Santo Domingo; 809/320-7621 in Puerto Plata.

TELEPHONES

COUNTRY & AREA CODES To call the D.R. from the United States, dial 1, then the area code 809 and the local number. From the D.R. there's also direct-dial service to the U.S.

INTERNATIONAL CALLS To reach the United States and Canada, dial 1, followed by the area code and number; to the United Kingdom dial 011, the country and city codes, and the number.

LOCAL CALLS To make a local call, dial the 7-digit number.

TIPPING

Generally, a 10% service charge is included. The bill will say, *propino incluido*. When in doubt, ask. If you found the service to your liking, tip an extra 5%–10%. It's customary to leave a dollar per day for the hotel maid regardless of whether or not your resort says that tips are included. Taxi drivers expect a 10% tip, especially if they've had to lift luggage or to wait for you. Skycaps and hotel porters expect at least RD$10 per bag.

TRANSPORTATION AROUND THE DOMINICAN REPUBLIC

AIR TRAVEL Air Century, flying out of Herrara Airport and La Romana/Casa de Campo Airport, offers charters, transfers, excursions, and sightseeing. Air Santo Domingo offers service between the capital (Las Américas and Herrera Airports) and Puerto Plata, Punta Cana, La Romana/Casa de Campo, El Portillo, and Santiago. Each hop is about $60. Jimmy and Irene Butler of Air Taxi charter planes for trips around the island or to neighboring islands. Caribar has both planes and helicopters and offers general air service, ambulance service, and aerial photography trips.

Air Century ✉ Herrara Airport, Santo Domingo ☎ 809/566-0888 or 809/567-6778 ✉ La Romana/Casa de Campo Airport, La Romana ☎ 809/550-6636 or 809/550-8201 ✉ Casa de Campo, La Romana ☎ 809/523-3333 Ext. 8351. **Air Santo Domingo** ✉ Herrara Airport, Santo Domingo ☎ 809/683-8020. **Air Taxi** ✉ Herrera Airport, Núñez de Cáceres 2, Santo Domingo ☎ 809/227-8333 or 809/567-1555. **Caribar** ✉ Herrara Airport, Av. Luperon, Santo Domingo ☎ 809/542-6688 ✉ La Romana/Casa de Campo Airport, La Romana ☎ 809/550-2585.

BUS TRAVEL Privately owned air-conditioned buses make regular runs to Santiago, Puerto Plata, and other destinations from Santo Domingo. You should make reservations by calling Metro Buses or Caribe Tours. One-way bus fare from Santo Domingo to Puerto Plata is about $6, and it takes four hours. Metro's buses have more of an upscale clientele. Although the coffee and cookies are complimentary, there are no movies. Caribe, which shows bilingual movies, is favored by locals and families; buses are often filled to capacity, especially on weekends.

Frequent service from Santo Domingo to the town of La Romana is provided by Express Bus. Buses depart from Revelos Street in front of Enriquillo Park every hour on the hour from 5 AM to 9 PM; the schedule is exactly the same from La Romana, where they leave from Camino Avenue. There is no office and no phone, but a ticket-taker will take your $3 just before departure. There is general chaos, a crazy kind of congestion (allow time in a taxi), horns blowing, diesel fumes, but it all comes together. Don't be dismayed, remember that you are spending $3 instead of $80 or $100 by taxi, which might be an aging vehicle without air-conditioning. Travel time is about 1¾ hours, and if luck is with you you'll get the larger bus, which will show a first-rate American movie. Once in town you can take a taxi from the bus stop to Casa de Campo ($7) or Casa del Mar or Iberostar Dominicus ($10).

🚍 **Caribe Tours** ☎ 809/221-4422. **Metro Buses** ☎ 809/566-7126 in Santo Domingo, 809/586-6062 in Puerto Plata, 809/587-4711 in Santiago.

OTHER OPTIONS Traditionally, *públicos* or *conchos* are small blue-and-white or blue-and-red cars that run regular routes, stopping to let passengers on and off. But now everyone is getting into the act. Anyone who owns a car can operate it as a *público*, and after 5 PM many do. The fare is RD$2. Competing with the públicos are the *colectivos* (privately owned vans), whose drivers coast around the major thoroughfares, leaning out of the window or jumping out to try to persuade you to climb aboard. It's a colorful if cramped way to get around. The fare is about RD$1.

Voladoras (fliers) are vans that run from Puerto Plata's Central Park to Sosúa and Cabarete a couple of times each hour for RD$10. They have a reliable schedule, but aren't always labeled with their destination.

Motoconchos are a popular, inexpensive mode of transportation in such areas as Puerto Plata, Sosúa, Cabarete, and Jarabacoa. You can flag one of these bikes down along rural roads and in town; rates vary from RD$3 to RD$20 per person, depending upon distance. You can find a pair of them, one to take you, the other your luggage. A typical motoconcho sight is, for example, a woman on a desperately dilapadated bike, with a massive stalk of green bananas in front of her. Then she picks up another woman with a tote bag overflowing with groceries. She jumps on the back and holds her little girl off to the side.

VISITOR INFORMATION

🚍 **Before You Leave** **Dominican Republic Tourist Office** ⊕ www.dr1.com/travel.shtml ✉ 136 E. 57th St., Suite 803, New York, NY 10022 ☎ 212/575-4966 or 888/374-6361 ✉ 248 W. Le Jeune Rd., Miami, FL 33126 ☎ 305/444-4592 or 888/358-9594 ✉ 1464 Crescent St., Montréal, Québec H3A 2B6, Canada ☎ 514/933-6126 ✉ 20 Hand Court, High Holborn, London WC1, U.K. ☎ 0171/723-1552.

🚍 **In the Dominican Republic** **Secretary of Tourism** ✉ Secretaria de Estado de Turismo, Edificios Guberbamentales, Av. México, esq. Av. 30 de Arzo, Gazcue Santo Domingo ☎ 809/221-4660. **Ministry of Tourism** ✉ Av. Mexico, Gazcue, Santo Domingo ☎ 809/221-4660. **Puerto Plata tourist office** ✉ Playa Long Beach, Puerto Plata ☎ 809/586-3676.

GRENADA

11

FODOR'S CHOICE

Ft. George, St. George's

Grand Anse Beach, Grand Anse

La Belle Creole, a restaurant in Grand Anse

The Nutmeg, a budget restaurant in St. George's

Shopping in St. George's Market Square

Spice Island Beach Resort, Grand Anse

HIGHLY RECOMMENDED

RESTAURANTS   Cicely's, L'Anse aux Épines

Coconut Beach Restaurant, Grand Anse

La Dolce Vita, Grand Anse

HOTELS   Blue Horizons Cottage Hotel, Grand Anse

Calabash Hotel, L'Anse aux Épines

Coyaba, Grand Anse

LaSOURCE, Pink Gin Beach

OUTDOORS   Boating & sailing to the Grenadines

Sandy Island Beach

It's cool, dark, and pungent inside the nutmeg co-op. In loose floral skirts and cotton shirts, bandanas around their heads, the ladies of Gouyave work hard for their money. Perched on stools, facing huge wooden chutes, they sort nutmegs all day. Fingers move like lightning, sorting thousands per hour. When sunlight briefly brightens the room, the chute wall reveals someone's hand-written message: GOD LOOKED AT MY WORK AND WAS PLEASED. THEN HE LOOKED AT MY SALARY, BOWED HIS HEAD, AND SADLY WALKED AWAY.

By Jane E.
Zarem

Grenada, just 21 mi (34 km) long and 12 mi (19 km) wide, has 45 beaches and countless secluded coves. Crisscrossed by nature trails and laced with spice plantations, its mountainous interior is lush rain forest. Select hotels cling to hillsides or skirt the sea; a mellow island spirit juxtaposes nicely with top facilities and sensible development. St. George's is one of the most picturesque capital cities in the Caribbean, and Grand Anse is one of the finest beaches. Nicknamed Isle of Spice, Grenada is a major producer of nutmeg, cinnamon, mace, cocoa, and other spices and flavorings. The aroma of spices fills the air in markets, in restaurants, and throughout the countryside.

Grenada lies in the southeastern Caribbean, 12 degrees north of the equator, and is the southernmost of the Windward Islands. The nation of Grenada consists of three islands: Grenada, the largest, with 120 square mi (311 square km) and a population of just over 90,000; Carriacou (*car*-ree-a-coo), 23 mi (37 km) north of Grenada, with 13 square mi (34 square km) and a population of about 5,000; and Petite Martinique, 2 mi (3 km) northeast of Carriacou, with just 486 acres and a population of only 700. Carriacou and Petite Martinique are popular for day trips, fishing adventures, or diving and snorkeling excursions, but most of the tourist activity is on Grenada. People interested in a really quiet, getaway-from-it-all vacation will, however, appreciate the simple pleasures of Carriacou during an extended stay.

Although he never set foot on the island, Christopher Columbus sighted Grenada in 1498 and named it Concepción. Spanish sailors following in his wake renamed it Granada, after the city in the hills of their homeland. Adapted to Grenade by French colonists, the transformation to Grenada was completed by the British in the 18th century.

Throughout the 17th century, Grenada was the scene of many bloody battles between indigenous Carib Indians and the French. Rather than surrender to the Europeans after losing their last battle in 1651, the Caribs committed mass suicide by leaping off a cliff in Sauteurs, at the island's northern tip. The French were later overwhelmed by the British in 1762, the beginning of a seesaw of power between the two nations. By the Treaty of Versailles in 1783, Grenada was granted to the British and, almost immediately, African slaves were brought in to work the sugar plantations. Slavery in Grenada actually began with the French colonization in 1650, and was finally abolished in 1834.

On February 7, 1974, Grenada was granted total independence within the British Commonwealth. The socialist New Jewel Movement (NJM) party seized power in 1979, formed the People's Revolutionary Government, and named Maurice Bishop prime minister. A division within the party led to the murder of Bishop and many of his supporters, after which NJM deputy prime minister Bernard Coard and Army Commander Hudson Austin took over the government. Days later, on October 25,

1983, at the request of Grenada's governor general and the heads of state of neighboring islands, U.S. troops intervened. American students attending St. George's University Medical School were evacuated, and the revolution was quickly quelled. Coard and Austin (and others) were arrested, found guilty of murder, and are currently serving life sentences in prison, high on a hill overlooking St. George's Harbour and the scene of the crime.

With U.S. and Canadian aid, government officials elected in 1984 reorganized Grenada's economy to emphasize agriculture, light manufacturing, and tourism. Grenada's modern Point Salines International Airport, which was begun with Cuban assistance prior to the intervention, was completed and opened in 1984. Over the ensuing years, the country has built a modern infrastructure that includes good roads, up-to-date technology, and reliable utilities.

Grenada's popularity as a vacation destination increases each year, as travelers seek friendly, exotic islands to visit. Hotels continue to renovate, improve, and expand, but growth in the tourism industry is carefully controlled: no building can stand taller than a coconut palm. Many hotels, resorts, and restaurants are family-owned, run by people whose guests often become their friends. Grenadians have a well-deserved reputation for their friendliness, hospitality, and entrepreneurial spirit.

WHAT IT COSTS In U.S. dollars				
$$$$	$$$	$$	$	¢
RESTAURANTS*				
over $30	$20–$30	$12–$20	$8–$12	under $8
HOTELS**				
Cost EP/BP/CP over $350	$250–$350	$150–$250	$80–$150	under $80
Cost AI over $450	$350–$450	$250–$350	$125–$250	under $125

*Restaurant prices are for a main course at dinner. **EP, BP, and CP prices are per night for a standard double room in high season, excluding taxes, service charges, and meal plans. AI (all-inclusive) prices are per person, per night based on double-occupancy during high season, excluding taxes and service charges.

Where to Stay

Grenada's tourist accommodations are, for the most part, in the southwest part of the island, primarily on or near Grand Anse Beach. Lodging options range from simply furnished, inexpensive apartments to elegant suites just steps from the sea. Hotels tend to be small and intimate, with friendly management and attentive staff. All guest rooms are equipped with air-conditioning, an in-room TV, and telephone unless indicated otherwise. During the off-season (April 15–December 15), prices may be discounted up to 40%.

Villa & Private-Home Rentals

For information about renting a villa or home on Grenada, contact **Villas of Grenada** (🖂 Box 218, St. George's ☎ 473/444–1896 🖷 473/444–4529 ⊕ www.grenadaexplorer.com/villa). In-season rates range from about $1,600 a week for a two-bedroom home with a pool to $8,000 a week for a six-bedroom home on the beach.

For Carriacou rental information, contact **Down Island Villa Rentals, Ltd.** (🖂 Craigston ☎ 473/443–8182 🖷 473/443–8290 ⊕ www.islandvillas.com). In-season rates range from $80 per day for a small cottage or in-town apartment suitable for two people to $200 per day for a villa with panoramic views and a swimming pool that accommodates up to six people.

Hotels on Grenada

$$$$ 🏨 **Bel Air Plantation.** On an 18-acre finger of land on Grenada's southeastern coast, gaily painted gingerbread cottages dot a verdant hillside. Beautifully constructed by local craftsmen, the spacious cottages are luxuriously decorated in a country-casual style, with teak and wicker furniture, coordinated Caribbean colors, and the works of local artisans. Each one- or two-bedroom cottage has a fully equipped kitchen, Bose entertainment system, CD/book library, and private verandah. Arrange fishing and boating charters next door at Grenada Marina, or simply relax in style. A deli and two restaurants are on-site; rent a car for sightseeing and going to town (a half-hour drive). ⊠ *St. David's Harbour St. David's* ☎ *Box 857 St. George's* ☎ *473/444–6305* ⊕ *www. belairplantation.com* ⇨ *25 cottages* ⚹ *2 restaurants, grocery, fans, in-room dataports, kitchens, 4 pools, beach, dock, snorkeling, boating, fishing, hiking, bar, shop, laundry facilities, Internet, airport shuttle, car rental, no kids under 12* ⊟ *AE, D, DC, MC, V* ❶❶ *EP.*

★ $$$$ 🏨 **Calabash Hotel.** Elegant suites are in two-story cottages distributed around 8 acres of garden that hug a curved beach. Each suite has a spacious bedroom and sitting area with rattan and wicker furniture, and a verandah where breakfast is freshly prepared and served by your maid. Twenty-two suites have whirlpool baths; eight have private plunge pools. Each room has a CD player, but you'll have to go to the library to watch TV. Complimentary fruit is served on the beach each morning; tea is served in the restaurant each afternoon; and canapés are delivered to your suite in the evening. Cicely's restaurant serves memorable cuisine. ⊠ *L'Anse aux Épines* ☎ *Box 382, St. George's* ☎ *473/444– 4334* 🖷 *473/444–5050* ⊕ *www.calabashhotel.com* ⇨ *30 suites* ⚹ *Restaurant, room service, fans, golf privileges, tennis court, pool, gym, spa, beach, snorkeling, boating, billiards, shuffleboard, 2 bars, library, shops, baby-sitting, dry cleaning, laundry service, concierge, car rental; no room TVs* ⊟ *AE, MC, V* ❶❶ *CP.*

$$$$ 🏨 **Laluna.** An upscale enclave hidden away on a remote, pristine beach near Grenada's Quarantine Point, Laluna's large thatched-roof cottages—each with its own plunge pool—line the beachfront, with the wooded hillside as a backdrop. Bedrooms open onto large verandahs that serve as indoor-outdoor sitting areas. Each room has a stereo CD player and coffeemaker. Bathrooms have custom-made tubs and showers that partially open to the natural environment. The restaurant, bar with weekly entertainment, a small CD and video library, and other services are in the main Club House. Nightly sunset meditation and yoga classes add to the peaceful mood. ⊠ *Morne Rouge* ☎ *Box 1500, St. George's* ☎ *473/439–0001* 🖷 *473/439–0600* ⊕ *www.laluna.com* ⇨ *16 cottages* ⚹ *Restaurant, fans, in-room data ports, in-room safes, minibars, in-room VCRs, pool, massage, beach, snorkeling, windsurfing, boating, bicycles, bar, library, shops, concierge, car rental* ⊟ *AE, DC, MC, V* ❶❶ *BP.*

★ $$$$ 🏨 **LaSOURCE.** Minutes from the airport, LaSOURCE unfolds on 40 acres facing Pink Gin Beach. A breezy courtyard leads to the Oasis spa, the Great House restaurant with its colonnaded terrace, a piano bar, and swimming pool. Guest quarters are in four-story buildings (lots of stairs) facing the beach. Bedrooms have Oriental-design rugs on Italian marble floors, Jamaican mahogany furniture and woodwork, king-size four-poster beds, balconies, and marble bathrooms. There's plenty to do day and night. The cuisine is memorable, with light and vegetarian choices always available. Best of all, rates include daily spa treatments—massages, wraps, aromatherapy, and more. ⊠ *Pink Gin Beach* ☎ *Box*

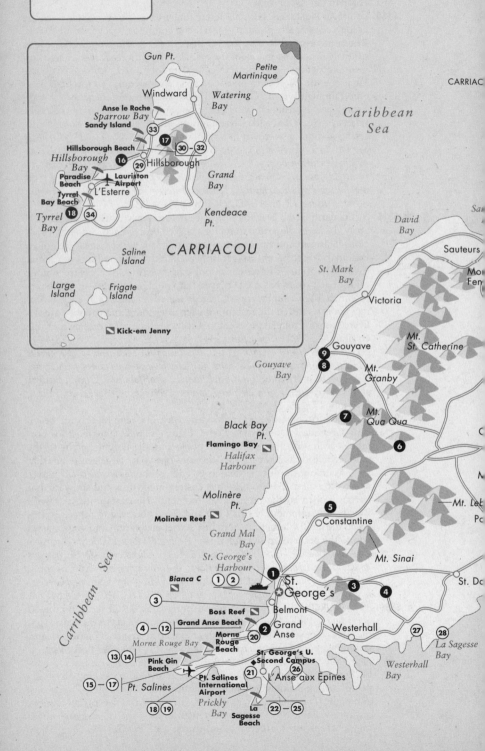

Grenada & Carriacou

CARRIACOU (inset map):

Gun Pt.

Petite Martinique

Windward

Watering Bay

Anse le Roche
Sparrow Bay
Sandy Island ㉝

㉗

㉚ – ㉜

Hillsborough Beach ⑯
Hillsborough Bay ㉙ Hillsborough

Paradise Beach
Tyrrel Bay Beach
L'Esterre
Lauriston Airport

Grand Bay

⑱ ㉞
Tyrrel Bay

Kendeace Pt.

Saline Island

CARRIACOU

Large Island

Frigate Island

🛶 Kick-em Jenny

Main map:

CARRIAC

Caribbean Sea

David Bay

Sa

Sauteurs

Mo
Fen

St. Mark Bay

Victoria

Mt. St. Catherine

❾ Gouyave
❽
Gouyave Bay

Mt. Granby

❼

Mt. Qua Qua

❻

Black Bay Pt.

Flamingo Bay 🛶
Halifax Harbour

Mt. Let
Po

Molinère Pt.

Molinère Reef 🛶

❺

Constantine

Mt. Sinai

Grand Mal Bay

St. George's Harbour

Bianca C 🛶

① ② ❶ St. George's

❸

❹

St. Do

③

Boss Reef 🛶

Belmont

Grand Anse Beach ②
④ – ⑫ ⑳ Grand Anse

Westerhall

㉗

㉘

Morne Rouge Bay
Morne Rouge Beach

La Sagesse Bay

⑬ ⑭
Pink Gin Beach

St. George's U. Second Campus

Westerhall Bay

⑮ – ⑰ Pt. Salines

㉑ L'Anse aux Epines

㉖

⑱ ⑲

Pt. Salines International Airport

Prickly Bay

La Sagesse Beach

㉒ – ㉕

Caribbean Sea

0 miles
4 miles
0
6 km

TO CARRIACOU

Isle la Ronde

The Sisters

Twin Sisters

Caille Island

London Bridge Island

Sauteurs Bay

Levera Beach

Green Island

Bathway Beach

Sauteurs

Mount Rodney Estate

Morne Fendre

Morne Fendue

Grenada Bay

Tivoli

Pearl's

Great River Bay

Grenville

Telescope Pt.

Marquis

Grenville Bay

Mt. Lebanon

Pomme Rose

Grand Bacolet Bay

St. David's

agesse

ATLANTIC OCEAN

Hotels ▼

Ade's Dream
Guest House **30**

Allamanda
Beach Resort **6**

Bel Air Plantation **27**

Blue Horizons
Cottage Hotel **10**

Calabash Hotel **22**

Caribbee Inn **33**

Carriacou Grand View
Hotel **32**

Coyaba **7**

Flamboyant Hotel
& Cottages **11**

Gem Holiday
Beach Resort **14**

Grenada Grand
Beach Resort **5**

Laluna **18**

La Sagesse
Nature Centre **28**

LaSOURCE **17**

Mariposa Beach
Resort **13**

Rex Grenadian **15**

Secret Harbour
Resort **26**

Silver Beach
Resort **31**

Spice Island
Beach Resort **8**

True Blue Bay
Resort & Marina **21**

Twelve Degrees
North **24**

Restaurants ▼

Aquarium Beach
Club and
Restaurant **16**

The Beach
House **19**

The Boatyard **24**

Callaloo By
The Sea **29**

Cicely's **22**

Coconut Beach **4**

La Belle Creole **10**

La Boulangerie **9**

La Dolce Vita **12**

La Sagesse
Nature Centre **28**

Fish 'n' Chick **20**

The Nutmeg **1**

Oliver's Restaurant **8**

The Red Crab **25**

Scraper's **34**

Tout Bagay **2**

Tropicana **3**

Exploring ▼

Annandale Falls **5**

Bay Gardens **3**

Belair **17**

Carib's Leap **11**

Carriacou Museum **16**

Concord Falls **7**

Dougaldston
Spice Estate **8**

Gouyave Nutmeg
Processing Coop **9**

Grand Anse **2**

Grand Étang
National Park **6**

Grenville Coop
Nutmeg Assn. **15**

Laura Herb and
Spice Garden **4**

Levera
National Park **12**

Mt. Rodney
Estate **10**

Pearl's Airport **14**

River Antoine
Rum Distillery **13**

St. George's **1**

Tyrrel Bay **18**

KEY

⌇ Beaches

🚢 Cruise Ship Terminal

◥ Dive Sites

❶ Exploring Sights

① Hotels & Restaurants

852, St. George's ☎ *473/444–2556* 🖶 *473/444–2561* ⊕ *www. lasourcegrenada.com* ⇌ *91 rooms, 9 suites* ⚭ *2 restaurants, fans, in-room safes, refrigerators, 9-hole golf course, 2 tennis courts, pool, aer-obics, hair salon, health club, hot tub, sauna, spa, beach, dive shop, snorkeling, windsurfing, boating, waterskiing, archery, badminton, Ping-Pong, volleyball, 2 bars, piano bar, piano, shops, laundry service, concierge, travel services; no kids under 16* 🖃 *AE, D, MC, V* ⦾ *AI.*

$$$$
Fodor'sChoice
★
🏨 **Spice Island Beach Resort.** The grand entrance to Grenada's premier resort leads straight to Grand Anse Beach. Exquisite suites in dozens of peach-colored buildings extend along 1,600 ft of beachfront. Guest rooms have dark rattan furniture and stylish fabrics; huge bathrooms have double-size whirlpool tubs. Beachfront suites are steps from the sand, and 13 ocean-view suites have private gardens, patios, and plunge pools. While all guests are treated royally, four Royal suites offer the ultimate luxury: a private pool and garden, sitting room, and private sauna. Janissa's Spa offers a full menu of beauty and therapeutic treat-ments. You won't want to go home. ⊠ *Grand Anse* 🕮 *Box 6, St. George's* ☎ *473/444–4258* 🖶 *473/444–4807* ⊕ *www.spicebeachresort. com* ⇌ *66 suites* ⚭ *2 restaurants, room service, fans, in-room safes, minibars, golf privileges, tennis court, pool, gym, hair salon, outdoor hot tub, spa, beach, dive shop, snorkeling, boating, bicycles, bar, library, recreation room, shops, laundry service, concierge, business services, meet-ing room; no kids under 5* 🖃 *AE, D, DC, MC, V* ⦾ *AI.*

$$–$$$$
🏨 **Grenada Grand Beach Resort.** Conveniently situated on 20 landscaped acres along a broad section of beautiful Grand Anse Beach, this resort offers comfortable rooms and extensive amenities. Freshwater swimmers enjoy the 300-ft pool with its waterfalls and swim-up bar. Besides in-dividual vacationers, groups sometimes frequent this resort, which has Grenada's largest convention center. Guest rooms all have attractive ma-hogany furniture, king-size or twin beds, and a large balcony or patio. Two suites have double-size whirlpool tubs. The restaurant offers table d'hôte and à la carte menus—you can even get a good New York–style steak. ⊠ *Grand Anse* 🕮 *Box 441, St. George's* ☎ *473/444–4371* 🖶 *473/444–4800* ⊕ *www.grandbeach.net* ⇌ *238 rooms, 2 suites* ⚭ *Restaurant, snack bar, room service, fans, 9-hole golf course, 2 ten-nis courts, 2 pools, gym, hair salon, beach, dive shop, snorkeling, boat-ing, 2 bars, shops, laundry service, business services, convention center, meeting rooms, car rental, travel services* 🖃 *AE, DC, MC, V* ⦾ *BP.*

$$–$$$$
🏨 **Rex Grenadian.** This massive resort on Tamarind Bay is minutes from the airport. Guests, many of whom are European, are welcomed into a glistening reception area with lofty ceilings, vast arched doorways, trel-lised walkways, and tiled terraces. Most rooms are in eight two-story buildings on a bluff overlooking the sea. Rooms have simple rattan fur-niture and balconies. The pool, casual restaurant, and bar are near the beach but separated from the guest rooms by a large lawn and lake. Ac-tivities abound—water sports, nature walks, dance classes, dive lessons, evening shows in the lounge, and happy hours. Buffet breakfast and din-ner are served at the International restaurant. ⊠ *Point Salines* 🕮 *Box 893, St. George's* ☎ *473/444–3333* 🖶 *473/444–1111* ⊕ *www. rexcaribbean.com* ⇌ *191 rooms, 21 suites* ⚭ *3 restaurants, café, fans, 2 tennis courts, pool, health club, sauna, 2 beaches, dive shop, snorkel-ing, windsurfing, boating, waterskiing, 4 bars, piano bar, cabaret, piano, shops, baby-sitting, business services, meeting rooms; no a/c in some rooms* 🖃 *AE, D, DC, MC, V* ⦾ *EP.*

$$–$$$
🏨 **Allamanda Beach Resort.** Right on Grand Anse Beach, this small hotel has some rooms with whirlpool baths; many rooms also have connect-ing doors, making it a good choice for families. All rooms have tile floors and a balcony or patio. The restaurant serves international cuisine, and

a poolside snack bar has great fresh-fruit smoothies. At the water-sports center you'll find Sunfish and snorkeling equipment. Shopping, restaurants, nightlife, and the minibus to town are right at the doorstep. An all-inclusive option is available, which also includes a massage. ⊠ *Grand Anse ⌂ Box 1025, St. George's* ☎ *473/444–0095* 🖷 *473/444–0126* ⊕ *www.allamandaresort.com* ⇝ *50 suites ♂ 2 restaurants, snack bar, fans, in-room safes, refrigerators, tennis court, pool, gym, massage, beach, snorkeling, boating, volleyball, meeting room* ⊟ *AE, MC, V* ⓘⓄⓘ *EP.*

★ **$$** 🏨 **Blue Horizons Cottage Hotel.** An especially good value, all suites and studios here have kitchenettes and private terraces. Deluxe suites have separate sitting-dining rooms and one king- or two queen-size beds; studios have dining alcoves and king-size beds. Handsome mahogany furniture is set off by white walls, floral prints, and white-tile floors with grass mats. Palm trees and tropical plants stud the 6 acres of grounds, where 21 species of birds can be found. Lunch is served poolside, dinner at La Belle Creole—renowned for its contemporary West Indian cuisine. It's a short walk from Grand Anse Beach, where Blue Horizons guests use sister hotel Spice Island's beach chairs, tennis court, fitness center, and water-sports equipment. ⊠ *Grand Anse ⌂ Box 41, St. George's* ☎ *473/444–4316 or 473/444–4592* 🖷 *473/444–2815* ⊕ *www.bluegrenada.com* ⇝ *26 suites, 6 studios ♂ Restaurant, fans, kitchenettes, golf privileges, pool, outdoor hot tub, 2 bars, library, recreation room, baby-sitting, laundry service, meeting rooms, car rental* ⊟ *AE, MC, V* ⓘⓄⓘ *EP.*

★ **$$** 🏨 **Coyaba.** Family-run Coyaba (Arawak for "heaven") is directly on Grand Anse Beach. Rooms, decorated with natural wood and Arawak-inspired folk art, are in eight two-story buildings surrounding 5½ acres of lawn and gardens. Nonmotorized water-sports equipment is complimentary; you can also play tennis and volleyball and enjoy pool with a swim-up bar. Excellent West Indian cuisine is served at the bamboo-walled Arawakabana restaurant or poolside at Pepperpot restaurant, with musical entertainment most nights. Each room has a king-size or two double beds, a balcony or patio, and most have a water view. ⊠ *Grand Anse ⌂ Box 336, St. George's* ☎ *473/444–4129 or 473/444–2011* 🖷 *473/444–4808* ⊕ *www.coyaba.com* ⇝ *70 rooms ♂ 2 restaurants, room service, golf privileges, tennis court, pool, beach, dive shop, snorkeling, shuffleboard, volleyball, 2 bars, shops, baby-sitting, laundry service, meeting room* ⊟ *AE, D, DC, MC, V* ⓘⓄⓘ *EP.*

$$ 🏨 **Flamboyant Hotel & Cottages.** Built on a steep hillside, the rooms at this friendly, Grenadian-owned hotel have private verandahs with fabulous panoramic views of Grand Anse Bay. Self-catering one-bedroom suites and two-bedroom, two-bath cottages each have a fully equipped kitchen and sitting room with sofa bed, making this an excellent value for families. Be prepared for lots of stairs—about 100 to get to Grand Anse Beach. But halfway down—or on the way back up—you can stop for a dip in the pool or grab a bite at the Beachside Terrace restaurant. ⊠ *Grand Anse ⌂ Box 214, St. George's* ☎ *473/444–4247* 🖷 *473/444–1234* ⊕ *www.flamboyant.com* ⇝ *38 rooms, 20 suites, 2 cottages ♂ Restaurant, grocery, room service, in-room safes, kitchenettes, minibars, golf privileges, pool, beach, snorkeling, billiards, bar, cabaret, recreation room, shop, baby-sitting, laundry service, meeting room, car rental* ⊟ *AE, D, DC, MC, V* ⓘⓄⓘ *EP.*

$$ 🏨 **Secret Harbour Resort.** Perched on a cliff above remote Mt. Hartman Bay, this resort attracts a yachting crowd. The on-site Moorings' Club Mariner Water-Sports Centre has a fleet of sailboats and yachts available for day or long-term charters. But this is also a small, romantic retreat. The 20 suites are beautifully decorated, with two antique, full-size four-poster beds and an Italian-tile bath. Water-sports equipment, including Windsurfers, Sunfish, and sailboats, can be used without charge.

Just offshore, Calvigny Island is a 10-minute ride by speedboat; bring a picnic and spend the afternoon on your own deserted isle. ⊠ *Mt. Hartman Bay* ⌖ *Box 11, St. George's* ☎ *473/444–4439* 🖷 *473/444–4819* ⊕ *www.secretharbour.com* 🛏 *20 suites* ⚭ *2 restaurants, room service, tennis court, pool, beach, dive shop, dock, snorkeling, windsurfing, boating, waterskiing, bar; no kids under 12* ▤ *AE, D, DC, MC, V* ⏀ *CP.*

☙ **$$** ▦ **True Blue Bay Resort & Marina.** The lawns and gardens at this family-run resort, a former indigo plantation, slope down to True Blue Bay. Three cottages are near the pool, and four spacious apartments are perched on a cliff. Each has a dining area, a living room with sofa bed, and a fully-equipped kitchen. Modern rooms, decorated in Caribbean colors, overlook the bay. The restaurant specializes in Mexican and Caribbean cuisine. Two beaches are on the bay, and Grand Anse Beach is a five-minute drive away. Arrange yacht charters at the marina or dive excursions at the on-site dive center. This is a perfect place for families ⊠ *Old Mill Ave., True Blue Bay* ⌖ *Box 1414, St. George's* ☎ *473/443–8783 or 866/325–8322* 🖷 *473/444–5929* ⊕ *www.truebluebay.com* 🛏 *19 rooms, 4 1-bedroom apartments, 3 2-bedroom cottages* ⚭ *Restaurant, fans, kitchens, kitchenettes, pool, gym, 2 beaches, dive shop, snorkeling, boating, marina, fishing, bar, shop, baby-sitting, laundry service, meeting room, car rental* ▤ *AE, MC, V* ⏀ *EP.*

$$ ▦ **Twelve Degrees North.** Named for the latitude at which it sits, this small secluded inn has one- and two-bedroom suites, all of which face the sea. Accommodations come with a personal housekeeper who cooks breakfast and lunch, cleans, and tends to your laundry. Groceries are stocked for your arrival, along with flowers, rum punch, and a spice basket. Apartments are bright and airy, with modern furniture and woven-grass rugs on the tile floors. The balcony or patio is perfect for breakfast (in the terry-cloth robes provided), a quiet lunch, sunset drinks, or a romantic dinner for two. Activities center on the private beach, pool, and tennis court. ⊠ *L'Anse aux Épines* ⌖ *Box 241, St. George's* ☎☎ *473/444–4580* ⊕ *www.twelvedegreesnorth.com* 🛏 *8 suites* ⚭ *Tennis court, pool, massage, beach, snorkeling, boating, library, laundry service; no a/c, no kids* ▤ *AE, V* ⏀ *EP.*

$–$$ ▦ **La Sagesse Nature Centre.** Secluded on La Sagesse Bay—10 mi (16 km) east of the airport (about a 30-minute drive)—the grounds here include a salt-pond bird sanctuary, thick mangroves, nature trails, and ½ mi (¾ km) of tree-shaded beach. Guest rooms are in the manor house, a beach cottage, and a newer building. All rooms are just 30 ft from the beach and all have screened verandahs. The restaurant is popular, the food excellent. Be content to relax here and enjoy the natural surroundings; you will probably need to rent a car. ⊠ *La Sagesse, St. David's* ⌖ *Box 44, St. George's* ☎ *473/444–6458* 🖷 *473/444–6458* ⊕ *www.lasagesse. com* 🛏 *12 rooms* ⚭ *Restaurant, fans, kitchenettes, beach, snorkeling, hiking, bar, laundry service; no a/c in some rooms* ▤ *MC, V* ⏀ *EP.*

$ ▦ **Gem Holiday Beach Resort.** Owner Miriam Bedeau and her family operate this friendly apartment hotel on Morne Rouge Beach. One- and two-bedroom self-catering apartments are small and simple, with a kitchenette, dining-living room with mahogany furniture, and private verandah overlooking the sea. If you don't want to cook, Sur La Mer beachside restaurant specializes in seafood and West Indian dishes for lunch and dinner. And for later, Fantazia, Grenada's premier dance club, is also on the property (and soundproof). ⊠ *Morne Rouge Bay* ⌖ *Box 58, St. George's* ☎ *473/444–2288* 🖷 *473/444–1189* ⊕ *www.gembeachresort.com* 🛏 *15 one-bedroom apartments, 4 two-bedroom apartments* ⚭ *Restaurant, grocery, fans, kitchenettes, beach, snorkeling, bar, dance club, baby-sitting, laundry service, car rental* ▤ *AE, D, DC, MC, V* ⏀ *EP.*

$ 🏨**Mariposa Beach Resort.** Over the hill from Grand Anse Beach, this colony of Mediterranean-style, coral-colored villas covers the side of a hill overlooking Morne Rouge Bay. Each stylishly decorated room or self-catering apartment has a water view, a covered verandah or garden, and an Italian-tile bathroom. It's a short walk downhill to Morne Rouge Beach or a water-taxi ride to the beach club. The restaurant specializes in seafood and international dishes. ⊠ *Morne Rouge Bay* ① *Box 857, St. George's* ☎ *473/444–3171* 🖷 *473/444–3172* ⊕ *www.mariposaresort.com* ⇆ *30 rooms, 15 apartments* ⚘ *Restaurant, room service, fans, in-room safes, kitchenettes, pool, beach, bar, laundry service* ▤ *AE, MC, V* �◎ *EP.*

Hotels on Carriacou

$–$$ 🏨**Caribbee Inn.** The views from this rambling country house high on a promontory overlooking the sea in northwest Carriacou are magnificent, particularly at sunset. Hillside suites are decorated by theme (Colonial, South American, West Indian) and have four-poster beds draped with netting, soft-pastel color schemes, and Italian-tile floors. One suite has a step-up shower with an open-air view of the bay; another has its own beach. Breakfast and dinner (French creole cuisine) are served in the dining room—and don't be surprised if a macaw joins you. The inn is isolated, and perfect for nature walks, meditation, romance, and total relaxation. ⊠ *Prospect* ☎ *473/443–7380* 🖷 *473/443–8142* ⊕ *www. caribbeeinn.com* ⇆ *6 rooms, 3 suites* ⚘ *Dining room, beach, snorkeling, hiking, bar, library, laundry service, airport shuttle; no a/c, no kids* ▤ *No credit cards* ◎ *EP.*

¢–$ 🏨**Carriacou Grand View Hotel.** The view is lovely, particularly at sunset, from this perch high above Hillsborough Harbour. Though the building is four stories high, its hillside location provides entrances at three levels, making stair-climbing a nonissue if you're on the top floor. Guest rooms are pleasant and comfortably furnished; suites have added sitting rooms (large enough for a roll-away bed) and full kitchens. Most bathrooms have showers only. The beach and the town are a 15-minute walk away—or rent a car and explore Carriacou during your stay. The friendly atmosphere extends to the restaurant, which attracts guests and locals alike. ⊠ *Beausejour* ☎☎ *473/443–6348* ⊕ *www.grenadines. net/carriacou/grandview.html* ⇆ *6 rooms, 7 suites* ⚘ *Restaurant, fans, kitchenettes, pool, piano bar, shop, Internet, meeting room; no a/c in some rooms* ▤ *MC, V* ◎ *EP.*

¢–$ 🏨**Silver Beach Resort.** Choose between a self-catering cottage with sitting room and kitchenette and an oceanfront double room at this laid-back beachfront resort a short walk from the jetty in Hillsborough. All quarters have a patio or balcony; most have an ocean view. You can arrange fishing or spearfishing excursions on the resort's 30-ft Chris-Craft. From the dock you can see Sandy Island, a deserted islet a stone's throw from shore, where you can picnic and snorkel. The open-air Shipwreck Restaurant serves hearty breakfasts and Caribbean and seafood dinners. Those who purchase MAP may dine around at other local restaurants. ⊠ *Beausejour Bay, Hillsborough* ☎ *473/443–7337* 🖷 *473/443–7165* ⊕ *www.silverbeachhotel.com* ⇆ *10 rooms, 6 cottages* ⚘ *Restaurant, fans, kitchenettes, tennis court, dive shop, dock, snorkeling, windsurfing, boating, fishing, bar, shops, laundry service, airport shuttle, car rental, travel services; no a/c* ▤ *AE, MC, V* ◎ *EP.*

¢ 🏨**Ade's Dream Guest House.** Adjacent to the jetty in Hillsborough, this small guest house is a convenient place to rest your weary head after a day touring Carriacou, snorkeling at Sandy Island, or scuba diving at some of Grenada's best dive spots. Enjoy a good meal at Sea Wave, the owner's restaurant across the street; next day, fall out of bed at your leisure to catch the boat back. Or hey, stay longer. The accommodations (7 of the

23 rooms have shared baths) are simple, with queen-size or twin beds and a writing table, but the view of the mountains, sea, neighboring islands, and all the harbor activity is great—and it's certainly priced right. ⊠ *Main St., Hillsborough* ☎ *473/443-7317* 🖷 *473/443-8435* ⊕ *grenadines.net/carriacoulade.htm* ⟿ *23 rooms* ⚭ *Restaurant, grocery, fans, kitchenettes, beach, laundry facilities, car rental* ⊟ *AE, MC, V* ⊚⎮*BP.*

Where to Eat

Grenada grows everything from lettuce and tomatoes to plantains, mangoes, papaya (called *pawpaw*), callaloo (similar to spinach), citrus, yams, christophenes (like squash), breadfruit—the list is endless. And all restaurants prepare dishes with local produce and season them with the many spices grown here. Be sure to try the local flavors of ice cream: mango, soursop, guava, rum raisin, coconut (the best), or nutmeg.

Soups—especially pumpkin and callaloo—are divine, and often start a meal. Pepper pot is a savory stew of pork, oxtail, vegetables, and spices simmered for hours. Oildown, the national dish, is salted meat, breadfruit, onion, carrot, celery, dasheen (a root vegetable), and dumplings all boiled in coconut milk until the liquid is absorbed and the savory mixture becomes "oily."

Fresh seafood of all kinds, including lobster, is plentiful. Conch, known here as *lambi,* is popular and often appears curried or in a stew. Crab back, though, is not seafood—it's land crab. Most Grenadian restaurants serve seafood and at least some native dishes.

Rum punches are ubiquitous and always topped with grated nutmeg. Clarke's Court and Westerhall are locally produced and marketed rums. Carib, the local beer, is refreshing, light, and quite good.

What to Wear

Dining in Grenada is casual. Collared shirts and long pants for men (even the fanciest restaurants don't require jacket and tie) and sundresses or slacks for women are appropriate. Beachwear, of course, should be reserved for the beach.

Grenada

CAFÉS ✕ **La Boulangerie.** This combination French bakery and Italian pizzaria,
¢–$ convenient to the Grand Anse hotels, is a great place for breakfast or a light meal—to eat in, take out, or have delivered. You'll find croissants and other special breads and pastries, espresso, juices, baguette sandwiches, focaccia, crêpes, pizza, various pasta dishes, and homemade gelati. ⊠ *Le Marquis Complex, Grand Anse* ☎ *473/444-1131* ⊟ *AE, MC, V.*

CARIBBEAN ✕ **Coconut Beach Restaurant.** Take local seafood, add butter, wine, and
★ $$ Grenadian spices, and you have excellent French creole cuisine. Throw in a beautiful location at the northern end of Grand Anse Beach, and this West Indian cottage becomes an even more delightful spot. Lobster is a specialty, perhaps wrapped in a crêpe, dipped in garlic butter, or added to pasta. There are also the seafood platter, lambi Calypso, and T-bone steak. Homemade coconut pie is a winner for dessert. Wander down the beach and stop by for an alfresco lunch. In season there's a beach barbecue with live music Wednesday and Sunday nights. ⊠ *Grand Anse* ☎ *473/444-4644* ⊟ *AE, D, MC, V* ⊘ *Closed Tues.*

¢–$ ✕ **The Nutmeg.** Fresh seafood, homemade West Indian dishes, great
FodorsChoice hamburgers, and the waterfront view make this a favorite with locals
★ and visitors alike. It's upstairs on the Carenage (above Sea Change bookstore), with large, open windows from which you can watch the harbor activity as you eat. Try the callaloo soup, curried lambi, lobster

thermidor, grilled filet mignon—or just stop by for a rum punch and a roti, a fish sandwich and a Carib beer, or a hamburger and a Coke. ⊠ *The Carenage, St. George's* ☎ *473/440–2539* ▭ *AE, MC, V.*

CHINESE ✕ **Tropicana.** The chef-owner here hails from Trinidad and specializes
¢–$$ in both Chinese and West Indian cuisine. Local businesspeople seem to be the best customers for the extensive menu of Chinese food, the tantalizing aroma of barbecued chicken notwithstanding. Eat in or take out— it's open from 7:30 AM until midnight. Tropicana is right at the Lagoon Road traffic circle, overlooking the marina. ⊠ *Lagoon Rd., St. George's* ☎ *473/440–1586* ▭ *AE, DC, MC, V.*

CONTEMPORARY ✕ **Oliver's Restaurant.** Diners tend to dress up for the five-course prix-
$$$$ fixe evening meal at the open-air, beachfront dining room of the Spice Island Beach Resort, where dozens of ceiling fans stir the sultry air. The menu combines international cuisine with local specialties. Roast beef or grilled pork are as likely to appear on the menu as, for instance, chicken stuffed with bread nuts or grapefruit consommé. You'll always find fresh seafood and a vegetarian choice. Live music accompanies dinner several nights each week, including a steel band on Fridays. ⊠ *Spice Island Beach Resort, Grand Anse* ☎ *473/444–4258 or 473/444–4423* ♢ *Reservations essential* ▭ *AE, D, DC, MC, V* ⊘ *No lunch.*

$$$ ✕ **La Belle Creole.** The marriage of Continental and West Indian cuisines
Fodor'sChoice and a splendid view of distant St. George's are the delights of this ro-
★ mantic hillside restaurant at the Blue Horizons Cottage Hotel. The always-changing five-course table d'hôte menu is based on original recipes from the owner's mother, a pioneer in incorporating local products into "foreign" cuisines. Try, for instance, Grenadian caviar (roe of the white sea urchin), cream of bread nut soup, lobster-egg flan, or callaloo quiche, followed by lobster à la creole or ginger pork chops. The inspired cuisine, romantic setting, and gracious service are impressive. ⊠ *Blue Horizons Cottage Hotel, Grand Anse* ☎ *473/444–4316 or 473/444– 4592* ♢ *Reservations essential* ▭ *AE, D, MC, V.*

$$–$$$ ✕ **The Beach House.** At this casual restaurant next door to the Laluna resort, the gleaming white sand and sea views are the perfect backdrop for a salad or pasta luncheon on the deck. At dinner, excellent steak and seafood—sashimi tuna, rack of lamb, blackened fish, or prime rib of beef— accompanied by a superb wine—give the term "beach party" new meaning. A kids' menu is available, too. ⊠ *Airport Rd., Point Salines* ☎ *473/ 444–4455* ♢ *Reservations essential* ▭ *AE, MC, V* ⊘ *Closed Sun.*

★ $$–$$$ ✕ **Cicely's.** The open-air restaurant at the Calabash Hotel, named for chef Cicely Roberts, is surrounded by palms, flowers, and twinkling lights. Cicely's culinary skills are complemented by those of Graham Newbould, former chef to British royals; the result is international cuisine with a Caribbean flair. The five-course table d'hôte dinner is a good bet; past menus have included chilled lobster mousse, cream of tannia (similar to potato) soup or christophene vichyssoise, followed by baked stuffed rainbow runner or charcoal-grilled pork fillet with piquant guava, garlic, and ginger sauce. Fresh-fruit sorbet or cheese and English biscuits top off your meal. ⊠ *Calabash Hotel, L'Anse aux Épines* ☎ *473/444– 4334* ♢ *Reservations essential* ▭ *AE, MC, V* ⊘ *No lunch.*

ECLECTIC ✕ **Tout Bagay Restaurant & Bar.** Its name means "everything is possible,"
$–$$$ and the eclectic menu proves the point. At lunch, for example, you might select a salad (lobster, shrimp, Caesar) or try a local specialty, such as a roti, flying-fish sandwich, or creole-style fish. At dinner, the menu is equally broad—lobster thermidor, cappellini with red-pepper pesto and shrimp, curry goat, or sweet and sour lambi. On the water at the northern end of The Carenage, the view (day or night) is spectacular. It's a

popular lunch choice for businesspeople, as well as those touring the capital or shopping on adjacent streets. ⊠ *The Carenage, St. George's* ☎ *473/440–1500* ⊟ *MC, V.*

$–$$ ✕ **The Boatyard.** As its name implies, boaters frequent this lively restaurant and its Tiki Bar at the Spice Island Marina. Burgers, fish-and-chips, and deep-fried shrimp are served at lunchtime. At dinner you can order charcoal-grilled club steaks, lobster, and meat or seafood brochettes. The menu always includes pasta, a vegetarian plate, West Indian dishes—and even some Mexican snacks. In season there's music and dancing on weekend nights. For quieter nights, there's a book-exchange library. ⊠ *L'Anse aux Épines* ☎ *473/444–4662* ⊟ *AE, D, DC, MC, V.*

FAST FOOD ✕ **Fish 'n' Chick.** All day and most of the night, this fast-food restaurant ¢ serves up snacks, sandwiches, burgers, salads, rotis, stewed or curried lambi—and, of course, fish or chicken (barbecued, baked, or jerk) and chips. Local folks and visitors alike drop by during the day for a bite to eat in or take away; it's also a popular place for a midnight snack. ⊠ *Old Sugar Mill, Grand Anse* ☎ *473/444–4132* ⊟ *No credit cards.*

ITALIAN ✕ **La Dolce Vita.** Hidden away at the southern end of Grand Anse Beach, ★ **$$$** overlooking the sea and the twinkling lights of St. George's in the distance, this is *the* place to come for fine dining and delicious Italian cuisine. The chef is noted for his homemade pasta, prepared fresh daily. Start with a selection of cold and hot antipasti, then try lobster spaghetti, gnocchi, or fresh seafood. The restaurant is at the bottom of the 100-step beach access at the Flamboyant Hotel. ⊠ *Grand Anse* ☎ *473/444–3456* ☖ *Reservations essential* ⊟ *AE, MC, V* ☾ *Closed Mon. No lunch.*

SEAFOOD ✕ **The Red Crab.** Locals and expats love to gather at this pub, especially **$$–$$$$** on Saturday night. The curried lambi and garlic shrimp keep the regulars coming back. Seafood, particularly lobster, and steak (imported from the U.S.) are staples of the menu; hot garlic bread comes with all orders. Eat inside or under the stars, and enjoy live music Monday and Friday in season. ⊠ *L'Anse aux Épines, near the Calabash* ☎ *473/444–4424* ☖ *Reservations essential* ⊟ *AE, MC, V* ☾ *Closed Sun.*

$–$$ ✕ **Aquarium Beach Club and Restaurant.** The beach club rents ocean kayaks and snorkeling equipment. When you come up for air, enjoy fresh seafood or luncheon salads and a cool drink at the restaurant. On Friday, happy hour at the Bamboo Bar is from 4:30 to 6:30, at which time dinner is served. Besides fresh fish and lobster, the menu might include callaloo cannelloni or pepper steak. Saturday is volleyball day, and on Sunday there's a lobster barbecue. It's a very congenial spot—and convenient to the airport, as well, for preflight meal. ⊠ *LaSource Rd., Point Salines* ☎ *473/444–1410* ☖ *Reservations essential* ⊟ *AE, D, DC, MC, V* ☾ *Closed Mon.*

¢–$$ ✕ **La Sagesse Nature Centre.** The perfect spot to soothe a frazzled soul, La Sagesse's open-air, mostly seafood restaurant is on a secluded cove in a nature preserve about 30 minutes from Grand Anse. You can combine your lunch or dinner with a hike or a day at the beach. Select from sandwiches, salads, or lobster for lunch. Lambi, smoked marlin, dolphinfish, and tuna steak may be joined on the dinner menu by chicken française and a daily vegetarian special. Wash down your meal with a cold beer or a fresh-fruit smoothie. Transportation is available. ⊠ *La Sagesse, St. David's* ☎ *473/444–6458* ☖ *Reservations essential* ⊟ *AE, MC, V.*

Carriacou

CARIBBEAN ✕ **Callaloo by the Sea Restaurant & Bar.** On the main road, south of **¢–$$** town, diners enjoy extraordinary views of Sandy Island and Hillsborough Bay. The emphasis is on West Indian dishes and excellent seafood, including lobster thermidor. The callaloo soup, of course, is outstanding. Don't miss it! ✉ *Hillsborough* ☎ *473/443–8004* ⊟ *AE, MC, V* ⊘ *Closed Sept.*

SEAFOOD ✕ **Scraper's.** Scraper's serves up lobster, conch, and the fresh catch of
¢–$ the day. It's a simple spot seasoned with occasional calypsonian sere-
nades (by owner Steven Gay "Scraper," who's a pro). Order a rum punch
and just enjoy yourself. ✉ *Tyrrel Bay* ☎ *473/443–7403* ⊟ *AE, D,
MC, V.*

Beaches

Grenada

Grenada has some 80 mi (130 km) of coastline, 65 bays, and 45 white-
sand (and a few black-sand) beaches—many in little coves. The best
beaches face the Caribbean, south of St. George's, where the resorts are
also clustered.

Bathway Beach. A beautiful strip of sand with a natural reef that protects swimmers from the rough Atlantic surf on Grenada's north shore,
this Levera National Park beach has changing rooms at the park headquarters.

Fodor'sChoice **Grand Anse Beach.** In the southwest, about 3 mi (5 km) south of St.
★   George's, is Grenada's loveliest and most popular beach. It's a gleam-
ing 2-mi (3-km) semicircle of white sand lapped by clear, gentle surf.
Sea grape trees and coconut palms provide shady escapes from the sun.
Brilliant rainbows frequently spill into the sea from the high green
mountains that frame St. George's Harbour to the north. The Grand
Anse Craft & Spice Market is at the midpoint of the beach.

La Sagesse Beach. Along the southeast coast, at La Sagesse Nature Center, is this lovely, quiet refuge with a strip of powdery white sand. Plan
a full day of nature walks, with lunch at the small inn adjacent to the
beach.

Levera Beach. This beach in Levera National Park at the north end of
the island is pretty and remote, but too rough for more than wading
(note that it's closed from April to June, when turtle eggs are hatching).

Morne Rouge Beach. Just 1 mi (1½ km) south of Grand Anse Bay, this ½-
mi-long (¾-km-long) crescent has a gentle surf that is excellent for swimming. Light meals are available nearby.

Pink Gin Beach. This beach is at Point Salines, near the airport.

Carriacou

Anse La Roche. Like all the beaches on Carriacou, this one—about a 15-
minute hike from the village of Prospect, in the north—has pure white
sand, sparkling clear water, and abundant marine life for snorkelers. It's
never crowded here.

Hillsborough. Day-trippers can take a dip at this beach adjacent to the
jetty. The beach stretches for quite a distance in each direction, so there
is plenty of room to swim without interference from the boat traffic.

Paradise Beach. This long, narrow stretch of sand between Hillsborough
and Tyrrel Bay has calm, clear, inviting water, but there are no changing facilities.

★ **Sandy Island.** This is a truly deserted island off Hillsborough—just a strip
of white sand with a few palm trees, surrounded by a reef and crystal-
clear waters. Anyone hanging around the jetty with a motorboat will
provide transportation for a few dollars. Bring your snorkeling gear and,
if you want, a picnic—and leave all your cares behind.

Tyrrel Bay. This swath of sand is popular with the sailing set, who use
the bay as an anchorage. But beware the manchineel trees here; they drop
poisonous green "apples," and their foliage can burn your skin.

Sports & the Outdoors

BOATING & SAILING

★

As the "Gateway to the Grenadines," Grenada attracts significant numbers of seasoned sailors to its waters. Large marinas are in the lagoon area of St. George's, at Prickly Bay and True Blue on Grenada's south coast, at St. David's in southeast Grenada, and at Tyrrel Bay in Carriacou. You can charter a yacht, with or without crew, for weeklong sailing vacations through the Grenadines or along the coast of Venezuela. Scenic half- or full-day sails along Grenada's coast cost $30–$60 per person (with a minimum of four passengers), including lunch or snacks and open bar; a full-day cruise from Grenada to Carriacou may cost $350–$700, depending on the boat, for one to six people.

On Grenada: **Carib Cats** (☎ 473/444–3222) departs from the lagoon area of St. George's for either a full-day sail along the southwest coast, a half-day snorkel cruise to Molinière Bay, or a two-hour sunset cruise along the west coast. **First Impressions** (☎ 473/440–3678) offers full-day, half-day, and sunset sailing trips along Grenada's southwest coast aboard *Starwind II,* a 43-ft sailing yacht, or the 42-ft catamaran *Starwind III.* **Footloose Yacht Charters** (☎ 473/440–7949) operates from the lagoon in St. George's and has both sailing or motor yachts available for day trips around Grenada or longer charters to the Grenadines. **Horizon Yacht Charters** (☎ 473/439–1000), at True Blue Bay Resort, will arrange bareboat or crewed charters, as well as day sails or three-day trips to the Grenadines. **Island Dreams** (☎ 473/443–3603) has a 45-ft sailing yacht available for private half- or full-day charters for up to 10 passengers or overnight sails around Grenada or to the Grenadines for two people. **Moorings "Club Mariner" Watersports Center** (☎ 473/444–4449 or 473/444–4549), at the Secret Harbour Resort, in L'Anse aux Épines, has half- and full-day skippered charters, rental sailboats, and a several sailing programs for beginning and experienced sailors. **SeaHawk Charters** (☎ 473/444–1126) operates *SeaHawk,* an 87-ft, U.S.-flagged, live-aboard dive vessel that accommodates 12 passengers. The 6-night/7-day voyage costs $1,750 per person and includes a shared cabin (with private head and a/c), meals and snacks, wine and beer, five dives daily (including night dives), and all equipment. **Tradewind Yacht Charters** (☎ 473/444–4924), at the Spice Island Marina on Prickly Bay, rents sailing or power yachts, with or without crew, by the day or week.

On Carriacou: **Carriacou Yacht Charters** (✉ Tyrrel Bay ☎ 473/443–6292) has a 76-ft ketch, *Suvetar,* which cruises the Grenadines on either long- or short-term charters or for day trips.

CYCLING

Level ground is rare in Grenada, but that doesn't stop the aerobically primed. Roads are narrow and winding, however, and sharing lanes with fast-moving vehicles can be hazardous. You can rent bikes at **Grenada Mountain Bike Club** (✉ Grand Anse ☎ 473/444–5985). **Trailblazers Mountain Bikes** (✉ Grand Anse ☎ 473/444–5337) rents bikes by the day or week, and also offers guided day tours at $60 per person, including lunch.

FISHING

Deep-sea fishing around Grenada is excellent, with marlin, sailfish, yellowfin tuna, and dolphinfish topping the list of good catches. You can arrange half- or full-day sportfishing trips for $250–$500, depending on the type of boat, number of people, and length of trip. **Bezo Charters** (☎ 473/443–5477 or 473/443–5021) has a tournament-equipped Bertram 31 Flybridge Sport Fisherman, called *Bezo,* with air-conditioned cabin, fighting chair, and an experienced crew just waiting to take you bluewater fishing. Charters can be customized; equipment and beverages are included. **Evans Fishing Charters** (☎ 473/444–4422 or 473/444–4217) has a Bertram 35 Sport Fisherman, *Xiphias Seeker,* with an air-conditioned cabin; equipment includes Penn International and Shimano reels. **True Blue Sportfishing** (📞 473/444–2048) offers big-game charters on its "purpose-built" 31-ft Sport Fisherman, *Yes Aye*. It has an enclosed cabin, fighting chair, and professional tackle. Refreshments and courtesy transport are included.

GOLF A major new development under construction at Levera Beach, at the northeastern tip of Grenada, will include an 18-hole, 7,250-yard, championship golf course and, eventually, two upscale resorts, 150 vacation villas, and shops. The golf course should be complete in late 2003 or early 2004; construction of the resorts will follow. Determined golfers might want to try the 9-hole course at the **Grenada Golf and Country Club** (📞 473/444–4128), about halfway between St. George's and Grand Anse. Greens fees are EC$7, and club rental is available; your hotel can make arrangements for you. It's the only truly public course on the island. **Grenada Grand Beach Resort** (📞 473/444–4371) in Grand Anse has a 9-hole, par-3 course. **LaSOURCE** (📞 473/444–2556), in Point Salines, has a 9-hole, par-3 course.

HIKING Mountain trails wind through **Grand Étang National Park and Forest Reserve** (📞 473/440–6160); if you're lucky, you may spot a Mona monkey or some exotic birds on your hike. There are trails for all levels—from a self-guided nature trail around Grand Étang Lake to a demanding one through the bush to the peak of Mt. Qua Qua (2,373 ft [724 m]) or a real trek up Mt. St. Catherine (2,757 ft [841 m]). Long pants and hiking shoes are recommended. The cost is $25 per person for a four-hour guided hike up Mt. Qua Qua, $20 each for two or more, or $15 each for three or more; the Mt. St. Catherine hike starts at $35 per person. **EcoTrek** (📞 473/444–7777) takes small groups on day trips to the heart of the rain forest, where you'll find hidden waterfalls and hot-spring pools. **Henry's Safari Tours** (📞 473/444–5313) offers hiking excursions through rich agricultural land and rain forest to Upper Concord Falls and other fascinating spots. **Telfor Bedeau, Hiking Guide** (📞 473/442–6200) is a Grenadian treasure. Over the years he has walked up, down, or across nearly every mountain, trail, and pathway on the island. His experience and knowledge make him an excellent guide, whether it's an easy walk with novices or the most strenuous hike with experts.

RUNNING At 4 PM on alternate Saturdays throughout the year, **Hash House Harriers** (📞 473/440–3343) welcomes not-so-serious runners and walkers to join them for exercise and fun in the countryside.

SCUBA DIVING & SNORKELING You can see hundreds of varieties of fish and more than 40 species of coral at more than a dozen sites off Grenada's southwest coast, only 15 to 20 minutes by boat, and another couple of dozen sites around Carriacou's reefs and neighboring islets. Depths vary from 20 ft to 120 ft, and visibility varies from 30 ft to 100 ft.

Off Grenada: A spectacular dive is *Bianca C*, a 600-ft cruise ship that caught fire in 1961, sank to 100 ft, and is now encrusted with coral and a habitat for giant turtles, spotted eagle rays, barracuda, and jacks. **Boss Reef** extends 5 mi (8 km) from St. George's Harbour to Point Salines, with a depth ranging from 20 to 90 ft. **Flamingo Bay** has a wall that drops to 90 ft (27½ m) and is teeming with fish, sponges, seahorses, sea fans, and coral. **Molinère Reef** slopes from about 20 ft below the surface to a wall that drops to 65 ft. It's a good dive for beginners, and advanced divers can continue farther out to view the wreck of the *Buccaneer*, a 42-ft sloop.

Off Carriacou: **Kick-em Jenny** is an active underwater volcano, with plentiful coral and marine life and visibility up to 100 ft. **Sandy Island,** in Hillsborough Bay, is especially good for night diving and has fish that feed off its extensive reefs 70 ft deep. For experienced divers, **Twin Sisters of Isle de Rhonde** is one of the most spectacular dives in the Grenadines, with walls and drop-offs of up to 185 ft and an underwater cave.

Most dive operators take snorkelers along on dive trips or have special snorkeling adventures. The best snorkeling in Grenada is at Molinère Point, north of St. George's; in Carriacou, Sandy Island is magnificent and just a few hundred yards offshore.

The PADI-certified dive operators listed below offer scuba and snorkeling trips to reefs and wrecks, including night dives and special excursions to the *Bianca C.* They also offer resort courses for beginning divers and certification instruction for more experienced divers. It costs about $40–$45 for a one-tank dive, $70–$75 for a two-tank dive, $50 for *Bianca C,* $75–$80 to dive Isle De Rhonde, and $50–$55 for night dives. Discounted 5- and 10-dive packages are also offered. Resort courses cost about $70, lifetime open-water certification about $350, and snorkeling trips about $15.

Aquanauts Grenada (⊠ Rendezvous Beach Resort, L'Anse aux Épines ☎ 473/444–1126 ⊠ Spice Island Beach Resort, Grand Anse ☎ 473/439–2500) has a multilingual staff, so instruction is available in English, German, Dutch, French, and Spanish. Two-tank dive trips, accommodating no more than eight divers, are offered each morning to both the Caribbean and Atlantic sides of Grenada. **Dive Grenada** (⊠ Flamboyant Hotel, Morne Rouge ☎ 473/444–1092) offers dive trips twice daily (at 10 AM and 2 PM), specializing in diving the *Bianca C.* **EcoDive** (⊠ Coyaba Beach Resort, Grand Anse ☎ 473/444–7777) offers two dive trips daily, both drift and wreck dives, as well as weekly day trips to dive Isle de Rhonde. The company also runs Grenada's marine conservation and education center, which conducts coral-reef monitoring and turtle projects. **EcoDive True Blue** (⊠ True Blue Bay Resort, True Blue ☎ 473/444–2133) offers trips to Atlantic sites. **Sanvics Scuba** (⊠ Grenada Grand Beach Resort, Grand Anse ☎ 473/444–4753) offers daily one- and two-tank dive trips to coral reefs, walls, and wreck sites. **Scuba World** (⊠ Rex Grenadian Resort, Point Salines ☎ 473/444–3684) offers daily trips to the *Bianca C.*

Arawak Divers (⊠ Tyrrel Bay, Carriacou ☎ 473/443–6906) has its own jetty at Tyrrel Bay; it takes small groups on daily dive trips and night dives, offers courses in German and English, and provides pick-up service from yachts. **Carriacou Silver Diving** (⊠ Main St., Hillsborough, Carriacou ☎ 473/443–7882) accommodates up to 12 divers on one of its dive boats and up to six on another. The center operates two guided single-tank dives daily, as well as individually scheduled excursions. **Tanki's Watersport Paradise Ltd.** (⊠ Paradise Beach, Carriacou ☎ 473/443–8406) offers dive trips to nearby reefs and snorkeling trips to Sandy Island.

TENNIS Those staying at a hotel without tennis on-site may play on the unattended, first come–first "serve" public courts in Grand Anse and in Tanteen, St. George's.

Shopping

The best souvenirs of Grenada are little spice baskets filled with cinnamon, nutmeg, mace, bay leaves, cloves, turmeric, and ginger. You can buy them for as little as $2 in practically every shop, at the open-air produce market at **Market Square** in St. George's, at the vendor stalls near the pier, and at the Craft & Spice Market on Grand Anse Beach. Vendors also sell inexpensive handmade fabric dolls, coral jewelry, seashells, and hats and baskets handwoven from green palm fronds. Bargaining is not appropriate in the shops, and it isn't customary with vendors—although most will offer you "a good price."

Areas & Malls

In St. George's, vendor stalls and gift shops along **The Carenage** are particularly convenient for cruise-ship passengers. On the north side of the harbor, **Young Street** is a main shopping thoroughfare; it rises steeply from the Carenage, then descends just as steeply to the market area.

In Grand Anse, a short walk from the resorts, the **Excel Plaza** has numerous shops and services to interest locals and tourists alike, including a full-service health club and a three-screen movie theater. **Grand Anse Shopping Centre** offers a supermarket–liquor store, a clothing store, a fast-food restaurant, a pharmacy, an art gallery, and several small gift shops. **Le Marquis Complex,** diagonally across the street, has restaurants, shops, an art gallery, and tourist services. **Spiceland Mall** has a modern supermarket (with a liquor section), clothing and shoe boutiques for men and women, housewares, a wine shop, gift shops, a food court, a bank, and a video-game arcade.

Specialty Items

ART **Art and Soul** (⊠ Spiceland Mall, Grand Anse ☎ 473/439–3450) is the personal gallery of Susan Mains, whose colorful paintings of island scenes grace the walls of many local hotels and businesses. **Art Grenada** (⊠ Suite 7, Grand Anse Shopping Centre, Grand Anse ☎ 473/444–2317) displays and sells paintings, drawings, and watercolors exclusively by Grenadian artists, among them Canute Caliste, Lyndon Bedeau, and Susan Mains. Exhibitions change monthly, and you can have your purchases shipped. At **United Artists Art Gallery** (⊠ No. 15, Le Marquis Complex, Grand Anse ☎ 473/444–5022), you'll find wood and stone carvings, painted masks, paintings, furniture, and other objets d'art created by artists from Grenada, Carriacou, and Petite Martinique. **Yellow Poui Art Gallery** (⊠ 9 Young St., St. George's ☎ 473/440–3001) displays and sells original paintings, sculpture, photography, lithographs, and antique engravings by artists from Grenada and elsewhere in the Caribbean.

BOOKS A colorful souvenir picture book, works on island culture and history, charming local stories for kids, a thick novel for the beach, or a paperback for the trip home are all good reasons to drop into one of Grenada's bookstores. **B&G Books** (⊠ Grand Anse Shopping Center, Grand Anse ☎ 473/439–3395) is a tiny shop next to the Food Fair. **Sea Change** (⊠ The Carenage, St. George's ☎ 473/440–3402) is nestled underneath the Nutmeg restaurant, right on the waterfront.

DUTY-FREE GOODS Duty-free shops at the airport sell liquor at impressive discounts of up to 50%, as well as perfumes, gifts, and crafts. You can shop duty free at some shops in town, but you must show your passport and outbound ticket to benefit from the duty-free prices. **Colombian Emeralds** (⊠ The Carenage, St. George's ☎ 473/440–1746 ⊠ Point Salines International Airport ☎ 473/444–1047) has a large selection of fine jewelry, watches, and gifts at its two shops. **The Gift Shop** (☎ 473/444–4408) sells crystal, china, watches, and leather goods at its shop at the Grand Anse Shopping Centre. **Gitten's** (⊠ The Carenage, St. George's ☎ 473/440–3174 ⊠ Spiceland Mall ☎ 473/439–0860 ⊠ Point Salines International Airport ☎ 473/444–2549) carries perfume and cosmetics at its three shops.

FOODSTUFFS **Marketing & National Importing Board** (⊠ Young St., St. George's ☎ 473/440–1791) stocks fresh fruits and vegetables, spices, hot sauces, and local syrups and jams at lower prices than you'll find in gift shops. **Market Square** (⊠ foot of Young St., St. George's) is a bustling, open-air produce market that's open mornings; Saturday is the best—and busiest—

Fodor's Choice ★

time to stock up on fresh fruit to enjoy during your stay. But it's a particularly good place to buy fresh, island-grown spices, perhaps the best such market in the entire Caribbean. Crafts, leather goods, and decorative objects are also for sale.

GIFTS **Arawak Islands** (⊠ Upper Belmont Rd., St. George's ☎ 473/444–3577) blends island perfumes, colognes, body oils, soaps, and herbal teas—all packaged for gift giving. The workshop is on-site. **Figleaf** (⊠ The Carenage, St. George's ☎ 473/440–9771 ⊠ Le Marquis Complex, Grand Anse ☎ 473/439–1824) is a small gift shop where you'll find an interesting selection of Caribbean arts and crafts, aromatherapy and herbal bath products, and resort wear. **Gifts Remembered** (⊠ Cross St., St. George's ☎ 473/440–2482 ⊠ Coyaba Beach Resort, Grand Anse ☎ 473/444–4129) is crammed with wonderful, inexpensive things, including hammocks, scrimshaw, wood carvings, beachwear, sundries, and hand-painted masks made from calabashes. **Imagine** (⊠ Grand Anse Shopping Centre, Grand Anse ☎ 473/444–4028) specializes in island handicrafts, including straw work, ceramics, island fashions, and batik fabrics. **Pssst Boutique** (⊠ Spiceland Mall, Grand Anse ☎ 473/443–8783) will catch your eye; it's chock full of unusual costume jewelry, colorful island clothing, and fascinating gift items for the home.

HANDICRAFTS **Art Fabrik** (⊠ 9 Young St., St. George's ☎ 473/440–0568) is a studio where you can watch artisans create batik before turning it into clothing or accessories. In the shop you'll find fabric by the yard or fashioned into dresses, shirts, shorts, hats, and scarves. The **Grand Anse Craft & Spice Market** (⊠ Grand Anse ☎ 473/444–3780), managed by the Grenada Board of Tourism, is between the main road and the beach. The facility has 82 booths for vendors who sell arts, crafts, spices, music tapes, clothing, produce, and refreshments. It's open daily 7–7. **Tikal** (⊠ Young St., St. George's ☎ 473/440–2310) is known for its exquisite baskets, artwork, jewelry, batik items, and fashions, both locally made and imported from Africa and Latin America.

RECORDS **Turbo Charge Records & Tapes** (⊠ St. John's St., St. George's ☎ 473/440–0586) is the place to buy the latest reggae, calypso, soca, and steel-band music.

Nightlife & the Arts

Nightlife
Grenada's nightlife is centered on the resort hotels and a handful of nightspots in the Grand Anse area. During the winter season many hotels have a steel band or other local entertainment several nights a week.

BARS **The Boatyard** (⊠ L'Anse aux Épines ☎ 473/444–4662), at the Spice Island Marina, is the place to be on Friday from 11 PM 'til sun-up, when there's a steel band and international discs are spun by a smooth-talkin' local DJ; on Saturday there's dancing to live band music. **Casablanca** (⊠ Grand Anse ☎ 473/444–1631) is a sports bar, upstairs above the banks, where you can play chess, cards, dominoes, darts, pool, or snooker, and watch games on a big-screen TV while having a drink and a snack; Monday to Saturday, from 5 PM to 3 AM, you can listen and dance to a DJ or live music. **Castaways** (⊠ L'Anse aux Épines ☎ 473/444–1250) is a friendly spot, with a DJ and dancing most nights, live music on Friday and Saturday in season, and snacks and meals served indoors or out, if you wish.

DANCE CLUBS **Dynamite Disco** (⊠ The Limes, Grand Anse ☎ 473/444–4056) has a party every weekend, with disco, reggae, and calypso music. **Fantazia** (⊠ Morne Rouge ☎ 473/444–2288) is a popular nightspot; disco, soca, reggae, and international pop music are played from 9:30 PM until the wee hours on Thursday, Friday, and Saturday nights. Wednesday is oldies night, and Friday night is a cultural cabaret designed to give visitors a taste of local folklore and traditional dances. There's a small cover charge of EC$10–EC$20 on weekends.

THEME NIGHTS **Rhum Runner** (⊠ The Carenage, St. George's ☎ 473/440–4386), a 60-ft twin-deck catamaran, leaves from the Carenage at 7:30 PM each Friday and Saturday for a moonlight cruise in the waters around St. George's and Grand Anse, returning about midnight. Tickets are $8 (EC$20), and reservations are recommended. On Wednesday from 6 to 9 there's a sunset dinner cruise for $40 (EC$107) per person; reservations must be made by 4:30 the day before. *Rhum Runner II,* a 72-ft sister ship, operates monthly moonlight cruises the Friday and Saturday nights nearest the full moon for $11 (EC$30) per person—add $2 (EC$6) for a barbecue dinner.

The Arts

ISLAND CULTURE **Marryshow Folk Theatre** (⊠ Herbert Blaize St., St. George's ☎ 473/440–2451) presents concerts, plays, and special cultural events. Call for a schedule.

Exploring Grenada

Numbers in the margin correspond to points of interest on the Grenada & Carriacou map.

Grenada

It may be hard to pull yourself away from the beach, but a day or more of exploring is time well spent: the scenery is stunning, and the scent of nutmeg fills the air. St. George's has a busy harbor, interesting shops, and several historic sites. Visit a spice plantation and a nutmeg processing plant, or if you're adventurous, take guided hikes into the rain forest, up a mountainside, or to hidden waterfalls.

WHAT TO SEE **Annandale Falls.** A mountain stream cascades 40 ft into a pool surrounded by exotic vines, such as liana and elephant ears. This is a lovely, cool spot for swimming and picnicking. ⊠ *Main interior road, 15 mins northeast of St. George's* ☎ 473/440–2452 🖃 *$1* ☉ *Daily 9–5.*

❸ **Bay Gardens.** Fifteen minutes from St. George's, on what was once a sugar plantation, some 450 species of flowers and plants have been cultivated in patterns mimicking their growth in the wild. Eight acres of paths are open to visitors. ⊠ *Morne Delice, St. Paul's* ☎ 473/435–1986 🖃 *$2* ☉ *Daily 7–6.*

⓫ **Carib's Leap.** At Sauteurs (the French word for "leapers"), on the island's northernmost tip, Carib's Leap (or Leapers Hill) is the 100-ft vertical cliff from which the last of the indigenous Carib Indians flung themselves into the sea in 1651. After losing several bloody battles with European colonists, they chose to exterminate their race rather than surrender to the French. A commemorative display recounts the event.

❼ **Concord Falls.** About 8 mi (13 km) north of St. George's, a turnoff from the West Coast Road leads to Concord Falls—actually three separate waterfalls. The first is at the end of the road; during the dry months (January–May), when the currents aren't too strong, you can take a dip under the cascade. Reaching the two other waterfalls requires an hour's hike into the forest reserve. The third and most spectacular waterfall, at Fontainbleu, thunders 65 ft over huge boulders and creates a small pool where you can cool off before hiking back down the trail. It's smart to hire a guide. The path is clear, but slippery boulders toward the end can be treacherous without assistance. ⊠ *West Coast Rd.* 🎫 *$2 for changing room.*

🐢 ❽ **Dougaldston Spice Estate.** Just south of Gouyave, this historic plantation, now primarily a living museum, still grows and processes spices the old-fashioned way. You can see cocoa, nutmeg, mace, cloves, and other spices laid out on giant racks to dry in the sun. A worker will be glad to explain the process (and will appreciate a small donation). You can buy spices for about $2 a bag. ⊠ *Gouyave* 🕾 *No phone* 🎫 *Free* ☉ *Weekdays 9–4.*

🐢 ❾ **Gouyave Nutmeg Processing Cooperative,** in the center of the west coast fishing village of Gouyave (pronounced *gwahve*), is a fragrant, fascinating way to spend a half-hour. Workers in the three-story plant, which turns out 3 million pounds of Grenada's most famous export each year, sort nutmegs by hand and pack them in burlap bags for shipping worldwide. ⊠ *Gouyave* 🕾 *473/444–8337* 🎫 *$1* ☉ *Weekdays 10–1 and 2–4.*

🐢 ❷ **Grand Anse.** A residential and commercial area about 5 mi (8 km) south of downtown St. George's, Grand Anse is named for the world-renowned beach it surrounds. Most of Grenada's tourist facilities—resorts, restaurants, some shopping, and most nightlife—are in this general area. **Grand Anse Beach** is a 2-mi (3-km) crescent of sand shaded by coconut palms and seagrape trees, with gentle turquoise surf. A handful of resort hotels line the beachfront, and there's a public entrance at Camerhogne Park, just a few steps from the main road. **St. George's University,** which for years held classes at its enviable beachfront location in Grand Anse, has a sprawling campus in True Blue, a nearby residential community. The university's Grand Anse property, from which the evacuation of U.S. medical students was a high priority of U.S. forces during the 1983 intervention, is currently used for administrative purposes.

🐢 ❻ **Grand Étang National Park and Forest Reserve.** Deep in the interior of lush, mountainous Grenada is a bird sanctuary and forest reserve with miles of hiking trails, lookouts, and fishing streams. **Grand Étang Lake** is a 36-acre expanse of cobalt-blue water that fills the crater of an extinct volcano 1,740 ft above sea level. Although legend has it the lake is bottomless, maximum soundings are recorded at 18 ft. The informative **Grand Étang Forest Center** has displays on the local wildlife and vegetation. A forest manager is on hand to answer questions. A small snack bar and souvenir stands are nearby. ⊠ *Main interior road, between Grenville and St. George's* 🕾 *473/440–6160* 🎫 *$1* ☉ *Daily 8:30–4.*

🐢 ⓯ **Grenville Cooperative Nutmeg Association** is open to the public for guided tours. You can see and learn about the entire process of receiving, drying, sorting, and packing nutmegs. ⊠ *Grenville* 🕾 *473/442–7241* 🎫 *$1* ☉ *Weekdays 10–1 and 2–4.*

🐢 ❹ **Laura Herb and Spice Garden.** The 6½-acre gardens are part of an old plantation in the village of Laura, in St. David's, just 6 mi (10 km) east of Grand Anse. On the 45-minute tour you'll learn all about Grenada's indigenous spices and herbs, including cocoa, clove, nutmeg, pimiento, cinnamon, turmeric, and tonka beans (vanilla). ⊠ *St. David's* 🕾 *473/443–2604* 🎫 *$2* ☉ *Weekdays 8–4.*

⓬ **Levera National Park and Bird Sanctuary.** This portion of Grenada's protected parkland encompasses 450 acres at the northeastern tip of the island, where the Caribbean Sea meets the Atlantic Ocean. Facilities include a visitor center, changing rooms, a small amphitheater, and a gift shop. A natural reef protects swimmers from the rough Atlantic surf at Bathway Beach. Thick mangroves provide food and protection for nesting seabirds and seldom-seen parrots. Some fine Arawak ruins and petroglyphs are on display, and the first islets of the Grenadines are visible from the beach. Entrance and use of the beaches and grounds are free; there's a small charge to view the displays in the visitor center. ⊠ *Levera* ☎ *473/442–1018* 🖃 *Free* ⊙ *Daily 8:30–4.*

⑩ **Mt. Rodney Estate.** When touring northern Grenada, plan to have lunch in Sauteurs. A road winds up a mountainside to an 1880s plantation house lovingly restored by Lin and Norris Nelson. Sugar, coffee, and cocoa grew on the plantation in its heyday, and there are still fabulous views north to the Grenadines. Buffet luncheon is served from noon to 2 on the dining terrace. (This lunch stop is often included on a guided island tour; or call 473/442–9420 for reservations.) ⊠ *Sauteurs.*

⑭ **Pearl's Airport.** Just north of Grenville, on the east coast, is the island's original airport, which was replaced in 1984 by Point Salines International Airport. Deteriorating Cuban and Soviet planes sit at the end of the old runway, abandoned after the 1983 intervention, when Cuban "advisors" helping to construct the airport at Point Salines were summarily removed from the island. There's a good view north to the Grenadines and a small beach nearby. ⊠ *Grenville.*

⑬ **River Antoine Rum Distillery.** At this rustic operation, kept open primarily as a museum, Rivers rum is produced by the same methods used since the distillery opened in 1785. The process begins with the crushing of sugarcane from adjacent fields in the River Antoine (pronounced an-*twine*) Estate. The result is a potent overproof rum that will knock your socks off. ⊠ *River Antoine Estate, St. Patrick's* ☎ *473/442–7109* 🖃 *$2* ⊙ *Guided tours daily 9–4.*

❶ **St. George's.** Grenada's capital is a busy West Indian city, most of which remains unchanged from colonial days. Narrow streets lined with shops wind up, down, and across steep hills. Pastel-painted warehouses with roofs covered in orange tiles (brought over from Europe as ballast in 18th-century ships) cling to the waterfront. Small rainbow-hue houses rise from the waterfront and disappear into steep green hills.

St. George's Harbour is the center of town. Schooners, ferries, and tour boats tie up along the seawall or at the small dinghy dock. Cruise ships dock at the large pier at the harbor entrance or anchor just outside and transport passengers ashore by tender. On weekends a tall ship is likely to be anchored in the middle of the harbor, giving the scene a 19th-century flavor.

The Carenage (pronounced car-a-*nahzh*), which surrounds horseshoe-shape St. George's Harbour, is the capital's main thoroughfare. Warehouses, shops, and restaurants line the waterfront. Near the cruise-ship welcome center, at the south end of The Carenage, the Grenada Board of Tourism has its offices, and you can buy inexpensive spices and crafts at vendor stalls nearby. At the center of The Carenage, on the pedestrian plaza, sits the *Christ of the Deep* statue. It was presented to Grenada by Costa Cruise Line in remembrance of its ship *Bianca C,* which burned and sank in the harbor in 1961 and is now a favorite dive site.

⟳ The **Grenada National Museum,** a block from The Carenage, is set in the foundation of a French army barracks and prison that was built in 1704. The small museum has exhibitions of news items, photos, and proclamations relating to the 1983 intervention, along with Empress Josephine's childhood bathtub and other memorabilia from earlier historical periods. ⊠ *Young and Monckton Sts.* ☎ *473/440–3725* 🖃 *$1* ⊙ *Weekdays 9–4:30, Sat. 10–1.* An engineering feat for its time, the 340-ft-long (103-m-long) **Sendall Tunnel** was built in 1895 and named for an early governor. It separates the harborside of St. George's from the Esplanade on the bay side of town, where you'll find the open-air meat, fish, and produce markets. The Esplanade is also the terminus of the minibus route. Don't miss St. George's picturesque **Market Square** (⊠ Granby St.), a block from The Esplanade. It's open every weekday morning, but really comes alive on Saturday from 8 to noon. Vendors sell baskets, spices, brooms, clothing, knickknacks, coconut water, and heaps of fresh produce. Market Square is historically where parades and political rallies take place—and the beginning of the minibus routes to all areas of the island. **St. Andrew's Presbyterian Church,** built in 1830, is at the intersection of Halifax and Church streets. Also known as Scots' Kirk, it was constructed with the help of the Freemasons. Built in 1825, the beautiful stone-and-pink-stucco **St. George's Anglican Church,** on Church Street, is filled with statues and plaques depicting Grenada in the 18th and 19th centuries. **St. George's Methodist Church,** on Green Street near Herbert Blaize Street, was built in 1820 and is the oldest original church in the city. The Gothic tower of **St. George's Roman Catholic Church** dates from 1818, but the current structure was built in 1884; the tower is the city's most visible landmark. On Church Street, **York House** (1801) is home to Grenada's Houses of Parliament and Supreme Court. It, the neighboring Registry Building (1780), and Government House (1802) are fine examples of early Georgian architecture.

Fodor$Choice **Ft. George** (⊠ Church St.) is high on the hill at the southern tip of Church
★ Street. The fort, which rises above the entrance to St. George's Harbour, is Grenada's oldest—built by the French in 1705 to protect the harbor. No shots were fired here until October 1983, when Prime Minister Bishop and some of his followers were assassinated in the courtyard. The fort now houses police headquarters, but is open to the public daily; admission is free. The 360-degree view of the capital city, St. George's Harbour, and the open sea is spectacular.

On Richmond Hill, high above the city of St. George's and the inland side of the harbor, historic **Ft. Frederick** provides a panoramic view of two-thirds of Grenada. The fort was completed in 1791; it was also the headquarters of the People's Revolutionary Government during the 1983 coup. Today you can get a bird's-eye view of the prison, on top of an adjacent hill, where the rebels remain incarcerated—and have, by all accounts, one of the most picturesque views in all of Grenada.

In St. Paul's, five minutes outside St. George's, **de la Grenade Industries** produces syrups, jams, jellies, and liqueurs made from nutmeg and other homegrown fruits and spices. It began in 1960 as a cottage industry. You're welcome to watch the process and purchase gifts from the retail operation on-site. ☎ *473/440–3241* ☒ *Free* ☉ *Weekdays 8– 5, Sat. 9–12:30.*

Carriacou

Carriacou, the land of many reefs, is a hilly island and (unlike its lush sister island of Grenada) has neither lakes nor rivers—only rainwater, caught in cisterns and purified with bleach. It gets arid during the dry season (January–May). Nevertheless, plenty of fruit is grown here, and the climate seems to suit the mahogany trees used for furniture-making and the white cedar critical to the boatbuilding that has made Carriacou famous.

Hillsborough is Carriacou's main town. Just offshore, Sandy Island is one of the nicest beaches around; almost anyone with a boat can give you a ride out, and you can leave your cares on the dock. Rolling hills cut a wide swath through the island's center, from Gun Point in the north to Tyrrel Bay in the south. The small town of Windward, on the northeast coast, is a boatbuilding community. You'll likely encounter half-finished hulls on the roadside. Originally constructed for interisland commerce, the boats are now built for fishing and pleasure sailing.

Interestingly, tiny Carriacou has several distinct cultures. Hillsborough is decidedly English; the southern region, around L'Esterre, reflects French roots; and the northern town of Windward has Scottish ties. African culture, of course, is the overarching influence.

WHAT TO SEE   **Belair.** For a wonderful bird's-eye view of Carriacou's west coast, drive
⑰   to Belair, 700 ft above sea level, in the north-central part of the island. On the way you'll pass the photogenic ruins of an old sugar mill. The Belair lookout is adjacent to Princess Royal Hospital, where patients surely find the view of Hillsborough, the harbor, and endless sea to be restorative.

⑯ **Carriacou Museum.** Housed in a building that once held a cotton gin, one block from the waterfront, the museum has exhibitions of Amerindian, European, and African artifacts, a collection of watercolors by native folk artist Canute Caliste, and a gift shop loaded with local items. ✉ *Paterson St., Hillsborough* ☎ *473/443–8288* 🎟 *$2* 🕙 *Weekdays 9:30–4, Sat. 10–4.*

⑱ **Tyrrel Bay.** Picturesque Tyrrel Bay is a large protected harbor in southwest Carriacou. The bay is almost always full of sailboats, powerboats, and working boats—coming, going, or bobbing at their moorings. Edging the bay is a beach with pure white sand; bars, restaurants, a guest house, and a few shops face the waterfront.

Petite Martinique

Petite Martinique (pronounced *pit*-ty mar-ti-*neek*), 10 minutes north of Carriacou by boat, is tiny and residential, with a guest house or two but no tourist facilities or attractions—just peace and quiet. Meander along the beachfront and watch the boatbuilders at work. And if by chance there's a boat launch, sailboat race, wedding, or cultural festival while you're there, you're in for a treat. The music is infectious, the food bountiful, the spirit lively.

GRENADA A TO Z

To research prices, get advice from other travelers, and book travel arrangements, visit www.fodors.com.

AIR TRAVEL

Air Jamaica has twice-weekly nonstop flights into Grenada's Point Salines International Airport from New York and connecting flights from its other gateway cities via Montego Bay, Jamaica, with a stop in St. Lucia. American Airlines/American Eagle has daily flights from major U.S. and Canadian cities via San Juan. BWIA flies to Grenada from New York, Miami, Washington, D.C., Toronto, London, and Manchester via Trinidad. British Airways flies from London/Gatwick twice a week. US Airways has weekly flights nonstop from Philadelphia. Virgin Atlantic flies nonstop each week from London/Heathrow. From other parts of the world, connections must be made through U.S. cities, San Juan, Toronto, or London.

Caribbean Star flies daily to Grenada from its Antigua hub, via Dominica, St. Lucia, St. Vincent, and Trinidad. LIAT has scheduled service between Grenada and several neighboring islands. SVG Air flies between Grenada and Carriacou and between both islands and St. Vincent and the Grenadines (St. Vincent, Union, Canouan, and Bequia).

🛪 **Air Jamaica** 🕾 473/444-5975. **American Airlines/American Eagle** 🕾 473/444-2222. **British Airways** 🕾 473/444-1664. **BWIA** 🕾 473/444-1221. **Caribbean Star** 🕾 473/439-4444. **LIAT** 🕾 473/440-2796 or 473/440-4121. **SVG Air** 🕾 473/444-0328, 473/444-3549, or 800/744-7285. **US Airways** 🕾 473/439-0681. **Virgin Atlantic** 🕾 473/439-0681.

AIRPORTS

Point Salines International Airport, at the southwestern tip of Grenada, is a modern facility suitable for the largest jets. Passenger amenities include a restaurant, snack bar, and several shops (including duty-free shopping in the departure lounge). Best of all, it's no more than a ten-minute drive from nearly all hotels and resorts.

On Carriacou, five minutes south of Hillsborough, Lauriston Airport is a lighted landing strip suitable only for light planes, with a small building for ticket sales and shelter.

There is no bus service between the Point Salines Airport and hotels, but taxis are always available. Fares to St. George's are $15; to the hotels of Grand Anse and L'Anse aux Épines, $10. Rides taken between 6 PM and 6 AM incur a $4 surcharge. At Carriacou's Lauriston Airport, taxis meet every plane; the fare to Hillsborough is $4.

🛪 **Lauriston Airport** 🕾 473/443-6306. **Point Salines Airport** 🕾 473/444-4101.

BOAT & FERRY TRAVEL

The high-speed power catamaran *Osprey Express* makes two round-trip voyages daily from Grenada to Carriacou and on to Petite Martinique. The fare for the 90-minute one-way trip between Grenada and Carriacou is is $19 per person; round trip, $35. For the 15-minute trip between Carriacou and Petite Martinique, the fare is $6 each way. The boat leaves Grenada from The Carenage in St. George's.

Passenger ferries and cargo schooners (that also take passengers) to Grenada's other islands, Carriacou and Petite Martinique, depart from The Carenage. The freighters *Alexia II, Alexia III,* and *Adelaide B* leave from The Carenage in St. George's in the morning (except Monday and Thursday), ferrying cargo and passengers on the four-hour voyage to Carriacou; they return to Grenada daily (except Tuesday and Friday). The *Adelaide B* continues on from Carriacou to Petite Martinique (about a 1½-hour trip) on Wednesday and Saturday afternoons, returning early on Monday and Thursday mornings. The fare between Grenada and Carriacou is $7.50 one way, $12 round trip; between Carriacou and Petite Martinique, it's about $5 each way. Reservations aren't necessary.

The mail boat between Carriacou and Petite Martinique makes one round trip on Monday, Wednesday, and Friday, leaving Petite Martinique at 8 AM and returning from Windward, Carriacou, at noon. The fare is about $5 each way.

🛪 *Osprey Express* 🕾 473/440-8126 ⊕ www.ospreyexpress.com.

BUSINESS HOURS

BANKS Banks are open Monday–Thursday 8–3, Friday 8–5.

POST OFFICES The main post office, at Burns Point by the port in St. George's, is open weekdays 8–3:30. Each town or village has a post office branch.

SHOPS Stores are generally open weekdays 8–4 or 4:30 and Saturday 8–1; some close from noon to 1 during the week. Most are closed Sunday, although tourist shops usually open if a cruise ship is in port.

CAR RENTALS

To rent a car, you need a valid driver's license and a local permit (available at the Central Police Station on The Carenage and at some car-rental firms), which costs $12 (EC$30). Some rental agencies impose a minimum age of 25 and a maximum age of 65 to rent a car. Rental cars (including four-wheel-drive vehicles) cost $55–$75 a day or $285–$375 a week with unlimited mileage. In high season there may be a three-day minimum rental.

On Grenada, Avis is at Spice Island Rentals, on Paddock and Lagoon roads in St. George's. David's has offices at Point Salines International Airport, The Grenada Grand Beach Resort, Rex Grenadian Hotel, and the Limes in Grand Anse. Dollar Rent-a-Car is at Point Salines Airport. In the True Blue area, call McIntyre Bros. Ltd. or Indigo Car Rentals. On Carriacou, Barba's Auto Rentals, at Tyrrel Bay, will meet you at the airport.

🚗 **Avis** ☎ 473/440-3936 or 473/440-2624; 473/444-5480 after hrs. **Barba's Auto Rentals** ☎ 473/443-7454. **David's** ☎ 473/444-3399 or 473/444-2323 ⊕ www.davidscars.com. **Dollar Rent-a-Car** ☎ 473/444-4786; 473/443-2330 after hrs. **Indigo Car Rentals** ☎ 473/439-3300 ⊕ www.indigocarsgrenada.com. **McIntyre Bros. Ltd.** ☎ 473/444-3944; 473/443-5319 after hrs ⊕ www.caribbeanhorizons.com.

CAR TRAVEL

Having a car or jeep is a convenience—particularly if you are staying at a resort in a location other than Grand Anse, which has frequent minibus service. Otherwise, round-trip taxi rides can get expensive if you plan to leave the resort frequently for shopping, meals, or visiting other beaches. Driving is also a reasonable option if you want to explore the island on your own.

GASOLINE   Gasoline costs about $2.80 per gallon, and filling stations are in St. George's, Grand Anse, Grenville, Gouyave, and Sauteurs.

ROAD
CONDITIONS   Driving is a constant challenge in the tropics, but most of Grenada's 650 mi (1,050 km) of paved roads are kept in fairly good condition—albeit steep and narrow beyond the Grand Anse area. The main road between St. George's and Grand Anse winds along the coast and is heavily traveled—and kept in good condition. Directions are clearly posted, but having a map on hand is certainly a good idea when traveling in the countryside.

RULES OF THE
ROAD   Driving is on the left, British style.

ELECTRICITY

Electric current on Grenada is 220 volts/50 cycles. Appliances rated at 110 volts (U.S. standard) will work only with a transformer and adapter plug. For dual-voltage computers or appliances, you'll still need an adapter plug; some hotels will loan adapters. Most hotels have 110 outlets for shavers.

EMBASSIES

🚩 **United Kingdom British High Commission** ✉ The Netherlands Building, St. George's ☎ 473/440-3536 or 473/440-3222.
🚩 **United States Embassy of the United States** ✉ L'Anse Aux Épines Stretch, Grand Anse ☎ 473/444-1173 or 473/444-1177.

EMERGENCIES

🚩 **Ambulance Carriacou Ambulance** ☎ 774. **St. Andrew's Ambulance** ☎ 724. **St. George's, Grand Anse, and L'Anse aux Épines Ambulance** ☎ 434.
🚩 **Coast Guard Coast Guard** ☎ 399 emergencies; 473/444-1931 for nonemergencies.

🔢 Hospitals **Princess Alice Hospital** ✉ Mirabeau ☎ 473/442–7251. **Princess Royal Hospital** ✉ Hillsborough, Carriacou ☎ 473/443–7400. **St. Augustine's Medical Services, Inc.** ✉ Grand Anse ☎ 473/440–6173. **St. George's General Hospital** ✉ St. George's ☎ 473/440–2051.

🔢 Pharmacies **Charles Pharmacy** ✉ Sea View, Carriacou ☎ 473/443–7933. **Gitten's** ✉ Halifax St., St. George's ☎ 473/440–2165 ✉ Spiceland Mall, Grand Anse ☎ 473/439–0863. **Gitten's Drugmart** ✉ Main Rd., Grand Anse ☎ 473/444–4954. **Mitchell's Pharmacy** ✉ Grand Anse Shopping Centre, Grand Anse ☎ 473/444–3845. **Parris' Pharmacy Ltd.** ✉ Victoria St., Grenville ☎ 473/442–7330. **People's Pharmacy** ✉ Church St., St. George's ☎ 473/440–3444

🔢 Police & Fire **Police and fire emergencies** ☎ 911.

ETIQUETTE & BEHAVIOR

A Grenadian will always greet you with a friendly "good morning," "good afternoon," or "good evening," and will be disappointed if the courtesy isn't returned. That's true whether it's a perfect stranger or someone you've met before. Though such greetings are common throughout the Caribbean, in Grenada they will often be followed by, "Are you enjoyin' it?" It seems everyone wants to make sure you're having a good time in Grenada.

Taking photos of local people, their boats, homes, or children isn't appreciated without first asking permission and offering a tip for the favor.

Dress appropriately and discreetly, saving swimwear for the beach. Shorts and T-shirts are fine for sightseeing and shopping but frowned upon in restaurants in the evening.

FESTIVALS & SEASONAL EVENTS

GRENADA In late January, during the Spice Island Billfish Tournament, sportfishermen vie for cash prizes for the biggest game fish (marlin, sailfish, yellowfin tuna). The Grenada Sailing Festival, held at the end of January and early February, includes six days of races and regattas and a day-long crafts market and street festival—all organized by the Grenada Yacht Club.

February 7 is Independence Day. Watch the float parade and fireworks at Queen's Park, on the north side of St. George's. Beginning around March 17 and lasting a week, the St. Patrick's Day Fiesta is celebrated in Sauteurs (St. Patrick's Parish), in the north of Grenada, with arts and crafts, agricultural exhibits, food and drink, and a cultural extravaganza with music and dancing.

Late April sees international triathletes compete in the annual Grenada International Triathlon. The competition starts and finishes at Grand Anse Beach. Participants swim 1½ km, cycle 25 km, and run 5 km on the first day. A three-person relay takes place on the second day. Teams must include at least one female and have a combined age of at least 100 years.

Each June 29 the Fisherman's Birthday Celebration is a sort of mini-Carnival in villages on Grenada's west coast, particularly in Gouyave. There are a blessing of the boats, boat racing, fishing contests, and music and dancing in the street. In early August the Rainbow City Festival is held in Grenville; it's primarily an agricultural fair, with local arts and crafts and livestock.

The Grenada to Carriacou Yacht Race is a highlight of the Carriacou Regatta in August. A month of calypso road shows culminates in the Grenada Carnival the second week of August. It's the biggest celebration of the year, with a beauty pageant, a soca monarch competition, continuous steel-pan and calypso music, and a huge Parade of the Bands on the last Tuesday.

CARRIACOU The biggest event of the year is the four-day Carriacou Carnival, held in mid-February. Revelers participate in parades, calypso contests, music and dancing, and general frivolity.

During the first weekend in August, the Carriacou Regatta attracts yachts and sailboats from throughout the Caribbean for three days of boat races. Festivities also include road relays, fashion shows, donkey rides, and greasy pole contests—and music and partying galore.

In December the week before Christmas, the Carriacou Parang Festival is a musical and cultural celebration. "Parang" is Spanish for ad-libbing. Costumed singers travel from village to village, creating spontaneous songs based on local gossip and accompanied by guitar, violin, and drums.

A highlight of most festivals on Carriacou is the Big Drum Dance, unique to this island (and neighboring Union Island). The term refers to the size of the gathering, not the drum. When the British took control of Carriacou in 1783 they banned the beating of drums for fear the former French slaves would use them to communicate and start a revolt. Despite the repression, the African tradition of drumming survived. Today on Carriacou costumed dancers move to the rhythmic beat of pounding drums at social events, harvests, boat launches, weddings, and other happy occasions.

HEALTH
Insects can be a nuisance after heavy rains, when mosquitoes emerge, and on the beach after 4 PM, when tiny sand flies begin to bite. Use repellent, especially when hiking in the rain forest. Tap water in hotels and restaurants is perfectly safe to drink.

HOLIDAYS
New Year's Day (Jan. 1), Independence Day (Feb. 7), Good Friday, Easter Monday, Labour Day (May 1), Whit Monday (7th Mon. after Easter), Corpus Christi (8th Thurs. after Easter), Emancipation Holidays (1st Mon. and Tues. in Aug.), Carnival (2nd Mon. in Aug.), Thanksgiving Day (Oct. 25), Christmas, and Boxing Day (Dec. 26).

LANGUAGE
English—spoken with a fetching lilt with British intonations—is the official language here. Creole patois isn't commonly heard except, perhaps, among older folks in the countryside.

Here's some local terminology you should know: if you want a refreshing drink of coconut water at the market, for EC$1 or so the "jelly man" will hack off the top of a fresh green "jelly" (coconut) for you with one swipe of his machete. And if someone asks if you'd like a "sweetie," they're offering you a candy. When you're buying spices, you may be offered "saffron" and "vanilla." The saffron is really turmeric, a ground yellow root rather than the fragile pistils of crocus flowers; the vanilla is an essence made from locally grown tonka beans, a close substitute but not the real thing. No one is trying to pull the wool over your eyes; these are common local terms.

MAIL & SHIPPING
Airmail rates for letters to the United States, Canada, and the United Kingdom are EC$1 for a half-ounce letter or postcard; airmail rates to Australia or New Zealand are EC$1.60 for a half-ounce letter or EC$1

for a postcard. When addressing a letter to Grenada, simply write "Grenada, West Indies" after the local address.

MONEY MATTERS
Prices quoted in this chapter are in U.S. dollars unless otherwise indicated.

First Caribbean International Bank (a merger of Barclay's Bank and CIBC) has a main office in downtown St. George's; branches are in Grand Anse, Grenville, and Carriacou. National Commercial Bank is a regional bank, with branches in St. George's, Grand Anse, Grenville, and Carriacou. Scotiabank (The Bank of Nova Scotia), an international bank, has its head office in Grenada in St. George's, with branches in Grand Anse and Grenville.

🏦 **FirstCaribbean International Bank** ⊠ Church and Halifax Sts., St. George's ☎ 473/440-3232 ✉ Grand Anse ☎ 473/444-3322 ✉ Grenville ☎ 473/442-7733 ✉ Carriacou ☎ 473/443-7232. **National Commercial Bank** ⊠ True Blue ☎ 473/444-2265 ✉ Halifax St., St. George's ☎ 473/440-3566 ✉ Grand Anse ☎ 473/444-2627 ✉ Grenville ☎ 473/442-7532 ✉ Carriacou ☎ 473/443-7289. **Scotiabank** ⊠ Halifax St., St. George's ☎ 473/440-3274 ✉ Grand Anse ☎ 473/444-1917 ✉ Victoria St. Grenville ☎ 473/442-5507.

ATMS ATMs are available 24 hours a day at bank branches, on The Carenage in St. George's, and at the airport.

CREDIT CARDS Major credit cards—including Access, American Express, Diners Club, Discover, Eurocard, MasterCard, and Visa—are widely accepted.

CURRENCY Grenada uses the Eastern Caribbean dollar (EC$). The official exchange rate is fixed at EC$2.67 to US$1; cabs, shops, and hotels sometimes have slightly lower rates (EC$2.50–EC$2.60). You can exchange money at banks and hotels, but U.S. and Canadian paper currency, traveler's checks, and major credit cards are widely accepted. You will usually receive change in EC$.

PASSPORTS & VISAS
A valid passport and a return or ongoing ticket are required. An original birth certificate with raised seal and a valid, government-issued photo I.D. are also acceptable instead of a passport for U.S., Canadian, and British citizens only.

SAFETY
Crime isn't a big problem, but it's a good idea to secure your valuables in the hotel safe and not leave articles unattended on the beach. Removing bark from trees, taking wildlife from the forest, and removing coral from the sea are all forbidden.

SIGHTSEEING TOURS
Guided tours offer the sights of St. George's, Grand Étang National Park, spice plantations and nutmeg processing centers, rain-forest hikes and treks to waterfalls, snorkeling trips to offshore islands, and day trips to Carriacou. A full-day sightseeing tour costs $55–$65 per person, including lunch; a half-day tour, $40–$45; a guided hike to Mt. Qua Qua, $45.

On Adventure Jeep Tours, you drive safari fashion along scenic coastal roads, trek in the rain forest, lunch at a plantation, take a swim, and skirt the capital.

Caribbean Horizons offers personalized tours of historic and natural island sites, market and garden tours, and excursions to Carriacou.

EkoTrek, based at Grand Anse Beach, offers adventurous tours to the rain forest, snorkeling trips, and tours of Carib caves and plantation houses.

Dennis Henry of Henry's Safari Tours knows Grenada like the back of his hand. He leads adventurous hikes and four-wheel-drive-vehicle safaris, or you can design your own tour.

Spiceland Tours has several five- and seven-hour island tours, from the Urban/Suburban tour of St. George's and the south coast to the Emerald Forest tour, highlighting Grenada's natural beauty. Sunsation Tours offers customized and private island tours to all the usual sites and "as far off the beaten track as you want to go." From garden tours or a challenging hike to a day sail on a catamaran, it's all possible.

Mandoo Tours offers half- or full-day tours following northern, southern, or eastern routes, as well as hikes to Concord Falls and the mountains.

Grenada taxi drivers will conduct island sightseeing tours for $25 to $55 per person, depending on the destinations selected. Carriacou minibus drivers will take up to four people on a four-hour island tour for about $65; extra people, $15 each.

Adventure Jeep Tours ☎ 473/444-5337 ⊟ 473/444-5681 ⊕ www.grenadajeeptours. com. **Caribbean Horizons** ☎ 473/444-1550 ⊟ 473/444-2899 ⊕ www.caribbeanhorizons. com. **EcoTrek** ☎ 473/444-7777 ⊟ 473/444-4808 ⊕ www.scubadivegrenada.com. **Henry's Safari Tours** ☎ 473/444-5313 ⊟ 473/444-4460. **Mandoo Tours** ☎⊟ 473/440-1428 ⊕ www.grenadatours.com. **Spiceland Tours** ☎ 473/440-5127 or 473/440-5180 ⊟ 473/440-5466. **Sunsation Tours** ☎ 473/444-1594 ⊟ 473/444-1103 ⊕ www. grenadasunsation.com.

TAXES & SERVICE CHARGES

DEPARTURE TAX The departure tax, collected at the airport, is $20 (EC$50) for adults and $10 (EC$25) for children ages 5–11, payable in cash in either currency. A $4 (EC$10) departure tax is collected when departing Carriacou.

SALES TAX An 8% government tax is added to all hotel and restaurant bills.

SERVICE CHARGES A 10% service charge is generally added to hotel and restaurant bills.

TAXIS

Taxis are plentiful, and rates are set by the government. The trip between Grand Anse and St. George's costs $10; between Point Salines and St. George's, $15. A $4 surcharge is added for rides taken between 6 PM and 6 AM. Taxis often wait for fares at hotels, at the cruise-ship welcome center, and on the north side of The Carenage. They can be hired at an hourly rate of $20.

Water taxis are available along The Carenage. For $4 (EC$10) a motorboat will transport you on a lovely cruise between St. George's and the jetty at Grand Anse Beach. Water taxis are privately owned, unregulated, and don't follow any particular schedule—so make arrangements for a pickup time if you expect a return trip.

In Carriacou the taxi fare from Hillsborough to Belair is $4; to Prospect, $6; and to Tyrrel Bay or Windward, $8.

TELEPHONES

COUNTRY & AREA CODES The area code is 473.

INTERNATIONAL CALLS You can place direct-dial calls from Grenada to anywhere in the world using pay phones, card phones, most hotel room phones, and some mobile phones. For international calls using a major credit card, dial 111; to place a collect call or use a calling card, dial 800/225–5872 from any telephone. Pay phones are available at the airport, the cruise-ship welcome center, or the Cable & Wireless office on The Carenage in St. George's, shopping centers, and other convenient locations. Pay phones accept EC25¢ and EC$1 coins, as well as U.S. quarters. Mobile phones that operate on a TDMA digital network can roam in Grenada—for outgoing calls only.

LOCAL CALLS Local calls are free from most hotels; for directory assistance, dial 411. Prepaid phone cards, which can be used in special card phones throughout the Caribbean for local or international calls, are sold in denominations of EC$20 ($7.50), EC$30 ($12), EC$50 ($20), and EC$75 ($28) at shops, attractions, transportation centers, and other convenient outlets.

TIPPING
If the usual 10% service charge is not added to your hotel or restaurant bill, a tip at that amount is appropriate. Additional tipping is discretionary.

VISITOR INFORMATION
Before You Leave Grenada Board of Tourism ⊕ www.grenadagrenadines.com ⊠ 317 Madison Ave., New York, NY 10017 ☎ 212/687-9554 or 800/927-9554 ⊟ 212/573-9731 ⊠ 439 University Ave., Suite 920, Toronto, Ontario M5G 1Y8, Canada ☎ 416/595-1339 ⊟ 416/595-8278 ⊠ 1 Battersea Church Rd., London SW11 3LY, U.K. ☎ 020/7771-7016 ⊟ 020/7771-7181. **Grenada Hotel Association** ☎ 473/444-1353, 800/322-1753 in the U.S. and Canada ⊟ 473/444-4847 ⊕ www.grenadahotelsinfo.com.
In Grenada Grenada Board of Tourism ⊠ Burns Pt., St. George's ☎ 473/440-2001 or 473/440-2279 ⊟ 473/440-6637 ⊠ Pointe Salines ☎ 473/444-4140 ⊠ Carriacou ☎ 473/443-7948.

GUADELOUPE

12

FODOR'S CHOICE
Sofitel Auberge de la Vieille Tour resort, Gosier

HIGHLY RECOMMENDED

RESTAURANTS
Le Genois, Terre-de-Haut, Iles des Saintes
L'Hibiscus Restaurant, Bas du Fort
La Terrasse du Port (Chez Mimi), Ste-Rose
La Varangue, St-François
Sofitel Auberge de la Vieille Tour Restaurant, Gosier

HOTELS
Habitation Grande Anse, Localité Ziotte
Le Jardin de Malanga, Trois-Rivières
Le Méridien La Cocoteraie, St-François
La Métisse, St-François
Paradis Saintois, Terre-de-Haut, Iles des Saintes

SIGHTS
Jardin Botanique, Basse-Terre
Marie-Galante
Musée du Café, Vieux Habitants
Parc National de la Guadeloupe, Saint-Claude
St-François
Terre-de-Haut, Iles des Saintes
Vernou

SHOPPING
Maogany Artisanat, Terre-de-Haut, Iles des Saintes

NIGHTLIFE
Lollapalooza, Gosier

Anyone who has read the Biblical story of Adam and Eve and tried to visualize the Garden of Eden will thrill to find it in Basse-Terre, the wild side of Guadeloupe, where the rains color everything green and where agriculture is still king. Over there is a colonial-style *habitation* secluded on a lush banana plantation. It houses a boutique hotel overlooking the sea and the Iles des Saintes. In the paradisiacal gardens the fruits of the earth grow in abundance. Breadfruit, avocados, and mangos drop from the trees. I watched at a discreet distance as one "Adam" picked grapefruits and mandarin oranges for his "Eve," who had adorned herself with ginger and yellow hibiscus, some of the tropics most prized flowers. Eden seduces lovers and lovers of nature's generosity.

Updated by
Eileen Robinson
Smith

Sprawling and changing by the mile—from jungle highlands to seaside resorts, from mall shopping to rustic dining—Guadeloupe is richly varied. At 629 square mi (1,629 square km), it looks like a giant butterfly resting on the sea between Antigua and Dominica. Its wings—Basse-Terre and Grande-Terre—are the two largest islands in the Guadeloupe archipelago. The Rivière Salée, a 4-mi (6½-km) channel flowing between the Caribbean and the Atlantic, forms the spine of the butterfly. Smaller, flatter Grande-Terre, at 218 square mi (565 square km), is dry and sandy. It has Guadeloupe's best beaches, restaurants, casinos, resorts, and clubs. Basse-Terre (Low Land) is wild, wet, and mountainous. It once lagged behind Grande-Terre, but today it is popular with those who love hiking, whale-watching, diving, or deep-sea fishing. Its lush west coast is as beautiful as any other place in the Caribbean. On the Iles des Saintes, La Désirade, Marie-Galante, and the other islands of the archipelago, you'll find places that have remained largely untouched by the world.

Guadeloupe was annexed by France in 1674. During the French Revolution, battles broke out between royalists and revolutionaries on the island. In 1794 Britain aided Guadeloupe royalists, and that same year France dispatched Victor Hugues to sort things out. (In virtually every town and village you'll run across a Victor Hugues street, boulevard, or park.) After his troops banished the British, Hugues abolished slavery and guillotined recalcitrant planters. Those who managed to keep their heads fled to Louisiana or hid in the hills of Grande-Terre, where their descendants now live. Hugues—"the Robespierre of the Isles"—was soon relieved of his command, slavery was reestablished by Napoléon, and the French and English continued to battle over the island. The 1815 Treaty of Paris restored Guadeloupe to France, and in 1848, thanks to Alsatian Victor Schoelcher, slavery was abolished. The island was made a *département* of France in 1946, and in 1974 was elevated to a *région,* administered by a prefect appointed from Paris. With Martinique, St. Barths, and St. Martin, it forms *les Antilles Françaises,* the French West Indies.

An old saying of the French Caribbean refers to *les grands seigneurs de la Martinique et les bonnes gens de la Guadeloupe* (the lords of Martinique and the bourgeoisie of Guadeloupe). Though there are few aristocrats left on Martinique, the saying still holds some truth in Guadeloupe. Middle-class French tourists come (most on package tours) to swim and sunbathe, scuba dive, or hike. But sugar is still Guadeloupe's primary source of income. Only 10% of the workforce is employed in the tourism industry—which thrives from mid-November through May and is quiet the rest of the year. At harvest time, in February, the fields teem with workers cutting cane, and the roads are clogged with trucks taking the harvest to factories or distilleries.

Everything about Guadeloupe—from the *franglais* (*le topless, le snack-bar*) to the zippy little cars and ubiquitous *vendeuses de la plage* (women who model bathing suits on *le beach* and do a strip-tease show in the process)—is French. The prices, however, are Parisian, and unlike St. Martin the island imposes stiff taxes on most goods. To really feel at home here, some *français* is indispensable, though you may receive a bewildering response in Creole patois. Still, you'll be welcomed in this land of volcanoes, French food, and 'ti punch (a heady concoction of white rum, sugarcane syrup, and lime juice).

WHAT IT COSTS In U.S. dollars				
$$$$	$$$	$$	$	¢
RESTAURANTS*				
over $30	$20–$30	$12–$20	$8–$12	under $8
HOTELS**				
Cost EP/BP/CP over $350	$250–$350	$150–$250	$80–$150	under $80
Cost AI over $450	$350–$450	$250–$350	$125–$250	under $125

*Restaurant prices are for a main course at dinner. **EP, BP, and CP prices are per night for a standard double room in high season, excluding taxes, service charges, and meal plans. AI (all-inclusive) prices are per person, per night based on double-occupancy during high season, excluding taxes and service charges.

Where to Stay

On Guadeloupe you can opt for a splashy hotel with a full complement of activities or a small *relais* (inn) for more personal attention or a more authentic island experience. Many of the island's chain hotels cater to French package groups. Gosier, St-François, and Bas-du-Fort are generally considered resort areas, as is Ste-Anne. First-time visitors often land in Gosier, but after touring the island some decide to move over to St-François or St. Anne, or plan to do so next time. A smaller property outside the large touristic areas can offer a real island experience, and force your French. There are small hotels on Les Saintes and Marie-Galante. More—and better—hotels are opening in Basse Terre. Most hotels include buffet breakfast in their rates. Prices decline 25%–40% in the off-season. Note that American Express is not widely accepted, and in many cases even where it is, the credit card machines are only equipped to take European AX cards. Ask first, and always have a second form of payment available.

Villas

For information about villas and apartments, contact **French Caribbean International** (☎ 800/322–22–23; 805/967–9850 in Santa Barbara, CA 🖷 805/967–7798 ⊕ www.frenchcaribbean.com) handles private villa rentals, from charming cottages in Basse-Terre ($100 to $300 a night) to deluxe sea-view villas in Grand Terre ($1,650 to $7,000 per week), all with pools. With more than 22 years of experience in the region and a reputation for honesty and professionalism, the company provides travelers with knowledgeable assistance and helpful, personal reservation services.

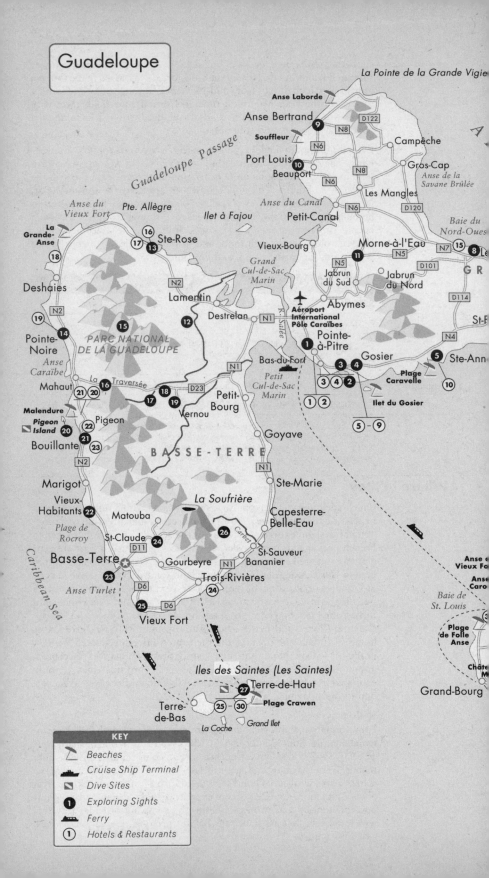

Guadeloupe

La Pointe de la Grande Vigie

Anse Laborde

Anse Bertrand **9**

Souffleur

N8 **D122**

Campêche

Port Louis **10**

Gros-Cap

Beauport

N6 **N8**

Anse de la
Savane Brûlée

Les Mangles

N6

Guadeloupe Passage

Anse du Canal

Petit-Canal

D120

Baie du
Nord-Oues

Anse du
Vieux Fort

Pte. Allègre

Ilet à Fajou

Vieux-Bourg

Morne-à-l'Eau **15**

N7 **8** Le

La Grande-
Anse

16 Ste-Rose

17 **13**

*Grand
Cul-de-Sac
Marin*

N5 **N5**

11 Jabrun
du Sud

Jabrun
du Nord

D101

GR

18

D114

Deshaies

N2

Lamentin

Abymes

St-F

19 **N2**

12

Destrelan

N1

Aéroport
International
Pôle Caraïbes

N4

14

Pointe-
Noire

15

*PARC NATIONAL
DE LA GUADELOUPE*

Pointe-
à-Pitre **1**

Gosier

5 Ste-Ann

Anse
Caraïbe

La Traversée

16

Bas-du-Fort

*Petit
Cul-de-Sac
Marin*

3 **4**

3 **4** **2**

Plage
Caravelle

10

Mahaut

21 **20**

17 **18**

D23

Petit-
Bourg

3 **4** **2**

Ilet du Gosier

Malendure

*Pigeon
Island*

20

21

Pigeon

22

19 Vernou

1 **2**

5 — **9**

Bouillante

23

N2

BASSE-TERRE

Goyave

Marigot

N1

Ste-Marie

Vieux-
Habitants **22**

Matouba

La Soufrière

Capesterre-
Belle-Eau

Anse d
Vieux Fo

*Plage de
Rocroy*

St-Claude

24

26

St-Sauveur

Anse
Caro

23

D11

Gourbeyre

N1

Bananier

Baie de
St. Louis

Basse-Terre

Anse Turlet

D6

Trois-Rivières

24

Plage
de Folle
Anse

25

D6

Vieux Fort

Châte
M

Iles des Saintes (Les Saintes)

Grand-Bourg

Terre-de-Haut **27**

25 **30** **Plage Crawen**

Terre-
de-Bas

La Coche *Grand Ilet*

KEY

	Beaches
	Cruise Ship Terminal
	Dive Sites
1	*Exploring Sights*
	Ferry
①	*Hotels & Restaurants*

0 10 miles

0 15 km

Hotels on Grande-Terre

★ ☾ $$$$ ⊞ **Le Méridien La Cocoteraie.** Like the Beatles song, "It just keeps getting better, better all the time!" The suites in this classy boutique hotel are lovely, particularly after a 2002 refurbishment. Each has two bathrooms and a Hermès octagonal tub set in the curve of bow windows. But it is the pool, traversed by a white footbridge, that is glorious, especially with lavender market umbrellas that complement the large Oriental urns and the wheeled chaise longues, as you would find on the Riviera. At the circular Indigo Bar, golfers relive their day spent on the neighboring, 18-hole Robert Trent Jones course. La Varangue is a gastronomic experience. ⊠ *Av. de l'Europe, St-François 97118* ☎ *0590/88–79–81* 🖷 *0590/88–78–33* ⊕ *www.lemeridien.com* ↘ *50 suites* ☖ *Restaurant, in-room safes, minibars, 2 tennis courts, pool, gym, beach, bar, baby-sitting, car rental* ⊟ *AE, DC, MC, V* ☺ *Sept. 15–Oct. 20* ⦵ *BP.*

$$$–$$$$ ⊞ **Sofitel Auberge de la Vieille Tour.** It has grown from six rooms fash-
Fodor's Choice   ioned around a 200-year-old stone sugar mill into a genuine luxury re-
★   sort. Guests love it, from the moment they drive up the impressive new, grand entrance with international flags waving a welcome to the juice and moist, scented towels dispensed by pretty, local girls in white eyelet and madras, to when they return "home" to their split-level suite with a glass-walled bathroom looking out to a winking lighthouse. A fabulous breakfast buffet is served poolside. The restaurant is unquestionably one of the island's finest. Shuttles run to the Novotel, which has a long beach and a host of water sports. ⊠ *Rte. de Montauban, Gosier 97190* ☎ *0590/84–23–23* 🖷 *0590/84–33–43* ⊕ *www.sofitel.com* ↘ *77 rooms, 102 suites* ☖ *2 restaurants, 2 tennis courts, pool, beach, bar, shops, Internet* ⊟ *AE, MC, V* ⦵ *BP.*

☾ $$$ ⊞ **Club Med La Caravelle.** This 1970s resort sits on 50 secluded acres on Caravelle Beach, one of the island's best white-sand beaches. Regular rooms have twin beds and are acceptable to the clientele, which is 80% European. Americans may want to pay the 20% extra for the Marie Galante wing. Nonguests can call for day passes (about $60), which include all sports and lunch or dinner, with complimentary wine and beer. Bar bills are paid for with coupons. Soft drinks, bottled water, and even coffee taken outside of meals, must be bought. The resort is great for children, who love the kids' club. ⊠ *Quartier Caravelle, Ste-Anne 97180* ☎ *0590/85–49–50* 🖷 *0590/85–49–70* ⊕ *www.clubmed.com* ↘ *340 rooms* ☖ *2 restaurants, 6 tennis courts, pool, aerobics, beach, windsurfing, boating, archery, volleyball, pub, nightclub, children's programs, Internet* ⊟ *AE, MC, V* ⦵ *AI.*

$$–$$$ ⊞ **Canella Beach Hotel-Residence.** Like a Creole village, all fretwork and pastels, this is one resort where people actually do move in because the monthly rates for the studios and duplex apartments are reasonable, particularly in low season. Weekly and daily rates are also available. The front desk clerks speak English and will care for you like family. On a semiprivate cove, there is a beach bar and water-sports center. The Veranda ($$$), looking like a white gingerbread house, serves creole, French, and lobster specialties and has prix-fixe menus with "mains" like a duo of tuna and dorado with a ginger velouté. More important, it has personality. Live music, great bar concoctions, and a fun crowd make it a happening nightspot. ⊠ *Pointe de la Verdure, Gosier 97190* ☎ *0590/90–44–00* 🖷 *0590/90–44–44* ↘ *86 studios, 59 suites* ☖ *Restaurant, kitchenettes, 2 pools, beach, snorkeling, windsurfing, boating, jet skiing, waterskiing, fishing, bar, Internet* ⊟ *AE, DC, MC, V* ⦵ *EP.*

$$ ⊞ **Novotel Coralia Bas du Fort.** This is a sprawling, water sports–oriented resort, offering everything from kayaking to knee-boarding. The clientele is mostly French package tourists, but Americans can be found, and business travelers have discovered it, too. Rooms are not luxurious, but

powder-blue fabrics and white tiles give them a pleasant, fresh look. All have terraces, most with sea views. Six bungalows are smack on the beach. The spacious grounds look magical when lighted at night. Delightful full-day catamaran cruises to the Iles des Saintes are popular. Sundays there are beach barbecues and live bands. ⊠ *Gosier 97190* ☏ *0590/ 90–40–00* 🖷 *0590/90–99–07* ⊕ *www.novotel.com* ⇆ *385 rooms, 48 bungalows* ♢ *4 restaurants, minibars, 2 pools, health club, beach, snorkeling, boating, waterskiing, bar* ☰ *AE, MC, V* ‖◯‖ *CP.*

$–$$ ▦ **La Créole Beach Hotel.** A large complex that includes a residential development as well as tourist accommodations, this resort spans 10 acres of tropical greenery and two beaches. The best rooms are those at the upscale Les Palmes. The oversize rooms are akin to those on a fine wooden yacht. Palm fronds, painted blue, are under glass and hung over the beds. Expensive white bedspreads carry on the crisp, minimalist look. An impressive, international buffet, Road of Spices, offers everything from curries to prime rib. La Créole Beach guests can sunbathe—topless or otherwise—on the expansive teak deck at Les Palmes. ⊠ *Pointe de la Verdure, Gosier* ⌖ *Box 61, 97190* ☏ *0590/90–46–46* 🖷 *0590/90–46– 66* ⊕ *www.creole-beach.gp* ⇆ *156 rooms* ♢ *2 restaurants, some kitchenettes, pool, 2 beaches, snorkeling, boating, volleyball, bar, meeting rooms, car rental* ☰ *AE, DC, MC, V* ‖◯‖ *EP.*

☺ **$** ▦ **Hotel Royal Caraïbes.** Le Moule, a major northern port on the Atlantic coast, was *the* seaside place to be 15 years ago, as was this hotel, located on its own peninsula. Both are making a comeback. Everything about the resort is spacious, from the 20 acres of landscaped grounds to the lobby and the bungalows—full-service, freestanding apartments. Many have a tranquil view of the lagoon with no other development in sight. Some of the units are time shares in the RCI system. When the renovation and expansion are complete there will be 200 units total. You'll find dual pools (one for children) raised on a teak deck, plus a lovely beach, and a creole restaurant. ⊠ *La Baie, Le Moule 97160* ☏ *0590/93–35–35* 🖷 *0590/23–17–39* ⇆ *50 apartments* ♢ *Restaurant, kitchenettes, 3-hole golf course, 2 tennis courts, 2 pools, beach, boating, billiards, Ping-Pong, bar, meeting rooms* ☰ *MC, V* ‖◯‖ *EP.*

★ ☺ **$** ▦ **La Métisse.** On a hilltop in an upscale residential neighborhood, a handful of rooms arc around a pool and an elevated hot tub. With pink stucco, white rattan furniture, and white and blue fretwork, it is honeymoon-pretty and immaculately clean. The caring owners give guests rides to town and the beach, which can eliminate the need for a rental car. Business travelers hide out here, loving the quiet and the free local calls. Connecting rooms are ideal for families. A lovely breakfast with house-made jam, is served poolside. The intrigue is that after you draw your drapes your breakfast appears on your terrace, thanks to a breakfast fairy sequestered in the garden. ⊠ *66, les Hauts de St-François, St-François 97118* ☏ *0590/88–70–00* 🖷 *0590/88–59–08* ⊕ *www. im-caraibes.com/metisse* ⇆ *7 rooms* ♢ *Minibars, pool, hot tub, playground* ☰ *AE, MC, V* ‖◯‖ *CP.*

Hotels on Basse-Terre

★ **$$–$$$** ▦ **Le Jardin de Malanga.** A hideaway for lovers and lovers of nature, this *hôtel de charme* is surrounded by tropical fruit and flower gardens. Accommodations are in traditional-but-contemporary Creole buildings of courbaril wood with patios and hammocks; the antiques-filled main house with three guest rooms was built in 1927. White-tile bathrooms gleam. A cliffside pool looks to the sea and faces the Iles des Saintes. French-creole meals with produce from the gardens are served for hotel guests only. Excursions, like a tour of the nearby national park, can be incorporated into special rates. You will want a car; the closest beach is Grand

Anse, 15 to 20 minutes away by car. ⊠ *Hermitage, Trois-Rivières 97114* ☎ *0590/92–67–57* 🖶 *0590/92–67–58* ⊕ *www.leader-hotels.gp* ➳ *3 rooms, 3 cottages* ⚬ *Dining room, fans, pool; no room TVs* ⊟ *AE, MC, V* ⎰⎱ *CP.*

☚ $ 🏨 **Domaine de Petite-Anse.** Above the sea, the red-roofed buildings of this complex spill down verdant hills. There's a terrific pool with adjacent bar. Rustic accommodations are either in simple and small rooms, which were refurbished in 2002 (ask for a sea view, which costs the same as one without) or bungalows with full baths, kitchenettes, and terraces. They cost $6 more and do not include breakfast The staff is friendly, but most speak only a little English. The resort is noted for its dive shop and nature tours of the national park. By night, guests gather around the piano bar or enjoy a folkloric show. ⊠ *Plage de Petite-Anse, Monchy, Bouillante 97125* ☎ *0590/98–78–78* 🖶 *0590/98–80–28* ➳ *135 rooms, 40 bungalows* ⚬ *Restaurant, in-room safes, some kitchenettes, refrigerators, pool, dive shop, snorkeling, boating, archery, hiking, volleyball, bar, shops* ⊟ *AE, DC, MC, V* ⎰⎱ *CP.*

★ $ 🏨 **Habitation Grande Anse.** With beautiful views of Baie Anse, the hills, and the atmospheric pool, this lovely property offers a mix of bungalows, apartments, studios, and standard rooms. The quality of accommodations and service is in striking contrast to that of similarly priced hotels. Units have rattan furnishings and radios; apartments house four to six people (Nos. 16 and 17 have the best views). The youthful Italian owners, brothers Claudio and Fulvio, speak English. Across the road is Grande Anse Beach. The hotel will help arrange fishing and diving excursions and rents Renaults at a reasonable price with full insurance. Ask about airport pickup. ⊠ *Localité Ziotte 97126* ☎ *0590/28–45–36* 🖶 *0590/28–51–17* ⊕ *www.grande-anse.com* ➳ *3 rooms, 39 studios, 3 apartments* ⚬ *Restaurant, bar, in-room safes, kitchenettes, pool, bar, car rental* ⊟ *AE, MC, V* ⎰⎱ *EP.*

$ 🏨 **Le Paradis Créole.** This *hôtel de charme* is certainly worth the long, single-lane drive up the hill for the expansive views of the mountains, the sea, and Pigeon Island. The grounds are lush and green, the rooms simple (go for a sea view). Of the bungalows, the newest one of dark wood is the best. Most of the fun Europeans come on week-long trips to dive in the nearby Jacques Cousteau Reserve; the hotel is associated with the well-respected Les Saintes Dive Centre. Happily, the renown restaurant provides more than just fuel for the diving machines. The pool bar blends up some concoctions that make the crimson setting of the sun truly celebratory. ⊠ *Route de Poirier, Pigeon-Bouillante 97132* ☎ *0590/98–71–62* 🖶 *0590/98–77–76* ⊕ *www.paradis-creole.gp* ➳ *10 rooms, 3 bungalows* ⚬ *Restaurant, pool, dive shop, bar* ⊟ *MC* ⎰⎱ *CP.*

$ 🏨 **Les Pavillons Ti' Anse.** A cluster of two-story bungalows makes its way up a flowering hillside, with the highest having views of the beach. The central complex houses a casual grill and small nightclub; a commendable creole restaurant is on the second floor. The facades and railed porches are of a beautiful hardwood. Buildings are capped with green copper roofs, detailed with fretwork. Interiors have the same dark, native mahogany and pine trim, beams, Dutch doors, and rustic floor tiles. Surrounded by frangipani trees, gardens with aromatic plants like citronella, and night-lit by lanterns, it's one nice place in this mountainous countryside. ⊠ *Baillargent, Pointe-Noire 97116* ☎ *0590/99–97–51* 🖶 *0590/ 99–97–57* ➳ *5 bungalows* ⚬ *2 restaurants, kitchenettes, beach, dance club* ⊟ *AE, MC, V* ⎰⎱ *EP.*

¢–$ 🏨 **La Sucrerie du Comté.** The ruins of a 19th-century sugar factory punctuate the lawns and gardens of this small resort; in fact, the historically significant grounds, along with the attractive public areas, are the main attractions. The bar re-creates a plantation feel with wood beams and stone walls. The restaurant is built with a Brazilian wood roof and serves creole and international food. Small, simple rooms are in 26 bungalows that duplicate the gingerbread architecture of the early 20th century. The nearest beach is a five-minute stroll through a tangle of greenery. Diving is nearby in Grand Cul Sac Marin. ⊠ *Comté de Lohéac, Ste-Rose 97115* ☎ *0590/28–60–17* 🖨 *0590/28–65–63* ⊕ *www.prime-invest-hotels.com* ⟿ *52 rooms* ◊ *Restaurant, fans, pool, bar* 🖃 *AE, DC, MC, V* ⧫ *CP.*

¢ 🏠 **Le Jardin Tropical.** The setting is one pretty, tropical picture: white and blue bungalows with gingerbread trim and landscaped gardens that topple down the hillside. The cluster of bungalows and the appealing, L-shaped pool enjoy an exceptional view of the Caribbean; the beach is a mile away. This small property is less than five years old and immaculately maintained. There is an attractive, open-air common area, furnished with white wicker, that has a bar, a breakfast area, billiards, and a wide-screen satellite TV. ⊠ *Route de Poirier Bouillante 97125* ☎ *0590/98–77–23* 🖨 *0590/98–74–33* ⊕ *www.rocher-de-malendure.gp* ⟿ *6 units* ◊ *Kitchenettes, fans, pool, bar; no room TVs* 🖃 *MC, V.*

Hotels on Iles des Saintes

$ 🏠 **Hôtel Cocoplaya.** This tasteful, two-story stucco hotel is still the island's newest, right in the heart of the village. Each room has its own theme—Chinese, African, Romantic, Provençal; sea views command the higher tariffs, but even the rooms facing the street are remarkably quiet. The soundproof double windows block out even the annoying drone of the motor scooters. The minimalist, open lobby, its bar, and the restaurant (dinner only) on the beach have been designed with characteristic French élan. English is spoken by the young and accommodating management. ⊠ *Terre-de-Haut 97137* ☎ *0590/92–40–00* 🖨 *0590/99–50–41* ⊕ *www.im-caraibes.com/cocoplaya* ⟿ *10 rooms* ◊ *Restaurant, cable TV, beach, bar* 🖃 *MC, V* ⧫ *CP.*

$ 🏠 **L'Auberge les Petits Saints aux Anarcadiers.** This distinctive inn is trimmed with trellises and topped by dormers. An ambitious and effective redo on the interior in 2002 put leather and other commodious furniture in the reception area, which is crammed with antiques, objets d'art, ornate French lighting, and Indonesian wood panels. Guest rooms have been transformed. Walls have come down, making small, single rooms into suites. Handsome, new king-size beds are in place, some with bamboo frames. American amenities have been added: satellite TV, air-conditioning, and phones with Internet plugs. Throughout, windows open to an enviable hillside view of the bay. This is the island's *in* place—and the one with charisma. ⊠ *La Savane, Terre-de-Haut 97137* ☎ *0590/99–50–99* 🖨 *0590/99–54–51* ⊕ *www.petitssaints.com* ⟿ *4 rooms, 3 suites, 1 guest house* ◊ *Restaurant, in-room data ports, pool, bar, airport shuttle* 🖃 *AE, MC, V* ⧫ *CP.*

★ ¢ 🏠 **Paradis Saintois.** These simple apartments are a superb value for the money and a real find, just a 10-minute walk from the beach. Although not luxurious, each is spacious and has a terrace. Feel like king of the hill as you lull yourself into a *sieste* in your hammock while watching the village and the Caribbean blue below. The newest units are embellished with attractive stonework and tiles. Ceiling fans cool sufficiently, and you won't miss a TV or phone, whether you rent for a day, week, or month. Guests share the large barbecue grill and picnic table. The resident managers see to all your needs. ⊠ *Route des Pres Cassin–B. P.I., Terre-de-Haut 97137* ☎ *0590/99–56–16* 🖨 *0590/99–56–11* ⊕ *www. antilles-info-tourisme.com/guadeloupe/paradis.htm* ⟿ *5 apartments, 3 studios, 1 room* ◊ *Fans, kitchenettes, 2 pools, bicycles, laundry service; no a/c, no room phones, no room TVs* 🖃 *MC, V* ⧫ *EP.*

Hotels on Marie-Galante

There are several small, simple lodgings (¢) on Marie-Galante. **Auberge de l'Arbre à Pain** (⊠ 32 Jeanne D'Arc du Docteur Marcel Enzol ☎ 0590/97–73–69) has nine basic rooms in two stories surrounding a courtyard and a recommendable creole restaurant, where complimentary breakfast is served. Centrally located in the center of Grand-Bourg, it is an easy walk from any place in town, but a hike from the beach. **Hôtel Hajo** (⊠ Section Bernard 140, Capesterre ☎ 0590/97–32–76) has six rooms and is a good location if you want to be in the country yet near the beaches. **Le Touloulou** (⊠ Plage de Petite Anse, Capesterre ☎ 0590/97–32–63) has four stucco bungalows with kitchenettes, which are simple but right there on the beach. The creole seafood restaurant is good and it's also a happening place, with atmospheric music from the beach bar vying with the slapping of the waves. The disco adjacent to the restaurant warms up to hot at night.

$ ▣ **Au Village de Ménard.** Care has gone into the gardens of this hotel, which sits cliffside at the island's north end (the beach is 1 mi [1½ km] away). Inexpensive, this is for the independent traveler. Simple and Euro-style, the bungalows are situated around a central pool. The owner speaks English. ⊠ *Vieux Fort, St-Louis 97134* ☎ *0590/97–09–45* 🖶 *0590/97–15–40* 🖙 *9 bungalows* ⚭ *Fans, kitchenettes, pool* ▤ *MC, V* ⦿⃓ *CP.*

👆 $ ▣ **Hôtel Cohoba.** Marie-Galante's only beach resort is named for a plant whose hallucinogenic red pods gave the earliest Caribbean peoples prophetic powers. Half of the basic suites are sky-blue and sea-green stucco bungalows; the rest are slightly larger studios. White walls and white-tile floors lend an air of space; cool and warm fabrics add cheer. In the dining room you can contemplate the past while studying the painstakingly reproduced cave paintings that decorate the walls. Although the sandy beach is just two minutes from the delightful pool area, there are no sea views from the bungalows because of dense tree cover. ⊠ *Grand-Bourg 97112* ☎ *0590/97–50–50* 🖶 *0590/97–97–96* ⊕ *www. cohoba.gp* 🖙 *100 suites* ⚭ *Restaurant, 2 tennis courts, pool, beach, windsurfing, boating, waterskiing, volleyball, bar, shops* ▤ *AE, MC, V* ⦿⃓ *CP.*

Hotels on La Désirade

An even more remote island than Marie-Galante or the Isles des Saintes, La Désirade has few lodging options. There's **L'Oasis** (⊠ Grande-Anse ☎ 0590/20–02–12), a six-room hotel whose simple restaurant serves excellent seafood. **Le Mirage** (⊠ Grand-Anse ☎ 0590/20–01–08 🖶 0590/ 20–07–45) is a tiny, eight-room establishment.

Where to Eat

Guadeloupe's fine creole dishes are made up of primarily local seafood and vegetables, such as christophenes (like a squash) and plantains, always with a healthy dose of pepper sauce. Favorite appetizers are *accras* (salted codfish fritters), *boudin* (highly seasoned blood sausage), and *crabes farcis* (stuffed land crabs). *Blaff* is a spicy fish stew. *Langouste* (lobster) and *lambi* (conch) are widely available, as is *souchy*, (like ceviche, it is fish "cooked" in lime juice). You'll find a diverse selection of dining options—from pizza to grilled Caribbean lobster, Vietnamese to contemporary *haute* French cuisine. And then there are Italian, African, Indian, and South American establishments—which, for the most part, aren't inexpensive; nothing is. At least menu prices include tax and service. Look for restaurants that belong to the gastronomic association, l'Union des Arts Culinaires (UAC); their pamphlet is widely distributed. For a quick and inexpensive bite to eat, visit a *boulangerie,* where you can buy luscious French pastries or basic sandwiches. And don't forget DeliFrance, a self-service deli chain that is in many of the larger towns—even on Les Saintes. As for rum, it's synonymous with the islands. and the ubiquitous rum libation is 'ti punch. (Now *that* you can buy for a song.)

What to Wear

Dining is casual at lunch, but beach attire is a no-no except at the more laid-back marina and beach eateries. Dinner is slightly more formal. Long pants, collared shirts, and skirts or dresses are appreciated, although not required.

Grande-Terre

CARIBBEAN
★ $$–$$$$

✕ **L'Hibiscus Restaurant.** Like its namesake flower, this restaurant is tropical and cheery, with yellow, blue, and coral decor, all very Guadeloupean. Overlooking the water, the tables are set with linen tablecloths; ocher linen napkins are coiled and set upon base plates. The gregarious chef/owner, Jocelyn Corvo, realized his dream after 24 years with the Accor Hotel Group, assigned to enviable posts in France. He puts his classical training into play, utilizing the freshest island products. Start with smoked marlin atop a seafood bisque reduction. The best main course is the incredible freshwater crayfish in a coconut cream sauce with saffron. ✉ *Bord de Mer, face au Zenith Bas du Fort* ☎ *0590/91–13–61* ⊟ *AE, V* ☉ *Closed Sept. 15–Oct. 15.*

CONTEMPORARY
★ $$–$$$$

✕ **Sofitel Auberge de la Vieille Tour Restaurant.** Tables are grouped around a historic whitewashed sugar mill; the conservatory-style extension has views up into lighted trees. No question, Chef George delivers some of the island's best, most contemporary food, like the starter lobster salad and crayfish with melon and avocado, followed by filet mignon with foie gras and sesame seeds. Dessert presentations are dazzling, with lots of puff pastry, towers, sauces, and glacés, like the floating islands with caramel anise. Consider the imaginative, three-course, prix-fixe menus for $38. Menus change biannually. From *la cave,* the selection includes muscadets, pinot noirs, Sancerres, pommerols, and Gewürztraminers. ✉ *Rte. de Montauban, Gosier* ☎ *0590/84–23–23* ⊟ *AE, MC, V* ☉ *No lunch. Reduced schedule June–Nov.*

$$–$$$$

✕ **Villa Fleur d'Epée.** The front-of-the-house man, humorless and snooty, will peer out from the locked iron door, and—with reservations confirmed— you will be allowed into this home in an upscale residential neighborhood. From the *amuse bouche* through the several courses, you'll have a global experience; you may have snapper in banana leaves or kangaroo steak with cèpe mushrooms. The chef/owner, Thierry Larade, is an *artiste* with food. Charming to boot, he visits each table. Although à la carte is best, the $30 discovery menu is a good value in an otherwise expensive restaurant. (Be certain to call for precise directions.) ✉ *Rue du Fort Fleur d'Epée, Bas du Fort* ☎ *0590/90–86–59* ⌕ *Reservations essential* 🎩 *Jacket required* ⊟ *AE, MC, V* ☉ *Closed Sun. No lunch.*

$$$

✕ **Iguane Café.** Sylvan and Marie Seronait serve innovative food at this classy restaurant. In an open kitchen a group of chefs busily prepare such specialties as roasted duck with mangoes and cinnamon. The wine list is outstanding, populated with Margaux, St. Juliens, and Sancerres. Iguanas are indeed the theme, and you will spy them in art forms in all the usual unsuspected places. Marie's *grandmere*'s portraits and antique French cherubs are juxtaposed with island artifacts, driftwood mirrors, and rotating shows of local artists. Cool music—jazz and French faves— set a mellow mood as you lovingly devour your dessert. ✉ *Rte. de La Pointe des Châteaux (½ mi [¾ km] from airport), St-François* ☎ *0590/ 88–61–37* ⊟ *AE, MC* ☉ *Closed Tues. No lunch Mon.–Sat.*

ECLECTIC
¢–$

✕ **Cha Cha Café.** A minute from the Hotel St. John, two from the ferry docks, and next to KFC, this is a fun, hip hangout. A bar, a breakfast and lunch place, and an ice-cream parlor, it's also a gift shop, with wares from exotic lands. This one-room emporium spills out to a terrace with umbrella tables. French belles sip espresso and tap their heels to the latest French, Latin, and American music collected by the French owner, Ricard. It adds to the milieu of this meeting place. Richard's English is excellent, and he will help you with your translations. ⊠ *2 Quai Layrie, Pointe-à-Pitre* ☎ *0590/89–61–94* ▤ *No credit cards* ⊘ *No dinner.*

FRENCH
$$–$$$$

✕ **La Mandarine.** In one of Gosier's original neighborhoods, this modest, unassuming spot is owned by a mature French couple—he's the chef, she's the hostess. Chef Alain's food is a pleasant gastronomic experience, with dishes like veal kidneys sautéed with port, which are impossible to find elsewhere. Tantalizing lobster profiteroles are one way to begin, as is the breast of duck and sautéed foie gras over greens with walnut oil and sherry vinegar. The wine list is intelligent. Desserts, a marriage of French classics and tropical fruit coulis, are luscious. You'll even find a cigar menu. ⊠ *4 rue Simon, Gosier* ☎ *0590/84–30–28* ▤ *MC, V* ⊘ *Closed Mon.*

★ $$–$$$$

✕ **La Varangue.** In beautiful surroundings overlooking the sea, this restaurant offers some of the island's most refined dining. A memorable repast begins with a thick cream of pumpkin soup flavored with orange and cumin. Chef Menad Berkani utilizes top-quality imported meats, the freshest fish and lobster, and fresh island produce. The rack of lamb needs only its simple thyme *jus* for flavor; it sits atop a potato pancake and comes with a spinach custard. Red snapper in pineapple broth with guava is a heart-healthy main course. Lighter Mediterranean plates are also on offer, from carpaccios to pasta and salads, including one with warm goat cheese, honey, and nuts. The wine list is appropriately upscale. ⊠ *Le Méridien La Cocoteraie, Av. de l'Europe, St-François* ☎ *0590/88–79–81* ▤ *AE, MC, V.*

INDIAN
$–$$$

✕ **Restaurant Maharajah Monty.** Ask directions at the tourism office; the restaurant is just a few blocks away and worth the walk. You'll know you're there when you see an orientalesque carpet on the sidewalk, running up the staircase to the second floor. It is done in red and gold and is wildly ornate. Here you will find all of your authentic Indian faves. The owner, the lovely Madame Manjit Kaur, with her bejeweled forehead and traditional costume, will guide you. She suggests that you start with a mix of *pakoras* (vegetable fritters), move on to the *tandoori* chicken or one of the big-ticket items, curried shrimp or lobster. ⊠ *Rue A. Rene Boisneuf, Angle Rue Jean Jaures, Pointe-à-Pitre* ☎ *0590/83–12–60* ▤ *MC, V* ⊘ *No dinner Sun.*

Basse-Terre

CARIBBEAN
★ $–$$$

✕ **La Terrasse du Port (Chez Mimi).** At this unassuming second-story restaurant with a view of the sea and breakwater the surprise is that the food is better than some of Guadeloupe's gastronomic landmarks, although almost as pricey. It is a mom-and-pop operation; Mimi, a Guadeloupean, reigns in the kitchen, while Bernard, her French husband, is "on the floor." Seafood is it. Start with a coquilles St. Jacques of tender conch. Go on to *vivaneau* (red snapper) with shrimp atop a sauce of reduced lobster bisque. It is amazing. Other winners are crayfish in coconut milk, shrimp flambéed in *vieux rhum,* and lobster creole. French music plays. ⊠ *Bd. Maritime, Ste-Rose* ☎ *0590/28–60–72* ▤ *MC, V* ⊘ *Closed Mon. and Sept.*

$$

✕ **Les Pavillons Restaurant.** This restaurant is on a terrace with views of Le Rouix Beach. Traditional Antilles specialties like lambi in butter sauce are joined by innovations like avocado with hot Roquefort cream sauce, and lamb with pine nuts. Finish with Tourment d'amour, Guadeloupe's famous coconut cake, and choose a homemade rum liqueur (punch) from the fascinating display (the best is aged with raisins, pistachios, or sea grapes). Downstairs a simple grill menu, from brochettes to lobster, is available for lunch. ⊠ *Les Pavillons Ti 'Anse Hotel, Baillargent, Pointe-Noire 97116* ☎ *0590/99–97–51* ⊟ *AE, MC, V.*

ECLECTIC
$
✕ **Carib Cocktail.** Does the name say it all? Well, yes and no. There is no rum here, just healthy fresh fruit drinks. The sign at this simple yet sophisticated "roadhouse" reads EVERYTHING MADE WITH PLENTY OF VITAMINS! Owned by a classy French woman and her husband, a sports medicine doctor, it offers 12 different fruits to chose from. Add yogurt, milk, or ice cream—say mango with vanilla bean—and the result is a delicious smoothie. Cool French CDs play as you belly up to the bar of blue-and-white wainscoting. Salads, sandwiches, and omelettes are offered, plus a $12 plat du jour. And yes, you can break training with beer or wine. ⊠ *Rte. 2, Pigeon* ☎ *0590/44–28–15* ⊟ *No credit cards.*

FRENCH
$$–$$$$
✕ **Le Rocher de Malendure.** Guests climb the yellow wooden stairs for the panoramic sea view at Le Jardin Tropical's restaurant. They return for the food. If you arrive before noon, when the divers pull in, you might snag the primo table under the gazebo. The fruits of the sea are the obvious specialities. A laudable selection of appetizers includes stuffed avocado or crabs and fish soup. An inexpensive cold plate encompasses smoked marlin and sushi *antilliaise*, which is actually a mixed-fish ceviche. Fish comes simply grilled, with either a vanilla-cream sauce or a classic poivre Nouilly sauce. You must end it all with a café Antillis. ⊠ *Le Jardin Tropical, Bord de Mer, Malendure de Pigeon, Bouillante* ☎ *0590/ 98–70–84* ⊟ *AE, MC, V* ☺ *Closed Wed.*

$$–$$$
✕ **Restaurant Paradis Creole.** At the hotel of the same name, this restaurant has a well-established reputation, which Fred, the new French chef, is capable of retaining given his global repertoire. The open-air dining is simple, with a panoramic sea view. Your gastronomic experience should begin at sunset at the bar with one of the amazing cocktail creations. Then savor the fish and crustaceans of the Caribbean, complemented by original sauces of fruit and local spices and the island's vegetables. Examples are dolphinfish with a vanilla bean–cream sauce, or medallions of pork with a cinnamon sauce. The prix-fixes are the the most affordable options ($23–$38) and here they are recommendable. ⊠ *Hotel Paradis Creole, Rte. de Poirier, Pigeon Bouillante* ☎ *0590/98– 71–62* ⊟ *MC, V* ☺ *Closed Sun., Wed. No lunch.*

Iles des Saintes

ECLECTIC
$$$
✕ **L'Auberge les Petits Saints aux Anarcadiers Restaurant.** Hotel guests and a few visitors have the privilege of dining at this verandah restaurant. The set *table d'hôte* menu constantly changes, but what's certain is that meat is no longer served because chef/proprietor Jean Paul Colas says he only wants what is fresh and available, and that means only seafood and produce. Dinner is consistently enjoyable, with the night sounds of the tropics and oldies like Bobby Darin's "Beyond the Sea." Didier Spindler, co-owner and pastry chef, makes a superb pastry with almonds from the overhanging trees and a sauce with local vanilla. ⊠ *L'Auberge les Petits Saints aux Anarcadiers, La Savane, Terre-de-Haut* ☎ *0590/99–50–99* ⊟ *AE, MC, V.*

$–$$
✕ **El Dorado.** This plant-filled Creole-style house with a double verandah—near Bourg's delightful main square—is a good place to stop for tasty creole fare. Go with the cod fritters with *chien* (dog sauce), the warm goat cheese on toast with salad, the chicken Columbo (curried

chicken), the fresh catch of the day, or lobster from the grill. The ice cream is the best—be it rum raisin or coffee. What makes this place special is that wife Roselle cooks and husband Guy is the very personable, English-speaking host. Breakfast, lunch, and dinner are available. ⊠ *Terre-de-Haut* ☎ *0590/99–54–31* 🖃 *AE, MC, V* ☺ *Closed Sun.*

$–$$ ✕ **La Saladerie.** The menu here is a sophisticated mélange of light plates and the freshest of fish. You can make a meal of the assortment of smoked fish served cold and a refreshing bowl of gazpacho, a perfect choice for those with light appetites. Shrimp in coconut milk with rice, coupled with a salad that you compose, is another light dinner. The wine list is pleasantly varied, and this is one place where you can find Calvados and Armagnac. Have a snifter full and just listen to the great French music and the waves lap the dock. Better yet, walk the pier and give in to the inclination to be romantic. ⊠ *Anse Mirre, Terre-de-Haut* ☎ *0590/99–53–43* ☺ *Closed Tues. No dinner Mon.* 🖃 *MC, V.*

FRENCH   ✕ **Le Genois.** On the water, this one has it all—location, creative French-★ **$–$$$** island cuisine, exceptional wine, and the personalities of its owners Philip, an English-speaking French lawyer, and his beautiful wife (and chef) Chantal. Lunch can be smoked fish, ceviche, or quiche—imagine one with two cheeses and vanilla. Duck breast in a fruit and wine sauce might be on the nightly prix-fixe. Kids go *oo la la* over Chantal's incredible desserts, like chocolate and green *crème de menthe fondant*. A fun place, it caters to yachties and sponsors the annual Genois Regatta. The emporium sells pastries, rum liqueurs. glassware, etc., and breakfast is also served. ⊠ *Terre-de-Haut* ☎ *0590/99–53–01* 🖃 *MC, V* ☺ *Closed Mon.*

Marie-Galante

SEAFOOD   ✕ **Le Touloulou.** On the curve of Petite-Anse beach, with tables in the sand, **$–$$** this ultracasual eatery serves sumptuous seafood at down-to-earth prices. Chef José Viator's standouts include conch and lobster specialities. Set menus start at about $9 and go to $22. Jose plays DJ with his fine collection of French and international music. The circular bar in the gazebo is a great place to savor the best in rum cocktails while contemplating the sun's descent. ⊠ *Petite-Anse* ☎ *0590/97–32–63* 🖃 *MC, V* ☺ *Closed Mon. and mid-Sept.–mid-Oct.*

Beaches

Guadeloupe's beaches are generally narrow and tend to be cluttered with cafés and cars (when the parking spots fill up, folks create impromptu lots in the sand). But all beaches are free and open to the public; for a small fee, hotels allow nonguests to use changing facilities, towels, and beach chairs. On the southern coast of Grande-Terre, from Ste-Anne to Pointe des Châteaux, you'll find stretches of soft white sand. Along the western shore of Basse-Terre you'll see signposts to many small beaches. The sand starts turning gray as you reach Ilet de Pigeon (Pigeon Island); it becomes volcanic black farther south. There is one official nudist beach, and topless bathing is common. Note that the Atlantic waters on the northeast coast of Grande-Terre are too rough for swimming.

Grand-Terre Beaches

Anse de la Gourde. This beautiful stretch of sand is popular on weekends.

Ilet du Gosier. On this little speck off the shore of Gosier you can bathe in the buff. Take along a picnic for an all-day outing. The beach is closed on weekends.

Plage Caravelle. Southwest of Ste-Anne is one of Grande-Terre's longest and prettiest (the occasional dilapidated shack aside) stretches of sand.

Protected by reefs, it's also a fine snorkeling spot. Club Med occupies one end of this beach; nude bathing is no longer permitted.

Pointe Tarare. This secluded, sandy strip just before the tip of Pointe des Châteaux is the island's only official nudist beach. There's a small bar-café in the parking area, a four-minute walk away.

Souffleur. On the west coast of Grande-Terre and north of Port-Louis, this beach has brilliant flamboyant trees that bloom in summer. There are no facilities on the beach, but you can buy picnic supplies from nearby shops.

Basse-Terre Beaches

La Grande-Anse. North of Deshaies on Basse-Terre's northwest coast you'll find soft beige sand sheltered by palms; it's probably the best beach on the island. There's a large parking area, but no facilities other than those at a nearby restaurant.

Malendure. This beach lies on Basse-Terre's west coast, in Bouillante across from Pigeon Island.

Beaches on Other Islands

Anse Canot. Like all the beaches on Marie-Galante, this is longer, wider, and less crowded than other beaches in Guadeloupe.

Anse Crawen. A secluded ½-mi (¾-km) stretch of white sand on Terre-de-Haut (one of the Isles des Saintes) is popular with families on Sunday.

Anse de Vieux Fort. On Marie-Galante, this is known as a beach for lovers.

Les Pompierres. A palm-fringed stretch of tawny sand, this is a popular beach on Terre-de-Haut in Isles des Saintes.

Petite-Anse. This long beach on Marie-Galante has golden sand that is crowded with locals on weekends. The only facilities are at the little seafood restaurant nearby.

Plage de Folle Anse. This beach on Marie-Galante is perfect for a sunset walk.

Sports & the Outdoors

ADVENTURE TRIPS
With hundreds of trails and countless rivers and waterfalls, the **Parc National de la Guadeloupe,** on Basse-Terre, is the main draw for hikers. Some of the trails should be attempted only with an experienced guide. All tend to be muddy, so wear a good pair of boots. Trips for as many as 12 people are arranged by **Guides de Montagne de la Caraïbe** (✉ Maison Forestière, Matouba, Basse-Terre ☎ 0590/99–28–92 or 590/92–06–10). A half-day guided tour costs $80, a full day $150. The acknowledged private-sector pros are at **Parfum d'Aventure** (✉ Roche Blonval, St-François, Grande-Terre ☎ 0590/88–47–62). They offer everything from hiking to four-wheel-drive safaris, sea kayaking, and white-water canoeing. The young and fun company has also become known for rappelling and canyoning. **Sport D'av** (✉ La Marina, Gosier, Grande-Terre ☎ 0590/32–58–41) is a reliable company that organizes both treks and canoe trips. **Vert Intense** (✉ Basse-Terre, Basse-Terre ☎ 0590/99–34–73) organizes both hikes and canyoning in the national park, to the volcano (with fascinating commentary), as well as to tropical forests and rivers. Guides speak some English and Spanish.

BICYCLING
The French are mad about *le cyclisme,* so if you want to feel like a native, take to two wheels. Pedal fever hits the island in August every year, when hundreds of cyclists converge here for the 10-day Tour de Guadeloupe, which covers more than 800 mi (1,290 km). On Grande-Terre you can rent bikes at **Eli Sport** (✉ Rond Point de Grand-Camp, Grand-Camp, Grande-Terre ☎ 0590/90–37–50). In St-François you can rent from **Espace VTT** (✉ St-François, Grande-Terre ☎ 0590/88–79–91). On the Iles

des Saintes, try **Localizes** (⊠ Place des Débarcadere, Terre-de-Haut, Iles des Saintes ☎ 0590/99–51–99).

BOATING & SAILING
If you plan to sail these waters, you should be aware that the winds and currents tend to be strong. There are excellent, well-equipped marinas in Pointe-à-Pitre, Bas-du-Fort, Deshaies, St-François, and Gourbeyre. You can rent a yacht (bareboat or crewed) from several companies. **Cap Sud** (⊠ 3 pl. Créole, Bas-du-Fort, Grande-Terre ☎ 0590/90–76–70) has a fleet of 8 yachts, including both monohulls and catamarans. The sailboats are generally rented as bareboats and by the week. **Sunsail** (⊠ Bas du Fort Marina, Bas-du-Fort, Grande-Terre ☎0590/90–92–02; 410/280–2553 or 207/253–5400 in the U.S. 🖷 0590/90–97–99 ⊕ www.sunsail.com) has joined forces with Stardust Yacht Charters to form one of the largest charter companies in the world. Although it is primarily a bareboat operation, skippers can be hired by the week for those with limited experience, or they are available to instruct charterers in sailing skills and local waters. Ocean kayaks, Windsurfers, and kite boards can be rented, too, but must be reserved in advance.

FISHING
You can go out for bonito, dolphinfish, captain fish, barracuda, kingfish, and tuna, or thrill to the challenge of the big billfish like marlin and swordfish. Expect to pay from $470 to $645 to charter a boat for a full day (about $100–$115 per person) which usually includes lunch and drinks. It is more than half those prices for a half-day charter. **Centre de Peche Sportive** (⊠ Malendure de Pigeon, Bouillante, Basse-Terre ☎ 0590/98–70–84) has state-of-the art boats with flying bridges and is known for success in showing fishermen where to pull in the big billfish. **Michel** (⊠ Plage de Malendure, Pigeon-Bouillante, Basse-Terre ☎ 0590/85–42–17) is a reliable fishing charter company near Pigeon Island.

GOLF
Golf Municipal St-François (⊠ St-François, Grande-Terre ☎ 0590/88–41–87), across from the Méridien and Cocoteraie hotels, is an 18-hole, par-71, Robert Trent Jones–designed course; it has an English-speaking pro, a clubhouse, a pro shop, and electric carts for rental. The greens fees are $40 for nine holes, $50 for the day; carts rent for $27 for nine holes and $40 for all day. Clubs can be rented for $30–$35.

HORSEBACK RIDING
The half- or full-day excursions offered by **La Manade** (⊠ St-Claude, Basse-Terre ☎ 0590/81–52–21) utilize trails through the rain forest, a fascinating place to ride. Lessons are also available.

SCUBA DIVING
The main diving area at the **Cousteau Underwater Park,** just off Basse-Terre near Pigeon Island, offers routine dives to 60 ft. But the numerous glass-bottom boats and day-trippers make the site feel like a crowded marine parking lot. That said, the underwater sights are spectacular. Guides and instructors here are certified under the French CMAS (and some have PADI, but none have NAUI). Most operators offer two-hour dives three times per day for about $40–$50 per dive. Hotels and dive operators usually rent snorkeling gear.

Caraïbes Plongées (⊠ Gosier, Grande-Terre ☎ 0590/90–44–90) is one of the best-known dive operations in the area. **Centre Nautique des Saintes** (⊠ Plage de la Coline, Terre-de-Haut, Iles des Saintes ☎ 0590/99–54–25) prides itself on the quality of its instruction; some English is spoken. **Chez Guy et Christian** (⊠ Plage de Malendure, Basse-Terre ☎ 0590/98–82–43) has a good reputation and is well-established among those who dive Pigeon Island. After 10 years of experience, dive master Cedric Phalipon of **Club de Plongeé Des Saintes, Pisquettes** (⊠ Le Mouillage, Terre-de-Haut, Iles des Saintes ☎ 0590/99–88–80) knows all the sites and islets and gives excellent lessons in English. Equipment is renewed frequently and is of a high caliber. Small tanks are available for kids, who are taken buddy diving. An all-day scuba-diving cruise on a catamaran to Iles des Saintes is offered by **Croisieres sous le vent** (✉ Plage de Malendure, Basse-Terre ☎ 0590/98–83–73). **Les Heures Saines** (✉ Plage de Malendure, Basse-Terre ☎ 0590/98–86–63) is the premier operator for dives in the Cousteau Reserve. Trips to Les Saintes offer one or two dives, for medium and advanced card holders, with time for lunch and sightseeing. Wreck, night, and Nitrox diving are also available. The instructors, many English-speaking, are excellent with children and the handicapped. Whale/dolphin watching with marine biologists as guides, aboard a catamaran equipped with hydrophones, is most fruitful in the winter.

SEA EXCURSIONS **Coralia** (✉ Novotel Coralia, Bas-du-Fort, Grande-Terre ☎ 0590/90–40–00), a sleek catamaran, sails to Marie-Galante, where guests tour the island then come back aboard for rum cocktails and a barbecue lunch. A second sea voyage is to Les Saintes, with a shipboard luncheon, drinks, music, and snorkeling. **Tip Top One** and **Tip Top Two** (✉ Section Leroux, Gosier, Grand-Terre ☎ 0590/84–66–36) are large, safe catamarans that fly through the water on their course to Les Saintes and other islands. It is a full day at sea, with snorkeling, lunch, rum libations, and shore excursions.

TENNIS Many hotels have courts (most lighted); if you're not a guest of a hotel with tennis facilities, call ahead for more information and to reserve a court. The **Auberge de la Vieille Tour** (✉ Rte. de Montauban, Gosier, Grande-Terre ☎ 0590/84–23–23) has two courts. **Club Med La Caravelle** (✉ Quart Carvelle, Ste-Anne, Grande-Terre ☎ 0590/85–49–50) has six courts. **Marina Club** (✉ Point-à-Pitre, Grand-Terre ☎ 0590/90–84–08) has seven courts. The **Tennis League of Guadeloupe** (✉ Centre Lamby-Lambert Stadium, Gosier, Grande-Terre ☎ 0590/90–90–97) has six courts.

WINDSURFING Most beachfront hotels can help you arrange lessons and rentals. **Alizée** (✉ Ste-Anne, Grande-Terre ☎ 0590/31–82–26) offers kitesurfing lessons and rentals. **Canella Beach Hotel** (✉ Gosier, Grande-Terre ☎ 0590/90–44–84) has a water-sports center that offers windsurfing, jet-skiing, and waterskiing. **LCS** (✉ Ste-Anne, Grande-Terre ☎ 0590/88–15–17) specializes in lessons for children six and older as well as adults, and has boards for rent. Windsurfing buffs congregate at the **UCPA Hotel Club** (✉ St-François, Grande-Terre ☎ 0590/88–64–80), where for moderate weekly rates of €440–€540, they sleep, eat, and windsurf. Windsurf lessons and boards (also available to nonguests) are included in the package, as are bikes, to pedal to the lagoon.

Shopping

You can find good buys on anything French—perfume, crystal, china, cosmetics, fashions, scarves. Many stores offer a 20% discount on luxury items purchased with traveler's checks or, in some cases, major credit cards. As for local handicrafts, you'll find fine wood carvings, madras table linens, island dolls dressed in madras, woven straw baskets and hats, and *salakos*—fishermen's hats made of split bamboo. Of course, there's the favorite Guadeloupean souvenir—rum—and, for foodies, great little baskets lined with madras and filled with aromatic, fresh spices.

Areas & Malls
Grande-Terre's largest shopping mall, **Destrelland,** has more than 70 stores and is just minutes from the Aéroport International Pôle Caraïbes,

which, with its duty-free stores, is a shopping destination in its own right. In **Pointe-à-Pitre** you can enjoy browsing in the street stalls around the harbor quay and at the two markets (the best is the Marché de Frébault). The town's main shopping streets are rue Schoelcher, rue de Nozières, and the lively rue Frébault. At the St-John Perse Cruise Terminal there's an attractive mall with about two dozen shops. **Bas-du-Fort**'s two shopping areas are the Cora Shopping Center and the marina, where there are 20 or so boutiques and quite a few restaurants. In **St-François** there are more than a dozen shops surrounding the marina, some selling sensual French lingerie, swimsuits, and fashions. A supermarket has incredibly good prices on French wines. Cheeses are many, and if you pick up some bread (fresh baguettes), you have a picnic. (Go get lost at a secluded beach.)

Specialty Items

ART **Brigitte Boesch** (✉ St-François, Grande-Terre ☎ 0590/88–48–94), a German-born painter who has exhibited all over the world, lives in St-François, and her studio is worth a visit. Call for directions. Guadeloupean painter **Joel Nankin** (✉ Baie Mahault, Basse-Terre ☎ 0590/23–28–24) specializes in masks and acrylic and sand paintings.

CHINA, CRYSTAL **Rosebleu** (✉ 5 rue Frébault, Pointe-à-Pitre, Grande-Terre ☎ 0590/82–
& SILVER 93–43 ✉ Aéroport International Pôle Caraïbes ☎ no phone) sells china, crystal, and silver by top manufacturers, including Christoffle.

COSMETICS, **L'Artisan Parfumeur** (✉ Centre St-John Perse, Pointe-à-Pitre, Grande-
LINGERIE & Terre ☎ 0590/83–80–25) sells top French and American brands as well
PERFUME as tropical scents. **Au Bonheur des Dames** (✉ 49 rue Frébault, Pointe-à-Pitre, Grande-Terre ☎ 0590/82–00–30) sells several different lines of cosmetics and skin-care products in addition to its perfumes. **Phoenicia** (✉ Bas-du-Fort, Grande-Terre ☎ 0590/90–85–56 ✉ 8 rue Frébault, Pointe-à-Pitre, Grande-Terre ☎ 0590/83–50–36 ✉ 121 bis rue Frébault, Pointe-à-Pitre, Grande-Terre ☎ 0590/82–25–75) sells various perfumes. **Vendôme** (✉ 8–10 rue Frébault, Pointe-à-Pitre, Grande-Terre ☎ 0590/ 83–42–84) is Guadeloupe's exclusive purveyor of Stendhal and Germaine Monteil cosmetics.

HANDICRAFTS **Boutique de la Plage** (✉ Bd. Général de Gaulle, Gosier, Grande-Terre ☎ 0590/84–52–51) offers a mind-boggling jumble of items ranging from tacky tchotchkes ("fertility" sculptures, for example) to sublime art naïf canvases for as little as $20. At **Kaz à Lorgé** (✉ 25 rue Benoit Cassin Terre-de-Haut Iles des Saintes ☎ 0590/99–59–60) you'll find an artistic jumble of handicrafts, both local and from around the world, that fills the two tiny rooms of this "gingerbread" shop: prints, mobiles, wall masks, Haitian woodcraft, miniature lobster traps, and cutesy things made from madras. **La Case à Soie** (✉ Ste-Anne, Grande-Terre ☎ 0590/88–11–31) sells flowing silk dresses and scarves in Caribbean colors. The **Centre d'Art Haitien** (✉ 65 Montauban, Gosier, Grande-Terre ☎ 0590/84–32–60) is the place to buy imaginative art. The **Centre Artisanat** (✉ Ste-Anne, Grande-Terre) offers a wide selection of local crafts.

Didier Spindler (✉ Terre-de-Haut, Iles des Saintes ☎ 0590/99–57–47) has his art gallery in the row of shops between the dock and the church. His oils depict Caribbean life. Posters are for sale as well as objets d'art, ★ small pieces of furniture, and lighting from foreign ports. At **Maogany Artisanat** (✉ Terre-de-Haut, Iles des Saintes ☎ 0590/99–50–12), Yves Cohen, an artist and designer, creates batiks and hand-painted T-shirts in luminescent seashell shades. Hand-loomed silk fabrics are embellished with gold thread; others are translucent, like his sensual women's collection, 1000 & One Nights. Silk shawls and scarves, hand-embroidered with tropical birds, and his children's collection make great gifts. **Pas-**

cal Foy (⊠ Rte. à Pompierres, Terre-de-Haut, Iles des Saintes ☎ 0590/99–52–29) produces stunning homages to traditional Creole architecture: paintings of houses that incorporate collage and marvelous wall hangings. As his fame has grown, his prices have risen.

LIQUOR & **Aéroport International Pôle Caraïbes** (⊠ Grande-Terre ☎ 0590/21–14–
TOBACCO 72) has a good selection of island rum and tobacco. **Délice Shop** (⊠ 45 rue Achille René-Boisneuf, Pointe-à-Pitre, Grande-Terre ☎ 0590/82–98–24) is the spot for island rum and edibles from France—from cheese to chocolate.

Nightlife

Cole Porter notwithstanding, Guadeloupeans maintain that the beguine began here (the Martinicans and St. Lucians make the same claim for their islands). Discos come, discos go, and the current music craze is zouk (music with an African-influenced Caribbean rhythm), but the beat of the beguine remains steady. Many resorts have dinner dancing, as well as entertainment by steel bands and folk groups.

BARS & Join Fidel Castro and Che Guevara, whose photos hang proudly on the
NIGHTCLUBS walls of **Lollapalooza** (⊠ 122 Montauban, Gosier, Grande-Terre ☎ 0590/
★ 84–58–58), for hot Latin dancing and genuine Cuban rum. On Iles des Saintes, **Jardin Creole** (⊠ Terre-de-Haut ☎ 0590/99–55–08), at the pier, serves up local food at lunch and dinner, ice cream, and cocktails, with CDs making the music except on Friday and Saturdays when live music makes it the happening spot.

CASINOS Both of the island's two casinos are on Grande-Terre, and both have American-style roulette, blackjack, and chemin de fer. The legal age is 18, and you'll need a photo ID. Jacket and tie aren't required, but "proper attire" means no shorts. **Casino de Gosier** (⊠ Gosier, Grande-Terre ☎ 0590/84–79–69) has a bar, restaurant, and cinema. There are a number of well-priced packages, for dinner and a movie, for example. The higher-stakes gambling is behind a closed door. You will have to pay $10 to be part of that action—or even to look on. It's open Monday to Saturday from 7:30 PM; slot machines open at 10 AM. **Casino de St-François** (⊠ Marina, St-François, Grande-Terre ☎ 0590/88–41–31) has a snack bar and nightclub with a piano bar, karaoke, and Elvis nights, and is open daily from 9 PM.

DISCOS Night owls should note that carousing isn't cheap. Most discos charge a cover of at least $20, which includes one drink (drinks cost about $10 each). **Le Barracuda** (⊠ Rte. du Club Méditerranée, Ste-Anne, Grande-Terre ☎ 0590/88–18–19) is really on fire with the hot dance rhythms of the tropics: zouk, funk, reggae, and salsa. **Caraïbes 2** (⊠ Carrefour de Blanchard, Bas-du-Fort, Grande-Terre ☎ 0590/90–85–27) plays Brazilian dance music and has erotic spectacles with charming girls from around the world; the ambience is like that of Parisian music halls. **La Plantation** (⊠ Gourbeyre, Basse-Terre ☎ 0590/81–23–37) is the top spot on Basse-Terre; couples dance to zouk, funk, and house music on the immense mezzanine dance floor. Outside Gosier, there's **Shiva 1** (⊠ Le Moule, Grande-Terre ☎ 0590/23–53–59) a tri-level club with the first floor like the loges in a theater; many local musicians perform here. **Le Sans Tabou** (⊠ 153 av. Charles de Gaulle, Gosier, Grande-Terre ☎ 0590/84–31–15) is a high-tech, chrome-covered dance club that plays the music that's hot in New York, London, and Paris to a cosmopolitan clientele. **Zenith** (⊠ Rte. de la Riviera, Gosier, Grande-Terre ☎ 0590/90–72–04) is one of the island's most exclusive clubs, featuring local creole salsa and remarkable service; there is a view of the sea and a terrace with a pool.

Exploring Guadeloupe

To see each "wing" of the butterfly, you'll need to budget at least one day. Grande-Terre has pretty villages along its south coast and the spectacular Pointe des Châteaux. You can see the main sights in Pointe-à-Pitre in a half day. Touring the rugged, mountainous Basse-Terre is a challenge. If time is a problem, head straight to the west coast; you could easily spend a day traveling its length, stopping for sightseeing, lunch, and a swim. You can make day trips to the islands, but an overnight works best.

Numbers in the margin correspond to points of interest on the Guadeloupe map.

Grande-Terre

WHAT TO SEE
Anse Bertrand. The northernmost village in Guadeloupe lies 4 mi (6½
❾ km) south of La Pointe de la Grande Vigie. It was the Caribs' last refuge and was prosperous in the days of sugar. Most excitement takes place in the St-Jacques Hippodrome, where horse races and cockfights are held. Anse Laborde is a good swimming beach.

❸ **Aquarium de la Guadeloupe.** The Caribbean's largest aquarium is a good place to spend an hour. The well-planned facility is in the marina near Pointe-à-Pitre and has an assortment of tropical fish, crabs, lobsters, moray eels, dorsal spines, trunkfish, and coral. ⊠ *Pl. Créole, off Rte. N4, Point-à-Pitre* ☎ *0590/90–92–38* ⊠ *€4.76* ☉ *Daily 9–7.*

❷ **Bas-du-Fort.** The main attraction in this town is the Fort Fleur d'Épée, an 18th-century fortress that hunkers down on a hillside behind a deep moat. It was the scene of hard-fought battles between the French and the English in 1794. You can explore its well-preserved dungeons and battlements and take in a sweeping view of the Iles des Saintes and Marie-Galante. **The Other End of the World** (☎ 0590/35–33–45 or 0590/55–38–52) is a 15-minute ferry ride from Bas-du-Fort Marina. This islet was a refuge from society for a French wine merchant and his bride, a Guadeloupean slave. Their lovely and talented granddaughter, the esteemed writer Simone Schwarz-Bart, has re-created their home, which was destroyed in the hurricane of 1928. In addition to the museum, there is a vast open-air restaurant with a buffet of authentic creole dishes and rum libations. Dancing and card-playing follow lunch. The excursion costs €37, including the round-trip ferry ride.

❹ **Gosier.** People stroll with baguettes over their shoulders or sit at sidewalk cafés reading *Le Monde* and drinking *planteurs punch* in the island's major tourist center, where you'll also find hotels, nightclubs, shops, a casino, and a long stretch of sand.

⓫ **Morne-à-l'Eau.** This agricultural town of about 16,000 people has an amphitheater-shaped cemetery, with black-and-white-checkerboard tombs, elaborate epitaphs, and multicolor (plastic) flowers. On All Saints' Day (November 1), it's the scene of a moving (and photogenic) candlelight service.

❽ **Le Moule.** On the Atlantic coast, and once the capital city of Guadeloupe, this port city of 24,000 has had more than its share of troubles: it was bombarded by the British in 1794 and 1809 and by a hurricane in 1928. A large East Indian population, which originally came to cut cane, lives here. Canopies of flamboyant trees hang over the narrow streets, where colorful vegetable and fish markets do a brisk business. The town hall, with graceful balustrades, and a small 19th-century neoclassical church, are on the main square. Le Moule's beach is protected by a reef, perfect for windsurfing.

❼ Pointe des Châteaux. The island's easternmost point offers a breathtaking view of the Atlantic crashing against huge rocks, carving them into pyramid-like shapes. The majestic cliffs are reminiscent of the headlands of Brittany. There are spectacular views of Guadeloupe's south and east coasts and the island of La Désirade. On weekends locals come in numbers to walk their dogs, surf, or look for romance.

❶ Pointe-à-Pitre. Although not the capital city, this is the largest commercial and industrial hub in the southwest of Grande-Terre. It's bustling, noisy, and hot—a place of honking horns and traffic jams and cars on sidewalks for want of a parking place. By day its pulse is fast, but at night, when its streets are almost deserted, you don't want to be there, when street crime can be a problem.

The city has suffered severe damage over the years from earthquakes, fires, and hurricanes. It took heavy hits by Hurricanes Frederick (1979), David (1980), and Hugo (1989). On one side of rue Frébault you can see the remaining French colonial structures; on the other, the modern city. Some of the downtown area has been rejuvenated. Completion of the Centre St-John Perse has transformed old warehouses into a cruise-terminal complex that consists of the Hotel St-John, restaurants, shops, ferry docks, and the port authority headquarters. An impressive new ferry terminal is within, for the ferries that depart for Iles des Saintes, Marie-Galante, Dominica, Martinique, and St. Lucia.

The heart of the old city is Place de la Victoire, surrounded by wooden buildings with balconies and shutters and by many sidewalk cafés. Place de la Victoire was named in honor of Victor Hugues's 1794 victory over the British. The sandbox trees in the park are said to have been planted by Hugues the day after. During the French Revolution, Hugues ordered the guillotine to be set up in the square so that the public could witness the bloody end of 300 recalcitrant royalists. Many were plantation owners, which put a fast end to the plantocracy.

Even more colorful is the bustling marketplace, between rues St-John Perse, Frébault, Schoelcher, and Peynier. It's a cacophonous place, where housewives bargain for spices, herbs (and herbal remedies), papayas, breadfruits, christophenes, tomatoes, and a bright assortment of other produce. For fans of French ecclesiastical architecture, there's the imposing **Cathédrale de St-Pierre et St-Paul** (⊠ Rue Alexandre Isaac at rue de l'Eglise), built in 1807. Although battered by hurricanes, it is reinforced with iron pillars and ribs that look like leftovers from the Eiffel Tower. The fine stained-glass windows and Creole-style balconies make it worth a look.

Anyone with an interest in French literature and culture won't want to miss the **Musée St-John Perse,** which is dedicated to Guadeloupe's most famous son and one of the giants of world literature, Alexis Léger, better known as St-John Perse, winner of the Nobel Prize for literature in 1960. Some of his finest poems are inspired by the history and landscape—particularly the sea—of his beloved Guadeloupe. The museum contains a complete collection of his poetry and some of his personal belongings. Before you go, look for his birthplace at 54 rue Achille René-Boisneuf. ⊠ *Corner of rues Noizières and Achille René-Boisneuf* ☎ *0590/ 90–01–92* ☎ *€1.25* ☼ *Thurs.–Tues. 8:30–12:30 and 2:30–5:30.*

Guadeloupe's other famous son is celebrated at the **Musée Schoelcher.** Victor Schoelcher, a high-minded abolitionist from Alsace, fought against slavery in the French West Indies in the 19th century. The museum contains many of his personal effects, and exhibits trace his life and work. ⊠ *24 rue Peynier* ☎ *0590/82–08–04* 🖃 *€1.68* ⊙ *Weekdays 8:30–11:30 and 2–5.*

🔟 **Port Louis.** This fishing village of about 7,000 is best known for the Souffleur Beach. It was once one of the island's prettiest, but it has become a little shabby. Still, the sand is fringed by flamboyant trees, and though the beach is crowded on weekends it's blissfully quiet during the week. There are also spectacular views of Basse-Terre.

❺ **Ste-Anne.** In the 18th century this town, 8 mi (13 km) east of Gosier, was a sugar-exporting center. Sand has replaced sugar as the town's most valuable asset. La Caravelle and the other beaches here are among the best in Guadeloupe. On a more spiritual note, Ste-Anne has a lovely cemetery with stark-white tombs.

★ ❻ **St-François.** This was once a simple little village primarily involved with fishing and harvesting tomatoes. Increasingly, though, St-François is overtaking Gosier as Guadeloupe's most fashionable tourist resort area. The fish and tomatoes are still here, but so is one of the island's ritziest hotels. Avenue de l' Europe runs between the well-groomed 18-hole Robert Trent Jones–designed municipal golf course and the marina. On the marina side, a string of shops, hotels, bars, and restaurants—even a truck selling pizza and crêpes—caters to tourists.

Basse-Terre

Yellow butterflies—clouds of them—are what you might see when you arrive on Basse-Terre. Rugged, green, and mysterious, this half of Guadeloupe is all mountain trails, lakes, waterfalls, and hot springs. It's the home of La Soufrière volcano, as well as the island's capital city, also called Basse-Terre. The northwest coast, between Bouillante and Grande-Anse, is magnificent; the road twists and turns up steep hills smothered in vegetation and then drops down and skirts deep blue bays and colorful seaside towns. Constantly changing light, towering clouds, and frequent rainbows only add to the beauty. The Parc National de la Guadeloupe is crisscrossed by numerous trails, many following the old *traces,* routes that porters once took across the mountains.

WHAT TO SEE   **Basse-Terre.** Because Pointe-à-Pitre is so much bigger, few people suspect
❷❸   that this little town of 15,000 inhabitants is the capital and administrative center of Guadeloupe. But if you have any doubts, walk up the hill to the state-of-the-art Théâtre Nationale, where some of France's finest theater and opera companies perform. Paid for by the French government, it's a sign that Basse-Terre is reinventing itself. The town has had a lot to overcome. Founded in 1640, it has endured not only foreign attacks and hurricanes but sputtering threats from La Soufrière as well. The last major eruption was in the 16th century, though the volcano seemed active enough to warrant evacuating more than 70,000 people in 1975.

Start exploring the city at the imposing 17th-century Fort Louis Delgrès. Its small museum gives a good outline of Basse-Terre's history. The Cathedral of Our Lady of Guadeloupe, to the north across the Rivière aux Herbes, is also worth a look. On boulevard Félix Eboué you can see the impressive colonial buildings housing government offices. Two main squares, both with gardens, Jardin Pichon and Champ d'Arbaud, give you a feel for how the city used to be. Not far from Champ d'Arbaud are the botanical gardens.

For shopping, walk down rue Dr. Cabre, with its brightly painted Creole houses and imposing church, Ste-Marie de Guadeloupe. For a flavor of local life, check out the daily vegetable and fruit market on boulevard Basse-Terre, which runs parallel to the ocean. The other main street is rue St-François. For a guided tour of Basse-Terre, climb aboard the **Pom, Pom** (☎ 0590/81–24–83), a miniature train that does a circuit of the major sights. The ride costs €7 and lasts 2½ hours.

★ ☺ The **Jardin Botanique,** an exquisitely tasteful 10-acre park populated with parrots and flamingos, has a circuitous walking trail that takes you by ponds with floating lily pads, cactus gardens, and every kind of tropical flower and plant, including orchids galore. A restaurant and another snack bar are housed in terraced, gingerbread buildings, one overlooking a waterfall, the other the mountains. The garden has a kiddie park and nature-oriented playthings in the shop. ⊠ *Deshaies* ☎ *0590/ 28–43–02* 🖃 *€8.50* ☻ *Daily 7 AM–5:30 PM.*

㉑ **Bouillante.** The name means "boiling," and so it's no surprise that hot springs were discovered here. However, today the biggest attraction is scuba diving on nearby Pigeon Island, which is accessed by boat from Plage de Malendure. There's an information office on the beach that can help you with diving and snorkeling arrangements.

⑱ **Cascade aux Ecrevisses.** Part of the Parc National de la Guadeloupe, Crayfish Falls is one of the island's loveliest (and most popular) spots. There's a marked trail (walk carefully—the rocks can be slippery) leading to this splendid waterfall that dashes down into the Corossol River—a good place for a dip. Come early, though, otherwise you definitely won't have it to yourself.

㉕ **Centre de Broderie.** Vieux Fort is renowned for its traditional lacework. In 1980, 40 local lace makers united to preserve—and display—the ancient tradition of lace-making. At the center, built into the ruins of Fort L'Olive, you can see these local ladies tat intricate handkerchiefs, tablecloths, and doilies. This kind of lacework is rare, so prices are *très cher* (about $30 for a doily). ⊠ *Bourg, Vieux Fort* ☎ *0590/92–04–14* 🖃 *Free* ☻ *8:30–6.*

㉖ **Chutes du Carbet.** You can reach three of the Carbet Falls (one drops from 65 ft [20 m], the second from 360 ft [110 m], the third from 410 ft [125 m]) via a long, steep path from the village of Habituée. On the way up you'll pass the Grand Étang (Great Pond), a volcanic lake surrounded by interesting plant life. For horror fans there's also the curiously named Étang Zombi, a pond believed to house evil spirits.

⑳ **Ilet de Pigeon.** This tiny, rocky island a few hundred yards off the coast is the site of the Jacques Cousteau Marine Reserve, the island's best scuba and snorkeling site, but it doesn't rank with the best Caribbean dive spots. Les Heures Saines and Chez Guy et Christian, both on Malendure Beach, conduct diving trips, and the glass-bottom *Aquarium* and *Nautilus* make daily trips to this spectacular site.

⑰ **Maison de la Forêt.** This part of the Parc National de la Guadeloupe is where you can park and explore various nature trails. The **Habitation Beausoleil** has a variety of displays that describe (in French) the flora, fauna, and topography of the national park. There are three marked botanical trails and picnic tables. It's open daily 9–4:30; admission is free.

⑯ **Les Mamelles.** Two mountains—Mamelle de Petit-Bourg, at 2,350 ft, and Mamelle de Pigeon, at 2,500 ft—rise in the Parc National de la Guadeloupe. *Mamelle* means "breast," and when you see the mountains, you'll understand why they are so named. Trails ranging from easy to arduous lace up into the surrounding mountains. There's a glorious view from the lookout point 1,969 ft up Mamelle de Pigeon. If you're a climber, plan to spend several hours exploring this area.

㉔ Le Musée Volcanologique. Inland from Basse-Terre, on the road to Matouba, is the village of St-Claude, where you can see this museum that will tell you everything you need to know about volcanoes. ⊠ *Rue Victor Hugo, St-Claude* ☎ *0590/78–15–16* 🖅 *€3* ☉ *Daily 9–5.*

★ **⑮ Parc National de la Guadeloupe.** This 74,100-acre park has been recognized by UNESCO as a Biosphere Reserve. Before going, pick up a *Guide to the National Park* from the tourist office; it rates the hiking trails according to difficulty (note: most mountain trails are in the southern half of the park). The park is bisected by the Route de la Traversée, a 16-mi (26-km) paved road lined with masses of tree ferns, shrubs, flowers, tall trees, and green plantains. It's the ideal point of entry to the park. Wear rubber-soled shoes and take along a swimsuit, a sweater, and perhaps food for a picnic. Try to get an early start to stay ahead of the hordes of cruise-ship passengers who are making a day of it. ⊠ *Administrative Headquarters, Rte. de la Traversée, Saint-Claude* ☎ *0590/80–86–00.*

⑭ Pointe-Noire. This town has two small museums devoted to local products. **La Maison du Bois** (☎ 0590/98–17–09) offers a glimpse into the traditional use of wood on the island. Superbly crafted musical instruments and furnishings are for sale. It's open Tuesday to Sunday from 9:30 to 5:30 and charges €1 admission. Across the road from La Maison du Bois is **La Maison du Cacao** (☎ 0590/98–21–23), where you can see a working cocoa plantation. It is open daily from 9 to 5 for a €4 admission fee. Pointe-Noire is a good jumping-off point from which to explore Basse-Terre's little-visited northwest coast. A road skirts magnificent cliffs and tiny coves, dances in and out of thick stands of mahogany and gommier trees, and weaves through unspoiled fishing villages with boats and ramshackle houses as brightly colored as a child's finger painting. One of the most attractive villages is Deshaies (pronounced "day").

⑬ Ste-Rose. In addition to a sulfur bath, there are two good beaches (Amandiers and Clugny) and several interesting small museums in Ste-Rose. **Le Domaine de Séverin** (☎ 0590/28–91–86), free and open daily 8:30–12:30, is a historic rum distillery with a working waterwheel; the restaurant in a colonial house is known for crayfish pulled from its river.

⑫ Station Thermale de Ravine Chaude René Toribio. It's not Vichy—or tourist-oriented—but this spa is a good place to soak after tackling the trails. It draws upon the area's healthful geothermal waters. If you do nothing but bathe in the vast, warm pool you will feel healed. If time allows, have a sauna, massage, algae mask, or hydrotherapy. Almost no English is spoken here, but then it's all in the touch. The surrounding landscape in the foothills of Grosse Montagne—with its cane fields, country lanes, and colorful little villages—is very pleasant. However, do get specific directions from your hotel concierge or someone who speaks English. Finding it is not like a day at the spa. ⊠ *Le Lamentin* ☎ *0590/25–75–92* 🖅 *€2.64* ☉ *Daily 8–8.*

★ **⑲ Vernou.** Many of the old mansions in this area remain in the hands of the original aristocratic families, the *bekés* (Creole for "whites"), who trace their lineage to before the French Revolution. Traipsing along a path that leads beyond the village through the forest, you'll come to the waterfall at Saut de la Lézarde (Lizard's Leap).

㉒ **Vieux-Habitants.** This was the island's first colony, established in 1635. Beaches, a restored coffee plantation, and the oldest church on the island (1666) make this village worth a stop. From the riverfront **Musée du Café** (☎ 0590/98–54–96), dedicated to the art of coffee-making, the tantalizing aroma of freshly ground beans reaches the highway. Plaques and photos tell of the island's coffee history. The shop sells excellent coffee and rum punches (liqueurs). Admission is €6.

Iles des Saintes

The eight-island archipelago of Iles des Saintes, usually referred to as Les Saintes, dots the waters off the south coast of Guadeloupe. The islands are Terre-de-Haut, Terre-de-Bas, Ilet à Cabrit, Grand Ilet, La Redonde, La Coche, Le Pâté, and Les Augustins. Columbus discovered them on November 4, 1493, and christened them Los Santos in honor of All Saints' Day.

Only Terre-de-Haut and Terre-de-Bas are inhabited, with a combined population of 3,260. Many of les Saintois, as the islanders are called, are fair-haired, blue-eyed descendants of Breton and Norman sailors. Fishing is their main source of income, and the shores are lined with their boats and *filets bleus* (blue nets dotted with burnt-orange buoys). For generations, the fishermen wore hats called *salakos,* which look like inverted saucers. They're patterned after a hat said to have been brought here by a seafarer from China or Indonesia. Now, you are more likely to see visors and French sunglasses.

★ ㉗ **Terre-de-Haut.** With 5 square mi (13 square km) and a population of about 1,500, Terre-de-Haut is the largest and most developed of Les Saintes. Its "big city" is Bourg, with one street and a few bistros, cafés, and shops. Clutching the hillside are trim white houses with bright red or blue doors, balconies, and gingerbread frills.

Terre-de-Haut's ragged coastline is scalloped with lovely coves and beaches, including the semi-nudist beach at Anse Crawen. The beautiful bay, complete with a "sugarloaf" mountain, has been called a mini Rio. There are precious few vehicles on island, so to get around you can get your exercise by walking. Terre-de-Haut is tiny, but it's also very hilly. Or you can add to the din and rent a motorbike. Take your time on these rutted roads. Around any bend there can be a herd of goats chomping on a fallen palm frond. This island makes a great day trip, but you'll really get a feel for Les Saintes if you stay over. It is much like St. Barths, but for a fraction of the price.

Fort Napoléon. This gallery holds a collection of 250 modern paintings, influenced by cubism and surrealism. However, this museum is noted for its exhaustive exhibit of the greatest sea battles ever fought. You can also visit the well-preserved barracks and prison cells, or admire the botanical gardens, which specialize in cacti of all sizes and descriptions. ⊠ *Bourg* ☎ *0590/37–99–59* 🖵 *€2.64* ☉ *Daily 9–12:30.*

Other Islands

㉙ **La Désirade.** According to legend, this is the "desired land" of Columbus's second voyage. Along with Marie-Galante, it was spotted on November 3, 1493. The 8-square-mi (21-square-km) island, 5 mi (8 km) east of St-François, was a leper colony for many years. Most of today's 1,700 inhabitants are fishermen and boatbuilders. The main settlement is Grande-Anse, which has a pretty church and a couple of lodgings. There are good beaches here, and there's little to do but loll around on them.

★ ㉘ **Marie-Galante.** Columbus sighted this 60-square-mi (155-square-km) island on November 3, 1493, the day before he landed at Ste-Marie on

Basse-Terre. He named it for his flagship, the *Maria Galanda,* and sailed on. It's dotted with ruined 19th-century sugar mills, and sugar is still its major product. With its rolling hills of green cane still worked by oxen and men with broad-brimmed straw hats, this island is a journey back to a time when all of Guadeloupe was an agrarian place. Only an hour by high-speed boat from Pointe-à-Pitre, this is where Guadeloupeans come for day trips; it has only just become a tourist destination. The country folk are still a bit shy and have a gentle sense of humor. You'll see yellow butterflies, pigs tethered by the side of the road, and some of the archipelago's best beaches. Ox-pulling contests, visits to distilleries, days at the beach, or country hikes await you. The main community on the island is Grand-Bourg; an entertainment complex here, called El Rancho, has a 400-seat movie theater, a restaurant, a terrace grill, a snack bar, a disco, and a few double rooms. Take time to explore the dramatic coast. You'll find soaring cliffs—such as the Gueule Grand Gouffre (Mouth of the Giant Chasm) and Les Galeries (where the sea has sculpted a natural arcade)—and enormous sun-dappled grottoes, such as Le Trou à Diable, whose underground river can be explored with a guide. After sunset, no-see-ums and mosquitoes can be a real aggravation, especially near beaches. Always be armed with repellant. The **Château Murat** (⊠ Grand-Bourg, Marie-Galante ☎ 0590/97–94–41) is a restored 17th-century sugar plantation and rum distillery housing exhibits on the history of rum making and sugarcane production and an admirable *ecomusée,* whose displays celebrate local crafts and customs. The château is open daily 9:15–5; admission is €2. **Le Moulin de Bézard** (⊠ Chemin de Nesmond, off D202, Marie-Galante) is the only rebuilt windmill in the Caribbean. There are two gift shops and a café here. They're housed in replicated slave quarters: tiny cabins (with wattle walls) of a type found only on this island. Admission is €1.25; it's open daily 10–2. You should make it a point to see the distilleries, especially **Père Labat** (⊠ Grand Bourg, Section Poisson, Marie-Galante ☎ 0590/97–03–79), whose rum is considered some of the finest in the Caribbean and whose atelier turns out lovely pottery; admission is free, and it's open daily 7–noon.

GUADELOUPE A TO Z

To research prices, get advice from other travelers, and book travel arrangements, visit www.fodors.com.

AIR TRAVEL

American Eagle has seasonal connections to Guadeloupe from San Juan, Puerto Rico. Air Canada has direct flights from Montréal on Saturday. Air France flies nonstop from Paris to Guadeloupe and has direct service from Miami and San Juan. Air Caraïbes flies in daily from Martinique, St. Martin, St. Barths, and Santo Domingo in the Dominican Republic. LIAT flies from St. Croix, Antigua, and St. Maarten in the north and is your best bet from Dominica, Martinique, St. Lucia, Grenada, Barbados, and Trinidad. Air Tropical, with two twin-engine aircraft with five-passenger seating capacity, flies into Pointe-à-Pitre's Le Raizet Airport. An air-charter operation (English-speaking) based at the St. François Airport, it has day tours to the neighboring islands and provides air-taxi and ambulance services.

🛧 Air Canada ☎ 0590/21-12-77. **Air Caraïbes** ☎ 0590/82-47-00 or 590/21-12-88. **Air France** ☎ 0590/21-13-00 or 590/21-13-28. **Air Tropical** ☎ 0590/88-89-90 or 0690/35-05-15. **American/American Eagle** ☎ 0590/87-70-40 or 0590/21-11-80. **LIAT** ☎ 0590/21-13-93.

AIRPORTS

Most airlines fly into Aéroport International Pôle Caraïbes, 3 mi (5 km) from Pointe-à-Pitre. Cabs meet flights at the airport. The metered fare is about $9 to Pointe-à-Pitre, $22 to Gosier, and $38 to St-François. Fares go up 40% on Sunday and holidays and from 9 PM to 7 AM. For $1 you can take a bus from the airport to downtown Pointe-à-Pitre. A local bus ($1) then runs from the capital to Gosier. If you have a lot of luggage, however, it's not advisable.

🚹 **Aéroport International Pôle Caraïbes** ☎ 0590/21-14-72 or 0590/21-14-00.

BIKE & MOPED RENTALS

You can rent a Vespa (motorbike) at Eli Sport and Equator Moto for about $29 per day, including insurance. You'll need to put down nearly $150 for a deposit. On Terre-de-Haut mopeds start at about €24. There are numerous vendors by the ferry dock; shop around for the best price. On Marie-Galante try Loca Sol or Magaloc.

🚹 **Eli Sport** ✉ Grand Camp, Grande-Terre ☎ 0590/90-37-50. **Equator Moto** ✉ Gosier, Grande-Terre ☎ 0590/90-36-77. **Loca Sol** ✉ Rue du Fort, Grand-Bourg, Marie-Galante ☎ 0590/97-76-58. **Magaloc** ✉ Grand-Bourg, Marie-Galante ☎ 0590/72-91-33.

BOAT & FERRY TRAVEL

Express des Isles and Transport Maritime Brudey Frères provide ferry service to Les Saintes and Marie-Galante. Schedules often change, especially on weekends, so phone first or check them at the tourist office or ferry terminal.

FARES & SCHEDULES

It's a choppy 45-minute crossing to Terre-de-Haut from Trois-Rivières on Basse-Terre; ferries leave at about 9:30 AM (7:30 AM on Sunday) and return about 4 PM. One way costs €10, €16 round trip. Parking is €2. From Pointe-à-Pitre on Grande-Terre, it's a 60-minute ride. Departure time is 8 AM, with return at 3:45 PM; the round-trip fare is €30, one-way €17.

The ferry to Grand-Bourg on Marie-Galante departs from Pointe-à-Pitre at 8 AM, and returns at 4 PM. It takes one hour and costs €17 one way and €30 round-trip. It is Brudey Freres that service these islands.

Ferries run between La Désirade and St-François on Grande-Terre, departing daily at 8 AM and 4 PM, returning at 3:30 PM. Companies change on this route, so check with the St. François Marina: 0590/88-47-28 or 0590/55-79-26.

Brudey Frères is the major ferry company with service from Pointe-a-Pitre to Fort-de-France, Martinique for €57, €87 round-trip, with a stopover in Dominica. The ferry departs at 1:00 PM Mon.–Thurs. and Sun., on Fri. and Sat. at 12:30 PM, and the crossing takes four hours. It is generally smooth sailing aboard these large car ferries, called motorized catamarans. It can be the most direct and least costly way to get to Martinique. If you have heavy luggage, you can check it, but steel yourself for the onslaught. It's chaos and there is no real line. Know also that you will not get a receipt, so try to be among the first to retrieve yours from where they drop it near customs. Make certain to ask for a green immigration card aboard the boat and fill it out so as not to slow down that process. Once under way, the ferries are better than many in the U.S. A movie is shown, the bar has drinks and sandwiches. Brudey also has service to St. Lucia from both Guadeloupe and Martinique.

Caribbean Ferries is yet another company now with service to Martinique for €57, €87 round-trip, but the trip takes just three hours because the stop in Dominica is a short one. Call or stop by the new ferry dock for the schedules.

Express des Isles has service to Dominica (about €59.84, 2½ hours) and Martinique (around €61.60, four hours) from Pointe-à-Pitre. The ferry departs at 8 AM four days a week. In all cases, check with the ferry companies for schedule changes, which happen with relative frequency.

⛴ Brudey Frères Transport Maritime ☎ 0590/91-60-87; 0590/92-69-74 in Trois Rivières. *Caribbean Ferries* ☎ 0590/82-05-05. *Express des Isles* ☎ 0590/83-12-45 or 0890/64-20-00.

BUSINESS HOURS

BANKS Banks are open weekdays 8–noon and 2–4. Crédit Agricole, Banque Populaire, and Société Générale de Banque aux Antilles have branches that are open Saturday. In summer most banks are open 8–3. Banks close at noon the day before a legal holiday that falls during the week.

POST OFFICES Post offices are open weekdays 8–noon and 2–4.

SHOPS Shops are open weekdays 8 or 8:30–noon and 2:30–6.

CAR RENTALS

There are rental offices at Aéroport International Pôle Caraïbes and the major resorts. Count on spending about $60 a day for a small car (usually Korean or French) with standard shift, in the winter season. Automatics are considerably more expensive, and normally have to be reserved in advance (especially the beautiful Peugeots). Try negotiating for better deals both from the states with the international agencies, like Avis, or on the Internet, and once again at the counters. Note: You must allow an extra 30 minutes to drop off your car at the end of your stay—the rental return sites are still at the old airport, Le Raizet, 2 mi (3 km) away.

⛴ Avis ☎ 0590/21-13-54 or 0590/85-00-11. **Budget** ☎ 0590/21-13-48. **Europcar** ☎ 0590/21-13-52. **Hertz** ☎ 0590/21-13-46. **Jumbo Car** ☎ 0590/91-42-17.

CAR TRAVEL

If you are based in Gosier or at a larger resort, you will probably not need a car for your entire stay, but rather for a day or two of sightseeing. If driving is not your forte—you need to be a keen driver to maneuver the roundabouts, the mountain roads, and go up against the fast, aggressive drivers—taxis are available.

GASOLINE Gas is expensive, at about $1 per liter (roughly $4 per gallon).

ROAD CONDITIONS Guadeloupe has 1,225 mi (1,976 km) of roads (marked as in Europe), and driving around Grande-Terre is relatively easy. On Basse-Terre it will take more effort to navigate the hairpin bends on the mountains and around the eastern shore. At night these scenic roads are poorly lit and treacherous. Guadeloupeans are skillful, fast, and sometimes impatient drivers. Avoid morning and evening rush hours, especially around Pointe-à-Pitre. If lost, know that the people on the side of the road are waiting for a lift and if you stop they will jump in. Try to find a gas station to ask directions.

RULES OF THE ROAD Driving is on the right, as in the U.S. and Europe. Your valid driver's license will suffice for up to 20 days, after which you'll need an international driver's permit.

ELECTRICITY

Electricity is 220 volts (though some hotels have 110 volts), so if you're visiting from North America, you'll need to pack an adapter and a converter to use any appliances you bring with you.

EMERGENCIES

Pharmacies alternate in staying open around the clock. The tourist offices or your hotel can help you locate a pharmacist who is on duty and/or find an English-speaking doctor. SAMU is a medical service, where you can get to see a doctor fast. However, the receptionists generally do not speak English. SOS Taxi Ambulance can get you to a hospital quickly, but you may need to have a French-speaking person make the call. SMUR is both an ambulance service and an emergency room.

🚹 **Ambulance & Fire** Ambulance ☎ 15. Fire ☎ 18. SAMU ☎ 0590/89-11-00. SMUR Ambulance of Basse-Terre ☎ 0590/80-54-00. SOS Taxi Ambulance ☎ 0590/82-89-33.

🚹 **Hospitals** Centre Hôpitalier de Pointe-à-Pitre ✉ Pointe-à-Pitre, Abymes, Grande-Terre ☎ 0590/89-10-10. Centre Hôpitalier ✉ Basse-Terre, Basse-Terre ☎ 0590/80-54-00.

🚹 **Police** Police emergencies ☎ 17. Police nonemergencies on Basse-Terre ☎ 0590/81-11-55. Police nonemergencies on Grande-Terre ☎ 0590/82-13-17.

ETIQUETTE & BEHAVIOR

Ask permission before taking a picture of an islander, and don't be surprised if the answer is a firm "No." Guadeloupeans are also deeply religious and traditional. Don't offend them by wearing short-shorts or swimwear off the beach.

FESTIVALS & SEASONAL EVENTS

Carnival starts in early January and continues until Lent, finishing with a parade of floats and costumes on Mardi Gras (Fat Tuesday) and a huge bash on Ash Wednesday. In October, the Union des Arts Culinaires sponsors an upscale food festival. On a Sunday in early August, Point-à-Pitre on Grande-Terre holds the Fête des Cuisinières, which celebrates the masters of creole cuisine with a five-hour banquet that's open to the public. The festival was started in 1916 by a guild of female cooks who wanted to honor the patron saint of cooks, St. Laurent. August also sees the Tour Cycliste de la Guadeloupe, a highly competitive bike race that begins in Point-à-Pitre and covers more than 800 mi (1,290 km) on both Grande-Terre and Basse-Terre.

HOLIDAYS

Public holidays are: New Year's Day, Ash Wednesday (beginning of Lent, usually Feb.), Good Friday, Easter Monday, Labor Day (May 1), Bastille Day (July 14), Assumption Day (August 15), All Saints' Day (Nov. 1), Armistice Day (Nov. 11), and Christmas.

LANGUAGE

The official language is French. Everyone also speaks a Creole patois, which you won't be able to understand even if you're fluent in French. In the major hotels most of the staff knows some English, but communicating may be more difficult in the countryside and in stores. Some taxi drivers speak a little English. Arm yourself with a phrase book, a dictionary, patience, and a sense of humor.

MAIL & SHIPPING

Postcards to the United States cost about €.44 and to Canada €.52; letters up to 20 grams, €.70. Postcards and letters to Europe cost around €.44. Stamps can be purchased at post offices, *café-tabacs,* hotel newsstands, and souvenir shops. When writing to Guadeloupe, be sure to include the name of the specific island in the archipelago (e.g., Grande-Terre, Basse-Terre, Iles des Saintes, etc.) as well as the postal code; then "Guadeloupe" followed by "French West Indies."

MONEY MATTERS

Prices quoted throughout the chapter are in U.S. dollars unless otherwise noted.

ATMS   There are ATMs that accept Visa and MasterCard at Aéroport International Pôle Caraïbes and at some banks—such as Crédit Agricole, Banque Populaire, and Société Générale de Banque aux Antilles, and BDAF; they dole out euros. Your home bank card, if it is a Plus card, should work at the above banks, but you will not be able to check your balance; you must have a four-digit PIN number. However, ATMs don't always work with foreign bank cards, particularly in smaller towns, and don't always work, period (especially on Les Saintes, where there is no longer a bank). Do not count on them. Have a back-up plan. The post office in Terre Haut, Les Saintes, will cash traveler's checks.

CURRENCY   As in Europe, the euro (€) is legal tender in the French West Indies. No more francs. Some places accept U.S. dollars, but it's best to change your money, which can be done at a bank or at your hotel (which will take a larger cut). You tend to get better rates at a bureau de change, such as Change Caraïbe, which is near both the tourist office and market in Point-à-Pitre. Sometimes the bank rate is the same, but they usually take a larger fee.

🏴 Change Caraïbe ⊠ 21 rue de Rene Frebault, Point-à-Pitre, Grande-Terre.

PASSPORTS & VISAS

All citizens of the United States, Canada, and the United Kingdom need a passport and a return or ongoing ticket.

SAFETY

Put your valuables in the hotel safe. Don't leave them unattended in your room or on the beach. It isn't a good idea to walk around Pointe-à-Pitre at night, since it's almost deserted after dark and street crime can be a problem there. If you rent a car, always lock it, with luggage and valuables stashed out of sight.

SIGHTSEEING TOURS

Guadeloupe has a number of fun, professional tour operators. However, much happens in French. Air Tropical has two twin-engine planes (five-passenger capacity) and organizes day trips to the neighboring islands; the most far-ranging is the Archipelago Air Cruise, which goes to Les Saintes in the morning and Marie Galante or Désirade in the afternoon. Emeraude Guadeloupe offers everything from hikes up the volcano to botanical tours and visits to Creole homes; guides are certified by the state, but you'll probably need some French to understand them.

🏴 Air Tropical ⊠ St-François, Grande-Terre ☎ 0590/88-89-90 or 0690/35-05-15. Emeraude Guadeloupe ⊠ St-Claude ☎ 0590/81-98-28.

TAXES & SERVICE CHARGES

SALES TAX   The *taxe de séjour* (room tax) varies from hotel to hotel, but never exceeds $1.80 per person per day.

SERVICE CHARGES   Most hotel prices include a 10%–15% service charge; if not, it will be added to your bill. A 15% service charge is included in all restaurant prices, as are taxes.

TAXIS

Taxis are metered and fairly pricey, and on Sunday, holidays, and between 9 PM and 7 AM, fares increase by 40%. Tourist offices or your hotel can arrange for an English-speaking taxi driver and even organize a small group for you to share the cost of a tour. Nicho—of Nicho's Reliable Taxi—speaks perfect English and knows every back way when the traffic backs up on the main highways. Call Narcisse Taxi for an English-speaking, professional taxi driver and tour guide. If your French is in order, you can call Radio Cabs.

🚕 Call **Narcisse Taxi** ☎ 0590/35-27-29 or 0590/83-24-79 on Grand-Terre ☎ 0590/ 81-79-70 on Basse-Terre. **Nicho's Reliable Taxi** ☎ 0590/74-86-85. **Radio Cabs** ☎ 0590/82-00-00, 0590/83-09-55, or 0590/20-74-74.

TELEPHONES

Coin-operated phones are rare. If you need to make many calls outside of your hotel, purchase a *télécarte* at the post office or other outlets marked TÉLÉCARTE EN VENTE ICI. Télécartes look like credit cards and are used in special booths labeled TÉLÉCOM. Local and international calls made with these cards are cheaper than operator-assisted calls. It is difficult, but not impossible, to put collect or credit-card calls through to the U. S. from Guadeloupe. Many Guadeloupeans have cell phones as their primary telephone service. In a pinch, you can ask someone to make a call for your from their "orange" (the name of the major cellular company) and offer to give them a euro.

COUNTRY & AREA CODES — To call Guadeloupe from the U.S., dial 011–590, another 590, and then the local number. If in one of the other French West Indies, you now must dial 0 then 590 and the six-digit local number.

LOCAL CALLS — To make on-island calls, simply dial the six-digit phone number.

TIPPING

Restaurants are legally required to include a 15% gratuity in the menu price, and no additional gratuity is necessary (although appreciated if service is particularly good). Tip skycaps and porters about €1 a bag. Many cab drivers own their own taxis and don't expect a tip. You won't have any trouble ascertaining if a 10% tip is expected. It's a look. Leaving the chamber maid a euro a night is always good form.

VISITOR INFORMATION

🚩 Before You Leave **French Government Tourist Office** ⊕ www.franceguide.com ✉ 9454 Wilshire Blvd., Beverly Hills, CA 90212 ☎ 310/276-2835 ✉ 645 N. Michigan Ave., Chicago, IL 60611 ☎ 312/337-6339 ✉ 1981 McGill College Ave., Suite 490, Montréal, Québec H3A 2W9, Canada ☎ 514/288-4264 ✉ 30 St. Patrick St., Suite 700, Toronto, Ontario M5T 3A3, Canada ☎ 416/593-6427 ✉ 178 Piccadilly, London W1V OAL, U.K. ☎ 0171/499-6911

🚩 In Guadeloupe **Office Départemental du Tourisme** ✉ 5 sq. de la Banque, Pointe-à-Pitre ☎ 0590/82-09-30. **Syndicats d'Initiatives** ✉ Av. de l'Europe, St-François ☎ 0590/88-48-74 ✉ Marie-Galante ☎ 0590/97-56-51.

JAMAICA

13

FODOR'S CHOICE
Grand Lido Negril resort, Negril
Negril Beach, Negril
Ocho Rios Village Jerk Centre, Ocho Rios
Playing golf at Tryall, Sandy Bay
Rockhouse, a hotel in Negril

HIGHLY RECOMMENDED

HOTELS   Couples Swept Away Negril, Negril
FDR, Franklyn D. Resort, Runaway Bay
Grand Lido Negril, Negril
Hedonism III, Runaway Bay
Round Hill Hotel and Villas, Montego Bay
Royal Plantation at Beaches, Ocho Rios
Starfish Trelawny, Falmouth
Strawberry Hill, Irishtown

SIGHTS   Doctor's Cave Beach, Montego Bay
Dunn's River Falls, Ocho Rios

*Many other great places enliven this area. For other
favorites, look for the black stars as you read this chapter.*

Around one bend of the winding North Coast Highway lies a palatial home; around another, a shanty without doors or windows. The towns are frenetic centers of activity, filled with pedestrians, street vendors, and neighbors visiting. Roads are crammed with vehicles and full of honking—not a chorus of hostility but notes of greeting or of friendly caution or just for the heck of it. Drivers wait patiently while groups of uniformed schoolchildren and women bearing loads on their heads cross the street, and a spirit of cooperation prevails amid chaos.

Updated by Paris Permenter and John Bigley

The cultural life of Jamaica is a wealthy one; its music, art, and cuisine have a spirit that's as hard to describe as the rhythms of reggae or an outburst of streetwise patois. Although 95% of the population traces its bloodlines to Africa, Jamaica is a stockpot of cultures, including those of other Caribbean islands, Great Britain, the Middle East, India, China, Germany, Portugal, and South America. The third-largest island in the Caribbean (after Cuba and Hispaniola), Jamaica enjoys a considerable self-sufficiency based on tourism, agriculture, and mining.

The island's physical attractions include jungle mountaintops, clear waterfalls, and unforgettable beaches, and its tourist areas are grouped around the northern and western coastlines. Ocho Rios (often just Ochi) is a major cruise port, resort center, and the home of Dunn's River Falls, probably the most photographed spot in the nation. Montego Bay (or MoBay, as it's affectionately known), destination of most tourist flights, is a sprawling blend of opulent beach resorts and commerce. At the island's western tip lies Negril, once a sleepy hangout for bohemian travelers; though now bigger and glitzier, it's still a haven for the hip and the hedonistic. In addition to these pleasure capitals, Jamaica has a real capital in Kingston. For all its congestion—and for all the disparity between city life and the bikinis and parasails to the north—Kingston is the true heart and head of the island. This is where politics, literature, music, and art wrestle for acceptance in the largest (800,000 people) English-speaking city in the Western hemisphere south of Miami.

The first group known to have reached Jamaica were the Arawak Indians, who paddled their canoes from the Orinoco region of South America around AD 1000. In 1494 Christopher Columbus stepped ashore at what is now called Discovery Bay. Having spent four centuries on the island, the Arawaks had little notion that his footsteps on their sand would mean their extinction within 50 years, thanks to overwork, cruelty, and European diseases. When the indigenous population died out, the Spanish brought African slaves to the island.

What is now St. Ann's Bay was established as New Seville in 1509 and served as the Spanish capital until the local government crossed the island to Santiago de la Vega (now Spanish Town). The Spaniards were never impressed with Jamaica; they found no precious metals, and they let the island fester in poverty for 161 years. When 5,000 British soldiers and sailors appeared in Kingston Harbor in 1655, the Spaniards didn't put up a fight.

The arrival of the English and the three centuries of rule that followed provided Jamaica with the genteel underpinnings of its present life—and a period of history enlivened by a rousing pirate tradition fueled by rum. The very British 18th century was a time of prosperity for Jamaican landholders. This was the age of the sugar baron, who ruled his plantation great house—and his slaves—and made the island the largest sugar-producing colony in the world.

The British were challenged soon after their arrival, however, by the Maroons, former slaves the Spanish had freed and armed to harass the island's new rulers. (Other accounts say the Maroons were actually escaped slaves, named for the Spanish word *cimarrón*: wild.) The Maroons took to the most rugged regions of the island, led by the runaway, slave and head of an Ashanti freedom-fighting family, Cudjoe. The First Maroon War (1690–1739) was played out across the island using guerrilla warfare. The island then remained quiet until 1760, when a slave rebellion broke out; later that century the Second Maroon War began. Tensions reached a peak in 1832 with the hanging of a Baptist minister, Sam Sharpe, in Montego Bay—punishment for his role as ringleader in an island-wide slave rebellion. Three years later slavery was abolished. Today the hanging is remembered at Sam Sharpe Square in the midst of bustling MoBay with a statue of the fallen leader; nearby, "the Cage," once used to imprison runaways, is another solemn reminder of this period in Jamaican history.

The second half of the 20th century brought independence to Jamaica. On August 6, 1962, the island became an independent nation, although still a member of the British Commonwealth. The government is headed by a freely elected prime minister. Two political parties, the People's National Party (PNP) and the Jamaica Labour Party (JLP), vie for position, and elections can become heated, even violent, events. Elections in 1980 resulted in many deaths, mostly in Kingston's ghettos; seven more recent elections were carefully monitored by a contingent that included Jimmy Carter and Colin Powell, and remained peaceful. But the 1990s brought high unemployment, low wages, and high interest rates as well as brief riots over an increase in the gasoline tax. Occasional rioting has continued to be a problem in Kingston, where gangs backing rival political parties have caused death.

Today's Jamaica is a place where poverty is rampant, and many citizens must work at the fringes of the tourist industry as unlicensed taxi drivers, hair braiders, and vendors who walk the beaches in search of a vacationer. Being hassled is one of the most common complaints by travelers to Jamaica, and the government has increased fines and even penalties of jail time for hassling tourists. Many problems involve attempts to sell marijuana, or *ganja*, an illegal product.

Smoking of sacramental ganja and flowing dreadlocks are the most recognized aspects of Rastafarianism, a religion that believes in the divinity of Haile Selassie, former emperor of Ethiopia. The Rastas gained strength in the 1960s, inspired in part by the 1930s movement led by Jamaican Marcus Garvey, founder of the U.S.-based Universal Negro Improvement Association. Garvey advocated black pride, which, along with his "back to Africa" message, was picked up by the Rastas, who embraced Ethiopia as their homeland. Today the Rastas are a small sector of the Jamaican population, but they are known internationally because of prominent Rastas such as the late reggae singer Bob Marley.

The reggae rhythms and lyrics for which Marley is known provide a peek at the Jamaican culture, but music is just one aspect of this rich island. Travelers here find a multitude of melodies—from the sizzle of jerk pork on a roadside grill to the lap of waves on a sandy beach, the call of the magnificent doctor bird flitting through the trees, or the quiet whistle of a breeze through the Blue Mountains.

WHAT IT COSTS In U.S. dollars				
$$$$	**$$$**	**$$**	**$**	**¢**
RESTAURANTS*				
over $30	$20–$30	$12–$20	$8–$12	under $8
HOTELS**				
Cost EP/BP/CP over $350	$250–$350	$150–$250	$80–$150	under $80
Cost AI over $450	$350–$450	$250–$350	$125–$250	under $125

*Restaurant prices are for a main course at dinner. **EP, BP, and CP prices are per night for a standard double room in high season, excluding taxes, service charges, and meal plans. AI (all-inclusive) prices are per person, per night based on double-occupancy during high season, excluding taxes and service charges.

Where to Stay

Jamaica was the birthplace of the Caribbean all-inclusive resort, a concept that took the Club Med idea and gave it an excess-in-the-tropics spin. The all-inclusive is the most popular vacation option here, offering incredible values. Prices usually include airport transfers, accommodations, three meals a day plus snacks, all bar drinks (often including premium liquors) and soft drinks, a plethora of sports options (from scuba diving to golf), nightly entertainment, and all gratuities and taxes. Usually the only surcharges are for such luxuries as massages, tours, and weddings or vow renewal ceremonies (though even these are often included at high-end establishments). The all-inclusives have branched out, some of them courting families, others going after an upper crust that wouldn't even have picked up a brochure a few years ago.

If you like to get out and explore, you may prefer an EP property. Many places offer MAP or FAP packages that include such extras as airport transfers and tours. Even if you don't want to be tied down to a meal plan, it pays to inquire, because the savings can be considerable.

Jamaica's resorts and hotels have varying policies about children; some don't accept children under 16 or 18 years old, but those that do often allow up to two to stay in their parents' room at no additional charge. Others allow kids to stay free in the off-season or offer discounted meal plans. Baby-sitting is readily available at properties that accept children, and several offer fully supervised kids' programs. If you plan to bring the kids, ask lots of questions before making a reservation, or have your travel agent find the best deal. In addition, some resorts are for male-female couples only. If you're a same-sex couple or a single parent traveling with one child, you simply won't be allowed to book a room in a couples-only establishment like a Sandals resort.

As a rule, rates are reduced anywhere from 10% to 30% from April 30 to December 15. All price categories are based on standard double rooms at the most comprehensive (and most expensive) meal-plan rate. Opting for a less comprehensive plan (if it's available in winter) can save you 20%–40%. The **Jamaica Reservations Service** (☎ 800/526-2422 in the U.S. and Canada) can book resorts, hotels, villas, and guest houses throughout the country.

Kingston

Some of the island's finest business hotels are in Kingston, and these high towers are filled with rooftop restaurants, English pubs, theater and dance presentations, art museums and galleries, jazz clubs, upscale supper clubs, and disco dives.

Jamaica

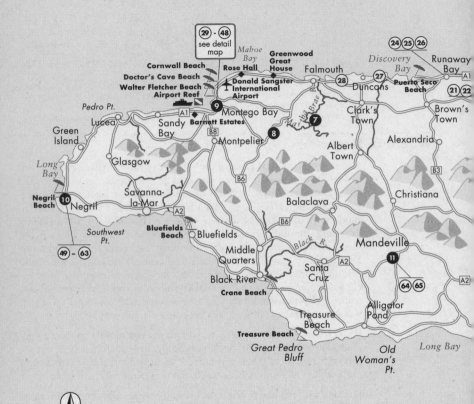

Mahoe Bay
Greenwood Great House
Rose Hall
Cornwall Beach
Doctor's Cave Beach
Walter Fletcher Beach
Airport Reef
Donald Sangster International Airport
Barnett Estates
Sandy Bay
Montego Bay
Montpelier
Falmouth
Duncans
Discovery Bay
Runaway Bay
Puerto Seco Beach
Brown's Town
Clark's Town
Albert Town
Alexandria
Christiana
Balaclava
Mandeville
Pedro Pt.
Lucea
Green Island
Glasgow
Savanna-la-Mar
Long Bay
Negril Beach
Negril
Southwest Pt.
Bluefields Beach
Bluefields
Middle Quarters
Black River
Crane Beach
Santa Cruz
Black R.
Alligator Pond
Treasure Beach
Great Pedro Bluff
Old Woman's Pt.
Long Bay
Martha Brae

29 - 48 see detail map

0   10 miles
0   15 km

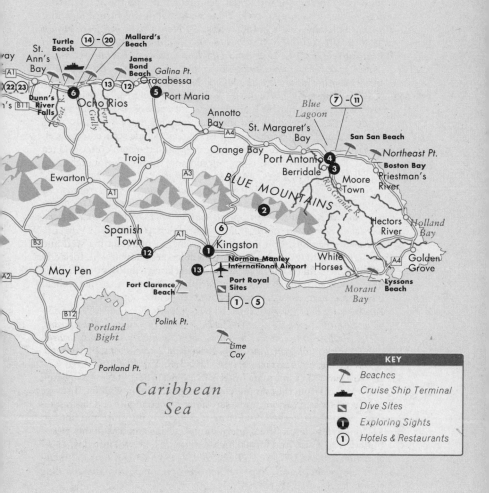

KEY

⊼	Beaches
⛴	Cruise Ship Terminal
◩	Dive Sites
●	Exploring Sights
①	Hotels & Restaurants

★ **$$$-$$$$**   ⊡ **Strawberry Hill.** One of many island properties owned by Chris Black-well, formerly the head of Island Records (the late Bob Marley's label), this Blue Mountains retreat 45 minutes north of Kingston offers refined luxury and absolute peace. Authors, musicians, and screenwriters come here to relax, rejuvenate the creative juices (perhaps in the Aveda spa), and work. The food is top-notch, as are the staff and the accommodations—elegant Georgian-style villas with mahogany furnishings and roomy balconies with grand vistas. ⊠ *New Castle Rd., Irishtown* ☎ *876/944–8400* ⊟ *876/944–8408* ⊕ *www.islandoutpost.com/ StrawberryHill* ⊲ *12 1-, 2-, and 3-bedroom villas* ⏶ *Restaurant, room service, fans, refrigerators, pool, sauna, spa, croquet, bar, meeting rooms, airport shuttle; no a/c* ⊟ *AE, MC, V* ⑩| *CP.*

$-$$$ ⊡ **Hilton Kingston.** This high-rise is the best of Kingston's business hotels. The expansive marble lobby leads to attractive, well-appointed guest rooms. The concierge floors include complimentary cocktails, hors d'oeuvres, and Continental breakfast. Extras include secured-access elevators, an American Airlines service desk, and in-room coffee and tea setups. Rates include admission to Jonkanoo, the hotel's hot nightclub; there's also an art gallery. ⊠ *77 Knutsford Blvd.* ⌂ *Box 112* ☎ *876/ 926–5430* ⊟ *876/929–7439* ⊕ *www.hilton.com* ⊲ *284 rooms, 13 suites, 6 1- and 2-bedroom units* ⏶ *2 restaurants, in-room data ports, in-room safes, 2 tennis courts, pool, health club, massage, sauna, 3 bars, nightclub, recreation room, shops, concierge* ⊟ *AE, DC, MC, V* ⑩| *EP.*

$$ ⊡ **Jamaica Pegasus.** You'll find an efficient, accommodating staff and modern furnishings at this 17-story complex near downtown, formerly the Méridien. All rooms have balconies and large windows that face the Blue Mountains, the pool, or the Caribbean. There's also an excellent business center, duty-free shops, and 24-hour room service. ⊠ *81 Knutsford Blvd.* ⌂ *Box 333* ☎ *876/926–3690* ⊟ *876/929–5855* ⊕ *www.jamaicapegasus.com* ⊲ *325 rooms, 16 suites* ⏶ *Restaurant, coffee shop, room service, in-room safes, minibars, 2 tennis courts, pool, wading pool, gym, hair salon, basketball, 2 bars, shops, playground, concierge, business services* ⊟ *AE, DC, MC, V* ⑩| *EP.*

$$ ⊡ **Terra Nova.** This intimate hotel is in a quieter part of New Kingston, 1 mi (1½ km) from the commercial district and within walking distance of Devon House, a historic home surrounded by boutiques and fine restaurants. Rooms are decked out in classic mahogany furniture and fine art. El Dorado restaurant offers international cuisine and reasonably priced buffets. You'll also find formal high-tea service here on Thursday. ⊠ *17 Waterloo Rd.* ☎ *876/926–2211* ⊟ *876/929–4933* ⊲ *35 rooms* ⏶ *Restaurant, coffee shop, grill, room service, in-room safes, pool, no-smoking rooms* ⊟ *AE, MC, V* ⑩| *EP.*

Port Antonio

Described by poet Ella Wheeler Wilcox as "the most exquisite port on earth," Port Antonio is a seaside town at the foot of verdant hills toward the east end of the north coast. The area's must-do activities include rafting the Rio Grande, snorkeling, or scuba diving in the Blue Lagoon, exploring the Nonsuch Caves, and stopping at the classy Trident resort for lunch or a drink.

$$$-$$$$ ⊡ **Trident Villas and Hotel.** The living here is truly gracious. Peacocks strut the manicured lawns, colonnaded walkways wind through whimsically sculpted topiaries that dot the 14 acres, and the pool—on a rocky bit of land that juts out into crashing surf—is a memory unto itself. The luxurious Laura Ashley–style rooms, many with turrets, bay windows, and balconies or verandahs, are awash in mahogany and local art; however, they do not have TVs or clocks. ⊠ *North Coast Hwy., Point Ann, Port Antonio* ⌂ *Box 119* ☎ *876/993–2602* ⊟ *876/993–2590* ⊕ *www.*

tridentvillas.com ☞ *8 rooms, 1 suite, 14 villas* ⚹ *Restaurant, in-room safes, minibars, 2 tennis courts, pool, fitness classes, massage, beach, snorkeling, boating, croquet, bar, library, concierge; no room TVs* ⊟ *AE, MC, V* ⫶⚬⫶ *MAP.*

$$ 🏨 **Goblin Hill Villas at San San.** This lush 12-acre estate is atop a hill overlooking San San Bay. Each attractively appointed villa comes with its own dramatic view, plus a staff member to do the grocery shopping, cleaning, and cooking for you. The rooms and villas come equipped with cable TV, ceiling fans, air-conditioning, and tropical furnishings. The beach is a 10-minute walk away. Excellent car-rental packages are available. ⊠ *San San* ⓓ *Box 26* ☎ *876/925–8108* 🖷 *876/925–6248* ⊕ *www.goblinhill.com* ☞ *12 rooms, 28 1- and 2-bedroom villas* ⚹ *Fans, kitchenettes, cable TV, 2 tennis courts, pool, beach, bar, library; no room phones* ⊟ *AE, MC, V* ⫶⚬⫶ *EP.*

$–$$ 🏨 **Dragon Bay Beach Resort.** On a private cove, Dragon Bay is an idyllic grouping of individually decorated villas surrounded by tropical gardens. Villa 35 has a private pool, a large living room, and two bedrooms with separate sitting rooms that have sofa beds. This place is popular with German and Italian tour groups. ⊠ *Dragon Bay* ⓓ *Box 176* ☎ *876/993–8751* 🖷 *876/993–8971* ⊕ *www.dragonbay.com* ☞ *30 1-, 2-, and 3-bedroom villas* ⚹ *2 restaurants, room service, refrigerators, tennis court, pool, fitness classes, gym, massage, beach, dive shop, snorkeling, volleyball, 3 bars* ⊟ *AE, MC, V* ⫶⚬⫶ *MAP.*

$–$$ 🏨 **Hotel Mocking Bird Hill.** With only 10 rooms, some overlooking the sea and all with views of lush hillsides, Mocking Bird Hill feels more like a cozy B&B than a hotel. Owners Barbara Walker and Shireen Aga run an environmentally sensitive operation: you'll find bamboo instead of hardwood furniture, solar-heated water, meals made with local produce in the Mille Fleurs dining terrace, locally produced toiletries and stationery sets, and seven naturally landscaped acres. Wedding packages are available. ⊠ *North Coast Hwy., Point Ann, Port Antonio* ⓓ *Box 254* ☎ *876/993–7267* 🖷 *876/993–7133* ⊕ *www.hotelmockingbirdhill.com* ☞ *10 rooms* ⚹ *Restaurant, in-room safes, pool, massage, bar, nosmoking rooms; no room phones, no room TVs* ⊟ *AE, MC, V* ⫶⚬⫶ *EP.*

$–$$ 🏨 **Jamaica Palace.** Built to resemble a 17th-century Italian mansion, this imposing white-columned hotel has oversize black-lacquer-and-gilt furniture throughout its common areas. Some rooms are more lavish than others, though each has a semicircular bed, European objets d'art, and Asian rugs; none is equipped with TV (you can, however, rent one). Although the hotel isn't on the beach, there's a 114-ft swimming pool that's shaped like Jamaica. ⊠ *Williamsfield* ⓓ *Box 279* ☎ *876/993–7720* 🖷 *876/993–7759* ⊕ *www.jamaicapalace.com* ☞ *24 rooms, 56 suites* ⚹ *2 restaurants, room service, in-room safes, pool, 2 bars, laundry service* ⊟ *AE, MC, V* ⫶⚬⫶ *CP, EP, MAP.*

Ocho Rios

On the northeast coast halfway between Port Antonio and MoBay, Ocho Rios is hilly and lush. Its resorts, hotels, and villas are all a short drive from a bustling crafts market, boutiques, duty-free shops, restaurants, and several scenic attractions.

$$$$ 🏨 **Beaches Grande Sport.** This expansive resort, formerly Ciboney, now welcomes those 16 and over in search of an active vacation. True to its sporty name, the resort offers a full menu of activities ranging from a rock-climbing wall to a running track to extensive water-sports facilities. Accommodations here vary from traditional hotel rooms to expansive villas; 88 villas come with their own courtyard swimming pools. Some villa suites are a distance from the public facilities and the beach, so the resort offers transportation to your door. ⊠ *North Coast Hwy.* ⓓ *Box*

2 ☎ 876/974–5601 🖷 876/974–5912 ⊕ *www.beaches.com* ⇆ *85 rooms, 200 suites* ⚲ *4 restaurants, 3 grills, in-room safes, 4 tennis courts, 3 pools, spa, beach, concierge; no kids under 16* ▭ *AE, MC, V* ⏍ *AI.*

$$$$ ▦ **Couples Ocho Rios.** This resort accepts reservations from only male-female couples. Each one-bedroom suite has a two-person hot tub in its bathroom that peeks through a window at the four-poster king-size bed. There's a lovely white beach for relaxation or water sports, and a private island where you can sunbathe in the buff. Weddings are included in the package as are five off-site excursions. If you plan to visit for seven nights, you can split your stay between this resort and Couples Negril. ⊠ *Tower Isle* ☎ *876/975–4271* 🖷 *876/975–4439* ⊕ *www.couples. com* ⇆ *201 rooms, 11 suites* ⚲ *4 restaurants, room service, in-room safes, 5 tennis courts, pool, 5 outdoor hot tubs, massage, sauna, beach, dive shop, snorkeling, windsurfing, horseback riding, squash, 4 bars* ⚲ *3-night minimum* ▭ *AE, MC, V* ⏍ *AI.*

$$$$ ▦ **Jamaica Inn.** A combination of class and quiet attracts a discerning crowd—not to mention such celebrities as Kate Moss and I. M. Pei—to this vintage property that was once a favorite of Winston Churchill. Each room has its own verandah (larger than most hotel rooms) on the private cove's powdery, champagne-colored beach. The dining room uses Wedgwood china; the inn has Jamaican antique furniture and terrazzo floors. The Full American Plan is available during summer months only. ⊠ *North Coast Hwy., east of Ocho Rios* ⍟ *Box 1* ☎ *876/974–2514* 🖷 *876/974–2449* ⊕ *www.jamaicainn.com* ⇆ *49 rooms, 4 suites* ⚲ *Restaurant, room service, pool, gym, beach, snorkeling, boating, croquet, 2 bars, library; no kids under 12* ▭ *AE, MC, V* ⏍ *MAP.*

★ **$$$$** ▦ **Royal Plantation at Beaches.** Formerly the Plantation Inn, this resort has been transformed into an ultra-luxurious all-inclusive for those 16 and over. The all-suites resort, built high atop a bluff, has the feel of a small, exclusive hotel; all rooms have ocean views. Steps lead to the beach, where the luxury continues with the services of a beach butler. You can play golf at the Sandals Golf and Country Club. ⊠ *North Coast Hwy.* ⍟ *Box 728* ☎ *876/974–5601* 🖷 *876/974–5912* ⊕ *www.beaches.com* ⇆ *80 suites* ⚲ *3 restaurants, room service, in-room safes, golf privileges, 2 tennis courts, pool, health club, outdoor hot tub, spa, beach, dive shop, windsurfing, concierge; no kids under 16* ▭ *AE, MC, V* ⏍ *AI.*

$$$$ ▦ **Sandals Dunn's River Golf Resort and Spa.** This luxury all-inclusive resort is exclusively for male-female couples. Twenty-five acres of lush, manicured grounds are fronted by a wide, sugary beach. With courteous service and posh rooms, it's the finest of Sandals's Jamaican properties. Rooms are light pink, blue, turquoise, and cream, and most have a balcony or patio that overlooks the sea or the grounds. The resort prides itself on catering to guests' every whim. You have access to a nearby golf course at the Sandals Golf and Country Club, with a free shuttle service. ⊠ *North Coast Hwy., Mammee Bay, 2 mi (3 km) east of Ocho Rios* ⍟ *Box 51* ☎ *876/972–1610* 🖷 *876/972–1611* ⊕ *www.sandals. com* ⇆ *256 rooms, 10 suites* ⚲ *4 restaurants, in-room safes, golf privileges, putting green, 4 tennis courts, 2 pools, 3 outdoor hot tubs, sauna, spa, steam room, beach, racquetball, 7 bars, concierge; no kids* ▭ *AE, MC, V* ⏍ *AI.*

$$$–$$$$ ▦ **Sans Souci Resort & Spa.** A stay at this pastel-pink cliffside resort is a wonderfully luxurious experience. Romantic oceanfront suites have oversize whirlpool tubs. Throughout, blond-wood furniture, cool tile floors, and sheer curtains are accented by pastel watercolors and Jamaican prints on the walls. A highlight is Charlie's Spa, which offers pampering massages, body scrubs, reflexology sessions, facials, and a complimentary manicure and pedicure (book treatments as soon as you arrive, if not before). Guests booking a four-night stay receive six complimentary spa treatments. ⊠ *North Coast Hwy., Mammee Bay, 2 mi (3 km) east of Ocho Rios* ☖ *Box 103* ☎ *876/994–1206* 🖶 *876/994–1544* ↪ *146 suites* ♨ *3 restaurants, 2 grills, room service, in-room safes, minibars, 2 tennis courts, 4 pools, 2 hot tubs, outdoor hot tub, spa, beach, 4 bars, library, complimentary weddings, laundry service, concierge, airport shuttle; no kids under 16* ☞ *2-night minimum* ▤ *AE, D, DC, MC, V* �🍽 *AI.*

$$ 🏨 **Renaissance Jamaica Grande.** The Renaissance, one of the largest conference hotels in Jamaica, attracts all types of travelers: families, couples, singles (there is no supplementary fee for singles), as well as conference attendees. Even though it's a beachfront resort, the focal point is definitely the tiered and winding pool, which has a waterfall, a swaying bridge, and a swim-up bar. Rooms in the south building are the largest, but those in the north building have slightly better views. Kids are kept busy in the daily Club Mongoose activity program. Children under 2 stay free. The hotel's disco, Jamaic'N Me Crazy, is *very* popular. ⊠ *Main St.* ☖ *Box 100* ☎ *876/974–2201* 🖶 *876/974–2289* ⊕ *www. renaissancehotels.com* ↪ *708 rooms, 19 suites* ♨ *5 restaurants, in-room safes, 2 tennis courts, 3 pools, 2 outdoor hot tubs, massage, beach, dive shop, snorkeling, windsurfing, boating, 8 bars, children's programs (ages 4–12), playground, concierge, convention center* ▤ *AE, DC, MC, V* �🍽 *AI.*

$–$$ 🏨 **The Crane Ridge Resort.** Families on a budget planning an extended stay should consider a suite here; the fully equipped kitchens can help keep the dining bills down. Each spacious, immaculate unit has white-tile floors, rattan furniture, and tropical floral prints. The two-bedroom suite has an open bathroom (it's divided from the main room by only a screen), as well as a whirlpool tub in its master-bedroom loft. This hotel is not on the beach, although it's close enough to walk—and a shuttle is provided. ⊠ *17 Da Costa Dr.* ☎ *876/974–8050* 🖶 *876/974–8070* ⊕ *www.craneridge.net* ↪ *87 suites* ♨ *Restaurant, room service, in-room safes, kitchenettes, refrigerators, tennis court, outdoor hot tub, bar, airport shuttle, no-smoking rooms* ▤ *AE, MC, V* �🍽 *EP.*

Runaway Bay

The smallest of the resort areas, Runaway Bay, west of Ocho Rios, has a handful of modern hotels, a few all-inclusive resorts, and an 18-hole golf course.

★ ♨ **$$$$** 🏨 **FDR, Franklyn D. Resort.** Upscale yet unpretentious, the beachside complex has spacious, well-planned one-, two-, and three-bedroom suites in pink villas set in a horseshoe around a pool. Best of all, a staff member is assigned to each suite, filling the role of nanny and housekeeper. Children and teens are kept busy with supervised activities and sports. Parents can join in or just lounge by the pool, play golf, or scuba dive. Children age 2 and under stay and eat free when staying in a room with their parents. ⊠ *Runaway Bay* ☖ *Box 201* ☎ *876/973–4591* 🖶 *876/973–3071* ⊕ *www.fdrfamily.com* ↪ *76 suites* ♨ *2 restaurants, kitchenettes, golf course, tennis court, pool, beach, dive shop, snorkeling, 3 bars, baby-sitting, children's programs (ages infant–16)* ▤ *AE, MC, V* �🍽 *AI.*

$$$–$$$$ 🏨 **Grand Lido Braco.** Just a 15-minute drive west of Runaway Bay, this all-inclusive, adults-only, gingerbread- and Georgian-style village focuses on the culture, crafts, music, and food of Jamaica. Boutiques, an art shop, and several restaurants—including a jerk grill and a sidewalk café—fan out from a central fountain in the "town square." The pool is one of the island's largest. Rooms are generous in size, and all but the garden-view rooms are steps from the 2,000-ft beach, including a nude beach and pool, or have a great view of the ocean from a patio. ✉ *Trelawny, between Duncans and Rio Bueno* ☎ *876/954–0000* 🖷 *876/954–0021* 🌐 *www.superclubs.com* ⇥ *232 rooms* ♨ *5 restaurants, café, room service, in-room safes, driving range, 9-hole golf course, 3 tennis courts, 2 pools, health club, 4 hot tubs, spa, beach, dive shop, snorkeling, windsurfing, fishing, hiking, soccer, 8 bars, dance club, shops, complimentary weddings, concierge, meeting rooms, airport shuttle; no kids under 16* ⚲ *2-night minimum* ▤ *AE, DC, MC, V* ⦿ *AI.*

★ **$$$–$$$$** 🏨 **Hedonism III.** Like its more spartan cousin in Negril, Hedonism is an adults-only hotel for travelers looking for fun that includes a circus clinic and waterslide (through the disco, no less). Unlike its Negril equivalent, however, Hedonism III offers luxurious rooms and Jamaica's first swim-up rooms. The guest rooms, each with mirrored ceilings, have Jacuzzi tubs and CD players. The beach is divided into "nude" and "prude" sides, although a quick look shows that most people leave the suits at home. Scheduled activities include nude body painting and volleyball; there's even shuffleboard in the buff as well as Jamaica's only nude weddings. ✉ *Main Rd., Runaway Bay* ⬡ *Box 250* ☎ *876/973–5029* 🖷 *876/973–5402* 🌐 *www.superclubs.com* ⇥ *225 rooms* ♨ *4 restaurants, grill, in-room safes, 2 tennis courts, 3 pools, health club, 3 outdoor hot tubs, beach, dive shop, snorkeling, windsurfing, boating, 6 bars, dance club, complimentary weddings, airport shuttle; no kids under 18* ⚲ *2-night minimum* ▤ *AE, DC, MC, V* ⦿ *AI.*

$$–$$$$ 🏨 **Breezes Runaway Bay.** This moderately priced SuperClubs resort emphasizes an active, sports-oriented vacation—from golf (at the resort's own course), tennis, and horse and carriage rides to an array of water sports. Expert instruction and top-rate equipment are part of the package. Guests—often Germans, Italians, and Japanese—flock here for the reef just off the beach, as well as for the superb golf school. ✉ *North Coast Hwy. Runaway Bay* ⬡ *Box 58* ☎ *876/973–2436* 🖷 *876/973–2352* 🌐 *www.superclubs.com* ⇥ *234 rooms* ♨ *2 restaurants, 2 grills, in-room safes, driving range, 18-hole golf course, 4 tennis courts, pool, 3 outdoor hot tubs, beach, dive shop, snorkeling, windsurfing, 4 bars, complimentary weddings, airport shuttle; no kids under 14* ⚲ *2-night minimum* ▤ *AE, DC, MC, V* ⦿ *AI.*

★ ♨ **$–$$** 🏨 **Starfish Trelawny.** This moderately priced all-inclusive resort by Superclubs offers something for almost any kind of traveler, but is a favorite with families. Several cottages are especially popular with larger groups. Nightly entertainment is for the whole family; a late-night disco is aimed at adults. Some motorized water sports, including waterskiing, the banana boat ride, and scuba diving, are not included in the all-inclusive price. The resort has a rock-climbing wall, a circus workshop, and "ice" skating on a special plastic surface. ✉ *North Coast Hwy., Falmouth* ☎ *876/954–2450* 🖷 *876/954–9923* 🌐 *www.starfishresorts.com* ⇥ *350 rooms* ♨ *4 restaurants, grill, 4 tennis courts, 4 pools, 3 outdoor hot tubs, beach, dive shop, snorkeling, windsurfing, waterskiing, badminton, 6 bars, dance club, baby-sitting, children's programs (ages 6 months–12 years), meeting rooms, airport shuttle* ⚲ *2-night minimum* ▤ *AE, DC, MC, V* ⦿ *AI.*

Montego Bay

MoBay has miles of hotels, villas, apartments, and duty-free shops. Although lacking much in the way of cultural stimuli, it presents a comfortable island backdrop for the many conventions it hosts.

★ **$$$$** 🏨 **Round Hill Hotel and Villas.** The Hollywood set frequents this peaceful resort 8 mi (13 km) west of town on a hilly peninsula. Twenty-seven villas dot 98 acres, and the Pineapple House, a building that overlooks the sea, houses 36 hotel rooms. Rooms are done in a refined Ralph

Lauren style, with mahogany furnishings and terra-cotta floors. Villas are leased back to the resort by private owners and vary in decor, but jungle motifs are a favorite. All come with a personal maid and a cook to make your breakfast, and several have private pools. ⊠ *North Coast Hwy.,* ⌂ *Box 64* ☎ *876/956–7050* 🖷 *876/956–7505* ⊕ *www. roundhilljamaica.com* ↦ *36 rooms, 27 villas* ⚒ *Restaurant, room service, 5 tennis courts, pool, fitness classes, gym, hair salon, massage, beach, dive shop, snorkeling, windsurfing, bar, shops, concierge, helipad* 🖃 *AE, DC, MC, V* ⦿ *EP.*

$$$$ 🏨 **Sandals Montego Bay.** The largest private beach in MoBay is the spark that lights this Sandals—one of the most popular upscale resorts in the Caribbean, though restricted to male-female couples. Its all-inclusive rate, nonstop activities, and rooms overlooking the bay make it a bit like a cruise ship that remains in port. It certainly feels like a great big party, despite the planes that zoom overhead (the airport is nearby). Rooms are done in tropical colors and have four-poster beds. The Oleander Room may well be the best fine-dining establishment in the Sandals chain. ⊠ *Kent Ave.* ⌂ *Box 100* ☎ *876/952–5510* 🖷 *876/952–0816* ⊕ *www.sandals. com* ↦ *244 rooms* ⚒ *5 restaurants, snack bar, in-room safes, 4 tennis courts, 4 pools, 4 outdoor hot tubs, sauna, beach, dive shop, dock, snorkeling, windsurfing, boating, racquetball, 4 bars, library, concierge; no kids* ⚘ *2-night minimum* 🖃 *AE, MC, V* ⦿ *AI.*

$$$$ 🏨 **Sandals Royal Caribbean.** Formerly Sandals Royal Jamaican, this upscale, all-inclusive resort, which is 4 mi (6½ km) east of airport, is exclusively for male-female couples. Rooms are in Jamaican-style buildings arranged in a semicircle around attractive gardens. Although there are plenty of activities here, the resort is quieter and more genteel than Sandals Montego Bay. Oceanfront rooms and suites are elegant and inviting, with floral-print fabrics and mahogany four-poster beds. A colorful "dragon boat" transports you to Sandals's private island for meals at an Indonesian restaurant. ⊠ *North Coast Hwy.* ⌂ *Box 167* ☎ *876/ 953–2231* 🖷 *876/953–2788* ⊕ *www.sandals.com* ↦ *176 rooms, 14 suites* ⚒ *4 restaurants, in-room safes, 3 tennis courts, 4 pools, fitness classes, hair salon, 5 outdoor hot tubs, sauna, beach, dive shop, snorkeling, windsurfing, 5 bars, concierge, airport shuttle; no kids* ⚘ *2-night minimum* 🖃 *AE, MC, V* ⦿ *AI.*

$$$$ 🏨 **Tryall Golf, Tennis, and Beach Club.** Part of a posh residential development 15 mi (24 km) west of MoBay, Tryall clings to a hilltop that overlooks a golf course and the Caribbean. Here you'll stay in one of the many villas—each with its own pool and full staff (butler, cook, maid, and gardener)—that dot the 2,200-acre island plantation or in a luxurious hilltop villa suite. All accommodations are individually and plushly decorated. The elegant dining room in the great house serves Continental and Jamaican cuisine. The beautiful seaside golf course is considered one of the meanest in the world and hosts big-money tournaments. ⊠ *North Coast Hwy., Sandy Bay* ⌂ *Box 1206* ☎ *876/956–5660* 🖷 *876/956–5673* ⊕ *www.tryallclub.com* ↦ *57 villas* ⚒ *Restaurant, refrigerators, driving range, 18-hole golf course, 9 tennis courts, pool, massage, beach, snorkeling, windsurfing, 4 bars, children's programs (ages 5–12)* 🖃 *AE, DC, MC, V* ⦿ *EP.*

$$$–$$$$ 🏨 **Coyaba Beach Resort and Club.** Owners Joanne and Kevin Robertson live on the property, interacting with their guests and giving this oceanfront retreat the feel of an intimate country inn. The plantation-style great house, just east of MoBay, successfully blends modern amenities with antique charm. Rooms are decorated with lovely colonial prints and hand-carved mahogany furniture. A basket with bottled spring water and freshly baked banana bread greets you at check-in; regular rates include afternoon tea and evening cocktail parties as well as tennis. It's a very family-friendly place. ⊠ *Montego Bay, Little River* ☎ *876/953–9150* 🖷 *876/953–2244* ⊕ *www.coyabaresortjamaica.com* ➪ *50 rooms* ᗷ *3 restaurants, tennis court, pool, gym, outdoor hot tub, massage, beach, dive shop, snorkeling, windsurfing, volleyball, 3 bars, library, recreation room, playground, airport shuttle* ⊟ *AE, MC, V* ⍥*EP.*

$$$–$$$$ 🏨 **Half Moon Golf, Tennis, and Beach Club.** Since 1962, this resort has been a destination unto itself. Although it has mushroomed from 30 to more than 400 units, it has maintained a luxurious feel with its black-and-white accents and such decorating touches as Asian rugs and antique radios. All villas (which come with a cook, a butler, a housekeeper, and a golf cart) have private pools, and the 2-mi-long (3-km-long) stretch of beach is just steps from every room. On the grounds are an upscale shopping mall, a nature reserve, a croquet lawn (considered one of the Caribbean's best), and a hospital. ⊠ *North Coast Hwy., 7 mi (11 km) east of Montego Bay* ᗒ *Box 80* ☎ *876/953–2211* 🖷 *876/953–2731* ⊕ *www.halfmoon-resort.com* ➪ *245 rooms, 174 suites, 32 villas* ᗷ *7 restaurants, 18-hole golf course, 13 tennis courts, 53 pools, fitness classes, gym, outdoor hot tub, sauna, spa, beach, dive shop, snorkeling, windsurfing, bicycles, badminton, croquet, horseback riding, Ping-Pong, squash, 3 bars, theater, shops, concierge, convention center* ⊟ *AE, DC, MC, V* ⍥ *EP.*

$$$–$$$$ 🏨 **Sandals Inn.** If they can forgo a private beach (there's a public one across the street), male-female couples can stay here for much less than at the other Sandals resorts. Rooms are compact, and most have balconies that face the pool. Dark carpet contrasts with white-lacquered furniture and tropical-print fabrics. Free hourly shuttles hop to the two other MoBay Sandals, but there's plenty to do here, too. The in-town location puts you close to shops and sights. ⊠ *Gloucester Ave.* ᗒ *Box 412* ☎ *876/952–4140* 🖷 *876/952–6913* ⊕ *www.sandals.com* ➪ *52 rooms* ᗷ *2 restaurants, in-room safes, tennis court, pool, hair salon, outdoor hot tub, 2 bars, concierge, airport shuttle; no kids* ᗢ *2-night minimum* ⊟ *AE, MC, V* ⍥ *AI.*

☾ $$–$$$$ 🏨 **Ritz-Carlton Golf and Spa Resort, Rose Hall, Jamaica.** Across the road from the historic Rose Hall estate, this expansive property is the newest addition to Jamaica's luxury hotels. The beige buildings span a large swath of beachfront east of Montego Bay, although most beach and watersports action takes place at the nearby Rose Hall Beach Club (transportation is provided for guests). Rooms here are subtly Caribbean with understated tropical florals, plus mahogany and rattan furniture. Along with a full-service spa, the resort offers a fully supervised children's club, making it a popular choice for families. ⊠ *1 Ritz Carlton Dr., St. James* ☎ *876/953–2800* 🖷 *876/953–2501* ⊕ *www.ritzcarlton. com* ➪ *427 rooms* ᗷ *4 restaurants, in-room safes, 18-hole golf course, pool, health club, spa, beach, dive shop, snorkeling, windsurfing, 3 bars, shops, children's programs (ages 5–12), concierge, meeting rooms* ⊟ *AE, DC, MC, V* ⍥ *EP.*

$–$$$ 🏨 **Breezes Montego Bay.** Like its cousin in Runaway Bay, this SuperClubs resort for adults emphasizes moderate prices and plenty of around-the-clock activities. It stands on the portion of Gloucester Avenue known as the "Hip Strip." Rooms have white-tile floors, cozy love seats, carved wooden headboards, and big marble bathrooms. The resort doesn't have a private beach, but sits on a stretch of Doctor's Cave Beach. Free weddings are also part of the package. ⊠ *Gloucester Ave.* ☎ *876/940–1150* 🖷 *876/940–1160* ⊕ *www.superclubs.com* ➪ *124 rooms* ᗷ *2 restaurants, grill, in-room safes, 2 tennis courts, pool, beach, dive shop, snorkeling, windsurfing, 4 bars, complimentary weddings, airport shuttle; no kids under 14* ᗢ *2-night minimum* ⊟ *AE, DC, MC, V* ⍥ *AI.*

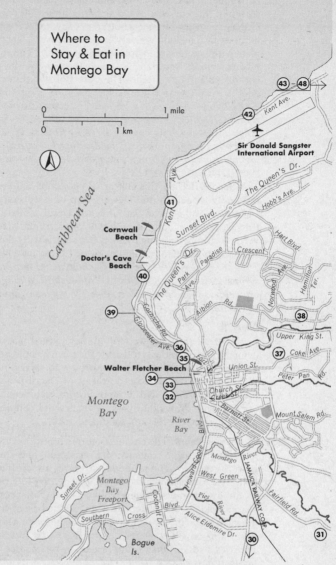

Where to Stay & Eat in Montego Bay

$–$$$ **Holiday Inn Sunspree Resort.** There are activities day and night at this family-oriented resort 6 mi (9½ km) east of the airport. Although the rooms—spread out in seven buildings—are cheerful enough, the hotel is big and can be noisy (rooms farthest from the pool and central dining-entertainment area are the quietest). However, adults can take a break in the quiet pool with a swim-up bar on the resort's west side. On the east end, a 9-hole miniature golf course is lit for night play. Children under 11 stay and eat free, and an all-inclusive plan is available. ⊠ *North Coast Hwy.* ☎ *Box 480* ☎ *876/953–2485* 📠 *876/953–2840* ⊕ *www. holiday-inn.com/montegobayjam* 🛏 *497 rooms, 27 suites* ⚓ *3 restaurants, 2 snack bars, room service, in-room safes, miniature golf, 4 tennis courts, 3 pools, beach, dive shop, snorkeling, windsurfing, 4 bars, children's programs (ages 6 months–12 years), playground, concierge, airport shuttle, no-smoking rooms* ▤ *AE, DC, MC, V* ❍¶ *EP.*

🖐 $$ 🏨 **Wyndham Rose Hall Resort and Country Club.** This self-contained resort 4 mi (6½ km) east of the airport, on the 400-acre Rose Hall Plantation, is a bustling business hotel popular with large groups. It has plenty of amenities, including a very large water park, Sugar Mill Falls, complete with lagoons and a towering water slide. You can enjoy lazy river rafting among waterfalls scattered throughout the park. Rooms are comfortable if a bit sterile. The waters off the thin crescent beach are good for sailing and snorkeling. ✉ *North Coast Hwy.* ⌂ *Box 999* ☎ *876/953–2650* 📠 *876/953–2617* ⊕ *www.wyndham.com* ☞ *470 rooms, 19 suites* ♨ *5 restaurants, room service, in-room safes, 18-hole golf course, 6 tennis courts, 3 pools, fitness classes, gym, massage, beach, dive shop, snorkeling, windsurfing, basketball, volleyball, 3 bars, nightclub, children's programs (ages 4–12), playground, meeting rooms* ⊟ *AE, DC, MC, V* ⊺ *EP.*

$ 🏨 **Richmond Hill Inn.** This hilltop inn—a quaint 200-year-old great house originally owned by the Dewars clan—has spectacular views of the Caribbean and a great deal of peace. Decor tends toward the dainty: frilly lace curtains and doilies, lots of lavenders and mauves, and crushed-velvet furniture here and there. A free shuttle will take you to shops and beaches, about 10 to 15 minutes away. ✉ *Union St.* ⌂ *Box 362* ☎ *876/ 952–3859* 📠 *876/952–6106* ⊕ *www.richmond-hill-inn.com* ☞ *17 rooms, 4 suites* ♨ *Restaurant, coffee shop, dining room, some microwaves, some refrigerators, cable TV, pool, bar, laundry service, meeting rooms* ⊟ *MC, V* ⊺ *EP.*

Negril

Some 50 mi (80 km) west of MoBay, Negril was long a sleepy bohemian retreat. In the last decade the town has blossomed and added a number of classy all-inclusive resorts, with several more on the drawing board for Bloody Bay (northeast of Negril Beach). Negril itself is only a small village with little of historic significance. But such sights are not what draws the sybaritic singles and couples. The young, hip crowd here comes for sun, sand, and sea.

$$$$ 🏨 **Couples Negril.** The emphasis at this resort, exclusively for male-female couples, is on romance and relaxation, and you will find neither hard to come by. The property's 18 acres are on Bloody Bay. Negril's bohemian nature is reflected throughout the nine low-rise buildings, where a rainbow of colors and lively art by local craftspeople peppers public spaces. All land and water activities, selected excursions, and weddings are included in the all-inclusive rates. ✉ *Norman Manley Blvd.* ☎ *876/ 957–5960* 📠 *876/957–5858* ⊕ *www.couples.com* ☞ *216 rooms, 18 suites* ♨ *3 restaurants, room service, in-room safes, 4 tennis courts, 2 pools, fitness classes, health club, 2 outdoor hot tubs, spa, beach, dive shop, snorkeling, windsurfing, 5 bars, complimentary weddings, concierge, airport shuttle; no kids* ⚲ *3-night minimum* ⊟ *AE, MC, V* ⊺ *AI.*

★ $$$$ 🏨 **Couples Swept Away Negril.** This adults-only resort is known for its emphasis on sports and healthful cuisine, attracting primarily the fitness-minded. The suites are in 26 two-story tropical villas—each with a private garden atrium—spread out along a ½-mi (¾-km) stretch of gorgeous beach. There's an outstanding 10-acre sports complex across the road. At the Feathers Continental restaurant, the chefs prepare dishes designed to keep you fit and trim, with lots of fish, white meat, fresh fruits, and vegetables. ✉ *Norman Manley Blvd., Long Bay* ☎ *876/957–4061* 📠 *876/957–4060* ⊕ *www.sweptaway.com* ☞ *134 suites* ♨ *2 restaurants, in-room safes, 10 tennis courts, 2 pools, fitness classes, health club, 2 outdoor hot tubs, 2 saunas, spa, 2 steam rooms, beach, dive shop, snorkeling, windsurfing, racquetball, squash, 4 bars, complimentary* *weddings, concierge, airport shuttle; no kids* ☞ *3-night minimum* ▭ *AE, DC, MC, V* ⦶ *AI.*

★ $$$$ ⊡ **Grand Lido Negril.** The dramatic entrance of marble floors and columns sets an elegant tone. The resort is geared to folks with some money in their pockets, attracting mostly mature couples and singles. The well-appointed split-level oceanfront and garden suites are spacious and stylish. For some, the pièce de résistance is a sunset cruise on the resort's 147-ft yacht, M/V *Zein*, a wedding gift from Aristotle Onassis to Prince Rainier and Princess Grace of Monaco. The Piacere restaurant is superb. The sprawling resort sits on one of Jamaica's top stretches of white-sand beach, including a clothing-optional beach. ✉ *Norman Manley Blvd.* ⌕ *Box 88* ☎ *876/957–5010* 🖷 *876/957–5517* ⊕ *www.superclubs. com* ⇆ *210 suites* ⇆ *5 restaurants, room service, in-room safes, mini-bars, 4 tennis courts, 2 pools, health club, 5 outdoor hot tubs, spa, beach, dive shop, snorkeling, windsurfing, 9 bars, library, shops, complimentary weddings, laundry service, concierge, convention center, airport shuttle, no-smoking rooms; no kids under 16* ☞ *2-night minimum* ▭ *AE, DC, MC, V* ⦶ *AI.*

$$$$ ⊡ **Sandals Negril Beach Resort and Spa.** Male-female couples looking for an upscale, sports-oriented getaway and a casual atmosphere (you can wear dressy shorts to dinner) flock to this resort on one of the best stretches of Negril Beach. Water sports, particularly scuba diving, are popular; the capable staff is happy to work with neophytes as well as certified veterans. There's a huge swim-up pool bar and a range of spacious accommodations. Both rooms and staff are sunny and appealing. ✉ *Norman Manley Blvd.* ⌕ *Box 12* ☎ *876/957–5216* 🖷 *876/957–5338* ⊕ *www.sandals.com* ⇆ *137 rooms, 86 suites* ⇆ *4 restaurants, in-room safes, 4 tennis courts, 2 pools, 2 outdoor hot tubs, sauna, spa, beach, dive shop, snorkeling, windsurfing, racquetball, squash, 4 bars, concierge; no kids* ▭ *AE, MC, V* ⦶ *AI.*

$$$–$$$$ ⊡ **Hedonism II.** Hedonism is best for uninhibited adults who like a robust mix of physical activities. The resort has a trampoline clinic, a rock-climbing wall, a gaming lounge with slots and table games, and an "ice" skating rink on a special surface. Handsome guest rooms, which do not include TVs, have mirrored ceilings above king or twin beds (those going solo either pay a hefty supplement or are assigned a roommate of the same sex). You'll find both "nude" and "prude" beaches. Most people prefer the nude beach, with its grill, pool, and swim-up bar plus activities ranging from nude body painting to volleyball to shuffleboard. ✉ *Norman Manley Blvd., Ruthland Point* ⌕ *Box 25* ☎ *876/957– 5200* 🖷 *876/957–5289* ⊕ *www.superclubs.com* ⇆ *280 rooms* ⇆ *4 restaurants, 2 grills, in-room safes, 6 tennis courts, 2 pools, 2 outdoor hot tubs, beach, dive shop, snorkeling, windsurfing, boating, squash, 6 bars, dance club, shops, complimentary weddings, airport shuttle; no room TVs, no kids* ☞ *2-night minimum* ▭ *AE, DC, MC, V* ⦶ *AI.*

$$–$$$ ⊡ **Point Village Resort.** This moderately priced resort is family friendly. Rooms have tile floors and basic furnishings, and each is individually decorated. The sprawling complex has two small crescent beaches, rocky grottoes to explore, and fine snorkeling offshore. If you don't want an all-inclusive plan, the one- and two-bedroom suites with kitchens are a good choice. One child age 13 and under stays free when sharing a room with parents. ✉ *Norman Manley Blvd.* ⌕ *Box 105* ☎ *876/957– 5170* 🖷 *876/957–5113* ⊕ *www.pointvillage.com* ⇆ *99 rooms; 66 1-, 2-, and 3-bedroom suites* ⇆ *3 restaurants, 2 grills, grocery, tennis court, pool, outdoor hot tub, massage, beach, snorkeling, windsurfing, 4 bars, children's programs (ages infant–12), playground* ▭ *AE, MC, V* ⦶ *AI.*

$$ ⊞ **Charela Inn.** Each quiet, elegantly appointed room here has a private balcony or a covered patio. The owners' French-Jamaican roots find daily expression in La Vendôme restaurant, where you can dine on local produce and seafood dressed up with French sauces; there's also an excellent selection of wines. The small beach is part of the glorious 7-mi (11-km) Negril crescent. On Saturday night many guests staying at other resorts come here to watch a folkloric show. ⊠ *Norman Manley Blvd.* ⬚ *Box 3033* ☎ *876/957–4277* 🖷 *876/957–4414* ⊕ *www.charela.com* ⇴ *49 rooms* ⚲ *Restaurant, pool, beach, windsurfing, boating, bar, laundry service* ⚲ *5-night minimum in high season, 3-night minimum summer* ▭ *MC, V* ⦿ *EP.*

$–$$ ⊞ **Coco La Palm.** This quiet seaside hotel has oversize rooms (junior suites average 525 square ft [49 square m]) in octagonal buildings set in a U-shape around the pool. Amenities include direct-dial phones, color TVs, coffeemakers, and private patios or terraces—most overlooking gardens (only seven rooms have ocean views). On Negril Beach, the sandy shoreline of Coco La Palm is dotted with palm trees. The beachside restaurant is open-air and casual. ⊠ *Norman Manley Blvd.* ☎ *876/957–4227* 🖷 *876/957–3460* ⊕ *www.cocolapalm.com* ⇴ *41 rooms* ⚲ *Restaurant, grill, fans, refrigerators, pool, outdoor hot tub, beach, bar* ▭ *AE, DC, MC, V* ⦿ *EP.*

$–$$ ⊞ **Negril Cabins Resort.** These elevated timber cottages are amid lush vegetation and towering royal palms. Rooms are open and airy, with floral bedspreads, gauzy curtains, natural-wood floors, and high ceilings. The most popular rooms have TVs and air-conditioning; others have no TV and are cooled by ceiling fans and breezes that come through slatted windows. The gleaming beach across the road is filled with sunbathers and water-sports enthusiasts; for shopping you can take the shuttle into town. A most convivial place, this property is popular with young Europeans. Children under 12 stay free in their parents' room. ⊠ *Norman Manley Blvd.* ⬚ *Box 118* ☎ *876/957–5350* 🖷 *876/957–5381* ⊕ *www.negril-cabins.com* ⇴ *82 rooms, 4 suites* ⚲ *2 restaurants, room service, in-room safes, tennis court, pool, gym, outdoor hot tub, beach, dive shop, snorkeling, 2 bars, recreation room, baby-sitting, playground; no a/c in some rooms, no TV in some rooms* ▭ *AE, MC, V* ⦿ *AI.*

$
Fodor'sChoice
★ ⊞ **Rockhouse.** You're side-by-side with nature at this stylish resort on Negril's rugged cliffs. Accommodations are built from rough-hewn timber, thatch, and stone, and are filled with furniture that echoes the nature theme. Regular rooms have private, indoor baths, but even these seem pleasantly rustic; villa rooms have private, enclosed outdoor showers. There's a thatch-roofed Jamaican restaurant, a spa, yoga, kayaking, and a cliff-top pool and bar. ⊠ *West End Rd.* ⬚ *Box 24* ☎ *876/ 957–4373* 🖷 *876/957–0557* ⊕ *www.rockhousehotel.com* ⇴ *16 rooms, 12 villas* ⚲ *Restaurant, fans, in-room safes, minibars, pool, snorkeling, 2 bars; no kids under 12* ▭ *AE, MC, V* ⦿ *EP.*

Mandeville

At 2,000 ft above the sea, Mandeville is noted for its cool climate and proximity to secluded south coast beaches. Most accommodations here don't have air-conditioning, but you really don't need it. Many are close to golf, tennis, horseback riding, and bird-watching areas.

¢–$ ⊞ **Mandeville Hotel.** Tropical gardens wrap around the building, and flowers spill onto the terrace restaurant, where breakfast and lunch are served. Rooms are simple and breeze-cooled; suites have full kitchens. You'll need a car to get around town, go out for dinner, and get to the beach, which is an hour away. ⊠ *4 Hotel St.* ⬚ *Box 78* ☎ *876/962– 2460* 🖷 *876/962–0700* ⊕ *www.mandevillehotel.com* ⇴ *46 rooms; 17 1-, 2-, and 3-bedroom suites* ⚲ *Restaurant, coffee shop, some kitchens,* *refrigerators, cable TV, golf course, tennis courts, pool, bar, baby-sitting, laundry service, meeting rooms, travel services; no a/c in some rooms* ▤ *AE, MC, V* ¶◎¶ *EP.*

¢ ▦ **Astra Country Inn & Restaurant.** "Country" is the key word in the name of this mountain retreat. The low price reflects the nature of the very basic rooms: they're spartan but immaculately clean. The small restaurant is open from 6:30 AM to 9 PM and serves snacks in addition to breakfast, lunch, and dinner. The food is billed as "home cooking," and emphasizes fresh produce—lots of vegetables and fruit juices. ✉ *62 Ward Ave.* ✆ *Box 60* ▩ *876/962–3725* ♔ *20 rooms, 1 suite* ♿ *Restaurant, kitchenettes, pool, sauna, bar, laundry service; no a/c* ▤ *MC, V* ¶◎¶ *MAP.*

Where to Eat

Although many cultures have contributed to Jamaica's cuisine, it has become a true cuisine in its own right. It would be a shame to travel to the heart of this complex culture without having at least one typical island meal.

Probably the most famous Jamaican dish is jerk pork—the ultimate island barbecue. The pork (purists cook a whole pig) is covered with a paste of Scotch bonnet peppers, pimento berries (also known as allspice), and other herbs and cooked slowly over a coal fire. Many aficionados believe the best jerk comes from Boston Beach, near Port Antonio. Jerk chicken and fish are also seen on many menus. The ever-so-traditional rice and peas, also known as "coat of arms," is similar to the *moros y christianos* of Spanish-speaking islands: white rice cooked with red kidney beans, coconut milk, scallions, and seasonings.

The island's most famous soup—the fiery pepper pot—is a spicy mixture of salt pork, salt beef, okra, and the island green known as callaloo. Patties (spicy meat pies) elevate street food to new heights. Although they actually originated in Haiti, Jamaicans excel at making them. Curried goat is another island standout: young goat is cooked with spices and is more tender and has a gentler flavor than the lamb for which it was substituted by immigrants from India. Salted fish was once the best that islanders could do between catches. Out of necessity, a breakfast staple (and the national dish of Jamaica) was invented. It joins seasonings with salt fish and ackee, a red fruit that grows on trees throughout the island. When cooked in this dish, ackee reminds most people of scrambled eggs.

Where restaurants are concerned, Kingston has the widest selection, with establishments that serve Italian, French, Cantonese, German, Thai, Indian, Korean, and Continental fare, as well as Rasta natural foods, also known as *I-tal.* There are also fine restaurants in all the resort areas, many in the resorts themselves. Most restaurants outside the hotels in MoBay and Ocho Rios will provide complimentary transportation.

What to Wear

Dress is usually casual chic (or just plain casual at many local hangouts). There are a few exceptions in Kingston and at the top resorts, some require semiformal wear in the evening during high season. People tend to dress up for dinner; men might be more comfortable in nice slacks, women in a sundress.

Kingston

CONTINENTAL

★ $$$–$$$$

✕ **Blue Mountain Inn.** The elegant Blue Mountain Inn is a 30-minute taxi ride from New Kingston and worth every penny of the fare. On a former coffee plantation, the antiques-laden inn complements its English colonial atmosphere with Continental cuisine. All the classic beef and seafood dishes are here, including chateaubriand béarnaise and lobster thermidor. ✉ *Gordon Town Rd., Gordon Town* ☎ 876/927–1700 or 876/927–2606 ⚓ *Reservations essential* 🍷 *Jacket required* 🚾 *AE, MC, V* ⊘ *Closed Sun. No lunch.*

$$–$$$ ✕ **Palm Court.** On the mezzanine floor of the Hilton Kingston, the elegant Palm Court is open for lunch and dinner. The menu is Continental; the rack of lamb, sautéed snapper almandine, and grilled salmon are delicious. ✉ *77 Knutsford Blvd.* ☎ 876/926–5430 🚾 *AE, DC, MC, V.*

Ocho Rios

ECLECTIC **$–$$$** ✕ **Almond Tree.** One of the most popular restaurants in Ocho Rios, the Almond Tree has a menu of Jamaican and Continental favorites: pumpkin soup, pepper pot, and wonderful preparations of fresh fish, veal *piccata,* and fondue. The swinging rope chairs of the terrace bar and the tables perched above a Caribbean cove are great fun. ✉ *83 Main St.* ☎ 876/974–2813 ⚓ *Reservations essential* 🚾 *AE, DC, MC, V.*

★ **$–$$$** ✕ **Evita's Italian Restaurant.** The large windows of this hilltop 1860s gingerbread house open to cooling mountain breezes and stunning views of city and sea. Over 30 kinds of pasta range from lasagna Rastafari (vegetarian) and fiery jerk spaghetti to *rotelle colombo* (crabmeat with white sauce and noodles). Other excellent choices include sautéed fillet of red snapper with orange sauce, scampi and lobster in basil-cream sauce, red snapper stuffed with crabmeat, and tasty grilled sirloin with mushroom sauce. Kids under 12 eat for half price, and light eaters will appreciate half-portion orders. The restaurant offers free transportation from area hotels. ✉ *Mantalent Inn, Eden Bower Rd.* ☎ 876/974–2333 🚾 *AE, MC, V.*

¢–$$ ✕ **Little Pub.** Relaxed alfresco dining awaits you at this charming restaurant. It also has a bustling sports bar and an energetic Caribbean revue several nights a week. Jamaican standards (jerk or curried chicken, baked crab, sautéed snapper) accompany surf-and-turf, lobster thermidor, pasta primavera, seafood stir-fry, crêpes suzette, and bananas flambé. Burgers and other standard pub fare are also available. ✉ *59 Main St.* ☎ 876/974–5825 🚾 *AE, MC, V.*

JAMAICAN **¢–$** Fodor'sChoice ★ ✕ **Ocho Rios Village Jerk Centre.** This blue-canopied, open-air eatery is a good place to park yourself for frosty Red Stripe beer and fiery jerk pork, chicken, or seafood. Milder barbecued meats, also sold by weight (typically, ¼ or ½ pound makes a good serving), turn up on the fresh daily chalkboard menu posted on the wall. It's lively at lunch, especially when passengers from cruise ships swamp the place. ✉ *DaCosta Dr.* ☎ 876/974–2549 🚾 *MC, V.*

Montego Bay

ECLECTIC **$$–$$$** ✕ **Day-O Plantation Restaurant.** Transport yourself back in time with a fine meal served on the garden terrace of this Georgian-style plantation house. You might start with smoked marlin and then segue into seafood ragoût, broiled rock lobster with lemon butter, or beef fillet with béarnaise sauce. Sweeten things up with one of the traditional Jamaican desserts (rum pudding, sweet cakes, or fruit salad). After dinner, tour the house. ✉ *Next door to Barnett Estate Plantation, Fairfield* ☎ 876/952–1825 🚾 *AE, MC, V* ⊘ *Closed Mon.*

★ **$$–$$$** ✕ **Sugar Mill.** Seafood is served with flair at this terrace restaurant on the golf course of the Half Moon Golf, Tennis, and Beach Club. Caribbean specialties, steak, and lobster are usually offered in a pungent sauce that blends Dijon mustard with Jamaica's own Pickapeppa sauce. Otherwise, choices are the daily à la carte specials and anything flame-grilled. Live music and a well-stocked wine cellar round out the experience. ✉ *Half*

*Moon Golf, Tennis, and Beach Club, North Coast Rd., 7 mi (11 km)
east of Montego Bay* ☎ *876/953–2228* ⌘ *Reservations essential* ▤ *AE,
MC, V.*

$$–$$$ ✕ **Town House.** Most of the rich and famous who have visited Jamaica
over the decades have eaten here. You'll find daily specials, delicious variations of standard dishes (red snapper *papillote* is a specialty, with lobster, cheese, and wine sauce), and many Jamaican favorites (curried chicken
with breadfruit and ackee). The 18th-century Georgian house is adorned
with original Jamaican and Haitian art. There's alfresco dining on the
stone patio. ✉ *16 Church St.* ☎ *876/952–2660* ⌘ *Reservations essential*
▤ *AE, DC, MC, V* ☾ *No lunch Sun.*

★ ¢–$$ ✕ **Le Chalet.** Don't let the French name fool you. This Denny's look-alike,
set in a nondescript shopping mall, serves heaping helpings of some of
the best Chinese and Jamaican food in MoBay. Tasty lobster Cantonese
costs only $15. ✉ *32 Gloucester Ave.* ☎ *876/952–6063* ▤ *AE, MC,
V* ☾ *No lunch Sun.*

¢–$$ ✕ **The Native.** Shaded by a large poinciana tree and overlooking Gloucester Avenue, this open-air stone terrace serves Jamaican and international
dishes. To go native, start with smoked marlin, move on to the
boonoonoonoos platter (a sampler of local dishes), and round out with
coconut pie or *duckanoo* (a sweet dumpling of cornmeal, coconut, and
banana wrapped in a banana leaf and steamed). Live entertainment and
candlelit tables make this a romantic choice for dinner on weekends.
The popular afternoon buffets on Friday and Sunday are family affairs.
✉ *29 Gloucester Ave.* ☎ *876/979–2769* ⌘ *Reservations essential*
▤ *AE, MC, V.*

¢–$ ✕ **Margueritaville Caribbean Bar and Grill.** This brightly painted bar-restaurant is tough to miss: just look for the slide that connects it with
the water. You'll find plenty of casual dishes on the menu, including burgers, chicken sandwiches, tuna melts, pizzas, and the like. This restaurant is a favorite with young travelers and the spring break crowd.
✉ *Gloucester Ave.* ☎ *876/952–4777* ▤ *AE, MC, V.*

ITALIAN ✕ **Julia's Italian Restaurant.** Couples flock to this romantic Italian restaurant in the hills overlooking MoBay. You can choose from an à la carte
$$–$$$$ menu or order a five-course prix-fixe meal ($33–$45 per person) that
includes homemade soups and pastas, entrées of fish, chicken, and veal,
and scrumptious desserts. Don't expect the meal to equal the stupendous view, and you won't be disappointed. ✉ *Bogue Hill* ☎ *876/952–
1772* ⌘ *Reservations essential* ▤ *AE, MC, V.*

SEAFOOD ✕ **Marguerites.** At this romantic pier-side dining room, "flambé" is the
$$–$$$ operative word. Lobster, shrimp, fish, and several desserts are prepared
in dancing flames as you sip an exotic cocktail. The Caesar salad, prepared tableside, is also a treat. ✉ *Gloucester Ave.* ☎ *876/952–4777*
⌘ *Reservations essential* ▤ *AE, MC, V* ☾ *No lunch.*

$$–$$$ ✕ **Pier 1.** After tropical drinks at the deck bar, you'll be ready to dig into
the international variations on fresh seafood; the best are the grilled lobster and any preparation of island snapper. Several party cruises leave
from the marina here, and on Friday night the restaurant is mobbed by
locals who come to dance. ✉ *Off Howard Cooke Blvd.* ☎ *876/952–
2452* ▤ *AE, MC, V.*

Negril

CARIBBEAN ✕ **Sweet Spice.** This mom-and-pop no-frills diner run by the Whytes serves
¢ inexpensive, generous plates of conch, fried or curried chicken, freshly
caught fish, oxtail in brown stew sauce, and other down-home specialties. The fresh juices are quite satisfying. Drop by for breakfast, lunch,
or dinner. ✉ *1 White Hall Rd.* ☎ *876/957–4621* ▤ *MC, V.*

ECLECTIC ✕ **Margueritaville Negril.** On a beautiful stretch of Negril Beach, this op-
$–$$ eration, a sibling of MoBay's wildly popular Margueritaville Caribbean
Bar and Grill, is a sports bar, disco, beach club, and restaurant. You'll
also find an art gallery, a gift shop, a five-star PADI dive shop, volleyball and basketball courts, and changing rooms. Lobster is the house
specialty. Far less expensive are the fish, chicken, and sandwich platters. There are also more than 50 varieties of margaritas. ⊠ *Norman
Manley Blvd.* ☎ *876/957–9180* ⊟ *MC, V.*

¢–$$ ✕ **Rick's Café.** Here it is—the local landmark complete with cliffs, cliff
divers, and powerful sunsets, all perfectly choreographed. Most folks
come for the drinks and the renowned sunset party, since the standard
pub menu is overpriced. In the sundown ritual the crowd toasts Mother
Nature with rum drinks amid shouts, laughter, and ever-shifting meet-
ing and greeting. When the sun slips below the horizon, there are more
shouts, more cheers, and more rounds of rum. ⊠ *West End Rd.* ☎ *876/
957–0380* ⊟ *MC, V.*

¢–$ ✕ **Kuyaba on the Beach.** This charming thatch-roofed eatery has an in-
ternational menu—including curried conch, kingfish steak, grilled lamb
with sautéed mushrooms, and several pasta dishes—plus a lively ambi-
ence, especially at the bar. There's a crafts shop on the premises, and
chaise longues line the beach; come prepared to spend some time, and
don't forget a towel and bathing suit. ⊠ *Norman Manley Blvd.* ☎ *876/
957–4318* ⊟ *AE, MC, V.*

SEAFOOD ✕ **Cosmo's Seafood Restaurant and Bar.** Owner Cosmo Brown has made
★ $–$$$ this seaside open-air bistro a pleasant place to spend the afternoon—
and maybe stay on for dinner. Fish is the main attraction, and the conch
soup—a house specialty—is a meal in itself. You'll also find lobster (grilled
or curried), fish-and-chips, and the catch of the morning. Customers often
drop cover-ups to take a dip before coffee and dessert and return to lounge
in chairs scattered under almond and sea grape trees (there's a small entrance fee for the beach). ⊠ *Norman Manley Blvd.* ☎ *876/957–4330*
⊟ *AE, MC, V.*

Beaches

Jamaica has 200 mi (325 km) of beaches, some of them relatively deserted. Generally, the farther west you go the lighter and finer the sand.
The beaches listed below are public (though there's usually a small admission charge) and are among the best Jamaica has to offer. In addition, nearly every resort has its own private beach, complete with towels
and water sports. Some of the larger resorts sell day passes to nonguests.

PORT ANTONIO **Boston Bay.** Approximately 11 mi (18 km) east of Pórt Antonio, beyond
the Blue Lagoon, is a small, intimate beach. It's a good place to buy the
famous peppery delicacy jerk pork, available at any of the shacks spew-
ing scented smoke along the beach.
San San Beach. About 5 mi (8 km) east of Port Antonio you'll find beautiful blue waters at this beach used mainly by area villa or hotel owners and their guests.

OCHO RIOS **Turtle Beach.** Stretching behind the Renaissance Jamaica Grande is the
busiest beach in Ocho Rios (where the islanders come to swim).
James Bond Beach. East of Ocho Rios in the quaint village of Oracabessa
is this beach, which is popular because of the live reggae performances
on its bandstand.

DISCOVERY BAY **Puerto Seco Beach.** This stretch of sand is frequented primarily by locals.
There's an admission charge of $5 for the beach, which is open daily

9–5. You'll find plenty of water-sports activities and some concessions that sell local foods.

MONTEGO BAY **Cornwall Beach.** A lively beach with lots of places that sell food and drink, Cornwall also has a water-sports concession.

★ **Doctor's Cave Beach.** The 5-mi (8-km) beach has been spotlighted in so many travel articles and brochures that it often resembles Florida during spring break. On the bright side, it has much to offer admirers beyond just sugary sand, including changing rooms, water sports, colorful if overly insistent vendors, and plenty of places to grab a snack.

Walter Fletcher Beach. Near the center of town, there's protection from the surf on a windy day and therefore unusually fine swimming here; the calm waters make it a good bet for children.

NEGRIL **Negril Beach.** Not too long ago, Negril was a beachcomber's Eden.
Fodor$Choice Today much of its 7 mi (11 km) of white sand is fronted by resorts, al-
★ though some stretches along Bloody Bay remain relatively untouched. A few resorts have built accommodations overlooking their nude beaches, adding a new twist to the notion of "ocean view."

THE SOUTHWEST To find a beach off the main tourist routes, head for Jamaica's unex-
COAST ploited southwest coast. These isolated beaches are some of the island's safest, because the population in this region is sparse, and hasslers are practically nonexistent. You should, however, use common sense; never leave valuables unattended on the beach.

Bluefields Beach. Near Savanna-La-Mar (or just Sav-La-Mar to locals), south of Negril, this is the south coast beach nearest to "civilization."

Crane Beach. At Black River, Crane Beach has retained its natural beauty and has—so far—remained undiscovered by most tourists.

Treasure Beach. This has to be the best that the south shore has to offer. By a quaint fishing village, this undeveloped beach has coves that are ideal for snorkeling explorations.

Sports & the Outdoors

The tourist board licenses all recreational activity operators and outfitters, which should ensure you of fair business practices as long as you deal with companies that display its decals.

BIRD-WATCHING Many bird-watchers flock here for the chance to see the vervian hummingbird (the second-smallest bird in the world, larger only than Cuba's bee hummingbird), the Jamaican tody (which nests underground), or another of the island's 27 unique species. A great place to spot birds is the **Rocklands Feeding Station** (✉ Anchovy ☎ 876/952–2009), which is south of Montego Bay. It costs about $8 for an afternoon's visit.

FISHING Port Antonio makes deep-sea fishing headlines with its annual Blue Marlin Tournament, and MoBay and Ocho Rios have devotees who exchange tales (tall and otherwise) about sailfish, yellowfin tuna, wahoo, dolphinfish, and bonito. Licenses aren't required, and you can arrange to charter a boat at your hotel. A boat (with captain, crew, and equipment) that accommodates four to six passengers costs about $400 for a half day.

GOLF Golfers appreciate both the beauty and the challenges offered by Jamaica's courses. Caddies are almost always mandatory throughout the island, and rates are $5–$15. Cart rentals are available at all courses except Constant Spring and Manchester Country Club; costs are $20–$35. Some of the best courses in the country are found near MoBay.

The Runaway Bay golf course is found at **Breezes Runaway Bay** (✉ North Coast Hwy., Runaway Bay ☎ 876/973–7319). This 18-hole course has hosted many championship events (greens fees are $80 for nonguests; guests play for free). Near Kingston, **Caymanas** (⊠ Mandela Hwy., halfway between Kingston and Spanish Town, Kingston ☎ 876/922–3386 ⊕ www.caymanasgolfclub.com), actually 6 mi (9½ km) west of the city center, was Jamaica's first major championship 18-hole course (greens fees are $24).

The golf course at **Sandals Golf and Country Club** (⊠ Ocho Rios ☎ 876/975–0119), is 700 ft above sea level (greens fees for 18 holes are $100, or $70 for 9 holes for nonguests). East of Falmouth, try **Grand Lido Braco Golf Club** (⊠ Trelawny ☎ 876/954–0010), between Duncans and Rio Bueno, a 9-hole course with lush vegetation (nonguests should call for fee information). Caddies are not mandatory on this course.

Half Moon Golf, Tennis, and Beach Club (⊠ Montego Bay ☎ 876/953–3105), a Robert Trent Jones–designed 18-hole course 7 mi (11 km) east of town, is the home of the Red Stripe Pro Am (greens fees are $90 for guests, $130 for nonguests). **Ironshore** (⊠ Montego Bay ☎ 876/953–2800), 3 mi (5 km) east of the airport, is an 18-hole links-style course (the greens fees are $50). **Tryall Golf, Tennis, and Beach Club** (⊠ North Coast Hwy., Sandy Bay ☎ 876/956–5681), 15 mi (24 km) west of Montego Bay, has an 18-hole championship course on the site of a 19th-century sugar plantation (greens fees are $80 for guests, $115 for nonguests). The **Wyndham Rose Hall Beach Resort** (⊠ North Coast Hwy., Montego Bay ☎ 876/953–2650), 4 mi (6½ km) east of the airport, hosts several invitational tournaments (greens fees run $115 for guests, $150 for nonguests). The newest course in Jamaica is the White Witch course at the **Ritz-Carlton Golf and Spa Resort, Rose Hall** (⊠ 1 Ritz Carlton Dr., Rose Hall, St. James ☎ 876/518–0174). The greens fees at this 18-hole championship course are $140 for guests of the resort, $160 for nonguests.

FodorsChoice
★

Great golf, rolling hills, and a "liquor mobile" go hand in hand at the 18-hole **Negril Hills Golf Club** (⊠ Sheffield Rd., Negril ☎ 876/957–4638), which is east of town; the greens fees are $28.75 for 9 holes or $57.50 for 18 holes. In the hills, the 9-hole **Manchester Club** (⊠ Caledonia Rd., Mandeville ☎ 876/962–2403) is the Caribbean's oldest golf course and charges greens fees of about $15.

HORSEBACK RIDING
Jamaica is fortunate to have an outstanding equestrian facility in **Chukka Cove** (⊠ Ocho Rios ☎ 876/972–2506 ⊕ www.chukkablue.com). This resort offers riding, polo, and jumping (starting at $50), as well as hourlong trail rides ($30) and three-hour beach rides ($55). During in-season weekends this is the place for polo (and social) action. **Prospect Plantation** (⊠ Ocho Rios ☎ 876/974–2058) offers horseback riding for $20 per hour, but advance reservations are required. You can saddle up for $30–$50 at the **Rocky Point Riding Stables at Half Moon** (⊠ Montego Bay ☎ 876/953–2286), which is east of the Half Moon Club.

SCUBA DIVING & SNORKELING
You'll find good scuba diving off the the the coasts of Ocho Rios, Port Antonio, and Negril. MoBay, known for its wall dives, has **Airport Reef** at its southwestern edge. The site is known for its coral caves, tunnels, and canyons. Near the Kingston airport is **Port Royal**, filled with sunken ships that are home to many different varieties of tropical fish. Prices on the island range from $30 to $60 for a single dive. All the large resorts rent equipment, and the all-inclusive places sometimes include scuba diving in their rates. To scuba dive, you need to show a certification card. Most dive operators licensed by the tourist board offer certification courses, dive trips, and snorkel gear rentals.

Dolphin Divers (⊠ Beach Rd., Negril ☎ 876/957–4944) offers scuba facilities for sites in western Jamaica. **Garfield Diving Station** (⊠ Shop 13,

Santa Maria, west of Renaissance Jamaica Grande, Ocho Rios ☎ 876/
974–5749) offers guided dives near Ocho Rios. **Negril Scuba Centre**
(✉ Negril Beach Club, Norman Manley Blvd., Negril ☎ 876/957–
9641) offers one-tank dives in the western end of Jamaica for $50. **North
Coast Marine Sports** (✉ Montego Bay ☎ 876/953–2211) has several locations, one of which is at Half Moon, offering dives to numerous
north coast sites. **Resort Divers** (✉ Gloucester Ave., Montego Bay ☎ 876/
940–1183 ✉ Island Plaza, Ocho Rios ☎ 876/974–5338) offers dives
from Montego Bay, Braco, and Ocho Rios.

TENNIS Many hotels have tennis facilities that are free to their guests, but some
will allow nonguests to play for a fee. Court fees generally run $5–$8
per hour for nonguests; lessons start at $12 an hour.

Breezes Runaway Bay (✉ North Coast Hwy., Runaway Bay ☎ 876/
973–2436) has four tennis courts. **Sandals Dunn's River Golf Resort and
Spa** (✉ North Coast Hwy., Ocho Rios ☎ 876/972–1610) has two courts
lit for night play as well as the services of a pro. **Sans Souci Resort & Spa**
(✉ North Coast Hwy., Ocho Rios, ☎ 876/974–2353) has two lighted
tennis courts and a pro.

Half Moon Golf, Tennis, and Beach Club (✉ Montego Bay ☎ 876/953–2211)
offers tennis buffs the use of 13 Laykold courts (7 lit for night play) along
with a resident pro and a pro shop. Tennis is a highlight at **Sandals Montego Bay** (✉ Kent Ave., Montego Bay ☎ 876/952–5510), with four
courts lit for night play and a tennis pro. **Tryall Golf, Tennis, and Beach
Club** (✉ North Coast Hwy. ☎ 876/956–5660), 15 mi (24 km) west of
MoBay, has nine courts.

You'll find five hard courts and five clay courts, all lit for night play, at
Couples Swept Away Negril (✉ Norman Manley Blvd., Negril ☎ 876/
957–4061).

Shopping

Jamaican crafts are made with style and skill and take the form of resort wear, hand-loomed fabrics, silk-screened articles, wood carvings,
paintings, and other fine arts. Jamaican rum is a great take-home gift.
So is Tia Maria, Jamaica's world-famous coffee liqueur. The same goes
for the island's prized coffees (both Blue Mountain and High Mountain) and its jams, jellies, and marmalades. If you shop around you'll
find good deals on such duty-free luxury items as jewelry, cameras, china,
Swiss watches, and Irish crystal. The top-selling French perfumes are
sold alongside Jamaica's own fragrances.

Areas & Malls

A shopping tour of the **Kingston** area should begin at Constant Spring
Road or King Street. The city's ever-growing roster of malls includes
Twin Gates Plaza, New Lane Plaza, the New Kingston Shopping Centre, Tropical Plaza, Manor Park Plaza, the Village, the Springs, and the
newest (and some say nicest), Sovereign Shopping Centre. Devon House
is the place to find things old and new made in Jamaica. The great house
is now a museum with antiques and furniture reproductions; boutiques
and an ice-cream shop—try one of the tropical flavors (mango, guava,
pineapple, and passion fruit)—now fill what were once the stables.

The crafts markets in **Port Antonio** and—unless there's a cruise ship in
port—**Ocho Rios** are less hectic than the one in MoBay. Ocho Rios shopping plazas are Pineapple Place, Ocean Village, the Taj Mahal, Coconut
Grove, and Island Plaza.

In **MoBay** you should visit the crafts market on Market Street; just be prepared for haggling over prices in the midst of pandemonium. If you want to spend serious money, head for City Centre Plaza, Half Moon Village, Holiday Inn Shopping Centre, St. James's Place, Westgate Plaza, and Montego Bay Shopping Centre, a favorite with locals. At **Negril**'s Rutland Point crafts market you'll find a plethora of T-shirts, straw hats, baskets, place mats, carved wood statues, colorful Rasta berets, and cheap jewelry. The most upscale shopping area in Negril is Time Square, filled with luxury wares from jewelry to watches to leather goods.

Specialty Items

COFFEE   Java lovers will find beans and ground coffee at **Hi-Lo Supermarket** (⊠ West End Rd., Negril ☎ 876/957–4546). But if the store is out of Blue Mountain, you may have to settle for High Mountain coffee, the locals' second-favorite brand.

HANDICRAFTS   **Gallery of West Indian Art** (⊠ 11 Fairfield Rd., Montego Bay ☎ 876/952–4547) is the place to find Jamaican and Haitian paintings. A corner of the gallery is devoted to hand-turned pottery (some painted) and beau-
★ tifully carved and painted birds and animals. **Harmony Hall** (⊠ Hwy. A1, Ocho Rios ☎ 876/975–4222), an 8-minute drive east of the main part of town, is a restored great house where Annabella Proudlock sells her unique wooden boxes (their covers are decorated with reproductions of Jamaican paintings). Also on sale—and magnificently displayed—are larger reproductions of paintings, lithographs, and signed prints of Ja-maican scenes and hand-carved wooden combs. In addition, Harmony Hall is well known for its shows by local artists. **Things Jamaican** (⊠ Devon House, 26 Hope Rd., Kingston ☎ 876/929–6602 ⊠ Sang-ster International Airport, Montego Bay ☎ 876/952–1936) sells some of the best Jamaican crafts—from carved wooden bowls and trays to reproductions of silver and brass period pieces.

LIQUOR &   As a rule, only rum distilleries, such as Appleton's and Sangster's, have
TOBACCO   better deals than the airport stores. Best of all, if you buy your rum or Tia Maria at either the Kingston or the MoBay airport before you leave, you don't have to tote all those heavy, breakable bottles to your hotel and then to the airport. There are several good cigar shops in Negril. Fine handmade cigars from Macanudo make great easy-to-pack gifts; you can pick some up at Montego Bay airport on your way home or at one of the island's many cigar stores. **Cigar World** (⊠ 11 Time Square Mall, Negril ☎ 876/957–3299) offers hand-made Jamaican cigars as well as Cubans. **Cigar King** (⊠ 7 Time Square Mall, Negril ☎ 876/957–3315) has a wide selection of cigars, along with a walk-in humidor.

RECORDS & CDS   Kingston has several good music stores, but there are also good stores in both Port Antonio and Montego Bay. If you like reggae by world fa-mous Jamaican artists—Bob Marley, Peter Tosh, and Third World, to name a few—a pilgrimage to **Randy's Record Mart** (⊠ 17 N. Parade, Kingston ☎ 876/922–4859) is a must. **Record Plaza** (⊠ Tropical Plaza, Kingston ☎ 876/926–7645) is a good place to stop for Jamaican tunes.

Record City (⊠ 1 William St., Port Antonio ☎ 876/993–2836) has many new sounds as well as popular favorites. You'll find the works of Ja-maican musical stars at **Top Ranking Records** (⊠ Westgate Plaza, Mon-tego Bay ☎ 876/952–1216).

SHOES   Cheap sandals are good buys in shopping centers throughout Jamaica. Although workmanship and leathers don't rival the craftsmanship of Italy or Spain, neither do the prices (about $20 a pair). **Lee's Fifth Av-enue Shoes** (⊠ Tropical Plaza, Kingston ☎ 876/926–7486) is a good store in the capital. In Ocho Rios, the **Pretty Feet Shoe Shop** (⊠ Ocean Village Shopping Centre, Ocho Rios ☎ 876/974–5040) is a good bet. In MoBay try **Best Ever Footwear** (⊠ 5 East St., Montego Bay ☎ 876/979–5095) if you find yourself in need of footwear during your trip.

Nightlife & the Arts

Nightlife

Jamaica—especially Kingston—supports a lively community of musicians. For starters there's reggae, popularized by the late Bob Marley and the Wailers and performed today by son Ziggy Marley, Jimmy Tosh (the late Peter Tosh's son), Gregory Isaacs, Jimmy Cliff, and many others. If your experience of Caribbean music has been limited to steel drums and Harry Belafonte, then the political, racial, and religious messages of reggae may set you on your ear; listen closely and you just might hear the heartbeat of the people.

Those who know and love reggae should visit between mid-July and August for the Reggae Sumfest. This four-night concert—at the Bob Marley Performing Center (a field set up with a temporary stage), in the Freeport area of MoBay—showcases local talent and attracts such big-name performers as Third World and Ziggy Marley and the Melody Makers.

DANCE & MUSIC CLUBS For the most part, the liveliest late-night happenings throughout Jamaica are in the major resort hotels, with the widest variety of spots probably in Montego Bay. Some of the all-inclusives offer a dinner and disco pass from about $50. Pick up a copy of the *Daily Gleaner,* the *Jamaica Observer,* or the *Star* (available at newsstands throughout the island) for listings on who's playing when and where.

Live jazz performances are offered on Saturday evenings at the **Blue Lagoon Restaurant** (⊠ San San Beach, Port Antonio ☎ 876/993–7646). If you have but one night to dance, do it at the **Roof Club** (⊠ 11 West St., Port Antonio ☎ 876/993–3817). On weekends from 11 PM on, this is where it's all happening. Dancers often head to **Shadows** (⊠ 40 West St., Port Antonio ☎ 876/993–3823).

One of the top dance clubs is **Jamaic'N Me Crazy** (⊠ Renaissance Jamaica Grande, Main St., Ocho Rios ☎ 876/974–2201); the popular club is a favorite with both locals and visitors who pay a hefty cover charge. The **Little Pub** (⊠ Main St., Ocho Rios ☎ 876/974–5826) produces Caribbean revues several nights a week. **Silks** (⊠ Shaw Park Beach Hotel, Shaw Park Ridge Rd., Ocho Rios ☎ 876/974–2552), 1½ mi (2½ km) south of town, has long been a favorite on the dance scene.

Brewery (⊠ Shop 4, Miranda Ridge, Gloucester Ave., Montego Bay ☎ 876/940–2433) is a popular sports bar. With its location right on what's deemed the "Hip Strip," **Hurricanes Disco** (⊠ Breezes Montego Bay Resort, Gloucester Ave., Montego Bay ☎ 876/940–1150) is packed with locals and visitors from other hotels willing to pay a hefty cover charge. ★ The colorful **Margueritaville Caribbean Bar and Grill** (⊠ Gloucester Ave., Montego Bay ☎ 876/952–4777 ⊠ Norman Manley Blvd., Negril ☎ 876/952–4777) throbs with a spring-break crowd during the season and with a fun-loving atmosphere any night of the year. After 10 PM on Friday night, the crowd gathers at **Pier 1** (⊠ Howard Cooke Blvd., Montego Bay ☎ 876/952–2452), opposite the straw market. **Walter's** (⊠ 39 Gloucester Ave., Montego Bay ☎ 876/952–9391) is a downtown favorite. The **Witches Disco** (⊠ Holiday Inn Sunspree Resort, North Coast Hwy., Montego Bay, 6 mi [9½ km] east of airport ☎ 876/953–2485) rocks with a Jamaican beat nightly.

★ You'll find the best live music at **Alfred's Ocean Palace** (✉ Norman Manley Blvd., Negril ☎ 876/957–4735), with live performances right on the beach. **De Buss** (✉ Norman Manley Blvd., Negril ☎ 876/957–4405) pulsates with a Jamaican sound, and it's impossible to miss; this joint is in a

★ former double decker bus. The sexy, always packed disco at **Hedonism II** (✉ Norman Manley Blvd., Negril ☎ 876/957–5200) is the wildest dance spot on the island; Tuesday (pajama night) and Thursday (toga night) are tops.

Exploring Jamaica

Touring Jamaica can be both thrilling and frustrating. Rugged (albeit beautiful) terrain and winding—often potholed—roads make for slow going. (In the rainy season from June through October, roads can easily be washed out; *always* check conditions prior to heading out.) Primary roads that loop around and across the island are two-lane, and signs are not prevalent. Numbered addresses are seldom used outside major townships, locals drive aggressively, and people and animals seem to have a knack for appearing on the street out of nowhere. That said, Jamaica's scenery shouldn't be missed. The solution? Stick to guided tours and licensed taxis—to be safe and avoid frustration.

If you're staying in Kingston or Port Antonio, set aside at least one day for the capital's highlights and another for a guided excursion to the Blue Mountains. If you have more time, head for Mandeville. You'll find at least three days' worth of activity right along MoBay's boundaries; you should also consider a trip to Cockpit Country or Ocho Rios. If you're based in Ocho Rios, be sure to visit Dunn's River Falls; you may also want to stop by Firefly or Port Antonio. If Negril is your hub, take in the south shore, including Y. S. Falls and the Black River.

Numbers in the margin correspond to points of interest on the Jamaica map.

WHAT TO SEE **Blue Mountains.** These lush mountains rise to the north of Kingston. Un-
② less you're traveling with a local, don't rent a car and go to the Blue Mountains on your own; the roads wind and dip, hand-lettered signs blow away, and you could easily get lost—not just for hours but for days. It's best to hire a taxi (look for red PPV license plates to identify a licensed taxi) or to take a guided tour. Another place worth a visit is **Mavis Bank** (✉ Mavis Bank ☎ 876/977–8005) and its Jablum coffee plant. A half-hour guided tour is available for $5; inquire when you arrive at the main office.

❽ **Cockpit Country.** Fifteen miles (24 km) inland from MoBay is one of the most untouched areas in the West Indies: a terrain of pitfalls and potholes carved by nature in limestone. For nearly a century after 1655 it was known as the Land of Look Behind, because British soldiers nervously rode their horses through here on the lookout for the guerrilla freedom fighters known as Maroons. Former slaves who refused to surrender to the invading English, the Maroons eventually won their independence. Today their descendents live in this area, untaxed and virtually ungoverned by outside authorities. Most visitors to the area stop in Accompong, a small community in St. Elizabeth Parish. You can stroll through town, take in the historic structures, and learn more about the Maroons—considered Jamaica's greatest herbalists.

❺ **Firefly.** About 20 mi (32 km) east of Ocho Rios in Port Maria, Firefly was once Sir Noël Coward's vacation home and is now maintained by the Jamaican National Heritage Trust. Although the setting is Eden-like, the house is surprisingly spartan, considering that he often entertained jet-setters and royalty. He wrote *High Spirits, Quadrille,* and other plays here, and his simple grave is on the grounds next to a small stage where his works are occasionally performed. Recordings of Coward singing about mad dogs and Englishmen echo over the lawns. Tours include time in the photo gallery and a walk through the house and grounds, the viewing of a video on Coward, and a drink in the gift shop. ✉ *Port Maria* ☎ *876/725–0920* 🖃 *$10* ☉ *Mon.–Sat. 8:30–5.*

❶ **Kingston.** The reaction of most newcomers to the capital is far from love at first sight. Yet the islanders themselves can't seem to let the city go. Everybody talks about it, about their homes or relatives there, about their childhood memories. Indeed, Kingston seems to reflect more of the true Jamaica—a wonderful cultural mix—than do the sunny havens of the north coast. As one Jamaican put it, "You don't really know Jamaica until you know Kingston." Parts of the city may be dirty, crowded, and raucous, yet it's still where international and local movers and shakers come to move and shake, where the arts flourish, and where the shopping is superb. It's also home to the University of the West Indies, one of the Caribbean's largest universities.

Sprawling Kingston spills over into communities in every direction. To the west, coming in from Spanish Town, lie some of the city's worst slums, in the neighborhoods of Six Miles and Riverton City. Farther south, Spanish Town Road skirts through a high-crime district that many Kingstonians avoid. In the heart of the business district, along the water, the pace is more peaceful, with a lovely walk and parks on Ocean Boulevard. Also here is the Jamaica Convention Centre, home of the U.N. body that creates all laws for the world's seas. From the waterfront you can look across Kingston Harbour to the Palisadoes Peninsula. This narrow strip is where you'll find Norman Manley International Airport and, farther west, Port Royal, the island's former capital, which was destroyed by an earthquake. Downtown Kingston is considered unsafe, particularly at night, so be careful whenever you go.

New Kingston, north of downtown, is bordered by Old Hope Road on the east and Half Way Tree Road (which changes to Constant Spring Road) on the west. The area is sliced by Hope Road, a major thoroughfare that connects this region with the University of the West Indies, about 15 minutes east of New Kingston. You may feel most comfortable in New Kingston, which glistens with hotels, office towers, apartments, and boutiques. But don't let your trip to the capital end here; away from the high-rises of the new city, Kingston's colonial history is recalled at many well-preserved sites.

North of New Kingston, the city gives way to steep hills and magnificent homes. East of here, the views are even grander as the road winds into the Blue Mountains. Hope Road, just after the University of the West Indies, becomes Gordon Town Road and starts twisting up through the mountains—it's a route that leaves no room for error.

Devon House, built in 1881 and bought and restored by the government in the 1960s, is filled with period furnishings, such as Venetian crystal chandeliers and period reproductions. You can see the inside of the two-story mansion (built with a South American gold miner's fortune) only on a guided tour. On the grounds you'll find some of the island's best crafts shops as well as one of the few mahogany trees to have survived Kingston's ambitious, but not always careful, development. ✉ *26 Hope Rd.* ☎ *876/929–7029 or 876/929–6602* 🖃 *$3 for house tour* ☉ *Devon House Tues.–Sat. 9–5, shops Mon.–Sat. 10–6.*

The artists represented at the **National Gallery** may not be household names in other countries, but their paintings are sensitive and moving. You'll find works by such Jamaican masters as intuitive painter John Dunkley and Edna Manley, a sculptor who worked in a cubist style. Among other highlights from the 1920s through 1980s are works by the artist Kapo, a self-taught painter who specialized in religious images. Reggae fans should look for Christopher Gonzalez's controversial statue of Bob Marley (it was slated to be displayed near the National Arena, but was placed here because many Jamaicans felt it didn't resemble Marley). ⊠ *12 Ocean Blvd., Kingston Mall, near the waterfront* ☎ *876/922–1561* ⌨ *$1* ⊘ *Tues.–Thurs. 10–4:30, Fri. 10–4.*

At the height of his career, Bob Marley built a recording studio. Today the structure—painted Rastafarian red, yellow, and green—houses the **Bob Marley Museum.** The guided tour takes you through the medicinal herb garden, his bedroom, and other rooms wallpapered with magazine and newspaper articles that chronicle his rise to stardom. The tour includes a 20-minute biographical film on him; there's also a reference library if you want to learn more. Certainly there's much here that will help you to understand Marley, reggae, and Jamaica itself. A striking mural by Jah Bobby, *The Journey of Superstar Bob Marley,* depicts the hero's life from its beginnings, in a womb shaped like a coconut, to enshrinement in the hearts of the Jamaican people. ⊠ *56 Hope Rd.* ☎ *876/927–9152* ⌨ *$10* ⊘ *Mon.–Sat. 9:30–4.*

⓫ **Mandeville.** At 2,000 ft above sea level, Mandeville is considerably cooler than the coastal areas 25 mi (40 km) to the south. Its vegetation is also lusher, thanks to the mists that drift through the mountains. But climate and flora aren't all that separate it from the steamy coast: Mandeville seems a hilly tribute to all that is genteel in the British character. The people here live in tidy cottages with gardens around a village green; there's even a Georgian courthouse and a parish church. The entire scene could be set down in Devonshire, were it not for the occasional poinciana blossom or citrus grove.

The **Manchester Club** (☎ 876/962–2403) has tennis courts and a well-manicured 9-hole golf course, the first golf course in the Caribbean. At **Lovers' Leap,** (☎ 876/965–6634) legend has it that two slave lovers chose to jump off the 1,700-ft-high (520-m-high) cliff rather than be recaptured by their master. At the **High Mountain Coffee Plantation** (⊠ Williamsfield ☎ 876/963–4211), free tours (by appointment only) show how coffee beans are turned into one of the world's favorite morning drinks. **Appleton Estate Rum Tour** (⊠ Siloah ☎ 876/963–9215 ⊕ www.jamaica-southcoast.com) is open Monday through Saturday from 9 to 3:30. You'll enjoy a tour of this expansive south coast factory for $12; samples are part of the tour.

❼ **Martha Brae River.** The gentle waterway takes its name from an Arawak Indian who killed herself because she refused to reveal the whereabouts of a local gold mine to the Spanish. According to legend, she agreed to take them there and, on reaching the river, used magic to change its course, drowning herself and the greedy Spaniards with her. Her *duppy* (ghost) is said to guard the mine's entrance. Rafting on this river is a very popular activity. Martha Brae River Rafting arranges trips downriver. Near the rafting company ticket office you'll find gift shops, a bar-restaurant, and a swimming pool.

❾ **Montego Bay.** Today many explorations of MoBay are conducted from a reclining chair—frothy drink in hand—on Doctor's Cave Beach. Believe it or not, the area had a history before all the resorts went up. If you can pull yourself away from the water's edge and brush the sand off your toes, you'll find some very interesting colonial sights.

The outstanding free tour of **Barnett Estates** is led by a charming guide in period costume who recites period poetry and sings period songs. The Kerr-Jarrett family has held the land here for 11 generations, and they still grow coconuts, mangoes, and sugarcane on 3,000 acres. ⊠ *Granville Main Rd.* ☎ *876/952–2382* ✉ *Free, but open only for diners at the Day-O Plantation Restaurant, next door* ☉ *Great house 9:30 AM–10 PM; tours daily 6:30 PM–11 PM.*

In the 1700s, **Rose Hall** may well have been the greatest of great houses in the West Indies. Today it's popular less for its architecture than for the legend surrounding its second mistress: Annie Palmer was credited with murdering three husbands and a *busha* (plantation overseer) who was her lover. The story is told in a novel that's sold everywhere in Jamaica: *The White Witch of Rose Hall.* There's a pub on-site. It's across the highway from the Wyndham Rose Hall resort. ⊠ *North Coast Hwy.* ☎ *876/953–2341* ✉ *$15* ☉ *Daily 9–6.*

The **Greenwood Great House** has no spooky legend to titillate, but it's much better than Rose Hall at evoking life on a sugar plantation. The Barrett family, from whom the English poet Elizabeth Barrett Browning descended, once owned all the land from Rose Hall to Falmouth; they built this and several other great houses on it. (The poet's father, Edward Moulton Barrett, "the Tyrant of Wimpole Street," was born at nearby Cinnamon Hill, currently the estate of country singer Johnny Cash.) Highlights of Greenwood include oil paintings of the Barretts, china made for the family by Wedgwood, a library filled with rare books from as early as 1697, fine antique furniture, and a collection of exotic musical instruments. There's a pub on-site as well. It's 15 mi (24 km) east of Montego Bay. ⊠ *Greenwood* ☎ *876/953–1077* ✉ *$12* ☉ *Daily 9–6.*

❿ Negril. In the 18th century, English ships assembled here in convoys for dangerous ocean crossings. The infamous pirate Calico Jack and his crew were captured right here while they guzzled rum. All but two of them were hanged on the spot; Mary Read and Anne Bonney were pregnant at the time, so their executions were delayed.

On the winding coast road 55 mi (89 km) southwest of MoBay, Negril was once Jamaica's best-kept secret. Recently, however, it has begun to shed some of its bohemian, ramshackle atmosphere for the attractions and activities traditionally associated with MoBay. One thing that hasn't changed around this west-coast center (whose only true claim to fame is a 7-mi [11-km] beach) is a casual approach to life. As you wander from lunch in the sun to shopping in the sun to sports in the sun, you'll find that swimsuits and cover-ups are common attire. Want to dress for a special meal? Slip on a caftan over your swimsuit.

Negril stretches along the coast south from horseshoe-shape Bloody Bay (named when it was a whale-processing center) along the calm waters of Long Bay to the Lighthouse section and landmark Rick's Café. Sunset at Rick's is a Negril tradition. Divers spiral downward off 50-ft-high cliffs into the deep green depths as the sun turns into a ball of fire and sets the clouds ablaze with color. Sunset is also the time when Norman Manley Boulevard, which intersects West End Road, comes to life with bustling bistros and ear-splitting discos.

Even nonguests can romp at **Hedonism II** (⊠ Norman Manley Blvd., Ruthland Point ☎ 876/957–5200). The resort beach is divided into "prude" and "nude" sides; a quick look around reveals where most guests pull their chaise longues. Nude volleyball, body-painting contests, and shuffleboard keep daytime hours lively; at night most action occurs in the high-tech disco or in the hot tub. Your day pass (10:30–5; $65) includes food and drink and participation in water sports, tennis, squash, and other activities. Night passes ($75) cover dinner, drinks, and entrance to the disco. Day or night, reservations are a must; bring a photo I.D. as well. West End Road leads to Negril's only structure of historical significance, the **Lighthouse,** which has guided ships past Jamaica's rocky western coast since 1895. You can stop by the adjacent caretaker's cottage 11–7 (except Tuesday) and, for the price of a tip, climb the spiral steps to the best view in town.

❻ Ocho Rios. Although Ocho Rios isn't near eight rivers as its name would seem to indicate, it does have a seemingly endless series of cascades that sparkle from limestone rocks along the coast. (The name Ocho Rios came about because the English misunderstood the Spanish *laschorreras*—"the waterfalls.")

Today Ocho Rios can be a traffic-clogged community, but a visit is worthwhile, if only to enjoy its two chief attractions—Dunn's River Falls and Prospect Plantation. A few steps from the main road in Ocho Rios are some of the most charming inns and oceanfront restaurants in the Caribbean. Lying on the sand of what seems to be your very own cove or swinging gently in a hammock while sipping a tropical drink, you'll soon forget the traffic that's just a stroll away.

The original "defenders" stationed at the Old Fort, built in 1777, spent much of their time sacking and plundering as far afield as St. Augustine, Florida, and sharing their booty with the local plantation owners who financed their missions. Fifteen miles (24 km) west is Discovery Bay, site of Columbus's landing, with a small museum of artifacts and such local memorabilia as ships' bells and cannons and iron pots used for boiling sugarcane. Other places nearby include Runaway Bay's Green Grotto Caves (and the boat ride on an underground lake); a ramble through the Shaw Park Botanical Gardens; a visit to Sun Valley, a working plantation with banana, coconut, and citrus trees; and a drive through Fern Gully, a natural canopy of vegetation filtered by sunlight. (Jamaica has the world's largest number of fern species, more than 570.)

★ Dunn's River Falls is an eye-catching sight: 600 ft of cold, clear mountain water splashing over a series of stone steps to the warm Caribbean. The best way to enjoy the falls is to climb the slippery steps: don a swimsuit, take the hand of the person ahead of you, and trust that the chain of hands and bodies leads to an experienced guide. The leaders of the climbs are personable fellows who reel off bits of local lore while telling you where to step; you can hire a guide's service for a tip of a few dollars. ✉ *Off A1, between St. Ann's and Ocho Rios* ☎ *876/974–2857* 🎟 *$6* ☉ *Daily 9–5.*

To learn about Jamaica's former agricultural economy, a trip to **Prospect Plantation,** just west of town, is a must. But it's not just a place for history lovers or farming aficionados; everyone seems to enjoy the views over the White River Gorge and the tour by jitney (a canopied open-air cart pulled by a tractor). The grounds are full of exotic fruits and tropical trees, some planted over the years by such celebrities as Winston Churchill and Charlie Chaplin. You can also go horseback riding on the plantation's 900 acres or play miniature golf, grab a drink in the bar, or buy souvenirs in the gift shop. If you want more time to really explore, you can rent one of the on-site villas. ✉ *Hwy. A1* ☎ *876/994–1058* ✉ *$12* ⊙ *Daily 8–5; tours Mon.–Sat. 10:30, 2, and 3:30, Sun. 11, 1:30, and 3.*

Jamaica's national motto is "Out of Many, One People," and at the **Coyaba River Garden and Museum** you'll see exhibits on the many cultural influences that have contributed to the creation of the one. The museum covers the island's history from the time of the Arawak Indians up to the present day. A guided 45-minute tour through the lush 3-acre garden, which is 1½ mi (2½ km) south of Ocho Rios, introduces you to the flora and fauna of the island. The complex includes a crafts and gift shop and a snack bar. ✉ *Shaw Park Estate, Shaw Park Ridge Rd.* ☎ *876/974–6235* ✉ *$4.50* ⊙ *Daily 8–5.*

You enjoy the North Coast rivers and flowers without the crowds at **Cranbrook Flower Forest**, filled with blooming orchids, ginger, and ferns. Nature trails lead into dense vegetation alongside undeveloped riverbanks. Donkey rides, picnicking, croquet, wading, and volleyball are also available here. The complex includes a snack shop and rest rooms. ✉ *5 mi (8 km) east of Runaway Bay, 1 mi (1½ km) off North Coast Hwy.* ☎ *876/770–8071* ⊙ *Daily 8:30–sunset.*

In Island Village, an open-air shopping and entertainment center opened by Island Records tycoon Chris Blackwell, **Reggae Explosion** traces the history of Jamaican music. Ska, mento, dancehall, reggae, and more are featured in a series of exhibits spanning two stories. Special sections highlight the careers of some of Jamaica's best known talents including Bob Marley, Peter Tosh, and Bunny Wailer. The museum also includes an extensive gift shop with recordings and collectibles. ✉ *North Coast Hwy.* ✉ *$10* ⊙ *Daily 9–5.*

❹ **Port Antonio.** Early in the 20th century the first tourists seeking a respite from New York winters arrived on the northeast coast, drawn by the exoticism of the island's banana trade. In time the area became fashionable among a fast-moving crowd and has counted J. P. Morgan, Rudyard Kipling, William Randolph Hearst, Clara Bow, Bette Davis, and Ginger Rogers among its admirers. Its most passionate devotee was the actor Errol Flynn, whose spirit still seems to haunt the docks, and you can almost imagine him devouring raw dolphinfish and swigging gin at 10 AM. Although the action has moved elsewhere, the area can still weave a spell. Robin Moore wrote *The French Connection* here, and Broadway's tall and talented Tommy Tune found inspiration for the musical *Nine* while being pampered at Trident.

Port Antonio has also long been a center for some of the Caribbean's finest deep-sea fishing. Dolphins (the delectable fish, not the lovable mammal) are the likely catch here, along with tuna, kingfish, and wahoo. In October the weeklong Blue Marlin Tournament attracts anglers from around the world. By the time they've all had their fill of beer, it's the fish stories—rather than the fish—that carry the day.

A good way to spend a day in Port Antonio is to laze in the deep azure water of the **Blue Lagoon**, 1 mi (1½ km) east of San San Beach. Although there's not much beach to speak of, you'll find a water-sports center, changing rooms, and a soothing mineral pool. Good, inexpensive Jamaican fare is served at a charming waterside terrace restaurant; it's open daily for lunch and dinner and has live jazz music on Saturday night. **DeMontevin Lodge** (✉ 21 Fort George St. ☎ 876/993–2604), on Titchfield Hill, is owned by the Mullings family. The late Gladys Mullings was Errol Flynn's cook, and you can still get great food here. The lodge, and a number of structures on nearby Musgrave Street (the crafts market is here), are built in a traditional seaside style that's reminiscent of New England. **Queen Street,** in the residential Titchfield area, a couple of miles north of downtown Port Antonio, has several fine examples of Georgian architecture.

A short drive east from Port Antonio puts you at Boston Bay, which is popular with swimmers and has been enshrined by lovers of jerk pork. The spicy barbecue was originated by the Arawaks and perfected by the Maroons. Eating almost nothing but wild hog preserved over smoking coals enabled them to survive years of fierce guerrilla warfare with the English.

Some 6 mi (9½ km) northeast of Port Antonio are the **Athenry Gardens,** a 3-acre tropical wonderland including the Nonsuch Caves, whose underground beauty has been made accessible by concrete walkways, railed stairways, and careful lighting. ⊠ *Nonsuch* ☎ *876/993–3740* ⌨ *$6* ⊙ *Daily 9–5.*

⑬ Port Royal. Just south of Kingston, Port Royal was called "the wickedest city in the world" until an earthquake tumbled much of it into the sea in 1692. The spirits of Henry Morgan and other buccaneers add energy to what remains. The proudest possession of St. Peter's Church, rebuilt in 1726 to replace Christ's Church, is a silver communion set said to have been donated by Morgan himself (who probably obtained it during a raid on Panama).

A ferry from the square in downtown Kingston goes to Port Royal at least twice a day, and the town is small enough to see on foot. If you drive out to Port Royal from Kingston, you'll pass several other sights, including remains of old forts virtually overgrown with vegetation, an old naval cemetery (which has some intriguing headstones), and a monument commemorating Jamaica's first coconut tree, planted in 1863 (there's no tree there now, just plenty of cactus and scrub brush). You can no longer down rum in Port Royal's legendary 40 taverns, but two small pubs still remain in operation.

You can explore the impressive remains of **Ft. Charles,** once the area's major garrison. Built in 1662, this is the oldest surviving monument from the British occupation of Jamaica. On the grounds are a maritime museum and the old artillery storehouse, Giddy House, that gained its name after being tilted by the earthquake of 1907: locals say its slant makes you giddy. ☎ *876/967–8438* ⌨ *$4* ⊙ *Daily 9–5.*

❸ Rio Grande. The Rio Grande (yes, Jamaica has a Rio Grande, too) is a granddaddy of river-rafting attractions: an 8-mi-long (13-km-long) swift, green waterway from Berrydale to Rafter's Rest (it flows into the Caribbean at St. Margaret's Bay). The trip of about three hours is made on bamboo rafts pushed along by a raftsman who is likely to be a character. You can pack a picnic lunch and eat it on the raft or on the riverbank; wherever you lunch, a Red Stripe vendor will appear at your elbow. A restaurant, a bar, and souvenir shops are at Rafter's Rest. The trip costs about $40 per two-person raft.

⑫ Spanish Town. Twelve miles (19 km) west of Kingston on A1, Spanish Town was the island's capital when it was ruled by Spain. The town has Georgian Antique Square, the Jamaican People's Museum of Crafts and Technology (in the Old King's House stables), and St. James, the oldest cathedral in the Western Hemisphere. Spanish Town's original name was Santiago de la Vega, meaning St. James of the Plains.

JAMAICA A TO Z

To research prices, get advice from other travelers, and book travel arrangements, visit www.fodors.com.

AIR TRAVEL

Air Canada offers direct service from Toronto, Winnipeg, and Montréal in conjunction with Air Jamaica. Air Jamaica provides the most frequent service from U.S. cities, including Atlanta, Baltimore, Boston, Chicago, Fort Lauderdale, Houston, Los Angeles, Miami, New York, Orlando, Philadelphia, Phoenix, San Francisco, and Washington, D.C.; flights are also available from London and Manchester. American Airlines flies nonstop daily from New York and Miami. British Airways connects Kingston with London. Copa offers service between Miami and Kingston. Northwest Airlines offers service to MoBay from Detroit, Minneapolis/St. Paul, and Memphis. US Airways has service to Jamaica from Charlotte, NC, and Philadelphia.

Air Canada ☎ 876/952-5160 in Montego Bay; 876/942-8211 in Kingston. **Air Jamaica** ☎ 876/952-4300 in Montego Bay; 876/924-8331 in Kingston. **American Airlines** ☎ 876/952-5950 in Montego Bay; 876/924-8248 in Kingston. **British Airways** ☎ 876/924-8187 in Kingston. **Copa** ☎ 876/926-1762 in Kingston. **Northwest Airlines** ☎ 876/952-9740 in Montego Bay. **US Airways** ☎ 876/952-5532 in Montego Bay.

AIRPORTS

Donald Sangster International Airport, in MoBay, is the most efficient point of entry for travelers destined for MoBay, Ocho Rios, Runaway Bay, and Negril. Norman Manley International Airport, in Kingston, is the best arrival point for travelers headed to the capital or Port Antonio.
Donald Sangster International Airport ☎ 876/952-3124. **Norman Manley International Airport** ☎ 876/924-8452.

BIKE & MOPED TRAVEL

Although the front desks of most major hotels can arrange the rental of bicycles, mopeds, and motorcycles, it isn't a very good idea. The strangeness of driving on the left, the less-than-cautious driving style that prevails on the island, the abundance of potholes, and the prevalence of vendors who will approach you at every traffic light are just a few reasons why.

BUSINESS HOURS

BANKS Banks are generally open Monday–Thursday 9–2, Friday 9–4.

POST OFFICES Post office hours are weekdays 9–5.

SHOPS Normal business hours for stores are weekdays 8:30–4:30, Saturday 8–1.

CAR RENTALS

Although Jamaica has dozens of car-rental companies (you'll find branches at the airports and the resorts among other places), rentals can be difficult to arrange once you've arrived. Make reservations and send a deposit before your trip. (Cars are scarce, and without either a confirmation number or a receipt you may have to walk.) You must be at least 25 years old, have a valid driver's license (from any country), and have a valid credit card. You may be required to post a security of several hundred dollars before taking possession of your car; ask about it when you make the reservation. Rates are quite expensive, averaging $65–$120 a day after the addition of the compulsory CDW coverage, which you must purchase even if your credit card offers it.

▪ **Budget** ☎ 876/952-3838 in Montego Bay; 876/924-8762 in Kingston. **Hertz** ☎ 876/979-0438 in Montego Bay; 876/924-8028 in Kingston. **Island Car Rentals** ☎ 876/952-5771 in Montego Bay; 876/926-5991 in Kingston. **Jamaica Car Rental** ☎ 876/952-5586 in Montego Bay; 876/974-2505 in Ocho Rios.

CAR TRAVEL

GASOLINE · Gas stations are open daily but accept cash only. Gas costs roughly $1.35–$1.60 a gallon.

ROAD CONDITIONS · Driving is a chore and can be extremely frustrating. You must constantly be on guard—for enormous potholes, people, and animals darting out into the street, as well as aggressive drivers.

RULES OF THE ROAD · Traffic keeps to the left in Jamaica.

ELECTRICITY

Like the electrical current in North America, the current in Jamaica is 110 volts but only 50 cycles, with outlets that take two flat prongs. Some hotels provide 220-volt plugs as well as special shaver outlets. If you plan to bring electrical appliances with you, it's best to ask when making your reservation.

EMBASSIES & CONSULATES

▪ Canada **Canadian High Commission** ⊠ 3 West Kings House Rd., Kingston ☎ 876/926-1500.

▪ United Kingdom **British High Commission** ⊠ Trafalgar Rd., Kingston ☎ 876/920-4361.

▪ United States **U.S. Embassy** ⊠ 32 Oxford Rd., Kingston ☎ 876/929-4850.

EMERGENCIES

▪ Air Rescue **Air rescue** ☎ 119.

▪ Ambulance & Fire **Ambulance and fire emergencies** ☎ 110.

▪ Hospitals **Cornwall Regional Hospital** ⊠ Mt. Salem, Montego Bay ☎ 876/952-5100. **Mo Bay Hope Medical Center** ⊠ Half Moon Resort, Montego Bay ☎ 876/953-3981. **Port Antonio Hospital** ⊠ Naylor's Hill, Port Antonio ☎ 876/715-5778. **St. Ann's Bay Hospital** ⊠ St. Ann's Bay ☎ 876/794-8565. **University Hospital of the West Indies** ⊠ Mona, Kingston ☎ 876/927-1620.

▪ Pharmacies **Great House Pharmacy** ⊠ Brown's Plaza, DaCosta Dr., Ocho Rios ☎ 876/974-2352. **Jamaica Pegasus** ⊠ 81 Knutsford Blvd., Kingston ☎ 876/926-3690.

▪ Police **Police emergencies** ☎ 119.

▪ Scuba Diving Emergencies **St. Ann's Bay Hospital** ⊠ St. Ann's Bay ☎ 876/972-2272.

ETIQUETTE & BEHAVIOR

As you travel the island, you'll see Rastafarians with their flowing dreadlocks (although some prefer to wear their hair beneath knitted caps). Rastas smoke marijuana as part of their religious rites, do not eat salt or pork (many are vegetarians), and often sell crafts. Always ask for permission before taking a photograph.

FESTIVALS & SEASONAL EVENTS

The biggest festival is Carnival, an event filled with lots of music and dancing in the streets. It's held in Kingston, Ocho Rios, and MoBay every March and April and in Negril every May. Music lovers also fill the island for the July and August Reggae Sumfest, which is getting hotter every year, because the best, brightest, and newest of the reggae stars gather to perform in open-air concerts in MoBay. Anglers come to Port Antonio to compete in the annual International Marlin Tournament, which is usually held in October.

▪ **Reggae Sumfest** ☎ 800/526-2422 ⊕ www.reggaesumfest.com.

HOLIDAYS

Public holidays include New Year's Day, Ash Wednesday (beginning of Lent, 6 weeks before Easter), Good Friday, Easter Monday, Labor Day (May 23), Independence Day (1st Mon. in Aug.), National Heroes Day (Oct. 15), Christmas, and Boxing Day (Dec. 26).

LANGUAGE

The official language of Jamaica is English. Islanders usually speak a patois among themselves, a lyrical mixture of English, Spanish, and various African languages. Some examples of patois are *me diyah* ("I'm here"; pronounced mee *de*-ya); *nyam* ("eat"; pronounced yam); and, if someone asks how your vacation is going, just say *irie* (pronounced *eye*-ree), which means "great."

MAIL & SHIPPING

Postcards may be mailed anywhere in the world for J$25. Letters to the United States and Canada cost J$25, to Europe J$12.50, to Australia J$40, and to New Zealand J$30.
🏠 **Kingston Post Office** ⊠ 13 King St. ☎ 876/922-2120. **Montego Bay Post Office** ⊠ 122 Barnett St. ☎ 876/952-7389.

MONEY MATTERS

Note that prices quoted throughout this chapter are in U.S. dollars, unless otherwise noted.

ATMS ATM machines do not accept American bank cards, although cash advances can be made using credit cards.

CREDIT CARDS Major credit cards are widely accepted throughout the island, although cash is required at gas stations, in markets, and in many small stores. Discover and Diners Club are accepted at many resorts.

CURRENCY The official currency is the Jamaican dollar. At this writing the exchange rate was about J$49.85 to US$1. U.S. money (currency only, no coins) is accepted at most establishments, although you'll often be given change in Jamaican money.

CURRENCY EXCHANGE Currency can be exchanged at airport bank counters, exchange bureaus, or commercial banks. Throughout the island you'll find branches of the Bank of Nova Scotia.
🏠 **Bank of Nova Scotia** ⊠ Sam Sharpe Sq., Montego Bay ☎ 876/952-4440 ⊠ Main St., Ocho Rios ☎ 876/974-2689 ⊠ Negril Sq., Negril ☎ 876/957-3040 ⊠ 35 King St., Kingston ☎ 876/922-1420.

PASSPORTS & VISAS

U.S. and Canadian citizens must have a passport (not expired beyond one year). Or, to prove citizenship, bring an original birth certificate (with a raised seal) or a naturalization certificate along with a government-issued photo I.D. (all documents must bear exactly the same name). British, Australian, and New Zealand travelers must have passports. Everyone must have a return or ongoing ticket. Declaration forms are usually distributed in flight to keep customs formalities to a minimum.

SAFETY

Don't let the beauty of Jamaica cause you to abandon the caution you would practice in any unfamiliar place. Crime in Jamaica is, unfortunately, a persistent problem. Although many of the headlines are grabbed by murders in Kingston, often gang-related, crime is an island-wide problem. Visitors should be extremely cautious about visiting many of the neighborhoods in Kingston that are outside the business district of New Kingston; Kingston visitors should also maintain an awareness of political situations that can trigger rioting. Never leave valuables in your room; use the safe-deposit boxes that most hotels make available. Carry your funds in traveler's checks, and keep a record of the check numbers in a secure place. Never leave a rental car unlocked, and never leave valuables in a locked car. Ignore efforts, however persistent, to sell you *ganja* (marijuana), which is illegal across the island. Independent travelers, especially those renting cars, need to take special precautions. Some travelers have been harassed by locals offering to "guard" cars and have experienced vandalism when requests for money were denied. The most common problem visitors encounter is hassling by vendors on the public beaches; offers of everything from hair braiding to ganja can be very persistent.

SIGHTSEEING TOURS

Half-day tours are offered by most tour operators in the important areas of Jamaica. The best great-house tours include Rose Hall, Greenwood, and Devon House. Plantations to tour are Prospect, Barnett Estates, and Sun Valley. The Appleton Estate Tour uses a bus to visit villages, plantations, and a rum distillery. The increasingly popular waterside folklore feasts are offered on the Dunn's, Great, and White rivers. The significant city tours are in Kingston, MoBay, and Ocho Rios. Caribic Tours offers tours of Jamaica, as well as to Cuba. Safari Tours offers guided jeep, bike, and horseback tours. Tourwise offers guided tours of top attractions including Dunn's River Falls, Black River Safari, Cockpit Country, Kingston, Mayfield Falls, and Blue Lagoon; tours are available in English, French, Spanish, German, Italian, and Dutch.
🚩 **Caribic Tours** ⊠ 1310 Providence Dr., Montego Bay ☎ 876/953-9878 ⊕ www.caribicvacations.com. **CS Tours** ⊠ 66 Claude Clarke Ave., Montego Bay ☎ 876/952-6260. **Glamour Tours** ⊠ Montego Freeport, Montego Bay ☎ 876/979-8207 ⊕ www.glamourtours.com. **Safari Tours** ⊠ Mammee Bay, Montego Bay ☎ 876/972-2639. **SunHoliday Tours** ⊠ Donald Sangster International Airport, Montego Bay ☎ 876/979-1061. **Tourwise** ⊠ 103 Main St., Ocho Rios ☎ 876/974-2323.

BOAT TOURS Calico Sailing offers snorkeling trips and sunset cruises on the waters of MoBay; costs are $35 and $25, respectively. Martha Brae River Rafting leads trips down the Martha Brae River, about 25 mi (40 km) from most hotels in MoBay. The cost is $35 (two per raft) for the 1½-hour river run. Mountain Valley Rafting runs trips down the River Lethe, approximately 12 mi (19 km) (a 50-minute trip) southwest of MoBay; the excursion costs about $36 per raft (two per raft) and takes you through unspoiled hill country. Bookings can also be made through hotel tour desks. Rio Grande Attractions Ltd. guides raft trips down the Rio Grande; the cost is $45 per raft. South Coast Safaris Ltd. has guided excursions up the Black River for some 10 mi (16 km) (round-trip), into the mangroves and marshlands to see alligators, birds, and plant life. The trip on the 25-passenger *Safari Queen* or *Safari Princess* costs around $15.
🚩 **Calico Sailing** ⊠ North Coast Hwy., Montego Bay ☎ 876/952-5860. **Martha Brae River Rafting** ⊠ Claude Clarke Ave., Montego Bay ☎ 876/952-0889. **Mountain Valley Rafting** ⊠ 31 Gloucester Ave., Montego Bay ☎ 876/952-0527. **Rio Grande Attractions Ltd.** ⊠ St. Margaret's Bay ☎ 876/993-5778. **South Coast Safaris Ltd.** ⊠ 1 Crane Rd., Black River ☎ 876/965-2513.

HELICOPTER TOURS Helitours Jamaica Ltd., 1 mi (1½ km) west of Ocho Rios, offers helicopter tours of Jamaica, ranging from 20 minutes to an hour, at prices from $65 to $225.
🚩 **Helitours Jamaica Ltd.** ⊠ North Coast Hwy., Ocho Rios ☎ 876/974-2265 or 876/974-1108.

SPECIAL-INTEREST TOURS Countrystyle offers unique, personalized tours of island communities. You're linked with community residents based on your interests; there are tours that include anything from bird-watching in Mandeville to nightlife in Kingston. Maroon Attraction Tours leads full-day tours from MoBay to Maroon headquarters at Accompong, giving you a glimpse of the society of Maroons who live in Cockpit Country. The cost is $50 per person.

⛏ **Countrystyle** ✉ 62 Ward Ave., Mandeville ☎ 876/962-7979. **Maroon Attraction Tours Co.** ✉ North Coast Hwy., Montego Bay ☎ 876/952-4546.

TAXES

DEPARTURE TAX The departure tax is $27 and must be paid in cash if it is not added to the cost of your airline tickets; this policy varies by carrier, although many ticket prices now include the departure tax. Be sure to ask.

SALES TAX Jamaica has replaced the room occupancy tax with a VAT of 15% on most goods and services, which is already incorporated into the prices of taxable goods.

TAXIS

Some but not all of Jamaica's taxis are metered. If you accept a driver's offer of his services as a tour guide, be sure to agree on a price before the vehicle is put into gear. (Note that a one-day tour should run about $100–$180, depending on distance traveled.) All licensed taxis display red Public Passenger Vehicle (PPV) plates. Cabs can be summoned by phone or flagged down on the street. Rates are per car, not per passenger, and 25% is added to the metered rate between midnight and 5 AM. Licensed minivans are also available and bear the red PPV plates. JUTA is the largest taxi franchise and has offices in all resort areas.

⛏ **JUTA** ☎ 876/974-2292 in Ocho Rios; 876/957-9197 in Negril; 876/952-0813 in Montego Bay.

TELEPHONES

Most hotels offer direct-dial telephone services; local businesses provide fax services for a fee. Pay phones are available in most communities.

COUNTRY & AREA CODES To dial Jamaica from the United States, just dial 1 + the area code 876.

INTERNATIONAL CALLS Some U.S. phone companies, such as MCI, won't permit credit-card calls to be placed from Jamaica because they have been victims of fraud. The best option is to purchase Jamaican phone cards, sold in most stores across the island.

LOCAL CALLS While on the island, calls from town to town are long-distance.

TIPPING

Most hotels and restaurants add a 10% service charge to your bill. When a service charge isn't included, a 10% to 20% tip is appreciated. Tips of 10% to 20% are customary for taxi drivers as well. However, many all-inclusives have a strict no-tipping policy.

TRANSPORTATION AROUND JAMAICA

Air Jamaica Express, a subsidiary of Air Jamaica, provides shuttle services on the island. Be sure to reconfirm your departing flight a full 72 hours in advance. Tropical Airlines offers service between Kingston and MoBay as well as flights to Cuba. Tim Air offers quick flights between resort areas as well as to Kingston.

⛏ **Air Jamaica Express** ☎ 876/952-5401 in Montego Bay, 876/923-8680 in Kingston ⊕ www.airjamaica.com. **Tim Air** ☎ 876/952-2516 in Montego Bay. **Tropical Airlines** ☎ 876/920-3770 in Kingston, 876/940-5917 in Montego Bay.

VISITOR INFORMATION

🔃 Before You Leave Jamaica Tourist Board ⊕ www.jamaicatravel.com ✉ 801 2nd Ave., 20th floor, New York, NY 10017 ☎ 212/856-9727 or 800/233-4582 ✉ 500 N. Michigan Ave., 10th Floor, Chicago, IL 60611 ☎ 312/527-1296 ✉ 1320 S. Dixie Hwy., Suite 1101, Coral Gables, FL 33146 ☎ 305/665-0557 ✉ 3440 Wilshire Blvd., Suite 805, Los Angeles, CA 90010 ☎ 213/384-1123 ✉ 303 Eglinton Ave. E, Suite 200, Toronto, Ontario M4P 1L3, Canada ☎ 416/482-7850 ✉ 1-2 Prince Consort Rd., London SW7 2BZ, U.K. ☎ 0441/207-224-0505.

🔃 In Jamaica Jamaica Tourist Board ✉ 2 St. Lucia Ave., Kingston ☎ 876/929-9200, 888/995-9999 for the on-island help line ✉ Hendriks Bldg., 2 High St., Black River ☎ 876/965-2074 ✉ Cornwall Beach, Montego Bay ☎ 876/952-4425 ✉ Coral Seas Plaza, Negril ☎ 876/957-4243 ✉ Ocean Village Shopping Centre, Ocho Rios ☎ 876/974-2570 ✉ City Centre Plaza, Port Antonio ☎ 876/993-3051.

MARTINIQUE

14

FODOR'S CHOICE
'Ti Plage, a restaurant in Anse-d'Artlets
Le Plein Soleil, a hotel in Le François

HIGHLY RECOMMENDED

RESTAURANTS
La Belle Epoque, Fort-de-France
La Canne á Sucre, Fort-de-France
Le Colibri, Ste-Marie
Le Fromager, St. Pierre
Le Plein Soleil, Le François
Mille Et Une Brindilles, Fort-de-France
Sapori d'Italia, Les Trois-Ilets

HOTELS
Cap Est Lagoon Resort & Spa, Le François
Sofitel Bakoua Coralia, Les Trois-Ilets

BEACHES
Les Salines Beach, Ste-Anne

SHOPPING
The boutiques of Fort-de-France

SIGHTS
Depaz Distillery, St-Pierre
Habitation Clément, Le François
Leyritz Plantation, Basse-Pointe
Musée de la Pagerie, Les Trois-Ilets
Musée Régional d'Histoire et d'Ethnographie, Fort-de-France
Musée Vulcanologique Frank Perret, St-Pierre
St-Pierre

One annual event that is celebrated simultaneously throughout France—yes, this little corner of the Caribbean is France, too—is the annual fête in honor of the arrival of the Beaujolais nouveau. Here, grape-colored balloons floated in clusters in an aquamarine pool overlooking the twinkle-lights of Fort-de-France. Servers placed the wine buckets in strategic locations as chic Martinicans filed in. The one-man band played his sax along with the synthesizer that spewed out melodies made famous by Edith Piaf and Johnny Mathis. What the female chef called a "typical country buffet" was a charcuterie of cold meats and patés, expensive French cheeses, and desserts made with the ubiquitous Beaujolais nouveau. On the way out, I brought a bottle of water for the drive home, and a Frenchman retorted: "L'eau! That's American wine!" And we laughed and told more stories.

Updated by
Eileen
Robinson Smith

The Arawak Indians named Martinique *Madinina* (Island of Flowers). Exotic wild orchids, frangipani, anthurium, jade vines, flamingo flowers, and hundreds of vivid varieties of hibiscus still grow on the island. But these days the scent of flowers competes with those of French perfume and espresso.

Martinique is like a tropical suburb of Paris; it has a definite sense of style that you first notice at the clean, contemporary airport. Fellow passengers, particularly *les femmes*, have that admirable chic; even the women at the airline and rental-car desks manage to accessorize their uniforms so that they look like French designer ensembles.

In their dealings with foreigners, Martinicans are polite and self-assured—qualities anchored in the privileged position the island has enjoyed historically. Martinique was the administrative, social, and cultural center of the French Antilles. Guadeloupe was an island of merchants and shopkeepers. Martinique was a rich, aristocratic island, famous for its beautiful women and gracious living, which gave birth to an empress, Napoléon's Josephine, and saw the full flowering of plantocracy, with servants and soirees, wine cellars and snobbery. Today the island has one of the highest standards of living in the Caribbean, and a fine educational system, with many young people going to study in France.

This 425-square-mi (1,101-square-km) island, the largest of the Windwards, has landscapes as varied as its culture and history. In the south, which holds most of the development and the best beaches, there are rolling hills and sugarcane fields. In the north look for lush, tropical vegetation, fields of bananas and pineapples, deep gorges, towering cliffs, and one of the Caribbean's most impressive volcanoes, Mont Pelée. Fort-de-France is the island's capital as well as its cultural and commercial hub. Most of the other towns—such as Ste-Anne and Vauclin, to the south, and Carbet and Marigot, to the north—are either small resorts or fishing villages.

Britain and France squabbled over Martinique until 1815, when the island was ceded by treaty to Paris. Today the French connection means French-influenced food from the motherland and wine, a wonderful élan, superb roads, Franco-Caribbean pop music, relatively high prices, and plenty of culture and arts (Martinique has one of the finest Caribbean jazz festivals). However, its tourism has suffered in recent decades. The chic upper-crust Europeans and Americans, the women in long dresses and men in dinner jackets, are not prevalent as in the 1970s. Everyone has high hopes for the new Cap Est Lagoon Resort & Spa in Le François, hope that the chic, international set that frequented Martinique in the 1970s will return. What continues to prevail are French package tours that attract a mass-market clientele. The result is that prices have fallen and the island is generally more affordable than in years past. Most Americans who come are Francophiles.

You'll need some French to feel truly at home, though the locals are more forthcoming with English here than in other places in the French-speaking world. Franglais is universal. This island is not *like* France—it *is* France. Most everything shuts down at midday and reopens sometime after 2:30. Topless bathing is almost de rigueur, driving is frenetic, and poodles are the pedigree pooch of choice. High season runs mid-November through May, and the island can be quiet the rest of the year, with some hotels closing down for months, particularly in September and October. Others discount tariffs significantly.

WHAT IT COSTS In U.S. dollars					
	$$$$	**$$$**	**$$**	**$**	**¢**
RESTAURANTS*					
	over $30	$20–$30	$12–$20	$8–$12	under $8
HOTELS**					
Cost EP/BP/CP	over $350	$250–$350	$150–$250	$80–$150	under $80
Cost AI	over $450	$350–$450	$250–$350	$125–$250	under $125

*Restaurant prices are for a main course at dinner. **EP, BP, and CP prices are per night for a standard double room in high season, excluding taxes, service charges, and meal plans. AI (all-inclusive) prices are per person, per night based on double-occupancy during high season, excluding taxes and service charges.

Where to Stay

Martinique's accommodations range from tiny inns called *relais créoles* to splashy tourist resorts—some all-inclusive—and restored plantation houses. A large number of hotels are clustered on Les Trois-Ilets peninsula, across the bay from Fort-de-France. There are only a few deluxe properties on the island. A number that lack mega-stellar ratings make up for it with charisma, hospitality, and French style. Most hotels have the busy, slightly frenetic feel that the French seem to like. The major establishments usually include a large buffet breakfast of fresh fruit, cheese, croissants, baguettes, jam, and café au lait. Many hotels can accommodate guests in wheelchairs.

VILLAS & CONDOMINIUMS It's possible to rent a villa or apartment if you are staying for a week or longer, so that you can save some money with a self-catering vacation. However, don't forget to add in the cost of a car rental to your vacation budget. **French Caribbean International** (☎ 800/322–2223 ⊕ www.frenchcaribbean.com), an English-speaking reservation service, represents many of the hotels in Martinique. It also handles villas for rent. At the **Villa Rental Service** (☎ 0596/71–56–11 ℻ 0596/63–11–64) an English-speaking staffer can help you find a home, a villa, or an apartment to rent for a week or a month. Most properties are in the south of the island near good beaches.

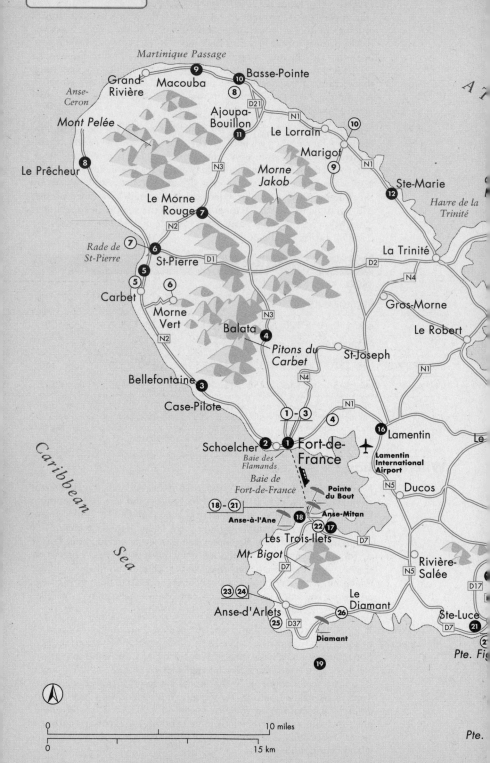

Martinique

Martinique Passage

Anse-Ceron

Grand-Rivière

Macouba

Basse-Pointe

Mont Pelée

Ajoupa-Bouillon

Le Lorrain

Marigot

Le Prêcheur

Morne Jakob

Ste-Marie

Havre de la Trinité

Le Morne Rouge

Rade de St-Pierre

St-Pierre

La Trinité

Carbet

Morne Vert

Gros-Morne

Le Robert

Balata

Pitons du Carbet

St-Joseph

Bellefontaine

Case-Pilote

Schoelcher

Fort-de-France

Lamentin

Lamentin International Airport

Baie des Flamands

Baie de Fort-de-France

Pointe du Bout

Ducos

Anse-à-l'Ane

Anse-Mitan

Les Trois-Ilets

Mt. Bigot

Rivière-Salée

Caribbean

Sea

Anse-d'Arlets

Le Diamant

Ste-Luce

Diamant

Pte. Fig

0
10 miles

0
15 km

Pte.

ATLANTIC OCEAN

Caravelle
Peninsula

de la
ité

Tartane **13**
14 Pointe
Caracoli

⑬ ⑫

Baie du Galion

Havre du Robert

Pte.
Larose

Le Plein Soleil

⑭ ⑮
15
Le François

⑯
⑰

Mt. Vauclin

N6

Le Vauclin

24

D17
20
Rivière-
Pilote
D18
N6

Luce
21
D18A
Le Marin

23

N5

27–**29**
te. Figuier
30
Pointe
Marin
D9
Cul-de-Sac
du Marin
22 Ste-
31
Anne
La Savane
(Petrified
Forest)
Cap
Chevalier
Baie des Anglais
Les Salines

Grande Anse
Anse-Trabaud
Pte. des Salines
Pte. d'Enfer
St. Lucia Channel

South of Fort-de-France

★ **$$$–$$$$** ⌖ **Cap Est Lagoon Resort & Spa.** Martinique's newest, most exclusive property debuted in 2002. Set on a beguiling green crystalline lagoon, all of the villas (some bi-level) have water views. A Franco-Caribbean design, with southeast Asian influences, the luxurious decor utilizes natural materials, including marble, hemp, exotic woods, and even Tibaume branches. Each suite is equipped with a DVD-CD player, plasma-screen satellite TV, and elaborate minibars; 36 have private plunge pools. Restaurant Le Bélem is staffed by a chef and manager with credentials from top restaurants in France. Discriminating clients self-indulge at the Euro Spa, and there's even a helipad for those who require a grand entrance. ⊠ *Quartier Cap Est, Le Francois 97240* ☎ *0596/54–80–80* 🖷 *0596/54–96–00* ⊕ *www.capest.com* ⇨ *50 suites* ♺ *2 restaurants, room service, in-room data ports, minibars, cable TV, in-room VCRs, tennis court, pool, gym, spa, beach, dock, snorkeling, windsurfing, boating, fishing, 2 bars, laundry service, concierge, Internet, meeting room, car rental, helipad* ⊟ *AE, MC, V* ⫧⦿⫧ *BP.*

★ **$$$–$$$$** ⌖ **Sofitel Bakoua Coralia.** A former family estate overlooking the bay of Fort-de-France is one of Martinique's finest hotels. Its impressive canopied entrance, with international flags hoisted, could be that of an embassy. Accommodations are in three hillside buildings, with a fourth on the white sand beach. Beach rooms, while small, are modern, light, quiet, and comfortable. All have a balcony or patio and a bathroom with hand-painted tiles. The rooms in the original residence are the largest and most charismatic. There is always an animated scene at the circular bar near the gorgeous infinity pool. Entertainment consists of live music and nightly shows. ⊠ *Pointe du Bout, Les Trois-Ilets 97229* ☎ *0596/66–02–02* 🖷 *0596/66–00–41* ⊕ *www.sofitel.com* ⇨ *133 rooms, 6 suites* ♺ *2 restaurants, minibars, 2 tennis courts, pool, hair salon, beach, snorkeling, boating, 2 bars, shops, business services, Internet, meeting rooms* ⊟ *AE, DC, MC, V* ⫧⦿⫧ *BP.*

$$ ⌖ **Club Med Les Boucaniers.** Occupying 48 acres, this village has plazas, cafés, restaurants, a boutique, and a marina. Pastel rooms have twin beds and a shower. Excursions (in French) are not included, nor are any drinks—even bottled water—outside of meals. Set on a picturesque cove, the resort offers a plethora of water sports and plenty of nightlife, with everything from karaoke to theme parties 'til dawn. It draws singles from their 20s to 40s, mainly French, as well as couples. Children are welcome, but there is no kids' club. The place is circa 1969, and although well maintained, it has never had a full renovation. ⊠ *Pointe du Marin, Ste-Anne 97227* ☎ *0596/76–72–72 or 800/258–2633* 🖷 *0596/76–83–36* ⊕ *www.clubmed.com* ⇨ *308 rooms* ♺ *2 restaurants, 7 tennis courts, pool, gym, beach, dive shop, dock, snorkeling, boating, waterskiing, basketball, volleyball, 2 bars, dance club, nightclub; no room TVs* ⊟ *AE, MC, V* ⫧⦿⫧ *AI.*

$$ ⌖ **L'Habitation de L'Ilet Thierry.** A dock with a palapa and a palm tree dead-ends at a steep, stone staircase that goes up to a primitive hotel, the only edifice on this remote, windswept island. Rooms in the white, two-story, colonial-style building are large, but forget creature comforts. Although they have basic bathrooms, low water pressure means you must shower on the first floor. The dining room looks like something from the movie *Key Largo*. Some come just for the prix-fixe lunch—$45 for fish, $55 for lobster; the ferry from Le François is not included (though it is for hotel guests) and costs $50 round-trip. ⊠ *Ilet Thierry 97240* ☎ *0596/65–88–54 or 0596/27–66–07* ⇨ *5 rooms* ♺ *Kitchenettes* ⊟ *No credit cards* ⫧⦿⫧ *CP.*

🖢 **$–$$** ⌖ **Hôtel Amyris.** In the south, this resort from the Karibéa Group is a stand out. Still the newest in the developing tourist area of Ste-Luce, it has a panoramic view of a natural cove. Four three-story buildings (sans elevators), housing the guest rooms, are situated within the park-like gardens around a beautifully designed pool. Each suite has two bathrooms. There are convertible couches in the living rooms, balconies and wood furniture. Garden rooms have full kitchenettes. The food served is of a high caliber; the front desk crew have young, smiling faces and are English-speaking. ⊠ *Ste-Luce 97228* ☎ *0596/62–12–00* 🖷 *0596/ 62–12–10* ⊕ *www.karibea.com* ↪ *110 jr suites* ⚒ *Restaurant, in-room safes, some kitchenettes, refrigerators, tennis court, pool, beach, snorkeling, children's programs (ages 4–11), Internet, meeting rooms, car rental* ⊟ *AE, MC, V* ⭗ *EP.*

$–$$ ▦ **Le Plein Soleil.** Chic, contemporary Creole, the scattering of ginger-bread cottages with fretwork and painted in pastels clings to the hill-side. As attractive as these terraced suites are, it is the inn's "great house" that captivates. It is a study in white with tropical furnishings, objets d'art and nature, and—up the wooden stairs—a loft, which is the designated TV room. Creative lighting plays up the artistic vignettes of pods, berries, and palm fronds in the terrace restaurant. The pool is on its own plateau, with views down the coastline. The caring owner, Jean Christophe, is a former creative talent for a Parisian ad agency. ⊠ *Villa Lagon Sarc, Pointe Thalemont, Le François 97240* ☎ *0596/38–07–77* 🖷 *0596/65–58–13* ⊕ *www.sasi.fr/pleinsoleil* ↪ *12 bungalows* ⚒ *Restaurant, kitchenettes, pool* ⊟ *MC, V* ⭗ *EP.*

FodorsChoice
★

$–$$ ▦ **Manoir de Beauregard.** Built in the 18th century, this plantation house has thick stone walls and mullioned windows like a medieval abbey. Where the nave would be is a drawing room with bentwood rockers, chandeliers, and checkerboard marble floors. The three rooms upstairs in the main building have wood-beam ceilings, antique furniture, and four-poster beds. Other rooms are in a modern annex. This property has history and personality, and it has received exactly what it needed in 2002— pool, lobby, and room renovations, plus three new, spacious bungalows of a rich Brazilian wood; another 18 are planned. ⊠ *Chemin des Salines, Ste-Anne 97227* ☎ *0596/76–73–40* 🖷 *0596/76–93–24* ↪ *11 rooms, 3 bungalows* ⚒ *Restaurant, pool, bar* ⊟ *AE, MC, V* ⭗ *CP* ⭗ *Closed Sept.–Dec.*

$–$$ ▦ **Relais Caraïbes.** Twelve bungalows are spread over the manicured grounds, and each has a hammock, a bedroom, a small salon with a pull-out bed for two, and a bathroom; there are also three rooms in the main house. The pool is on the edge of a cliff that overlooks the sea and adjacent to the appealing terrace restaurant. Even nonguests come for the good French food, wine, and music. The present owner, Eric Bordiere, is maintaining the inn's charisma while sprucing it up. The tiny beach is a short walk away, and there's scuba and boating instruction available at the nearby Diamant-Novotel. ⊠ *Pointe de la Chery, Le Diamant 97223* ☎ *0596/76–44–65* 🖷 *0596/76–21–20* ↪ *3 rooms, 12 bungalows* ⚒ *Restaurant, some refrigerators, pool, boating, bar* ⊟ *MC, V* ⭗ *CP* ⭗ *Closed Sept.–Oct.*

$ ▦ **Hôtel Caribia.** Of the trio of Karibéa hotels in Ste-Luce, the Caribia's "junior" suites are the largest (in Manhattan, they would be considered huge one-bedroom apartments). Here the kitchen is on the terrace, which looks out onto the tropical gardens. Alas, there is no beach or restaurant (though a fine breakfast buffet is available for an additional cost near the bar) but both are across the street at the sister properties. A small but ample commissary is on-site. The real draw here is a feeling of family—the staff makes you feel as if you are a part of theirs. ⊠ *Quartier Desert, St. Luce 97228* ☎ *0596/62–20–62* 🖷 *0596/62–59– 52* ⊕ *www.karibea.com* ↪ *75 jr suites* ⚒ *Kitchenettes, children's programs (ages 6–11), bar* ⊟ *AE, MC, V* ⭗ *EP.*

☾ $ 🖾 **Pierre & Vacances.** This self-contained village, the largest resort in Ste-Luce, is a happening place, with TV and good music in the lobby, which has attractive plantation-style furnishings. An outdoor amphitheater is the setting for many *serious* parties and concerts—P.V. has a large fun quotient. The accommodations, particularly on the third and fourth floors (sans elevators) are true apartments, attractive with dormers and eaves and exterior turrets and balconies overlooking the large pool complex and, beyond, the sea. Outdoor terrace kitchens are well-equipped with dishwashers and small ovens. Children thrive in this safe compound. ⊠ *Pointe Philippeau, Lieu-dit "Pavillon," St. Luce, 97228* ☎ *0596/62–12–62* 🖷 *0596/62–12–63* ⟿ *337 apartments* ⚇ *3 restaurants, kitchens, tennis court, pool, 2 beaches, dive shop, snorkeling, jet skiing, 3 bars, children's programs (ages 3–12), shop, car rental* ▭ *AE, MC, V* ¶◎¶ *EP* ⊘ *Closed Sept.–Oct. 12.*

☾ ¢–$ 🖾 **La Résidence Village Créole.** Vacation rentals from studios to two-bedroom apartments are on the ground and second floors (no elevator) of this fun, attractive, nouveau Creole complex. Most have French doors that open onto the courtyard. Simple modern tropical furniture and bright floral fabrics give these units a clean, uncluttered look. Each has a fully equipped kitchen and TV. With convertible couches, the units are ideal for families. Kids can maneuver safely within the area. A large apartment with a loft for five to seven persons is $190. Laundry facilities are nearby. ⊠ *Pointe du Bout, Les Trois-Ilets 97229* ☎ *0596/66–03–19* 🖷 *0596/66–07–35* ⊕ *www.villagecreole.com* ⟿ *35 apartments* ⚇ *Kitchens* ▭ *AE, DC, MC, V.*

Fort-de-France & Points North

$$–$$$ 🖾 **Habitation Lagrange.** Nowhere on the island do you feel the style, romance, and elegance of the old plantation society more than in this 19th-century manor house, which is in a rain forest. Everything in the rooms in this main building—from the dual antique shaving mirrors to the flowered commodes in the "water closets"—bespeaks another era. Lunch, like dinner, is served in the formal room with its wall mural of early Martinique, but a successor to the former chef, who left to start his own restaurant, had not been named at this writing. Money is being spent on minor renovations and maintenance, and mercifully, the road was redone in 2002. ⊠ *Marigot 97225* ☎ *0596/53–60–60 or 800/322–2223* 🖷 *0596/53–50–58* ⊕ *www.habitation-lagrange.com* ⟿ *14 rooms, 1 suite* ⚇ *Dining room, tennis court, pool, bar, library* ▭ *AE, DC, MC, V* ¶◎¶ *CP.*

$ 🖾 **Hôtel Squash.** This accommodating, well-maintained hotel is a good base for business or for touring the capital (a 10-minute drive away) or if you need to stay the night after arriving at the airport (just 15 minutes away), before heading out to your hotel in the country. Set in a fashionable suburb, its open-air restaurant and bar enjoy a panorama of the sea and Fort-de-France, as do some of the guest rooms. The French chef knows her way around the kitchen. Rates are lower in the older building without elevators. ⊠ *3 bd. de la Marne, Fort-de-France 97200* ☎ *0596/72–80–80* 🖷 *0596/63–00–74* ⊕ *www.karibea.com* ⟿ *105 rooms, 3 suites* ⚇ *Restaurant, pool, gym, spa, squash, bar, business services, meeting rooms, Internet, car rental* ▭ *AE, DC, MC, V* ¶◎¶ *EP.*

$ 🖾 **Leyritz Plantation.** Sleeping on a former sugar plantation, be it in a cottage or one of the renovated slave cabins, is a novelty. The isolated Leyritz sits on 16 lush acres. Cottages have rough-wood beams, (some) mahogany four-posters, and secretaries. Ironically, it's 10 of the 20 newer bungalows that are smaller and lack individuality, but they do have sea views. Except when tours come through, it's very quiet here. A taxi will charge $75 from the airport, so most people pick up a rental car. However, if the sun has set, stay closer to the airport and chart your course in the morning. ✉ *Basse-Pointe 97218* ☎ *0596/78–53–92* 🖷 *0596/78–92–44* ➘ *70 rooms* ⚭ *Restaurant, tennis court, pool, bar* 🖶 *AE, MC, V* ⏐◉⏐ *BP.*

$ ⚏ **Résidence Oceane.** This fanciful Creole inn overlooks the Atlantic, with an unobstructed panorama of cliffs that meet blue ocean. The bungalows are many steps down a hillside splashed with bouganvillea. This patch of ocean is Tartane, the wild side of Caravelle peninsula. Each bungalow has five rooms decorated with yellow and blue fabrics (there are a few bunk beds). Air-conditioning is extra, about $5 a day; televisions are also available. A surfing school is on-site, and surfers and the young love this fun, friendly place, as do families. English is spoken. Although the hotel is only 20 minutes from the airport, a taxi is $55. ✉ *Anse Bonneville Trinité, Tartane 97220* ☎ *0596/58–73–73* 🖷 *0596/58–33–95* ➘ *24 bungalows* ⚭ *Fans, kitchenettes, pool, beach; no TV in some rooms* 🖶 *MC, V* ⏐◉⏐ *EP.*

$ ⚏ **Valmenière.** The hotel closest to the airport, it is ideal for first-night stays, when your flight arrives too late to navigate a long drive to a remote hotel. Perched on a hilltop overlooking Fort-de-France, it is squeaky clean, efficient, and wired for work. Suites are large, with smoky blue shades and coral marble lamps and mirrors, desks, and a separate entrance to the living room. Business rooms have beds you can fold up, turning the room into a flexible office space. The hotel offers most business services, including translation. A good restaurant, an infinity pool, and a sun roof share the top floors. ✉ *Av. des Arawaks, Fort-de-France 97200* ☎ *0596/75–75–75* 🖷 *0596/75–69–70* ⊕ *www.karibea.com* ➘ *116 rooms, 4 suites* ⚭ *2 restaurants, pool, gym, bar, shop, business services, meeting rooms, Internet* 🖶 *AE, MC, V* ⏐◉⏐ *CP.*

¢ ⚏ **La Caravelle.** This simple hotel built in 1985 and lovingly maintained by the Combaluziers, the hands-on owners, was totally renovated in 2002. Now it's new everything, from floor tiles and wall paint to furniture and bathrooms, and the prices have remained pleasantly low. The lack of a pool is compensated for by vistas of Tartane's beach, L'Anse L'Etang, which is many steps down, and by extra-special food at the restaurant. Most guests rent a car to get here, but Nicole can arrange a taxi for the initial transfer from the airport. Jean Luc, a Frenchman with the king's English, willingly helps you plot your course. ✉ *L'Anse L'Etang, Trinité Route de Chateau Dubuc, Tartane 97220* ☎ *0596/58–07–32* 🖷 *0596/ 58–07–90* ➘ *14 studios, 1 1-bedroom apartment* ⚭ *Restaurant, fans, kitchenettes, car rental* ⊕ *http://perso.wanadoo.fr/hotelcaravelle* 🖶 *AE, MC, V* ⏐◉⏐ *CP.*

Where to Eat

Martinique's restaurants serve classic French, contemporary, and creole cuisines, and their cellars are generally filled with fine French wines. You can find some great spots in the countryside that serve a savory combination of creole and French cuisines, using local produce such as breadfruit, yucca, and christophenes. The farther you venture from tourist hotels, the less likely you are to discover English-speaking islanders, but don't let that stop you.

The local creole specialties are *colombo* (curry), *accras* (cod or vegetable fritters), *crabes farcis* (stuffed land crab), *écrevisses* (freshwater crayfish), *boudin* (creole blood sausage), *lambi* (conch), *langouste* (clawless Caribbean lobster), *blaff* (fish or shellfish plunged into seasoned stock). And, if you like your *poisson* (fish) or any other dish with a little hit of hot, try the *chien* sauce; it literally means "dog" sauce. It's made from onions, shallots, peppers, oil, and vinegar. The favorite local libation is 'ti punch—four parts white rum and one part sugarcane syrup.

Most restaurants offer a prix-fixe menu, often with several choices of appetizers and main courses, sometimes with wine. Finding a cheap American-style bite for lunch is not impossible. The supermarkets often have snack bars with sandwiches, as do the bakeries. DeliFrance, the French deli chain, has locations in most touristic areas. And there are crêperies and pizza shacks, even an African pizza place in Le François.

WHAT TO WEAR   For dinner, casual resort wear is appropriate. Generally, men do not wear jackets and ties, as they did in decades past, but they do wear collared shirts. Women typically wear light cotton sundresses, short or long. At dinnertime, beach attire is too casual for most restaurants. Nice shorts are okay for lunch, depending on the venue. Keep in mind, in Martinque lunch is usually a wonderful three-course, two-hour affair.

South of Fort-de-France

BARBECUE
$$
✕ **Le Grange Inn.** Nearly every item is cooked over the open grill, top-quality meats, fish, and fresh jumbo crayfish, and with five sauces, from *chien* to *beurre blanc,* available. A fun starter is the chicken wings done in a Bacardi–brown sugar sauce. The prix-fixe menus, at several price levels, represent a good value. A kids' menu offers crispy fried fish or chicken tenders rub-a-dub style (that means with peanut sauce). You'll find a large and good selection of French wines. The circular red-brick bar has promoted many friendships. ⊠ *Village Créole, Pointe du Bout, Les Trois-Ilets* ☎ *0596/66–01–66* ▤ *AE, MC, V.*

ECLECTIC
$$
✕ **Fatzo.** Despite the connotations of its name, this former 1890 residence is one grande dame that has it all: food, service, hospitality, history, and a good crowd of interesting types, from fun locals to yachties. Chef Pascal is Swiss, and has a global repertoire from his many travels. He puts a contemporary twist on his preparations and his pairings such as the duo of veal and pork filets in a wild mushroom sauce. Shrimp with a garlic confit and coconut is yet another surprise pairing. His plate presentations are works of art. And then there's the *gratin de fruits* (layered and baked fruits with white chocolate) for dessert. ⊠ *11 rue Felix Eboue, Anse d'Arlet* ☎ *0596/68–62–79* ▤ *MC, V* ☽ *Closed Mon.*

$–$$
✕ **Les Passagers du Vent.** In a pretty brick building on the main street of the village, the chef/owners, Frenchman Stephane Ourey and his wife Aurelie, create superb Franco-Caribbean dishes: *filet de merou* (a local white fish) poached in coconut milk; fried breadfruit; duck breast in raspberry sauce; and bouillabaisse creole. Perfect profiteroles and premium ice creams in tropical flavors are dessert bests. Funky and fun—there's a fish skeleton encased in plexiglass—the place presents hip music and rotating art shows. ⊠ *27 rue de l'Impératrice Joséphine, Les Trois-Ilets* ☎ *0596/68–42–11* ▤ *AE, MC, V* ☽ *Closed Sun. and Sept.*

¢–$$
Fodor$Choice
★
✕ **'Ti Plage.** This is one fun beach bar, from the Continental "breakfast club" attended by those about to go down deep with the nearby dive center to the Friday-night "couscous royale," (reservations needed). The good-time sounds echo across the quiet, mint-green lagoon. "Beach food" is taken to another level at this creole-style restaurant surrounded by coconut palms. Painted in Caribbean colors—celery green, guava, and saffron—with a wooden bar, it is *inches* from the water. Menu favorites are crêpes, salads, prawns flambéed with pastis, and shish kebabs. Owner—and bartender—Alain is a true mixologist and makes incredible cocktails with skewered fruit as a garnish. ⊠ *Anse-d'Artlets* ☎ *0696/29–59–89* ▤ *No credit cards* ☽ *Closed Mon.*

FRENCH
★ $$
✕ **Le Plein Soleil.** Chef Francois Xavier Gayalin creates one memorable prix-fixe after another. He graduated from the École Superieure de Cuisine Française in Paris, where he last worked at the esteemed Le Parc au Cerfs. Xavier is a rising star and, at 25, his cuisine has a multi-lay-

ered complexity that usually comes only with decades of experience. For example, try the soup of puréed white beans and foie gras with bacon; a pork tenderloin rolled in black walnuts with a reduction of balsamic vinegar, red wine, tomatoes, raisins, and honey; or a mousse of prunes with almond milk. The cuisine is as artistic as the surroundings. ⊠ *Hôtel Le Plein Soleil, Villa Lagon Sarc, Pointe Thalemont, Le François* ☎ *0596/ 38–07–77* ⌘ *Reservations essential* ▭ *MC, V.*

ITALIAN
★ $$$
✕ **Sapori d'Italia.** Valentina, the Milanese owner of this terrace restaurant, is confident that her Italian food is the island's most authentic. It is. The quality of product shows through in every dish from the beef carpaccio to the homemade gnocchi with a Gorgonzola–crème fraîche sauce. The marinara is like grandmama's. The long wine list is a good mix of Italian and French vintages, with many half-bottles. You will be too curious not to try the chocolate salami. Finish with a perfect espresso and a grappa and listen to Valentina sing after supper, in both Italian and Creole. ⊠ *Village Créole, Pointe du Bout, Les Trois-Ilets* ☎ *0596/ 66–15–85* ▭ *AE, MC, V* ☉ *Closed Tues. and 3 weeks in June.*

SEAFOOD
$$–$$$
✕ **La Maison de l'Ilet Oscar.** You must be fetched by yawl ($50 for 1-6 persons) from Le François to land at this Robinson Crusoe bistro. You will be taken to Joséphine's bath, a gorgeous shallow area with white sand, where Napoléon's wife would swim in the emerald water, for 'ti punch and accras. Then chose from three prix-fixe menus created by a French chef–served at the water's edge: chicken (the cheapest), fresh fish, or lobster (the most expensive). This vintage Creole hotel, won by the owner's grand-uncle in a poker game in 1935, has four atmospheric guest rooms ($). ⊠ *La Maison de l'Ilet Oscar, Baie de François, Ilet Oscar* ☎ *0696/45–33–30* ⌘ *Reservations essential* ▭ *MC, V.*

Fort-de-France & Points North

CAFÉS
★ $$
✕ **Mille Et Une Brindilles.** At this trendy salon, aromatic pots of tea come in flavors like vanilla and black current, as well as Darjeeling and other favorites. These complement some of the best-ever desserts, like the cocoa-dusted marquise au chocolat. Several *fraicheurs* offer a litany of tapenades, olive cakes, flans, couscous, etc. for lunch. Fred, the cute, bubbly Parisian who is both chef and proprietress, is the queen of terrines and can make a delicious paté out of anything—vegetable, fish, or meat. For non-tea-totalers, there are cocktails, beer, and wine. With red walls, the decor is Morroccan à la Paris flea market. ⊠ *27 rue du Prof. R. Garcin, Rte. de Didier, Didier, Fort-de-France* ☎ *596/71–75–61* ▭ No credit cards ☉ *No dinner except on the last Fri. of each month.*

CARIBBEAN
$–$$
✕ **Couleurs Locales.** As the name suggests, this is a local restaurant, with colorful food, plus views of a church and its steeple and of the luxuriant mountains. Chef René may tell you that he doesn't speak English, but he can cook from the heart. Happily, someone has translated the menu, and you will find such delicacies as shrimp fritters, callalou and pumpkin soups, smoked chicken with pineapple sauce, breadfruit patties, stewed fish, crayfish, lobster, duck fillet with passion-fruit sauce, and sautéed pork with dark rum and cinnamon. As the bell tolls, a favorite American oldie plays "500 miles, 500 miles from my home." ⊠ *Morne-Vert* ☎ *0596/55–59–12* ▭ *AE, MC, V* ☉ *Closed Mon. No dinner Sun.*

★ $–$$
✕ **Le Colibri.** Gregarious Joel Paladino is lovingly continuing a family culinary tradition with this little local spot in the island's northeastern reaches. His beautiful twin sisters are the chefs. Begin with deep green callalou soup with crab, conch pie, or avocado and crab salad, and go on to grilled lobster with a side of christophene gratin, or the rabbit blanquette. Some of the traditional creole dishes, like pigeon stuffed with pureed

chicken and veal, and *cochon au lait* (suckling pig), are favorites on Sundays. There's a good wine list. The view across the ocean is spectacular: if you're lucky, you'll see a rainbow. ⊠ *4 rue des Colibris, Morne-des-Esses, Ste-Marie* ☎ *0596/69–91–95* ⊟ *AE, MC, V* ⊙ *Closed Mon.*

★ ¢–$$ ✕ **Le Fromager.** To reach this restaurant from the port, take a left at Font St. Denis and ask your car to climb the steep hill. Then, once you park and walk down a long set of stairs, you will be rewarded with a superb, 360-degree harbor view and cooling breezes. Tables in the open-air dining room are covered in white lace, in contrast to the big bamboo wall adornments. And the food: Chef Nancy's avocado stuffed with saltfish and farina rests on banana leaves and is *the* best. However, the *ecrivesses Columbo* (curried crayfish) are remarkable. Her husband René happily dispenses pastis, punch coco, or that perfect half-bottle of Sancerre. ⊠ *Quartier St. James, St. Pierre* ☎ *0596/78–19–07* ⊟ *MC, V.*

CONTEMPORARY ✕ **La Canne á Sucre.** This tiny restaurant on the road to Schoelcher seats
★ $$–$$$ only 40 people, but you are treated with a sincere, personalized hospitality. Chef Gerard Virginus puts his heart into his *haute nouvelle* Antilles gastronomy, which he presents at lunch and dinner with artistry. *Foie gras* is sautéed with tropical fruits, a fabulous rabbit and prune terrine comes with an onion confit, duck breast with *vieux rhum* sauce, local fish—a fillet of *vivaneau*—with vanilla sauce. The wine list includes varietals from Sancerres to St-Émilions. The pastry chef turns out delicate creations, studies in flavors, colors, and shapes. ⊠ *Patio de Cluny,* *Fort-de-France* ☎ *0596/63–33–95* ⌘ *Reservations essential* ⊟ *AE, MC, V* ⊙ *Closed Sun.*

FRENCH ✕ **La Belle Epoque.** The glasses are crystal and the cutlery proper silver
★ $$–$$$$ in this antiques-filled dining room of a century-old, white-pillared mansion in the upscale suburb of Didier. The ever-popular garden-view terrace has been expanded and covered with a canopy. The food is divine—and French. Giant prawns in a Scotch cream sauce segue to lamb fillet with carmelized shallots, tonka beans, and a rich wine sauce with herbes de Provence. Owner Martine, a statuesque blonde who interjects Motown classics between French ballads, makes this a personality palace. Finish with a *vieux rhum* from the 1930s, '50s, or '90s. ⊠ *97 rte. de Didier, Didier, Fort-de-France* ☎ *0596/64–41–19* ⊟ *MC, V* ⊙ *Closed Sun.*

$$–$$$ ✕ **Le Dôme.** The word needs to get out about this spot on the top floor of the Valmenière with a panorama of Fort-de-France by night. Dinner here is definitely a gastronomic experience. The most appealing items are à la carte: cream of breadfruit soup with bacon; marinated salmon with cythere plums and shredded chayote remoulade; foie gras served on a pineapple Tartin; a salad of maché and crayfish with a mango vinaigrette—and those are just for starters. Mains might be pan-fried sea scallops with lemongrass and carrot pudding, or grilled salmon with asparagus coulis. However, the prix-fixe is a super deal. ⊠ *Hôtel Valmeniere, av. des Arawaks, Fort-de-France* ☎ *0596/75–75–75* ⊟ *AE, MC, V.*

$–$$$ ✕ **Cocoaplage.** Waves pummel the jagged cliffs and you can better witness that if you ask your waiter to pull your table onto the sand. On weekends and Wednesday night you'll hear live salsa bands, and on Sundays jazz. But the food is far better than that of the usual fun beach-front restaurant. Chef/owner Eric Melenec was previously the chef at Plein Soleil, and his repertoire is global, with contemporary French dishes like Camembert with apricots and prunes; creole crayfish with coconut milk and vieux rhum; and veal kidneys in port. Five salads are on the lunch menu. ⊠ *L'Anse L'Etang, Tartane* ☎ *0696/33–39–86* ⊟ *MC, V* ⊙ *No dinner Sun. No lunch Mon.*

$–$$ ✕ **La Caravelle.** At this gastronomic find in Tartane the amicable chef/ owner Jean Luc puts a French twist on local produce and dishes and puts country music from the 1950s on the sound system. Start with callalou, a local soup of greens with a crab base, then move on to avocado with smoked salmon and lime crème fraîche. Fresh fish is given a simple sauté and set upon a passion-fruit sauce, with rollades of fresh spinach. Finish with an anise-flavored crème brûlée. Enjoy the sea view from the terrace or call for take-out. Lunch is served topside: simple and delicious crêpes and salads. ⊠ *Hotel La Caravelle, rte. du Château Dubuc, Tartane* ☎ *0596/58–07–32* ▤ *MC, V* ◠ *Reservations essential.*

SEAFOOD ✕ **Chez Les Pecheurs.** This is the kind of beach restaurant you expect but
$–$$ seldom find anymore in the islands. It all began when owner Palmont, who made his living fishing, would come back in and grill a fish or two for his own lunch. He now devotes most of his energies to fish farming. Thursdays, Fridays, and Saturdays are crayfish nights. The fisherman's platter (which might be tuna, marlin, or loup) with two special sauces is served for lunch and dinner with red beans and rice. On weekend nights local bands play. The bar opens daily at 10:30 AM. ⊠ *Le Bord de Mer, Carbet* ☎ *0696/23–95–59 or 0596/78–05–72* ▤ *MC, V.*

Beaches

All of Martinique's beaches are open to the public, but hotels charge a fee for nonguests to use changing rooms and facilities. There are no official nudist beaches, but topless bathing is prevalent. Unless you're an expert swimmer, steer clear of the Atlantic waters, except in the area of Cap Chevalier and the Caravelle Peninsula. The soft white-sand beaches are south of Fort-de-France; to the north, the beaches are hard-packed gray volcanic sand. Some of the most pleasant beaches are around Ste-Anne and Ste-Luce.

Anse-à-l'Ane. There are picnic tables and a nearby shell museum. Cool off in the bar of Le Calalou hotel.

Anse-Mitan. You'll find golden sand and excellent snorkeling. Small, family-owned bistros are half hidden among palm trees nearby.

Anse-Trabaud. On the Atlantic side, across the southern tip of the island from Ste-Anne, there's nothing here but white sand and the sea.

Baie des Anglais. Drive through a plantation in Ste-Anne and pay the owner two bucks to get to this huge, quiet, sandy beach with a bit of surf.

Diamant. The island's longest beach (2½ mi [4 km]) has a splendid view of Diamond Rock, but the waters are rough.

★ **Les Salines.** A 1½-mi (2½-km) cove of soft white sand lined with coconut palms is a short drive south of Ste-Anne. Les Salines is awash with families and children during holidays and on weekends but quiet and uncrowded during the week—even at the height of the winter season. This beach, especially the far end, is most appealing.

Pointe du Bout. The beaches here are small, man-made, and lined with luxury resorts, including the Sofitel Bakoua.

Pointe Marin. Stretching north from Ste-Anne, this is a good windsurfing and waterskiing spot with restaurants, campsites, sanitary facilities, and a $3 charge. Club Med is on the northern edge.

Sports & the Outdoors

BOATING & Only people very familiar with handling marine craft should consider
SAILING striking out on the rough Atlantic side. The Caribbean side is much calmer—more like a vast lagoon rather than an actual sea. If you are unsure of your nautical prowess, cruises can be arranged through sev-

eral companies. You can rent Hobie Cats, Sunfish, and Sailfish by the hour from hotel beach shacks. As an example of bareboat prices, a Dufour 38-ft costs $2,335 a week in high season through Sunsail, $1,505 in low season. A Sunodyssey 45.2-ft charters for $3,270 or $2,110, depending on the season. **Club Nautique du Marin** (✉ Le François ☎ 0596/74–92–48) rents Hobie Cats, Windsurfers, small boats, and a large monohull, a 45-ft Gypsy. This yacht club has a sailing school as well, for both kids and adults; although most instruction is in French, the school will try to accommodate English-speakers. **Moorings Antilles Françaises** (✉ Le Marin ☎ 0596/74–75–39 🖷 0596/74–76–44 ⊕ www.moorings. com), one of the largest bareboat operations in the world, has a fleet of some 30 boats in Martinique, including catamarans and monohulls. Boats can also be rented fully crewed, and provisioning is another option. **Sunsail** (✉ Le Marin ☎ 0596/74–77–61, 800/889–2248, 866/644–2327 in the U.S. ⊕ www.sunsail.com) has joined with Stardust Yacht Charters to form one of the largest yacht-charter companies in the world. Although it's primarily a bareboat operation, skippers can be hired by the week by those with limited experience or are available to instruct charterers in sailing skills and local waters. Ocean kayaks can be rented, too, and must be reserved in advance. **Turquoise Yachting Location** (✉ Pointe du Bout Marina, Trois-Ilets ☎ 0596/66–10–74 ⊕ www.turquoise-yachting. com) specializes in runabouts, starting with a Merry Fisher 450 with a 6-h.p. motor, for which you do not need a boating license. It rents for $30 an hour, $130 a day. It's up from there with Boston Whalers for $150 for four hours. Prices are without gas, which is about $40 for a half-day. A license or *permis* is needed for anything over 9 h.p. **Windward Island Cruising Company** (✉ Marina du Marin, Le Marin ☎ 0596/74–31–14 ⊕ www.sailing-adventure.com) has sailboats from 30 ft to a commodious 70-ft catamaran.

CYCLING Mountain biking is popular in mainland France, and now it has reached Martinique. You can rent a VTT (Vélo Tout Terrain), a bike specially designed with 18 speeds to handle all terrains for $15 with helmet, delivery, and pick-up from your hotel, though it requires a $150 credit card deposit. **V.T.Tilt** (✉ Les Trois-Ilets ☎ 0596/66–01–01) has an English-speaking owner who loves to put together groups for fun tours, either half-day or full, which include lunch. They can be beach, river, or mountain rides, tours of plantations or horse ranches, historic, adventure, and nature experiences.

DAYSAILS *Le Creole/Cata Kreyol* (✉ Pointe du Boute Marina, Les Trois-Ilets ☎ 0596/66–10–23), two sister catamarans, offer a variety of options for half- ($36) or full-day ($75.50) excursions, including a 4x4 adventure through sugarcane and banana plantations, or a sail to St. Pierre with a side trip to the Depaz Distillery. Those aboard all day enjoy unlimited rum libations, a good, multicourse lunch (half-lobsters are $9 extra) with wine, and great CD sounds in four languages.

FISHING Fish cruising these waters include tuna, barracuda, dolphinfish, kingfish, and bonito, and the big game—white and blue marlins. **Bleu Marine Evasion** (✉ Le Diamant ☎ 0596/76–46–00) offers fishing excursions as well as day sails. The owner of the *Limited Edition* (✉ Marina du Marin, Le Marin ☎ 0596/76–24–20 or 0696/98–48–68), a fully loaded Davis 47-ft fishing boat, goes out with five anglers for $150 per person for a half day, or a $260 for a full day. Charters can be arranged for up to five days on Captain René Alaric's 37-ft *Rayon Vert* (✉ Auberge du Vare, Case-Pilote ☎ 0596/78–80–56 or 0696/98–48–68).

GOLF The **Golf Country Club de la Martinique** (✉ Les Trois-Ilets ☎ 0596/68–32–81) has a par-71, 18-hole Robert Trent Jones course with an English-

slots are open Monday–Saturday noon–3 AM; for the other games things start rolling at 8 PM.

DANCE CLUBS Your hotel or the tourist office can put you in touch with the current "in" places. It's also wise to check on opening and closing times and cover charges. For the most part, the discos draw a mixed crowd—Martinicans and tourists, and although predominately a younger crowd, all ages go dancing here. **Crazy Nights** (⊠ Ste-Luce ☎ 0596/68–56–68) remains popular because it is all about having one crazy night. With upward to 1,000 partying people, your chances are good here. **Le Cheyenne** (⊠ 6/8 rue Joseph Compere, Fort-de-France ☎ 0596/70–31–19) is like a glittery Miami disco with international music and zouk—and dancing until the wee hours. **Le Top 50** (⊠ Zone Artisanale, La Trinité ☎ 0596/58–61–43) is one of the few night spots in the area where tourists, surfers, and locals all come together to party. **Yucca Bar** (⊠ Zac de Rivière Roche, Fort-de-France ☎ 0596/60–48–36), with a Mexican motif and Tex-Mex food, is known for its piano bar and for the innovative local bands that perform, usually on Wednesdays.

MUSIC CLUBS Jazz musicians, like their music, tend to be informal and independent. They rarely hold regular gigs. Zouk music mixes Caribbean rhythm and an Occidental tempo with Creole words. Jacob Devarieux is the leading exponent of this style and is occasionally on the island. You'll hear zouk played by one of his followers at the hotels and clubs.

Calembesse Cafe (⊠ 19 bd. Allegre Le Marin ☎ 0596/74–69–27) pleases a diverse crowd—mostly older types. Jazz is the norm, and often it is background for a talented local songbird. Funky and hip, the interior is a bit rough, but civilized. Lunch and dinner are served, and on Saturday nights if you don't reserve for dinner you will not have a seat. Best, there's no cover charge. At **La Case de Da Paulette** (⊠ Village Créole, Pointe du Bout, Les Trois-Ilets ☎ 0596/66–15–15), with corrugated aluminum walls papered with vintage newspapers like an old Criollo cottage, you might see anything from a ventriloquist to musicians playing limbo and samba to the crooner Alex Rosa. **Havana Café** (⊠ Village Créole, Pointe du Bout, Les Trois-Ilets ☎ 0596/66–15–93) often has singing guitarists. **Le Molokoi** (⊠ Le Diamant ☎ 0596/76–48–63) is a hot spot for zouk and pop music. When owner Valentina of **Sapori D'Italia** (⊠ Village Créole, Pointe du Bout Les Trois-Ilets ☎ 0596/66–15–85) turns her talents to the microphone, she turns on the electronic keyboard and sings like an angel in Italian, French, and even Creole. **Les Soirees de l'Amphore** (⊠ Anse-Mitan ☎ 0596/66–03–03), a piano bar, is a mini-restaurant, too. You might hear anything from funk, soul, and disco to international music from the 1970s and '80s. Wednesdays there are live soirees and Thursday is karaoke night. **La Villa Créole** (⊠ Anse-Mitan ☎ 0596/66–05–53) is a bistro whose owner, Guy Dawson, strums nightly on the guitar—everything from Piaf to Sting, and some original ditties. His understudy is a handsome Frenchman who might first appear as your waiter. In season you'll find one or two combos playing at clubs and hotels, but it's only at **West Indies** (⊠ Bd. Alfassa, Fort-de-France ☎ 0596/63–77), next to the tourist office, that there are regular jazz sessions.

ISLAND CULTURE **L'Atrium** (⊠ Bd. Général de Gaulle, Fort-de-France ☎ 0596/70–79–29 or 0596/60–78–78), Martinique's cultural center, is where large-scale theater, dance, and musical performances take place.

Exploring Martinique

The north of the island will appeal to nature lovers, hikers, and mountain climbers. The drive from Fort-de-France to St-Pierre is particularly

speaking pro, a pro shop, bar, and restaurant. The club offers special greens fees to cruise-ship passengers. Normal greens fees are $46; an electric cart costs another $46. For those who don't mind walking while admiring the Caribbean view between the palm trees, club trolleys are $6. There are no caddies.

HIKING The island has 31 marked hiking trails. At the beginning of each, a notice is posted advising on the level of difficulty, the duration of a hike, and any interesting points to note. The **Parc Naturel Régional de la Martinique** (⊠ 9 bd. Général de Gaulle, Fort-de-France ☎ 0596/73–19–30) organizes inexpensive guided excursions year-round.

HORSEBACK Excursions and lessons are available at several places on the island. At
RIDING **Black Horse Ranch** (⊠ Les Trois-Ilets ☎ 0596/68–37–80), 1-hr trail rides ($22) go into the countryside and across waving cane fields, two hours on the trail ($32) bring riders near the beach. Only western saddles are used. Semi-private lessons ($32 a person) are in French or English. **Ranch Jack** (⊠ Anse-d'Arlets ☎ 0596/68–37–69) has trail rides (English saddle) across the countryside for $22 an hour; half-day excursions go through the country and forests to the beach. Beverages are included for $43. Little English is spoken at **Ranch de Trois Caps** (⊠ Cap Macré, Le Marin ☎ 0596/74–70–65), but for two hours you can ride (western) on the wild southern beaches and across the countryside for $36. Rides go out in the morning and afternoon, every day but Monday. Reserve in advance.

SCUBA DIVING & Martinique has several dive operators who explore the old shipwrecks,
SNORKELING coral gardens, and other undersea sites. **Okeanos Club** (⊠ Village Pierre et Vacances, Ste-Luce ☎ 0596/62–52–36) has a morning trip close to shore; in the afternoon, dive boats go out to open water. A single dive is $41, a package of three dives, including the initial "baptism," is $111. Lessons (including children's) with a PADI certified instructor, can be held in English. **Plongee Passion** (⊠ Le Plage, St. Pierre ☎ 0596/68–71–78) has two bases and is a PADI center. One dive is $39, and there are packages available for 3, 6, or 10 dives.

SPORTS CENTERS The **La Basse de Plein Air et Loisirs** (☎ 0596/58–24–32), on the Caravelle Peninsula, is an open-air sports and leisure center offering tennis, windsurfing, waterskiing, and other activities.

TENNIS & There are two courts at **Le Bakoua** (⊠ Pointe du Bout ☎ 0596/66–02–
SQUASH 02). The **Diamant-Novotel** (⊠ Pointe de la Chery, Le Diamant ☎ 0596/76–42–42) has two tennis courts. There are six excellent courts at **Framissima** (⊠ La Batelière, Schoelcher ☎ 0596/61–64–52). In addition to its links, the **Golf Country Club de la Martinique** (⊠ Les Trois-Ilets ☎ 0596/68–32–81) has three lighted tennis courts. **La Ligue Régionale de Tennis** (⊠ Petit Manoir, Lamentin ☎ 0596/51–50–01) is a tennis club where an hour's court time averages $8 for nonmembers. **Le Mercure Diamant** (⊠ Pointe de la Chery, Le Diamant ☎ 0596/76–46–00) has two tennis courts. There is one court at **Leyritz Plantation** (⊠ Bourg, Basse-Pointe ☎ 0596/78–53–92). There are three squash courts at the aptly named **Squash Hotel** (⊠ 3 bd. de la Marine, Fort-de-France ☎ 0596/72–80–80).

WINDSURFING At **Ecole du Surf Français** (⊠ Anse Bonneville Trinité, Tartane ☎ 0596/58–0096 ⊕ www.surfmartinique.com), near Residence Oceane, individual ($28) or group lessons ($19) are given to ages five and up. English and Spanish are spoken. Surf- and bodyboards (with fins) can be rented for three hours for $14, or for the day for $23. **UPCA Hotel Club** (⊠ Le Plage, Le Vauclin ☎ 0596/74–33–68) rents out windsurfing boards.

Shopping

French fragrances and designer scarves, fine china and crystal, leather goods, wine (amazingly inexpensive at supermarkets), liquors, and liqueurs are all good buys in Fort-de-France. Purchases are further sweetened by the 20% discount on luxury items when paid for with traveler's checks or certain major credit cards. Among local items, look for Creole gold jewelry, such as hoop earrings and heavy bead necklaces; white and dark rum; and handcrafted straw goods, pottery, and tapestries.

Areas & Malls

★ The area around the cathedral in Fort-de-France has a number of small shops that carry luxury articles. Of particular note are the shops on **rue Victor Hugo, rue Moreau de Jones, rue Antoine Siger,** and **rue Lamartine.** The **Galleries Lafayette** department store on rue Schoelcher in downtown Fort-de-France sells everything from perfume to paté. On the outskirts of Fort-de-France, the **Centre Commercial de Cluny, Centre Commercial de Dillon, Centre Commercial de Bellevue,** and **Centre Commercial la Rond Point** are among the major shopping malls.

You'll find more than 100 boutiques at **La Galleria** in Le Lamentin. In Pointe du Bout there are a number of appealing tourist shops, both in **Village Créole** and on the surrounding streets.

Specialty Items

CHINA & CRYSTAL **Cadet Daniel** (⊠ 72 rue Antoine Siger, Fort-de-France ☎ 0596/71–41–48) sells Lalique, Limoges, and Baccarat. **Roger Albert** (⊠ 7 rue Victor Hugo, Fort-de-France ☎ 0596/71–71–71) carries designer crystal.

CLOTHING **Cannelle** (⊠ Pointe du Bout, Les Trois-Ilets ☎ 0596/66–05–33), across the street from the Village Créole, has smashing French maillots and bikinis, name-brand resort wear for women and men, sandals, watches, and backpacks. **Mounia** (⊠ rue Perrinon, near the old House of Justice, Fort-de-France ☎ 0596/73–77–27), owned by a former Yves St. Laurent model, carries the top French designers for women and men. **Toi & Moi** (⊠ Pointe du Bout, Les Trois-Ilets ☎ 0596/66–05–02) specializes in his-and-hers sportswear with French élan, in cotton and natural fabrics. It is also the exclusive purveyor of Maogany Artisanat of Les Saintes, which includes women's tops, skirts, and dresses, as well as men's loose, lightweight tropical pants, shorts, and shirts.

HANDICRAFTS Following the roadside signs advertising ATELIERS ARTISANALES (art studios) can yield unexpected treasures, many of them reasonably priced. **Atelier Céramique** (⊠ Le Diamant ☎ 0596/76–42–65), which is just outside of the main part of town, displays the ceramics, paintings, and miscellaneous souvenirs of owners and talented artists David and Jeannine England, members of the island's small British expat community. **Art et Nature** (⊠ Ste-Luce ☎ 0596/62–59–19) carries Joel Gilbert's unique wood paintings, daubed with 20–30 shades of earth and sand. **Artisanat & Poterie des Trois-Ilets** (⊠ Les Trois-Ilets ☎ 0596/68–18–01) allows you to watch the creation of Arawak- and Carib-style pots, vases, and jars. **Bois Nature** (⊠ La Semair, Le Robert ☎ 0596/65–77–65) is all about mood—and mystique. The gift items begin with scented soap, massage oil, aromatherapy sprays, and perfumes. Then there are mosquito netting, wind chimes, and sun hats made of coconut fiber. The big stuff includes natural wood-framed mirrors and furniture à la Louis XV. **Centre des Métiers d'Art** (⊠ Rue Ernest Deproge, Fort-de-France ☎ 0596/70–25–01) exhibits authentic local arts and crafts. **Galerie Arti-Bijoux** (⊠ 89 rue Victor Hugo, Fort-de-France ☎ 0596/63–10–62) has some unusual and excellent Haitian art—paintings, sculptures, ceramics, and intricate

jewelry cases. **Galerie de Sophen** (⊠ Pointe du Bout, Les Trois-Ilets ☎ 0596/66–13–64), across from the Village Créole, is a combination of Sophie and Henry, both in name and content. This art gallery showcases the work of a French husband and wife team who live aboard their sailboat and paint the beauty of the sea and the island. At **Galerie du Village Créole** (⊠ Village Créole, Pointe du Bout, Les Trois-Ilets ☎ 0596/66–15–75), watercolors, oil paintings, and other works by local artists and the gallery owner—as well as reproductions—rotate weekly. **La Paille Caraibe** (⊠ Morne des Esses ☎ 0596/69–83–74) is where you can watch artisans weave straw baskets, mats, and hats. **L'Éclat de Verre** (⊠ La Trinité ☎ 0596/58–34–03) specializes in all manner of glittering glass-work. **Victor Anicet** (⊠ Schoelcher ☎ 0596/52–04–40) fashions lovely ceramic masks and vases.

LIQUOR **Depaz Distillery** (⊠ Plantation de la Montagne Pelée, St. Pierre ☎ 0596/78–13–14) owes its fine reputation to consistency of production (rum is produced like vintage wine) and to the volcanic soil and abundant water supply. One of the best rums on the island is the *vieux rhum* from **JM Distillery** (⊠ Macouba ☎ 0596/78–92–55). It was purchased in 2002 by Habitation Clément. You can get some great rum and also tour the grounds of the bucolic 32-acre **Habitation Clément** (⊠ Le François ☎ 0596/54–62–07 ☎ 0596/54–63–50). It is the most popular site among tourists and has produced fine rum for centuries. **Niesson Distillery** (⊠ Carbet ☎ 0596/78–07–90) is a "Mercedes"—a small, family-run operation whose rum is produced from pure sugarcane juice rather than molasses. It is open for tours and tastings, and the shop sells *vieux rhum* that truly rivals cognac. **St. James Distillery** (⊠ Ste-Marie ☎ 0596/69–30–02) is a somewhat wild scene when some dozen tour buses pull in, but the two-story, gingerbread mansion showcases some rum-related antiques, and as at the others, the tasting is on the house.

PERFUMES **Roger Albert** (⊠ 7 rue Victor Hugo, Fort-de-France ☎ 0596/71–71–71) stocks such popular scents as those by Dior, Chanel, and Guerlain.

Nightlife & the Arts

Although Martinique is dotted with lively discos and nightclubs, nightlife isn't confined to partying. Most leading hotels offer nightly entertainment in season, including the marvelous **Les Grands Ballets de Martinique,** one of the finest folkloric dance troupes in the Caribbean. Consisting of about 30 musicians and dancers dressed in traditional costume, the ballet revives the Martinique of yesteryear through dance rhythms such as the beguine or the mazurka. This folkloric group appears Fridays at the hotel Sofitel Bakoua Coralia and Mondays at the Novotel Diamant. **Tche Kreyal,** another folkloric ballet group, which has some 20 performers—many of them children—performs at Les Almandiers in St. Luce on Saturdays. At the Hotel Amyris, the **Kalenda Ballet** dances on Wednesday nights. In addition, many restaurants offer live entertainment, usually on weekends. The Sofitel Bakoua has a Caribbean band at its circular bar; the dancing begins at 8 PM and goes 'til 10 PM. The **Village Créole** complex itself has a good line-up of entertainment in season that includes music, theater, and art expos.

CASINOS The **Casino Batelière Plaza,** (⊠ Schoelcher, Fort-de-France ☎ 596/61–91–51), on the outskirts of Fort-de-France, is divided into two areas: to the left are more than 100 slot machines; to the right you'll need $10, a passport (you must be 18 to play), and the proper attire (jacket and tie for men, dresses for women) to play blackjack, roulette, or baccarat. There are two restaurants; fine dining is offered in an area about the size of a boxing ring. Bands provide even more entertainment on weekends. The

impressive, as is the one across the island, via Morne Rouge, from the Caribbean to the Atlantic. This is Martinique's wild side—a place of waterfalls, rain forest, and mountains. The highlight is Mont Pelée. The south is the more developed half of the island, where the resorts and restaurants are, as well as the beaches.

Numbers in the margin correspond to points of interest on the Martinique map.

WHAT TO SEE **Ajoupa-Bouillon.** This flower-filled 17th-century village amid pineapple
⓫ fields is the jumping-off point for several sights. The Saut Babin is a 40-ft waterfall, half an hour's walk from Ajoupa-Bouillon. The Gorges de la Falaise is a river gorge where you can swim. **Les Ombrages** botanical gardens has marked trails through the rain forest. ⊠ *Ajoupa-Bouillon* ☒ €3.36 ☉ *Daily 9–5:30.*

❹ **Balata.** This quiet little town has two sights worth visiting. Built in 1923 to commemorate those who died in World War I, **Balata Church** is an exact replica of Paris's Sacré-Coeur Basilica. The **Jardin de Balata** (Balata Gardens), created more than 20 years ago by Jean-Philippe Thoze, a professional landscaper and horticulturist, has thousands of varieties of tropical flowers and plants. There are shaded benches from which to take in the mountain view. You can order anthurium and other tropical flowers to be delivered to the airport. ⊠ *Rte. de Balata* ☎ *0596/64–48–73* ☒ €7 ☉ *Daily 9–5.*

❿ **Basse-Pointe.** On the route to this village on the Atlantic coast at the island's northern end you pass many banana and pineapple plantations—agriculture for as far as the eye can see. Just south of Basse-Pointe is a **Hindu temple** built by descendants of the East Indians who settled in this area in the 19th century. The view of the eastern slope of Mont Pelée
★ is terrific. The highlight of Basse-Pointe is the estimable **Leyritz Plantation,** which has been restored as a hotel. When tour groups aren't swarming, the rustic setting, complete with sugarcane factory and gardens, is delightful, and includes the Musée des Figurines Végétales. Local artisan Will Fenton has used bananas, *balisier* (a tall grass), and other local plants to make dolls of famous French women—from Marie Antoinette to Madame Curie—in period costumes. Admission is waived if you are having lunch. ⊠ *Leyritz Plantation, Basse-Pointe* ☎ *0596/78–53–92* ☒ €2.60 ☉ *Daily 10–6.*

❸ **Bellefontaine.** This colorful fishing village has pastel houses on the hillsides and beautifully painted *gommiers* (fishing boats) bobbing in the water. Look for the restaurant built in the shape of a boat.

⓳ **Diamond Rock.** This volcanic mound is 1 mi (1½ km) offshore from the small, friendly village of Le Diamant and is one of the island's best diving spots. In 1804, during the squabbles over possession of the island between the French and the English, the latter commandeered the rock, armed it with cannons, and proceeded to use it as a warship. The British held the rock for nearly a year and a half, attacking any French ships that came along. The French got wind that the British were getting cabin fever on their isolated ship-island, and arranged for barrels of rum to float up on the rock. The French easily overpowered the inebriated sailors, ending one of the most curious engagements in naval history.

⓮ **Dubuc Castle.** At the eastern tip of the Presqu'île du Caravelle are the ruins of this castle, once the home of the Dubuc de Rivery family, who owned the peninsula in the 18th century. According to legend, young Aimée Dubuc de Rivery was captured by Barbary pirates, sold to the Ottoman Empire, became a favorite of the sultan, and gave birth to Mahmud II. You can park your car right after the turn-off for Residence Oceane and walk the dirt road to the ruins.

⑳ Forêt de Montravail. A few miles north of Ste-Luce, this tropical rain forest is ideal for a short hike. Look for the interesting group of Carib rock drawings.

❶ Fort-de-France. With its historic fort and superb location beneath the towering Pitons du Carbet on the Baie des Flamands, Martinique's capital—home to about one-third of the island's 360,000 inhabitants—should be a grand place. It isn't. The most pleasant districts, such as Didier, Belle-vue, and Schoelcher, are on the hillside, and you need a car to reach them. But if you come here by car, you may find yourself trapped in gridlock in the warren of narrow streets in the center of town, especially on cruise-ship days. Parking is difficult, and its best to try for one of the parking garages or—as a second choice—outside public parking areas. A taxi is a good alternative.

There are some good shops with Parisian wares (at Parisian prices) and lively street markets that sell, among other things, human hair for wigs (starting price: €40). Near the harbor is a marketplace where local crafts and souvenirs are sold. Town can be fun, and you probably should just do it. But the heat, exhaust fumes, and litter tend to make exploring here a chore rather than a pleasure. At night the city feels dark and gloomy, with little street life except for the extravagantly dressed prostitutes who openly parade the streets after 10 PM. If you plan to go out, it is best to go with a group.

The heart of Fort-de-France is **La Savane,** a 12½-acre park filled with trees, fountains, and benches. It's a popular gathering place and the scene of promenades, parades, and impromptu soccer matches. Along the east side are numerous snack wagons. Alas, it is no longer a desirable oasis, what with a lot of litter and other problems often found in urban parks. A statue of Pierre Belain d'Esnambuc, leader of the island's first settlers, is unintentionally upstaged by Vital Dubray's vandalized—now head-less—white Carrara marble statue of the empress Joséphine, Napoléon's first wife. The most imposing historic site is **Fort St-Louis,** which runs along the east side of La Savane. It is open Monday–Saturday 9–3, and admission is €4. Across from La Savane, you can catch the ferry *La Vedette* for the beaches at Anse-Mitan and Anse-à-l'Ane and for the 20-minute run across the bay to Pointe du Bout. It costs just €6 and is stress-free—much safer, more pleasant, and faster than by car.

The **Bibliothèque Schoelcher** is the wildly elaborate Romanesque pub-lic library. It was named after Victor Schoelcher, who led the fight to free the slaves in the French West Indies in the 19th century. The eye-popping structure was built for the 1889 Paris Exposition, after which it was dismantled, shipped to Martinique, and reassembled piece by or-nate piece. ⊠ *Corner of rue de la Liberté (runs along west side of La Savane) and rue Perrinon* ☎ *0596/70–26–67* ⊠ *Free* ☉ *Mon. 1–5:30, Tues.–Fri. 8:30–5:30, Sat. 8:30–noon.*

★ Le Musée Régional d'Histoire et d'Ethnographie is a learning experi-ence that is best undertaken at the beginning of your vacation, so you can better understand the history, background, and people of the island. Housed in an elaborate former residence (circa 1888) with balconies and fretwork, it has everything from displays of the garish gold jewelry that prostitutes wore after emancipation to reconstructed rooms of a home of proper, middle-class Martinicans. There is even a display of madras, Creole headdresses with details of how they were tied to indicate if a woman was single, married, or otherwise occupied. ⊠ *10 bd. General* *de Gaulle* ☎ *0596/72–81–87* ✉ *€4* ☉ *Tues. 8–5, Mon.–Fri. 2–5, Sat. 8–noon.*

Rue Victor Schoelcher runs through the center of the capital's primary shopping district, a six-block area bounded by rue de la République, rue de la Liberté, rue de Victor Severe, and rue Victor Hugo. Stores sell Paris fashions and French perfume, china, crystal, and liqueurs, as well as local handicrafts. The Romanesque **St-Louis Cathedral** (⊠ Rue Victor Schoelcher) with its lovely stained-glass windows, was built in 1878, the sixth church on this site (the others were destroyed by fire, hurricane, and earthquake). The Galerie de Biologie et de Géologie at the **Parc Floral et Culturel,** in the northeastern corner of the city center, will acquaint you with the island's exotic flora. There's also an aquarium. The park contains the island's official cultural center, where there are sometimes free evening concerts. ⊠ *Pl. José-Marti, Sermac* ☎ *0596/71–66–25* ✉ *Grounds free; aquarium €5.60; botanical and geological gallery €1.12* ☉ *Park daily dawn–10 PM; aquarium daily 9–7; gallery Tues.–Fri. 9:30–12:30 and 3:30–5:30, Sat. 9–1 and 3–5.*

⑮ Le François. With some 16,000 inhabitants, this is the main city on the Atlantic coast. Many of the old wooden buildings remain and are juxtaposed with concrete structures. The classic West Indian cemetery, with its black-and-white tiles, is still here and a marina is at the end of town. Two of Martinique's best hotels are in this area, as well as some of the most upscale residences. Le François is also noted for its snorkeling. Offshore are the privately owned Les Ilets de l'Impératrice. The islands received that name because, according to legend, this is where Empress Joséphine came to bathe in the shallow basins known as *fonds blancs* because of their white-sand bottoms. Group boat tours leave from the harbor and include lunch and drinks. Prices vary. You can also haggle with a fisherman to take you out for a while on his boat to indulge in the uniquely Martinican custom of standing waist-deep in warm water, sipping a 'ti punch, eating accras, and smoking. Their prices keep going up however, and $50 for one to six persons is what they usually command. There's a fine bay 6 mi (9½ km) farther along the coast at Le Robert, though the town is lackluster.

★ The **Habitation Clément** offers a glimpse into Martinique's colonial past, into the elegance and privilege of plantation society, and is complete with Creole ladies in traditional dresses moving about the grounds. The acreage named the Palm Grove is delightful, with an avenue of palms and park benches. It was all built with the wealth generated by its rum distillery, and its 18th-century splendor has been lovingly preserved. There is fine art displayed and soothing French music plays. Framed vintage labels from rum bottles track the changes in the marketing of rum and the island over the centuries. Enjoy the free tastings at the bar and wander into their retail shop. Consider the Canne Bleu, or an aged rum. ⊠ *Domaine de l'Acajou* ☎ *0596/54–62–07* ⊕ *www.rhum-clement.com* ✉ *€4* ☉ *Daily 9–6.*

⑯ Lamentin. There's nothing pretty about Lamentin; the multibillion-franc airport is its most notable landmark. The rest of the town is a sprawling industrial and commercial zone. But you come here for shopping in the big, fancy shopping mall Euromarché. La Galleria, a megamall of roughly 100 shops and boutiques, offers everything from pâté de foie gras and Camembert to CDs and sunglasses.

⑨ Macouba. Named after the Carib word for "fish," this village was a prosperous tobacco town in the 17th century. Today its clifftop location affords magnificent views of the sea, the mountains, and—on clear days—the neighboring island of Dominica. The **JM Distillery** produces some of the best *vieux rhum* on the island here. A tour and samples are free. Macouba is the starting point for a spectacular drive, the 6-mi (9½-km) **route to Grand' Rivière** on the northernmost point. This is Martinique at its greenest: groves of giant bamboo, cliffs hung with curtains of vines, and 7-ft tree ferns that seem to grow as you watch them. Literally, at the end of the road, is Grand' Rivière, a colorful sprawling fishing village at the foot of high cliffs.

㉓ Le Marin. The yachting capital of Martinique is also known for its colorful August carnival and its Jesuit church, circa 1766. From Le Marin a narrow road leads to picturesque Cap Chevalier (Cape Knight), about 1 mi (1½ km) from town. Most of the buildings are white and very Euro. The marina is lively, and there are waterfront restaurants and clubs.

❼ Le Morne Rouge. This town sits on the southern slopes of the volcano that destroyed it in 1902. Today it's a popular resort spot and offers hikers some fantastic mountain scenery. From Le Morne Rouge you can start the climb up the 4,600-ft **Mont Pelée** volcano. But don't try it without a guide unless you want to get buried alive under pumice stones. Instead, drive up to the Refuge de l'Aileron. From the parking lot it's a mile (1½ km) up a well-marked trail to the summit. Bring a sweatshirt, because there's often a mist that makes the air damp and chilly. From the summit follow the route de la Trace (Route N3), which winds south of Le Morne Rouge to St-Pierre. It's steep and winding, but that didn't stop the *porteuses* of old: balancing a tray, these women would carry up to 100 pounds of provisions on their heads for the 15-hour trek to the Atlantic coast.

❺ Musée Gauguin. Martinique was a brief station in Paul Gauguin's wanderings but a decisive moment in the evolution of his art. He arrived from Panama in 1887 with friend and fellow painter Charles Laval and, having pawned his watch at the docks, rented a wooden shack on a hill above the village of Carbet. Dazzled by the tropical colors and vegetation, Gauguin developed a style, his Martinique period, that directly anticipated his Tahitian paintings. Disappointingly, this modest museum has no originals, only reproductions. There is an exhibit of letters and documents relating to the painter. Also remembered here is the writer Lafcadio Hearn. In his endearing book *Two Years in the West Indies* he provides the most extensive description of the island before St-Pierre was buried in ash and lava. ✉ *Anse-Turin, Carbet* ☎ *0596/78–22–66* 🎟 *€4* ☉ *Daily 9–5:30.*

⑱ Pointe du Bout. This touristic area has resort hotels, among them the Sofitel Bakoua, and a marina. The ferry to Fort-de-France leaves from here. A cluster of boutiques, ice-cream parlors, and rental-car agencies forms the hub from which restaurants and hotels of varying caliber radiate. The beach at Anse-Mitan is one of the best on the island. At Anse-à-l'Ane, a little to the west, is a pretty white-sand beach with picnic tables. There are also numerous small restaurants and inexpensive guest-house hotels here. Ten miles (16 kilometers) south is Anse-d'Arlets, a quiet, unspoiled fishing village.

❽ Le Prêcheur. This quaint town, the last on the northern Caribbean coast, is surrounded by volcanic hot springs. The village itself was the childhood home of Françoise d'Aubigné, who later became the Marquise de Maintenon and the second wife of Louis XIV. At her request, the Sun King donated a handsome bronze bell to the village, which still hangs outside the church. On the way from St-Pierre, the Tomb of the Carib Indians commemorates a sadder event. It is actually a formation of limestone cliffs from which the last of the Caribs are said to have flung themselves to avoid capture by the Marquise's forebears.

Presqu'île du Caravelle. Much of the Caravelle Peninsula, which juts 8 mi (13 km) into the Atlantic Ocean, is under the protection of the Regional Nature Reserve and offers places for trekking, swimming, and sailing. This is also the site of Anse-Spoutourne, an open-air sports and leisure center operated by the reserve. Tartane has a popular beach with cool Atlantic breezes.

Ste-Anne. A lovely white-sand beach and a Catholic church are the highlights of this town on the island's southern tip. To the south of Ste-Anne is Pointe des Salines, the southernmost tip of the island and site of Martinique's best beach. Near Ste-Anne is **La Savane des Pétrifications**, the Petrified Forest. This desertlike stretch was once swampland and is a veritable geological museum, where a few specimens of petrified wood can still be found.

Ste-Luce. This quaint fishing village has a sleepy main street that's deserted at midday, panoramic views across to the island of St. Lucia, and excellent beaches; several resorts are nearby. To the east is Pointe Figuier, an excellent spot for scuba diving. On the way from Ste-Luce to Pointe Figuier is **Ecomusée de Martinique** (⊠ Anse Figuier ☎ 0596/62–79–14), showcasing artifacts from Arawak and Carib settlements through the plantation years. Admission is €4, and it's open Tuesday through Sunday 9–1:30 and 2:30–5.

Ste-Marie. This town has a population of about 20,000 and is the commercial capital of the island's north. There's a lovely mid-19th-century church here. The **Musée du Rhum,** operated by the St. James Rum Distillery, is housed in a graceful, galleried Creole house. Guided tours take in displays of the tools of the trade and include a visit and tasting at the distillery. ⊠ *Ste-Marie* ☎ *0596/69–30–02* ☎ *Free* ☉ *Weekdays 9–5, weekends 9–1, except during the harvest period, Feb.–June (call first).*

Le Musée de la Banane. You probably won't find more cordial hostesses than those here. After navigating the extremely narrow road, you'll arrive at the compound. Excellent graphics and beautiful prints tell the story of the banana (Martinique's primary export) as it makes its way from the fields to your table. A vintage Creole cottage serves as a well-stocked retail shop, and there's a bar and lunch counter—lots of edibles made from bananas. ⊠ *Habitation Limbé* ☎ *0596/69–45–52* ☎ €6 ☉ *Daily 9–5.*

St-Pierre. The rise and fall of St-Pierre is one of the most remarkable stories in the Caribbean. Martinique's modern history began here in 1635. By the turn of the 20th century St-Pierre was a flourishing city of 30,000, known as the Paris of the West Indies. As many as 30 ships at a time stood at anchor. By 1902 it was the most modern town in the Caribbean, with electricity, phones, and a tram. On May 8, 1902, two thunderous explosions rent the air. As the nearby volcano erupted, Mont Pelée split in half, belching forth a cloud of burning ash, poisonous gas, and lava that raced down the mountain at 250 mph. At 3,600°F, it instantly vaporized everything in its path; 30,000 people were killed in two minutes. One man survived. His name was Cyparis, and he was a prisoner in an underground cell in the town's jail. He was later pardoned and afterward was a sideshow attraction in the Barnum & Bailey Circus.

Today St-Pierre is trying to reinvent itself. An Office du Tourisme has been built, as well as a seafront promenade. There are plenty of sidewalk cafés, and you can stroll the main streets and check the blackboards before deciding where to lunch, or go up the hill to a restaurant where the view is spectacular. At night some places will have live music. Like stage sets for a dramatic opera, there are the ruins of the island's first church (built in 1640), the imposing theater, the toppled statues. This city, situated on its naturally beautiful harbor and with its narrow, winding streets, has the feel of a European seaside hill town. Although a lot of the oldest buildings need work, stark modernism has not invaded this burg. As much potential as it has, this is one town in Martinique where real estate is cheap—for obvious reasons.

★ ☾ For those interested in the eruption of 1902, the **Musée Vulcanologique Frank Perret** is a must. Established in 1932, it houses photographs of the old town, documents, and a number of relics—some gruesome—excavated from the ruins, including molten glass, melted iron, and contorted clocks stopped at 8 AM. ✉ *Rue de Victor Hugo* ☎ *0596/78–15–16* 🖅 *€3* ☉ *Daily 9–5.*

The *Cyparis Express* is a small tourist train that runs through the city, hitting the important sights with a running narrative (in French). ✉ *Pl. des Ruines du Figuier* ☎ *0596/55–50–92* 🖅 *€9* ☉ *Departs hourly, weekdays 9:30–1 and 2:30–5:30.*

★ An excursion to **Depaz Distillery** is one of the island's nicest treats. For four centuries it has been at the foot of the volcano. In 1902 the great house was destroyed in the eruption, but soon after it was courageously rebuilt and the fields replanted. A self-guided tour includes the workers' gingerbread cottages, and an exhibit of art and sculpture made from wooden casks and parts of distillery machinery. The tasting room sells their rums, including golden and aged rum (notably Rhum Dore) and distinctive liqueurs made from ginger and basil. ✉ *Mt. Pelée Plantation* ☎ *0596/78–13–14.*

❷ **Schoelcher.** Pronounced "shell-*share*," this suburb of Fort-de-France is home to the University of the French West Indies and Guyana and the site of Martinique's largest convention center, Madiana.

⑰ **Les Trois-Ilets.** Named after the three rocky islands nearby, this lovely little village (population 3,000) has unusual brick and wood buildings roofed with antique tiles. It's known for its pottery, straw, and woodwork, but above all as the birthplace of Napoléon's empress Joséphine. In the square, where there's also a market and a fine *mairie* (town hall), you can visit the simple church where she was baptized Marie-Joseph Tascher de la Pagerie. The Martinicans have always been enormously proud of Joséphine, even though her husband reintroduced slavery on the island and most historians consider her to have been rather shallow.

★ A stone building that held the kitchen of the estate where she grew up houses the **Musée de la Pagerie.** It contains an assortment of memorabilia pertaining to her life and rather unfortunate loves, including a marriage certificate, a love letter written straight from the heart by Napoléon in 1796, and various antiques. The main house blew down in the hurricane of 1766, when Joséphine was three, and the family lived for years above the sugarcane factory, a hot, odiferous and fly-ridden existence. At 16 she was wed (an arranged marriage because her father was a gambling man in need of money) to Alexandre de Beauharnais. After he was assassinated during the Revolution she married Napoléon, but despite his love for her, he divorced her, as she was unable to produce children. She was, however, able to keep her titles, various castles and the equivalent of millions of dollars. ✉ *Les Trois-Ilets* ☎ *0596/68–34–55* 🖅 *€5* ☉ *Tues.–Fri. 9–5, weekends 9–1 and 1:30–5:30.*

The **Maison de la Canne** will teach you everything you ever wanted to know about sugarcane. Exhibits take you through three centuries of cane production, with displays of tools, scale models, engravings, and photographs. ⊠ *Les Trois-Ilets* ☎ *0596/68–32–04* 🎟 *€3* ☯ *Tues.– Sun. 9–5.*

24 **Le Vauclin.** The return of the fishermen at noon is the big event in this important fishing port on the Atlantic. There's also the 18th-century Chapel of the Holy Virgin. Nearby is the highest point in the south, Mont Vauclin (1,654 ft [504 m]). A hike to the top rewards you with one of the best views on the island.

MARTINIQUE A TO Z

To research prices, get advice from other travelers, and book travel arrangements, visit www.fodors.com.

AIR TRAVEL

It's not always easy to get to Martinique from the U.S. At this writing, Air France, which flies daily from Miami with a stopover in Guadeloupe or Port-au-Prince, Haiti, is the only airline with direct connections between the U.S. and Martinique. LIAT flies from San Juan and Barbados, Air Caraïbes from Santo Domingo, both of which have good air connections from the U.S.

Air Caraïbes flies from Guadeloupe and the Guadeloupean islands of Les Saintes, Marie-Galante, and La Désirade, St. Maarten, St. Barths, the Dominican Republic, and St. Lucia. LIAT flies in from Antigua, Barbados, Dominica, Grenada, Guadeloupe, San Juan, St. Lucia, St. Maarten, and Trinidad and Tobago.

🚩 **Air Caraïbes** ☎ 0590/82-47-00 for reservations; 0596/42-18-25 ⊕ www.aircaraibes. com. **Air France** ☎ 0820/820-820. **LIAT** ☎ 0590/21-13-93 ⊕ www.liatairline.com.

AIRPORTS

The contemporary Lamentin International Airport is about a 15-minute taxi ride from Fort-de-France and some 40 minutes from Les Trois-Ilets peninsula.

🚩 **Lamentin International Airport** ☎ 0596/42-16-00.

BOAT & FERRY TRAVEL

Weather permitting, *vedettes* (ferries) operate daily (about every 15 minutes) between Fort-de-France and the marina in Pointe du Bout, as well as between Fort-de-France and Anse-Mitan and Anse-à-l'Ane, and take 15 minutes. Two companies, Madinina and Somatour, operate these ferries. Fares are €3.80 one-way, €6 round-trip. The Quai d'Esnambuc, just minutes from the tourist office, is the arrival and departure point in Fort-de-France. Without question, this is *the* best way to go into the capital, where traffic and parking is a bad tropical dream.

Caribbean Ferries has service to Martinique from Pointe-à-Pitre, Guadeloupe, for €57, €87 round trip; the trip takes about three hours, including a short stop in Dominica. Call or stop by the ferry dock for the schedules.

The **Express des Isles** offers scheduled (though not daily) interisland service aboard a 128-ft, 227-passenger motorized catamaran, linking Martinique with Dominica, Guadeloupe, Les Saintes (with a separate ferry), and St. Lucia. It can be the most pleasurable way to travel, with great views of the islands. Fares run approximately 25% below economy airfares.

Transport Maritime Brudey Freres is the major ferry company, with service from Fort-de-France to Pointe-a-Pitre, Guadeloupe, for €57, € 87 round trip, with a stopover in Dominica. It is generally smooth sailing aboard these large car ferries, called motorized catamarans, and Brudey's are the newest and most impressive. The trip takes four hours. Brudey's also sails to St. Lucia.

⏏ Caribbean Ferries ☎ 0596/63-68-88. **Express des Isles** ☎ 0596/63-12-11. **Madinina** ☎ 0596/63-06-46. **Somatour** ☎ 0596/73-05-53. **Transport Maritime Brudey Ferries** ☎ 0590/90-04-48 in Guadeloupe.

BUSINESS HOURS

BANKS   Banks are open weekdays 7:30–noon and 2:30–4.

POST OFFICES   Post offices are generally open Monday–Saturday 7 AM–6 PM, though many close on Wednesday at 1 PM.

SHOPS   Stores that cater to tourists are generally open weekdays 8:30–6, Saturday 8:30–1. Many stores in Fort-de-France close 12:30–2 for lunch.

CAR RENTALS

A valid U.S. driver's license is needed to rent a car for up to 20 days. After that, you'll need an International Driver's Permit. U.K. citizens can use their EU licenses, since Martinique is a *département* of France.

Rates are about $60 per day (unlimited mileage) for a manual shift, during "season," but always question agents thoroughly about possible discounts. Although the car-rental companies have some automatics, they are substantially more expensive. If you book from the U.S. at least 48 hours in advance by phone or Internet, you can qualify for a hefty discount. If you wait until you arrive, you will be able to negotiate a weekly rate discount. Should you have a gold or platinum credit card, which allows you to safely waive insurance, you can use it here. A hefty deposit—as much as $2,500—will be put on your credit card until the car is returned safely. Lowest prices are $225 per week in low season, $330 in high season. Among the many agencies in Fort-de-France are Avis, Budget, Hertz, Europcar, and JumboCar. You might want to start with Jumbo; they are the most likely to cut a deal. There is a feeling of security in going with a stateside "major" like Avis. The lowest rate for their smallest manual, peak season, is $71; it's $105 for an Opel automatic, $147 for an Audi automatic.

⏏ Avis ☎ 0596/42-11-00 or 800/331-1212. **Budget** ☎ 0596/51-22-88 or 800/472-3325. **Europcar** ☎ 0596/42-42-42. **Hertz** ☎ 0596/42-16-90 or 800/654-3131. **JumboCar** ☎ 0596/42-22-22.

CAR TRAVEL

It's useful to rent a car to discover Martinique, if for only a day or two. But be aware that almost all cars on the island are manuals because of the steep hills. Even on some of the automatics, you still have gears and shift without a clutch. Be aware that traffic jams often occur on steep inclines that will necessitate the deft use of clutch, gas pedal, and emergency brake. And then it will inevitably rain. It can be worth the additional cost to rent an automatic for both the stress and safety factors.

Martinique, especially around Fort-de-France and environs, has become plagued with heavy traffic. Streets in the capital itself are narrow and choked with traffic during the day. It is wiser to tour it on the weekends, certainly not on cruise-ship days. Absolutely avoid the Lamentin Airport area and Fort-de-France during weekday rush hours, roughly 7–10 AM and 4–7:30 PM, or on Sunday nights. Even the smaller towns like Trinité have rush hours. Pay particular attention late on Friday and Saturday nights. Martinicans love to party and those are the big nights.

Watch out, too, for *dos d'ânes* (literally, donkey backs), speed bumps that are extremely hard to spot—particularly at night—though if you hit one, you'll know it.

GASOLINE Gas is costly, the equivalent of about $4 per gallon. Beware of exorbitant charges if you do not fill up the tank of your rental car (the agency will happily do it for you at about $6.50 a gallon).

ROAD CONDITIONS The main highways, about 175 mi (280 km) of well-paved and well-marked roads are excellent, but only in certain areas are they illuminated at night. And many hotels are on roads that are barely passable, so get wherever you are going by nightfall or prepare to be lost. If you can find someone to ask, say: *"Je suis perdu"*(I am lost)! It elicits sympathy.

RULES OF THE ROAD Pay attention at the roundabouts, always a good source of collision possibilities. And drive defensively: although Martinicans are polite and lovely people, they drive with aggressive abandon.

ELECTRICITY
Most tourist locations are equipped with 220-volt electrical outlets. If you're coming from North America and plan to use your own appliances, bring a converter kit with adapters.

EMERGENCIES
🎐 Ambulance & Fire **Ambulance** ☎ 0596/70-36-48 or 0596/71-59-48. **Fire** ☎ 18.
🎐 Hospitals **Hôpital Pierre Zabla Quitman** ✉ Lamentin ☎ 0596/55-20-00.
🎐 Pharmacies **Pharmacie Cypria** ✉ Bd. Général de Gaulle, Fort-de-France ☎ 0596/63-22-25. **Pharmacie de la Paix** ✉ Corner rue Victor Schoelcher and rue Perrinon, Fort-de-France ☎ 0596/71-94-83.
🎐 Police **Police emergencies** ☎ 17.

FESTIVALS & SEASONAL EVENTS
Martinique's Carnival begins in early January and runs through the first day of Lent. About 20 days into Lent there's a mini-Carnival called Mi-carême. This one-day hiatus from what is traditionally 40 days of abstinence brings parties, dances, and the like; after it, however, everyone returns to the somber (and often sober) business of penance until Easter. Early August sees the Tour des Yoles Rondes point-to-point yawl race. On November 21 the arrival of Beaujolais nouveau is celebrated. In odd-numbered years in early December the island hosts its jazz festival, Jazz à la Martinique; in addition to showcasing the best musical talent of the islands, it has attracted such top American performers as Branford Marsalis.

HOLIDAYS
Public holidays are: New Year's Day, Ash Wednesday (6 weeks before Easter), Good Friday, Easter Monday, Labor Day (May 1), Bastille Day (July 14), Assumption Day (August 15), All Saints' Day (Nov. 1), Armistice Day (Nov. 11), and Christmas.

LANGUAGE
Martinicans speak a lovely French, and many speak Creole, a mixture of Spanish, French, and some African languages, all pronounced with a Caribbean accent. Even if you do speak fluent French, you may have a problem understanding the accent. Try *sa ou fe* for "hello" in Creole. In major tourist areas you'll find someone who speaks English, but using a few French words—even if it's only to say, *"Parlez-vous anglais?"*—will be appreciated. Most menus are written in French. But rest assured that these people are typically courteous and will work with you on your French—or lack thereof.

MAIL & SHIPPING

Airmail letters to the U.S. and Canada cost €.74 for up to 20 grams; postcards, about €.58. For Great Britain the costs are €.69 and €.50, respectively. Stamps may be purchased from post offices, café-tabacs, and hotel newsstands. Letters to Martinique should include the name of the business, street (if available), town, postal code, island, and French West Indies. Be forewarned, however, that mail is extremely slow both coming and going.

MONEY MATTERS

Prices quoted here are in U.S. dollars, unless otherwise indicated.

ATMS There are ATMs at the airport and at branches of the Crédit Agricole Bank, which is on the Cirrus and Plus systems and also accepts Visa and MasterCard. If the change bureau at the airport is closed when you arrive and you need euros for a taxi, you can use the ATM machine and put in your American debit or credit card to withdraw and, *voilà,* out will come euros. You will not be able to check your bank balance, however. Keep a certain amount of cash on you because some places don't even accept traveler's checks.

CREDIT CARDS Major credit cards are accepted in hotels and restaurants in Fort-de-France and the Pointe du Bout areas, and you will generally get a favorable exchange rate on purchases; few establishments in the countryside accept them. Many establishments are no longer accepting American Express because its fees are too high, so be certain not to leave home without it, but also carry a second or third card, a MasterCard or Visa. There's generally a 20% discount on luxury items paid for with traveler's checks or with certain credit cards.

CURRENCY The French franc is no longer. It has been replaced by the euro. U.S. dollars are accepted in some hotels, but it's better to convert your money. Banks give a more favorable rate than hotels. A currency exchange service that also offers a favorable rate is Change Caraïbes. If you are cashing less than a $100, it is usually better to go to the exchange or to use your ATM card.

🖅 **Change Caraïbes** ⊠ Lamentin International Airport, Lamentin ☎ 0596/42-17-11 ⊠ Rue Ernest Deproge, Fort-de-France, across from tourist office ☎ 0596/60-28-40.

PASSPORTS & VISAS

All visitors must have a valid passport and a return or ongoing ticket.

SAFETY

Martinique is a reasonably safe island, where crime is not a major concern. In Fort-de-France, however, exercise the same safety precautions you would in any large city. And never leave jewelry or money unattended on the beach or in your car. Except for the area around Cap Chevalier and the Caravelle Peninsula, the Atlantic waters are rough and should be avoided by all but expert swimmers.

SIGHTSEEING TOURS

The terrific staff at the tourist office can help you arrange a personalized island tour with an English-speaking driver. There are set rates for certain tours, and if you share the ride with others the per-person price will be whittled down.

Madinina Tours offers half- and full-day jaunts (lunch included). Boat tours are also available, as are air excursions to the Grenadines and St. Lucia. Madinina has tour desks in most of the major hotels. Parc Naturel Régional de la Martinique organizes inexpensive guided hiking tours. Descriptive folders are available at the tourist office.

On Saturdays, Somatour has excursions to St. Pierre, departing three times a day, on one of their bigger ferry boats for just €10, from Fort-de-France, Schoelcher, and the marina at Pointe du Bout, with commentary by a guide. Once in St-Pierre, passengers can go to Depaz Distillery or take a thrilling but pricey helicopter ride with Heli Blue.

🛈 Madinina Tours ✉ 111–113 rue Ernest Deproge, Fort-de-France ☎ 0596/70-65-25. **Parc Naturel Régional de la Martinique** ✉ 9 bd. Général de Gaulle, Fort-de-France ☎ 0596/73-19-30. **Somatour** ✉ 14 Rue Blenac, Fort du France ☎ 0596/73-05-53.

TAXES & SERVICE CHARGES

HOTEL TAX A resort tax varies from city to city. Each has its own tax, with most between €.50 and €1.25 per person per day; the maximum is €2.25.

SERVICE CHARGES Rates quoted by hotels usually include a 10% service charge; some hotels add 10% to your bill.

TAXIS

Taxis, which are metered, are expensive. From the airport to Fort-de-France is about €25–€30; from the airport to Pointe du Bout, about €35, and to Les Trois-Ilets, €32. A 40% surcharge is levied between 7 PM and 6 AM and on Sunday. This means that if you arrive at night, depending on where your hotel is, it may be cheaper (although not safer) to rent a car from the airport and keep it for 24 hours than to take a taxi to your hotel. Drivers of M. Marital Mercedes taxis speak English and Spanish as well as French.

🛈 Regular taxis ☎ 0596/63-63-62 or 0596/63-10-10. **M. Marital Mercedes taxis** ☎ 0596/64-20-24; 0696/45-69-07 mobile.

TELEPHONES

There are no coin-operated phone booths. Public phones now use a *télécarte*, which you can buy at post offices, café-tabacs, hotels, and at *bureaux de change*.

COUNTRY & AREA CODES To call Martinique from the United States, dial 011 + 596 + 596 + the local six-digit number (you must dial 596 *twice*). If calling from Guadeloupe you should dial 0596 and the six digits. Numbers with the 0696 prefix are for cell phones.

INTERNATIONAL CALLS To call the United States from Martinique, dial 00 + 1, the area code, and the local number. You can now make collect calls to Canada through the Bell operator; you can get the AT&T or MCI operators from special service phones at the cruise ports and in town. These phones are blue, and one such is at the Super Sumo snack bar, on rue de la Liberté, near the library. Or you can call the access numbers from your hotel phone. To call Great Britain from Martinique, dial 00 + 44, the area code (without the first zero), and the number.

🛈 AT&T ☎ 800/99-00-11. **Bell** ☎ 800/99-00-16. **MCI** ☎ 800/99-00-19.

INTERNET SERVICE In Fort-de-France there is the Cyber Café Blénac, open weekdays 10 AM–1 PM and Saturday 6 PM–1 AM. There is also Internet service at the main post office and in some of the branches in other towns like Le François. In Le Marin, the Calebasse Cafe, a music venue by night, has an Internet station; it's closed Mondays but opens early, at 7 AM.

🛈 Calebasse Cafe ✉ 19 Bd. Allegre, Le Marin ☎ 0596/74-84-20. **Cyber Café Blénac** ✉ Rue Blénac, Fort-de-France ☎ 0596/70-31-62.

LOCAL CALLS To place a local or inter-island call you have to dial all 10 numbers, beginning with 0596 and then the six-digit number.

TIPPING
All restaurants include a 15% service charge in their menu prices. You can always add to this if you feel that service was particularly good.

VISITOR INFORMATION
🛈 **Before You Leave Martinique Promotion Bureau** ⊕ www.martinique.org ✉ 444 Madison Ave., New York, NY 10022 ☎ 800/391-4909 ✉ 9454 Wilshire Blvd., Beverly Hills, CA 90212 ☎ 310/271-6665 ✉ 676 N. Michigan Ave., Chicago, IL 60611 ☎ 312/751-7800 ✉ 1981 McGill College Ave., Suite 490, Montréal, Québec H3A 2W9, Canada ☎ 514/288-4264 ✉ 1 Dundas St. W, Suite 2405, Toronto, Ontario M5G 1Z3, Canada ☎ 416/593-4723 or 800/361-9099 ✉ 178 Piccadilly, London W1V 0AL, U.K. ☎ 0181/124-4123. 🛈 **In Martinique Martinique Tourist Office** ✉ Bd. Alfassa, Fort-de-France ☎ 0596/63-79-60 🖷 0596/73-66-93.

PUERTO RICO

15

FODOR'S CHOICE

Bahía Mosquito, a bioluminiscent bay in Vieques
Historic San Germán
Horned Dorset Primavera, a resort in Rincón
Playing at one of the Hyatt golf courses, Dorado
Shopping in Old San Juan

HIGHLY RECOMMENDED

HOTELS Casa Isleña Inn, Rincón
El Convento Hotel, Old San Juan
Hostería del Mar, San Juan
Inn on the Blue Horizon, Esperanza
Ritz-Carlton San Juan Hotel, Spa & Casino, San Juan
The Water Club, San Juan
Villa Montaña Beach Resort, Isabela
Wyndham El Conquistador Resort and Country Club, Fajardo

SIGHTS Bosque Estatal de Guánica
Cabo Rojo
El Yunque
Fuerte San Felipe del Morro, Old San Juan
Museo de Arte de Puerto Rico, San Juan
Observatorio de Arecibo
Parque Ceremonial Indígena de Caguana
Parque de las Cavernas del Río Camuy

Many other great places enliven this area. For other
favorites, look for the black stars as you read this chapter.

At night, flickering night flies are little lanterns in the misty mountains; the warm ocean turns into luminescent aqua-blue speckles on your skin; and everywhere you go, tiny frogs sing their legendary sweet lullaby to the moon. When you walk out of your room in the morning, the day moves rhythmically around you. The sun mildly toasts your body, and you are immediately healed by soft waves and cool breezes. Cool papaya bites slip into your mouth, and the smell of yummy fritters is followed by the promised gulp of a cold, light beer. Known as the Island of Enchantment, Puerto Rico—somehow, somewhere—will surely put a spell on you.

Updated by
Isabel
Abislaimán

Few Caribbean cities are as steeped in Spanish tradition as Puerto Rico's Old San Juan. Originally built as a fortress, the old city's myriad attractions include restored 16th-century buildings and 200-year-old houses with balustraded balconies of filigreed wrought iron that overlook narrow cobblestone streets. Spanish traditions are also apparent in the countryside—from the festivals celebrated in honor of small-town patron saints to the *paradores,* inexpensive but accommodating inns whose concept originated in Spain.

Puerto Rico, 110 mi (177 km) long and 35 mi (56 km) wide, was populated by several tribes of Indians (primarily the Taíno) when Columbus landed during his second voyage in 1493. In 1508 Juan Ponce de León, the frustrated seeker of the Fountain of Youth, established a settlement on the island and became its first governor; in 1521 he founded what would become known as Old San Juan. For three centuries the French, Dutch, and English tried unsuccessfully to wrest the island from Spain. In 1897 Spain granted the island dominion status and a year later—as a result of the Spanish-American War—ceded the island to the United States. In 1917 Puerto Ricans became U.S. citizens, and in 1952 Puerto Rico became a semiautonomous commonwealth.

The years since have brought several referenda to determine whether the island should remain a commonwealth, become a state, or gain independence. It may be true that all the latest American TV programs are broadcast here, that *el béisbol* (baseball) is a major pastime, that San Juan has the trappings of any American city, and that many islanders have family stateside. But life *en la isla* (on the island) is far more traditional. A strong Latin sense of community and family prevails, and *puertorriqueños* are fiercely proud of both their Spanish and African heritages.

Music is another source of Puerto Rican pride. The brash Latin sound is best characterized by salsa—referring both to the music and the dance—which shares not only its name with the Spanish word for "sauce" but also has a zesty, hot flavor. This fusion of West African percussion, jazz (especially swing and big band), and other Latin beats (mambo, merengue, flamenco, cha-cha, rumba) is sexy and primal. Dancing to it is a chance to let go of inhibitions. You may also go for some clubbing *à la vida loca* espoused by Puerto Rican pop star Ricky Martin. Nightlife options are of the variety available in any metropolitan environment—and then some. In San Juan's sophisticated Condado and Isla Verde areas you'll find flashy cabaret shows and casinos.

By day you can step into the Old World—in Old San Juan, in a quiet colonial town, or on a coffee plantation. If you're the athletic type, you'll appreciate the island's many acres of golf courses, its abundant tennis courts, and its hundreds of beaches that offer every imaginable water sport. In the extraordinary 28,000-acre Caribbean National Forest (known as El Yunque) you'll find 100-ft-high trees and dramatic mountain ranges. For more adventures off the beaten track, you can head to the outlying islets of Culebra and Vieques where the snorkeling and scuba diving are fine.

	$$$$	**$$$**	**$$**	**$**	**¢**
WHAT IT COSTS In U.S. dollars					
RESTAURANTS*					
	over $30	$20–$30	$12–$20	$8–$12	under $8
HOTELS**					
Cost EP/BP/CP	over $350	$250–$350	$150–$250	$80–$150	under $80
Cost AI	over $450	$350–$450	$250–$350	$125–$250	under $125

*Restaurant prices are for a main course at dinner. **EP, BP, and CP prices are per night for a standard double room in high season, excluding taxes, service charges, and meal plans. AI (all-inclusive) prices are per person, per night based on double-occupancy during high season, excluding taxes and service charges.

Where to Stay

San Juan's high-rise beachfront hotels cater primarily to the cruise-ship and casino crowd, though several target business travelers. Outside San Juan, particularly on the east coast, you'll find self-contained luxury resorts that cover hundreds of acres. In the west, southwest, and south—as well as on the islands of Vieques and Culebra—smaller inns, villas, and condominiums for short-term rentals are the norm. Also look into government-sponsored paradores. Some of these are rural inns, some offer no-frills apartments, and some are large hotels, but all must meet certain standards, such as proximity to an attraction or beach.

Most hotels operate on the EP, although larger establishments often offer other meal plans or even all-inclusive packages. In the off-season, or summer months, rates at some hotels can drop 20% or more. For hotels outside of San Juan rates most often don't include airport transfers. Be sure to ask when you book.

For information on paradores, contact the **Puerto Rico Tourism Company** (🖰 Box 902-3960, Old San Juan Station, San Juan 00902-3960 ☎ 787/721–2400 ⊕ www.gotopuertorico.com). **Small Inns of Puerto Rico** (✉ Av. Ponce de León 954, Suite 702, 00907 ☎ 787/725–2901 🖷 787/725–2913), a branch of the Puerto Rico Hotel and Tourism Association, is a marketing arm for some 25 small hotels island-wide.

For condos or villas on Vieques, contact **Connections** (🖰 Box 358, Esperanza, Vieques 00765 ☎ 787/741–0023). **Island West Properties & Beach Rentals** (✉ Rte. 413, Km 1.3, Rincón 🖰 Box 700, 00677 ☎ 787/823–2323 🖷 787/823–3254) can you help you rent condos in Rincón by the week or the month. **Puerto Rico Vacation Apartments** (✉ Marbella del Caribe Oeste S-5, Isla Verde, San Juan 00979 ☎ 787/727–1591 or 800/266–3639 🖷 787/268–3604) represents some 200 condo properties in San Juan's Condado and Isla Verde areas.

Old San Juan

★ $$$–$$$$ ⊡ **El Convento Hotel.** Once a Carmelite convent, this 350-year-old building is a prime example of the right way to blend Old World gentility with modern luxury. Much of the original architecture is intact, including a colonial interior courtyard. Rooms have a Spanish-deco look, with dark woods, wrought-iron lamps, and ornate furniture. Complimentary wine and hors d'oeuvres are served before dinner, and there's an honor bar that's open until 4 AM. The courtyard's Café del Níspero and street-side Café Bohemio are among the dining choices. ⊠ *Calle Cristo 100, Old San Juan* ✆ *Box 1048, 00902* ☎ *787/723–9020 or 800/468–2779* 🖷 *787/721–2877* ⊕ *www.elconvento.com* ↻ *54 rooms, 4 suites* ♨ *4 restaurants, in-room safes, minibars, pool, gym, massage, 2 bars, library, shops, meeting room, parking (fee)* ⊟ *AE, D, DC, MC, V* ⦿ *CP.*

$$$ ⊡ **Wyndham Old San Juan Hotel & Casino.** The gleaming Wyndham blends classic Spanish colonial lines with a modern, triangular shape that subtly echoes the cruise ships docked nearby. The lobby, adjacent to the casino, shines with multihued tiles and mahogany. Each standard room—with honey-colored rugs, floral prints, and light woods—has a two-line phone, a coffeemaker, and a hair dryer. Spacious suites also have sitting rooms and extra TVs. On the ninth floor you'll find a small patio pool and whirlpool bath; the seventh-floor concierge level provides hassle-free check-ins, Continental breakfasts, and evening hors d'oeuvres. ⊠ *Calle Brumbaugh 100, Old San Juan 00901* ☎ *787/721–5100 or 800/ 996–3426* 🖷 *787/721–1111* ⊕ *www.wyndham.com* ↻ *185 rooms, 55 suites* ♨ *Restaurant, some minibars, cable TV, pool, gym, hot tub, massage, 2 bars, casino, concierge floor, business services, meeting rooms, parking (fee)* ⊟ *AE, D, DC, MC, V* ⦿ *CP.*

$–$$$ ⊡ **Gallery Inn.** Jan D'Esopo and Manuco Gandía have transformed this rambling colonial house into an inn that's full of comforts and quirky details: winding, uneven stairs; a music room with a Steinway grand piano; courtyard gardens, where Jan's pet macaws and cockatoos hang out. Each room has a look all its own; several have whirlpool baths. From the rooftop deck there's a spectacular view of the forts and the Atlantic. The first-floor Galería San Juan displays artwork by Jan and others. There's no restaurant, but meals for groups can be prepared upon request. ⊠ *Calle Norzagaray 204–206, Old San Juan 00901* ☎ *787/ 722–1808* 🖷 *787/724–7360* ⊕ *www.thegalleryinn.com* ↻ *13 rooms, 10 suites* ♨ *Dining room, some in-room hot tubs, piano, free parking; no room TVs* ⊟ *AE, DC, MC, V* ⦿ *CP.*

San Juan

★ $$$$ ⊡ **Ritz-Carlton San Juan Hotel, Spa & Casino.** The Ritz's signature elegance won't undermine the feeling that this is a true beach getaway. The hotel's sandy stretch is lovely, as is the free-form pool, which is surrounded by a garden overlooking the ocean. Works by local artists adorn the lobby lounge and the hallways leading to the well-equipped business center. A full-service spa begs to pamper you with aloe body wraps and *parcha* (passion-fruit juice) massages. Though most room windows are sealed shut to muffle airport noise, many suites open onto terraces. ⊠ *Av. Las Gobernadores (Rte. 187), Isla Verde 00979* ☎ *787/253–1700 or 800/ 241–3333* 🖷 *787/253–0700* ⊕ *www.ritzcarlton.com* ↻ *403 rooms, 11 suites* ♨ *3 restaurants, in-room data ports, minibars, cable TV, 2 tennis courts, pool, gym, hair salon, health club, hot tub, spa, beach, 3 bars, casino, nightclub, shop, children's programs (ages 4–12), concierge floor, business services, meeting rooms, parking (fee), no-smoking floor* ⊟ *AE, D, DC, MC, V* ⦿ *EP.*

★ $$$$ ⊡ **The Water Club.** Every inch of this boutique hotel will soothe you. Aromatherapy scents waft through corridors, candles light your way, and

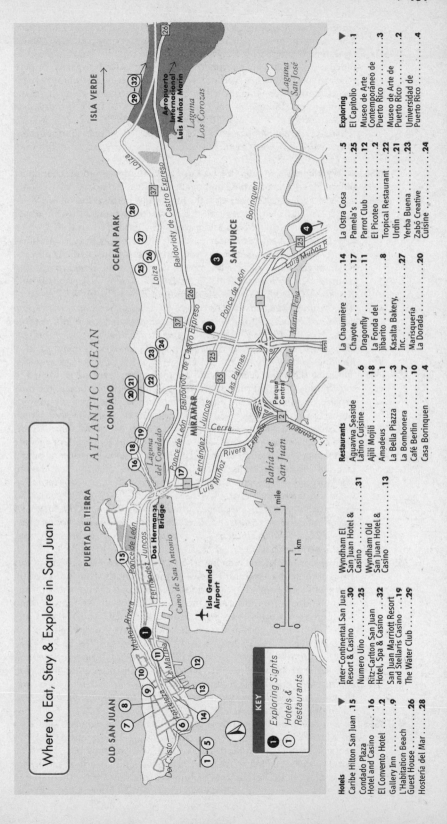

Where to Eat, Stay & Explore in San Juan

KEY

▼ Exploring Sights

① Hotels & Restaurants

Hotels

Caribe Hilton San Juan	.15
Condado Plaza Hotel and Casino	.16
El Convento Hotel	.2
Gallery Inn	.9
L'Habitation Beach Guest House	.26
Hostería del Mar	.28
Inter-Continental San Juan Resort & Casino	.30
Numero Uno	.25
Ritz-Carlton San Juan Hotel, Spa & Casino	.32
San Juan Marriott Resort and Stellaris Casino	.19
The Water Club	.29
Wyndham El San Juan Hotel & Casino	.31
Wyndham Old San Juan Hotel & Casino	.13

Restaurants

Aguaviva Seaside Latino Cuisine	.6
Ají Mojili	.18
Amadeus	.1
La Bella Piazza	.3
La Bombonera	.7
Café Berlin	.10
Casa Borinquen	.4
La Chaumière	.14
Chayote	.17
Dragonfly	.11
La Fonda del Jibarito	.8
Kasalta Bakery, Inc.	.27
Marisquería La Dorada	.20
La Ostra Cosa	.5
Pamela's	.25
Parrot Club	.12
El Picoteo	.2
Tropical Restaurant	.22
Urdin	.21
Yerba Buena	.23
Zabó Creative Cuisine	.24

Exploring

El Capitolio	.1
Museo de Arte Contemporáneo de Puerto Rico	.3
Museo de Arte de Puerto Rico	.2
Universidad de Puerto Rico	.4

water runs inside the glass walls of elevators that glow with blue neon. They seem the proper ride for trips to the rooftop pool or to the rooms, all of which have ocean views and such contemporary amenities as CD players. Four suites are equipped with telescopes for star-gazing or people-watching along Isla Verde beach. The Tangerine Restaurant is sensuous; and water is again a literal and a decorative element in the lobby's Liquid lounge and the rooftop's Wet bar. ⊠ *Calle Tartak 2, Isla Verde, 00979* ☎ *787/728–3666 or 888/265–6699* 🖷 *787/728–3610* ⊕ *www.waterclubsanjuan.com* ➥ *84 rooms* ⅋ *Restaurant, in-room data ports, cable TV, pool, gym, hot tub, massage, beach, 2 bars, Internet, parking (fee)* ⊟ *AE, D, DC, MC, V* ⅋⊙⅋ *EP.*

$$$$ 🛏 **Wyndham El San Juan Hotel & Casino.** An immense antique chandelier illuminates the hand-carved mahogany paneling, Italian rose marble, and 250-year-old French tapestries in the huge lobby of this resort on Isla Verde beach. You'll be hard pressed to decide whether you want a main tower suite with a whirlpool bath and a wet bar; a garden room with a whirlpool bath and a patio; or a casita with a sunken Roman bath. All guest quarters have such amenities as walk-in closets, irons, and CD players. Relax at the lobby's Cigar Bar or take dinner at the Ranch, a rooftop country-western bar and grill. ⊠ *Av. Isla Verde 6063, Isla Verde 00902* ☎ *787/791–1000, 800/468–2818, or 800/996–3426* 🖷 *787/791–0390* ⊕ *www.wyndham.com* ➥ *332 rooms, 57 suites* ⅋ *8 restaurants, in-room data ports, minibars, in-room VCRs, 3 tennis courts, 2 pools, wading pool, gym, health club, 5 hot tubs, spa, beach, 14 bars, casino, nightclub, shops, children's programs (ages 5–17), business services, parking (fee), no-smoking rooms* ⊟ *AE, DC, MC, V* ⅋⊙⅋ *CP.*

$$$–$$$$ 🛏 **Caribe Hilton San Juan.** Beyond the lobby, your eyes are gently led to the Atlantic blue past the edge of the infinity pool. The beach, the only private one in San Juan, has been expanded. The open-air lobby's sunken bar looks out over the gentle cascades of a tri-level pool, which is adjacent to a wading pool and an area with whirlpool tubs. Rooms have ocean or lagoon views, and those on the executive floor include such services as private check-in and check-out and free Continental breakfast and evening cocktails. Local businesspeople often frequent the on-site Morton's of Chicago restaurant. ⊠ *Calle Los Rosales, San Gerónimo Grounds, Puerta de Tierra, 00901* ☎ *787/721–0303 or 800/468–8585* 🖷 *787/725–8849* ⊕ *www.caribehilton.com* ➥ *602 rooms, 44 suites* ⅋ *3 restaurants, 3 tennis courts, pool, wading pool, health club, hot tub, spa, beach, 2 bars, shops, children's programs (ages 4–12), business services, meeting rooms, parking (fee)* ⊟ *AE, D, DC, MC, V* ⅋⊙⅋ *BP.*

$$$–$$$$ 🛏 **Inter-Continental San Juan Resort & Casino.** The spacious rooms in this 16-story hotel have pleasant views of the ocean, the San José Lagoon, or the city; suites overlook the pool. The jangling casino is just off the lobby, and on-site restaurants include the poolside Restaurant Ciao Mediterraneo; Ruth's Chris Steak House; and the Grand Market Café, with deli favorites you can eat on the spot or have packed up for a picnic on the beach. ⊠ *Av. Isla Verde 187, Isla Verde 00914* ☎ *787/791–6100 or 800/443–2009* 🖷 *787/253–2510* ⊕ *www.intercontinental.com* ➥ *381 rooms, 19 suites* ⅋ *6 restaurants, in-room safes, pool, gym, health club, hot tub, spa, beach, boating, 3 bars, casino, nightclub, shops, concierge floor, business services, meeting rooms, parking (fee), no-smoking rooms* ⊟ *AE, D, MC, V* ⅋⊙⅋ *EP.*

$$$–$$$$ 🛏 **San Juan Marriott Resort and Stellaris Casino.** The red neon sign atop the Marriott seems like a beacon, beckoning you to beautiful Condado beach. The hotel's soundproofed rooms have soothing pastel carpets, floral spreads, and attractive tropical art; balconies overlook the ocean, the pool, or both. Restaurants include the Tuscany, for northern Italian cuisine, and the casual La Vista, which is open 24 hours. On weekends, there's live entertainment in the enormous lobby, which, combined with the ringing of slot machines from the adjoining casino, makes the area noisy. A large pool area and a gorgeous beach are right outside. ⊠ *Av. Ashford 1309, Condado 00907* ☎ *787/722–7000 or 800/228–9290* 🖷 *787/722–6800* ⊕ *www.marriott.com* ⌁ *512 rooms, 17 suites* ♿ *3 restaurants, 2 tennis courts, pool, gym, hair salon, health club, hot tub, spa, beach, 1 bar, 2 lounges, casino, shops, children's programs (ages 4–12), business services, meeting rooms, parking (fee), no-smoking rooms* ⊟ *AE, D, DC, MC, V* ⦿⎸ *CP.*

$$–$$$$ 🏨 **Condado Plaza Hotel and Casino.** The Atlantic and the Laguna del Condado border this high-rise, whose wings—fittingly named Ocean and Lagoon—are connected by an enclosed, elevated walkway. Standard rooms have walk-in closets and dressing areas. There's a variety of suites, including some with oversize hot tubs. A stay on the Plaza Club floor entitles you to 24-hour concierge service, use of a private lounge, and complimentary Continental breakfast and refreshments all day. Find your own place in the sun on the beach or beside one of four pools. Dining options include the poolside Tony Roma's as well as Max's Grill, which is open 24 hours. ⊠ *Av. Ashford 999, Condado 00902* ☎ *787/721–1000 or 800/624–0420* 🖷 *787/722–7955* ⊕ *www.condadoplaza.com* ⌁ *570 rooms, 62 suites* ♿ *7 restaurants, some in-room hot tubs, 2 tennis courts, 3 pools, wading pool, health club, 3 hot tubs, beach, dock, boating, 2 bars, 2 lounges, casino, shops, children's programs (ages 5–12), concierge floor, business services, parking (fee)* ⊟ *AE, D, DC, MC, V* ⦿⎸ *MAP.*

$–$$ 🏨 **Numero Uno.** Former New Yorker Esther Feliciano bought this three-story, red-roofed guest house, spruced it up, and made it a very pleasant place to stay. It's in a quiet residential area, and its rooms are simple and clean; three have ocean views. Two apartments come with kitchenettes. A walled-in patio provides privacy for sunning or hanging out by the small pool. Reserve a table in the torch-lit outdoor sections of Pamela's restaurant and caress the sand with your toes to complement the sensuous experience of the delicious food and soft ocean breezes. The wide, sandy beach beckons; if you're a guest here, you're provided with beach chairs and towels. ⊠ *Calle Santa Ana 1, Ocean Park 00911* ☎ *787/726–5010* 🖷 *787/727–5482* ⌁ *11 rooms, 2 apartments* ♿ *Restaurant, fans, some kitchenettes, minibars, pool, beach, bar, free parking* ⊟ *AE, MC, V* ⦿⎸ *CP.*

¢–$ 🏨 **L'Habitation Beach Guest House.** Alain Tasca—who is from Paris by way of Guadeloupe and Key West—has created a very relaxed and oh-so-French ambience at this guest house, which has a primarily gay clientele. Rooms are simple and comfortable; Nos. 8 and 9 are the largest and have ocean views. A combined bar and snack bar sits in the corner of a palm-shaded patio between the guest house and the sands of Ocean Park. Beach chairs and towels are provided: get your gear together before having one of Alain's margaritas, which will knock your sandals off. ⊠ *Calle Italia 1957, Ocean Park 00911* ☎ *787/727–2499* 🖷 *787/727–2599* ⊕ *www.habitationbeach.com* ⌁ *10 rooms* ♿ *Snack bar, fans, beach, bar, library, laundry facilities, free parking* ⊟ *AE, D, MC, V* ⦿⎸ *CP.*

★ ¢–$ 🏨 **Hostería del Mar.** Condado's high-rises are far to the west of this small, white inn on the beach in Ocean Park. Rooms are attractive and simple, with tropical prints and rattan furniture. Many rooms have ocean views, and four apartments have kitchenettes. The staff is courteous and helpful, and the ground-floor restaurant, which serves many vegetarian dishes and fruit shakes as well as seafood and steaks, faces the trade winds and has breathtaking beach views. ⊠ *Calle Tapia 1, Ocean Park 00911* ☎ *787/727–3302 or 800/742–4276* 🖷 *787/268–0772* ⊕ *www. prhtasmallhotels.com* ⌁ *8 rooms, 4 apartments, 1 suite* ♿ *Restaurant, some kitchenettes, beach, free parking* ⊟ *AE, D, DC, MC, V* ⦿⎸ *EP.*

Puerto Rico

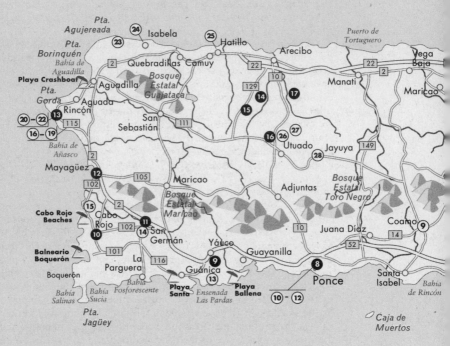

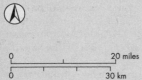

Caribbean Sea

20 miles
30 km

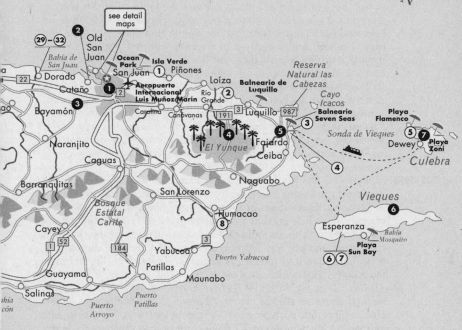

KEY

- Beaches
- Exploring Sights
- Ferry
- Hotels & Restaurants
- Rain Forest

Eastern Puerto Rico

★ **$$$–$$$$** ⊞ **Wyndham El Conquistador Resort and Country Club.** What many consider Puerto Rico's loveliest resort is on a bluff above the ocean. The colossal hotel and the villas in Las Casitas Village and Las Olas Village have Moorish and Spanish colonial architectural details. Cobblestone streets and fountain-filled plazas enhance the feeling that this place is more like a community than a complex. The resort's beach is on Palomino Island just offshore; a free shuttle boat takes you there and back. The staff prides itself on its attentive service. If the place seems familiar, it may be because the James Bond movie *Goldfinger* was filmed here. ⊠ *Av. El Conquistador 1000, Fajardo* ♻ *Box 70001, 00738* ☎ *787/863–1000, 800/996–3426, or 800/468–5228* 🖷 *787/253–0178* ⊕ *www.wyndham.com* ♻ *750 rooms, 16 suites* ♻ *11 restaurants, minibars, cable TV with movies and video games, 18-hole golf course, 8 tennis courts, 5 pools, gym, health club, spa, beach, dive shop, dock, snorkeling, windsurfing, boating, jet skiing, marina, 4 bars, casino, nightclub, shop, children's programs, business services, meeting rooms, airport shuttle* ⊟ *AE, MC, V* ⦿ *CP.*

$$–$$$$ ⊞ **Westin Río Mar Beach Resort.** Golf, biking, tennis, and playing in the waters off a mile-long beach are just some of the attractions at this top-notch resort. Every room in the seven-story hotel, which anchors the complex, has a balcony that faces the sea or the golf courses and mountains. There are also one- and two-bedroom villas for guests who want more space and privacy. Tropical color schemes are used throughout, as are such luxurious touches as natural woods, Italian tile, and marble accents. ⊠ *Río Mar Blvd. 6000 (Rte. 968, Km 1.4), Río Grande* ♻ *Box 2006, 00745* ☎ *787/888–6000* 🖷 *787/888–6600* ⊕ *www. westinriomar.com* ♻ *528 rooms, 72 suites* ♻ *7 restaurants, room service, in-room data ports, in-room safes, minibars, cable TV with movies and video games, in-room VCRs, 2 18-hole golf courses, 13 tennis courts, 3 pools, gym, hair salon, health club, spa, beach, dive shop, snorkeling, windsurfing, boating, jet skiing, fishing, bicycles, 3 bars, 4 lounges, casino, dance club, shop, children's programs, dry cleaning, laundry service, concierge, business services, meeting rooms, airport shuttle, car rental, no-smoking rooms* ⊟ *AE, MC, V* ⦿ *FAP.*

$$–$$$ ⊞ **Candelero Resort at Palmas del Mar.** Shuttle buses scoot you around, and parking attendants and other personnel are good about giving directions. You need such assistance: with 3,000 acres, the grounds are seemingly endless. Accommodations include a 100-room hotel with 110 villas. There are also 85 privately owned condos, a 106-unit time-share complex, myriad bars and restaurants, and a casino. The hotel's rooms and public spaces are open and airy; many have balconies. If you want more space, inquire about the villas, which can be rented by the day, the week, or longer. There's no shortage of activity, from water sports to tennis and golf. ⊠ *Rte. 906 Humacao* ♻ *Box 2020, 00792* ☎ *787/852–6000* 🖷 *787/852–6320* ⊕ *www.palmasdelmar.com* ♻ *100 rooms, 110 villas* ♻ *13 restaurants, room service, minibars, cable TV with movies, 2 18-hole golf courses, 20 tennis courts, pool, gym, beach, dive shop, dock, snorkeling, windsurfing, fishing, horseback riding, 15 bars, casino, shop, children's programs, airport shuttle* ⊟ *AE, MC, V* ⦿ *BP.*

Vieques Island

★ **$$–$$$** ⊞ **Inn on the Blue Horizon.** One of Puerto Rico's most expensive small hotels, which has been featured in *Architectural Digest*, consists of 17 villas and a main house near the sea on a former plantation. You truly feel away from it all at this gorgeous, 20-acre complex. Sit on white Adirondack chairs at the edge of a rocky cliff and enjoy the Caribbean breezes at sunset. Then move over for pre-dinner cocktails at the Blue

Bar. End your long day of sun and fun at the elegant dining room. For your own good, rooms don't have phones. ⊠ *Rte. 996, Km 4.3* ⊙ *Box 1556, Esperanza, 00765* ☎ *787/741–3318* ♨ *787/741–0522* ⊕ *www. innontheBluehorizon.com* ↪ *65 rooms* ♢ *2 Restaurants, bar, fans, pool, gym, massage; no a/c in some rooms, no room phones, no kids under 14* ⊟ *AE, MC, V* ⫤⊙⫤ *BP.*

$–$$ 🏨 **Hacienda Tamarindo.** Interior designer Linda Vail and her husband Burr are the charming hosts at this hilltop guest house, which is named after the venerable tamarind tree that rises three stories in the lobby. The panoramic views include grounds landscaped with coconut palms and mahogany trees as well as tropical flowers. Half the guest rooms—which have terra-cotta floors, light pastel color schemes, and antiques—are airconditioned. The rest are cooled by overhead fans and trade winds. ⊠ *Rte. 996, Km 4.5* ⊙ *Box 1569, Esperanza, 00765* ☎ *787/741–8525* ♨ *787/ 741–3215* ⊕ *www.enchanted-isle.com/tamarindo* ↪ *16 rooms* ♢ *Dining room, fans, pool, bar; no a/c in some rooms, no kids under 15* ⊟ *AE, MC, V* ⫤⊙⫤ *BP.*

Culebra Island

¢–$$ 🏨 **Harbour View Villas.** Jane and Druso Daubon are your hosts in this wonderful lodging overlooking the Culebra harbor and the Vieques Sound. These private, but not isolated, wood villas boast 12-ft-high exposed-beam ceilings, handsome French doors, and ample balconies with splendid views. This five-acre property is within walking distance of the town and Melones Beach and its reef, which is known for good snorkeling. ⊠ *Barrio Melones 1, Culebra* ⊙ *Box 216, 00775* ☎ *787/742–3855 or 800/440–0070* ♨ *787/742–3171 or 787/742–3855* ⊕ *www. harbourviewvillas.com* ↪ *1 room, 1 suite, 2 villas* ♢ *Fans, some kitchens; no a/c in some rooms* ⊟ *AE, MC, V* ⫤⊙⫤ *EP.*

Southern Puerto Rico

$$$ 🏨 **Hilton Ponce & Casino.** Black-sand beaches border the south coast's biggest resort, a cream-and-turquoise complex on 80 acres, 4 mi (6 km) outside of Ponce. Guest rooms have a tropical decor. The romantic, dark-paneled La Cava ($$–$$$) has a menu that blends different international cuisines—try the beef tenderloin with goose liver or the vegetable spring rolls. Near the lobby's spectacular waterfall is La Terraza ($$–$$$), a casual buffet serving breakfast and lunch. If the shopping arcade doesn't keep you busy, the many outdoor activities will. At this writing, plans for two golf courses were on the table. ⊠ *Av. Caribe 1150, La Guancha, Ponce* ⊙ *Box 7419, 00732* ☎ *787/259–7676, 800/445–8667, or 800/981–3232* ♨ *787/259–7674* ⊕ *www.ponce-hilton.com* ↪ *148 rooms, 5 suites* ♢ *2 restaurants, in-room safes, minibars, cable TV with movies and video games, driving range, 4 tennis courts, pool, gym, hot tub, sauna, spa, beach, bicycles, basketball, Ping-Pong, volleyball, 3 bars, casino, dance club, video game room, shops, baby-sitting, playground, business services, meeting rooms, parking (fee)* ⊟ *AE, DC, MC, V* ⫤⊙⫤ *EP.*

$$ 🏨 **Copamarina Beach Resort.** On one side of the Copamarina's 16 acres of flowers and fruit trees is the Caribbean; on the other, is dry tropical forest. If the resort's beach is too crowded with other guests and their children, several equally beautiful stretches are minutes away. Rooms are basic but spacious; all have balconies or patios and at least partial ocean views. The red snapper is a must at the Coastal Cuisine restaurant ($$–$$$); you'll need to rent a car for outings to other area eateries and nightspots. ⊠ *Rte. 333, Km 6.5, Guánica* ⊙ *Box 805, 00653* ☎ *787/821–0505 or 800/468–4553* ♨ *787/821–0070* ⊕ *www. copamarina.com* ↪ *106 rooms, 2 villas* ♢ *Restaurant, refrigerators, cable TV, 2 tennis courts, 2 pools, 2 wading pools, gym, 2 hot tubs, spa, beach,* *dive shop, snorkeling, windsurfing, boating, bicycles, volleyball, bar, shop, playground, meeting rooms, water sports* ⊟ *AE, DC, MC, V* ⟨○⟩ *CP.*

$ 🏨 **Hotel Meliá.** In the heart of Ponce, near Plaza las Delicias, this family-owned hotel is a good, low-key base for exploring downtown's landmark buildings and museums. The lobby, with its high ceilings and blue-and-beige tile floors, is well worn but charming. Rooms have a somewhat dated, European feel. Breakfast is served on the rooftop terrace, which overlooks the city and mountains. Six suites have balconies with terrific views of Ponce's historic district. ⊠ *Calle Cristina 75, Ponce Centro, Ponce* ✆ *Box 1431, 00733* ☎ *787/842–0260 or 800/742–4276* 📠 *787/841–3602* ⊕ *http://home.coqui.net/melia* ⬧ *75 rooms* ⟨& *Restaurant, cable TV, bar, parking (fee)* ⊟ *AE, MC, V* ⟨○⟩ *CP.*

$ 🏨 **Parador Baños de Coamo.** On weekends, musicians play in the interior patio of this rustic country inn, portions of which date from the 19th century. Rooms—in four modern two-story buildings—open onto latticed wooden verandahs and have a cozy, lodgelike feel. Thermal water flows from sulfur springs into a swimming pool a few steps away from a cool-water pool, where you can still see walls dating from 1843. In the dining room ($–$$), portions of delicious *churrasco* (barbecued meats) with rice and beans are generous. ⊠ *Rte. 546, Km 1, Coamo* ✆ *Box 540, 99769* ☎ *787/825–2186 or 787/825–2239* 📠 *787/825–4739* ⬧ *48 rooms* ⟨& *Restaurant, cable TV, 2 pools, bar, video game room* ⊟ *AE, D, MC, V* ⟨○⟩ *EP.*

Northwestern Puerto Rico

$$$$ 🏨 **Horned Dorset Primavera.** This hotel caters to adults seeking privacy
Fodor's Choice   and peace and quiet. Rooms are individually furnished with antiques,
★ including four-poster beds; some have private plunge pools. But you'll find no radios, TVs, or phones in the rooms. The main house has elegant plantation-style furniture and glistening chandeliers. The Casa Escondida is designed to resemble a Puerto Rican hacienda. The main restaurant offers an exquisite 5-course prix-fixe with tropical touches and a Cordon Bleu influence; dress is formal—no shorts allowed—and reservations are required. The new Florentine-tiled Blue Room offers a more intimate ocean-front dining option. ⊠ *Rte. 429, Km 3, Rincón* ✆ *Box 1132, 00677* ☎ *787/823–4030, 787/823–4050, or 800/633–1857* 📠 *787/725–6068* ⊕ *www.horneddorset.com* ⬧ *30 rooms* ⟨& *2 restaurants, fans, 3 pools, gym, beach, library; no room phones, no room TVs, no kids under 12* ⊟ *AE, MC, V* ⟨○⟩ *BP.*

$$$$ 🏨 **Hyatt Dorado Beach Resort & Country Club.** Sprawling over 1,000 acres on a secluded white-sand beach, the Hyatt Dorado is a former plantation. Most rooms have four-poster beds, patios or balconies, and marble baths. For the requisite romantic dinner, ask for a table on the balcony at Su Casa ($$$–$$$$), one of the resort's five restaurants. Its creative cuisine includes such dishes as pork chops with *adobe* (a garlic-oregano marinade) and mahimahi in spicy corn sauce served with corn fritters. Free trolleys take you to the Dorado's sister property, the Regency Cerromar Beach, where you have access to all the facilities including the casino. MAP is compulsory from mid-December through February. ⊠ *Rte. 693, Km 10.8, Dorado, 00646* ☎ *787/796–1234 or 800/233–1234* 📠 *787/796–2022* ⊕ *www.doradobeach.hyatt.com* ⬧ *298 rooms* ⟨& *5 restaurants, minibars, 2 18-hole golf courses, 7 tennis courts, 2 pools, wading pool, health club, spa, beach, snorkeling, windsurfing, boating, bicycles, hiking, 2 lounges, casino, children's programs (ages 3–12)* ⊟ *AE, D, DC, MC, V* ⟨○⟩ *MAP.*

$$$$ 🏨 **Hyatt Regency Cerromar Beach Resort & Casino.** Of the twin Hyatt resorts, this hotel is livelier, both night and day. The complex is very sports- and family-oriented and its famous river pool is one of the longest in

the world, flowing some 1,776 ft under bridges and over waterfalls and waterslides. Most rooms have balconies with ocean views. The casino and Club Bacchus disco are centers of nightlife. At the Steak Co. ($$$–$$$$), try the pan-seared swordfish; the Zen Garden serves Japanese and Chinese cuisine and has a sushi bar. A trolley takes you next door to the Dorado Beach Resort. ☒ *Rte. 693, Km 11.8, Dorado, 00646* ☎ *787/796–1234 or 800/233–1234* ☒ *787/796–4647* ⊕ *www. cerromarbeach.hyatt.com* ➮ *506 rooms* ☾ *4 restaurants, minibars, 2 18-hole golf courses, 10 tennis courts, 3 pools, gym, health club, hot tub, spa, beach, snorkeling, bicycles, hiking, 6 bars, casino, dance club, shops, children's programs* ▤ *AE, D, DC, MC, V* ⊙ *EP.*

$$–$$$$ 🏨 **Rincón Beach Resort.** This beachfront resort is both family- and business-oriented. Most rooms have balconies with ocean views. The open lobby has high ceilings and Indonesian chaises inviting a view of the palms and almond trees. The choice rooms are Nos. 108 and 109, which face the pool and beach. A beach chair–lined deck stretches along the shore at the end of the infinity pool. You will have a handful of nonmotorized water sports and activities to pick from; during the whale-watching and turtle-nesting seasons, you'll have added possibilities. Brasas Restaurant offers an interesting variety of contemporary Caribbean grill specialties emphasizing yucca instead of plaintains as complements, and guava and mango flavorings. ☒ *Rte. 115, Km 5.8, Añasco, 00610* ☎ *787/589–9000 or 866/598–0009* ☒ *787/598–9010 or 787/598–9020* ⊕ *www.rinconbeach.com* ➮ *118 rooms* ☾ *Restaurant, room service, fans, in-room dataports, some kitchenettes, refrigerators, in-room safes, cable TV, pool, gym, beach, dive shop, boating, snorkeling, 2 bars, baby-sitting, business services, free parking* ▤ *AE, D, DC, MC, V* ⊙ *EP.*

★ $$–$$$$ 🏨 **Villa Montaña Beach Resort.** The creativity and homemaking skills of general manager Alain Tiphaine and his wife Jessica have joyfully spilled over to their surroundings in this unique Caribbean condominium resort. You're likely to want to make this your home away from home, too, considering the considerable comfort and fun quotient. The bougainvilleas lead your way through the airy garden to the beach. In the evening, the sound of Spanish guitar will lure you to the candle- and torch-lit beachfront Eclipse Restaurant and Bar, where the daily menu varies but will surely include an irresistible version of marinated tuna or lobster with avocado accompaniment. ☒ *Rte. 4466, Km 1.9 Interior, Barrio Bajuras Isabela, 00662* ☎ *787/872–9554 or 888/780–9195* ☒ *787/872–9553* ⊕ *www.villamontana.com* ➮ *55 rooms* ☾ *Restaurant, in-room data ports, cable TV, 3 tennis courts, massage, 2 pools, beach, snorkeling, boating, bicycles, hiking, horseback riding, bar* ▤ *AE, D, MC, V* ⊙ *FAP.*

$$–$$$ 🏨 **Embassy Suites Hotel Dorado del Mar Beach & Golf Resort.** With hotel, condo, and time-share options, Embassy offers an affordable beachfront alternative in the exclusive Dorado Beach area. The concept is to make sure you can fulfill all your family and business needs in a pleasant environment. To guarantee comfort, the hotel has only two-room suites with ocean or mountain views. The courtyard is an indoor tropical garden surrounded by shops and facilities. The suites are comfortable and well-equipped, and have all the features of a small apartment. The Paradise Café boasts an award-winning crusted sea bass. ☒ *Dorado del Mar Blvd. 201, Dorado 00646-6125* ☎ *787/796–6125 or 800–362–2779* ☒ *787/796–6145* ⊕ *www.embassysuitesdorado.com* ➮ *179 suites* ☾ *2 restaurants, in-room data ports, microwaves, refrigerators, in-room safes, cable TV, in-room VCRs, 18-hole golf course, 2 tennis courts, pool, gym, hot tub, beach, shops, 2 bars, video game room, children's programs* *(ages 3–14), laundry facilities, convention center, parking (fee)* ⊟ *AE, D, DC, MC, V* 🍴 *EP.*

★ $–$$ 🏨 **Casa Isleña Inn.** The wraparound wall and the wooden gate make this small inn feel like a private Mexican villa, where once inside, small mysteries seem to unfold. The secret of Casa Isleña is in the simplicity it achieves without compromising elegance. This inn has a private stretch of beach, a pool and Jacuzzi, as well as an indoor patio with a soothing, burbling fountain. All rooms have queen-size beds. Rooms 254 and 203 have private balconies, which makes them special. Breakfast is not included, but is served on the verandah, as is lunch. ⊠ *Rte. 413, Km 4.8, Barrio Puntas, Rincón 00677* 📞 *787/823–1525 or 888/289–7750* 🖷 *787/823–1530* ⊕ *www.casa-islena.com* 🛏 *9 rooms* ♻ *Restaurant, cable TV, some refrigerators, pool, hot tub, beach, snorkeling, surfing, shop, free parking* ⊟ *AE, D, DC, MC, V* 🍴 *EP.*

$ 🏨 **Hostal Villas del Lago Caonillas.** On the shore of Lake Caonillas, 17 villas can each sleep up to six people comfortably. Surrounded by the densely forested mountains of Utuado, this hostel is designed for those who seek to get outdoors and enjoy nature in a quiet, rural setting. The bar and restaurant are open only during the weekends, but you can make your own meals and snacks in the fully-equipped kitchen. And there are a few nearby options for meals outside the hostel, too. All villas have balconies with views of the lake, and prices reflect their proximity to the shore. ⊠ *Rte. 140, Km 28.1, Barrio Caonillas, Utuado 00641* 📞 *787/894–3481 or 787/894–3464* 🖷 *787/894–3464* ⊕ *www. hostalvillaslago.com* 🛏 *17 villas* ♻ *Restaurant, fans, kitchens, lake, boating, fishing, horseback riding, shop, bar, free parking* ⊟*AE, MC, V* 🍴*EP.*

$ 🏨 **Hotel La Casa Grande.** The main house of this small resort contains a restaurant, bar, and reception area. The other five wooden buildings hold 20 guest rooms. There are no TVs, phones, or radios in the rooms, but a chorus of tiny tree frogs provides symphonies at night. And you can start the day off with a morning yoga class. Dining is on an outdoor patio at Jungle Jane's restaurant ($–$$); the menu includes such offerings as lemon-garlic chicken breast and Puerto Rican specialties including shrimp *asopao* (a soupy rice gumbo). ⊠ *Rte. 612, Km 0.3, Utuado* 🕮 *Box 1499, 00641* 📞 *787/894–3939 or 800/343–2272* 🖷 *787/ 894–3900* ⊕ *www.hotelcasagrande.com* 🛏 *20 rooms* ♻ *Restaurant, fans, pool, bar, meeting room; no room TVs* ⊟ *AE, MC, V* 🍴 *EP.*

$–$$ 🏨 **Lemontree Waterfront Cottages.** These large, sparkling-clean apartments sit right on the beach. Each unit is decorated with bright tropical colors and local artwork and has a deck with a wet bar and grill. Choose from one three-bedroom unit with two baths, one two-bedroom unit, two one-bedroom units, or two newer studios with kitchenettes. Maid service can be arranged. The beach here is small, but larger ones are nearby. ⊠ *Rte. 429, Km 4.1, Rincón* 🕮 *Box 200, 00677* 📞 *787/ 823–6452* 🖷 *787/823–5821* ⊕ *www.lemontreepr.com* 🛏 *6 apartments* ♻ *Fans, some kitchens, some kitchenettes, cable TV, beach, laundry service* ⊟ *AE, MC, V* 🍴 *EP.*

$ 🏨 **Parador Hacienda Gripiñas.** Built on the grounds of a coffee plantation, this elegant inn is surrounded by gardens and mountain peaks. Rooms have balconies overlooking the lush scenery. Across from the house are a bar and a swimming pool filled with cool mountain water. One hiking trail near the property leads to Cerro de Punta, about a 2½-hour climb. The restaurant serves steaks, lobster, shrimp, and criollo fare such as chicken with rice and beans. For dessert, try the *tembleque*—a custard made from coconut milk and sugar. ⊠ *Rte. 527, Km 2.7, Jayuya* 🕮 *Box 387, 00664* 📞 *787/828–1717* 🖷 *787/828–1718* ⊕ *www. haciendagripinas.com* 🛏 *19 rooms* ♻ *Restaurant, pool, hiking, bar, lounge* ⊟ *AE, MC, V* 🍴 *MAP.*

$–$$ ▦ **Villas del Mar Hau.** The hub of the Villas del Mar Hau is a fanciful row of pastel one-, two-, and three bedroom cottages overlooking Montones Beach. They aren't luxurious, but if you're looking for comfort and seclusion in an unpretentious atmosphere, you'll have a hard time doing better. There are also 16 suites, some with kitchens. The popular restaurant, Olas y Arena ($–$$; closed Mon.), is known for fish and shellfish; the paella is especially good. ⊠ *Rte. 4466, Km 8.3, Isabela* ⬤ *Box 510, 00662* ☎ *787/872–2045 or 787/872–2627* 🖷 *787/872–0273* ⊕ *www.villahau.com* ⟿ *40 rooms* ⚘ *Restaurant, fans, some kitchenettes, tennis court, pool, massage, basketball, horseback riding, volleyball, laundry facilities; no a/c in some rooms, no TV in some rooms* ▭ *AE, MC, V* ⦿ *EP.*

Where to Eat

In San Juan you'll find everything from Italian to Thai, as well as superb local eateries serving *comida criolla* (traditional Caribbean creole food). All of San Juan's large hotels have fine restaurants, but some of the city's best eateries are stand-alone, and smaller hotels also often present good options. There is also a mind-boggling array of U.S. chain restaurants. No matter your price range or taste, San Juan is a great place to eat.

Mesónes gastronómicos are restaurants recognized by the government for preserving culinary traditions. There are more than 40 island-wide. (Although there are fine restaurants in the system, the *mesón gastronómico* label is not an automatic symbol of quality.) Wherever you go, it's *always* good to make reservations in the busy season, mid-November–April, in restaurants where they are accepted.

Puerto Rican cooking uses a lot of local vegetables: plantains are cooked a hundred different ways—as *tostones* (fried green), *amarillos* (baked ripe), and chips. Rice and beans with tostones or amarillos are accompaniments to every dish. Locals cook white rice with *habichuelas* (red beans), *achiote* (annatto seeds), or saffron; brown rice with *gandules* (pigeon peas); and *morro* (black rice) with *frijoles negros* (black beans). Yams and other root vegetables, such as yucca and *yautía*, are served baked, fried, stuffed, boiled, and mashed. *Sofrito*—a garlic, onion, sweet pepper, coriander, oregano, and tomato puree—is used as a base for practically everything.

Beef, chicken, pork, and seafood are rubbed with *adobo*, a garlic-oregano marinade, before cooking. *Arroz con pollo* (chicken with rice), *sancocho* (beef or chicken and tuber soup), *asopao* (a soupy rice gumbo with chicken or seafood), and *encebollado* (steak smothered in onions) are all typical plates. Also look for fritters served along highways and beaches. You may find *empanadillas* (stuffed fried turnovers), *surrullitos* (cheese-stuffed corn sticks), *alcapurias* (stuffed green-banana croquettes), and *bacalaitos* (codfish fritters). Caribbean lobster, available mainly at coastal restaurants, is sweeter and easier to eat than Maine lobster, and there is always plentiful fresh dolphinfish and red snapper. Conch is prepared in a chilled ceviche salad or stuffed with tomato sauce inside fritters.

Puerto Rican coffee is excellent black or *con leche* (with hot milk). The origin of the piña colada is attributed to numerous places, from the Caribe Hilton to a Fortaleza Street bar. Puerto Rican rums range from light mixers to dark, aged liqueurs. Look for Bacardí, Don Q, Ron Rico, Palo Viejo, and Barrilito.

What to Wear

Dress codes vary greatly, though a restaurant's price category is a good indicator of its formality. For less expensive places, anything but beachwear is fine. Ritzier eateries will expect collared shirts for men (jacket and tie requirements are rare) and chic attire for women. When in doubt, do as the Puerto Ricans often do and dress up.

Old San Juan

CAFÉS
¢–$$
✕ **Café Berlin.** This casual café, bakery, and delicatessen overlooks the Plaza Colón. Tasty vegetarian fare prevails—try one of the creative salads—but nonvegetarian dishes are also available. The café's pastries, desserts, fresh juices, and Puerto Rican coffees are the perfect elixir after a day of touring Old San Juan. ⊠ *Calle San Francisco 407* ☎ *787/722–5205* ▣ *AE, MC, V.*

¢–$$
✕ **La Bombonera.** Strong coffee and excellent pastries make this café, a landmark established in 1903, very popular in the morning—particularly on Sunday. All this despite the fact that the waiters are grumpy and give the appearance of having worked here since day one. It's open from 7:30 AM to early evening, and full breakfasts are served 'til 11 AM. ⊠ *Calle San Francisco 259, Old San Juan* ☎ *787/722–0658* ▣ *AE, MC, V.*

CARIBBEAN
$$–$$$
✕ **Casa Borinquen.** A portrait of independence leader Pedro Albizu Campos adorns the building's facade, a holdover from before restoration work, when a group of artists turned the crumbling walls into the "Museo sin Techo" ("Roofless Museum"). Today it's a bright, attractive restaurant serving radically delicious local cuisine. The vegetarian dishes are made with local produce, shrimp is served with *acerola* (a local fruit similar to a cherry but not as sweet) sauce and mashed cassava, and pork loin comes with fresh corn relish. ⊠ *Calle San Sebastián 109, Old San Juan* ☎ *787/725–0888* ▣ *AE, D, MC, V* ☉ *Closed Mon.*

$–$$
✕ **La Fonda del Jíbarito.** Sanjuaneros have favored this casual, family-run restaurant for years. The back porch is filled with plants, the dining room is filled with fanciful depictions of Calle Sol (the street outside), and the ever-present owner, Pedro J. Ruiz, is filled with the desire to ensure that everyone's happy. The conch ceviche and chicken fricasse are among the specialties. ⊠ *Calle Sol 280, Old San Juan* ☎ *787/725–8375* ⚐ *Reservations not accepted* ▣ *AE, MC, V.*

CONTEMPORARY
★ $$$$
✕ **Aguaviva Seaside Latino Cuisine.** Chef Roberto Treviño's seafood extravaganza is taking Old San Juan by storm, from the oyster and ceviche bar to the menu accented with contemporary Latin flavors. Try the *calamares rellenos* with ox tail *ropa vieja* (calamari filled with shredded, seasoned beef), or the spectacularly moist swordfish chop with roasted pozole and mushroom *escabeche* (marinade of oil and vinegar, peppers, onions, and garlic). Ocean-blue lighting and the lamps in the shape of *aguavivas* (jellyfish) are contrasted by white seating, and the room is decorated with seashells and starfish. At the bar, a beach cooler (watermelon lemonade with Bacardí Limon) throws you back on your beach chair. ⊠ *Calle Fortaleza 364, Old San Juan* ☎ *787/722–0665* ⚐ *No reservations accepted* ▣ *AE, MC, V.*

$$–$$$
✕ **Amadeus.** A trendy crowd enjoys such nouvelle Caribbean appetizers as buffalo wings or plantain mousse with shrimp and entrées such as ravioli with a goat cheese–and-walnut sauce or Cajun-grilled mahimahi. The front dining room is attractive—whitewashed walls, dark wood, white tablecloths, ceiling fans—and an interior courtyard leads to a romantic back dining room with printed tablecloths, candles, and exposed brick. There's also a seating area on Plaza San José. ⊠ *Calle San Sebastián 106, Old San Juan* ☎ *787/722–8635* ▣ *AE, MC, V* ☉ *No lunch Mon.*

$$–$$$ ✗ **Parrot Club.** The cuisine is inventive, the decor is colorful, and the staff is casual but efficient. Stop by the bar for the speciality passion-fruit drink before moving to the adjacent dining room or the back courtyard. The menu has contemporary variations of Cuban and Puerto Rican classics. You might start with mouthwatering crabcakes or tamarind-barbecued ribs, followed by blackened tuna in a dark-rum sauce or churrasco with *chimichurri* (a green sauce made with herbs, garlic, and tomatoes). ⊠ *Calle Fortaleza 363, Old San Juan* ☎ *787/725–7370* ⌦ *Reservations not accepted* ⊟ *AE, DC, MC, V.*

$–$$$ ✗ **Dragonfly.** Don't leave town without eating here. With Chinese-red furnishings and a charming staff outfitted in kimonos and satin shirts, this hip little restaurant has the feel of an elegant opium den. Surely the frequent lines outside its door attest to the seductive power of chef Roberto Treviño's Latin-Asian cuisine. The *platos* (large appetizers) are meant to be shared and include pork-and-plantain dumplings with an orange dipping sauce; spicy, perfectly fried calimari; and Peking-duck nachos with wasabi sour cream. ⊠ *Calle Fortaleza 364, Old San Juan* ☎ *787/ 977–3886* ⌦ *Reservations not accepted* ⊟ *AE, MC, V.*

ECLECTIC **$$** ✗ **La Ostra Cosa.** The menu here includes everything from oysters to burgers, but most people come for the large, succulent prawns, which are grilled and served with garlic butter. Opt for a seat in the back courtyard: with bougainvillea and moonlight, it's one of the city's prettiest alfresco dining spots. The gregarious owner, Alberto Nazario, brother of pop star Ednita Nazario, truly enjoys seeing his guests satisfied. ⊠ *Calle Cristo 154, Old San Juan* ☎ *787/722–2672* ⊟ *AE, MC, V.*

FRENCH **$$$–$$$$** ✗ **La Chaumière.** With black-and-white floor tiles, a beamed ceiling, and floral-print curtains, this two-story restaurant evokes rural France. It has been under the same management since 1969, and with all that experience the service is smooth. Daily specials augment a menu of stellar French classics, including onion soup, rack of lamb, scallops Provençale, and chateaubriand for two. ⊠ *Calle Tetuan 367, Old San Juan* ☎ *787/722–3330* ⊟ *AE, DC, MC, V* ☻ *Closed Sun. No lunch.*

ITALIAN **$$–$$$** ✗ **La Bella Piazza.** The narrow dining room has Roman columns, gold-leaf flourishes, and arched doorways that lead to an interior terrace. You'll find such quintessentially Italian appetizers as calamari *in padella* (lightly breaded and sautéed in olive oil, parsley, and garlic) and such archetypal pasta dishes as fusilli *amatriciana* (in a crushed bacon, tomato, and red-pepper sauce). Main courses include *saltinbocca alla romana* (veal and prosciutto in a sage, white-wine, and butter sauce) and *medaglioni al Chianti* (beef medallions in a spicy Chianti sauce). ⊠ *Calle San Francisco 355, Old San Juan* ☎ *787/721–0396* ⊟ *AE, MC, V* ☻ *Closed Wed.*

SPANISH **$–$$$** ✗ **El Picoteo.** Many patrons make a meal of the appetizers that dominate the menu at this chic tapas bar. Entrées such as paella are also noteworthy. There's a long, lively bar inside; one dining area overlooks the hotel El Convento's courtyard, and the other takes in the action along Calle Cristo. Even if you have dinner plans elsewhere, consider stopping here for a cocktail or a nightcap. ⊠ *El Convento Hotel, Calle Cristo 100, Old San Juan* ☎ *787/723–9621* ⊟ *AE, D, DC, MC, V.*

San Juan

CAFÉ **$–$$** ✗ **Kasalta Bakery, Inc.** Make your selection from the display cases full of luscious pastries and other tempting treats. Walk up to the counter and order a sandwich (try the Cubano) or such items as the meltingly tender octopus salad and the savory *caldo gallego* (a soup of fresh vegetables, sausage, and potatoes). Wash everything down with a cold drink or a café con leche that's guaranteed to be strong. ⊠ *Calle McLeary 1966, Ocean Park* ☎ *787/727–7340* ▤ *AE, MC, V.*

CARIBBEAN ✕ **Pamela's.** For the ultimate tropical dining experience, Pamela's is the
★ **$$$$** only city restaurant that offers outdoor seating at simple wooden tables with umbrellas right on the sand, just steps away from the ocean water. The contemporary Caribbean menu is as memorable as the alfresco setting, though it's also possible to dine indoors in air-conditioned comfort. Daily specials might include a blackened salmon glazed with honey and mandarin sauce, or Jamaican jerk shrimp and coconut corn arepa with tamarind barbecue sauce and guava coulis. ⊠ *Numero Uno Guesthouse, Calle Santa Ana 1, Ocean Park* ☎ *787/726–5010* ▤ *AE, MC, V.*

★ **$$–$$$$** ✕ **Ajili Mojili.** Traditional Puerto Rican food is prepared with a flourish and served in an attractive plantation-style setting. Sample the fried cheese and yautía dumplings with the house sauce, a tomato, herb, garlic, and shaved almond concoction. The *mofongo* (a mashed plantain casserole with seafood or meat), is wonderful, as is the plantain-crusted shrimp in a white-wine herb sauce. The restaurant is in a beautifully restored, historic mansion with terraces and views over the Condado lagoon. ⊠ *Av. Ashford 1006, Condado* ☎*787/725–9195* ▤*AE, MC, V* ⌂ *Reservations essential* ⊙ *No lunch Sat.*

$$–$$$ ✕ **Yerba Buena.** This "corner of South Beach in the Condado" serves Latin Caribbean food in contemporary trappings. The Cuban classic *ropa vieja* (meat cooked so slowly that it becomes tender shreds) comes in a stylish plantain nest. The shrimp has a coconut-and-ginger sauce, the halibut fillet one of mango and Grand Marnier. The restaurant claims to use the "original" recipe for its *mojito*, Cuba's tasty rum, lime, and mint drink. ⊠ *Av. Ashford 1350, Condado* ☎ *787/721–5907* ▤ *AE, MC, V* ⊙ *Closed Sun.*

$–$$$ ✕ **Tropical Restaurant.** For years, locals have favored this unpretentious Cuban restaurant for its reasonably priced, lovingly prepared Latin classics. Years of experience at preparing steak in brandy sauce, lobster stew, and chicken in rice shows up in the final product. For dessert, the *dulce de leche* (a sweet milk pudding) and the flan are good bets. ⊠ *Av. Ashford 1214, Condado* ☎ *787/724–3760* ▤ *AE, MC, V.*

CONTEMPORARY ✕ **Chayote.** Although it's slightly off the beaten path, this chic eatery—
$$–$$$ all earth tones and contemporary Puerto Rican art—is definitely an "in" spot. The chef gives haute international dishes a tropical panache. Starters include *sopa del día* (soup of the day) made with local produce, chayote stuffed with prosciutto, and corn tamales with shrimp in a coconut sauce. Many of the entrées are seafood dishes, including an excellent pan-seared tuna with Asian ginger sauce. The ginger flan is a must for dessert. ⊠ *Hotel Olimpo Court, Av. Miramar 603, Miramar* ☎ *787/722–9385* ▤ *AE, MC, V* ⊙ *Closed Sun.–Mon. No lunch Sat.*

$$–$$$ ✕ **Zabó Creative Cuisine.** In a restored plantation home with a pastoral front yard, this inventive restaurant seems as if it's out on the island somewhere. One of the main pastimes here is grazing—that is, sharing such appetizers as breaded calamari in a tomato-basil sauce with your dinner companions. Of the notable main courses, try the veal chops stuffed with provolone, pancetta, and herbs and served with a garlic-merlot sauce, or the catch of the day over yellow-raisin couscous in a mango-rosemary curry. ⊠ *Calle Candina 14, Condado* ☎ *787/725–9494* ▤ *AE, D, DC, MC, V* ⊙ *Closed Sun.–Mon. No lunch Tues.–Thurs. and Sat.*

SEAFOOD ✕ **Marisquería La Dorada.** This fine seafood establishment on Condado's
$$–$$$$ restaurant row is surprisingly affordable. The grilled seafood platter is the specialty, but there are also excellent pastas and other fish dinners, including mahimahi in caper sauce and codfish in green sauce. The

friendly waitstaff makes you feel genuinely welcome. ⊠ *Av. Magdalena 1105, Condado* ☎ 787/722–9583 ⊟ AE, D, MC, V.

SPANISH
$$–$$$$ ╳ **Urdin.** The owners, who include Julián Gil, a local celebrity, describe the menu here as Spanish with a Caribbean touch. The soup and seafood appetizers are particularly good, and a highly recommended main course is *chillo urdin de lujo* (red snapper sautéed with clams, mussels, and shrimp in a tomato, herb, and wine sauce). The name of the restaurant comes from the Basque word for "blue," which is the dining room's dominant color. ⊠ *Av. Magdalena 1105, Condado* ☎ 787/724–0420 ⊟ AE, MC, V.

Eastern Puerto Rico

CONTEMPORARY
$$–$$$$ ╳ **Hermès Creative Cuisine.** The menu at this restaurant in the Palmas del Mar Country Club is distinctive. Chef Hermés Vargas, from the Condado restaurant that also bears his name, likes to experiment with game, including wild boar and venison. You can eat yours alfresco on the terrace or by candlelight in the dining room. ⊠ *Palmas del Mar, Rte. 906, Km 86.4, Humacao* ☎ 787/285–2277 or 787/285–2266 ⚖ *Reservations essential* ⊟ AE, MC, V ☉ *No dinner Mon.*

SEAFOOD
$–$$$ ╳ **Anchor's Inn.** Seafood is the specialty at this meson gastronómico. Clever maritime decor and superb cooking have made it a local favorite; the convenient location down the road from El Conquistador Resort lures visitors. Try the *chillo entero* (fried whole red snapper) or the paella. ⊠ *Rte. 987, Km 2.7, Fajardo* ☎ 787/863–7200 ⚖ *Reservations not accepted* ⊟ AE, MC, V ☉ *Closed Tues.*

$–$$$ ╳ **Pulpo Loco By the Sea.** Octopus, oysters, mussels, and crab lead the lineup here, though many locals come for a beer or a cocktail as much as for the food. If your thirst is greater than your hunger, you can opt for a lighter snack. ⊠ *Rte. 187, Km 4.5, Piñones* ☎ 787/791–8382 ⚖ *Reservations not accepted* ⊟ AE, MC, V.

Southern Puerto Rico

CARIBBEAN
$–$$$ ╳ **Cilantro's.** In a 120-year-old mansion called Casa Real, chef Carlos Rosario serves new Puerto Rican cuisine in an intimate, second-floor dining room (reservations are a good idea). Under an arched ceiling and surrounded by stained-glass windows and decorative Spanish tiles, you can try dorado with a black-bean sauce or squid stuffed with sausage and lobster. There are also vegetarian dishes, and on Tuesday nights sushi is added to the menu. ⊠ *Calle Luna 85, San Germán* ☎ 787/264–2735 ⊟ D, MC, V ☉ *Closed Wed.*

ECLECTIC
★ $$–$$$ ╳ **Mark's at the Meliá.** One of the island's best restaurants is off the lobby of the Meliá hotel. Chef Mark French has won praise from the Caribbean Chefs Association, and his menu lives up to that honor. The menu changes often, but you'll find a long list of appetizers that includes a three-cheese onion soup or a bacon, lettuce, and tomato salad. Entrées range from plantain-crusted dorado with congri to medallions of tenderloin with a shrimp and béarnaise sauce. The chocolate truffle cake draws diners all the way from San Juan. ⊠ *Calle Cristina 75, Ponce* ☎ 787/284–6275 ⊟ AE, MC, V ☉ *Closed Mon.–Tues.*

SEAFOOD
$$–$$$ ╳ **El Bohío.** Watch tarpon play in the water while you dine on the enclosed deck at this informal restaurant. The long list of seafood is prepared in a variety of ways: shrimp comes breaded, stewed, or in a salad; conch is served as a salad or cooked in a butter and garlic sauce. ⊠ *Rte. 102, Km 9.7, Playa Joyuda, Cabo Rojo* ☎ 787/851–2755 ⊟ AE, DC, MC, V.

$–$$$ ╳ **El Ancla.** Families favor this restaurant at the edge of the sea. The kitchen serves generous and affordable plates of fish, crab, and other fresh seafood with tostones, *papas fritas* (french fries), and garlic bread. Try the shrimp in garlic sauce, the salmon fillet with capers, or the delectable mofongo. The piña coladas—with or without rum—and the flan are exceptional. There are two dining rooms—one for those who smoke and another for those who don't. ✉ *Av. Hostos Final 9, Ponce Playa, Ponce* ☎ *787/840–2450* 🖃 *AE, MC, V.*

Northwestern Puerto Rico

CARIBBEAN
¢–$$

✕ **El Buen Café.** Between Arecibo and the neighboring town of Hatillo, this diner attached to a parador is a local favorite and is often packed on the weekends. Favorites dishes include *carne mechada* (stuffed pot roast), chicken and rice soup, and seafood. Breakfast is also served. The restaurant opens at 5 AM and closes at 10:30 PM. ✉ *381 Rte. 2, Km 84, Hatillo* ☎ *787/898–3495* 🖃 *AE, MC, V.*

ECLECTIC
$$–$$$

✕ **The Landing.** This spacious restaurant and club has a large, beautiful wooden bar that's often filled with a mix of people, from surfers to retirees. You can dine on pasta, steaks, and burgers inside or on a back terrace overlooking the ocean. There's also a children's menu with junior burgers and chicken fingers. On weekend nights when live bands play, the place often fills with a younger crowd. ✉ *Rte. 413, Km 4.7, Rincón* ☎ *787/823–3112* 🖃 *AE, MC, V.*

$$–$$$

✕ **Larry B's.** Tucked next to the bar at Beside the Point Inn is a wooden patio where you can watch the surf crash against the beach while dining on steaks, shrimp, pasta, salads, and fresh fish, all simply prepared and served in generous helpings. Larry himself serves up the food, and he's happy to regale guests with tales of his wave-seeking exploits. ✉ *Beside the Point Inn, Rte. 413, Barrio Puntas, Rincón* ☎ *787/823–3210* 🖃 *MC, V* ☺ *Closed Mon.–Wed.*

ITALIAN
$$

✕ **Mangére.** You'll find a long menu of Italian favorites and 86 wines at this spacious restaurant decorated in pastel colors. Entrées include veal medallions with Portobello and porcini mushrooms, smoked Norwegian salmon with capers, and linguine carbonara. ✉ *Rte. 693, Km 8.5, Dorado* ☎ *787/796–4444* 🖃 *AE, D, MC, V.*

LATIN
$–$$$

✕ **El Molino del Quijote.** This family-run restaurant and bar serves Spanish and Puerto Rican cuisine in a charming thatch-roof building. Additional tables in the garden overlook the water. The paellas, mofongo, and sangría are superb. The service is warm and friendly. You may end up on one of its magic garden's hammocks after a Sancho Panza (the house drink made of orange juice, pineapple juice, peach schnapps, rum 151, and grenadine). The family also rents two comfortable and very affordable rooms ($) with cable TV. ✉ *Rte. 429, Km 3.3, Rincón* ☎ *787/823–4010* 🖃 *MC, V* ☺ *Closed Mon.–Thurs.*

Beaches

An island visit isn't complete without some time in the sand and sun. By law, everyone is welcome on Puerto Rico's *playas* (beaches), some of which—called *balnearios*—are maintained by the government. There are more than a dozen such beaches around the island, with dressing rooms, lifeguards, parking, and, in some cases, picnic tables, playgrounds, and camping facilities. Admission is free, parking is $2–$3. Hours vary, but most balnearios are open 9–5 daily in summer and Tuesday–Sunday the rest of the year.

SAN JUAN AREA

Playa de Isla Verde. Like Condado to its west, this beach is bordered by resorts and has plenty of places to rent chairs and sports equipment or grab a bite to eat. There aren't any lifeguards, but the sands are white, and the snorkeling is good.

Playa del Condado. East of Old San Juan and west of Ocean Park and Isla Verde, the long, wide Playa del Condado is often full of guests from the hotels that tower over it. Beach bars, sports outfitters, and chair-rental places abound, but there are no lifeguards.

Playa de Ocean Park. A residential neighborhood just east of Condado and west of Isla Verde is home to this wide, 1-mi-long (1½-km-long) stretch of golden sand. The waters are often choppy but still swimmable—take care, however, as there are no lifeguards.

EASTERN PUERTO RICO   **Balneario de Luquillo.** Coconut palms line crescent-shaped Luquillo, and coral reefs protect its crystal-clear lagoon from Atlantic waters, making it an ideal place to swim. Amenities include changing rooms, lockers, showers, picnic tables, tent sites, and stands that sell cocktails and island savories. It also has a ramp that allows wheelchair users water access.

Balneario Seven Seas. Near the Reserva Natural Las Cabezas de San Juan, Seven Seas is a long stretch of powdery sand with a smattering of shade. Facilities include food kiosks, picnic and camping areas, changing rooms, bathrooms, and showers. On weekends, the beach attracts crowds keen on its calm, clear waters—perfect for swimming.

Playa Flamenco. On the north shore of Culebra Island, Flamenco has shade trees, clear, shallow water, picnic tables, and rest rooms. In winter, storms in the Atlantic often create great waves for bodysurfing.

Playa Sun Bay. Of Vieques's more than three dozen beaches, Sun Bay is one of the most popular. Its white sands skirt a mile-long, crescent-shape bay. You'll find food kiosks, picnic tables, camping areas, and a bathhouse; on weekdays, when the crowds are thin, you might also find wild horses grazing among the palm trees.

SOUTHERN PUERTO RICO   **Balneario Boquerón.** This broad beach of hard-packed sand is fringed with coconut palms. You'll find changing facilities, cabins, showers, rest rooms, and picnic tables. Nearby, Playa Santa and Ballena beaches are often deserted.

Cabo Rojo beaches. Of the beaches near Cabo Rojo, El Combate, Buyé, and the more secluded La Playuela are the most gorgeous.

NORTHWESTERN PUERTO RICO   **Balneario de Rincón.** Swimmers enjoy the tranquil waters of this beach, which has parking facilities and rest rooms. Surfers and snorkelers swear by the waters off the nearby beach, Tres Palmas.

Playa Crashboat. The beach near Aguadilla is famous for the colorful fishing boats docked on its shores; its long, beautiful stretch of sand; and its clear water, which often looks like glass. Named after rescue boats that were docked here when Ramey Air Force Base was in operation, the beach has picnic huts, showers, and rest rooms.

Sports & the Outdoors

BASEBALL   The late, great Roberto Clemente is just one of many Puerto Rican ballplayers to find success in the U.S. major leagues after honing their skills at home. The island's pro season runs from October to February. Santurce, Ponce, Carolina Caguas, Arecibo, and Mayagüez all have teams. Contact the tourist office for details on baseball games, or call **Professional Baseball of Puerto Rico** (☎ 787/765–6285).

BOATING & SAILING   **Eco Action Tours** (✉ Condado Plaza Hotel, Av. Ashford 999, Laguna Wing, Condado, San Juan ☎ 787/791–7509 or 787/640–7385) rents kayaks, Sunfish, and Jet Skis; and offers kayaking trips to other parts of the island. In eastern Puerto Rico, **Puerto del Rey Marina** (✉ Rte. 3, Km 51.2, Fajardo ☎ 787/860–1000 ⊕ www.marinapuertodelrey.com), home to 750 ships, is one of the Caribbean's largest marinas. It's the place to arrange for a charter or find out about excursions to Vieques's biolumi-nescent Bahía Mosquito.

CYCLING Selected areas lend themselves to bike travel. In general, however, the roads are congested and distances are vast. Avoid main thoroughfares in San Juan: the traffic is heavy and the fumes are thick. The Paseo Piñones is an 11-mi bike path that skirts the ocean east of San Juan. The entire southwest coast of Cabo Rojo also makes for good biking, particularly the broad beach at Boquerón. Road bike events are organized year-round by the **Federación Puertorriqueña de Ciclismo** (⊕ www.federacionciclismopr. com). The **Puerto Rico Mountain Bike Association** (⊕ www.prmtb.com) sched-ules mountain-bike events from March to October.

Hot Dog Cycling (⊠ Av. Isla Verde 5916, Isla Verde, San Juan ☎ 787/ 982–5344 ⊕ www.hotdogcycling.com) rents Cannondale bicycles for $30 a day and organizes group excursions to El Yunque and other places out on the island. You can rent bikes for about $5 an hour from **Pulpo Loco By the Sea** (⊠ Rte. 187, Km 4.5, Piñones ☎ 787/791–8382).

FISHING Puerto Rico's waters are home to large game fish such as marlin, wahoo, dorado, tuna, and barracuda; as many as 30 world records for catches have been set off the island's shores. Half-day, full-day, split-charter, and big- and small-game fishing can be arranged through **Benitez Deep-Sea Fishing** (⊠ Club Náutico de San Juan, Miramar, San Juan ☎ 787/723–2292). **Moondog Charters** (⊠ Black Eagle Marina, off Rte. 413, Rincón ☎ 787/823–7168) organizes fishing charters and whale-watching trips. **Shiraz Charters** (⊠ Rte. 906, Candelero Resort at Palmas del Mar, Site 6, Humacao ☎ 787/285–5718 ⊕ www.charternet.com/fishers/shiraz) specializes in deep-sea fishing charters in search of tuna. **Tour Marine** (⊠ Rte. 101, Km 14.1, Joyuda Sector, Puerto Real, Cabo Rojo ☎ 787/851–9259) takes anglers out to waters off Cabo Rojo's coast.

GOLF Aficionados may know that Puerto Rico is the birthplace of golf legend Chi Chi Rodríguez—and he had to hone his craft somewhere. Currently, you'll find nearly 20 courses on the island, including many championship links. Be sure to call ahead for tee times; hours vary, and several hotel courses give preference to guests. Greens fees start at about $30 and go up as high as $150. The **Puerto Rican Golf Association** (⊠ Calle Caribe 58, San Juan ☎ 787/721–7742 ⊕ www.prga.org) is a good source for information on courses and tournaments.

Developed on what was once a coconut plantation, the public, 18-hole course at the **Bahía Beach Plantation** (⊠ Rte. 187, Km 4.2, Río Grande ☎ 787/256–5600) is an old-time favorite that skirts a slice of the east coast. **Candelero Resort at Palmas del Mar** (⊠ Rte. 906, Humacao ☎ 787/ 285–2256) has two courses: the Rees Jones–designed Flamboyán course, named for the flamboyant trees that pepper its fairway, winds around a lake, over a river, and to the sea before turning toward dunes and wet-lands. The Gary Player–designed Palmas course has a challenging par 5 that scoots around wetlands. The 7,100-yard course at **Dorado Del Mar** (⊠ Rte. 693, Dorado ☎ 787/796–3065) is a Chi Chi Rodríguez signa-ture course with narrow fairways that can be a challenge to hit when the wind picks up. Four world-class Robert Trent Jones–designed 18-hole courses are shared by Hyatt's two resorts in the Dorado area west

Fodor'sChoice of San Juan, the **Hyatt Dorado Beach Resort** and the **Hyatt Regency Cer-**
★ **romar Beach** (⊠ Rte. 693, Km 10.8 and Km 11.8, Dorado ☎ 787/796–1234 Ext. 3238). With El Yunque as a backdrop, the two 18-hole courses at the **Westin Río Mar Beach Resort** (⊠ Río Mar Blvd. 6000, Río Grande ☎ 787/888–6000) are inspirational. The River Course was de-signed by Greg Norman, the Ocean course by George and Tom Fazio.

The 18-hole Arthur Hills–designed course at **Wyndham El Conquistador Resort and Country Club** (✉ Av. El Conquistador 1000, Fajardo ☎ 787/863–6784) is famous for its 200-ft changes in elevation. The trade winds make every shot challenging.

HORSE RACING Thoroughbred races are run year-round at **Hipódromo El Comandante** (✉ Av. 65th Infantry, Rte. 3, Km 15.3, Canóvanas ☎ 787/724–6060 ⊕ www.comandantepr.com) a racetrack about 20 minutes east of San Juan. On race days the dining rooms open at 12:30 PM. Post time is 2:15 or 2:45 (depending on the season) Wednesday and Friday through Monday.

HORSEBACK RIDING **Campo Allegre** (✉ Rte. 127, Km 5.1, Yauco ☎ 787/856–2609) is a 204-acre horse ranch in southern Puerto Rico that conducts half-hour, one-hour, and two-hour rides through the hills surrounding Yauco. There are also pony rides for children. The family-run **Hacienda Carabali** (✉ Rte. 992, Km 4, at Mameyes River Bridge, Barrio Mameyes, Río Grande ☎ 787/889–5820 or 787/889–4954) in eastern Puerto Rico is a good place to see Puerto Rico's Paso Fino horses in action. You can even jump in the saddle yourself. Riding excursions ($45 an hour) include a one-hour jaunt along Río Mameyes and the edge of El Yunque and a two-hour ride along Balneario de Luquillo. Marlene Steck Jones of **Rancho de Caballos de Utuado** (✉ Rte. 612, across from Casa Grande, Utuado ☎ 787/894–0240) takes adults and children on friendly rides along the rivers and lakes of Utuado, greeting all the local townspeople along the way. **Tropical Trail Rides** (✉ Rte. 4466, Km 1.8, Isabela ☎ 787/872–9256), in the northwest, offers guided tours of secluded beaches, tropical trails, and cliff caves, with stops for swimming and exploring. **Tropical Paradise Horse Back Riding** (✉ Off Rte. 690, west of Hyatt Regency Cerromar, Dorado ☎ 787/720–5454) arranges rides along a north-coast beach on Paso Fino horses.

SCUBA DIVING & SNORKELING The diving is excellent off Puerto Rico's south, east, and west coasts, as well as its offshore islands. Particularly striking are dramatic walls created by a continental shelf off the south coast between La Parguera and Guánica. It's best to choose specific locations with the help of a guide or outfitter. Escorted half-day dives range from $45 to $95 for one or two tanks, including all equipment; in general, double those prices for night dives. Packages that include lunch and other extras start at $100; those that include accommodations are also available.

Snorkeling excursions, which include transportation, equipment rental, and sometimes lunch, start at $50. Equipment rents at beaches for about $5–$7. (Caution: coral-reef waters and mangrove areas can be dangerous. Unless you're an expert or have an experienced guide, stay near the water-sports centers of hotels and avoid unsupervised areas.)

Aquatica Underwater Adventures (✉ Rte. 110, Km 10, Gate 5, Aguadilla ☎ 787/890–6071) offers scuba-diving certification courses and dives off Aguadilla and Isabela beaches in the northwest. You can also rent snorkeling equipment. **Blue Caribe Dive Center** (✉ Calle Flamboyán, Esperanza, Vieques ☎ 787/741–2522 ⊕ www.enchanted-isle.com/bluecaribe) offers scuba excursions to several sites and night dives in Bahía Mosquito. **Divers' Outlet** (✉ Calle Fernández Garcia 38, Luquillo ☎ 787/889–5721 or 888/746–3483) is a full-service dive shop on the northeast coast. It offers PADI certification, rents equipment, and can arrange scuba outings. **Ocean Sports** (✉ Av. Ashford 1035, Condado, San Juan ☎ 787/723–8513 ⊕ www.osdivers.com) offers certified scuba dives, air tank fill-ups; and equipment repairs, sales, and rentals. **Parguera Divers** (✉ Posada Porlamar, Rte. 304, La Parguera ☎ 787/899–4171) offers scuba and snorkeling expeditions and basic instruction on the southwest coast. At **Sea Ventures Pro Dive Center** (✉ Puerto del Rey Marina, Rte. 3, Km 51.4, Fajardo ☎ 787/863–3483 or 800/739–3483 ⊕ www.divepuertorico.com) you can get PADI certified and arrange dive trips to 20 offshore sites.

SURFING Although the west-coast beaches are considered *the* places to surf, San Juan was actually where the sport got its start on the island, back in 1958 thanks to legendary surfers Gary Hoyt and José Rodríguez Reyes. In San Juan many surfers head to La Punta, a reef break behind the Ashford Presbyterian Hospital, or the Sheraton, a break named after the hotel (it's now the Marriott) with either surf or boogie boards. In Isla Verde, white water on the horizon means that the waves are good at the beach break near the Ritz-Carlton, known as Pine Grove.

East of the city, in Piñones, the Caballo has deep-to-shallow-water shelf waves that require a big-wave board known as a "gun." Playa La Pared, near Balneario de Luquillo is a surfer haunt with medium-range waves. Numerous local competitions are held here throughout the year. The very best surfing beaches are along the western coast from Isabela south to Rincón, which gained notoriety by hosting the World Surfing Championship in 1968. Today the town draws surfers from around the globe, especially in winter when the waves are at their best.

La Selva Surf (✉ Calle Fernández Garcia 250, Luquillo ☎ 787/889–6205 ⊕ www.rainforestsafari.com), near Playa La Pared, has anything a surfer could need, including news about current conditions. At Ocean Park beach, famous surfer Carlos Cabrero, proprietor of **Tres Palmas** (✉ Av. McLeary 1911, Ocean Park, San Juan ☎ 787/728–3377), rents boards (daily rates are $25 for short boards, $30 for long boards), repairs equipment, and sells all sorts of hip beach and surfing gear. Pick up new and used surfboards, body boards, kayaks, and snorkeling gear, or rent equipment at **West Coast Surf Shop** (✉ Calle Muñoz Rivera 2E, Rincón ☎ 787/823–3935).

TENNIS If you'd like to use courts at a property where you aren't a guest, call in advance for information. Hotel guests usually get first priority, and you are likely to have to pay a fee. Courts at the following hotels are open to nonguests: Candelero Resort at Palmas del Mar, Caribe Hilton, Condado Plaza, Copamarina Beach Resort, Hilton Ponce, Hyatt Dorado Beach, Hyatt Regency Cerromar Beach, San Juan Marriott, Westin Río Mar Beach Resort, Wyndham El Conquistador, and Wyndham El San Juan. The four lighted courts of the **Isla Verde Tennis Club** (✉ Calles Ema and Delta Rodriguez, Isla Verde, San Juan ☎ 787/727–6490) are open for nonmember use at $4 per hour, daily 8 AM–10 PM. The **Parque Central Municipo de San Juan** (✉ Calle Cerra, exit on Rte. 2, Santurce, San Juan ☎ 787/722–1646) has 17 lighted courts. Fees are $3 per hour 8 AM–6 PM and $4 per hour 6 PM–10 PM.

WINDSURFING You'll get the best windsurfing advice and equipment from Jaime Torres at **Velauno** (✉ Calle Loíza 2430, Punta Las Marías, San Juan ☎ 787/728–8716 ⊕ www.velauno.com), the second-largest, full-service windsurfing center in the United States. Lisa Penfield, a former windsurfing competitor, teaches beginners at the **Watersports Center at the Dorado Beach Resort & Country Club** (✉ Rte. 693, Km 10.8, Dorado ☎ 787/796–2188).

Shopping

FodorsChoice San Juan, the island's shopping mecca, isn't a free port, so you won't
★ find bargains on electronics and perfumes. You can, however, find excellent prices on china, crystal, fashions, and jewelry. Shopping for local crafts can also be gratifying: you'll run across a lot that's tacky, but you

can also find treasures, and in many cases you can watch the artisans at work. Popular items include *santos* (small carved figures of saints or religious scenes), hand-rolled cigars, handmade *mundillo* lace from Aguadilla, *vejigantes* (colorful masks used during Carnival and local festivals) from Loíza and Ponce, and fancy men's shirts called guayaberas. For guidance on finding genuine craftspeople, contact the **Puerto Rico Tourism Company's Asuntos Culturales** (☎ 787/723–0692 Cultural Affairs Office).

Areas & Malls

In Old San Juan—especially on Calles Fortaleza and San Francisco— you'll find everything from T-shirt emporiums to selective crafts stores, bookshops, art galleries, jewelry boutiques, and even shops that specialize in made-to-order Panama hats. Calle Cristo is lined with factory-outlet stores, including Coach, Dooney & Bourke Factory Store, Polo/ Ralph Lauren Factory Store, Guess Factory Story, and Tommy Hilfiger.

With many stores selling luxury items and designer fashions, the shopping spirit in the San Juan neighborhood of Condado is reminiscent of that in Miami. Avenida Condado is a good bet for souvenirs and curios as well as art and upscale jewelry or togs. Avenida Ashford is considered the heart of San Juan's fashion district. There's also a growing fashion scene in the business district of Hato Rey.

Look for vendors selling crafts from kiosks at the **Artesanía Puertorriqueña** (⊠ Plaza Dársenas, Old San Juan, San Juan ☎ 787/722–1709) in the tourism company's La Casita near Pier 1. Several vendors also set up shop to sell articles such as belts, handbags, and toys along Calle San Justo in front of Plaza Dársenas. Right off the highway east of San Juan, the **Belz Factory Outlet World** (⊠ Rte. 3, Km 18.4, Canóvanas ☎ 787/ 256–7040 ⊕ www.belz.com) has more than 75 stores, including Nike, Guess, Mikasa, Gap, Levi's, Liz Claiborne, and Tommy Hilfiger. There's also a large food court. Just outside of the southern city of Ponce, **Plaza del Caribe Mall** (⊠ Rte. 2, Km 227.9 ☎ 787/259–8989), one of the island's largest malls, has stores such as Sears, JCPenney, and Gap. For a mundane albeit complete shopping experience, head to **Plaza Las Américas** (⊠ Av. Franklin Delano Roosevelt 525, Hato Rey, San Juan ☎ 787/767–1525), which has 200 shops, including the world's largest JCPenney store, Gap, Sears, Macy's, Godiva, and Armani Exchange, as well as restaurants and movie theaters. About 20 minutes from Dorado via Highway 22 at Exit 55 is Puerto Rico's first factory-outlet mall. **Prime Outlets Puerto Rico** (⊠ Rte. 2, Km 54.8, Barceloneta ☎ 787/846–9011) is a pastel village of more than 40 stores selling discounted merchandise from such familiar names as Liz Claiborne, Polo, Calvin Klein, Brooks Brothers, the Gap, Reebok, and Tommy Hilfiger.

Specialty Items

ART Artists show and sell their work at **Casa Vieja Gallery** (⊠ Rte. 996, outside Esperanza, Vieques ☎ 787/741–3078), in a Caribbean-style building at the entrance to the grounds of Inn on the Blue Horizon. **Galería Botello** (⊠ Av. Franklin Delano Roosevelt 314, Hato Rey, San Juan ☎ 787/250–8274 ⊕ www.botello.com) offers a broad range of works, from traditional santos to pieces by such up-and-coming Puerto Rican artists as María del Mater O'Neill, whose large formats and bold strokes and colors give familiar home-and-garden themes a twist. **Galería Raíces** (⊠ Av. José de Diego 314, Santurce, San Juan ☎ 787/723–8909) has works by such emerging Puerto Rican artists as Nayda Collazo Llorens, whose cerebral and sensitive multimedia installations examine connections and patterns in games, codes, and human memory. **OBRA** (⊠ Calle Tetuán 301, Old San Juan, San Juan ☎ 787/723–3206), is a visually pleasing space with museum-quality paintings, drawings, and sculptures by such Puerto Rican masters as Augusto Marín, Myrna Baez, and Rafael Tufiño. The picturesque **Treehouse Studio** (⊠ Unmarked road off Rte. 3, Río Grande ☎ 787/888–8062), not far from El Yunque, sells vibrant watercolors by Monica Laird, who also gives workshops. Call for an appointment and directions.

CLOTHES   After many years of catering to a primarily local clientele, **Clubman** (⊠ Av. Ashford 1351, Condado, San Juan ☎ 787/722–1867) is the

★   classic choice for gentlemen's clothing. **La Femme** (⊠ Av. Franklin Delano Roosevelt 320, Hato Rey, San Juan ☎ 787/753–0915) sells attractive (and sexy) women's clothes and accessories. **Matahari** (⊠ Calle San Justo 202, Old San Juan, San Juan ☎ 787/724–5869) sells unusual clothes for men and women as well as accessories, jewelry, and trinkets that proprietor Fernando Sosa collects during his trips around the world.

Monsieur (⊠ Av. Ashford 1126, Condado, San Juan ☎ 787/722–0918) has casual, contemporary designs for men. The window displays at

★   **Nativa Boutique** (⊠ Calle Cervantes 55, Condado, San Juan ☎ 787/724–
★   1396) are almost as daring as the clothes it sells. **Nono Maldonado** (⊠ Av. Ashford 1051, Condado, San Juan ☎ 787/721–0456) is well known for his high-end, elegant linen designs for men and women.

HANDICRAFTS   Among the offerings at **Artesanías Castor Ayala** (⊠ Rte. 187, Km 6.6, Loíza ☎ 787/876–1130), in eastern Puerto Rico, are the coconut-shell festival masks dubbed "Mona Lisas" because of their elongated smiles. Craftsman Raúl Ayala Carrasquillo has been making these museum-quality pieces for more than 40 years, following in the footsteps of his late father, the esteemed craftsman for whom the store is named. Masks, priced from $50 to $350, are often snapped up by collectors. At the **Convento de los Dominicos** (⊠ Calle Norzagaray 98, Old San Juan, San Juan ☎ 787/721–6866)—the Dominican Convent on the north side of the old city that houses the offices of the Instituto de Cultura Puertorriqueña—you'll find baskets, masks, the famous *cuatro* guitars, santos, and reproductions of Taíno artifacts. At El Conquistador Resort, Maria Elba Torres runs the **Galería Arrecife** (⊠ Av. El Conquistador 1000, Fajardo ☎ 787/863–3972), which shows only works by artists living in the Caribbean. Look for ceramics by Rafael de Olmo and jewelry made from fish scales.

JEWELRY   **Aetna Gold** (⊠ Calle Gilberto Concepción de Gracia 111, Old San Juan, San Juan ☎ 787/721–4756), adjacent to the Wyndham Old San Juan Hotel, sells exquisite gold jewelry designed in Greece. For a wide array of watches and jewelry, visit the two floors of **Bared** (⊠ Calle Fortaleza and Calle San Justo, Old San Juan, San Juan ☎ 787/724–4811). Diamonds and gold galore are found at **Joseph Manchini** (⊠ Calle Fortaleza 101, Old San Juan, San Juan ☎ 787/722–7698). **Joyería Cátala** (⊠ Plaza de Armas, Old San Juan, San Juan ☎ 787/722–3231) is distinguished for its large selection of pearls. **Joyería Riviera** (⊠ Calle Cruz 205, Old San Juan, San Juan ☎ 787/725–4000) sells fine jewelry by David Yurman and Rolex watches.

SOUVENIRS   Carnival masks, hammocks, Puerto Rican coffee, and rum fill the shelves of **Mi Coquí** (⊠ Calle Marina 9227, Ponce Centro, Ponce ☎ 787/841–0216). Chocolate-loving Laurie Humphrey had trouble finding a supplier for her sweet tooth, so she opened the **Paradise Store** (⊠ Hwy. 194, Km 0.4, Fajardo ☎ 787/863–8182). Lindt and other gourmet chocolates jam the shop, which also sells flowers and such gift items as Puerto Rican–made soaps. Buy a recording of the tree frog's song, pick up a coffee-table book about the rain forest, and check out the books for eco-minded children at the large, lovely **El Yunque Gift Shop** (⊠ Rte. 191, Km 4.3 ☎ 787/888–1880). Tucked among the rain-forest gifts are other Puerto Rican goods, including note cards, maps, soaps, jams, and coffee.

Nightlife & the Arts

Qué Pasa, the official visitor's guide, has listings of events in San Juan and out on the island. For up-to-the-minute listings, pick up a copy of the English-language edition of the *San Juan Star,* the island's oldest daily. The Thursday edition's weekend section is especially useful. You can also check with local tourist offices and the concierge at your hotel to find out what's doing.

Nightlife

In Old San Juan, Calle San Sebastián is lined with bars and restaurants. Salsa music blaring from jukeboxes in cut-rate pool halls competes with mellow Latin jazz in top-flight nightspots. Evenings begin with dinner and stretch into the late hours at the bars of the more upscale, so-called SoFo (south of Fortaleza) end of Old San Juan. Well-dressed visitors and locals alike often mingle in the lobby bars of large hotels, many of which have bands in the evening. An eclectic crowd heads to the Plaza del Mercado off Avenida Ponce de León at Calle Canals in Santurce after work to hang out in the plaza or enjoy drinks and food in one of the small establishments skirting the farmers market. Condado and Ocean Park have their share of nightlife, too. Most are restaurants and bar environments.

Just east of San Juan, funky Piñones has a collection of open-air seaside eateries that are popular with locals. On weekend evenings, many places have merengue combos, Brazilian jazz trios, or reggae bands. In the southern city of Ponce, people embrace the Spanish tradition of the *paseo,* an evening stroll around the Plaza las Delicias. The boardwalk at La Guancha in Ponce is also a lively scene. Live bands often play on weekends. Elsewhere *en la isla,* nighttime activities center on the hotels and resorts.

Wherever you are, dress to party. Puerto Ricans have flair, and both men and women love getting dressed up to go out. Bars are usually casual, but if you have on jeans, sneakers, and a T-shirt, you may be refused entry at nightclubs and discos.

BARS & MUSIC CLUBS
Café Bohemio (⊠ El Convento Hotel, Calle Cristo 100, Old San Juan, San Juan ☎ 787/723–9200), a Latin restaurant, turns into a live jazz and Bohemian music club from 11 PM to 2 AM Tuesday through Friday (after the kitchen closes); Thursday night is best. Power brokers indulge in fine smokes while mingling with local starlets and smartly attired visitors at the **Cigar Bar** (⊠ Wyndham El San Juan, Av. Isla Verde 6063, Isla Verde, San Juan ☎ 787/791–1000). **Dunbar's** (⊠ Calle McCleary 1954, Ocean Park, San Juan ☎ 787/728–2920), a classic pub for locals and visitors alike, is very popular from Wednesday to Sunday night. They have live bands, chicken wings, and a pool table. **El Batey** (⊠ Calle Cristo 101, Old San Juan, San Juan ☎ 787/725–1787) is a hole-in-the-wall run by crusty New Yorker Davydd Gwilym Jones III; it looks like a military bunker, but it has the best oldies jukebox in the city and is wildly popular. With a large dance and stage area and smokin' Afro-Cuban bands, **Rumba** (⊠ Calle San Sebastián 152, Old San Juan, San Juan ☎ 787/725–4407) is one of the best parties in town.

CASINOS
By law, all casinos are in hotels, primarily in San Juan. The government keeps a close eye on them. Dress for the larger casinos is on the formal side, and the atmosphere is refined. Casinos set their own hours but are

generally open from noon to 4 AM. In addition to slot machines, typical games include blackjack, roulette, craps, Caribbean stud (a five-card poker game), and *pai gow* poker (a combination of American poker and the Chinese game pai gow). Hotels with casinos have live entertainment most weekends, as well as restaurants and bars. The minimum age to gamble is 18.

Among the San Juan hotels that have casinos are the Condado Plaza Hotel, Ritz-Carlton San Juan, Inter-Continental San Juan Resort and Casino, San Juan Marriott, Wyndham El San Juan Hotel, and Wyndham Old San Juan Hotel. Elsewhere on the island there are casinos at the Hyatt Regency Cerromar, the Candelero Resort at Palmas del Mar, Hilton Ponce and Casino, Westin Río Mar Beach Resort and Country Club, and Wyndham El Conquistador Resort & Country Club.

DANCE CLUBS A long line of well-heeled patrons usually runs out the door of **Babylon** (⊠ Wyndham El San Juan Hotel, Av. Isla Verde 6063, Isla Verde, San Juan ☎ 787/791–1000). Those with the staying power to make it inside step out of the Caribbean and into the ancient Middle East. Those who tire of waiting often head to El Chico Lounge, a small room with live entertainment right off the hotel lobby. An older, dressy crowd frequents **Martini's** (⊠ Inter-Continental San Juan Resort & Casino, Av. Isla Verde 187, Isla Verde, San Juan ☎ 787/791–6100 Ext. 356), which is known for its Las Vegas–style reviews; acts have included celebrity impersonators and flamenco music and dance troupes. Record parties and fashion shows are also held here from time to time.

GAY & LESBIAN The oceanfront deck bar of the **Atlantic Beach** hotel (⊠ Calle Vendig 1,
CLUBS Condado, San Juan ☎787/721–6100) is famed for its early-evening happy hours, with pulsating tropical music, a wide selection of exotic drinks, and ever-pleasant ocean breezes. The music is terrific at **Eros** (⊠ Av. Ponce de León 1257, Santurce, San Juan ☎ 787/722–1390), a club that's popular with the gay community but is just as welcoming to those who aren't gay. The lighting is dim, the dance floor is large, and the balcony bar overlooks all the drama.

The Arts

The renaissance of the music and dance form known as *bomba* dates from 1961, when a TV producer showed up in the eastern town of Loíza searching for residents who remembered it. In response, mask-maker Castor Ayala put together the **Ballet Folklórico Hermanos Ayala** (⊠ Rte. 187, Km 6.6, Loíza ☎ 787/876–1130), a folk group that performs around the island and elsewhere in Latin America. The group has no headquarters, but you can get its schedule at the mask-making shop, Artesanías Castor Ayala.

There's something going on nearly every night at the **Centro de Bellas Artes Luis A. Ferré** (Luis A. Ferré Center for the Performing Arts; ⊠ Av. José de Diego and Av. Ponce De León, Santurce, San Juan ☎ 787/725–7334), from pop or jazz concerts to plays, opera, and ballet. It's also the home of the San Juan Symphony Orchestra. If you're in Old San Juan on the first Tuesday of the month (September–December and February–May), take advantage of **Gallery Night** (☎ 787/723–6286). Galleries and select museums open their doors after hours for viewings accompanied by refreshments and music. Named for Puerto Rican playwright Alejandro Tapia, **Teatro Tapia** (⊠ Calle Fortaleza at Plaza Colón, Old San Juan, San Juan ☎ 787/722–0247) hosts theatrical and musical productions.

The **Museo de Arte de Ponce** (⊠ Av. Las Américas 2325, Sector Santa María, Ponce ☎ 787/848–0505) occasionally sponsors chamber music concerts and recitals by members of the Puerto Rico Symphony Orchestra. Check for theater productions and concerts at the **Teatro La Perla** (⊠ Calle Mayor and Calle Cristina, Ponce Centro, Ponce ☎ 787/843–4322 information, 787/843–4080 ticket office).

Exploring Puerto Rico

Old San Juan

Old San Juan, the original city founded in 1521, contains carefully preserved examples of 16th- and 17th-century Spanish colonial architecture. More than 400 buildings have been beautifully restored. Graceful wrought-iron balconies with lush hanging plants extend over narrow streets paved with *adoquines* (blue-gray stones originally used as ballast on Spanish ships). The Old City is partially enclosed by walls that date from 1633 and once completely surrounded it. Designated a U.S. National Historic Zone in 1950, Old San Juan is chockablock with shops, open-air cafés, homes, tree-shaded squares, monuments, pigeons, and people. You can get an overview on a morning's stroll (bear in mind that this "stroll" includes some steep climbs). However, if you plan to immerse yourself in history or to shop, you'll need two or three days.

SIGHTS TO SEE *Numbers in the margin correspond to points of interest on the Old San Juan Exploring map.*

⑪ **Alcaldía.** The city hall was built between 1604 and 1789. In 1841 extensive renovations were done to make it resemble Madrid's city hall, with arcades, towers, balconies, and a lovely inner courtyard. A tourist information center and an art gallery are on the first floor. ⊠ *Calle San Francisco 153, Plaza de Armas, Old San Juan* ☎ *787/724–7171 Ext. 2391* ⌨ *Free* ☉ *Weekdays 8–4.*

⑧ **Capilla del Cristo.** According to legend, in 1753 a young horseman named Baltazar Montañez got carried away during festivities in honor of San Juan Bautista (St. John the Baptist), raced down the street, and plunged over the steep precipice. A witness to the tragedy promised to build a chapel if the young man's life could be saved. Historical records maintain the the man died, though legend contends he lived. Regardless, this chapel was built, and inside it is a small silver altar dedicated to the Christ of Miracles. ⊠ *Calle Cristo, Old San Juan* ☎ *no phone* ⌨ *Free* ☉ *Tues. 10–3:30.*

⑤ **Casa Blanca.** The original structure on this site, not far from the ramparts of El Morro, was a frame house built in 1521 as a home for Ponce de León. But Ponce de León died in Cuba without ever having lived in it, and it was virtually destroyed by a hurricane in 1523, after which his son-in-law had the present masonry home built. His descendants occupied it for 250 years. From the end of the Spanish-American War in 1898 to 1966 it was the home of the U.S. Army commander in Puerto Rico. The home now contains several rooms decorated with colonial-era furnishings and an archaeology exhibit. The lush garden, cooled by spraying fountains, is a tranquil spot. ⊠ *Calle San Sebastián 1, Old San Juan* ☎ *787/724–4102* ⌨ *$2* ☉ *Tues.–Sat. 9–noon and 1–4:30.*

⑥ **Catedral de San Juan.** The Catholic shrine of Puerto Rico had humble beginnings in the early 1520s as a thatch-topped wooden structure. Hurricane winds tore off the thatch and destroyed the church. It was reconstructed in 1540, when the graceful circular staircase and vaulted Gothic ceilings were added, but most of the work was done in the 19th century. The remains of Ponce de León are in a marble tomb near the transept. ⊠ *Calle Cristo 153, Old San Juan* ☎ *787/722–0861* ⌨ *$1*

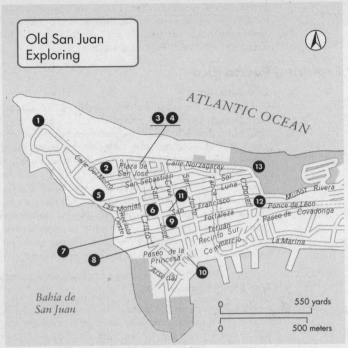

donation suggested ☉ Weekdays 8:30–4; masses Sat. at 7 PM, Sun. at
9 and 11 AM, weekdays at 12:15 PM.

❸ Convento de los Dominicos. Built by Dominican friars in 1523, this convent often served as a shelter during Carib Indian attacks and, more recently, as headquarters for the Antilles command of the U.S. Army. Now
home to some offices of the Institute of Puerto Rican Culture, the beautifully restored building contains religious manuscripts, artifacts, and
art. The institute also maintains a craft store and bookstore here.
⊠ Calle Norzagaray 98, Old San Juan ☎ 787/721–6866 ☒ Free
☉ Mon.–Sat. 9–5.

❼ La Fortaleza. On a hill overlooking the harbor, La Fortaleza, the western hemisphere's oldest executive mansion in continuous use and official residence of Puerto Rico's governor, was built as a fortress. The original
primitive structure, constructed in 1540, has seen numerous changes over
the past four centuries, resulting in the present collection of marble and
mahogany, medieval towers, and stained-glass galleries. Guided tours
are conducted every hour on the hour in English, on the half hour in
Spanish. ⊠ Calle Recinto Oeste, Old San Juan ☎ 787/721–7000 Ext.
2211 or 2358 ☒ Free ☉ Weekdays 9–4.

☙ ❽ Fuerte San Cristóbal. This 18th-century fortress guarded the city from
land attacks. Even larger than El Morro, San Cristóbal was known in
its heyday as the Gibraltar of the West Indies. ⊠ Calle Norzagaray, Old
San Juan ☎ 787/729–6960 ⊕ www.nps.gov/saju/ ☒ $2 ☉ Daily 9–5.

★ ☙ ❶ Fuerte San Felipe del Morro. On a rocky promontory at the Old City's
northwestern tip is El Morro, which was built by the Spaniards between
1540 and 1783. Rising 140 ft above the sea, the massive six-level fortress
covers enough territory to accommodate a 9-hole golf course. It's a
labyrinth of dungeons, barracks, turrets, towers, and tunnels. Its small,
air-conditioned museum traces the history of the fortress. Tours and a

video show are available in English. ✉ *Calle Norzagaray, Old San Juan* ☎ *787/729–6960* ⊕ *www.nps.gov/saju/* ✉ *$2.*

② Museo de las Américas. The Museum of the Americas is on the second floor of the imposing former military barracks, Cuartel de Ballajá. Most exhibits rotate, but the focus is on the popular and folk art of Latin America. The permanent exhibit, "Las Artes Populares en las Américas," has religious figures, musical instruments, basketwork, costumes, and farming and other implements of the Americas. ✉ *Calle Norzagaray and Calle del Morro, Old San Juan* ☎ *787/724–5052* ⊕ *www.museolasamericas. org* ✉ *Free* ☽ *Tues.–Fri. 10–4, weekends 11–5.*

④ Museo de Nuestra Raíz Africana. The Institute of Puerto Rican Culture created this museum to help Puerto Ricans understand African influences in island culture. On display over two floors are African musical instruments, documents relating to the slave trade, and a list of African words that have made it into popular Puerto Rican culture. ✉ *Calle San Sebastián 101, Plaza de San José, Old San Juan* ☎ *787/724–0700 Ext. 4239* ⊕ *www.icp.gobierno.org* ✉ *Free* ☽ *Tues.–Sat. 9:30–5, Sun. 11–5.*

⑩ Paseo de la Princesa. This street down at the port is spruced up with flowers, trees, benches, street lamps, and a striking fountain depicting the various ethnic groups of Puerto Rico. Take a seat and watch the boats zip across the water. At the west end of the paseo, beyond the fountain, is the beginning of a shoreline path that hugs Old San Juan's walls and leads to the city gate at Calle San Juan.

⑨ Plaza de Armas. This is the original main square of Old San Juan. The plaza, bordered by Calles San Francisco, Fortaleza, San José, and Cruz, has a lovely fountain with 19th-century statues representing the four seasons.

⑫ Plaza de Colón. A statue of Christopher Columbus is atop a high pedestal in this bustling square. Originally called St. James Square, it was renamed in honor of Columbus on the 400th anniversary of the discovery of Puerto Rico. On the plaza's north side is a terminal for buses to and from San Juan. ✉ *East of Calle O'Donell between Calles San Francisco and Fortaleza.*

San Juan

You'll need to resort to taxis, buses, *públicos* (public cars), or a rental car to reach the points of interest in "new" San Juan. Avenida Muñoz Rivera, Avenida Ponce de León, and Avenida Fernández Juncos are the main thoroughfares that cross Puerta de Tierra, east of Old San Juan, to the business and tourist districts of Santurce, Condado, and Isla Verde. Dos Hermanos Bridge connects Puerta de Tierra with Miramar, Condado, and Isla Grande. Isla Grande Airport, from which you can take short hops, is on the bay side of the bridge. On the other side, the Condado Lagoon is bordered by Avenida Ashford, which threads past the high-rise Condado hotels and Avenida Baldorioty de Castro Expreso, which barrels east to the airport and beyond. Due south of the lagoon is Miramar, a residential area with fashionable turn-of-the-20th-century homes and a few hotels and restaurants. South of Santurce is the Golden Mile—Hato Rey, the financial hub. Isla Verde, with its glittering beachfront hotels, casinos, discos, and public beach, is to the east, near the airport.

Numbers in the margin correspond to points of interest on the Where to Stay, Eat & Explore in San Juan map.

SIGHTS TO SEE **El Capitolio.** Puerto Rico's capitol is a white-marble building that dates
① from the 1920s. The grand rotunda, with mosaics and friezes, was completed a few years ago. The seat of the island's bicameral legislature,

the capitol contains Puerto Rico's constitution and is flanked by the modern buildings of the Senate and the House of Representatives. There are spectacular views from the observation plaza on the sea side of the capitol. Pick up a booklet about the building from the House Secretariat on the second floor. Guided tours are by appointment only. ⊠ *Av. Ponce de León, Puerta de Tierra* ☎ *787/724–8979* 🖃 *Free* ⊘ *Daily 8:30–5.*

❸ Museo de Arte Contemporáneo de Puerto Rico. In February 2003, the Museum of Contemporary Puerto Rican Art inaugurated its new facilities in a historic building ceded by the government of Puerto Rico, along with a $6.8 million investment in restoration. The red-brick, Georgian-style structure displays a dynamic range of painting, sculpture, photography, and new-media art by both established and up-and-coming Puerto Rican and Latin American artists. Exhibits, movies, conferences, and workshops are scheduled throughout the year. ⊠ *Av. Ponce de León, corner of Av. R. H. Todd, Santurce* ☎ *787/268–0049 or 787/727–5249* ⊕ *www.museocontemporaneopr.org* 🖃 *Free* ⊘ *Mon.–Sat. 9–5.*

❷ Museo de Arte de Puerto Rico. The west wing of this ambitious 130,000-square-ft museum is the former San Juan Municipal Hospital, a 1920s neoclassical building that contains a permanent collection of Puerto Rican art dating from the 17th century to the present. The east wing is dominated by a five-story-tall stained-glass window, the work of local artist Eric Tabales, that towers over the museum's Grand Hall and faces a 5-acre garden. In the east wing there are galleries for changing exhibits, an interactive Family Gallery, and a 400-seat theater that's worth seeing for the stage's remarkable lace curtain alone. The garden has a sculpture trail, a pond, and a variety of native flora. ⊠ *Av. José de Diego 300, Santurce* ☎ *787/977–6277* ⊕ *www.mapr.org* 🖃 *$5* ⊘ *Tues. and Thurs.–Sun. 10–5, Wed. 10–8.*

❹ Universidad de Puerto Rico. The southern district of Río Piedras is home to the University of Puerto Rico, between Avenida Ponce de León and Avenida Barbosa. The campus is one of the two performance venues for the Puerto Rico Symphony Orchestra. (The other is the Centro de Bellas Artes Luis A. Ferré in Santurce.) Theatrical productions and other concerts are also scheduled here.

The university's **Museo de Historia, Antropología y Arte** (Museum of History, Anthropology, and Art) has archaeological and historical exhibits that deal with the Native American influence on the island and the Caribbean, the colonial era, and the history of slavery. Art displays are occasionally mounted; the museum's prize exhibit is the painting *El Velorio* (*The Wake*), by the 19th-century artist Francisco Oller. ⊠ *Next to main university entrance on Av. Ponce de León, Río Piedras* ☎ *787/764–0000 Ext. 2452* 🖃 *Free* ⊘ *Mon.–Wed. and Fri. 9–4:30, Thurs. 9–9, weekends 9–3.*

The university's main attraction is the **Jardín Botánico** (Botanical Garden), a 75-acre forest of more than 200 species of tropical and subtropical vegetation. Gravel footpaths lead to a graceful lotus lagoon, a bamboo promenade, an orchid garden with some 30,000 plants, and a palm garden. Signs are in Spanish and English. Trail maps are available at the entrance gate, and groups of 10 or more can arrange guided tours ($25). ⊠ *Intersection of Rtes. 1 and 847, at entrance to Barrio Venezuela, Río Piedras* ☎ *787/767–1710* 🖃 *Free* ⊘ *Daily 9–4:30.*

San Juan Environs

Numbers in the margin correspond to points of interest on the Puerto Rico map.

SIGHTS TO SEE   **Bacardí Rum Plant.** The first Bacardí rum distillery was built in 1862 in
② Cuba, but it was confiscated by the Castro regime in 1960, and the Bacardí family was exiled. The Puerto Rico plant was built in the 1950s and is one of the world's largest, with the capacity to produce 100,000 gallons of spirits a day and 221 million cases a year. You can take a 45-minute tour of the bottling plant, museum (called the Cathedral of Rum), and distillery, and there's a gift shop. Yes, you'll be offered a sample. ☒ *Bay View Industrial Park, Rte. 888, Km 2.6, Cataño* ☎ *787/788–1500 or 787/788–8400* ☎ *Free* ☉ *Tours every 30 mins Mon.–Sat. 9–10:30 and noon–4.*

① **Caparra Ruins.** In 1508 Ponce de León established the island's first settlement here. The ruins—a few crumbling walls—are what remains of an ancient fort, and the small Museo de la Conquista y Colonización de Puerto Rico (Museum of the Conquest and Colonization of Puerto Rico) contains historical documents, exhibits, and excavated artifacts, though you can see the museum's contents in less time than it takes to say the name. ☒ *Rte. 2, Km 6.6, Guaynabo* ☎ *787/781–4795* ⊕ *www. icp.gobierno.pr* ☎ *Free* ☉ *Tues.–Sat. 8:30–4:30.*

③ **Parque de las Ciencias Luis A. Ferré.** The 42-acre Luis A. Ferré Science Park contains a collection of intriguing activities and displays. The Transportation Museum has antique cars and the island's oldest bicycle. In the Rocket Plaza, children can experience a flight simulator, and in the planetarium, the solar system is projected on the ceiling. On-site as well are a small zoo and a natural science exhibit. The park is popular with Puerto Rican schoolchildren, and, although it's a bit of a drive from central San Juan, it's a good activity for the family. ☒ *Rte. 167, Bayamón* ☎ *787/740–6878* ☎ *$5* ☉ *Wed.–Fri. 9–4, weekends and holidays 10–6.*

Eastern Puerto Rico

⑦ **Culebra.** There's archaeological evidence that small groups of pre-Columbian people lived on the islet of Culebra, and certainly pirates landed here from time to time. But Puerto Rico's Spanish rulers didn't bother laying claim to it until 1886; its dearth of freshwater made it unattractive for settlement. At one point it was controlled, like its neighbor Vieques, by the U.S. Navy. When the military withdrew, it turned much of the land into a wildlife reserve. Although the island now has modern conveniences, its pace seems little changed from a century ago. There's only one town, Dewey, named after U.S. Admiral George Dewey. When the sun goes down, Culebra winds down as well. But during the day it's a delightful place to stake out a spot on Playa Flamenco or Playa Soní and read, swim, or search for shells. So what causes stress on the island? Nothing.

★ ④ **El Yunque.** In the Luquillo mountain range, the 28,000-acre Caribbean National Forest (known popularly as El Yunque after the good Indian spirit Yuquiyú), didn't gain its "rain forest" designation for nothing. More than 100 billion gallons of precipitation fall over it annually, spawning rushing streams and cascades, 240 tree species, and oversize impatiens and ferns. In the evening, millions of inch-long *coquís* (tree frogs) begin their calls. El Yunque is also home to the *cotorra,* Puerto Rico's endangered green parrot, as well as 67 other types of birds.

Your best bet is to visit with a tour. If you'd rather drive here yourself, take Route 3 east from San Juan and turn right (south) on Route 191, about 25 mi (40 km) from the city. The forest's 13 hiking trails are well maintained; many of them are easy to walk and less than a mile long. Before you begin exploring, check out the high-tech interactive displays—explaining forests in general and El Yunque in particular—at **Centro de Información El Portal** (⊠ Rte. 191, Km 4.3, off Hwy. 3 ☎ 787/ 888–1880 ⊕ www.southernregion.fs.fed.us/caribbean), the information center near the northern entrance. Test your sense of smell at an exhibit on forest products; inquire about the day's ranger-led activities; and pick up trail maps, souvenirs, film, water, and snacks. All exhibits and publications are in English and Spanish. The center is open daily 9–5; admission is $3.

❺ Fajardo. Founded in 1772, Fajardo has historical notoriety as a port where pirates stocked up on supplies. It later developed into a fishing community and an area where sugarcane flourished. (There are still cane fields on the city's fringes.) Today it's a hub for the yachts that use its marinas; the divers who head to its good offshore sites; and for the day-trippers who travel by catamaran, ferry, or plane to the off-islands of Culebra and Vieques. With the most significant docking facilities on the island's eastern side, Fajardo is a bustling city of 37,000—so bustling, in fact, that its unremarkable downtown is often congested and difficult to navigate.

★ ❻ **Vieques.** This island off Puerto Rico's east coast is famed for its Playa Sun Bay, a gorgeous stretch of sand with picnic facilities and shade trees. In May 2003, the U.S. Navy withdrew from its military operations and turned in two-thirds of Vieques to the local government. Some 9,300 civilians call Vieques home, many of them expatriate artists and guesthouse or vacation-villa owners from the mainland United States. Other islanders fish for a living or work in tourism-related fields. It has two communities—Isabel Segunda, where the ferries dock, and the smaller Esperanza. Aside from its military firing range, Vieques does have one

FodorśChoice attraction that draws visitors from all over the world. **Bahía Mosquito**
★ (Mosquito Bay) is best experienced on moonless nights, when millions of bioluminescent organisms glow when disturbed—it's like swimming in a cloud of fireflies. If you are on the island, this is a not-to-be-missed experienced, and any hotel on the island can help you arrange a trip.

Southern Puerto Rico

★ ❾ **Bosque Estatal de Guánica.** The 9,200-acre Guánica State Forest, a United Nations Biosphere Reserve, is a great place for hikes and bird-watching expeditions. It's an outstanding example of a tropical dry coastal forest, with some 700 species of plants and more than 100 types of birds. There are 12 major trails through the sun-bleached hills, from which you'll see towering cacti and gumbo limbo trees. There are also several caves to explore. You can enter on Route 333, which skirts the forest's southwestern portion, or at the end of Route 334, where there's a park office. ⊠ *Rte. 333 or 334* ☎ *787/821–5706* ⊠ *Free* ☉ *Daily 9–5.*

★ ❿ **Cabo Rojo.** Named for the pinkish cliffs that surround it, Cabo Rojo was founded in 1771 as a port for merchant vessels—and for the smugglers and pirates who inevitably accompanied ocean-going trade. Today it's known as a family resort destination, and many small, inexpensive hotels line its shores. Seaside settlements such as Puerto Real and Joyuda— the latter has a strip of more than 30 seafood restaurants overlooking the water—are found along the coast. Although you can hike in wildlife refuges at the outskirts of town, there aren't any area outfitters, so be sure to bring along water, sunscreen, and all other necessary supplies.

8 **Ponce.** Puerto Rico's second-largest urban area (population 194,000) shines in 19th-century style with pink-marble-bordered sidewalks, painted trolleys, and horse-drawn carriages. Stroll around the main square, Plaza las Delicias, with its perfectly pruned India-laurel fig trees, graceful fountains, gardens, and park benches. View the Catedral de Nuestra Señora de la Guadalupe (Our Lady of Guadalupe Cathedral), perhaps even attend the 6 AM mass, and walk down Calles Isabel and Cristina to see turn-of-the-20th-century wooden houses with wrought-iron balconies.

You haven't seen a firehouse until you've seen the **Parque de Bombas,** a structure built in 1882 for an exposition and converted to a firehouse the following year. Today it is a museum tracing the history—and glorious feats—of Ponce's fire brigade ⊠ *Plaza las Delicias, Ponce Centro* ☎ *787/284–4141 Ext. 342* ⊠ *Free* ◷ *Wed.–Mon. 9:30–6.*

The neoclassical **Casa Armstrong-Poventud** houses the Ponce offices of the Institute of Puerto Rican Culture. You can walk through several rooms that display antique furnishings. ⊠ *Calle Union, across from Catedral, Ponce Centro* ☎ *787/844–2540 or 787/840–7667* ⊠ *Free* ◷ *Weekdays 8–4:30.*

Two superlative examples of early 20th-century architecture house the **Museo de la Historia de Ponce** (Ponce History Museum), where 10 rooms of exhibits vividly re-create Ponce's golden years, providing fascinating glimpses into the worlds of culture, high finance, and journalism in the 19th century. Hour-long tours in English and Spanish are available, but there's no set time when they start. ⊠ *Calle Isabel 51–53, Ponce Centro* ☎ *787/844–7071 or 787/843–4322* ⊠ *$3* ◷ *Wed.–Mon. 9–5.*

Be sure to allow time to visit the **Museo de Arte de Ponce** (Ponce Museum of Art). The architecture alone is worth seeing: the modern two-story building designed by Edward Durrell Stone (one of the designers of New York's Museum of Modern Art) has seven interconnected hexagons, glass cupolas, and a pair of curved staircases. The collection includes late Renaissance and baroque works from Italy, France, and Spain, as well as contemporary art by Puerto Ricans. ⊠ *Av. Las Américas 2325, Sector Santa María* ☎ *787/848–0505* ⊕ *www.museoarteponce. org* ⊠ *$4* ◷ *Daily 10–5.*

The **Castillo Serrallés** is a splendid Spanish Revival mansion on Vigía Hill. This former residence of the owners of the Don Q rum distillery has been restored with a mix of original furnishings and antiques that recalls the era of the sugar barons. A short film details the history of the sugar and rum industries; tours are given every half hour in English and Spanish. The 100-ft-tall cross (La Cruceta del Vigía) behind the museum has a windowed elevator; you can ascend for views of Ponce and the coast for $1. ⊠ *El Vigía 17, El Vigía Hill* ☎ *787/259–1774* ⊕ *www. castilloserralles.com* ⊠ *$3* ◷ *Tues.–Thurs. 9:30–5, Fri.–Sun. 10–5:30.*

Just outside the city, **Hacienda Buena Vista** is a 19th-century coffee plantation restored by the Conservation Trust of Puerto Rico, with authentic machinery and furnishings intact. Reservations are required for the 90-minute Spanish-language tours (at 8:30, 10:30, 1:30, and 3:30). Tours in English are at 1:30, also by reservation only. ⊠ *Rte. 10, Km 16.8, Sector Corral Viejo* ☎ *787/722–5882 weekdays, 787/284–7020 weekends* ⊕ *www.fideicomiso.org/hacienda.htm* ⊠ *$5* ◷ *Wed.–Fri. morning open to tour groups; Fri. afternoon–Sun. open to public.*

At the **Centro Ceremonial Indígena de Tibes** (Tibes Indian Ceremonial Center), you'll find pre-Taíno ruins and burials dating from AD 300 to AD 700. Some archaeologists, noting the symmetrical arrangement of stone pillars, surmise the cemetery may have been of great religious significance. The complex includes a detailed re-creation of a Taíno village and a museum. ✉ *Rte. 503, Km 2.2, Barrio Tibes* ☎ *787/840–2255 or 787/840–5685* ⊕ *http://ponce.inter/edu/tibes/tibes.html* ≊ *$2* ◷ *Tues.– Sun. 9–4.*

⑪ **San Germán.** Around San Germán's (population 39,000) two main
Fodor's Choice squares—Plazuela Santo Domingo and Plaza Francisco Mariano Quiñones
★ (named for an abolitionist)—are buildings done in every conceivable style of architecture found on the island including mission, Victorian, Creole, and Spanish colonial. The city's tourist office offers a free guided trolley tour. Students and professors from the Inter-American University often fill the center's bars and cafés.

The **Museo de Arte y Casa de Estudio** is an early 20th-century home that has been turned into a museum. Displays include colonial furnishings, religious art, and Taíno artifacts; there are also changing art exhibits. ✉ *Calle Esperanza 7* ☎ *787/892–8870* ≊ *Free* ◷ *Wed.–Sun. 10–noon and 1–3.*

One of the oldest Christian religious structures in the Americas, the **Capilla de Porta Coeli** (Heaven's Gate Chapel) overlooks the Plazuela de Santo Domingo. The original complex, which included a convent, was built in 1606; much of it was demolished in 1866, leaving only the chapel and a vestige of the convent's front wall. The chapel was restored and reopened for services in 1878. It functions as a museum of religious art, displaying painted wooden statuary by Latin American and Spanish artists. ✉ *Plazuela Santo Domingo* ☎ *787/892–5845* ≊ *$1* ◷ *Wed.– Sun. 9–4:45.*

Northwestern Puerto Rico

⑰ **Bosque Estatal de Río Abajo.** In the middle of karst country, the Río Abajo State Forest spans some 5,000 acres and includes huge bamboo stands and silk-cotton trees. It also has several plantations of Asian teaks, Dominican and Honduran mahogany, and Australian pines, which are part of a government tree management program that supplies wood for the local economy (primarily for artisans and fence building). Walking trails wind through the forest, which is one of the habitats of the rare Puerto Rican parrot. An information office is near the entrance, and a recreation area with picnic tables is farther down the road. ✉ *Rte. 621, Km 4.4* ☎ *787/817–0984* ≊ *Free* ◷ *Daily.*

⑫ **Mayagüez.** With a population of slightly more than 100,000, this is the largest city on Puerto Rico's west coast. Although bypassed by the mania for restoration that has spruced up Ponce and Old San Juan, Mayagüez is graced by some lovely turn-of-the-20th-century architecture, such as the landmark Art Deco Teatro Yagüez and the Plaza de Colón.

Just north of town, visit the **Tropical Research Station,** run by the U.S. Department of Agriculture, contains a plant collection that has been nurtured for more than half a century. More than 2,000 species from all over the tropical world are found here, including teak, mahogany, cinnamon, nutmeg, rubber, and numerous exotic flowers. Free maps are available for self-guided tours. ✉ *Intersection of Rte. 2 and Rte. 108* ☎ *787/831–3435* ≊ *Free* ◷ *Weekdays 7–4.*

★ ⑭ **Observatorio de Arecibo.** Hidden among fields and hills is the world's largest radar–radio telescope, operated by the National Astronomy and Ionosphere Center of Cornell University. A 20-acre dish, with a 600-ton suspended platform hovering eerily over it, lies in a 563-ft-deep sinkhole in the karst landscape. The observatory has been used to look for extraterrestrial life, and if it looks familiar it may be because scenes from the movie *Contact* were filmed here. You can walk around the platform and view the huge dish, and tour the visitor center, which has two levels of interactive exhibits on planetary systems, meteors, and weather phenomena. ⊠ *Rte. 625, Km 3.0* ☎ *787/878–2612* ⊕ *www.naic.edu* ☜ *$4* ☉ *Wed.–Fri. noon–4, weekends 9–4.*

★ **⑯ Parque Ceremonial Indígena de Caguana.** The 13 acres of this park were used more than 800 years ago by the Taíno tribes for worship and recreation, including a game—thought to have religious significance—that resembled modern-day soccer. Today you can see 10 *bateyes* (courts) of various sizes, large stone monoliths (some with petroglyphs), and re-creations of Taíno gardens. ⊠ *Rte. 111, Km 12.3* ☎ *787/894–7325* ☜ *$2* ☉ *Daily 8:30–4.*

★ **⑮ Parque de las Cavernas del Río Camuy.** This 268-acre park contains an enormous cave network and the third-longest underground river in the world. A tram takes you down a mountain covered with bamboo and banana trees to the entrance of Cueva Clara de Empalme. Hour-long guided tours in English and Spanish lead you on foot through the 180-ft-high cave, which has large stalactites and stalagmites and blind fish. The visit ends with a tram ride to Tres Pueblos sinkhole, where you can see the river passing from one cave to another, 400 ft below. Tours are first-come, first-serve; plan to arrive early on holidays and weekends. ⊠ *Rte. 129, Km 18.9* ☎ *787/898–3100* ☜ *$10* ☉ *Wed.–Sun. 8–4, last tour at 3:45.*

⑬ Rincón. Jutting out into the ocean along the rugged western coast, Rincón, meaning corner in Spanish, may have gotten its name because of how it is nestled in a "corner" of the coastline. Some, however, trace the town's name to Gonzalo Rincón, a 16th-century landowner who let poor families live on his land. Whatever the history, the name suits the town, which is like a little world unto itself.

The town jumped into the surfing spotlight after hosting the World Surfing Championship in 1968. Although the beat here picks up from October through April, when the waves are the best, Rincón is basically laid-back and unpretentious. If you visit between December and February you might get a glimpse of the humpback whales that winter off the coast. Because of its unusual setting, Rincón's layout can be a little disconcerting. The main road, Route 413, loops around the coast, and many beaches and sights are on dirt roads intersecting with it. Most hotels and restaurants hand out detailed maps of the area.

PUERTO RICO A TO Z

To research prices, get advice from other travelers, and book travel arrangements, visit www.fodors.com.

AIR TRAVEL

San Juan is the regional hub of American Airlines, which flies nonstop from New York, Newark, Boston, Miami, Orlando, Fort Lauderdale, Los Angeles, and St. Louis. Other major U.S. carriers serving San Juan include Continental, with daily nonstop service from Newark, Houston, and Cleveland; Delta, with nonstop service from Atlanta; JetBlue, with two daily flights from JFK to San Juan; Northwest, with daily nonstop flights from Detroit, Memphis, and Minneapolis; Spirit Air, which has two daily nonstop flights from Fort Lauderdale with connections from New York, Atlantic City, and Detroit; United, which flies nonstop daily from Chicago and on weekends from New York and Washington, D.C.; and US Airways, flying nonstop daily from Pittsburgh, Philadelphia, and Charlotte.

Continental Airlines has five direct flights a week direct from Newark to the northwestern town of Aguadilla, and daily direct flights during high season.

Air Canada has flights to San Juan from Montréal and Toronto, and Canadian Airlines has service—with a stop in Miami—from Toronto, Vancouver, and Calgary. British Airways serves San Juan from London, and Lufthansa's partner, Condor, flies out of Germany. LACSA connects San Juan to San José, Costa Rica.

Puerto Rico is also a good spot from which to hop to other Caribbean islands. American Airlines' American Eagle serves many of the Lesser Antilles islands; Cape Air connects San Juan to St. Thomas and St. Croix; ALM travels to Jamaica, Aruba, Bonaire, and its base in Curaçao; and Leeward Islands Air Transport (LIAT), based in Antigua, flies to nearly all the Lesser Antilles islands. Vieques Air-Link connects San Juan with Vieques and Culebra.

☎ Major U.S. Airlines American Airlines/American Eagle ☎ 797/749-1747. Continental ☎ 787/890-2990. Delta ☎ 787/282-6783. JetBlue ☎ 800/538-2583. Northwest ☎ 787/253-0206, 787/253-1505, or 787/791-4337. Spirit Air ☎ 787/772-7117. United ☎ 787/253-2776. US Airways ☎ 787/725-4895.

☎ Smaller Airlines ALM ☎ 800/327-7230. Cape Air ☎ 787/253-1121 or 800/352-0714. LIAT ☎ 787/791-0800. Vieques Air-Link ☎ 787/723-9882 or 888/901-9247.

☎ From Elsewhere in the World Air Canada Vacations ☎ 800/774-8993 in North America. British Airways ☎ 787/723-4327. Canadian Airlines ☎ 800/426-7000 in North America. Condor ☎ 800/645-3880. LACSA-Group Taca ☎ 787/724-3444, 787/791-6400, or 800/225-2272.

AIRPORTS

The Aeropuerto Internacional Luis Muñoz Marín (SJU) is minutes east of downtown San Juan in the coastal section of Isla Verde. San Juan's other airport is the small Fernando L. Ribas Dominicci Airport in Isla Grande, near the city's Miramar section. From here you can catch Vieques Air-Link flights to Culebra, Vieques, and other destinations on Puerto Rico and throughout the Caribbean. (Note that although the Dominicci airport was still operating at this writing, its future was uncertain.) Other Puerto Rican airports include Mercedita in the south coast town of Ponce, Eugenio María de Hostos in the west coast community of Mayagüez, Rafael Hernández in the northwestern town of Aguadilla, and Antonio Rivera Rodríguez on Vieques.

☎ Aeropuerto Antonio Rivera Rodríguez ☎ 787/741-8358 in Vieques. Aeropuerto Eugenio María de Hostos ☎ 787/833-0148 in Mayagüez. Aeropuerto Fernando L. Ribas Dominicci ☎ 787/729-8711 in Isla Grande, San Juan. Aeropuerto Mercedita ☎ 787/842-6292 in Ponce. Aeropuerto Internacional Luis Muñoz Marín ☎ 787/791-3840 in San Juan. Aeropuerto Rafael Hernández ☎ 787/891-2286 in Aguadilla.

BOAT & FERRY TRAVEL

The Autoridad de los Puertos (Port Authority) ferry between Old San Juan (Pier 2) and Cataño costs a mere 50¢ one-way. It runs every half hour from 6 AM to 10 PM, and every 15 minutes during peak hours. The Fajardo Port Authority's 400-passenger ferries run between that east coast town and the out islands of Vieques and Culebra; both trips take 90 minutes. The vessels carry cargo and passengers to Vieques three times daily ($2 one-way) and to Culebra twice a day Sunday through Friday and three times a day on Saturday ($2.25 one-way).

Get schedules for the Culebra and Vieques ferries by calling the Port Authority in Fajardo, Vieques, or Culebra. You buy tickets at the ferry dock. Reservations aren't necessary unless you're transporting a vehicle, in which case you should not only make a reservation but also arrive 1½ hours before the departure time.

🔼 **Autoridad de los Puertos** ☎ 787/788-1155 in San Juan, 787/863-4560 in Fajardo, 787/742-3161 in Culebra, 787/741-4761 in Vieques.

BUSINESS HOURS

BANKS & OFFICES Bank hours are generally weekdays 8–4 or 9–5, though a few branches are open Saturday 9–noon or 1. Post offices are open weekdays 7:30–4:30 and Saturday 8–noon. Government offices are open weekdays 9–5.

GAS STATIONS Most stations are open daily from early in the morning until 10 or 11 PM. Numerous stations in urban areas are open 24 hours.

MUSEUMS & As a rule, San Juan area museums are closed on Monday, and in some
SIGHTS cases, Sunday. Hours otherwise are 9 or 10 AM to 5 PM, often with an hour off for lunch between noon and 2. Sights managed by the National Parks Service, such as Fuerte San Felipe del Morro and San Cristóbal, are open daily 9–5.

PHARMACIES In cities, pharmacies are generally open 9–6 or 7 weekdays and on Saturday. Walgreens operates numerous pharmacies around the island; some are open 24 hours.

SHOPS Street shops are open Monday through Saturday 9 to 6 (9–9 during Christmas holidays); mall stores tend to stay open to 9 or so. Count on convenience stores staying open late into the night, seven days a week. Supermarkets are often closed on Sunday, although some remain open 24-hours, seven days a week.

BUS TRAVEL

The Autoridad Metropolitana de Autobuses (AMA, or Metropolitan Bus Authority) operates *guaguas* (buses) that thread through San Juan, running in exclusive lanes on major thoroughfares and stopping at signs marked PARADA or PARADA DE GUAGUAS. The main terminals are at the Covadonga parking lot and Plaza de Colón in Old San Juan and the Capetillo Terminal in Río Piedras, next to the central business district. Most buses are air-conditioned and have wheelchair lifts and lockdowns.

Bus travel to outlying areas is less than comprehensive. Your best bet for travel to other parts of the island is by rental car or by *públicos*—"public cars," though most are actually 17-passenger vans. They have yellow license plates ending in "P" or "PD," and they scoot to towns throughout the island, stopping in each community's main plaza. They operate primarily during the day; routes and fares are fixed by the Public Service Commission, but schedules aren't set, so you have to call ahead.

In San Juan, the main terminals are at the airport and at Plaza Colón on the waterfront in Old San Juan. San Juan–based público companies include Blue Line for trips to Aguadilla and the northwest coast, Choferes Unidos de Ponce for Ponce, Línea Caborrojeña for Cabo Rojo and the southwest coast, Línea Boricua for the interior and the southwest, Línea Sultana for Mayagüez and the west coast, and Terminal de Transportación Pública for Fajardo and the east.

FARES & In San Juan, bus fares are 25¢ or 50¢, depending on the route, and are
SCHEDULES paid in exact change upon entering the bus. Buses adhere to their routes, but schedules are fluid, to say the least. Count on a bus passing your stop every 20–30 minutes, less frequently on Sunday and holidays. Service starts

at around 6 AM and generally continues until 9 PM. For more information, call the AMA or pick up a schedule at the nearest bus station.

AMA ☎ 787/729-1512 or 787/767-7979. **Blue Line** ☎ 787/765-7733. **Choferes Unidos de Ponce** ☎ 787/764-0540. **Línea Boricua** ☎ 787/765-1908. **Línea Caborrojeña** ☎ 787/723-9155. **Línea Sultana** ☎ 787/765-9377. **Terminal de Transportación Pública** ☎ 787/250-0717.

CAR RENTALS

If you rent a car, a good road map will be helpful in remote areas. A valid driver's license from your country of origin can be used in Puerto Rico for three months. Rates start as low as $35 a day (plus insurance), with unlimited mileage. Discounts are often offered for long-term rentals and for cars that are booked more than 72 hours in advance. All major U.S. car-rental agencies are represented on the island, though many reliable local companies offer competitive rates.

You'll find offices for dozens of agencies at San Juan's airports, and a majority of them have shuttle service to and from the airport and the pickup point. Most rental cars are available with automatic or standard transmission. Four-wheel-drive vehicles aren't necessary unless you plan to go way off the beaten path or along the steep, rocky roads of Culebra or Vieques; in most cases a standard compact car will do the trick. Always opt for air-conditioning, though.

Major Agencies Avis ☎ 787/721-4499. **Budget** ☎ 787/791-3685. **Hertz** ☎ 787/791-0840. **National** ☎ 787/791-1805. **Thrifty** ☎ 787/253-2525.

Local Agencies Charlie Car Rental ☎ 787/791-1101 or 800/289-1227. **L & M Car Rental** ☎ 787/791-1160 or 800/666-0807. **Target** ☎ 787/728-1447 or 800/934-6457.

CAR TRAVEL

Several well-marked multilane highways link population centers. Route 26 is the main artery through San Juan, connecting Condado and Old San Juan to Isla Verde and the airport. Route 22, which runs east–west between San Juan and Camuy, and the Luis A. Ferré Expressway (Route 52), which runs north–south between San Juan and Ponce, are toll roads (35¢–50¢). Route 2, a smaller highway, travels along the west coast, and routes 3 and 53 traverse the east shore. Distances are posted in kilometers (1.6 km to 1 mi), whereas speed limits are posted in miles per hour. Speeding and drunk-driving penalties are much the same here as on the mainland.

GASOLINE All types of fuel—unleaded regular, unleaded super-premium, diesel—are available by the liter. At this writing, the cost for regular gas was 32¢ a liter, which works out to roughly $1.22 a gallon. Most stations have both full- and self-service. Hours vary, but stations generally operate daily from early in the morning until 10 or 11 PM; in metro areas many are open 24 hours. Stations are few and far between in the central mountains and other rural areas; plan accordingly. In cities you can pay with cash and bank or credit cards; in the hinterlands cash is often your only option.

ROAD CONDITIONS Roads are in generally good condition, although you may want to keep an eye out for potholes, especially after heavy rains. Some roads in the mountains are very curvy and take longer to cover than the distance on a map might suggest. Not every road is marked, but most Puerto Ricans are happy to help with directions.

ELECTRICITY

Puerto Rico uses the same electrical current as the U.S. mainland, namely 110 volts.

EMERGENCIES

☑ General Contacts **Ambulance, police, and fire** ☎ 911. **Air Ambulance Service** ☎ 800/ 633-3590 or 787/756-3424. **Dental Emergencies** ☎ 787/722-2351 or 787/795-0320. **San Juan Tourist Zone Police** ☎ 787/726-7020, 787/726-7015 for Condado, 787/728-4770, 787/726-2981 for Isla Verde. **Travelers' Aid** ☎ 787/791-1054 or 787/791-1034.

☑ Hospitals **Ashford Presbyterian Memorial Community Hospital** ☒ Av. Ashford 1451, Condado, San Juan ☎ 787/721-2160. **General Hospital Dr. Ramón Emeterio Betances** ☒ Rte. 2, Km 157, Mayagüez ☎ 787/834-8686. **Hospital de la Concepción** ☒ Calle Luna 41, San Germán ☎ 787/892-1860. **Hospital Damas** ☒ Ponce Bypass Rd. 2213, Ponce ☎ 787/840-8686. **Hospital Dr. Dominguez** ☒ Font Martello 300, Humacao ☎ 787/ 852-0505. **Hospital Gubern** ☒ Antonio R. Barcelo 11, Fajardo ☎ 787/863-0294.

ETIQUETTE & BEHAVIOR

Puerto Ricans have, in general, a strong sense of religion—as evidenced by the numerous Catholic patron-saint festivals held throughout the year. Many islanders are somewhat conservative in dress and manners despite a penchant for frenetic music and sexually charged dance. There's also a strong sense of island identity, marked by often-ferocious debates over Puerto Rico's political destiny.

FESTIVALS & SEASONAL EVENTS

Puerto Rico's festivals are colorful and inclined toward lots of music and feasting. The towns and villages are particularly fond of their patron saints, and every year each of the island's 78 municipalities celebrates its *fiesta patronal* (patron saint's festival). The festivities are religious in origin and feature processions, sports events, folklore shows, feasts, music, and dance. They last about 10 days, with more activities on weekends than on weekdays. San Juan's *fiesta patronal* honors San Juan Bautista in late June; Ponce honors Nuestra Señora de la Guadalupe in mid-December. Several towns and regions also have pre-Lenten carnivals, complete with parades, folk music, local dishes, a Carnival Queen pageant, and music competitions. Ponce's carnival, celebrated the week before Ash Wednesday, is the most famous. Contact the tourist office for a complete list of fiestas patronales and other events.

In addition to the patron saints' festivals, Old San Juan holds an annual San Sebastián Street Festival in January. Emancipation Day on March 22 honors the abolition of slavery. Mid-April's Sugar Harvest Festival, in San Germán, celebrates the crop with exhibitions, music, and feasts. The Casals Festival, held at the Luis A. Ferré Performing Arts Center in San Juan in early June, honors the late, great cellist with 10 days of classical music. In mid-November you can find the annual Festival of Puerto Rican Music in San Juan and other venues, celebrating the vibrancy of Puerto Rico's *plena* and *bomba* folk music, highlighted by a contest featuring the cuatro, a traditional guitar. During Christmas week you can join the residents of Hatillo for the Hatillo Masks Festival, when they retell the Biblical tale of King Herod's attempt to find and kill the infant Jesus. Men in masks move about town all day, representing Herod's soldiers, and the town brings out music and crafts.

HOLIDAYS

Public holidays in Puerto Rico include: New Year's Day, Three Kings Day (Jan. 6), Eugenio María de Hostos Day (Jan. 8), Dr. Martin Luther King Jr. Day (3rd Mon. in Jan.), Presidents' Day (3rd Mon. in Feb.), Palm Sunday, Good Friday, Easter Sunday, Memorial Day (last Mon. in May), Independence Day (July 4), Luis Muñoz Rivera Day (July 16), Constitution Day (July 25), José Celso Barbosa Day (July 27), Labor Day (1st Mon. in Sept.), Columbus Day (2nd Mon. in Oct.), Veteran's

Day (Nov. 11), Puerto Rico Discovery Day (Nov. 19), Thanksgiving Day, and Christmas.

LANGUAGE
Puerto Rico is officially bilingual, but Spanish predominates. Although English is widely spoken, you'll probably want to take a Spanish phrase book along on your travels about the island.

MAIL & SHIPPING
Puerto Rico uses the U.S. postal system, and all addresses on the island carry Zip codes. You can buy stamps and aerograms and send letters and parcels in post offices. Stamp-dispensing machines can occasionally be found in airports, office buildings, and drugstores. Major post office branches are at Calle Fortaleza 153 in Old San Juan, Avenida Fernández Juncos 163 in San Juan, Calle Garrido Morales 102 in Fajardo, Calle Atocha 94 in Ponce, and Calle McKinley 60 in Mayagüez.
🛈 **Postal Services** ☎ 787/622-1756.

MONEY MATTERS
ATMS   Automated Teller Machines (ATMs; known as ATHs here), are readily available and reliable in the cities; many are attached to banks, but you can also find them on the streets and in supermarkets. Just about every casino has one—the better to keep people in the game—as do many of the larger hotels. ATMs are found less frequently in rural areas. Look to local banks such as Banco Popular.

CREDIT CARDS   Credit cards, including Diner's Club and Discover, are widely accepted, especially in tourist areas. Some stateside gasoline credit cards may not be accepted at gas stations here.

CURRENCY   Puerto Rico, as a commonwealth of the United States, uses the U.S. dollar as its official currency.
🛈 **Banco Popular de Puerto Rico** ✉ Calle Tetuán 206, Old San Juan, San Juan ☎ 787/725-2636 ✉ Av. Ashford 1060, Condado, San Juan ☎ 787/725-4197 ✉ Muñoz Rivera 115, Isabel Segunda, Vieques ☎ 787/741-2071 ✉ Rte. 3, Km 42.4, Fajardo ☎ 787/860-1570 ✉ Plaza las Delicias, Ponce ☎ 787/843-8000 or 787/848-2410 ✉ Mayagüez Mall, Rte. 2, Km 159.4, Mayagüez ☎ 787/834-4750.

PASSPORTS & VISAS
Puerto Rico is a commonwealth of the United States, so U.S. citizens don't need passports to visit the island (they must have a valid photo I. D., however). Canadians need proof of citizenship (preferably a valid passport; otherwise bring a birth certificate with a raised seal along with a government-issued photo I.D.). Citizens of Australia, New Zealand, and the United Kingdom must have passports.

SAFETY
San Juan, like any other big city, has its share of crime, so guard your wallet or purse on the city streets. Puerto Rico's beaches are open to the public, and muggings can occur at night even on the beaches of the posh Condado and Isla Verde tourist hotels. Although you certainly can—and should—explore the city and its beaches, use common sense. Don't leave anything unattended on the beach. Leave your valuables in the hotel safe, and stick to the fenced-in beach areas of your hotel. Always lock your car and stash valuables and luggage out of sight. Avoid deserted beaches at night.

SIGHTSEEING TOURS
In Old San Juan, free trolleys can take you around, and the tourist board can provide you with a copy of *Qué Pasa,* which contains a self-guided

walking tour. The Caribbean Carriage Company gives Old City tours in horse-drawn carriages. Look for these buggies at Plaza Dársenas near Pier 1; the cost is $30–$60 per couple. If you'd like to explore other parts of the island, several companies offer tours. Leading San Juan operators include Cordero Caribbean Tours, Normandie Tours, Rico Suntours, Tropix Wellness Outings, and United Tour Guides.

🚌 **Caribbean Carriage Company** ☎ 787/797-8063. **Cordero Caribbean Tours** ☎ 787/786-9114, 787/780-2442 evenings. **Normandie Tours, Inc.** ☎ 787/722-6308. **Rico Suntours** ☎ 787/722-2080 or 787/722-6090. **Tropix Wellness Outings** ☎ 787/268-2173. **United Tour Guides** ☎ 787/725-7605 or 787/723-5578.

TAXES

SALES TAX Accommodations incur a tax: for hotels with casinos it's 11%, for other hotels it's 9%, and for government-approved paradores it's 7%. Ask your hotel before booking. The tax, in addition to the standard 5%–12% service charge applied by most hotels, can add a hefty 20% or more to your bill. There's no sales tax on Puerto Rico. Any departure taxes are included in your airline ticket.

TAXIS

The Puerto Rico Tourism Company has instituted a well-organized taxi program. Taxis painted white and displaying the *garita* (sentry box) logo and TAXI TURISTICO label charge set rates depending on the destination; they run from the airport or the cruise-ship piers to Isla Verde, Condado/Ocean Park, and Old San Juan, with rates ranging from $6 to $16. City tours start at $30 per hour. Metered cabs authorized by the Public Service Commission start at $1 and charge 10¢ for every additional ⅓ mi, 50¢ for every suitcase. Waiting time is 10¢ for each 45 seconds. The minimum charge is $3 and there is an extra $1 night charge between 10 PM and 6 AM.

In other Puerto Rican towns, you can flag down cabs on the street, but it's easier to have your hotel call one for you. Either way, make sure the driver is clear on whether he or she will charge a flat rate or use a meter to determine the fare. In most places, the cabs are metered.

LINÉAS *Linéas* are private taxis you share with three to five other passengers. There are more than 20 companies, each usually specializing in a certain region. Most will arrange door-to-door service. Check local Yellow Pages listings under *Linéas de Carros*. They're affordable and are a great way to meet people, but be prepared to wait: they usually don't leave until they have a full load.

🚕 **Atlantic City Taxi** ☎ 787/268-5050 in San Juan. **Fajardo Taxi Service** ☎ 787/860-1112. **Lolo Felix Tours** ☎ 787/485-5447 on Vieques. **Major Taxicabs** ☎ 787/723-2460 in San Juan. **Ponce Taxi Association** ☎ 787/842-3370. **Public Service Commission** ☎ 787/751-5050. **Ruben's Taxi** ☎ 787/405-1209 on Culebra. **White Taxi** ☎ 787/832-1115 in Mayagüez.

TELEPHONES

COUNTRY & AREA Puerto Rico's area codes are 787 and 939. Toll-free numbers (prefix 800,
CODES 888, or 877) are widely used in Puerto Rico, and many can be accessed from North America (and vice versa). For North Americans, dialing Puerto Rico is the same as dialing another U.S. state or a Canadian province.

INTERNATIONAL Dial 011, the country code, the city code, and the number. Dial 00 for
CALLS an international long-distance operator. Phone cards are not required, but can be useful and are widely available (most drug stores carry them). The Puerto Rico Telephone Company sells its "Ring Cards" in various denominations.

LOCAL CALLS To make a local call in Puerto Rico you must dial 1, the area code, and the seven-digit number.

TIPPING

Tips are expected, and appreciated, by restaurant waitstaff (15%–20% if a service charge isn't included), hotel porters ($1 per bag), maids ($1–$2 a day), and taxi drivers (15%–18%).

TROLLEYS

If your feet fail you in Old San Juan, climb aboard the free open-air trolleys that rumble and coast through the narrow streets. Departures are from La Puntilla and from the marina, but you can board anywhere along the route. Ponce has free trolleys that leave from Plaza las Delicias and stop at major tourist attractions.

VISITOR INFORMATION

🚹 Before You Leave **Puerto Rico Tourism Company** ⊕ www.gotopuertorico.com ⌂ Box 902-3960, Old San Juan Station, San Juan, PR 00902-3960 ☎ 787/721-2400 ☎ 800/223-6530 New York office toll-free ✉ 3575 W. Cahuenga Blvd., Suite 560, Los Angeles, CA 90068 ☎ 213/874-5991 ✉ 901 Ponce de León Blvd., Suite 101, Coral Gables, FL 33134 ☎ 305/445-9112

🚹 In Puerto Rico **Culebra Tourism Office** ✉ 250 Calle Pedro Marquez, Dewey ☎ 787/742-3521. **Fajardo Tourism Office** ✉ Av. Munoz Rivera 6 ☎ 787/863-4013 Ext. 274. **Mayagüez City Hall** ☎ 787/834-8585. **Ponce Municipal Tourist Office** ✉ 2nd floor of Citibank, Plaza las Delicias [Box 1709], Ponce 00733 ☎ 787/841-8160 or 787/841-8044. **Puerto Rico Tourism Company** ✉ Box 902-3960, Old San Juan Station, San Juan 00902-3960 ☎ 787/721-2400 ✉ Plaza Dársenas, near Pier 1, Old San Juan ☎ 787/722-1709 ✉ Aeropuerto Internacional Luis Muñoz Marín ☎ 787/791-1014 or 787/791-2551 ✉ Rte. 101, Km 13.7, Cabo Riojo ☎ 787/851-7070 ✉ Vallas Torres 291, Ponce ☎ 787/843-0465. **Rincón Tourism Office** ☎ 787/823-5024. **Vieques Tourism Office** ✉ Calle Carlos Lebrón 449, Isabel Segunda ☎ 787/741-5000 Ext. 26.

SABA

16

FODOR'S CHOICE
Scuba Diving & Snorkeling in Saba Marine Park
Taking in the views from the top of Mt. Scenery

HIGHLY RECOMMENDED

RESTAURANTS Brigadoon Restaurant, Windwardside
Gate House Café, Hell's Gate
YIIK, Windwardside

HOTELS Queens Garden Resort, Troy Hill
Lily Pond Cottage, Windwardside

SHOPPING Shopping for lace at Saba Artisan Foundation, The Bottom

SIGHTS Saba Museum, Windwardside

Just after daybreak, the street sweepers begin their task, brooms in hand, up and down the winding roads that zigzag around the mountains—steep and dramatic. Every day they follow these concrete ribbons that twist and turn—connecting the villages on the island—sweeping them all by hand until no dirt or litter remains. This tradition of cleanliness makes Saba special, and by nightfall the streets are pristine again.

Updated by
Roberta
Sotonoff

Tiny Saba (pronounced *say*-ba) has some of the Caribbean's most dramatic scenery, with sweeping, steep mountainsides and sheer cliffs. The breeze is always pleasant, the 1,500 friendly Sabans even more so. Everyone knows everyone—indeed, there are fewer than a dozen family names on the island (Johnson, Hassell, and Peterson being the most popular) so many people are also related—and unemployment and crime are virtually nonexistent. The island is a perfect hideaway, a challenge for hikers (Mt. Scenery rises to 2,855 ft [871 m]), a haven for seasoned divers, and heaven on water. It's no wonder Sabans call their island "the unspoiled queen."

Despite all its glories, however, this 5-square-mi (13-square-km) fairytale isle isn't for everybody. If you want exciting nightlife or lots of shopping, forget Saba (or make it a one-day excursion from St. Maarten). There are only a handful of shops, a few inns and eateries, and cable TV has replaced the movie theater. Sun worshipers should note that Saba is an essentially beachless volcanic island: steep cliffs ring the island and plummet sharply to the sea. Saba's famous disappearing black-sand beach at Well's Bay, on the northwestern coast, is usually only around for a few months in summer (the sand is washed in and out by rough winter surf). And because of precarious overhanging rocks above, it's no longer recommended as a place to swim.

The capital of Saba is The Bottom, which some believe is the bottom of the extinct volcano. In Windwardside, the island's second-largest village, the streets have no names. On the Road (and there's really only one), meandering goats have right of way, though chickens cross at their own risk. In toylike villages, flower-draped walls and neat picket fences border narrow paths. Tidy, sturdy white houses with gingerbread trim, green shutters, and red roofs are planted on the mountainsides among the bromeliads, palms, hibiscus, orchids, and Norwegian pines. Despite such modern additions as TVs (since 1965, when there was electricity only four hours per day) and full-time electricity (since 1970), this immaculate, picturesque island's uncomplicated lifestyle has persevered, giving it a make-believe air. Saban ladies still produce handmade lace—a genteel art that has flourished since the 1870s—and brew a potent 151-proof rum-based liquor, Saba Spice, that's flavored with herbs and spices. Families still follow the generations-old tradition of burying their dead in their neatly tended gardens.

Saba is part of the Netherlands Antilles' Windward Islands and is 28 mi (45 km)—a 12-minute flight—from St. Maarten, with a hair-raising landing on the world's smallest commercial airstrip. Though it is only the size of an aircraft carrier—sans catapult—it boasts a 100% safety record. The island is a volcano that has been extinct for 5,000 years. Columbus spotted the little speck in 1493, but except for the Carib Indians who may have lived here around AD 800, Saba remained uninhabited until Dutch settlers arrived from St. Eustatius (Statia) in 1640. From that time on, until the early 19th century, the French, Dutch,

English, and Spanish vied for control, and Saba changed hands 12 times before permanently raising the Dutch flag in 1816. Today the Kingdom of the Netherlands comprises three entities: Holland, the Netherlands Antilles (Saba, St. Maarten, St. Eustatius, Bonaire, and Curaçao), and Aruba. Saba's local administration supervises internal affairs, and the island elects representatives and sends them to the capital of the Netherlands Antilles, Willemstad in Curaçao, to attend to regional issues.

Sabans are a hardy lot. To get from Fort Bay to The Bottom, early settlers carved 900 steps out of the mountainside. Everything that arrived on the island, from a pin to a piano, had to be hauled up. Those rugged steps were the only way to travel until the Road was built by Josephus Lambert Hassell (a carpenter who took correspondence courses in engineering) in the 1940s. An extraordinary feat, the Road—known as the "road that couldn't be built"—took 25 years to construct. If you like roller coasters, you'll love the 9-mi (14½-km) white-knuckle route, which begins at sea level in Fort Bay, zigs up to 1,968 ft, and zags down to 131 ft above sea level at the airport, constructed on the island's only flat point, called (what else?) Flat Point.

WHAT IT COSTS In U.S. dollars				
$$$$	$$$	$$	$	¢
RESTAURANTS*				
over $30	$20–$30	$12–$20	$8–$12	under $8
HOTELS**				
Cost EP/BP/CP over $350	$250–$350	$150–$250	$80–$150	under $80
Cost AI over $450	$350–$450	$250–$350	$125–$250	under $125

*Restaurant prices are for a main course at dinner. **EP, BP, and CP prices are per night for a standard double room in high season, excluding taxes, service charges, and meal plans. AI (all-inclusive) prices are per person, per night based on double-occupancy during high season, excluding taxes and service charges.

Where to Stay

Saba's stock of hotel rooms are in tidy inns or guest houses perched on ledges or tucked into tropical gardens. There are also more than a dozen apartments, cottages, and villas—all with hot water and modern conveniences—for daily, weekly, and monthly rental.

$$$$ ▦ **Willard's of Saba.** From this luxury hotel's cliffside perch at 2,000 ft, breathtaking views reveal the faint profiles of neighboring isles. The property also has a large solar-heated pool and the island's only tennis court. Rooms have tile floors, ceiling fans, rattan furniture, and balconies. Though isolated from town, it offers privacy and tranquillity. (Note: because of its location, this hotel isn't recommended for families with children under 12 years old.) ⊠ *Windwardside* ☖ *Box 515* ☏ *599/416–2498* 🖷 *599/416–2482* ⊕ *www.willardsofsaba.com* ⇨ *7 rooms* ⚲ *Restaurant, fans, tennis court, pool, exercise equipment, hot tub, bar* 🖿 *AE, D, MC, V* ❚❍❚ *EP.*

★ $$$–$$$$ ▦ **Queens Garden Resort.** This classy resort is an elegant addition to Saba's collection of intimate inns. Three four-story buildings hug the mountain and house 12 suites with antique Dutch colonial and Indonesian furnishings, four-poster beds, TVs, kitchens, and verandahs that have breathtaking ocean views. Sit inside the Mango Royale Restaurant or on the patio beside the island's largest pool—which is particularly nice when the torches are lighted and soft music plays in the background.

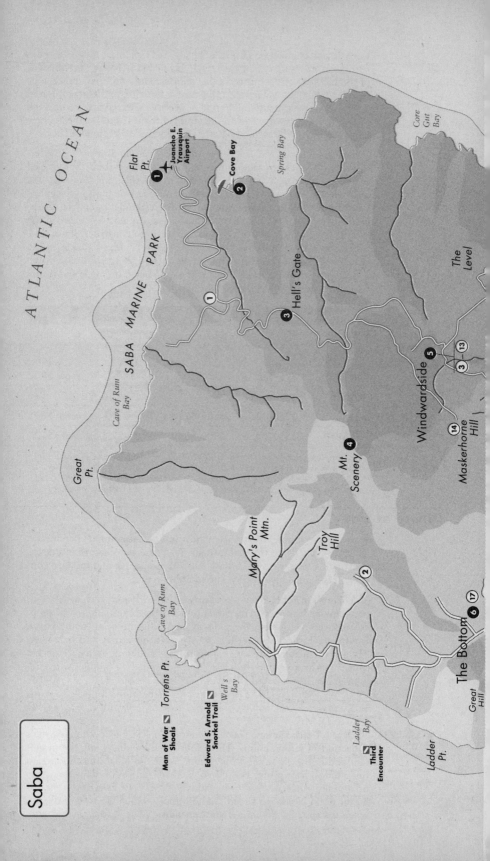

Saba

ATLANTIC OCEAN

SABA MARINE PARK

Flat Pt.

Juancho E. Yrausquin Airport ✈ 1

Cove Bay 2

Spring Bay

Core Gut Bay

Great Pt.

Cave of Rum Bay

1

Hell's Gate 3

The Level

Windwardside 5

13

3

Maskerhorne Hill 14

Cave of Rum Bay

Mt. Scenery 4

Mary's Point Mtn.

Troy Hill

2

The Bottom 6 17

Torrens Pt. ◢

Man of War Shoals ◢

Edward S. Arnold Snorkel Trail ◢

Well's Bay

Ladder Bay

Third Encounter ◢

Ladder Pt.

Great Hill

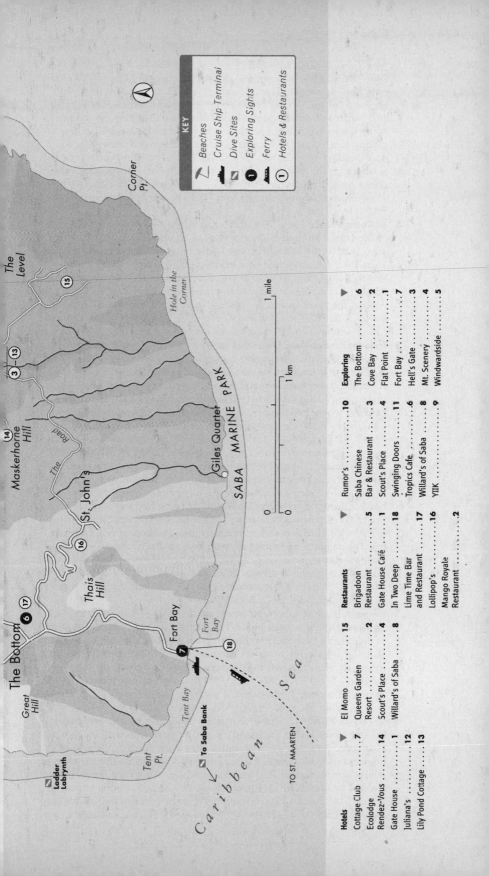

KEY

⌐ Beaches
⚓ Cruise Ship Terminal
◰ Dive Sites
❶ Exploring Sights
⚓ Ferry
① Hotels & Restaurants

Corner Pt.

The Level

⑮

Hole in the Corner

Maskerhorne Hill

③ — ⑬

The Road

St. John's

⑯

SABA MARINE PARK

Giles Quarter

Thais Hill

Great Hill

The Bottom

⑰

⑥

Fort Bay

❼

⑱

Fort Bay

Tent Bay

Tent Pt.

Ladder Labrynth

◰ To Saba Bank

Caribbean Sea

TO ST. MAARTEN

0 ___ 1 km
0 ___ 1 mile

Hotels

Cottage Club	.... **7**
Ecolodge Rendez-Vous	.... **14**
Gate House	.... **1**
Juliana's	.... **12**
Lily Pond Cottage	.... **13**
El Momo	.... **15**
Queens Garden Resort	.... **2**
Scout's Place	.... **4**
Willard's of Saba	.... **8**

Restaurants

Brigadoon Restaurant	.... **5**
Gate House Café	.... **1**
In Two Deep	.... **18**
Lime Time Bar and Restaurant	.... **17**
Lollipop's	.... **16**
Mango Royale Restaurant	.... **2**
Rumor's	.... **10**
Saba Chinese Bar & Restaurant	.... **3**
Scout's Place	.... **4**
Swinging Doors	.... **11**
Tropics Cafe	.... **6**
Willard's of Saba	.... **8**
YIIK	.... **9**

Exploring

The Bottom	.... **6**
Cove Bay	.... **2**
Flat Point	.... **1**
Fort Bay	.... **7**
Hell's Gate	.... **3**
Mt. Scenery	.... **4**
Windwardside	.... **5**

✉ *1 Troy Hill Dr., Troy Hill* ☏ *Box 4* ☎ *599/416–3494 or 599/416– 3496* 🖷 *599/416–3495* ⊕ *www.queenssaba.com* 🛏 *12 suites* ♿ *Restaurant, fans, kitchenettes, pool, hot tub, bar* ▤ *AE, D, MC, V* ⫶◯⫶ *EP.*

★ **$$** **Lily Pond Cottage.** Though most people stop just to admire the lily pond and gardens of this delightful little 200-year-old cottage, its interior is really worth exploring. The kitchen has a hearth and an old-fashioned pump, which conceals a modern faucet, while the bathroom is an indoor/outdoor tropical rain forest. The bed, with four-posters that resemble tropical foliage, sits atop a re-creation of a lily pond. Cottage guests have breakfast at Tropics Cafe ✉ *Windwardside* ☎ *599/466– 2745* ⊕ *www.lilypondcottage.com* 🛏 *1 cottage* ♿ *Kitchen, cable TV* ▤ *No credit cards* ⫶◯⫶ *BP.*

$ ▦ **Cottage Club.** These 10 gingerbread bungalows overlooking the sea or the village of English Quarter (Nos. 1, 2, and 6 have the best views) are owned by the Johnson brothers. Spacious and breezy, rooms are furnished in a basic style and have beamed ceilings, cable TV, and kitchens that the Johnsons will stock for you. Below the stone colonial-style main house, there's a lovely secluded pool area, where you can just catch the edge of the runway and see planes landing and taking off. ✉ *Windwardside* ☎ *599/416–2486 or 599/416–2386* 🖷 *599/416–2476* ⊕ *www. cottage-club.com* 🛏 *10 units* ♿ *Kitchens, pool* ▤ *MC, V* ⫶◯⫶ *EP.*

$ **Ecolodge Rendez-Vous.** On a small section of the Crispeen Track, Brownie, the donkey/bellman, transports luggage to this new inn on once-terraced farmland that has been reclaimed by rain forest. Sparse but adequate, colorful cottages have lofts and sleep up to four people. Some have kitchenettes, but all are solar-powered and surrounded by herb and vegetable gardens, whose products are used in the inn's restaurant, the Rainforest Cafe (¢–$), which serves beer and liquor. ✉ *Windwardside* ☎ *599/ 416–3348* 🖷 *599/416–3299* ⊕ *www.ecolodge-saba.com* 🛏 *12 cottages* ♿ *Restaurant; no a/c, no TV, no room phones* ▤ *MC, V* ⫶◯⫶ *EP.*

$ ▦ **Gate House.** Owners Lyliane and Michel Job, formerly of France and Boston, preside over this whimsical, two-story hideaway in the tiny village of Hell's Gate, a place where the silent night is broken only by the howl of the wind and the bell-like sound of grasshoppers and tree frogs. Bright color schemes created by the former owner, Jim Siegal, are accented with tile floors and crisp pinstripe or checked fabrics. One room has a kitchenette, and there is a two-person cottage. The pool is a great place to relax as the sun goes down. Eat indoors or out at the Gate House Café, which overlooks the sea. ✉ *Hell's Gate* ☎ *599/416–2416* 🖷 *599/ 416–2550* ⊕ *www.sabagatehouse.com* 🛏 *5 rooms, 1 villa, 1 cottage* ♿ *Restaurant, pool* ▤ *D, MC, V* ⫶◯⫶ *CP.*

$ **Juliana's.** It is just a short, but steep, uphill stroll to Main Street in Windwardside from this guest house. Private balconies offer sweeping vistas of the ocean and the surrounding tropical gardens. Owners Juliana and Franklin Johnson treat guests like one of the family. Included is a full American breakfast, which is served at Tropics Restaurant. ✉ *Windwardside* ☎ *599/416–2269* 🖷 *599/416–2389* ⊕ *www.julianas-hotel. com* 🛏 *9 rooms, 1 apartment, 2 cottages* ♿ *Restaurant, fans, refrigerators, cable TV, pool* ▤ *DC, MC, V* ⫶◯⫶ *BP.*

$ ▦ **Scout's Place.** German dive masters Wolfgang Tooten and Barbara Schafer have created the island's first dive operation with its own accommodations. You can take initial dive instruction at the property's pool and take advantage of special dive packages through Saba Divers, which Wolfgang and Barbara operate here. All rooms have private baths; 11 rooms have four-poster beds, as well as balconies and refrigerators. The Scout's Place restaurant serves three meals daily. ✉ *Windwardside* ☎ *599/416–2740* 🖷 *599/416–2741* ⊕ *www.sabadivers.com*

⛴ *13 rooms ᓬ Restaurant, fans, some refrigerators, cable TV, pool, dive shop, bar, shop, car rental* ▤ *MC, V* ⦿ *BP.*

¢–$ 🛏 **El Momo.** This funky inn amid tropical gardens is about 1,500 ft up Jimmy's Hill, near Windwardside, and is a 70-step climb—a good reason to pack light. But the views from the gingerbread cottages are well worth the trek. Rooms use solar power, and most share a communal bathroom; one ecocottage has a full kitchen, a private bathroom with composting toilet, and a bedroom with a sea view. Claim a hammock or chair in the snack bar (with honor bar) in the main house to watch the sunset. The property has the only bridge on Saba—a footbridge across its pool. Breakfast is available for $6. ⊠ *Booby Hill* ⓓ *Box 542, Windwardside* ☎☎ *599/416–2265* ⊕ *www.elmomo.com* ⛴ *7 cottages, 3 with private bath* ᓬ *Snack bar, pool, shop; no a/c* ▤ *D, MC, V* ⦿ *EP.*

Where to Eat

The quality of the restaurants on this tiny island is surprising. Several restaurants serve wonderfully fresh seafood and such Caribbean dishes as stuffed crabs, goat stew, and grilled lobster. A decent selection of wines is available at the better restaurants. Reservations aren't usually necessary, but it wouldn't hurt to call ahead to confirm hours and stake your claim to a table (some of the restaurants are quite small). In addition, some places provide transportation.

What to Wear

Restaurants are informal. Shorts are fine during the day, but for dinner you may want to put on pants or a casual sundress. Just remember that nights in Windwardside can be cool due to the elevation.

ASIAN ✕ **Saba Chinese Bar & Restaurant.** In this plain little house with plastic
$$ cloths on its tables you can get, among other things, sweet-and-sour pork or chicken, cashew chicken, and curried dishes. ⊠ *Windwardside* ☎ *599/416–2353* ▤ *MC, V* ⊘ *Closed Mon.*

CARIBBEAN ✕ **Lollipop's.** Under new management as of 2002, Lollipop's now serves
$–$$$ mostly seafood and vegetarian, with take-out and longer hours, but the later hours (9 PM–2 AM on weekends) is party time. No reservations are necessary, but if you call, someone will pick you up and drop you off after dinner—a sweet touch, indeed. ⊠ *St. John's* ☎ *599/416–3330* ▤ *MC, V* ⊘ *Closed Sun.*

$$ ✕ **Lime Time Bar and Restaurant.** A Saban house has been spruced up to create this lively bar-eatery. You can eat on the front porch with a view of the Governor's House. Sample such local favorites as spare ribs, burgers, garlic shrimp, and conch chowder. The music here is lively and modern. ⊠ *The Bottom* ☎ *599/416–3351* ▤ *AE, MC, V.*

CONTEMPORARY ✕ **Willard's of Saba.** On a cliff high above Windwardside, Saba's most
$$$–$$$$ expensive restaurant, in the Willard's of Saba hotel, has views of the sea at a dizzying 2,000 ft below. Chef Corazon de Johnson, an enthusiastic, charming cook, fuses international and Asian cuisine to offer such dishes as drunken pork loin, Shanghai rolls, and fresh lobster; Corazon also fills requests to fit most any dietary need, including kosher and vegetarian. Access to the restaurant is up a steep drive; only a few taxis will make the climb, but you can call the restaurant to arrange transport. ⊠ *Willard's of Saba, Windwardside* ☎ *599/416–2498* ▤ *AE, D, MC, V.*

★ $$$–$$$$ ✕ **YIIK.** Latticework, plants, tiny lights, and wind chimes add considerable charm to this rooftop restaurant in the heart of town. During the day, folks are drawn to this relaxed café for the pastries and the coffee. Local chefs Rudolph Hassell and Carl Buncamper also offer tasty shrimp and lobster dishes for dinner and lunch specialties such as curried goat. ⊠ *Windwardside* ☎ 599/416–2539 ⊟ *MC, V* ⊘ *Closed Sun.*

¢–$$ ✕ **Tropics Cafe.** Tropics has a "you are what you eat" theme, so it is the place for fresh fruit, smoothies, salads, fresh baked goodies, and tasty vegetarian dishes. Three meals a day are served alongside the pool of Juliana's hotel or in the terraced dining room. ⊠ *Windwardside* ☎ 599/ 416–2469 ⊟ *MC, V* ⊘ *No lunch or dinner Mon.*

ECLECTIC ✕ **Brigadoon Restaurant.** This friendly, local favorite lets you take in the
★ $–$$$ passing action on the street—which may not mean a whole lot on Saba, but it's still a nice thought. The varied menu includes sushi and a $10 schwarma plate (Lebanese gyros). Owners Michael and Trish Chammaa also offer local fresh fish and vegetables as well as a $10 weekly chef's special and home-made desserts. There's also a popular steak night. ⊠ *Windwardside* ☎ 599/416–2380 ⊟ *AE, DC, MC, V* ⊘ *Closed Tues. No lunch.*

$–$$$ ✕ **Scout's Place.** At Scout's Place, the outdoor verandah overlooks stunning water views and the tiny houses and lush forest that create Saba's fairyland. Chef and dive master Wolfgang Tooten creates cuisine that runs the gamut from local goat stew to Italian pasta dishes to German specialties, and always includes fresh lobster and a catch of the day. Every three weeks there is Mexican Monday; Wednesday and Saturday are gyros nights, and at Wednesday breakfast many American expatriates gather for their unofficial town meeting. ⊠ *Scout's Place, Windwardside* ☎ 599/416–2740 ⚹ *Reservations essential* ⊟ *MC, V.*

$ ✕ **In Two Deep.** The owners of the Saba Deep dive shop run this lively harborside spot, with its stained-glass window and mahogany bar. The soups and sandwiches (especially the Reuben) are excellent, and the customers are usually high-spirited—most have just come from a dive. Dinner is occasionally served on some holidays. ⊠ *Fort Bay* ☎ 599/ 416–3438 ⊟ *MC, V* ⊘ *No dinner.*

¢–$ ✕ **Swinging Doors.** A cross between an English pub and an Old West saloon (yes, there are swinging doors), this lively watering hole serves good, ample burgers, jalapeño poppers (a deep-fried flour puffball seasoned with hot peppers), parrotfish sandwiches, and plenty of brew daily from 9 AM until late at night. There's also barbecue on Tuesday and Friday nights and Saturday lunch, as well as plenty of conversation, including some local gossip. ⊠ *Windwardside* ☎ 599/416–2506 ⊟ *No credit cards.*

FRENCH ✕ **Gate House Café.** It is worth the slightly out of the way trip to sam-
★ $$–$$$ ple owner Michel Job's tasty French cuisine. To complement his chicken, seafood, or beef, choose from the extensive wine list, which won a 2002 Wine Spectator Award, and don't miss the tantalizing "Queen of Saba" chocolate cake, complete with Michel's explanation of how it represents the island. Both lunch and dinner are served seven days a week, and pickup service is available. ⊠ *Gate House Hotel, Hell's Gate* ☎ 599/416–2416 ⊟ *D, MC, V.*

★ $$–$$$ ✕ **Mango Royale Restaurant.** This elegant spot in the Queens Garden Resort serves the creative cuisine of chef Algernon Charles, whose specialties are Italian cuisine but also include Creole, French, and seafood dishes. Try lobster thermidor or seafood chowder, or chicken scallopini in a delicate basil-cream sauce. In these magical hillside surroundings you can dine inside or out. After dinner you can dance under the stars; poolside barbecues, musical events, and theme nights with international flavors are also on offer. ⊠ *Queens Garden Resort, 1 Troy Hill Dr., Troy Hill* ☎ 599/416–3494 ⊟ *AE, D, MC, V.*

ITALIAN ✕ **Rumor's.** Students at the Saba University School of Medicine love this
$–$$ place. And what's not to love? In addition to fresh soup, pizza, and lasagna,

there are a pool table, a few rooms to rent, and a fitness center. ⊠ *Windwardside* ☎ *599/416–2230* ▤ *No credit cards* ☉ *Closed Sun.*

Sports & the Outdoors

HIKING On Saba you can't avoid some hiking, even if you just go to mail a postcard. The big deal, of course, is Mt. Scenery, with 1,064 steps leading to its top. Many of the trails, including the Mt. Scenery trail, have signs that describe the flora. For information about Saba's 18 recommended botanical hikes, check with the **Saba Conservation Foundation** (⊠ behind tourist office, Windwardside ☎ 599/416–2630), which maintains trails, or the foundation's **trail shop** (☎ 599/416–2630 or 599/416–3307) across the street. Botanical tours are available upon request. Crocodile James (James Johnson) will explain the local flora and fauna. A guided, strenuous full-day hike through the undeveloped back side of Mt. Scenery costs about $50.

SCUBA DIVING & Saba is one of the world's premier scuba-diving destinations. Visibility
SNORKELING is extraordinary, and dive sites are alive with corals and other sea crea-
Fodor's Choice tures. Within ½ mi (¾ km) from shore, sea walls drop to depths of more
★ than 1,000 ft. The Saba Marine Park, which includes shoals, reefs, and sea walls alive with corals and other sea creatures, is dedicated to preserving its marine life.

Divers have a pick of 28 sites, including **Third Encounter,** a top-rated pinnacle dive (usually to about 110 ft [34 m]) for advanced divers, with plentiful fish and spectacular coral; **Man of War Shoals,** another hot pinnacle dive (70 ft [21 m]), with outstanding fish and coral varieties; and **Ladder Labyrinth,** a formation of ridges and alleys (down to 80 ft [24 m]), where likely sightings include grouper, sea turtles, and sharks. **Saba Bank,** a fertile fishing ground 3 mi (5 km) southwest of Saba, has coral gardens and undersea mountains.

Snorkelers need not feel left out: the marine park has several marked spots where reefs or rocks sit in shallow water. Among these sites are **Torrens Point,** on the northwest side of the island, and the **Edward S. Arnold Snorkel Trail**—a self-guided underwater tour (off the northwest coast near Well's Bay) with 11 numbered and marked sites. Waterproof maps are available from the marine park, the Saba Conservation Foundation, or dive shops.

Expect to pay about $50 for a one-tank dive, around $90 for a two-tank dive. Here are some dive operators that can help get you started: **Caradonna Caribbean Tours** (⊠ 435 Douglas Ave., Suite 2205, Altamonte Springs, FL 32714 ☎ 407/774–9000 or 800/328–2288 ⊕ www.caradonna.com) puts together packages at the hotel of your choice. **Saba Deep** (⊠ Fort Bay ☎ 599/416–3347 or 888/348–3722 🖷 599/416–3497 ⊕ www.sabadeep.com) offers both PADI- and/or NAUI-certified instructors, directed by owner Mike Myers. **Saba Divers** (⊠ Windwardside ☎ 599/416–2740 ⊕ www.sabadivers.com) was founded by a German state registered instructor and offers multilingual instruction. **Sea Saba** (⊠ Windwardside ☎ 599/416–2246 ⊕ www.seasaba.com) takes you to all of Saba's dive sites.

Shopping

Saba lace, one of the island's most popular purchases, goes back more than a century. Gertrude Johnson learned lace-making at a Caracas convent school. She returned to Saba in the 1870s and taught the art that has endured ever since. Saban ladies display and sell their creations at the community center in Hell's Gate and from their houses; just follow .

the signs. Collars, tea towels, napkins, and other small articles are relatively inexpensive; larger ones, such as tablecloths, can be pricey. The fabric requires some care—it's not drip-dry. Saba Spice is another island buy. Although it *sounds* as delicate as Saba lace and the aroma is as sweet as can be, the base for this liqueur is 151-proof rum. You'll find souvenirs, gifts, and *Saban Cottages: A Book of Watercolors,* in almost every shop.

Around the Bend (⊠ Windwardside ☎ 599/416–2259) carries souvenirs and clothing as well as "gifts, oddments, and pretties." The **Breadfruit Gallery** (⊠ Windwardside ☎ 599/416–2509) showcases and sells local artists' work. **Jobean Designs** (☎ 599/416–2490) sells intricate handmade glass-bead jewelry as well as sterling silver and gold pieces by artist-owner Jo Bean. She also offers workshops in beadwork. **Katherine's Windwardside Gallery** (⊠ Windwardside ☎ 599/416–2360) was Saba's first gallery for works by local artist Katherine Maeder, who now works out of Meadowview Cottage on Park Lane. The **Lynn Gallery** (⊠ Windwardside ☎ 599/416–2435) is open by appointment or by chance. It sells artwork by the multitalented Lynn family, which also has a gallery in St. Martin's Grand Case. **El Momo Folk Art** (⊠ Windwardside ☎ 599/ 416–2518) has silk-screened T-shirts and souvenirs. The **Saba Artisan Foundation** (⊠ The Bottom ☎ 599/416–3260) turns out hand-screened fabrics that you can buy by the yard or that are already made into resort clothing, and it's also a central location where you can buy the famous Saba lace. It also sells T-shirts and spices. **Sea Saba** (⊠ Windwardside ☎ 599/416–2246) carries T-shirts, diving equipment, clothing, and books. The **Yellow House** (⊠ Windwardside ☎ 599/416–2334) sells local books, souvenirs, and lace.

Nightlife

Check the bulletin board in each village for a list of events, which often include parties. **Scout's Place** (⊠ Windwardside ☎ 599/416–2740) is a popular evening gathering place, with special prices on desserts and coffee from 8 to 10 PM. The convivial bar can get crowded and sometimes there's even dancing.

Exploring Saba

Getting around the island means negotiating the narrow, twisting roadway that clings to the mountainside and rises from sea level to almost 2,000 ft. Although driving isn't difficult, just be sure to go slowly and cautiously. If in doubt, leave the driving to a cabbie so you can enjoy the scenery. You won't need long to tour the island by car—if you don't stop, you can cover the entire circuitous length of the Road in the space of a morning. If you want to shop, have lunch, and do some sightseeing, plan on a full day.

Numbers in the margin correspond to points of interest on the Saba map.

WHAT TO SEE **The Bottom.** Sitting in a bowl-shape valley 820 ft above the sea, this town ❻ is the seat of government and the home of the lieutenant governor. The gubernatorial mansion, next to Wilhelmina Park, has fancy fretwork, a high-pitched roof, and wraparound double galleries. Saba University School of Medicine runs a two-year **medical school** in The Bottom, at which about 200 students are enrolled.

On the other side of town is the Wesleyan Holiness Church, a small stone building with white fretwork. It dates from 1919, and although it's no longer used, you can go inside and look around. Stroll by the church, beyond a place called the Gap, to a lookout point where you can see the 400 rough-hewn steps leading down to Ladder Bay. This and Fort

Bay were the two landing sites from which Saba's first settlers had to haul themselves and their possessions up to the heights. Sabans sometimes walk down to Ladder Bay to picnic. Think long and hard before you do: going back requires 400 steps *up* to the Road.

② Cove Bay. Near the airport on the island's northeastern side, a 20-ft-long (6-m-long) strip of rocks and pebbles laced with gray sand is really the only place for sunning. There's also a small tidal pool here for swimming.

① Flat Point. This is the only place on the island where planes can land. The runway here is one of the world's shortest, with a length of 1,200 ft. Only STOL (short takeoff and landing) prop planes dare land here, as each end of the runway drops off more than 100 ft into the crashing surf below.

⑦ Fort Bay. The end of the Road is also the jumping-off place for all of Saba's dive operations and the location of the St. Maarten ferry dock. The island's only gas station is here, as is a 277-ft deep-water pier that accommodates the tenders from ships. On the quay are a decompression chamber, one of the few in the Caribbean, and three dive shops. Saba Deep's restaurant, In Two Deep, is a good place to catch your breath while enjoying some refreshments and the view of the water.

③ Hell's Gate. The Road makes 14 hairpin turns up more than 1,000 vertical ft to Hell's Gate. Holy Rosary Church, on Hell's Gate's Hill, is a stone structure that looks medieval but was built in 1962. In the community center behind the church, village ladies sell their Saba lace wares. The same ladies make the potent rum-based Saba Spice, each according to her old family recipe. The intrepid can venture to Lower Hell's Gate, where the Old Sulphur Mine Walk leads to bat caves (with a sulfuric stench) that can—with caution—be explored.

④ Mt. Scenery. Stone and concrete steps—1,064 of them—rise to the top
Fodor'sChoice of Mt. Scenery. En route to the mahogany grove at the summit, the steps
★ pass giant elephant ears, ferns, begonias, mangoes, palms, and orchids; there are six identifiable ecosystems in all. Signs name the trees, plants, and shrubs, and the staff at the trail shop in Windwardside can provide a field guide. Have your hotel pack a picnic lunch, wear nonslip shoes, and take along a jacket and a canteen of water. The round-trip excursion will take about three hours and is best begun in the early morning.

Saba Marine Park. Established in 1987 to preserve and manage the island's marine resources, the park circles the entire island, dipping down to 200 ft, and is zoned for diving, swimming, fishing, boating, and anchorage. One of the unique aspects of Saba's diving is the submerged pinnacles of land at about the 70-ft depth mark. Here all forms of sea creatures rendezvous. The information center offers talks and slide shows for divers and snorkelers and provides literature on marine life. (Divers are requested to contribute $3 a dive to help maintain the park facilities.) Before you visit, call first to see if anyone is around. ⊠ *Harbor Office, Fort Bay* ☎ *599/416–3295* ☉ *Weekdays 8–5.*

⑤ Windwardside. The island's second-largest village, perched at 1,968 ft, commands magnificent views of the Caribbean. Here amid the oleander bushes are rambling lanes and narrow alleyways winding through the hills, and clusters of tiny, neat houses and shops as well as the Saba Tourist Office. At the village's northern end is the Church of St. Paul's Conversion, a colonial building with a red-and-white steeple.

★ Small signs mark the way to the **Saba Museum.** This 150-year-old house, surrounded by lemongrass and clover, replicates a sea captain's home. Period pieces on display include a handsome mahogany four-poster bed, an antique organ, and, in the kitchen, a rock oven. You can also look at old documents, such as a letter a Saban wrote after the hurricane of 1772, in which he sadly says, "We have lost our little all." Don't miss the delightful stroll to the museum down the stone-walled Park Lane, one of the prettiest walks in the Caribbean. ⊠ *Windwardside* ☎ *no phone* 🖃 *$1 (suggested donation)* ⊙ *Weekdays 10–4.*

SABA A TO Z

To research prices, get advice from other travelers, and book travel arrangements, visit www.fodors.com.

AIR TRAVEL

Winair is the only airline that flies to Saba—from St. Eustatius and St. Maarten.

🚹 **Winair** ☎ 599/416-2255 or 800/634-4907 ⊕ www.fly-winair.com.

AIRPORTS

The approach to Saba's tiny airstrip is as thrilling as a roller-coaster ride. The strip is the shortest in the world, but the STOL aircraft are built for it, and the pilot needs only half of that length to land properly. Try not to panic; remember that the pilot knows what he's doing and wants to live just as much as you do. (If you're nervous, don't sit on the right. The wing just misses grazing the cliff side on the approach.) Once you've touched down on the airstrip, the pilot taxis an inch or two, turns, and deposits you just outside a little shoe box called the Juancho E. Yrausquin Airport, which opened in 2002 and is a full-fledged airport—the runway has been widened and resurfaced to increase safety and a new terminal has been added. The airport had its grand opening on Saba Day (December 6) in 2002. Taxi fare from the airport to Hell's Gate is $6; to Windwardside it's $8; and to The Bottom it's $12.50.

🚹 **Juancho E. Yrausquin Airport** ☎ 599/416-2255.

BOAT & FERRY TRAVEL

FARES & SCHEDULES
The Edge, a high-speed ferry, leaves St. Maarten's Pelican Marina in Simpson Bay for Fort Bay on Saba Wednesdays through Sundays at 9 AM, and boards for the return trip at about 3:45 PM. The trip, which can be rough, takes just over an hour each way. Round-trip fare is $60, plus 5% extra if you pay by credit card.

Other options for a trip to or from St. Maarten are the *Voyager I,* a large catamaran that holds 150 people and runs on Tuesdays and Thursdays between Marigot or Philipsburg and Fort Bay, and the *Voyager II,* a large powerboat that can take 100 people and runs on Tuesdays and Thursdays between Marigot and Philipsburg and Fort Bay. The fare on either Voyager boat is $57, port fees included, from Marigot. Call ahead to check current schedules.

🚹 ***The Edge*** ☎ 599/544-2640. ***Voyager I and II*** ☎ 599/542-4096 ⊕ www.voyager-st-barths.com.

BUSINESS HOURS

BANKS
The island's two banks open at 8:30. Barclays closes at 2, the Royal Bank of Trinidad and Tobago at 3 (4 on Friday).

POST OFFICES
There are two post offices, one at Windwardside, open 7:30 AM–noon, and one at The Bottom, open 1:30–4:30.

SHOPS
Shops are open weekdays and Saturday 8–5.

CAR RENTALS

The Road—Saba's one and only—is serpentine, with many a hairpin (read: hair-raising) curve. However, if you dare to drive, you can rent a car (about $45 a day with a full tank of gas and unlimited mileage). If you run out of gas, call the island's only gas station, down at Fort Bay, but remember that it closes at 3 PM. Gas costs roughly NAf 1.03 per liter ($2.72 per gallon).

🚗 Car Rentals **Hardiana** ⊠ The Bottom ☎ 599/416-2388. **Johnson's Rent A Car** ⊠ Juliana's Cottages, Windwardside ☎ 599/416-2269.

🚗 Gasoline **Gas Station** ⊠ Fort Bay ☎ 599/416-3272.

ELECTRICITY
Saba's current is 110 volts, 60 cycles, and visitors from North America should have no trouble using their travel appliances.

EMERGENCIES
🚑 Ambulance & Fire **Ambulance** ☎ 599/416-3288 or 599/416-3289 **Fire** ☎ 599/416-2222

🚑 Hospitals The **A. M. Edwards Medical Center** ⊠ The Bottom ☎ 599/416-3289.

🚑 Pharmacies The **Pharmacy** ⊠ A. M. Edwards Medical Center, The Bottom ☎ 599/416-3289.

🚑 Police **Police** ⊠ The Bottom ☎ 599/416-3237 or 599/416-3238.

🚑 Scuba Diving Emergencies **Saba Marine Park Hyperbaric Facility** ⊠ Fort Bay ☎ 599/416-3295.

FESTIVALS & SEASONAL EVENTS
Saba's Carnival might not be as big as those of other Caribbean islands, but it *is* energetic. This weeklong celebration, which starts in late July and runs through early August, has many special events, local and imported steel-pan bands, food booths, and parades (including the final Grand Carnival Parade). And just so Sabans don't forget what fun is, they hold a Saba Day the first weekend in December—three days of band contests, food tastings, and other events.

HOLIDAYS
Public holidays are: New Year's Day, Good Friday, Easter Monday, Coronation Day and the Queen's Birthday, celebrating the birthday and coronation of Holland's Queen Beatrix, Labor Day (May 1), Ascension Day, Christmas, and Boxing Day (Dec. 26).

LANGUAGE
Saba's official language is Dutch, but everyone on the island speaks English. Sabans are always willing to help, and they enjoy conversation. If you're open to chatting, you may get some good local advice.

MAIL & SHIPPING
An airmail letter to North America or Europe costs NAf 2.25; a postcard, NAf 1.10. Book reservations through a travel agent or over the phone; mail can take a week or two to reach the island. The main branch of the post office is in The Bottom in the government administration building; a second office is in Windwardside, near Scout's Place. Both branches offer express mail service. When writing to Saba, don't worry about addresses without post-office box numbers or street locations—on an island this size, all mail finds its owner. However, do make sure to include "Netherlands Antilles" and "Caribbean" in the address.

MONEY MATTERS
Prices quoted throughout the chapter are in U.S. dollars unless otherwise noted.

ATMS There are no ATMs on the island.

CURRENCY U.S. dollars are accepted everywhere, but Saba's official currency is the Netherlands Antilles florin (NAf; also called the guilder). The exchange rate fluctuates slightly but was around NAf 1.80 to US$1 at press time. The island's two banks provide foreign-exchange services.

f Barclays Bank ⊠ Windwardside ☎ 599/416-2216. **Royal Bank of Trinidad and Tobago** ⊠ Windwardside ☎ 599/416-2631.

PASSPORTS & VISAS

U.S. and Canadian citizens need proof of citizenship. A valid passport is preferred, but a birth certificate with a raised seal along with a government-issued photo I.D. will do. British citizens must have a British passport. All visitors must have an ongoing or return ticket.

SAFETY

Take along sunscreen and sturdy, no-nonsense shoes that get a good grip on the ground. You may encounter the harmless racer snake while hiking. Don't be alarmed; these snakes lie on rocks to sun themselves, but skitter off when people approach.

SIGHTSEEING TOURS

The taxi drivers who meet the planes at the airport or the boats at Fort Bay conduct tours of the island. Tours can also be arranged by dive shops or hotels. A full-day trek costs $40 for one to four passengers and $10 per person for groups larger than four. If you're in from St. Maarten for a day trip, you can do a full morning of sightseeing, stop off for lunch (have your driver make reservations before starting), complete the tour afterward, and return to the airport in time to make the last flight back to St. Maarten. Guides are available for hiking; arrangements may be made through the tourist office or the trail shop in Windwardside.

TAXES & SERVICE CHARGES

DEPARTURE TAX You must pay a $5 departure tax when leaving Saba by plane for either St. Maarten or St. Eustatius, or $22 when continuing on an international flight. (Note: when flying home through St. Maarten from here, list yourself as "in transit" and avoid repaying the tax in St. Maarten, which is $20.) There's no departure tax when you leave by boat.

SALES TAX Several of the larger hotels will tack on a 10%–15% service charge, others will build it into the rates. Call ahead to inquire about service charges. Hotels add a 5% government tax plus a 3% turnover tax to the cost of a room (sometimes it's tacked on to your bill, other times it's built into the room rate). Restaurants on Saba sometimes add service charges of 10%–15%.

TAXIS

Taxis meet planes, the ferry, and *Voyager I* and *Voyager II,* which run seasonally beginning in December, and take you to your destination. They charge a set rate for up to four people per taxi, with an additional cost for each person more than four. The fare from the airport to Hell's Gate is $6, to Windwardside it's $8, and to The Bottom it's $12.50. The fare from the Fort Bay ferry docks to Windwardside is $9.50. A taxi from Windwardside to The Bottom is $6.50.

TELEPHONES

Telephone communications are excellent on the island, and you can dial direct long-distance. There are public phone booths in The Bottom and Windwardside They take prepaid phone cards, which can be bought at stores throughout the island, or local coins.

COUNTRY & AREA CODES To call Saba from the United States, dial 011/599/416, followed by the four-digit number.

TIPPING
Even if service charges have been added into your bill, it's customary but not necessary to tip hotel personnel and restaurant waitstaff; you should tip taxi drivers, as well. About 10%–15% should do it.

TRANSPORTATION AROUND SABA
Carless Sabans get around the old-fashioned ways—walking and hitch-hiking (very popular and safe). If you choose to thumb rides, you'll need to know the rules of the Road. To get a lift from The Bottom (which actually is near the top of the island), sit on the wall opposite the Anglican church; to catch one in Fort Bay, sit on the wall opposite the Saba Deep dive center, where the road begins to twist upward.

VISITOR INFORMATION
The tourist office is open Monday through Friday 8 to 5.
🚹 Saba Tourist Office ⊕ www.sabatourism.com ⏍ Box 527, Windwardside ☎ 599/416-2231, 599/416-232, or 800/722-2394 🖨 599/416-2350.

ST. BARTHÉLEMY

FODOR'S CHOICE

Grande Saline Beach

Hôtel Isle de France, Baie des Flamands

La Route des Epices, a restaurant in Colombier

Shopping, especially for French fashions

HIGHLY RECOMMENDED

RESTAURANTS
Do Brazil, Gustavia

L'Orchidée, Pointe Milou

Le Rivage, Grand Cul de Sac

Le Tamarin, Salines

Le Ti St. Barth Caribbean Tavern, Pointe Milou

Maya's, Gustavia

Restaurant des Trois Forces, Morne Vitet

HOTELS
Carl Gustaf, Gustavia

François Plantation, Colombier

Guanahani, Grand Cul de Sac

Hostellerie des Trois Forces, Morne Vitet

Hotel La Banane, Quartier Lorient

La Paillote, Grand Cul de Sac

Le Toiny, Anse à Toiny

Les Mouettes, Quartier Lorient

Village St-Jean Hôtel, Baie de St-Jean

OUTDOORS
Anse du Gouverneur Beach

It's 3:30 PM. Sun-kissed youngsters tumble into the tanned arms of their *mamans* after a twirl on the school-yard carousel. Traffic along the narrow road stops while the children hop into waiting cars. Nobody cares much about the delay, preferring instead to enjoy the afternoon air perfumed by sea spray and jasmine. The red-tiled roofs along the hillsides glitter in the sun and seem to tumble into the sapphire water. It feels more like a small town in the south of France than an island in the Caribbean.

Updated by
Elise Meyer

St. Barthélemy blends the essence of the Caribbean with the essence of France. A sophisticated but unstudied approach to relaxation and respite prevails: you can spend the day on a beach, try on the latest French fashions, and watch the sun set while nibbling tapas over Gustavia Harbor, then choose from nearly 100 excellent restaurants for an elegant evening meal. You can putter around the island, explore the shops, scuba dive, windsurf on a quiet cove, or just admire the lovely views.

A mere 8 square mi (21 square km), St. Barths has lots of hills and sheltered inlets. The town of Gustavia wraps itself neatly around a lilliputian harbor lined with impressive yachts and rustic fishing boats. Red-roofed bungalows dot the hillsides, and beaches run the gamut from calm to "surfable," from deserted to packed. The cuisine is tops in the Caribbean, part of the French *savoir vivre* that prevails throughout the island.

Longtime visitors speak wistfully of the old, quiet St. Barths. Development has quickened the pace of life here, but the island hasn't yet been overbuilt, and a 1982 ordinance limited new tourist lodgings to 12 rooms. The largest hotel still has fewer than 100 rooms, and the remaining accommodations are divided among about 40 small hotels and guest houses. The tiny planes that arrive with regularity still land at the refurbished airport only during daylight hours. And "nightlife" usually means a leisurely dinner and a stargazing walk on the beach.

Christopher Columbus discovered the island—called "Ouanalao" by its native Carib Indians—in 1493; he named it for his brother Bartholomé. The first group of French colonists arrived in 1648, drawn by the ideal location on the West Indian Trade Route, but they were wiped out by the Carib Indians who dominated the area. Another small group from Normandy and Brittany arrived in 1694. This time the settlers prospered—with the help of French buccaneers, who took advantage of the island's strategic location and protected harbor. In 1784 the French traded the island to King Gustav III of Sweden in exchange for port rights in Göteborg. The king dubbed the capital Gustavia, laid out and paved streets, built three forts, and turned the community into a prosperous free port. The island thrived as a shipping and commercial center until the 19th century, when earthquakes, fire, and hurricanes brought financial ruin. Many residents fled for newer lands of opportunity, and Oscar II of Sweden decided to return the island to France. After briefly considering selling it to America, the French took possession of Saint-Barthélemy again on August 10, 1877.

Today the island is still a free port and, as a dependency of Guadeloupe, is part of an overseas department of France. Arid, hilly, and rocky, St. Barths was unsuited to sugar production and thus never developed an extensive slave base. Most of the 3,000 current residents are descendants of the tough Norman and Breton settlers of three centuries ago. They are feisty, industrious, and friendly—but insular. However, you will find many new, young French arrivals, predominantly from north-western France and Provence, who speak English well.

WHAT IT COSTS In U.S. dollars				
$$$$	$$$	$$	$	¢
RESTAURANTS*				
over $30	$20–$30	$12–$20	$8–$12	under $8
HOTELS**				
Cost EP/BP/CP over $350	$250–$350	$150–$250	$80–$150	under $80
Cost AI over $450	$350–$450	$250–$350	$125–$250	under $125

*Restaurant prices are for a main course at dinner. **EP, BP, and CP prices are per night for a standard double room in high season, excluding taxes, service charges, and meal plans. AI (all-inclusive) prices are per person, per night based on double-occupancy during high season, excluding taxes and service charges.

Where to Stay

There is no denying that hotel rooms carry high prices. You're paying for the privilege of staying on the island, and even at $500 a night the bedrooms tend to be small. Still, if you're flexible—in terms of timing and in your choice of lodgings—you can enjoy a holiday in St. Barths and still afford to send the kids to college.

The most expensive season falls during the holidays (mid-December to early January), when hotels are booked far in advance and may require a 10- or 14-day stay, and can be double the high-season rates. Most quoted hotel rates are per-room, not per-person, and include tax and service charges and transfers from the airport. More hotels and restaurants here have seasonal closings (from August to September or October) than on other islands, but some places are still open in August. If you're on a budget, look into an off-season stay, when rates can drop by as much as 50% and many properties offer attractive packages. Most top hotels are on four northern beaches: Anse des Flamands, Anse des Cayes, Baie de St-Jean, and Grand Cul de Sac. In the hills away from the beaches are a number of surprisingly reasonable small hotels, guest houses, rental villas, and bungalows that significantly broaden your options. And regardless of the lodgings you choose, you'll need a car to explore the island.

On St. Barths, the term "villa" is used to describe anything from a small cottage to a sprawling manor. Today almost half of St. Barths' accommodations are in villas, and rentals make a lot of sense, especially for longer stays or groups traveling together. Most houses include a small private swimming pool and maid service daily except Sunday. Houses are well furnished with linens, kitchen utensils, and such electronic playthings as CD players, satellite TV, and VCRs. In-season rates range from $700 to $25,000 a week. Peak periods are usually booked far in advance. Villa-rental companies have extensive Web sites with virtual tours that simplify the rental process, as most of the companies schedule from off the island. Local offices oversee maintenance and housekeeping. Some provide concierge services to clients.

VILLAS & **St. Barth Properties, Inc.** (☎ 508/528–7727 or 800/421–3396 🖷 508/528–
CONDOMINIUMS 7789 ⊕ www.stbarth.com), owned by American Peg Walsh—a regular on St. Barths since 1986—represents more than 100 properties here and can guide you to the perfect place to stay. Weekly peak-season rates range from $1,400 to $40,000 depending on the property's size, location, and

amenities. The excellent Web site offers virtual tours of most of the properties and details of availability. An office in Gustavia can take care of any problems you may have and offers some concierge-type services. **ParadiseLodging.com** (☎ 888/349–7800 🖷 770/426–5716 ⊕ www. paradiselodging.com) is an American company that arranges rentals of private villas. You can search and view the panoramic pictures of the offerings on their Web site. **WIMCO** (☎ 800/932–3222 🖷 401/847–6290 ⊕ www.wimco.com), which is based in Rhode Island, oversees bookings for more than 200 properties on St. Barths that are represented by SiBarth Real Estate. Rents range from $1,000 to $3,500 per week for one-bedroom villas and $1,800 to $7,000 for two- and three-bedroom villas. Larger villas rent for $7,000 per week and up. Properties can be previewed and reserved on WIMCO's Web site, or you can obtain a catalogue by mail.

Hotels

★ $$$$ 🖼 **Carl Gustaf.** One- and two-bedroom suites with private decks and plunge pools spill down a hill overlooking quaint Gustavia Harbor. High ceilings and gleaming white rooms are stylishly decorated with nautical prints, marble baths, tiny kitchens, and such welcome extras as fax machines, two satellite TVs, and stereos. Summer package rates and an excellent honeymoon package are available. The Carl Gustaf restaurant, known for its classic French cuisine, is spectacular. ⊠ *Rue des Normands, Gustavia* 🗗 *Box 700, 97133* ☎ *0590/29–79–00* 🖷 *0590/27–82–37* ⊕ *www. hotelcarlgustaf.com* 🗨 *14 suites* ☙ *Restaurant, kitchenettes, minibars, refrigerators, in-room VCRs, pool, health club, sauna, piano bar* 🖃 *AE, DC, MC, V* 🍴 *CP.*

$$$$ 🖼 **Eden Rock.** On a craggy bluff that splits Baie de St-Jean is St. Barths' first hotel, originally opened in the 1950s. Cozy, antiques-filled rooms have draped four-poster beds, fine art, sparkling silver fixtures, terracotta floors, and stunning bay views in suites, cabins, or beach cottages. The beach has comfortable chaises, umbrellas, and a seawater whirlpool. The breakfast buffet is terrific. The Rock, Michael's, and the Sand Bar restaurants are also all first-rate. ⊠ *Baie de St-Jean 97133* ☎ *0590/29–79–89* 🖷 *0590/27–88–37* ⊕ *www.edenrockhotel.com* 🗨 *15 rooms* ☙ *3 restaurants, minibars, pool, snorkeling, windsurfing, 2 bars, library* 🖃 *AE, MC, V* 🍴 *BP.*

$$$$ 🖼 **Filao Beach.** Charming service and a location on Baie de St-Jean keep them coming back to this casual mini-resort. Two-room bungalows are in a tropical garden. Quarters closer to the beach are the most expensive, but affordable garden rooms are only steps from the sand. Rooms are simple and smallish, with rattan furniture, pastel prints, a compact but tidy bath, and a patio. The deservedly popular restaurant serves breakfast, lunch, and drinks. ⊠ *Baie de St-Jean 97012* ☎ *0590/27–64–84* 🖷 *0590/27–62–24* ⊕ *www.filaobeach.com* 🗨 *30 rooms* ☙ *Restaurant, refrigerators, pool, beach, bar* 🖃 *AE, MC, V* 🍴 *CP.*

★ $$$$ 🖼 **François Plantation.** A colonial-era graciousness pervades this intimate, exquisite hillside complex of West Indian–style cottages. Owner and longtime island habitué François Beret is a passionate gardener, discriminating gourmand, and oenophile. A hint of shared interest may result in a tour of the grounds, or of the exceptional wine cellar. The pristine rooms have queen-size mahogany four-poster beds and colorful fabrics. Two larger rooms can accommodate an extra bed. The pool is atop a very steep hill, with magnificent views. La Route Des Epices restaurant, one of the best on the island, serves dinner on a romantic veranda. Low-season packages are available. ⊠ *Colombier 97133* ☎ *0590/29–80–22* 🖷 *0590/27–61–26* ⊕ *www.francois-plantation.com* 🗨 *12 rooms* ☙ *Restaurant, refrigerators, pool, gym* 🖃 *AE, MC, V* 🍴 *CP* ⊙ *Closed Aug.–Oct.*

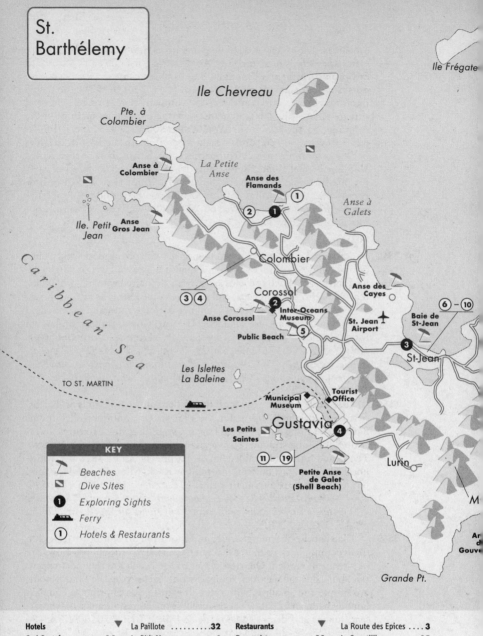

St. Barthélemy

Ile Frégate

Ile Chevreau

Pte. à Colombier

Anse à Colombier

La Petite Anse

Anse des Flamands

Anse à Galets

Anse Gros Jean

Ile. Petit Jean

Colombier

Corossol

Anse des Cayes

Inter-Oceans Museum

St. Jean Airport

Baie de St-Jean

Anse Corossol

Public Beach

St-Jean

Caribbean Sea

Les Islettes La Baleine

TO ST. MARTIN

Municipal Museum

Tourist Office

Les Petits Saintes

Gustavia

Lurin

Petite Anse de Galet (Shell Beach)

Grande Pt.

Ar d Gouv

M

KEY

- Beaches
- Dive Sites
- ① Exploring Sights
- Ferry
- ① Hotels & Restaurants

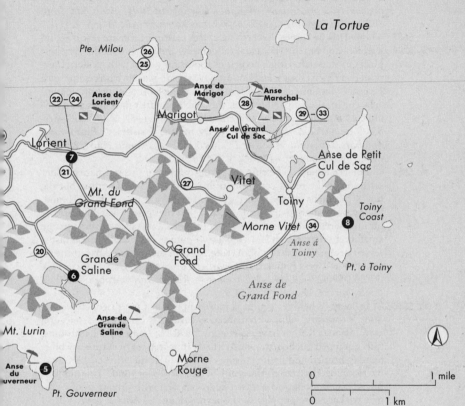

ile Toc Vers

ATLANTIC OCEAN

Les Grenadiers

La Tortue

Pte. Milou   26
              25

22 – 24   Anse de
          Lorient   Anse de   Anse
                            Marigot   Marechal
                  Marigot   28   29 – 33
Lorient   Anse de Grand
          7   Cul de Sac
       21   Anse de Petit
                            Vitet   Cul de Sac
                    27   Toiny
          Mt. du   Toiny
          Grand Fond   Coast
                                    Morne Vitet   34   8
          20   Anse à
                  Grand   Toiny
      6   Grande   Fond
          Saline   Pt. à Toiny
Mt. Lurin   Anse de   Anse de
                Grande   Grand Fond
                Saline
Anse   Morne
du   5   Rouge
Gouverneur
       Pt. Gouverneur

0   1 mile
0   1 km

★ $$$$ ⊡ **Guanahani.** The only full-service resort on the island has lovely rooms and suites (some with private pools) in brilliantly colored Creole cottages, all with big bathrooms. Rooms are decorated either in pretty pastel fabrics and stylish rattan furnishings, or luxurious, deep tropical colors complemented by plantation-style wood. Units vary in price, privacy, view, and distance from activities; make your preferences known. Service is impeccable. The hotel has two well-regarded restaurants. The hair salon is now run by Clarins. ⊠ *Grand Cul de Sac 97133* ☎ *0590/27–66–60* 🖷 *0590/27–70–70* ⊕ *www.guanahani-hotel.com* ⤴ *56 rooms, 21 suites* ⟶ *2 restaurants, room service, cable TV, in-room VCRs, 2 tennis courts, 2 pools, hair salon, windsurfing, boating, piano bar, shop, children's programs (ages 2–6), meeting room* ⊟ *AE, MC, V* ⥈ *CP.*

$$$$
Fodor's Choice
★   ⊡ **Hôtel Isle de France.** Everything at this pristine, intimate resort set on a white-sand beach says casual refinement, and it is among the very best places in St. Barth. Huge, luxurious rooms furnished with modern four-posters, French fabrics, and fine art have superb marble baths (some with Jacuzzis). La Case de l'Isle restaurant, serving tropics-appropriate nouvelle cuisine, is in a pavilion over the beach. Summer packages are available. ⊠ *Baie des Flamands 97098* ☎ *0590/27–61–81* 🖷 *0590/27–86–83* ⊕ *www.isle-de-france.com* ⤴ *24 rooms, 5 suites* ⟶ *Restaurant, minibars, refrigerators, cable TV, in-room VCRs, tennis court, 2 pools, gym, squash, bar* ⊟ *AE, MC, V* ⥈ *CP.*

★ $$$$ ⊡ **Hotel La Banane.** The chic simple decoration of this intimate garden-set resort will remind you more of New York City or London, but the high-style and hard-edge luxury will please fans of Starwood's "W" brand. Ebony walls, mahogany furniture, and sisal rugs give private bungalows unusual serenity. Private baths with outdoor showers have every upscale amenity. Lorient Beach is within a two-minute walk away. Breakfast is served around the shady pool. K'fe Massaï, the on-site African-theme restaurant, is very popular. ⊠ *Quartier Lorient 97133* ☎ *0590/52–03–00* 🖷 *0590/27–68–44* ⤴ *9 rooms* ⟶ *Restaurant, in-room VCRs, 2 pools, bar* ⊟ *AE, MC, V* ⥈ *CP.*

★ $$$$ ⊡ **Le Toiny.** When perfection is more important than price, choose Le Toiny's romantic villas with mahogany furniture, yards of red toile, and private pools. Rooms have every convenience of home: lush bathrooms, fully equipped kitchenettes, and either a stair-stepper or stationary bike. Sunday brunch and haute cuisine can be had at the alfresco Le Gaiac, overlooking the Italian-tile pool to the ocean beyond. The highest-priced accommodation is a two-bedroom villa with private pool. Summer packages are popular for honeymooning. ⊠ *Anse à Toiny 97133* ☎ *0590/27–88–88* 🖷 *0590/27–89–30* ⊕ *www.letoiny.com* ⤴ *12 1-bedroom villas, 1 3-bedroom villa, 1 cottage* ⟶ *Restaurant, in-room safes, minibars, cable TV, in-room VCRs, pool, exercise equipment, bar, laundry service* ⊟ *AE, DC, MC, V* ⥈ *CP.*

$$$$ ⊡ **Sofitel Christopher.** This Sofitel Coralia hotel, with oversize rooms, sunset views, and an especially gracious staff, is one of the island's bargains. Two-story buildings in exceptional gardens house spacious, nicely furnished if simple rooms with tiled baths, and either a balcony or terrace. The hotel's infinity swimming pool, which hangs over the ocean, is the largest on the island, with a wading area. The well-equipped gym has occasional yoga and fitness classes. L'Orchidée restaurant serves superb French-creole cuisine. ⊠ *Pointe Milou 97133* ☎ *0590/27–63–63* 🖷 *0590/27–92–92* ⊕ *www.accor.com* ⤴ *41 rooms, 1 suite* ⟶ *2 restaurants, room service, pool, gym* ⊟ *AE, DC, MC, V* ⥈ *BP* ⊗ *Closed Sept. 1–Oct. 1.*

$$$–$$$$ ⊡ **St-Barths Beach Hotel and Les Residences Saint-Barths.** Athletic Europeans and families love this simple, comfortable hotel for its location on a wide, calm beach ideal for wind-borne water sports (kite-surfing,

windsurfing), the complete on-site gym, the nice boutique, and its excellent restaurant, Le Rivage. The very favorably priced 8 hillside villas (one with a private pool) can accommodate up to seven guests and include a car. ⊠ *Grand Cul de Sac* ⬧ *Box 580, 97098* ☎ *0590/27–60–70* 🖷 *0590/27–75–57* ⊕ *www.saintbarthbeachhotel.com* 📞 *36 rooms, 8 villas* ⚭ *Some kitchens, refrigerators, pool, gym, beach, windsurfing* 🖃 *AE, MC, V* ⑩ *CP.*

$$$–$$$$ 🖾 **Le Tom Beach Hôtel.** Carole Gruson's pretty, compact "boutique" hotel on the St-Jean beach continues to raise its level of chic. A garden winds around the brightly painted suites, over the pool via a small foot-bridge, into the hopping open-air restaurant La Plage. Big, plantation-style rooms have high ceilings, exposed beams, cozy draped beds, nice baths, a TV with both VCR and DVD players, Internet, direct-dial phones, and patios. Oceanfront suites are expensive, but all the rooms are clean and cozy. ⊠ *Plage St-Jean 97133* ☎ *0590/27–53–13* 🖷 *0590/27–53–15* ⊕ *www.tombeach.com* 📞 *12 rooms* ⚭ *Restaurant, in-room safes, minibars, refrigerators, in-room VCRs, pool, beach, bar, Internet* 🖃 *AE, MC, V* ⑩ *CP.*

★ **$$–$$$$** 🖾 **Village St-Jean Hôtel.** For two generations, the Charneau family has seen to the high quality of service and the reasonable rates at their small hotel. Handsome, airy stone-and-redwood cottages have high ceilings, sturdy furniture, modern baths, open-air kitchenettes, and lovely terraces; one has a Jacuzzi. The five hotel-style rooms have refrigerators, and most have king-size beds. There is also a three-bedroom villa available. The location is great—you can walk to the beach and town from here—and most accommodations have views. ⊠ *Baie de St-Jean* ⬧ *Box 623, 97098* ☎ *0590/27–61–39 or 800/651–8366* 🖷 *0590/27–77–96* ⊕ *www.villagestjeanhotel.com* 📞 *5 rooms, 20 cottages* ⚭ *Restaurant, grocery, some kitchenettes, pool, hot tub, bar, library, shops* 🖃 *AE, MC, V* ⑩ *EP.*

$$$ 🖾 **Emeraude Plage.** Right on Baie de St-Jean, these modern and clean bungalows with outdoor kitchenettes on their patios are convenient, well located, and pleasant. Nice bathrooms add to the comfort. Hotel guests often gather to socialize in the comfortable library-lounge. ⊠ *Baie de St-Jean 97113* ☎ *0590/27–64–78* 🖷 *0590/27–83–08* ⊕ *www. emeraudeplage.com* 📞 *24 bungalows, 3 suites, 1 villa* ⚭ *Fans, beach* 🖃 *MC, V* ⑩ *EP.*

$$$ 🖾 **Hôtel Baie des Anges.** Ten clean, fresh, and nicely decorated rooms are right on serene Flamands beach. Each has a kitchenette and private terrace. Everyone is treated like family at this casual retreat. The food at La Langouste, the hotel's restaurant, is tasty and reasonable. ⊠ *Flamands 97095* ☎ *0590/27–63–61* 🖷 *0590/27–83–44* ✉ *annie. ange@wanadoo.fr* 📞 *10 rooms* ⚭ *Restaurant, pool, beach, car rental* 🖃 *AE, MC, V* ⑩ *EP.*

★ **$$–$$$** 🖾 **La Paillote.** Perched high above the glittering crescent of Grand Cul de Sac, which is home to some of the most expensive properties on the island, this tiny compound of five private and meticulous, exotic mini-villas has been restored by two young entrepreneurs and avid gardeners, Christine and Hubert Bonnet. Accommodations vary from a tiny studio to a spacious two-bedroom villa with a private pool, but all have new, fully-equipped kitchenettes, sitting and dining areas, and the comfort and elegance of much more costly island digs. Prices include a rental car. ⊠ *Grand Cul de Sac* ⬧ *97133* ☎ *0590/27–57–95* ✉ *la-paillote-st-barth@voila.fr* 📞 *5 bungalows* ⚭ *Kitchenettes, pool,* 🖃 *AE, MC, V* ⑩ *EP.*

$–$$$ 🖾 **Le Manoir.** History lovers—or those seeking something really eclectic—can try a stay in an actual 17th-century Norman cottage. This entire complex was dismantled in France and rebuilt here in 1984. Set in a pleasant garden with a small pool, the half-timbered cottages, three of which have kitchens, are whimsically decorated in a vaguely Victorian style, with high, beamed ceilings and the white crochet hammocks typical of St. Barth. ⊠ *Lorient* 🖰 *97113* ☎ *0590/27–79–27* 🖶 *0590/27–65–75* ⊕ *www.lemanoirstbarth.com* ↗ *7 cottages, 1 2-bedroom house* ⚿ *Some kitchens, pool* ⊟ *AE, MC, V* ⌘ *EP.*

★ $$ ⌦ **Hostellerie des Trois Forces.** High atop the island, this charming "holistic New Age inn" is an idiosyncratic delight. Each gingerbread cottage has an astrological color scheme (Libra: blue, Leo: red) and handcrafted furnishings chosen by personable owner/astrologer/international chef Hubert de la Motte, who, when not in the kitchen, may do your chart or lead a yoga session beside the pool. Don't miss a leisurely lunch or dinner at the superb Restaurant des Trois Forces. The views are breathtaking, but a four-wheel-drive vehicle is imperative. ⊠ *Morne Vitet 97133* ☎ *0590/27–61–25* 🖶 *0590/27–81–38* ⊕ *www.3forces.net* ↗ *8 rooms* ⚿ *Restaurant, fans, minibars, pool, bar* ⊟ *AE, MC, V* ⌘ *EP.*

★ $–$$ ⌦ **Les Mouettes.** This budget guest house features six clean, simply furnished and economical bungalows that open directly onto the beach. They are also quite close to the road, which can be either convenient for a quick shopping excursion or a bother on account of the noise. Each bungalow has a bathroom with a shower only, a kitchenette, a patio, two double beds, and a twin bed or fold-out sofa, making this place a good bet for families. ⊠ *Quartier Lorient 97133* ☎ *0590/27–77–91* 🖶 *0590/27–68–19* ✉ *hotel.lesmouettes@wanadoo.fr* ↗ *7 rooms* ⚿ *Kitchenettes, beach, shops, car rental* ⊟ *No credit cards* ⌘ *EP.*

$–$$ ⌦ **Tropical Hôtel.** Straight up the hill from Baie de St-Jean is a classic example of what the French affectionately call a *hôtel bourgeois*: a simple, stylish place that's also a good value. You'll find well-maintained rooms (those with lower numbers are the best) in a one-story L-shaped building. All rooms open onto patios with views of either the ocean or thick tropical foliage and have pristine white walls, linens, and furnishings, beamed ceilings, and beds swathed in mosquito netting. Continental breakfast is included in the price. ⊠ *Baie de St-Jean* 🖰 *Box 147, 97133* ☎ *0590/27–64–87* 🖶 *0590/27–81–74* ⊕ *www.st-barths.com/tropical-hotel* ↗ *21 rooms* ⚿ *Snack bar, refrigerators, pool, bar, recreation room* ⊟ *AE, MC, V* ⌘ *CP.*

$ ⌦ **Le P'tit Morne.** Each of the modestly furnished mountainside studios has a private balcony with panoramic views of the coastline. The small kitchenettes are adequate for creating picnic lunches and other light meals. The snack bar serves breakfast. It's relatively isolated here, however, and the beach is a 10-minute drive away. ⊠ *Colombier* 🖰 *Box 14, 97133* ☎ *0590/52–95–50* 🖶 *0590/27–84–63* ✉ *leptitmorne@wanadoo.fr* ↗ *14 rooms* ⚿ *Snack bar, kitchenettes, pool, library* ⊟ *AE, MC, V* ⌘ *CP.*

¢   ⌦ **La Normandie.** This cozy family-run hotel offers modestly furnished rooms (some with a TV) for well under $100 a night, making it one of the best deals on St. Barths. There's a small pool here, and the beach is within a five-minute walk. ⊠ *Quartier Lorient 97133* ☎ *0590/27–73–78* 🖶 *0590/27–98–83* ↗ *8 rooms* ⚿ *Pool; no TVs in some rooms* ⊟ *MC, V* ⌘ *EP.*

Where to Eat

Dining on St. Barths compares favorably to almost anywhere in the world. Varied and exquisite cuisine, breathtaking natural beauty, a French flair in the decorations, sensational wine, and attentive but unobtrusive service make for a wonderful epicurean experience. St. Barths' style is expressed in dozens of charming places to eat, from beachfront grills to serious establishments serving five-course meals. Freshly caught local seafood mingles on the plate with top-quality provisions that arrive every afternoon from Paris. Myth has it that St. Barths' restaurants are frightfully expensive—and, certainly, you can spend a small fortune in a number of restaurants by choosing rare vintages and luxury ingredients. However, you can also dine superbly on the island without breaking the bank.

Lunch is usually a less costly meal than dinner, and many casual restaurants are inexpensive. Be sure to sample such local specialties as *accras* (salt cod fritters), usually served with one or more varieties of creole sauce (herbs and crushed, spicy peppers in oil); spiced *christophene* (similar to acorn squash, usually stuffed); *boudin créole* (blood sausage); and lusty *soupe de poissons* (fish soup). Available local fish include *dorade* (mahimahi) and tuna; also look for langouste (spiny lobster). Delicious and interesting variations on *gazpacho* (cold tomato soup) are common, and a refreshing starter at lunch. Most meat in St. Barths comes from the United States or Argentina.

Reservations are always appreciated and, in high season, essential. If you enter a restaurant without a reservation and find there are empty tables, do not automatically assume the owner will seat you. Restaurant owners on St. Barths take great pride in their service as well as in their food, and they would rather turn you away than slight you on an understaffed evening. You are not being ignored at the end of a leisurely meal; as in France, it is considered rude to present a bill too promptly. Linger at the table and enjoy the complimentary vanilla rum that is sure to appear. Check restaurant bills carefully. A service charge (*service compris*) is always added by law, but you should leave the server 5%–10% extra. It is generally advisable to charge restaurant meals on a credit card, as the issuer will offer a better exchange rate than the restaurant. Many restaurants serve locally caught lobster (*langoustine*); priced by weight, it is usually the most expensive item on a menu, and depending on its size and the restaurant, will range in price from $40 to $60. In noting menu prices below, it has been left out of the range.

What to Wear

A bathing suit and *pareu* (sarong) are acceptable at beachside lunch spots. Jackets are never required and rarely worn, but people dress fashionably for dinner. Casual chic is the idea; women wear whatever is hip, current, and, well, sexy. Nice shorts, (not beachy ones) at the dinner table may label a man *américain*, but many locals have adopted the habit, and nobody cares much. Pack a light sweater or shawl for an after-dinner beach stroll. Shopkeepers in a few of the higher-end stores in Gustavia understandably prefer that customers not come come directly from the beach.

CARIBBEAN

★ $$$–$$$$ ✕ **L'Orchidée.** Come here for French-creole haute-cuisine in Sofitel's Hôtel Christopher: sunsets and moonlight vistas, friendly and solicitous service, live music, and serious, beautifully presented food. Try the chef's foie gras, roast duck in demi-glace, or grilled mahimahi with lime. A prix-fixe tasting menu for about $40 changes daily and is an excellent choice. Also, check to see if any theme nights, such as an Around the World Buffet or a Barbecue Night, are scheduled. They are casual fun. Or just sit at the outdoor bar for a first-rate piña colada. ⊠ *Sofitel Christopher, Pointe Milou* ☎ *0590/27–63–63* ▤ *AE, MC, V.*

$$–$$$ ✕ **Gloriette.** This friendly beachside spot serves delicious local creole dishes, such as crunchy accras and a cassoulet of local lobster, grilled fresh fish, meats, and light salads. A daily tasting menu for about $30 features lobster specialties. ⊠ *Grand Cul de Sac* ☎ *0590/27–75–66* ▤ *AE, MC, V* ☽ *Closed Wed.*

$$–$$$ ✕ **Pipiri Palace.** Tucked into a tropical garden, this popular in-town restaurant is known for its barbecued ribs, beef fillet, and rack of lamb. Fish choices include creole fish steamed in a banana leaf. Daily specials like mussels and foie gras are always a good choice here. Pierrot, the friendly owner, is sure to take good care of you. ⊠ *Rue Général-de-Gaulle, Gustavia* ☎ *0590/27–53–20* ⌳ *Reservations essential* ⊟ *AE, MC* ☾ *Closed Sept.*

★ $$ ✕ **Le Ti St. Barth Caribbean Tavern.** Chef-owner Carole Gruson captures the funky spirit of the island in her wildly popular hilltop hot spot, as much house party as restaurant. Dance to great music with the attractive crowd lingering at the bar, lounge at one of the pillow-strewn banquettes at Indian silk–topped tables, or chat on the torchlit terrace—by the time your appetizers arrive, you'll be best friends with the next table. Next come a warm, honey-drizzled chèvre salad, house-smoked fish, grilled duck fillet with mango chutney, ribs, and the best beef on the island. There is an extensive wine list. Check to see if one of the famously raucous full-moon parties will be held during your stay. ⊠ *Pointe Milou* ☎ *0590/27–97–71* ⌳ *Reservations essential* ⊟ *MC, V.*

★ $–$$ ✕ **Le Rivage.** This popular, affordable restaurant serves wonderful gazpacho and huge salads, like warm chèvre (goat cheese) with bacon, cold mixed seafood, and classic *salade niçoise* (with tuna, olives, green beans, and hard-boiled eggs). There are grilled fresh seafood and steaks for heartier appetites—but save room for the warm apple pastry or warm chocolate cake with vanilla sauce. Come for lunch and spend the rest of the afternoon sunning or windsurfing on the beautiful beach. ⊠ *St. Barths Beach Hôtel, Grand Cul de Sac* ☎ *0590/27–82–42* ⊟ *AE, MC, V.*

CONTEMPORARY ✕ **La Mandala.** Boubou, the owner, has popular restaurants all over the
$$$–$$$$ island. All are excellent, fun, attractive, and reasonable, with cute, friendly staff. Enjoy tasty Thai-influenced food on the sweeping terrace over Gustavia Harbor. Try the Chinese chicken with wasabi, rack of lamb with caramel-soy glaze, or the various curries. ⊠ *Rue de la Sous-Préfecture, Gustavia* ☎ *0590/27–96–96* ⊟ *AE, MC, V.*

$$ ✕ **K'fe Massaï.** Stunning ethnotropical decor and inventive food can be found at this romantic restaurant. The theme is African, but the food is basically French. Salmon tartare with grapefruit or creole-sausage tart are good starters. Main courses include thyme-roasted veal and sesame chicken brochettes. However, these fade into memory the minute your fork hits the decadent chocolate dessert medley. ⊠ *Lorient* ☎ *0590/29–76–78* ⊟ *No credit cards.*

ECLECTIC ✕ **Do Brazil.** At this cozy restaurant nestled at the cliff side of Gustavia's
★ $$$–$$$$ Shell Beach, you'll be able to sample more of restaurateur Boubou's delicious fusion creations. The not-exactly-Brazilian cuisine is served in a vaguely jungle-chic decor—romantic at night, lively at lunch. Choose between varied salads, ceviche, hand-chopped steak and fish tartares, grilled fresh-caught fish, and barbecue specialties; many are served with great fries. ⊠ *Shell Beach, Gustavia* ☎ *0590/29–06–66* ⌳ *Reservations essential* ⊟ *AE, MC, V.*

$$–$$$ ✕ **Buenavista.** Although the restaurant calls its cuisine "Pacific-Rim fusion," it offers mainly a grazing menu of various, well-prepared small dishes, including good guacamole with fresh tortilla chips, sushi, Thai-style spring rolls, mozzarella salad, and fresh grilled fish. The bar, right on the harbor, is a pretty "happening" place, well into the night, and there is often either a DJ or a live band. f4: ⊠ *Poet de Gustavia, Gustavia* ☎ *0590/27–51–51* ⊟ *MC, V.*

★ $$–$$$ ✕ **Maya's.** New Englander Randy Gurly and his French chef-wife Maya provide a warm welcome and a delicious dinner on their cheerful dock decorated with big round tables and crayon-color canvas chairs, all overlooking Gustavia Harbor. A market-inspired menu that changes daily assures the ongoing popularity of a restaurant that seems to be on everyone's favorites list. ✉ *Public, Gustavia* ☎ *0590/27–75–73* ⌘ *Reservations essential* ▭ *AE, MC, V.*

$$–$$$ ✗ **Le Repaire.** This friendly brasserie overlooks Gustavia's harbor and is a popular spot from its early-morning opening at 6 AM to its late-night closing at 1 AM. Grab a cappuccino, pull a captain's chair to the streetside rail, and watch the pretty girls. The menu ranges from cheeseburgers with the island's best fries to foie gras, grilled fish, and lobster. The *assiette creole* (creole assortment platter) is a great introduction to this fine cuisine. Try your hand at the billiards table or show up on weekends for live music. ✉ *Quai de la République, Gustavia* ☎ *0590/27–72–48* ▭ *MC, V.*

$$ ✗ **La Marine.** In-the-know islanders settle at the popular dockside picnic tables for mussels that arrive from France every Wednesday. The menu also includes fish, oysters, hamburgers, steaks, and omelets. Many think that meals here are the best buys on the island. ✉ *Rue Jeanne d'Arc, Gustavia* ☎ *0590/27–68–91* ▭ *AE, MC, V.*

FRENCH ✗ **Le Gaiac.** If you are in the mood to dress up, you can do it at this elegant, sophisticated restaurant at Le Toiny hotel. Starched napery and impeccable service complement the blue bay view. Lunch includes chilled, spicy mango soup, salads, and grilled seafood. The dinner menu showcases really serious food: free-range chicken baked in a clay shell, sparkling fresh fish in a refined beurre blanc, saddle of lamb in a red-wine reduction, braised duck, and velvety foie gras. Tableside crêpes suzettes are de rigueur. There's a buffet brunch on Sunday. ✉ *Le Toiny, Anse à Toiny* ☎ *0590/29–77–47* ▭ *AE, DC, MC, V* ☾ *Closed Sept.–mid-Oct.*

$$$–$$$$ ✗ **Lafayette Club.** This true St. Barth classic (reopened after a yearlong closing) is famous for its fabulous, if not irrational, priciness, but lunch in the pale pink pavilion beside the turquoise lagoon inspires loyal patronage from those who don't object to spending a fortune for chance to nibble country-French specialties like ratatouille, lobster bisque, grilled duck breast, and tart Tatin in the company of whichever celebrities might be in residence on the island. Informal modeling of fashions from the on-site boutique provides a great cover for not-so-discreet people-peering. ✉ *Grand Cul de Sac* ☎ *0590/27–75–69* ⌘ *Reservations essential* ▭ *AE, DC, MC, V* ☾ *Closed Sept.–Oct.*

$$$–$$$$ ✗ **La Route des Epices.** Follow the arbor lanterns to one of the island's FodorsChoice culinary treasures, a lovely verandah with sparkling white paint, luxuri-★ ant greenery, and buffed mahogany trim. Owner François Beret is justifiably proud of his wine cellar. You will be lucky, indeed, if he helps choose wines to enhance the sublime and serious cuisine. Offerings include terrine of foie gras with caramel, served with a perfect sauternes, smoked salmon and leek "lasagna," and grilled sea bass served with wild-rice risotto and roasted tomato. A vanilla soufflé with chocolate sauce elicits swooning. ✉ *Colombier* ☎ *0590/29–80–22* ⌘ *Reservations essential* ▭ *AE, DC, MC, V* ☾ *Closed Sept.–Oct. No lunch.*

★ **$$$–$$$$** ✗ **Restaurant des Trois Forces.** Make your way to the top of Vitet, the highest hill on the island, for a memorable meal at the hands of owner-chef Hubert de la Motte. Heady *émincés de veau,* homemade bread, chateaubriand, and exquisite desserts are complemented by rare vintages. ✉ *Hostellerie des Trois Forces, Morne Vitet* ☎ *0590/27–62–25* ⌘ *Reservations essential* ▭ *AE, MC, V.*

$$$–$$$$ ✗ **Le Sapotillier.** The brick walls, hand-painted wooden chairs, exquisite white-linen tablecloths, and vivid Creole paintings evoke an old-style private island home. But this is not the cooking of your *maman.* This long-established restaurant serves classic French cuisine like rack of lamb and roasted Bresse chicken with potato gratin. The sumptuous chocolate mousse and raspberry soufflé are longtime favorites. ⊠ *Rue de Centenaire, Gustavia* ☎ *0590/27–60–28* ⌕ *Reservations essential* ▤ *MC, V* ⊘ *Closed Mon. May–mid-Oct. No lunch.*

★ **$$–$$$** ✕ **Le Tamarin.** A leisurely lunch here en route to Grand Saline beach is a St. Barths *must.* Delicious French and creole cuisine is served at this sophisticated open-air restaurant. Get to know the parrot, or relax in a hammock after the house-special carpaccios of salmon, tuna, and beef. The lemon tart deserves its excellent reputation. ⊠ *Salines* ☎ *0590/27–72–12* ▤ *AE, MC, V* ⊘ *Open erratically May–Nov. Call to confirm.*

SEAFOOD ✕ **La Langouste.** This tiny beachside restaurant in the pool-courtyard of
$$–$$$$ Hôtel Baie des Anges lives up to its name by serving fantastic, fresh grilled lobster. Simple, well-prepared fish, pastas, and soups are also available. ⊠ *Hôtel Baie des Anges, Flamands Beach* ☎ *0590/27–63–61* ⌕ *Reservations essential* ▤ *MC, V* ⊘ *Closed May–Oct.*

Beaches

There are many *anses* (coves) and nearly 20 *plages* (beaches) scattered around the island, each with a distinctive personality and each open to the general public. Even in season you can find a nearly empty beach. Topless sunbathing is common, but nudism is forbidden—although both Saline and Gouverneur are de facto nude beaches. Bear in mind that the rocky beaches around Anse à Toiny are not swimmable.

Anse à Colombier. The beach here is the least accessible, thus the most private, on the island; to reach it you must take either a rocky footpath from Petite Anse or brave the 30-minute climb down (and back up) a steep, cactus-bordered trail from the top of the mountain behind the beach. Boaters favor this beach and cove for its calm anchorage.

Anse Corossol. This is a top boat- and sunset-watching spot.

★ **Anse du Gouverneur.** Because it's so secluded, nude sunbathing is popular here; the beach is truly beautiful, with blissful swimming and views of St. Kitts, Saba, and St. Eustatius.

Anse Marechal. Next to the Guanahani Hotel is this tiny beach, which offers some of the island's best snorkeling.

Baie de St-Jean. Like a mini Côte d'Azur—beachside bistros, bungalow hotels, bronzed bodies, windsurfing, and lots of day-trippers—the reef-protected strip is divided by Eden Rock promontory, and there's good snorkeling west of the rock.

Flamands. This is the most beautiful of the hotel beaches—a roomy strip of silken sand.

Grand Cul de Sac. The shallow, reef-protected beach is especially nice for small children, fly fishermen, and windsurfers; it has excellent lunch spots and lots of pelicans.

Fodor'sChoice **Grande Saline.** Secluded, with its sandy ocean bottom, this is just about
★ everyone's favorite beach and great for swimmers, too. Without any major development, it's an ideal Caribbean strand, though it can be a bit windy here, so you'll enjoy yourself more if you go on a calm day. In spite of the prohibition, young and old alike go nude.

Lorient. This beach is popular with St. Barths families and surfers, who like its rolling waves. Be aware of the level of the tide, which can come in very fast. Hikers and avid surfers like the walk over the hill to Point Milou in the late afternoon sun when the waves roll in.

Marigot. This tiny, calm beach has good snorkeling along the rocky far end.

Petite Anse de Galet. A five-minute walk from Gustavia, this one is named for the tiny shells on its shore.

Sports & the Outdoors

BOATING & SAILING

St. Barths is a popular yachting and sailing center, thanks to its location mid-way between Antigua and St. Thomas. Gustavia's harbor, 13 to 16 ft deep, has mooring and docking facilities for 40 yachts. There are also good anchorages available at Public, Corossol, and Colombier.

Marine Service (⊠ Gustavia ☎ 0590/27–70–34) offers full-day outings on a 40-ft catamaran to the uninhabited Ile Fourchue for swimming, snorkeling, cocktails, and lunch; the cost is $100 per person. The company also arranges deep-sea fishing trips, with a full-day charter of a 30-ft crewed cabin cruiser running $800; an unskippered motor rental runs about $260 a day. Marine Service can also arrange an hour's cruise ($32) on the glass-bottom boat *L'Aquascope*. **Océan Must Marina** (⊠ Gustavia ☎ 0590/27–62–25) offers all kinds of boat charters. **Ship Chandler du Port Franc** (⊠ Gustavia ☎ 0590/27–89–27) is the place for yachting information and supplies.

FISHING

Most fishing is done in the waters north of Lorient, Flamands, and Corossol. Popular catches are tuna, marlin, wahoo, and barracuda. There is an annual St. Barth Open Fishing Tournament, organized by Ocean Must, in mid-July.

Caraïbes Yachting (⊠ Gustavia ☎ 0590/27–52–48) rents boats and Jet Skis and can organize all kinds of boat excursions, including a picnic lunch. **Marine Service** (⊠ Gustavia ☎ 0590/27–70–34) arranges ocean fishing excursions. **Océan Must Marina** (⊠ Gustavia ☎ 0590/27–62–25) arranges deep-sea fishing expeditions as well as boat charters.

HORSEBACK RIDING

Two-hour horseback trail-ride excursions in the morning or the afternoon led by Coralie Fournier are about $40 per person at St. Barth Equitation. Instruction is also available. **Ranch des Flamands** (⊠ Anse des Flamands ☎ 0690/62–99–30).

SCUBA DIVING

Several dive shops arrange scuba excursions to local sites. Depending on weather conditions, you may dive at **Pain de Sucre, Coco Island,** or toward nearby **Saba.** There is also an underwater shipwreck to explore, plus sharks, rays, sea tortoises, coral, and the usual varieties of colorful fish. The waters on the island's leeward side are the calmest. Most of the waters surrounding St. Barths are protected in the island's **Réserve Marine de St-Barth** (⊠ Gustavia ☎ 0590/27–88 18), which also provides information at its office in Gustavia.

Marine Service operates the only five-star, PADI-certified diving center on the island, called **West Indies Dive** (☎ 0590/27–70–34); scuba trips, packages, resort dives, and certifications start at $50, gear included. **Ocean Master Dive** (☎☎ 0590/27–61–37) schedules three excursions a day, including one for beginners, during high season. **Odysée Caraïbe** (☎☎ 0590/27–55–94) is recommended for its up-to-the-minute equipment and dive boat.

TENNIS

If you wish to play tennis at a hotel at which you are not a guest, call ahead to inquire about fees and reservations. There are two lighted tennis courts at the **Guanahani** (⊠ Grand Cul de Sac ☎ 0590/27–66–60). **Hôtel Isle de France** (⊠ Baie des Flamands ☎ 0590/27–61–81) has a lighted tennis court. **Hôtel Manapany Cottages** (⊠ Anse de Cayes ☎ 0590/27–66–55) has a lighted court. **Le Flamboyant Tennis Club** (⊠ Anse à Toiny ☎ 0590/27–69–82) has two courts.

WINDSURFING

Windsurfing fever has definitely caught on here. You can rent boards for about $20 an hour at water-sports centers along Baie de St-Jean and Grand Cul de Sac beaches. Lessons are offered for about $40 an hour at **Eden Rock Sea Sport Club** (✉ Eden Rock Hotel, Baie de St-Jean ☎ 0590/29–79–93), which also rents boards. **Mat Nautic** (✉ Quai du Yacht Club, Gustavia ☎ 0690/49–54–72) can help you arrange to tour the island on a Jet Ski or Waverunner. On an hour's notice you can have a lesson, then rent by the hour or the half day. **Wind Wave Power** (✉ St. Barth Beach Hotel, Grand Cul de Sac ☎ 0590/27–82–57) offers an extensive, six-hour training course.

Shopping

Fodor'sChoice
★

St. Barths is a duty-free port and, with its sophisticated crowd of visitors, shopping in the island's 200-plus boutiques is a definite delight, especially for beachwear, accessories, jewelry, and casual wear. It would not be an overstatement to say that shopping for fashionable clothing, accessories, and decorative items for the home is better in St. Barth than anywhere else in the Caribbean. New shops open all the time, so there is always something new to discover. Note that stores often close from noon to 2, and many on Wednesday afternoon as well, but they are open until about 7 in the evening. A popular afternoon pastime is strolling about the two major shopping areas in Gustavia and St. Jean.

Areas

In Gustavia, boutiques line the two major shopping streets, and the **Carré d'Or** plaza is great fun to explore. Shops are also clustered in **La Savane Commercial Center** (across from the airport), **La Villa Créole** (in St-Jean), and **Espace Neptune** (on the road to Lorient). It's worth working your way from one end to the other at these shopping complexes—just to see or, perhaps, be seen. Boutiques in all three areas carry the latest in French and Italian sportswear and some haute couture. Prices, although still on the high side, are often well below those for comparable merchandise in France or the United States.

Specialty Items

CLOTHES **Black Swan** (✉ Le Carré d'Or, Gustavia ☎ 0590/27–65–16 ✉ La Villa Créole, St-Jean) has an unparalleled selection of bathing suits. **Calypso** (✉ Le Carré d'Or, Gustavia ☎ 0590/27–69–74) carries resort wear for women by Chloé. **Dovani** (✉ Rue de la République, Gustavia ☎ 0590/29–84–77) has elegant leather goods and Baccarat jewelry. Fans of Longchamp handbags and leather goods will find a good selection at about 20% off stateside prices at **Elysée Caraïbes** (✉ Le Carré d'Or, Gustavia ☎ 0590/52–00–94). The **Hermès** (✉ Rue de la République, Gustavia) store in St. Barths is an independently owned franchise, and prices are about 20% below those in the States. **Laurent Effel** (✉ Rue Général-de-Gaulle, Gustavia) sells beautiful leather belts, colorful linen shirts, bags, and shoes. Don't miss **Lolita Jaca** (✉ Le Carré d'Or, Gustavia ☎ 0590/27–59–98) for trendy tailored sportswear by Paul and Joe and other fresh names. **Mia Zia** (✉ La Villa Créole, St-Jean ☎ 0590/27–55–48) imports wonderful accessories from Morocco, including multicolored, tassled linen shawls, caftans, and colorful 6-ft-long silk cords to wrap around your wrists, waist, or neck. **Morgan's** (✉ La Villa Créole, St-Jean ☎ 0590/27–57–22) has a line of popular and wearable casual wear in the trendy vein. **Paradoxe St-Barth** (✉ La Villa Créole, St-Jean ☎ 0590/27–84–98 ✉ Rue de la Républic, Gustavia ☎ 0590/29–21–86) stocks flattering patterned stretch jeans by TARK'1, and pretty chiffon tops. The Gustavia branch features dressier evening styles. **Pati de Saint Barth** (✉ Passage de la Crémaillière, Gustavia ☎ 0590/29–78–04) is the largest of the three shops that stock the chic, locally made T-shirts that have practically become the "logo" of St. Barths. The newest styles have hand-done graffiti lettering. **Quiksilver Boatriders Club** (✉ Rue de la République, Gustavia ☎ 0590/29–76–66) has the best T-shirts on St. Barths and is a great source for attractive and popular surfer-inspired beachwear, sunglasses, and waterwear for all ages. **Raffia** (✉ Rte. de Saline St-Jean ☎ 0590/27–78–39) has great handbags, resort accessories, and current fashions, including chic infant wear. **Stéphane & Bernard** (✉ Rue de la République, Gustavia ☎ 0590/27–69–13) stocks a large selection of French fashion designers, including Rykiel, Tarlazzi, Kenzo, Feraud, and Mugler. Look to **St. Tropez KIWI** (✉ St-Jean ☎ 0590/27–57–08 ✉ Gustavia ☎ 0590/27–68–97) for resort wear. **SUD SUD.ETC** (✉ Galerie du Commerce, St-Jean ☎ 0590/27–98–75) stocks hippie-chic styles from Betty Boom, and shell and mother of pearl jewelry. Cute sandals and raffia accessories complete the look. **Terra** (✉ Pelican Plage ☎ 0590/27–57–50) has pretty, classic styles of resort wear you can even wear back home.

COSMETICS Don't miss the superb skin-care products made on-site from local tropical plants by **Ligne de St. Barths** (✉ Rte. de Saline, Lorient ☎ 0590/27–82–63).

FOODSTUFFS **Match** (✉ St-Jean), a supermarket across from the airport, has a wide selection of French cheeses, pâtés, cured meats, produce, and fresh bread. **A.M.C.** (✉ Quai du République, Gustavia) is a bit older than Match but able to supply anything you might need for housekeeping in a villa, or for a picnic. **JoJo Supermarché** (✉ Lorient) is the well-stocked counterpart to Gustavia's two supermarkets and gets daily deliveries of bread and fresh produce. For exotic groceries or picnic fixings, stop by St. Barths' gourmet *traiteur* (take-out) **La Rotisserie** (✉ Rue du Roi Oscar II, Gustavia ☎ 0590/27–63–13 ✉ Centre Vaval, St-Jean ☎ 0590/29–75–69) for salads, prepared meats, groceries from Fauchon, and Iranian caviar. **Vitolive** (✉ Rte. de Saline, Lorient ☎ 0590/52–96–22) is a tiny shop with olives, tapas, and other provisions from the south of France, and a selection of organic groceries.

HANDICRAFTS The ladies of Corossol produce intricate straw work, wide-brim beach hats, and decorative ornaments by hand. Call the tourist office, which can provide information about the studios of other island artists: Christian Bretoneiche, Robert Danet, Nathalie Daniel, Patricia Guyot, Rose Lemen, Aline de Lurin, and Marion Vinot.

Look for Fabienne Miot's unusual gold jewelry at **L'Atelier de Fabienne** (✉ Rue de la République, Gustavia ☎ 0590/27–63–31). **Chez Pompi** (✉ On the road to Toiny ☎ 0590/27–75–67) is a cottage whose first room is a gallery for the naive paintings of Pompi (also known as Louis Ledée). **Kayali** (✉ Rue de la République, Gustavia ☎ 0590/27–64–48) shows varied works by local artists. Local works of art, including paintings, are sold in the bright **Made in St-Barth La Boutique** (✉ La Villa Créole, St-Jean ☎ 0590/27–56–57). Find local stoneware, raku pottery, and other crafts at **St. Barth Pottery** (✉ Gustavia ☎ 0590/27–69–81), next to the Post Office on the harbor.

JEWELRY **Carat** (✉ Quai de la République, Gustavia) has Chaumet and a large selection of Breitling watches. For fine jewelry, visit **Cartier** (✉ Quai de la République, Gustavia). A good selection of watches, including Patek Phillippe and Chanel, can be found at **Diamond Genesis** (✉ Rue Général-de-Gaulle, Gustavia). Next door to Cartier, **Oro del Sol** (✉ Quai de la République, Gustavia) carries beautiful fine accessories by Bulgari, Ebel, and others. **Sindbad** (✉ Carré d'Or, Gustavia ☎ 0590/27–52–29), at the top, is a tiny shop with "couture" fashion jewelry by Poggi and vintage-inspired, chunky, multicolored, Swarovski crystal-and-bead pieces, Nomination bracelets, and other up-to-the-minute styles.

LIQUOR &
TOBACCO **La Cave du Port Franc** (✉ Rue de la République, Gustavia ☎ 0590/27–65–27) has a good selection of wine, especially from France. **La Cave de Saint-Barths** (✉ Marigot ☎ 0590/27–63–21) has an excellent collection of French vintages stored in temperature-controlled cellars. **Couleur des Isles Cuban Cigar** (✉ Rue de Général-de-Gaulle, Gustavia ☎ 0590/27–79–60) has many rare varieties of smokeables, and good souvenir T-shirts too. **Le Comptoir du Cigare** (✉ Rue de Général-de-Gaulle, Gustavia ☎ 0590/27–50–62), run by Jannick and Patrick Gerthofer, is a top purveyor of cigars. The walk-in humidor has an extraordinary selection. Try the Cubans while you are on the island, and take home the Davidoffs. They will ship refills stateside. Be sure to try on the Panama hats.

Nightlife

"In" clubs change from season to season, so you might ask around for the hot spot of the moment. **Bar de l'Oubli** (✉ Rue du Roi Oscar II, Gustavia ☎ 0590/27–70–06) is where young locals gather for drinks. **Carl Gustaf** (✉ Rue des Normands, Gustavia ☎ 0590/27–82–83) lures those in search of quiet conversation and sunset watching. **Le Deck Cocktail and Music Bar** (✉ Gustavia ☎ 0590/27–86–07), on the Gustavia waterfront, is open every night until 2 AM. **La Licorne** (✉ Lorient ☎ 0590/27–83–94) is hot with a local crowd but open only on Saturday night. **New Feeling** (✉ Lurin ☎ 0590/27–88–67) is a disco in the Lurin Hills that has special theme nights on Thursday. **Le Petit Club** (✉ rue Courbet, Gustavia ☎ 0590/27–66–33) is the place to head for late-night dancing. **Le Repaire** (✉ Rue de la République, Gustavia ☎ 0590/27–72–48) lures a crowd for cocktail hour and its pool table. **Le Santa Fé** (✉ Lurin ☎ 0590/27–61–04), in the Lurin Hills, features a rowdy crowd, billiards, and satellite-TV sports. **Le Sélect** (✉ Rue du Centenaire, Gustavia ☎ 0590/27–86–87) is St. Barths' original hangout, commemorated by Jimmy Buffet's "Cheeseburger in Paradise." The boisterous garden is where the barefoot boating set gathers for a brew.

Exploring St. Barthélemy

With a little practice, negotiating St. Barths' narrow, steep roads soon becomes fun. Free maps are everywhere, roads are well marked, and painted signs will point you where you want to be. Take along a towel, sandals, and a bottle of water on your explorations, and you will surely find a beach upon which to linger.

Numbers in the margin correspond to points of interest on the St. Barthélemy map.

WHAT TO SEE
❶ Anse des Flamands. From this wide, white-sand, hotel-lined beach you can take a brisk hike to the top of the now-extinct volcano believed to have given birth to St. Barths.

❺ Anse du Gouverneur. Legend has it that pirates' treasure is buried at this beautiful beach. The road here from Gustavia offers spectacular vistas. If the weather is clear you'll be able to see the islands of Saba, St. Eustatius, and St. Kitts from the beach.

❷ Corossol. The island's French-provincial origins are most evident in this two-street fishing village with a little rocky beach. Older local women weave lantana straw into handbags, baskets, hats, and delicate strings of birds. Ingenu Magras's **Inter Oceans Museum** has more than 9,000 seashells and an intriguing collection of sand samples from around the world. You can buy souvenir shells. ✉ Corossol ☎ 0590/27–62–97 ⛶€3 ☉ Tues.–Sun. 9–12:30 and 2–5.

⑥ **Grande Saline.** The big salt ponds of Grande Saline are no longer in use, and the place looks a little desolate. Still, you should climb the short hillock behind the ponds for a surprise—the long arc of Anse de Grande Saline.

④ **Gustavia.** You can easily explore all of Gustavia during a two-hour stroll. Street signs in both French and Swedish illustrate the island's history. Shops close from noon to 2, so plan lunch accordingly. A good spot to park your car is Rue de la République, where catamarans, yachts, and sailboats are moored. The **tourist office** (☎ 0590/27–87–27) on the pier can provide maps and a wealth of information. It's open Monday from 8:30 to 12:30, Tuesday through Friday from 8 to noon and 2 to 5, and Saturday from 9 to noon. On the far side of the harbor known as La Pointe is the charming **Municipal Museum**, where you will find watercolors, portraits, photographs, and historic documents detailing the island's history as well as displays of the island's flowers, plants, and marine life. ☎ 599/29–71–55 ☜ €2 ⊙ *Mon.–Thurs. 8:30–12:30 and 2:30–6, Fri. 8:30–12:30 and 3–6, Sat. 9–11.*

⑦ **Lorient.** Site of the first French settlement, Lorient is one of the island's two parishes; a restored church, a school, and a post office mark the spot. Note the gaily decorated graves in the cemetery. One of St. Barths' treasured secrets is **Le Manoir** (☎ 0590/27–79–27), a 1610 Norman manor, now a guest house, that was painstakingly shipped from France and reconstructed in Lorient in 1984. Look for the entrance by the Ligne St. Barth building.

③ **St-Jean.** The ½-mi (¾-km) crescent of sand at St-Jean is the island's most popular beach. Windsurfers skim along the water here, catching the strong trade winds. A popular activity is watching and photographing the hair-raising airplane landings. You'll also find some of the best shopping on the island here, as well as several restaurants.

⑧ **Toiny coast.** Over the hills beyond Grand Cul de Sac is this much-photographed coastline. Stone fences crisscross the steep slopes of Morne Vitet, one of many small mountains on St. Barths, along a rocky shore that resembles the rugged coast of Normandy. It is one island beach that is often described as a "washing machine" because of its turbulent surf.

ST. BARTHS A TO Z

To research prices, get advice from other travelers, and book travel arrangements, visit www.fodors.com.

AIR TRAVEL

The principal gateway from North America is St. Maarten's Juliana International Airport. Although it's only 10 minutes by air to St. Barths, the last two may take your breath away. Don't worry when you see those treetops out your window. You're just clearing a hill before dropping down to the runway of Aéroport de St-Jean (St-Jean Airport). Flights leave at least once an hour between 7:30 AM and 5:30 PM on Winair. Air Caraïbes, based in Guadeloupe, flies among the French West Indies and to Dominican Republic. Air St. Thomas has daily flights to St. Barths from both St. Thomas and Puerto Rico. Inter Island Express, St. Barth Commuter, Tyden Air, Carib Aviation, and Nevis Express are small, private charter companies that can also arrange service. You must confirm your return interisland flight, even during off-peak seasons, or you may very well lose your reservation. Be prepared to fly at a more convenient time for one of the airlines if it doesn't have enough passengers to justify a previously scheduled flight. Do not be upset if your luggage has

504 < **St. Barthélemy**

not made the trip with you. It frequently will arrive on a later flight, and your hotel will send a porter to receive it. It's a good idea to pack a change of clothes, required medicines, and a bathing suit in your carry-on, and if travelling with a companion, put some clothes in each other's bags.

🛈 Air Caraïbes ☎ 0890/64-47-00; 877/772-1005 in the U.S. ⊕ www.aircaraibes. com. **Air St. Thomas** ☎ 0590/27-71-76. **Carib Aviation** ☎ 264/497-2719 in Antigua. **Inter Island Express** ☎ 787/253-1400 in the French West Indies ⊕ www. interislandairways.com **Nevis Express** ☎ 869/469-9065 in Nevis. **St. Barth Commuter** ☎ 0590/27-54-54 ⊕ www.stbarth-commuter.com. **Tyden Air (Anguilla)** ☎ 268/462-3147 in Anguilla. **Winair** ☎ 0590/27-61-01 or 800/634-4907 ⊕ www.fly-winair.com.

AIRPORTS

Many hotels offer free airport transfers. When you make your reservations, specify your arrival time. Hotels can be called from a free telephone in the arrivals building. Unmetered taxis cost $5–$20, depending on distance. Drivers set a fare before leaving, and it's usually not negotiable. There are taxi stands at the airport and in Gustavia on the pier. The taxi dispatcher will help. If you have reserved a rental car, your name will be on a blackboard at the appropriate counter.

🛈 **Aéroport de St-Jean** ☎ 0590/27-75-81. **Taxi dispatcher** ☎ 0590/27-66-31.

BIKE & MOPED TRAVEL

Several companies rent motorbikes, scooters, mopeds, and mountain bikes. Motorbikes go for about $30 per day and require a $100 deposit. Helmets are required. Scooter and motorbike rental places are located mostly along rue de France in Gustavia and around the airport in St. Jean. They tend to shift locations slightly.

🛈 **Barthloc Rental** ⊠ rue de France, Gustavia ☎ 0590/27-52-81. **Chez Béranger** ⊠ rue de France, Gustavia ☎ 0590/27-89-00. **Ets Denis Dufau** ⊠ St. Jean ☎ 0590/27-70-59.

BOAT & FERRY TRAVEL

Voyager offers ferry service for day trips between St. Barths, St. Martin (Marigot), and Saba. Round-trips for two are offered for about $60. All service is from the Quai de la République. However, the schedules generally will not accommodate you well if you are coming to St. Barths from St. Martin to stay for more than a day, since trips are generally scheduled only once a day in each direction.

🛈 *Voyager* ☎ 0590/87-10-68 ⊕ www.voyager-st-barths.com.

BUSINESS HOURS

BANKS Banks are generally open weekdays 8–noon and 2–3:30. There are 24-hour cash machines at most of them.

POST OFFICES The main post office on Rue Jeanne d'Arc in Gustavia is open Monday–Tuesday and Thursday–Friday 8–3, Wednesday and Saturday 8–noon. The branch in Lorient is open weekdays 7 AM–11 AM and Saturday 8 AM–10 AM. The post office in St-Jean opens Monday–Tuesday 8–2 and Wednesday–Saturday 8–noon.

SHOPS Stores are generally open weekdays 8:30–noon and 2–5, Saturday 8:30–noon. Some of the shops across from the airport and in St-Jean stay open on Saturday afternoon and until 7 PM on weekdays. A few around St. Jean even stay open on Sunday afternoon during the busy season. Although some shops are closed on Wednesday afternoon, most are open 8:30–noon and 3–6.

CAR RENTALS In the last two years the dune-buggy-ish minimoke has largely been replaced with small four-wheel-drive vehicles, which provide a welcome increase of power and maneuverability on steep, narrow roads. Be sure to check the brakes before you head out, and make a careful inventory of the existing dents and scrapes on the rental agreement.

You'll find major rental agencies at the airport, and all accept credit cards. Check with several counters for the best price. You must have a valid driver's license to rent, and in high season there may be a three-day minimum. Be sure to supply the licenses of all who might drive the car. During peak periods, such as Christmas week and February, be sure to arrange for your car rental ahead of time. Charges average about $55 a day; you may be able to bargain if you plan a stay longer than a week. When you make your hotel reservations, ask if the hotel has its own cars available to rent. Though the choice of vehicles may be limited, some hotels provide 24-hour emergency road service—something most rental companies don't offer. Smart of St. Barth rents the tiny, colorful two-seaters called "Smart Cars" that are the rage.

🚗 **Avis** ☎ 0590/27-71-43. **Budget** ☎ 0590/27-66-30. **Europcar** ☎ 0590/27-73-33. **Gumbs** ☎ 0590/27-75-32. **Hertz** ☎ 0590/27-71-14. **Smart of St. Barth** ☎ 0590/29-71-31. **Turbe** ☎ 0590/27-71-42.

CAR TRAVEL

Roads are sometimes unmarked, so be sure to get a map. Instead of road signs, look for signs pointing to a destination. These will be nailed to posts at all crossroads. Roads are narrow and sometimes very steep, so check the brakes and gears of your rental car before you drive away. Some hillside restaurants and hotels have steep entranceways and difficult steps that require a bit of climbing or negotiating.

GASOLINE There are two gas stations on the island, one near the airport and one in Lorient. They aren't open after 5 PM or on Sunday, but you can use the one near the airport at any time with some credit cards, including Visa, JCB, or Carte Blanche. A full tank of gas runs $13–$15; considering the short distances, this should last you most of a week.

RULES OF THE ROAD Maximum speed on the island is 50 kph. Driving is on the right, as in the United States and Europe. St. Barths drivers often seem to be in an unending grand prix, and thus tend to keep their cars maxed out, especially and inexplicably when in reverse. Parking is an additional challenge.

ELECTRICITY

Voltage is 220 AC, 60 cycles, as in Europe. You can sometimes use American appliances with French plug converters and transformers. Most hotel rooms are conveniently supplied with hair dryers.

EMERGENCIES

The tourist office can provide an up-to-date list of local health professionals.

🚑 Ambulance & Fire **Ambulance and Fire emergencies** ☎ 18.

🏥 Hospitals **Hospital De Bruyn** ✉ Gustavia ☎ 0590/27-60-35.

💊 Pharmacies **Island Pharmacie** ✉ Centre Commercial Vaval, St. Jean ☎ 0590/29-02-12 🖶 0590/29-06-17. **Pharmacie de L'Aéroport** ✉ St. Jean ☎ 0590/27-61-66 🖶 0590/27-73-21. **Pharmacie St. Barth** ✉ Quai de la République, Gustavia ☎ 0590/27-61-82 🖶 0590/27-75-44. 🚓 Police **Police emergencies** ☎ 0590/27-66-66.

FESTIVALS & SEASONAL EVENTS

In January, St. Barths hosts an international collection of musicians as part of the St. Barths Music Festival. February brings a flood of feasting, dancing, music, and parades during Carnival season. The Caribbean Film Festival takes place in early April. On July 14 Bastille Day is celebrated with a parade, a regatta, parties, and a fireworks display. In early December the annual St. Barths Marble Tournament attracts contestants of all ages.

HITCHHIKING
Hitching rides is a popular, legal, and interesting way to get around. It's widely practiced in the more heavily trafficked areas on the island. But there is more and more traffic, so be careful.

HOLIDAYS
Public holidays include New Year's Day, Easter weekend, Labor Day (May 1), Pentecost (mid- to late May), Bastille Day (July 14), Pitea Day (commemorates the joining of St. Barths with Pitea in Sweden, Aug. 15), All Saints' Day (Nov. 1), Armistice Day (Nov. 11), and Christmas.

LANGUAGE
French is the official language, so it can't hurt to pack a phrase book and/or French dictionary. If you speak any French at all, don't be shy. You may also hear Creole, the regional French dialect called patois, and even the Creole of Guadeloupe. Most hotel and restaurant employees speak some English—at least enough to help you find what you need.

MAIL & SHIPPING
Mail is slow. Correspondence between the United States and the island can take up to three weeks to arrive. The main post office is in Gustavia, but smaller post offices are in St-Jean and Lorient. When writing to an establishment on St. Barths, be sure to include "French West Indies" at the end of the address. Because of the slow mail service, faxes are widely used.

🛈 **Main post office** ✉ Rue Jeanne d'Arc Gustavia ☎ 0590/27-62-00.

MONEY MATTERS
Prices quoted in this chapter are in U.S. dollars, unless otherwise noted.

ATMS There are 24-hour cash machines at most banks.

CREDIT CARDS Credit cards are accepted at most shops, hotels, and restaurants. Paying with a credit card will generally yield a better exchange rate than what the individual restaurant or shop will offer.

CURRENCY The official currency in St. Barth is the euro, which at this writing is worth slightly more than a U.S. dollar. However, dollars are accepted in almost all shops and in many restaurants, though you will probably receive euros in change. All credit-card transactions are charged in euros.

PASSPORTS & VISAS
All foreign citizens need a passport and a return or ongoing ticket.

SAFETY
There is relatively little crime on St. Barths. Visitors can travel anywhere on the island with confidence. Most hotel rooms have mini-safes.

SIGHTSEEING TOURS
You can arrange island tours by minibus or car at hotel desks, through the tourist office, or through any of the island's taxi operators in Gustavia or at the airport. Wish Agency can arrange customized tours, as well as take care of airline ticketing, event planning, maid service, and private party arrangements.

🛈 **Wish Agency** ☎ 0590/29-83-74 ⊕ wish.agency@wanadoo.fr.

TAXES & SERVICE CHARGES

DEPARTURE TAX The island charges a $5 departure tax when your next stop is another French island, $10 if you're off to anywhere else. This is payable in cash only, dollars or euros, at the airport.

SALES TAX Some hotels add an additional 10%–15% service charge to bills; but most include it in their tariffs.

TAXIS

Taxis are expensive and not particularly easy to arrange, especially in the evening. There's a taxi station at the airport and another in Gustavia; from elsewhere you must contact a dispatcher in Gustavia or St. Jean. Technically, there's a flat rate for rides up to five minutes long. Each additional three minutes is an additional amount. In reality, however, cabbies usually name a fixed rate—and will not budge. Fares are 50% higher from 8 PM to 6 AM and on Sunday and holidays.
🚕 **Gustavia taxi dispatcher** ☎ 0590/27-66-31. **St. Jean taxi dispatcher** ☎ 0590/27-75-81.

TELEPHONES

MCI and AT&T services are available. Public telephones do not accept coins; they accept *télécartes,* prepaid calling cards that you can buy at the gas station next to the airport and at post offices in Lorient, St-Jean, and Gustavia. Making an international call using a télécarte is much less expensive than making it through your hotel. If you bring a cell phone to the island and wish to activate it for local use, visit St. Barth Eléctronique across from the airport, as many alternatives are possible depending on the model and service. Alternatively, inquire there about the purchase of an inexpensive, pre-paid, renewable phone, which sells for as little as €20 including some initial air time.

If you would like to retrieve e-mail while you're on the island, the best bet is a visit to the Internet Service at Centre Alizes, which has fax service and 10 computers on line. They are open weekdays, 8:30–12:30 and 2:30–7, as well as Saturday morning. France Télécom can provide you with temporary Internet access that may let you connect your laptop. They can also arrange cellular phone service.
🖥 **Centre Alizes** ✉ Rue de la République, Gustavia ☎ 0590/29-89-89. **France Télécom** ✉ Espace Neptune, St-Jean ☎ 0590/27-67-00. **St. Barth Eléctronique** ✉ St-Jean ☎ 0590/27-50-50.

COUNTRY & AREA CODES The country code for St. Barths is 590. Thus, to call St. Barths from the U.S., dial 011 + 590 + 590 and the local 6-digit number (dial 590 *twice* but omit the 0, which you must dial within the country, before the second 590).

INTERNATIONAL CALLS To call the United States from St. Barths, dial 001 + the area code + the local 7-digit number.

LOCAL CALLS For calls on St. Barths, you must dial 0590 + the 6-digit local number; for St. Martin dial just the six-digit number for the French side, for the Dutch side (Sint Maarten) dial 00–599–54 + the five-digit number, but remember that this is an international call and will be billed accordingly.

TIPPING

Restaurants include a 15% service charge in their published prices, but it is common French practice to leave 5%–10% *pourboire* (literally: for a drink)—in cash, even if you have paid by credit card—and no more on top of this. Keep this in mind that when your credit-card receipt is presented to be signed, the tip space should be blank—just draw a line through it—or you could end up paying a 30% service charge. Most taxi drivers don't expect a tip.

VISITOR INFORMATION

A daily news sheet called *NEWS* lists local happenings like special dinners or music and is available at markets and newsstands. You will also find free, weekly *Journal de Saint-Barth*—mostly in French—is useful for current events. The small *Ti Gourmet Saint-Barth* is a free pocket-sized guidebook that is invaluable for addresses and telephone numbers of restaurants and services; pick one up anywhere.

🛂 Before You Leave **French West Indies Tourist Board** ⊕ www.franceguide.com ✉ 610 5th Ave., New York, NY 10020. **French Government Tourist Office** ✉ 444 Madison Ave., 16th Floor, New York, NY 10022 ☎ 900/990–0040 [charges a fee] ✉ 9454 Wilshire Blvd., Suite 303, Beverly Hills, CA 90212 ☎ 213/272–2661 ✉ 645 N. Michigan Ave., Suite 3360, Chicago, IL 60611 ☎ 312/337–6301 ✉ in Canada: ✉ 1981 McGill College Ave., Suite 490, Montréal, Québec H3A 2W9, Canada ☎ 514/288–4264 ✉ 30 St. Patrick St., Suite 700, Toronto, Ontario M5T 3A3, Canada ☎ 416/593–4723 ✉ in the U.K.: ✉ 178 Piccadilly, London W1V 0AL, U.K. ☎ 0171/629–9376.

🛂 In St. Barths **Office du Tourisme** ✉ Quai Général-de-Gaulle ☎ 0590/27–87–27 🖷 0590/27–74–47.

ST. EUSTATIUS

FODOR'S CHOICE

Historic Fort Oranje, Oranjestad

Hiking in the Quill

King's Well Hotel, a budget hotel in Oranjestad

Scuba Diving and Snorkeling the Double Wreck

HIGHLY RECOMMENDED

RESTAURANTS   Blue Bead Bar & Restaurant, Oranjestad

HOTELS   The Old Gin House, Oranjestad

Down a country road that seems to lead to nowhere, the rural dwelling of the Berkel family appears. Ismael Berkel wanders through, showing guests his family's heirlooms, photos of his ancestors from a century ago. It's easy to see why he's proud of this property, part of the original 82-acre plantation. The charming clapboard houses, each with only a single room, hold the past: the family Bible, old glasses, even the old Singer that Pa gave Ma in 1944. Such was life in Statia's past, but the times here haven't changed all that much.

Updated by
Roberta
Sotonoff

The tiny Dutch island of St. Eustatius, commonly called Statia (pronounced *stay*-sha), in the Netherlands Antilles, is ideal for those with a penchant for quiet times and strolls through history. It was once one of the most powerful mercantile centers in the Caribbean; today you'll find only remnants of those times—forts, narrow cobblestone streets, and historic buildings. Statians themselves are reason enough to visit. So is the landing approach: in the distance looms the Quill, an extinct volcano with a primeval rain forest in its crater.

This 11.8-sq mi (30.5-sq km) island that Columbus sailed past in 1493 prospered from the day the Dutch Zeelanders colonized it in 1636. In the 1700s a double row of warehouses crammed with goods stretched 1 mi (1½ km) along the bay, and there were sometimes as many as 200 ships tied up at the duty-free port. The island was called the Emporium of the Western World and Golden Rock. There were almost 8,000 Statians in the 1790s (today the population is about 2,800). Holland, England, and France fought over the island, which changed hands 22 times. It has been a Dutch possession, however, since 1816.

During the American War of Independence, when the British blockaded the North American coast, food, arms, and other supplies for the revolutionaries were diverted to the West Indies, notably to neutral Statia (Benjamin Franklin had his mail routed through the island to ensure its safe arrival in Europe). On November 16, 1776, the brigantine *Andrew Doria,* commanded by Captain Isaiah Robinson of the Continental Navy, sailed into Statia's port flying the Stars and Stripes. The ship fired a 13-gun salute to the Royal Netherlands standard, and Governor Johannes de Graaff ordered the cannons of Ft. Oranje to return the salute. That first official acknowledgment of the new American flag by a foreign power earned Statia the nickname America's Childhood Friend. In retaliation, British admiral George Rodney looted the island, destroying much of its economy, in 1781. Statia has yet to recover its prosperity, which, ironically, ended partly because of the American Revolution's success: the island was no longer needed as a trans-shipment port, and its bustling economy gradually came to a stop.

Statia is in the Dutch Windward Triangle, 150 mi (241 km) east of Puerto Rico and 38 miles (61 km) south of St. Maarten. Oranjestad, the capital and only "city," is on the western side, facing the calm Caribbean. On the eastern side are the often rough waters of the Atlantic. The island is anchored at the north and the south by extinct volcanoes separated by a central, dry plain. The higher elevations are alive with greenery and abloom with flowers—bougainvillea, oleander, and hibiscus.

Statia is a playground for divers and hikers. Colorful coral reefs and a myriad ships rest on the ocean floor alongside 18th-century warehouses that were slowly absorbed by the sea. On land, much of the activity involves archaeology and restoration; students come here to study pre-Columbian artifacts dating back to 500 BC, and the island's historical foundation restores local landmarks. Statia is also home to an accredited, two-year medical school, the University of St. Eustatius School of Medicine, as well as a way-station for oil, with a 16-million-barrel storage bunker encased in the Boven, an extinct volcano on the island's northern end. On any given day there are several oil tankers at anchor waiting to give or receive the liquid gold.

Most visitors will be content with a day-trip from nearby St. Maarten, exploring some of the historical sights and maybe enjoying a meal. Those who stay longer tend to be collectors of unspoiled islands with a need to relax and a taste for history. Statians are mindful of the potential gold mine of tourism, and, in addition to preserving many historical buildings and forts, they're expanding the island's pier and improving its infrastructure. But it may be the locals themselves who make coming here such a pleasure. Folks in these parts still say hello to strangers, and drivers wave or beep to one another.

WHAT IT COSTS In U.S. dollars				
$$$$	**$$$**	**$$**	**$**	**¢**
RESTAURANTS*				
over $30	$20–$30	$12–$20	$8–$12	under $8
HOTELS**				
Cost EP/BP/CP over $350	$250–$350	$150–$250	$80–$150	under $80
Cost AI over $450	$350–$450	$250–$350	$125–$250	under $125

*Restaurant prices are for a main course at dinner. **EP, BP, and CP prices are per night for a standard double room in high season, excluding taxes, service charges, and meal plans. AI (all-inclusive) prices are per person, per night based on double-occupancy during high season, excluding taxes and service charges.

Where to Stay

None of Statia's accommodations could be considered luxurious. Cheerful, tidy, and homey are the best you can expect, and all (at this writing, Statia had only three hotels and one small B&B) have at most 20 units. Room decor and furnishing are eclectic but comfortable. If there's a philosophy to owning and running a hostelry on Statia, it's "do what you can with what you have."

Renting an apartment is another lodging alternative. Although Statia has only a handful of them, several are available for $50 or less per night, but don't expect much beyond a bathroom and kitchenette. Check with the tourist office for options.

★ $–$$$ 🏨 **The Old Gin House.** This gracious, historic waterfront building, which was once a cotton warehouse, is a wonderful part of Statia's hotel scene. Most rooms face a courtyard and pool, but four rooms across the street open directly on the waterfront. The Old Gin House restaurant and oceanside Beach Bar Cocopelli, across from the main building, serve three meals daily. MAP is available. ⊠ Bay Rd., Lower Town, Oranjestad ☎ 599/318–2319 🗎 599/318–2135 ⊕ www.oldginhouse. com ⇱18 rooms ⟁ Restaurant, cable TV, pool, bar ⊟AE, MC, V ⍾EP.

★ ¢–$ 🏨 **King's Well Hotel.** Perched on the cliffs between Upper Town and Lower Town, this small hotel has 14 pleasant rooms with balconies (four have queen-size waterbeds and French doors that open to the sea), mini-re-

St. Eustatius

KEY

‌Beaches
Dive Sites
① Exploring Sights
① Hotels & Restaurants
Rain Forest

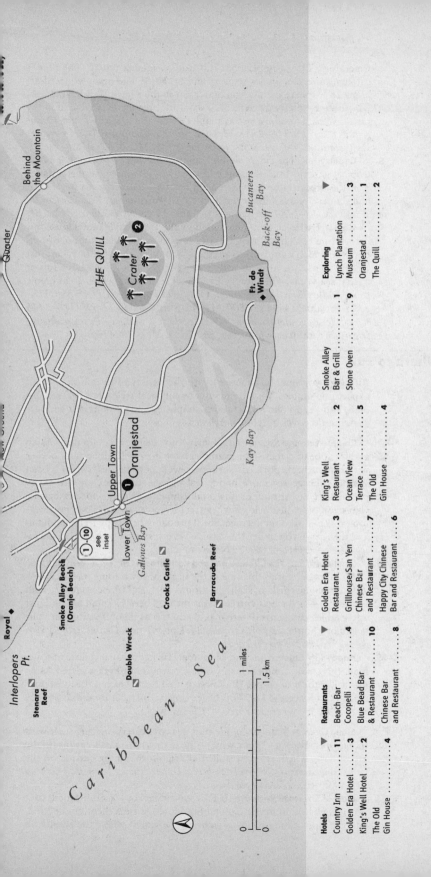

Hotels

Country Inn	**11**
Golden Era Hotel	**3**
King's Well Hotel	**2**
The Old Gin House	**4**

Restaurants

Beach Bar	
Cocopelli	**4**
Blue Bead Bar & Restaurant	**10**
Chinese Bar and Restaurant	**8**
Golden Era Hotel Restaurant	**3**
Grillhouse San Yen Chinese Bar and Restaurant	**7**
Happy City Chinese Bar and Restaurant	**6**
King's Well Restaurant	**2**
Ocean View Terrace	**5**
The Old Gin House	**4**
Smoke Alley Bar & Grill	
Stone Oven	**9**

Exploring

Lynch Plantation	**1**
Museum	**3**
Oranjestad	**1**
The Quill	**2**

frigerators, TVs, a pool, a hot tub, and an iguana refuge. The hotel's catamaran ferries guests to Saba and St. Kitts. The make-yourself-at-home atmosphere includes an honor bar in the King's Well Restaurant, which serves guests three meals a day (full breakfast is included in the rates). Weekly rates are also available. ⊠ *Bay Rd., Lower Town, Oranjestad* ☎☎ *599/318–2538* ⊕ *www.turq.com/kingswell* ➾ *14 rooms* ⚒ *Restaurant, refrigerators, pool, bar* ▭ *D, MC, V* ⧆ *BP.*

$ ⊡ **Country Inn.** The clean, simple rooms of this inn are surrounded by a tropical garden. In a pleasant part of town, it is just walking distance from the airport, close to the Statia Oil Terminal and Zeelandia Bay. Lunch and dinner are available on request. ⊠ *3 Passionfruit Rd., Concordia* ☎☎ *599/318–2484* ➾ *6 rooms* ⚒ *Cable TV* ▭ *No credit cards* ⧆ *BP.*

¢ ⊡ **Golden Era Hotel.** Don't be put off by the 1960s-style motel look: this harborfront hotel has a friendly staff and a central seaside location. Rooms have tile floors, mini-refrigerators, TVs, phones, and little terraces. Just be sure to ask for a room with a view; only half of them have full or partial sea vistas. The Golden Era Hotel restaurant serves great creole food. ⊠ *Bay Rd., Lower Town, Oranjestad* ⊘ *Box 109* ☎ *599/318–2345 or 800/223–9815; 800/344–0023 in Canada* ⧆ *599/318–2445* ✎ *goldera@goldenrock.net* ➾ *19 rooms, 1 suite* ⚒ *Restaurant, refrigerators, saltwater pool, bar* ▭ *AE, D, MC, V* ⧆ *EP.*

Where to Eat

Although you may be surprised with the variety of restaurants, don't expect fine dining. Your best bet is to eat local style; that is, West Indian, and keep your expectations simple. All restaurants are very casual, but do cover up your beachwear.

ASIAN ✗ **Chinese Bar and Restaurant.** Owner Kim Cheng serves up tasty Asian
$$ and Caribbean dishes—for example, *bami goreng* (Indonesian noodles with bits of beef, pork, or shrimp as well as tomatoes, carrots, bean sprouts, cabbage, soy sauce, and spices) and Spanish pork chop—in hearty portions at his unpretentious establishment. Dining indoors can be claustrophobic; just ask your waitress if you may tote your Formica-top table out onto the terrace. She'll probably be happy to lend a hand and then serve you under the stars. ⊠ *Prinseweg, Upper Town, Oranjestad* ☎ *599/318–2389* ▭ *No credit cards.*

$–$$ ✗ **Grillhouse/San Yen Chinese Bar and Restaurant.** One of several Chinese restaurants on Statia, this one in the heart of town touts its special—a dish combining chicken, scallops, shrimp, beef, and Chinese sausage with vegetables—as the best entrée on the menu. There's a small bar and just a few tables, and a meal here makes you feel as if you're eating at your neighbor's house. ⊠ *Fort Oranjestad, Upper Town, Oranjestad* ☎ *599/318–2915* ▭ *No credit cards.*

¢–$$ ✗ **Happy City Chinese Bar and Restaurant.** Tucked away in a little in-town mall, this small, simple, clean Chinese restaurant offers a varied Asian menu. Try the *nasi goreng* (Indonesian fried rice), which is the most popular local choice. ⊠ *De Windtweg, Upper Town, Oranjestad* ☎ *599/318–2540* ▭ *No credit cards* ⊙ *Closed Wed.*

CARIBBEAN ✗ **Stone Oven.** A Spanish couple runs this cozy eatery offering such West
$$ Indian specialties as "goat water" (goat stew). You can eat inside the little house, which is in a residential neighborhood, or outside on the palm-fringed patio. ⊠ *16A Feaschweg, Upper Town, Oranjestad* ☎ *599/318–2809* ▭ *No credit cards.*

$–$$ ✗ **Golden Era Hotel Restaurant.** This somewhat stark establishment (not surprisingly found in the Golden Era Hotel) has excellent creole food, and the large dining room is right on the water, where the sounds of crashing waves serve as dinner music. ☒ *Bay Rd., Lower Town, Oranjestad* ☎ *599/318–2345* ▤ *AE, D, MC, V.*

ECLECTIC ✕**The Old Gin House.** Chef Jan Buyens from Belgium has taken the
$$$ reigns of this charming, old-fashioned restaurant inside The Old Gin
House hotel, turning out his fabulous sauces, homemade breads, rack
of lamb, and his specialty, lobster. Prix-fixe three- and four-course meals
are available in the main dining room and in the courtyard bordering
the pool. ☒ *Bay Rd., Lower Town, Oranjestad* ☎ *599/318–2319*
▤ *AE, MC, V* ☺ *Closed Mon.–Tue. No lunch.*

$–$$$ ✕**Beach Bar Cocopelli.** Part of The Old Gin House hotel, this outdoor
eatery on the sea is relaxing and fun. Chef Jan Buyens serves his home-
made breads, pastas, salads, and light meals on a casual, umbrella-
shaded terrace, where you'll find lots of local conversation. ☒ *Old Gin
House Hotel, Bay Rd., Lower Town, Oranjestad* ☎ *599/318–2319*
▤ *AE, MC, V.*

$–$$$ ✕**Smoke Alley Bar & Grill.** Lunch and dinner are cooked to order at this
open-air beach restaurant. The burgers are good, the food is homemade,
and there is live music every Friday and Saturday nights. ☒ *Lower
Town, Gallows Bay* ☎ *599/318–2002* ▤ *MC, V* ☺ *Closed Sun.*

★ $$ ✕**Blue Bead Bar & Restaurant.** Pizzas as well as French and West Indian
cuisine are served on a cheery, bright, blue-and-yellow-trimmed veran-
dah decked with potted plants, just across from the waterfront. Fried calamari, French-creole stuffed crab, the local squash (christophene), daily
specials, and salt cod fritters are recommended, as well as a nip of the
after-dinner special, homemade vanilla rum, served by the bottle. Fridays
are seafood nights, and Saturdays are for families, when the kids (of any
age) can enjoy the Blue Bead Baby Bimmer Burger. ☒ *Bay Rd., Lower
Town, Oranjestad* ☎ *599/318–2873* ▤ *AE, D, MC, V* ☺ *Closed Mon.*

$$ ✕**King's Well Restaurant.** It's like watching mom and dad make dinner
to see owners Win and Laura Piechutzki scurry around their open
kitchen preparing the night's meal in this breezy terrace eatery. And don't
expect to eat alone, because a meal here makes you part of the family
at the King's Well Hotel. Overlooking the sea, the restaurant is run by
this fun-loving expatriate couple. The steaks are from Colorado, the lob-
ster is fresh, and the *Rostbraten* (roast beef) and schnitzels are authen-
tic: Win is German. ☒ *King's Well Hotel, Bay Rd., Lower Town,
Oranjestad* ☎▤ *599/318–2538* ▤ *D, MC, V.*

$$ ✕**Ocean View Terrace.** This patio spot in the courtyard overlooking the
beautiful stone Fort Oranje, serves sandwiches and burgers at lunch, and
local cuisine—baked snapper with shrimp sauce, spicy chicken, tenderloin
steak—at dinner (you can get breakfast here, too). Every now and then,
owner Lauris Redan prepares a succulent barbecue. ☒ *Oranjestraat,
Upper Town, Oranjestad* ☎ *599/318–2934* ▤ *No credit cards* ☺ *No
lunch Sun.*

Beaches

Beachcombing on Statia is for the intrepid: the beaches are pristine, un-
maintained, and occasionally rocky. The Atlantic side is generally too
rough for swimming. You can (though it's not recommended) hike
around the coast at low tide; but driving is the best way to reach remote Atlantic stretches. Searching the beaches for Statia's famed blue-
glass beads is a big deal. Manufactured in the 17th century by the
Dutch West Indies Company, these beads were traded for rum, slaves,
cotton, and tobacco. Although they're found only on Statia, some re-
searchers believe that it was beads like these that were traded for Manhattan. They're best unearthed after a heavy rain, but as the locals
chuckle, "If you find one, it's a miracle, man."

Corre Corre Bay. A 30-minute hike down an easy marked trail behind the Mountain Road will bring you to this gold-sand cove.

Lynch Bay. Two bends north of Corre Corre Bay, this beach is somewhat protected from the wild swells. On the Atlantic side, especially around Concordia Bay, the surf is rough, and there's sometimes an undertow, making beaches better for sunning than swimming.

Smoke Alley Beach. Also called Oranje Beach, the beige-and-black-sand, somewhat rocky beach is on the Caribbean off Lower Town, and is relatively deserted until late afternoon, when the locals arrive.

Zeelandia Beach. This 2-mi (3-km) strip of black sand on the Atlantic side has a dangerous undertow, but a small section is considered okay for swimming. It's a lovely, deserted stretch for sunning, walking, and wading.

Sports & the Outdoors

FISHING   By and large, deep-sea fishing is not a major activity off Statia's shores. But it's nice to be out on the water. **Golden Rock Dive Center** (⊠ Bay Rd., Lower Town, Oranjestad ☎☎ 599/318–2964) offers half- and full-day trips for $400 and $600, respectively, including gear and bait.

HIKING   Trails range from the easy to the "Watch out!" The big thrill here is the Quill, the 1,968-ft extinct volcano with its crater full of rain forest. Give yourself two to four hours to do the hike. The tourist office has a list of 12 marked trails and can put you in touch with a guide. The Quill National Park includes a trail into the crater, which is a long, windy, but safe walk. Maps and the necessary $3 permit are available at the Saba Marine Park headquarters on Bay Road. Wear layers: it can be cool on the summit and steamy in the interior.

SCUBA DIVING,   Statia has more than 30 dive sites protected by the Saba Marine Park,
SNORKELING   which has an office on Bay Road in Lower Town. Barracudas swim around
Fodor'sChoice   colorful coral walls at **Barracuda Reef,** off the island's southwest coast.
★   At **Double Wreck,** just offshore from Lower Town, you'll find two tall-masted ships that date from the 1700s. The coral has taken on the shape of these two disintegrated vessels, and the site attracts large schools of fish, sting rays, and moray eels. A new dive site has been created off the south end of the island with the recent sinking of the Charles L. Brown, a 1957 cable-laying vessel. Off the island's western shore, **Stenapa Reef** is an artificial reef created from the wrecks of barges, a harbor boat, and other ship parts. Large grouper and turtles are among the marine life you'll spot here. For snorkelers, **Crooks Castle** has several stands of pillar coral, giant yellow sea fans, and sea whips just southwest of Lower Town.

The island's three dive shops along Bay Road in Lower Town rent all types of gear (including snorkeling gear for about $20 a day), offer certification courses, and organize dive trips. The average cost of a one-tank dive is $35; two-tank dives run around $65. All three of Statia's dive operators will also take you waterskiing. The cost is $30–$50 per half-hour, $60–$80 per hour. Both the Saba Marine Park and Quill National Park are under the supervision of **STENAPA** (St. Eustatius National Parks Foundation; ☎ 599/318–2884 ⊕ www.statiapark.org). The marine tag fee, which all divers must buy, is used to help offset the costs of preserving the coral and other sea life here; the cost is $6 per day or $15 annually.

Dive Statia (⊠ Bay Rd., Lower Town, Oranjestad ☎ 599/318–2435 ⊕ www.divestatia.com), a fully equipped and PADI-certified dive shop, has received PADI's five-star Gold Palm Designation. It is operated by

Rudy and Rinda Hees out of a warehouse. In addition to offering standard courses, Dive Statia also offers underwater photography courses and night and multilevel dives and Nitrox diving. **Golden Rock Dive Center** (⊠ Bay Rd., Lower Town, Oranjestad ☎☎ 599/318–2964; 800/311–6658 direct to center. ⊕ www.goldenrockdive.com), operated by Glenn and Michel Faires, is another of Statia's PADI facilities. The staff here specializes in custom dive trips. A former Swiss pilot, Ronald Metrox, operates **Scubaqua** (⊠ Golden Era Hotel, Bay Rd., Lower Town, Oranjestad ☎☎ 599/318–2160), which caters to Europeans as well as Americans. It has dive courses, which are offered in various languages.

Shopping

The very limited shopping here is duty-free. Other than the predictable souvenirs, there's not much to buy. Look for the wonderful book by Saban artist Heleen Cornett *St. Eustatius: Echoes of the Past,* sold in several stores. **Mazinga Gift Shop** (⊠ Fort Oranjestreet, Upper Town, Oranjestad ☎ 599/318–2245) is a small department store of sorts, selling basic necessities. The **Paper Corner** (⊠ Van Tonningenweg, Upper Town, Oranjestad ☎ 599/318–2208) sells magazines, a few books, and stationery supplies.

Nightlife

Statia's nightlife consists of local bands playing weekend gigs and quiet drinks at hotel bars. The island's oldest bar, **Cool Corner** (⊠ Wilhelminaweg, Upper Town, Oranjestad ☎ 599/318–2523), a tiny corner bar in the heart of town across from the St. Eustatius Historical Foundation Museum, is a lively after-work and weekend hangout. **Smoke Alley Bar & Grill** (⊠ Lower Town, Gallows Bay ☎ 599/318–2002) has live music on Friday and Saturday nights.

Exploring St. Eustatius

Statia is an arid island consisting of a valley between two mountain peaks. Most sights lie in the valley, making touring the island easy. From the airport you can rent a car or take a taxi and be in historic Oranjestad in minutes; to hike the Quill, Statia's highest peak, you can drive to the trailhead in less than 15 minutes from just about anywhere.

Numbers in the margin correspond to points of interest on the St. Eustatius map.

WHAT TO SEE **Lynch Plantation Museum.** Also known as the Berkel Family Plantation, ❸ this museum consists of two one-room buildings, set up as they were almost 100 years ago. A remarkable collection preserves this family's history—pictures, Bibles, spectacles, original furniture, and farming and fishing implements give a detailed perspective of life on Statia. You'll need either a taxi or a car to visit, and it's well worth the trouble. ⊠ *Lynch Bay* ☎ *599/318–2209 to arrange tour* 🎫 *Free* ⊗ *Saturday.*

❶ **Oranjestad.** Statia's capital and only town sits on the west coast facing the Caribbean. Both Upper Town and Lower Town are easy to explore on foot. Some Dutch colonial buildings are being restored by the historical foundation. At the **tourist office,** right in the charming courtyard of the government offices, you can pick up maps, brochures, advice, and a listing of 12 marked trails, and arrange for guides and tours. With its Fodor's Choice three bastions, **Fort Oranje** has clutched these cliffs since 1636. In 1976 ★ Statia participated in the U.S. bicentennial celebration by restoring the fort, and now the black cannons point out over the ramparts. In the parade grounds a plaque, presented in 1939 by Franklin D. Roosevelt, reads,

HERE THE SOVEREIGNTY OF THE UNITED STATES OF AMERICA WAS FIRST FOR-
MALLY ACKNOWLEDGED TO A NATIONAL VESSEL BY A FOREIGN OFFICIAL.

Built in 1775, the partially restored **Dutch Reformed Church,** on Kerkweg (Church Way), has lovely stone arches that face the sea. Ancient
tales can be read on the gravestones in the adjacent 18th-century cemetery. On Synagogepad (Synagogue Path), off Kerkweg, is **Honen Dalim**
("She Who Is Charitable to the Poor"), one of the Caribbean's oldest
synagogues. Dating from 1738, its exterior is partially restored.

Lower Town sits below Ft. Oranjestraat (Fort Orange Street) and some
steep cliffs and is reached from Upper Town on foot via the zigzagging,
cobblestone Fort Road or by car via Van Tonningenweg. Warehouses
and shops that were piled high with European imports in the 18th century are either abandoned or simply used to store local fishermen's
equipment. Along the waterfront is a lovely park with palms, flowering shrubs, and benches—the work of the historical foundation. Peeking out from the shallow waters are the crumbling ruins of 18th-century
buildings, from Statia's days as the merchant hub of the Caribbean. The
sea has slowly advanced since then, and it now surrounds many of the
stone and brick ruins, making for fascinating snorkeling.

In the center of Upper Town is the **St. Eustatius Historical Foundation
Museum** in Doncker House, former headquarters of British admiral Rodney during the American Revolution. While here, he confiscated everything from gunpowder to port in retaliation for Statia's gallant support
of the fledgling country. The completely restored house is Statia's most
important intact 18th-century dwelling. Exhibits trace the island's history from the pre-Columbian 6th century to the present. Statia is the
only island thus far where ruins and artifacts of the Saladoid, a newly
discovered tribe, have been excavated. ⊠ *3 Wilhelminaweg, Upper
Town, Oranjestad* ☎ *599/318–2288* ⊠ *$2* ⊙ *Weekdays 9–5, weekends
9–noon.*

❷ **The Quill.** This extinct, perfectly formed, 1,968-ft-high (602-m-high)
Fodor's Choice   volcano has a primeval rain forest in its crater. If you like to hike, you'll
★   want to head here to see giant elephant ears, ferns, flowers, wild orchids,
fruit trees, and the endangered *iguana delicatissima* (a large—sometimes
several feet long—greenish-gray creature with spines down its back). The
volcanic cone rises 3 mi (5 km) south of Oranjestad on the main road.
Local boys go up to the Quill by torchlight to catch delectable land crabs.
The tourist board or Statia Marine Park will help you make hiking arrangements. You must buy a permit to hike here.

ST. EUSTATIUS A TO Z

*To research prices, get advice from other travelers, and book travel ar-
rangements, visit www.fodors.com.*

AIR TRAVEL
Winair makes the 16-minute flight from St. Maarten to Statia's Franklin
Delano Roosevelt Airport several times a day, the 10-minute flight from
Saba daily, and the 15-minute flight from St. Kitts twice a week in high
season. Reconfirm your flight because schedules can change abruptly.
You can buy tickets from the airline directly or from Rainbow Travel
on Statia.

🖪 **Airlines Rainbow Travel** ☎ 599/318–2811 **Winair** ☎ 599/318–2303 or 800/634–4907
🌐 www.fly-winair.com.
🖪 **Airport Information Franklin Delano Roosevelt Airport** ☎ 599/318–2887.

BUSINESS HOURS
Banks have varying hours: Barclays Bank is open weekdays 8:30–3:30; Windward Islands Bank is open weekdays 8:30–noon and 1–3:30.

Post offices are open weekdays 7:30–noon and 1–4 or 5.

Shops are open 8–6, and grocery stores often stay open until 7.

CAR RENTALS
To explore the island (and there isn't very much of it), car rentals, which cost about $40 to $45 a day, do the job.
🔢 Brown's ✉ White Wall Rd. 8, Oranjestad ☎ 599/318-2266. **Rainbow Car Rental** ✉ Statia Mall, Oranjestad ☎ 599/318-2811. **Walter's** ✉ Chapel Piece, Oranjestad ☎ 599/318-2719.

GASOLINE The island has two gas stations—one at the south end of Lower Town on the waterfront and Godfrey's in Upper Town. Both are open daily 7:30–7. Gas costs about $.74 per liter ($3.13 per gallon).

ROAD CONDITIONS Statia's roads, somewhat pocked with potholes, are undergoing resurfacing, but the going can be slow and bumpy.

ELECTRICITY
Statia, like the other islands of the Netherlands Antilles, uses a 110/120-volt system, the same as in North America.

EMERGENCIES
🔢 Ambulance & Fire **Fire** ☎ 699/318-2360 or 120. **Ambulance** ☎ 599/318-2371, 599/318-2211 or 140.
🔢 Hospitals **Queen Beatrix Medical Center** ✉ 25 Prinsesweg, Oranjenstad ☎ 599/318-2211 or 599/318-2371.
🔢 Pharmacies **Pharmacy** ✉ Queen Beatrix Medical Center, 25 Prinsesweg, Oranjenstad ☎ 599/318-2211 or 599/318-2371.
🔢 Police **Police emergencies** ☎ 599/318-2333 or 111.
🔢 Scuba Diving Emergencies **Saba Marine Park Hyperbaric Facility** ✉ Fort Bay ☎ 599/416-4395.

FESTIVALS & SEASONAL EVENTS
Statia celebrates Carnival for a week in July, and the events include parades (culminating in the Grand Carnival Parade), street parties called "jump-ups," local and imported steel-pan bands, sports activities, and food tastings.

HOLIDAYS
Public holidays for the year are: New Year's Day, Good Friday, Easter Monday, Coronation Day and the Queen's Birthday (celebrating the birthday and coronation of Holland's Queen Beatrix, Apr. 30), Labor Day (May 1), Ascension Day (Apr. or May, 3 days after Easter), Emancipation Day (July 1), Statia-America Day (commemorating the events of 1776, when Statia became the first foreign government to salute the American flag, Nov. 16), Christmas, and Boxing Day (Dec. 26).

LANGUAGE
Statia's official language is Dutch (it's used in government documents), but everyone speaks English. Dutch is taught as the primary language in the schools, and street signs are in both Dutch and English.

MAIL & SHIPPING
The post office is in Upper Town, on Cottageweg. Airmail letters to North America and Europe are NAf 2.25; postcards, NAf 1.10. When sending letters to the island, be sure to include "Netherlands Antilles" and "Caribbean" in the address.

MONEY MATTERS

Prices quoted throughout this chapter are in U.S. dollars, unless noted otherwise.

ATMS There are no ATMs on the island.

CURRENCY U.S. dollars are accepted everywhere, but legal tender is the Netherlands Antilles florin (NAf), also referred to as the guilder, and you shouldn't be surprised to receive change in them. The exchange rate fluctuates slightly but was about NAf 1.80 to US$1 at press time. The island's two banks in Upper Town provide foreign-exchange services.
🚹 Barclays Bank ☎ 599/318–2392. Windward Islands Bank ☎ 599/318–2846, 599/318–2845, or 599/318–2857.

PASSPORTS & VISAS

U.S. and Canadian citizens must have proof of citizenship. A valid passport is best, but a birth certificate with a raised seal along with a government-authorized photo I.D. will do. British citizens need a valid passport. All visitors need a return or ongoing ticket.

SAFETY

Statia is relatively crime-free, but common sense should prevail. Lock your rental car when leaving it, store valuables in the hotel safe, and lock your hotel room door behind you. When driving, particularly at night, be on the lookout for goats and other animals that have wandered onto the road. While hiking you might see the harmless racer snake sunning itself. These snakes are afraid of people and will promptly leave when you arrive.

SIGHTSEEING TOURS

Statia's five taxis, a minibus, and two large buses are available for island tours. A two- to three-hour outing costs $40 per vehicle for five people (extra persons are $5 each), usually including airport transfer. One of the better taxi tour operators is driver-historian Josser Daniel; ask him to show you his citation from President Clinton for rescuing an American tourist from drowning. The St. Eustatius Historical Foundation Museum sells a booklet detailing the sights for $3. The tour begins in Lower Town at the marina and ends at the museum. You can take it on your own using the booklet (numbered blue signs on most of the sights correspond to signs in the booklet), but a guide may prove more illuminating.
🚹 Josser Daniel ☎ 599/318–2358. St. Eustatius Historical Foundation Museum ✉ 3 Wilhelminaweg, Oranjestad ☎ 599/318–2288.

TAXES & SERVICE CHARGES

DEPARTURE TAX The departure tax is $5.65 for flights to other islands of the Netherlands Antilles and $12 to foreign destinations, payable in cash only. Note: when flying home through St. Maarten, list yourself as "in transit" and avoid paying the $20 tax levied in St. Maarten if you are there for less than 24 hours.

SALES TAX Hotels collect a 7% government tax and 3% turnover tax. Restaurants charge a 3% government tax and a 10% service charge.

TAXIS

Taxis meet all flights from Franklin Delano Roosevelt Airport and charge about $3.50 per person for the drive into town.

TELEPHONES

Statia has microwave telephone service to all parts of the world. Direct dial is available. There are two pay phones on the island, one near the airport and one in Landsradio. They work with phone cards that you can buy at stores throughout the island.

COUNTRY &
AREA CODES
To call Statia from North America, dial 011 + 599 + 318, followed by the four-digit number.

TIPPING
Although your hotel or restaurant might add a 10%–15% service charge, it's customary to tip maids, waitstaff, and other service personnel, including taxi drivers. About 10% for taxi drivers should do it; hotel maids will appreciate about a dollar or two per day, and members of the waitstaff will be grateful for an extra 5%–10%.

VISITOR INFORMATION
In St. Eustatius **Tourist Office** ⊕ www.statiatourism.com ⊠ Fort Oranjestraat, Oranjestad ☎ 599/318-2433 or 318-2107 🖷 599/318-2433 🕙 Mon.-Fri. 8-12 and 1-5.

ST. KITTS
AND NEVIS

FODOR'S CHOICE

Four Seasons Golf Course, Pinney's Beach, Nevis

Montpelier Plantation Inn, Montpelier Estate, Nevis

Ottley's Plantation Inn, Ottley's, St. Kitts

HIGHLY RECOMMENDED

RESTAURANTS Bananas, Tamarind Bay, Nevis

Le Bistro, Charlestown, Nevis

Miss June's Cuisine, Jones Bay, Nevis

Nisbet Plantation Beach Club, Newcastle Beach, Nevis

Royal Palm, Ottley's, St. Kitts

Sunshine's, Pinney's Beach, Nevis

Turtle Beach Bar and Grill, Turtle Beach, St. Kitts

HOTELS Four Seasons Resort Nevis, Pinney's Beach, Nevis

Golden Lemon, Dieppe Bay, St. Kitts

Hermitage Plantation Inn, Gingerland, Nevis

Montpelier Plantation Inn, Montpelier Estate, Nevis

Mount Nevis Hotel and Beach Club, Mt. Nevis

Nisbet Plantation Beach Club, Newcastle Beach, Nevis

Ocean Terrace Inn, Basseterre, St. Kitts

Rawlins Plantation Inn, St. Paul's, St. Kitts

Timothy Beach Resort, Frigate Bay, St. Kitts

Many other great places enliven this area. For other
favorites, look for the black stars as you read this chapter.

Several couples—men in blazers and slacks, women in flowing cotton dresses—sip cocktails on the patio of a magnificently restored 18th-century plantation great house. A mountain carpeted in lush rain forest towers over the building, and a flawlessly green croquet lawn sweeps down to the sea. Some people sit quietly; others speak into cell phones, checking on stocks or tots back home. It's an incongruous, anachronistic, utterly delightful scene: a Gatsby-esque party transplanted to today's Caribbean.

Updated by
Suzanne
Gordon

The sister islands of St. Kitts and Nevis (pronounced *nee*-vis) have developed a sibling rivalry. They're competing for increasingly upscale visitors, and it's a tight race: both islands have uncrowded beaches, lush rain forests, historic ruins; charming if slightly dilapidated capitals in Basseterre (St. Kitts) and Charlestown (Nevis), and restored 18th-century plantation inns. And yet, despite their rivalry, these blissful islands have remained mellow retreats for both well-heeled and barefoot travelers who appreciate local culture.

Mountainous St. Kitts, the first English settlement in the Leeward Islands, crams some stunning scenery into its 65 square mi (168 square km). Its shape has been compared to that of a whale, a cricket bat, and a guitar; suffice it to say, it's roughly an oval, with a narrow peninsula trailing off toward Nevis, just 2 mi (3 km) southeast across the strait. Vast, brilliant green fields of sugarcane run to the shore. The fertile, lush island has some fascinating natural and historical attractions: a rain forest replete with waterfalls, thick vines, and secret trails; a central mountain range dominated by the 3,792-ft (1,378-m) Mt. Liamuiga, whose crater has long been dormant; and Brimstone Hill, known in the 17th century as the Gibraltar of the West Indies.

St. Kitts is known as the mother colony of the West Indies, because it was from here that English settlers sailed to Antigua, Barbuda, Tortola, and Montserrat and French settlers dispatched colonizing parties to Martinique, Guadeloupe, St. Martin, and St. Barths. The French, who inexplicably brought a bunch of green vervet monkeys—an African species—with them as pets (the creatures now outnumber the 36,000 residents), arrived on St. Kitts a few years after the British. Still developing tourism, St. Kitts hosts some 75,000 overnight visitors annually—no doubt drawn by the island's rare combination of natural and historic attractions and great beaches.

In 1493, when Columbus spied a cloud-crowned volcanic isle during his second voyage to the New World, he named it Nieves—the Spanish word for "snows"—because it reminded him of the snow-capped peaks of the Pyrenees. Nevis rises from the water in an almost perfect cone, the tip of its 3,232-ft central mountain smothered in clouds. Even less developed than St. Kitts, Nevis is known for its long beaches with white and black sand, its lush greenery, and its restored sugar plantations that now house charming inns. In 1628 settlers from St. Kitts sailed across the 2-mi (3-km) channel that separates the two islands. At first they grew tobacco, cotton, ginger, and indigo, but with the introduction of sugarcane in 1640 Nevis became the island equivalent of a boomtown. Slaves were brought from Africa to work on magnificent estates, many of them high in the mountains amid lavish tropical gardens.

Restored plantation homes that now operate as inns are true sybaritic lures. Though there's plenty of activity for the energetic—mountain climbing, swimming, tennis, horseback riding, rain-forest walks, snorkeling—the going is easy here, with hammocks for snoozing and candlelit dinners in stately dining rooms and on romantic verandahs. Each inn has its own ambience, thanks to the delightful, often eccentric owners—either British or American expatriates.

St. Kitts and Nevis, along with Anguilla, achieved self-government as an associated state of Great Britain in 1967. In 1983 St. Kitts and Nevis became an independent nation. Nevis papers sometimes run fiery articles advocating independence, though one plebiscite has already failed. The sister islands may separate someday, but meanwhile they continue to wage war in speeches, ad campaigns, and political chat.

WHAT IT COSTS IN U.S. DOLLARS				
$$$$	**$$$**	**$$**	**$**	**¢**
RESTAURANTS*				
over $30	$20–$30	$12–$20	$8–$12	under $8
HOTELS**				
Cost EP/BP/CP over $350	$250–$350	$150–$250	$80–$150	under $80
Cost AI over $450	$350–$450	$250–$350	$125–$250	under $125

*Restaurant prices are for a main course at dinner. **EP, BP, and CP prices are per night for a standard double room in high season, excluding taxes, service charges, and meal plans. AI (all-inclusive) prices are per person, per night based on double-occupancy during high season, excluding taxes and service charges.

ST. KITTS

Where to Stay

St. Kitts has an appealing variety of places to stay—beautifully restored plantation inns (where MAP is encouraged, if not mandatory), full-service affordable hotels, simple beachfront cottages, and two all-inclusive resorts. There are also several guest houses and self-serve condos. Increasing development has been touted (or threatened) for years. As the new Marriott resort opened up in Frigate Bay, the Paradise Beach Resort and Conference Center was also scheduled for completion in 2003. With these two new properties, the room base will double, making St. Kitts a more popular tourist destination. On these islands, where breezes generally keep things cool (and sometimes blankets are needed at night), many, but not all hotels, have air-conditioning.

★ $$$$ 🏨 **Rawlins Plantation Inn.** The views at this idyllic plantation inn, caught between lush Mt. Liamuiga and the cobalt Caribbean, are spectacular. Rooms occupy restored estate buildings (including the original sugar mill) scattered amid 20 acres of manicured grounds dotted with hammocks and the plantation's original copper syrup vats. Guest quarters have mahogany four-poster or brass beds, wicker chairs, hardwood floors, grass mats, and local artworks. Rawlins's seclusion, charming owners (Claire and Paul Rawson), and peerless tranquillity invite total relaxation. ✉ *St. Paul's* 📫 *Box 340* ☎ *869/465–6221 or 800/346–5358* 📠 *869/465–4954* ⊕ *www.rawlinsplantation.com* ➥ *10 rooms* ⚭ *Restaurant, fans, tennis court, pool, croquet, laundry service; no a/c* ⊘ *Closed mid-Aug.–mid-Oct.* ⊟ *AE, MC, V* ⑩ *MAP.*

★ $$$–$$$$ 🏨 **Golden Lemon.** Arthur Leaman, a former decorating editor for *House and Garden,* created this world-renowned retreat. Rooms in the restored 17th-century great house are impeccably decorated with wrought-iron and four-poster beds, armoires, and rocking chairs. Fully equipped one- or two-bedroom town houses (some have a private pool) are equally stylish. The palm-shaded gray-sand beach oversees St. Maarten and St. Eustatius. Repeat guests cherish the serene ambience, almost telepathic service from long-time staffers, and romantically remote location. All-inclusive packages (just food and beverages) are great value. ⊠ *Dieppe Bay* ⑪ *Box 17* ☎ *869/465–7260 or 800/633–7411* 🖶 *869/465–4019* ⊕ *www.goldenlemon.com* ⟿ *9 rooms, 22 villas* ⌂ *Restaurant, fans, tennis court, pool, beach, bar, shop; no a/c in some rooms, no kids* ⊘ *Closed Sept.–mid Oct.* ⊟ *AE, MC, V* ⏀ *BP.*

$$$–$$$$
Fodor'sChoice
★
Ottley's Plantation Inn. Towering royal palms frame the wild Atlantic at this former sugar plantation. The 18th-century great house and stone cottages hold spacious guest rooms with hardwood floors, Laura Ashley–esque fabrics, and wicker and antique furnishings. Higher-end suites have private plunge pools. You can ramble through the exquisite 35-acre gardens or the luxuriant adjacent rain forest. Thoughtful extras include beach and town shuttles, on-call spa services, and TV/DVDs for rent. Ottley's is the model Caribbean inn: historic yet contemporary, elegant yet unpretentious. ⊠ *Ottley's, southwest of Nicola Town* ⑪ *Box 345* ☎ *869/465–7234 or 800/772–3039* 🖶 *869/465–4760* ⊕ *www. ottleys.com* ⟿ *24 rooms* ⌂ *Restaurant, fans, in-room safes, minibars, tennis court, pool, croquet, bar, shop, Internet; no TV in some rooms* ⊟ *AE, D, MC, V* ⏀ *EP.*

$$$–$$$$
Rex Papillon. Despite such spiffy touches as an art deco-ish piano bar and a waterfall pool, this all-inclusive can't overcome its predecessor's three distinct styles of architecture, from Antillean-style gingerbreads to ugly "institutional" concrete buildings. Families appreciate the bright one-bedroom cottages. Huge oceanfront rooms gleam with white-tile floors and blond-wood and rattan furnishings. Breezes overlooks the golf course and serves buffets. The fancier, vaguely nautical Nautilus offers a United Nations of dishes (from thyme-scented rack of lamb to chili con carne). Though the property borders Frigate Bay's wilder Atlantic beach, it lacks water-sports facilities—a definite minus for an all-inclusive. ⊠ *Frigate Bay* ⑪ *Box 341* ☎ *869/465–8037 or 800/255–5859* 🖶 *869/465–6745* ⟿ *78 rooms, 22 1-bedroom cottages* ⌂ *2 restaurants, grocery, fans, cable TV, tennis court, pool, wading pool, gym, beach, 2 bars, shops, children's programs (ages 4–12), meeting rooms* ⊟ *AE, D, MC, V* ⏀ *AI.*

★ **$$–$$$**
Ocean Terrace Inn. This stylish, intimate hotel, nicknamed OTI, offers many amenities attractive to both business and leisure travelers. Room blocks, lovingly tended gardens, and a man-made lagoon that feeds the large free-form waterfall pool spill down the hill to the sea. Attractively decorated units vary widely in size and style. Several deluxe rooms, including handsome junior suites, have kitchenettes or whirlpool tubs, while one- and two-bedroom condos down the hill have marvelous ocean views. Both the waterfront Fisherman's Wharf and more elegant hilltop Ocean Restaurant lure lively local crowds. Extras include a shuttle to nearby beaches. ⊠ *Bay Rd., Basseterre* ⑪ *Box 65* ☎ *869/465–2754 or 800/ 524–0512* 🖶 *869/465–1057* ⊕ *www.oceanterraceinn.net* ⟿ *70 rooms, 8 condominiums* ⌂ *3 restaurants, in-room safes, some kitchens, some kitchenettes, refrigerators, cable TV, 3 pools, hair salon, health club, 2 outdoor hot tubs, massage, sauna, dock, windsurfing, boating, water-skiing, 4 bars, shop, Internet, meeting rooms* ⊟ *AE, D, MC, V* ⏀ *EP.*

$$
Frigate Bay Resort. The cheerful yellow buildings house standard rooms and condos. Poolside units have nicer views but tend to be noisier. Higher-numbered rooms in the blocks have partial ocean views at the same price. All accommodations have tile floors and sliding glass doors that open onto a terrace or balcony. A thatched, split-level, oc-

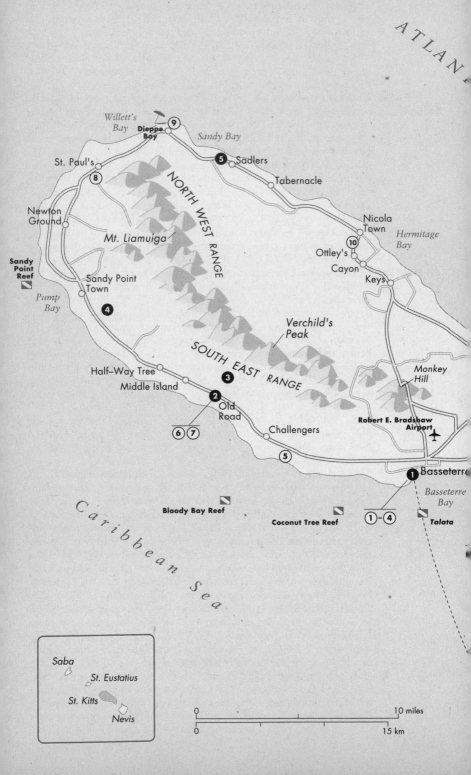

St. Kitts

Willett's Bay
Dieppe Bay ⑨
Sandy Bay
⑤ Sadlers
St. Paul's
⑧
Tabernacle
Newton Ground
Nicola Town
Hermitage Bay
Sandy Point Reef
Mt. Liamuiga
NORTH WEST RANGE
Ottley's ⑩
Cayon
Keys
Pump Bay
Sandy Point Town
④
Verchild's Peak
SOUTH EAST RANGE
Monkey Hill
Half-Way Tree
③
Middle Island
② Old Road
⑥ ⑦
Challengers
Robert E. Bradshaw Airport
⑤
① Basseterre
Basseterre Bay
Bloody Bay Reef
Coconut Tree Reef
① -④
Talata

Caribbean Sea

ATLANTIC

Saba
St. Eustatius
St. Kitts
Nevis

0 _____ 10 miles
0 _____ 15 km

KEY

⚲ Beaches
◩ Dive Sites
❶ Exploring Sights
⛴ Ferry
① Hotels & Restaurants

ATLANTIC OCEAN

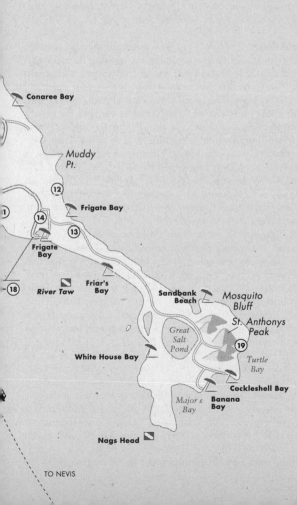

Conaree Bay

Muddy Pt.

⑫

Frigate Bay

①

⑭

⑬

Frigate
Bay

⑱   River Taw

Friar's
Bay

Sandbank
Beach

Mosquito
Bluff

St. Anthonys
Peak

⑲

Great
Salt
Pond

Turtle
Bay

White House Bay

Cockleshell Bay

Major's
Bay

Banana
Bay

Nags Head ◩

TO NEVIS

tagonal restaurant overlooks the pool and swim-up bar; it features raucous buffets, with live entertainment in season, but also serves creative
Caribbean/Continental fare. A complimentary shuttle runs to nearby
Caribbean and Atlantic beaches, though the former is within walking
distance. ⊠ *Frigate Bay* ⌂ *Box 137* ☎ *869/465–8935 or 800/266–2185*
⌨ *869/465–7050* ⊕ *www.frigatebay.com* ⤳ *40 rooms, 24 studios*
⟐ *Restaurant, fans, some kitchens, refrigerators, cable TV, golf privi-*
leges, pool, bar, shop, meeting rooms ⊟ *AE, D, MC, V* |◎| *EP.*

$$ ⊞ **St. Kitts Marriott Royal Beach Resort.** St. Kitts's first international-stan-
dard resort, which opened in February 2003, is a mélange of Mediter-
ranean and neoclassical elements (red barrel-tile roofs, interior gardens,
circular stairways, and bas reliefs). The main building contains a replica
of Christopher Columbus's *Santa Maria* plus waterfalls, restaurants, in-
door shops, a large casino, and half of the guest rooms. The rest are in
15 three-story buildings nestled amid lavishly landscaped courtyards with
fountains, arcaded walkways, and three free-form swimming pools.
Beige-tiled rooms have Italian-walnut furnishings, cushy carmine arm-
chairs, gold lamps, marble accents, peach walls, parrot-green rugs, and
floral spreads. ⊠ *Frigate Bay* ☎ *869/466–1200 or 800/228–9290*
⊕ *www.marriott.com* ⤳ *237 rooms, 234 villa suites* ⟐ *5 restaurants,*
grill, room service, in-room safes, refrigerators, cable TV, golf privileges,
5 tennis courts, 3 pools, health club, spa, beach, snorkeling, boating, 6
bars, piano bar, casino, nightclub, video game room, shops, baby-sit-
ting, children's programs (ages 4–12), laundry service, Internet, busi-
ness services, convention center, meeting rooms ⊟ *AE, D, MC, V*
|◎| *EP.*

$–$$ ⊞ **Bird Rock Beach Resort.** This plain but well-maintained resort perched
on a bluff consists of pastel two-story buildings snaking through gar-
dens. Rooms have tile floors, rattan and wicker furnishings, and ocean-
view balconies. Newer rooms are more stylish, with throw rugs and
mahogany two-poster beds. The tiered sundeck and pool, replete with
swim-up bar, offer sterling views of Basseterre, the sea, and the mountains. A complimentary shuttle whisks guests to Frigate Bay and its beach.
Dining choices are the alfresco Sunburst or the more informal Tipsy Lobster Cafe. The mix of divers and young Europeans on a budget gives
Bird Rock a pleasant international flavor. ⊠ *Basseterre Bay* ⌂ *Box 227,*
Basseterre ☎ *869/465–8914 or 800/621–1270* ⌨ *869/465–1675* ⊕ *www.*
birdrockbeach.com ⤳ *31 rooms, 19 studios* ⟐ *2 restaurants, grill,*
fans, some kitchenettes, cable TV, tennis court, 2 pools, beach, dive shop,
snorkeling, volleyball, 2 bars, shops ⊟ *AE, D, MC, V* |◎| *EP.*

$–$$ ⊞ **Fairview Inn.** This simple inn's main building is an 18th-century French
great house, with graceful white verandahs and Asian rugs on
hardwood floors. Though the smallish, motel-like rooms lack period flair
and unimpeded ocean views, they're cozy. Each has a beamed wood ceiling, white-tile floors, wicker furnishings, and light pastel or floral fabrics. Ask for the more atmospheric rooms, like No. 11: they're built into
original foundations and have partial fieldstone walls. The dining room
serves authentic island fare. Management lowers rates for longer stays
and offers periodic specials. ⊠ *Boyd's* ⌂ *Box 212* ☎ *869/465–2472*
or 800/223–9815 ⌨ *869/465–1056* ✉ *wall@caribsurf.com* ⤳ *30*
rooms ⟐ *Restaurant, room service, fans, refrigerators, pool, bar* ⊟ *AE,*
D, DC, MC, V |◎| *EP.*

★ $–$$ ⊞ **Timothy Beach Resort.** The cordial management is attentive at the sole
St. Kitts property directly on the Caribbean. Simple, powder-blue stucco
buildings hold comfortable, fully equipped, town house–style units,
which can be blocked off to form standard rooms. The original buildings right on the beach are larger and airier and have better views. Apartments are outfitted with new tropical prints and rattan furnishings in

fresh cool blue hues. The beachfront Sunset Café serves tasty Caribbean-Continental fare, and just steps away is an unaffiliated water-sports concession. ✉ *Frigate Bay* ✆ *Box 1198* ☎ *869/465–8597* 🖷 *869/466–7085* 🌐 *www.timothybeach.com* 🛏 *60 apartments* ⚭ *Restaurant, some kitchens, refrigerators, cable TV, pool, beach, bar, shop* ☰ *AE, MC, V* ❧ *EP.*

$ 🏠 **Rock Haven Bed and Breakfast.** Judith and Keith Blake have converted their gingerbread house, a two-minute drive from Frigate Bay beaches, into a relaxing, homey B&B. The living and dining rooms have carved mahogany doors, crystal chandeliers, English rugs, and hardwood floors. Two rooms have brass beds draped with mosquito netting. The larger one has a full kitchen and its own patio and entrance. The vast, breezy terrace beckons with white-wicker chaise longues, hammocks, and majestic sea views. Judith prepares sumptuous breakfasts of banana pancakes, Spanish omelets, and pumpkin fritters. Islanders also cherish her homemade ice creams made on-site. ✉ *Frigate Bay* ✆ *Box 821* ☎🖷 *869/ 465–5503* 🌐 *www.rock-haven.com* 🛏 *2 rooms* ⚭ *Dining room, fans, laundry service; no a/c* ☰ *No credit cards* ❧ *BP.*

Where to Eat

St. Kitts restaurants range from funky beachfront bistros to elegant plantation dining rooms (most with prix-fixe menus); most fare is tinged with the flavors of the Caribbean. Many restaurants offer West Indian specialties such as curried mutton, pepper pot (a stew of vegetables, tubers, and meats), and Arawak chicken (seasoned and served with rice and almonds on breadfruit leaf).

What to Wear

Throughout the island, dress is casual at lunch (but no bathing suits). Dinner, although not necessarily formal, definitely calls for long pants and sundresses.

CARIBBEAN   ✕ **Manhattan Gardens.** Even the tangerine, peach, and blueberry exterior
$–$$ rior of this 17th-century gingerbread Creole house looks appetizing. Inside, it's homey, with batik hangings, lace tablecloths, and wood carvings. The rear garden overlooking the sea comes alive for Saturday's Caribbean Food Fest and Sunday's barbecue. The regular menu includes lobster in lemon butter (the one pricey entrée), and wahoo in creole sauce; specials might consist of goat water (goat stew), souse (pickled pigs' trotters), and saltfish. Open only when there are reservations. ✉ *Old Road Town* ☎ *869/465–9121* ☰ *No credit cards* ⚭ *Reservations essential* ⊘ *No dinner Sun.*

¢–$ ✕ **Chef's Place.** Two things are the draw at this restaurant in a charmingly dilapidated 19th-century house: inexpensive West Indian meals and eavesdropping opportunities (the clientele runs toward local cops, cabbies, and mid-level government workers). Try the St. Kitts version of jerk chicken, the kingfish creole, pig tail and snout soup, or the goat stew. The best tables are outside on the wide, white verandah. ✉ *Upper Church St., Basseterre* ☎ *869/465–6176* ☰ *No credit cards* ⊘ *Closed Sun.*

CONTEMPORARY   ✕ **Golden Lemon.** Evenings at the Golden Lemon hotel's restaurant begin
$$$$ with cocktails and hors d'oeuvres on the bougainvillea-draped flagstone patio. A set three-course dinner is served in a tasteful room with crystal chandeliers, white rattan furnishings, Delft porcelain, and arched doorways. Tempting dishes range from breadfruit puffs in peanut sauce to grilled snapper with eggplant-and-sweet-pepper relish. Sunday brunch packs the patio with such offerings as banana pancakes and beef stew made with rum. Owner Arthur Leaman and his partner Martin Kreiner hold clever court (ask them for anecdotes about running a Caribbean

hostelry). ⊠ *Golden Lemon, Dieppe Bay* ☎ *869/465–7260* ⚱ *Reservations essential* ⊟ *AE, MC, V.*

$$$$ ✕ **Rawlins Plantation.** The refined dining room at the Rawlins Plantation Inn has fieldstone walls, lovely family antiques and period furnishings, and high vaulted ceilings. Owner Claire Rawson is one of the island's most sophisticated chefs. Her prix-fixe four-course dinner emphasizes local ingredients: witness conch ravioli in lobster sauce or shrimp ceviche with coriander and sour oranges, capped by banana puffs with lime sauce or chocolate terrine with passion-fruit sauce. The bountiful lunch buffet offers such classic West Indian items as breadfruit salad, shrimp fritters with mango salsa, and lobster and spinach crêpes. ⊠ *Rawlins Plantation Inn, St. Paul's* ☎ *869/465–6221* ⚱ *Reservations essential* ⊟ *AE, MC, V.*

★ **$$$$** ✕ **Royal Palm.** The 65-ft spring-fed pool stretches from the remaining walls of the sugar factory beside the elegant, alfresco restaurant at Ottley's Plantation Inn. Four-course extravaganzas from imaginative chef Pam Yahn blend indigenous ingredients with Pacific Rim, Mediterranean, southwestern, and Latin touches: for example, Caribbean lobster atop a chili-shrimp corn cake with passion-fruit butter. An à la carte "Le Bistro" option offers more casual fare like roasted vegetable torte and creative lobster wraps. The combination of superb food, artful presentation, and warm bonhomie here is unbeatable. ⊠ *Ottley's Plantation Inn, Ottley's, southwest of Nicola Town* ☎ *869/465–7234* ⚱ *Reservations essential* ⊟ *AE, D, MC, V.*

$$–$$$ ✕ **Marshall's.** The pool area of Horizons Villa Resort is transformed into a romantic eatery thanks to smashing ocean views, potted plants, and elegantly appointed tables. (The venue may change as the owner requires more parking.) Jamaican chef Verral Marshall fuses ultrafresh local ingredients with global influences. Delectable offerings include conch cutlets with white-rum lime sauce and black bean salad or Portobello-stuffed tortellini with lobster and shrimp in creamy tomato-basil sauce. Most dishes are regrettably more orthodox, but the execution is invariably excellent. ⊠ *Horizons Villa Resort, Frigate Bay* ☎ *869/466–8245* ⚱ *Reservations essential* ⊟ *AE, MC, V.*

$$–$$$ ✕ **Stonewall's.** Affable owners Garry and Wendy Steckles practically built this lush tropical courtyard restaurant by hand. "Our sweat is varnished into the bar," Garry swears. Banana trees, bougainvillea, and bamboo grow everywhere. Selections depend on what's fresh and the cook's mood: it could be a proper roast beef and Yorkshire pudding, tapenade-crusted wahoo, or chicken breast in sun-dried tomato sauce. Try the house drink, Stone Against the Wall, concocted from Cavalier rum, amaretto, coconut rum, triple sec, pineapple and orange juices, and grenadine. ⊠ *5 Princes St., Basseterre* ☎ *869/465–5248* ⊟ *AE, MC, V* ⊗ *No lunch.*

ECLECTIC ✕ **Ballahoo.** This second-floor terrace restaurant draws a crowd for
$$–$$$ breakfast, lunch, and dinner. Lilting calypso and reggae on the sound system, whirring ceiling fans, potted palms, and colorful island prints are appropriately tropical. Specialties include chili shrimp, conch simmered in garlic butter, Madras beef curry, lobster stir-fry, and a toasted rum-and-banana sandwich. Go at lunchtime, when you can watch the bustle of the Circus, and the prices for many dishes are slashed nearly in half. ⊠ *Fort St., Basseterre* ☎ *869/465–4197* ⊟ *AE, MC, V* ⊗ *Closed Sun.*

★ **$–$$** ✕ **Turtle Beach Bar and Grill.** Treats at this popular daytime watering hole include honey-mustard ribs, coconut-shrimp salad, grilled lobster, and the freshest fish in town. Business cards and pennants from around the world plaster the bar; the room is decorated with a variety of nautical accoutrements. You can snorkel here, spot hawksbill turtles, feed the tame monkeys that boldly belly-up to the bar, laze in a palm-shaded hammock, or rent a kayak or snorkel gear. On Sunday afternoon, locals come for dancing to live bands and volleyball. It's at the south end of S.E. Peninsula Road, but it's open only until 6 PM. ⊠ *S.E. Peninsula Rd., Turtle Beach* ☎ *869/469–9086* ⊟ *AE, MC, V* ☉ *No dinner.*

ITALIAN ✕ **PJ's Pizza.** "Garbage pizza"—topped with everything but the kitchen
$–$$ sink—is a favorite, or you can create your own pie. Sandwiches and simple but lustily flavored pastas are also served. Finish your meal with delicious, moist rum cake. This casual spot, bordering the golf course and open to cooling breezes, is always boisterous, despite—or perhaps because of—its ironic location atop the Frigate Bay police station. ⊠ *Frigate Bay* ☎ *869/465–8373* ⊟ *AE, MC, V* ☉ *Closed Mon. and Sept. No lunch.*

SEAFOOD ✕ **Fisherman's Wharf.** Part of the Ocean Terrace Inn, this extremely ca-
$$–$$$ sual waterfront eatery is decorated in swaggering nautical style, with rustic wood beams, rusty anchors, cannons, and buoys. Try the excellent conch chowder, followed by fresh grilled lobster or other ship-shape seafood, and finish off your meal with a slice of the memorable banana cheesecake. The tables are long, wooden affairs, and the place is generally hopping, especially on weekend nights. ⊠ *Ocean Terrace Inn, Fortlands, Basseterre* ☎ *869/465–2754* ⊟ *AE, D, MC, V* ☉ *No lunch.*

$–$$ ✕ **Sprat Net.** This simple cluster of picnic tables, sheltered by a brilliant turquoise corrugated-tin roof and decorated with driftwood and fishnets, sits on a sliver of sand. Nonetheless, it's an island hot spot. There's nothing fancy on the menu: just grilled fish, lobster, and meats—served with mountains of coleslaw and peas and rice. But the fish is amazingly fresh: the fishermen-owners heap their catches on a center table, where you choose your own dinner, as if you were at market, and then watch it grilled to your specification. ⊠ *Old Road Town* ☎ *no phone* ⊟ *No credit cards* ☉ *Closed Sun. No lunch.*

Beaches

The powdery white-sand beaches, free and open to the public (even those occupied by hotels), are in the Frigate Bay area or on the lower peninsula.

Banana Bay. One of the island's loveliest beaches stretches over a mile (1½ km) at the southeastern tip of the island. Several large hotels were abandoned in the early stages of development—their skeletal structures marring an otherwise idyllic scene.

Cockleshell Bay. Banana Bay's twin beach, another eyebrow of glittering sand backed by lush vegetation, is reachable on foot.

Conaree Bay. On the Atlantic side of the island, this narrow strip of gray-black sand is a good spot for bodysurfing.

Dieppe Bay. Snorkeling and windsurfing are good at this black-sand beach on the north coast, home of the Golden Lemon Hotel.

★ **Friar's Bay.** Locals consider the Caribbean (southern) side the island's finest beach, where you will find two hopping beach bars, Monkey and Sunset, which serve excellent inexpensive grilled and barbecued food. You can haggle with fishermen here to take you snorkeling off the eastern point. The waters on the Atlantic (northern) side are rougher, but the beach has a wild, desolate beauty.

Frigate Bay. On the Caribbean side you'll find talcum powder–fine sand, while on the Atlantic side, the 4-mi-wide (6½-km-wide) stretch is a favorite with horseback riders.

Sandbank Beach. A tiny dirt road, nearly impassable after heavy rains, leads to a long taupe crescent on the Atlantic. The shallow coves are

protected here, making it ideal for families, and it's usually deserted.
White House Bay. The beach is rocky, but the snorkeling, taking in several reefs surrounding a sunken tugboat, is superb.

Sports & the Outdoors

BIKING   Mountain-biking is growing in popularity. **Fun Bikes** (☎ 869/466–3202 or 869/662–2088) provides three 3-hour excursions daily on all-terrain quad bikes that hold two people. You'll wind through cane fields, rain forest, abandoned plantation ruins, and local villages. Free taxi transfers from Frigate Bay and Basseterre and a complimentary drink are included in the $65 rate.

BOATING   Most operators are on Frigate Bay, known for its gentle currents. Turtle Bay offers stronger winds and stunning views of Nevis. **Mr. X Watersports** (✉ Frigate Bay ☎ 869/465–0673) rents small craft, including motorboats (waterskiing and jet-skiing are available). Paddleboats are $15 per hour, sailboats (with one free lesson) $20–$25 per hour. Mr. X and his cohorts are usually hanging out at the adjacent open-air Monkey Bar. **Turtle Beach Bar and Grill** (✉ Turtle Beach ☎ 869/469–9086) rents kayaks from the restaurant and can also arrange fishing trips.

FISHING   The waters surrounding St. Kitts aren't renowned for their big game fish. Still, you can angle for yellowtail snapper, wahoo, mackerel, tuna, dolphinfish, shark, and barracuda. Rates are occasionally negotiable. Figure approximately $350 for a four-hour excursion with refreshments. Most of the large day-sail operators can arrange private charters, usually through the knowledgeable Todd Leypoldt of **Leeward Island Charters** (✉ Basseterre ☎ 869/465–7474), who takes you out on his charter boat, *Island Lore*. He's also available for snorkeling charters, beach picnics, and sunset-moonlight cruises.

GOLF   The **Royal St. Kitts Golf Club** (✉ Frigate Bay ☎ 869/465–8339) is an 18-hole, par-72 championship course that underwent a complete redesign to maximize Caribbean and Atlantic views and increase the number of hazards. A branch of the Nick Faldo Gold Academy will open. At this writing the course was expected to open by late 2003; greens fees with cart rental will likely be around $120 for 18 holes, $80 for nine.

HIKING   Trails in the central mountains vary from easy to don't-try-it-by-yourself. Monkey Hill and Verchild's Peak aren't difficult, although the Verchild's climb will take the better part of a day. Don't attempt Mt. Liamuiga without a guide. You'll start at Belmont Estates on horseback, then proceed on foot to the lip of the crater, at 2,600 ft. You can go down into the crater—1,000 ft deep and 1 mi (1½ km) wide, with a small freshwater lake—clinging to vines and roots. Tour rates range from $40 for a rain-forest walk to $65 for a volcano expedition and usually include round-trip transportation from your hotel and picnic lunch.

Addy of **Addy's Nature Tours** (☎ 869/465–8069) offers a picnic lunch and cold drinks during treks through the rain forest; she also discusses the history and folklore relating to native plants. Greg Pereira of **Greg's Safaris** (☎ 869/465–4121), whose family has lived on St. Kitts for well over a century, takes groups on half-day trips into the rain forest and on full-day hikes up the volcano and through the grounds of a private 250-year-old great house, followed by excursions down canyons and past petroglyphs. He and his staff relate fascinating historical, folkloric, and botanical information. **Kriss Tours** (☎ 869/465–4042) takes small groups up to the crater, through the rain forest, and to Dos d'Anse Pond, on Verchild's Mountain, heading off-road for trips in a customized Jeep truck. **Oliver Spencer's Off the Beaten Track** (☎ 869/465–6314) leads treks to ruins of an abandoned coffee plantation taken over by sprawling banyan trees.

HORSEBACK RIDING
Wild North Frigate Bay and desolate Conaree Beach are great for riding. Guides from **Trinity Stables** (☎ 869/465–3226) offers beach rides ($35) and trips into the rain forest ($45).

SCUBA DIVING & SNORKELING
St. Kitts has more than a dozen excellent dive sites. **Bloody Bay Reef** is noted for its network of underwater grottoes daubed with purple anemones, sienna bristle worms, and canary-yellow sea fans that seem to wave you in. **Coconut Tree Reef,** one of the largest in the area, includes sea fans, sponges, and anemones. **Nags Head** has strong currents, but experienced divers might spot gliding rays, lobsters, turtles, and reef sharks. Since it sank just over a decade ago in 50 ft of water, the *River Taw* makes a splendid site for less-experienced divers. **Sandy Point Reef** has been designated a National Marine Park, including Paradise Reef, with swim-through 90-ft sloping canyons, and Anchors Away, where anchors have been encrusted with coral formations. The 1985 wreck of the *Talata* lies in 70 ft of water; barracudas, rays, groupers, and grunts dart through its hull.

Kenneth Samuel of **Kenneth's Dive Centre** (☎ 869/465–2670) is a PADI-certified dive master who takes small groups of divers with C cards to nearby reefs. Rates average $50 for single-tank dives, $80 for double-tank dives; add $10 for equipment. Night dives, including lights, are $50, and snorkeling trips (four-person minimum) are $35, drinks included. Austin Macleod, a PADI-certified dive master–instructor and owner of **Pro-Divers** (☎ 869/466–3483), offers resort and certification courses. His prices are the lowest on the island: $50 less than anyone else for an open-water certification course. **St. Kitts Scuba** (✉ Frigate Bay, 2 mi [3 km] east of Basseterre ☎ 869/465–1189) offers competitive prices, friendly dive masters, and a more international clientele.

TENNIS
Unfortunately, options are quite limited unless you're staying at a hotel with a tennis court. However, most of the hotels do have courts, including Rawlins Plantation Inn, Golden Lemon, Ottley's Plantation Inn, Rex Papillon, and the new Marriott.

Shopping

St. Kitts has limited shopping, but there are a few small duty-free shops with good deals on jewelry, perfume, china, and crystal. Several galleries sell excellent paintings and sculptures. The batik fabrics, scarves, caftans, and wall hangings of Caribelle Batik are well known. British expat Kate Spencer is an artist who has lived on the islands for years, reproducing its vibrant colors on everything from silk *pareu* (beach wraps) to note cards to place mats. Other good island buys include crafts, jams, and herbal teas. Don't forget to pick up some CSR, a cane spirit drink that's distilled from fresh sugarcane right on St. Kitts.

Areas & Malls

Most shopping plazas are in downtown Basseterre, on the streets radiating from the Circus. **All Kind of Tings,** a peppermint-pink edifice on Liverpool Row at College Street Ghaut, functions as a de facto vendor's market where several booths sell local crafts and cheap T-shirts. Its courtyard frequently hosts folkloric dances, fashion shows, poetry readings, and steel pan concerts. The **Pelican Mall**—a shopping arcade designed to look like a traditional Caribbean street—has 26 stores, a restaurant, tourism offices, and a bandstand near the cruise-ship pier. Directly behind Pelican Mall, on the waterfront, is **Port Zante,** the deep-water cruise-ship pier; a much-delayed upscale shopping-dining complex is on its way to becoming a 25-shop area. **Shoreline Plaza** is next to the Treasury Building, right on Basseterre's waterfront. **TDC Mall** is just off the Circus in downtown.

Specialty Items

ART   **Chattel House Gallery at Paradise By Design** (⊠ Feinnes Ave. at Bay Rd., Basseterre ☎ 869/465–8109) exhibits and sells the work of owner Tom Jones, who made a name for himself as a painter of colorful chattel-style houses and Caribbean scenes. Now he's also building Caribbean-style furniture. **Spencer Cameron Art Gallery** (⊠ 10 N. Independence Sq., Basseterre ☎ 869/465–1617) has historical reproductions of Caribbean island charts and prints, in addition to owner Rosey Cameron's popular Carnevale clown prints and a wide selection of exceptional artwork by Caribbean artists. They will mail anywhere.

CDS & TAPES   **MusicUnltd** (⊠ TDC Mall, Basseterre ☎ 869/465–1998) offers a vast selection of island rhythms—lilting *soca* (a mix of soul and calypso) and *zouk* (a bopping beguine from Martinique and Guadeloupe), pulsating salsa and merengue, wicked hip-hop, and mellow reggae and calypso. You can also buy the CDs of some rocking local bands: hard-driving exponents of soca such as Nu-Vybes, Grand Masters, and Small Axe, and the "heavy dancehall" reggae group, House of Judah.

HANDICRAFTS   **Caribelle Batik** (⊠ Romney Manor, Old Road ☎ 869/465–6253) sells batik wraps, T-shirts, dresses, wall hangings, and the like. The **Crafthouse** (⊠ Bay Rd., Southwell Industrial Site, Basseterre, ½ mi [1 km] east of Shoreline Plaza ☎ 869/465–7754) is one of the best sources for local dolls, woodcarvings, and straw work. **Glass Island** (⊠ 4–5 Princes St., Basseterre ☎ 869/466–6771) sells frames, earrings, and handblown glass vases, bowls, and plates in sinuous shapes and seductive colors. **Island Hopper** (⊠ The Circus, Basseterre ☎ 869/465–2905) is a good place for island crafts, especially wood carvings, pottery, textiles, and colorful resort wear, as well as humorous T-shirts and trinkets. **Kate Design** (⊠ Bank St., Basseterre ☎ 869/465–5265) showcases the highly individual style of Kate Spencer, whose original paintings, serigraphs, note cards, and other pieces that she regularly introduces, are also available from her studio outside the Rawlins Plantation. **The Potter's House** (⊠ West Bay Rd., Basseterre ☎ 869/465–5947) is the atelier-home of Carla Astaphan, whose beautifully glazed ceramics and masks celebrate the Afro-Caribbean heritage. **Stonewall's Tropical Boutique** (⊠ 7 Princes St., Basseterre ☎ 869/466–9124) carries top-of-the-line products from around the Caribbean: hand-painted Jamaican pottery, West Indian photos and artworks, brass jewelry, hand-painted T-shirts, and flowing resort wear by leading Caribbean designer John Warden.

Nightlife

Most nightlife revolves around the hotels, which host folkloric shows and calypso and steel bands of the usual limbo-rum-and-reggae variety. Check with your hotel or the tourist board for schedules.

BARS   **Bambu's** (⊠ Bank St., off The Circus, Basseterre ☎ 869/466–5280) incorporates bamboo everywhere to create an "outdoorsy interior": in the ceiling, railings, bar, lamps, mirrors, benches. The rest is splashed in wild hues such as lemon, lime, tangerine, and raspberry. Local artworks adorn the walls, and the split-level warren of rooms accommodates those who seek intimate conversation, rooting for teams on the big-screen TV, and dancing on a tiny floor weekends. You can order both sophisticated single-malt scotches and down-home island food amid the Peace Corps hip ambience. The local gang flocks to **Bobsy's** (⊠ Bay Road, between

Sprott and Cayon Sts., Basseterre ☎ 869/466–6133), especially on Friday nights, for karaoke and a DJ spinning favorite dance tunes. A favorite happy-hour watering hole is the **Circus Grill** (✉ Bay Rd., Basseterre ☎ 869/465–0143), a second-floor eatery whose verandah offers views of the harbor and the activity on The Circus.

CASINOS   The **St. Kitts Marriott Royal Beach Resort** occupies a glitzy 35,000-sq-ft space, including *salons privés* for high rollers.

DANCE & MUSIC   Popular local disc jockey Ronnie Rascal entertains at his own night spot,
CLUBS   **Club Atmosphere** (✉ Canada Estate ☎ 869/465–3655), on Friday and Saturday nights. Locals disco down Friday and Saturday nights at **Henry's Night Spot** (✉ Dunn's Cottage, Main St., Cayon ☎ 869/465–3508).

Exploring St. Kitts

You can explore Basseterre, the capital city, in half an hour or so; allow three to four hours for an island tour. Main Road traces the northwestern perimeter through seas of sugarcane and past breadfruit trees and stone walls. Villages with tiny pastel-color houses of stone and weathered wood are scattered across the island, and the drive back to Basseterre around the island's other side passes through several of them. The most spectacular stretch of scenery is on Dr. Kennedy Simmonds Highway to the tip of the Southeast Peninsula. This ultrasleek modern road twists and turns through the undeveloped grassy hills that rise between the calm Caribbean and the windswept Atlantic, past the shimmering pink Great Salt Pond, a volcanic crater, and seductive beaches.

Numbers in the margin correspond to points of interest on the St. Kitts map.

WHAT TO SEE   **Basseterre.** On the south coast, St. Kitts's walkable capital is graced with
❶   tall palms, and although many of the buildings appear run-down, there are interesting shops, excellent art galleries, and some beautifully maintained houses.

The octagonal Circus, built in the style of London's famous Piccadilly Circus, has duty-free shops along the streets and courtyards off from it. There are lovely gardens on the site of a former slave market at **Independence Square** (✉ off Bank St.). The square is surrounded on three sides by 18th-century Georgian buildings. **St. George's Anglican Church** (✉ Cayon St.) is a handsome stone building with a crenellated tower originally built by the French in 1670 and called Nôtre-Dame. The British burned it down in 1706 and rebuilt it four years later, naming it after the patron saint of England. Since then it has suffered a fire, an earthquake, and hurricanes, and was once again rebuilt in 1869. **Port Zante** (✉ Waterfront, behind The Circus) is an ambitious, much-delayed, 27-acre cruise-ship pier-marina reclaimed from the sea. The domed welcome center features an imposing neoclassical design, with columns and stone arches; when completed (construction will continue through 2003), it will have walkways, fountains, and West Indian–style buildings housing luxury shops, galleries, and restaurants.

National Museum. In the restored former Treasury Building, the museum, which opened in 2002, presents an eclectic collection reflecting the history and culture of the island. It will expand and develop in future years— as a collaboration of the St. Christopher Heritage Society and the island government. *✉ Bay Rd. Basseterre ☎ 869/465-5584 ⊡ EC$1 residents, U.S.$1 nonresidents ⊙ Mon and Sat., 9:30–2, Tues.–Fri. 9–1 and 2–5.*

⑤ Black Rocks. This series of lava deposits was spat into the sea ages ago when the island's volcano erupted. It has since been molded into fanciful shapes by centuries of pounding surf. ⊠ *Atlantic coast, outside town of Sadlers, Sandy Bay.*

★ **④ Brimstone Hill.** The well-restored 38-acre fortress, a UNESCO World Heritage Site, is part of a national park dedicated by Queen Elizabeth in 1985. The steep walk up the hill from the parking lot is well worth it if military history and/or spectacular views interest you. After routing the French in 1690, the English erected a battery here, and by 1736 the fortress held 49 guns. In 1782, 8,000 French troops laid siege to the stronghold, which was defended by 350 militia and 600 regular troops of the Royal Scots and East Yorkshires. When the English finally surrendered, the French allowed them to march from the fort in full formation out of respect for their bravery (the English afforded the French the same honor when they surrendered the fort a mere year later). A hurricane severely damaged the fortress in 1834, and in 1852 it was evacuated and dismantled. The beautiful stones were carted away to build houses.

The citadel has been partially reconstructed and its guns remounted. A seven-minute orientation film recounts the fort's history and restoration. You can see what remains of the officers' quarters, the redoubts, the barracks, the ordinance store, and the cemetery. Its museum collections were depleted by hurricanes, but some pre-Columbian artifacts, objects pertaining to the African heritage of the island's slaves (masks, ceremonial tools, etc.), weaponry, uniforms, photographs, and old newspapers remain. The view from here includes Montserrat and Nevis to the southeast; Saba and St. Eustatius to the northwest; and St. Barths and St. Maarten to the north. Nature trails snake through the tangle of surrounding hardwood forest and savanna (a fine spot to catch the green vervet monkeys skittering about). ⊠ *Main Rd., Brimstone Hill* ☎ 869/ 465–2609 ⌛ *$5* ⊙ *Daily 9:30–5:30.*

② Old Road. This site marks the first permanent English settlement in the West Indies, founded in 1624 by Thomas Warner. Take the side road toward the interior to find some Carib petroglyphs, testimony of even earlier habitation. The largest depicts a female figure on black volcanic rock, presumably a fertility goddess. Less than a mile east of Old Road along Main Road is **Bloody Point,** where French and British soldiers joined forces in 1629 to repel a mass Carib attack; reputedly so many Caribs were massacred that the stream ran red for three days. ⊠ *Main Rd., west of Challengers.*

★ **③ Romney Manor.** The ruins of this somewhat restored house and surrounding cottages that duplicate the old chattel-house style are set in 6 acres of gardens, with exotic flowers, an old bell tower, and an enormous gnarled 350-year-old *saman* tree (sometimes called a rain tree). Inside, at **Caribelle Batik,** you can watch artisans hand-printing fabrics by the 2,500-year-old process known as batik. Look for signs indicating a turnoff for Romney Manor near Old Road.

NEVIS

Where to Stay

Most lodgings are in restored manor or plantation houses scattered throughout the island's five parishes (counties). The owners often live at these inns, and it's easy to feel as if you've been personally invited down for a visit. Before dinner you may find yourself in the drawing room having a cocktail and conversing with the family, other guests, and visitors who have come for a meal in the restaurant. Most inns operate on MAP (including complimentary afternoon tea) and offer a free shuttle service to their private stretch of beach. If you require TVs and air-conditioning, you're better off staying at hotels, then dining with the engaging inn owners.

For approximate costs, *see* the dining and lodging price chart at the beginning of this chapter.

★ **$$$$** ▦ **Four Seasons Resort Nevis.** This beachfront beauty offers exemplary business and recreational facilities while exuding romance, from the clubby library bar to 300 acres of exquisitely landscaped grounds. Impeccable services include a beach concierge, dispensing everything from reading materials to CDs. Spacious rooms are furnished with mahogany armoires and beds, marble bathrooms, and cushioned rattan sofas and chairs. The spa, with 12 treatment rooms, has a relaxation garden with two pools, a sugar-mill ruin with a waterfall into a Jacuzzi, and a chilled dipping pool. The resort admirably combines world-class elegance with West Indian hospitality. ✉ *Pinney's Beach* ☏ *Box 565, Charlestown* ☎ *869/ 469–1111; 800/332–3442 in the U.S.; 800/268–6282 in Canada* 🖷 *869/ 469–1112* ⊕ *www.fourseasons.com* ⇆ *179 rooms, 17 suites, 43 villas* ⌁ *2 restaurants, grill, room service, fans, in-room safes, minibars, in-room VCRs, 18-hole golf course, 10 tennis courts, pro shop, 2 pools, hair salon, health club, hot tub, spa, beach, dive shop, snorkeling, windsurfing, boating, bicycles, 2 bars, pub, library, video game room, shops, baby-sitting, children's programs (ages 2–12), laundry facilities, laundry service, Internet, business services, meeting rooms, car rental* ▭ *AE, D, MC, V* ⦿ *EP.*

★ **$$$–$$$$** ▦ **Hermitage Plantation Inn.** A 300-year-old great house—reputedly the Caribbean's oldest wooden house—is the heart of this breeze-swept hillside complex overlooking the distant ocean (beach shuttles are complimentary). The vivacious owners, Maureen and Richard "Loopy" Lupinacci, will introduce you to everyone who's anyone on Nevis. Individually decorated, bougainvillea-draped cottages have hardwood floors, antiques (including four-poster canopy beds swaddled in mosquito netting), and hammock-slung patios or balconies. The Hermitage appreciates life's finer things, from the elegant horse-drawn carriage rides to engaging conversation at the bar. ✉ *Gingerland* ☎ *869/469–3477* 🖷 *869/469–2481* ⊕ *www.hermitagenevis.com* ⇆ *8 rooms, 8 cottages, 1 house* ⌁ *Restaurant, fans, in-room safes, some kitchens, refrigerators, tennis court, pool, horseback riding, bar, shops; no a/c, no TV in some rooms* ▭ *AE, MC, V* ⦿ *BP.*

★ **$$$$** ▦ **Nisbet Plantation Beach Club.** From the patio of this 18th-century plantation manor house you can see the Atlantic and an old, flower-bedecked sugar mill while enjoying complimentary high tea. Three categories of impeccably maintained accommodations occupy several pale yellow Bermudian-style cottages staggered along a stately coconut palm-lined grass avenue that sweeps to the beach. All are tastefully appointed with patios, vaulted ceilings, gleaming tile floors, whitewashed wicker and rattan, and grass mats, all done in soothing sea-foam and peach fabrics. In addition to the refined great-house restaurant, you'll find a deck bar (terrific sunset watching) and two casual beach eateries. ✉ *Newcastle Beach* ☎ *869/469–9325 or 800/742–6008* 🖷 *869/469–9864* ⊕ *www.nisbetplantation.com* ⇆ *38 rooms* ⌁ *3 restaurants, fans, in-room safes, refrigerators, tennis court, pool, massage, beach, snorkeling, croquet, 2 bars, library, shop, laundry service; no room TVs* ▭ *AE, MC, V* ⦿ *MAP.*

★ **$$$$** ▦ **Montpelier Plantation Inn.** This grand lady of Nevis, created by James and Celia Gaskell, has been wonderfully reincarnated by new owners,

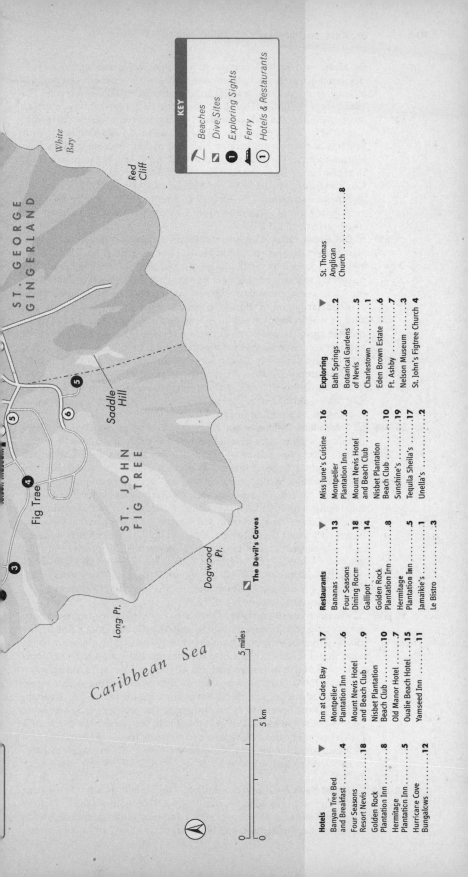

KEY

Beaches
Dive Sites
Exploring Sights
Ferry
Hotels & Restaurants

ST. GEORGE GINGERLAND

White Bay

Red Cliff

Saddle Hill

ST. JOHN FIG TREE

Fig Tree

Long Pt.

Dogwood Pt.

The Devil's Caves

Caribbean Sea

0   5 km
0   5 miles

Hotels

Banyan Tree Bed and Breakfast	4
Four Seasons Resort Nevis	18
Golden Rock Plantation Inn	8
Hermitage Plantation Inn	5
Hurricane Cove Bungalows	12
Inn at Cades Bay	17
Montpelier Plantation Inn	6
Mount Nevis Hotel and Beach Club	9
Nisbet Plantation Beach Club	10
Old Manor Hotel	7
Oualie Beach Hotel	15
Yamseed Inn	11

Restaurants

Bananas	13
Four Seasons Dining Rocm	18
Gallipot	14
Golden Rock Plantation Inn	8
Hermitage Plantation Inn	5
Jamaikie's	1
Le Bistro	3
Miss June's Cuisine	16
Montpelier Plantation Inn	6
Mount Nevis Hotel and Beach Club	9
Nisbet Plantation Beach Club	10
Sunshine's	19
Tequila Sheila's	17
Unella's	2

Exploring

Bath Springs	2
Botanical Gardens of Nevis	5
Charlestown	1
Eden Brown Estate	6
Ft. Ashby	7
Nelson Museum	3
St. John's Figtree Church	4
St. Thomas Anglican Church	8

the Hoffman family. The understated re-do with stunning use of fabrics, bamboo, and tasteful furnishings, makes Montpelier's civilized demeanor even more apparent. The fieldstone great house re-creates the 18th-century original (Horatio Nelson and Fanny Nisbet were married on the grounds); the old windmill is now a prix-fixe restaurant that seats just 12. The hillside cottages display an almost Asian simplicity, with bamboo or four-poster canopy beds and baskets of fresh flowers. The Hoffmans have given the inn a fresh look while keeping unpretentious, elegant touches like afternoon tea. ✉ *Montpelier Estate* 🗋 *Box 474, Charlestown* ☎ *869/469–3462* 🖷 *869/469–2932* ⊕ *www. montpeliernevis.com* ⇌ *17 rooms* ↳ *3 restaurants, fans, tennis court, pool, beach, shop, 2 bars; no room TVs* ▤ *AE, MC, V* ⊘ *Closed late Aug.–early Oct.* ⦿ *BP.*

$$$ 🏨 **Old Manor Hotel.** Vast tropical gardens surround this former sugar plantation in the shadow of Mt. Nevis. The outbuildings have been imaginatively restored as public spaces; the old cistern is now the pool, and rusting sugar-factory equipment forms a virtual sculpture garden. Many enormous guest rooms have exposed wood beams, gorgeous stone walls, polished hardwood or tile floors, marble vanities, four-poster beds, and antique wardrobes. Others have a monochromatic haute-1970s bachelor-pad look. The respected Cooperage restaurant has splendid sea views and an excellent nouvelle Continental menu. Of all the Nevisian inns, Old Manor probably best re-creates the old-time plantation feel. ✉ *Charlestown* 🗋 *Box 70, Charlestown* ☎ *869/469–3445 or 800/ 892–7093* 🖷 *869/469–3388* ⊕ *www.oldmanornevis.com* ⇌ *14 rooms* ↳ *2 restaurants, fans, refrigerators, pool, 2 bars, library, shops; no a/ c, no room TVs* ▤ *AE, MC, V* ⦿ *BP.*

$$–$$$ 🏨 **Golden Rock Plantation Inn.** More than 200 years ago, co-owner Pam Barry's great-great-great-grandfather built this estate. It straddles 96 mountainous acres crisscrossed by trails. Rusting cannons placed about the grounds add a sense of history, as do Pam's family heirlooms and the magnificent Eva Wilkin mural in the bar. Oceanview rooms have mahogany or bamboo four-poster beds and native grass mats. The former sugar mill is a spectacular bi-level suite, the old cistern a spring-fed swimming pool. Free transportation accesses the inn's beach bar on Pinney's. Green vervet monkeys skitter about, and La Rue, a gloriously colored, wolf-whistling Amazona parrot, perches wherever he pleases. ✉ *Gingerland* 🗋 *Box 493, Charlestown* ☎ *869/469–3346* 🖷 *869/469–2113* ⊕ *www.golden-rock.com* ⇌ *16 rooms, 1 suite* ↳ *Restaurant, grill, fans, tennis court, pool, hiking, bar; no a/c, no room TVs* ▤ *AE, MC, V* ⊘ *Closed Sept.–early Oct.* ⦿ *EP.*

$$–$$$ 🏨 **Hurricane Cove Bungalows.** These one-, two-, and three-bedroom bungalows cling precariously to a cliff overlooking lovely Oualie Beach. The glorified treehouse interiors are charmingly rustic, with gleaming terracotta floors, hand-carved wood furnishings, batik wall hangings, and beds swaddled in mosquito netting. All have full kitchens and an enormous enclosed beached-wood patio with breathtaking ocean views (most in-demand, especially for honeymooners, are Sea Biscuit, Baobab, and Williwah). Several have private pools. The postage-stamp-size hotel pool is in the foundation of a 250-year-old fort, under the shade of a baobab tree. The beach is within a five-minute walk. ✉ *Hurricane Hill* ⊕ *www.hurricanecove.com* 🏠🏠 *869/469–9462* ⇌ *11 cottages* ↳ *Fans, kitchens, pool, laundry service; no a/c* ▤ *AE, MC, V* ⊘ *Closed Sept.* ⦿ *EP.*

★ $$–$$$ 🏨 **Mount Nevis Hotel and Beach Club.** The Maguid family blends contemporary accommodations with typical Nevisian warmth. Deluxe rooms and suites have large balconies, handsome white and natural-wicker furnishings, apricot, mint, and white fabrics, and colorful island prints.

Suites have full kitchens and sofa beds, making them fine value for families; standard hotel rooms are comparatively cramped. There are also three fully equipped, individually decorated, oceanview houses. The beach club (free transportation) serves scrumptious pizzas and grilled meats. The hotel's verdant site was once a lime plantation; the wild trees' perfume wafts through the air. Invigorating hikes on-site include the 18th-century ruins of the Thomas Cottle Church, unusual in that owners and slaves worshiped together. ☒ *Shaw's Rd., Mt. Nevis* ☎ *Box 494, Newcastle* ☎ *869/469–9373 or 800/756–3847* ☏ *869/469–9375* ⊕ *www. mountnevishotel.com* ⤳ *28 suites, 3 houses* ♢ *Restaurant, grill, fans, some kitchens, refrigerators, in-room VCRs, golf course, tennis courts, pool, gym, bar, Internet, business services, meeting rooms* ⊟ *AE, D, MC, V* ⏋⊙⏛ *EP.*

$$–$$$ ⊞ **Oualie Beach Hotel.** These cozy gingerbread cottages have views of St. Kitts. Bright, airy rooms are tastefully furnished: deluxe rooms have mahogany four-posters and polished granite vanities; studios have full kitchens. Hammocks dangle everywhere, but most guests are active types, and families with young children especially love the beach. The on-site dive shop (fine packages available) offers NAUI-certified instruction, and you can rent Sunfish and Windsurfers, charter a sailboat, take sea-kayaking or turtle-watching tours, or head out to explore on a mountain bike. All meals are served at the informal hotel restaurant, best known for its West Indian–themed Saturday nights, with live music. ☒ *Oualie Beach* ☎ *869/469–9735 or 800/682–5431* ☏ *869/469–9176* ⊕ *www.oualie.com* ⤳ *34 rooms* ♢ *Restaurant, fans, in-room safes, some kitchens, refrigerators, some in-room VCRs, beach, dive shop, snorkeling, windsurfing, boating, fishing, bar, meeting room* ⊟ *AE, D, MC, V* ⏋⊙⏛ *EP.*

$$ ⊞ **Inn at Cades Bay.** At this complex, each of the tidy peach-colored cottages with sage-green gabled roofs has its own tiny lawn. Sizable rooms have high ceilings, bleached-wood paneling, rattan beds, smart, abstract Spanish fabrics, and terra-cotta patios that overlook the sea. The lovingly tended grounds include 10 varieties of palm trees and a cactus garden. The beach is lined with gazebos with hammocks. Ask about special "low" high-season rates in January and February and Internet deals. ☒ *Cades Bay* ☎ *869/469–8139* ☏ *869/469–8129* ⊕ *www.cadesbayinn. com* ⤳ *16 rooms* ♢ *Restaurant, fans, minibars, pool, bar* ⊟ *AE, MC, V* ⏋⊙⏛ *BP.*

$–$$ ⊞ **Banyan Tree Bed and Breakfast.** As the name implies, this inn sits in the shadow of a huge 300-year-old banyan tree–and nearby a wonderful stand of bamboo. Tucked into the hills, Banyan Tree offers two comfortable rooms or your own cottage, the gingerbread-bedecked yellow Bamboo House, with mahogany four-poster bed and kitchen. The Roses—Jonathan, an architect/artist, and Anne, a New Hampshire travel agent and former commercial herb gardener—turned the house into a B&B in search of a retirement haven. Guests are treated to fruit grown in the garden and simple dinners if they choose. In winter months the couple hosts retreats for artists by the week. ☒ *Morningstar* ☎ *869/ 469–6109* ⊕ *www.banyantreebandb.com* ⤳ *2 rooms and cottage* ♢ *Kitchen, fans, honor bar; no a/c* ⊟ *MC, V* ☞ *3-night minimum* ⏋⊙⏛ *BP.*

$ ⊞ **Yamseed Inn.** With lovely gardens and the beach nearby, Yamseed could be the perfect place. Sybil Siegfried, the friendly innkeeper and expert gardener, has created a masterful garden and comfortable inn. The first thing you meet entering the stylish, open reception area are orchids in full bloom, surrounded by hummingbirds. Each room is handsomely appointed with a mahogany bed, wood-paneled ceiling, throw rugs, white-tile floors, and antiques. Breakfasts include homemade muffins and muesli with grated coconut, fresh bread, French toast, or banana pancakes. The serene white-sand beach stares right at St. Kitts. Though it is near the airport's flight path, air traffic is fortunately sparse. ⊠ *Newcastle Beach* ☎ *869/469–9361* ⇥ *4 rooms* ♻ *Beach, fans; no a/c* ⊟ *No credit cards* ⟳ *3-night minimum* ¶⊙∣ *BP.*

Where to Eat

Dinner options range from intimate dinners at plantation guest houses (where the menu is often prix-fixe) to casual eateries. Seafood is ubiquitous, and many places specialize in West Indian fare.

What to Wear

Dress is casual at lunch, although beach attire is unacceptable. Dress pants and sundresses are appropriate for dinner.

For approximate costs, *see* the dining and lodging price chart at the beginning of this chapter.

CARIBBEAN $$$$ ✗ **Golden Rock Plantation Inn.** The romantic, dimly lit room's fieldstone walls date from the Golden Rock Inn's plantation days. Enchanting Eva Wilkin originals grace the walls, copper sugar-boiling pots are used as planters, and straw mats and unglazed local pottery provide island interest; distressed French highback chairs, maroon linens, and gold napery contribute colonial accents. The prix-fixe menu might include house favorites like velvety pumpkin soup, raisin curry chicken, and grilled local snapper with *tania* (a type of tuber) fritters. Don't miss the homemade juices, like passion fruit, soursop, and ginger beer. ⊠ *Gingerland* ☎ *869/ 469–3346* ♻ *Reservations essential* ⊟ *AE, MC, V* ⊘ *Closed Sun.*

★ $$$$ ✗ **Miss June's Cuisine.** The evening begins with cocktails in the ornate living room, followed by dinner in an elegant dining room. Hors d'oeuvres and three courses, including soup and fish, precede the grand feast of many international dishes. Known for her Trinidadian curries, local vegetable dishes, and meats, Miss June Mestier entertains in her home two or three nights per week. "I invite people into my home for dinner and then my manager has the audacity to charge them as they leave!" quips Miss June, who joins the guests after dinner for coffee and brandy. The price includes all you can eat and drink. ⊠ *Jones Bay* ☎ *869/469– 5330* ♻ *Reservations essential* ⊟ *MC, V.*

$–$$$ ✗ **Unella's.** It's nothing fancy here—just tables on a second-floor porch overlooking Charlestown's waterfront. Stop for exceptional lobster (more expensive than the rest of the menu), curried lamb, island-style spareribs, and steamed conch, all served with local vegetables, rice, and peas. Unella opens shop around 9 AM, when locals and boaters appear eager for their breakfast, and stays open all day. ⊠ *Waterfront, Charlestown* ☎ *869/469–5574* ⊟ *No credit cards.*

$–$$ ✗ **Jamakie's** Tucked away in the downstairs of a quaint gingerbread-trimmed former residence, this humble eatery serves such good, honest Jamaican-inspired fare as stewed saltfish (with sides of "real" rice and peas and ratatouille) and baked chicken, and whatever else is scribbled on the blackboard. The decor is similarly no-frills, save for a striking mural of marine life splashed across one wall. ⊠ *Prince William St., Charlestown* ☎ *869/469–8748* ⊟ *No credit cards* ⊘ *Closed Sun.*

★ ¢–$$ ✗ **Sunshine's.** Everything about this beach shack is larger than life, including the Rasta man Llewelyn "Sunshine" Caines himself. Flags from around the world drape the lean-to and complement the international patrons (including an occasional movie star), who wander over from the adjacent Four Seasons. Picnic tables are splashed with bright sunrise-to-sunset colors; even the palm trees are painted. Fishermen cruise up with their catch—you might savor lobster rolls or snapper creole.

Don't miss the lethal house specialty, Killer Bee rum punch. As Sunshine boasts, "One and you're stung, two you're stunned, three it's a knockout." ⊠ *Pinney's Beach* ☎ *869/469–1089* ▭ *No credit cards.*

CONTEMPORARY
$$$$
✕ **Hermitage Plantation Inn.** After cocktails in the inn's antiques-filled parlor (incomparable bartender Shabba's rum punches are legendary, and you could meet all Nevisian society, high and low, at the postage-stamp-size bar), dinner is served on the verandah. The four-course prix-fixe menu might include lemongrass and pumpkin soup, conch cakes with lobster sauce, tuna with guava and rosemary, and a rum soufflé—all lovingly prepared by the local chef, Lovey. Expect an evening of bon mots and bonhomie: the conversation is always lively, thanks to witty, gregarious owners Maureen and Richard Lupinacci. ⊠ *Gingerland* ☎ *869/469–3477* ⚄ *Reservations essential* ▭ *AE, MC, V.*

$$$$
Fodor'sChoice
★
✕ **Montpelier Plantation Inn.** New owners Tim and Meredith Hoffman preside over an elegant evening, starting with hors d'oeuvres. A candlelit walkway leads diners into the stone building, where dinner is served on the west verandah. The inventive chef, Mark Roberts, utilizes the property's herb gardens and fruit trees and occasionally even hauls in the day's catch. The changing menu might present lobster terrine with tarragon-chive sauce, seared swordfish in papaya–black bean salsa, and a proper herb-crusted rack of lamb in rosemary mustard jus. Simpler lunches (order the lobster salad) are served on the refreshing patio. ⊠ *Montpelier Estate* ☎ *869/469–3462* ⚄ *Reservations essential* ▭ *AE, MC, V* ⊘ *Closed late Aug.–early Oct.*

★ $$$$
✕ **Nisbet Plantation Beach Club.** The great house—an oasis of polished hardwood floors, mahogany and cherry-wood furnishings, straw mats, wicker furnishings, and stone walls—has long been a popular dinner spot. Tables on the verandah look down the palm tree–lined fairway to the sea. Kevin Hall's five-course menu combines Continental, Pacific Rim, and Caribbean cuisines with local ingredients. Sumptuous choices include blue-cheese-pumpkin quiche with avocado relish, ginger-crusted mahimahi with lemon-parsley rice and beet sauce, and chocolate-truffle torte. Enjoy cocktails or coffee with silky-soft live music in the civilized front bar. ⊠ *Newcastle Beach* ☎ *869/469–9325* ⚄ *Reservations essential* ▭ *AE, MC, V.*

$$$–$$$$
✕ **Four Seasons Dining Room.** The main restaurant at the Four Seasons is imposing yet romantic: beamed cathedral ceiling, imported hardwood paneling, parquet floors, ornate white-iron chandeliers, flagstone hearth, china-filled cabinets, hand-carved mahogany chairs, towering floral arrangements, and picture windows overlooking the sea. Chef Joseph Oldham's Southwest/Asian menu changes daily, stressing fresh, often organic, produce. Stellar offerings might include green tea–smoked salmon with tropical fruit salad and vanilla-bean dressing and lemongrass-poached lobster with banana spring roll and ginger-butter sauce. Numerous "spa selections" grace the menu, while the adjacent, less formal Grill Room provides a more classic meat-and-potatoes experience. ⊠ *Four Seasons Resort, Pinney's Beach* ☎ *869/469–1111* ⚄ *Reservations essential* ▭ *AE, D, DC, MC, V* ⊘ *No lunch.*

$$–$$$$
✕ **Mount Nevis Hotel and Beach Club.** The hotel's airy dining room opens onto the terrace and pool with a splendid view of St. Kitts. The elegant yet light menu deftly blends local ingredients with a cornucopia of cuisines, from Mexican to Thai. Excellent starters are calamari tempura with red peppers and saffron aioli, or Caribbean conch cake with mild basil-chili mayonnaise; excellent entrées include pan-seared salmon with garlic-lime butter sauce and superb flambé specials. The service is attentive, the dining room sublime (with lovely Fauvist-hued artworks). ⊠ *Shaws Rd., Mt. Nevis Estates* ☎ *869/469–9373* ▭ *AE, D, MC, V.*

ECLECTIC X **Bananas.** Gillian Smith, who has worked for Disney and Relais et
★ **$$–$$$** Châteaux, has reopened her funky eatery/bazaar perched atop a cliff with
stunning sunset views. She's added splashes of vivid colors, as well as
Turkish copper pots, kilims, and artwork (much of it for sale). Food prepared by Montréal-born chef Ben Goldberg includes starters like zucchini cakes with yogurt sauce and crab quesadillas; follow with
bourbon-glazed ribs or lobster tails with pineapple and ginger salsa. Jazzy
sounds and the scent of wild orchids commingled with Cubanos waft
through the lounge. No wonder Gillian fittingly calls it a "Caribbean
bistro." ⊠ *Tamarind Bay* ☎ *869/469–1891* ▤ *MC, V* ◷ *Closed Sun.*
No lunch.

$$ X **Tequila Sheila's.** Right next door to the Inn at Cades Bay, this thatched
shack of corrugated tin and wood sits on a beach (there are even pala-
pas) next to a colorful abandoned boat. It has been gussied up with plant-
filled baskets, terra-cotta floors, turquoise accents, and billowing
windsocks, but the laid-back air remains. The Caribbean-tinged Mediter-
ranean cuisine runs from paella to coconut shrimp to filet mignon in
béarnaise sauce. The popular Sunday brunch (the crab Benedict is a must)
draws locals and tourists alike. ⊠ *Cades Bay* ☎ *869/469–1633* ▤ *MC,*
V ◷ *Closed Mon. No lunch Tues.*

$–$$ X **Gallipot.** A two-family venture, Gallipot, with its octagonal bar and
casual atmosphere, attracts locals with fresh seafood at reasonable
prices. Large Sunday lunches with ample portions (only one dish per
week) are a big draw. The Fosbery's built the bar as an addition to their
small beach house on quiet Tamarind Bay, while their daughter and son-
in-law, Tracy and Julian Rigby, provide fish through Nevis Water Sports,
a charter fishing company. Aside from their local customers, Gallipot
attracts sailors with its moorings, showers, garbage-collection service,
and laundry. ⊠ *Tamarind Bay* ☎ *869/469–8430* ▤ *MC, V* ◷ *Closed*
Mon.–Wed. No dinner Sun.

★ **$–$$** X **Le Bistro.** Known informally as "Matt's," after owner/chef Matt Lloyd
(former chef at Montpelier), this minuscule boîte, in a 1930s chattel house,
is wildly popular, especially during Friday-night happy hour. Fare ranges
from quiches to curries; coconut chicken's a standout, but opt for the
fresh-fish specials (Matt usually hauls in the catch himself on his 30-
footer, *Deep Venture,* which is available for rent). The impeccable presentation is as colorful as the decor (persimmon floors, plaid tablecloths,
and vine-strangled trellises). Local chefs flock here on their nights off—
always a promising sign. ⊠ *Chapel St., Charlestown* ☎ *869/469–5110*
▤ *MC, V* ◷ *Closed weekends. No lunch.*

Beaches

All beaches are free to the public, but there are no changing facilities,
so wear a swimsuit under your clothes.

Newcastle Beach. This broad swath of soft ecru sand shaded by coconut
palms sits at the northernmost tip of the island by Nisbet Plantation, on
the channel between St. Kitts and Nevis. It's popular with snorkelers.

Oualie Beach. South of Mosquito Bay and north of Cades and Jones bays,
this beige-sand beach is where the folks at Oualie Beach Hotel can mix
you a drink and fix you up with water-sports equipment.

★ **Pinney's Beach.** The island's showpiece has almost 4 mi (6½ km) of soft,
golden sand on the calm Caribbean, lined with a magnificent grove of
palm trees. The Four Seasons Resort is here, as are the private cabanas
and pavilions of several mountain inns and casual beach bars.

Windward Beach. This windswept stretch on the "wild side" of the island faces Montserrat, tiny Redonda, and Antigua. Long and wide, it's
great for exploring, beachcombing, picnicking, and body surfing—not

at all like the calm Caribbean side. It's particularly popular with locals, who gather for Sunday picnics and beach barbecues.

Sports & the Outdoors

★ One of the Caribbean's most unusual events is the almost monthly Day at the Races, sponsored by the **Nevis Turf and Jockey Club** (☎ 869/469–3477). The races, which attract a "pan-Caribbean field" (as the club likes to boast), are held on a windswept course called Indian Castle, overlooking the "white horses" of the Atlantic. Last-minute changes and scratches are common; a party atmosphere prevails, with local ladies dispensing heavenly fried chicken and gossip.

BIKING **Windsurfing Nevis** (✉ Oualie Beach ☎ 869/469–9682) offers mountainbike rentals as well as specially tailored tours on its state-of-the-art Gary Fisher, Trek, and Specialised bikes. The tours, led by Winston Crooke, a master windsurfer and competitive bike racer, encompass lush rain forest, majestic ruins, and spectacular views. Rates vary according to itinerary and ability level, but are aimed generally at experienced riders.

BOATING The seas are usually uncommonly calm, with light breezes. The northwest side of Nevis is particularly delightful, thanks to the sterling views of St. Kitts. **Nevis Water Sports** (✉ Oualie Beach ☎ 869/469–9060) rents everything from Sunfish ($20 per hour) to powerboats ($100 per hour). You can rent kayaks, Hobie Cats, and Sunfish from **Windsurfing Nevis** (✉ Oualie Beach ☎ 869/469–9682), which also provides excellent instruction.

FISHING Fishing here focuses on kingfish, wahoo, grouper, tuna, and yellowtail snapper, with marlin occasionally spotted. The best areas are Monkey Shoals and around Redonda. Charters are $350 per half day. *Deep Venture* (✉ Oualie Beach ☎ 869/469–5110), run by fisherman/chef Matt Lloyd of Le Bistro, does day-fishing charters. **Nevis Water Sports** (✉ Jones Estate ☎ 869/469–9060) offers sport fishing aboard its tournament-winning boats, the 31-ft *Sea Brat* and *Sea Troll,* under the supervision of Captain Julian Rigby and Ian Gonzaley. *Venture II* (✉ Newcastle ☎ 869/469–9837). Capt. Claude Nisbett leads half- and full-day charters for $350 and $675, respectively, on a U.S. 28-ft Seasport, including drinks and snacks.

GOLF Duffers doff their hats to the beautiful, impeccably maintained Robert Trent Jones, Jr.–designed 18-hole, par-72, 6,766-yard championship
Fodor'sChoice course at the **Four Seasons Resort Nevis** (✉ Pinney's Beach ☎ 869/469–
★ 1111). The signature hole is the 15th, a 660-yard monster that encompasses a deep ravine; other holes include bridges, steep drops, rolling pitches, and fierce doglegs. The virtual botanical gardens surrounding the fairways almost qualify as a hazard themselves. Greens fees are $100 per person for nine holes, $150 for 18. For the frugal golfer, Nevis has **Golf at Cat Ghaut** (✉ Shaw's Rd., Newcastle ☎ 869/469–9826). This privately owned and operated par-3 "executive course" across from the Mount Nevis Hotel was built by Philadelphians Roger and Peggy Staiger over the last 10 years at their Nevis home. In 2002 they added 3 holes to the existing 9, and Roger says if he lives long enough, there will be 18. A wonderful outing for those who don't take their golf—or themselves—too seriously, and the price is right. Admission is $20, including a round of play, equipment, and a golf cart.

HIKING The center of the island is Nevis Peak—also known as Mount Nevis—which soars 3,232 ft and is flanked by Hurricane Hill on the north and Saddle Hill on the south. If you plan to scale Nevis Peak, a day-long affair, it is highly recommended that you go with a guide. Your hotel can arrange it (and a picnic lunch) for you. The **Upper Round Road Trail** is a 9-mi (14½-km) road constructed in the late 1600s and cleared and restored by the Nevis Historical and Conservation Society. It connects the Golden Rock Hotel, on the east side of the island, with Nisbet Plantation Beach Club, on the northern tip. The trail encompasses numerous vegetation zones, including pristine rain forest, and impressive plantation ruins. The original cobblestones, walls, and ruins are still evident in many places.

Eco-Tours Nevis (☎ 869/469–2091), headed by David Rollinson, rambles through 18th-century estates and explores what remains of Nevis's last working sugar factory as well as archaeological evidence of pre-Columbian settlements. David also offers treks up Mountravers, a spectacular greathouse ruin, and historical walks through Charlestown. The fee is $20 per person, $10 for the Charlestown walk. **Michael Herbert** (☎ 869/469–2856) leads 4-hr nature hikes up to Herbert Heights, where he offers fresh local juices as you drink in the views of Montserrat; his powerful telescope makes you feel as if you're staring right into that island's simmering volcano. The price is $20; for $25 you can ride one of Herbert's donkeys. Michael also brings people up by appointment to Saddle Hill Battery and Nelson's Lookout, where he has constructed a thatched hut. The festive activities includes crab races, refreshments, rock climbing, and whale-watching in season through a telescope donated by Greenpeace. The **Nevis Historical and Conservation Society** (☎ 869/469–5786) sells an informational guidebook on the Upper Round Road Trail at various shops and the island museums. **Sunrise Tours** (☎ 869/469–3512), run by Lynell and Earla Liburd, offers a range of hiking tours, but their most popular is Devil's Copper, a rock configuration full of ghostly legends. Local people gave it its name because at one time the water was hot—a volcanic thermal stream. They also do a Nevis village walk, a Hamilton Estate Walk, and trips to the rain forest and Nevis Peak. Hikes range from $20 to $40 per person. **Top to Bottom** (☎ 869/469–9080), run by Jim and Nikki Johnston, offers ecorambles (slower tours) and hikes that emphasize Nevis's volcanic and horticultural heritage (including pointing out folkloric herbal medicines). The Johnstons are also keen star- and bird-watchers. Three-hour rambles or hikes are $20 per person (snacks and juice included); it's $30 for a more strenuous climb up Mount Nevis.

HORSEBACK
RIDING
You can arrange for leisurely beach rides, more demanding trail rides through the lush hills ($50 per person), and lessons ($20 per hour) through **Nevis Equestrian Centre** (✉ Clifton Estate, Pinney's Beach ☎ 869/469–8118). Kids will love the petting zoo, with donkeys, goats, peacocks, and tortoises.

SCUBA DIVING &
SNORKELING
The Devil's Caves are a series of grottoes where divers can navigate tunnels, canyons, and underwater hot springs while viewing lobsters, sea fans, sponges, squirrel fish, and more. The village of Jamestown, which washed into the sea around Fort Ashby, just south of Cades Bay, makes for superior snorkeling and diving. Reef-protected Pinney's Beach offers especially good snorkeling. Single-tank dives are usually $50, two-tank dives $80.

Scuba Safaris (✉ Oualie Beach ☎ 869/469–9518) is a PADI five-star facility, NAUI Dream Resort, and NASDS Examining Station, whose experienced dive masters offer everything from a resort course to full certification. They also provide a snorkeling-learning experience that enables you to not only see but listen to sealife, including whales and dolphins. **Under the Sea** (✉ Oualie Beach ☎ 869/469–1291) is the brainchild of Barbara Whitman, a marine biologist from Connecticut. Barbara's mission is to orient snorkelers and divers of all ages about the sea life so they'll appreciate what they see. Using "touch tanks" with more than 50 species, she then offers snorkeling lessons and tours to see the creatures in the wild. Her programs range from $25.

TENNIS   Many hotels have their own tennis courts. There are 10 tennis courts (3 lighted), 6 clay, and 4 all-weather hardcourts at the **Four Seasons Resort Nevis** (⊠ Pinney's Beach ☎ 869/469–1111), which also offers instruction by Peter Burwash International pros.

WINDSURFING   Waters are generally calm and winds steady yet gentle, making Nevis an excellent spot for beginners and intermediates. **Windsurfing Nevis** (⊠ Oualie Beach ☎ 869/469–9682) offers top-notch instructors (Winston Crooke is one of the best in the islands) and equipment for $25 per half-hour.

Shopping

Nevis is certainly not the place for a shopping spree, but there are some unusual and wonderful surprises, notably the island's stamps, batik, and hand-embroidered clothing. Other than a few hotel boutiques and isolated galleries, virtually all shopping is concentrated on or just off Main Street in Charlestown. The lovely old stonework and wood floors of the waterfront Cotton Ginnery Complex make an appropriate setting for stalls of local artisans.

Specialty Items

ART   Nevis has produced one artist of some international repute, the late Dame Eva Wilkin, who for more than 50 years painted island people, flowers, and landscapes in an evocative art naïf style. Her originals are now quite valuable, but prints are available in some local shops. The **Eva Wilkin Gallery** (⊠ Clay Ghaut, Gingerland ☎ 869/469–2673) occupies her former atelier. If the paintings, drawings, and prints are out of your price range, consider buying the lovely note cards based on her designs. The front rooms of **Café des Arts** (⊠ Main St. and Samuel Hunkins Dr., Charlestown ☎ 869/469–7098) show the works of 15 Caribbean artists, including St. Kitts's Kate Spencer, plus teak furnishings, hand-crafted straw handbags, locally-made linen clothing, and gourmet delicacies. Breakfast, lunch, and espresso are served in the back yard, overlooking the Charlestown harbor, adjacent to the Museum of Nevis History. **Robert Humphreys** (⊠ Zetlands ☎ 869/469–3326) sells his work, flowing bronze sculptures of pirouetting marlins and local birds and animals at Café des Arts, where it's possible to watch the artist at work in his studio.

CLOTHING   Most hotels have their own specialized boutiques. **Fanny's Closet** (⊠ Hermitage Plantation Inn, Gingerland) sells St. Kitts designer John Warden's line of flowing, breathable linen resortwear in eggshell to earth tones, as well as hand-painted baubles and bibelots. **Island Fever** (⊠ Main St., Charlestown ☎ 869/469–0867) has become the island's classiest boutique, with an excellent selection of everything from bathing suits and dresses to straw bags and jewelry. You'll find colorful Caribelle Batik clothing, as well as T-shirts and other Nevis souvenirs at **Island Hopper** (⊠ Main St., Charlestown ☎ 869/469–5430). **Jerveren's Fashions** (⊠ Cotton Ginnery, Charlestown ☎ 869/469–0062) carries still more batik resortwear and light cotton sundresses in pastel colors.

FOOD & WINE   At **Caribbean Wine** (⊠ Prospect Rd., Fig Tree ☎ 869/469–3908), Dominique Nelson Ashley, a chemist by trade, produces surprisingly tasty wines by traditional methods from local plants such as soursop, white sorrel, ginger, guava, red plum, passion fruit, cane, mango, and star apple. He then corks and seals them in recycled bottles. Beekeeping is a buzzing biz, and you'll find beeswax candles (which burn longer than those made of regular wax) and fragrant, tropically flavored honey at many stores. Quentin Henderson, the amiable head of the **Nevis Beekeeping Cooperative** (⊠ Gingerbread ☎ 869/469–5521), will even arrange trips by appointment to various hives for demonstrations of beekeeping procedures.

HANDICRAFTS   **AAAC** (⊠ Main St., Charlestown ☎ 869/469–0657) is the acronym for Adams Afro-Caribbean Art & Craft; the name's promise is fulfilled with such striking pieces as drums from Mozambique, hand-carved elephant and lion walking sticks, Nigerian warri boards, Guyanese painted gourds, and various masks and straw mats. **Bocane Ceramics** (⊠ Main St., Charlestown ☎ 869/469–5437) stocks beautifully designed and glazed local pottery, such as platters painted with marine life. **Caribco Gifts** (⊠ Main St., Charlestown ☎ 869/469–1432) sells affordable T-shirts, candles, and pottery emblazoned with Nevis logos. **Knick Knacks** (⊠ Between Waterfront and Main Sts., next to Unella's Restaurant, Charlestown ☎ 869/469–5784) showcases top local artisans, including Marvin Chapman (stone and wood carvings) and Jeannie Rigby (exquisite dolls). The **Nevis Handicraft Co-op Society** (⊠ Main St., Charlestown ☎ 869/469–1746), next to the tourist office, offers work by local artisans (clothing, ceramic ware, woven goods) and locally produced honey, hot sauces, ★ and jellies. The **Nevis Pottery** (⊠ Main Road, Newcastle ☎ 869/469–1746), a cooperative, has continued the age-old tradition of hand-built red-clay pottery fired over burning coconut husks. It's possible to watch the potters and purchase wares at their small Newcastle factory. Stamp collectors should head for the **Philatelic Bureau** (⊠ Off Main St., Charlestown ☎ 869/469–0617), opposite the tourist office. St. Kitts and Nevis are famous for their decorative, and sometimes valuable, stamps. Real beauties include the butterfly, hummingbird, and marine life series.

Nightlife

In season it is usually easy to find a local calypso singer or a steel or string band performing at one of the hotels. Such performances are often in tandem with a special buffet dinner. Scan the posters plastered on doorways announcing informal jump-ups. Though Nevis (blessedly) lacks high-tech discos, many restaurants and bars have live bands or DJs on weekends. On Saturday nights, **Bananas** (⊠ Tamarind Bay ☎ 869/469–1891) heats up with live dance music after dinner. The local band Caribbean Roots plays nightly on the Ocean Terrace at the **Four Seasons Resort Nevis** (⊠ Pinney's Beach ☎ 869/469–1111).

BARS   **Eddy's Bar and Restaurant** (⊠ Main St., Memorial Sq., Charlestown ★ ☎ 869/469–5958) opens Wednesday nights for a raucous West Indian happy hour featuring half-price snacks, including tannia and conch fritters served with terrific hot sauce made by Eddy's mom, Eulalie Williams (you can buy a bottle down the block at the Main Street Supermarket). The evening will go on and on to the wee hours with karaoke and dancing with a local DJ. **The Water Department Barbecue** (⊠ Pump Rd., Charlestown ☎ no phone) is the informal name for a lively Friday-night jump-up that's run by two fellows from the local water department to raise funds for department trips. Friday afternoons the tents go up and the grills are fired. Cars line the streets and the guys dish up fabulous barbecue ribs and chicken—as certain customers lobby to get their water pressure adjusted. It's a classic Caribbean scene.

Exploring Nevis

Nevis's main road makes a 21-mi (32-km) circuit through the five parishes; various offshoots of the road wind into the mountains. You can tour Charlestown, the capital, in a half hour or so, but you'll need three to four hours to explore the entire island. Part of the island's charm is its rusticity: there are no traffic lights, goats still amble through the streets of Charlestown, and local grocers announce whatever's in stock on a blackboard (anything from pig snouts to beer).

Numbers in the margin correspond to points of interest on the Nevis map.

WHAT TO SEE **Bath Springs.** The springs and the Bath Hotel, built by businessman ❷ John Huggins in 1778, sustained hurricane and most likely some earthquake damage over the years, but the government is using parts of it now for offices. The first hotel in the Caribbean, the Bath Hotel was so popular in the 19th century that visitors traveled two months by ship to "take the waters" in the hot thermal springs on the property. Local volunteers have cleaned up the spring, built a stone pool and steps to enter the waters, and residents and visitors enjoy the springs, which range from 104°F–108°F. This is a fascinating site, with much promise for the future. Follow Main Street south from Charlestown. ⊠ *Charlestown outskirts.*

★ ❺ **Botanical Gardens of Nevis.** In addition to terraced gardens and arbors, this remarkable 7.8-acre site in the glowering shadow of Mt. Nevis has natural lagoons, streams, and waterfalls, as well as superlative bronze mermaids, egrets, and herons, old copper pots used as floral centerpieces, and extravagant fountains. You'll find a proper rose garden, sections devoted to orchids and bromeliads, cacti, and flowering trees and shrubs—even a bamboo garden. The entrance to the Rain Forest Conservatory—which attempts to include every conceivable Caribbean ecosystem and then some—duplicates an imposing Mayan temple. A splendid re-creation of a plantation-style great house contains a tearoom with sweeping sea views and a souvenir shop that sells teas, teapots, jams, botanical oils, candles, Caribbean cookbooks, and the like. ⊠ *Montpelier Estate* ☎ *869/469–3509* 💲 *$9* ⊙ *Mon.–Sat. 9–4:30.*

★ ❶ **Charlestown.** About 1,200 of Nevis's 10,000 inhabitants live in the capital. The town faces the Caribbean, about 12½ mi (20 km) south of Basseterre on St. Kitts. If you arrive by ferry, as most people do, you'll walk smack onto Main Street from the pier. It's easy to imagine how tiny Charlestown, founded in 1660, must have looked in its heyday. The weathered buildings still have their fanciful galleries, elaborate gingerbread fretwork, wooden shutters, and hanging plants. The stonework building with the clock tower (1825) houses the courthouse and the second-floor **library** (a cool respite on sultry days). A fire in 1873 damaged the building and destroyed valuable records; much of the present building dates from the turn of the 20th century. The little park next to the library is Memorial Square, dedicated to the fallen of World Wars I and II. Down the street from the square, archaeologists have discovered the remains of a Jewish cemetery and synagogue (Nevis reputedly had the Caribbean's second-oldest congregation), but there's little to see. The **Alexander Hamilton Birthplace,** which contains the Museum of Nevis History, is on the waterfront, covered in bougainvillea and hibiscus. This Georgian-style house is a reconstruction of what is believed to have been the American patriot's original home, built in 1680 and thought to have been destroyed during an earthquake in the mid-19th century. Hamilton was born here in 1755 and moved to St. Croix when he was about 12. A few years later, at 17, he moved to the American colonies to continue his education; he became Secretary of the Treasury to George Washington and died in a duel with political rival Aaron Burr. The Nevis House of Assembly occupies the second floor of this building, and the museum downstairs contains Hamilton memorabilia, documents pertaining to the island's history, and displays on island geology, politics, architecture, culture, and cuisine. ⊠ *Low St.* ☎ *869/469–5786* ⊕ *www.nevis-nhcs.com* ⊠ *$3; $2 if admission already paid to affiliated Nelson Museum* ◷ *Weekdays 9–4, Sat. 9–noon.*

❻ Eden Brown Estate. This government-owned mansion, built around 1740, is known as Nevis's haunted house, or haunted ruins. In 1822 a Miss Julia Huggins was to marry a fellow named Maynard. However, on the day of the wedding, the groom and his best man had a duel and killed each other. The bride-to-be became a recluse, and the mansion was closed down. Local residents claim they can feel the presence of "someone" whenever they go near the eerie old house with its shroud of weeds and wildflowers. You're welcome to drop by; it's always open, and it's free. ⊠ *East Coast Rd., between Lime Kiln and Mannings, Eden Brown Bay* ☎ *no phone.*

❼ Ft. Ashby. Overgrown with tropical vegetation, this site overlooks the place where the settlement of Jamestown fell into the sea after a tidal wave hit the coast in 1680. Needless to say, this is a favorite scuba-diving site. ⊠ *Main Rd., 1½ mi (2½ km) southwest of Hurricane Hill, Fort Ashby Beach.*

❸ Nelson Museum. This collection merits a visit for its memorabilia of Lord Nelson, including letters, documents, paintings, and even furniture from his flagship. Historical archives of the Nevis Historical and Conservation Society are housed here and are available for public viewing. Nelson was based in Antigua but on military patrol came to Nevis, where he met and eventually married Frances Nisbet, who lived on a 64-acre plantation here. ⊠ *Bath Rd., outside Charlestown* ☎ *869/469–0408* ⊠ *$3; $2 if admission already paid to affiliated Museum of Nevis History* ◷ *Weekdays 9–4, Sat. 9–noon.*

❹ St. John's Figtree Church. Among the records of this church built in 1680 is a tattered, prominently displayed marriage certificate that reads: HO-RATIO NELSON, ESQUIRE, TO FRANCES NISBET, WIDOW, ON MARCH 11, 1787. ⊠ *Church Ground* ☎ *no phone.*

❽ St. Thomas Anglican Church. The island's oldest church was built in 1643 and has been altered many times over the years. The gravestones in the old churchyard have stories to tell, and the church itself contains memorials to Nevis's early settlers. ⊠ *Main Rd., Jessups, just south of Cotton Ground* ☎ *no phone.*

ST. KITTS & NEVIS A TO Z

To research prices, get advice from other travelers, and book travel arrangements, visit www.fodors.com.

AIR TRAVEL
American flies into San Juan, Puerto Rico, from where its commuter arm, American Eagle, flies several times daily to St. Kitts. US Airways flies each Saturday from Philadelphia to St. Kitts. Other major domestic airlines fly from their eastern hubs either into Antigua or St. Maarten, where connections to St. Kitts (and, less frequently, to Nevis) can be made on American Eagle, LIAT, Caribbean Star, Carib Aviation, and Winair. If you are traveling from the U.K. or Canada, you will probably fly first into Antigua before connecting on a smaller aircraft to St. Kitts or

Nevis. Nevis Express is currently the only carrier with regularly sched-uled flights between St. Kitts and Nevis.

⚑ American/American Eagle ☎ 869/465-0500. **Carib Aviation** ☎ 869/469-9185 in Nevis. **Caribbean Star** ☎ 800/247-9297. **LIAT** ☎ 869/465-8613. **Nevis Express** ☎ 869/469-9755. **US Airways** ☎ 800/428-4322. **Winair** ☎ 869/465-8010.

AIRPORTS

Taxis meet every flight at the newly expanded and modernized Robert L. Bradshaw Golden Rock Airport on St. Kitts, and at Vance W. Amory International Airport on Nevis. The taxis are unmetered, but fixed rates, in EC dollars, are posted at the airport and at the jetty. Note that rates are the same for one to four passengers. On St. Kitts the fare from the airport to the closest hotel in Basseterre is EC$18, to Frigate Bay's resorts EC$29, and to the farthest point EC$72. From the airport on Nevis it costs EC$20 to Nisbet Plantation, EC$37 to the Four Seasons, and EC$55 to Montpelier. Before setting off in a cab, be sure to clarify whether the rate quoted is in EC or U.S. dollars. There's a 50% sur-charge for trips made between 10 PM and 6 AM.

⚑ Robert L. Bradshaw Golden Rock Airport ⊠ Golden Rock, St. Kitts ☎ no phone. **Vance W. Amory International Airport** ⊠ Newcastle, Nevis ☎ no phone.

BOAT & FERRY TRAVEL

There are three services between St. Kitts and Nevis, all with byzantine schedules that are subject to change. Call the ferry information lines for the most up-to-date schedules. The 150-passenger government-operated ferry M/V *Caribe Queen* makes the 45-minute crossing from Nevis to St. Kitts two to three times daily, except Thursday and Sunday. The for-mer cargo ship *Sea Hustler* is larger and makes the trip twice daily. Round-trip fare for both is $8. The faster, air-conditioned, 110-passenger ferry M/V *Caribe Breeze* makes the run twice daily Thursday and Sunday, more frequently other days. The fare is $12 ($15 first class) round-trip.

Sea-taxi service between the two islands is operated by Kenneth Samuel, Nevis Water Sports, Leeward Island Charters, and Austin Macleod of Pro-Divers for $20 one-way in summer, $25 in winter; discounts can be negotiated for small groups. There is an additional EC$1 tax for port security, paid separately upon departure.

FARES & SCHEDULES · **⚑ Ferry information** ☎ 869/466-4636 or 869/469-9373. **Kenneth's Dive Cen-tre** ☎ 869/465-2670. **Leeward Island Charters** ☎ 869/465-7474. **Nevis Water Sports** ☎ 869/469-9060. **Pro-Divers** ☎ 869/465 3223. *Sea Hustler* ☎ 869/467-9702 or 869/467-9826.

BUS TRAVEL · Privately owned minibuses–many with colorful names like "Dem Say" and "Rumors"–circle both St. Kitts and Nevis. They usually charge only about $1 to go most anywhere. Catch buses by standing on the side of the road in the direction you want to go, and flag them down. Check with the tourist office for further schedules and fares.

BUSINESS HOURS

BANKS · Hours vary somewhat for banks but are typically Monday–Thursday 8–3 and Friday 8–5. The Bank of Nevis and St. Kitts and Nevis National Bank are also open Saturday 8:30–11 AM.

POST OFFICES · Post offices are open Monday–Wednesday and Friday 8–3, Thursday and Saturday 8–noon.

SHOPS · Although shops used to close for lunch from noon to 1, more and more establishments are remaining open Monday–Saturday 8–4. Some shops close earlier on Thursday.

CAR RENTALS

On St. Kitts you'll need a local driver's license, which you can get by presenting yourself, your valid driver's license, and $25 at the police station on Cayon Street in Basseterre (on Nevis the car-rental agency will help you obtain a local license at the police station). The license is valid for one year. Car rentals start at about $35 per day for a compact; expect to pay a few extra bucks for a/c. Most agencies offer substantial discounts when you rent by the week.

Agencies include Avis, which has the best selection of Suzuki and Daihatsu four-wheel-drive vehicles on St. Kitts. Delise Walwyn also provides an excellent selection and the option of a replacement car for one day on Nevis if you rent for three days or more on St. Kitts. Agencies such as Noel's Courtesy Garage and Striker's Car Rentals offer a wide variety of cars and jeeps for exploring Nevis. TDC Rentals has a wide selection of vehicles and outstanding service; it offers a three-day rental that includes a car on both islands. **Avis** ⊠ S. Independence Sq., Basseterre, St. Kitts ☎ 869/465-6507. **Delise Walwyn** ⊠ Liverpool Row, Basseterre, St. Kitts ☎ 869/465-8449 ⊕ www.delisleco.com. **Nevis Car Rentals** ⊠ Newcastle, Nevis ☎ 869/469-9837. **Noel's Courtesy Garage** ⊠ Farms Estate, Nevis ☎ 869/469-5199. **Striker's Car Rental** ⊠ Hermitage Rd., Gingerland Nevis ☎ 869/469-2634. **TDC Rentals** ⊠ W. Independence Sq., Basseterre, St. Kitts ☎ 869/465-2991 ⊠ Bay Rd., Charlestown, Nevis ☎ 869/469-5430 ⊕ www.tdcltd.com.

CAR TRAVEL

One well-kept main road circumnavigates St. Kitts and is usually clearly marked, making it difficult to get lost. If you'd like to dine at the various inns and sight-see for more than one day, a car is advisable. If you plan to stay in the Frigate Bay–Basseterre area on St. Kitts, you can get by using taxis and doing a half-day island tour. Most roads on Nevis are new and in terrific shape, at least around three-quarters of the island; though driving is on the left, you may be given a right-drive vehicle. And if you deviate from Main Street in Charlestown, you're likely to have trouble finding your way.

GASOLINE Gasoline is expensive, about $2.60 per gallon.

ROAD CONDITIONS The main roads on St. Kitts are in admirable condition, especially in the more developed southwestern part, though the northeast can get a bit bumpy, and the access roads to the plantation inns are notoriously rough. The roads on Nevis are new and beautifully smooth, at least on the most-travelled north, west, and south sides of the island. The east coast has some potholes, and pigs, goats, and sheep still insist on the right-of-way all around the island.

RULES OF THE ROAD Driving is on the left.

ELECTRICITY

St. Kitts and Nevis hotels function on 110 volts, 60 cycles, making all North American appliances safe to use.

EMERGENCIES

There are no 24-hour pharmacies on St. Kitts or Nevis, but several pharmacies are open seven days a week, usually until at least 5 PM. Call ahead if it's late in the afternoon. **Ambulance & Fire Ambulance** ☎ 911. **Fire emergencies on St. Kitts** ☎ 869/465-2333. **Fire emergencies on Nevis** ☎ 869/469-5391. **Hospitals Joseph N. France General Hospital** ⊠ Cayon St., Basseterre, St. Kitts ☎ 869/465-2551. **Alexandra Hospital** ⊠ Government Rd., Charlestown, Nevis ☎ 869/469-5473.

Pharmacies City Drug ⊠ Fort St., Basseterre, St. Kitts ☎ 869/465-2156 ⊠ Rex Papillon, Frigate Bay, St. Kitts ☎ 869/465-1803. **Claxton Medical Centre Pharmacy** ⊠ Main St., Charlestown, Nevis ☎ 869/469-5357. **Evelyn's Drugstore** ⊠ Main St., Charlestown, Nevis ☎ 869/469-5278. **Parris Pharmacy** ⊠ Central St., Basseterre, St. Kitts ☎ 869/465-8569.

Police Police emergencies ☎ 911.

ETIQUETTE & BEHAVIOR
People are friendly but shy; always ask before you take photographs. Also, be sure to wear wraps or shorts over beach attire when you're in public places. Both topless and nude bathing are prohibited.

FESTIVALS & SEASONAL EVENTS
ST. KITTS Carnival is held for 10 days immediately following Christmas Eve and is the usual riot of color and noise, with steel-band and Calypso Monarch competitions and flamboyant parades of the various troupes. The St. Kitts Music Festival, held the last week of June, celebrates everything from R&B to reggae. Among the top international acts to perform have been Chaka Khan, Earl Klugh, Kool and the Gang, and Peabo Bryson. Much of September is devoted to various independence celebrations (contact the Government Information Service for information), ranging from beach picnics to military parades and theatrical events.

NEVIS Nevis's version of carnival—Culturama—is a summer event, held the end of July and beginning of August, and includes music competitions, queen shows, art exhibits, and cultural events. It culminates in the day-long last day jump-up, a colorful parade around the island. A special Tourism Week is usually held in winter, including horse races, bartender competitions, and community-wide picnics. In mid-September, Heritage Week includes pageants, jump-ups, and celebrations of local culture, from food fairs to craft exhibitions.

HOLIDAYS
Public holidays are: New Year's Day, Ash Wednesday (usually during Feb.), Easter Monday (usually Apr. to mid-May), Labour Day (1st Mon. in May), Whit Monday (usually mid-May to late June), Emancipation Day (1st Mon. in Aug.), Independence Day (Sept. 19), Christmas Day, and Boxing Day (Dec. 26).

LANGUAGE
The official language of St. Kitts and Nevis is English, which is spoken with a strong West Indian lilt.

MAIL & SHIPPING
Airmail letters to the United States and Canada cost EC$.90 per half ounce; postcards require EC$.80; to the United Kingdom letters cost EC$1.20, postcards EC$1; to Australia and New Zealand, letters cost EC$1.60, postcards EC$1.20. Mail takes at least 7 to 10 days to reach the United States. St. Kitts and Nevis issue separate stamps, but each honors the other's.

MONEY MATTERS
Prices quoted throughout this chapter are in U.S. dollars unless otherwise noted.

ATMS The Royal Bank of St. Kitts has an ATM. There are ATMs on Nevis at the airport, at the Bank of Nova Scotia, at Barclay's Bank, and at the St. Kitts-Nevis National Bank. They all accept CIRRUS and PLUS cards.

CREDIT CARDS Most large hotels, restaurants, and shops accept major credit cards, but small inns and shops often do not.

CURRENCY Legal tender is the Eastern Caribbean (EC) dollar. The rate of exchange at press time was EC$2.70 to US$1. U.S. dollars are accepted practically everywhere, but you'll usually get change in EC currency.

CURRENCY EXCHANGE Exchanging currency is usually not necessary.

PASSPORTS & VISAS

U.S. and Canadian citizens need a valid passport or must prove citizenship with a birth certificate (with a raised seal) accompanied by a government-issued photo I.D. British citizens must have a passport. A return or ongoing ticket is mandatory.

SAFETY

On these islands, safety is not a major concern. But as anywhere, visitors, especially women, should not jog on lonely roads or visit beaches alone. It is wise to lock cars, hotel rooms, and houses, and to travel with a minimum of valuables.

SIGHTSEEING TOURS

The taxi driver who picks you up will probably offer to act as your guide to the island. Each driver is knowledgeable and does a three-hour tour of Nevis for $50 and a four-hour tour of St. Kitts for $60. He can also make a lunch reservation at one of the plantation restaurants, and you can incorporate this into your tour.

BOAT TOURS In addition to the usual snorkeling, sunset, and party cruises (ranging in price from $35 to $65), most companies offer whale-watching excursions during the winter migrating season, January–April. On St. Kitts, Blue Water Safaris offers half-day snorkeling trips or beach barbecues on deserted cays, as well as sunset and moonlight cruises on its 65-ft catamaran *Irie Lime*. Leeward Island Charters offers day and overnight charters on three catamarans—the 47-ft *Caona*, and two 70-footers, the *Eagle* and *Spirit of St. Kitts*. Day sails are from 9:30 to 4:30 and include a barbecue, an open bar, and use of snorkeling equipment. Banana Boat Tours provides snorkeling and sunset cruises from Turtle Beach on its 34-ft inflatable, Coast Guard–certified Scarib boat. Private charters, Nevis–St. Kitts shuttles, and deep-sea fishing can be arranged. Turtle Tours Nevis offers sea kayaking along the Nevis coast, stopping at an otherwise inaccessible beach underneath a towering cliff for snorkeling and at Pinney's for refreshments and a refreshing view of St. Kitts. Turtle Tours on St. Kitts runs trips from Whitehouse Bay to Friars Bay. On Nevis, Sea Nevis Charters offers its 44-ft *Sea Dreamer* for snorkeling and island sunset cruises.

🚢 St. Kitts **Banana Boat Tours** ☎ 869/465-0645 or 869/469-9086. **Blue Water Safaris** ☎ 869/466-4933. **Leeward Island Charters** ☎ 869/465-7474. **Turtle Tours (St. Kitts)** ☎ 869/465-9094.

🚢 Nevis **Sea Nevis Charters** ☎ 869/469-9239. **Turtle Tours Nevis** ☎ 869/465-8503.

TRAIN TOURS One of the most memorable things in the Caribbean is the sugar-train tour around St. Kitts. A group of American investors—railroad and tourism experts—have revitalized the old narrow-gauge train that was used to transport sugarcane to the central sugar factory since 1912. New two-story, 28-passenger cars make the journey around the island in slightly more than three hours, through tall cane fields, over trestles spanning gorges, and over 23 bridges, in complete comfort. The Wingfield Bridge actually carries the trains right across the canopy of the rain forest. Each passenger gets a downstairs air-conditioned seat and an upstairs observation spot. Drinks are served while you get a history lesson on St. Kitts and Nevis. Tickets are $89 and can be purchased at the station at

Needsmust (near the airport), where the ride begins. The project is not just a profit-making venture; the owners help support the St. Kitts Sugar Manufacturing Corporation (SSMC), which is struggling for survival, and soon may close, causing sugarcane production to end.

🏠 St. Kitts Scenic Railway ✉ Needsmust ☎ 869/465-7263

ORIENTATION Kantours offers general island tours. Tropical Tours can run you around St. Kitts and take you to the rain forest for $45 per person. Norris Martin's Liamuiga Tours offers several tour options and will customize tours as well. On Nevis, Fitzroy "Teach" Williams is recommended: he's the former president of the taxi association—even older cabbies call him "the Dean." TC, a Yorkshire lass who used to drive a double-decker bus in England and has been married to a Nevisian for over a decade, offers entertaining explorations via TC's Island Tours. Jan's Travel Agency arranges half- and full-day tours of the island. You can also stop by the Nevis Tourism Authority office for the historical society's self-guided island tour.

🏠 St. Kitts **Kantours** ☎ 869/465-2098. **Liamuiga Tours** ☎ 869/465-4128. **Tropical Tours** ☎ 869/465-4167.

🏠 Nevis **Fitzroy "Teach" Williams** ☎ 869/469-1140. **Jan's Travel Agency** ☎ 869/469-5578. **Nevis Tourism Authority** ☎ 869/469-7550. **TC's Island Tours** ☎ 869/469-2911.

TAXES

DEPARTURE TAX The departure tax is $16.50, payable in cash only.

SALES TAX There is no sales tax on either St. Kitts or Nevis. Hotels collect a 7% government tax (8% on Nevis).

TAXIS

Taxi rates are government regulated and are posted at the airport, the dock, and in the free tourist guide. There are fixed rates to and from all the hotels and to and from major points of interest. In St. Kitts you can call the St. Kitts Taxi Association. In Nevis, taxi service is available at the airport, by the dock in Charlestown, and through arrangements made at your hotel. Sample fares from the dock: EC$40 to Nisbet Plantation, EC$18 to the Four Seasons, and EC$27 to Hermitage.

🏠 St. Kitts **Taxi Association** ☎ 869/465-8487, 869/465-4253, 869/465-7818 after hrs. **Nevis taxi service** ☎ 869/469-5621, 869/469-9790, 869/469-5515 after dark.

TELEPHONES

Phone cards, which you can buy in denominations of $5, $10, and $20, are handy for making local phone calls, calling other islands, and accessing U.S. direct lines.

COUNTRY & AREA CODES To call St. Kitts and Nevis from the United States, dial the area code 869, then access code 465, 466, 468, or 469 and the local four-digit number.

INTERNATIONAL CALLS A warning for both islands: many private lines and hotels charge access rates if you use your AT&T, Sprint, or MCI calling card; there's no regularity, so phoning can be frustrating. Pay phones, usually found in major town squares, take EC coins or phone cards.

LOCAL CALLS To make a local call, dial the seven-digit number.

TIPPING

Hotels add up to a 12% service charge to your bill. Restaurants occasionally do the same; ask just in case if it isn't printed on the menu; a 15% tip is appropriate when it isn't included. Taxi drivers typically receive a 10% tip, porters and bellhops $1 per bag; if you feel the service was exemplary, leave $3–$4 per night for the housekeeping staff.

VISITOR INFORMATION

🗂 Before You Leave **Nevis Tourism Authority** ⊕ www.nevisisland.com ✉ Elm House, Park Lane, Lower, Froyle, Alton, Hampshire, England GU34 4LT ☎ 44(0)1420 520810. **St. Kitts Tourism Authority** ⊕ www.stkitts-tourism.com ✉ 414 E. 75th St., New York, NY 10021 ☎ 212/535-1234, 800/582-6208, 866/556-3847 for Nevis alone ✉ 365 Bay St., Suite 806, Toronto, Ontario M5H 2V1, Canada ☎ 416/368-6707 or 888/395-4887 ✉ 10 Kensington Ct., London W8 5DL, U.K. ☎ 0171/376-0881.

🗂 In St. Kitts & Nevis **Nevis Tourism Authority** ✉ Main St., Charlestown, Nevis ☎ 869/469-7550 or 869/469-1042. **St. Kitts Tourism Authority** ✉ Pelican Mall, Bay Rd., Basseterre, St. Kitts ᴆ Box 132 ☎ 869/465-2620 or 869/465-4040. **St. Kitts-Nevis Hotel Association** ✉ Liverpool Row, Basseterre, St. Kitts ᴆ Box 438 ☎ 869/465-5304.

ST. LUCIA

20

FODOR'S CHOICE
Anse Chastanet Beach Hotel, Anse Chastanet
Auberge Seraphine, Vigie Cove
Dasheene Restaurant and Bar, Soufrière
The Pitons

HIGHLY RECOMMENDED

RESTAURANTS Great House, Cap Estate
Tao, Cap Estate
The Coal Pot, Castries

HOTELS Jalousie Hilton Resort & Spa, Anse des Pitons
Ladera, Soufrière
The Body Holiday at LeSPORT, Cap Estate

SIGHTS Diamond Botanical Gardens, Soufrière
La Soufrière Drive-In Volcano, Soufrière
Pigeon Island, Rodney Bay

ACTIVITIES Scuba Diving and Snorkeling

Watching the festivities from the porch of the corner bar, the lady seems disappointed with the Friday-night street party. The pounding beat sounds more disco than Caribbean. "Where's the reggae, the calypso?" she wonders aloud. "It's down there, Miss," offers a wiry young man with a broad smile and smooth moves. "You have to be dancing, near the speakers. Come on." Taking her hand, he leads her to the middle of the street, where the melody is loud and clear and the rhythm definitely Caribbean. To really enjoy the Gros Islet jump-up, you must first jump in.

Updated by
Jane E. Zarem

Historians feel certain that the intrepid Christopher Columbus never set foot—let alone danced—on St. Lucia. That was his loss. Today the eye-popping scenery and pristine beaches that Columbus missed are sprinkled with sprawling resorts, small hideaways, and friendly villages—all of which draw more and more visitors to this lush, tropical island.

Settled between Martinique and St. Vincent, and 100 mi (160 km) due west of Barbados, the 27 mi by 14 mi (43½ km by 22½ km) island of St. Lucia (pronounced *loo*-sha) occupies a prime position in the Caribbean, its striking natural beauty easily earning it the moniker "Helen of the West Indies." The capital city of Castries and nearby villages in the north are home to 40% of the population and the destination of most vacationers, who stay at posh resorts and play on honey-colored beaches. The south, on the other hand, is dominated by dense jungle and vast banana plantations that blanket the hills. A torturously winding road follows the coastline, cutting through mountains, rain forest, and fertile valleys. On the southwest coast, Petit Piton and Gros Piton, the island's unusual twin peaks, rise from the sea to more than 2,600 ft and are familiar navigational landmarks for sailors and aviators alike. Divers are attracted to the reefs found just offshore north of Soufrière, the island's picturesque French-colonial capital. Most of the natural tourist attractions are, in fact, in this area. "If you haven't been to Soufrière," the local people will tell you, "you haven't been to St. Lucia."

The Arawaks, St. Lucia's first inhabitants, paddled up from South America sometime before AD 200. The aggressive Caribs followed, conquering the Arawaks around AD 800. The Caribs, who named the island Hewanorra (Land Where the Iguana Is Found), still lived on the island when Europeans attempted to establish a settlement. François Le Clerc, a pirate nicknamed Jambe de Bois (Wooden Leg), was actually the first European settler. In the late 16th century he holed up on Pigeon Island, just off St. Lucia's northernmost point, and attacked passing ships. In 1605, 67 English settlers bound for Guiana were blown off course and landed at the island's southern tip, near Vieux Fort. Within a few weeks the Caribs had killed all but 19, who escaped in a canoe. More English settlers arrived 30 years later and were met with a similar lack of hospitality. The French arrived in 1651 after the French West India Company purchased the island.

For the next 150 years, battles between the French and the English for possession of the island were frequent, with a dizzying 14 changes in power before the British took possession in 1814. The Europeans established sugar plantations, using slaves from West Africa to work the fields. By 1838, when the slaves were emancipated, more than 90% of the population was of African descent—also the approximate proportion of today's 170,000 St. Lucians. Indentured East Indian laborers were brought over in 1882 to help bail out the sugar industry, which suffered when slavery was abolished and all but died in the 1960s, when bananas became the major crop. On February 22, 1979, St. Lucia became an independent state within the British Commonwealth of Nations, with a resident governor-general appointed by the queen. Still, there are many relics of French occupation, notably the island patois (spoken in addition to English), the cuisine, the place names, and surnames.

WHAT IT COSTS In U.S. dollars				
$$$$	$$$	$$	$	¢
RESTAURANTS*				
over $30	$20–$30	$12–$20	$8–$12	under $8
HOTELS**				
Cost EP/BP/CP over $350	$250–$350	$150–$250	$80–$150	under $80
Cost AI over $450	$350–$450	$250–$350	$125–$250	under $125

*Restaurant prices are for a main course at dinner. **EP, BP, and CP prices are per night for a standard double room in high season, excluding taxes, service charges, and meal plans. AI (all-inclusive) prices are per person, per night based on double-occupancy during high season, excluding taxes and service charges.

Where to Stay

Virtually all St. Lucia's lodgings are along the calm Caribbean coast, concentrated between Castries and Cap Estate in the north, at Marigot Bay a few miles south of Castries, and around Soufrière on the southwest coast. Low-rise resorts and small inns are tucked into lush surroundings on secluded coves, along unspoiled beaches, or in forested hillsides.

A group of small, locally owned and operated hotels and guest houses market themselves as The Inns of St. Lucia. Ranging in size from 3 to 71 rooms, with rates starting at just $20 per room at some guest houses, these small inns are a delightful alternative. For more information, contact the **St. Lucia Tourist Board** (✉ Sureline Bldg., Vide Bouteille ⌖ Box 221, Castries ☎ 758/452–4094 ☎ 758/453–1121 ⊕ www.stlucia.org). For villa rentals, contact **Tropical Villas** (⌖ Box 189, Castries ☎ 758/452–8240 ☎ 758/450–8089 ⊕ www.tropicalvillas.net).

Castries & the North

★ $$$$ 🏨 **The Body Holiday at LeSPORT.** Even before arrival, you can design your own "body holiday"—from robe size to tee time. Indulge in aromatherapy, a dozen different massages, wraps, yoga, personal trainer services, and more at the splendid Oasis; daily treatments are included. Otherwise, enjoy the beach, scuba diving, golf, and other sports—with instruction provided, if needed. The concept is to combine an active beach vacation with revitalization for both body and mind. Rooms have marble floors and king-size four-poster or twin beds. The food is excellent at Cariblue (the main dining room), the casual buffet restaurant, the deli, or top-of-the-line Tao. ✉ *Cariblue Beach, Cap Estate ⌖ Box 437, Castries ☎ 758/450–8551 ☎ 758/450–0368 ⊕ www.thebodyholiday. com ⇨ 152 rooms, 2 suites ⌂ 3 restaurants, deli, refrigerators, golf privileges, putting green, tennis court, 3 pools, gym, hair salon, health club, spa, beach, dive shop, snorkeling, windsurfing, waterskiing, archery, croquet, hiking, Ping-Pong, volleyball, 2 bars, piano bar, shops, concierge, Internet, airport shuttle; no room TVs. no kids under 16 ▭ AE, DC, MC, V* ⏺ *AI.*

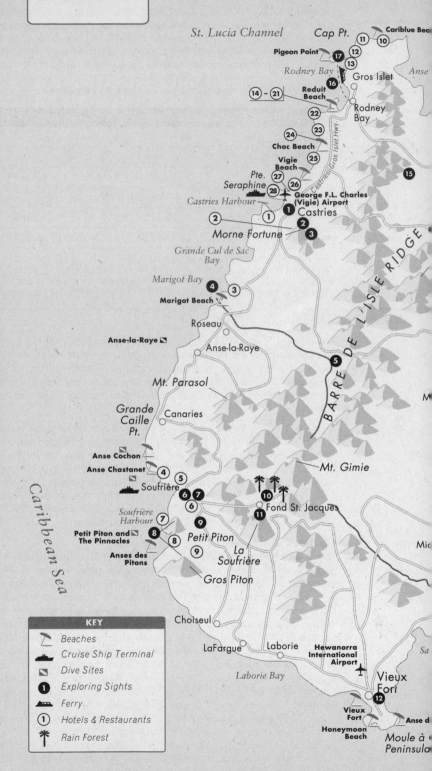

St. Lucia

St. Lucia Channel

Cap Pt.

Cariblue Bea

Pigeon Point

11

10

17

12

13

16

Gros Islet

Anse

Rodney Bay

Reduit
Beach

14 – 21

22

Rodney
Bay

15

23

24

Choc Beach

25

Vigie
Beach

Pte.
Seraphine

27

26

28

George F.L. Charles
(Vigie) Airport

Castries Harbour

1

1

Castries

2

2

3

Morne Fortune

*Grande Cul de Sac
Bay*

Marigot Bay

4

3

Marigot Beach

Roseau

Anse-la-Raye

Anse-la-Raye

5

BARRE DE L'ISLE RIDGE

Mt. Parasol

Grande
Caille
Pt.

Canaries

Anse Cochon

Anse Chastanet

4

5

Mt. Gimie

Soufrière

6

7

10

Fond St. Jacques

6

11

*Soufrière
Harbour*

7

9

Petit Piton and
The Pinnacles

8

8

9

Petit Piton

La
Soufrière

Anses des
Pitons

9

*Caribbean
Sea*

Gros Piton

Choiseul

Mi

LaFargue

Laborie

Hewanorra
International
Airport

Laborie Bay

Sa

Vieux
Fort

12

Vieux
Fort

Anse d

Honeymoon
Beach

Moule à
Peninsula

KEY

↗ *Beaches*

⛴ *Cruise Ship Terminal*

◪ *Dive Sites*

❶ *Exploring Sights*

⛴ *Ferry*

① *Hotels & Restaurants*

✳ *Rain Forest*

ach

avouette

sperance Harbour

Cape
Marquis

A T L A N T I C

Grand Anse
Bay

rande
Anse

a Sorcière

O C E A N

Fond d'or
Bay

nnery

ndéle Pt.

14 *Praslin*
Bay

Vierge
Pt.

ud

nes Bay

Maria Islands

13

ables

ique

0 _____ 4 miles

0 _____ 6 km

$$$$ ▦ **East Winds Inn.** On a private beach 10 minutes north of Castries, 15 gingerbread-style bungalows, each with two guest rooms, are scattered around 8 acres of gardens. Rooms have king-size beds and patios or terraces; deluxe rooms have TVs, VCRs, and indoor-outdoor showers. Mingle at the clubhouse, in the pool with its swim-up bar, on the sundeck, and on the beach—where kayaks, snorkeling gear, and other water-sports equipment are provided. The international and creole creations of a French chef are served in the thatched-roof restaurant, picnic hampers are available for outings, or dine around in the evening at participating restaurants. ⊠ *Labrelotte Bay, Gros Islet* ☏ *Box 1477, Castries* ☎ *758/452-8212* ☐ *758/452-9941* ⊕ *www.eastwinds.com* ⇗ *30 rooms* ♨ *Restaurant, fans, in-room safes, refrigerators, pool, beach, snorkeling, boating, croquet, lawn bowling, shuffleboard, 2 bars, shop, babysitting, dry cleaning, laundry service* ⊟ *AE, MC, V* ◯▮ *AI.*

$$$$ ▦ **Rendezvous.** This all-inclusive resort (for male-female couples only) sprawls along Malabar Beach amid 7 acres of gardens opposite the George F. L. Charles Airport runway. The distraction of prop aircraft taking off at the nearby airport is made up for by the luxurious accommodations. Rooms and suites have marble floors, king-size four-poster beds, large marble baths, and balconies or terraces (some with hammocks) facing the sea. Lounge lazily on the beach or actively participate in a host of land and water sports—your choice. Enjoy buffet-style meals at the beachfront terrace restaurant or fine dining at The Trysting Place. ⊠ *Malabar Beach, Vigie* ☏ *Box 190, Castries* ☎ *758/452-4211* ☐ *758/452-7419* ⊕ *www.rendezvous.com.lc* ⇗ *81 rooms, 11 suites, 8 cottages* ♨ *2 restaurants, fans, 2 tennis courts, 2 pools, health club, massage, beach, dive shop, boating, waterskiing, bicycles, archery, volleyball, 2 bars, piano bar, shops, complimentary weddings, concierge, airport shuttle; no room TVs, no kids* ⊟ *AE, MC, V* ◯▮ *AI.*

$$$$ ▦ **Royal St. Lucian.** This classy resort, facing Reduit Beach, caters to your every whim. The stunning reception area has a vaulted atrium, marble walls, a fountain, and a sweeping grand staircase. The free-form pool has Japanese-style bridges, a waterfall, and a swim-up bar. Sumptuous guest suites have sitting areas, luxurious bathrooms, large patios or balconies, soothing pastel color schemes, and background music systems. Massages, hydrotherapy, and other treatments can be arranged at the Royal Spa. Dine at the elegant Chic!, the sea-view L'Epicure, or two casual restaurants. Tennis and water-sports facilities are shared with the adjacent Rex St. Lucian. ⊠ *Reduit Beach, Rodney Bay* ☏ *Box 977, Castries* ☎ *758/452-9999* ☐ *758/452-9639* ⊕ *www.rexcaribbean.com* ⇗ *96 suites* ♨ *3 restaurants, room service, in-room safes, minibars, golf privileges, 2 tennis courts, pool, health club, spa, beach, dive shop, snorkeling, windsurfing, boating, waterskiing, fishing, 2 bars, shops, babysitting, children's programs (ages 4–12), laundry service, business services, meeting rooms* ⊟ *AE, DC, MC, V* ◯▮ *EP.*

$$$$ ▦ **St. James Club Morgan Bay Resort.** Eight three-story buildings fan out from a central activity area at this all-inclusive resort on 22 landscaped acres along Choc Bay. Rooms, attractively decorated in wicker and tropical pastel florals, have comfortable king-size beds and marble bathrooms. Each room has a verandah or balcony with either a garden or partial sea view. Two open-air restaurants offer informal buffet meals or à la carte French Caribbean cuisine. There's plenty to do—whether you look forward to the early morning fitness classes and daily watersports activities or prefer to relax under a palm tree and anticipate the nightly entertainment. ⊠ *Choc Bay, Gros Islet* ☏ *Box 2167, Castries* ☎ *758/450-2511* ☐ *758/450-1050* ⊕ *www.wyndhamstlucia.com* ⇗ *238 rooms* ♨ *2 restaurants, in-room safes, golf privileges, 4 tennis courts, pool, fitness classes, gym, hot tub, sauna, steam room, beach,* *snorkeling, windsurfing, boating, waterskiing, archery, billiards, Ping-Pong, volleyball, 2 bars, recreation room, shops, baby-sitting, children's programs (ages 5–12), dry cleaning, laundry service, concierge, meeting rooms, airport shuttle, car rental* ⊟ *AE, D, MC, V* ⫯◯⫯ *AI.*

$$$$ ⊞ **Sandals Grande St. Lucian Spa & Beach Resort.** Perched on the narrow Pigeon Island Causeway at St. Lucia's northern tip, the newest Sandals property (for male-female couples only) offers panoramic views of Rodney Bay on one side and the Atlantic on the other. Luxurious accommodations, decorated with colorful fabrics and mahogany furniture, all have king-size beds; 24 lagoon-side rooms have swim-up verandahs. With a plethora of land and water sports, a European-style full-service spa (additional cost), five excellent restaurants, nightly entertainment, and romance in the air, there's never a dull moment. Yet a shuttle service operates between St. Lucia's three Sandals for additional fun with full exchange privileges. ⊠ *Pigeon Island Causeway, Gros Islet* ⫯ *Box 2247, Gros Islet* ☎ *758/455–2000* ⊞ *758/455–2001* ⊕ *www.sandals. com* ⫯ *271 rooms, 11 suites* ⫯ *5 restaurants, room service, fans, in-room dataports, in-room safes, golf privileges, 2 tennis courts, 5 pools, fitness classes, hair salon, health club, spa, beach, dive shop, snorkeling, windsurfing, boating, basketball, billiards, croquet, horseshoes, Ping-Pong, shuffleboard, volleyball, 4 bars, nightclub, recreation room, shops, complimentary weddings, dry cleaning, laundry service, concierge floor, Internet, business services, meeting rooms, airport shuttle, car rental; no kids* ⊟ *AE, D, DC, MC, V* ⫯◯⫯ *AI.*

$$$$ ⊞ **Sandals Halcyon St. Lucia.** This beachfront resort (for male-female couples only) is 10 minutes north of Castries and a bit more low-key than its two sister resorts on St. Lucia. Rooms are surrounded by gardens and have king-size mahogany four-poster beds with colorful spreads. You can enjoy water sports, working out in the gym, nightly entertainment, and more. A shuttle runs hourly between the three Sandals resorts, so you can "stay at one, play at three." That also means a choice of dining at a dozen restaurants—including Halcyon's own picturesque seafood restaurant, The Pier. Seaside weddings are frequent. ⊠ *Choc Bay* ⫯ *Box GM 910, Castries* ☎ *758/453–0222 or 800/223–6510* ⊞ *758/451–8435* ⊕ *www.sandals.com* ⫯ *170 rooms* ⫯ *3 restaurants, snack bar, golf privileges, 2 tennis courts, 3 pools, gym, hair salon, beach, snorkeling, windsurfing, boating, waterskiing, basketball, billiards, croquet, horseshoes, Ping-Pong, shuffleboard, volleyball, 2 bars, nightclub, complimentary weddings, meeting rooms, airport shuttle; no kids* ⊟ *AE, DC, MC, V* ⫯◯⫯ *AI.*

$$$$ ⊞ **Sandals St. Lucia Golf Resort & Spa.** This expansive and colorful resort (for male-female couples only) covers a steep hillside overlooking the sea south of Castries. Guest rooms are lavishly decorated with rich mahogany furniture, king-size four-poster beds, and colorful fabrics. Many have private plunge pools. The main pool, with its waterfall and bridges, and a long crescent beach are focal points for socializing and water sports. Massages (single or duet), scrubs, and wraps are available at the full-service spa (for an additional charge). Six restaurants serve Asian, Continental, French, Mediterranean, Southwestern, or Caribbean cuisine. A free shuttle transports guests between the three Sandals properties. ⊠ *La Toc Rd., Castries* ⫯ *Box 399* ☎ *758/452–3081* ⊞ *758/453–7089* ⊕ *www.sandals.com* ⫯ *212 rooms, 116 suites* ⫯ *6 restaurants, room service, in-room safes, 9-hole golf course, 5 tennis courts, 3 pools, gym, hair salon, 2 hot tubs, sauna, spa, beach, dive shop, snorkeling, windsurfing, boating, waterskiing, basketball, billiards, boccie, croquet, horseshoes, Ping-Pong, shuffleboard, volleyball, 9 bars, nightclub, recreation room, shops, complimentary weddings, laundry service, concierge* floor, *Internet, business services, meeting rooms, airport shuttle; no kids* ▤ *AE, DC, MC, V* ¶ *AI.*

$$$ ▦ **Club St. Lucia by Splash.** This sprawling family resort has a village concept. Rooms and suites are in color-coordinated buildings on the hillside; each village has its own concierge, or "mayor." Guests enjoy free use of the adjacent St. Lucia Racquet Club and golf privileges nearby. Children's activities are grouped by age, starting at 6 months. The Jump Club for teenagers has a roller-blade track and an e-mail system for keeping in touch with parents. Live entertainment is scheduled nightly. In addition to on-site dining and all-day snacks at poolside food carts, resort guests receive a discount at the Great House restaurant. ⊠ *Cap Estate* ⌖ *Box 915, Gros Islet* ☎ *758/450–0551* ⌨ *758/450–0281* ⊕ *www.splashresorts.com* ↝ *297 rooms, 72 suites* ⚗ *5 restaurants, pizzeria, golf privileges, 9 tennis courts, 5 pools, gym, hair salon, health club, hot tub, spa, beach, snorkeling, windsurfing, boating, waterskiing, 5 bars, dance club, nightclub, shops, baby-sitting, children's programs (ages 6 mos–17 yrs), laundry service, concierge, airport shuttle, car rental, travel services* ▤ *AE, DC, MC, V* ¶ *AI.*

$$$ ▦ **Papillon St. Lucia.** The all-inclusive Papillon and the Rex St. Lucian, its sister hotel next door, both spill onto lovely Reduit Beach. Rooms are furnished with rattan furniture, tile floors, and tropical-print fabrics in blue and peach. Beachfront rooms have full baths, sitting areas, minibars, and ocean views; rooms with garden or ocean views have a shower only. The pool is shaped like a butterfly (*papillon*). Meals are served at the Monarch, the main restaurant, or the Clipper Bar, the informal beachside snack bar. Evening entertainment is presented at Tropigala lounge. ⊠ *Reduit Beach, Rodney Bay* ⌖ *Box 512, Castries* ☎ *758/452–0984* ⌨ *758/452–9332* ⊕ *www.rexcaribbean.com* ↝ *140 rooms* ⚗ *Restaurant, snack bar, in-room safes, golf privileges, 2 tennis courts, pool, gym, beach, snorkeling, windsurfing, boating, waterskiing, shuffleboard, volleyball, bar, shop, baby-sitting, children's programs (ages 4–12), laundry service* ▤ *AE, DC, MC, V* ¶ *AI.*

$$–$$$ ▦ **Windjammer Landing Villa Beach Resort.** White-stucco villas crowned with tile roofs climb the sun-kissed hillside on one of St. Lucia's prettiest bays. The reception area opens to shops, restaurants, and two pools. Huge, stylishly decorated villas have tile floors and wicker furniture loaded with richly colored pillows. Two- and three-bedroom villas have plunge pools. Eat in the restaurants, make your own meals, or have dinner prepared and served in your villa. Shuttles whoosh you between villas and activity areas—including two hillside pools connected by a waterfall. Perfect for families or for a romantic getaway, there's lots to do yet plenty of privacy. ⊠ *Labrelotte Bay* ⌖ *Box 1504, Castries* ☎ *758/452–0913* ⌨ *758/452–9454* ⊕ *www.windjammer-landing.com* ↝ *131 villas* ⚗ *3 restaurants, grocery, room service, fans, in-room safes, some kitchens, 2 tennis courts, 2 pools, gym, hair salon, massage, beach, dive shop, snorkeling, windsurfing, boating, waterskiing, 3 bars, shops, children's programs (ages 4–12), laundry service, concierge, car rental* ▤ *AE, MC, V* ¶ *EP.*

$$ ▦ **Rex St. Lucian.** A broad lobby leads to 10 acres of gardens, a pool, and beautiful Reduit Beach. Rooms, each with a patio or balcony, are decorated in rattan and tropical prints. Deluxe rooms have one king-size bed or two twin beds, full baths, sitting areas, and ocean views. Garden-view rooms are similar but smaller. Poolside rooms have showers only and no TV. Water sports—including swimming, scuba diving, boating, and fishing—are a major attraction. You can also book spa treatments at the sister Royal St. Lucian resort. Enjoy dining at the Oriental restaurant or stroll to any of several area restaurants and nightspots. ⊠ *Reduit Beach, Rodney Bay* ⌖ *Box 512, Castries* ☎ *758/452–8351,*

800/255–5859, or 800/223–9868 🖷 *758/452–8331* ⊕ *www. rexcaribbean.com* 📨 *120 rooms ♨ 2 restaurants, minibars, golf privileges, 2 tennis courts, pool, beach, dive shop, snorkeling, windsurfing, boating, waterskiing, bar, shops, baby-sitting, children's programs (ages 4–12), laundry service, business services, meeting rooms; no TV in some rooms* 🖃 *AE, DC, MC, V* 🍽 *EP.*

\$
FodorśChoice
★

🖭 **Auberge Seraphine.** This small, elegant inn overlooking Vigie Cove is minutes from George F. L. Charles Airport, Pointe Seraphine, and downtown Castries. Popular among business travelers, it's also a good choice for vacationers who don't require a beachfront location or the breadth of activities found at a resort. Accommodations are spacious, cheerful, and bright. Most have a view of the nearby marina. A broad tiled sundeck, the center of activity, surrounds a small pool. A shuttle service transports you to and from a nearby beach. The popular restaurant offers fine Caribbean, French, and Continental cuisine and a well-stocked wine cellar. ⊠ *Vigie Cove* 🕮 *Box 390, Castries* ☎ *758/453–2073* 🖷 *758/451–7001* ⊕ *www.aubergeseraphine.com* 📨 *22 rooms ♨ Restaurant, pool, bar, shop, meeting room* 🖃 *AE, MC, V* 🍽 *EP.*

\$

🖭 **Bay Gardens.** This boutique inn at Rodney Bay—near beautiful Reduit Beach, several popular restaurants, and shops at Rodney Bay Marina—is a favorite of vacationers and regional business travelers alike. Modern and colorful, the lime-green building is surrounded by flower gardens. Rooms encircle a courtyard with a serpentine pool and Jacuzzi. All are furnished with white wicker furniture and king or twin beds with colorful print spreads in tropical colors. Executive suites are larger, with double or king-size beds, sitting areas, and kitchenettes. Spices restaurant offers a varied menu, along with a weekly barbecue, Caribbean buffet, and Sunday brunch. ⊠ *Rodney Bay* 🕮 *Box 1892, Castries* ☎ *758/ 452–8060* 🖷 *758/452–8059* ⊕ *www.baygardenshotel.com* 📨 *59 rooms, 12 suites ♨ Restaurant, ice cream parlor, fans, some in-room data ports, in-room safes, some kitchenettes, minibars, refrigerators, 2 pools, hair salon, hot tub, 2 bars, library, recreation room, shops, business services, meeting rooms* 🖃 *AE, MC, V* 🍽 *EP.*

Soufrière

\$\$\$\$
FodorśChoice
★

🖭 **Anse Chastanet Beach Hotel.** Spectacular hillside rooms blend into the mountainside, with entire walls that are open to stunning vistas. Each deluxe room has a balcony, tile floor with straw mats, madras cotton fabrics, handmade wooden furniture, and impressive artwork. Other rooms are octagonal gazebos or beachfront cottages, all with similar decor but less drama. This place is magical, as long as you're fit to climb the 100 steps from the beach to the Pitons Restaurant and Bar, followed by another steep climb to most rooms. Diving is a premier draw here. So is lunch at the picturesque Trou au Diable beach restaurant. ⊠ *Anse Chastanet* 🕮 *Box 7000, Soufrière* ☎ *758/459–7000* 🖷 *758/459–7700* ⊕ *www.ansechastanet.com* 📨 *49 rooms ♨ 2 restaurants, fans, in-room safes, refrigerators, tennis court, gym, spa, beach, dive shop, snorkeling, windsurfing, boating, bicycles, mountain bikes, hiking, 2 bars, shops, airport shuttle, car rental; no a/c, no room phones, no room TVs* 🖃 *AE, DC, MC, V* 🍽 *MAP.*

★ \$\$\$\$

🖭 **Jalousie Hilton Resort & Spa.** Built on the remains of an 18th-century sugar plantation 2 mi (3 km) south of Soufrière, the hillside villas are all but hidden by lush foliage. Sugar Mill rooms are large, luxurious, and close to the beach. Villas have elegant furnishings, king-size beds, and huge bathrooms; villa suites also have sitting rooms and plunge pools. Shuttle service transports you around the grounds, a blessing given the steep hillside. Meals range from fine dining to a beach buffet. The spa offers outdoor massage, aromatherapy, and beauty treatments; there are also fitness classes, weight-training sessions, and exercise classes. The views here are perhaps the most dramatic in all of St. Lucia. ⊠ *Anse des Pitons* ⌖ *Box 251, Soufrière* ☎ *758/459–7666* 🖷 *758/459–7667* ⊕ *www.jalousie-hilton.com* ⟿ *12 rooms, 65 villas, 35 villa suites* ♧ *4 restaurants, room service, fans, in-room data ports, in-room safes, minibars, in-room VCRs, 3-hole golf course, putting green, 4 tennis courts, pool, fitness classes, hair salon, health club, spa, beach, dive shop, dock, snorkeling, windsurfing, boating, marina, waterskiing, fishing, basketball, billiards, hiking, racquetball, squash, 4 bars, nightclub, shops, baby-sitting, children's programs (ages 5–17), business services, meeting rooms, airport shuttle, car rental, helipad, no-smoking rooms* 🖃 *AE, D, DC, MC, V* ⊌*OI EP.*

★ **$$$$** 🏨 **Ladera.** Nestled high in the mountains, Ladera is one of the most sophisticated small inns in the Caribbean. Each suite or villa is furnished with French colonial antiques and local crafts and has a dazzling view. Villas have private pools fed by waterfalls; eight suites have plunge pools. Dasheene is one of St. Lucia's best restaurants—with a spectacular view of the Pitons. The inn provides shuttle service to Soufrière and nearby beaches and will arrange diving and other activities. Though children 8–15 stay free when sharing a room with an adult, the resort is unsuitable for really young children. ⊠ *2 mi (3 km) south of Soufrière* ⌖ *Box 225, Soufrière* ☎ *758/459–7323, 800/223–9868, or 800/738–4752* 🖷 *758/459–5156* ⊕ *www.ladera-stlucia.com* ⟿ *18 suites, 6 villas* ♧ *Restaurant, pool, 2 bars, refrigerators, library, shops, airport shuttle; no a/c, no room TVs* 🖃 *AE, MC, V* ⊌*OI EP.*

$$ 🏨 **Stonefield Estate Villa Resort.** A plantation house and several quaint cottages (with one, two, or three bedrooms) dot this former cocoa plantation at the base of Petit Piton, just a mile south of town. Accommodations all have antique furniture, including some four-poster beds, and one or two bathrooms—some with outdoor garden showers. Living/dining rooms open onto verandahs with double hammocks and panoramic views of the Pitons and the sea, perfectly romantic at sunset. A nature trail leads to ancient petroglyphs and palm-lined Malgretoute Beach. A complimentary shuttle takes guests to town or to Jalousie Hilton's beach, which offers snorkeling, windsurfing, and scuba diving. ⊠ *1 mi south of Soufrière* ⌖ *Box 228, Soufrière* ☎ *758/459–5648 or 758/459–7037* 🖷 *758/459–5550* ⊕ *www.stonefieldvillas.com* ⟿ *12 villas* ♧ *Restaurant, fans, in-room safes, kitchens, refrigerators, pool, massage, beach, snorkeling, hiking, bar, baby-sitting, laundry service, car rental; no a/c, no phones in some rooms, no room TVs* 🖃 *AE, MC, V* ⊌*OI EP.*

$–$$ 🏨 **Hummingbird Beach Resort.** This delightful little inn is on Soufrière Harbour. Rooms are in small seaside cabins; most have magnificent views of the Pitons. Rooms are simple—a primitive motif emphasized by African wood sculptures. Four rooms have mahogany four-poster beds hung with sheer mosquito netting. Most rooms have modern baths; two rooms and a suite share a bath. The two-bedroom country cottage—with a sitting room, kitchenette, and spectacular Piton view—is suitable for a family or two couples vacationing together. The Hummingbird Restaurant is a favorite lunch stop for locals and visitors touring Soufrière. ⊠ *Anse Chastanet Rd., Soufrière* ⌖ *Box 280* ☎ *758/459–7232 or 800/223–9815* 🖷 *758/459–7033* ⊕ *www.nvo.com/pitonresort* ⟿ *9 rooms (7 with private bath), 1 suite, 1 cottage* ♧ *Restaurant, pool, beach, bar, shops; no a/c in some rooms, no room TVs* 🖃 *D, MC, V* ⊌*OI EP.*

¢–$ 🏨 **Still Plantation & Beach Resort.** The simple, inexpensive studios and one- or two-bedroom apartments with sitting rooms and kitchenettes at Still Plantation are a five-minute walk from the waterfront. There are a swimming pool, a boutique, and the Still restaurant, well known for its Caribbean cuisine. The separate Still Beach Resort is also simple and inexpensive, with three small one-bedroom apartments and two studios; all share a verandah with a partial sea view. If you prefer hiking and nature walks, choose the Plantation; if you prefer sand and sea, choose the Beach Resort. A stay at one allows you to use the facilities of the other. ⊠ *Lewis St. and Anse Chastanet Rd., Soufrière* ☎ *Box 246* ☎ *758/459–7224 or 800/223–9815* ☎ *758/459–7301* ⊕ *www.thestillresort.com* ⇆ *13 apartments, 6 studios* ♨ *2 restaurants, some kitchenettes, pool, beach, 2 bars, shops, laundry service; no a/c in some rooms, no room TVs* ☰ *MC, V* ⊚ *EP.*

Where to Eat

Mangoes, plantains, breadfruit, avocados, limes, pumpkins, cucumbers, papaya, yams, christophenes (a squash-like vegetable), and coconuts are among the fresh local produce that graces St. Lucian menus. The French influence is strong, and most chefs cook with a creole flair. Resort buffets and restaurant fare run the gamut, from steaks and chops to pasta and pizza. Every menu lists fresh fish along with the ever-popular lobster. Caribbean standards include callaloo, stuffed crab back, pepper-pot stew, curried chicken or goat, and *lambi* (conch). The national dish of salt fish and green fig—a stew of dried, salted codfish and boiled green banana—is, let's say, an acquired taste. Soups and stews are traditionally prepared in a coal pot, a rustic clay casserole on a matching clay stand that holds the hot coals. Chicken and pork dishes and barbecues are also popular here. As they do throughout the Caribbean, local vendors who set up barbecues along the roadside, at street fairs, and at Friday night "jump ups," do a land-office business selling grilled chicken legs, bakes (biscuits), and beer—all for about $5. Most other meats are imported—beef from Argentina and Iowa, lamb from New Zealand. Piton is the local brew, Bounty the local rum.

With so many all-inclusive resorts, guests take most meals at hotel restaurants—which are generally quite good and, in some cases, exceptional. It's fun when vacationing, however, to try some of the local restaurants, as well—for lunch when sightseeing or for a special night out.

What to Wear
Dress on St. Lucia is casual but conservative. Shorts are usually fine during the day, but bathing suits and immodest clothing are frowned on anywhere but at the beach. In the evening the mood is casually elegant, but even the fanciest places generally expect only a collared shirt and long pants for men and a sundress or slacks for women.

Castries & the North

CARIBBEAN ✕ **J. J.'s Paradise.** Not only are the prices right, but the local fare is among
$ the best on the island. Superbly grilled fish with fresh vegetables gets top honors. The welcome is friendly, and the atmosphere is casual. Wednesday is Seafood Night, when owner-chef J. J. prepares an enormous selection of local fish and shellfish. On Friday night the music blares and the locals come to lime (hang out), eat barbecue, and dance the night away. ⊠ *Marigot Bay Rd., Marigot* ☎ *758/451–4076* ☰ *No credit cards.*

CREOLE ✕ **La Creole, The French Restaurant.** French West Indian cuisine—direct
$–$$ from St. Lucia's neighbor island Martinique—is the specialty at this Rodney Bay establishment. Choices include wonderful pumpkin or fish soup to start; curried goat, conch, fresh lobster that you select from the tank; and exotic seafood such as octopus and shark. Everything is

served with a hot, spicy sauce, but a delicious French pastry or homemade ice cream will quell the fire on your tongue. A creole buffet is the special at lunch. ✉ *Rodney Bay* ☎ *758/450–0022* ▭ *D, MC, V* ⊙ *Closed Tues.*

ECLECTIC $$ ✕ **Green Parrot.** Atop the Morne, acclaimed Chef Harry Edwards prepares a menu of West Indian, creole, and international dishes. There's lively entertainment—a floor show with a belly dancer on Wednesday night and limbo dancing on Saturday—but the best reasons to dine here are the seafood specialties and the romantic view of the twinkling lights in Castries and the harbor. On Monday night, if a lady wears a flower in her hair and is accompanied by a "well-dressed" gentleman, she might receive a free dinner. ✉ *Morne Fortune, Castries* ☎ *758/452–3399* ✍ *Reservations essential* *Jacket required* ▭ *AE, MC, V.*

¢–$$ ✕ **The Lime.** A casual bistro with lime-green gingham curtains, straw hats decorating the ceiling, and hanging plants, the Lime specializes in chargrilled steaks and fresh-caught fish, along with spicy jerk chicken or pork. The meals are well prepared, the portions are plentiful, and the prices are reasonable, which is perhaps why you often see St. Lucians and visitors alike "liming" at this popular all-day (and most of the night) restaurant. The Late Lime, a club where the crowd gathers as night turns to morning, is next door. ✉ *Rodney Bay* ☎ *758/452–0761* ▭ *MC, V.*

FRENCH ★ $$$ ✕ **Great House.** Elegant, gracious, and romantic, the Great House was reconstructed on the foundation of the original Cap Estate plantation house. The grandeur of those early days has been revived as well. The waitstaff wear traditional St. Lucian costumes. The chef adds a piquant creole touch to traditional French cuisine. The menu, which changes nightly, might include pumpkin-and-potato soup, local crab back with lime vinaigrette, sautéed Antillean shrimp in a creole sauce, and broiled sirloin with thyme butter and sweet-potato chips. Cocktails at the open-air bar are especially enjoyable at sunset. The Derek Walcott Theatre is next door. ✉ *Cap Estate* ☎ *758/450–0450 or 758/450–0211* ✍ *Reservations essential* ▭ *AE, DC, MC, V* ⊙ *No lunch.*

★ $$ ✕ **The Coal Pot.** Popular since the early 1960s, this tiny waterfront restaurant (only 10 tables) is managed by Michelle Elliott, daughter of the original owner, and her French husband, Chef Xavier. For a light lunch opt for Greek or shrimp salad, or broiled fresh fish with creole sauce. Dinner might start with divine pumpkin soup, followed by fresh seafood accompanied by one (or more) of the chef's fabulous sauces—ginger, coconut-curry, lemon–garlic butter, or wild mushroom. Hearty eaters may prefer duck, lamb, beef, or chicken laced with peppercorns, red wine, and onion or Roquefort sauce. ✉ *Vigie Marina, Castries* ☎ *758/452–5566* ✍ *Reservations essential* ▭ *AE, D, MC, V* ⊙ *Closed Sun. No lunch Sat.*

ITALIAN $–$$ ✕ **Capone's.** The French chef at this two-in-one restaurant lends a Gallic twist and Caribbean spice to some of your favorite Italian dishes. Paper-thin carpaccio is drizzled with olive oil and lime before being treated to shavings of Parmesan cheese. Polenta and local vegetables accompany delicate slices of calves' liver that have been gently sautéed with onions. And fresh Caribbean snapper is blessed with ginger and rum en route to your plate. The extensive menu includes pasta dishes, seafood, and Black Angus beef. At the adjacent La Piazza, diners enjoy casual meals of burgers, sandwiches, and pizza from noon to midnight. ✉ *Rodney Bay, across from St. Lucian hotel* ☎ *758/452–0284* ▭ *AE, MC, V* ⊙ *Closed Mon.*

¢–$ ✕ **Key Largo.** Gourmet pizzas baked in a wood-fired oven and a long list of pasta dishes are the specialties at this casual eatery near Rodney Bay's many hotels. You're welcome to stop in for an espresso or cappuccino, but the popular Pizza Key Largo—topped with shrimp, artichokes, and what seems like a few pounds of mozzarella—is tough to pass up. Kids love Key Largo, too. ⊠ *Rodney Heights* ☎ *758/452–0282* ⊟ *MC, V.*

PAN-ASIAN
★ $$$

✕ **Tao.** For exquisite dining, this small restaurant at The Body Holiday at LeSPORT welcomes nonguests. Perched on a second-floor balcony at the edge of Cariblue Beach, you're guaranteed a pleasant breeze and a starry sky while you enjoy fusion cuisine—a marriage of Asian tastes (borrowed from China, Japan, Indonesia, the Philippines) with a Caribbean touch. Tender slices of pork loin satay accompanied by *nasi goreng* rice, scallops steamed in rice paper, hibachi-grilled strip steak—the choices are mouthwatering. Fine wines accompany the meal, desserts are extravagant, and service is superb. Seating is limited since hotel guests have priority. ⊠ *Cap Estate* ☎ *758/450–8551* ⚓ *Reservations essential* ⊟ *AE, DC, MC, V* ☺ *No lunch.*

Soufrière

CARIBBEAN
$–$$

✕ **The Hummingbird.** The chef at this cheerful restaurant-bar in the Hummingbird Beach Resort specializes in French creole cuisine, starting with fresh seafood or chicken seasoned with local herbs and accompanied by a medley of vegetables just picked from the Hummingbird's garden. Sandwiches and salads are also available. If you stop for lunch, be sure to visit the batik studio and art gallery of proprietor Joan Alexander and her son, adjacent to the dining room. ⊠ *Hummingbird Beach Resort, Anse Chastanet Rd., Soufrière* ☎ *758/459–7232* ⊟ *AE, D, MC, V.*

$–$$

✕ **The Still.** If you're visiting Diamond Waterfall, this is a good lunch spot. The two dining rooms of the Still Plantation & Beach Resort seat up to 400 people, so it's a popular stop for tour groups and cruise passengers. The emphasis is on creole cuisine using local vegetables—christophenes, breadfruits, yams, callaloo—and seafood, but there are also pork and beef dishes. All fruits and vegetables used in the restaurant are organically grown on the estate. ⊠ *Still Plantation & Beach Resort, Bay St., Soufrière* ☎ *758/459–7232* ⊟ *MC, V.*

¢–$

✕ **Trou au Diable at Anse Chastanet.** Just 1 mi (1½ km) north of Soufrière, this beach restaurant is the perfect place to take a lunch break after diving, boating, touring, or sunbathing. The West Indian cuisine is delicious; many specialties are grilled right before your eyes. Outstanding *rotis* (turnovers filled with curried meat and/or vegetables) are served with homemade mango chutney you could eat by the jar. Try the pepper pot—pork, beef, or lamb stewed for hours with local veggies and spices—or have a tuna melt if you're homesick. Stick around for the beach barbecue and creole buffet Tuesday and Friday evenings. ⊠ *Anse Chastanet Beach Hotel, Anse Chastanet* ☎ *758/459–7000* ⊟ *AE, DC, MC, V.*

CONTEMPORARY
$$$
Fodor'sChoice
★

✕ **Dasheene Restaurant and Bar.** The terrace restaurant at Ladera Resort has breathtaking close-up views of the Pitons and the sea between them, especially at sunset. Casual by day and magical at night, the restaurant offers a creative menu best described as nouvelle Caribbean. Appetizers may include smoked kingfish crêpes and spicy seafood gazpacho. Typical entrées are shrimps Dasheene, pan-fried with peppers and herbs, or poulet supreme Ladera, stuffed with seafood and served on a green-banana risotto. Light dishes, salads, and sandwiches are served at lunchtime. ⊠ *Ladera Resort, 2 mi (3 km) south of Soufrière* ☎ *758/459–7323* ⊟ *AE, DC, MC, V.*

Beaches

Beaches are all public, but many of those north of Castries are flanked by hotels. A few secluded stretches of beach on the west coast south of Marigot Bay are accessible only by boat and are a popular stop on catamaran or powerboat sightseeing trips. Don't swim along the windward (east) coast, as the Atlantic Ocean is too rough—but the views are spectacular.

Anse Chastanet. In front of the resort of the same name, just north of Soufrière, this palm-studded dark-sand beach has a backdrop of green hills, brightly painted fishing skiffs bobbing at anchor, and the island's best reefs for snorkeling and diving. The resort's wooden gazebos are nestled among the palms; its dive shop, restaurant, and bar are on the beach and open to the public.

Anse Cochon. This remote black-sand beach 3 mi (5 km) south of Marigot Bay is accessible only by boat. The waters and adjacent reef are superb for swimming, diving, and snorkeling, but there are no facilities.

Anse des Pitons. South of Soufrière, between the Pitons on Jalousie Bay, is a crescent of white sand that was imported by Jalousie Hilton Resort and spread over the natural black sand. Accessible from the resort or by boat, the beach offers good snorkeling, diving, and a magnificent location.

Anse de Sables. At Vieux Fort, on the southeastern tip of St. Lucia, is a long stretch of white sand with crystal-clear waters protected by reefs.

Choc Beach. In the north, just below Rodney Bay, this beach is easily accessible from the road.

Marigot Beach. Calm waters rippled only by passing yachts lap the finger of sand studded with palm trees at Marigot Bay; dive trips can be arranged nearby, and refreshments are available at adjacent restaurants.

Pigeon Point. At this small beach within Pigeon Island National Historic Park, a restaurant serves snacks and drinks, but this is also a perfect spot for picnicking.

Reduit Beach. This long stretch of golden sand is next to Rodney Bay. The Rex St. Lucian Hotel, which faces the beach, has a water-sports center. Many feel that Reduit (pronounced red-*wee*) is the island's finest beach.

Vigie Beach. This 2-mi (3-km) stretch of white sand runs parallel to the George F. L. Charles Airport runway, in Castries, and continues on to become Malabar Beach, the beachfront for the Rendezvous resort.

Sports & the Outdoors

BOATING &
SAILING

Rodney Bay and Marigot Bay are centers for bareboat and crewed yacht charters. Their marinas offer safe anchorage, shower facilities, restaurants, groceries, and maintenance for yachts sailing the waters of the eastern Caribbean. **Destination St. Lucia (DSL) Ltd.** (✉ Rodney Bay Marina, Gros Islet ☎ 758/452–8531) offers bareboat yacht charters; vessels range in length from 38 ft to 51 ft. The **Moorings Yacht Charters** (✉ Marigot Bay ☎ 758/451–4357 or 800/535–7289) rents bareboat or crewed yachts ranging from Beneteau 39s to Morgan 60s.

CAMPING

Bay of Freedom Camp Site (☎ 758/452–5005 or 758/454–5014), St. Lucia's only campsite, is 133 acres of sloping terrain at Anse La Liberté (French for "Bay of Freedom"), on the west coast near the village of Canaries—accessible by boat or by car (a 45-minute drive south from Castries or 15 minutes north from Soufrière). Rough campsites and platforms for tents are available, along with communal toilets and showers, a cooking center, a small secluded beach, and 4 mi of hiking trails. Camping fees are inexpensive, and reservations are required. The facility is on one of the many sites where former slaves celebrated their emancipation in 1834; it is administered by the St. Lucia National Trust.

CRICKET & SOCCER Cricket and soccer—both national pastimes—are played at Mindoo Philip Park in Marchand, 2 mi (3 km) east of Castries. Contact the tourist board for details on schedules and tickets.

FISHING Among the deep-sea creatures you can find in St. Lucia's waters are dolphinfish (dorado), barracuda, mackerel, wahoo, kingfish, sailfish, and white or blue marlin. Sportfishing is generally done on a catch-and-release basis, but the captain may permit you to take a fish back to your hotel to be prepared for your dinner. Neither spearfishing nor collecting live fish in coastal waters is permitted. Half- or full-day deep-sea fishing excursions can be arranged at either Vigie Cove or Rodney Bay Marina. A half-day of fishing on a scheduled trip runs about $80 per person. Beginners are welcome. **Captain Mike's** (⊠ Vigie Cove ☎ 758/452–1216 or 758/452–7044) has a fleet of Bertram fishing boats (up to 38-ft long) that accommodate as many as eight passengers; all equipment and cold drinks are supplied. **Mako Watersports** (⊠ Rodney Bay Marina, Rodney Bay ☎ 758/452–0412) takes fishing enthusiasts out on the well-equipped six-passenger *Annie Baby.*

GOLF Courses on St. Lucia are scenic and enjoyable, but they're not championship quality. **St. Lucia Golf and Country Club** (⊠ Cap Estate ☎ 758/452–8523), the island's only public course, is at the island's northern tip and offers panoramic views of both the Atlantic and Caribbean. It's an 18-hole course (6,829 yards, par 72). The clubhouse has a bar and a pro shop where you can rent clubs and shoes and arrange lessons. Greens fees are $70 for nine holes or $95 for 18 holes; carts are included. Reservations are essential.

HIKING The island is laced with trails, but you shouldn't attempt the challenging peaks on your own. The **St. Lucia Forestry Department** (☎ 758/450–2231) manages trails throughout the rain forest and provides guides who explain the plants and trees you'll encounter and keep you on the right track for a small fee—about $10 per person. The **St. Lucia National Trust** (☎ 758/452–5005) maintains two trails: one is at Anse La Liberté, near Canaries on the Caribbean coast; the other is on the Atlantic coast, from Mandélé Point to the Fregate Islands Nature Reserve. Full-day excursions with lunch cost about $50–$60 per person and can be arranged through hotels or tour operators.

HORSEBACK RIDING Creole horses, an indigenous breed, are fairly small, fast, sturdy, and even-tempered animals suitable for beginners. Established stables can accommodate all skill levels and offer countryside trail rides, beach rides with picnic lunches, plantation tours, carriage rides, and lengthy treks. Prices run about $40 for one hour, $50 for two hours, and $70 for a three-hour beach ride and barbecue. Transportation is usually provided between the stables and nearby hotels. Local people sometimes appear on beaches with their steeds and offer 30-minute rides for $10; ride at your own risk.

Country Saddles (⊠ Marquis Estate, Babonneau ☎ 758/450–5467), 45 minutes east of Castries, guides beginners and advanced riders through banana plantations, forest trails, and along the Atlantic coast. **International Riding Stables** (⊠ Beauséjour Estate, Gros Islet ☎ 758/452–8139 or 758/450–8665) offers either English- or western-style riding. Their beach-picnic ride includes time for a swim—with or without your horse. **Trim's National Riding Stable** (⊠ Cas-en-Bas, Gros Islet ☎ 758/452–8273 or 758/450–9971), the island's oldest establishment, offers four riding sessions per day, plus beach tours, trail rides, and carriage tours to Pigeon Island.

Anse Chastanet, near the Pitons on the southwest coast, is the best beach-entry dive site. The underwater reef drops off from 20 ft to nearly 140 ft in a stunning coral wall. A 165-ft freighter, *Lesleen M,* was deliberately sunk in 60 ft of water near **Anse Cochon** to create an artificial reef; divers can explore the ship in its entirety and view huge gorgonians, black coral trees, gigantic barrel sponges, lace corals, schooling fish, angelfish, sea horses, spotted eels, stingrays, nurse sharks, and sea turtles. **Anse-La-Raye,** midway up the west coast, is one of St. Lucia's finest wall and drift dives and a great place for snorkeling. At the base of the **Petit Piton,** a spectacular wall drops to 200 ft. You can view an impressive collection of huge barrel sponges and black coral trees; strong currents ensure good visibility. At **The Pinnacles,** four coral-encrusted stone piers rise to within 10 ft of the surface.

Depending on the season and the particular trip, prices range from about $40 to $60 for a one-tank dive, $175 to $260 for a 6-dive package over 3 days, and $265 to $450 for a 10-dive package over 5 days. Dive shops provide instruction for all levels (beginner, intermediate, and advanced). For beginners, a resort course (pool training), followed by one open-water dive, runs about $65. Snorkelers are generally welcome on dive trips and usually pay about $25, which includes equipment.

Buddies (✉ Rodney Bay Marina, Rodney Bay ☎ 758/452–9086) offers wall, wreck, reef, and deep dives; resort courses and open-water certification with advanced and specialty courses are taught by PADI-certified instructors. **Dive Fair Helen** (✉ St. James Club Morgan Bay Resort, Choc Bay ☎ 758/450–1640) is a PADI center that offers half-day excursions to wreck, wall, and marine reserve areas, as well as night dives. **Frogs** (✉ Windjammer Landing Villa Beach Resort, Labrelotte Bay ☎ 758/452–0913 ✉ Jalousie Hilton, Anse des Pitons ☎ 758/452–0913 or 758/459–7666 Ext. 4024) provides resort courses and open-water certification. Two-tank and night dives are also offered, and rental equipment is available. **Rosemond's Trench Divers** (✉ Marigot Bay ☎ 758/451–4761) offers PADI training, wreck dives, night dives, and special dive packages for yachties. **Scuba St. Lucia** (✉ Anse Chastanet, Soufrière ☎ 758/459–7755 ✉ Rex St. Lucian Hotel, Rodney Bay ☎ 758/452–8009) is a PADI five-star training facility. Daily beach and boat dives and resort and certification courses are offered; underwater photography and snorkeling equipment are available. Day trips from the north of the island include round-trip speedboat transportation.

A day sail or sea cruise to Soufrière and the Pitons is a wonderful way to see St. Lucia and, perhaps, the perfect way to get to the island's distinctive natural sites. Prices for a full-day sailing excursion to Soufrière run about $70–$85 per person and include a land tour to the Sulphur Springs and the Botanical Gardens, lunch, a stop at Anse Cochon for swimming and snorkeling, and a visit to pretty Marigot Bay. Two-hour sunset cruises along the northwest coast cost about $40 per person. Most boats leave from either Vigie Cove in Castries or Rodney Bay. The 140-ft tall ship *Brig Unicorn* (✉ Vigie Cove, Castries ☎ 758/452–8644), used in the filming of the TV miniseries *Roots,* is a replica of a 19th-century sailing ship. Day trips along the coast are fun for the whole family. Several nights each week a sunset cruise, with drinks and a live steel band, sails to Pigeon Point and back. Customized pleasure trips and snorkeling charters can be arranged for small groups (four to six people) through **Captain Mike's** (✉ Vigie Cove, Castries ☎ 758/452–0216 or 758/452–7044). On *Endless Summer* (✉ Rodney Bay Marina, Rodney Bay ☎ 758/450–8651), a 56-ft "party" catamaran, you can take a day trip to Soufrière or a half-day swimming and snorkeling trip. For romantics, there's a weekly sunset cruise, with dinner and entertainment. *Surf Queen* (⊠ Vigie Cove, Castries ☎ 758/452–8232), a trimaran, runs a fast, sleek sail and has a special tour for German-speaking passengers. From Pigeon Island, north of Rodney Bay, you can take a more intimate cruise to the Pitons aboard the 57-ft luxury cruiser **MV** *Vigie* (☎ 758/452–8232).

TENNIS & SQUASH All large resorts have their own tennis courts; most are lighted for night play and often have pros who offer lessons. People staying at small inns without tennis courts or those who wish to play squash can access a few private facilities for a fee. The **Rex St. Lucian** (⊠ Reduit Beach, Rodney Bay ☎ 758/452–8351) has two tennis courts open to the public at $20 per half hour or $30 per hour; reservations are required. **St. Lucia Racquet Club** (⊠ Club St. Lucia, Cap Estate ☎ 758/450–0106), the site of the St. Lucia Open each December, has seven lighted tennis courts, a pro shop, a restaurant-bar, and a squash court. The club charges $10 per person per hour for use of the facilities; reservations are required. **St. Lucia Yacht Club** (⊠ Rodney Bay ☎ 758/452–8350) has two air-conditioned, wood-floored, glass-backed squash courts; rackets can be rented. The club charges $10 per hour, and you'll need to make reservations. **Windjammer Landing Villa Beach Resort** (⊠ Labrelotte Bay ☎ 758/452–0913) permits nonguests to use its tennis courts for $10 per hour; reservations are required.

WINDSURFING Major resorts generally offer Windsurfers and instruction. Cas-en-Bas, on the northeast coast, and Vieux Fort, at the southeast tip, are the most popular windsurfing locations for advanced and intermediate windsurfers. Reduit Beach, near Rodney Bay, and elsewhere along the calmer west coast are the best areas for beginners. Note that from August to October the wind loses strength island-wide. **Island Windsurfing Ltd.** (⊠ Anse de Sables Beach, Vieux Fort ☎ 758/454–7400) has board rentals and instruction; it's open daily from 10 AM until dusk. The **Rex St. Lucian** (⊠ Reduit Beach, Rodney Bay ☎ 758/452–8351) offers board rentals and instruction to nonguests for a fee.

Shopping

The island's best-known products are artwork and wood carvings; clothing and household articles made from batik and silk-screened fabrics, designed and printed in island workshops; and clay pottery. You can also take home straw hats and baskets and locally grown cocoa, coffee, and spices.

Areas & Malls

Along the harbor in Castries, you can see the rambling structures with bright orange roofs that house several markets, which are open from 6 AM to 5 PM Monday through Saturday. Saturday morning is the busiest and most colorful time to shop. For more than a century, farmers' wives have gathered at the **Castries Market** to sell produce—which, alas, you can't import to the United States. But you can bring back spices (such as cocoa, turmeric, cloves, bay leaves, ginger, peppercorns, cinnamon sticks, nutmeg, mace, and vanilla essence), as well as bottled hot pepper sauces—all of which cost a fraction of what you'd pay back home. The **Craft Market**, adjacent to the produce market, has aisles and aisles of baskets and other handmade straw work, rustic brooms made from palm fronds, wood carvings and leather work, clay pottery, and souvenirs—all at affordable prices. The **Vendor's Arcade**, across the street from the Castries Craft Market, is a maze of stalls and booths where you can find handicrafts among the T-shirts and costume jewelry.

Gablewoods Mall, on the Gros Islet Highway in Choc Bay, a couple of miles north of downtown Castries, has about 35 shops that sell groceries, wines and spirits, jewelry, clothing, crafts, books and foreign newspapers, music, souvenirs, household goods, and snacks. At the grocery or liquor store at Gablewoods, you might pick up a bottle of Bounty Rum, the local firewater made at a distillery in Roseau, just south of Castries. Along with 54 boutiques, restaurants, and other businesses that sell services and supplies, a large supermarket is the focal point of each **J. Q.'s Shopping Mall**; one is at Rodney Bay, and the other is at Vieux Fort. If you're a diehard shopper, be sure to visit **Pointe Seraphine,** an attractive Spanish-motif complex on Castries Harbour with more than 20 shops that sell duty-free goods, clothing, and local artwork. **La Place Carenage,** on the opposite side of the harbor, is also a duty-free shopping complex with some of the same stores as at Pointe Seraphine. The origin of its French name dates back to its waterfront location, where ships were "careened" in order to clean, repair, and paint the bottom of their hulls. What was once an old cargo shed is now two floors of inviting boutiques. A contemporary three-story addition has more shops, an arcade of indigenous products (sauces, jams, and confections), artisan studios, a restaurant, and an interactive Interpretation Centre. **William Peter Boulevard,** the capital's main shopping street, is primarily where locals shop for household goods.

Most shops in **Soufrière** provide goods for local consumption, although you can also find gift shops, boutiques, and studios at local inns and attractions.

Specialty Items

ART **Artsibit Gallery** (✉ Brazil and Mongiraud Sts., Castries ☎ 758/452–7865) exhibits and sells moderately priced pieces by St. Lucian painters and sculptors. **Caribbean Art Gallery** (✉ Rodney Bay Yacht Marina, Rodney Bay ☎ 758/452–8071) sells original artwork by world-renowned local artist Llewellyn Xavier, along with antique maps and prints and hand-painted silk. St. Lucian artist **Llewellyn Xavier** (✉ Cap Estate ☎ 758/450–9155) creates modern art, ranging from vigorous oil abstracts that take up half a wall to small objects made from beaten silver and gold. Much of his work has an environmental theme, created from recycled materials. Xavier's work is on permanent exhibit at major museums in New York and Washington, D.C. Call to arrange a visit. **Modern Art Gallery** (✉ Gros Islet Highway, Bois d'Orange ☎ 758/452–9079) is a home studio, open by appointment only, where you can buy contemporary and avant-garde Caribbean art. **Snooty Agouti** (✉ Rodney Bay ☎ 758/452–0321) sells original Caribbean artwork, wood carvings, prints, and maps; it's adjacent to the bar and restaurant of the same name.

BOOKS & MAGAZINES **Sunshine Bookshop** (✉ Gablewoods Mall, Castries ☎ 758/452–3222) has novels and titles of regional interest, including books by Caribbean authors—among them the works of the St. Lucian Nobel laureate, poet Derek Walcott. You can also find current newspapers and magazines. **Valmont Books** (✉ Corner of Jeremie and Laborie Sts., Castries ☎ 758/452–3817) has West Indian literature and picture books, as well as stationery.

CLOTHES & TEXTILES **Bagshaw Studios** (✉ La Toc Rd., La Toc Bay, Castries ☎ 758/452–2139 or 758/451–9249) sells clothing and table linens in colorful tropical patterns using Stanley Bagshaw's original designs. The fabrics are silk-screened by hand in the adjacent workroom. You can also find Bagshaw boutiques at Pointe Seraphine, La Place Carenage, and Rodney Bay, and a selection of items in gift shops at Hewanorra Airport. to see how Stanley Bagshaw's original tropical designs are turned into colorful silk-screened fabrics, which are fashioned into clothing and household articles that are created and sold on site. Admission is free; it's open weekdays 8:30–5, Saturday 8:30–4, and Sunday 10–1. Weekend hours may be extended if a cruise ship is in port. **Batik Studio** (⊠ Hummingbird Beach Resort, on the bayfront, north of wharf, Soufrière ☎ 758/459–7232) has superb batik sarongs, scarves, and wall panels designed and created on-site by Joan Alexander and her son David. At **Caribelle Batik** (⊠ Howelton House, Morne Fortune, Castries ☎ 758/452–3785), craftsmen demonstrate the art of batik and silk-screen printing. Meanwhile, seamstresses create clothing and wall hangings, which you can purchase in the shop. The studio is in an old Victorian mansion, high atop the Morne overlooking Castries. There's a terrace where you can have a cool drink, and there's a garden full of tropical orchids and lilies. Caribelle Batik creations are featured in many gift shops throughout St. Lucia. **Sea Island Cotton Shop** (⊠ Bridge St., Castries ☎ 758/452–3674 ⊠ Gablewoods Mall, Choc Bay ☎ 758/451–6946 ⊠ J. Q.'s Shopping Mall, Rodney Bay ☎ 758/458–4220) sells quality T-shirts, Caribelle Batik clothing and other resort wear, and colorful souvenirs.

DUTY-FREE GOODS Pointe Seraphine and La Place Carenage in Castries, the arcade at the Rex St. Lucian hotel in Rodney Bay, and Hewanorra International Airport are where duty-free goods are sold. You must present your passport and airline ticket to get the duty-free price. If you can forget for a moment that you're in the tropics, try on beautiful wool sweaters at **Benetton** (⊠ Pointe Seraphine, Castries ☎ 758/452–7685). **Colombian Emeralds** (⊠ Pointe Seraphine, Castries ☎ 758/453–7721 ⊠ La Place Carenage, Castries ☎ 758/452–4288 ⊠ Hewanorra Airport, Vieux Fort ☎ 758/454–7774) has fine-quality gems set in beautiful pieces of jewelry. **Little Switzerland** (⊠ Pointe Seraphine, Castries ☎ 758/452–7587 ⊠ La Place Carenage, Castries ☎ 758/451–6785) specializes in imported china and crystal, jewelry, and leather goods. **Studio Images** (⊠ Pointe Seraphine, Castries ☎ 758/452–6883 ⊠ La Place Carenage, Castries ☎ 758/452–0887 ⊠ Hewanorra Airport, Vieux Fort ☎ 758/454–7884) sells designer fragrances; they also stock watches, cameras, sunglasses, electronics, and gifts.

GIFTS & SOUVENIRS **Caribbean Perfumes** (⊠ Morne Fortune, Castries ☎ 758/453–7249) blends a half-dozen lovely scents for women and two aftershaves for men from exotic flowers, fruits, tropical woods, and spices. Fragrances are all made in St. Lucia, reasonably priced, and available at the perfumery and at many hotel gift shops. **Noah's Arkade** (⊠ Jeremie St., Castries ☎ 758/452–2523 ⊠ Pointe Seraphine, Castries ☎ 758/452–7488) has hammocks, wood carvings, straw mats, T-shirts, books, and other regional goods. Take home a cassette recording or CD by a local band, which you can find at **Sights 'n Sounds** (⊠ 46 Micoud St., Castries ☎ 758/451–9600 ⊠ Gablewoods Mall, Castries ☎ 758/451–7300). The **St. Lucia Philatelic Bureau** supplies collectors and stamp dealers throughout the world with beautiful St. Lucian commemoratives. They can be found in the **General Post Office** (⊠ Bridge St., Castries ☎ 758/452–3774).

HANDICRAFTS On the southwest coast, halfway between Soufrière and Vieux Fort, you can find locally made clay and straw pieces at the **Choiseul Arts & Crafts Centre** (⊠ La Fargue ☎ 758/454–3226). Many of St. Lucia's artisans come from this area. At Marigot Bay, **Cinnamon Batiks** (⊠ Marigot Bay Beach Club, Marigot Bay ☎ 758/451–4974) has colorful handmade batik wall hangings and pillow covers depicting island themes, such as fish, parrots, and flowers, which are reasonably priced. **Eudovic Art Studio** (⊠ Morne Fortune, Castries ☎ 758/452–2747) is a workshop and studio where you can buy trays, masks, and figures sculpted from local mahogany, red cedar, and eucalyptus wood. At **Zaka** (✉ Rodney Bay ☎ 758/452–0946), next to Shamrock's Pub, you can find contemporary Caribbean masks and totems carved from local driftwood and painted in brilliant colors. All pieces are created in a home studio, just down the road, by London-born woodcarver Simon Gajadhar and his wife, St. Lucian artist Sophie Barnard.

Nightlife & the Arts

Nightlife

The large, all-inclusive resort hotels have nightly entertainment—island music, calypso singers, and steel bands, as well as disco, karaoke, and talent shows. Many offer entertainment packages, including dinner, to nonguests. Otherwise, Rodney Bay is the best bet for nightlife. The many restaurants and bars there attract a crowd nearly every night.

BARS The **Captain's Cellar** (✉ Pigeon Island, Rodney Bay ☎ 758/450–0253) is a cozy Old English pub with live jazz on weekends. **Shamrocks Pub** (✉ Rodney Bay ☎ 758/452–8725) is an Irish-style pub with pool tables and darts, lots of beer, and music. **The Wharf** (✉ Choc Bay ☎ 758/450–4844) has a happy hour every evening, followed by live music or karaoke.

DANCE CLUBS Most dance clubs with live bands have a cover charge of $6–$8 (EC$15–EC$20), and the music usually starts at 11 PM. **Doolittle's** (✉ Marigot Bay ☎ 758/451–4974) has live bands and dance music—calypso, soul, salsa, steel-band, reggae, limbo, and jump-up—that changes nightly. At **Indies** (✉ Rodney Bay ☎ 758/452–0727) you can dance to the hottest rhythms Wednesday, Friday, and Saturday; dress is casual though smart—no hats or sandals, no shorts or sleeveless shirts for men. There's shuttle bus service to and from most major hotels. The **Late Lime** (✉ Reduit Beach, Rodney Bay ☎ 758/452–0761) is a particular favorite of St. Lucians; it's air-conditioned and intimate, with live music, a DJ, or karaoke every night but Tuesday.

THEME NIGHTS For a taste of St. Lucian village life, head south from Castries to the **Anse La Raye "Fish Feast"** on a Friday night. Beginning at 6:30 PM, streets in this tiny fishing village are closed to vehicles and the residents prepare what they know best: fish cakes for about 40¢ each, fried or stewed fish for $3 a portion, even a whole lobster for $10–$15, depending on size. Walk around, eat, chat with the local people, and listen to live music in the village square until the wee hours of the morning.

The **Green Parrot** (✉ Morne Fortune, Castries ☎ 758/452–3399) is in a class all by itself. On Wednesday and Saturday, Chef Harry Edwards hosts the floor show—singing, dancing, and shimmying under the limbo pole himself. Dress semiformally for these evenings of frolic. **J. J.'s Friday Night Street Jam** (✉ Marigot Bay ☎ 758/451–4076) is the south-side alternative to Gros Islet, with an outdoor barbecue and a band that plays island music.

The Arts

THEATER The small, open-air **Derek Walcott Center Theatre** (✉ Cap Estate ☎ 758/450–0551 or 758/450–0450), next to the Great House restaurant in Cap Estate, seats just 200 people for monthly productions of music, dance, and drama, as well as Sunday brunch programs. The Trinidad Theatre Workshop also presents an annual performance here. For schedule and ticket information, contact the **Great House.**

Exploring St. Lucia

One main route circles all of St. Lucia, except for a small area in the extreme northeast. The road snakes along the coast, cuts across mountains, makes hairpin turns and sheer drops, and reaches dizzying heights. It would take five or six hours to drive the whole loop. Even at a leisurely pace with frequent sightseeing stops, it would be a tiring drive.

The West Coast Road between Castries and Soufrière (a 1½- to 2-hour journey) has steep hills and sharp turns, but it's well marked and incredibly scenic. South of Castries, the road tunnels through Morne Fortune, skirts the island's largest banana plantation (more than 127 varieties of bananas, called "figs" in this part of the Caribbean, are grown on the island), and passes through tiny fishing villages. Just north of Soufrière is the island's fruit basket, where most of the mangoes, breadfruit, tomatoes, limes, and oranges are grown. In the mountainous region that forms a backdrop for Soufrière, you can see Mt. Parasol and 3,118-ft Mt. Gimie (pronounced Jimmy), St. Lucia's highest peak. As you approach Soufrière, you'll also have spectacular views of the Pitons.

The landscape changes dramatically between the Pitons and Vieux Fort (also a 1½- to 2-hour journey), on the island's southeastern tip. Along the South Coast Road, the terrain starts as steep mountainside with dense vegetation, progresses to undulating hills that drop into sleepy fishing villages, and finally becomes rather flat and comparatively arid. Anyone arriving at Hewanorra International Airport and staying at a resort near Soufrière will travel along this route, a journey of just over an hour.

From Vieux Fort north to Castries, a 1¼-hour drive, the East Coast Road twists through Micoud, Dennery, and other villages. It winds up, down, and around mountains, crosses Barre de l'Isle Ridge, and slices through the rain forest. The scenery is breathtaking. The Atlantic pounds against rocky cliffs, and acres and acres of bananas and coconut palms cover the hillsides. If you arrive at Hewanorra and stay at a resort near Castries, you'll travel along the East Coast Road.

Numbers in the margin correspond to points of interest on the St. Lucia map.

Castries & the North

Castries, the capital, and the area north of it are the island's most developed areas. The roads are straight, flat, and easy to navigate. The beaches are some of the island's best. Rodney Bay Marina and most of the resorts are in this area. Pigeon Island, one of the important historical sites, is at the island's northwestern tip.

WHAT TO SEE
⑤ **Barre de l'Isle Forest Reserve.** St. Lucia is divided into eastern and western halves by Barre de L'Isle Ridge. A mile-long (1½-km-long) trail cuts through the reserve, and four lookout points provide panoramic views. Visible in the distance are Mt. Gimie, immense green valleys, both the Caribbean and the Atlantic, and coastal communities. The reserve is about a half-hour drive from Castries; it takes about an hour to walk the trail and another hour to climb Mt. La Combe Ridge. Permission from the **Forest and Lands Department** (☎ 758/450–2231 or 758/450–2078) is required to access the trail in Barre de L'Isle; a naturalist or forest officer guide will accompany you.

① **Castries.** The capital, a busy commercial city of about 65,000 people, wraps around a sheltered bay. Morne Fortune rises sharply to the south of town, creating a dramatic green backdrop. The charm of Castries lies almost entirely in its liveliness, since most of the colonial buildings were destroyed by four fires that occurred between 1796 and 1948. Freighters (exporting bananas, coconut, cocoa, mace, nutmeg, and citrus fruits) and cruise ships come and go daily, making Castries Harbour one of the Caribbean's busiest ports. **Pointe Seraphine** is a duty-free shopping complex on the north side of the harbor, about a 20-minute walk or two-minute cab ride from the city center; a launch ferries passengers across the harbor when ships are in port. Pointe Seraphine's attractive Spanish-style architecture houses more than 20 upscale duty-free shops, a tourist information kiosk, a taxi stand, and car-rental agencies. **Derek Walcott Square** is a green oasis bordered by Brazil, Laborie, Micoud, and Bourbon streets. Formerly Columbus Square, it was renamed to honor the hometown poet who won the 1992 Nobel prize for literature—one of two Nobel laureates from St. Lucia (the late Sir W. Arthur Lewis won the 1979 Nobel prize in economics). Some of the 19th-century buildings that have survived fire, wind, and rain can be seen on Brazil Street, the square's southern border. On the Laborie Street side, there's a huge, 400-year-old *samaan* tree with leafy branches that shade a good portion of the square. Directly across Laborie Street from Derek Walcott Square is the Roman Catholic **Cathedral of the Immaculate Conception,** which was built in 1897. Though it is rather somber on the outside, its interior walls are decorated with colorful murals reworked by St. Lucian artist Dunstan St. Omer in 1985, just prior to the pope's visit. This church has an active parish and is open daily for both public viewing and religious services. At the corner of Jeremie and Peynier streets, spreading beyond its brilliant orange roof, is the **Castries Market.** Full of excitement and bustle, the market is open every day except Sunday. It is liveliest on Saturday morning, when farmers bring their fresh produce and spices to town, as they have for more than a century. Next door to the produce market is the **Craft Market,** where you can buy pottery, wood carvings, and handwoven straw articles. Across Peynier Street from the Craft Market, at the **Vendor's Arcade,** there are still more handicrafts and souvenirs.

❷ **Ft. Charlotte.** Begun in 1764 by the French as the Citadelle du Morne Fortune, Ft. Charlotte was completed after 20 years of battling and changing hands. Its old barracks and batteries are now government buildings and local educational facilities, but you can drive around and look at the remains, including redoubts, a guardroom, stables, and cells. You can also walk up to the Inniskilling Monument, a tribute to the 1796 battle in which the 27th Foot Royal Inniskilling Fusiliers wrested the Morne from the French. At the military cemetery, which was first used in 1782, faint inscriptions on the tombstones tell the tales of French and English soldiers who died here. Six former governors of the island are buried here as well. From this point atop Morne Fortune you can view Martinique to the north and the twin peaks of the Pitons to the south.

❹ **Marigot Bay.** This is one of the prettiest natural harbors in the Caribbean. In 1778 British Admiral Samuel Barrington sailed into this secluded bay-within-a-bay and covered his ships with palm fronds to hide them from the French. Today this picturesque community—where parts of the original movie *Doctor Doolittle* were filmed more than 30 years ago—is a favorite anchorage. You can charter a yacht, swim, snorkel, or mingle with the yachting crowd at one of the bars. There are several small inns and restaurants here. A 24-hour ferry connects the bay's two shores.

❶❺ **Marquis Estate.** If you want a close-up view of a working plantation and are willing to get a little wet and muddy in the process, you can tour the island's largest one. The 600-acre Marquis Estate, situated on the northern Atlantic coast, began as a sugar plantation. Now it produces bananas and copra (dried coconut processed for oil) for export, as well as a number of other tropical fruits and vegetables for local consumption. St. Lucia Representative Services Ltd. conducts the tour and will pick you up at your hotel in an air-conditioned bus. You can see the estate by bus or on horseback; a river ride to the coast and lunch at the plantation house are both included. Self-drive or private taxi tours aren't permitted. Wear casual clothes. ⊠ *Marquis Bay* ☎ *758/452–3762.*

③ Morne Fortune. Morne Fortune forms a striking backdrop for the capital. This "Hill of Good Luck" has overlooked more than its share of bad luck over the years—including devastating hurricanes and four fires that leveled Castries. The drive to Morne Fortune from Castries will take you past **Government House,** on Government House Road, the official residence of the governor-general of St. Lucia and one of the island's few remaining examples of Victorian architecture.

★ ☺ ⑰ Pigeon Island. Jutting out from the northwest coast, Pigeon Island is connected to the mainland by a causeway. Tales are told of the pirate Jambe de Bois (Wooden Leg), who once hid out on this 44-acre hilltop islet— a strategic point during the struggles for control of St. Lucia. Now, it's a national landmark and a venue for concerts, festivals, and family gatherings. There are two small beaches with calm waters for swimming and snorkeling, a restaurant, and picnic areas. Scattered around the grounds are ruins of barracks, batteries, and garrisons that date from 18th-century French and English battles. In the Museum and Interpretative Centre, housed in the restored British officers' mess, a multimedia display explains the island's ecological and historical significance. ⊠ *Pigeon Island, St. Lucia National Trust, Rodney Bay* ☎ *758/452– 5005* ⊕ *www.slunatrust.org* ☞ *$4* ⊙ *Daily 9–5.*

⑯ Rodney Bay. About 15 minutes north of Castries, the 80-acre man-made lagoon—surrounded by hotels and many popular restaurants—is named for British admiral George Rodney, who sailed the English Navy out of Gros Islet Bay in 1780 to attack and ultimately decimate the French fleet. Rodney Bay Marina is one of the Caribbean's premier yachting centers and the destination of the Atlantic Rally for Cruisers (trans-Atlantic yacht crossing) each December. Yacht charters and sightseeing day trips can be arranged at the marina. The Rodney Bay Ferry makes hourly crossings between the marina and the shopping complex, as well as daily excursions to Pigeon Island.

Soufrière & the South

The southwest coast is the destination of most sightseeing trips. This is where you can view the landmark Pitons and explore the French-colonial town of Soufrière, with its drive-in volcano, botanical gardens, working plantations, and countless other examples of the natural beauty for which St. Lucia is deservedly famous.

WHAT TO SEE **Diamond Botanical Gardens.** These splendid gardens are part of Soufrière
★ ☺ ⑦ Estate, a 2,000-acre land grant made in 1713 by Louis XIV to three Devaux brothers from Normandy in recognition of their services to France. The estate is still owned by their descendants; the gardens are maintained by Joan Du Bouley Devaux. Bushes and shrubs bursting with brilliant flowers grow beneath towering trees and line pathways that lead to a natural gorge. Water bubbling to the surface from underground sulfur springs streams downhill in rivulets to become Diamond Waterfall, deep within the botanical gardens. Through the centuries, the rocks over which the cascade spills have become encrusted with minerals and tinted yellow, green, and purple. Adjacent to the falls, curative mineral baths are fed by the underground springs. For $2.50 you can slip into your

swimsuit and bathe for 30 minutes in one of the outside pools; a private bath costs $3.75. King Louis XVI of France provided funds in 1784 for the construction of a building with a dozen large stone baths to fortify his troops against the St. Lucian climate. It is claimed that Joséphine Bonaparte bathed here as a young girl while visiting her father's plantation nearby. During the Brigand's War, just after the French Revolution, the bathhouse was destroyed. In 1930 the site was excavated by André Du Boulay, and two of the original stone baths were restored for his use. The outside baths were added later. ⊠ *Soufrière Estate, Soufrière* ☎ *758/452–4759 or 758/454–7565* ☒ *$2.75* ☉ *Mon.–Sat. 10–5, Sun. and holidays 10–3.*

⑭ Fregate Island Nature Reserve. A mile-long (1½-km) trail encircles the nature reserve, which you reach from the East Coast Road near the fishing village of Praslin. In this area, boat builders still fashion traditional fishing canoes, called *gommiers* after the trees from which the hulls are made. The ancient design was used by the original Amerindian people who populated the Caribbean. A natural promontory at Praslin provides a lookout from which you can view the two small islets Fregate Major and Fregate Minor, and—with luck—the frigate birds that nest here from May to July. Guided tours of Fregate Island Nature Reserve, which include a ride in a gommier to Fregate Minor for a picnic lunch and swim, are arranged through the **St. Lucia National Trust** (⌖ Box 595, Castries ☎ 758/452–5005 ⊕ www.slunatrust.org). All hikers must be accompanied by a guide. The cost is $18 per person (minimum of two), and trips are by appointment only.

⑬ Maria Islands Nature Reserve. Two tiny islands in the Atlantic, off St. Lucia's southeast coast, comprise the reserve, which has its own interpretive center. The 25-acre Maria Major and the 4-acre Maria Minor, its little sister, are inhabited by two rare species of reptiles (the colorful Maria Island ground lizard and the harmless grass snake) that share their home with frigate birds, terns, doves, and other wildlife. There's a small beach for swimming and snorkeling, as well as an undisturbed forest, a vertical cliff covered with cacti, and a coral reef for snorkeling or diving. Tours, including the boat trip, cost $35 per person and are arranged by the **St. Lucia National Trust** (⌖ Box 595, Castries ☎ 758/452–5005 ⊕ www.slunatrust.org). Bring a picnic lunch.☉ *Aug.–mid-May, Wed.–Sun. 9:30–5.*

✋⑨ Morne Coubaril Estate. This 250-acre coconut and cocoa plantation in Soufrière, the first major estate established on St. Lucia, has a rich French history that dates from 1713, when Crown land was granted by King Louis XIV to three St. Lucian brothers. Authentic 18th-century plantation life is explained as a guide escorts you along an original mule-carriage pathway and through reconstructed slave quarters. On the interesting 90-minute tour you see how cocoa, copra, and manioc were processed in the days before mechanization. The foliage is thick and green, and the tropical flowers are beautiful. The plantation house has been renovated and furnished according to the original plans. You can purchase freshly made cocoa, straw goods, and hand-carved wooden pieces. If you wish to have lunch, a delicious creole buffet is available by reservation for about $10 per person. ⊠ *Soufrière* ☎ *758/459–7340* ☒ *$6* ☉ *Daily 9–5.*

⑧ The Pitons. These incredible mountains have become the symbol of St. **Fodor'sChoice** Lucia. The road south from Soufrière offers a magnificent view of the ★ twin peaks, which rise precipitously from the cobalt blue Caribbean. The two pyramidal cones, covered with thick tropical vegetation, were formed by lava from a volcanic eruption 30 to 40 million years ago. They are not identical twins since—confusingly—2,619-ft Petit Piton is taller than 2,461-ft Gros Piton, though Gros Piton is, as the word translates, broader. Gros Piton is currently the only one where climbing is permitted, though the trail up even this shorter Piton is one very tough trek and requires the permission of the **Forest and Lands Department** (☎ 758/450–2231 or 758/450–2078) and a knowledgeable guide—whose services cost about $45.

⑩ **St. Lucia National Rain Forest.** Dense tropical rain forest stretches from one side of the island to the other, sprawling over 19,000 acres of mountains and valleys. It's home to a multitude of exotic flowers and plants, as well as rare birds—including the brightly feathered Jacquot parrot. The Edmund Forest Reserve, on the island's western side, is most easily accessible from just east of Soufrière, on the road to Fond St. Jacques. A trek through the lush landscape, with spectacular views of mountains, valleys, and the sea beyond, can take a full day. It takes an hour or so just to reach the reserve by car from the north end of the island. You'll also need plenty of stamina and sturdy hiking shoes. Permission from the **Forest and Lands Department** (☎ 758/450–2231 or 758/450–2078) is required to access reserve trails, and the department requires that a naturalist or forest officer guide you ($10 per person) because the vegetation is so dense.

⑥ **Soufrière.** The oldest town in St. Lucia and the former French-colonial capital, Soufrière was founded by the French in 1746 and named for its proximity to the volcano. The wharf is the center of activity in this sleepy town (which currently has a population of about 9,000), particularly when a cruise ship is moored in pretty Soufrière Bay. French-colonial influences can be noticed in the architecture of the wooden buildings, with second-story verandahs and gingerbread trim, that surround the market square. The market building itself is decorated with colorful murals. The **Soufrière Tourist Information Centre** (✉ Bay St., Soufrière ☎ 758/459–7200) provides information about area attractions.

★ ☞ ⑪ **La Soufrière Drive-In Volcano.** As you approach, your nose will pick up the strong scent of the sulfur springs—more than 20 belching pools of muddy water, multicolored sulfur deposits, and other assorted minerals baking and steaming on the surface. Actually, you don't drive in. You drive up within a few hundred feet of the gurgling, steaming mass, then walk behind your guide—whose service is included in the admission price—around a fault in the substratum rock. It's a fascinating, educational half hour that can also be pretty stinky on a hot day. ✉ *Bay St., Soufrière* ☎ *758/459–5500* ✉ *$1.25* ☉ *Daily 9–5.*

⑫ **Vieux Fort.** St. Lucia's second-largest port is the location of Hewanorra International Airport. From the Moule à Chique Peninsula, the island's southernmost tip, you can see all of St. Lucia to the north and the island of St. Vincent 21 mi (34 km) south. This is where the clear Caribbean waters blend with those of the deeper blue Atlantic.

ST. LUCIA A TO Z

To research prices, get advice from other travelers, and book travel arrangements, visit www.fodors.com.

AIR TRAVEL

Air Canada has direct weekend service to Hewanorra from Toronto and Montréal. Air Jamaica flies daily from New York, via Montego Bay or Barbados, to Hewanorra and from London via Barbados. American Airlines/American Eagle has daily service to George F. L. Charles via San

Juan from New York and other major U.S. cities. British Airways has direct service to Hewanorra from London via Barbados. BWIA has direct service to George F. L. Charles, via either Barbados or Trinidad, from Miami, New York, Washington, D.C., and London. US Airways flies twice-weekly between Philadelphia and Hewanorra. Virgin Atlantic flies nonstop to Hewanorra from London. From other parts of the world, connections must be made through U.S. cities, San Juan, Toronto, or London.

Air Caraïbes flies into George F. L. Charles Airport from Martinique and other islands in the French West Indies. Caribbean Star connects George F. L. Charles with Antigua, Dominica, St. Vincent, and Grenada. HelenAir flies charter service between Barbados and George F. L. Charles. LIAT operates at Hewanorra, as well as at George F. L. Charles, linking St. Lucia with Barbados, Trinidad, Antigua, Martinique, Dominica, Guadeloupe, and other islands.

⑦ Air Canada ☎ 758/452-3051 or 758/452-2550. **Air Caraïbes** ☎ 758/452-2463 or 758/453-6660. **Air Jamaica** ☎ 758/453-6611. **American Airlines/American Eagle** ☎ 758/452-6777. **British Airways** ☎ 758/452-3951. **BWIA** ☎ 758/452-3778, 758/451-7700, or 758/454-5075. **Caribbean Star** ☎ 758/452-5898. **HelenAir** ☎ 758/453-2777. **LIAT** ☎ 758/452-3051 or 758/452-2348. **US Airways** ☎ 758/454-8186. **Virgin Atlantic** ☎ 758/454-3610.

AIRPORTS

St. Lucia has two airports. Hewanorra International Airport, at Vieux Fort on the southern tip of the island, is a modern airport with a long runway capable of handling wide-body jets. George F. L. Charles Airport, in Castries, is a short airstrip that accommodates small, propeller-driven aircraft used for interisland and charter flights.

The drive from Hewanorra to Castries takes about 1¼ hours; to Soufrière, just over an hour. Although both are long rides to take after long flights, either route follows a picturesque coastline and traverses lush rain forest—and is a beautiful introduction to St. Lucia. George F. L. Charles Airport (also referred to as Vigie Airport) is only 10 to 20 minutes from resorts in or near Castries; it's about 30 minutes from Marigot and 1¼ hours from Soufrière. Another option is to take a boat between George F. L. Charles Airport (from Vigie Cove Marina) and Soufrière, which shortens the trip to about 40 minutes.

Many resorts include airport transfers in their rates. Taxis are always available at the airports. If you take one, be sure to agree on the fare (and on which currency it's being quoted in) before you get in. Between Hewanorra and Soufrière expect to pay $55–$60 each way; between Hewanorra and the resorts near Castries, $70–$75; between George F. L. Charles (Vigie) Airport and nearby resorts, $15–$20; between Vigie and Soufrière, $70–$75.

⑦ George F. L. Charles Airport ☎ 758/452-1156. **Hewanorra International Airport** ☎ 758/454-6355.

BOAT & FERRY TRAVEL

Cruise ships from major lines call at Castries and Soufrière. At Port Castries, ships tie up at berths right in town and are convenient to duty-free shops, the market, and transportation for sightseeing excursions. In Soufrière, ships anchor offshore, and passengers are transferred ashore by tenders.

Visitors arriving on private or chartered yachts can find full-service facilities—including duty-free fuel, ship's chandlery, sail and engine repair, telecommunications, groceries, and other services—at the island's two main yachting centers, action-packed Rodney Bay or picturesque Marigot Bay. Along with Port Castries (including Vigie Cove Marina), all are official ports of entry to St. Lucia.

FARES & SCHEDULES The Rodney Bay Ferry makes the trip between the marina and the shopping complex daily on the hour from 9 to 4 for $4 round-trip. Ferry service to Pigeon Island from Rodney Bay (adjacent to The Lime restaurant) is available twice daily for $50 round-trip, including the entrance fee to Pigeon Island and lunch; snorkel equipment can be rented for $12. ⚑ **Castries Yacht Centre** ☎ 758/452-6234. **Moorings Yacht Charters** ☎ 758/451-4357. **Port Castries** ☎ 758/452-3036. **Rodney Bay Ferry** ☎ 758/452-8816. **Rodney Bay Marina Boatyard** ☎ 758/452-0324. **St. Lucia Yacht Services** ☎ 758/452-5057.

BUSINESS HOURS

BANKS Banks are open Monday–Thursday 8–3, Friday 8–5; a few branches in Rodney Bay are also open Saturday 9–noon.

POST OFFICES Post offices are open weekdays 8:30–4:30.

SHOPS Most stores are open weekdays 8:30–12:30 and 1:30–4:30, Saturday 8–12:30; Gablewoods Mall shops are open Monday–Saturday 9–7; J. Q.'s Shopping Mall shops are open from 9–8; Pointe Seraphine shops are open weekdays 9–5, Saturday 9–2. Some hotel gift shops may be open on Sunday.

CAR RENTALS

To rent a car you must be at least 25 years old and provide a valid driver's license and a credit card. If you don't have an international driver's license, you must buy a temporary St. Lucian driving permit at car-rental firms, the immigration office at either airport, or the Gros Islet police station. The permit costs $20 (EC$54) and is valid for three months. Car-rental rates are usually quoted in U.S. dollars and range from $45 to $80 per day or $250–$400 per week, depending on the car.

Car-rental agencies generally include free pickup at your hotel and unlimited mileage. Many major U.S. car-rental firms have agencies in St. Lucia. Avis has a main office in Castries and desks at both airports, at the Pointe Seraphine transportation center, and at Rodney Bay Marina. Budget has its main office in Castries and a desk at Hewanorra International Airport. Hertz has desks at both airports.

Local agencies offer competitive service and rates. C. T. L. Rent-a-Car is convenient for people staying at resorts near Rodney Bay or who arrive in St. Lucia by private yacht. Cool Breeze Jeep/Car Rental is convenient for people staying at resorts in the southwest near Soufrière. Courtesy Car Rental has an office north of Rodney Bay and a rental desk at the Bay Gardens Hotel in Rodney Bay. Gibin Rent A Car is convenient for people staying in the north, near Gros Islet. St. Lucia National Car Rental has desks at both airports, at the Pointe Seraphine transportation center, and a desk at The Body Holiday at LeSPORT resort and a few other hotels. ⚑ **Avis** ✉ Vide Bouteille, Castries ☎ 758/452-2700 ✉ Rodney Bay ☎ 758/452-0782 ✉ Vieux Fort ☎ 758/454-6325 ✉ Vigie ☎ 758/452-2046 **Budget** ✉ Castries ☎ 758/452-0233 ✉ Vieux Fort ☎ 758/454-5311. **C. T. L. Rent-a-Car** ✉ Rodney Bay Marina ☎ 758/452-0732. **Cool Breeze Jeep/Car Rental** ✉ Soufrière ☎ 758/459-7729. **Courtesy Car Rental** ✉ Bois d'Orange, Gros Islet ☎ 758/452-8140. **Gibin Rent A Car** ✉ Beausejour, Gros Islet ☎ 758/452-9528. **Hertz** ✉ Castries ☎ 758/452-0679 ✉ Vieux Fort ☎ 758/454-9636 ✉ Vigie ☎ 758/451-7351. **St. Lucia National Car Rental** ✉ Castries ☎ 758/450-8721 ✉ Vieux Fort ☎ 758/454-6699 ✉ Vigie ☎ 758/452-3050 ✉ Pointe Seraphine ☎ 758/453-0085.

CAR TRAVEL

Driving yourself is a fine idea if you want to do a lot of exploring and try lots of restaurants during your stay. If you're staying at an all-inclusive resort and plan limited excursions off the property, however, taxis would be a better bet. The drive from Castries to Soufrière is magnificent, but the winding roads can be exhausting for the uninitiated; local drivers are accustomed to the trek. You might even prefer to make that trip by boat, which is a popular option.

GASOLINE Gasoline is expensive: about EC$2 per liter (the equivalent of $2.75 per gallon).

ROAD CONDITIONS St. Lucia has about 500 mi (800 km) of roads, but only about half (281 mi [450 km]) are paved. All towns and villages are connected by major routes. The highways on both coasts are winding and steep—and often scarred by potholes.

RULES OF THE ROAD Driving in St. Lucia is on the left, British style. Observe speed limits, particularly the 30-mph limit within Castries. Respect no-parking zones; police issue tickets, and penalties start at about $15 (EC$40). Wear your seat belts.

ELECTRICITY

The electric current on St. Lucia is 220 volts, 50 cycles, with a square three-pin plug. A few large hotels have 110-volt outlets—at least for shavers. To use most North American appliances, however, you'll need a transformer to convert voltage and a plug adapter; dual-voltage computers or appliances will still need a plug adapter. Hotels will sometimes lend you one for use during your stay.

EMBASSIES & CONSULATES

🚩 United Kingdom **British High Commission** ⊠ N.I.S. Building, Waterfront Second Floor, Castries ☎ 758/452-2482.

EMERGENCIES

Victoria Hospital is St. Lucia's main hospital, on the southwest side of Castries harbor heading toward La Toc. Regional medical facilities are located at Dennery Hospital, on the island's east coast, St. Jude's Hospital, near Hewanorra International Airport, and Soufrière Hospital, in the southwest.

🚩 Ambulance & Fire **Ambulance and fire emergencies** ☎ 911.

🚩 Hospitals **Dennery Hospital** ⊠ Main Rd., Dennery ☎ 758/453-3310. **St. Jude's Hospital** ⊠ Airport Rd., Vieux Fort ☎ 758/454-6041. **Soufrière Hospital** ⊠ W. Quinlan St., Soufrière ☎ 758/459-7258. **Victoria Hospital** ⊠ Hospital Rd., Castries ☎ 758/452-2421.

🚩 Pharmacies **M & C Drugstore** ⊠ Bridge St., Castries ☎ 758/452-2811 ⊠ J. Q.'s Shopping Mall, Rodney Bay ☎ 758/458-0178 ⊠ Gablewoods Mall, Gros Islet Hwy., Choc ☎ 758/451-7808 ⊠ New Dock Rd., Vieux Fort ☎ 758/454-3760. **Williams Pharmacy** ⊠ Bridge St., Castries ☎ 758/452-2797.

🚩 Police Dial 999. **Marine police** ☎ 758/453-0770 or 758/452-2595. **Sea-air Rescue** ☎ 758/452-2894, 758/452-1182, or 758/453-6664.

ETIQUETTE & BEHAVIOR

Dress conservatively in town and in restaurants. In St. Lucia, as well as throughout the Caribbean, beachwear should be reserved for the beach. If you wish to take photographs of local people or their property, be sure to ask permission first and offer a small gratuity in appreciation. Note that souvenir vendors can be persistent, particularly outside some of the popular attractions in and around Soufrière. Be polite but firm if you're not interested.

FESTIVALS & SEASONAL EVENTS

In March, the St. Lucia Golf Open, a two-day tournament held at the St. Lucia Golf and Country Club in Cap Estate, is open to amateurs; it's a handicap event, and prizes are awarded.

For two days in May, the St. Lucia National Trust holds its annual fund-raiser, the Festival of Comedy; adult comedy shows are held at the Cultural Centre in Castries, and there's a day of family entertainment, with storytellers and comedians, at Pigeon Island.

In early May the weeklong St. Lucia Jazz Festival, one of the premier events of its kind in the Caribbean, sees international jazz greats entertain at outdoor venues on Pigeon Island and at various hotels, restaurants, and nightspots throughout the island; free concerts are also held at Derek Walcott Square in downtown Castries.

St. Lucia's Carnival, the most extravagant two days of the year, is held on the third Monday and Tuesday in July; a costume parade winds through Castries, prizes are awarded for the best band, the calypso king and queen are crowned, and there is endless music and dancing in the streets.

The St. Lucia Billfishing Tournament, held in late September or early October, attracts anglers from all over the Caribbean, with prizes awarded for the biggest fish and the largest catch; the blue marlin is the most sought-after fish, and everyone hopes to find one that beats the 1,000-lb mark.

The last Sunday in October marks Jounen Kweyol Etenasyonnal (International Creole Day), the grand finale of Creole Heritage month; festivities are held in several communities, but musicians always do their stuff at Pigeon Point Park and in the streets in Castries, where vendors set up stalls and sell food and handicrafts.

The annual Atlantic Rally for Cruisers, or ARC, is the world's largest ocean-crossing race. It starts in Las Palmas, Canary Islands, and ends in late November or early December at Rodney Bay; the event is marked by a week of festivities and parties.

HEALTH

Tap water is perfectly safe to drink throughout the island, but you should be sure that fruit is peeled or washed thoroughly before eating it. Insects can be a real bother during the wet season (July–November), particularly in the rain forest; bring along repellent to ward off mosquitoes and sand flies.

HOLIDAYS

Public holidays are: New Year's Day (Jan. 1), Independence Day (Feb. 22), Good Friday, Easter Monday, Labour Day (May 1), Whit Monday (7th Mon. after Easter), Corpus Christi (8th Thurs. after Easter), Emancipation Day (1st Mon. in Aug.), Carnival (3rd Mon. and Tues. in July), Thanksgiving Day (Oct. 25), National Day (Dec. 13), Christmas, and Boxing Day (Dec. 26).

LANGUAGE

English is the official language of St. Lucia and is spoken everywhere, but you'll often hear local people speaking a French Creole patois (Kweyol) among themselves. If you're interested in learning some patois words and phrases, pick up a copy of *A Visitor's Guide to St. Lucia Patois*, a small paperback book sold in local bookstores for $4.

As in many of the Caribbean islands, to "lime" is to hang out and a "jump-up" is a big party with lots of dance music (often in the street, as in the village of Gros Islet every Friday night). Don't be surprised if people in St. Lucia call you "darling" instead of "ma'am" or "sir"—they're being friendly not forward.

MAIL & SHIPPING

The General Post Office is on Bridge Street in Castries and is open week-days 8:30–4:30; all towns and villages have branches. Postage for air-mail letters to the U.S., Canada, and the U.K. is EC95¢ per ½ ounce; postcards are EC65¢. Airmail letters to Australia and New Zealand cost EC$1.35; postcards, EC70¢. Airmail can take two or three weeks to be delivered—even longer to Australia and New Zealand.

MONEY MATTERS

Prices quoted in this chapter are in U.S. dollars unless otherwise indicated.

The international Bank of Nova Scotia, or Scotiabank, has its head of-fice in central Castries and branch offices at Rodney Bay and Vieux Fort. Barclays Bank offers international banking services from its two offices in Castries and branches in major towns. National Commercial Bank of St. Lucia is a large regional bank, with two offices in Castries and branches at Hewanorra Airport, Gros Islet, and Soufrière. Royal Bank of Canada has its main office in downtown Castries and a branch at Rodney Bay Marina.

🏦 **Bank of Nova Scotia** ✉ Wm. Peter Blvd., Castries ☎ 758/452–2100 ✉ Rodney Bay ☎ 758/452–8805 ✉ Vieux Fort ☎ 758/454–6314. **FirstCaribbean International Bank** ✉ Bridge St., Castries ☎ 758/456–2100 ✉ Rodney Bay Marina, Rodney Bay ☎ 758/452–9384 ✉ Hewanorra Airport, Vieux Fort ☎ 758/454–6255 ✉ Soufrière ☎ 758/459–7255. **National Commercial Bank of St. Lucia** ✉ Bridge St., Castries ☎ 758/456–6000 ✉ Pointe Seraphine, Castries ☎ 758/452–4787 ✉ Hewanorra Airport ☎ 758/454–7780 ✉ Gros Islet ☎ 758/450–9851 ✉ Soufrière ☎ 758/459–7450. **Royal Bank of Canada** ✉ William Peter Blvd., Castries ☎ 758/452–2245 ✉ Rodney Bay Marina, Rodney Bay ☎ 758/452–9921.

ATMS   Automated teller machines (ATMs) are available 24 hours a day at bank branches, transportation centers, and shopping malls, where you can use major credit cards to obtain cash (in local currency only).

CREDIT CARDS   Major credit cards and traveler's checks are widely accepted.

CURRENCY   The official currency is the Eastern Caribbean dollar (EC$). It's linked to the U.S. dollar at EC$2.67, but stores and hotels often exchange at EC$2.50 or EC$2.60. U.S. currency is readily accepted, but you'll prob-ably get change in EC dollars.

PASSPORTS & VISAS

U.S., Canadian, and British citizens whose stay does not exceed six months must have a valid passport or prove citizenship with a birth certificate (with a raised seal) and a government-issued photo I.D. Visitors from other countries must present a valid passport. Everyone must have a re-turn or ongoing ticket.

SAFETY

Although crime isn't a significant problem, take the same precautions you would at home—lock your door, secure your valuables, and don't carry too much money or flaunt expensive jewelry on the street.

SIGHTSEEING TOURS

Guided half- and full-day land and/or sea tours depart from the Cas-tries area (Pointe Seraphine and Vigie Cove) or Rodney Bay and head north to Pigeon Island or south along the picturesque west coast to the Pitons and the sights in and around Soufrière. Half-day land tours range in price from $35 to $40 per person; full-day land tours, from $120 to $140 for one to four people. Cruises include refreshments and range in price from $40 per person at sunset to $85 for a full day.

BICYCLE   Although the terrain can get pretty rugged, several tour operators have put together fascinating bicycle and combination bicycle-hiking tours that appeal to novice riders as well as those who enjoy a good workout. It's a marvelous way to enjoy the spectacular scenery in the St. Lucia countryside. Prices range from $60 to $100 per person.

Bike St. Lucia takes small groups of bikers on Jungle Biking™ tours along trails that meander through the remnants of an 18th-century plantation near Soufrière. Stops are made to explore the French colonial ruins, study the beautiful tropical plants and fruit trees, enjoy a picnic lunch, and take dip in a river swimming hole or a swim at the beach. For those staying in the north, transportation to and from the facility is provided by land taxi and boat from Vigie Marina, in Castries.

Island Bike Hikes is suitable for all fitness levels. Jeep or bus transportation is provided across the central mountains to Dennery, on the east coast. After a 3-mi ride through the countryside, bikes are exchanged for shoe leather. The short hike into the rain forest ends with a picnic and a refreshing swim next to a sparkling waterfall—then the return leg to Dennery. All gear is supplied.

🚲 **Bike St. Lucia** ✉ Anse Chastanet, Soufrière ☎ 758/451-2453 ⊕ www.bikestlucia. com. **Island Bike Hikes** ✉ Box GM785, Castries ☎ 758/458-0908.

BOAT   Board the 140-ft *Brig Unicorn* for a full-day sail to Soufrière or a sunset cruise under full sail, accompanied by champagne, snacks, and live music. Endless Summer Cruises (Cats Inc.) offers full-day tours and champagne sunset cruises aboard its 56-ft catamaran party boat, *Endless Summer*. The 56-ft motor cruiser MV *Vigie* takes passengers for half-day cruises to Pigeon Island or full-day tours to the Pitons and the sights around Soufrière, with lunch, swimming, and snorkeling at Anse Cochon included.

🚤 **Brig Unicorn** ✉ Vigie Cove, Castries ☎ 758/452-8811. **Endless Summer** ✉ Cats Inc., Rodney Bay ☎ 758/450-8651. **MV Vigie** ✉ Rodney Bay Marina, Rodney Bay ☎ 758/452-9423 or 758/452-8232.

HELICOPTER   Helicopter sightseeing tours are fascinating ways to get a bird's-eye view of the island. A 10-minute North Island tour ($45 per person) leaves from Pointe Seraphine, in Castries, continues up the west coast to Pigeon Island, then flies along the rugged Atlantic coastline before returning inland over Castries. The 20-minute South Island tour ($85 per person) starts at Pointe Seraphine and follows the western coastline, circling picturesque Marigot Bay, Soufrière, and the majestic Pitons before returning inland over the volcanic hot springs and tropical rain forest. A complete island tour combines the two and lasts 30 minutes ($120 per person). To arrange a helicopter sightseeing trip, contact St. Lucia Helicopters.

🚁 **St. Lucia Helicopters** ✉ Pointe Seraphine ☎ 758/453-6950 🖶 758/452-1553 ⊕ www.stluciahelicopters.com.

ORIENTATION   Taxi drivers are well informed and can give you a full tour—and often an excellent one, thanks to government-sponsored training programs. From the Castries area, full-day island tours cost $140 for up to four people; sightseeing trips to Soufrière, $120. If you plan your own day, expect to pay the driver $20 per hour plus tip.

St. Lucia Heritage Tours has put together an "authentic St. Lucia experience," specializing in the local culture and traditions. Groups are small, and some of the off-the-beaten-track sites visited are a 19th-century plantation house surrounded by nature trails, a 20-ft waterfall hidden away on private property, and a living museum presenting Creole practices and traditions. Plan on paying $65 per person for a full-day tour.

Jungle Tours specializes in rain-forest hiking tours for all levels of ability. You're only required to bring hiking shoes or sneakers and have a willingness to get wet and have fun! Prices range from $80 to $90 and include lunch, fees, and transportation via open Land Rover truck.

Sunlink Tours offers dozens of land, sea, and combination sightseeing tours, as well as shopping tours, plantation, and rain-forest adventures via Jeep safari, deep-sea fishing excursions, and day trips to other islands. Prices range from $20 for a half-day shopping tour to $120 for a full-day land-and-sea Jeep safari to Soufrière.

⬛ Jungle Tours ⊠ Cas en Bas, Gros Islet ☎ 758/450-0434 ⊕ www.jungletoursstlucia. com. **St. Lucia Heritage Tours** ⊠ Pointe Seraphine, Castries ☎ 758/451-6058 ⊕ www. heritagetoursstlucia.com. **Sunlink Tours** ⊠ Reduit Beach Ave., Rodney Bay ☎ 758/ 452-8232 or 800/786-5465 ⊕ www.sunlinktours.com.

TAXES & SERVICE CHARGES

DEPARTURE TAX The departure tax is $20 (EC$54), payable in cash only (either Eastern Caribbean or U.S. dollars).

SALES TAX A government tax of 8% is added to all hotel and restaurant bills. There is no sales tax on goods purchased in shops.

SERVICE CHARGES Most restaurants add a service charge of 10% to restaurant bills in lieu of tipping.

TAXIS

Taxis are always available at the airports, the harbor, and in front of major hotels. They're unmetered, although nearly all drivers belong to a taxi cooperative and adhere to standard fares. Sample fares for up to four passengers are: Castries to Rodney Bay, $16; Rodney Bay to Cap Estate, $10; Castries to Cap Estate, $20; Castries to Marigot Bay, $24; Castries to Soufrière, $70. Always ask the driver to quote the price *before* you get in, and be sure that you both understand whether it's in EC or U.S. dollars. Drivers are knowledgeable and courteous.

TELEPHONES

COUNTRY & AREA CODES The area code for St. Lucia is 758.

INTERNATIONAL CALLS You can make direct-dial overseas and interisland calls from St. Lucia, and the connections are excellent. You can charge an overseas call to a major credit card with no surcharge by dialing a simple 3-digit number. From public phones and many hotels, you can dial AT&T or MCI Worldcom and charge the call to your calling card to avoid expensive rates or hotel surcharges. Phone cards can be purchased at many retail outlets and used from any touch-tone telephone (including pay phones) in St. Lucia. Cell phones can be rented from Cable & Wireless.

⬛ AT&T ☎ 800/872-2881 **Cable & Wireless** ☎ 758/453-9922 **Credit Card Charge Call** ☎ 811 **MCI Worldcom** ☎ 800/888-8000

LOCAL CALLS You can dial local calls throughout St. Lucia directly from your hotel room by connecting to an outside line and dialing the seven-digit number. Some hotels charge a small fee (usually about EC50¢) for local calls. Pay phones accept EC25¢ and EC$1 coins. Phone cards can be used for local calls, as well as for international calls.

TIPPING

Most restaurants add a 10% service charge to your bill in lieu of tipping; if one has not been added, a 10%–15% tip is appropriate for good service. Tip porters and bellhops $1 per bag, although many of the all-inclusive resorts have a no-tipping policy. Taxi drivers also appreciate a 10%–15% tip.

TRANSPORTATION AROUND ST. LUCIA

Privately owned and operated minivans constitute St. Lucia's bus system, an inexpensive and efficient means of transportation used primarily by local people. Minivan routes cover the entire island and run from early morning until approximately 10 PM. You may find this method of getting around most useful for short distances, between Castries and the Rodney Bay area, for example; longer hauls can be uncomfortable. The fare between Castries and Gablewoods Mall is EC$1; Castries and Rodney Bay, EC$1.50; Castries and Vieux Fort (a trip that takes more than two hours), EC$7. Minivans follow designated routes (signs are displayed on the front window); ask at your hotel for the appropriate route number for your destination. Wait at a marked bus stop or hail a passing minivan from the roadside. In Castries, buses depart from the corner of Micoud and Bridge streets, behind the markets.

Each minivan has a driver and usually a conductor, a young man whose job it is to collect fares, open the door, and generally take charge of the passenger area. If you're sure of where you're going, simply knock twice on the metal window frame to signal that you want to get off at the next stop. Otherwise, just let the conductor or driver know where you're going, and he'll stop at the appropriate place.

Helicopter transfers are much more expensive but a much quicker mode of transport. For the 10-minute straight flight between Castries (Pointe Seraphine, Windjammer Landing, or Rodney Bay) and either Hewanorra or Soufrière (Jalousie Hilton helipad), St. Lucia Helicopters charges $90 per person, including luggage; for the 7-minute flight between Soufrière and Hewanorra, $80 per person.

🚁 **St. Lucia Helicopters** ⊠ Pointe Seraphine ☎ 758/453-6950 🖷 758/452-1553 ⊕ www.stluciahelicopters.com.

VISITOR INFORMATION

🚁 Before You Leave **St. Lucia Tourist Board** ⊕ www.stlucia.org ⊠ 800 2nd Ave., Suite 400-], New York, NY 10017 ☎ 212/867-2950 or 800/456-3984 🖷 212/867-2795 ⊠ 8 King St. E, Suite 700, Toronto, Ontario M5C 1B5 ☎ 416/362-4242 🖷 416/362-7832 ⊠ 421A Finchley Rd., London NW3 6H] ☎ 0171/431-3675 🖷 0171/431-7920.
🚁 In St. Lucia **St. Lucia Tourist Board** ⊠ Sureline Bldg., Vide Bouteille ☎ Box 221, Castries ☎ 758/452-4094 or 758/452-5968 🖷 758/453-1121 ⊠ Jeremie St., Castries ☎ 758/452-2479 ⊠ Pointe Seraphine, Castries ☎ 758/452-7577 ⊠ Bay St., Soufrière ☎ 758/459-7419 ⊠ George F. L. Charles Airport, Vigie, Castries ☎ 758/452-2596 ⊠ Hewanorra International Airport, Vieux Fort ☎ 758/454-6644.

ST. MAARTEN/ ST. MARTIN

21

FODOR'S CHOICE

Baie Orientale beach

The Horny Toad, a hotel in Simpson Bay

Ric's Place, a budget restaurant in Simpson Bay

Shopping

Turtle Pier Bar & Restaurant, Simpson Bay

HIGHLY RECOMMENDED

RESTAURANTS   Antoine, Philipsburg

Bay Watch, Orient Beach

Bistrot Nu, Marigot

La Main Á La Páte, Marigot

Le Pressoir, Grand Case

Mario's Bistro, Sandy Ground

Paradise View, Orient Bay

Saratoga, Simpson Bay

The Rainbow, Grand Case

HOTELS   Green Cay Village, Baie Oriental

Hôtel L'Esplanade Caraïbes, Grand Case

La Vista, Simpson Bay

Le Méridien, Anse Marcel

Mary's Boon Beach Plantation, Simpson Bay

SIGHTS   Le Fort Louis, Marigot

Loterie Farm, Pic du Paradis

OUTDOORS   Dawn Beach

Baie Rouge Beach

It sounded like a joyous Tower of Babel. At least six languages competed in the lively conversation around the crumb-strewn dinner table in the restaurant on the Marigot waterfront. Aruban-born Elio—raised speaking the Caribbean tongue of Papiamento but also fluent in Dutch, French, English, and Spanish—mediated serious translation impasses. Walter, Vietnamese by birth, Canadian by circumstances, and now a resident of St. Maarten by choice, preferred English, that is except when going tête-à-tête with Alice, his Parisian-raised wife. We, the expatriate Americans, struggled with our loudest English and très très rusty, high-school French. When in doubt of being understood, the speakers would repeat themselves, using ever-widening hand gestures, or I lean in close, pinching words between thumb and forefinger for emphasis.

Updated by
John and Judy
Ingrisano

Welcome to tiny St. Maarten/St. Martin, home to people from 90 countries and speaking dozens of languages, a rich and unique cultural crossroads of the world, all on just 37 square miles (96 square km), making it the world's smallest land mass to host two separate governments—French and Dutch—separated by a meandering non-border that nobody notices. Though English always works, you'd have to walk the halls of the United Nations to hear so many different languages or find more cultural diversity in such close proximity.

Every stroll along one of the island's more than 37 beautiful beaches or streets in Caribbean-style Philipsburg or very French Marigot is an opportunity for a multicultural encounter with someone from one of the four corners of the globe. The island's diversity is reflected in hundreds of world-class eateries, from Parisian bistros to American sports bars, to restaurants serving German, Indian, creole, Vietnamese, and Italian fare.

Enjoy the food, but first and foremost come to St. Maarten for the sand and the sea, the friendly people, and wonderful weather—where the temperature is almost always 87 degrees, with cooling trade winds, which make the island a good vacation spot all year round.

Whatever can be done in or on the water—snorkeling, scuba, sailing, windsurfing and more—can be found here. There's even a golf course, and many resorts have tennis courts. The duty-free shopping is as good as anywhere in the Caribbean, and the nightlife is second to none, whether your preference is cool and mellow or loud and wild. Day trips are available by ship or plane to the nearby islands of Anguilla, Saba, St. Eustatius, and St. Barthélemy. There are hotels for every budget—from motel-type units to some of the Caribbean's most exclusive resort accommodations. The standard of living is one of the highest in the Caribbean.

On the negative side, St. Maarten/St. Martin has been heavily developed in recent years, so the quaint island culture is becoming harder to find. Especially in the high season, traffic can be difficult. Still, the beaches are clean, the water blue, and the weather intoxicating.

WHAT IT COSTS In U.S. dollars				
$$$$	**$$$**	**$$**	**$**	**¢**
RESTAURANTS*				
over $30	$20–$30	$12–$20	$8–$12	under $8
HOTELS**				
Cost EP/BP/CP over $350	$250–$350	$150–$250	$80–$150	under $80
Cost AI over $450	$350–$450	$250–$350	$125–$250	under $125

*Restaurant prices are for a main course at dinner. **EP, BP, and CP prices are per night for a standard double room in high season, excluding taxes, service charges, and meal plans. AI (all-inclusive) prices are per person, per night based on double-occupancy during high season, excluding taxes and service charges.

Where to Stay

On the Dutch side the main resort areas are along beaches such as Maho Bay, where the restaurants and nightlife activities are abundant; at Simpson Bay, southeast of the airport, where traffic can be heavy; and along Front Street in downtown Philipsburg, where shops and eateries abound.

The French side's attractive Baie Nettlé and busy, popular Baie Orientale (Orient Bay, with its sports outfitters and beachside bistros) are two resort areas. Others include secluded Anse Marcel (Marcel Cove); Mont Vernon, which has a nice beach a bit removed from the crowds; Marigot, with shops, an open-air market, and fine dining; and Grand Case, which has an excellent beach and dozens of charming restaurants.

In general, the French resorts are more intimate. Most large Dutch resorts have time-share annexes; the units are often available for rental to those who prefer the condo lifestyle.

Hotels

DUTCH SIDE 🏨 **Maho Beach Resort & Casino.** Whatever your pleasure—sunning or swim-
$$$–$$$$ ming, sailing or shopping, dancing to dawn or being pampered in the full-service spa—the island's largest resort also has the largest list of vacation activities. Plus the casino theater has circus acts, Chinese acrobats, and other entertainment. Comfortable rooms have balconies with sea or garden views. Besides the resort's three restaurants, other eateries, a cybercafé, and shops are just across the street. ⊠ *Airport Rd., Maho Bay* ✆ *Box 834* ☎ *599/545–2115 or 800/223–0757* 🖷 *599/545–3180* ⊕ *www.mahobeach.com* ⇨ *570 rooms, 25 suites* ⚹ *3 restaurants, 4 tennis courts, 2 pools, health club, spa, beach, 3 bars, casino, dance club, shops, baby-sitting, business services, meeting rooms, car rental* ⊟ *AE, D, DC, MC, V* ⛧ *EP.*

$$–$$$$ 🏨 **Sunterra Royal Palm Beach Club.** All rooms have an ocean view in this well-maintained complex of suites on Kimsha Beach. The resort has a pool with a swim-up bar and an adjoining outdoor restaurant, plus a large, well-equipped workout center, jewelry store, beauty salon, Internet café, and mini-deli. ⊠ *Airport Rd., Simpson Bay* ✆ *Box 3035* ☎ *599/544–3732* 🖷 *599/544–3727* ⊕ *www.sunterra.com* ⇨ *141 suites* ⚹ *Restaurant, kitchens, in-room VCRs, pool, beach, 2 bars, shops, baby-sitting, laundry service* ⊟ *AE, D, MC, V* ⛧ *EP.*

$$$ 🏨 **Princess Heights.** In the hills above Dawn Beach, with a sweeping view of St. Barths, this resort offers plenty of privacy, though it is only a ten-minute drive from Philipsburg. Suites, which have separate bedrooms, are spacious and elegantly furnished, including granite countertops and

marble floors; all have balconies. The beach is just across the road. ⊠ *156 Oyster Pond Rd. Oyster Pond* ☎ *599/543–6906 or 800/441–7227* 🖷 *599/543–6007* ⊕ *www.princessheights.com* ⬚ *15 suites* ⬧ *Fans, kitchens, minibars, in-room safes, cable TV, pool, gym, massage, beach, baby-sitting, dry cleaning, laundry service, concierge, car rental* ☰ *AE, MC, V* ⫟◌⫞ *EP.*

$$–$$$ 🎫 **Great Bay Beach Hotel & Casino.** A 10-minute walk from the heart of Philipsburg, this resort on Great Bay, with its own beach, offers a splen-did view of town, bay, ocean, mountains, and ships as they enter port. Rooms are comfortable, though not richly appointed. Be sure to ask for an ocean view. The Golden Casino is part of the resort. ⊠ *Little Bay Rd., Great Bay* ⬤ *Box 910, Philipsburg* ☎ *599/542–2446 or 800/ 223–0757* 🖷 *599/542–3859* ⊕ *www.greatbayhotel.com* ⬚ *275 rooms, 10 suites* ⬧ *2 restaurants, tennis court, 2 pools, gym, hair salon, beach, snorkeling, boating, 2 bars, casino, nightclub, shops, car rental* ☰ *AE, D, DC, MC, V* ⫟◌⫞ *EP.*

★ $$–$$$ 🎫 **La Vista.** Thirty-two wood-frame bungalow suites connected by brick walkways lined with hibiscus and bougainvillea create a tranquil haven in the heart of bustling Pelican Key; suites, which have balconies, have dazzling Caribbean views. There are also 18 rooms on the beach, so be sure to ask about available options. The beach is rocky but good for snorkeling. Guests of La Vista may use the facilities, including the pool, tennis courts, and spa, at the nearby Pelican Resort, which is within walk-ing distance. ⊠ *Pelican Key Simpson Bay* ⬤ *Box 2086* ☎ *599/544– 3005* 🖷 *599/544–3010* ⊕ *www.lavistaresort.com* ⬚ *18 rooms, 32 suites* ⬧ *Restaurant, fans, some kitchens, some kitchenettes, in-room safes, cable TV, pool, beach, shop, laundry facilities* ☰ *AE, MC, V* ⫟◌⫞ *EP.*

★ $$–$$$ 🎫 **Mary's Boon Beach Plantation.** This charming, Caribbean-style guest house, though right across from the airport, sits on one of the prettiest stretches of Simpson Bay Beach. The lobby has shelves stuffed with books, plus a self-serve honor bar and open-air dining room. Rooms have four-poster king-size beds, verandahs, and air-conditioning. The courtyard pool has a swim-up bar. The restaurant is known island-wide for its chef's-choice menu (Fridays the specialty is lobster creole). ⊠ *17 Simpson Bay Rd., Simpson Bay* ☎ *599/545–4235* 🖷 *599/545–3403* ⊕ *www. marysboon.com* ⬚ *21 rooms* ⬧ *Restaurant, in-room data ports, fans, some kitchens, some kitchenettes, cable TV, pool, beach, 2 bars, Inter-net* ☰ *AE, MC, V* ⫟◌⫞ *EP.*

$$ 🎫 **Divi Little Bay Beach Resort.** Jutting out on a peaceful peninsula at the end of Great Bay, this resort has a panoramic view of Philipsburg to one side and is steps from a private beach on the other, though the sand is gravelly. Rooms and suites are comfortable, though not plush, with king-size beds, wide balconies with sea views, and refrigerators or kitchenettes. ⊠ *Little Bay Rd., Philipsburg* ⬤ *Box 961* ☎ *599/542–2333 or 800/ 367–3484* 🖷 *599/542–4336* ⊕ *www.diviresorts.com* ⬚ *235 rooms* ⬧ *2 restaurants, grocery, some kitchenettes, some refrigerators, tennis court, 3 pools, gym, hair salon, beach, dive shop, snorkeling, boating, 3 bars, shops, laundry facilities, laundry service, car rental* ☰ *AE, D, DC, MC, V* ⫟◌⫞ *EP.*

$$ 🎫 **Holland House Beach Hotel.** This oasis in the heart of Philipsburg is a good value if you like being close to duty-free shopping and don't mind the hustle and bustle of being in town. The shops of Front Street are at this hotel's doorstep, and the mile-long (1½-km-long) Great Bay Beach is out back. Each room (ask for one with a beach view) has a balcony and most have kitchenettes. The open-air restaurant overlooking the water serves reasonably priced dinners, and the indoor-outdoor patio lounge is a popular spot for a quiet breakfast and sunset views. There is free 24-hour Internet access in the lobby. ⊠ *43 Front St., Philipsburg (Box*

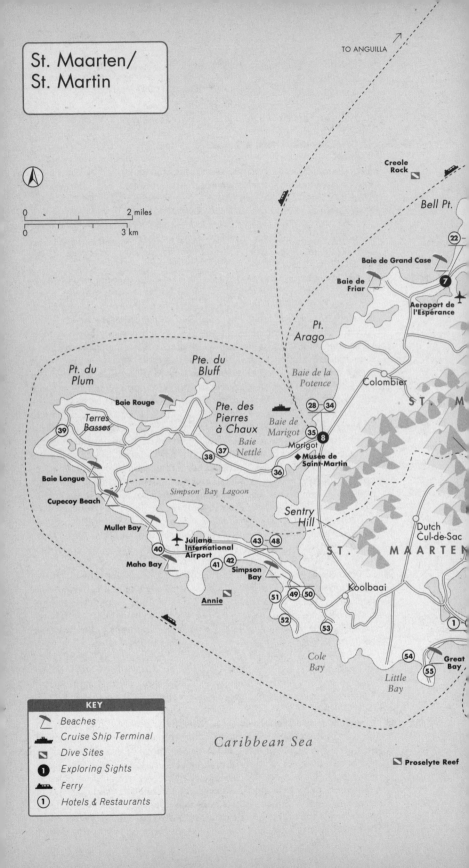

St. Maarten/ St. Martin

TO ANGUILLA

Creole Rock

Bell Pt.

22

Baie de Grand Case

Baie de Friar

7

Aeroport de l'Espérance

Pt. Arago

Baie de la Potence

Colombier

S T. M

Pt. du Plum

Pte. du Bluff

Baie Rouge

Terres Basses

Pte. des Pierres à Chaux

39

Baie de Marigot

28 34

35

8

Marigot

◆ Musée de Saint-Martin

Baie Nettlé

38 37

36

Baie Longue

Cupecoy Beach

Simpson Bay Lagoon

Sentry Hill

Dutch Cul-de-Sac

Mullet Bay

Juliana International Airport

43 48

ST. MAARTEN

Maho Bay

40

41

42

Simpson Bay

49 50

Koolbaai

1

Annie

51

52

53

Cole Bay

54

55

Great Bay

Little Bay

Caribbean Sea

▧ Proselyte Reef

KEY

⌐ Beaches
⛴ Cruise Ship Terminal
▧ Dive Sites
❶ Exploring Sights
🚢 Ferry
① Hotels & Restaurants

0   2 miles
0   3 km

TO ST. BARTHÉLEMY →

Pt. des
Froussards

Anse
Marcel

Red
Rock

Grandes
Cayes

Ile →
Tintamarre

Ilet
Pinel

Baie
Orientale

Green
Key

Orléans

Galion
Beach

Etang
aux Poissons

Baie de
L'Embouchure

Flagstaf

Babit
Pt.

en
en

Boven
Prinsen

Sucker Garden Road

Dawn
Beach

Philipsburg

Geneve Bay

Pelican
Key

ATLANTIC
OCEAN

Pt. Blanche

TO ST. BARTHÉLEMY →

Hotels ▼
Alizéa **19**
Captain Oliver's **11**
Divi Little Bay
Beach Resort **54**
Esmeralda Resort **18**
Grand Case
Beach Club **25**
Great Bay Beach
Hotel & Casino **55**
Green Cay
Village **16**
Holland House
Beach Hotel **7**
The Horny Toad **42**
Hôtel l'Atlantide **26**
Hôtel L'Esplanade
Caraïbes **27**
Hôtel Mont Vernon . . . **17**
Maho Beach
Resort & Casino **40**
Mary's Boon
Beach Plantation **41**
Mercure Coralia
Simson Beach **38**
Le Méridien **21**
Nettlé Bay
Beach Club **37**
Oyster Bay
Beach Resort **10**
Pasanggrahan
Royal Inn **8**
Le Privilege
Resort & Spa **20**
Princess Heights **10**
La Résidence **30**
Le Royale
Louisiana **33**
La Samanna **39**
Sunterra Royal
Palm Beach Club **43**
La Vista **46**

Restaurants ▼
Antoine **1**
Bay Watch **15**
Bistrot Nu **28**
Captain's Cove at
Pelican Reef **52**
Chesterfield's **2**
Claude
Mini-Club **29**
Enoch's Place **32**
L'Escargot **3**
The French Corner **4**
The Green House **9**
Hot Tomatoes **49**
Indiana Beach **47**
La Main À La Paté **34**
Mario's Bistro **35**

Paradise View **14**
Le Perroquet **44**
Le Poulet
d'Orléans **13**
Le Pressoir **22**
The Rainbow **24**
Ric's Place **50**
Le Santal **36**
Saratoga **48**
Shiv Sagar **5**
Spartaco **53**
Le Tastevin **23**
Top Carrot **51**
Turtle Pier Bar
& Restaurant **45**
La Vie En Rose **31**
Wajang Doll **6**
Yvette's **12**

Exploring ▼
Butterfly Farm **4**
French Cul de Sac **6**
Grand Case **7**
Guana Bay Point **2**
Le Fort Louis **9**
Marigot **8**
Orléans **3**
Philipsburg **1**
Pic du Paradis **5**

393) ☎ *599/542–2572 or 800/223–9818* 🖷 *599/542–4673* ⊕ *www.hhbh. com* 🖙 *48 rooms, 6 suites* ⚐ *Restaurant, some in-room faxes, in-room safes, some kitchenettes, refrigerators, cable TV, beach, lounge, Internet, meeting room* 🖃 *AE, D, DC, MC, V* ¶○¶ *EP.*

\$\$
Fodor's Choice
★

🖸 **The Horny Toad.** This marvelous little eight-room, beachfront guest house with a funky name offers the island's best value for those who want to experience a traditional Caribbean vacation at a reasonable cost. Owner Betty Vaughan has been pampering guests as if they were family for more than 20 years, with personal service and casual fun including barbecues under the stars. Rooms are comfortable and meticulous maintained, overlook the white-sand beach at Simpson Bay, and have kitchens. Restaurants and nightlife are a five-minute walk away, so a car is not a necessity. Be sure to book early, because the place fills up fast each year with repeat guests. ⊠ *2 Vlaun Drive Simpson Bay* ☎ *599/545–4323 or 800/ 417–9361* 🖷 *599/545–3316* ⊕ *www.thehornytoadguesthouse.com* 🖙 *8 rooms* ⚐ *Fans, kitchens, beach, laundry service; no a/c in some rooms, no kids under 7* 🖃 *AE, V, MC, D* ¶○¶ *EP.*

\$\$
🖸 **Oyster Bay Beach Resort.** Formerly known as Radisson Vacation Villas, this modern apartment resort is nestled between the ocean and the Oyster Bay Marina on the quieter east side of the island. The pool overlooks the sea from a dramatic drop-off, and you're only steps away from Dawn Beach, which has one of the nicest strips of white sand on St. Maarten as well as snorkeling reefs. You're also just a two-minute walk from the French side and a ten-minute drive from bustling Philipsburg. ⊠ *10 Emerald Merit Rd., Oyster Pond* ⓓ *Box 239, Philipsburg* ☎ *599/543– 6042 or 877/478–6669* 🖷 *599/543–6695* ⊕ *www.oysterbaybeachresort. com* 🖙 *190 condos* ⚐ *Restaurant, some kitchenettes, some kitchens, some in-room VCRs, pool, beach, bicycles, gym, hot tub, massage, bar, shops, laundry service, car rental* 🖃 *AE, D, MC, V* ¶○¶ *EP.*

\$–\$\$
🖸 **Pasanggrahan Royal Inn.** Formerly the governor's home, this is the oldest colonial-style inn on St. Maarten. Though set in the heart of bustling Philipsburg, it oozes romance and 19th-century ambience. Wicker peacock chairs, balconies shaded by tropical greenery, and four-poster beds with mosquito nets add to the relaxed, tropical allure. The patio restaurant has excellent meals for a reasonable price: try an \$8 omelet for breakfast or \$9 pasta special for lunch while looking out over the beach on Great Bay. ⊠ *15 Front St., Philipsburg* ⓓ *Box 151* ☎ *599/542–3588 or 599/542–2743* 🖷 *599/542–2885* 🖙 *27 rooms, 1 suite* ⚐ *Restaurant, in-room safes, refrigerators, beach, bar* 🖃 *AE, MC, V* ¶○¶ *EP.*

FRENCH SIDE
\$\$\$\$
🖸 **La Samanna.** Overlooking a perfect white beach and set on 55 acres of lush gardens, this Mediterranean-style retreat is pure luxury. The designer rooms are furnished with mahogany and teak imports, and there are also ultraluxurious penthouses and suites for the chic set. The service is impeccable, the food exquisite. ⊠ *Baie Longue* ⓓ *Box 4007, Marigot 97064* ☎ *590/87–64–00 or 800/854–2252* 🖷 *590/87–87–86* ⊕ *www.lasamanna.orient-express.com* 🖙 *81 units* ⚐ *Restaurant, 3 tennis courts, pool, health club, spa, beach, windsurfing, waterskiing, bar, shops* 🖃 *AE, MC, V* ⊘ *Closed Sept.–Oct.* ¶○¶ *BP.*

★ \$\$\$\$
🖸 **Le Méridien.** Nestled on the secluded north shore, Le Méridien is simply the island's finest resort. Though pricey, it offers high value for those who desire a peaceful retreat, fine dining, and a private beach. The resort consists of two smaller complexes, L'Habitation and Le Domaine. Popular with couples and families, Le Méridien has 1,600 ft of white-sand beach and acres of beautifully landscaped gardens on enchanting Anse Marcel Cove. All rooms have balconies, and those on the marina have fully equipped kitchens and patios. Guests also have free access to the facilities at Le Privilege Resort & Spa. ⊠ *Anse Marcel* ⓓ *Box 581,*

97150 ⊕ *bear north at French Cul de Sac, follow signs to Anse Mar-cel* ☎ *590/87–67–00 or 800/543–4300* 🖶 *590/87–30–38* ⊕ *www. lemeridien-hotels.com* ⇨ *396 rooms, 37 suites* ⚤ *4 restaurants, some kitchens, refrigerators, 6 tennis courts, 2 pools, aerobics, gym, beach, dive shop, dock, snorkeling, boating, jet skiing, waterskiing, racquet-ball, squash, 3 bars, shops, car rental* 🖃 *AE, DC, MC, V* ⏀ *BP.*

$$$$ 🖽 **Le Privilege Resort & Spa.** This resort, perched above Marcel Cove and Le Méridien on the remote, northern tip of the island, is for those who want a pampered, restful getaway. The health spa, fitness and workout center, and aerobics classes are among the island's best. Rooms and suites, many with ocean views, are spacious and comfortably furnished, with tile floors, marble baths, and CD players. There's a free shuttle down to the beach and the resort's marina. Though Marcel Cove is isolated from the rest of the island by a mountain, you are only a 15-minute drive from Grand Case or Orient Bay. ⊠ *Anse Marcel 97150, bear left at French Cul de Sac, follow signs over the mountain* ☎ *590/87–38–38 or 800/ 874–8541* 🖶 *590/87–44–12* ⊕ *www.privilege-spa.com* ⇨ *31 rooms* ⚤ *2 restaurants, in-room safes, in-room VCRs, 6 tennis courts, 3 pools, hair salon, health club, spa, dive shop, dock, windsurfing, boating, fishing, racquetball, squash, bar, nightclub* 🖃 *AE, D, MC, V* ⏀ *BP.*

$$$–$$$$ 🖽 **Esmeralda Resort.** Above Orient Bay, this upscale villa complex has private pools, restaurants, and ocean views; in addition, it offers as full a range of activities and services as any resort, including snorkeling, car rental, tennis, and baby-sitting. All rooms and suites, which are in 18 villas, have fully-equipped kitchenettes. Each villa has a private pool, which the rooms in that villa share, and all rooms have terraces. Five beachfront restaurants in the area let you charge meals to your room. Though pricey, this resort offers excellent value for money, with many amenities, including a free 2-hour tennis clinic. ⊠ *Baie Orientale* ⓓ *Box 5141, 97064* ☎ *590/87–36–36 or 800/622–7836* 🖶 *590/87–35–18* ⊕ *www.esmeralda-resort.com* ⇨ *65 rooms in 18 villas* ⚤ *2 restaurants, room service, fans, in-room safes, some kitchenettes, some kitchens, cable TV, 2 tennis courts, 17 pools, massage, beach, snorkeling, windsurfing, parasailing, waterskiing, shops, baby-sitting, laundry service, business services, Internet* 🖃 *AE, MC, V* ⏀ *EP.*

$$$–$$$$ 🖽 **Grand Case Beach Club.** This gated condo complex combines the best view of the Grand Case beachfront with its own "secret" crescent of sand looking toward Anguilla and Creole Rock. For pampered restau-rant service on the beach, just raise the blue flag by your beach chair, and a waiter from the Sunset Café will come to take your order. Or go on a two-minute trip into Grand Case for a choice of excellent water-front restaurants, among the finest in the Caribbean. The tastefully fur-nished studios and one- and two-bedroom apartments have balconies or patios; the 62 oceanfront units are in greatest demand, so be sure to ask for them specifically. ⊠ *21 Rue de Petit Plage, at the north end of Blvd. de Grand Case, Grand Case* ⓓ *Box 339, 97150* ☎ *590/87–51– 87 or 800/537–8483* 🖶 *590/87–59–93* ⊕ *www.grandcasebeachclub.com* ⇨ *69 condos* ⚤ *Restaurant, kitchens, in-room safes, cable TV, tennis court, beach, dive shop, snorkeling, waterskiing, bar, shops, laundry fa-cilities, laundry service, Internet, car rental* 🖃 *AE, MC, V* ⏀ *CP.*

★ $$$–$$$$ 🖽 **Green Cay Village.** This elegant collection of villas, located high above Orient Bay facing the Atlantic Ocean trade winds, is ideal for small groups or families. Each of the spacious one-, two-, and three-bedroom villas— some as large as 4,500 square feet—has its own pool, large deck, full kitchen, and dining patio. The area is quiet and safe. The beach and restau-rants are a ten-minute walk away. Daily maid service is included. Al-though all villas have plenty of privacy, those highest on the hill enjoy the most seclusion—and the best views. ⊠ *Parc de la Baie Orientale,*

*Baie Oriental ✆ Box 3006, 97064 ☎ 590/87–38–63 or 888/843–4760
🖷 590/87–39–27 ⊕ www.greencayvillage.com ✎ 16 villas ⚲ Kitchens,
cable TV, in-room VCRs, tennis court, 16 pools, baby-sitting, laundry
service, airport shuttle ⊟ AE, MC, V ⫶⊘⫶ EP.*

$$–$$$$ ⊞ **Hotel Mont Vernon.** Creole-inspired architecture marks this rambling,
first-class hotel, which sits on a 70-acre bluff above Orient Bay in one
of the quietest, most beautiful spots on St. Martin. It has one of the largest
freshwater swimming pools on the island. Oceanfront rooms are slightly
larger, but all the rooms have balconies. This is a big resort that attracts
many package-tour groups as well as business seminars. Complimen-
tary transportation is provided to casinos and nightlife in Philipsburg.
⊠ *French Cul de Sac, Baie Orientale ✆ Box 1174, 97062 ☎ 590/87–
62–40 🖷 590/87–37–27 ⊕ www.hotelmontvernon.com ✎ 394 rooms
⚲ 2 restaurants, in-room safes, refrigerators, 2 tennis courts, 2 pools,
gym, beach, snorkeling, windsurfing, badminton, Ping Pong, volleyball,
2 bars, shops, baby-sitting, children's programs (ages 5–12), meeting
rooms, car rental, some pets allowed ⊟ AE, DC, MC, V ⫶⊘⫶ BP.*

★ $$$ ⊞ **Hôtel L'Esplanade Caraïbes.** This intimate, 24-unit Mediterranean-
style complex, with its breathtaking view from a hilltop overlooking the
village of Grand Case and the bay, is ideal for those looking for a relaxing getaway. Still, you are only a short walk down the hillside from
town or beach. Two curved stone staircases with inlaid tile and brick
lead up to the open-air reception area. Tastefully decorated suites are
large, and duplexes have cathedral ceilings and mahogany staircases as
well as an extra half-bath and a loft bedroom. Grand Case's roster of
fine restaurants is a three-minute walk away. Marigot or Orient Bay are
ten-minute drives. ⊠ *Grand Case ✆ Box 5007, 97150 ☎ 590/87–
06–55 🖷 590/87–29–15 ⊕ www.lesplanade.com ✎ 24 units ⚲ Kitchens,
in-room safes, cable TV, 2 pools, wading pool, laundry service, car
rental ⊟ AE, MC, V ⫶⊘⫶ EP.*

$$–$$$ ⊞ **Alizéa.** The view of Orient Bay from this peaceful hilltop resort is stun-
ning. An open-air feeling pervades the hotel, starting with the paperback honor library at the reception desk to the patio terrace, with a
sweeping view that includes the island of St. Barths, several miles off
shore. The 26 guest apartments offer a pick of Creole or West Indian
decor. All rooms are tasteful, with large balconies, kitchens, ceiling
fans, and air-conditioning. There's a path to the beach, a 10-minute walk
away. Some rooms have fold-out sofas for children or a third person;
bungalows can accommodate four. ⊠ *Mont Vernon 97150, bear right
on road to French Cul de Sac ☎ 590/87–33–42 🖷 590/87–41–15
⊕ www.alizeahotel.com ✎ 8 1-bedroom bungalows, 18 studios
⚲ Restaurant, fans, kitchens, cable TV, pool, bar ⊟ AE, D, MC, V ⫶⊘⫶ CP.*

$$–$$$ ⊞ **Hôtel l'Atlantide.** This homey 10-unit boutique hotel in the heart of
Grand Case is more like a trim, well-maintained residence than a resort. Grab your own beach chair and step through the ship's-hatch
door in the lobby right onto the sands of Grand Case Bay. Apartments
range in size from a studio to a two-bedroom suite. They are airy, with
gleaming white-tile floors, crisp pastel-striped or floral upholstery, and
balconies that overlook Grand Case Bay and the beach. In the heart of
Grand Case, it is just steps from some of the best dining in all the
Caribbean. ⊠ *Blvd. de Grand Case, Grand Case ✆ Box 5140, 97150
☎ 590/87–09–80 🖷 590/87–12–36 ✎ 10 apartments ⚲ Kitchenettes,
beach ⊟ MC, V ⫶⊘⫶ EP ⊘ Closed Sept.*

$$–$$$ ⊞ **Mercure Coralia Simson Beach.** A five-minute drive from Marigot,
this resort is a favorite among budget-conscious Europeans for its huge
breakfast buffet and nightly local entertainment. Rooms and suites are
basic and comfortable, with kitchenettes on the balconies. Many have
water views. The lagoon is placid, but the beach is thin and the water

rocky. The location is peaceful, with grocery stores and night spots a short walk away. ⊠ *Sandy Ground Rd., Baie Nettlé* ☎ *Box 172, 97052* ☎ *590/87-54-54* 📠 *590/87-92-11* ⊕ *www.mercure-simson-beach. com* ➥ *132 studios, 46 1-bedroom duplexes* ♿ *Restaurant, grocery, kitchenettes, tennis court, 2 pools, hair salon, beach, dive shop, snorkeling, windsurfing, boating, jet skiing, waterskiing, bicycles, bar, shops, laundry facilities, car rental* ⊟ *AE, DC, MC, V* ❑ *BP.*

$$–$$$ 🏨 **Nettlé Bay Beach Club.** Tile floors, rattan furniture, sandy walkways, and breezy, aqua colors give the beach club a distinct Caribbean flavor. About five minutes from Marigot, facing the open sea, Nettlé Bay has four sets of villa suites (one- or two-bedroom) and a set of garden bungalows, each with its own pool. Rooms and suites are furnished simply but comfortably and have kitchens, as well as patios or balconies. The on-site restaurants serve South American and French cuisine. ⊠ *Sandy Ground Rd., Baie Nettlé* ☎ *Box 4081, Marigot 97064* ☎ *590/87-68-68* 📠 *590/87-21-51* ➥ *45 rooms, 105 suites* ♿ *2 restaurants, some kitchens, 3 tennis courts, 4 pools, beach, snorkeling, jet skiing, bar, shops, laundry service* ⊟ *AE, MC, V* ❑ *EP.*

$$ 🏨 **Captain Oliver's.** This marina-resort-restaurant on the island's laid-back east side near Dawn Beach straddles the Dutch–French border. Stay in France, and dine in the Netherlands—literally. The bungalow suites are comfortable and reasonably priced. Sail-and-stay packages are popular. The four-star restaurant, with roped walkways on the marina, serves fresh-baked breads and a Caribbean menu. The creole conch and sautéed shrimp are excellent. Although there is no beach, the pool is available for both hotel and restaurant guests. ⊠ *Oyster Pond 97150, on the east side of Oyster Pond* ☎ *590/87-40-26* 📠 *590/87-40-84* ⊕ *www. captainolivers.com* ➥ *50 suites* ♿ *Restaurant, grill, snack bar, in-room safes, some kitchenettes, minibars, pool, dive shop, marina, 2 bars, shops* ⊟ *AE, DC, MC, V* ❑ *CP.*

¢–$ 🏨 **La Résidence.** The downtown location, low cost, and soundproof rooms of this Marigot hotel make it a popular place for business travelers and the budget conscious. The spartan rooms are reflected in the reasonable rates. An intimate restaurant offers a good $28 three-course menu. You're in the heart of Marigot, just a minute's walk from the city's beautiful waterfront and marina. However, you'll have to take a cab or drive to the beach. ⊠ *Rue du Général de Gaulle, Marigot* ☎ *Box 679, 97150* ☎ *590/87-70-37 or 800/223-9815* 📠 *590/87-90-44* ➥ *22 rooms* ♿ *Restaurant, minibars, lounge, shops* ⊟ *AE, D, MC, V* ❑ *CP.*

¢–$ 🏨 **Le Royale Louisiana.** This inexpensive and basic hotel's white-and-pale-green galleries overlook a flower-filled courtyard. There's a selection of simply-furnished, no-frills rooms, but the New Orleans–inspired courtyard offers a quiet haven for relaxation. Although you may need to take a taxi to the beach (the nearest one is a 20-minute walk away), you'll find plenty of shopping just steps from your door in downtown Marigot's boutique area. ⊠ *Rue du Général de Gaulle, Marigot* ☎ *Box 476, 97055* ☎ *590/87-86-51* 📠 *590/87-96-49* ➥ *58 rooms* ♿ *Restaurant, snack bar, hair salon* ⊟ *AE, D, MC, V* ❑ *CP.*

Villas

Both sides of the island have villas of different sizes and for different budgets. On the island, contact **Carimo** (☎ Rue du Général de Gaulle, ☎ Box 220, Marigot 97150 ☎ 590/87-57-58), which has villas for rent in the tony Terres Basses area. **French Caribbean International** (☎ 5662 Calle Real, No. 333, Santa Barbara, CA 93117-2317 ☎ 805/967-9850 or 800/322-2223 ⊕ www.frenchcaribbean.com) offers island condos and villas. **St. Martin Rentals** (☎ 26 Beacon Hill St. Martin ☎ 599/545-4330 ⊠ Box 10300, Bedford, NH 03110 ☎ 800/308-8455) represents several rental properties. With over 25 years experience, it is the oldest villa-rental company on the island. **Villas of Distinction** (⌾ Box 55, Armonk, NY 10504 ☎ 914/273–3331 or 800/289–0900 ⊕ www. villasofdistinction.com) is one of the oldest villa rental companies serving the island. **WIMCO** (⌾ Box 1461, Newport, RI 02840 ☎ 401/849–8012 or 800/932–3222 ⊕ www.wimco.com) has more villa, apartment, and condo listings in the Caribbean than just about anyone else.

Where to Eat

St. Maarten's identity as a cultural crossroads is reflected in the many different types of excellent restaurants. Whether your tastes run to Italian, Tex-Mex, Vietnamese, French, Bavarian, Caribbean, or even downhome American, it could take months to eat your way across the island. Prices can be steep, a reflection both of the island's high culinary reputation and the difficulty of obtaining fresh ingredients. In high season, **make reservations.** A month's notice is needed for many of the island's top restaurants, especially on the French side. Many restaurants close during summer months; call ahead to check hours. Some restaurants include a 15% service charge, so go over your bill before tipping.

What to Wear

Appropriate dining attire on this island ranges from swimsuits to sport jackets. For men, a jacket and khakis or jeans will take you anywhere; for women, dressy pants, a skirt, or even fancy shorts are usually acceptable. Jeans are de rigueur in the less formal and trendier eateries. In the listings below dress is casual (and chic) unless otherwise noted, but ask when making reservations if you're unsure.

Dutch Side

AMERICAN ✕ **Ric's Place.** This airy, American-style café and sports bar on Simpson
¢–$ Bay Lagoon is popular with island residents and visitors hungry for Texas-
Fodor'sChoice sized black Angus burgers and Tex-Mex fare at low prices. Owners Ric
★ and Kathy Hetzel have kept most meals around $8, and they serve breakfast, lunch, and dinner. Try the nachos *grande* with a couple of friends while you watch one (or two) of six satellite televisions. ⊠ *12 Airport Rd., Simpson Bay* ☎ *599/545–3630* ▭ *No credit cards.*

ASIAN ✕ **Wajang Doll.** Indonesian dishes are served in the garden of this West
$$ Indian–style house. *Nasi goreng* (fried rice) and red snapper in a sweet soy glaze are standouts, as is *rijsttafel,* a traditional Indonesian meal of rice accompanied by 15 to 20 dishes. (The restaurant's name comes from the *wajang* doll, which is used in Indonesian shadow plays, a traditional art form.) ⊠ *167 Front St., Philipsburg* ☎ *599/542–2687* ▭ *AE, MC, V* ☉ *Closed Sun. No lunch Sat.*

CAFÉ ✕ **The French Corner.** A rich selection of Italian ice cream, fresh crêpes,
¢–$ hearty salads, and hot or cold sandwiches on fresh bread makes this little, out-of-the-way café just off Back Street worth the visit for a quick, inexpensive snack when you are in Philipsburg. Watching employees make the crêpes is half the fun; eating them is the other half. It opens at 11 AM ⊠ *120 Old St., Philipsburg* ☎ *059/027–0200* ▭ *No credit cards.*

CARIBBEAN ✕ **Hot Tomatoes.** This casual gourmet Caribbean café on Simpson Bay
$$–$$$ Lagoon has such traditional island favorites as jerk chicken, tequila-lime shrimp, and curried mahimahi, plus spicy pasta dishes, steak, pizza, and lobster, all served in a spacious, cantinalike atmosphere. The chargrilled New York strip is good and tender, with a hint of wood smoke. The spot is open seven days from 3 PM, with live contemporary and jazz music every night during the the high season, and lots of off-street park-

ing. ⊠ *46 Airport Rd. Simpson Bay* ☎ *599/545–2223* ▭ *AE, MC, V*
⊘ *No lunch.*

$$
Fodor'sChoice
★
✕ **Turtle Pier Bar & Restaurant.** The atmosphere at this restaurant on the Simpson Bay Lagoon waterfront is pure Caribbean, though the menu runs the gamut from steak to seafood to duck. Uncertain what to order? You'll always be safe with the coconut shrimp. Or choose your own live lobster on the way in. Open seven days a week for breakfast, lunch, and dinner, Turtle Pier has daily specials, including all-you-can-eat Sunday rib dinners, dinner-cruise specials, and live music several nights a week. ⊠ *114 Airport Rd., Simpson Bay* ☎ *599/545–2562* ▭ *AE, D, MC, V.*

CONTEMPORARY
$$–$$$
✕ **Le Perroquet.** This romantic restaurant overlooking the lagoon has a relaxing, green-and-white West Indian decor and offers good quality for a good price. Specialties include pastas, fresh seafood (try the red snapper in garlic-cream sauce), Long Island duck, and grilled steaks (the filet mignon with green peppercorn sauce is for diners who appreciate a good cut of meat). ⊠ *106 Airport Rd., Simpson Bay* ☎ *599/545–4339* ▭ *AE, MC, V* ⊘ *Closed Mon., June, and Sept. No lunch.*

CONTINENTAL
$$
✕ **Chesterfield's.** On the Great Bay waterfront, a five-minute walk from the ship pier in Philipsburg, nautically themed "Chesty's" serves breakfast, lunch, and dinner at reasonable prices. The main fare is steak and seafood, though the dinner menu includes French onion soup, roast duckling with fresh pineapple and banana sauce, and several different shrimp dishes. The Mermaid Bar is popular with yachties. ⊠ *Great Bay Marina, Philipsburg* ☎ *599/542–3484* ▭ *MC, V.*

ECLECTIC
$$–$$$$
✕ **Indiana Beach.** This light-hearted restaurant and bar is fronted by Kimsha Beach at Simpson Bay. The motif is exotic jungle, with cavernous arches and terra-cotta walls painted with designs based on pre-Columbian petroglyphs. You can swim at Kimsha or at the restaurant's own pool. Meals are hearty and reasonably priced, including sandwiches, steaks, and seafood. ⊠ *8 Billy Folly Rd., Simpson Bay* ☎ *599/544–2797* ▭ *AE, MC, V.*

$$–$$$
✕ **Captain's Cove at Pelican Reef.** Go for the spectacular sunset, then stay for the fine food. At Pelican Key marina, with a sweeping view of Kimsha Bay and Saba, this elegant restaurant serves fine steak, ribs, and seafood along with a wide selection of quality wines. The Gaucho prime Argentine beef tenderloin is especially recommended. The Cove also has a daily prix-fixe menu (Monday is Scampi Platter night). ⊠ *Waterfront Marina Plaza, below the Pelican Resort Club, Simpson Bay* ☎ *599/544–2616* ▭ *AE, D, MC, V* ⊘ *No lunch.*

★ $$–$$$
✕ **Saratoga.** An island favorite for 15 years, Saratoga has built a loyal following of return patrons, so make reservations. The handsome mahogany-paneled dining room in the yacht club's stucco and red-tile building overlooks the Simpson Bay Marina. The menu changes daily, but you can never go wrong with one of the fresh fish dishes. You might start with a spicy ceviche of snapper with mango and tortilla chips, then segue into grilled grouper fillet or a cured pork tenderloin. The wine list includes 10 to 12 choices by the glass. ⊠ *Simpson Bay Yacht Club, Airport Rd., Simpson Bay* ☎ *599/544–2421* ⌖ *Reservations essential* ▭ *AE, MC, V* ⊘ *Closed Sun. and Aug.–Sept. No lunch.*

¢–$$
✕ **The Green House.** This open-air harborfront restaurant in Philipsburg balances a relaxed atmosphere, reasonable prices, and quality food with a just-right, flavorful bite. All beef dishes are black Angus, and some people say the burgers and steaks are the best on the island. For the spicy palate, try the black-bean soup or Jamaica jerked chicken wrap. The Green House is nestled between Bobby's Marina and the start of Front Street at the marina on Great Bay. ⊠ *Knaalsteeg, Philipsburg* ☎ *599/542-2941* ▭ *AE, D, MC, V.*

FRENCH
★ $$–$$$$

✕ **Antoine.** This elegant Philipsburg landmark overlooks Great Bay, with an airy view of the mountains and cruise ships as they enter and leave port. Candles glow on tables set with crisp blue-and-white table-cloths and gleaming silver, and the sound of the surf drifts up from the beach. You might start your meal with a rich, flavorful lobster bisque, then move on to lobster thermidor, the house favorite. You can also get a excellent steak. Valet parking is available in season. You can also lunch in the thatched roof huts right on the sand. Say hello to accommodating owner Jean-Pierre. ✉ *119 Front St., Philipsburg* ☎ *599/542–2964* ⌨ *Reservations essential* 🖃 *AE, MC, V.*

$$–$$$$

✕ **L'Escargot.** One of the oldest restaurants on the island, L'Escargot has passed the test of time: it is also one of St. Martin's finest and friendliest places to dine, known for great food and friendly atmosphere. Enter the 19th-century verandah-wrapped house on Philipsburg's Front Street, and you could be dining in the heart of Provence. The restaurant is famous for snails imported from Burgundy, as its name might suggest. If you're not sure how you would like them, ask owners Jöel and Sonya for an escargot sampler appetizer. Or try one of the many lobster, shrimp, duck, or melt-in-your-mouth steak dishes. The rack of lamb is Sonya's favorite. If you have Friday evening free, make reservations for the cabaret-style floor show. ✉ *84 Front St. Philipsburg* ☎ *599/542–2483* 🖃 *AE, MC, V.*

INDIAN
$$

✕ **Shiv Sagar.** This large second-floor restaurant in Philipsburg emphasizes Kashmiri and Mughal specialties. Marvelous tandooris (boneless chicken) and curry dishes are on offer, but try one of the less familiar preparations such as *madrasi machi* (red snapper with hot spices). ✉ *20 Front St., opposite Barclay's Bank, Philipsburg* ☎ *599/542–2299* 🖃 *AE, D, DC, MC, V* ☾ *Closed Sun.*

ITALIAN
$$–$$$

✕ **Spartaco.** Whether you dine on the verandah or inside the 200-year-old stone plantation house, every table shares in the intimate, warm atmosphere of this northern Italian restaurant. For nearly 20 years, Spartaco himself has been greeting his customers at the steps and recommending such house specialties as the black angel-hair pasta with shrimp and garlic or veal Vesuviana with mozzarella, oregano, and tomato sauce. ✉ *Almond Grove, Cole Bay* ☎ *599/544–5379* 🖃 *AE, MC, V* ☾ *Closed Mon. and June–Oct. No lunch.*

VEGETARIAN
¢

✕ **Top Carrot.** This vegetarian café and juice bar serves sandwiches, salads, and homemade pastries for breakfast and lunch, until closing time at 6 PM. The signature Top Carrot sandwich is a pita or French bread stuffed with roasted bell peppers, tomato, mozzarella, and tuna, with balsamic vinegar dressing, well worth the $6 price tag. You can also get health-food ingredients such as homemade granola and yogurt, plus books on eating healthy. ✉ *Airport Rd., near Simpson Bay Yacht Club, Simpson Bay* ☎ *599/544–3381* ☾ *Closed Sun.*

French Side

AMERICAN-
CASUAL
★ ¢–$$

✕ **Bay Watch.** This ultra-casual beachfront eatery on Orient Bay is like a Jersey Shore bar and grill, with owners Cheryl and Andy serving up hot wings and sausage and pepper sandwiches, along with the friendliest, neighborhood-bar atmosphere on the island. Ask Cheryl to rattle off the daily specials. Try the grouper Caesar salad for $13. They're open for breakfast, too. ✉ *Orient Beach* ☎ *690/66–22–27* ☾ *No dinner.*

CARIBBEAN
$$–$$$

✕ **Claude Mini-Club.** This brightly decorated upstairs restaurant on Marigot Harbor has served traditional creole and French cuisine for more than 30 years. The chairs and madras tablecloths are a mélange of sun-yellow and orange, and the whole place is built (tree house–style) around the trunks of coconut trees. It's the place to be on Wednesday and Saturday nights, when the dinner buffet includes roast pig, lobster, roast beef, and all the trimmings. ⊠ *Front de Mer, Marigot* ☎ *590/87–50–69* ⊟ *AE, MC, V* ☉ *No lunch Sun.*

★ $$–$$$ ✕ **Paradise View.** The view is indeed breathtaking from this aerie perched atop one of the island's most scenic lookouts, where you look out over Orient Beach, the coast, and St. Barths. The atmosphere is relaxed, open-air, and very Caribbean. Owner Claudette Davis is an island native, willing to share local history and the stories behind her spicy dishes, which include conch and dumplings, ribs, traditional beef stew, and the house drink, mango madness colada (free with lunch). ⊠ *Hope Hill, Orient Bay* ☎ *590/29–45–37* ⊟ *AE, MC, V.*

$–$$$ ✕ **Yvette's.** Though short on atmosphere, this cozy little Caribbean restaurant serves such creole specialties as *accras*(spicy fish fritters), stewed chicken with rice and beans, and conch and dumplings, making Yvette's an island favorite. ⊠ *Off Orléans Rd., Orléans* ☎ *590/87–32–03* ⊟ *No credit cards* ☉ *Closed Wed.*

$$ ✕ **Le Poulet d'Orléans.** Chef Tony and his children serve up warm service and quality food in their four-table restaurant in their roadside gingerbread home. The local specialties include seafood, conch, dumplings, and ribs. ⊠ *Orient Bay Hwy., French Quarter* ☎ *590/87–48–24* ⊟ *No credit cards* ☉ *Closed Mon. No lunch except Sun.*

¢–$ ✕ **Enoch's Place.** Enoch's cooking draws crowds of locals and visitors each day to the blue-and-white-striped awning on a corner of the Marigot Market. Local specialties include garlic and creole shrimp, and fresh lobster. For breakfast, try cod in fried johnnycakes. Enoch's Place is one of about a dozen mini-restaurants—all worth visiting—in this unusual open-air building on the waterfront. ⊠ *Marigot Market, Front de Mer, Marigot* ☎ *590/29–29–88* ⊟ *No credit cards* ☉ *Closed Sun.*

CONTEMPORARY ✕ **Le Tastevin.** This chic pavilion lookout out on Grand Case Bay is filled
$$$–$$$$ with tropical plants and cooled by ceiling fans. Owner Daniel Passeri, a native of Burgundy, also founded the homey Auberge Gourmande across the street. The menu here is more ambitious, including foie gras in Armagnac sauce, duck breast in banana-lime sauce, and red snapper fillet with curry and wild-mushroom sauce. ⊠ *86 bd. de Grand Case, Grand Case* ☎ *590/87–55–45* ⚐ *Reservations essential* ⊟ *AE, MC, V.*

ECLECTIC ✕ **The Rainbow.** In a town of splendid seaside dining spots, this is one
★ $$$–$$$$ of the best. The cobalt-blue-and-white, split-level dining room is strikingly simple. Lapping waves and gentle breezes make for a highly romantic mood. Fleur and David are the stylish, energetic hosts. Specialties include shrimp and scallop fricassee with Caribbean chutney, and dishes are dressed with such fanciful touches as red-cabbage crisps. ⊠ *176 bd. de Grand Case, Grand Case* ☎ *590/87–55–80* ⊟ *AE, MC, V* ☉ *Closed Sun.*

★ $$$ ✕ **Le Pressoir.** Many say that presentation is everything. Combine that with excellent food and a setting in a charming West Indian house, where the bill won't break the bank, and you have a great restaurant. French and creole cuisine reign, especially fresh local fish. Try the grilled snapper in vanilla sauce, followed by a dessert of crème brûlée. 30 bd. de Grand Case, Grand Case ☎ *590/87–76–62* ⊟ *AE, MC, V* ☉ *Closed Sun. No lunch.*

★ $–$$$ ✕ **La Main á La Páte.** This Marina Royale restaurant offers a world-ranging menu with everything from pizza to French cuisine, fish to pasta, plus daily specials to please most palates. It combines impeccable service (all waitstaff speak at least two languages) with exceptional food, making it one of the outstanding, must-try restaurants on St. Martin. A highlight is the lobster-tail salad, which is a light combination of firm lobster meat. La palette Caraïbes, which includes three different fish, includes the tastiest tuna steak on the island. Be sure to ask about passion pie with mango ice cream for dessert. You'll get a free drink if you come in with your Fodor's guide. ⊠ *Marina Royale on the waterfront, Marigot* ☎ *590/87–71–19* ⊟ *D, MC, V.*

FRENCH   ✕ **Le Santal.** The location of this fine restaurant is out of the way (turn
$$$–$$$$ left immediately before the bridge heading into Marigot from Sandy Ground), and the neighborhood is a bit scruffy, but the interior is transformed by soft lighting, china, and crystal. Specialties by chef Marc Daniel, who trained at Paris's Lasserre restaurant, include roasted lobster with shallots and tomatoes, foie gras sautéed in cassis, and lacquered duck. Reserve one of the five cherished waterside tables. ⊠ *Sandy Ground Rd., Sandy Ground* ☎ *590/87–53–48* ⊟ *AE, MC, V* ☽ *No lunch.*

$$–$$$$ ✕ **La Vie En Rose.** This bustling curbside café on the Marigot waterfront serves classic French cuisine with an occasional Caribbean twist, as in the filet of red snapper in a puff pastry served with fresh herbs and lime sauce. The food is excellent and the service attentive. For lunch, start off with the cold mango soup and follow with a baked-goat-cheese salad ($11). For dinner, you can't go wrong with anything on the menu, from fish to meat to poultry. ⊠ *On the waterfront, at rue de la République, Marigot* ☎ *590/87–54–42* ⊟ *AE, D, MC, V.*

★ $$–$$$ ✕ **Mario's Bistro.** This fabulous, romantic eatery earns raves for its fine service and high-quality cuisine. Didier Gonnon and Martyne Tardif are out front, while chef Mario Tardif is in the kitchen creating dishes such as baked salmon in a caramelized onion crust. The open-air country French–style restaurant is on the canal as you enter Marigot from Sandy Ground, and if you didn't know better you might think you were in Venice. ⊠ *Sandy Ground* ☎ *590/87–06–36* ⌕ *Reservations essential* ⊟ *MC, V* ☽ *Closed Sun. and mid-June–July. No lunch.*

★ $–$$ ✕ **Bistrot Nu.** It's hard to top the simple, unadorned fare and reasonable prices you'll find at this intimate restaurant tucked in a Marigot alley. Traditional brasserie-style food—coq au vin, fish soup, snails—is served in a friendly, intimate dining room. The place is enormously popular, and the tables are routinely packed until it closes at midnight. ⊠ *Rue de Hollande, Marigot* ☎ *590/87–97–09* ⊟ *MC, V* ☽ *Closed Sun. No lunch.*

Beaches

The island's 10 mi (16 km) of beaches—all open to the public—range from powder-soft sand and gentle surf for sun lounging to rocky and rough, with reefs for snorkeling; from romantically secluded to beach-bar bustling. Take your pick. Topless bathing is virtually de rigueur on the French side. Don't leave valuables unattended on the beach or in your rental car—even in the trunk.

Dutch Side
Cupecoy Beach. Near the Dutch–French border and south of Baie Longue, this small clothing-optional strip is one of the finest beaches on the island, with soft, white sand. Though the beach is a bit secluded, vendors sell cold drinks and rent chairs and umbrellas.

★   **Dawn Beach–Oyster Pond.** On the rustic east side of the island, this stretch of white sand has one of the finest beaches for sunning, snorkeling, and body surfing. It is not well marked, so follow the signs for either Mr. Busby's or Scavenger's restaurant.

Great Bay. This long stretch of white sand runs behind Philipsburg's Front Street. There are many beachside bistros, restaurants, and shops, some renting water-sports equipment. The bay is a favorite with cruise-ship passengers, but swim with caution; the water isn't always as clean as that of other beaches.

Mullet Bay. Though rocky in places where you enter the water (listen for the "whispering pebbles" as the waves wash up), this beach, with its powdery-white sands, is a favorite with locals and students from the nearby medical school. Open-air concessions sell drinks, burgers, and ribs.

Simpson Bay. This long half-moon of white sand on the Caribbean Sea is tucked just southeast of the airport. Follow the signs to Mary's Boon and the Horny Toad guesthouses. Most of the properties on the beach are locally owned private residences, so there are no commercial spots for refreshments.

French Side

Baie de Friar. This unexceptional beach at Friar's Bay is at the end of a poorly maintained dirt road. On a small, picturesque cove between Marigot and Grand Case, it attracts a casual crowd of locals and has a small snack bar and restaurant.

Baie de Grand Case. A gentle surf and plenty of fine restaurants are the draws of the thin beach at Grand Case Bay. You'll find water-sports activities, and, at the north end, small coves. The snorkeling is best at the south end. On the north end you'll find several *lolos,* barbecue huts that serve inexpensive local fare.

Baie Longue. Getting to this generally secluded, mile-long curve of white sand on the island's westernmost tip requires a bumpy, ten-minute, we-must-be-lost drive off the main road, with just one small, unmarked entry down to the water. Though the beach is gravely in places, this is a good place for snorkeling and swimming, but beware of a strong undertow when the waters are rough. If you want privacy, visit this isolated spot. There are no facilities or vendors, so bring a picnic.

FodorśChoice **Baie Orientale.** By far the most beautiful beach on the island, Orient Bay
★ Beach has something for everyone, with its clean, white sand, clear, blue water, and an assortment of beach bars dotting its mile-long length and serving Mexican, Caribbean, American, and even kosher fare. There are plenty of places to rent equipment for water activities. Note the demographics: the north end tends to be conservative and family-oriented, while the far south is almost exclusively for nudists.

★ **Baie Rouge.** Red Bay is right off the main western road, five minutes from Marigot. Some consider this crescent sweep of sand the prettiest beach on the island. You'll find refreshment stands and places to rent beach chairs and umbrellas, though the beach is not too commercial. Listen for the sound of the conch at 3 PM, which signals happy hour at the open-air, beachfront bistros.

Ilet Pinel This little speck of land—with gently sloping beaches and a nature preserve—is a treat for nature lovers and families with young children. Take the five-minute ferry ride from French Cul de Sac ($5 per person round-trip). The soft-sand beach is protected, and you can wade out about a hundred yards in the shallows. There are basic facilities, including a beach restaurant, some shops, and chair-rental facilities. If you want a break from the beach, take a walk through the protected nature preserve, the first on St. Martin.

Sports & the Outdoors

BOATING &
SAILING
The island's waters and winds make it ideal for exploring or relaxing by boat. It'll cost you around $500 per day to rent a 20-ft power boat, less for smaller boats. A 35-ft sailboat runs about $700 per day, or you can get a 20-ft day sailer for as little as $150. You can rent motorboats, speedboats, Jet Skis, and sailboats at **Aquamania Watersports** (⊠ Pelican Marina, Simpson Bay ☎ 599/544–2640). **Bobby's Marina** (⊠ Yrausquin Blvd., Philipsburg ☎ 599/542–4096) has numerous water-sports and boat rental options. **Lagoon Sailboat Rental** (⊠ Airport Rd., near Uncle

Harry's, Simpson Bay ☎ 599/557–0714) has 20-ft day sailers for rent within Simpson Bay Lagoon for $150 per day. **The Moorings** (✉ Captain Oliver's Marina, Oyster Pond ☎ 590/87–32–54 or 800/521–1126) has a fleet of Beneteau yachts as well as bareboat and crewed catamarans. **Sunsail** (✉ Captain Oliver's Marina, Oyster Pond ☎ 590/87–83–41 or 800/327–2276) has a fleet of sailboats for hire. **Westport Water Sports** (✉ Simpson Bay ☎ 599/544–2557), at Kimsha Beach, has Jet Skis for rent and offers parasailing excursions.

Both landlubbers and old salts enjoy the thrill of sailboat racing with the daily **St. Maarten 12-Metre Challenge** (✉ Bobby's Marina, Philipsburg ☎ 599/542–0045 or 800/786–2278). Participants compete on 68-ft racing yachts, including Dennis Connor's *Stars and Stripes,* the actual boat that won the America Cup in 1987, and the *Canada II.* The cost to participate in the two-plus hour race is $65.

FISHING You can angle for yellowtail snapper, grouper, marlin, tuna, and wahoo on deep-sea excursions. Costs (for four people) range from $400 for a half day to $700 for a full day. Prices usually include bait and tackle, instruction for novices, and refreshments. Ask about licensing and insurance. **Lee Deepsea Fishing** (✉ 84 Welfare Rd., Simpson Bay ☎ 599/544–4233 or 599/544–4234) organizes excursions. **Rudy's Deep Sea Fishing** (✉ 14 Airport Rd., Simpson Bay ☎ 599/545–2177 ⊕ www.rudysdeepseafishing.com) has been around for years and is one of the more experienced sport angling outfits. **Sailfish Caraïbes** (✉ Anse Marcel ☎ 590/87–31–94 or 590/27–40–90) is your best bet on the north side of the island.

GOLF St. Maarten is not a golf destination. **Mullet Bay Resort** (✉ Airport Rd., north of the airport ☎ 599/545–3069), on the Dutch side, has an 18-hole course—the island's *only* one. The course, which is in poor shape, nonetheless offers duffers a unique experience: playing through the eerie ruins of Mullet Bay Resort, once the island's largest, but destroyed by a hurricane and never rebuilt. Greens fees, with cart, are $55 for 9 holes, $88 for 18.

HORSEBACK RIDING Island stables offer riding packages—from novice to expert—for $25 to $40 per hour for a beach ride. Ask about full-moon and sunset rides. You can arrange rides directly or through most hotels. **Bayside Riding Club** (✉ Galion Beach Rd., Baie Orientale ☎ 590/87–36–64), on the French side, is a long-established outfit. **Lucky Stables** (✉ Traybay Dr., Cay Bay ☎ 599/544–5255) offers mountain- and beach-trail rides, including a romantic champagne night ride.

PARASAILING On the French side, **Kontiki Watersports** (✉ Northern beach entrance, Baie Orientale ☎ 590/87–46–89) offers parasailing rides. On the Dutch side, **Westport Water Sports** (✉ Simpson Bay ☎ 599/544–2557) has parasailing available off Kimsha Beach.

SCUBA DIVING The water temperature here is rarely below 70°F (21°C), and visibility is usually excellent, averaging about 100 ft. Beginners and night divers will appreciate the tugboat *Annie,* which lies in 25 ft–30 ft of water in Simpson Bay. Off the north coast, in the protected and mostly current-free Grand Case Bay, is **Creole Rock.** The water here ranges in depth from 10 ft to 25 ft, and visibility is excellent. Other sites off the north coast include **Ilet Pinel,** for its good shallow diving; Green Key, with its vibrant barrier reef; and Tintamarre (Flat Island), for its sheltered coves and geologic faults. One of the most popular sites is **Proselyte Reef,** named for the British frigate HMS *Proselyte.* The ship, initially a Dutch frigate, was captured by the British in 1796 and sank about 1 mi (1½ km) south of Great Bay in 1801. Today the hulk lies 15 ft–45 ft below the surface and is almost completely covered with coral. On average, one-tank dives start at $50, two-tank dives start at $80, and certification courses start at $350.

On the Dutch side, **Dive Safaris** (⊠ Bobby's Marina, Yrausquin Blvd., Philipsburg ☎ 599/544–4056) is a full-service outfit for divers. SSI- (Scuba Schools International) and PADI-certified dive centers include **Ocean Explorers Dive Shop** (⊠ 113 Welfare Rd., Simpson Bay ☎ 599/544–5252).

On the French side, **Blue Ocean** (⊠ Sandy Ground Rd., Baie Nettlé ☎ 590/87–89–73) is a PADI-certified dive center. **Octoplus** (⊠ Bd. de Grand Case, Grand Case ☎ 590/87–20–62) is a complete PADI-certified dive center. **O2 Limit** (⊠ Blvd. de Grand Case, Grand Case ☎ 690/50–04–00), in the Grand Case Beach Club, is PADI-certified.

SNORKELING   Some of the best snorkeling on the Dutch side can be found around the rocks below Fort Amsterdam off Little Bay Beach, in the west end of Maho Bay, off Pelican Key, and around the reefs off Dawn Beach and Oyster Pond. On the French side, the area around Orient Bay, Caye Verte (Green Key), Ilet Pinel, and Flat Island is especially lovely and is officially classified, and protected, as a regional underwater nature reserve. The average cost of an afternoon snorkeling trip is $25 per person. **Blue Ocean** (⊠ Sandy Ground Rd., Baie Nettlé ☎ 590/87–89–73) offers snorkeling trips. Arrange equipment rentals and snorkeling trips through **Kontiki Watersports** (⊠ Northern beach entrance, Baie Orientale ☎ 590/87–46–89).

SEA EXCURSIONS   The 50-ft catamaran *Bluebeard II* (⊠ Simpson Bay ☎ 599/545–2898) sails around Anguilla's south and northwest coasts to Prickly Pear, where there are excellent coral reefs for snorkeling and powdery white sands for sunning. The cost is $45–$65 per person. You can take a day-long picnic sail to nearby islands or secluded coves aboard the 45-ft ketch *Gabrielle* (☎ 599/542–3170). The sleek 76-ft catamaran *Golden Eagle* (☎ 599/543–0068) takes day sailors to outlying islets and reefs for snorkeling and partying. The *Laura Rose* (☎ 599/547–0710) offers half- and full-day sails ranging from $25 to $65 per person.

For low-impact sunset and dinner cruises, contact skipper Neil of the catamaran *Celine* (⊠ Simpson Bay ☎ 599/545–3961), which is moored behind Turtle Pier Bar and Restaurant. The *Tango* (⊠ Pelican Marina, Simpson Bay ☎ 599/544–2640), operated by Aqua Mania Watersports, and her sister boats offer a full range of cruise options—everything from dinner cruises to day-long snorkeling trips to Anguilla.

A cross between a submarine and a glass-bottom boat, the 34-passenger *Seaworld Explorer* (⊠ Bd. de Grand Case, Grand Case ☎ 599/542–4078) crawls along the water's surface while you, submerged in a lower chamber, view marine life and coral through large windows. Divers jump off the boat and feed the fish and eels. The cost is $30 for adults, $20 for kids; transport to and from your hotel costs an extra $10 per adult, $7 per child.

Sailing, snorkeling, and picnic excursions to nearby islands can be arranged through **Kontiki Watersports** (⊠ Northern beach entrance, Baie Orientale ☎ 590/87–46–89). **Le Méridien's L'Habitation** (⊠ Anse Marcel ☎ 590/87–33–33) is a good choice for those staying in the north.

TENNIS   Many of the larger resorts have tennis courts, though nonguests may have to pay a fee. There are two lighted courts at the **Blue Bay Club Mont Vernon** (⊠ East off road to French Cul de Sac, Baie Orientale ☎ 590/87–62–00). You'll find four lighted courts at the **Maho Beach Resort & Casino** (⊠ Airport Rd., Maho Bay ☎ 599/545–2115). Anyone can use the four lighted courts at the **Pelican Resort & Casino** (✉ Airport Rd., Pelican Key, Simpson Bay ☎ 599/544–2503). The six lighted courts at **Le Privilege Resort & Spa** (✉ Anse Marcel ☎ 590/87–38–38) are available to nonguests, as are its four squash and two racquetball courts.

WATERSKIING   Expect to pay $50 per half hour for waterskiing, and $40–$45 per half hour for jet-skiing. On the Dutch side, rent waterskiing and jet-skiing equipment through **Aquamania Watersports** (✉ Pelican Marina, Simpson Bay ☎ 599/544–2640), a full-service water-sports activity center. On the French side, **Kontiki Watersports** (✉ Northern beach entrance, Baie Orientale ☎ 590/87–46–89) rents windboards, takes water-skiers out, and provides instruction. **Grand Case Beach Club Activities** (✉ 21 rue de Petit Plage, Grand Case ☎ 590/87–51–87) provides instruction for novice water-skiers.

WINDSURFING   The **Nathalie Simon Windsurfing Club** (✉ Northern beach entrance, Baie Oriental ☎ 590/29–41–57) offers rentals and lessons. Lessons are $25–$30 per hour. **Windy Reef** (✉ Galion Beach, past the Butterfly Farm ☎ 590/87–08–37) has provided windsurfing lessons and rentals since 1991.

Shopping

Fodor'sChoice   Nearly 500 cruise ships call at Philipsburg each year. Two reasons are
★   the number and the variety of duty-free shops on the island. Prices can be 25% to 50% below those in the United States and Canada on perfumes, jewelry, liquor, tobacco, Swedish crystal, Irish linen, Italian leather, electronics, cameras, designer fashions, Swiss watches, and more. Most shopkeepers are courteous, and a little haggling may bring down the price. Philipsburg has a bustling Caribbean flavor, while Marigot, on the French side, is distinctly southern European. On both sides of the island, be alert for idlers alert for unwatched purses.

Prices are quoted in florins, euros, and dollars; many shops take credit cards and traveler's checks.

Areas

Front Street, Philipsburg, is one long, often-congested street lined with dozens of sleek boutiques and colorful shops. **Old Street,** near the end of Front Street, has stores, boutiques, and open-air cafés offering French crêpes, rich chocolates, and island mementos. Shops are a bit more upscale at the **Maho** shopping plaza and the **Plaza del Lago**, at the Simpson Bay Yacht Club complex, which also has an excellent choice of restaurants. On the French side, wrought-iron balconies, colorful awnings, and gingerbread trim decorate Marigot's smart shops, tiny boutiques, and bistros in the **Marina Royale** complex and on the main streets, **rue de la Liberté** and **rue de la République.** Also in Marigot is the chic and pricy **West Indies Mall.**

Specialty Items

ART GALLERIES   **Dona Bryhiel Art Gallery** (✉ Oyster Pond ☎ 590/87–43–93), on the French side before the turnoff to Captain Oliver's Marina, deals mostly in modern figurative paintings by the owner, who will delight you with stories of her life and the paintings, which are steeped in romantic French and Caribbean traditions. **Galerie Lynn** (✉ 83 bd. de Grand Case, Grand Case ☎ 590/87–77–24) sells stunning paintings and sculptures. **Gingerbread Galerie** (✉ Marina Royale, Marigot ☎ 590/87–73–21) specializes in Haitian art. **Greenwith Galleries** (✉ 33 Front St., Philipsburg ☎ 599/542–3842) has a broad selection of Caribbean artists. **Minguet Art Gallery** (✉ Rambaud Hill ☎ 590/87–76–06), between Marigot and Grand Case, is managed by the daughter of the late artist Alexandre Minguet. The gallery carries original paintings, lithographs, posters, and postcards depicting island flora and landscapes by Minguet, as well as original works by Robert Dago and Loic BarBotin. **Roland Richardson Gallery** (✉ 6 rue de la République, Marigot ☎ 590/87–32–24) sells oil and watercolor paintings by well-known local artist Roland Richardson. The gallery, with a garden studio in the rear, is worth visiting even if you don't intend to buy a painting, and you may meet the artist himself or his stepmother.

DUTY-FREE GOODS   **Carat** (✉ 16 rue de la République, Marigot ☎ 590/87–73–40 ✉ 73 Front St., Philipsburg ☎ 599/542–2180) sells china and jewelry. **Havane** (✉ Marina Royale, Marigot ☎ 590/87–70–39) is a good place for designer fashions. **Lipstick** (✉ Plaza Caraïbes, rue du Kennedy, Marigot ☎ 590/87–73–24 ✉ 31 Front St., Philipsburg ☎ 599/542–6051) has an enormous selection of perfume and cosmetics. **Little Europe** (✉ 80 Front St., Philipsburg ☎ 599/542–4371 ✉ 1 rue de Général de Gaulle, Marigot ☎ 590/87–92–64) sells fine jewelry, crystal, and china. **Little Switzerland** (✉ 6 rue de la Liberté, Marigot ☎ 590/87–09–02 ✉ 52 Front St., Philipsburg ☎ 599/542–3530) purveys fine crystal and china as well as perfume and jewelry. **Oro Diamante** (✉ 62 Front St., Philipsburg ☎ 599/543–0343) carries loose diamonds, jewelry, watches, perfume, and cosmetics. **Manek's** (✉ Rue de la République, Marigot ☎ 590/87–54–91) sells, on two floors, luggage, perfume, jewelry, Cuban cigars, duty-free liquors, and tobacco products.

HANDICRAFTS   **Frodes Paradise** (✉ 7 PaLaPa Marina, Simpson Bay ☎ 599/545–3379) is a little shop loaded with original island and African art, crystals, and jewelry. The **Guavaberry Emporium** (✉ 8 Front St., Philipsburg ☎ 599/542–2965 ⊕ www.guavaberry.com) is the small factory where the the island's own guavaberry liqueur is made by the Sint Maarten Guavaberry Company; on sale are myriad versions of the liqueur (including one made with jalapeño peppers), as well as bottled hot sauces. Ask for free samples. **Shipwreck Shop** (✉ 42 Front St., Philipsburg ☎ 599/542–2962 ✉ Marina Royale, Marigot ☎ 590/87–27–37) stocks Caribelle batiks, hammocks, handmade jewelry, the local guavaberry liqueur, and herbs and spices.

Nightlife

★   St. Maarten has lots of evening and late-night action. To find out what's doing on the island, pick up *St. Maarten Nights, St. Maarten Quick Pick Guide,* or *St. Maarten Events,* all of which are distributed free in the tourist office and hotels. The glossy *Discover St. Martin/St. Maarten* magazine, also free, has articles on island history and on the newest shops, discos, and restaurants. Or for 50¢ buy a copy of Thursday's *Daily Herald* newspaper, which lists all the week's entertainment.

BARS   **Axum Café** (✉ 7L Front St., Philipsburg ☎ no phone), a bar and 1960s-style coffee shop, offers cultural activities, dancing, open-mike night, and art exhibits. It's open daily, 11:30 AM until the wee hours. **Cheri's Café** (✉ Airport Rd., Simpson Bay ☎ 599/545–3361), across from Maho Beach Resort & Casino, is a local institution, with reasonably priced food and great live bands. **Le Bar de la Mer** (✉ Market Sq., Marigot ☎ 590/87–81–79), on the harbor, is a popular gathering spot in the evening (it's open until 2 AM). **Sunset Beach Bar** (✉ Beacon Hill ☎ 599/545–3998), at the south end of the airport runway, has live music Wednesday through Sunday and a relaxed, anything-goes atmosphere. Enjoy a beer and watch planes take off and land directly over your head.

CASINOS   All the island's casinos—found only on the Dutch side—have craps, blackjack, roulette, and slot machines. You must be 18 years or older to gamble. Dress is casual (except for bathing suits or skimpy beachwear). Most are found in hotels, but there are also some independents. **Casino Royale** (⊠ Maho Beach Resort & Casino, Maho Bay ☎ 599/545–2115) is in bustling Maho, near restaurants and nightlife, and offers valet parking. **Dolphin Casino** (⊠ Caravanserai Beach Resort, 2 Beacon Hill Rd., Maho Bay ☎ 599/545–3707) has friendly dealers, easy parking, and a Blues Brothers bar. **Golden Casino** (⊠ Great Bay Beach Hotel, Little Bay Rd., Great Bay ☎ 599/542–2446) is conveniently located on the road that leads into the west side of Philipsburg. **Hollywood Casino** (⊠ Pelican Resort, Pelican Key, Simpson Bay ☎ 599/544–2503) has an upbeat, celebrity theme and a nice late-night buffet.

The **Lightning Casino** (⊠ Airport Rd., Cole Bay ☎ 599/544–3290) is easily recognized by its gaudy, flashing sign. The **Rouge et Noir Casino** (⊠ Front St., Philipsburg ☎ 599/542–2952) is small but busy, catering mostly to cruise-ship passengers.

DANCE CLUBS **Club One** (⊠ Marina Royale, Marigot Bay ☎ 590/87–98–41) is a late-night (really, all-night every night but Sunday and Monday) happening spot on the marina. **Greenhouse** (⊠ Front St., Philipsburg ☎ 599/542–2941) has canned DJ music and a two-for-one happy hour that lasts all night Tuesday. **L'Atmo** (⊠ Marina Royale, Marigot ☎ 590/87–98–41) is where French nationals and locals flock for salsa and soca on Friday. It's open every night but Monday. **Pink Mango** (⊠ Sandy Ground Rd., Baie Nettlé ☎ 590/87–91–75) at the Hotel Laguna, is a popular gay spot with a young, mixed crowd. **Q Club** (⊠ Airport Rd., Maho Bay ☎ 599/545–2115) is a popular disco upstairs from the casino at the Maho Beach Resort & Casino.

Exploring St. Maarten/St. Martin

The best way to explore St. Maarten/St. Martin is by car. Though often congested, especially around Philipsburg and Marigot, the roads are fairly good, though narrow and winding, with some planned speed bumps, unplanned pot holes and an occasional wandering goat herd. Few roads are marked with their names, but destination signs are good. Besides, the island is so small that it's hard to get really lost.

A scenic "loop" around the island can take just half a day, including plenty of stops. If you head up the east shoreline from Philipsburg, follow the signs to Dawn Beach and Oyster Pond. The road winds past soaring hills, turquoise waters, quaint West Indian houses, and wonderful views of St. Barths. As you cross over to the French side, the road leads to Grand Case, Marigot, and Sandy Ground. Completing the loop brings you past Cupecoy Beach, through Maho and Simpson Bay, and back over the mountain road into Philipsburg.

Numbers in the margin correspond to points of interest on the St. Maarten/St. Martin map.

Sights to See

❹ **Butterfly Farm.** Visitors enter a serene, tropical environment when they walk through the terrarium-like Butterfly Sphere amid dozens of colorful butterfly varieties at the farm. At any given time, some 40 species of butterflies, numbering as many as 600, flutter inside the garden under a tented net. Butterfly art and memorabilia are for sale in the gift shop. ⊠ *Rte. de Le Galion, Quartier d'Orleans* ☎ *590/87–31–21* ⊕ *www.thebutterflyfarm.com* ☞ *$10* ☉ *Daily 9–3:30.*

❻ **French Cul de Sac.** North of Orient Bay Beach, the French-colonial mansion of St. Martin's mayor is nestled in the hills. Little red-roof houses look like open umbrellas tumbling down the green hillside. The area is peaceful and good for hiking. There's a lot of construction, however, as the surroundings are slowly being developed. From the beach here, shuttle boats make the five-minute trip to **Ilet Pinel**, an uninhabited island that's fine for picnicking, sunning, and swimming.

⑦ Grand Case. The island's most picturesque town is set in the heart of the French side on a beach at the foot of green hills and pastures. Though it has only a 1-mi-long (1½-km-long) main street, it's known as the "restaurant capital of the Caribbean." More than 27 restaurants serve French, Italian, Indonesian, and Vietnamese fare here. The budget-minded love the half-dozen *lolos*—kiosks at the far end of town that sell savory barbecue and seafood. Grand Case Beach Club is at the end of this road and has two beaches where you can take a dip.

② Guana Bay Point. On the rugged, windswept east coast about ten minutes north of Philipsburg, Guana Bay Point offers isolated, untended beaches and a spectacular view of St. Barths.

★ **⑨ Le Fort Louis.** Though not much remains of the structure itself, the fort, completed by the French in 1789, commands a sweeping view of Marigot, its harbor, and the English island of Anguilla, which alone makes it worth the climb. There are few signs to show the way, so the best way to find the fort is to go to Marigot and look up. ⊠ *Marigot*.

⑧ Marigot. This town has a very southern European flavor, especially its beautiful harborfront, with shopping stalls, open-air cafés, and fresh-food vendors. It is well worth a few hours to explore if you are a shopper, a gourmand, or just a Francophile. Marina Royale is the shopping complex at the port, but rue de la République and rue de la Liberté, which border the bay, are also filled with duty-free shops, boutiques, and bistros. The West Indies Mall offers a deluxe shopping experience. There is less bustle here than in Philipsburg, and the open-air cafés are tempting places to sit and people-watch. Marigot doesn't die at night, so you might wish to stay here into the evening—particularly on Wednesdays, when the market opens its art, crafts, and souvenir stalls, and on Thursdays, when the shops of Marina Royale remain open until 10 and shoppers enjoy live music. From the harborfront you can catch the ferry for Anguilla or St. Barths. Overlooking the town is Le Fort Louis, from which you get a breathtaking, panoramic view of Marigot and the surrounding area. The small, ambitious **Musée de Saint-Martin** (St. Martin Museum), south of town, has artifacts from the island's pre-Columbian days. Included are pottery exhibits, rock carvings, and petroglyphs, as well as displays from colonial and sugar-plantation days. Upstairs is a small art gallery, where you'll find locally produced art, including lithographs and posters. ⊠ *Sandy Ground Rd.* ☎ *590/29–22–84* ⌨ *$5* ⊙ *Mon.–Sat. 9–1 and 3–6.*

③ Orléans. North of Oyster Pond and the Étang aux Poissons (Fish Lake) is the island's oldest settlement, also known as the French Quarter. You'll find classic, vibrantly painted West Indian–style homes with elaborate gingerbread fretwork.

① Philipsburg. The capital of Dutch St. Maarten stretches about a mile (1½ km) along an isthmus between Great Bay and the Salt Pond and has five parallel streets. Most of the village's dozens of shops and restaurants are on Front Street, narrow and cobblestoned, closest to Great Bay. It is generally congested when cruise ships are in port. It features many duty-free shops and several casinos. Little lanes called *steegjes* connect Front Street with Back Street, which has fewer shops and considerably less congestion.

Wathey Square (pronounced watty), is in the heart of the village. Directly across from the square are the town hall and the courthouse, in the striking white building with the cupola. The structure was built in 1793 and has served as the commander's home, a fire station, a jail, and a post office. The streets surrounding the square are lined with hotels, duty-free shops, fine restaurants, and cafés—most of them in West Indian cottages gussied up with gingerbread trim. Alleys lead to arcades and flower-filled courtyards where there are yet more boutiques and eateries. The **Captain Hodge Pier,** just off the square, is a good spot to view Great Bay and the beach that stretches alongside. The **Sint Maarten Museum** hosts rotating cultural exhibits and a permanent historical display called Forts of St. Maarten/St. Martin. The artifacts range from Arawak pottery shards to objects salvaged from the wreck of the HMS *Proselyte.* ⊠ *7 Front St.* ☎ *599/542–4917* 🖃 *Free* ⊙ *Weekdays 10–4, Sat. 10–2.*

❺ Pic du Paradis. From Friar's Bay Beach, a bumpy, tree-canopied road leads inland to this peak. At 1,492 ft, it's the island's highest point. Though the vistas from it are breathtaking, the road is quite isolated, so it is best

★ to travel in groups. Near the bottom of Pic du Paradis is **Loterie Farm,** a peaceful 150-acre private nature preserve opened to the public in 1999 by American expat B. J. Welch. Designed to preserve island habitats, Loterie Farm offers a rare glimpse of Caribbean forest and mountain land. Welch has renovated an old farmhouse and welcomes visitors for horseback riding, hiking, mountain biking, ecotours, or such nonactivities as meditation and yoga. The Hidden Forest Café is open for lunch and dinner Tuesday through Sunday. ⊠ *Route de Pic du Paradis* ☎ *590/87–86–16* ⊕ *www.loteriefarm.com* 🖃 *$5, 1½-hr tour $25, 4-hr tour $35* ⊙ *Daily sunrise–sunset.*

ST. MAARTEN/ST. MARTIN A TO Z

To research prices, get advice from other travelers, and book travel arrangements, visit www.fodors.com.

AIR TRAVEL

KLM and its affiliates offer service from Curaçao, Aruba, Bonaire, and Caracas, and other islands, as well as from numerous European cities. Air France offers daily nonstop flights from Paris, with connections from other European cities, as well as connections to and from Martinique and Antigua. Air Caraïbes offers daily flights to St. Barths; the airline flies mainly out of L'Espérance, on the French side.

American Airlines has daily nonstop flights from New York and Miami, and connections via its San Juan hub. Delta offers daily nonstops from Atlanta. BWIA has service from Trinidad, Jamaica, and Antigua. Continental Airlines has daily nonstop flights from Newark and connections from San Juan. LIAT has daily service from San Juan and several Caribbean islands, including Antigua, the USVI, the BVI, and St. Kitts & Nevis. US Airways has nonstop service from Philadelphia and Charlotte. Windward Islands Airways (a.k.a. Winair), based on St. Maarten, has daily service to Anguilla, Saba, St. Barths, St. Eustatius, and St. Kitts & Nevis, as well as several weekly flights to Tortola. The company also offers tour and charter services.

🔰 Air Caraïbes ☎ 599/545-2568. Air France ☎ 599/545-4212. American Airlines ☎ 599/545-2040. BWIA ☎ 599/545-4646. Continental Airlines ☎ 599/545-3444. Delta Airlines ☎ 599/545-4344. KLM ☎ 599/545-4747. LIAT ☎ 599/545-4203. US Airways ☎ 599/545-4344. Windward Islands Airways ☎ 599/545-4237.

AIRPORTS

Aeroport de L'Espérance, on the French side, is small and handles only island hoppers. Jumbo jets fly into Princess Juliana International Airport, on the Dutch side.

🛈 **Aeroport de L'Espérance** ☎ 590/87-53-03. **Princess Juliana International Airport** ☎ 599/545-4211.

BIKE & MOPED TRAVEL

Though traffic can be heavy, road speeds are generally slow, so a moped can be a good way get around. Parking is easy, filling the tank with gas is affordable, and you've got that sea breeze in your hair. Scooters rent for as low as $23 a day and motorbikes for $37 a day at Eugene Moto, on the French side. At Go Scoot the bikes are in good repair and the counter clerks are helpful. If you're in the mood for a more substantial bike, contact the Harley-Davidson dealer, on the Dutch side, where you can rent a big hog for $112 a day.

🛈 **Eugene Moto** ✉ Sandy Ground Rd., Sandy Ground ☎ 590/87-13-97. **Go Scoot** ✉ 20 Airport Rd.Simpson Bay ☎ 599/545-4533. **Harley-Davidson** ✉ Cole Bay ☎ 599/544-2779.

BOAT & FERRY TRAVEL

FARES & SCHEDULES

The *Voyager II* offers daily service from Marigot to St. Barths Tuesday through Saturday. The cost for the 75-minute ride is $57 per person roundtrip, including an open bar, snacks, and port fees. Children under 12 are roughly half price, and children under five travel free. The high-speed passenger ferries *Edge I* (47 passengers) and *Edge II* (62 passengers) motor from Simpson Bay's Pelican Marina to Saba on Wednesday, Friday, and Sunday in just an hour ($60 round-trip) and to St. Barths on Tuesday, Thursday, and Saturday in 45 minutes ($50 round-trip, plus $7 port fee). The trips depart at 9 and return by 5 the same day. The Link ferries make the 20-minute trip between the Marigot piers, on the Marigot waterfront, and Blowing Point, on Anguilla, departing and returning every half-hour from 8 AM until 7 PM daily. The fare is $10 one-way plus $3 departure tax, or $26 round-trip.

🛈 *Edge II* ☎ 599/544-2640. **Link Ferries** ☎ 264/497-2231 ⊕ www.link.ai *Voyager II* ☎ 599/542-4096 or 590/87-10-68 ⊕ www.voyager-st-barths.com.

BUSINESS HOURS

BANKS

Banks on the Dutch side are open Monday–Thursday 8:30–3:30 and Friday 8:30–4:40. French banks are open weekdays 8:30–12:30 and 2:30–4 and close afternoons preceding holidays.

POST OFFICES

Dutch-side post offices are open Monday–Thursday 7:30–5 and Friday 7:30–4:30. On the French side, post offices are open weekdays 7:30–4:45 and Saturday 7:30–11:30.

SHOPS

Shops on the Dutch side are generally open Monday–Saturday 8–noon and 2–6; on the French side, Monday–Saturday 9–noon or 12:30 and 2–6. Increasingly, however, shops on both sides remain open during lunch. Some of the larger shops are open on Sunday and holidays when cruise ships are in port.

CAR RENTALS

The best and most economical way to get around St. Maarten is by car. You can book a car at Juliana International Airport, where all major rental companies have booths. Rates, in general, are low for the Caribbean—between $25 and $50 a day with unlimited mileage for a subcompact car. All foreign driver's licenses are honored, and major credit cards are accepted. Avis, Budget, Dollar, and Hertz have good selections. Also try locally owned Unity Car Rental.

🚹 **Avis** ☎ 599/545-2319. **Budget** ☎ 599/545-4030; **Dollar** ☎ 599/545-3281. **Hertz** ☎ 599/545-4541. **Unity Car Rental** ☎ 599/557-6760 or 800/836-4529.

CAR TRAVEL

GASOLINE Gas costs about 60¢ per liter ($2.27 per gallon) on the Dutch side, about 55¢ per liter ($2.10 per gallon) on the French side.

ROAD CONDITIONS Most roads are paved and in generally good condition. However, they can be narrow and often crowded. Be alert for potholes and speed bumps, as well as the island tradition of stopping in the middle of the road to chat with a friend or let someone into traffic. Few roads are identified by name, so use a map and follow destination signs. International symbols are used.

ELECTRICITY
Generally, the Dutch side operates on 110 volts AC (60-cycle) and has outlets that accept flat-prong plugs—the same as in North America. The French side operates on 220 volts AC (60-cycle), with round-prong plugs; you'll need an adapter and a converter for North American appliances.

EMERGENCIES
🚹 **Ambulance & Fire** Ambulance or fire emergencies Dutch side ☎ 130 or 120. Ambulance or fire emergencies French side ☎ 15.
🚹 **Hospitals** Hospital de Marigot ✉ Rue de l'Hôpital, Marigot ☎ 590/29-57-57. St. Maarten Medical Center ✉ Cay Hill ☎ 599/543-1111.
🚹 **Pharmacies** Central Drug Store ✉ Camille Richardson St., Philipsburg ☎ 599/542-2321. Friendly Drug Store ✉ Plaza del Lago, Simpson Bay ☎ 599/544-3653 Pharmacie du Port ✉ Rue de la Liberté, Marigot ☎ 590/87-50-79.
🚹 **Police** Police emergencies Dutch side ☎ 911. Police emergencies French side ☎ 590/87-88-33.

ETIQUETTE & BEHAVIOR
Religion plays an important part in island life, and churches are packed on Sunday. On the streets and in shops, conservative dress is the norm. Take the cue. In addition, a smile and a simple greeting go a long way toward establishing good relations with locals.

FESTIVALS & SEASONAL EVENTS
The French side's Carnival is a pre-Lenten bash of costume parades, music competitions, and feasts. On the Dutch side, Carnival takes place after Easter—usually in early May— with a parade and music competition. On the French side, the Calypso Festival is held in early July. The Caribbean Quest Musical Awards, a festival of regional music from around the islands, is held in early August on the French side. On the Dutch side, early March has the Heineken Regatta, with as many as 300 sailboats competing from around the world. (For the experience of a lifetime, some visitors can purchase a working berth aboard a regatta vessel.)

HEALTH
The island is surprisingly bug-free, thanks to the trade winds. You may encounter mosquitoes, but usually not in droves. The biggest problem might be sun exposure. Even on seemingly cloudy days, the sun can cause painful burns, so use sunscreen and monitor your sunbathing time. Drinking water is generally safe, except immediately following a hurricane or storm. Still, most locals use bottled drinking water, which is plentiful at shops throughout the island.

HOLIDAYS
Both sides of the island celebrate specific holidays related to their government and culture, and some, such as New Year's, the Easter holidays

(moveable, Apr. or May), Labor Day (the first Monday in Sept.), Christmas, and Boxing Day (Dec. 26) are celebrated together.

Other French-side holidays are Ascension Day (May 25), Bastille Day (July 14), Schoelcher Day (July 21), All Saints' Day (Nov. 1), and the Feast of St. Martin (Nov. 11). Other Dutch-side holidays are Antillean Day (Oct. 21) and St. Maarten Day (Nov. 11; this coincides with Feast of St. Martin on the French side). On many holidays, government offices, shops, and even gas stations may be closed.

LANGUAGE
Dutch is the official language of St. Maarten, and French is the official language of St. Martin, but almost everyone speaks English. If you hear a language you can't quite place, it may be Papiamento—a mix of Spanish, Portuguese, Dutch, French, and English—spoken throughout the Netherlands Antilles.

MAIL & SHIPPING
The main Dutch-side post office is on Walter Nisbeth Road in Philipsburg. Other branches are at Captain Hodge Wharf in Philipsburg and Simpson Bay on Airport Road. The main post office on the French side is in Marigot, on rue de la Liberté. Letters from the Dutch side to North America and Europe cost NAf 2.85, and to New Zealand NAf 3.80; postcards to all destinations are NAf 1.45. A standard letter to Australia is NAf 2.75. From the French side, letters up to 20 grams and postcards are €.58 to North America and €.79 to Europe, New Zealand, and Australia. When writing to Dutch St. Maarten, call it "Sint Maarten" and make sure to add "Netherlands Antilles" to the address. When writing to the French side, the proper spelling is "St. Martin," and you add "French West Indies" to the address. Postal codes are used only on the French side.

MONEY MATTERS
Prices quoted in this chapter are in U.S. dollars unless otherwise noted.

ATMS All banks now have automatic teller machines (ATMs) that accept international cards. On the Dutch side, try RBTT. Windward Islands Bank has several branches on the island. On the French side, try Banque des Antilles Françaises or Banque Française Commerciale, but they will issue only euros.
🚩 RBTT ✉ Emnaplein, Philipsburg ☎ 599/542-3344 ✉ Union Rd., Cole Bay ☎ 599/544-3078 🌐 www.rbttantilles.com. **Windward Islands Bank** ✉ Wathey Sq., Front St., Philipsburg ☎ 599/542-2313 🌐 www.wib-bank.net. **Banque des Antilles Françaises** ✉ Rue de la République, Marigot ☎ 590/29-13-30. **Banque Française Commerciale** ✉ Rue de la République, Marigot ☎ 590/87-53-80.

CREDIT CARDS MasterCard, Visa, and Amex are accepted all over the island, Diners Club and Discover on occasion.

CURRENCY Legal tender on the Dutch side is the Netherlands Antilles florin (guilder), written NAf; on the French side, the euro (€). The exchange rates fluctuate, but at this writing they're about NAf 1.82 to US$1 and about €1 to US$1.10. On the Dutch side, prices are usually given in both NAf and U.S. dollars, which are accepted all over the island.

PASSPORTS & VISAS
U.S. and Canadian citizens need proof of citizenship. A passport (valid or not expired more than five years) is always the best document with which to travel, particularly for children. Barring a passport, an original birth certificate with raised seal (or a photocopy with notary seal) *plus* a government-issued photo I.D., such as a driver's license, is also acceptable. This is why children are best served by passports, since they

are unlikely to have other types of photo I.D. British citizens need a valid passport or a national I.D. card. Citizens of Australia and New Zealand require a valid passport. All visitors must have a confirmed room reservation and an ongoing or return ticket.

SAFETY

Always lock your valuables and travel documents in your room safe or your hotel's front desk safe. When sightseeing in a rental car, keep valuables locked in the trunk or car, and never leave your things unattended at the beach. Despite the romantic imagery of the Caribbean, it's not good policy to take long walks along the beach at night.

SIGHTSEEING TOURS

ORIENTATION A 2½-hour taxi tour of the island costs $30 for one or two people, $10 for each additional person. Your hotel or the tourist office can arrange it for you. On the Dutch side, Calypso Tours has, among other things, three-hour island tours for $20 per person. Elle Si Belle offers tours by van or bus. You can also contact St. Maarten Sightseeing Tours. On the French side, R&J Tours will show you the island; a three-hour tour (minimum of five people) is $15 per person.

🚹 **Elle Si Belle** ✉ Airport Blvd., Simpson Bay ☎ 599/545-2271. **R&J Tours** ✉ north of Marigot, Colombier ☎ 590/87-56-20. **St. Maarten Sightseeing Tours** ✉ Maho Plaza at Maho Beach Hotel & Casino, Airport Rd., Simpson Bay ☎ 599/545-2115.

TAXES

DEPARTURE TAX Departure tax from Juliana Airport is $7 to destinations within the Netherlands Antilles and $20 to all other destinations. This tax is not included in your airline ticket, but must be paid in cash (dollars, euros, or NAf) at a booth before you get on your plane. If you arrive on the island by plane and depart within 24 hours, you will be considered "in transit" and not required to pay the $20 departure tax. It will cost you €3 (usually included in the ticket price) to depart by plane from L'Espérance Airport, and $4 by ferry to Anguilla from Marigot's pier.

SALES TAX Hotels on the Dutch side add a 15% service charge to the bill as well as a 5% government tax, for a total of 20%. Hotels on the French side add 10%–15% for service and a *taxe de séjour*; the amount of this visitor tax differs from hotel to hotel, and can be as high as 5%.

TAXIS

The government regulates taxi rates. You can hail cabs on the street or call the Dutch taxi dispatch on the Dutch side. On the French side of the island, contact the French taxi dispatch for pickups. There's a taxi service at the Marigot port near the tourist information bureau. Fixed fares apply from Juliana International Airport and the Marigot ferry to the various hotels around the island. Fares are 25% higher between 10 PM and midnight, 50% higher between midnight and 6 AM.

🚹 **Dutch taxi dispatch** ☎ 147. **French taxi dispatch** ☎ 590/87-56-54.

TELEPHONES

COUNTRY & To call the Dutch side from the U.S., dial 011–599/54 plus the local num-
AREA CODES ber; for the French side, 011–590–590 plus the six-digit local number.

INTERNATIONAL At the Landsradio in Philipsburg, there are facilities for overseas calls
CALLS and an AT&T USADirect phone, where you are directly in touch with an AT&T operator who will accept collect or credit-card calls. On the French side, you can't make collect calls to the U.S., and there are no coin phones. If you need to use public phones, go to the special desk at Marigot's post office and buy a *telecarte*. There's a public phone at the tourist office in Marigot where you can make credit-card calls: the op-

erator takes your card number (any major card) and assigns you a PIN (Personal Identification Number), which you then use to charge calls to your card.

LOCAL CALLS   To phone from the Dutch side to the French, dial 00–590–590 plus the local number; from the French side to the Dutch, 00–599 plus local number. Note that a call from one side to the other is considered an overseas call and billed at international rates. To call a French side local number from the French side, dial 0590 plus the six-digit number.

TIPPING
Often without consistency, service charges of between 10% and 15% may be added to hotel and restaurant bills. Especially in restaurants, be sure to ask if a tip is included; that way, you are not either double tipping or short-changing the staff. Taxi drivers, porters, chambermaids, and restaurant waitstaff depend on tips. The guideline is 10%–15% for waitstaff and cabbies, a dollar per bag for porters, and $1–$5 per night for chambermaids.

TRANSPORTATION AROUND ST. MARTIN
The island has approximately 200 privately owned licensed buses; many are eight-seat Toyota vans. At a flat rate of $1 to $1.50 (as high as $2 after 8 PM), payable when you get out, buses are the island's best bargains. They operate casually but frequently between 7 AM and midnight from Philipsburg through Cole Bay to Marigot and on to Grand Case. There are only a few official stops: just stand beside the road and flag down the vehicle (the license plate says "BUS").

VISITOR INFORMATION
🚺 Before You Leave St. Maarten Tourist Office ⊕ www.st-maarten.com ⊠ 675 3rd Ave., Suite 1806, New York, NY 10017 ☎ 800/786-2278 or 212/953-2084. St. Maarten Tourist Information ⊕ www.st-martin.org ⊠ 703 Evans Ave., Suite 106, Toronto, Ontario M9C 5E9, Canada ☎ 416/622-4300. St. Martin Office of Tourism ⊠ 675 3rd Ave., Suite 1807, New York, NY 10017 ☎ 877/956-1234 or 212/475-8970 🖶 212/260-8481 ⊠ 9454 Wilshire Blvd., Suite 715, Beverly Hills, CA 90212 ☎ 310/271-6665 ⊠ 676 N. Michigan Ave., Suite 3360, Chicago, IL 60611 ☎ 312/751-7800 ⊠ 1981 McGill College Ave., Suite 490, Montréal, Québec H3A 2W9, Canada ☎ 514/288-4264 ⊠ 30 St. Patrick St., Suite 700, Toronto, Ontario M5T 3A3, Canada ☎ 416/593-6427.
🚺 In St. Maarten/St. Martin Dutch-side Tourist Information Bureau ⊠ Cyrus Wathey Sq., Philipsburg ☎ 599/542-2337. Dutch-side tourist bureau administrative office ⊠ 33 W. G. Buncamper Rd., Philipsburg, in the Vineyard Park Bldg. ☎ 599/542-2337. French-side Tourist Information Office ☎ 590/87-57-21.

ST. VINCENT AND THE GRENADINES

22

FODOR'S CHOICE

Basil's Bar, a restaurant in Mustique

Macaroni Beach, Mustique

Scuba diving in the Tobago Cays

Young Island Resort, St. Vincent

HIGHLY RECOMMENDED

RESTAURANTS   Frangipani, Port Elizabeth, Bequia

Gingerbread, Port Elizabeth, Bequia

Great Room, Mustique

HOTELS   Camelot Inn, Kingstown, St. Vincent

Cotton House, Mustique

Gingerbread Apartments, Port Elizabeth, Bequia

Grand View Beach Hotel, Villa Point, St. Vincent

Palm Island Resort, Palm Island

Petit St. Vincent Resort, Petit St. Vincent

SIGHTS   Falls of Baleine, St. Vincent

Ft. Charlotte, St. Vincent

Port Elizabeth, Bequia

Saltwhistle Bay Beach, Mayreau

*Many other great places enliven this area. For other
favorites, look for the black stars as you read this chapter.*

Standing on Dorsetshire Hill, above Kingstown, the wily old gentleman points to an island just offshore. On it is a large white cross that glimmers in the sun. "Know what that's about?" he asks. The grin on his weathered face fades to a wry smile as, without pause, he tells the tale. A local land developer, it seems, bought the island and put up the cross. Later, when he died, his body was placed upright inside it so that he could always face his life's work. "You see," says the gent with a shrug, "Vincentians love their country with a passion."

Updated by
Jane E. Zarem

The island of St. Vincent and the string of 32 islands and cays that make up the Grenadines are a single nation—one that's loved passionately by its inhabitants as much for its interesting history as for its natural beauty. SVG, as it's abbreviated, is in the Windward Islands chain in the southern Caribbean. Mountainous St. Vincent, only 18 mi (29 km) by 11 mi (18 km) and just 13° north of the equator, is the largest and northernmost of the group; the Grenadines extend southwest in a 45-mi (73-km) arc toward Grenada. While the island of St. Vincent will appeal to anyone interested in exploring nature, regional history, and ecotourism, the islands of the Grenadines will dazzle you with their secluded white-sand beaches, fine sailing waters, and get-away-from-it-all atmosphere.

St. Vincent's major export is bananas, and these plants, along with coconut palms and breadfruit trees, crowd more of the island than the 110,500 inhabitants (another 10,000 live on the Grenadines). This has obvious charm for nature lovers, who can spend days walking or hiking St. Vincent's well-defined trails, catching a glimpse of the rare St. Vincent parrot in the Vermont Valley, or climbing the active volcano La Soufrière, which last erupted in 1979. Below sea level, snorkeling and scuba landscapes are similarly intriguing.

Historians believe that the Ciboney Indians were the first to journey from South America to St. Vincent, which they called Hairoun (Land of the Blessed). The Ciboney ultimately moved on to Cuba and Haiti, leaving St. Vincent to the agrarian Arawak tribes, who journeyed from coastal South America to islands throughout the Lesser Antilles. Not long before Columbus sailed by in 1492, the Arawaks succumbed to the powerful Carib Indians, who had also paddled their way north from South America, conquering one island after another en route.

St. Vincent's mountains and forests thwarted European settlement. As colonization advanced elsewhere in the Caribbean, many Caribs fled to St. Vincent—making it even more of a Carib stronghold. In 1626 the French managed to settle on the island, but their success was short-lived; England took over a year later. Although "possession" of the island see-sawed between France and England for years, the Caribs continued to make complete European colonization impossible. Ironically it was a rift in the Carib community itself that enabled the Europeans to gain a foothold.

In 1675 African slaves who had survived a Dutch shipwreck were welcomed into the Carib community. Over time the Carib nation became, for all intents and purposes, two nations—one composed of the so-called Yellow Caribs, the other of the so-called Black Caribs. Relations between the two groups were often strained. In 1719 tensions rose so high that the Yellow Caribs united with the French (who were the colonizers that year) against the Black Caribs in what is called the First Carib War. The Black Caribs ultimately retreated to the hills, but they continued to resist the Europeans.

The French went on to establish plantations, importing African slaves to work the fertile land. In 1763 the British claimed the island yet again, and a wave of Scottish slave masters and indentured servants from India and Portugal arrived. Although the ethnic groups have mixed over the years to give Vincentians their unique heritage, communities of direct descendents of the Scots live near St. Vincent's Dorsetshire Hill and on Bequia. In 1779 the French surprised the British and reclaimed the island without a struggle; but four years later St. Vincent was back in the British grip. The determined French backed the Black Caribs against the British in 1795's Second Carib War (also known as the Brigands War). British plantations were ravaged and burned on the island's windward coast, and Black Carib chief Chatoyer pushed British troops down the leeward coast to Kingstown. On Dorsetshire Hill, high above the town, Chatoyer subsequently lost a duel with a British officer. The 5,000 remaining Black Caribs were rounded up and shipped off to Honduras and present-day Belize, where their descendents (the Garifuna people) remain to this day. The few remaining Yellow Caribs retreated to the remote northern tip of St. Vincent, near Sandy Bay, where many of their descendents now live. A monument to Chatoyer has been erected on Dorsetshire Hill, where there's a magnificent view over Kingstown and the Caribbean Sea toward Central America.

The Grenadines were historically as free from war and politics as their pristine beaches are today free from crowds. Just south of St. Vincent is Bequia, the largest of the Grenadines. Its Admiralty Bay is one of the most popular anchorages in the Caribbean. With superb views, snorkeling, hiking, and swimming, the island has much to offer the international mix of backpackers and luxury-yacht owners who frequent its shores.

South of Bequia, on the exclusive, private island of Mustique, posh villas are tucked into lush hillsides. Mustique does not encourage wholesale tourism, least of all to those hoping for a glimpse of the rich and famous who own villas here. The appeal of Mustique is its seclusion.

Boot-shape Canouan, just over 3 square mi (8 square km) in area, is an unspoiled island where you can relax on the beach, snorkel, or hike. Its 1,000 residents earn their living mainly from farming and fishing. Tiny Mayreau has fewer than 200 residents and one of the area's most beautiful beaches—where the Caribbean Sea is often mirror calm, and just yards away at the narrow northern tip of the island, the rolling Atlantic surf washes the shore.

Union Island is the transportation center of the southern Grenadines, with a busy airport for landlubbers and yacht services for sailors. It took decades to turn the 100-acre, mosquito-infested mangrove swamp called Prune Island into the private resort of Palm Island; now well-heeled vacationers lounge on the island's five palm-fringed white-sand beaches. Petit St. Vincent is another private island, reclaimed from the overgrowth by owner-manager Hazen K. Richardson II. The luxury resort's cobblestone cottages are so private that, if you wish, you could spend your vacation completely undisturbed.

The Tobago Cays, five uninhabited islands south of Canouan and east of Mayreau, draw snorkelers and divers who are mesmerized by the marine life and boaters who are equally impressed with the sheer beauty of the area. Surrounded by a shallow reef, the tiny islands have rustling palm trees, pristine beaches, the clearest water in varying shades of brilliant blue—and plenty of resident fish.

Although SVG has its share of the poor and unemployed, the super-fertile soil allows everyone to grow enough food to eat and trade for necessities. Villages are busy and clean, homes are painted in tropical hues, and colorful flowers and bright green foliage grow in profusion. The issue of "possession" of St. Vincent has long since been resolved; fully independent since 1979 (but still a part of the British Commonwealth), it belongs to a diverse, culturally rich people now known only as Vincentians—who truly have good reason to love their homeland with a passion.

WHAT IT COSTS In U.S. dollars				
$$$$	**$$$**	**$$**	**$**	**¢**
RESTAURANTS*				
over $30	$20–$30	$12–$20	$8–$12	under $8
HOTELS**				
Cost EP/BP/CP over $350	$250–$350	$150–$250	$80–$150	under $80
Cost AI over $450	$350–$450	$250–$350	$125–$250	under $125

*Restaurant prices are for a main course at dinner. **EP, BP, and CP prices are per night for a standard double room in high season, excluding taxes, service charges, and meal plans. AI (all-inclusive) prices are per person, per night based on double-occupancy during high season, excluding taxes and service charges.

ST. VINCENT

Where to Stay

With a few exceptions, tourist accommodations and facilities on St. Vincent are in either Kingstown or the Villa Beach area. Most hotels offer the EP, with the MAP available as an option; at resorts in the Grenadines, the FAP or all-inclusive is common. All guest rooms have air-conditioning, TV, and telephone, unless stated otherwise.

$$$$

Fodor's Choice ★

Young Island Resort. St. Vincent's premier resort is 200 yards offshore (a five-minute ride from Villa Beach by hotel launch). Airy hillside cottages are decorated in ecru, ocher, and green, with bamboo and rattan furniture. Walls of stone and glass have louvered windows surrounding the sitting areas. Each room has a terrace, and bathrooms have garden showers. All cottages have water views despite being hidden in lush tropical vegetation. Two beachfront cottages have private plunge pools. Enjoy fine dining in the terrace dining room or in a private thatched-roof gazebo. Sailaway packages include two nights touring the Grenadines on a 44-ft sailing yacht. ⌧ Young Island ✆ Box 211 ☎ 784/458–4826 ☎ 784/457–4567 ⊕ www.youngisland.com ✈ 30 cottages ⌂ Restaurant, room service, fans, in-room safes, refrigerators, tennis court, pool, beach, snorkeling, windsurfing, boating, 2 bars, baby-sitting, laundry service, meeting room, airport shuttle; no a/c, no room TVs ☰ AE, MC, V ⷩ⌽ MAP.

$$$

Petit Byahaut. Soft adventure aficionados love this 50-acre retreat. Accommodations are in large deluxe tents, complete with wood floors, private decks, queen-size beds, hammocks, solar-powered lighting, and bathrooms with solar-heated, alfresco showers. Meals, including candlelit dinners, are served in the bayfront dining room. This adults-only camp is accessible only by a 20-minute boat ride from Kingstown (com-

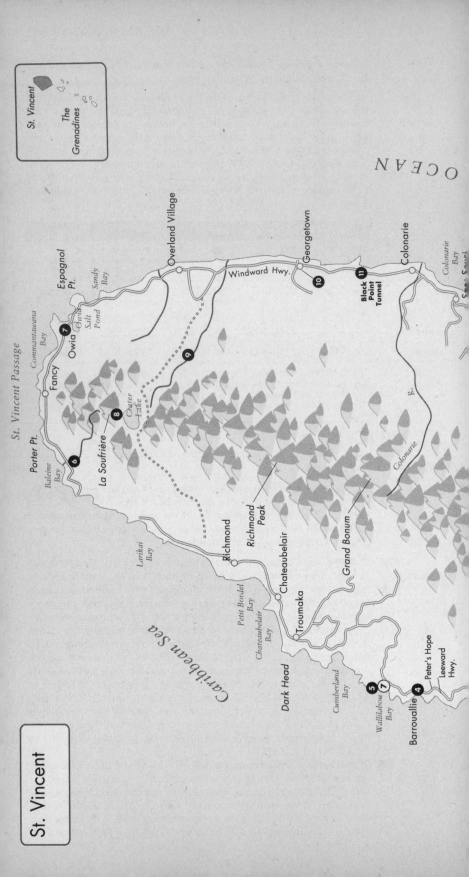

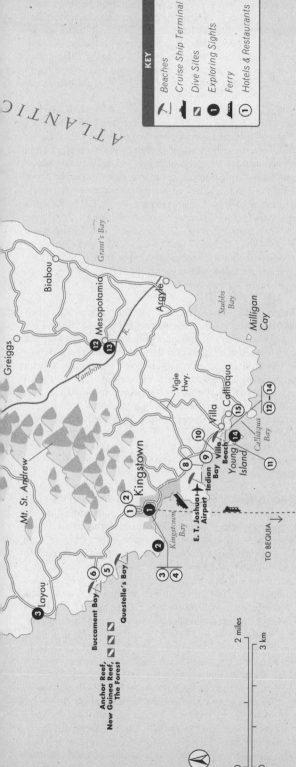

ATLANTIC

KEY

⚓	Beaches
⚓	Cruise Ship Terminal
◢	Dive Sites
●	Exploring Sights
⚓	Ferry
①	Hotels & Restaurants

Hotels ▶

Beachcombers **9**
Camelot Inn **1**
Cobblestone Inn **3**
Grand View Beach
Hotel **8**
Lagoon Marina
& Hotel **15**
The New
Montrose Hotel **2**

Petit Byahaut **5**
Sunset Shores
Beach Hotel **10**
Young Island
Resort **11**

Restaurants ▶

Basil's Bar and
Restaurant **3**
Buccama
On the Bay **6**
The French
Restaurant **12**
King Arthur
Dining Room **1**

Lime Restaurant
& Pub **13**
Slick's Restaurant
& Bar **14**
Vee Jay's Rooftop
Diner & Pub **4**
Wallilabou Bay Hotel
Restaurant **7**
Young Island
Resort **11**

Exploring ▶

Barrouallie **4**
Black Point
Tunnel **11**
Falls of Baleine **6**
Ft. Charlotte **2**
Ft. Duvernette **7**
Georgetown **10**
Kingstown **1**

La Soufrière **8**
Layou **3**
Mesopotamia
Valley **12**
Montreal Gardens **13**
Owia **7**
Rabacca Dry River **9**
Wallilabou Bay **5**

plimentary for guests). Once you've settled in, you'll find a selection of other boats with which to play, along with scuba and snorkeling equipment and a private black-sand beach. If you tire of the seclusion, excursions are easily arranged. Weekly rates are available. ⊠ *Petit Byahaut Bay* 🏠 *784/457–7008* ⊕ *www.petitbyahaut.com* ⇌ *6 tents* ⚹ *Restaurant, dining room, beach, dive shop, snorkeling, boating, hiking, bar, shop, meeting room, airport shuttle; no a/c, no room phones, no room TVs, no kids* ▤ *MC, V* ⊘ *Closed July–Oct.* ⊜ *3-night minimum* ⭐ *FAP.*

★ $$ 🏨 **Camelot Inn.** Snuggled in the hills overlooking Kingstown, this stylish inn sits on the site of the island's first French governor's residence. It's an elegant place with impeccable service and magnificent views. Guest rooms are spacious, with a soothing white-and-deep-green color scheme, rattan furniture, antique mirrors and prints, parquet floors, and private patios; bathrooms have hand-painted porcelain sinks imported from France. Meals are served in the King Arthur dining room or on the terrace, afternoon tea in the garden. Guests may use Young Island Resort's beach and water-sports facilities (transportation included). A city tour and one massage are complimentary. ⊠ *Kingstown Park, Kingstown* 🅿 *Box 787* ☎ *784/456–2100* 🖷 *784/456–2233* ⊕ *www.vincy.com/camelot* ⇌ *19 rooms, 3 suites* ⚹ *2 restaurants, fans, in-room safes, tennis court, pool, gym, hair salon, massage, sauna, 2 bars, library, shop, laundry service, meeting rooms, airport shuttle* ▤ *AE, DC, MC, V* ⭐ *EP.*

★ $$ 🏨 **Grand View Beach Hotel.** This 19th-century great house perched just above Indian Bay has both extensive facilities and intimate charm—all set on 8 acres that beckon you to explore. Rooms are attractive but not fussy, with plain white walls and hardwood floors, and most offer a sweeping vistas of the Grenadines. Luxury rooms have broad terraces with ocean views; two honeymoon suites have king-size beds and whirlpool tubs. Enjoy West Indian and Continental-style cuisine at Wilkie's restaurant. Sailboats, Windsurfers, and snorkeling equipment are complimentary, but you have to hike down a rather steep hill to the beach. ⊠ *Villa Point* ☎ *784/458–4811* 🖷 *784/457–4174* ⊕ *www.grandviewhotel. com* ⇌ *17 rooms, 2 suites* ⚹ *2 restaurants, fans, tennis court, pool, health club, massage, beach, snorkeling, windsurfing, boating, squash, 3 bars, library, baby-sitting, laundry service, meeting room* ▤ *AE, MC, V* ⭐ *EP.*

$$ 🏨 **Sunset Shores Beach Hotel.** Down a long, steep driveway off the main road, this lemon-yellow low-rise surrounds a small pool and a gigantic and prolific mango tree (help yourself from January through July). It also faces a lovely curve of Indian Bay beachfront. All rooms are large and comfortable, with patios or balconies. Opt for a room with a water view; otherwise you'll have to amble over to the poolside bar to get a glimpse of the gorgeous sunsets. The restaurant is good, with a small but varied menu featuring fresh local fish and lobster (in season); service is friendly and efficient. ⊠ *Villa Beach* 🅿 *Box 849* ☎ *784/458– 4411* 🖷 *784/457–4800* ⊕ *www.sunsetshores.com* ⇌ *32 rooms* ⚹ *Restaurant, room service, pool, beach, snorkeling, boating, Ping-Pong, 2 bars, baby-sitting, laundry service, meeting room* ▤ *AE, D, MC, V* ⭐ *EP.*

$ 🏨 **Beachcombers.** This small, family-owned beachfront hotel is modest but delightful. Half the guest rooms face the sea; the others overlook the Mango Tree Lounge or the garden's frenzy of flowers. Rooms with air-conditioning cost extra, and bathrooms have showers only—insignificant privations when the welcome here is so warm and the rates so low. Best of all, an on-site health spa offers aromatherapy, facials, sauna, steam baths, and fitness classes. On weekend evenings you'll usually find a live band and dancing on the sundeck adjacent to the restaurant and bar. ⊠ *Villa Beach* ① *Box 126* ☎ *784/458–4283* 🖷 *784/458–4385* ⊕ *www.beachcombershotel.com* ➲ *18 rooms, 2 suites, 1 apartment* ⚘ *Restaurant, room service, fans, kitchenettes, refrigerator, pool, fitness classes, sauna, spa, steam room, Turkish bath, beach, bar, library, baby-sitting, laundry service, Internet, meeting room; no a/c in some rooms* 🖃 *AE, MC, V* ⦿ *CP.*

$ 🖭 **The Lagoon Marina & Hotel.** This hotel overlooking sheltered Blue Lagoon Bay may well be the island's busiest. Thanks to its marina, there are usually seafaring types liming (hanging out) in the terrace bar and plenty of yacht traffic to watch from one of two couches on your big balcony. Sliding patio doors lead onto these perches from the wood-ceilinged, carpeted rooms. Basic wooden furniture, twin beds, dim lighting, tiled bathrooms, and ceiling fans provide an adequate level of comfort, but don't expect luxury. Sloping garden grounds contain a secluded two-level pool, a strip of beach, and a pretty terrace restaurant. ⊠ *Blue Lagoon, Ratho Mill* ① *Box 133* ☎ *784/458–4308* 🖷 *784/457–4308* ⊕ *www.lagoonmarina.com* ➲ *19 rooms, 2 apartments* ⚘ *Restaurant, grocery, room service, fans, kitchenettes, pool, beach, dock, snorkeling, windsurfing, boating, marina, bar, baby-sitting, laundry service, Internet, meeting room; no a/c in some rooms* 🖃 *AE, V* ⦿ *EP.*

¢–$ 🖭 **The New Montrose Hotel.** Despite the lack of a beach, pool, or activities, this is a fine choice for comfortable and reasonable lodgings. Painted a delightful lemon-yellow, the rambling hotel is on the northern outskirts of Kingstown. All suites are modern, with fully equipped kitchenettes, table and chairs, and two queen-size beds. The restaurant serves a limited menu of West Indian cuisine, but the food is good, and service is pleasant. This is a quiet, residential part of Kingstown, yet it's just a few minutes from downtown, the beach, the airport, and the botanical gardens. Long-term rates are available. ⊠ *New Montrose, Kingstown (Box 215)* ☎ *784/457–0172* 🖷 *784/457–0213* ⊕ *www.newmontrosehotel.com* ➲ *25 suites* ⚘ *Restaurant, room service, fans, kitchenettes, refrigerators, bar* 🖃 *AE, MC, V* ⦿ *EP.*

¢   🖭 **Cobblestone Inn.** On the waterfront in "the city," as Vincentians call Kingstown, this small hotel occupies a stone structure formerly used as a warehouse for sugar and arrowroot. Converted to a hotel in 1970, the building (1814) has original Georgian architecture, a sunny interior courtyard, and winding cobblestone walkways and arches. Rooms are tiny, but each has stone walls, rattan furniture, and a private bath. No. 5, at the front, is lighter and bigger than most of the others—but noisier, too. A rooftop bar-restaurant serves breakfast and light lunches. The popular Basil's Bar and Restaurant is at ground level. ⊠ *Upper Bay St., Kingstown* ① *Box 867* ☎ *784/456–1937* 🖷 *784/456–1938* ⊕ *www.cobblestoneinnsvg.com* ➲ *21 rooms* ⚘ *Restaurant, bar, shops, baby-sitting, laundry service, meeting room* 🖃 *AE, D, MC, V* ⦿ *EP.*

Where to Eat

Nearly all restaurants in St. Vincent specialize in West Indian cuisine, although you'll find chefs with broad culinary experience at the posher places. Local dishes to try include *callaloo* (similar to spinach) soup, curried goat or chicken, *rotis* (turnovers filled with curried meat or vegetables), seasonal seafood (lobster, kingfish, snapper, and mahimahi), local vegetables (avocados, breadfruit, christophene, and pumpkin) and "provisions" (roots such as yams or dasheen) and tropical fruit (from mangoes and soursop to pineapples and papaya). Fried or baked chicken is available everywhere, often accompanied by "rice 'n' peas" or *pelau* (seasoned rice). The local beer, Hairoun, is brewed according to a German recipe at Campden Park, just north of Kingstown. Sunset is the local rum.

What to Wear

Restaurants are casual. You may want to dress up a little—long pants and collared shirts for gents, summer dresses or dress pants for the ladies—for an evening out at a pricey restaurant, but none of the places listed below requires gentlemen to wear a jacket or tie. Beachwear should always be reserved for the beach.

CARIBBEAN
$-$$

✕ **Basil's Bar and Restaurant.** It's not just the air-conditioning that makes this restaurant cool. Downstairs at the Cobblestone Inn, it is owned by Basil Charles, whose Basil's Beach Bar on Mustique is a hangout for the vacationing rich and famous. This is the Kingstown power-lunch venue. Local businesspeople gather for the daily buffet or a full menu of salads, sandwiches, barbecued chicken, or fresh seafood platters. Dinner entrées of pasta, local seafood, and chicken (try it poached in fresh ginger and coconut milk) are served at candlelit tables. There's a Chinese buffet on Friday, and takeout is available that night only. ⊠ *Cobblestone Inn, Upper Bay St., Kingstown* ☎ *784/457–2713* ⊟ *AE, MC, V.*

$-$$

✕ **Buccama On the Bay.** You'll find Buccama in a quaint Caribbean-style building surrounded by tropical gardens and Carib petroglyphs and facing a black-sand beach. Just 20 minutes north of Kingstown, it's a perfect spot for a special dinner or a relaxing lunch when touring the leeward coast. Local food is the specialty, particularly seafood, along with grilled or roasted meat and other international favorites. Steel-pan, calypso, or jazz music often accompanies dinner. Changing facilities are available for beachgoers. ⊠ *Leeward Hwy., Buccament Bay* ☎ *784/456–7831* ⊟ *AE, MC, V.*

¢-$$

✕ **Vee Jay's Rooftop Diner & Pub.** This eatery above Roger's Photo Studios (have your pix developed while you eat) and opposite the Cobblestone Inn offers downtown Kingstown's best harbor view from beneath a green corrugated-plastic roof. Among the "authentic Vincy cuisine" specials chalked on the blackboard are mutton or fish stew, chicken or vegetable rotis, curried goat, souse, and *buljol* (sautéed codfish, breadfruit, and vegetables). Not-so-Vincy sandwiches, fish-and-chips, and burgers can be authentically washed down with *mauby,* a bittersweet drink made from tree bark; linseed, peanut, passion-fruit, or sorrel punch; local Hairoun beer; or cocktails. Lunch is buffet style. ⊠ *Upper Bay St., Kingstown* ☎ *784/457–2845* ⚭ *Reservations essential* ⊟ *AE, MC, V* ☉ *Closed Sun.*

¢-$

✕ **Wallilabou Bay Hotel.** Halfway up the Caribbean coast of St. Vincent, this is a favorite anchorage for folks sailing the Grenadines as well as day-trippers returning from a visit to the Falls of Baleine. Pretty as a picture, it's open all day (from 8 AM), and it's a particularly perfect luncheon or sunset-viewing spot for landlubbers touring the leeward coast. The bar-and-restaurant serves snacks, sandwiches, tempting West Indian dishes, and lobster in season. Ice, telephones, business services, and shower facilities are available to boaters. ⊠ *Leeward Hwy., Wallilabou Bay* ☎ *784/458–7270* ⊟ *AE, MC, V.*

CONTEMPORARY
$$-$$$

✕ **King Arthur Dining Room.** Expect fine cuisine and elegant service when supping at this intimate dining room downstairs in the Camelot Inn. The chef's table d'hôte menu offers you a choice of two to three starters and entrées, which change daily. Dishes—such as filet mignon, grilled fish with herb sauce, chicken sautéed in white wine—are served with local vegetables. The homemade soups are memorable, and so is the rum-raisin ice cream. There's entertainment in season and a weekly barbecue on the breezy Guinevere Terrace, which overlooks the harbor. ⊠ *Camelot Inn, Kingstown Park* ☎ *784/456–2100* ⚭ *Reservations essential* ⊟ *AE, D, MC, V.*

CONTINENTAL ✕ **Young Island Resort.** Take the ferry (a five-minute ride from Villa
$$$ Beach) to Young Island for a picturesque lunch or a very special romantic
evening. Stone paths lead to candlelit tables, some in breezy, thatch-roof
huts. Tiny waves lap against the shore. Five-course table d'hôte, prix-
fixe dinners of grilled seafood, roast pork, beef tenderloin, and sautéed
chicken are accompanied by local vegetables; a board of fresh breads is
offered for your selection. Two or three choices are offered for each course.
Lunch is à la carte—soups, salads, grilled meats, or fish—and served on
the beachfront terrace. ⊠ *Young Island* ☎ *784/458–4826* ⚹ *Reservations
essential* ▤ *AE, MC, V.*

ECLECTIC ✕ **Slick's Restaurant & Bar.** On the second floor above the Kingstown
$$–$$$$ Produce Market, Slick's offers main courses culled from Italian, American, French, and West Indian cuisines. Whether you choose shrimp,
lobster, steak, lamb chops, or chicken, the dish is ultimately determined
that day by the chef's preparation and accompanying sauces.
⊠ *Kingstown Produce Market, 2nd floor, Villa Harbour* ☎ *784/451–
2756* ▤ *AE, MC, V.*

$–$$$ ✕ **Lime Restaurant & Pub.** Named for the *pursuit* of liming, this sprawl-
ing waterfront restaurant also includes a great deal of green in its decor.
An extensive all-day menu caters to beachgoers and boaters, who drop
by for a roti and a bottle of Hairoun—or burgers, curries, sandwiches,
gourmet pizzas, pastas, soups, and salads. Dinner choices include fresh
seafood, volcano chicken (with a creole sauce that's as spicy as lava is
hot), curried goat, and pepper steak. Casual and congenial by day, it's
candlelit and romantic at night—enhanced by the twinkling lights of an-
chored boats and the soft sound of waves quietly breaking against the
seawall. ⊠ *Young Island Channel, Villa Harbour* ☎ *784/458–4227*
▤ *AE, D, DC, MC, V.*

FRENCH ✕ **The French Restaurant.** Yachties come here for a quiet waterfront
$$–$$$ breakfast or lunch—and also when they're in the mood for lobster.
There's a lobster pool on the terrace, where the staff fishes for your sup-
per. As befits a bistro called "The French," most dishes are Gallic ver-
sions of local cuisine. Stuffed crab back, for instance, comes in a pastry
shell, not a crab shell; steak—au poivre, with garlic butter or with béar-
naise—is imported; the onion soup and lemon tart are French, the way
they should be; and the warm, fresh bread is a genuine Parisienne-style
baguette. ⊠ *Young Island Channel, Villa Harbour* ☎ *784/458–4972*
▤ *AE, MC, V.*

Beaches

St. Vincent's origin is volcanic, so its beaches range in color from golden
brown to black. Young Island has the only truly white-sand beach; but
since the island is private, it's reserved for hotel guests. Otherwise, all
beaches are public. On the windward coast, dramatic swaths of broad
black sand are strewn with huge black boulders, but the water is rough
and unpredictable. Swimming is recommended only in the lagoons and
bays along the leeward coast.

Buccament Bay. Good for swimming, this tiny black-sand beach is 20 min-
utes north of Kingstown.
Indian Bay. South of Kingstown, it has golden sand but is slightly rocky—
a good place for snorkeling.
Questelle's Bay. This beach (pronounced keet-*ells*), north of Kingstown
and next to Campden Park, has a black-sand beach.
Villa Beach. Opposite Young Island and 10 minutes south of Kingstown
is the island's main beach (although it's hardly big enough to merit such

a title). Boats bob at anchor in the channel; dive shops and restaurants line the shore.

Sports & the Outdoors

BICYCLING   Bicycles can be rented for about $10 per day, but roads are not particularly conducive to leisurely cycling. Serious bicyclists, however, will enjoy a day of mountain biking in wilderness areas. **Sailor's Wilderness Tours** (✉ Middle St., Kingstown ☎ 784/457–1712; 784/457–9207 after hours) takes individuals or groups on half-day bike tours for $25 per person (which includes bike rental).

BOATING,   From St. Vincent you can charter a monohull or catamaran (bareboat
FISHING &   or complete with captain, crew, and cook) to weave you through the
SAILING   Grenadines for a day or a week of sailing—or a half-day, full-day, or overnight fishing trip. Boats of all sizes and degrees of luxury are available. Charter rates run about $250 per day and up. **Barefoot Yacht Charters** (✉ Blue Lagoon, Ratho Mill ☎ 784/456–9526 🖷 785/456–9238) has a fleet of yachts in the 32- to 50-ft range. **Blue Water Charters** (✉ Aquatic Club, Villa Beach ☎ 784/456–1232 🖷 784/456–2382) will take you on full-day, half-day, or overnight fishing or sightseeing excursions on its modern 55-ft Sport Fisherman. **Crystal Blue Charters** (✉ Indian Bay ☎ 784/457–4532 🖷 784/456–2232) offers sportfishing charters on a 34-ft pirogue for amateur and serious fishermen. **Sunsail** (✉ Blue Lagoon, Ratho Mill ☎🖷 784/458–4308) charters bareboat and crewed yachts ranging from 30 ft to 50 ft.

HIKING   St. Vincent offers hikers and trekkers a choice of experiences: easy, picturesque walks near Kingstown; moderate-effort nature trails in the central valleys; and exhilarating climbs through a rain forest to the rim of an active volcano. Bring a hat, long pants, and insect repellent if you plan to hike in the bush.

A hike up **Dorsetshire Hill,** about 3 mi (5 km) from Kingstown, rewards you with a sweeping view of city and harbor. You can also see the monument to Black Carib chief Chatoyer, who lost his life in a duel at this site.

La Soufrière, the queen of climbs, is St. Vincent's active volcano (which last erupted, appropriately enough, on Friday the 13th, April 1979). Approachable from either the windward or leeward coast, this is *not* a casual excursion for inexperienced walkers—the massive mountain covers nearly the entire northern third of the island. Climbs are all-day excursions. You'll need stamina and sturdy shoes to reach the top and peep into the mile-wide (1½-km-wide) crater at just over 4,000 ft. Be sure to check the weather before you leave; hikers have been sorely disappointed to find a cloud-obscured view at the summit. A guide ($25–$30) can be arranged through your hotel, the Ministry of Tourism & Culture, or tour operators. The eastern approach is more popular. In a four-wheel-drive vehicle you pass through Rabacca Dry River, north of Georgetown, and the Bamboo Forest; then it's a two-hour, 3½-mi (5½-km) hike to the summit. Approaching from the west, near Châteaubelair, the climb is longer—10–12 mi (6–7 km)—and rougher, but even more scenic. If you hike up one side and down the other, arrangements must be made in advance to pick you up at the end.

Trinity Falls, in the north, requires a trip by four-wheel-drive vehicle from Richmond to the interior, then a steep two-hour climb to a crystal-clear river and three waterfalls, one of which forms a whirlpool where you can take a refreshing swim.

Vermont Nature Trails are two hiking trails that start near the top of the Buccament Valley, 5 mi (8 km) north of Kingstown. A network of 1½-mi (2½-km) loops passes through bamboo, evergreen forest, and rain forest. In the late afternoon you may be lucky enough to see the rare St. Vincent parrot, *Amazona guildingii*.

SCUBA DIVING & SNORKELING ★ Novices and advanced divers alike will be impressed by the marine life in the waters around St. Vincent—brilliant sponges, huge deepwater coral trees, and shallow reefs teeming with colorful fish. Many sites in the Grenadines are still virtually unexplored.

Most dive shops offer 3-hour beginner "resort" courses, full certification courses, and excursions to reefs, walls, and wrecks throughout the Grenadines. A single-tank dive costs about $50; a two-tank, $95; a 10-dive package, $400. All prices include equipment. It can't be emphasized enough, however, that the coral reef is extremely fragile, and you must only look and never touch.

St. Vincent is ringed by one long, almost continuous reef. The best dive spots are in the small bays along the coast between Kingstown and Layou; many are within 20 yards of shore and only 20–30 ft down. **Anchor Reef** has excellent visibility for viewing a deep-black coral garden, schools of squid, seahorses, and maybe a small octopus. **The Forest**, a shallow dive, is still dramatic, with soft corals in pastel colors and schools of small fish. **New Guinea Reef** slopes to 90 ft and can't be matched for its quantity of corals and sponges. **Young Island** is also a good place for snorkeling. If you're not a resort guest, phone for permission to take the ferry from Villa Beach over to the island and rent snorkeling equipment from the resort's water-sports center. The pristine waters surrounding the **Tobago Cays,** in the Southern Grenadines, will give you a world-class diving experience.

Dive Fantasea (✉ Villa Beach ☎ 784/457–5560 or 784/457–5577) offers dive and snorkeling trips to the St. Vincent coast and the Tobago Cays. **Dive St. Vincent** (✉ Young Island Dock, Villa Beach ☎ 784/457–4714 or 784/547–4928) is where NAUI- and PADI-certified instructor Bill Tewes and his staff offer beginner and certification courses and dive trips to the St. Vincent coast and the southern Grenadines. **Wallilabou Dive Experience** (✉ Wallilabou ☎ 784/456–0355) offers PADI-certified courses and daily one- or two-tank dives to sites on St. Vincent.

TENNIS **Haddon Tennis Club** (✉ Murrays Rd., Kingstown ☎ 784/456–1897) has two outdoor courts lighted for night use. **St. Vincent and the Grenadines National Tennis Centre** (✉ Villa ☎ 784/457–4090) has four lighted outdoor courts.

Shopping

The 12 blocks that hug the waterfront in downtown Kingstown comprise St. Vincent's main shopping district. Among the shops that sell goods to fulfill household needs are a few that sell local crafts, gifts, and souvenirs. Bargaining is neither expected nor appreciated.

CDS, TAPES & RECORDS To bring back sounds of the islands, stop by **Music World** (✉ Egmont St., Kingstown ☎ 784/547–1884), where you'll find the latest reggae, soca, and calypso music on CD or tape.

DUTY-FREE GOODS The best place for duty-free shopping is at the **Cruise Ship Terminal** (✉ Upper Bay St., Kingstown ☎ 784/456–1830). Among its 20 shops are several that specialize in duty-free goods. At **Gonsalves Duty-Free Liquor** (✉ Airport Departure Lounge, Arnos Vale ☎ 784/456–4781), spirits and liqueurs are available at discounts of up to 40%.

HANDICRAFTS At **FranPaul's Selections** (✉ 2nd floor, Bonadie's Plaza, Bay St., Kingstown ☎ 784/456–2662), Francelia St. John fashions dresses, pants, and shirts from colorful fabrics she selects in Trinidad. The emphasis is on African, Afro-Caribbean, and casual wear. **Nzimbu Browne** (✉ Bay St., in front of the Cobblestone Inn, Kingstown ☎ 784/457–1677) creates original art from dried banana leaves, carefully selecting and snipping bits and arranging them on pieces of wood to depict local scenes. He sets up shop on Bay Street, near the Cobblestone Inn. **St. Vincent Craftsmen's Centre** (✉ Frenches St., Kingstown ☎ 784/457–2516), three blocks from the wharf, sells locally made grass floor mats, place mats, and other straw articles, as well as batik cloth, handmade West Indian dolls, hand-painted calabashes, and framed artwork. The large grass mats can be rolled and folded for easy transport home. No credit cards are accepted.

Nightlife

Nightlife here consists mostly of once-a-week hotel barbecue buffets with local music and jump-ups, so called because the lively steel-band and calypso music makes listeners jump up and dance. At nightspots in Kingstown and at Villa Beach, you can join Vincentians for late-night dancing to live or recorded reggae, hip-hop, and soca music.

CASINO **Emerald Valley Casino** (✉ Peniston Valley ☎ 784/456–7824) combines the hominess of a small English pub with the gaming of Vegas—roulette, blackjack, Caribbean stud poker, craps, and slots. It's generally open Wednesday–Monday 9 PM–3 AM, and until 4 AM on Saturday. Call ahead for free transportation.

DANCE & MUSIC Dance clubs generally charge a cover of $4 (EC$10), slightly more for
CLUBS headliners. At the **Aquatic Club** (✉ Villa Beach ☎ 784/458–4205), the rhythmic sounds of soca and reggae reverberate on the waterfront on Saturday night as locals and visitors dance to live music. The **Attic** (✉ 1 Melville St., Kingstown ☎ 784/457–2558) is above the KFC; you'll hear international jazz and blues on Thursday night; weekend parties begin at 10 PM. **Touch Entertainment Centre** (✉ Grenville St., Kingstown ☎ 784/457–1825) is a dance hall with disco music on Friday and live music on Saturday. It attracts a local crowd of mostly young people.

THEME NIGHTS **Calliaqua Culture Pot** (✉ Main Rd., Calliaqua ☎ no phone) is a community street party held every Friday evening at 8 PM. Join the crowd for barbecue, beer, dancing to local music, arts and crafts, and cultural performances. On Wednesday and Friday evenings at **Vee Jay's Rooftop Diner & Pub** (✉ Bay St., Kingstown ☎ 784/457–2845), karaoke accompanies dinner, drinks, and the open-air harbor view. **Young Island Resort** (✉ Young Island ☎ 784/458–4826) hosts sunset cocktail parties with hors d'oeuvres every Friday evening at adjacent Ft. Duvernette. Hotel guests and nonguests (with reservations) are ferried from Young Island Resort to the tiny island, where the 100 steps up the hill are lighted by flaming torches. The National String Band plays infectious music on guitars and instruments made of bamboo, bottles, and gourds.

Exploring St. Vincent

Kingstown's shopping and business district, historic churches and cathedrals, and other points of interest can easily be seen in a half day, with another half day for the Botanical Gardens. The coastal roads of St. Vincent offer spectacular panoramas and scenes of island life. The Leeward Highway follows the scenic Caribbean coastline; the Windward Highway follows the more dramatic Atlantic coast. A drive along the windward coast or a boat trip to the Falls of Baleine each requires a full day.

Exploring La Soufrière and the Vermont Trails are also major under-takings, requiring a very early start and a full day's strenuous hiking.

Numbers in the margin correspond to points of interest on the St. Vincent map.

Sights to See

④ Barrouallie. This was once an important whaling village; now, however, the fishermen of Barrouallie (pronounced *bar*-relly) earn their livelihoods trawling for blackfish, which are actually small pilot whales. The one-hour drive north from Kingstown, on the Leeward Highway, takes you along ridges that drop to the sea, through small villages and lush val-leys, and beside picturesque bays with black-sand beaches and safe bathing.

⑪ Black Point Tunnel. In 1815, under the supervision of British colonel Thomas Browne, Carib and African slaves drilled this 300-ft tunnel through solid volcanic rock to facilitate the transportation of sugar from estates in the north to the port in Kingstown. The tunnel, an en-gineering marvel for the times, links Grand Sable with Byrea Bay, just north of Colonarie (pronounced con-a-*ree*).

★ ⑥ Falls of Baleine. They're impossible to reach by car, so book an escorted, all-day boat trip from Villa Beach or the Lagoon Marina. The boat ride along the coast offers scenic island views. When you arrive, you have to wade through shallow water to get to the beach. Then local guides help you make the easy five-minute trek to the 60-ft falls and the rock-enclosed freshwater pool the falls create—plan to take a dip.

★ ☁ ② Ft. Charlotte. Started by the French in 1786 and completed by the British in 1806, the fort was named for King George III's wife. It sits on Berk-shire Hill, a dramatic promontory 636 ft above sea level, with a stun-ning view of Kingstown and the Grenadines. Interestingly, cannons face inward—the fear of attack by native peoples was far greater than any threat approaching from the sea, though, truth be told, the fort saw no action. Nowadays the fort serves as a signal station for ships; its ancient cells house paintings, by Lindsay Prescott, depicting early island history.

⑭ Ft. Duvernette. The fort was built around 1800, on a massive rock be-hind Young Island, to defend Calliaqua Bay. Views from the 195-ft sum-mit are terrific, but you'll have to climb about 100 steps carved into the rock to get here. Two complete batteries of rusting armaments remain near the top. Arrange your visit at the Young Island Resort—their lit-tle ferry will transport you to the fort and bring you back.

⑩ Georgetown. St. Vincent's second-largest city (and former capital), halfway up the island's east coast, is surrounded by acres and acres of coconut groves. This is also the site of the now defunct Mount Bentinck sugar factory. A small, quiet town—with a few streets, small shops, a restaurant or two, and modest homes—it is completely untainted by tourism. It's also a convenient place to stop for a cool drink or snack or other essential shopping while traveling along the windward coast.

① Kingstown. The capital city of St. Vincent and the Grenadines is on the island's southwestern coast. The town of 25,000 residents, about a fourth of the nation's population, wraps around Kingstown Bay; a ring of green hills and ridges, studded with homes, forms a backdrop for the city. This is very much a working city, with a busy harbor and few con-cessions to tourists. Kingstown Harbour is the only deepwater port on the island.

What few gift shops there are can be found on and around **Bay Street**, near the harbor. Upper Bay Street, which stretches along the bayfront, bustles with daytime activity—workers going about their business and housewives doing their shopping. Many of Kingstown's downtown buildings are built of stone or brick brought to the island in the holds of 18th-century ships as ballast (and replaced with sugar and spices for the return trip to Europe). The Georgian-style stone arches and second-floor overhangs on former warehouses create shelter from midday sun and the brief, cooling showers common to the tropics.

Grenadines Wharf, at the south end of Bay Street, is busy with schooners loading supplies and ferries loading people bound for the Grenadines. The **Cruise Ship Terminal,** south of the commercial wharf, has a duty-free mall with 20 shops, plus restaurants, a post office, communications facilities, and a taxi/minibus stand.

An almost infinite selection of produce fills the **Kingstown Produce Market,** a three-story building that takes up a whole city block on Upper Bay, Hillsboro, and Bedford streets in the center of town. It's noisy, colorful, and open Monday through Saturday—but the busiest times (and the best times to go) are Friday and Saturday mornings. In the courtyard, vendors sell local arts and crafts. On the upper floors, merchants sell clothing, household items, gifts, and other products.

Little Tokyo, so called because funding for the project was a gift from Japan, is a waterfront shopping area with a bustling indoor fish market and dozens of stalls where you can buy inexpensive homemade meals, drinks, ice cream, bread and cookies, clothing, and trinkets, and even get a haircut.

St. George's Cathedral, on Grenville Street, is a pristine, creamy-yellow Anglican church built in 1820. The dignified Georgian architecture includes simple wooden pews, an ornate chandelier, and beautiful stained-glass windows; one was a gift from Queen Victoria, who actually commissioned it for London's St. Paul's Cathedral in honor of her first grandson. When the artist created an angel with a red robe, she was horrified and sent it abroad. The markers in the cathedral's graveyard recount the history of the island. Across the street is **St. Mary's Cathedral of the Assumption** (Roman Catholic), built in stages beginning in 1823. The strangely appealing design is a blend of Moorish, Georgian, and Romanesque styles applied to black brick. Nearby, freed slaves built the **Kingstown Methodist Church** in 1841. The exterior is brick, simply decorated with quoins (solid blocks that form the corners), and the roof is held together by metal straps, bolts, and wooden pins. **Scots Kirk** (1839–80) was built by and for Scottish settlers but became a Seventh-Day Adventist church in 1952.

A few minutes north of downtown by taxi is St. Vincent's famous ☪ **Botanical Garden.** Founded in 1765, it is the oldest botanical garden in the western hemisphere. Captain Bligh—of *Bounty* fame—brought the first breadfruit tree to this island for landowners to propagate. The prolific bounty of the breadfruit tree was used to feed the slaves. You can see a direct descendant of this original tree among the specimen mahogany, rubber, teak, and other tropical trees and shrubs in the 20 acres of gardens. Two dozen rare St. Vincent parrots live in the small aviary. Guides explain all the medicinal and ornamental trees and shrubs; they also appreciate a tip at the end of the tour. ⊠ *Off Leeward Hwy., Montrose* ☎ *784/457–1003* 🖃 *$3* ۞ *Daily 6–6.*

❽ **La Soufrière.** The volcano, which last erupted in 1979, is 4,000 ft high and so huge in area that it covers virtually the entire northern third of the island. The eastern trail to the rim of the crater, a two-hour ascent, begins at Rabacca Dry River.

3 **Layou.** Just beyond this small fishing village, about 45 minutes north of Kingstown, are petroglyphs (rock carvings) left by pre-Columbian peoples 13 centuries ago. Arrange a visit through the Ministry of Tourism & Culture. For $2, Victor Hendrickson, who owns the land, or his wife will escort you to the site.

12 **Mesopotamia Valley.** The rugged, ocean-lashed scenery along St. Vincent's windward coast is the perfect counterpoint to the lush, calm west coast. The fertile Mesopotamia Valley (nicknamed "Mespo") offers a panoramic view of dense rain forests, streams, and endless banana and coconut plantations. Breadfruit, sweet corn, peanuts, and arrowroot also grow in the rich soil here. The valley is surrounded by mountain ridges, including 3,181-ft Grand Bonhomme Mountain, and overlooks the Caribbean.

13 **Montreal Gardens.** Welsh-born landscape designer Timothy Vaughn renovated 7½ acres of neglected commercial flower beds and a falling-apart plantation house into a stunning, yet informal, garden spot. Anthuriums, ginger lilies, birds-of-paradise, and other tropical flowers are planted in raised beds; tree ferns create a canopy of shade along the walkways. The gardens are in the shadow of majestic Grand Bonhomme mountain, deep in the Mesopotamia Valley, about 12 mi from Kingstown. ⊠ *Montreal St., Mesopotamia* ☎ *784/458–1198* ✉ *$3* ☉ *Mon.–Fri. 9–4* ☉ *Closed Sept.–Nov.*

7 **Owia.** The Carib village of Owia, on the island's far northeast coast about two hours from Kingstown, is the home of many descendents of the Carib people of St. Vincent. It is also the location of the Owia Arrowroot Processing Factory. Used for generations to thicken sauces and flavor cookies, arrowroot is now in demand as a finish for computer paper. Close to the village is the **Owia Salt Pond,** created by the pounding surf of the Atlantic Ocean, which flowed over a barrier reef of lava rocks and ridges. Have a picnic and take a swim before the long, scenic ride to Kingstown.

9 **Rabacca Dry River.** This rocky gulch just beyond the village of Georgetown was carved out of the earth by the lava flow from the 1902 eruption of nearby **La Soufrière.** When it rains on La Soufrière, the river is no longer dry—and you can be stranded on one side or the other for an hour or two or, in rare cases, longer.

5 **Wallilabou Bay.** You can sunbathe, swim, picnic, or buy your lunch at Wallilabou (pronounced wally-la-*boo*) Anchorage, on the bay. This is a favorite stop for day-trippers returning from the Falls of Baleine and boaters anchoring for the evening. Nearby there's a river with a small waterfall where you can take a freshwater plunge.

THE GRENADINES

The Grenadine Islands offer excellent spots for sailing, fine diving and snorkeling, magnificent beaches, and unlimited chances to relax with a picnic, watch boats, and wait for the sun to set. Whether you're seeking peace and quiet or active water sports and informal socializing, you'll be happy in the Grenadines—though each island has a different appeal.

Bequia

Bequia (pronounced *beck*-way) is the Carib word for "island of the cloud." Hilly and green, with several gold-sand beaches, Bequia is just 9 mi (14½ km) south of St. Vincent's southwestern shore; with a population of 5,000, it's the largest of the Grenadines.

While boatbuilding, whaling, and fishing have been industries here for generations, sailing and Bequia have become almost synonymous. Be-

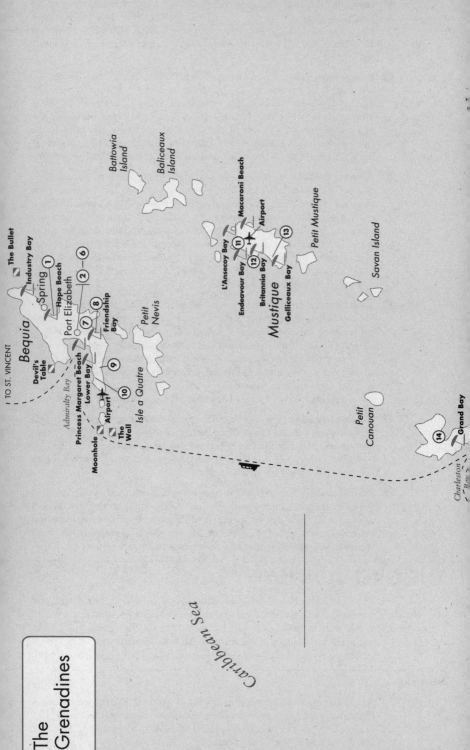

The Grenadines

TO ST. VINCENT

Caribbean Sea

Bequia
Devil's Table
Admiralty Bay
Princess Margaret Beach
Lower Bay
Moonhole
Airport
The Wall
Isle a Quatre
Petit Nevis
Port Elizabeth
Spring
Hope Beach
Industry Bay
The Bullet
Friendship Bay

① ② ⑥ ⑦ ⑧ ⑨ ⑩

Battowia Island
Baliceaux Island

Mustique
L'Ansecoy Bay
Endeavour Bay
Britannia Bay
Gelliceaux Bay
Macaroni Beach
Airport
Petit Mustique

⑪ ⑫ ⑬

Savan Island

Petit Canouan

Charleston Bay
Grand Bay

⑭

quia's picturesque Admiralty Bay is a favored anchorage for private or chartered yachts. Lodgings range from comfortable resorts to cozy West Indian inns. Bequia's airport and regular, frequent ferry service from St. Vincent make this a favorite destination for day-trippers as well. The ferry docks in Port Elizabeth, a tiny town with waterfront bars, restaurants, and shops where you can buy handmade souvenirs, including the exquisitely detailed model sailboats for which Bequia is famous.

Where to Stay

For approximate costs, *see* the lodging price chart *in* St. Vincent.

$$$ 🏨 **Plantation House.** The peach-pink Plantation House sits on 20 manicured acres facing Admiralty Bay, with lawn and gardens punctuated by swaying palms, alabaster statuary, hammocks, and lounge chairs. Standard rooms each have a dressing room, twin beds, and a verandah. Deluxe rooms are in the main building, five suites in two beachfront cottages. Buffet breakfast and candlelight dinners are served at the Verandah restaurant in the main house. The informal beachfront Green Flash bar/restaurant serves lunch and is a convivial gathering place in the evening. Taxi-boat service to Princess Margaret Beach (a three-minute ride) is complimentary. ⊠ *Admiralty Bay, Port Elizabeth* 🗄 *Box 16* ☎ *784/458–3425* 🖷 *784/458–3612* ⊕ *www.hotel-plantation.com* ➾ *5 rooms, 5 suites, 17 cabanas* ⚲ *2 restaurants, room service, fans, in-room safes, refrigerator, in-room VCRs, tennis court, pool, beach, snorkeling, windsurfing, boating, waterskiing, mountain bikes, 2 bars, piano, shops, baby-sitting, laundry service, meeting room, airport shuttle* ⊟ *AE, MC, V* ⑩ *BP.*

$$ 🏨 **Friendship Bay Beach Resort.** This sprawling hillside complex hugs a mile-long (1½-km-long) arc of white-sand beach. Accommodations are in the main building, with a sweeping view of the sea, and in a group of coral-stone cottages that dot the spacious landscaped grounds. Rooms are small, but each has a terrace with an ocean panorama. The open-air Spicy 'n' Herby beach bar and restaurant serves seafood and creole cuisine. On Saturday night there's a barbecue and jump-up, and the rope-swing seats at the bar will keep you upright even after a potent rum punch. Breakfast and special dinners are served in the Oceanside restaurant. ⊠ *Friendship Bay* 🗄 *Box 9* ☎ *784/458–3222* 🖷 *784/458–3840* ➾ *27 rooms, 1 suite* ⚲ *2 restaurants, room service, fans, tennis court, beach, dive shop, dock, snorkeling, windsurfing, boating, waterskiing, volleyball, 2 bars, shops, baby-sitting, laundry service, meeting room; no a/c, no room phones, no room TVs* ⊟ *AE, MC, V* ⑩ *BP.*

★ $–$$ 🏨 **Gingerbread Apartments.** Identified by its decorative woodwork, the Gingerbread faces the busy Admiralty Bay waterfront. Suites—suitable for three—are large, modern, and stylishly decorated, with bedroom alcoves, adjoining salons, and full kitchens. Downstairs rooms have twin beds and large bayfront porches; upper rooms have king-size four-poster beds and verandahs with harbor views. Decorated and furnished in a sophisticated tropical style, rooms have Italian tile floors, blue-and-white geometric-print bed quilts, sheer mosquito netting gathered over beds, and natural wood and rattan furniture throughout. Bathrooms are large and modern. Gingerbread restaurant serves full meals; for snacks head to the waterfront café. ⊠ *Admiralty Bay, Port Elizabeth* 🗄 *Box 1* ☎ *784/458–3800* 🖷 *784/458–3907* ⊕ *www.gingerbreadhotel.com* ➾ *9 suites* ⚲ *Restaurant, café, ice-cream parlor, room service, fans, in-room safes, kitchens, tennis court, beach, dive shop, snorkeling, boating, bar, baby-sitting, travel services; no a/c* ⊟ *AE, MC, V* ⑩ *EP.*

$–$$ 🏨 **The Old Fort Country Inn.** Otmar Schaedle turned this sugar estate's stone great house into an intimate inn reminiscent of something you might see in Provence. It is perched high on a cliff and cooled by trade winds, in a spot both remote and stunning. Each guest room has thick stone walls, and windows that overlook a panoramic Grenadine vista. Because the nearest beach, Ravine, is nearly 450 ft down a rather steep path and the water is too rough for swimming, the inn is a good choice for romantics and getaway purists who are content with a pool. The Old Fort restaurant is well worth the 10-minute trek from town by car. ⊠ *Mt. Pleasant* ☎ *784/458–3440* 🖷 *784/457–3340* ⊕ *www.theoldfort.com* ⤸ *5 rooms* ⟁ *Restaurant, room service, kitchenettes, pool, hiking, bar, baby-sitting, laundry service, airport shuttle; no a/c* ▭ *MC, V* ⦿ *EP.*

$–$$ 🏨 **Spring on Bequia.** Nestled on 20 acres of green hills belonging to a 200-year-old plantation, this small hotel is about 1 mi (1½ km) north of Port Elizabeth. Two spacious guest rooms with balconies are in a stone-and-wood building called Fort, highest on the hill, with beautiful views of countless coconut palms and the sea. Four large units are in Gull, halfway up the hill, and have similar full or partial ocean views. Three more rooms are convenient to the pool, garden, open-air bar, and restaurant. Strolling down to the beach—a 10-minute walk—you'll pass the ruins of a sugar mill, now a potter's studio. ⊠ *Spring Bay* ☎ *784/458– 3414* 🖷 *784/457–3305* ⊕ *www.springonbequia.com* ⊠ *U.S. agent:* ⌖ *Spring on Bequia, Box 19251, Minneapolis, MN 55419* 🖷 *612/823– 1202* ⤸ *9 rooms* ⟁ *Restaurant, tennis court, pool, beach, snorkeling, hiking, bar; no a/c* ☾ *Closed mid-June–Oct.* ▭ *AE, D, MC, V* ⦿ *EP.*

¢–$$ 🏨 **Frangipani Hotel.** The venerable Frangipani, owned by former prime minister James Mitchell, is also known for its friendly waterfront bar and excellent restaurant—both hangouts for the yachting crowd. Five simple, inexpensive rooms in the original shingle-sided sea captain's home have painted-wood walls and floors, grass rugs, and plain furniture; all but one share a bath. Luxurious garden units, built of local stone and hardwoods, rise on a gentle slope filled with fragrant frangipani trees. These rooms have tile floors, louvered windows and doors, canopy beds, spacious baths with dressing rooms, and verandahs with spectacular sunset views of the harbor. ⊠ *Admiralty Bay, Port Elizabeth* ⌖ *Box 1* ☎ *784/458–3255* 🖷 *784/458–3824* ⊕ *www.frangipanibequia.com* ⤸ *15 rooms (1 with private bath)* ⟁ *Restaurant, room service, fans, refrigerator, tennis court, beach, dive shop, snorkeling, boating, bar, shops, baby-sitting, laundry service; no a/c* ▭ *MC, V* ⦿ *EP.*

Where to Eat

Dining on Bequia ranges from casual meals to more elaborate cuisine, and the food and service are consistently good. Barbecues at Bequia's hotels mean spicy West Indian seafood, chicken, or beef, plus a buffet of side salads and vegetable dishes and sweet desserts.

For approximate costs, *see* the dining price chart *in* St. Vincent.

CARIBBEAN ✕ **Old Fort.** Otmar and Sonja Schaedle, owners of The Old Fort Coun-
$$–$$$ try Inn, restored this mid-1700s estate to its current bougainvillea-shaded, stone-arched, candlelit beauty and continue to serve food good enough to attract nonguests to its romantic atmosphere with one of the best views—and coolest breezes—on the island. At lunch, feast on pumpkin or callaloo soup, crêpes, sandwiches, salads, or pasta. At dinner the French creole cuisine focuses on entrées such as spring lamb, tuna steak, langouste Grenadines, or chargrilled whole snapper, accompanied by fresh, homemade bread and curried pigeon peas. ⊠ *Old Fort Country Inn, Mt. Pleasant* ☎ *784/458–3440* ⟁ *Reservations essential* ▭ *MC, V.*

$–$$$ ✕ **Dawn's Creole Garden.** It's worth the walk uphill to the Creole Garden Hotel for the delicious West Indian food and the view. Lunch options include sandwiches, rotis, fresh mutton, "goat water" (a savory soup with bits of goat meat and root vegetables), fresh fish, or conch. At dinner, the five-course creole seafood, lobster, or vegetarian specials include the christophene and breadfruit accompaniments for which Dawn's is known. Barbecue is always available on request. The dinner menu changes daily. There's live guitar music most Saturday nights and a barbecue lunch, with live music, right on the beach on Sundays. ⊠ *Creole Garden Hotel, Lower Bay* ☎ *784/458–3154* ⚲ *Reservations essential* ▤ *AE, MC, V.*

★ $$ ✕ **Frangipani.** Just before sunset, yachties come ashore to what is arguably the most popular gathering spot in Bequia—the Frangipani Hotel's waterfront bar. After a drink and a chat, the mood turns romantic, with candlelight and excellent Caribbean cuisine in the open-air dining room. The à la carte menu emphasizes seafood and local dishes. On Monday nights in high season, a local string band plays catchy tunes on both usual (mandolin, guitar) and unusual instruments (bamboo, bottles, gourds); on Friday nights, folksingers entertain. The Thursday Frangi barbecue buffet (about $30) is accompanied by steel-band music and a jump-up. ⊠ *Frangipani Hotel, Belmont Walkway, Admiralty Bay, Port Elizabeth* ☎ *784/458–3255* ⚲ *Reservations essential* ▤ *MC, V.*

¢–$ ✕ **De Reef.** This café-restaurant on Lower Bay is the primary feeding station for long, lazy beach days. When the café closes at dusk, the restaurant takes over—if you've made reservations, that is. For breakfast (from 7) or light lunch, the café bakes its own breads, croissants, coconut cake, and cookies—and blends fresh juices to accompany them. For a full lunch or dinner, conch, lobster, whelks, and shrimp are treated the West Indian way, and the mutton curry is famous. Every other Saturday in season there's a seafood buffet dinner accompanied by live music; on Sunday afternoons there's a music jam. ⊠ *Lower Bay* ☎ *784/458–3484* ⚲ *Reservations essential* ▤ *No credit cards.*

CONTINENTAL ✕ **Green Flash.** The informal waterfront restaurant at the posh Planta-
$$–$$$ tion House hotel has an à la carte menu that ranges from pizza and cold buffet at lunch to French, Italian, and local specialties (lobster and fresh grilled fish with regional vegetables) at dinner. On Tuesday evenings check out the creole buffet—a feast of barbecued meats and fish, side salads, vegetable dishes, and excellent pastries—accompanied by live band music. ⊠ *Plantation House, Belmont Beach, Admiralty Bay, Port Elizabeth* ☎ *784/458–3425* ▤ *AE, MC, V.*

ECLECTIC ✕ **Gingerbread.** The airy dining room verandah at the Gingerbread
★ $$–$$$ Apartments overlooks Admiralty Bay and the waterfront activity. The lunch crowd can enjoy barbecued beef kebabs or chicken with fried potatoes or onions, grilled fish, homemade soups, salads, and sandwiches. In the evening, steaks, seafood, and curries are specialties of the house. Save room for warm, fresh gingerbread—served here with lemon sauce. In season, dinner is often accompanied by live music. ⊠ *Gingerbread Apartments, Belmont Walkway, Admiralty Bay, Port Elizabeth* ☎ *784/ 458–3800* ⚲ *Reservations essential* ▤ *AE, MC, V.*

FRENCH ✕ **L'Aubergine des Grenadines.** Owned by the same couple who oper-
$$–$$$ ated The French Restaurant on St. Vincent for years, this quaint restaurant and guest house on the waterfront facing Admiralty Bay is convenient for the yachting crowd, day-trippers, and anyone staying a while. The extensive menu marries French and West Indian cuisines: fresh seafood and local vegetables prepared with a French twist. Lobster is a specialty; select your own from the lobster pool to be prepared to taste. Light salads and sandwiches are available at lunch. Delicious baguettes and delicate pastries round out any meal. ⊠ *Belmont Walk-*

way, Admiralty Bay, Port Elizabeth ☎ 784/458–3201 ⚓ *Reservations essential* ▤ *AE, MC, V.*

PIZZA $ ✗ **Mac's Pizzeria.** Overheard at the dock in Mustique: "We're sailing over to Bequia for pizza." The two-hour sunset sail to Admiralty Bay is worth the trip for Mac's pizza. Choose from 14 mouthwatering toppings (including lobster), or select quiche, pita sandwiches, lasagna, or soups and salads. Mac's home-baked cookies and muffins are great for dessert or a snack. To complement your meal, the outdoor terrace offers fuchsia bougainvillea and water views. ✉ *Belmont Walkway, Admiralty Bay, Port Elizabeth* ☎ 784/458–3474 ⚓ *Reservations essential* ▤ *No credit cards.*

Beaches

Bequia has clean, uncrowded white-sand beaches. Some are a healthy walk from the jetty at Port Elizabeth; others require transportation.

Friendship Bay. This beach can be reached by land taxi. You can rent windsurfing and snorkeling equipment at Friendship Bay Resort and also grab a bite to eat or a cool drink.

Hope Beach. Getting to this beach on the Atlantic side involves a long taxi ride (about $7.50) and a mile-long (1½-km-long) walk downhill on a semi-paved path. Your reward is a magnificent crescent of white sand, total seclusion, and—if you prefer—nude bathing. Be sure to ask your taxi driver to return at a prearranged time. Bring your own lunch and drinks; there are no facilities. Even though the surf is fairly shallow, swimming can be dangerous because of the undertow.

Industry Bay. A nearly secluded beach fringed with towering palms is on the northeast side of the island and requires transportation from Port Elizabeth. This is a good beach for snorkelers, but there could be a strong undertow. Bring a picnic; the nearest facilities are at Spring on Bequia resort, a 10- to 15-minute walk from the beach.

Lower Bay. This wide, palm-fringed beach, reachable by taxi or hiking beyond Princess Margaret Beach, is an excellent location for swimming and snorkeling. There are facilities to rent water-sports equipment here, as well as De Reef restaurant.

Princess Margaret Beach. Quiet and wide, with a natural stone arch at one end, the beach is a half-hour hike over rocky bluffs from Belmont Walkway—or you can take a water or land taxi. Though it has no facilities, it's a popular spot for swimming, snorkeling, or snoozing under the palm and sea grape trees.

Sports & the Outdoors

BOATING & SAILING With regular trade winds, visibility for 30 mi (48 km), and generally calm seas, Bequia is a center for some of the best blue-water sailing you'll find anywhere in the world, with all kinds of options: day sails or weekly charters, bareboat or fully crewed, monohulls or catamarans—whatever's your pleasure. Prices for day trips run $50–$75 per person, depending on the destination.

Friendship Rose (✉ Port Elizabeth ☎ 784/458–3373), an 80-ft schooner that spent its first 25 years as a mail boat, was subsequently refitted to take passengers on day trips from Bequia to Mustique and the Tobago Cays. The 60-ft catamaran *Passion* (✉ Belmont ☎ 784/458–3884), custom-built for day sailing, offers all-inclusive daylong snorkeling and/or sportfishing trips from Bequia to Mustique, the Tobago Cays, and St. Vincent's Falls of Baleine. It's also available for private charter. The Frangipani Hotel owns the *S. Y. Pelangi* (✉ Port Elizabeth ☎ 784/458–3255), a 44-ft cutter, for day sails or longer charters; four people can be accommodated comfortably, and the cost is $200 per day.

SCUBA DIVING & SNORKELING   About 35 dive sites around Bequia and nearby islands are accessible within 15 minutes by boat. The leeward side of the 7-mi (11-km) reef that fringes Bequia has been designated a marine park. **The Bullet,** off Bequia's north point, is a good spot for spotting rays, barracuda, and the occasional nurse shark. **Devil's Table** is a shallow dive that's rich in fish and coral and has a sailboat wreck nearby at 90 ft. **Moonhole** is shallow enough in places for snorkelers to enjoy. **The Wall** is a 90-ft drop off West Cay. Expect to pay dive operators $50 for a one-tank and $95 for a two-tank dive. Dive boats welcome snorkelers, but for the best snorkeling in Bequia, take a water taxi to the bay at Moonhole and arrange a pickup time.

Bequia Dive Adventures (⊠ Belmont Walkway, Admiralty Bay, Port Elizabeth ☎ 784/458–3826 ᗌ 784/458–3964) offers PADI instruction courses and takes small groups on three dives daily; harbor pickup and return is included for customers staying on yachts. **Dive Bequia** (⊠ Belmont Walkway, Admiralty Bay, Port Elizabeth ☎ 784/458–3504 ᗌ 784/458–3886), at the Gingerbread complex, offers dive and snorkel tours, night dives, and full equipment rental. Resort and certification courses are available. **Dive Paradise** (⊠ Friendship Bay ☎ 784/458–3563 ᗌ 784/457–3115) has two modern dive boats and offers dive packages and certified instruction for beginners and advanced divers, equipment rental, night and wreck dives, and snorkeling packages (but they don't take credit cards). **Friendship Divers** (⊠ Friendship Bay ☎ᗌ 784/458–3422), near the Bequia Beach Club, offers one- and two-tank dives, instruction, and equipment rental; the dive boat accommodates up to 16 people.

TENNIS   The **public tennis courts** are next to the Bequia airport and can be used by anyone at no charge on a first-come, first-served basis.

Shopping

Bequia's shops are mostly on Front Street and Belmont Walkway, its waterfront extension, just steps from the jetty where the ferry arrives in Port Elizabeth. North of the jetty there's an open-air market and farther along the road are the model-boat builders' shops. Opposite the jetty, at Bayshore Mall, shops sell ice cream, baked goods, stationery, gifts, and clothing; a liquor store, pharmacy, travel agent, and bank are also here. On Belmont Walkway, south of the jetty, shops and studios showcase gifts and handmade articles. Shops are open weekdays from 8 to 5, Saturday 8 to noon.

HANDICRAFTS   Long renowned for their boatbuilding skills, Bequians have translated that craftsmanship to model-boat building. In their workshops in Port Elizabeth you can watch as hair-thin lines are attached to delicate sails or individual strips of wood are glued together for decking. Other Bequian artisans create scrimshaw, carve wood, crochet, or work with fabric—designing or hand-painting it first, then creating clothing and gift items for sale.

At **Banana Patch Studio** (⊠ Paget Farm ☎ 784/458–3865), you can view and purchase paintings and scrimshaw work by artist Sam McDowell and shellcraft created by his wife Donna, by appointment only. You can visit the studio of French artist **Claude Victorine** (⊠ Lower Bay ☎ 784/458–3150) and admire her delicate hand-painted silk wall hangings and scarves. Large wall hangings cost $100, scarves $50. Her studio is open

★   from noon to 7 PM; closed Fridays. **Mauvin's Model Boat Shop** (⊠ Front St., Port Elizabeth ☎ no phone) is where you can purchase the handmade model boats for which Bequia is known. You can even special-order a replica of your own yacht. They're incredibly detailed and quite expensive—from a few hundred to several thousand dollars. The sim-

★   plest ones take about a week to make. **Sargeant Brothers Model Boat Shop**

(✉ Front St., Port Elizabeth ☎ 758/458–3312) sells handmade model boats and will build special requests on commission. Housed in the ruins of an old sugar mill, **Spring Pottery & Studios** (✉ Spring ☎ 784/457–3757) is the working pottery of Mike Goddard and Maggie Overal, with gallery exhibits of ceramics, paintings, and crafts—their own and those of other local artists. All works are for sale.

SOUVENIRS **Bequia Bookshop** (✉ Belmont Walkway, Port Elizabeth ☎ 784/458–3905) has Caribbean literature, plus cruising guides and charts, Caribbean flags, beach novels, souvenir maps, and exquisite scrimshaw and whalebone pen knives hand-carved by Bequian scrimshander Sam McDowell. **Local Color** (✉ Belmont Walkway, Port Elizabeth ☎ 784/458–3202), above the Porthole restaurant, has an excellent and unusual selection of handmade jewelry, wood carvings, and resort clothing. **Noah's Arkade** (✉ Frangipani Hotel, Belmont Walkway, Port Elizabeth ☎ 784/458–3424) sells gifts, souvenirs, and contemporary arts and crafts from all over the Caribbean.

Exploring Bequia

To see the views, villages, beaches, and boatbuilding sites around Bequia, hire a taxi at the jetty in Port Elizabeth. Several usually line up under the almond trees to meet each ferry from St. Vincent. The driver will show you the sights in a couple of hours, point out a place for lunch, and drop you (if you wish) at a beach for swimming and snorkeling and pick you up later on. Negotiate the fare in advance, but expect to pay about $15 per hour.

Water taxis are available for transportation between the jetty in Port Elizabeth and the beaches. The cost is only a couple of dollars per person each way, but keep in mind that most of these operators are not insured: ride at your own risk.

SIGHTS TO SEE **Admiralty Bay.** This huge sheltered bay on the leeward side of Bequia is a favorite anchorage of yachtsmen. Throughout the year it's filled with boats; in season they're moored cheek by jowl. It's the perfect spot for watching the sun dip over the horizon each evening—either from your boat or from the terrace bar of one of Port Elizabeth's bayfront hotels.

Hamilton Battery. Just north of Port Elizabeth, high above Admiralty Bay, the 18th-century battery was built to protect the harbor from marauders. Today it's a place to enjoy a magnificent view.

Mt. Pleasant. Bequia's highest point (881 ft [270 m]) is a reasonable goal for a hiking trek. Alternatively, it's a pleasant drive. The reward is a stunning view of the island and surrounding Grenadines.

☺ **Oldhegg Turtle Sanctuary.** In the far northeast of the island, Orton "Brother" King, a retired skin-diving fisherman, tends to endangered hawksbill turtles. He'll be glad to show you around and tell you how his project has increased the turtle population in Bequia. ✉ *Park Beach, Industry* ☎ *784/458–3245* ✆ *$5 donation requested* ☽ *By appointment only.*

★ **Port Elizabeth.** Bequia's capital is on the northeast side of Admiralty Bay. The ferry from St. Vincent docks at the jetty, in the center of the tiny town that's only a few blocks long and a couple of blocks deep. Walk north along Front Street, which faces the water, to the open-air market, where you can buy local fruits and vegetables and some handicrafts; farther along, you'll find the model-boat builders' workshops for which Bequia is renowned. Walk south along Belmont Walkway, which meanders along the bay front past shops, cafés, restaurants, bars, and hotels.

Canouan

Halfway down the Grenadines chain, this tiny boot-shaped island—just 3½ mi (5½ km) long and 1¼ mi (2 km) wide—has only about 1,000 residents; however, it does have three resort hotels (though at this writing Carenage Bay Beach & Golf Club, the largest, is closed) and an airstrip—with night-landing facilities and regularly scheduled flights from both St. Vincent and Puerto Rico. Canouan (pronounced *can*-no-wan), which is the Carib word for "turtle," also claims some of the most pristine white-sand beaches in the Caribbean. Walk, swim, sail, dive, snorkel, or just relax—these are your options. At this writing, **Carenage Bay Beach & Golf Club** ($$$$ ⊠ Carenage Bay ☎ 784/458–8000 🖷 784/458–8885 ⊕ www.canouan.com) is expected to make a long-awaited and highly anticipated reopening in late 2003 or early 2004 after a two-year closure.

Where to Stay

For approximate costs, *see* the lodging price chart *in* St. Vincent.

$$$ 🏨 **Tamarind Beach Hotel & Yacht Club.** Thatched roofs are a trademark of this beachfront hotel. Accommodations are in three buildings facing reef-protected Grand Bay Beach. Rooms have natural wood walls and white-wicker furniture; louvered wooden doors open onto a spacious verandah and a beautiful Caribbean vista. Ceiling fans keep you cool. The alfresco Palapa Restaurant serves Caribbean specialties, grilled meat or fish, pizzas, and pasta prepared by a European chef. Barbecues and themed dinners rotate throughout the week. Live Caribbean music is featured fairly regularly at the Pirate Cove bar. A 55-ft catamaran is available for day sails to the Tobago Cays. ⊠ *Charlestown* ☎ *784/458–8044* 🖷 *784/458–8851* ⊕ *www.tamarindbeachhotel.com* ⤧ *42 rooms* ♢ *2 restaurants, ice-cream parlor, fans, in-room safes, golf privileges, beach, dive shop, snorkeling, windsurfing, boating, marina, fishing, bicycles, 2 bars, shops, baby-sitting, laundry service, meeting room, airport shuttle, car rental, travel services; no a/c, no room TVs* ⊟ *AE, MC, V* ⫴⃘ *CP.*

$ 🏨 **Canouan Beach Hotel.** Perched on a lovely beach at the southwest end of the island, within walking distance of the airport, this all-inclusive hotel attracts repeat French tourists most of the year. Small, very simply furnished whitewashed cottages with pastel roofs and trim are just steps from the sand. An open-air restaurant specializes in French cuisine, mainly seafood. Included in the rates are soft drinks from the bar, rum punch each evening, and French wine with dinner—as well as all water sports, including a catamaran day sail to the Tobago Cays. Twice a week the hotel hosts live music and dancing. ⊠ *S. Glossy Bay* ⫶ *Box 520* ☎ *784/458–8888* 🖷 *784/458–8875* ⊕ *www.grenadines.net/#canouan* ⤧ *30 cottages* ♢ *Restaurant, grocery, some fans, driving range, tennis court, beach, dive shop, snorkeling, windsurfing, boating, marina, Ping-Pong, volleyball, bar, shop, complimentary weddings, airport shuttle* ⊟ *AE, MC, V* ⫴⃘ *AI.*

Beaches

Glossy Bay. This and other beaches along the southwest (windward) coast of Canouan are absolutely spectacular. To reach them, you cross a narrow ridge that runs the length of the island.

Godahl Beach. This lovely beach is at the south end of the Carenage Bay property.

Grand Bay. In the center of the island on the leeward side is the main beach and the site of Charlestown, the largest settlement, where ferries dock; it's also called Charlestown Bay.

Mahault Bay. This lovely but remote expanse of beach (pronounced *ma*-ho) is at the northern tip of the island.

Sports & the Outdoors

BOATING The Grenadines offer sailors some of the most superb cruising waters in the world. Canouan is at the mid-point of the Grenadines, an easy sail north to Bequia and Mustique or south to Mayreau, the Tobago Cays, and beyond. **The Moorings** (✉ Charlestown Bay ☎ 784/482–0653 🖷 784/482–0654) operates out of Tamarind Beach Hotel & Yacht Club. It offers bareboat and crewed yacht charters of monohulls and catamarans ranging in size from 38 ft to 52 ft. Also available are one-way charters between Canouan and The Moorings operations in St. Lucia and Grenada.

GOLF Tiny Canouan has a challenging golf course, belonging to the Carenage Bay Beach & Golf Club at the northern tip of the island. While the resort and golf course have been closed to the public for two years, at this writing the course was expected to reopen by early 2004.

SCUBA DIVING & The mile-long (1½-km-long) reef and waters surrounding Canouan offer
SNORKELING excellent snorkeling as well as spectacular sites for both novice and experienced divers. **Gibraltar,** a giant stone almost 30 ft down, is a popular site; plenty of colorful fish and corals are visible. The crystalline waters surrounding the **Tobago Cays** offer marvelous diving and snorkeling.

Blue Wave Dive Centre (✉ Tamarind Beach Hotel, Charlestown ☎ 784/458–8044 🖷 784/458–8851), a full-service dive facility, offers resort and certification courses and dive and snorkel trips to the Tobago Cays, Mayreau, and Palm Island. **Glossy Dive Club** (✉ Canouan Beach Hotel, Charlestown ☎ 784/458–8888 🖷 784/458–8875) is a full-service PADI facility offering dive and snorkel trips to the Tobago Cays and other nearby sites.

Mayreau

Privately owned Mayreau (pronounced *my*-row) is minuscule—just 1½ square mi (4 square km). Only 200 or so residents live in the hilltop village, and there are no proper roads. Guests at the resort on Saltwhistle Bay enjoy the natural surroundings in one of the prettiest locations in the Grenadines—one of the few spots where the calm Caribbean is separated from the Atlantic surf by only a narrow strip of beach. It's a favorite stop for boaters, as well. Except for water sports and hiking, there's not much to do—but everyone prefers it that way. For a day's excursion, you can hike up Mayreau's only hill (wear sturdy shoes) to a stunning view of the Tobago Cays. Then stop for a drink at Dennis's Hideaway and enjoy a swim at Saline Bay Beach, where you may be joined by a few boatloads of cruise-ship passengers. This pretty little island is a favorite stop for small ships that ply the waters of the Grenadines and anchor just offshore for the day. The only access to Mayreau is by boat (ferry, private, or hired), which you can arrange at Union Island.

Where to Stay

For approximate costs, *see* the lodging price chart *in* St. Vincent.

$$$–$$$$ 🏨 **Saltwhistle Bay Club.** This resort is so cleverly hidden within 22 acres of lush foliage that sailors need binoculars to be sure it's there at all. Gorgeous Saltwhistle Bay is a half-moon of crystal-clear water rimmed by almost a mile of sparkling white sandy beach. Each roomy cottage is decked out with wooden shutters, ceiling fans, and a circular stone shower. You can dry your hair on the breezy second-story verandah atop each bungalow. At the restaurant, individual dining cabanas with stone tables are protected from sun and the occasional raindrop by thatched roofs. You'll relish turtle steak, duckling, lobster, and à la carte lunches. ✉ *Saltwhistle Bay* ☎ *784/458–8444* 🖷 *784/458–8944* ⊕ *www.saltwhistlebay.com*

⊃ *10 cottages* ⚒ *Restaurant, fans, beach, dive shop, snorkeling, wind-surfing, boating, Ping-Pong, volleyball, bar, baby-sitting; no a/c, no room TVs* ☐ *AE, MC, V* ⦶ *EP* ⊘ *Closed Sept.–Oct.*

¢ ⊡ **Dennis's Hideaway.** Dennis (who plays guitar two nights a week) is a charmer, the seafood at the restaurant is great, the drinks are strong, and the view is heavenly. The rooms in his guest house, about a three-minute walk from the beach, are clean but very simple: a bed, a night-stand, a chair, a private bath, and a place to hang some clothes. Also, they each have a private balcony, with a perfect view of the sun as it sets over Saline Bay. ✉ *Saline Bay* ☎☎ *784/458–8594* ⊃ *7 rooms* ⚒ *Restaurant, boating, bar* ☐ *No credit cards* ⦶ *EP.*

Beaches
Saline Bay Beach. This beautiful 1-mi (1½-km) curve on the southwest coast has no facilities, but you can walk up the hill to Dennis's Hide-away for lunch or drinks. The dock here is where the ferry from St. Vin-cent ties up, and small cruise ships and windjammers occasionally anchor offshore to give passengers a beach break.

★ **Saltwhistle Bay Beach.** In the north, this beach takes top honors—it's an exquisite crescent of powdery white sand, shaded by perfectly spaced palms, sea grapes, and flowering bushes. It's also a popular anchorage for the yachting crowd, who stop for a swim and lunch or dinner at the beachfront Saltwhistle Bay Resort.

Sports & the Outdoors
BOATING, FISHING & SAILING Yacht charters, drift fishing trips, and day sails on the 44-ft sailing yacht *Georgia* can be arranged at **Dennis's Hideaway** (✉ Saline Bay ☎ 784/458–8594). Expect to pay $40 per person for drift fishing for 1½ hours and $120–$200 per person (depending on the number of passengers) for a full day of sailing, swimming, and snorkeling—lunch included.

Mustique

This upscale hideaway, 18 mi (29 km) southeast of St. Vincent, is only 3 mi (5 km) by 1½ mi (2 km) at its widest point. The island is hilly and has several green valleys, each with a sparkling white-and beach facing an aquamarine sea. The permanent population is about 300.

Britain's late Princess Margaret put this small, private island on the map after owner Colin Tennant (Lord Glenconner) presented her with a 10-acre plot of land as a wedding gift in 1960 (Tennant had purchased the entire 1,400-acre island in 1958 for $67,500). The Mustique Com-pany—which Tennant formed in 1968 to develop the copra, sea-island cotton, and sugarcane estate into the glamorous hideaway it has become—now manages the privately owned villas, provides housing for all island employees, and operates Mustique Villa Rentals. Arrangements must be made about a year in advance to rent one of the luxury villas that now pepper the northern half of the island.

Sooner or later, stargazers see the resident glitterati at Basil's Bar, the island's social center. Proprietor Basil Charles also runs a boutique crammed with clothes and accessories specially commissioned from Bali. A pair of candy-colored, gingerbread-style buildings, the center-piece of the tiny village, houses a gift shop and clothing boutique. There's a delicatessen-grocery to stock yachts and supply residents with fresh Brie and Moët; an antiques shop is stocked with fabulous *objets d'art* for those extraordinary villas.

Where to Stay
For approximate costs, *see* the lodging price chart *in* St. Vincent.

★ **$$$$** ⊞ **Cotton House.** Mustique's classy (and only real) hotel was once an 18th-century cotton warehouse and sugar mill. Today, oceanfront rooms and suites have private walkways leading to the beach, while a quartet of elegant ocean-view suites and three poolside cottages have sunken baths, king-size beds with mosquito nets, and terraces affording stunning views. All accommodations have dressing areas, French doors and windows, desks, bathrooms with marble fittings, your choice of bed pillows, and perfect peace. The restored plantation house has the Great Room restaurant, whose wraparound porch functions as lounge, bar, tearoom, and social center. TV/VCRs are available at your request. ⊠ *Endeavour Bay* ⌂ *Box 349* ☎ *784/456–4777* 🖷 *784/456–5887* ⊕ *www.cottonhouse.net* ⇄ *12 rooms, 5 suites, 3 cottages* ⌖ *2 restaurants, fans, in-room safes, minibars, 2 tennis courts, pool, spa, 2 beaches, dive shop, snorkeling, windsurfing, boating, horseback riding, 2 bars, library, shops, baby-sitting, concierge, meeting room, airport shuttle* ⊟ *AE, D, MC, V* ⟋⟍ *MAP.*

$$$$ ⊞ **Firefly.** Tiny and charming, this exclusive, reclusive three-story aerie is wedged into dense tropical foliage on a hillside above Britannia Bay. Each room is unique: one has a private deck with hot tub; another, a plunge pool; yet another, an open-air shower. The inn's two pools are connected by a waterfall, and the beach is just down the (rather steep) garden path. Firefly restaurant serves Caribbean cuisine, gourmet pizza, and pasta dishes. A small motorized buggy is included in the room rate. ⊠ *Britannia Bay* ⌂ *Box 349* ☎ *784/456–3414* 🖷 *784/456–3514* ⊕ *www.mustiquefirefly.com* ⇄ *4 rooms* ⌖ *Restaurant, room service, fans, minibars, 2 pools, beach, snorkeling, bar, piano, airport shuttle; no a/c in some rooms, no kids under 12* ⊟ *AE, MC, V* ⟋⟍ *FAP.*

$$$$ ⊞ **Mustique Villas.** Villa rentals are arranged solely through Mustique Villa Rentals, even though the villas are privately owned. Villas have two to seven bedrooms, and rentals include a full staff (with a cook), laundry service, and a vehicle or two. Houses range from "rustic" (albeit with en suite bathrooms for every bedroom, phones, pools, cable TVs, VCRs, CD players, and faxes) to extravagant, expansive, faux-Palladian follies with resident butler. All are designer-elegant and immaculately maintained. Weekly rentals run from $3,000 for a two-bedroom villa in the off-season to $30,000 for a palatial seven-bedroom, five-staff, two-jeep, one-whirlpool villa in winter. ⌂ *The Mustique Co., Ltd., Box 349, St. Vincent* ☎ *784/458–4621* 🖷 *784/456–4565* ⊕ *www.mustique-island.com* ⇄ *55 villas* ⊟ *AE, DC, MC, V* ⟋⟍ *EP.*

Where to Eat

For approximate costs, *see* the dining price chart *in* St. Vincent.

★ **$$$–$$$$** ✕ **Great Room.** Expect a memorable experience when dining at the fine Cotton House resort. The chef pairs fresh island ingredients with excellent wines. Appetizers of conch Napoléon or tuna carpaccio are every bit as tempting as the entrées—which might include grilled barracuda with thyme-braised potatoes or curry-rubbed chicken breast with coconut rice. A vegetarian choice is always available. Homemade ice cream or sorbet may be enough for dessert, if you can blink when the warm chocolate cake is offered. Luncheon pastas, sandwiches, and salads are served by the pool bar or packed in a picnic basket. ⊠ *Endeavour Bay* ☎ *784/456–4777* ⌖ *Reservations essential* ⊟ *AE, D, MC, V.*

$–$$$ ✕ **Basil's Bar.** Basil's is *the* place to be—and only partly because it is the **FodorsChoice** *only* place to be aside from the two hotel restaurants. This rustic eatery ★ has a wooden deck built over the waves, a thatched roof, a congenial bar, and a dance floor that's open to the stars—in every sense. You never know what recognizable face may show up at the next table. The food is simple and good—mostly fish hauled from the water 100 yards away, homemade ice cream, burgers and salads, great French toast, the usual cocktails, and unusual wines. Wednesday is barbecue and party night; on Monday there's live music. ⊠ *Britannia Bay* ☎ *784/458–4621* ⚓ *Reservations essential* ▭ *AE, MC, V.*

Beaches

Britannia Bay. This beach is best for day-trippers, since it's next to the jetty, and Basil's Bar is convenient for lunch.

Endeavour Bay. On the northwest coast is the site of the Cotton House, as well as a dive shop and water-sports equipment rental.

Gelliceaux Bay. On the southwest coast is a good beach for snorkelers.

L'Ansecoy Bay. At the island's very northern tip is a broad crescent of white sand with brilliant turquoise water.

Fodor'sChoice
★
Macaroni Beach. Macaroni is Mustique's most famous stretch of fine white sand—offering swimming (no lifeguards) in moderate surf that's several shades of blue, along with a few palm huts and picnic tables in a shady grove of trees.

Sports & the Outdoors

Water-sports facilities are at the Cotton House, and most villas have equipment of various sorts. Four floodlit tennis courts are near the airport for those whose villa lacks its own; there's a cricket field for the Brits (matches on Sunday afternoon), and motorbikes or "mules" (beach buggies) to ride around the bumpy roads rent for $45 per day.

HORSEBACK RIDING
Mustique is one of the few islands in the Grenadines where you can find a fine horse. Daily excursions leave from the **Equestrian Centre** (☎ 784/458–4316), which is one block from the airport. Rates are $50 per hour for an island trek, $60 per hour for a surf ride, and $45 per hour for lessons. All rides are accompanied, and children over five years are allowed to ride.

SCUBA DIVING & SNORKELING
Mustique is surrounded by coral reefs. **Mustique Watersports** (⊠ Cotton House, Endeavour Bay ☎ 784/456–3486 🖷 784/456–4565) offers PADI instruction and certification and has a 28-ft, fully equipped dive boat. Rates are $65 for a one-tank dive, and multidive packages are available.

Palm Island

A private speck of land only 100 acres in area, exquisite Palm Island used to be an uninhabited, swampy, mosquito-infested spot called Prune Island. One intrepid family put heart and soul—as well as muscle and brawn—into taking the wrinkles out of the prune and rechristened it as Palm Island. They cleaned the five surrounding beaches, built bungalows, planted palm trees, and irrigated the swamp with seawater to kill the mosquitos. The rustic getaway existed for 25 years. Palm Island has been dolled up by its current owners to be one of the finest resorts in the Caribbean. Other than the resort, the island has only a handful of private villas. Access is via Union Island, 1 mi (1½ km) to the west and a 10-minute ride in the resort's launch.

Where to Stay

For approximate costs, *see* the lodging price chart *in* St. Vincent.

★ $$$$
🏨 **Palm Island Resort.** Perfect for a honeymoon, rendezvous, or luxurious escape, this palm-studded resort offers pristine white-sand beaches, a calm aquamarine sea for swimming and water sports, nature trails for quiet walks, a pool with waterfall, sophisticated dining, impeccable service, and exquisite accommodations. Choose a beachfront room with stone bathroom, palm-view room or suite, or an "Island Loft"—

a remote cottage on stilts. All have custom-designed wicker and bamboo furniture, rich fabrics, wooden louvers on three walls to catch every breeze, and original artwork. The dining room, for guests only, offers a varied menu, while the restaurant near the dock serves seafood, light fare, and drinks and is open to the public. ⊠ *Palm Island* 🕾 *784/458–8824* 🖷 *784/458–8804* ⊕ *www.palmislandresorts.com* 🖙 *36 rooms, 4 suites, 7 cottages* ♢ *Restaurant, dining room, room service, fans, in-room safes, refrigerator, 5-hole golf course, tennis court, pool, gym, massage, 5 beaches, dock, snorkeling, windsurfing, boating, bicycles, croquet, hiking, Ping-Pong, 2 bars, library, recreation room, shop, airport shuttle; no room TV* 🖃 *AE, D, DC, MC, V* ⊺◯⊺ *AI.*

Petit St. Vincent

The southernmost of St. Vincent's Grenadines, tiny (113-acres), private Petit St. Vincent, affectionately called PSV, is ringed with white-sand beaches and covered with tropical foliage. To get here you fly from Barbados to Union Island, where the resort's motor launch meets you for the 30-minute trip.

Where to Stay

For approximate costs, *see* the lodging price chart *in* St. Vincent.

★ **$$$$** 🏨 **Petit St. Vincent Resort.** No phones, no TVs, and no outside interference are appealing, when you can indulge in shipwreck fantasies without foregoing luxury. Each secluded cobblestone cottage has a large bedroom, separate sitting room with sliding glass walls facing the ocean, a patio with double hammock, and beach access. Bathrooms have cobblestone showers, robes, and beach bags. A system of signal flags conveys whims to the staff. Hoist your red flag and nobody *dreams* of approaching; hoist the yellow and you can promptly receive a meal, drinks, a picnic lunch, or a lift to the dining room. Relax, read, swim, get away from it all in rustic elegance. The entire island is yours. ⊠ *Petit St. Vincent* 🕾 *784/458–8801* 🖷 *784/458–8428* ⊕ *www.psvresort.com* ⊠ *U.S. Agent:* 🖅 *PSV, Box 841338, Pembroke Pines, FL 33084* 🕾 *954/963–7401 or 800/654–9326* 🖷 *954/963–7402* 🖙 *22 cottages* ♢ *Restaurant, room service, tennis court, beach, snorkeling, boating, bar, shop; no a/c, no room phones, no TVs* 🖃 *AE, MC, V* ⊺◯⊺ *FAP* ⊗ *Closed Sept.–Oct.*

Tobago Cays

FodorsChoice
★

A trip to this small group of uninhabited islands in the southern Grenadines east of Mayreau will allow you to experience some of the best snorkeling in the world. Horseshoe Reef surrounds five uninhabited islets, each with tiny palm-lined, white-sand beaches. The brilliantly colored water (alternating shades of azure and turquoise) is studded with sponges and coral formations and populated with countless colorful fish. All the major dive operators go here, whether they are based in St. Vincent or anywhere in the Grenadines. Diving here is truly unforgettable.

Union Island

The jagged peak of The Pinnacle soars 995 ft in the air, distinguishing Union Island from its neighbors. Union is a particularly popular anchorage for French vacationers sailing the Grenadines and a crossroads for others heading to surrounding islands (Palm, Mayreau, and Petit St. Vincent) just minutes away by speedboat. Clifton, the main town, is small and commercial, with a bustling harbor, three simple beachfront inns, a few restaurants, businesses that cater to yachts, and the regional airstrip—perhaps the busiest in the Eastern Caribbean. Taxis and minibuses are available.

Where to Stay

For approximate costs, *see* the lodging price chart *in* St. Vincent.

$ ▦ **Anchorage Yacht Club.** Between the airstrip and the waterfront, comfortably furnished seaside rooms and beach bungalows with concealed outdoor showers and terraces offer great bay views. Grounds have flower gardens, palm trees, and a large fish pool. You'll find water sports and yacht charters galore. The full-service marina creates a cosmopolitan buzz throughout the resort. Rates include breakfast at Les Pieds dans l'Eau, the adjoining restaurant, which also serves a barbecue lunch and French and creole cuisine at dinner. There's a pizza and sandwich counter as well. Each night guests and stranded sailors are serenaded by steel-band, reggae, or piano music in the bar. ⊠ *Clifton* ☎ *784/458-8221* 📠 *784/458-8365* ⊕ *www.ayc-hotel-grenadines.com* ⤶ *10 rooms, 6 bungalows* ♢ *Restaurant, snack bar, beach, dock, snorkeling, boating, marina, fishing, bar, shops* ▭ *MC, V* ⦿❙ *CP.*

Where to Eat

For approximate costs, *see* the dining price chart *in* St. Vincent.

CARIBBEAN ✕ **Lambi's.** Overlooking the waterfront in Clifton, enjoy Lambi's spe-
$–$$ cialty—delicious conch creole. Lambi is Creole patois for "conch," and the restaurant's walls are even constructed from conch shells. The menu also offers other local seafood and grilled meats. Yachts and dinghies can tie up at the wharf, and there's steel-band music every night in season. ⊠ *Clifton* ☎ *784/458-8549* ▭ *No credit cards.*

Beaches

Big Sand. Union has relatively few good beaches, but the trek to this one on the north shore is worth the effort.
Chatham Bay. The desolate but lovely beach offers good swimming.

Sports & the Outdoors

BOATING & Union is a major base for yacht charters and sailing trips. At **Anchorage**
SAILING **Yacht Club** (⊠ Clifton ☎ 784/458–8221) you can arrange crewed yacht or sailboat charters for a day sail or longer treks around the Grenadines. For example, sailing out of Union to the nearby islands of Mayreau, Canouan, and the Tobago Cays for a full day of snorkeling, fishing, and swimming costs about $200 per person for two people or $120 per person for four or more—lunch and drinks included. The marina is also a good place to stock up on fresh-baked bread and croissants, ice, water, food, and other boat supplies.

SCUBA DIVING & **Grenadines Dive** (⊠ Sunny Grenadines Hotel, Clifton ☎ 784/458–8138
SNORKELING 📠 784/458–8122), run by NAUI-certified instructor Glenroy Adams, offers Tobago Cays snorkeling trips and wreck dives at the *Purina*, a sunken World War I English gunboat. A single-tank dive costs $60; multidive packages are discounted. Beginners can take a four-hour resort course, which includes a shallow dive, for $85. Certified divers can rent equipment by the day or week.

ST. VINCENT & THE GRENADINES A TO Z

To research prices, get advice from other travelers, and book travel arrangements, visit www.fodors.com.

AIR TRAVEL

Travelers from North America and Europe arrive at airports in St. Vincent and the Grenadines via connecting service to major airlines that serve six gateways: Barbados, Grenada, Martinique, St. Lucia, Puerto Rico, or Trinidad. Connections are via Air Caraïbe, American Eagle, BWee Express, Caribbean Star, LIAT, Mustique Airways, SVG Air, and Trans Island Air (TIA).

Air Caraïbe flies between Martinique and St. Vincent, Canouan, and Union islands. American Eagle flies nonstop from San Juan, Puerto Rico, to Canouan. BWIA's BWee Express flies to SVG from Barbados and Trinidad. Caribbean Star flies to St. Vincent from St. Lucia or Grenada. LIAT connects St. Vincent, Bequia, and Union with Grenada and St. Lucia. Mustique Airways operates frequent shared-charter service linking Barbados with St. Vincent and the four airports in the Grenadines. SVG Air has daily scheduled service between Barbados and St. Vincent, Bequia, and Mustique; between Grenada/Carriacou and Bequia, Canouan, and Union; and between St. Vincent and Mustique, Canouan, and Union. TIA provides regular shared-charter service between Barbados and The Grenadines.

From other parts of the world, connections must be made through major U.S. cities, Toronto, London, or one of the Caribbean hubs, such as San Juan or Barbados.

🛪 **Air Caraïbe** ☎ 784/458-4528 in St. Vincent; 784/458-8888 in Canouan; 784/458-8826 in Union. **American Eagle** ☎ 784/456-5555. **BWee Express** ☎ 784/627-6222. **Caribbean Star** ☎ 784/456-5800. **LIAT** ☎ 784/458-4841 in St. Vincent; 784/457-1821 in Bequia; 784/458-8230 in Union. **Mustique Airways** ☎ 784/458-4380; 784/458-3183 in Bequia; 784/458-8325 in Canouan. **SVG Air** ☎ 784/457-5124 in St. Vincent; 784/458-3713 in Bequia; 784/458-8329 in Canouan; 784/458-8882 in Union; 800/744-5777 toll-free in the Caribbean. **Trans Island Air (TIA)** ☎ 784/485-8306 or 784/485-8440.

AIRPORTS

St. Vincent's E. T. Joshua Airport is in Arnos Vale, about halfway between Kingstown and Villa Beach. It's a busy airport with night-landing equipment, although it only accommodates turboprop aircraft. The St. Vincent Ministry of Tourism and Culture has an information desk in the arrivals hall, where arriving passengers can ask questions or collect maps, brochures, and other information. Departing passengers will find a snack bar and a few shops that sell souvenirs, handicrafts, and sundry items. The departure lounge has a duty-free liquor shop.

In the Grenadines, Bequia has a small, modern airport with night-landing equipment. Mustique, Canouan, and Union islands each have an airstrip with frequent commercial service.

Taxis and buses are readily available at the airport on St. Vincent. The taxi fare to hotels in either Kingstown or the Villa Beach area is about $8–$10 (EC$20–$25). Taxi service is available from the airports on Bequia, Mustique, Canouan, and Union islands.

🛪 **Canouan Airport** ✉ Canouan ☎ 784/458-8049. **E. T. Joshua Airport** ✉ Arnos Vale, St. Vincent ☎ 784/458-4011. **James F. Mitchell Airport** ✉ Bequia ☎ 784/458-3948. **Mustique Airport** ✉ Mustique ☎ 784/458-4621. **Union Airport** ✉ Union ☎ 784/458-8750.

BOAT & FERRY TRAVEL

St. Vincent's Cruise Ship Terminal is in Port Kingstown. The berths can accommodate two ships at one time; a broad landing stage accommodates passengers arriving by launch from ships at anchor. The facility has all clearance services; a bank, post office, communications facility, and tourism office; a restaurant and food courts; and 20 retail shops offering local goods (spices and seasonings, shellwork, leather goods, art and wood carvings, clothing, and straw mats) and duty-free items.

Tour buses depart from the terminal, and those opting for a day in Bequia can board the ferry at an adjacent wharf.

Cruise ships that call at Port Elizabeth on Bequia, Mayreau, and elsewhere in the Grenadines anchor offshore and tender passengers to beaches or waterfront jetties.

FARES & SCHEDULES In St. Vincent, interisland ferries dock at Grenadines Wharf in Kingstown; in Bequia they dock at Port Elizabeth. The one-way trip between St. Vincent and Bequia takes 60 minutes and costs $6 (EC$15) each way or $11 (EC$28) round-trip.

MV *Admiral I* and MV *Admiral II* make three or four round-trips each day between Bequia and Kingstown Monday–Saturday beginning at 6:30 AM in Bequia and 9 AM in St. Vincent; the latest departure each day is at 5 PM from Bequia and 7 PM from St. Vincent. On Sunday two round-trips operate in each direction, one in the morning and one in the evening.

MV *Barracuda* leaves St. Vincent on Monday and Thursday mornings, stopping in Bequia, Canouan, Mayreau, and Union Island. It makes the return trip Tuesday and Friday. On Saturday it does the round-trip from St. Vincent to each island and returns in a day. Including stopover time, the trip from St. Vincent takes 2¾ hours (via Bequia) to Canouan ($5), 4½ hours to Mayreau ($6), and 5¼ hours to Union Island ($8).

MV *Bequia Express* travels between Kingstown and Bequia, making one or two round-trips daily, including holidays.
🚢 MV *Admiral I* and MV *Admiral II* 🕾🕾 784/458-3348. MV *Barracuda* 🕾 784/456-5180. MV *Bequia Express* 🕾 784/458-3472.

BUSINESS HOURS

BANKS Banks are open Monday–Thursday 8–1, 2, or 3, Friday until 5. The bank at the airport is open Monday–Saturday 7–5. Bank branches on Bequia, Canouan, and Union are open Monday–Thursday 8–1 and Friday 8–5.

POST OFFICES The General Post Office, on Halifax Street in Kingstown, is open daily 8:30–3, Saturday 8:30–11:30.

SHOPS Shops and businesses in Kingstown are open weekdays 8–4; many close for lunch noon–1. Saturday hours are 8–noon. Shops are closed on Sunday, but supermarkets in Kingstown and Arnos Vale are open Sunday mornings.

BUS TRAVEL

Public buses on St. Vincent are really privately owned, brightly painted minivans with colorful names like *Confidence, Fully Loaded, Irie,* and *Who to Blame.* Bus fares range from EC$1 to EC$6 (40¢ to $2.25) on St. Vincent; the 10-minute ride from Kingstown to Villa Beach, for example, costs EC$1.50 (60¢). Buses operate from early morning until about midnight, and routes are indicated on a sign on the windshield. Just wave from the road or point your finger to the ground as a bus approaches, and the driver will stop. When you want to get out, signal by knocking twice on a window. A conductor rides along to open the door and collect fares; it's helpful to have the correct change in EC coins. In Kingstown the central departure point is the bus terminal at the New Kingstown Fish Market. Buses serve the entire island, although trips to remote villages are infrequent.

CAR RENTALS

Rental cars cost about $55 per day or $300 a week, with some free miles. Unless you already have an international driver's license, you'll need to buy a temporary local permit for EC$50 (US$20), valid for six months. To get one you'll need to present your valid driver's license at the police station on Bay Street or the Licensing Authority on Halifax Street, both in Kingstown, St. Vincent, or the Revenue Office in Port Elizabeth, Bequia.

Among the car-rental firms on St. Vincent are Avis Rent-A-Car—the one international agency represented on St. Vincent. Avis offers rates that are competitive with local firms. Ben's Auto Rental is located two minutes from the airport and offers all-terrain vehicles as well as cars. David's Auto Clinic, just south of Kingstown and not far from the airport, offers reliable vehicles at reasonable rates. Kims Rentals has been renting cars and jeeps on St. Vincent since the early 1960s. Star Garage is right in town and rents minivans and buses, in addition to cars and four-wheel-drive vehicles. If you'd prefer "the slow lane," two-seater scooters or mopeds can be rented for $30 per day or $180 per week from Speedway Bike & Scooter Rental.

In Bequia, you can rent a four-wheel drive vehicle from B&G Jeep Rental. For a car during your stay on Bequia, check out Phil's Car Rental.

🔝 St. Vincent **Avis Rent-A-Car** ✉ Airport, Arnos Vale, St. Vincent ☎ 784/456-4389. **Ben's Auto Rental** ✉ Arnos Vale, St. Vincent ☎ 784/456-2907. **David's Auto Clinic** ✉ Sion Hill, St. Vincent ☎ 784/456-4026. **Kims Rentals** ✉ Arnos Vale, St. Vincent ☎ 784/456-1884. **Speedway Bike & Scooter** ✉ Arnos Vale, St. Vincent ☎ 784/456-4894. **Star Garage** ✉ Grenville St., Kingstown, St. Vincent ☎ 784/456-1743.

🔝 Bequia **B&G Jeep Rental** ✉ Port Elizabeth, Bequia ☎ 784/458-3760. **Phil's Car Rental** ✉ Port Elizabeth, Bequia ☎ 784/458-3304.

CAR TRAVEL

About 360 mi (580 km) of paved roads wind around St. Vincent's perimeter, except for a section in the far north with no road at all, precluding a circle tour of the island. A few roads jut into the interior a few miles, and only one east–west road (through the Mesopotamia Valley) bisects the island. It's virtually impossible to get lost.

GASOLINE Gasoline costs about $2.80 per gallon.

ROAD CONDITIONS Although major improvements are being made, roads are usually unmarked and not always well maintained. Roads are narrow in the country, often not wide enough for two cars to pass, and people (including schoolchildren), dogs, goats, and chickens often share the roadway. Outside populated areas, roads can be bumpy and potholed; be sure your rental car has proper tire-changing equipment and a spare in the trunk.

RULES OF THE ROAD Be sure to drive on the left, and honk your horn before you enter blind curves out in the countryside—you'll encounter plenty of steep hills and hairpin turns.

ELECTRICITY

Electricity is generally 220/240 volts, 50 cycles; Petit St. Vincent has 110 volts/60 cycles (U.S. standard). Some resorts also have 110-volt current; most have 110-volt shaver outlets. Dual-voltage computers or small appliances will still require a plug adapter (three rectangular pins). Some hotels will lend transformers and/or plug adapters.

EMBASSIES

🔝 United Kingdom **British High Commission** ✉ Grenville St., Kingstown, St. Vincent 📮 Box 132 ☎ 784/457-1701 or 784/458-4381.

EMERGENCIES

ST. VINCENT   **⚠ Ambulance & fire Ambulance and fire emergencies** ☎ 911.
⚠ Coast Guard Coast Guard emergencies ☎ 911. **Coast Guard non-emergencies**
☎ 784/457-4578.
⚠ Hospitals Kingstown General Hospital ⊠ Kingstown ☎ 784/456-1185.
⚠ Pharmacies Davis Drugmart ⊠ Tyrrell and McCoy Sts., Kingstown, St. Vincent
☎ 784/456-1174. **Deane's** ⊠ Middle St., Kingstown ☎ 784/457-2877. **People's Pharmacy** ⊠ Bedford St., Kingstown ☎ 784/456-1170.
⚠ Police Police emergencies ☎ 911. **Police nonemergencies** ☎ 784/457-1211.

THE GRENADINES   **⚠ Ambulance & fire Ambulance and fire** ☎ 911.
⚠ Hospitals Bequia Casualty Hospital ⊠ Port Elizabeth, Bequia ☎ 784/458-3294.
Canouan Clinic ⊠ Charlestown, Canouan ☎ 784/458-8305. **Mustique Company Island Clinic** ⊠ Adjacent to Mustique Airport, Mustique ☎ 784/458-4621 Ext. 353.
Union Island Health Centre ⊠ Clifton, Union ☎ 784/458-8339.
⚠ Pharmacies Imperial Pharmacy ⊠ Front St., Port Elizabeth, Bequia ☎ 784/458-3373.
⚠ Police Police emergencies ☎ 911.

ETIQUETTE & BEHAVIOR

People are friendly, helpful, and photogenic. But if you wish to photograph them, their families, or their property, ask permission first—and offer a small tip as a gesture of appreciation.

Except in the evenings at the fanciest hotel restaurants, dress is extremely casual—particularly in the Grenadines. Keep in mind, however, that in St. Vincent, as throughout the Caribbean, local people dress modestly and expect visitors to do the same. T-shirts and shorts are fine for shopping or sightseeing, but swimsuits and short-shorts should be reserved for beach and boat.

FESTIVALS & SEASONAL EVENTS

The National Music Festival is held at Kingstown's Memorial Hall during March and April. The best in Vincentian music and song is presented—folk songs and calypso, solos and duets, choirs and group ensembles. Fisherman's Day (Labour Day, which falls on the first Monday in May) marks the end of a week's activities honoring the fisherman's contribution to the economy. All kinds of fishing competitions take place. Vincy Mas, St. Vincent's Carnival, is the biggest cultural festival of the year, with street parades, costumes, calypso, steel bands, food and drink, and the crowning of Miss Carnival and the Soca Monarch. It begins in late June, builds in intensity through the first two weeks in July, and culminates in a calypso competition on the final Sunday (Dimanche Gras), a huge street party (Jouvert) on the final Monday and a Parade of Bands on the final Tuesday. The National Dance Festival is held in September each year at Kingstown's Memorial Hall, with presentations of traditional, folk, ballroom, ballet, and tap dancing. Bicycle racing, arts and crafts exhibitions, caroling, and street parties with music and dancing mark Nine Mornings, a pre-Christmas tradition, which occurs during the nine days immediately before Christmas.

On Bequia, the Easter Regatta is held during the four-day Easter weekend. Revelers gather to watch boat races and celebrate Bequia's seafaring traditions with food, music, dancing, and competitive games. The Bequia Carnival, with calypso music and revelry, is a four-day celebration held in late June, just prior to St. Vincent's Carnival.

On Canouan, the Canouan Regatta is held in mid-May. Besides competitive boat races and sailing events, there are fishing contests, calypso competitions, donkey and crab races, and a beauty pageant.

On Mustique, the Mustique Blues Festival, held during the last week of January, features artists from North America, Europe, and the Caribbean. Shows are held nightly at Basil's Bar.

On Union, the Easterval Regatta occurs during the Easter weekend. Festivities include boat races, sports and games, a calypso competition, a beauty pageant, and a cultural show featuring the Big Drum Dance (derived from French and African traditions). Union is one of the few islands (along with Grenada's Carriacou) that perpetuates this festive dance.

HEALTH
Water from the tap is safe to drink, but bottled water is available. Fresh fruits and vegetables from the market are safe to eat, but (as at home) you should wash them first. Cooked food purchased at the market, in small shops, or at village snackettes is wholesome and safe to enjoy.

HOLIDAYS
New Year's Day (Jan. 1), National Heroes Day (Mar. 13), Good Friday, Easter Monday, May Day (1st Mon. in May), Whit Monday (7th Mon. after Easter), Caricom Day/Carnival Monday (2nd Mon. in July), Carnival Tuesday (2nd Tues. in July), Emancipation Day (1st Mon. in Aug.), Independence Day (Oct. 27), Christmas, and Boxing Day (Dec. 26).

LANGUAGE
English is spoken throughout St. Vincent and the Grenadines. Although there's certainly a Caribbean lilt, you won't hear the Creole patois common on other islands that have a historical French background. One term to listen for is "jump-up," in which case you can expect a party with music and dancing. And if you're going to "lime" at the next "gap," you'll be hanging out (probably at a rum shop) down the road.

MAIL & SHIPPING
The General Post Office is on Halifax Street in Kingstown, St. Vincent. Most villages on St. Vincent have branch offices. Bequia's post office is in Port Elizabeth, across from the jetty. Airmail postcards cost EC.60 to the United States, Canada, the United Kingdom, Australia, and New Zealand; airmail letters cost EC.90 per ounce to the United States and Canada; EC$1.10 to the United Kingdom, Australia, and New Zealand. When writing to a location in the Grenadines, the address on the envelope should always indicate the specific island name followed by "St. Vincent and the Grenadines, West Indies."

MONEY MATTERS
Prices quoted in this chapter are in U.S. dollars unless otherwise noted.

ATMS ATMs are located at banks in Kingstown and at their branches.

BANKS Branches of several regional and international banks are in Kingstown, with other branches elsewhere on St. Vincent and in the Grenadines.
🔁 St. Vincent **Bank of Nova Scotia** (Scotiabank) ✉ Halifax St., Kingstown ☎ 784/457-1601. **First Caribbean International Bank** ✉ Halifax St., Kingstown ☎ 784/456-1706. **National Commercial Bank of St. Vincent** ✉ Bedford St., Kingstown ☎ 784/457-1844 ✉ E. T. Joshua Airport, Arnos Vale, Kingstown ☎ 784/458-4943.
🔁 The Grenadines **National Commercial Bank of St. Vincent** ✉ Port Elizabeth, Bequia ☎ 784/458-3700 ✉ Charlestown, Canouan ☎ 784/458-8595 ✉ Clifton, Union ☎ 784/458-8347.

CREDIT CARDS Major credit cards—including Access, American Express, Diners Club, Discover, Eurocard, MasterCard, and Visa—and traveler's checks are accepted by hotels, car-rental agencies, and some shops and restaurants.

CURRENCY   Although U.S. dollars are accepted nearly everywhere, Eastern Caribbean currency (EC$) is the official currency and preferred. The exchange rate is fixed at EC$2.67 to US$1. Price quotes in shops are often given in both currencies. Large U.S. bills may be difficult to change in small shops. U.S. coins are not accepted anywhere.

PASSPORTS & VISAS

U.S., Canadian, and U.K. citizens need a valid passport or a birth certificate with a raised seal and a government-issued photo I.D. Travelers from other countries must present a valid passport. Everyone must hold return or ongoing tickets.

SAFETY

There's relatively little crime here, but don't tempt fate by leaving your valuables lying around or your room or rental car unlocked. Also, be alert and mindful of your belongings around the wharf areas in Kingstown; it's congested when passengers are disembarking from ferries or cruise ships.

SIGHTSEEING TOURS

Several operators offer sightseeing tours on land or by sea. Per-person prices range from $20 for a two-hour tour to St. Vincent's Botanical Gardens to $140 for a day sail to the Grenadines. A full-day tour around Kingstown and either the leeward or windward coast, including lunch, will cost about $50 per person.

You can arrange informal land tours through taxi drivers, who double as knowledgeable guides. Expect to pay $25 per hour for up to four people.

On St. Vincent, Baleine Tours offers scenic coastal trips to the Falls of Baleine as well as charters to Bequia and Mustique, deep-sea fishing trips, and snorkeling excursions to the Tobago Cays. Calypso Tours has a 42-ft tour boat for trips to the Falls of Baleine, Bequia, Mustique, and the Tobago Cays. Fantasea Tours will take you on a 38-ft power cruiser to the Falls of Baleine, Bequia, and Mustique, or to the Tobago Cays for snorkeling. For bird-watchers, hikers, and ecotourists, HazECO Tours offers wilderness tours and hikes to enjoy the natural beauty and see historic sites throughout St. Vincent. Preference Tours has a 55-ft catamaran for sunset cruises and day trips out of Bequia to the Falls of Baleine and the Grenadines. Sailor's Wilderness Tours run the gamut, from a comfortable sightseeing drive (by day or by moonlight) to mountain biking on remote trails or a strenuous hike up the La Soufrière volcano. Sam Taxi Tours offers half- or full-day tours of St. Vincent, as well as hiking tours to La Soufrière and scenic walks along the Vermont Nature Trails. Sam's also operates on Bequia, where a sightseeing tour includes snorkeling at Friendship Bay. SVG Tours has several hiking itineraries for St. Vincent and sailing day trips to the Grenadines.

🚩 **Baleine Tours** ☒ Villa Beach, St. Vincent ☎ 784/457–4089. **Calypso Tours** ☒ Blue Lagoon, St. Vincent ☎ 784/456–1746. **Fantasea Tours** ☒ Villa Beach, St. Vincent ☎ 784/457–5555 ⊕ www.fantaseatours.com. **HazECO Tours** ☒ Kingstown, St. Vincent ☎ 784/457–8634 ⊕ www.begos.com/hazecotour. **Preference Tours** ☒ Port Elizabeth, Bequia ☎ 784/458–3197. **Sailor's Wilderness Tours** ☒ Middle St. Kingstown, St. Vincent ☎ 784/457–1712. **Sam Taxi Tours** ☒ Cane Garden, St. Vincent ☎ 784/456–4338, 784/458–3686 in Bequia. **SVG Tours** ☒ Kingstown, St. Vincent ☎ 784/458–4534.

TAXES & SERVICE CHARGES

DEPARTURE TAX   The departure tax from St. Vincent and the Grenadines is $12 (EC$30), payable in either U.S. or EC currency; children under 12 are exempt.

SALES TAX A government tax of 7% is added to hotel bills.

SERVICE A service charge of 10% is generally added to both hotel and restau-
CHARGES rant bills.

TAXIS
Fares are set by the government, but it's smart to settle on the price before entering the taxi—and be sure you know what currency is being
quoted. On St. Vincent, the one-way fare between Kingstown and Villa
is about $10 (EC$25).

On some islands, most notably Bequia, water taxis can take you between
Port Elizabeth and the beaches for a couple of dollars each way. Keep
in mind that these taxi operators aren't regulated or insured, so travel
at your own risk.

TELEPHONES
St. Vincent and the Grenadines has a fully digitized telephone system,
with international direct dialing available throughout the entire area.
Pay phones are readily available and best operated with the prepaid phone
cards that are sold at many stores and can be used on many Caribbean
islands. Cell phones that are compatible with the TDMA digital network
can roam in St. Vincent and the Grenadines—for outgoing calls only.

COUNTRY & AREA The area code for St. Vincent and the Grenadines is 784.
CODES

E-MAIL Internet access is available so you can check your e-mail or look up a
Web site at Office Essentials in Kingstown.
🚩 **Office Essentials, Ltd.** ✉ Bonadie's Plaza, Middle St., Kingstown ☎ 784/457-
2235.

INTERNATIONAL 🚩 **International Operator** ☎ 115. **Operator-assisted Credit Card Calls** ☎ 117.
CALLS

LOCAL CALLS Local calls are free from private phones and most hotels. Prepaid phone
cards, which can be used in special card phones throughout St. Vincent
and other Caribbean islands, are sold at shops, transportation centers,
and other convenient outlets. (The phone cards can be used for local or
international calls.)

TIPPING
Hotels and restaurants generally add a 10% service charge to the tab.
If the charge hasn't been added, a gratuity at that rate is appropriate.
Otherwise, tipping is expected only for special service.

VISITOR INFORMATION
🚩 Before you leave **St. Vincent and the Grenadines Tourist Office** 🌐 www.svgtourism.
com ✉ 801 2nd Ave., 21st floor, New York, NY 10017 ☎ 212/687-4981 or 800/729-1726
🖨 212/949-5946 ✉ 32 Park Rd. Toronto Ontario Canada ☎ 416/924-5796 🖨 416/924-
5844 ✉ 10 Kensington Ct., London W8 5DL, U.K. ☎ 0207/937-6570 🖨 0207/937-3611.
St. Vincent Hotels & Tourism Association 🌐 www.svghotels.com.
🚩 In St. Vincent & the Grenadines **St. Vincent and the Grenadines Ministry of Tourism
& Culture** ✉ Cruise Ship Terminal, Harbour Quay, Kingstown, St. Vincent ☎ 784/457-
1502 🖨 784/451-2425. **Tourist information desks** ✉ E. T. Joshua Airport, Arnos Vale,
St. Vincent ☎ 784/458-4685 ✉ Union airport, Clifton, Union ☎ 784/458-8350. **Be-
quia Tourism Association** 🌐 www.bequiatourism.com ✉ Main Jetty Port Elizabeth,
Bequia ✏ Box 164 ☎ 784/458-3286 🖨 784/458-3964.

TRINIDAD AND TOBAGO

FODOR'S CHOICE

Bird-watching in the Asa Wright Nature Centre, Trinidad

Veni Mangé, a restaurant in Port-of-Spain, Trinidad

HIGHLY RECOMMENDED

RESTAURANTS Blue Crab, Scarborough, Tobago

Kariwak Village, Crown Point, Tobago

La Tartaruga, Buccoo, Trinidad

Solimar, Port-of-Spain, Trinidad

HOTELS Asa Wright Nature Centre, Arima Valley, Trinidad

Blue Waters Inn, Speyside, Tobago

Carnetta's Inn, Maraval, Trinidad

Coco Reef Resort, Scarborough, Tobago

Hilton Trinidad and Conference Centre, Port-of-Spain, Trinidad

Kapok Hotel, Port-of-Spain, Trinidad

Kariwak Village, Crown Point, Tobago

Mt. Plaisir Estate, Grande Riviere, Trinidad

NIGHTLIFE Bonkers, Crown Point, Tobago

Carnival in Trinidad

Pier 1, Chaguaramas, Trinidad

HiRpm, La Romain, Trinidad

OUTDOORS Bird-watching in Tobago

Englishman's Bay Beach, Tobago

Maracas Bay Beach, Trinidad

Mt. Irvine Golf Club, Mt. Irvine Bay, Tobago

The boat slides lazily through the brackish waters of the Caroni Bird Sanctuary. On either side of the channel the twisted fairy-tale roots of the mangrove trees seem locked in some eternal struggle. Curious caimans slice noiselessly through the water, snakes shimmer in the branches of the trees. In the distance the emerald-clad Northern Range rises imperiously toward a cloudless sky. All the world seems at peace. The small boat turns a corner and you're suddenly in a large lake surrounded by the mangrove forest. Then, as if on cue, the sky turns red—confusing the senses—the scarlet ibis have returned home in their thousands to settle in for the evening. Every tree is now cloaked with birds—what was green is now red—squawking in appreciation of their own magnificent show. Thousands of performances behind them and no end in sight.

Updated by Vernon O'Reilly-Ramesar

From the beat of calypso and *soca* (an upbeat, sexy variation of calypso) to the steady tapping of raindrops accompanied by birdsong, Trinidad and Tobago's cultural and natural diversions are refreshing, vivid, and alive. This two-island republic—T&T, as it's commonly called—is the southernmost link in the Antillean island chain, lying some 9 mi (14½ km) off the coast of Venezuela and safely outside the path of all those devastating Caribbean hurricanes. Both Trinidad and Tobago are more geologically akin to continental South America than they are to other Caribbean islands: Tobago's Main Ridge and Trinidad's Northern Range are believed to represent the farthest reaches of the Andes Mountains. But although the two islands are linked geographically and politically, in some ways they could not be more dissimilar.

Trinidad's growth arose out of oil prosperity—it remains one of the largest petroleum producers in the western hemisphere—which makes it a prime destination for business travelers. They enjoy the sophisticated shopping, restaurants, and hotels in the republic's lively capital, Port-of-Spain, partying late into the night to the syncopated steel-band sounds that originated in Trinidad.

Port-of-Spain is still one of the most active commercial cities in the Caribbean. The cultural scene is as vital as ever, especially during the country's riotous Carnival—a period of festivities, concerts, and shows that begins after Christmas and culminates in a two-day street parade that ends on Ash Wednesday. The capital is home to around 300,000 of Trinidad's 1.3 million residents—Africans, Indians, Americans, Europeans, and Asians, each culture with its own language and customs (though the official language is English). About a quarter of the population is Hindu, which is why there's an abundance of East Indian festivals, religious celebrations, and delicious East Indian food. Outside Port-of-Spain you can find good beaches and many other natural attractions, though there are currently few hotels that offer more than bare-bones comfort.

On Tobago, 22 mi (35 km) away, the pace of life is slower, and seclusion easier to find. Though seaside resorts may beckon, you can still lazily explore unspoiled rain forests, coral reefs, and a largely undeveloped coastline—for now, anyway. Tourism is a growing industry, and the number of hotel rooms has been growing dramatically.

Trinidad was called *Iere* (Land of the Hummingbird) by the original Amerindian population. Columbus reached these islands on his third voyage, in 1498. Three prominent peaks around the southern bay of Trinidad prompted him to name the land La Trinidad, after the Holy Trinity. Trinidad was captured by British forces in 1797, ending 300 years of Spanish rule. Tobago's history is more complicated. It was "discovered" by the British in 1508. The Spanish, Dutch, French, and British all fought for it until it was ceded to England under the Treaty of Paris in 1814. In 1962 both islands gained their independence within the British Commonwealth, finally becoming a republic in 1976.

WHAT IT COSTS In U.S. dollars				
$$$$	$$$	$$	$	¢
RESTAURANTS*				
over $30	$20–$30	$12–$20	$8–$12	under $8
HOTELS**				
Cost EP/BP/CP over $350	$250–$350	$150–$250	$80–$150	under $80
Cost AI over $450	$350–$450	$250–$350	$125–$250	under $125

*Restaurant prices are for a main course at dinner. **EP, BP, and CP prices are per night for a standard double room in high season, excluding taxes, service charges, and meal plans. AI (all-inclusive) prices are per person, per night based on double-occupancy during high season, excluding taxes and service charges.

TRINIDAD

Where to Stay

Trinidad accommodations range from charming guest houses to large business hotels; most acceptable establishments, however, are within the vicinity of Port-of-Spain, far from any beach. Most places will include breakfast and dinner for an additional flat rate (MAP). Port-of-Spain has a small downtown core—with a main shopping area along Frederick Street—and is surrounded by inner and outer suburbs. The inner areas include Belmont, Woodbrook, Newtown, St. Clair, St. Ann's, St. James, and Cascade. Regardless of the type of accommodation, be prepared to book far in advance (and to pay a good deal more) for stays during Carnival season.

★ $$-$$$ ▣ **Hilton Trinidad and Conference Centre.** Beautifully landscaped grounds and a singular setting are among the draws here. The complex stretches across the top and down the side of a hill overlooking the Gulf of Paria and Queen's Park Savannah. You take an elevator *down* to your room. Each room has a balcony with a fine view of Queen's Park Savannah, the city, the mountains, and the sea or the large, inviting pool. The Hilton is the most upscale hotel in the city. On most nights there is poolside entertainment ranging from calypso to Latin jazz. Two rooms have facilities for people with disabilities. ✉ *Lady Young Rd., Port-of-Spain* 🖃 *Box 442* ☎ *868/624–3211; 800/445–8667 in the U.S.* 🖷 *868/624–4485* 🌐 *www.trinidadhilton.com* 🛏 *394 rooms, 25 suites* ♿ *2 restaurants, room service, in-room safes, minibars, 2 tennis courts, pool, wading pool, health club, massage, sauna, Ping-Pong, 3 bars, shops, baby-sitting, playground, dry cleaning, laundry service, business services, meeting rooms, car rental, travel services, no-smoking rooms* 🖃 *AE, DC, MC, V* ❚⊙❙ *EP.*

$-$$ ▣ **Crowne Plaza Trinidad.** Proximity to the port and Independence Square is both the draw and the drawback here. From any upper-floor room you have a lovely pastel panorama of the Old Town and of ships idling in the Gulf of Paria, and you're within walking distance of the downtown sights and shops. Bear in mind, however, that with the action comes traffic and noise. Rooms are spacious and tastefully decorated. La Ronde, a revolving rooftop restaurant, offers a striking view of the city at night, which compensates for the generally uninspired food. ⊠ *Wrightson Rd., Port-of-Spain* ☎ *Box 1017* ☎ *868/625–3361 or 800/465–4329* 🖷 *868/625–4166* 📨 *235 rooms, 10 suites* 🖒 *2 restaurants, room service, pool, gym, 3 bars, shops, baby-sitting, laundry service, business services, meeting rooms, travel services, no-smoking rooms* ▭ *AE, MC, V* ⦿◎ *MAP.*

★ ¢–$$ ▦ **Asa Wright Nature Centre.** In this mountain retreat you can swim in cool waterfall pools, explore dim caverns populated by nocturnal oilbirds, or simply sip a cup of tea while enjoying the view from the lodge verandah. Built in 1908, this 200-acre mountain estate is in a rain forest (about two hours east of Port-of-Spain) populated by 400 species of birds. The elegant lounge has mahogany floors, bookcases, antiques, and ornithological artifacts. To reach the nature center, drive east from Port-of-Spain past Arima, heading for Wallerfield; turn left at Emmaus Centre after pillars designating Ft. Read; cross Eastern Main Rd. and bear right; drive about ½ hr until you see the sign for the Centre. ⊠ *Arima Valley* ☎ *Box 4710* ☎ *868/667–4655 or 800/426–7781* 🖷 *868/667–4540* ⊕ *www.asawright.org* 📨 *24 rooms, 1 bungalow* 🖒 *Dining room, fans, pond, hiking, shops; no a/c, no kids under 14* ▭ *MC, V* ⦿◎ *FAP.*

★ $ ▦ **Carnetta's Inn.** When Winston Borrell retired as director of tourism for T&T, he and his wife Carnetta opened this inn on their suburban property in Maraval. All rooms have a bath (with shower), a phone, a radio, and cable TV; most have kitchenettes. Although there's air-conditioning, cool breezes usually do the trick. Carnetta uses her garden-grown herbs in her cooking and prepares excellent dinners. The hotel does not serve lunch during low season. ⊠ *99 Saddle Rd., Maraval* ☎ *868/628–2732* 🖷 *868/628–7717* ⊕ *www.carnettas-tt.com* 📨 *14 rooms* 🖒 *Restaurant, dining room, some kitchenettes, cable TV, bar, lounge, laundry service, airport shuttle, car rental* ▭ *AE, DC, MC, V* ⦿◎ *EP.*

$ ▦ **The Chancellor Hotel.** This beautiful, small hotel has Internet access in all rooms and full business services. Rooms are large and well appointed (each with cable TV) and are decorated with original batik hangings. The waterfall cascading into the nearby swimming pool adds a relaxing air to the bar and restaurant area. ⊠ *5 St. Ann's Ave., St. Ann's, Port-of-Spain* ☎☎ *868/623–0883* ⊕ *www.thechancellorhotel.com* 📨 *15 rooms, 7 suites* 🖒 *Restaurant, in-room data ports, cable TV, pool, bar, business services, meeting rooms* ▭ *AE, MC, V* ⦿◎ *EP.*

★ $ ▦ **Kapok Hotel.** Leave it to business travelers to find a well-run hotel that's a good value for the money. Sunlight (front rooms have views of Queen's Park Savannah) complements the pastel color schemes and rattan furniture. If you're into cooking for yourself, take one of the studios, which have kitchenettes. Otherwise, the Tiki Village Asian restaurant has terrific views of the city and is popular with locals. On the second floor, the alfresco coffee and wine bar, Bois Cano, is lovely and relaxed. ⊠ *16–18 Cotton Hill, St. Clair, Port-of-Spain* ☎ *868/622–5765 or 800/344–1212* 🖷 *868/622–9677* ⊕ *www.kapok.co.tt* 📨 *75 rooms, 12 suites, 9 studios* 🖒 *Restaurant, room service, some kitchenettes, pool, gym, hair salon, shops, dry cleaning, laundry facilities, laundry service, business services, meeting rooms, no-smoking rooms* ▭ *MC, V* ⦿◎ *EP.*

★ $ ▦ **Mt. Plaisir Estate.** If getting away from it all appeals to you, then this gem of a hotel is a perfect choice. In remote Grande Riviere, with the ocean on one side and the peaks of the rain forest in the backdrop, you

Trinidad

ATLANTIC OCEAN

Caribbean Sea

Dragon's Mouth

Gulf of Paria

TO TOBAGO

Galera Pt.
Salibea Bay
Sans Souci
Redhead
Balandra Bay
Toco
Grande Rivière
Matelot
Mt. Oropuche
Salinè Bay
Matura
Manzanilla Beach
Matura Bay
Cocos Bay
Guataro Pt.
Pierreville
Madamas Bay
El Cerro del Aripo
Valencia
Sangre Grande
Rio Claro
Blanchisseuse Bay
Chupara Pt.
Las Cuevas Bay
Eastern Main Rd.
Churchill-Roosevelt Hwy.
Cyril Bay
Arima
Tunapuna
Chaguanas
Flanigin Town
Tabaquite
Tableland
New
Tyrico Bay
Maracas Bay
La Vache Bay
El Tucuche
San Juan
Piarco International Airport
Uriah Butler Hwy.
Couva
Princes
Chaguaramas
Port-of-Spain
California
Pointe-a-Pierre
San Fernando
Oropouche

2 **16** **17** **15** **3** **1** **14** **4**

TOBAGO
Scarborough
TRINIDAD
Port-of-Spain
VENEZUELA

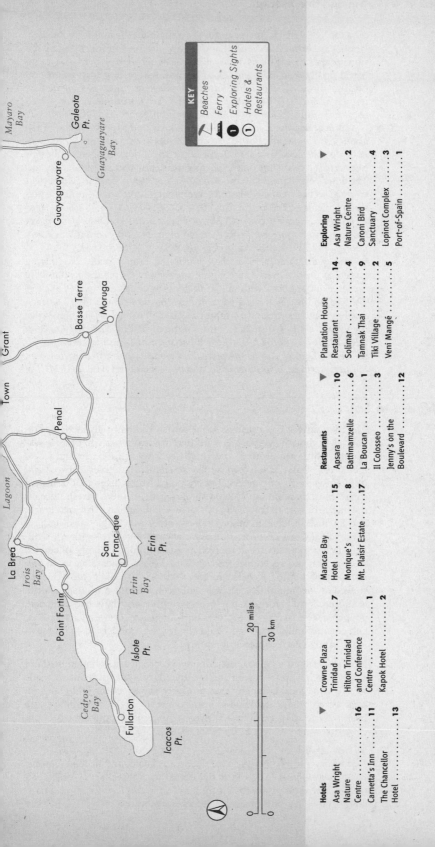

KEY

- Beaches
- Ferry
- ● Exploring Sights
- ① Hotels & Restaurants

Hotels

Asa Wright Nature Centre	16
Carnetta's Inn	11
The Chancellor Hotel	13
Crowne Plaza Trinidad	7
Hilton Trinidad and Conference Centre	1
Kapok Hotel	2
Maracas Bay Hotel	15
Monique's	8
Mt. Plaisir Estate	17

Restaurants

Apsara	10
Battimamzelle	6
La Boucan	1
Il Colosseo	3
Jenny's on the Boulevard	12
Plantation House Restaurant	14
Solimar	4
Tamnak Thai	9
Tiki Village	2
Veni Mangé	5

Exploring

Asa Wright Nature Centre	2
Caroni Bird Sanctuary	4
Lopinot Complex	3
Port-of-Spain	1

20 miles

30 km

may see leatherback turtles nesting by the hundreds in this idyllic spot. Rooms are homey and clean, and the on-site restaurant serves exceptional meals. Meal plans are available. Owner Piero Guerrini is an internationally renowned photographer and will be happy to advise you on your shots. All in all, this hotel is an excellent value. ⊠ *Grande Riviere* ☎ *868/670–8381* 🖷 *868/670–0057* ⊕ *www.mtplaisir.com* ✑ *13 rooms, 2 suites* ⚫ *Dining room, beach, lounge* ▤ *AE, MC, V* ⚫ *CP.*

¢–$ 🖻 **Maracas Bay Hotel.** This hotel sits on the island's most popular beach about ½ hour outside Port-of-Spain. Rooms are simple and clean, with firm double beds and cool terra-cotta tile floors (but no radios or phones); the two suites have refrigerators, but regular rooms do not. The hotel's open-air restaurant, Bandanya, has been redesigned with bright tropical scenes on the walls and serves imaginative and beautifully presented meals. ⊠ *Maracas Bay* ☎ *868/669–1914* 🖷 *868/669–1643* ⊕ *www.maracasbay.com* ✑ *28 rooms, 2 suites* ⚫ *Dining room, refrigerators in some rooms, beach, lounge, meeting rooms; no room phones, no TV in some rooms* ▤ *AE, MC, V* ⚫ *EP, MAP.*

¢   🖻 **Monique's.** Members of the Charbonné family really *like* having guests, as they've been proving for more than two decades. Rooms here are large and spotless, with solid teak floors and furniture as well as cable TV and phones. Ask for a room in "Monique's on the Hill," as each one has a kitchenette and a sizable balcony. All rooms are equipped with data ports. ⊠ *114–116 Saddle Rd., Maraval* ☎ *868/628–3334 or 868/628–2351* 🖷 *868/622–3232* ⊕ *www.moniquestrinidad.com* ✑ *20 rooms* ⚫ *Dining room, in-room data ports, some kitchenettes, bar, laundry service, airport shuttle, travel services* ▤ *AE, DC, MC, V* ⚫ *EP.*

Where to Eat

The food on T&T is a delight to the senses and has a distinctively creole touch, though everyone has a different idea about what creole seasoning is (just ask around, and you'll see). Bountiful herbs and spices include bay leaf, *chadon beni* (similar to cilantro), nutmeg, saffron, and different varieties of peppers. The cooking also involves a lot of brown sugar, rum, plantain, and local fish and meat. If there's fresh juice on the menu, be sure to try it. You can taste Asian, Indian, African, French, and Spanish influences, among others, often in a single meal. Indian-inspired food is a favorite: *rotis* (sandwiches of soft dough with a filling, similar to a burrito) are served as a fast food; a mélange of curried meat or fish and vegetables frequently makes an appearance as do *vindaloos* (spicy meat, vegetable, and seafood dishes). *Pelau* (chicken stewed in coconut milk with peas and rice), a Spanish-influenced dish, is another local favorite. Crab lovers will find large blue-backs curried, peppered, or in callaloo, a stew made with green dasheen leaves, okra, and coconut milk. Shark-and-bake (lightly seasoned, fried shark meat) is the sandwich of choice at the beach.

No Trinidadian or Tobagonian dining experience is complete without a rum punch with fresh fruit and the legendary Angostura bitters, made by the same local company that produces the excellent Old Oak rum (just watch out for the fiendish sugar content). Light, refreshing Carib beer is the local lager; Stag is an even stronger lager, and dark-beer aficionados can try Royal Extra Stout (R. E.).

What to Wear

Restaurants are informal: you won't find any jacket-and-tie requirements. Beachwear, however, is a little too casual for most places. A nice pair of shorts is appropriate for lunch; for dinner you'll probably feel most comfortable in a pair of slacks or a casual sundress.

ASIAN
$$–$$$$ ✕ **Tamnak Thai.** In a beautifully renovated former colonial house on Queen's Park Savannah, you'll find the best Thai cuisine on Trinidad. You may choose to sit outside on the patio surrounded by flowing water and lush foliage or pick the elegant inside dining room for a more intimate (and cooler) dining experience. You might well start with the hors d'oeuvres *Tamnak Thai,* a delightful selection of Thai appetizers, and if you can stand the heat move on to *gai pad med manuang, prik tod* (chicken with cashew nuts and fiery chilies). ✉ *13 Queen's Park East, Belmont, Port-of-Spain* ☎ *868/623–7510* 🖷 *868/628–4783* ▭ *AE, MC, V.*

$$–$$$ ✕ **Tiki Village.** Port-of-Spainers in the know flock to the eighth floor of the Kapok Hotel, where the views of the city day and night are simply spectacular. The dining room is lined with teak, and the menu includes the best of Polynesian and Chinese fare. The dim sum—with tasting-size portions of dishes such as pepper squid and tofu-stuffed fish—is very popular. ✉ *Kapok Hotel, 16–18 Cotton Hill, St. Clair, Port-of-Spain* ☎ *868/622–5765* ▭ *AE, MC, V.*

CARIBBEAN
$$$–$$$$ ✕ **Plantation House Restaurant.** This elegant gem in a late-19th-century building is furnished in colonial style with wrought iron and chintz. The menu concentrates on game and seafood dishes, all beautifully presented and served. Beware of the massive portions. The truly adventurous can order alligator tails (creole style, of course) or stewed agouti (a large local rodent). The conch-souse appetizer (conch strips marinated in a spicy lime-juice mixture) is a must-try. ✉ *38 Ariapita Ave., Woodbrook, Port-of-Spain* ☎ *868/628–5551* ▭ *AE, DC, MC, V* ☾ *Closed Sun.*

$–$$
Fodor$Choice ✕ **Veni Mangé.** The best lunches in town are served upstairs in this tra-
★ ditional West Indian house decorated with local art. Credit Allyson Hennessy—a Cordon Bleu–trained chef and local television celebrity—and her friendly, flamboyant sister and partner Rosemary (Roses) Hezekiah. The creative creole menu changes regularly, and there's always an unusual and delicious vegetarian entrée. This place is popular, so reservations are advised; dinner is served only on Wednesday from 7:30 to 10. The bar area is a fun hangout on a Friday evening (5 to midnight), when Allyson and Roses hold court. ✉ *67A Ariapita Ave., Woodbrook, Port-of-Spain* ☎ *868/624–4597* 🕮 *Reservations essential* ▭ *AE, MC, V* ☾ *Closed weekends. No dinner except Wed.*

ECLECTIC
$$–$$$$ ✕ **La Boucan.** Trinidadian dancer Geoffrey Holder painted the large mural of a social idyll in Queen's Park Savannah that dominates one wall of this room at the Hilton Trinidad and Conference Centre. A more leisurely Trinidad is also reflected in the old-fashioned charm of silver service, uniformed waiters, soft lighting, and pink tablecloths. The menu is international, including steaks, seafood grills, and other simple preparations, but you can also find such local specialties as callaloo soup, shrimp creole, and West Indian chicken curry. ✉ *Hilton Trinidad and Conference Centre, Lady Young Rd., Port-of-Spain* ☎ *868/624–3211* ▭ *AE, DC, MC, V* ☾ *Closed Sun.*

★ $$–$$$$ ✕ **Solimar.** In a series of dimly lit, plant-filled dining areas, chef Joe Brown offers a menu that travels the world in one meal: there's always a choice of a European, Asian, or North American main course. Solimar is popular with expats and is known for being a relaxed and informal spot. Valet parking is available. ✉ *6 Nook Ave., St. Ann's, Port-of-Spain* ☎ *868/ 624–6267* ▭ *AE, MC, V.*

$$–$$$ ✕ **Battimamzelle.** When skilled chef Khalid Mohammed decided to open his own restaurant, he named it using the local name for a dragonfly and painted it in colors to match. The decor of this lovely little establishment—tucked away in a small inn—is truly beautiful. It seems that Mr. Mohammed wanted the food to compete with the decor, since he

serves the most beautifully presented meals on the island. Be sure to try the geera- (cumin-) crusted rack of lamb. ⊠ *Coblentz Inn, 44 Coblentz Ave., Cascade, Port-of-Spain* 🕾 *868/621–10541* ⌖ *Reservations essential* 🖃 *AE, MC, V* ⊗ *Closed Sun.*

$$–$$$ ✕ **Jenny's on the Boulevard.** Jenny's is in a beautifully restored, grand old art nouveau–style home near Port-of-Spain's Queen's Park Savannah. The decidedly eclectic (almost dizzying) interior is filled with antiques, but the excellent American steak-house food and true Cantonese cuisine shine. The Cellar Pub, a blend of British tradition and Hollywood kitsch, is fun, raucous, and upscale—but also tends to be smoke-filled and congested. A no-smoking room and a private dining room are available. ⊠ *6 Cipriani Blvd., Newton, Port-of-Spain* 🕾 *868/625–1807* ⌖ *Reservations essential* 🖃 *AE, MC, V* ⊗ *Closed Sun.*

INDIAN ✕ **Apsara.** The name means "celestial dancer," and the food here is indeed heavenly. The elegant maroon interior is decorated with modern interpretations of Mughal art by local artist Sarah Beckett. Choosing dishes from the comprehensive menu is a bit daunting, so don't be afraid to ask for help. The boneless chicken curry with spinach and fennel is an excellent choice. Owner Marie Kavanagh is a delightful hostess and would be thrilled to give you the history of the restaurant. ⊠ *13 Queen's Park E, Belmont, Port-of-Spain* 🕾 *868/627–7364 or 868/623–7659* 🖃 *AE, MC, V* ⊗ *Closed Sun.*

$$–$$$

ITALIAN ✕ **Il Colosseo.** Calabrian chef Angelo Cofone married a Trinidadian and soon found himself co-owning the island's best Italian restaurant, popular with locals and visiting businesspeople alike. His success has led him to move the restaurant into bigger and more lavish quarters in the heart of Port-of-Spain. The innovative Italian menu changes monthly. ⊠ *16 Rust St., St. Clair, Port-of-Spain* 🕾 *868/622–8418* 🖃 *AE, MC, V* ⊗ *Closed Sun. No lunch Sat.*

$$–$$$$

Beaches

Although Trinidad is not the beach destination Tobago is, it has its share of fine shoreline along the North Coast Road, within an hour's drive of Port-of-Spain. To reach the east coast beaches you must drive for an hour and take the detour road to Arima. But "goin' behind God's back," as the Trinis say, rewards the persistent traveler with gorgeous vistas and secluded stretches of sand. And, best of all, Trinidad's beaches are all open to the public and free of charge.

Balandra Bay. On the northeast coast, the beach is sheltered by a rocky outcropping and is popular with bodysurfers.

Blanchisseuse Bay. On the North Coast Road you'll find this narrow, palm-fringed beach. Facilities are nonexistent, but it's an ideal spot for a romantic picnic. You can haggle with local fishermen to take you out in their boats to explore the coast.

Grande Riviere. At the end of the road on Trinidad's rugged northeast coast, Grand Riviere is well worth the drive. Swimming is good and there are several guest houses nearby for refreshments, but the main attraction here is turtles. Every year up to 500 giant leatherback turtles come onto the beach to lay their eggs. If you're here at night, run your hand through the black sand to make it glow—a phenomenon caused by plankton.

Las Cuevas Bay. This narrow, picturesque strip on North Coast Road is named for the series of partially submerged and explorable caves that ring the beach. A food stand offers tasty snacks, and vendors hawk fresh fruit across the road. You can also buy fresh fish and lobster from the fishing depot near the beach. There are basic changing and toilet facilities. It's less crowded here than at nearby Maracas Bay and seemingly serene, although, as at Maracas, the current can be treacherous.

Manzanilla Beach. You'll find picnic facilities and a pretty view of the Atlantic here, though its water is occasionally muddied by the Orinoco River, which flows in from South America. The Cocal road running the length of this beautiful beach is lined with stately palms, whose fronds vault like the arches at Chartres. This is where many well-heeled Trinis have vacation homes.

★ **Maracas Bay.** This long stretch of sand has a cove and a fishing village at one end. It's *the* local favorite, so it can get crowded on weekends. Lifeguards will guide you away from strong currents. Parking sites are ample, and there are snack bars and rest rooms. Try a shark-and-bake ($2, to which you can add any of dozens of toppings, such as tamarind sauce and coleslaw) at one of the huts at the beach or in the nearby car park. Richard's is by far the most popular shark-and-bake stand.

Salibea Bay. Past Galera Point, which juts toward Tobago, this gentle beach has shallows and plenty of shade—perfect for swimming. Snack vendors abound in the vicinity.

Tyrico Bay. This small beach is right next door to Maracas Beach. The strong undertow may be too much for some swimmers. Be sure to pack insect repellent, as the sand flies and mosquitoes can be a nuisance in the rainy season.

Sports & the Outdoors

BIRD-WATCHING Trinidad and Tobago are among the top 10 spots in the world in terms of the number of species of birds per square mile—more than 430 altogether, many living within pristine rain forests, lowlands and savannas, and fresh- and saltwater swamps. If you're lucky, you might spot the collared trogon, Trinidad piping guan (known locally as the common pawi), or rare white-tailed Sabrewing hummingbird. Restaurants often hang feeders outside on their porches, as much to keep the birds away from your food as to provide a chance to see them.

You can fill up your books with notes on Trinidad's native species at the island's major bird sanctuaries. **Asa Wright Nature Centre** (⊠ Arima Valley ☎ 868/667–4655), a half-hour drive from Blanchisseuse, has more than 170 bird species in residence. **Caroni Bird Sanctuary** (☎ 868/645–1305), a half-hour from Port-of-Spain, is a habitat for the scarlet ibis, Trinidad's national bird. The **Point-a-Pierre Wildfowl Trust** (⊠ Petrotrin Complex, Point-a-Pierre ☎ 868/658–4200 Ext. 2512) is a haven for rare bird species on 26 acres within the unlikely confines of a petrochemical complex; you must call in advance for a reservation. **Winston Nanan** (☎ 868/645–1305) runs the highly regarded Nanan's Bird Sanctuary Tours to nearby Guyana and Venezuela.

FISHING The islands off the northwest coast of Trinidad have excellent waters for deep-sea fishing; you may find wahoo, king fish, and marlin, to name a few. The ocean here was a favorite angling spot of Franklin D. Roosevelt's. Through **Bayshore Charters** (⊠ 29 Sunset Dr., Bayshore, Westmoorings ☎ 868/637–8711) you can fish for an afternoon or hire a boat for a weekend; the *Melissa Ann* is fully equipped for comfortable cruising, sleeps six, and has an air-conditioned cabin, refrigerator, cooking facilities, and, of course, fishing equipment. Captain Sa Gomes is one of the most experienced charter captains on the islands. Members of the **Trinidad and Tobago Yacht Club** (⊠ Western Main Rd., Bayshore, Westmoorings ☎ 868/637–4260) may be willing to arrange a fishing trip for you.

GOLF The best course in Trinidad is the 18-hole **St. Andrew's Golf Club** (⊠ Moka, Saddle Rd., Maraval, Port-of-Spain, ☎ 868/629–2314), just outside

Port-of-Spain. Greens fees are approximately $35 for 18 holes. The most convenient tee times are available on weekdays.

TENNIS Several establishments allow nonmembers or nonguests to play tennis on their courts, but you will need to call to make reservations. There is usually a fee for nonguests (and sometimes for guests) to use tennis courts; expect to pay around $30TT–$40TT per hour. The **Hilton Trinidad and Conference Centre** (✉ Lady Young Rd., Port-of-Spain ☎ 868/624–3211) has two asphalt courts and charges both guests and nonguests for the use of the courts. The **Tranquility Square Lawn Tennis Club** (✉ Victoria Ave., Port-of-Spain ☎ 868/625–4182) has four asphalt courts. The **Trinidad Country Club** (✉ Long Circular Rd., Maraval, Port-of-Spain ☎ 868/ 622–3470) has six asphalt courts. The club allows foreign visitors to purchase a daily membership for $40TT, which allows you use of all facilities, including the courts (bring your passport as proof).

Shopping

Good buys in Trinidad include Angostura bitters, Old Oak or Vat 19 rum, and leather goods, all widely available throughout the country. Thanks in large part to Carnival costumery, there's no shortage of fabric shops. The best bargains for Asian and East Indian silks and cottons can be found in downtown Port-of-Spain, on Frederick Street, and around Independence Square. Recordings of local calypsonians and steel-pan performances as well as *chutney* (a local East Indian music) are available throughout the islands and make great gifts.

Areas & Malls

Downtown Port-of-Spain, specifically **Frederick, Queen,** and **Henry streets,** is full of fabrics and shoes. **Ellerslie Plaza** is an attractive outdoor mall well worth a browse. **Excellent City Centre** is set in an old-style oasis under the lantern roofs of three of downtown's oldest commercial buildings. Look for cleverly designed keepsakes, trendy cotton garments, and original artwork. The upstairs food court overlooks bustling Frederick Street. **Long Circular Mall** has upscale boutiques that are great for window-shopping. **The Market** is a small collection of shops that specialize in indigenous fashions, crafts, jewelry, basketwork, and ceramics. You can also have afternoon tea in the elegant little café.

Specialty Items

CLOTHING A fine designer clothing shop, **Meiling** (✉ Kapok Hotel, Maraval, Port-of-Spain ☎ 868/627–6975), sells classically detailed Caribbean resort clothing. **Radical** (✉ West Mall, Western Main Rd., Westmoorings ☎ 868/632–5800 ✉ Long Circular Mall, Long Circular Rd., St. James, Port-of-Spain ☎ 868/628–5693 ✉ Excellent City Centre, Independence Square, Port-of-Spain ☎ 868/627–6110), which carries T-shirts and original men's and women's clothing, is something like the Gap of the Caribbean.

DUTY-FREE Duty-free goods are available only at the airport upon departure or ar-
GOODS rival. **De Lima's** (✉ Piarco International Airport, Piarco ☎ 868/669–4738) sells traditional duty-free luxury goods. **Stecher's** (✉ Piarco International Airport, Piarco ☎ 868/669–4793) is a familiar name for those seeking to avoid taxes on fine perfumes, china, crystal, handcrafted pieces, and jewelry.

HANDICRAFTS The tourism office can provide a list of local artisans who specialize in everything from straw and cane work to miniature steel pans. The **101 Art Gallery** (✉ 101 Tragarete Rd., Woodbrook, Port-of-Spain ☎ 868/ 628–4081) is Trinidad's foremost gallery, showcasing local artists such as Sarah Beckett (semi-abstracts in oil, some of which are featured on local stamps); Jackie Hinkson (figurative watercolors); Peter Sheppard (stylized realist local landscapes in acrylic); and Sundiata (semi-abstract watercolors). Openings are usually held Tuesday evenings year-round; the gallery is closed Sunday and Monday. For painted plates, ceramics, aromatic candles, wind chimes, and carved wood pieces and instruments, check out **Cockey** (✉ Long Circular Mall, Long Circular Rd., St. James, Port-of-Spain ☎ 868/628–6546). **Poui Boutique** (✉ Ellerslie Plaza, Long Circular Rd., Maraval, Port-of-Spain ☎ 868/622–5597) has stylish handmade batik articles, Ajoupa ware (an attractive, local terra-cotta pottery), and many other gift items. The miniature ceramic houses and local scenes are astoundingly realistic, and are all handcrafted by owners Rory and Bunty O'Connor.

JEWELRY The design duo of Barbara Jardine and Rachel Ross creates the Alchemy jewelry line. Their handmade works of art with sterling silver, 18K gold, and precious and semiprecious stones are for sale at **Precious Little** (✉ West Mall, Western Main Rd., Westmoorings ☎ 868/632–1077).

MUSIC **Just CDs and Accessories** (✉ Long Circular Mall, Long Circular Rd., St. James, Port-of-Spain ☎ 868/622–7516) has a good selection of popular local musicians as well as other music genres. **Rhyner's Record Shop** (✉ 54 Prince St., Downtown, Port-of-Spain ☎ 868/625–2476 ✉ Piarco International Airport, Piarco ☎ 868/669–3064) has a decent (and duty-free) selection of calypso and soca music.

Nightlife & the Arts

Nightlife

There's no lack of nightlife in Port-of-Spain, and spontaneity plays a big role—around Carnival time look for the handwritten signs announcing the PANYARD, where the next informal gathering of steel-drum bands is going to be.

Two of the island's top nightspots are on a former American Armed Forces base in Chaguaramas. **The Anchorage** (✉ Point Gourde Rd., Chaguaramas ☎ 868/634–4334) is a good spot for early evening cocktails and snacks. **Pier 1** (✉ Western Main Rd., Chaguaramas ☎ 868/634–4426) is *the* place for lively late-night action. You can dance through the night on a large wooden deck jutting into the ocean with gentle sea breezes to cool you down. It's about 20 minutes west of Port-of-Spain, so get a party together from your hotel and hire a cab. It opens at 9 PM, Wednesday–Sunday. For the serious partiers, Pier 1 offers a "party boat" that leaves on Friday, Saturday, and Sunday night for a floating party for $10.

At **Club Coconuts** (✉ Cascadia Hotel, St. Ann's, Port of Spain ☎ 868/623–6887) you can dance 'til the wee hours with a fun crowd. **Mas Camp Pub** (✉ Corner of Ariapata Ave. and French St., Woodbrook, Port-of-Spain ☎ 868/627–4042) is Port-of-Spain's most dependable nightspot. Along with a bar and a large stage where a DJ or live band reigns, the kitchen dishes up hearty, reasonably priced creole lunches, and if one of the live bands strikes your fancy, chances are you can also buy their tape here. **Pelican** (✉ 2–4 Coblentz Ave., St. Ann's, Port-of-Spain ☎ 868/624–7486), an English-style pub with a mixed gay and straight crowd, gets increasingly frenetic as the week closes. The biggest nights are Wednesday, Friday, and Sunday, when the crowd overflows into the parking lot. There is also seasonal entertainment with calypso at carnival time and *parang* (Spanish-influenced music) at Christmas time. **Smokey and Bunty** (✉ Western Main Rd., St. James, Port-of-Spain) is a unique Port-of-Spain phenomenon. This is the late-night spot to visit when everything else is closed, and although it doesn't amount to much more than standing around on the sidewalk, the people are fun and the drinks are very cheap. **Trotters** (⊠ Corner of Maraval and Sweet Briar Rd., St. Clair, Port-of-Spain ☎ 868/627–8768) is a sports bar in a 2-story atrium. There is an abundance of TV monitors, and you'll find over 30 varieties of beer from around the globe. It is incredibly popular on weekends despite the pricey drinks.

★ **HiRpm** (⊠ Gulf City Mall, 2nd floor, South Trunk Rd., La Romain ☎ 868/652–3760) is a great alternative if you want something out of town. Just take the main highway south to the end of the line and then follow South Trunk Road to the mall. This lively, laid-back establishment is a good place to listen to pop music, and you can hear live local pop/rock bands on Wednesday nights performing their covers of the latest hits. The large oval bar (it takes up half the room) is a great place to meet talkative southerners. The owner Selwyn "Bunny" Persad is a race-car driver and enthusiast and will be happy to talk to you about his favorite sport.

The Arts

Trinidad always seems to be either anticipating, celebrating, or recovering from a festival. Visitors are welcome at these events, which are a great way to explore the island's rich cultural traditions.

CARNIVAL
★ Trinidad's version of the pre-Lenten bacchanal is reputedly the oldest in the western hemisphere; there are festivities all over the country, but the most lavish are in Port-of-Spain. Trinidad's Carnival has the warmth and character of a massive family reunion, and is billed by locals (not unreasonably) as "The Greatest Show on Earth".

The season begins right after Christmas, and the parties, called fêtes, don't stop till Ash Wednesday. Listen to a radio station for five minutes, and you'll find out where the action is. The Carnival event itself officially lasts only two days, from *J'ouvert* (2 AM) on Monday to midnight the following day, Carnival Tuesday. It's best to arrive in Trinidad a week or two early to enjoy the preliminary events. (Hotels fill up quickly, so be sure to make reservations months in advance, and be prepared to pay premium prices for a minimum five-night stay. Even private homes have been known to rent bedrooms for as much as $225 per night.) If you visit during Carnival, try to get tickets to one of the all-inclusive parties where thousands of people eat and drink to the sound of soca music all night long. The biggest Carnival party in Trinidad is **UWI Fete,** which raises money for the university and attracts several thousand people. A ticket will cost you about $70, but includes all drinks and food.

Carnival is about extravagant costumes. Colorfully attired *mas* (troupes), whose membership sometimes numbers in the thousands, march to the beat set by massive music trucks and steel bands. You can visit the various mas "camps" around Port-of-Spain where these elaborate getups are put together—the addresses are listed in the newspapers—and perhaps join one that strikes your fancy. Fees run anywhere from $35 to $200; you get to keep the costume. You can also buy your costume online at the tourist board's Web site, which has links to all the major camps. Children can parade in a kiddie carnival that takes place on the Saturday morning before the official events.

Carnival is also a showcase for performers of calypso, music that mixes dance rhythms with social commentary—sung by characters with such evocative names as Shadow, the Mighty Sparrow, and Black Stalin—and soca, which fuses calypso with a driving dance beat. As Carnival approaches, many of these singers perform nightly in calypso tents around the city. Many hotels also have special concerts by popular local musicians. You can also visit the city's "panyards," where steel orchestras such as the Renegades, Desperadoes, Neal and Massy All-Stars, Invaders, and Phase II rehearse their musical arrangements (most can also be heard during the winter season).

For several nights before Carnival, costume makers display their work, and the steel bands and calypso singers perform in competitions at Queen's Park Savannah. Here the Calypso Monarch is crowned on the Sunday night before Carnival (Dimanche Gras). The city starts to fill with metal-frame carts carrying steel bands, trucks hauling sound systems, and revelers who squeeze into the narrow streets. At midnight on Carnival Tuesday, Port-of-Spain's exhausted merrymakers go to bed. The next day feet are sore, but spirits have been refreshed. Lent (and theoretical sobriety) takes over for a while.

MUSIC   Trinidadian culture doesn't end with music, but it definitely begins with it. Although both calypso and steel bands are at their best during Carnival, steel bands play at clubs, dances, and fêtes throughout the year. At Christmas time the music of the moment is a Venezuelan-derived folk music called *parang,* sung in Spanish to the strains of a stringed instrument called a *quattro.* The Lopinot Complex in Arouca is a parang center. If you can stomach the steep uphill drive, Paramin, near Port-of-Spain (take Maracas Road and turn off on Paramin Road), is another spectacular place to hear this music.

THEATER   There are always a few plays being performed by local groups. You might be better off visiting one of the many "comedy tents," where local comedians usually have locals rolling in the aisles. Consult local newspapers for listings.

Exploring Trinidad

The intensely urban atmosphere of Port-of-Spain belies the tropical beauty of the countryside surrounding it. You'll need a car and three to eight hours to see all there is to see. Begin by circling the Queen's Park Savannah to Saddle Road, in the residential district of Maraval. After a few miles the road begins to narrow and curve sharply as it climbs into the Northern Range and its undulating hills of dense foliage. Stop at the lookout on North Coast Road; a camera is a must-have here. You'll pass a series of lovely beaches, starting with Maracas. From the town of Blanchisseuse there's a winding route to the Asa Wright Nature Centre that takes you through canyons of towering palms, mossy grottoes, and imposing bamboo. In this rain forest keep an eye out for vultures, parakeets, hummingbirds, toucans, and if you're lucky, maybe red-bellied, yellow-and-blue macaws. Trinidad also has more than 600 native species of butterflies and well over 1,000 varieties of orchids.

Numbers in the margin correspond to points of interest on the Trinidad map.

What to See

② **Asa Wright Nature Centre.** Nearly 500 acres here are covered with plants, trees, and multi-hued flowers, and the surrounding acreage is atwitter with more than 400 species of birds, from the gorgeous blue-green motmot to the rare nocturnal oilbird. If you stay at the center's inn for two nights or more, take one of the guided hikes (included in your room price if you are staying here) to the oilbirds' breeding grounds in Dunston Cave (reservations for hikes are essential). Those who don't want to hike can relax on the inn's verandah and watch birds swoop about the porch feeders—an armchair bird-watcher's delight. This stunning

Fodor'sChoice
★

plantation house looks out onto the lush, untouched Arima Valley. Even if you're not staying over, book ahead for lunch (TT$37.50) Monday–Saturday or for the noontime Sunday buffet (TT$62.50). The center is ½ hr outside Blanchisseuse; take a right at the fork in road (signposted to Arima) and drive another ½ hr (the sign for the center is at milepost 7¾) on Blanchisseuse Rd.; turn right there. ⊠ *Arima Valley* 🖃 *Box 4710* 📞 *868/667–4655* ⊕ *www.asawright.org* 🖃 *$6* ⊙ *Daily 9–5. Guided tours at 10:30 and 1:30.*

❹ Caroni Bird Sanctuary. This large swamp with maze-like waterways is bordered by mangrove trees, some plumed with huge termite nests. If you're lucky, you may see lazy caimans idling in the water and large snakes hanging from branches on the banks taking in the sun. In the middle of the sanctuary are several islets that are home to Trinidad's national bird, the scarlet ibis. Just before sunset the ibis arrive by the thousands, their richly colored feathers brilliant in the gathering dusk, and as more flocks alight they turn the mangrove foliage a brilliant scarlet. Bring a sweater and insect repellent.

The only official tour operator for the sanctuary is **Winston Nanan** (📞 868/645–1305). Tours are $10, children over 5 years old are half price, and ages 5 and under are free. Phone or write him in advance for reservations. ✛ *½ hr from Port-of-Spain; take Churchill Roosevelt Hwy. east to Uriah Butler south; turn right and in about 2 mins, after passing Caroni River Bridge, follow sign for sanctuary* 🖃 *Free.*

❸ Lopinot Complex. It's said that the ghost of the French count Charles Joseph de Lopinot prowls his former home on stormy nights. Lopinot came to Trinidad in 1800 and chose this magnificent site to plant cocoa. His restored estate house has been turned into a museum—a guide is available from 10 to 6—and a center for parang, the Venezuelan-derived folk music. ✛ *Take Eastern Main Rd. from Port-of-Spain to Arouca; look for sign that points north* 📞 *no phone* 🖃 *Free* ⊙ *Daily 6–6.*

❶ Port-of-Spain. Most tours begin at the port. If you're planning to explore on foot, which will take two to four hours, start early in the day; by midday the port area can be as hot and packed as Calcutta. It's best to end your tour on a bench in the Queen's Park Savannah, sipping a cool coconut water bought from one of the vendors operating out of flatbed trucks. For about 35¢ he'll lop the top off a green coconut with a deft swing of the machete and, when you've finished drinking, lop again, making a bowl and spoon of coconut shell for you to eat the young pulp. As in most cities, take extra care at night; women should not walk alone.

The town's main dock, **King's Wharf,** entertains a steady parade of cruise and cargo ships, a reminder that the city started from this strategic harbor. When hurricanes threaten other islands it's not unusual to see as many as five large cruise ships taking advantage of the safety of the harbor. It's on Wrightson Road, the main street along the water on the southwest side of town.

Across Wrightson Road and a few minutes' walk from the south side of King's Wharf, the busy **Independence Square** has been the focus of the downtown area's major gentrification. Flanked by government buildings and the familiar twin towers of the Financial Complex (they adorn all T&T dollar bills), the square (really a long rectangle) is a lovely park with trees, flagstone walkways, chess tables, and the Brian Lara Promenade (named after Trinidad's world-famous cricketer). On its south side the Cruise Ship Complex, full of duty-free shops, forms an enclave of international anonymity with the Crowne Plaza Trinidad. On the eastern end of the square is the Cathedral of the Immaculate Conception; it was by the sea when it was built in 1832, but subsequent land-fill around the port gave it an inland location. The imposing Roman Catholic structure is made of blue limestone from nearby Laventille.

Frederick Street, Port-of-Spain's main shopping drag, starting north from the midpoint of Independence Square, is a market street of scents and sounds—perfumed oils sold by sidewalk vendors and music tapes being played from vending carts—and crowded shops.

At Prince and Frederick streets, **Woodford Square** has served as the site of political meetings, speeches, public protests, and occasional violence. It's dominated by the magnificent Red House, a Renaissance-style build-ing that takes up an entire city block. Trinidad's House of Parliament takes its name from a paint job done in anticipation of Queen Victo-ria's Diamond Jubilee in 1897. The original Red House was burned to the ground in a 1903 riot, and the present structure was built four years later. The chambers are open to the public.

The view of the south side of the square is framed by the Gothic spires of Trinity, the city's Anglican cathedral, consecrated in 1823; its ma-hogany-beam roof is modeled after that of Westminster Hall in London. On the north are the impressive Public Library, the Hall of Justice, and City Hall.

If the downtown port area is the pulse of Port-of-Spain, the great green expanse of **Queen's Park Savannah,** roughly bounded by Maraval Road, Queen's Park West, Charlotte Street, and Saddle Road, is the city's soul. You can walk straight north on Frederick Street and get there within 20 minutes. Its 2-mi (3-km) circumference is a popular jogger's track. The grandstand on the southern end is a popular venue for Calypso and cultural shows. The northern end of the Savannah is devoted to plants. A rock garden, known as the The Hollows, and a fishpond add to the rusticity. In the middle of the Savannah you will find a small graveyard where members of the Peschier family– who originally owned the land– are buried.

A series of astonishing buildings constructed in several 19th-century styles—known collectively as the **Magnificent Seven**—flanks the west-ern side of the Savannah. Notable are Killarney, patterned (loosely) after Balmoral Castle in Scotland, with an Italian-marble gallery surround-ing the ground floor, Whitehall, constructed in the style of a Venetian palace by a cacao-plantation magnate and currently the office of the prime minister; Roomor, a flamboyantly baroque colonial house with a pre-ponderance of towers, pinnacles, and wrought-iron trim that suggests an elaborate French pastry; and the Queen's Royal College, in German Renaissance style, with a prominent tower clock that chimes on the hour. Sadly, several of these fine buildings have fallen into advanced decay.

Head over to the southeast corner of the Savannah to see the **National Museum and Art Gallery,** especially its Carnival exhibitions, the Amerindian collection and historical re-creations, and the fine 19th-cen-tury paintings of Trinidadian artist Cazabon. ⊠ *117 Upper Frederick St.* ☎ *868/623–5941* ☒ *Free* ☉ *Tues.–Sat. 10–6.* The cultivated expanse of parkland north of the Savannah is the site of the president's and prime minister's official residences and also the **Emperor Valley Zoo and the Botanical Gardens.** A meticulous lattice of walkways and local flora, the parkland was first laid out in 1820 for Governor Ralph Woodford. In the midst of the serene wonderland is the 8-acre zoo, which exhibits mostly birds and animals of the region—from the brilliantly plumed scar-let ibis to slithering anacondas and pythons; you can also see (and hear) the wild parrots that breed in the surrounding foliage. The zoo draws a quarter of a million visitors a year, and more than half of them are children, so admission is priced accordingly—a mere TT$2 for folks under 12. ⊠ *Botanical Gardens* ☎ *868/622–3530 or 868/622–5343* ☞ *TT$4 for the zoo, gardens free* ۩ *Daily 9:30–5:30.*

TOBAGO

Where to Stay

On Tobago there are a few modest lodgings in the towns, but the trend is toward seaside resorts, many of them appealingly low-key. If you're staying on the east side of Tobago, accommodations with meal plans are almost essential due to the dearth of restaurants.

For approximate costs, *see* the dining and lodging price chart at the beginning of this chapter.

$$$$ ▦ **Le Grand Courlan Resort and Spa.** This hotel, under the same ownership as—and right next door to—the Grafton Beach Resort, is aiming for a *very* upscale clientele. The spacious rooms have pink-tile floors, oak furniture, and large balconies with fantastic views; the beach is one of the best on the island; and the staff is gracious. The spa offers a variety of services, from aromatherapy with essential-oil extracts to Swedish massage. Several packages are available, including scuba, spa, and golf. ⊠ *Shirvan Rd., Black Rock* ☎ *868/639–9667 or 800/468–3750; 800/ 424–5500 in Canada* 🖷 *868/639–9292* ☞ *68 rooms, 10 suites* ♿ *3 restaurants, room service, in-room safes, minibars, golf privileges, 2 tennis courts, pool, hair salon, health club, hot tub, spa, beach, dive shop, windsurfing, boating, fishing, bicycles, squash, 2 bars, shops, laundry service, business services, meeting rooms, car rental, travel services, no-smoking rooms* ▤ *AE, MC, V* ᵀᴼᴵ *EP, MAP.*

$$$$ ▦ **Plantation Beach Villas.** Nestled on a hillside above a palm-fringed beach, these pink-and-white villas are comfortably furnished in plantation style—four-poster beds, rocking chairs, louvered doors, and lots of West Indian fretwork. Each two-story villa has three bedrooms, three baths, and a teak verandah with a view of the sea. ⊠ *Scarborough* ✑ *Box 434* 🖷 *868/639–9377* ⊕ *www.plantationbeachvillas.com* ☞ *6 villas* ♿ *Kitchenettes, pool, bar, baby-sitting, laundry service* ▤ *AE, MC, V* ᵀᴼᴵ *EP.*

$$$–$$$$ ▦ **Stonehaven Villas.** This property perches on a hillside adjacent to a bird sanctuary and commands an impressive view of the Caribbean. The complex consists of 14 French-style villas and a club house, which serves as the restaurant and social gathering area. Each villa has three large bedrooms with en suite bathrooms and a private vanishing-edge pool. Have no fear about cleaning, cooking, or ironing, because each villa comes complete with all-day maid service. ⊠ *Bon Accord, Grafton Estate, Shirvan Rd., Black Rock* ✑ *Box 1079* ☎ *868/639–9887* 🖷 *868/ 639–0102* ⊕ *www.stonehavenvillas.com* ☞ *14 villas* ♿ *Restaurant, kitchenettes, pool, bar, laundry service, meeting rooms* ▤ *AE, MC, V* ᵀᴼᴵ *EP.*

$$–$$$$ ▦ **Blue Haven Hotel.** Tobago's newest hotel is also, strangely, one of its oldest. This was *the* place to be in the 1950s, when movie stars like Robert Mitchum and Rita Hayworth stayed here during film shoots. It fell into ruin but has now been brilliantly restored. The hotel stands on a small peninsula surrounded by ocean on three sides. Rooms are exquisitely furnished with wood floors and a glass wall separating the bathroom from the bedroom, with special touches like Venetian glass ornaments in the bathroom. The secluded beach is one of the nicest on the island. ⊠ *Bacolet Bay, Scarborough* 🖷 *868/660–7400* ⊕ *www.bluehavenhotel.*

com ⇆ *43 rooms, 8 suites, 1 villa* ⚓ *Restaurant, tennis court, pool, gym, massage, beach, 2 bars, playground* ▤ *AE, MC, V* ⑩ *EP.*

★ **$$$** ⌨ **Coco Reef Resort.** Elements of Caribbean, colonial, and Mediterranean architecture blend in an abundance of arches, tiles, and fretwork flourishes; harsh angles have been eliminated to create soothing spaces. Rooms have cool, calming tiles, pretty wall stencils, and handcrafted wicker furniture. If you want to venture off the resort's small beach, Coco Bay, Pigeon Point, and Store Bay are nearby. ✉ *Coconut Bay, Scarborough* ☖ *Box 434* ☎ *868/639–8571 or 800/221–1294* 🖷 *868/639–8571 or 305/639–2717* ⊕ *www.cocoreef.com* ⇆ *135 rooms, 35 suites* ⚓ *2 restaurants, room service, 2 tennis courts, pool, gym, hair salon, spa, beach, dive shop, snorkeling, windsurfing, 2 bars, baby-sitting, business services, meeting rooms, car rental, travel services* ▤ *AE, D, DC, MC, V* ⑩ *EP.*

$$$ ⌨ **Grafton Beach Resort.** The palm-fringed hotel has a huge lobby-bar-restaurant-pool area, and the in-room amenities and furnishings (solid-teak furniture and terra-cotta floors) are all first class. A walkway leads directly to a fine beach, where there's another bar. You can learn to dive, play squash, work out in the gym at the Le Grand Courlan Resort next door, or go canoeing and sailing, among other things—all included in the rates. Guests here can also use the spa facilities at Le Grand Courlan for a fee. ✉ *Shirvan Rd., Black Rock* ☎ *868/639–0191* 🖷 *868/639–0030* ⊕ *www.grafton-resort.com* ⇆ *101 rooms, 4 suites* ⚓ *2 restaurants, pool, beach, dive shop, snorkeling, windsurfing, boating, squash, 3 bars, dance club, shops, business services, meeting rooms* ▤ *AE, MC, V* ⑩ *AI.*

$$$ ⌨ **Hilton Tobago.** This dazzling resort sets a high standard for Tobago. The hotel occupies 20 beachfront acres, and has, among other things, an 18-hole championship par-72 golf course and a massive pool. The huge atrium lobby has floor-to-ceiling windows that manage to blur the line between hotel and ocean. Rooms are spacious and comfortable, offering amenities that you would expect from any world-class hotel. All rooms are oceanfront; ground floor rooms have a small patio that opens onto the gardens. ✉ *Scarborough* ☖ *Box 633* ☎ *868/660–8500* 🖷 *868/660–8503* ⊕ *www.tobago.hilton.com* ⇆ *178 rooms, 22 suites* ⚓ *2 restaurants, minibars, in-room safes, 18-hole golf course, 2 tennis courts, 3 pools, hair salon, gym, sauna, beach, dive shop, snorkeling, windsurfing, waterskiing, fishing, 3 bars, shops, meeting rooms, no-smoking rooms* ▤ *AE, MC, V* ⑩ *EP.*

$$–$$$ ⌨ **Mt. Irvine Bay Hotel.** The advantage of this low-key resort is golf—guests of the hotel get special rates on the 18-hole, par-72 Mt. Irvin Bay Golf Course. Since opening in 1972, this resort has had many repeat customers (who rave about the staff). The main restaurant, the Sugar Mill, is set inside a 17th-century mill, and there are two more restaurants—a dressy French one, Le Beau Rivage, and the Jacaranda, which serves true Caribbean dishes. You can swim in the large pool, play tennis on the flood-lit courts, or take the private trail across the road to the beach and its bar. ✉ *Shirvan Rd., Mt. Irvine Bay* ☖ *Box 222* ☎ *868/639–8871* 🖷 *868/639–8800* ⊕ *www.mtirvine.com* ⇆ *105 rooms, 6 suites, 46 cottages* ⚓ *3 restaurants, 18-hole golf course, 2 tennis courts, pool, hair salon, sauna, beach, snorkeling, windsurfing, waterskiing, fishing, 6 bars, shops, meeting rooms, no-smoking rooms* ▤ *AE, MC, V* ⑩ *EP.*

★ **$$** ⌨ **Blue Waters Inn.** A 90-minute drive from Scarborough and a trek down a bumpy driveway bring you to this beach hotel, with villas set amid 46 acres of greenery on the northeast Atlantic coast. You're guaranteed the sound of waves all night in each room. The bungalows have one or two bedrooms, a living room, and a kitchen. You can fax in an order for provisions and have the staff stock your room. The restaurant serves

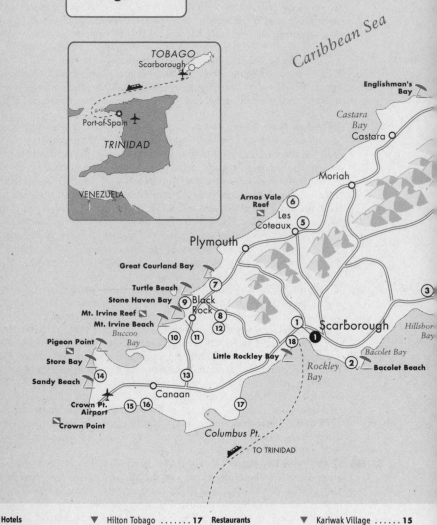

Tobago

Caribbean Sea

TOBAGO
Scarborough

Port-of-Spain
TRINIDAD

VENEZUELA

Englishman's Bay

Castara Bay
Castara

Moriah

Arnos Vale Reef
6
Les Coteaux
5

Plymouth

Great Courland Bay

Turtle Beach
7
Stone Haven Bay
9
Mt. Irvine Reef
Mt. Irvine Beach
Black Rock
8
12
3

Pigeon Point
10 11
Buccoo Bay

Store Bay
Little Rockley Bay
1
Scarborough
Hillsbor Bay

Sandy Beach
14
13
18
Bacolet Bay
Rockley Bay
2
Bacolet Beach

Crown Pt. Airport
15 16
Canaan
17

Crown Point

Columbus Pt.

TO TRINIDAD

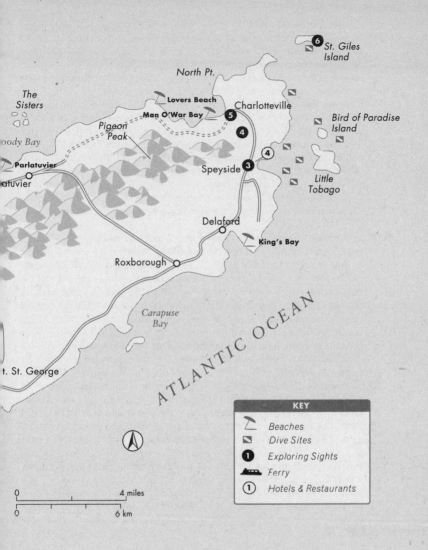

KEY

⚓	Beaches
◥	Dive Sites
1	Exploring Sights
🚢	Ferry
①	Hotels & Restaurants

the freshest of fish, and the lively bar specializes in exotic drinks. Barbecue dinners are cooked up on the beach patio. ⊠ *Bateaux Bay, Speyside* ☎ *868/660–4077 or 800/742–4276* ☒ *868/660–5195* ⊕ *www.bluewatersinn.com* ⇨ *28 rooms, 3 suites, 4 bungalows* ⚘ *Restaurant, tennis court, beach, dive shop, snorkeling, boating, bar, baby-sitting, meeting rooms, car rental* ☰ *AE, MC, V* ⦿ *EP.*

$ 🏨 **Arnos Vale Hotel.** Romance isn't hard to find at this Mediterranean-style complex on 450 lush acres (the late Princess Margaret honeymooned here). Rooms are in white-stucco cottages on a hill; from your quarters you can take a winding path down to a secluded beach, a pool, and a bar. The hilltop restaurant—furnished with antiques, iron-lattice tables, and a chandelier—has a magnificent patio with sweeping sea views. ⊠ *Arnos Vale and Franklin Rds., Scarborough* ⬠ *Box 208* ☎ *868/639–2881* ☒ *868/639–4629* ⊕ *www.arnosvalehotel.com* ⇨ *35 rooms, 3 suites* ⚘ *Restaurant, tennis court, pool, beach, snorkeling, bar, shops* ☰ *AE, DC, MC, V* ⦿ *CP.*

★ $ 🏨 **Kariwak Village.** People tend to return to Allan and Cynthia Clovis's charming, reasonably priced cabana village, which the owners describe as the "hotel and holistic haven." This peaceful atmosphere, all-natural cuisine (vegetarians love this place), an outdoor hot tub, and weekly yoga classes in the open-air conference area keep them coming back. A bamboo pavilion houses the highly respected Kariwak Village restaurant. All accommodations are in nicely appointed cabanas featuring high ceilings (designed to maximize your energy potential). The complex is near the airport, Store Bay, and Pigeon Point. ⊠ *Crown Point* ⬠ *Box 27* ☎ *868/639–8442* ☒ *868/639–8441* ⊕ *www.kariwak.co.tt* ⇨ *24 rooms* ⚘ *Restaurant, pool, outdoor hot tub, bar* ☰ *AE, MC, V* ⦿ *EP.*

¢ 🏨 **Toucan Inn.** This charming 20-room hotel is in the midst of beautiful gardens. You may choose from garden rooms or the less private cabanas around the pool. Immaculate rooms are well-appointed with beautiful local teak furniture. The rates, excellent service, and proximity to the airport make this hotel an unbeatable value. There's great live entertainment Monday, Wednesday, and Friday nights. One of the main advantages of staying here is that the hotel's restaurant and bar, Bonkers, is one of Tobago's most popular hangouts. ⊠ *Store Bay Local Rd., Crown Point* ☎ *868/639–7173* ☒ *868/639–8933* ⊕ *www.toucan-inn.com* ⇨ *20 rooms* ⚘ *Restaurant, pool, bar* ☰ *AE, MC, V* ⦿ *CP.*

Where to Eat

Curried crab and dumplings is Tobago's Sunday dinner favorite. Oil-down—a local dish—tastes better than it sounds: it's a gently seasoned mixture of boiled breadfruit and salt beef or pork flavored with coconut milk. Mango ice cream or a sweet and sour tamarind ball makes a tasty finish. You may want to take home some hot-pepper sauce or chutney to a spice-loving friend or relative.

For approximate costs, *see* the dining and lodging price chart at the beginning of this chapter.

CARIBBEAN ✕ **Shirvan Watermill.** For a quiet, romantic dinner, this elegant alfresco
$$–$$$$ restaurant surrounded by lush foliage and a winding fishpond filled with carp is an essential dining experience. The daily-changing menu, the bouquets of anthuriums, and the starched navy tablecloths and white napkins add even more charm. A regular specialty is "river lobster" (crayfish) with garlic butter (a mess is expected). ⊠ *Shirvan Rd., Mt. Pleasant* ☎ *868/639–0000* ☰ *AE, MC, V* ☯ *No lunch.*

★ $$–$$$ ✕ **Kariwak Village.** Recorded steel-band music plays gently in the background at this romantic, candlelit spot in the Kariwak Village complex.

In a bamboo pavilion that resembles an Amerindian round hut, Cynthia Clovis orchestrates a very original menu. Whatever the dish, it will be full of herbs and vegetables picked from Cynthia's organic garden. Saturday buffets, with live jazz or calypso, are a Tobagonian highlight. ⊠ *Crown Point* ☎ *868/639–8442* ☐ *AE, DC, MC, V.*

★ $–$$$ ╳ **Blue Crab.** Alison Sardinha is Tobago's most ebullient and kindest hostess, and her husband Ken one of its best chefs. The menu may include kingfish, curried chicken, or suckling pig. You'll always find callaloo, rotis, and *cou-cou* (a cornmeal dish); sometimes you may find a "cookup"—a pelau-type rice dish with *everything* in it. The place is officially open only on Wednesday and Friday nights, but Miss Alison will open up on other evenings and for weekend lunches if you call in the morning. ⊠ *Robinson and Main Sts., Scarborough* ☎ *868/639–2737* ☐ *AE, MC, V* ☉ *Closed weekends. No dinner Mon., Tues., and Thurs.*

¢ ╳ **Café Petunia.** This little gem is a true delight—the sort of place that you will brag to your friends that you "discovered." On a little hill and simply decorated in what can only be described as "mauve retro," it's a great place to while away the hours sipping on cappuccino or wine. Owner Petunia Thomas offers light snacks, salads, and fresh juices that she prepares herself. Friday evenings are lively, with a band performing jazz, pop, and calypso standards and featuring the song stylings of Petunia herself. It's near the Signal Hill turnoff, between Crown Point and Scarborough. ⊠ *Old Milford Rd.* ☎ *868/639–6878* ☐ *No credit cards.*

¢ ╳ **First Historical Café/Bar.** This funky little roadside eatery in a traditional West Indian building in the Studley Park area en route to Charlotte is owned by the Washington family. The back-porch dining area overlooking the sea has a crushed-rock-and-coral floor, brightly painted yellow, green, and red bamboo walls, time-line posters that present historical tidbits on Tobago, and a thatch roof. The food is simple but good, featuring such island delights as fruit plates, coconut bread, and fish sandwiches. ⊠ *Mile Marker 8, Windward Main Rd.* ☎ *868/660–2233* ☐ *No credit cards.*

CONTEMPORARY ╳ **Tamara's.** Here, at the elegant Coco Reef Resort, you dine on contemporary cuisine with an island twist. The peach walls and whitewashed wooden ceiling make the place feel airy and light, and island breezes waft through the palm-tree-lined terrace. The prix-fixe menu changes seasonally, but the fish dishes are sure to please. A full tropical buffet breakfast is served daily; dinner is served nightly. ⊠ *Coco Reef Resort, Pigeon Point, Scarborough* ☎ *868/639–8571* ☐ *AE, MC, V* ☉ *No lunch.*

$$–$$$ ╳ **Arnos Vale Waterwheel Restaurant.** At this popular eatery on landscaped grounds in a rain-forest nature park, gleaming hardwood walkways take you past remnants of an old sugar mill. There's a roof overhead, but otherwise you're completely outdoors (insect repellent is a good idea). Tables and chairs are green wrought iron, the lights overhead fashioned in the shape of large pineapples. The crayfish and caviar salad with raspberry vinaigrette is a good choice. When you arrive at the park entrance, let the attendants know you're dining here to save the park admission fee. ⊠ *Arnos Vale Estate, Franklyn Rd., Scarborough* ☎ *868/660–0815* ☐ *MC, V.*

ECLECTIC ╳ **Pinnacle.** The main dining room at Le Grand Courlan Resort and Spa
$$$–$$$$ serves pleasant local dishes and international favorites in a large open, airy space facing the beach. Light dinner music is performed nightly, starting at 8, and service is friendly. ⊠ *Le Grand Courlan Resort and Spa, Shirvan Rd., Black Rock* ☎ *868/639–9667* ☐ *AE, MC, V.*

$–$$$ ╳ **Bonkers.** Despite the rather odd name, this restaurant at the Toucan Inn is atmospheric and excellent. Designed by expatriate British co-owner Chris James, the architecture is a blend of Kenyan and Caribbean styles, executed entirely in local teak and open on all sides. The menu is huge; Chris claims it pains him to remove any items, so he just keeps adding more. You can savor your lobster Rockefeller while enjoying the nightly entertainment. Open for breakfast and lunch seven days a week, this is the busiest eatery on the island. ⊠ *Toucan Inn, Store Bay Local Rd., Crown Point* ☎ *868/639–7173* 🖷 *868/639–8933* ▭ *AE, MC, V.*

ITALIAN   ✗ **La Tartaruga.** Milanese owner Gabriele de Gaetano has created one
★ **$$$$**   of the island's most delightful dining experiences. Sitting on the large patio surrounded by lush foliage with Gabriele rushing from table to table chatting in Italian-laced English is all the entertainment you'll need. The tagliatelli with lobster and capers in wine and cream will give your tastebuds fond memories to last for years to come. The restaurant has an impressive wine cellar stocked with only Italian wines. ⊠ *Buccoo Rd., Buccoo* ☎ *868/639–0940* ⚱ *Reservations essential* ▭ *AE, MC, V* ☉ *Closed Sun.*

Beaches

You won't find manicured country-club sand here. But those who enjoy feeling as though they've landed on a desert island will relish the untouched quality of these shores.

Bacolet Beach. This dark-sand beach was the setting for the films *Swiss Family Robinson* and *Heaven Knows, Mr. Allison.*

★ **Englishman's Bay.** This charming beach is usually completely deserted.

Great Courland Bay. Near Fort Bennett, the bay has clear, tranquil waters. Along the sandy beach—one of Tobago's longest—you'll find several glitzy hotels. A marina attracts the yachting crowd.

King's Bay. Surrounded by steep green hills, this is the most visually satisfying of the swimming sites off the road from Scarborough to Speyside—the bay hooks around so severely you'll feel like you're in a lake. The crescent-shape beach is easy to find because it's marked by a sign about halfway between the two towns. Just before you reach the bay there's a bridge with an unmarked turnoff that leads to a gravel parking lot; beyond that, a landscaped path leads to a waterfall with a rocky pool. You may meet locals who'll offer to guide you to the top of the falls; however, you may find the climb not worth the effort.

Little Rockley Bay. West of Scarborough (take Milford Road off the main highway) the beach is craggy and not much good for swimming or sunbathing, but it's quiet and offers a pleasing view of Tobago's capital across the water.

Lovers Beach. So called because of its pink sand and its seclusion—you have to hire a local to bring you here by boat—it's an isolated and quiet retreat.

Man O' War Bay. In the pretty little fishing village of Charlotteville (just northwest of Speyside) you can lounge on the sand and purchase the day's catch for your dinner.

Mt. Irvine Beach. Across the street from the Mt. Irvine Bay Hotel is this unremarkable beach, but it has great surfing in July and August; the snorkeling is excellent, too. It's also ideal for windsurfing in January and April. There are picnic tables surrounded by painted concrete pagodas and a snack bar.

Parlatuvier. On the north side of the island, the beach is best approached via the road from Roxborough. It's a classic Caribbean crescent, a scene peopled by villagers and fishermen.

Pigeon Point. This stunning locale is often displayed on Tobago travel brochures. Although the beach is public, it abuts part of what was once a large coconut estate, and you must pay a token admission (about TT$10) to enter the grounds and use the facilities. The beach is lined with towering royal palms, and there are food stands, gift shops, a diving concession, and paddleboats for rent. The waters are calm.

Sandy Beach. Along Crown Point, this beach is abutted by several hotels. You won't lack for amenities around here.

Stone Haven Bay. A gorgeous stretch of sand is across the street from the luxurious Grafton Beach Resort.

Store Bay. The beach, where boats depart for Buccoo Reef, is little more than a small sandy cove between two rocky breakwaters, but the food stands here are divine: six huts licensed by the tourist board to local ladies who sell roti, pelau, and the world's messiest dish—crab and dumplings. Miss Jean's is the most popular; but you should try Miss Esmie's crab.

Turtle Beach. Named for the leatherback turtles that lay their eggs here at night between February and June, it's on Great Courland Bay. (If you're very quiet, you can watch; the turtles don't seem to mind.)

Sports & the Outdoors

BIRD-WATCHING ★ Some 200 varieties of birds have been documented on Tobago: look for the yellow oriole, scarlet ibis, and the comical motmot—the male of the species clears sticks and stones from an area and then does a dance complete with snapping sounds to attract a mate. The flora is as vivid as the birds. Purple and yellow *poui* trees and spectacular orange immortelles splash color over the countryside, and something is blooming virtually every season. Naturalist and ornithologist David Rooks operates **Rooks Nature Tours** (⊠ 462 Moses Hill, Lambeau ☎ 868/639–4276 ⊕ www.pariasprings.com/rookstours/tours.html), offering bird-watching walks inland and trips to offshore bird colonies. Pat Turpin or Renson Jack at **Pioneer Journeys** (☎ 868/660–4327 or 868/660–5175) can give you information about their bird-watching tours of Bloody Bay rain forest and Louis D'Or River valley wetlands.

BOATING **Hew's Glass Bottom Boat Tours** (⊠ Pigeon Point ☎ 868/639–9058) are perfect excursions for those who neither snorkel nor dive. Boats leave daily at 11:30 AM. **Kalina Kats** (⊠ Scarborough ☎ 868/639–6304) has a 50-ft catamaran on which you can sail around the Tobago coastline with stops for snorkeling and exploring the rain forest. The romantic sunset cruise with cocktails is a great way to end the day.

FISHING **Dillon's Fishing Charter** (⊠ Crown Point ☎ 868/639–8765) is excellent for full- and half-day trips for kingfish, barracuda, wahoo, mahimahi, blue marlin, and others. Trips start at $165 for four hours, including equipment. With **Hard Play Fishing Charters** (⊠ 13 The Evergreen, Auchenskeoch, Buccoo ☎ 868/639–7108), colorful skipper Gerard "Frothy" De Silva helps you bag your own marlin. Cost is for $275 for two hours on the 38-ft *Hard Play* or $200 on the 31-ft *Hard Play Lite*.

GOLF ★ The 18-hole course at the **Mt. Irvine Golf Club** (⊠ Mt. Irvine Bay Hotel, Shirvan Rd., Mt. Irvine Bay ☎ 868/639–8871) has been ranked among the top five in the Caribbean and among the top 100 in the world. Greens fees are $30 for 9 holes; $48 for 18 holes (note that these rates are subject to 15% VAT tax). The 18-hole, PGA-designed championship par-72 course at **Tobago Plantations Golf & Country Club** (⊠ Lowlands ☎ 868/631–0875) is spanking new and set amidst rolling greens and mangroves. It offers some amazing views of the ocean as a bonus. Greens fees are $95 for 1 round; $150 for 2 rounds (these rates include a golf cart and taxes).

HIKING Eco-consciousness is strong on Tobago, where the rain forests of the Main Ridge were set aside for protection in 1764, creating the first such preserve in the western hemisphere. Natural areas include Little Tobago and St. Giles islands, both major seabird sanctuaries. In addition, the endangered leatherback turtles maintain breeding grounds on some of Tobago's leeward beaches.

Private-tour guide **AJM Tours** (✉ Crown Point Airport, Crown Point ☎ 868/639–0610 ⊕ www.ajmtours.com) offers tours of the Arnos Vale Waterwheel complex, as well as guided tours of Tobago and even nearby Venezuela. They groomed some of the rain forest around the **Arnos Vale Waterwheel** (✉ Arnos Vale Estate, Franklyn Rd. ☎ 868/660–0815) to insert a series of shiny wooden walkways that take you past the remnants of an old sugar factory. The walkways allow you to see much of the ruins without disturbing nature. There's also a small museum, an excellent restaurant, and several hiking trails around the property, including a 2½-mi (4-km) loop. The remnants of the Buckra Estate house are on a hilltop that has spectacular views of Tobago. There are also two Amerindian sights, remains of a slave village, and a tomb. Guides are available and can make your nature-history walk truly come alive. There's a TT$10 admission charge unless you're dining at the restaurant, so let the attendants know if you plan to have a meal here.

SCUBA DIVING   An abundance of fish and coral thrives on the nutrients of South America's Orinoco River, which are brought to Tobago by the Guyana current. Off the west coast is **Arnos Vale Reef**, with a depth of 40 ft and several reefs that run parallel to the shore. Here you can spot French and queen angelfish, moray eels, southern stingrays, and even the Atlantic torpedo ray. Much of the diving is drift diving in the mostly gentle current. **Crown Point**, on the island's southwest tip, is a good place for exploring the Shallows—a plateau at 50 ft to 100 ft that's favored by turtles, dolphins, angelfish, and nurse sharks. Just north of Crown Point on the southwest coast, **Pigeon Point** is a good spot to submerge. North of Pigeon Point, long sandy beaches line the calm western coast; it has a gradual offshore slope and the popular **Mt. Irvine Wall**, which goes down to about 60 ft.

A short trip from Charlotteville, off the northeast tip of the island, is **St. Giles Island.** Here are natural rock bridges—London Bridge, Marble Island, and Fishbowl—and underwater cliffs. The **waters off Speyside** on the east coast draw scuba-diving aficionados for the many manta rays in the area. Exciting sites in this area include Batteaux Reef, Angel Reef, Bookends, Blackjack Hole, and Japanese Gardens—one of the loveliest reefs, with depths of 20 ft to 85 ft and lots of sponges.

There are several places in Tobago to get information, supplies, and instruction. **AquaMarine Dive Ltd.** (✉ Blue Waters Inn, Batteaux Bay, Speyside ☎ 868/639–4416) is on the northeast coast. **Man Friday Diving** (✉ Windward Rd., Charlotteville ☎ 868/660–4676) is on the northwest coast. **Tobago Dive Experience** (✉ Manta Lodge, Speyside ☎ 868/639–7034) is a west coast scuba-diving operation. **Tobago Dive Masters** (✉ Windward Rd., Speyside ☎ 868/639–4697) is on the northeastern end of the island.

SNORKELING   Tobago offers many wonderful spots for snorkeling. Although the reefs around Speyside in the northeast are becoming better known, **Buccoo Reef**, off the island's southwest coast, is still the most popular—perhaps too popular. Over the years the reef has been damaged by the ceaseless boat traffic and by the thoughtless visiting divers who take pieces of coral for souvenirs. Still, it's worth experiencing, particularly if you have children. Daily 2½-hour tours by flat glass-bottom boats let you snorkel at the reef, swim in a lagoon, and gaze at Coral Gardens—where fish and coral are as yet untouched. The trip usually costs about $8, and masks, snorkeling equipment, and reef shoes are provided. Departure is at 11

AM from Pigeon Point. Most dive companies in the Black Rock area also arrange snorkeling tours. There is also good snorkeling near the **Arnos Vale Hotel** and the **Mt. Irvine Bay Hotel.**

TENNIS The remote enclave of **Blue Waters Inn** (⊠ Batteaux Bay, Speyside ☎ 868/ 660–4341), on the northeast Atlantic coast, has two of the best courts on the island and also allows nonresidents to play. If you're in the Mt. Irvine area, the **Mt. Irvine Bay Hotel** (⊠ Shirvan Rd., Mt. Irvine Bay ☎ 868/639–8871) has great lighted courts and a splendid view (if you can take your eye off the ball). Guests and nonguests can play on one of the two lighted, all-weather courts at **Rex Turtle Beach** (⊠ Courland Bay, Black Rock ☎ 868/639–2851). Lessons are available for $30 per hour.

Shopping

The souvenir-bound will do better in Trinidad than in Tobago, but determined shoppers should manage to ferret out some things to take home. Scarborough has the largest collection of shops, and Burnett Street, which climbs sharply from the port to St. James Park, is a good place to browse.

FOODSTUFFS **Forro's Homemade Delicacies** (⊠ The Andrew's Rectory, Bacolet St., opposite the fire station, Scarborough ☎ 868/639–2485) sells its own fine line of homemade tamarind chutney, lemon or lime marmalade, hot sauce, and guava or golden-apple jelly. Eileen Forrester, wife of the Anglican Archdeacon of Trinidad and Tobago, supervises a kitchen full of good cooks who boil and bottle the condiments and pack them in little straw baskets—or even in bamboo. Most jars are small, easy to carry, and inexpensive.

HANDICRAFTS **Cotton House** (⊠ Bacolet St., Scarborough ☎ 868/639–2727) is a good bet for jewelry and imaginative batik work. Paula Young runs her shop like an art school. You can visit the upstairs studio; if it's not too busy, you can even make a batik square at no charge. **Souvenir and Gift Shop** (⊠ Port Mall, Wrightson Rd., Scarborough ☎ 868/639–5632) stocks straw baskets and other crafts.

Nightlife

Tobago is not the liveliest island after dark, but there's usually some form of nightlife to be found. Whatever you do the rest of the week, don't miss the huge impromptu party affectionately dubbed "Sunday School," that gears up after midnight on all the street corners of Buccoo and breaks up around dawn. Pick your band, hang out for a while, then move on. In downtown Scarborough on weekend nights you can also find competing sound systems blaring at informal parties that welcome extra guests. In addition, "blockos" (spontaneous block parties) spring up all over the island; look for the hand-painted signs. Tobago also has harvest parties on Sunday throughout the year, when a particular village extends its hospitality and opens its doors to visitors.

★ **Bonkers** (⊠ Store Bay Local Rd., Crown Point ☎ 868/639–7173) is lively on most evenings with live entertainment every night except Sunday. **Diver's Den Bar & Grill** (⊠ Corner Mt. Pleasant Rd. and Robert St., Crown Point ☎ 868/639–8533), near the gas station, is the newest hangout on the island and the only one that consistently stays open really late. **Grafton Beach Resort** (⊠ Shirvan Rd., Black Rock ☎ 868/639– 0191) has some kind of organized cabaret-style event every night. Even if you hate that touristy stuff, check out Les Couteaux Cultural Group, which does a high-octane dance version of Tobagonian history. **Kariwak Village** (⊠ Crown Point ☎ 868/639–8442) has hip hotel entertainment and is frequented as much by locals as visitors on Friday and Saturday nights—one of the better local jazz-calypso bands almost always plays.

Exploring Tobago

A driving tour of Tobago, from Scarborough to Charlotteville and back, can be done in about four hours, but you'd never want to undertake this spectacular, and very hilly, ride in that time. The switchbacks can make you wish you had motion-sickness pills (take some along if you're prone). Plan to spend at least one night at the Speyside end of the island, and give yourself a chance to enjoy this largely untouched country and seaside at leisure.

Numbers in the margin correspond to points of interest on the Tobago map.

WHAT TO SEE **⑤ Charlotteville.** This delightful fishing village in the northeast is enfolded in a series of steep hills. Fishermen here announce the day's catch by sounding their conch shells. A view of Man O' War Bay with Pigeon Peak (Tobago's highest mountain) behind it at sunset is an exquisite treat.

④ Flagstaff Hill. One of the highest points of the island sits at the northern tip of Tobago. Surrounded by ocean on three sides and with a view of other hills, Charlotteville, and St. Giles Island, this was the site of an American military lookout and radio tower during World War II. It's an ideal spot for a sunset picnic. The turnoff to the hill is at the major bend on the road from Speyside to Charlotteville. It is largely unpaved, so the going may be a bit rough.

② Ft. King George. On Mt. St. George, a short drive up the hill from Scarborough, Tobago's best-preserved historic monument clings to a cliff high above the ocean. Ft. King George was built in the 1770s and operated until 1854. It's hard to imagine that this lovely, tranquil spot commanding sweeping views of the bay and landscaped with lush tropical foliage was ever the site of any military action, but the prison, officers' mess, and several stabilized cannons attest otherwise. Just to the left of the tall wooden figures dancing a traditional Tobagonian jig is the former barrack guardhouse, now housing the small **Tobago Museum.** Exhibits include weapons and other pre-Colombian artifacts found in the area; the fertility figures are especially interesting. Upstairs are maps and photographs of Tobago's past. Be sure to check out the gift display cases for the perversely fascinating jewelry made from embalmed and painted lizards and sea creatures; you might find it hard to resist a pair of bright-yellow shrimp earrings. The **Fine Arts Centre** at the foot of the Ft. King George complex shows the work of local artists. ⌧ *84 Fort St., Scarborough* ☎ *868/639–3970* ⌧ *Fort free; museum TT$5* ☉ *Weekdays 9–5.*

⑥ St. Giles Island. The underwater cliffs and canyons here off the northeastern tip of Tobago draw divers to this spot where the Atlantic meets the Caribbean. ✣ *Take Windward Rd. inland across mountains from Speyside.*

① Scarborough. Around Rockley Bay on the island's leeward hilly side, this town is both the capital of Tobago and a popular cruise-ship port, but it conveys the feeling that not much has changed since the area was settled two centuries ago. It may not be one of the delightful pastel-color cities of the Caribbean, but Scarborough does have its charms, including several interesting little shops. Whatever you do, be sure to check out the busy Scarborough Market, an indoor and outdoor affair featuring everything from fresh vegetables to live chickens and clothing.

Note the red-and-yellow Methodist church on the hill, one of Tobago's oldest churches.

❸ **Speyside.** At the far reach of Tobago's windward coast, this small fishing village has a few lodgings and restaurants. Divers are drawn to the unspoiled reefs in the area and to the strong possibility of spotting giant manta rays. The approach to Speyside from the south affords one of the most spectacular vistas of the island. Glass-bottom boats operate between Speyside and **Little Tobago Island,** one of the most important seabird sanctuaries in the Caribbean.

TRINIDAD & TOBAGO A TO Z

To research prices, get advice from other travelers, and book travel arrangements, visit www.fodors.com.

AIR TRAVEL

American Airlines offers daily direct flights from both New York and Miami to Trinidad. The national carrier, BWIA West Indies Airways, offers direct flights to Trinidad from Atlanta, Miami, New York, and Washington, D.C., in the U.S.; from Toronto in Canada; and from London in the U.K.; and from many Caribbean islands. There are regular flights between Tobago and Trinidad on Tobago Express and Caribbean Star. Air Canada flies nonstop from Toronto to Trinidad; British Airways offers weekly flights to Tobago from London (the number of flights increases in peak season). LIAT offers numerous flights to Trinidad from other Caribbean islands; it also has service from the eastern Caribbean islands to Tobago. Air DCA has direct flights from Curaçao to Trinidad on Tuesday, Thursday, and Sunday; flights from Aruba and Bonaire connect with this Curaçao flight.

🛪 **Air Canada** 🕾 868/664-4065. **Air DCA** 🕾 868/623-6522. **American Airlines** 🕾 868/664-4661. **British Airways** 🕾 800/744-2997. **BWIA West Indies Airways** 🕾 868/625-1010 or 868/669-3000. **Caribbean Star** 🕾 800/744-7827. **LIAT** 🕾 868/627-2942 or 868/623-1838. **Tobago Express** 🕾 868/625-1010 or 868/669-3000.

AIRPORTS

Trinidad's Piarco International Airport, located about 30 minutes east of Port-of-Spain (take Golden Grove Road north to Arouca and then follow Eastern Main Road west for about 10 mi [16 km] to Port-of-Spain), is a thoroughly modern facility complete with 16 airbridges. To bago's small Crown Point Airport is the gateway to the island. Taxis are readily available at Piarco Airport; the fare to Port-of-Spain is set at $20 ($30 after 10 PM) and $24 to the Hilton. In Tobago the fare from Crown Point Airport to Scarborough is fixed at $8, to Speyside at $36.

🛪 **Crown Point Airport** 🕾 868/639-0509 ⊕ www.airporttnt.com. **Piarco International Airport** 🕾 868/669-4101 ⊕ www.airporttnt.com.

BOAT & FERRY TRAVEL

FARES & SCHEDULES The Port Authority maintains ferry service every day except Saturday between Trinidad and Tobago, although flying is preferable because the seas can be very rough. The ferry leaves once a day (from St. Vincent Street Jetty in Port-of-Spain and from the cruise-ship complex in Scarborough); the trip takes about five hours. The round-trip fare is TT$50. Cabins, when available, run TT$160 (round-trip, double occupancy).

🛪 **Port-of-Spain, Trinidad** 🕾 868/625-3055 ⊕ www.patnt.com/ferry.htm. **Scarborough, Tobago** 🕾 868/639-2181 ⊕ www.patnt.com/ferry.htm.

BUSINESS HOURS

BANKS Banks are open Monday–Thursday 8–3, and Friday 8–noon and 3–5. Banks in malls will often stay open until 7 PM.

POST OFFICES   Post offices are open 8–noon and 1–4:30 on weekdays.

SHOPS   Most shops are open weekdays 8–4:30, Saturday 8–noon; malls stay open later during the week and operate all day Saturday.

CAR RENTALS

All agencies require a credit-card deposit, and in peak season you must make reservations well in advance of your arrival. Figure on paying $40–$60 per day in both Trinidad and Tobago (much more during Carnival). In addition to Thrifty, an international company, there are several local agencies operating on either Trinidad or Tobago or both; Auto Rentals is a local company with many locations on Trinidad.

🚗 Trinidad **Auto Rentals** ✉ Piarco International Airport, Piarco, Trinidad ☎ 868/669–2277. **Kalloo's Auto Rentals** ✉ Piarco International Airport, Piarco, Trinidad ☎ 868/669–5673. **Southern Sales Car Rentals** ✉ Piarco International Airport, Piarco, Trinidad ☎ 868/669–2424, or 269 from a courtesy phone in airport baggage area. **Thrifty** ✉ Piarco International Airport, Piarco, Trinidad ☎ 868/669–0602.

🚗 Tobago **Rattan's Car Rentals** ✉ Crown Point Airport, Crown Point, Tobago ☎ 868/639–8271. **Rollock's Car Rentals** ✉ Crown Point Airport, Crown Point, Tobago ☎ 868/639–0328. **Singh's Auto Rentals** ✉ Grafton Beach Resort, Shirvan Rd., Black Rock, Tobago ☎ 868/639–0191 Ext. 53. **Thrifty** ✉ Rex Turtle Beach Hotel, Courland Bay, Black Rock, Tobago ☎ 868/639–8507.

CAR TRAVEL

It's not worth renting a car if you're staying in Port-of-Spain, where the streets are often jammed with drivers who routinely play chicken with one another; taxis are your best bet. If you're planning to tour Trinidad, you'll need some wheels. In Tobago you're better off renting a four-wheel-drive vehicle than relying on expensive taxi service. Be cautious driving on either island, as the country has very lax and seldom enforced drinking and driving laws.

GASOLINE   Gas runs about TT$2.85 per liter. There are plenty of gas stations in Trinidad, but in Tobago don't let your tank get low, because there aren't many gas stations on the island.

ROAD CONDITIONS   Trinidad has excellent roads throughout the island. Be careful when driving during the rainy season, as roads often flood. Never drive into downtown Port-of-Spain during afternoon rush hour (generally from 3 to 6:30).

In Tobago, many roads, particularly in the interior or on the coast near Speyside and Charlotteville, are bumpy, pitted, winding, and/or steep (though the main highways are smooth and fast).

RULES OF THE ROAD   Driving is on the left, in the British style, so remember to look to your right when pulling out into traffic.

ELECTRICITY

Electric current is usually 110 volts/60 cycles, but some establishments provide 220-volt outlets.

EMBASSIES

🏛 Canada **Canadian High Commission** ✉ 3–3A Sweet Briar Rd., St. Clair, Port-of-Spain, Trinidad ☎ 868/622–6232.

🏛 United Kingdom **British High Commission** ✉ 19 St. Clair Ave., St. Clair, Port-of-Spain, Trinidad ☎ 868/622–2748.

🏛 United States **U.S. Embassy** ✉ 15 Queen's Park West, Port-of-Spain, Trinidad ☎ 868/622–6371.

EMERGENCIES

🚑 Ambulance & Fire **Ambulance and fire emergencies** ☎ 990.

◪ Hospitals **Port-of-Spain General Hospital** ⊠ 169 Charlotte St., Port-of-Spain, Trinidad ☏ 868/623-2951. **St. Clair Medical Centre** ⊠ 18 Elizabeth St., St. Clair, Port-of-Spain, Trinidad ☏ 868/628-1451. **Scarborough Hospital** ⊠ Fort St., Scarborough, Tobago ☏ 868/639-2551.
◪ Pharmacies **Bhaggan's** ⊠ Charlotte and Oxford Sts., Port-of-Spain, Trinidad ☏ 868/627-4657. **Kappa Drugs** ⊠ Roxy Round-a-bout, St. James, Port-of-Spain, Trinidad ☏ 868/622-2728. **Scarborough Drugs** ⊠ Carrington St. and Wilson Rd., Scarborough, Tobago ☏ 868/639-4161.
◪ Police **Police emergencies** ☏ 999.

ETIQUETTE & BEHAVIOR

Religious and racial tolerance are important to the people of Trinidad and Tobago. You may hear a word used in public that elsewhere might constitute a slur; on these islands, chances are it's being used in jest—but only by locals who know one another well. Many islanders are well educated and well traveled; don't assume they're unfamiliar with international politics and customs. As in many British-influenced Caribbean nations, beach attire isn't appreciated on the streets, in stores, restaurants, or hotel lobbies.

FESTIVALS & SEASONAL EVENTS

In addition to the incomparable Trinidad Carnival, there are a number of celebrations throughout the year. During the Tobago Heritage Festival (usually held in late July), villages throughout the island hold events and activities that portray one aspect (music, dance, drama, cooking, costuming) of island arts or culture. Divali, held in October or November and known as the Festival of Lights, is the climax of long spiritual preparation in the Hindu community. Small lamps beautifully illuminate the night, and there are events involving music, dancing, gift exchange, and much hospitality.

HEALTH

Insect repellent is a must during the rainy season (June–December) and is worth having around anytime. Trinidad is only 11 degrees north of the equator, and the sun here is intense; bring a strong sun block. If you have a sensitive stomach, you're better off drinking bottled water, though tap water on the islands is generally safe. In case of illness, treatment at public hospitals is free but conditions are often poor. Most people opt for one of the private medical establishments.

HOLIDAYS

Public holidays are: New Year's Day, Good Friday, Easter Monday, Spiritual Baptist Liberation Day (March 30), Indian Arrival Day (May 30), Corpus Christi (June 10), Labour Day (June 19), Emancipation Day (Aug. 1), Independence Day (Aug. 31), Republic Day (Sep. 24), Divali (date is announced by government a few months before, but it's usually in October or November), Eid (a Muslim festival whose actual date varies), Christmas, and Boxing Day (Dec. 26). Carnival Monday and Tuesday are not official holidays, but don't expect anything to be open.

LANGUAGE

The official language of Trinidad and Tobago is English, but there's no end of idiomatic expressions used by the loquacious locals (who tend to speak English very fast). If someone invites you for a "lime," by all means go—you're being invited to a party; "limin' " means relaxing and having a good time. To "beat pan" is to play the steel drum; "wine" is a sexy dance style done by rotating the hips. You'll also hear smatterings of French, Spanish, Chinese, and Hindi (Trinidad's population is about 40% Indian).

MAIL & SHIPPING

Postage to the United States and Canada is TT$3.45 for first-class letters and TT$2.25 for postcards; prices are slightly higher for other destinations. The main post offices are on Wrightson Road (opposite the Crowne Plaza) in Port-of-Spain, and in the NIB Mall on Wilson Street (near the docks) in Scarborough. There are no zip codes on the islands. To write to an establishment here, you simply need its address, town, and "Trinidad and Tobago, West Indies."

MONEY MATTERS

Prices quoted in this chapter are in U.S. dollars unless otherwise noted.

ATMS   Banks (many with ATMs that accept international cards) are plentiful in the towns and cities (branches of the Republic Bank and the Royal Bank are a common sight) but much less so in the countryside. In addition to the banks in Scarborough and Tobago's airport, a couple of grocery stores in the southwest part of Tobago have ATMs.

BANKS   There are four major banks operating on the islands: First Citizens Bank, Republic Bank, RBTT, and Scotiabank. Each of these banks has dozens of branches (there are far fewer branches in Tobago and most of those are in Scarborough). Banking hours are 8 AM–2 PM Monday to Thursday, 9–noon and 3–5 on Fridays. Bank branches in shopping malls are usually open until 6 PM on weekdays. First Citizens Bank operates branches at both Piarco and Crown Point airports.
🗂 **First Citizens Bank** ☎ 868/623-2576. **RBTT** ☎ 868/623-1322. **Republic Bank** ☎ 809/625-3611. **Scotiabank** ☎ 809/625-3566.

CREDIT CARDS   Credit cards and ATM cards are almost universally accepted for payment by businesses, hotels, and restaurants. VISA and MasterCard are ubiquitous, American Express much less so, and Diners Club and Discover rarely accepted. Cash is necessary only in the smallest neighborhood convenience shops and roadside stalls.

CURRENCY   The current exchange rate for the Trinidadian dollar (TT$) is about TT$6.20 to US$1. Most businesses on the island will accept U.S. currency if you're in a pinch.

PASSPORTS & VISAS

Citizens of the United States, the United Kingdom, and Canada who expect to stay for less than six weeks may enter the country with a valid passport. Citizens of Australia and New Zealand must also obtain a visa before entering the country.

SAFETY

Travelers should exercise reasonable caution in Trinidad, especially in the highly populated east–west corridor and downtown Port-of-Spain, where walking on the streets at night is not recommended unless you're with a group. As a general rule, Tobago is safer than its larger sister island, though this should not lure you into a false sense of security. Petty theft occurs on both islands, so don't leave cash in bags that you check at the airport, and use hotel safes for valuables.

SIGHTSEEING TOURS

IN TRINIDAD   Almost any taxi driver in Port-of-Spain will take you around town and to beaches on the north coast. It costs around $70 for up to four people to go to Maracas Bay beach, plus $20 per hour extra if you decide to go farther; but you should haggle for a cheaper rate. For a complete list of tour operators and sea cruises, contact the tourism office. Kalloo's offers tours ranging from a fascinating 3-hr tour of Port-of-Spain to an overnight turtle watching tour.

🚩 **Kalloo's** ✉ Piarco International Airport, Piarco ☎ 868/669–5673 or 868/622–9073.

IN TOBAGO   Frank's Glass Bottom Boat and Birdwatching Tours offers glass-bottom-boat and snorkeling tours of the shores of Speyside; Frank also conducts guided tours of the rain forest and Little Tobago. As a native of Speyside, he's extremely knowledgeable about the island's flora, fauna, and folklore. Tobago Travel is the island's most experienced tour operator, offering a wide variety of services and tours.

🚩 **Frank's Glass Bottom Boat and Birdwatching Tours** ✉ Speyside ☎☎ 868/660–5438. **Tobago Travel** ✉ Scarborough ☎ 868/639–8778.

TAXES

DEPARTURE TAX   Departure tax, payable in cash at the airport, is TT$100. At this writing there were plans in the works to add an additional TT$100 "airport maintenance tax."

SALES TAX   All hotels add a 15% government tax.

VALUE ADDED   Prices for almost all goods and services include a 15% V.A.T.
TAX (V.A.T.)

TAXIS

Taxis in Trinidad and Tobago are easily identified by their license plates, which begin with the letter *H*. Passenger vans, called Maxi Taxis, pick up and drop off passengers as they travel and are color-coded according to which of the six areas they cover. Rates are generally less than $1 per trip. (Yellow is for Port-of-Spain, red for eastern Trinidad, green for south Trinidad, and black for Princes Town. Brown operates from San Fernando to the southeast—Erin, Penal, Point Fortin. The only color for Tobago is blue.) They're easy to hail day or night along most of the main roads near Port-of-Spain. For longer trips you'll need to hire a private taxi. Cabs aren't metered, and hotel taxis can be expensive. A taxi service available in Trinidad, called 628–TAXI, will take you to and from the airport for $11 each way, to the beach for $10, and around town for $4.

🚩 **628-TAXI** ☎ 868/628-8294.

TELEPHONES

A digital phone system is in place, bringing with it direct-dial service, a comprehensive cell-phone network, and easy Internet access. Pay phones take phone cards or "companion" cards (that let you call from any phone—even from your hotel), which you can buy in different denominations at gift shops and newsagents.

COUNTRY & AREA   The area code for both islands is 868 ("TNT" if you forget). This is also
CODES   the country code if you're calling to Trinidad and Tobago from another country. From the U.S., just dial "1" plus the area code and number.

INTERNATIONAL   Most hotels and guest houses will allow you to dial a direct international
CALLS   call. To dial a number in North America or the Caribbean simply dial "1" and the area code before the number you're calling, but be warned that most hotels add a hefty surcharge for overseas calls. Calls to Europe and elsewhere can be made by checking for the appropriate direct dial codes in the telephone directory. To make an international call from a pay phone you must first purchase a "companion" card, which is readily available from most convenience shops—then simply follow the instructions on the card. Cards are available in various denominations.

LOCAL CALLS   To make a local call to any point in the country simply dial the seven-digit local number.

TIPPING

Almost all hotels will add a 10%–15% service charge to your bill. Most restaurants include a 10% service charge, which is considered standard on these islands. If it isn't on the bill, tip according to service: 10%–15% is fine. Cabbies expect a token tip of around 10%. At drinking establishments tipping is optional, and the staff at smaller bars may tell you on your way out that you forgot your change.

VISITOR INFORMATION

🚩 Before You Leave **Tourism Hotline** ☎ 888/595-4868. **Trinidad and Tobago Tourism Office** ⊕ www.visitTNT.com ✉ 331 Almeria Ave., Coral Gables, FL 33134 ☎ 800/748-4224 ✉ Mitre House, 66 Abbey Rd., Bush Park Hill, Enfield, Middlesex EN1 2RQ ☎ 208/350-1000 ✉ Taurus House, 512 Duplex Ave., Toronto, Ontario M4R 2E3 ☎ 416/535-5617 or 416/485-8724.

🚩 In Trinidad **TIDCO** ✉ 10-14 Phillips St., Port-of-Spain, Trinidad ☎ 868/623-6023 or 868/623-1932 ✉ Piarco International Airport, Piarco, Trinidad ☎ 868/669-5196.

🚩 In Tobago **Tobago Division of Tourism** ✉ N.I.B. Mall, Level 3, Scarborough, Tobago ☎ 868/639-2125 ✉ Crown Point Airport, Crown Point, Tobago ☎ 868/639-0509.

TURKS AND CAICOS ISLANDS

24

FODOR'S CHOICE

Parrot Cay Resort, Parrot Cay

HIGHLY RECOMMENDED

RESTAURANTS Anacaona, Providenciales

HOTELS Beaches Turks & Caicos, Providenciales
Coral Gardens, Providenciales
Grace Bay Club, Providenciales
Meridian Club, Pine Cay
Ocean Club, Providenciales
Ocean Club West, Providenciales
Point Grace, Providenciales
Prospect of Whitby Hotel, North Caicos
The Sands at Grace Bay, Providenciales
Windmills Plantation, Salt Cay

OUTDOORS Governor's Beach, Grand Turk
North Coast Beaches, Providenciales
Beaches on Salt Cay
Scuba diving and snorkeling in Providenciales

"Everything cool, man?" Shadow asks with a laugh as he cuts the speedboat through Crocodile Pass en route to Middle Caicos. A Caribbean renaissance man, Shadow took his nickname from an uncanny ability to sneak up on bonefish. He also bats .500 for the local all-star team, fishes for trophy-size blue marlin in the annual rodeo, plays a mean guitar, and tells a great story. When he reaches the shore, he plans to whip up a batch of seviche using fresh conch, onion, sweet peppers, lime juice, and Tabasco—thus adding "cook" to an impressive, island-style résumé.

Updated by
Kathy Borsuk

Sportfishermen, scuba divers, and beach aficionados have long known about the Turks and Caicos (pronounced *kay*-kos). To them this British Crown colony of more than 40 islands and small cays (only ten of which are inhabited) is a gem that offers dazzling turquoise seas, priceless stretches of fine ivory sand, and reefs rich in marine life. Whether you're swimming with the fishes or attempting to catch them from the surface, the Turks and Caicos won't disappoint. In an archipelago 575 mi (927 km) southeast of Miami and 90 mi (145 km) north of Haiti, the total landmass of these two groups of islands is 193 square mi (500 square km); the total population less than 25,000.

The Turks Islands include Grand Turk, which is the capital and seat of government, and Salt Cay. It's claimed that Columbus's first landfall was at Guanahani Beach on Grand Turk. Legend also has it that these islands were named by early settlers who thought the scarlet blossoms on the local cactus resembled the Turkish fez.

Approximately 22 mi (35½ km) west of Grand Turk, across the 7,000-ft-deep (2,141-m-deep) Columbus Passage, is the Caicos group: South, East, West, Middle, and North Caicos and Providenciales (nicknamed Provo). All but East Caicos are now inhabited, along with Pine, Parrot, and Ambergris Cays. "Caicos" is derived from *cayos,* the Spanish word for "cay" and is believed to mean, appropriately, "string of islands."

In the mid-1600s, Bermudians began to rake salt from the salinas on the Turks Islands, returning to Bermuda to sell their crop. Despite French and Spanish attacks and pirate raids, the Bermudians persisted and established a trade that became the bedrock of the islands' economy. In 1766 Andrew Symmers settled here to hold the islands for England. The American Declaration of Independence left British loyalists from South Carolina and Georgia without a country, causing many to take advantage of British Crown land grants in the Turks and Caicos. Cotton plantations were established and prospered for nearly 25 years until the boll weevil, soil exhaustion, and a terrible hurricane in 1813 devastated the land. Left behind to make their living off the land and sea were the former slaves, who remained to shape the islands' culture.

Today the Turks and Caicos are known as a reputable offshore tax haven whose company formation, banking, trusts, and insurance institutions lure investors from North America and beyond. Provo, in particular, is becoming a popular Caribbean tourist destination, and real-estate sales—especially for luxury beachfront condominiums—are booming. Mass tourism, however, shouldn't be in the cards; government guidelines promote a quality, not quantity policy, including conservation awareness. However, for the first time, regular cruise ship stops were scheduled to begin in Grand Turk in mid-2003. If proposed plans come to fruition, Grand Turk's quaint, quiet atmosphere is likely to change drastically.

WHAT IT COSTS In U.S. dollars					
	$$$$	$$$	$$	$	¢
	RESTAURANTS*				
	over $30	$20–$30	$12–$20	$8–$12	under $8
	HOTELS**				
Cost EP/BP/CP	over $350	$250–$350	$150–$250	$80–$150	under $80
Cost AI	over $450	$350–$450	$250–$350	$125–$250	under $125

*Restaurant prices are for a main course at dinner. **EP, BP, and CP prices are per night for a standard double room in high season, excluding taxes, service charges, and meal plans. AI (all-inclusive) prices are per person, per night based on double-occupancy during high season, excluding taxes and service charges.

THE TURKS

Grand Turk

Bermudian colonial architecture abounds on this string bean of an island (just 7 mi [11 km] long and 1½ mi [2½ km] wide). Buildings have walled-in courtyards to keep wandering horses from nibbling on the foliage. The island caters to divers, and it's no wonder: the Wall, a slice of vertical coral mountain, is less than 300 yards from the beach.

Where to Stay

Throughout the islands, accommodations range from small (sometimes non-air-conditioned) inns to splashy resorts and hotels that are the ultimate in luxury. Most medium and large hotels offer a choice of EP and MAP. Almost all hotels offer dive packages, which are an excellent value.

$$ **The Arches of Grand Turk.** If you're looking for a home away from home, these immaculate vacation town houses offer space, privacy, and a loving touch. Each of the four two-story suites is fully furnished in clean-cut country style. Kitchen/dining areas are on the lower levels, with two huge, air-conditioned bedrooms upstairs. Arched balconies front and back promise breathtaking sunrises and sunsets. Since the buildings sit atop the ridge northeast of town, steady breezes are refreshing, and there is an eagle's-eye view of the island. ✉ *Lighthouse Rd.* *Box 226* ☎ 📠 *649/946–2941* 🌐 *www.grandturkarches.com* *4 town houses* *Kitchens, microwaves, cable TV with movies, pool, bicycles, laundry facilities* 💳 *D, MC, V* 🍽 *EP.*

$ **Island House.** Perched on a breezy hill overlooking North Creek, about 1 mi (1½ km) outside of town, this Mediterranean-style all-suites inn offers romantic comfort and panoramic views from large porches. Gas-powered golf carts are provided free of charge so you can get around easily. Relax in the expansive, palm-shaded pool/patio area with barbecue grill. Fishing from the dock and bird-watching are popular at this peaceful retreat, and kayaks, small sailboats, and dive packages are available for more active types. ✉ *Lighthouse Rd., Grand Turk* *Box 36* ☎ *649/946–1519* 📠 *649/946–2646* 🌐 *www.islandhouse-tci.com* *9 suites* *Kitchenettes, microwaves, cable TV with movies, pool, dock, fishing, bicycles, laundry facilities, Internet, some pets allowed* 💳 *AE, MC, V* 🍽 *EP.*

$ **Salt Raker Inn.** Across a quaint, foliage-lined street from the beach, this inn—once the home of a Bermudian shipwright—was built in the

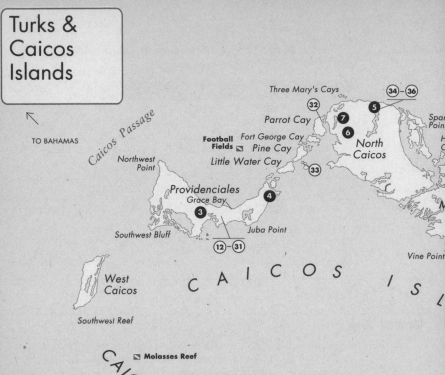

Turks & Caicos Islands

TO BAHAMAS

Caicos Passage

Three Mary's Cays

Parrot Cay

Fort George Cay

Football Fields ▨

Pine Cay

Little Water Cay

Northwest Point

Providenciales

Grace Bay

Southwest Bluff

Juba Point

⑫—㉛

④

㉝

㉜

⑦

⑥

⑤

㉞—㊱

North Caicos

Spani

Hi
Co

M

Vine Point

CAICOS ISL

West Caicos

Southwest Reef

③

C A I C O S   I S L

▨ Molasses Reef

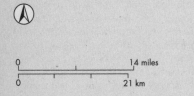

CAICOS BANK

0 ——— 14 miles
0 ——— 21 km

White Ca

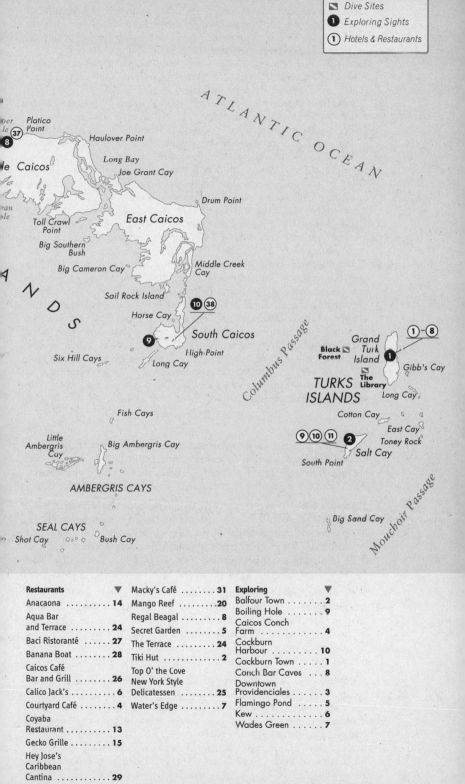

KEY
◤ Dive Sites
① Exploring Sights
① Hotels & Restaurants

ATLANTIC OCEAN

Platico Point
❽ �37
Haulover Point
Long Bay
Joe Grant Cay
Drum Point
le Caicos
Toll Crawl Point
East Caicos
Big Southern Bush
Big Cameron Cay
Middle Creek Cay
Sail Rock Island
Horse Cay
❿ ㊳
❾
South Caicos
High Point
Six Hill Cays
Long Cay

LANDS

Columbus Passage

Black Forest ◤
Grand Turk Island
① — ❽
①
Gibb's Cay
The Library ◤
Long Cay

TURKS ISLANDS

Cotton Cay

Fish Cays

Little Ambergris Cay
Big Ambergris Cay

AMBERGRIS CAYS

❾ ❿ ⑪ ❷
South Point
Salt Cay

East Cay
Toney Rock

SEAL CAYS
Shot Cay
Bush Cay

Big Sand Cay

Mouchoir Passage

early 19th century. The renovated rooms are clean and comfortable, all with the original pine floors. Upstairs suites have balconies overlooking the ocean; lush tropical gardens at back envelop the Secret Garden restaurant. Hotel service is unpretentious and friendly. ⊠ *Duke St., Grand Turk* ⊡ *Box 1* ☎ *649/946–2260* 🖷 *649/946–2817* ⊕ *www.saltraker. com* ➫ *10 rooms, 3 suites* ⚬ *Restaurant, refrigerators, cable TV, bicycles, bar, Internet, some pets allowed* ⊟ *MC, V* ⦿| *EP.*

$ 🏨 **Turks Head Hotel.** Although thoroughly modernized, the historical Turks Head Hotel has maintained its romantic charm and tranquil ambience. The two-story structure, filled with antique furnishings, was built in 1823 as the home of a prosperous shipwright and has also served as the American consulate and governor's guest house. Rooms are a comfortable blend of old and new, with a coffeemaker and minibar beside the canopied four-poster bed. The hotel bar and Calico Jack's restaurant bustle at night; the beach is only a few strides away, and dive packages are available. ⊠ *Duke St., Grand Turk* ⊡ *Box 58* ☎ *649/946–2466* 🖷 *649/946–1716* ⊕ *www.grand-turk.com* ➫ *8 rooms* ⚬ *Restaurant, minibars, refrigerators, cable TV with movies, golf privileges, beach, bicycles, bar, pub* ⊟ *MC, V* ⦿| *CP.*

¢–$ 🏨 **Osprey Beach Hotel.** Rooms in this two-story oceanfront building open onto a private verandah overlooking the beach; there are airy cathedral ceilings on the top floors. Deluxe units have brand-new furnishings with king-size four-poster beds; suites include sitting rooms and full kitchens. The pool bar/restaurant serves drinks, tapas, and barbecue specials to the sound of breaking waves just steps away. A pleasant touch is the lush foliage lining the walkways. ⊠ *Duke St., Grand Turk* ⊡ *Box 1* ☎ *649/946–2888* 🖷 *649/946–2817* ⊕ *www.ospreybeachhotel.com* ➫ *28 rooms* ⚬ *Restaurant, some kitchens, some kitchenettes, microwaves, refrigerators, cable TV with movies, golf privileges, pool, beach, snorkeling, bar, meeting rooms, some pets allowed* ⊟ *AE, MC, V* ⦿| *EP.*

Where to Eat

Like everything else on these islands, dining out is a very laid-back affair, which is not to say it's cheap. Because of the high cost of importing all edibles, the price of a meal is higher than in the United States. Reservations are generally not required, and dress tends to be casual.

AMERICAN ✕ **Water's Edge.** This pleasantly rustic eatery would have to float to be
$$–$$$ any closer to the ocean. Here you'll find conch served in any way, shape, or form—conch salad, cracked conch, conch creole, curried conch, and even conch po'boys. Other choices include giant, juicy Goo Burgers, made-from-scratch pizza, and homemade pies. ⊠ *Duke St., Cockburn Town* ☎ *649/946–1680* ⊟ *MC, V* ⊗ *Closed Sun.*

CAFÉS ✕ **Courtyard Café.** Homemade waffles with fresh fruit and whipped
¢–$ cream? Huge omelets and blueberry muffins? Submarine sandwiches and pasta salad? It's all at this casual café, where you can enjoy your meal in the cool shade of the garden courtyard. Prices are reasonable, and daily specials range from lasagna and quiche to island-style beef patties. ⊠ *Duke St., Cockburn Town* ☎ *649/946–1453* ⊟ *AE, MC, V.*

ECLECTIC ✕ **Calico Jack's.** The menu changes daily at this lively restaurant—touted
$$–$$$ by many residents as the best on the island—in the Turks Head Hotel. Look for lobster, steaks, chicken curry, lamb shanks, pizza, and homemade soups on the menu, as well as an excellent selection of wines. On Friday nights there's a courtyard barbecue, with live music by local musicians. The English pub is usually abuzz with local gossip and mirthful chatter. ⊠ *Turks Head Hotel, Duke St., Cockburn Town* ☎ *649/946–2466* ⊟ *MC, V.*

SEAFOOD ✕ **Secret Garden.** Menu highlights at the Salt Raker Inn's restaurant in-
$–$$$ clude local conch and fish dishes, grilled lobster tail, and a different in-
ternational specialty every night. For dessert try the Caribbean bread
pudding or key lime pie. Morning offerings include a full English break-
fast and an island favorite, fish-and-grits. Wednesday-night sing-alongs,
featuring local guitarist/divemaster Mitch Rolling, are popular, as are
the Saturday-night barbecues. ⊠ *Salt Raker Inn, Duke St., Cockburn
Town* ☎ *649/946–2260* ⊟ *MC, V.*

¢–$ ✕ **Regal Beagal.** Drop by this local eatery for island specialties such as
cracked conch, minced lobster, and fish-and-chips. It's a casual place with
unmemorable decor, but the portions are large and the prices easy on
your wallet. ⊠ *Hospital Rd.* ☎ *649/946–2274* ⊟ *No credit cards.*

Beaches

There are more than 230 mi (370 km) of beaches in the Turks and Caicos
Islands, ranging from secluded coves to miles-long stretches, and most
beaches are soft coralline sand. Tiny cays offer complete isolation for
nude sunbathing and skinny-dipping. Many are accessible only by boat.

★ **Governor's Beach,** a long white strip on the west coast of Grand Turk,
is one of the island's nicest, with plenty of sparkling, powder-soft sand
on which to stroll.

Sports & the Outdoors

CYCLING The island's flat terrain isn't very taxing, and most roads have hard sur-
faces. Take water with you: there are few places to stop for refreshment.
Most hotels in Cockburn Town, Grand Turk's only town, have bicycles
available, but you can also rent them for $10–$15 a day from **Sea Eye
Diving** (⊠ Duke St., Grand Turk ☎☎ 649/946–1407).

SCUBA DIVING & In these waters you can find undersea cathedrals, coral gardens, and count-
SNORKELING less tunnels, but note that you must carry and present a valid certificate
★ card before you'll be allowed to dive. As its name suggests, the **Black
Forest** offers staggering black-coral formations as well as the occasional
black-tip shark. In the **Library** you can study fish galore, including large
numbers of yellowtail snapper. At the Columbus Passage separating South
Caicos from Grand Turk, each side of a 22-mi-wide (35-km-wide) chan-
nel drops more than 7,000 ft. From January through March, thousands
of Atlantic humpback whales swim through en route to their winter breed-
ing grounds.

Dive outfitters can all be found in Cockburn Town. Two-tank boat dives
generally cost $60–$75. **Blue Water Divers** (⊠ Salt Raker Inn, Duke St.,
Grand Turk ☎☎ 649/946–1226) has been in operation on Grand Turk
since 1983. **Oasis Divers** (⊠ Duke St., Grand Turk ☎☎ 649/946–1128)
specializes in complete gear handling and pampering treatment. It also
supplies NITROX. Owner Everette Freites is a local authority on hump-
back whales and leads whale-watching trips in season. Besides daily dive
trips to the Wall, **Sea Eye Diving** (⊠ Duke St., Grand Turk ☎☎ 649/946–
1407 ⊕ www.seaeyediving.com) offers encounters with friendly stingrays
on a popular snorkeling trip to nearby Gibbs Cay.

Nightlife

A fun crowd gathers at **Turks Head Hotel** (⊠ Duke St., Grand Turk
☎ 649/946–2466) almost every night. On weekends and holidays the
younger crowd heads over to the **Nookie Hill Club** (⊠ Nookie Hill, Grand
Turk ☎ no phone) for late-night wining and dancing. There's folk and
pop music at the **Salt Raker Inn** (⊠ Duke St., Grand Turk ☎ 649/946–
2260) on Wednesday nights.

Exploring Grand Turk

Pristine beaches with vistas of turquoise waters, small local settlements, historic ruins, and native flora and fauna are among the sights on Grand Turk. Fewer than 5,000 people live on this 7½-square-mi (19-square-km) island, and it's hard to get lost, as there aren't many roads.

Numbers in the margin correspond to points of interest on the Turks & Caicos Islands map.

① **Cockburn Town.** The buildings in the colony's capital and seat of government reflect a 19th-century Bermudian style of architecture. Narrow streets are lined with low stone walls and old street lamps, now powered by electricity. The once-vital salinas have been restored, and covered benches along the sluices offer shady spots for observing wading birds, including flamingos that frequent the shallows. Be sure to pick up a copy of the Tourist Board's new Heritage Walk guide to discover Grand Turk's rich history. In one of the oldest stone buildings on the islands, the **Turks & Caicos National Museum** (✉ Duke St., Cockburn Town ☎ 649/946–2160) houses the Molasses Reef wreck of 1513, the earliest shipwreck discovered in the Americas. The natural history exhibits include artifacts left by Taíno, African, North American, Bermudian, French, and Latin American settlers. An impressive addition to the museum is the coral-reef and sea-life exhibit, faithfully modeled on a popular dive site just off the island. The museum is open Monday–Tuesday and Thursday–Friday 9–4, Wednesday 9–5, and Saturday 9–1. Admission is $5.

Salt Cay

Fewer than 100 people live on this 2½-square-mi (6-square-km) dot of land, maintaining an unassuming lifestyle against a backdrop of quaint stucco cottages, stone ruins, and weathered wooden windmills standing sentry in the abandoned salinas. There's not much in the way of development, but there are splendid beaches on the north coast. The most spectacular sights are beneath the waves: 10 dive sites are just minutes from shore.

Where to Stay

For approximate costs, *see* the dining and lodging price chart at the beginning of this chapter.

★ $$$–$$$$ 🏨 **Windmills Plantation.** The attraction here is the lack of distraction. The hotel resembles a romantic's version of a colonial-era plantation—placed on over two miles of deserted beach. The great house has four suites, each with a sitting area, a four-poster bed, ceiling fans, and a verandah or balcony with a sea view. All are furnished in a mix of antique English and wicker furniture. Four other rooms are housed in adjacent buildings. Managers Jim and Sharon Shafer bring a sterling reputation as gracious hosts. ✉ *North Beach Rd., Salt Cay* ☎ *649/946–6962* 🖷 *649/946–6930* ⊕ *www.windmillsplantation.com* ⇆ *4 rooms, 4 suites* ⚭ *Restaurant, pool, beach, snorkeling, fishing, hiking, horseback riding, bar, library; no a/c, no room phones, no room TVs, no kids* ▤ *AE, MC, V* ⚭ *EP.*

$ 🏨 **Mount Pleasant Guest House.** This simple, somewhat rustic hotel was a former salt-plantation home, now serving as a guest house catering to divers. Rooms, renovated in 2002, are bright, clean, and simply furnished. The premises are filled with memorabilia and artifacts, and the gazebo bar overlooks a cut-stone cistern pit converted into a palm grove for hammocks. Meals are superb, with dinners including whelk soup, grilled fresh fish and lobster, buttery cracked conch, and New York strip steaks. ⊠ *Balfour Town* 🕾🕾 *649/946–6927* ⊕ *www.turksandcaicos.tv/mtpleasant* 📠 *8 rooms ⚓ Restaurant, fans, bicycles, horseback riding, bar, library; no a/c in some rooms, no room phones, no room TVs* ▤ *MC, V* ⦿ *EP.*

$ 🕮 **Salt Cay Sunset House.** Built in 1832, this historic bed-and-breakfast and oceanfront café is housed in the oldest salt-plantation home on Salt Cay, lovingly restored by enthusiastic owners Michele Wells and Paul Dinsmore. All three bedrooms have en suite baths; there's a shared living room. Period furnishings can be found throughout. Michelle serves hearty local and Continental fare for breakfast, lunch, and dinner on the breezy verandah at the Blue Mermaid Café. ⊠ *Balfour Town* 🕾🕾 *649/946–6942* ⊕ *www.seaone.org* 📠 *3 rooms ⚓ Restaurant, fans, beach, snorkeling, horseback riding, Internet; no a/c, no room phones, no room TVs* ▤ *MC, V* ⦿ *BP.*

Beaches

★ There are superb beaches on the north coast of **Salt Cay. Big Sand Cay,** 7 mi (11 km) south of Salt Cay, is also known for its long, unspoiled stretches of open sand.

Sports & the Outdoors

SCUBA DIVING & SNORKELING Scuba divers can explore the ***Endymion,*** a 140-ft wooden-hull British warship that sank in 1790. It's off the southern point of Salt Cay. **Reef Runners** (🕾 649/946–6901) conducts daily trips and rents all the necessary equipment. It costs around $80 for a two-tank dive.

Exploring Salt Cay

Numbers in the margin correspond to points of interest on the Turks & Caicos Islands map.

Salt sheds and salinas are silent reminders of the days when the island was a leading producer of salt. Island tours are often conducted by motorized golf cart. From January through March, whales pass by on the way to their winter breeding grounds.

➋ **Balfour Town.** What little development there is on Salt Cay is found here. It's home to several small hotels and a few stores that sell hand-woven baskets, T-shirts, convenience foods, and beach items.

THE CAICOS

West Caicos

The 2002 dredging of the previously uninhabited island's natural harbor was the first step in the proposed "Isle of West Caicos" project. Plans are for a very exclusive island retreat centering around a harbor town (re-created with 18th-century atmosphere) and three coastal residential settlements. For many years the island was accessible only by boat, but developers have restored an old 3,000-ft airport runway. Fortunately, offshore diving here remains among the most exotic in the islands. The "Wilds of West Caicos" encompass a pristine wall, about ¼ mi (½ km) from shore, which starts at 35 ft to 45 ft and cascades to 7,000 ft. Sharks, eagle rays, and turtles are commonly seen on the many dive sites. It's about an hour's boat ride from Provo, but well worth the trip. Most dive operators depart from satellite locations on the south side of Provo for the journey.

Providenciales

In the mid-18th century, so the story goes, a French ship was wrecked near here, and the survivors were washed ashore on an island they gratefully christened La Providentielle. Under the Spanish, the name was changed to Providenciales. Today about 25,000 people live on Provo (as everybody calls it); a considerable number are expatriate British, Canadian, and American businesspeople and retirees, or refugees from nearby Haiti. The island's 44 square mi (114 square km) are by far the most developed in the Turks and Caicos.

Along the beach-lined north shore there are no fewer than a dozen high-end condominium hotels (some currently under construction), three all-inclusive resorts, and the country's first time-share resort. Residential development is also booming, especially in the upscale Leeward and Chalk Sound areas. Although roads are in desperate need of upgrading, power, water, telecommunications, and cable TV utilities are modern and well-serviced.

Where to Stay

For approximate costs, *see* the dining and lodging price chart at the beginning of this chapter.

A popular option on Provo is renting a self-catering villa or private home. For the best villa selection, plan to make your reservations three to six months in advance.

Elliot Holdings and Management Company (⌂ Box 235, Providenciales ☎ 649/946–5355 ⊕ www.ElliotHoldings.com) offers a wide selection of modest to magnificent villas in the Leeward, Grace Bay, and Turtle Cove areas of Providenciales. **T. C. Safari** (⌂ Box 64, Providenciales ☎ 649/941–5043 ⊕ www.tcsafari.tc) has exclusive oceanfront properties in the beautiful and tranquil Sapodilla Bay/Chalk Sound neighborhood on Provo's southwest shores.

★ ☺ $$$$ 🏨 **Beaches Turks & Caicos Resort & Spa.** There's plenty to satisfy families at this member of the Sandals chain, including a children's park complete with a video-game center, water slides, a swim-up soda bar, a 1950s-style diner, and a teen disco. Nice rooms, lots of activities, extravagant meals, and many kinds of water sports (with scuba diving included in the price) make this beachfront all-inclusive resort an indulgent experience. Rooms are furnished in rich mahogany and warm tropical tones, with king-size beds; honeymoon villas include a Jacuzzi in the bedroom. The spa offers body wraps, massages, and facials. ⊠ *Lower Bight Rd., Grace Bay* ☎ *649/946–8000 or 800/726–3257* 🖷 *649/946–8001* ⊕ *www.beaches.com* 🛏 *359 rooms, 103 suites* ♨ *9 restaurants, in-room safes, cable TV with movies, miniature golf, 4 tennis courts, 6 pools, hair salon, health club, spa, beach, dive shop, snorkeling, windsurfing, boating, parasailing, fishing, bicycles, 12 bars, nightclub, recreation room, theater, video game room, shops, baby-sitting, children's programs (ages 0–5), concierge, meeting rooms, car rental* ⊟ *AE, MC, V* ⊚ *AI.*

★ $$$$ 🏨 **Grace Bay Club.** Every room is a suite at the island's original luxury property—and all have breathtaking views of stunning Grace Bay. A recent change in ownership led to a number of enhancements, including upgrading linens, upholstery, and rugs, adding large TVs and DVD players, and freshening the entire look of the gracious, Mediterranean-style resort. There is also a new business center with Internet access. Future plans include the construction of 30 ultra-upscale, beachfront condominium residences. Activities range from diving to golf to catered picnics on surrounding islands, but relaxing remains the major pastime. Elegant European-Caribbean meals are served in the Anacaona restaurant. ⊠ *Grace Bay* ⌂ *Box 128* ☎ *649/946–5050 or 800/946–5757* 🖷 *649/946–5758* ⊕ *www.gracebayclub.com* 🛏 *21 suites* ♨ *Restaurant,* *room service, in-room data ports, in-room fax, in-room safes, kitchens, cable TV with movies, in-room VCRs, 2 tennis courts, 2 pools, hot tub, spa, beach, snorkeling, windsurfing, boating, parasailing, bicycles, bar, shop, laundry service, concierge, business services, Internet; no kids under 12* ⊟ *AE, MC, V* ☉ *Closed Sept.* ⦿ *CP.*

★ $$$$ ⊞ **Point Grace.** This boutique hotel raises the bar for luxury resorts on the islands. Majestically designed in British colonial style, two ocean-front buildings house magnificent two- and three-bedroom suites. All have expansive terraces overlooking Grace Bay and are furnished with Indonesian hardwood and teak. Hand-painted tiles line the bathrooms, and Frette linens cover the king-size four-poster beds. The four-bedroom penthouse suite has a separate massage room and rooftop Jacuzzi. Expanded spa services, featuring thallasotherapy, are offered in private cottages on the dunes overlooking the sea. Rolls-Royce airport transfers can be arranged. ⊠ *Grace Bay* ⬤ *Box 700* ☎ *888/682–3705 or 649/ 946–5096* 🖷 *649/946–5097* ⊕ *www.pointgrace.com* ⤼ *23 suites, 9 cottages, 2 villas* ⟐ *2 restaurants, room service, in-room fax, in-room safes, some in-room hot tubs, kitchenettes, microwaves, cable TV with movies, in-room VCRs, pool, spa, beach, snorkeling, windsurfing, boating, parasailing, fishing, bicycles, 2 bars, library, baby-sitting, laundry service, concierge, Internet, business services, car rental* ⊟ *AE, D, MC, V* ☉ *Closed Sept.* ⦿ *CP.*

$$$–$$$$ ⊞ **Allegro Resort and Casino Turks & Caicos.** This sprawling beachfront property is an all-inclusive resort that caters primarily to adults (though it still welcomes children). The oversize oceanfront rooms have rattan furniture, a rich Caribbean color scheme, and private balcony or terrace. A pool-patio area and a PADI 5-star dive facility are on site. Meals range from Caribbean fare to Italian specialties, with unlimited beverages. The American Casino, the island's only gaming facility, is here. ⊠ *Grace Bay* ⬤ *Box 205* ☎ *649/946–5555 or 800/858–2258* 🖷 *649/ 946–5522* ⊕ *www.allegroresorts.com* ⤼ *186 rooms* ⟐ *3 restaurants, in-room safes, cable TV with movies, 3 tennis courts, pool, fitness classes, gym, hot tub, massage, beach, dive shop, snorkeling, windsurfing, boating, fishing, bicycles, volleyball, 3 bars, casino, theater, shops, baby-sitting, children's programs (ages 4–12), laundry service, concierge, Internet, meeting rooms, car rental, travel services* ⊟ *AE, MC, V* ⦿ *AI.*

★ $$–$$$$ ⊞ **Coral Gardens.** This intimate beachfront resort fronts one of Provo's most popular snorkeling reefs and is in a tranquil area well west of bustling Grace Bay. The deluxe suites have terraces and floor-to-ceiling walls of sliding glass. Gourmet kitchens open into the dining areas, and bedrooms and baths overlook the luxurious gardens. A dramatic waterfall cascades down the face of each building. Fine dining alfresco is offered at Coyaba Restaurant, with creatively casual fare (including sushi) served at the beachside bar and grill Ripples. The European-style Serenity Spa, specializing in tropical indulgence, was added in 2002. ⊠ *Penn's Rd., The Bight* ⬤ *Box 281* ☎ *649/941–3713 or 800/532–8536* 🖷 *649/ 941–5171* ⊕ *www.coralgardens.com* ⤼ *30 suites* ⟐ *2 restaurants, room service, in-room data ports, in-room safes, kitchens, kitchenettes, microwaves, cable TV with movies, 2 pools, fitness classes, spa, beach, dive shop, snorkeling, boating, fishing, boccie, 2 bars, laundry facilities, concierge, Internet, car rental* ⊟ *AE, MC, V* ⦿ *EP.*

★ $$–$$$$ ⊞ **Ocean Club.** These luxury all-suites condominiums are on a 12-mi (19-km) stretch of pristine beach, a short walk from Provo's only golf course. Units range from efficiency studios to three-bedroom suites with living rooms, dining rooms, kitchens, and screened balconies. Management and service are consistently superb. You can take a free shuttle to use the facilities of sister property, Ocean Club West. The on-site Gecko Grille serves creative island dishes. ✉ *Grace Bay* ⌖ *Box 240* ☎ *649/946–5880 or 800/457–8787* 🖷 *649/946–5845* ⊕ *www.oceanclubresorts.com* ☞ *86 suites* ♨ *2 restaurants, in-room data ports, in-room safes, some kitchens, some kitchenettes, microwaves, cable TV with movies, golf privileges, tennis court, 2 pools, gym, spa, beach, dive shop, snorkeling, boating, 2 bars, shops, laundry facilities, concierge, Internet, meeting room, car rental* ▭ *AE, MC, V* ⏁ *EP.*

★ **$$–$$$$** 🏨 **Ocean Club West.** This sister property to the Ocean Club maintains signature details of the original—breathtaking seascapes, large balconies, and exquisite landscaping—while expanding the oceanfront central courtyard area to include a gazebo-capped island, winding free-form pool, and seaside café and swim-up bar. Interiors are decorated in subdued sophistication, utilizing whites, light woods, and wicker. Junior one-bedrooms and get-away packages are especially good values. ✉ *Grace Bay* ⌖ *Box 640* ☎ *649/946–5880 or 800/457–8787* 🖷 *649/946–5845* ⊕ *www.oceanclubresorts.com* ☞ *90 suites* ♨ *1 restaurant, in-room data ports, in-room safes, some kitchens, some kitchenettes, microwaves, cable TV with movies, golf privileges, tennis court, 2 pools, gym, spa, beach, dive shop, snorkeling, boating, bar, laundry facilities, concierge, Internet, meeting room, car rental* ▭ *AE, MC, V* ⏁ *EP.*

$$–$$$$ 🏨 **Royal West Indies Resort.** Distinctive British colonial architecture and extensive gardens highlight this well-run luxury condominium resort. Private balconies front all units to make the most of the sea view, and interiors are an eclectic blend of wood and fabrics from Central and South America. Although the beach is steps away, the 80-ft-long pool surrounded by tropical fruit trees is a peaceful place to relax and sip a drink from the superb on-site Mango Reef restaurant and bar. ✉ *Grace Bay* ⌖ *Box 482* ☎ *649/946–5004 or 800/332–4203* 🖷 *649/946–5008* ⊕ *www.royalwestindies.com* ☞ *99 suites* ♨ *Restaurant, fans, in-room data ports, in-room safes, kitchenettes, microwaves, refrigerators, cable TV with movies, 2 pools, beach, snorkeling, boating, fishing, bar, baby-sitting, laundry facilities, laundry service, car rental* ▭ *AE, MC, V* ⏁ *EP.*

★ **$$–$$$$** 🏨 **The Sands at Grace Bay.** "Simply breathtaking" describes the sparkling ocean views from the huge screened patios and floor-to-ceiling windows of units at this beach lover's haven. The upscale condominium resort offers accommodations ranging from studios to three-bedroom suites; larger suites have two TVs, extra sleeper sofas, and washer-dryers. Contemporary furnishings combine Indonesian wood, wrought iron, and wicker with seaside-tone fabrics to emphasize the resort's theme of sophisticated simplicity. Hemingway's, an excellent oceanfront cabana restaurant and bar, is on site. Look for senior discounts from May 1 to December 15. ✉ *Grace Bay* ⌖ *Box 681* ☎ *649/941–5199 or 877/777–2637* 🖷 *649/946–5198* ⊕ *www.thesandsresort.com* ☞ *116 suites* ♨ *Restaurant, in-room data ports, in-room safes, some kitchens, some kitchenettes, microwaves, refrigerators, cable TV with movies, tennis court, 3 pools, gym, spa, beach, snorkeling, boating, bicycles, bar, shop, baby-sitting, laundry facilities, laundry service, concierge, car rental* ▭ *AE, MC, V* ⏁ *EP.*

$$$ 🏨 **Club Med Turkoise.** This village is a major water-sports center, with scuba diving, windsurfing, sailing, and waterskiing on the turquoise waters at its doorstep. Two- and three-story bungalows line a 1-mi (1½-km) beach, and all the usual sybaritic pleasures are here. This all-inclusive (except drinks) club is geared toward couples, singles age 18 and over, and divers. There are also a flying trapeze, nightly entertainment, dive packages, and excursions offered to sites in the Turks and Caicos. ✉ *Grace Bay* ☎ *649/946–5500 or 888/932–2582* 🖷 *649/946–5497* ⊕ *www.clubmed.com* ☞ *293 rooms* ♨ *2 restaurants, cable TV with movies, 8 tennis courts, pool, fitness classes, gym, hot tub, massage, beach,* *dive shop, snorkeling, windsurfing, boating, fishing, bicycles, billiards, soccer, volleyball, 3 bars, dance club, theater, shops, laundry service; no kids* ⊟ *AE, MC, V* ⏣ *AI.*

$$ ⊞ **Sibonné.** Just steps from the peaceful waters and soft sand of Grace Bay Beach, this small, quiet "boutique hotel" is especially popular with honeymooners and older couples. The comfortable rooms, each with a patio or balcony, surround a lush courtyard, with hammocks nestled within and a circular pool overlooking the beach. Oceanfront Bay Bistro is known for its creative international cuisine, including tapas-style entrées and luscious chocolate desserts. With longtime island aficionados Ken and Sandra McLeod at the helm, hospitality is superb. ⊠ *Grace Bay* ⏃ *Box 144* ☎ *649/946–5547 or 800/528–1905* 🖷 *649/946–5770* ⊕ *www.sibonne.com* ⤿ *26 rooms, 1 apartment* ⚲ *Restaurant, bar, in-room data ports, in-room safes, cable TV, pool, beach, snorkeling, boating, bicycles, laundry service* ⊟ *AE, MC, V* ⏣ *EP.*

$–$$ ⊞ **Comfort Suites.** Although Comfort Suites is the island's only "franchise" hotel, the property's exceptional hospitality and superior performance are anything but standard. Suites are housed in two three-story buildings built around an Olympic-size pool and landscaped patio area; frosty drinks are served at the tiki bar. Like the rest of the hotel, rooms are spotless and furnished in bright Caribbean colors. Grace Bay's pearly white beach is just across the street. The hotel flanks the Ports of Call shopping village. ⊠ *Grace Bay* ⏃ *Box 590* ☎ *649/946–8888 or 888/678–3483* 🖷 *649/946–5444* ⊕ *www.comfortsuitesci.com* ⤿ *100 suites* ⚲ *Fans, in-room data ports, in-room safes, refrigerators, cable TV with movies, pool, bar, shops, travel services* ⊟ *AE, MC, V* ⏣ *CP.*

$ ⊞ **Back of Beyond.** As the name suggests, this retreat is set apart from Provo's hustle and bustle on the quiet south shore. A burnished-orange stucco, pueblo-style inn houses the nine rooms, each charmingly decorated by proprietress Coleen Darragh, who with husband Ed designed and built the distinctive building to complement the surrounding cactus-dotted terrain. Rooms and the dining patio overlook the turquoise-green hues of the ocean beyond; a secluded white-sand beach is just a stroll away. Coleen's hospitality extends to the on-site restaurant and bar, where she cooks and serves home-style "comfort" fare. ⊠ *Venetian Rd., Discovery Bay* ☎ *649/941–4555* ⊕ *www.backofbeyond.tc* ⤿ *9 rooms* ⚲ *Restaurant, fans, pool, bar; no a/c, no room TVs* ⊟ *No credit cards* ⏣ *BP.*

$ ⊞ **Turtle Cove Inn.** This pleasant two-story inn offers affordable, comfortable lodging much in favor with scuba, boating, and fishing enthusiasts. All rooms include a private balcony or patio overlooking either the courtyard's lush tropical gardens and pool or Turtle Cove Marina. Besides the dockside Aqua Bar and Terrace, the inn has a souvenir shop, liquor store, and local artisan's gallery. You can readily stroll to the snorkeling at Smith's Reef, and access the remaining miles of north shore beach from there. ⊠ *Turtle Cove Marina, Turtle Cove* ⏃ *Box 131* ☎ *649/946–4203 or 800/887–0477* 🖷 *649/946–4141* ⊕ *www.turtlecoveinn.com* ⤿ *28 rooms, 2 suites* ⚲ *Restaurant, bar, in-room safes, refrigerators, cable TV with movies, pool, marina, fishing, bicycles, shops, car rental, no-smoking rooms* ⊟ *AE, MC, V* ⏣ *EP.*

Where to Eat

There are more than 50 restaurants on Provo, ranging from casual to elegant, with cuisine from Continental to Asian (and everything in between). You can spot the islands' own Caribbean influence no matter where you go, exhibited in fresh seafood specials, colorful presentations, and a tangy dose of spice.

For approximate costs, *see* the dining and lodging price chart at the beginning of this chapter.

CARIBBEAN ✕ **Mango Reef.** Third-generation restaurateur Doug Camozzi (of Tiki Hut
$$–$$$ fame) was determined to spotlight Caribbean ingredients when he created the menu for his newest venture, in the Royal West Indies Resort. The end result is a marvelous medley of flavors, colors, and textures made by marinating meats and seafood prior to grilling and pairing them with inventive fruit- and vegetable-based chutneys and salsas. Meals are served throughout the day, and the separate bar area is a popular evening spot for residents. ⊠ *Royal West Indies Resort, Grace Bay* ☏ *649/946–8200* ⊟ *AE, MC, V.*

¢–$ ✕ **Macky's Café.** This is where the locals go for their favorite fare, served hot and tasty from the impossibly small kitchen. Daily specials include steamed grouper, cracked conch, barbecued ribs and stewed beef, all hearty helpings complete with peas 'n' rice, coleslaw, and fried plantains. You can enjoy a cold beer or soda along with your meal at the outdoor seating in the courtyard of a small shopping plaza. ⊠ *Leeward Hwy., The Market Place* ☏ *649/941–3640* ⊟ *No credit cards.*

DELI ✕ **Top o' the Cove New York Style Delicatessen.** You can walk to this tiny
¢–$ café on Leeward Highway, just south of Turtle Cove. Order breakfast, deli sandwiches, salads, and enticingly rich desserts and freshly baked goods. From the deli case you can buy the fixings for a picnic; the shop's shelves are stocked with an eclectic selection of fancy foodstuffs. It's open at 6:30 AM on weekdays and Saturday and from 8 to 2 on Sunday. ⊠ *Leeward Hwy., Turtle Cove* ☏☏ *649/946–4694* ⊟ *No credit cards* ☉ *No dinner.*

ECLECTIC ✕ **Anacaona.** At the Grace Bay Club, this *palapa*-style restaurant (with
★ $$$–$$$$ tables clustered under large thatch-roof structures) offers a memorable dining experience minus the tie, the air-conditioning, and the attitude. Start with a bottle of fine wine and then enjoy a three- or four-course meal of the chef's light but flavorful cooking, which combines traditional European recipes with Caribbean fare. Oil lamps on the tables, gently circulating ceiling fans, and the murmur of the trade winds add to the Eden-like environment. Children under 12 are not allowed. ⊠ *Grace Bay Club, Grace Bay* ☏ *649/946–5050* ⌘ *Reservations essential* ⊟ *AE, MC, V.*

$$$–$$$$ ✕ **Coyaba Restaurant.** As the founding member of the local chapter of the Chaîne des Rôtisseurs, chef Paul Newman lets his talent soar at Coral Gardens' elegantly appointed, terrace-style restaurant. A typical meal (served on Royal Doulton china, no less) might start with truffle mousse, follow with chipotle-glazed maple-leaf duck breast, and finish with upside-down apple pie, all complemented by wines from the outstanding list. The careful attention to detail makes an evening here live up to its name's translation from the Arawak Indian tongue, "heavenly." New and very popular is the seven-course tasting menu. ⊠ *Penn's Rd., The Bight* ☏ *649/946–5186* ⊟ *AE, MC, V* ☉ *Closed Tues.*

$$–$$$$ ✕ **Gecko Grille.** At this Ocean Club resort restaurant, you can eat indoors surrounded by tropical murals or out on the garden patio, where the trees are interwoven with tiny twinkling lights. Creative "Floribbean" fare combines native specialties with exotic fruits and zesty island spices and includes Black Angus steaks grilled to order. ⊠ *Ocean Club, Grace Bay* ☏ *649/946–5885* ⊟ *AE, MC, V* ☉ *Closed Mon.–Tues.*

$$$ ✕ **Caicos Café Bar and Grill.** There's a pervasive air of celebration in the tree-shaded outdoor dining terrace of this popular eatery across from the Allegro Resort. Choose from grilled seafood, steak, lamb, and chicken served hot off the outdoor barbecue. Owner-chef Pierrik Marziou

adds a French accent to his appetizers, salads, and homemade desserts. ⊠ *Grace Bay* ☎ 649/946–5278 ▭ *AE, MC, V.*

$–$$ ✕ **Tiki Hut.** From its new location overlooking the marina, the ever-popular Tiki Hut continues to serve consistently tasty, value-priced meals in a fun atmosphere. Locals take advantage of the Wednesday night $10 chicken and rib special, and the lively bar is a good place to sample local Turks Head brew. There's a special family-style menu and kid's seating. Don't miss pizzas made with their signature white sauce. ⊠ *Turtle Cove Marina, Turtle Cove* ☎ 649/941–5341 ▭ *AE, MC, V.*

ITALIAN ✕ **Baci Ristoranté.** Aromas redolent of the Mediterranean waft from the
$$–$$$ open kitchen as you walk into this intimate eatery east of Turtle Cove. Outdoor seating is on a romantic canal-front patio. The menu offers a small, varied selection of Italian delights. Main courses focus on veal, but also include pasta, chicken, fresh fish dishes, and brick-oven pizza. House wines are personally selected by the owners and complement the tasteful wine list. Try the tiramisu for dessert with a flavored coffee drink. ⊠ *Harbour Town, Turtle Cove* ☎ 649/941–3044 ▭ *AE, MC, V.*

SEAFOOD ✕ **Aqua Bar and Terrace.** Formerly The Terrace, this popular dining spot
$$–$$$ shifted its position on the grounds of the Turtle Cove Inn and added a waterfront dining deck. Specializing in locally caught seafood and farm-raised conch, the menu retains many favorite dishes, including wahoo sushi, conch fillets encrusted with ground pecans, and grilled fish served with flavorful sauces. A selection of more casual entrées, including salads and burgers, has been added to broaden the appeal to the budget-conscious. Top it all off with a scoop of homemade ice cream. ⊠ *Turtle Cove Inn, Turtle Cove Marina, Turtle Cove* ☎ 649/946–4763 ▭ *AE, MC, V.*

$–$$ ✕ **Banana Boat.** Buoys and other sea relics deck the walls of this lively restaurant/bar on the wharf. Grilled grouper, lobster salad sandwiches, conch fritters, and conch salad are among the options. Tropical drinks include the rum-filled Banana Breeze—a house specialty. ⊠ *Turtle Cove Marina, Turtle Cove* ☎ 649/941–5706 ▭ *AE, MC, V.*

TEX-MEX ✕ **Hey Jose's Caribbean Cantina.** Frequented by locals, this restaurant,
$–$$ just south of Turtle Cove, claims to serve the island's best margaritas. Customers also return for the tasty Tex-Mex treats: tacos, tostadas, nachos, burritos, fajitas, and special-recipe hot chicken wings. Thick, hearty pizzas are another favorite—especially the Kitchen Sink, with a little bit of everything thrown in. ⊠ *Leeward Hwy., Central Square* ☎ 649/ 946–4812 ▭ *MC, V* ☉ *Closed Sun.*

Beaches

There are good beaches at **Sapodilla Bay** and **Malcolm Roads,** at North West Point, which is accessible only by four-wheel-drive vehicles. A fine ★ white-sand beach stretches 12 mi (19 km) along Provo's **north coast,** where most of the hotels are.

Sports & the Outdoors

BICYCLING Provo has a few steep grades to conquer, but they're short. Unfortunately, traffic on Leeward Highway and rugged road edges make pedaling here a less than relaxing experience. Instead, try the less-traveled roads through the native settlements of Blue Hills, The Bight, and Five Cays. Most hotels have bikes available. You can rent mountain bikes at **Provo Fun Cycles** (⊠ Ports of Call, Grace Bay ☎ 649/946–5868) for $16 a day.

BOATING & Provo's calm, reef-protected turquoise seas combine with constant east-
SAILING erly trade winds for excellent sailing conditions. Several multihull vessels offer charters with snorkeling stops, food and beverage service, and sunset vistas. Prices range from $39 for group trips to $600 or more for

private charters. *Atabeyra* (☎ 649/941–5363) is a retired rum runner and the choice of residents for special events. **Sail Provo** (☎ 649/946–4783) runs 52-ft and 48-ft catamarans on scheduled half-day, full-day, and sunset cruises.

FISHING   The island's fertile waters are great for angling—anything from bottom- and reef fishing (most likely to produce plenty of bites and a large catch) to bonefishing and deep-sea fishing (among the finest in the Caribbean). You're required to purchase a $15 visitor's fishing license; operators generally furnish all equipment, drinks, and snacks. Prices range from $100 to $375, depending on the length of trip and size of boat. You can rent a boat with a captain for a half or full day of bottom- or bonefishing through **J&B Tours** (✉ Leeward Marina, Leeward ☎ 649/ 946–5047). For deep-sea fishing trips in search of marlin, sailfish, wahoo, tuna, barracuda, and shark, look up *Sakitumi* (✉ Turtle Cove Marina, Turtle Cove ☎ 649/946–4065). Captain Arthur Dean at **Silver Deep** (✉ Leeward Marina, Leeward ☎ 649/946–5612) is said to be among the Caribbean's finest bonefishing guides.

GOLF   The par-72, 18-hole championship course at **Provo Golf and Country Club** (✉ Governor's Rd., Grace Bay ☎ 649/946–5991), designed by Karl Litten, is a combination of lush greens and fairways, rugged limestone outcroppings, and freshwater lakes. Fees are $120 for 18 holes with shared cart.

HORSEBACK   Provo's long beaches and secluded lanes are ideal for trail rides on
RIDING   horseback. **Provo Ponies** (☎ 649/946–5252) offer morning and afternoon rides for all levels of experience. A 45-minute ride costs $45; an 80-minute ride is $65.

PARASAILING   A 15-minute parasailing flight over Grace Bay is available for $60 (single) or $110 (tandem) from **Captain Marvin's Watersports** (☎ 649/231– 0643), who will pick you up at your hotel for your flight.

SCUBA DIVING &   The island's many shallow reefs offer excellent and exciting snorkeling
SNORKELING   relatively close to shore. Try **Smith's Reef**, over Bridge Road east of Tur-
★   tle Cove.

Scuba diving in the crystalline waters surrounding the islands ranks among the best in the Caribbean. The reef and wall drop-offs thrive with bright, unbroken coral formations and lavish numbers of fish and marine life. Mimicking the idyllic climate, waters are warm all year, averaging 76°F– 78°F in winter and 82°F–84°F in summer. With minimal rainfall and soil runoff, visibility is naturally good and frequently superb, ranging from 60 ft to more than 150 ft. An extensive system of marine national parks and boat moorings, combined with an ecoconscious mindset among dive operators, contributes to an uncommonly pristine underwater environment.

Dive operators in Provo regularly visit sites at **Grace Bay** and **Pine Cay** for spur-and-groove coral formations and bustling reef diving. They make the longer journey to the dramatic walls at **North West Point** and **West Caicos** depending on weather conditions. Instruction from the major diving agencies is available for all levels and certifications. An average one-tank dive costs $45; a two-tank dive, $90. There are also two live-aboard dive boats available for charter working out of Provo.

Art Pickering's Provo Turtle Divers (☎ 649/946–4232 or 800/833–1341), at the Ocean Club, Ocean Club West, and in Turtle Cove Marina, has been on Provo for more than 30 years. The staff is friendly, knowledgeable, and unpretentious. **Big Blue Unlimited** (✉ Leeward Marina, Leeward ☎ 649/946–5034) specializes in eco-diving adventures, with a certified marine biologist on staff. It also offers Nitrox, Trimix, and rebreathers. **Caicos Adventures** (✉ Caicos Cafe Plaza, Grace Bay ☎☎ 649/941–3346) is run by friendly Frenchman Fifi Kuntz, and offers daily trips to West Caicos, French Cay, and Molasses Reef. **Dive Provo** (✉ Allegro Resort Turks and Caicos, Ports of Call, Grace Bay ☎ 649/946–5040 or 800/234–7768) is a resort-based, PADI 5-star operation that runs daily one- and two-tank dives to popular Grace Bay sites. **Flamingo Divers** (✉ Provo Marine Biology Centre, Discovery Bay ☎ 649/946–4193 or 800/204–9282) focuses on small groups and personalized service for the discerning diver.

Sea Dancer (☎ 800/932–6237) offers live-aboard diving to individuals and groups, with weekly trips out of Provo. The *Turks and Caicos Aggressor* (☎ 800/348–2628), a live-aboard dive boat, plies the islands' pristine sites with weekly charters from Turtle Cove Marina. It's sometimes possible to buy a berth instead of chartering the entire boat.

TENNIS Several hotels have courts open to nonguests. Prices vary, so call before you go. **Club Med Turkoise** (✉ Grace Bay ☎ 649/946–5491) has eight courts; four of them are lit for night games. **Miramar Resort** (✉ Turtle Cove ☎ 649/946–4240) has clay courts, both of them lit. **Grace Bay Club** (✉ Grace Bay ☎ 649/946–5754) has two lighted courts. The **Ocean Club** (✉ Grace Bay ☎ 649/946–5880) resort has one lighted court, and its sister resort, Ocean Club West, has two. You can rent equipment at **Provo Golf and Country Club** (✉ Grace Bay ☎ 649/946–5991) and play on their two lighted courts.

WATERSKIING & Windsurfers find the calm, turquoise water of Grace Bay ideal. **Wind-**
WINDSURFING **surfing Provo** (✉ Ocean Club, Grace Bay ☎ 649/946–5649 ✉ Ocean Club West, Grace Bay ☎ 649/231–1687) rents Windsurfers, kayaks, motorboats, and Hobie Cats and offers windsurfing instruction.

Shopping

Don't expect the variety of goods offered in more developed Caribbean island destinations. There are several main shopping areas in Provo: Market Place and Central Square, on the Leeward Highway about ½ mi to 1 mi (1 to 1½ km) east of downtown, and the shopping village Ports of Call, in Grace Bay. Hand-woven straw baskets, polished conch shells, paintings, wood carvings, handmade dolls, and small metalwork are the only crafts native to the area.

Bamboo Gallery (✉ Market Place, Leeward Hwy., Downtown Providenciales ☎☎ 649/946–4748) sells Caribbean art, from vivid Haitian paintings to wood carvings and local metal sculptures. For a large selection of duty-free liquor, visit **Discount Liquors** (✉ Leeward Hwy., east of Suzie Turn Rd., Providenciales ☎ 649/946–4536). **Greensleeves** (✉ Central Square, Leeward Hwy., Turtle Cove ☎☎ 649/946–4147) offers paintings and pottery by local artists, baskets, jewelry, and sisal mats and bags. **Marilyn's Craft** (✉ Ports of Call, Grace Bay ☎ no phone) sells handmade dolls, rag rugs, and wood carvings, plus tropical clothing and knickknacks. **Royal Jewels** (✉ Providenciales International Airport ☎ 649/941–4513 ✉ Allegro Resort Turks and Caicos, Grace Bay ☎ 649/946–5311 ✉ Arch Plaza ☎ 649/946–4699 ✉ Beaches Turks & Caicos Resort & Spa, Grace Bay ☎ 649/946–8285 ✉ Club Med Turkoise, Grace Bay ☎ 649/946–5602) sells gold and jewelry, designer watches, perfumes, fine leather goods and cameras—all duty-free—at several outlets. **The Tourist Shoppe** (✉ Central Square, Leeward Hwy., Turtle Cove ☎ 649/946–4627) has a large selection of souvenirs, including quality T-shirts, CDs, cards and postcards, beach toys, and sunglasses.

With more than 20,000 items, including a large fresh produce section, on-site bakery, and extensive meat counter, **IGA Supermarket** (✉ Leeward

Hwy., Grace Bay ☎ 649/941–5000), Provo's largest, is likely to have what you're looking for. Be prepared: prices are much higher than you would expect at home. If you need to supplement your beach-reading stock or are looking for island-specific materials, visit **The Unicorn Bookstore** (⊠ Market Place, Leeward Hwy., Downtown Providenciales ☎ 649/941–5458) for a wide assortment of books and magazines, including a large children's section.

Besides having a licensed pharmacist on duty, **Lockland Trading Co.** (⊠ Neptune Plaza, Grace Bay ☎ 649/946–8242), sells flavored coffees, snacks, ice cream, and a selection of T-shirts and souvenirs. Termed "the best little water-sports shop in Provo," **Seatopia** (⊠ Ports of Call, Grace Bay ☎ 649/941–3355) sells reasonably priced scuba and snorkeling equipment, swimwear, beachwear, sandals, hats, and related water gear and swim toys.

Nightlife

Residents and tourists flock to **Lattitudes** (⊠ Ports of Call, Grace Bay ☎ 649/946–5832) to let their hair down. There are billiards and satellite sports on five TVs in the bar, and it delivers pizza in the Grace Bay area. On Friday nights you can find a local band and lively crowd at **Calico Jack's Restaurant & Bar** (⊠ Ports of Call, Grace Bay ☎ 649/946–5129). A popular gathering spot for locals to shoot pool, play darts, slam dominoes, and catch up on gossip is **Club Sodax Sports Bar & Grill** (⊠ Leeward Hwy., Grace Bay ☎ 649/941–4540). You won't go hungry with snacks such as conch and fish fingers, jerk pork, and typical native dishes.

The only casino on the island is the **American Casino** (⊠ Allegro Resort, Grace Bay ☎ 649/946–5508). It's open to all and includes 80 slot machines and several table games, including blackjack, Caribbean stud poker, and roulette. Drinks are free for all players.

Exploring Providenciales

Numbers in the margin correspond to points of interest on the Turks & Caicos Island map.

❸ **Downtown Providenciales.** Near Providenciales International Airport, downtown Provo is really an extended strip mall that houses a grocery store, car-rental and travel agencies, law offices, banks, and other businesses.

❹ **Caicos Conch Farm.** On the northeast tip of Provo, this is a major mariculture operation where mollusks are farmed commercially (more than 3 million conch are here). Guided tours are available; call to confirm times. The small gift shop sells conch-related souvenirs. ⊠ *Leeward-Going-Through, Leeward* ☎ *649/946–5330* ☎ *$6* ☉ *Mon.–Sat. 9–4.*

Little Water Cay

This small, uninhabited cay is a protected area under the Turks and Caicos National Trust. On these 150 acres are two trails, small lakes, red mangroves, and an abundance of native plants. Boardwalks protect the ground and interpretive signs explain the habitat. The cay is home to about 2,000 rare, endangered rock iguanas. They say the iguanas are shy, but these creatures actually seem rather curious. They waddle right up to you, as if posing for a picture.

Parrot Cay

Once said to be a hideout for pirate Calico Jack Rackham and his lady cohorts Mary Reid and Anne Bonny, the 1,000-acre cay, between Fort George Cay and North Caicos, is now the site of an ultra-exclusive hideaway resort, a holistic health spa, and upscale homesites. Bordered by a wild stretch of pristine beach to the north and mangrove-lined wetlands to the south, tiny Parrot Cay is a natural wonder.

Where to Stay

For approximate costs, *see* the dining and lodging price chart at the beginning of this chapter.

$$$$
FodorsChoice
★

⊞ Parrot Cay Resort. Frequented by celebrities and the international ultra-chic, this exclusive resort combines natural beauty and elegant simplicity to create a rarified atmosphere of tranquillity. Mediterranean-style hillside structures house one- and two-bedroom suites, all with private terraces overlooking the ocean. Seaside villas include some private pools, butler service, and fully equipped kitchens, complete with chef and waitstaff on request. Three new villas on Rocky Point offer the ultimate in seclusion for $4,000 per night. International cuisine is served in the main dining room, while the poolside restaurant specializes in authentic Thai, Indonesian and Malaysian dishes. The on-site Shambhala Spa has been ranked among the top 10 in the world. The resort can only be accessed by private boat from Leeward Marina. ⌕ *Box 164, Providenciales* ☎ *649/946–7788* ☐ *649/946–7789* ⊕ *www.parrot-cay.com* ↪ *58 rooms* ♿ *2 restaurants, room service, in-room data ports, in-room safes, some kitchens, some kitchenettes, minibars, cable TV with movies, in-room VCRs, 2 tennis courts, pool, gym, hot tub, Japanese baths, sauna, spa, Turkish bath, beach, snorkeling, windsurfing, boating, waterskiing, fishing, mountain bikes, 2 bars, library, baby-sitting, laundry service* ▤ *AE, MC, V* ◯| *BP.*

Pine Cay

One of a chain of small cays linking North Caicos and Provo, 800-acre Pine Cay is where you'll find the Meridian Club—a retreat for people seeking peaceful seclusion. Its 2½-mi (4-km) beach is among the most beautiful in the archipelago. The island has a 3,800-ft airstrip and electric golf carts for getting around. Offshore is the **Football Fields** dive site, which has been called the Grand Central Station of the fish world.

Where to Stay

For approximate costs, *see* the dining and lodging price chart at the beginning of this chapter.

★ **$$$$**
⊞ Meridian Club. Here you can enjoy an unspoiled cay with vast stretches of soft, white sand and a 500-acre nature reserve that lures bird-watchers and botanists. A stay here is truly getting away from it all, as there are no air-conditioners, phones, or TVs. Accommodations are in spacious rooms with king-size beds and patios, as well as cottages that range from rustic to well appointed. Meals and activities are included in the room rate, as is your boat or air-taxi trip from Provo. ⊠ *Pine Cay* ☎ *800/ 331–9154; 203/602–0300 for reservations only* ☐ *649/941–7010 direct to hotel; 203/602–2265 U.S. reservations number* ⊕ *www. meridianclub.com* ↪ *12 rooms, 38 cottages* ♿ *Restaurant, bar, fans, pool, beach, snorkeling, windsurfing, boating, fishing, bicycles, hiking, tennis court, library, airstrip; no a/c, no room phones, no room TVs, no kids under 12* ▤ *No credit cards* ◯| *AI.*

North Caicos

Thanks to abundant rainfall, this 41-square-mi (106-square-km) island is the lushest of the Turks and Caicos. Bird lovers can see a large flock of flamingos here, and fishermen can find shallow creeks full of bonefish. Bring all your own gear; this quiet island has no water-sports shops. Although there's no traffic, almost all the roads are paved, so bi-cycling is an excellent way to sightsee.

Where to Stay

For approximate costs, *see* the dining and lodging price chart at the beginning of this chapter.

★ $$$-$$$$ 🏨 **Prospect of Whitby Hotel.** This secluded, all-inclusive retreat is run by an Italian resort chain, Club Vacanze. Miles of beach are yours for sunbathing, windsurfing, or snorkeling. Spacious rooms have elegant Tuscan floor tiles and pastel pink paneling; in true chic getaway fashion, rooms lack TVs but include minibars. The restaurant, on a verandah overlooking the sea, is excellent, with a selection of local, Italian, and international dishes served buffet style. Scuba diving and daily excursions to nearby natural wonders are included. ⊠ *Whitby* ☎ *649/946–7119* 🖷 *649/946–7114* ⊕ *www.prospectofwhitby.com* ☜ *24 rooms, 4 suites* ⚅ *Restaurant, in-room safes, minibars, tennis court, pool, beach, dive shop, snorkeling, windsurfing, boating, fishing, bicycles, bar, piano bar; no room TVs* ▤ *AE, MC, V* ⏐◯⏐ *AI.*

$-$$ 🏨 **Ocean Beach Hotel Condominiums.** This unpretentious place provides family-style accommodations on a 10-mi (16-km) stretch of sheltered beach. The spacious units, with full kitchens, face the ocean and are cooled by the constant trade winds. You can learn about local plants from the botanical walk encircling the premises. Tasty meals, featuring local seafood and homemade breads and desserts, are served in the common dining room. Diving, snorkeling, and exploring trips are arranged through Beach Cruiser Charters, at the hotel. ⊠ *Whitby* ☎ *649/946–7113 or 800/710–5204; 905/690–3817 in Canada* 🖷 *649/946–7386* ⊕ *www.turksandcaicos.tc/oceanbeach* ☜ *3 rooms, 7 suites* ⚅ *Restaurant, bar, fans, kitchenettes, pool, beach, dive shop, snorkeling, boating, fishing, bicycles, car rental; no a/c* ▤ *AE, MC, V* ⊙ *Closed June–Oct.* ⏐◯⏐ *EP.*

$-$$ 🏨 **Pelican Beach Hotel.** Built and operated by Clifford Gardiner (the Islands' first licensed solo pilot) and his family, this laid-back hotel fronts beautiful expanses of deserted, windswept beach. Large rooms are done in pastels and dark-wood trim; the sound of breaking waves will soothe you in the first-floor beachfront units. Excellent local dishes and homemade bread are served in the airy dining room shaded by a grove of whispering casuarina pines. ⊠ *Whitby* ☎ *649/946–7112* 🖷 *649/946–7139* ☜ *14 rooms, 2 suites* ⚅ *Restaurant, beach, snorkeling, fishing, bar; no room TVs* ▤ *MC, V* ⏐◯⏐ *EP.*

Beaches

The beaches of North Caicos are superb for shelling and lolling, and the waters offshore have excellent snorkeling and scuba diving.

Exploring North Caicos

Numbers in the margin correspond to points of interest on the Turks & Caicos Island map.

⑤ Flamingo Pond. This is a regular nesting place for the beautiful pink birds. They tend to wander out in the middle of the pond, so bring binoculars.

⑥ Kew. This settlement has a small post office, a school, a church, and ruins of old plantations—all set among lush tropical trees bearing limes, papayas, and custard apples. Visiting Kew will give you a better understanding of the daily life of many islanders.

⑦ Wades Green. Visitors can view well-preserved ruins of the great house, overseer's house, and surrounding walls of one of the most successful plantations of the loyalist era. A lookout tower provides views for miles. Contact the National Trust for tour details. ⊠ *Kew* ☎ *649/941–5710.*

Middle Caicos

At 48 square mi (124 square km) and with fewer than 300 residents, this is the largest and least developed of the inhabited Turks and Caicos. A limestone ridge runs to about 125 ft above sea level, creating dramatic cliffs on the north shore and a cave system farther inland. Middle Caicos is best suited to those looking to unwind and who enjoy nature.

Where to Stay

For approximate costs, *see* the dining and lodging price chart at the beginning of this chapter.

$$ 🏨 **Blue Horizon Resort.** Breathtaking scenery and sweet seclusion abound in this 50-acre retreat. Cottages (and two villas) come in several sizes; all have screened-in porches, bleached-wood furniture, comfortable beds, and spectacular views of the beachfront cliff, where there's a hillside cave and private swimming cove. Fax a (basic) grocery list ahead of time, and management will stock your refrigerator. Activities by request include spelunking, fishing, and snorkeling with local guides. ⊠ *Mudjin Harbor, Conch Bar* ☎ *649/946–6141* 🖷 *649/946–6139* ⊕ *www.bhresort.com* ⊅ *5 cottages, 2 villas* ♨ *Fans, some kitchenettes, refrigerators, cable TV with movies, beach, snorkeling, fishing, bicycles, hiking, laundry service; no a/c in some rooms, no phones in some rooms, no TV in some rooms* ⊟ *AE, MC, V* ⦿ *EP.*

Exploring Middle Caicos

Numbers in the margin correspond to points of interest on the Turks & Caicos Island map.

❽ Conch Bar Caves. These limestone caves have eerie underground lakes and milky-white stalactites and stalagmites. Archaeologists have discovered Lucayan Indian artifacts in the caves and the surrounding area. It's an easy walk through the main part of the cave, but wear sturdy shoes to avoid slipping. You'll hear, see, and smell some bats, but they don't bother visitors. J&B Tours in Providenciales offers boat trips to the caves from Provo (*see* Sightseeing Tours *in* Turks & Caicos A to Z).

South Caicos

This 8½-square-mi (21-square-km) island was once an important salt producer; today it's the heart of the fishing industry. Nature prevails, with long, white beaches, jagged bluffs, quiet backwater bays, and salt flats. Diving and snorkeling on the pristine wall and reefs are a treat enjoyed by only a few.

Where to Stay

For approximate costs, *see* the dining and lodging price chart at the beginning of this chapter.

$$ 🏨 **South Caicos Ocean Haven.** On Cockburn Harbour, a protected marine sanctuary, this hotel operates as the base from which divers can discover a pristine underwater paradise minutes from the dock. Comfortable, air-conditioned rooms are oceanside; evenings bring spectacular sunsets over the harbor. The restaurant emphasizes local seafood. Instructors on staff offer PADI courses, with economical dive packages available. ⊠ *West St., Cockburn Harbour* ☎ *649/946–3444* 🖷 *649/946–3446* ⊕ *www.oceanhaven.tc* ⊅ *22 rooms* ♨ *Restaurant, saltwater pool, beach, dive shop, snorkeling, windsurfing, boating, fishing, bar* ⊟ *MC, V* ⦿ *AI.*

Beaches

Due south of South Caicos is **Big Ambergris Cay,** an uninhabited cay about 14 mi (23 km) beyond the Fish Cays, with a magnificent beach at Long Bay. To the north of South Caicos, uninhabited **East Caicos** has a beautiful 17-mi (27-km) beach on its north coast. The island was once a cattle range and the site of a major sisal-growing industry. Both places are accessible only by boat.

Exploring South Caicos

Numbers in the margin correspond to points of interest on the Turks & Caicos Island map.

At the northern end of the island are fine white-sand beaches; the south coast is great for scuba diving along the drop-off; and there's excellent snorkeling off the windward (east) coast, where large stands of elkhorn and staghorn coral shelter several varieties of small tropical fish. Spiny lobster and queen conch are found in the shallow Caicos Bank to the west, and are harvested for export by local processing plants. The bonefishing here is some of the best in the West Indies. **Beyond the Blue** (✉ Cockburn Harbour ☎ 649/231–1703 ⊕ www.beyondtheblue.com) offers bonefishing charters on a specialized airboat, which can operate in less than a foot of water.

⑨ Boiling Hole. Abandoned salinas make up the center of this island—the largest, across from the downtown ball park, receives its water directly from an underground source connected to the ocean through this boiling hole.

⑩ Cockburn Harbour. The best natural harbor in the Caicos chain hosts the South Caicos Regatta, held each year in May.

TURKS & CAICOS A TO Z

To research prices, get advice from other travelers, and book travel arrangements, visit www.fodors.com.

AIR TRAVEL

American Airlines flies three times daily between Miami and Provo, Thursdays through Sundays between New York/JFK and Provo, and on Saturdays between Boston and Provo. US Airways flies on Mondays, Wednesdays, Fridays, and Saturdays between Charlotte and Provo. Delta Air Lines travels on Saturdays between Atlanta and Provo. British Airways connects London/Heathrow and Provo on Sundays. Air Canada flies between Toronto and Provo on Saturdays. Bahamasair flies between Nassau and Provo on Tuesdays, Thursdays, and Sundays. Air Jamaica Express travels between Provo and Montego Bay daily except Wednesdays. Turks & Caicos Airways, the national flag carrier, offers regularly scheduled flights between Provo, Grand Turk, and the outer Turks and Caicos Islands. SkyKing connects Provo with Grand Turk and South Caicos several times daily and also offers flights to Cuba, the Dominican Republic, and Haiti. Additionally, in season there are weekly charter flights from a number of North American cities, including Boston, Chicago, Detroit, New York, Philadelphia, Montréal, and Toronto.
🛪 Air Canada ☎ 888/247-2262 or 800/361-8071. Air Jamaica Express ☎ 800/523-5585. American Airlines ☎ 649/946-4948. Bahamasair ☎ 649/946-4999 or 800/222-4262. British Airways ☎ 649/941-3352 or 800/247-9297. Delta Air Lines ☎ 800/241-4141. SkyKing ☎ 649/941-5464. Turks & Caicos Airways ☎ 649/946-4255. US Airways ☎ 800/622-1015.

AIRPORTS

All international flights arrive at Providenciales International Airport. Then you use domestic carriers to fly on to airports in Grand Turk and the out islands of North Caicos, Middle Caicos, South Caicos, and Salt Cay. All have paved runways in good condition. Providenciales International Airport has modern, secure arrival and check-in services. You'll find taxis at the airports, and most resorts provide pickup service. A trip between Provo's airport and most major hotels runs about $15. On Grand Turk a trip from the airport to Cockburn Town is about $5; it's $5–$8 to hotels outside town.

For private planes, Provo Air Center is a full service FBO (Fixed Base Operator) offering refueling, maintenance, and short-term storage, as well as on-site customs and immigration clearance, a lounge, and concierge services.

🔁 **Grand Turk International Airport** ☎ 649/946–2233. **Providenciales International Airport** ☎ 649/941–5670. **Provo Air Center** ☎ 649/946–4181 ⊕ www.provoaircenter.com.

BIKE & MOPED TRAVEL

Although scooters and bicycles are available for rental on Provo, the option has dwindled in popularity with the deteriorating condition of the roads and an increase in auto traffic. If you choose to ride a scooter or bicycle, take extra care around steep shoulder drop-offs. Scooter Bob's in Providenciales rents double-seater scooters and bicycles (as well as jeeps, SUVs, vans, and cars). Rates are $40 per day for scooters and $20 per day for bicycles.

🔁 **Bike & Moped Rentals Scooter Bob's** ✉ Turtle Cove Marina, Turtle Cove ☎ 649/946–4684.

BOAT & FERRY TRAVEL

Surprisingly, there is no scheduled boat or ferry service between Provo and the other Turks and Caicos Islands. Instead, islanders tend to catch rides leaving from the marina at Leeward-Going-Through.

BUSINESS HOURS

BANKS Banks are open Monday–Thursday 9 to 3, Friday 9 to 5.

POST OFFICES Post offices are open weekdays from 8 to 4.

SHOPS Shops are generally open weekdays from 8 or 8:30 to 5.

CAR RENTALS

Car- and jeep-rental rates average $35–$80 per day, plus a $15-per-rental-agreement government tax. Reserve well ahead of time during the peak winter season. Most agencies offer free mileage and airport pickup service. Tony's Car Rental is the only player on Grand Turk. Several agencies, including Avis, Budget, Provo Rent-a-Car, Rent a Buggy, and Tropical Auto Rentals, operate on Provo.

🔁 **Avis** ☎ 649/946–4705. **Budget** ☎ 649/946–4079. **Provo Rent-a-Car** ☎ 649/946–4404 ⊕ www.provo.net/rentacar. **Rent a Buggy** ☎ 649/946–4158 ⊕ www.rentabuggy. tc. **Tony's Car Rental** ☎ 649/231–1806. **Tropical Auto Rentals** ☎ 649/946–5300 ⊕ www.provo.net/TropicalAuto.

CAR TRAVEL

GASOLINE Gasoline is expensive, running around $3 per gallon.

ROAD CONDITIONS There are paved, two-lane roads connecting the resort areas, airport, and major settlements on Providenciales. However, they're often pocked with potholes and have steep shoulder drop-offs. A major road rehabilitation project is reportedly in the making. Dusty, rutted side roads are in worse condition. Ironically, the little-traveled roads in Grand Turk and the out islands are, in general, smooth and paved.

RULES OF THE ROAD Driving here is on the left side of the road, British style; when pulling out into traffic, remember to look to your right. The maximum speed is 40 mph, 20 mph through settlements, and limits, as well as the use of seat belts, are enforced.

ELECTRICITY

Electricity is fairly stable throughout the islands, and the current is suitable for all U.S. appliances (120/240 volts, 60 Hz).

EMERGENCIES

Ambulance & Fire **Ambulance and Fire** ☎ 999 or 911.

Hospitals **Associated Medical Practices** ✉ Leeward Hwy., Glass Shack, Providenciales ☎ 649/946-4242. **Grand Turk Hospital** ✉ Hospital Rd., Grand Turk ☎ 649/946-2333.

Pharmacies **Grand Turk Hospital** ✉ Grand Turk Hospital, Grand Turk ☎ 649/946-2040. **Grace Bay Medical Center** ✉ Neptune Plaza, Grace Bay, Providenciales ☎ 649/941-5252.

Police **Police Emergencies** ☎ 649/946-2499 in Grand Turk; 649/946-7116 in North Caicos; 649/946-4259 in Provo; 649/946-3299 in South Caicos.

Scuba Diving Emergencies **Associated Medical Practices** ✉ Leeward Hwy., Glass Shack, Providenciales ☎ 649/946-4242.

HOLIDAYS

Public holidays are: New Year's Day, Commonwealth Day (second Monday in March), Good Friday, Easter Monday, National Heroes Day (last Monday in May), Queen's Birthday (third Monday in June), Emancipation Day (first Monday in August), National Youth Day (last Monday in September), Columbus Day (second Monday in October), International Human Rights Day (last Monday in October), Christmas Day, and Boxing Day (Dec. 26).

LANGUAGE

The official language of the Turks and Caicos is English. Native islanders (termed "Belongers") are of African descent, though the population—especially on cosmopolitan Provo—also consists of Canadian, British, American, European, Haitian, and Dominican expats.

MAIL & SHIPPING

The post office is in downtown Provo at the corner of Airport Road. Collectors will be interested in the wide selection of stamps sold by the Philatelic Bureau. It costs 50¢ to send a postcard to the United States, 60¢ to Canada and the United Kingdom, and $1.25 to Australia and New Zealand; letters, per ½ ounce, cost 60¢ to the United States, 80¢ to Canada and the United Kingdom, and $1.40 to Australia and New Zealand. When writing to the Turks and Caicos Islands, be sure to include the specific island and "Turks and Caicos Islands, BWI" (British West Indies). Delivery service is provided by FedEx, with offices in Provo and Grand Turk.

FedEx ☎ 649/946-2542 on Grand Turk; 649/946-4682 on Provo. **Philatelic Bureau** ☎ 649/946-1534.

MONEY MATTERS

Prices quoted in this chapter are in U.S. dollars. Barclays Bank, Scotiabank and CIBC have offices on Provo, with branches on Grand Turk. Many larger hotels and the casino can take care of your money requests. Bring small denominations to the less-populated islands.

Barclays Bank ☎ 649/946-4245. **CIBC** ☎ 649/946-5303. **Scotiabank** ☎ 649/946-4750.

ATMS There are few ATMs on the islands.

CREDIT CARDS Major credit cards and traveler's checks are accepted at many establishments.

CURRENCY The unit of currency is the U.S. dollar.

PASSPORTS & VISAS

U.S. and Canadian citizens need some proof of citizenship, such as a birth certificate (original or certified copy), plus a photo I.D. or a current passport. All other travelers, including those from the United Kingdom, Australia, and New Zealand, require a current passport. Everyone must have an ongoing or return ticket.

SAFETY

Although crime is not a major concern in the Turks & Caicos Islands, petty crime does occur here, and you're advised to leave your valuables in the hotel safe-deposit box and lock doors in cars and rooms when unattended.

SIGHTSEEING TOURS

Whether by taxi, boat, or plane, you should try to venture beyond your resort's grounds and beach. Global Airways specializes in trips to North Caicos. If you want to island-hop on your own schedule, air charters are available through Inter-Island Airways. Nell's Taxi offers taxi tours of the islands, priced between $25 and $30 for the first hour and $25 for each additional hour. J&B Tours offers sea and land tours, including trips to Middle Caicos, the largest of the islands, for a visit to the caves, or to North Caicos to see flamingos and plantation ruins. Aerial photo safaris are provided by Provo Air Charter.

🔰 **Global Airways** ☎ 649/941-3222. **Inter-Island Airways** ☎ 649/941-5481 🌐 www. interislandairways.com. **J&B Tours** ☎ 649/946-5047 🌐 www.jbtours.com. **Nell's Taxi** ☎ 649/231-0051. **Provo Air Charter** ☎ 649/941-0685.

TAXES & SERVICE CHARGES

DEPARTURE TAX The departure tax is $23, payable only in cash or traveler's checks.

SALES TAX Hotels add 10%–15% to your bill for service, and restaurants and hotels add a 10% government tax.

TAXIS

Cabs (actually large vans) are now metered, and rates are regulated by the government at $2 per person per mile traveled. In Provo call the Provo Taxi and Bus Group for more information. Many resorts and car-rental agencies offer complimentary airport transfers. Ask ahead of time.

🔰 **Provo Taxi and Bus Group** ☎ 649/946-5481.

TELEPHONES

All telephone service is provided by Cable & Wireless. Many U.S.–based cell phones work on the islands; use your own or rent one from Cable & Wireless. Internet access is available via hotel-room phone connections or Internet kiosks on Provo and Grand Turk. You can also connect to the World Wide Web from any telephone line by dialing C-O-N-N-E-C-T to call Cable & Wireless and using the user name *easy* and the password *access*. Calls from the islands are expensive, and many hotels add steep surcharges for long-distance. Talk fast.

🔰 **Cable & Wireless** ☎ 649/946-2200; 800/744-7777 for long distance; 649/266-6328 for Internet access; 811 for mobile service 🌐 www.tcimall.tc.

AREA CODE The area code for the Turks and Caicos is 649. Just dial 1 plus the 10-digit number, including area code, from the U.S.

INTERNATIONAL CALLS To make calls from the Turks and Caicos, dial 0, then 1, the area code, and the number.

LOCAL CALLS To make local calls, dial the seven-digit number.

TIPPING

At restaurants, tip 15% if service isn't included in the bill. Taxi drivers also expect a token tip, about 10% of your fare.

VISITOR INFORMATION

The Turks and Caicos Islands Tourist Board maintains a comprehensive Web site covering each of the islands. Another excellent source of information is TCISearch, which—besides all the basics and information about resorts, restaurants, and activities—includes weather information, maps, a business directory, downloadable postcards, and video clips and a helpful "chat" forum of island-related topics. Times Publications publishes a quarterly magazine on all aspects of life in the islands. Subscriptions are available.

🛪 Before You Leave **Turks and Caicos Islands Tourist Board** ⊕ www.turksandcaicostourism.com ⊠ 2715 E. Oakland Park Blvd., #101, Fort Lauderdale, FL 33316 ☎ 954/568-6588 or 800/241-0824. **TCISearch** ⊕ www.tcisearch.com.

🛪 In Turks & Caicos Islands **Government Tourist Board** ⊠ Front St., Cockburn Town, Grand Turk ☎ 649/946-2321 ⊠ Stubbs Diamond Plaza, The Bight, Providenciales ☎ 649/946-4970 **Times Publications** ⊕ www.timespub.tc.

UNITED STATES VIRGIN ISLANDS

FODOR'S CHOICE

Caneel Bay Resort, St. John

Carringtons Inn, a budget hotel in St. Croix

Historic Christiansted, St. Croix

Island View Guest House, a budget hotel in St. Thomas

Magens Bay Beach, St. Thomas

Playing on Mahogany Run Golf Course, St. Thomas

Ritz-Carlton Resort, St. Thomas

Shopping in St. Thomas

Skinny Legs Bar and Restaurant, a budget choice in St. John

Top Hat, a restaurant in Christiansted, St. Croix

Virgilio's, a restaurant in Charlotte Amalie, St. Thomas

Virgin Islands National Park, St. John

HIGHLY RECOMMENDED

HOTELS   Bed & Breakfast Caribbean Style, St. Thomas

Blazing Villas, St. Thomas

Hotel 1829, Charlotte Amalie, St. Thomas

Maho Bay Camps, St. John

Renaissance Grand Beach Resort, St. Thomas

The Anchorage, St. Thomas

Villa Madeleine, Teague Bay, St. Croix

Villa Santana, Charlotte Amalie, St. Thomas

Wyndham Sugar Bay, St. Thomas

Many other great places enliven this area. For other
favorites, look for the black stars as you read this chapter.

Mornings at Lillian's on St. Thomas aren't much different from those in coffee shops back home. A cop stops by to joke with the waitress and collect his first cup of coffee; a high-heeled secretary runs in for the paper and some toast; a store clerk lingers over a cup of tea to discuss politics with the cook. But is the coffee shop back home in a ballast-brick-walled 19th-century building, steps from a park abloom with frangipani—in January? Are bush tea and johnnycake served alongside oatmeal and omelets?

Updated by
Carol
Bareuther and
Lynda Lohr

It's the combination of the familiar and the exotic found in St. Thomas, St. Croix, and St. John—the United States Virgin Islands (USVI)—that defines this "American paradise" and explains much of its appeal. The effort to be all things to all people—while remaining true to the best of itself—has created a sometimes paradoxical blend of island serenity and American practicality in this U.S. territory 1,000 mi (1,600 km) from the southern tip of the U.S. mainland.

The images you'd expect from a tropical island are here: stretches of beach arc into the distance, and white sails skim across water so blue and clear it stuns the senses. Red-roofed houses color the green hillsides as do the orange of the flamboyant tree, the red of the hibiscus, the magenta of the bougainvillea, and the blue stone ruins of old sugar mills. Towns of pastel-tone villas decorated with filigree wrought-iron terraces line narrow streets that climb from the harbor. Amid all the images you can find moments of exquisite tranquillity: an egret standing in a pond at dawn, palm trees backlit by a full moon, sunrises and sunsets that send your spirits soaring with the frigate bird flying overhead.

Chances are that on one of the three islands you'll find your own idea of an ideal Caribbean vacation spot. Check into a beachfront condo on the east end of St. Thomas, eat burgers and watch football at a beachfront bar and grill. Or stay at an 18th-century plantation great house on St. Croix, dine on Danish delicacies, and go horseback riding at sunrise. Rent a tent or a cottage in the pristine national park on St. John, take a hike, kayak off the coast, read a book, or just listen to the sounds of the forest. Or dive deep into "island time" and learn the art of limin' (hanging out, Caribbean-style) on all three islands.

Idyllic though they may be, these bits of volcanic rock in the middle of the Caribbean Sea haven't entirely escaped such worries of overdevelopment as trash, crime, and traffic. Isolation and limited space have, in fact, accentuated these problems. What, for example, do you do with 76 million cans and bottles imported annually when the nearest recycling plant is across 1,000 mi (1,600 km) of ocean? Despite these dilemmas, wildlife has found refuge here. The brown pelican is on the endangered list worldwide but is a common sight in the USVI. The endangered native boa tree is protected, as is the hawksbill turtle, whose females lumber onto the beaches to lay eggs.

Preserving native culture while progressing as a tourist destination is another problem. The islands have been inhabited by Taíno Indians (on St. John and St. Thomas); Carib Indians (on St. Croix); Danish settlers and Spanish pirates; traders and invaders from all the European powers; Africans brought in as slaves; migrants from other Caribbean islands; and, finally, Americans, first as administrators, then as businesspeople and tourists. But the influence of America is creating a more homogeneous culture, and with each passing year the USVI lose more of their rich, spicy, Caribbean personality.

Sailing into the Caribbean on his second voyage in 1493, Christopher Columbus came upon St. Croix before the group of islands that would later be known as St. Thomas, St. John, and the British Virgin Islands (BVI). He named St. Croix "Santa Cruz" (called Ay Ay by the Carib Indians already living there), but moved on quickly after he encountered the fierce residents. As he approached St. Thomas and St. John he was impressed enough with the shapely silhouettes of the numerous islands and cays (including the BVI) to name them after Ursula and her 11,000 virgins, but he found the islands barren and moved on to explore Puerto Rico.

Over the next century, as it became clear that Spain couldn't defend the entire Caribbean, other European powers began to settle the islands. In the 1600s the French were joined by the Dutch and the English on St. Croix, and St. Thomas had a mixture of European residents in the early 1700s. By 1695 St. Croix was under the control of the French, but the colonists had moved on to what is today Haiti. The island lay virtually dormant until 1733, when the Danish government bought it—along with St. Thomas and St. John—from the Danish West India Company. At that time settlers from St. Thomas and St. John moved to St. Croix to cultivate the island's gentler terrain. St. Croix developed a plantation economy, but St. Thomas's soil was ill suited to agriculture. There the harbor became internationally known because of its size and ease of entry; it's still hailed as one of the most beautiful seaports in the world.

Plantations depended on slave labor, of which there was a plentiful supply in the Danish West Indies. As early as 1665, agreements between the Brandenburger Company (which needed a base in the West Indies from which to ship the slaves it had imported from Africa) and the West India Company (which needed the kind of quick cash it could collect in duties, fees, and rents from the slave trade) established St. Thomas as a primary slave market.

It's from the slaves who worked the plantations that most Virgin Islanders are descended. More than likely the sales clerk who sells you a watch and the waitress who serves your rum punch can trace their lineage to ancestors captured in Africa some 300 years ago and brought to the West Indies, where they were sold on the block, priced according to their comeliness and strength. Most were captured along Africa's Gold Coast, from the tribes of Asante, Ibo, Mandika, Amina, and Wolof. They brought with them African rhythms in music and language, herbal medicine, and such crafts as basketry and wood carving. The West Indian–African culture comes to full bloom at Carnival time, when playing *mas* (with abandon) takes precedence over all else.

Yet you can still see the influence of the early Danish settlers here, too. It's reflected in the language and architecture; in common surnames such as Petersen, Jeppesen, and Lawaetz; and in street names such as Kongen's Gade (King Street) and Kronprindsen's Gade (Prince Street). The town of Charlotte Amalie was named after a Danish queen. The Lutheran Church is the state church of Denmark, and Frederick Lutheran Church on St. Thomas dates from 1666. Other peoples have left their marks on the USVI as well. Jewish settlers came to the territory as early as 1665; they were shipowners, chandlers, and brokers in the slave trade. Today their descendants coexist with nearly 1,500 Arabs—95% of whom are Palestinian. There are also many East Indians, who are active members

United States
Virgin Islands

ATLANTIC OCEAN

BRITISH
VIRGIN ISLANDS

Jost van Dyke

TORTOLA
West End

Great Thatch
Island

Mary
Cinnamon
Bay

The Narrows

Cruz Bay   ST. JOHN

East End
Pt.

Long
Pt.

Privateer Pt.

Flanagan
Island

Salt
Pond
Bay

Reef
Bay

Great
St. James
Island

Little St. James
Island

Pillsbury
Sound

Red
Hook

Thatch Cay

Big Hans
Lollick

Loveland Bay

Nadir

Long
Pt.

Borowo
Bay

Frenchman
Bay

Picara Pt.

Magens
Bay

ST. THOMAS

Charlotte
Amalie

Water
Island

Inner
Brass

Dorothea

Brewers
Bay

Cyril E. King
International
Airport

Santa
Maria
Bay

Stumpy
Bay

Fortuna

David
Pt.

Britany
Bay

TO
PUERTO RICO

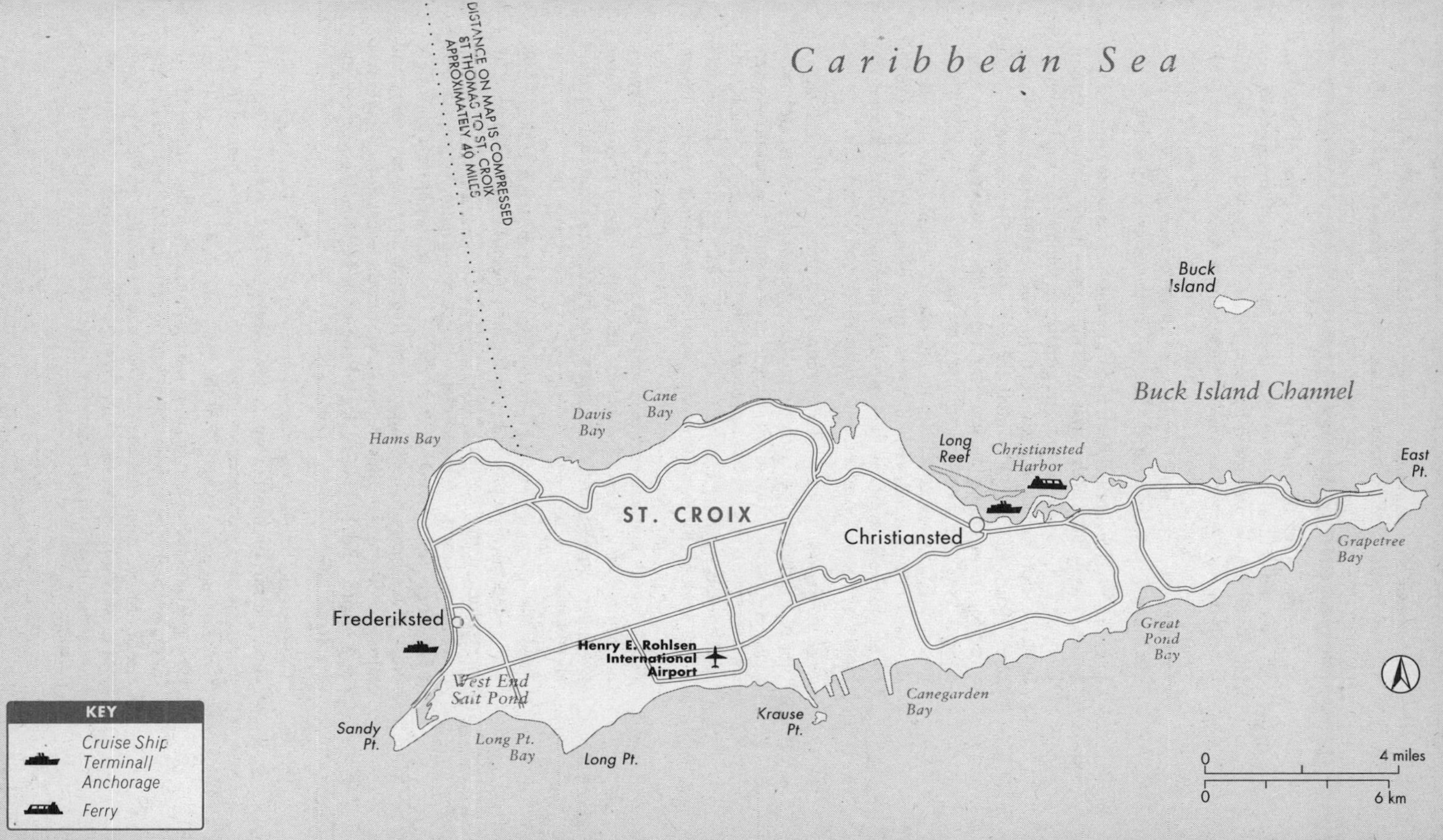

Caribbean Sea

Buck Island Channel

East Pt.

Grapetree Bay

Great Pond Bay

Buck Island

Long Reef

Christiansted Harbor

Canegarden Bay

Christiansted

Krause Pt.

ST. CROIX

Cane Bay

Davis Bay

Henry E. Rohlsen International Airport

Long Pt.

Hams Bay

West End Salt Pond

Long Pt. Bay

DISTANCE ON MAP IS COMPRESSED
ST THOMAS TO ST. CROIX
APPROXIMATELY 40 MILES

Frederiksted

Sandy Pt.

4 miles

6 km

KEY

Cruise Ship
Terminal/
Anchorage

Ferry

of the business community. Immigrants from Puerto Rico and the Dominican Republic make up close to half of St. Croix's population. Transplants from Caribbean countries to the south continue to arrive, seeking better economic opportunities.

St. Thomas, St. Croix, and St. John were known collectively as the Danish West Indies until the United States bought the territory in 1917 during World War I, prompted by fears that Germany would establish a U-boat base in the western hemisphere. The name was changed to the United States Virgin Islands, and almost immediately thereafter British-held Tortola and Virgin Gorda—previously known simply as the Virgin Islands—hastily inserted "British" on the front of their name.

In the 1960s, Pineapple Beach Resort (today Renaissance Grand Beach Resort) was built on St. Thomas, and the Caneel Bay Resort on St. John, built in 1956, was expanded; and with direct flights from the U.S. mainland, the tourism industry was born. In 1960 the total population of all three islands was 32,000. Today there are about 50,000 people living on 32-square-mi (83-square-km) St. Thomas (about the same size as Manhattan), 51,000 on the 84 square mi (216 square km) of pastoral St. Croix, and about 5,000 on 20-square-mi (52-square-km) St. John, two-thirds of which is a national park. The per capita income in the USVI is the highest in the West Indies. Just over 25% of the total labor force is employed by the government, and about 10% work in tourism.

Agriculture hasn't been a major economic factor since the last sugarcane plantation on St. Croix ceased operating in the 1960s, and today most foods are imported. The islands' cuisine reflects a tradition where root vegetables such as sweet potato, slave rations of cornmeal, and stick-to-your-ribs breads were staples 200 years ago. Their influence is still evident in the sweet-potato stuffing (mashed potatoes, spices, and raisins), *fungi* (cornmeal and okra), and johnnycakes (deep-fried dough rounds made of cornmeal and white flour) that are ever-present on menus today. Beverages include not only rum but coconut water, fruit juices, and *maubi*, made from tree bark, and reputedly a virility enhancer.

The backbone of the economy is tourism, but at the heart of the islands is an independent, separate being: a rollicking hodgepodge of West Indian culture with a sense of humor that puts sex and politics in almost every conversation. Lacking a major-league sports team, Virgin Islanders follow the activities and antics of their 15 elected senators with the rabidity of Washingtonians following the Redskins. Loyalty to country and faith in God are the rules in the USVI, not the exceptions. Prayer is a way of life, and ROTC is one of the most popular high-school extracurricular activities.

The struggle to preserve the predominantly black Caribbean-influenced culture is heating up in the Virgin Islands. Native Virgin Islanders say they want access to more than just the beach when big money brings in big development. But the three islands are far from united in their goals, especially in light of a $1 billion deficit that threatens the autonomy of the local government and protection of the territory's number-one resource—scenic beauty. The ongoing conflict between progress and preservation here is no mere philosophical exercise, and attempts at resolutions display yet another aspect of the islands' unique blend of character.

WHAT IT COSTS In U.S. dollars				
$$$$	**$$$**	**$$**	**$**	**¢**
RESTAURANTS*				
over $30	$20–$30	$12–$20	$8–$12	under $8
HOTELS**				
Cost EP/BP/CP over $350	$250–$350	$150–$250	$80–$150	under $80
Cost AI over $450	$350–$450	$250–$350	$125–$250	under $125

*Restaurant prices are for a main course at dinner. **EP, BP, and CP prices are per night for a standard double room in high season, excluding taxes, service charges, and meal plans. AI (all-inclusive) prices are per person, per night based on double-occupancy during high season, excluding taxes and service charges.

ST. THOMAS

Updated by
Carol
Bareuther

If you fly to the 32-square-mi (83-square-km) island of St. Thomas, you land at its western end; if you arrive by cruise ship, you come into one of the world's most beautiful harbors. Either way, one of your first sights is the town of Charlotte Amalie. From the harbor you see an idyllic-looking village that spreads into the lower hills. If you were expecting a quiet hamlet with its inhabitants hanging out under palm trees, you've missed that era by about 300 years. Although other islands in the USVI developed plantation economies, St. Thomas cultivated its harbor, and it became a thriving seaport soon after it was settled by the Danish in the 1600s.

The success of the naturally perfect harbor was enhanced by the fact that the Danes—who ruled St. Thomas with only a couple of short interruptions from 1666 to 1917—avoided involvement in some 100 years' worth of European wars. Denmark was the only European country with colonies in the Caribbean to stay neutral during the War of the Spanish Succession in the early 1700s. Thus, products of the Dutch, English, and French islands—sugar, cotton, and indigo—were traded through Charlotte Amalie, along with the regular shipments of slaves. When the Spanish wars ended, trade fell off, but by the end of the 1700s Europe was at war again, Denmark again remained neutral, and St. Thomas continued to prosper. Even into the 1800s, while the economies of St. Croix and St. John foundered with the market for sugarcane, St. Thomas's economy remained strong. This prosperity led to the development of shipyards, a well-organized banking system, and a large merchant class. In 1845 Charlotte Amalie had 101 large importing houses owned by the English, French, Germans, Haitians, Spaniards, Americans, Sephardim, and Danes.

Charlotte Amalie is still one of the most active cruise-ship ports in the world. On almost any day at least one and sometimes as many as eight cruise ships are tied to the dock or anchored outside the harbor. Gently rocking in the shadows of these giant floating hotels are just about every other kind of vessel imaginable: sleek sailing mono- and multi-hulls that will take you on a sunset cruise complete with rum punch and a Jimmy Buffett soundtrack, private megayachts that spirit busy executives away, and barnacle-bottom sloops—with laundry draped to dry over the lifelines—that are home to world-cruising gypsies. Huge container ships pull up in Sub Base, west of the harbor, bringing in everything from cornflakes to tires. Anchored right along the waterfront are picturesque down-island barges that ply the waters between the Greater Antilles and the Leeward Islands, transporting goods like refrigerators, VCRs, and disposable diapers.

The waterfront road through Charlotte Amalie was once part of the harbor. Before it was filled to build the highway, the beach came right up to the back door of the warehouses that now line the thoroughfare. Two hundred years ago those warehouses contained indigo, tobacco, and cotton. Today the stone buildings house silk, crystal, linens, and leather. Exotic fragrances are still traded—but by island beauty queens in air-conditioned perfume palaces instead of through open market stalls. The pirates of old used St. Thomas as a base from which to raid merchant ships of every nation, though they were particularly fond of the gold- and silver-laden treasure ships heading to Spain. Pirates are still around, but today's versions use St. Thomas as a drop-off for their contraband: illegal immigrants and drugs.

Where to Stay

Of the USVI, St. Thomas has the most rooms and the greatest number and variety of resorts. You can let yourself be pampered at a luxurious resort—albeit at a price of from $300 to more than $500 per night, not including meals. If your means are more modest, there are fine hotels (often with rooms that have a kitchen and a living area) in lovely settings throughout the island. There are also guest houses and inns with great views (if not a beach at your door) and great service at about half the cost of the beachfront pleasure palaces. Learn more about these properties from the St. Thomas–St. John Hotel & Tourism Association. Many of these are east and north of Charlotte Amalie or overlooking hills—ideal if you plan to get out and mingle with the locals. There are also inexpensive lodgings (most right in town) that are perfect if you just want a clean room to return to after a day of exploring or beachbumming.

Families often stay at an east end condominium complex. Although condos are pricey (winter rates average $350 per night for a two-bedroom unit, which usually sleeps six), they have full kitchens, and you can definitely save money by cooking for yourself—especially if you bring your own nonperishable foodstuffs. (Virtually everything on St. Thomas is imported, and restaurants and shops pass shipping costs on to you.) Though you may spend some time laboring in the kitchen, many condos ease your burden with daily maid service and on-site restaurants; a few also have resort amenities, including pools and tennis courts. The east end is convenient to St. John, and it's a hub for the boating crowd, with some good restaurants. The prices below reflect rates in high season, which runs from December 15 to April 15. Rates are 25% to 50% lower the rest of the year.

Hotels

CHARLOTTE
AMALIE
$$

🏖 **Best Western Emerald Beach Resort.** On a white-sand beach across from the airport, this mini-resort has the feel of its much larger east-end cousins. Each room in the four pink three-story buildings has its own terrace or balcony, palms, and colorful flowers that frame an ocean view. Rooms have modern tropical prints and rattan furniture. A minus: the noise from nearby jets taking off and landing can be heard intermittently over a three-hour period each afternoon. ✉ *8070 Lindberg Bay, 00802* 🕿 *340/777–8800 or 800/233–4936* 🖷 *340/776–3426* ⊕ *www.emeraldbeach.com* ➦ *90 rooms* ♨ *Restaurant, in-room data ports, refrigerators, tennis courts, pool, gym, beach, boating, volleyball, bar; no room TVs* ▤ *AE, D, MC, V* ⼀ *CP.*

$$ ⌂ **Bluebeard's Castle.** Though not exactly a castle, this large red-roofed complex offers kingly comforts on a steep hill above town. All rooms, many of which are rented as timeshares, are air-conditioned and have terraces. The hotel is a short ride from the shops of Charlotte Amalie and Havensight Mall, and there's free transportation to Magens Bay Beach and to town. Its sister property, Bluebeard's Beach Club & Villas, is directly on Limetree Beach. ⊠ *Bluebeard's Hill ⌂ Box 7480, 00801* ☎ *340/774–1600 or 800/524–6599* 🖶 *340/774–5134* 🛏 *170 rooms* 🍴 *3 restaurants, minibars, 2 tennis courts, pool, gym, bar, shops, concierge, meeting rooms, car rental* ☰ *AE, D, DC, MC, V* ⎮○⎮ *EP.*

$$ ⌂ **Holiday Inn St. Thomas.** This harborfront property is comfortable for business travelers as well as vacationers who want to be close to the duty-free shopping. Contemporarily furnished rooms have such amenities as coffeemakers, hair dryers, ironing boards, and irons. A daily beach shuttle and an introductory dive lesson are also complimentary. ⊠ *Waterfront Hwy. ⌂ Box 640, 00804* ☎ *340/774–5200 or 800/524–7389* 🖶 *340/774–1231* ⊕ *www.holidayinn.st-thomas.com* 🛏 *140 rooms, 11 suites* 🍴 *2 restaurants, room service, in-room data ports, in-room safes, refrigerators, room TVs with movies and video games, pool, gym, hair salon, dive shop, bar, shops, laundry service, business services, meeting rooms, car rental* ☰ *AE, D, DC, MC, V* ⎮○⎮ *EP.*

★ **$–$$** ⌂ **Hotel 1829.** This historic Spanish-style inn is popular with visiting officials conducting business at Government House down the street. Rooms, on several levels (no elevator), range from elegant and roomy to quite small, but are priced accordingly. Author Graham Greene is said to have stayed here, and it's easy to imagine him musing over a drink in the small, dark bar. The second-floor botanical gardens and open-air champagne bar make a romantic spot for sunset viewing. The shops of Charlotte Amalie are within walking distance. ⊠ *Government Hill ⌂ Box 1567, 00804* ☎ *340/776–1829 or 800/524–2002* 🖶 *340/776–4313* ⊕ *www.hotel1829.com* 🛏 *14 rooms* 🍴 *Refrigerators, pool, bar; no room phones* ☰ *AE, D, MC, V* ⎮○⎮ *CP.*

$–$$ ⌂ **Inn at Blackbeard's Castle.** This cozy hilltop inn is laid out around a tower from which, it's said, Blackbeard kept watch for invaders sailing into Charlotte Amalie harbor. Mahogany furnishings, including four-poster beds, lend a 17th-century feel to the place, yet each room has many modern conveniences. ⊠ *Blackbeard's Hill ⌂ Box 6227, 00804* ☎ *340/776–1234 or 800/334–5771* 🖶 *340/776–4521* ⊕ *www.blackbeardscastle.com* 🛏 *16 rooms* 🍴 *Restaurant, fans, pool, bar; no room phones* ☰ *AE, D, DC, MC, V* ⎮○⎮ *CP.*

★ **$–$$** ⌂ **Villa Santana.** Built by General Santa Anna of Mexico, this six-villa landmark (circa 1857) still provides a panoramic view of the harbor and plenty of West Indian charm. Dark-wood furniture, plaster-and-stone walls, shuttered windows, cathedral ceilings, four-poster or cradle beds, and interesting nooks contribute to the sense of romance and history. Villas La Torre and La Mansion are split-level quarters with spiral staircases. ⊠ *2D Denmark Hill, 00802* ☎ *340/776–1311* 🖶 *340/776–1311* ⊕ *www.st-thomas.com/villasantana* 🛏 *6 rooms* 🍴 *Fans, kitchenettes, pool, croquet; no a/c in some rooms, no room phones* ☰ *AE* ⎮○⎮ *CP.*

$ ⌂ **Island View Guest House.** In tropical foliage 545 ft up on the face of Crown Mountain, this simply furnished bed-and-breakfast offers sweeping views of Charlotte Amalie harbor from the pool and shaded terraces. Continental breakfast is served daily; however, six rooms have kitchenettes. The friendly office staff can arrange tours. ⊠ *Rte. 332, Estate Contant ⌂ Box 1903, 00801* ☎ *340/774–4270 or 800/524–2023* 🖶 *340/774–6167* ⊕ *www.st-thomas.com/islandviewguesthouse* 🛏 *15 rooms* 🍴 *Fans, kitchenettes, pool; no a/c, no kids under 14* ☰ *AE, MC, V* ⎮○⎮ *CP.*

Fodor's Choice ★

St. Thomas

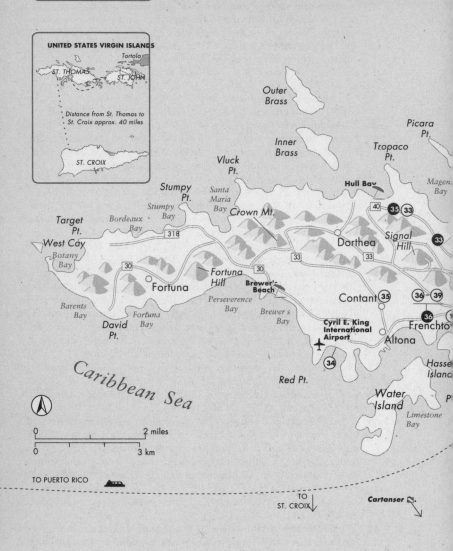

UNITED STATES VIRGIN ISLANDS

Tortola

ST. THOMAS

ST. JOHN

Distance from St. Thomas to
St. Croix approx. 40 miles

ST. CROIX

Outer
Brass

Inner
Brass

Picara
Pt.

Tropaco
Pt.

Vluck
Pt.

Hull Bay

Magen
Bay

Stumpy
Pt.

Santa
Maria
Bay

Crown Mt.

40 · 35 · 33

Stumpy
Bay

Bordeaux
Bay

Dorthea

Signal
Hill

33

Target
Pt.

318

33

33

West Cay

Botany
Bay

30

Fortuna
Hill

30

Brewer's
Beach

Contant · 35

36 — 39

Fortuna

36

Perseverence
Bay

Frenchto

Barents
Bay

Fortuna
Bay

Brewer s
Bay

Cyril E. King
International
Airport

Altona

David
Pt.

Hasse
Island

Caribbean Sea

Red Pt.

34

Water
Island

P

Limestone
Bay

0 ——— 2 miles
0 ——— 3 km

TO PUERTO RICO

TO
ST. CROIX

Cartanser

KEY

- ⚓ Beaches
- 🚢 Cruise Ship Terminal
- 🔲 Dive Sites
- ① Exploring Sights
- ⚓ Ferry
- ① Hotels & Restaurants

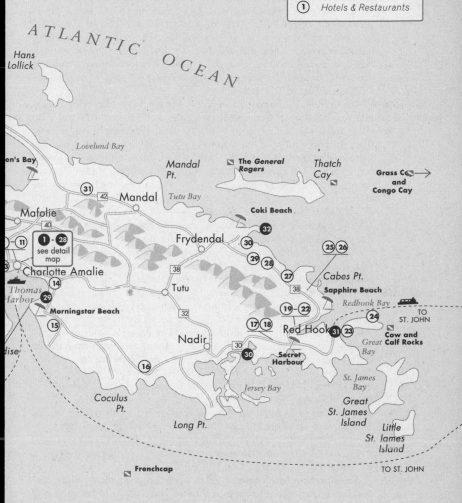

ATLANTIC OCEAN

Hans Lollick

en's Bay

Loveland Bay

Mandal Pt.

🔲 **The General Rogers**

Thatch Cay

Grass C◁→ and Congo Cay

③① 42 Mandal

Tutu Bay

Coki Beach

Mafolie

40

① · ㉘ see detail map

⑪

Frydendal

㉜

㉚

㉙ ㉘

㉗

⑬

Charlotte Amalie

⑭

Thomas Harbor

㉙

Morningstar Beach

Tutu

38

⑮

Nadir

30

㉚

25 26

Cabes Pt.

Sapphire Beach

Redhook Bay

TO ST. JOHN

⑲-㉒

㉔

Cow and Calf Rocks

⑰ ⑱

Red Hook

㉛ ㉓

Secret Harbour

Great Bay

dise'

⑯

Coculus Pt.

Jersey Bay

Long Pt.

St. James Bay

Great St. James Island

Little St. James Island

🔲 **Frenchcap**

TO ST. JOHN

EAST END   ⚏ **Wyndham Sugar Bay Beach Club & Resort.** Most rooms at this terra-
★ **$$$$**   cotta hillside resort overlook water. All are spacious and comfortable
and have balconies, hair dryers, and coffeemakers. The beach is small,
but there's a giant pool with waterfalls. Health buffs will enjoy the full-
service spa and fitness center, as well as a ⅓-mi Fit Trail equipped with
10 strengthening exercise stations. ✉ *Rte. 38 No. 6500, Estate Smith
Bay 00802* ☎ *340/777–7100 or 800/927–7100* 🖷 *340/777–7200*
⊕ *www.wyndham.com* ⇆ *300 rooms, 9 suites* ⚘ *2 restaurants, snack
bar, room service, 5 tennis courts, pool, health club, spa, beach, snorkeling, windsurfing, boating, bar, shop, baby-sitting, children's programs
(ages 4–12), laundry service, concierge, business services, meeting rooms*
⊟ *AE, D, DC, MC, V* ⏐◯⏐ *AI.*

$$$–$$$$ ⚏ **Ritz-Carlton, St. Thomas.** This premier luxury resort resembles a Vene-
FodorsChoice   tian palazzo. Guest rooms, in six buildings that fan out from the main
★   villa, are spacious and tropically furnished. Elegance is everywhere,
from the beautiful pool that appears to become one with the sea to the
superior dinner restaurant. A $75 million renovation and expansion proj-
ect, completed in the fall of 2002, added 48 additional rooms, a full-
service spa and fitness center, and 80 two- and three-bedroom private
club residences. ✉ *Rte. 317, No. 6900, Estate Great Bay 00802* ☎ *340/
775–3333 or 800/241–3333* 🖷 *340/775–4444* ⊕ *www.ritzcarlton.com*
⇆ *200 rooms* ⚘ *4 restaurants, room service, in-room safes, minibars,
2 tennis courts, 2 pools, hair salon, health club, spa, beach, windsurf-
ing, boating, 5 bars, shops, baby-sitting, children's programs (ages 4–
12), laundry service, concierge, Internet, business services, meeting
rooms, airport shuttle, no-smoking rooms* ⊟ *AE, D, DC, MC, V* ⏐◯⏐ *EP.*

★ **$$–$$$$**   ⚏ **Renaissance Grand Beach Resort.** The zigzag architectural angles spell
luxury, and it's everywhere—from the marble atrium lobby to the one-
bedroom suites with whirlpool baths. The beach is excellent, and there's
a fitness center with Nautilus machines. The resort is favored by convention groups. Families are welcome, and daily activities for children
include iguana hunts, T-shirt painting, and sand-castle building. ✉ *Rte.
38, Estate Smith Bay* ⚏ *Box 8267, 00801* ☎ *340/775–1510 or 800/
468–3571* 🖷 *340/775–2185* ⊕ *www.renaissancehotels.com/sttsr* ⇆ *290
rooms, 36 suites* ⚘ *2 restaurants, snack bar, room service, in-room
data ports, in-room safes, minibars, cable TV with movies, 6 tennis courts,
2 pools, hair salon, health club, beach, dock, boating, jet skiing, parasailing, volleyball, 2 bars, shops, baby-sitting, children's programs (ages
4–12), laundry service, concierge, business services, convention center,
car rental* ⊟ *AE, D, DC, MC, V* ⏐◯⏐ *EP.*

$$–$$$$ ⚏ **Secret Harbour Beach Resort & Villas.** These beige buildings, which con-
tain low-rise studios and suites, are tucked into the hillsides and along
an inviting sandy cove. Watch marvelous sunsets from the balconies or
the casual restaurant. All units have air-conditioning and maid service.
Children under age 13 stay free, making this a family-friendly resort.
✉ *Rte. 317, No. 6280, Estate Nazareth 00802-1104* ☎ *340/775–6550
or 800/524–2250* 🖷 *340/775–1501* ⊕ *www.secretharbourvi.com* ⇆ *49
suites, 15 studios* ⚘ *Restaurant, fans, kitchenettes, 4 tennis courts,
pool, health club, beach, dive shop, snorkeling, windsurfing, boating,
bar, shop* ⊟ *AE, MC, V* ⏐◯⏐ *CP.*

$$$ ⚏ **Point Pleasant Resort.** Stretching up a steep, tree-covered hill and af-
fording a great view of Drake's Channel, this resort offers a choice of
accommodations from simple bedrooms to multiroom suites. Although
the "beach" is almost nonexistent, three good-size pools surrounded by
decks are placed at different levels on the hill. The property also has a
labyrinth of well-marked nature trails to explore. If you like seafood,
don't miss dinner at the Agave Terrace restaurant. ✉ *Rte. 38, No.
6600, Estate Smith Bay 00802* ☎ *340/775–7200 or 800/524–2300*

☎ *340/776–5694* ⊕ *www.pointpleasantresort.com* 🛏 *132 suites* 🍴 *2 restaurants, in-room data ports, in-room safes, kitchenettes, tennis court, 3 pools, gym, beach, bar, shops, laundry facilities, concierge* ▭ *AE, D, DC, MC, V* �’⊙❙ *EP.*

$$–$$$ 🏨 **Sapphire Beach Resort & Marina.** On a clear day the lush, green mountains of the neighboring British Virgin Islands seem close enough to touch from this picturesque, red-roofed resort. Rooms have bold-patterned rugs, comforters, and full kitchenettes. This is a fun, family-oriented resort, where highlights are the Sunday beach party and a kid's club, which offers activities like arts and crafts, sing-alongs, and sand-castle building. Children under 12 eat free, and teens up to 18 can sleep in their parents' room at no additional charge. In mid-2004, 150 new rooms, plus a convention center, shops, deli and entertainment area are expected to open. ✉ *Rte. 38, Sapphire Bay* ✆ *Box 8088, 00801* ☎ *340/775–6100 or 800/330–8272* 🖷 *340/775–2403* ⊕ *www.sapphirebeachstthomas.com* 🛏 *171 suites* 🍴 *2 restaurants, snack bar, room service, kitchenettes, microwaves, refrigerators, 4 tennis courts, pool, health club, beach, dock, snorkeling, windsurfing, boating, jet skiing, marina, parasailing, volleyball, bar, shop, baby-sitting, children's programs (ages 4–12), playground, concierge, meeting room, car rental* ▭ *AE, MC, V* ❘⊙❙ *EP.*

SOUTH SHORE 🏨 **Marriott Frenchman's Reef and Morning Star Beach Resorts.** On a prime
$$$$ harbor promontory east of Charlotte Amalie, you'll find these two sprawling, full-service superhotels. Frenchman's Reef suites have ocean and harbor views, although trees often get in the way at lower levels. Many rooms are in need of refurbishment. The more elegant Morning Star rooms are in buildings nestled surfside along the fine white sand of Morning Star Beach. Dining is alfresco on American or Caribbean fare or oceanfront at the Tavern on the Beach; there's also a lavish buffet served, overlooking the sparkling lights of Charlotte Amalie. Live entertainment and dancing, scheduled activities for all ages, and a shuttle boat to town make having fun easy. ✉ *Rte. 315, Estate Bakkeroe (Box 7100, 00801)* ☎ *340/776–8500 or 800/524–2000* 🖷 *340/715–6191* ⊕ *www.offshoreresorts.com/stthomas.html* 🛏 *504 rooms, 27 suites* 🍴 *6 restaurants, snack bar, room service, in-room data ports, in-room safes, minibars, cable TV with movies, 4 tennis courts, 2 pools, hair salon, health club, spa, beach, boating, volleyball, bar, piano bar, dance club, shops, baby-sitting, concierge, business services, convention center* ▭ *AE, D, DC, MC, V* ❘⊙❙ *EP.*

$$–$$$$ 🏨 **Bolongo Bay Beach Club & Villas.** This beachfront resort also includes the 20-room Bolongo Villas next door and the six-room Bolongo Bayside Inn across the street. All rooms—which include minisuites and one- and two-bedroom units—have kitchens and balconies and are just steps from a stretch of white-sand beach. The resort offers a choice of all-inclusive or semi-inclusive plan, which means you can pay less if you opt for fewer activities and no included meals. There's a three-night minimum for the all-inclusive plan. ✉ *Rte. 30, No. 50, Estate Bolongo 00802* ☎ *340/775–1800 or 800/524–4746* 🖷 *340/775–3208* ⊕ *www.bolongobay.com* 🛏 *75 rooms, 26 suites* 🍴 *2 restaurants, snack bar, kitchenettes, 2 tennis courts, 3 pools, health club, beach, dive shop, dock, snorkeling, windsurfing, boating, jet skiing, volleyball, bar, nightclub, shop, baby-sitting, children's programs (ages 4–12), playground* ▭ *AE, D, DC, MC, V* ❘⊙❙ *AI.*

Villas & Condominiums

EAST END 🏨 **The Anchorage.** Next to the St. Thomas Yacht Club and facing Cow-
★ **$$$$** pet Bay, these two- and three-bedroom villas are right on the beach. They have washing machines and dryers, and the complex has two lighted tennis courts, a freshwater pool, and an informal restaurant. ✉ *Rte. 317,*

Estate Nazareth ⬠ *Antilles Resorts, Box 8529, 00801* ☎ *340/775–2600 or 800/874–7897* 🖷 *340/775–5901* ⊕ *www.antillesresorts.com* ⬒ *30 rooms* ♿ *Restaurant, dining room, kitchenettes, 2 tennis courts, pool, beach, bar, laundry facilities* ▭ *AE, D, MC, V* ⦿ *EP.*

\$\$–\$\$\$ ⊞ **Sapphire Village.** A stay in these high-rise units may take you back to the swinging-singles days of apartment-house living, since many of the units are rented out long-term to refugees from northern winters. The best units overlook the marina and St. John; the beach is in sight and just a short walk down the hill. ⊠ *Rte. 38, Sapphire Bay* ⬠ *Antilles Resorts, Box 8529, 00801* ☎ *340/775–2600 or 800/874–7897* 🖷 *340/775–5901* ⊕ *www.antillesresorts.com* ⬒ *35 units* ♿ *Restaurant, kitchenettes, 2 tennis courts, 2 pools, beach, dock, snorkeling, windsurfing, boating, jet skiing, marina, parasailing, volleyball, bar, pub, laundry facilities* ▭ *AE, D, MC, V* ⦿ *EP.*

★ \$\$ ⊞ **Blazing Villas.** On the Renaissance Grand Beach Resort property, these cool pastel yellow, pink, green, and blue villas have their own garden patios and can be combined with other villas to create a four-bedroom, four-bath unit. Children under 12 are free when staying with parents. You can use all the resort's facilities. ⊠ *Rte. 38, Estate Smith Bay* ⬠ *Box 502697, 00805* ☎ *340/776–0760 or 800/382–2002* 🖷 *340/776–3603* ⊕ *www.blazingvillas.com* ⬒ *19 rooms* ♿ *2 restaurants, snack bar, room service, microwaves, refrigerators, 6 tennis courts, 2 pools, health club, beach, dock, boating, jet skiing, parasailing, volleyball, 2 bars, shops, baby-sitting, children's programs (ages 4–12), laundry service, concierge, business services, convention center, car rental* ▭ *AE, MC, V* ⦿ *EP.*

★ \$–\$\$ ⊞ **Bed & Breakfast Caribbean Style.** Honeymooners will enjoy the romantic feel of these private, elegantly decorated condos. Each unit has a king-size bed, a reading and video library, and a porch with hammock. The kitchen comes stocked with a tempting selection of breakfast foods. There's a small pool on the property, and the beach and water sports are a five-minute walk away. Those seeking to tie the knot will find that making wedding arrangements, including professional photography, is a specialty of the owner. ⊠ *Rte. 317 at Cabrita Point, Estate Vessup Bay* ⬠ *6501 Red Hook Plaza, Suite 201, 00802* ☎ *340/715–1117* ⊕ *www.cstyle. co.vi* ⬒ *4 units* ♿ *Kitchenettes, pool, beach, snorkeling, windsurfing, boating; no kids, no smoking* ▭ *AE, MC, V* ⦿ *CP.*

Private Homes

You can arrange private-home rentals through various agents that represent luxury residences and usually have both Web sites and brochures that show photos of the properties they represent. Some villas are suitable for travelers with disabilities. **Calypso Realty** (⬠ Box 12178, 00801 ☎ 340/774–1620 or 800/747–4858 ⊕ www.calypsorealty.com) specializes in rental properties in St. Thomas. **McLaughlin-Anderson Villas** (⬠ 100 Blackbeard's Hill, Suite 3, 00802 ☎ 340/776–0635 or 800/537–6246 ⊕ www.mclaughlinanderson.com) handles rental villas throughout the U.S. Virgin Islands, British Virgin Islands, and Grenada.

Where to Eat

The beauty of St. Thomas and its sister islands has attracted a cadre of professionally trained chefs who know their way around fresh fish and local fruits. You can dine on everything from terrific, cheap local dishes such as goat water (a spicy stew) and fungi (a cornmeal polentalike side dish), to imports such as hot pastrami sandwiches and raspberries in crème fraîche.

In large hotels the prices are similar to those in New York City or Paris. Fancy restaurants may have a token chicken or pasta dish under $20, but otherwise, main courses are pricey. You can, however, find good inexpensive Caribbean restaurants. To snack on some local fare, order a johnnycake or a thick slice of dumb bread (a dense round loaf often cut into triangles and filled with cheddar cheese) from any of the mobile food vans parked all over the island. Familiar fast-food franchises also abound.

If your accommodations have a kitchen and you plan to cook, there's good variety in St. Thomas's mainland-style supermarkets. Note, however, that grocery prices are about 20% higher than those on the mainland United States. As for drinking, outside the hotels a beer in a bar will cost between $2 and $3 and a piña colada $4 or more.

What to Wear

Dining on St. Thomas is informal. Few restaurants require a jacket and tie. Still, at dinner in the snazzier places shorts and T-shirts are inappropriate; men would do well to wear slacks and a shirt with buttons. Dress codes on St. Thomas rarely require women to wear skirts, but you'll never go wrong with something flowing.

Charlotte Amalie

AMERICAN
$$–$$$
✕ **Greenhouse Bar and Restaurant.** Watch the waterfront wake up at this large, bustling open-air restaurant. An eight-page menu offers burgers, omelets, salads, sandwiches, and pizza served all day long, along with more upscale entrées like peel-'n'-eat shrimp, Maine lobster, and certified Black Angus prime rib that are reasonably priced. This is generally a family-friendly place, though the Friday night live reggae band that starts thumping at 10 PM draws a lively young-adult crowd. ⊠ *Waterfront Hwy. at Storetvaer Gade* ☎ *340/774–7998* ▤ *AE, D, MC, V.*

$–$$
✕ **Hard Rock Cafe.** A hot spot from the day it opened, this waterfront restaurant is pretty much like its namesakes around the world. Rock-and-roll memorabilia abound, and the menu offers hamburgers, sandwiches, salads, and great desserts. Jerk pork tenderloin is a delicious Caribbean addition. Doors are open from 11 AM until 2 AM; there's always a wait for a table during prime meal times. ⊠ *International Plaza on Waterfront* ☎ *340/777–5555* ⊕ *www.hardrock.com/locations/cafes/Cafes.asp?Lc=STTH* ▤ *AE, MC, V.*

CARIBBEAN
★ $ $$
✕ **Gladys' Cafe.** Even if the local specialties—conch in butter sauce, saltfish and dumplings, hearty red bean soup—didn't make this a recommended café, it would be worth coming for Gladys's smile. While you're here, pick up a $5 or $10 bottle of her hot sauce. ⊠ *Waterfront at Royal Dane Mall* ☎ *340/774–6604* ▤ *AE* ☯ *No dinner.*

$–$$
✕ **Lillian's Caribbean Grill.** This is where the local business community fuels up for their day of selling in Main Street stores. Specialties include dumb bread and cheese, spicy oatmeal and bush tea for breakfast, with everything from hamburgers to conch in butter sauce, fish and fungi, curried chicken and stewed mutton served for lunch. ⊠ *Grand Galleria* ☎ *340/774–7900* ⊕ *pws.prserv.net/lillian/* ▤ *AE, MC, V* ☯ *No dinner. Closed Sun.*

CONTINENTAL
$
✕ **Texas Pit BBQ.** The smell of smoky barbecued ribs, beef brisket and chicken wafts enticingly from these mobile stands that set up daily around 4 PM. Austin native and long-time Virgin Islands resident Bill Collins perfected his sauce recipe, which received a thumbs-up from the late culinary great, James Beard. Choice of homemade rice, coleslaw or potato salad, plus roll, completes the meal. Take-outs only. ⊠ *Waterfront, near the Edward Wilmoth Blyden Marine Terminal* ☎ *340/776–9579* ⊠ *Wheatley Center* ☎ *340/714–5775* ⊠ *Red Hook, next to Marina Market* ☎ *no phone* ▤ *No credit cards* ☯ *No lunch.*

ECLECTIC
$$$–$$$$

✕**Hervé Restaurant & Wine Bar.** In the glow of candlelight—at tables impeccably dressed with linen cloths, silver settings, and fine crystal—you can start off with French-trained Hervé Chassin's crispy conch fritters served with a spicy-sweet mango chutney, then choose from such entrées as fresh tuna encrusted with sesame seeds or succulent roast duck with a ginger and tamarind sauce. The passion-fruit cheesecake is to die for. ✉ *Government Hill* ☎ *340/777–9703* ⊕ *www.st-thomas.com/herve/* ⌕ *Reservations essential* ▤ *AE, MC, V.*

$$$–$$$$

✕**Tavern on the Waterfront.** White linen tablecloths, silver and crystal table settings, and a rich mahogany interior set the scene for an elegant meal at this second-floor, air-conditioned restaurant that overlooks the harbor. Tiger Woods, Michael Jordan, and Walter Cronkite have all supped here. The menu offers flavors from every corner of the globe. Try the salmon Margarita flavored with tequila and lime or spiced marinated pork loin with a rum-soaked raisin sauce. Sunday is Latin night. ✉ *Waterfront at Royal Dane Mall* ☎ *340/776–4328* ⊕ *www.tavernonthewaterfront.com* ▤ *AE, MC, V.*

ITALIAN
$$$–$$$$
Fodor'sChoice
★

✕**Virgilio's.** For the island's best northern Italian cuisine, don't miss this intimate, elegant hideaway tucked on a quiet side street. Eclectic art covers the two-story-high brick walls, and the sound of Italian opera sets the stage for a memorable meal. Come here for more than 40 homemade pastas complemented by superb sauces—*cappellini* (very thin spaghetti) with fresh tomatoes and garlic or spaghetti peasant style (in a rich tomato sauce with mushrooms and prosciutto). House specialties include osso buco as well as tiramisu for dessert, expertly prepared by chef Ernesto Garrigos. ✉ *18 Main St.* ☎ *340/776–4920* ⌕ *Reservations essential* ▤ *AE, MC, V* ⊙ *Closed Sun.*

East End

AMERICAN
$$–$$$

✕**Blue Moon Cafe.** Watch the serene scene of sailboats floating at anchor while supping; sunsets are especially spectacular here. Enjoy piña colada pancakes for breakfast, a grilled mahimahi sandwich with Thai sesame slaw at lunch, or Caribbean rum-glazed salmon for dinner. ✉ *Rte. 32, Red Hook* ☎ *340/779–2080* ⊕ *www.bluemooncafevi.com* ▤ *No credit cards.*

ECLECTIC
★ $$–$$$

✕**Old Stone Farmhouse.** Dine in the splendor of a beautifully restored plantation house. Signature dishes include three-day Mango Asian duck and mahogany-smoked New York strip steak. Tropical fruit sorbets are a must for dessert. Crusty breads are baked fresh daily. There's a full sushi menu for lunch. ✉ *Rte. 42, 1 mi (1½ km) west of the entrance to the Mahogany Run Golf Course, Estate Lovenlund* ☎ *340/777–6277* ⌕ *Reservations essential* ▤ *AE, MC, V.*

$

✕**Duffy's Love Shack.** If the floating bubbles don't attract you to this zany eatery, the lime-green shutters, loud rock music, and fun-loving waitstaff surely will. It's billed as the "ultimate tropical drink shack," and the bartenders shake up such exotic concoctions as the Love Shack Volcano—a 50-ounce flaming extravaganza. Dining selections are just as trendy. Try the grilled mahimahi taco salad or jerk Caesar wrap. Thursday night is usually a theme party complete with giveaways. ✉ *Rte. 32, Red Hook* ☎ *340/779–2080* ⊕ *www.duffysloveshack.com* ▤ *No credit cards.*

IRISH
$$–$$$

✕**Molly Molone's.** This casual alfresco restaurant has a devout following among locals who live and work on boats docked nearby. Traditional Irish dishes include stew and bangers and mash (sausage and mashed potatoes), as well as fresh fish, oversize deli sandwiches, and rich soups. Beware: the iguanas like to beg for table scraps—bring your camera. Upstairs, the same owners run A Whale of a Tale, a pricier seafood eatery that also serves freshly made pasta and fine wines. ☒ *Rte. 32 at American Yacht Harbor, Bldg. D, Red Hook* ☎ *340/775–1270* ▭ *MC, V.*

ITALIAN
★ **$$$–$$$$**
✕**Romanos.** Inside this huge old stucco house is a delightful surprise: a spare yet elegant restaurant serving superb northern Italian cuisine. Try the pastas, either with a classic sauce or a more unique creation such as cream sauce with mushrooms, prosciutto, pine nuts, and Parmesan. You can also take advantage of Tony's private chef services. Either visit his home, where you can watch his culinary wizardry at work, or he'll come cook at your vacation villa. ☒ *Rte. 388 at Coki Point, Estate Frydendal* ☎ *340/775–0045* ⊕ *www.romanosrestaurant.com* ⌖ *Reservations essential* ▭ *MC, V* ☯ *No lunch; closed Sun.*

SEAFOOD
$$$–$$$$
✕**Agave Terrace.** At this open-air pavilion restaurant in the Point Pleasant Resort, fresh fish is the specialty, served as steaks or fillets, and the catch of the day is listed on the blackboard. There are more than a dozen fish sauces to choose from, including teriyaki-mango and lime-ginger. If you get lucky on a sportfishing day charter, the chef will cook your catch if you bring the fish in by 3 PM. Come early and have a drink at the Lookout Lounge, which has breathtaking views of the British Virgins. ☒ *Rte. 38 at the Point Pleasant Resort, Estate Smith Bay* ☎ *340/775–4142* ⊕ *www.agaveterrace.com* ▭ *AE, MC, V* ☯ *No lunch.*

$$–$$$
✕**Off The Hook.** The fish is so fresh at this open-air eatery that you may see it coming in from one of the boats tied up at the dock just steps away. For starters, try the crispy conch fritters with sweet-hot banana-chili chutney. Entrées include a rib-sticking fish stew with scallops, shrimp, mahimahi, mussels, conch, and calamari swimming in a coconut curry broth. Steak, poultry, and pasta lovers will find something to please on the menu, too. There's also a children's menu. ☒ *Rte. 32, Red Hook* ☎ *340/775–6350* ▭ *AE, MC, V* ☯ *No lunch.*

Frenchtown

AUSTRIAN
★ **$$–$$$**
✕**Alexander's Café.** This place is a favorite with the people in the restaurant business on St. Thomas—always a sign of quality. Alexander is Austrian, and the schnitzels are delicious. His recent trip to the Orient has infused the menu with outstanding selections like seared ginger tuna and banana fried shrimp with sweet and sour sauce. Save room for strudel. ☒ *24-A Honduras* ☎ *340/774–4349* ▭ *AE, MC, V* ☯ *Closed Sun.*

CARIBBEAN
$$–$$$
✕**Victor's New Hide-Out.** Although it's a little hard to find—it's up the hill between the Nisky shopping center and the airport—this landmark restaurant is worth the search. Native food—steamed fish, marinated pork chops, and local lobster—and native music are offered in a casual, friendly West Indian spot. ☒ *Sub Base* ☎ *340/776–9379* ▭ *AE, MC, V.*

ECLECTIC
★ **$$–$$$**
✕**Craig & Sally's.** In the heart of Frenchtown, culinary wizard Sally Darash creates menus with a passionate international flavor using fresh ingredients and a novel approach that makes for a delightful dining experience at this friendly casual eatery. Husband Craig maintains a 300-bottle wine list that's received accolades. ☒ *22 Honduras* ☎ *340/777–9949* ▭ *AE, MC, V* ☯ *Closed Mon.–Tues. No lunch weekends.*

$$–$$$
✕**The Pointe at Villa Olga.** Set in the old Russian consulate great house at the tip of the Frenchtown peninsula, this restaurant offers superb views along with fresh fish, teriyaki dishes, lobster, and steaks grilled to order. A large salad bar brimming with traditional salad fare, along with Mediterranean-style roasted vegetables and fresh-baked rustic breads, offers a meal in itself. ☒ *Villa Olga* ☎ *340/774–4262* ▭ *AE, D, MC, V* ☯ *No dinner Sun.*

Northside

AMERICAN ✕ **Sib's Mountain Bar and Restaurant.** Here you'll find live music, foot-
$$–$$$ ball, burgers, barbecued ribs and chicken, and beer. It's the perfect place
for a casual dinner after a day at the beach. ⊠ *Rte. 35, Estate Mafolie*
☎ *340/774–8967* ⊟ *AE, MC, V.*

ECLECTIC ✕ **Bryan's Bar & Restaurant.** The dramatic views are of Hull Bay and Inner
$$–$$$$ Brass Cay. Tuna, wahoo, and dolphinfish—caught daily by the island's
French fishermen—are served grilled, fried, or broiled. Baby-back ribs,
9-ounce beef burgers, gourmet pizza, and a kids' menu are the major
draws. Sunday brunch attracts a big local crowd for choices ranging from
steak and eggs to salmon quesadillas. Live music and lively billiard
games keep the place jumping on weekends. ⊠ *Rte. 37, Estate Hull*
☎ *340/777–1262* ⊟ *AE, MC, V* ⊘ *No lunch.*

Beaches

All 44 St. Thomas beaches are open to the public, although you can reach
some of them only by walking through a resort. Hotel guests frequently
have access to lounge chairs and floats that are off-limits to nonguests;
for this reason you may feel more comfortable at one of the beaches not
associated with a resort, such as Magens Bay (which charges an entrance
fee to cover beach maintenance) or Coki. Whichever one you choose,
remember to remove your valuables from the car and keep them out of
sight when you go swimming.

Brewer's Beach. This long stretch of powdery white sand is on Route 30
near the airport. Trucks that sell lunch, snacks, and drinks often park
along the road bordering the beach.

Coki Beach. Next to Coral World (turn north off Route 38) is this pop-
ular snorkeling spot for cruise-ship passengers; it's common to find a
group of them among the reefs on the east and west ends of the beach.
Colorful beachside shops rent water-sports equipment. Some also sell
snack foods, cold drinks, and even fish food (dry dog food).

Hull Bay. This beach on the north shore (Route 37) faces Inner and Outer
Brass cays and attracts fishermen and beachcombers. With its rough At-
lantic surf and relative isolation, Hull Bay is one of the island's best surf-
ing spots. Take a break from the rigors of sightseeing at the Hull Bay
Hideaway, a laid-back beach bar where a local band plays rock on Sun-
day afternoon.

Fodor'sChoice **Magens Bay.** On Route 35, Magens Bay is usually lively because of its
★ spectacular crescent of white sand, more than ½ mi (¾ km) long, and its
calm waters, which are protected by two peninsulas. It's often listed among
the world's most beautiful beaches. (If you arrive between 8 AM and 5
PM, you have to pay an entrance fee of $3 per person, $1 per vehicle,
and 25¢ per child under age 12.) The bottom is flat and sandy, so this
is a place for sunning and swimming rather than snorkeling. On week-
ends and holidays the sounds of groups partying under the sheds fill the
air. There's also a bar, snack bar, and bathhouses with toilets and salt-
water showers. East of the beach is Udder Delight, a one-room shop of
the St. Thomas Dairies that serves a Virgin Islands tradition—a milk shake
with a splash of Cruzan rum. Kids can enjoy virgin shakes, which have
a touch of soursop, mango, or banana flavoring.

★ **Morning Star Beach.** Close to Charlotte Amalie and fronting the Mar-
riott Frenchman's Reef Hotel, this pretty curve of sand is where many
young locals bodysurf or play volleyball. Snorkeling is good near the
rocks when the current doesn't affect visibility.

★ **Sapphire Beach.** There's a fine view of St. John and other islands here.
The snorkeling is excellent at the reef to the right, or east, near Petty-

klip Point. The constant breeze makes this a great spot for windsurfing.
Secret Harbor. The condo resort here doesn't at all detract from the attractiveness of the cove-like beach. Not only is this East End spot pretty, it also has superb snorkeling—head out to the left, near the rocks.

Sports & the Outdoors

Participant Sports

BOATING &
SAILING

Calm seas, crystal waters, and nearby islands (perfect for picnicking, snorkeling, and exploring) make St. Thomas a favorite jumping-off spot for day- or week-long sails or powerboat adventures. With more than 100 vessels from which to choose, St. Thomas is the charter-boat center of the U.S. Virgin Islands. You can go through a broker to book a sailing vessel with a crew or contact a charter company directly. Crewed charters start at $1,200 per person per week, while bareboat charters can start at $1,700 for a 32-ft boat (not including provisioning), which can comfortably accommodate up to four people.

Island Yachts (⊠ 6100 Red Hook Quarter, 18B Red Hook ☎ 340/775–6666 or 800/524–2019 ⊕ www.islandyachts.com) offers sail- or power-boats on either a bareboat or crewed basis. **Paradise Connections** (⊠ No. 41, Water Island ☎ 340/774–1111 or 877/567–9350 ⊕ www.paradiseconnections.com) is run by long-time sailors Bob and Sheila Wise, who are expert at matching clients with yachts for a week-long crewed charter holidays. Bareboat sail and power boats, including a selection of stable trawlers, are available at **VIP Yacht Charters** (⊠ South off Rte. 32, Estate Frydenhoj ☎ 340/774–9224 or 866/847–9224 ⊕ www.vipyachts.com), at Compass Point Marina.

Awesome Powerboat Rentals (⊠ 6100 Red Hook Quarter, Red Hook ☎ 340/775–0860 ⊕ www.powerboatrentalsvi.com), at "P" dock next to the Off the Hook restaurant, offers 22-ft to 26-ft twin-engine catamarans for day charters. Rates range from $185 to $375 for half- or full-day. A captain can be hired, if desired, for $75 to $100 for half- or full-day. **Nauti Nymph** (⊠ 6501 Red Hook Plaza, Suite 201 Red Hook ☎☎ 340/775–5066 ☎ 800/734–7345 ⊕ www.st-thomas.com/nautinymph/) has a large selection of powerboats for rent. Rates vary from $255 to $380 a day, including snorkel gear, water skis, and out-riggers.

CYCLING

Water Island Bike Tours (⊠ Water Island ☎ 340/714–2186 or 340/775–5770) is a cycling adventure to the USVI's "newest" Virgin. You'll take a 10-minute ferry ride from Crown Bay Marina to Water Island before jumping on a Cannondale M-200 18-speed mountain bike for a three-hour tour over rolling hills on mostly paved roads. Explore the remains of the Sugar Bird Hotel, the inspiration for Herman Wouk's book *Don't Stop the Carnival,* the site of a 17th-century plantation, and beautiful Honeymoon beach for a cooling swim. Helmets, water, a guide, and ferry fare are included in the $50 cost.

FISHING
★

Fishing here is synonymous with blue marlin angling—especially from June through October. Four 1,000-pound-plus blues, including three world records, have been caught on the famous North Drop, about 20 mi (32 km) north of St. Thomas. If you're not into marlin fishing, try hooking up sailfish in the winter, dolphinfish come spring, and wahoo in the fall. To really find the trip that will best suit you, walk down the docks at either American Yacht Harbor or Sapphire Beach Marina in the late afternoon and chat with the captains and crews.

Captain Red Bailey's *Abigail III* (☎ 340/775–6042 ⊕ www.sportfishvi.com) operates out of the Sapphire Beach Resort & Marina. At the

American Yacht Harbor (✉ 6100 Red Hook Plaza, Red Hook ☎ 340/775–6454) you can charter two boats: the *Marlin Prince* and *Prowler*. The **Charter Boat Center** (✉ 6300 Red Hook Plaza, Red Hook ☎ 340/775–7990 or 800/866–5714 ⊕ www.charterboat.vi) is a major source for sportfishing charters.

GOLF
Fodor'sChoice
★
The **Mahogany Run Golf Course** (✉ Rte. 42, Estate Lovenlund ☎ 340/777–5000 ⊕ www.mahoganyrungolf.com) attracts golfers for its spectacular view of the British Virgin Islands and the challenging 3-hole Devil's Triangle on this Tom and George Fazio–designed par-70, 18-hole course. There's a fully stocked pro shop, snack bar, and open-air club house. The course is open daily and there are frequently informal weekend tournaments.

PARASAILING
The Caribbean waters are so clear here that the outlines of coral reefs are visible from high in the sky. Parasailers sit in a harness attached to a parachute that lifts them off a boat deck until they're sailing up in the air. Parasailing trips average a 10-minute ride in the sky that costs $60 per person. Friends who want to ride along and watch pay $15 for the boat trip. **Caribbean Parasail and Watersports** (✉ 6501 Red Hook Plaza, Red Hook ☎ 340/775–9360) makes parasailing pickups from 10 locations around the island, including many major beachfront resorts. They also rent Jet Skis, kayaks, and floating battery-powered chairs.

SCUBA DIVING &
SNORKELING
Popular dive sites include such wrecks as the *Cartanser Sr.,* a beautifully encrusted World War II cargo ship sitting 35-ft deep (11-m deep), and the *General Rogers,* a 65-ft-deep (21-m-deep) Coast Guard cutter with a gigantic resident barracuda. Reef dives offer hidden caves and archways at **Cow and Calf Rocks,** coral-covered pinnacles at **Frenchcap,** and tunnels where you can explore undersea from the Caribbean to the Atlantic at **Thatch Cay, Grass Cay,** and **Congo Cay.** Many resorts and charter yachts offer dive packages. A one-tank dive starts at $50; two-tank dives are $70 or more. Call the USVI Department of Tourism to obtain a free 8-page guide to Virgin Islands dive sites. There are plenty of snorkeling possibilities, too.

Admiralty Dive Center (✉ Waterfront Hwy., Charlotte Amalie ☎ 340/777–9802 or 888/900–DIVE ⊕ www.admiraltydive.com), at the Holiday Inn St. Thomas, provides boat dives, rental equipment, and a retail store. Six-tank to 12-tank packages are available if you want to dive over several days. **Aqua Action** (✉ 6501 Red Hook Plaza, Red Hook ☎ 340/775–6285 or 888/775–6285 ⊕ www.aadivers.com) is a full-service, PADI five-star shop that offers all levels of instruction at Secret Harbour Beach Resort. **Aqua Adventures** (✉ Rte. 314 at Yacht Haven Marina, Charlotte Amalie ☎ 340/715–0348) offers an alternative to traditional diving in the form of an underwater motor scooter called BOB, or Breathing Observation Bubble. A half-day tour, including snorkel equipment, guided BOB excursion, rum punch, and towels is $99 per person. **Blue Island Divers** (✉ Rte. 304 at Crown Bay Marina, Estate Contant ☎ 340/774–2001 ⊕ www.blueislanddivers.com) is a full-service dive shop that offers both day and night dives to wrecks and reefs. **Chris Sawyer Diving Center** (☎ 340/775–7320 or 877/929–3483 ⊕ www.sawyerdive.vi) is a PADI five-star outfit that specializes in dives to the 310-ft-long *Rhone,* in the British Virgin Islands. Hotel/dive packages are offered through the Renaissance Grand Beach Resort and Wyndham Sugar Bay Beach Club & Resort. **Snuba of St. Thomas** (✉ Rte. 388 at Coki Point, Estate Frydendal ☎ 340/693–8063 ⊕ www.visnuba.com) offers a cross between snorkeling and scuba diving: a 20-ft air hose connects you to the surface. The cost is $59 per person. Children must be 8 years or older.

SEA EXCURSIONS Landlubbers and seafarers alike will enjoy the wind in their hair and salt spray in the air while exploring the waters surrounding St. Thomas. Several businesses can book you on a half-day inshore light-tackle fishing trip for $325 to $400 for two anglers; a snorkel-and-sail to a deserted cay for the day that costs on the average $75 to $90 per person; or an excursion over to the British Virgin Islands starting at $100 per person plus $12 custom's fees. For a soup-to-nuts choice of sea tours, contact the **Adventure Center** (⊠ Rte. 315 at Marriott French's Reef Hotel, Estate Bakkeroe ☎ 340/774–2990). The **Charter Boat Center** (⊠ 6300 Red Hook Plaza, Red Hook ☎ 340/775–7990 or 800/866–5714 ⊕ www. charterboat.vi) specializes in day trips to the British Virgin Islands and day- or week-long sailing charters. **Limnos Charters** (⊠ 6100 Red Hook Plaza, Red Hook ☎ 340/775–3203 ⊕ www.limnoscharters.com) offers one of the most popular British Virgin Islands day trips, complete with lunch, open bar, and snorkel gear. Jimmy Loveland at **Treasure Isle Cruises** (⊠ Rte. 32, No. 6616 Estate Nadir ☎ 340/775–9500 ⊕ www. treasureislecruises.com) can set you up with everything from a half-day sail to a 7-day U.S. and British Virgin Islands trip that combines sailing with accommodations and sightseeing trips onshore.

SEA KAYAKING Fish dart, birds sing, and iguanas lounge on the limbs of dense mangroves deep within a marine sanctuary on St. Thomas's southeast shore. Many resorts on St. Thomas's eastern end have kayaks. **Virgin Islands Ecotours** (⊠ Rte. 32, Estate Nadir ☎ 340/779–2155 ⊕ www.viecotours.com) offers 2½-hour guided trips on two-person sit-atop ocean kayaks; there are stops for swimming and snorkeling. The cost is $50 per person.

STARGAZING Without the light pollution so prevalent in more densely populated areas, the heavens appear supernaturally bright. On a **Star Charters Astronomy Adventure** (☎ 340/774–9211) you can peer into the Caribbean's largest telescope—an 18-inch Newtonian reflector—and learn the science and lore of the stars from a well-informed celestial guide.

SUBMARINING Dive 90 ft under the sea to one of St. Thomas's most beautiful reefs without getting wet. The *Atlantis* **Adventures** (⊠ Havensight Shopping Mall, Bldg. VI, Charlotte Amalie ☎ 340/776–5650 ⊕ www.goatlantis.com/ stthomas) submarine is a 46-passenger, air-conditioned conduit to a watery world teeming with brightly colored fish, vibrant sea fans, and an occasional shark. A guide narrates the one-hour underwater journey, while a diver makes a mid-tour appearance for a fish-feeding show. The cost is $72. No children shorter than 36 inches tall are allowed.

TENNIS The Caribbean sun is hot, so be sure to hit the courts before 10 AM or after 5 PM (many courts are lighted). You can indulge in a set or two even if you're staying in a guest house without courts, since most hotels rent time to nonguests. **Marriott Frenchman's Reef and Morning Star Beach Resorts** (⊠ Rte. 315, Estate Bakkeroe ☎ 340/776–8500 Ext. 6818) has two courts, with nonguests charged $10 per hour per court. There are six courts at **Renaissance Grand Beach Resort** (⊠ Rte. 38, Estate Smith Bay ☎ 340/775–1510) that are lighted until 8 PM and rent for $8 per hour. Tennis pro George Newton offers lessons for $45 per hour, $25 per ½-hour. Two courts are available at the **Ritz-Carlton, St. Thomas** (⊠ Rte. 317, No. 6900, Estate Great Bay ☎ 340/775–3333), where nonguests can reserve lessons for $80 per hour and $40 per ½ hour. **Sapphire Beach Resort & Marina** (⊠ Sapphire Bay ☎ 340/775–6100 Ext. 8135) has four courts that fill up fast in the cool early morning hours. The cost for nonguests is $10 per hour. At **Wyndham Sugar Bay Beach Club & Resort** (⊠ Rte. 38, No. 6500, Estate Smith Bay ☎ 340/777–7100) nonguests can rent any of the 5 courts for $10 per hour. Lessons are by appointment and rates start at $40 for a half-hour.

Lindberg Bay Park (⊠ Rte. 302, Estate Lindberg Bay) has two courts that are open to the public; it's opposite the Cyril E. King Airport. There are two public tennis courts at **Sub Base** (⊠ Rte. 306, next to the Water and Power Authority, Estate Contant), open on a first-come, first-served basis at no cost. Lights are on until 10 PM.

WINDSURFING Expect some spills, anticipate the thrills, and try your luck clipping through the seas. Most beachfront resorts rent Windsurfers and offer one-hour lessons for about $35 to $50. One of the island's best-known independent windsurfing companies is **West Indies Windsurfing** (⊠ Vessup Beach, No. 9, Estate Nazareth ☎ 340/775–6530). Owner John Phillips is the far-sighted board buff who introduced the sport of kite-boarding, which entails using a kite to lift a board sailor off the water for an airborne ride. A two-hour land-based kite-boarding lesson costs $75, while a two-hour lesson with on-the-water time is $150.

Spectator Sports

HORSE RACING The **Clinton Phipps Racetrack** (⊠ Rte. 30, Estate Nadir ☎ 340/775–4555) schedules races—especially on local holidays—with sanctioned betting. Be prepared for large crowds.

Shopping

Fodor'sChoice St. Thomas lives up to its billing as a duty-free shopping destination.
★ Even if shopping isn't your idea of how to spend a vacation, you still may want to slip in on a quiet day (check the cruise-ship listings—Monday and Sunday are usually the least crowded) to browse. Among the best buys are liquor, linens, china, crystal (most stores will ship), and jewelry. The amount of jewelry available makes this one of the few items for which comparison shopping is worth the effort. Local crafts include shell jewelry, carved calabash bowls, straw brooms, woven baskets, fragrances, and dolls. Creations by local doll maker Gwendolyn Harley— like her costumed West Indian market woman—have been goodwill ambassadors bought by visitors from as far away as Asia. Spice mixes, hot sauces, and tropical jams and jellies are other native products.

There's no sales tax in the USVI, and you can take advantage of the $1,200 duty-free allowance per family member (remember to save your receipts). Although you'll find the occasional salesclerk who will make a deal, bartering isn't the norm.

Areas & Malls

The prime shopping area in **Charlotte Amalie** is between Post Office and Market squares; it consists of three parallel streets that run east–west (Waterfront Highway, Main Street, and Back Street) and the alleyways that connect them. Particularly attractive are the historic **A. H. Riise Alley, Royal Dane Mall, Palm Passage,** and pastel-painted **International Plaza**— quaint alleys between Main Street and the Waterfront.

Vendors Plaza, on the waterfront side of Emancipation Gardens in Charlotte Amalie, is a central location for vendors selling handmade earrings, necklaces, and bracelets; straw baskets and handbags; T-shirts; fabrics; African artifacts; and local fruits. Look for the many brightly colored umbrellas.

West of Charlotte Amalie, the pink-stucco **Nisky Center,** on Harwood Highway about ½ mi (¾ km) east of the airport, is more of a hometown shopping center than a tourist area, but there's a bank, pharmacy, record shop, and Radio Shack.

★ **Havensight Mall,** next to the cruise-ship dock, may not be as charming as downtown Charlotte Amalie, but it does have more than 60 shops.

It has an excellent bookstore, a bank, a pharmacy, a gourmet grocery, and smaller branches of many downtown stores. The shops at **Port of Sale**, which adjoins the Havensight Mall (its buildings are pink instead of the brown of the Havensight shops), sell discount goods.

East of Charlotte Amalie on Route 38, **Tillett Gardens** is an oasis of artistic endeavor across from the Tutu Park Shopping Mall. The late Jim Tillett and then-wife Rhoda converted this old Danish farm into an artists' retreat in 1959. Today you can watch artisans produce silk-screen fabrics, pottery, candles, watercolors, jewelry, and other handicrafts. Something special is often happening in the gardens as well: the Classics in the Gardens program is a classical music series presented under the stars, and the Pistarckle Theater holds its performances here.

Tutu Park Shopping Mall, across from Tillett Gardens, is the island's one and only enclosed mall. The 47 stores and food court are anchored by a Kmart and the Plaza Extra grocery store. Archaeologists have discovered evidence that Arawak Indians once lived near the mall grounds.

Red Hook has **American Yacht Harbor,** a waterfront shopping area with a dive shop, a tackle store, a clothing and jewelry boutique, and a few restaurants. Don't forget **St. John.** A ferry ride (an hour from Charlotte Amalie or 20 minutes from Red Hook) will take you to the charming shops of **Mongoose Junction** and **Wharfside Village,** which specialize in unusual, often island-made articles.

Specialty Items

ART **Blue Turtle Gallery.** Best known for her vivid tropical landscapes, local artist Lucinda Schutt not only exhibits her artwork but uses the gallery to teach and showcase watercolor paintings by students. ⊠ *Government Hill, two buildings west of Hotel 1829, Charlotte Amalie* ☎ *340/774–9440* ⊕ *www.blueturtlegallery.net.*

Camille Pissarro Art Gallery. This second-floor gallery, in the birthplace of St. Thomas's famous artist, offers a fine collection of original paintings and prints by local and regional artists. ⊠ *14 Main St., Charlotte Amalie* ☎ *340/774–4621.*

Mango Tango. Works by popular local artists—originals, prints, and notecards—are displayed (there's a one-person show at least one weekend a month) and sold here. It also has the island's largest humidor and a brand name cigar gallery. ⊠ *Al Cohen's Plaza, atop Raphune Hill, ½ mi (¾ km) east of Charlotte Amalie* ☎ *340/777–3995.*

MAPes MONDE. Historic and contemporary prints, posters, and photo notecards depicting West Indian life are sold at two downtown locations. ⊠ *Grand Galleria, Tolbod Gade at Norre Gade* ☎ *340/776–2160* ⊠ *37 Main St., at Riise's Alley* ☎ *340/776–2886* ⊕ *www.mapesmonde. com.*

BOOKS **Dockside Bookshop.** This place is packed with books for children, travelers, cooks, and historians, as well as a good selection of paperback mysteries, best-sellers, art books, calendars, and prints. It also carries a selection of books written in and about the Caribbean and the Virgin Islands. ⊠ *Rte. 30 at Havensight Mall, Charlotte Amalie* ☎ *340/774–4937.*

CAMERAS & **Boolchand's.** Brand-name cameras, audio and video equipment, and
ELECTRONICS binoculars are sold here. ⊠ *31 Main St., Charlotte Amalie* ☎ *340/776–0794* ⊠ *Rte. 30 at Havensight Mall, Charlotte Amalie* ☎ *340/776–0302.*

Royal Caribbean. Shop here for cameras, camcorders, stereos, watches, and clocks. ⊠ *23 Main St., Charlotte Amalie* ☎ *340/776–5449* ⊠ *33*

Main St., Charlotte Amalie ☎ *340/776–4110* ✉ *Rte. 30 at Havensight Mall, Charlotte Amalie* ☎ *340/776–8890* ⊕ *www.royalcaribbean.vi.*

CHINA & CRYSTAL **The Crystal Shoppe.** All is glitter at this family-run store that sells Swarovski and Waterford crystal, figurines by Hummel, Daum, and Royal Copenhagen, and china by Belleek, Kosta Boda, and several Limoges factories. ✉ *14 Main St., Charlotte Amalie* ☎ *340/777–9835.*

The English Shop. This store offers figurines, cutlery, and china and crystal from major European and Japanese manufacturers, including Spode, Royal Doulton, Portmeirion, Noritaki, and Wedgwood. You can choose what you like from the catalogs here, and shopkeepers will order and factory-ship it for you. (Be sure to keep your receipts in case something goes awry.) ✉ *106–108 Drake's Passage, Charlotte Amalie* ☎ *340/ 776–3776.*

Little Switzerland. All of this establishment's shops carry crystal from Baccarat, Waterford, and Orrefors; china from Kosta Boda, Rosenthal, and Wedgwood, among others. There's also an assortment of Swarovski cut-crystal animals, porcelain figurines—including Lladro, gemstone globes, and many other affordable collectibles. They also do a booming mail-order business; ask for a catalog. ✉ *Tolbod Gade, across from Emancipation Garden, Charlotte Amalie* ☎ *340/776–2010* ✉ *3B Main St., Charlotte Amalie* ☎ *340/776–2010* ✉ *Rte. 30 at Havensight Mall, Charlotte Amalie, located dockside* ☎ *340/776–2198* ⊕ *www. littleswitzerland.com.*

CLOTHING **Cosmopolitan.** At this sophisticated clothing emporium, look for such top lines as Paul and Shark, Bally, Timberland, Sperry Topsider, Givenchy, and Nautica. ✉ *Drake's Passage at the Waterfront, Charlotte Amalie* ☎ *340/776–2040* ⊕ *www.cosmopolitan.vi.*

Local Color. Men, women, and children will find something to choose from among brand-name wear like Jams World and Urban Safari, and St. John artist Sloop Jones's colorful, hand-painted island designs on cool dresses, T-shirts, and sweaters. There are also tropically oriented accessories like big-brimmed straw hats, bold-color bags, and casual jewelry. ✉ *Royal Dane Mall, Charlotte Amalie, at the Waterfront* ☎ *340/ 774–2280.*

Lover's Lane. With the motto "Couples that play together, stay together," this romantic second-floor shop sells sensuous lingerie, sexy menswear, and provocative swimwear. ✉ *Waterfront Hwy. at Raadets Gade, Charlotte Amalie* ☎ *340/777–9616* ⊕ *www.loverslane.com.*

Pusser's Tropical & Nautical Co. Store. Tropical sports and travel clothing for men, women, and children here all have a nautical theme. Look for bottles of Pusser's rum at the sales counter. ✉ *Waterfront Hwy. at Riise's Alley, Charlotte Amalie* ☎ *340/777–9281.*

Tommy Hilfiger Boutique. Stop by this shop for classic American jeans and sportswear, as well as trendy bags, belts, ties, socks, caps, and wallets. ✉ *Waterfront Hwy. at Trompeter Gade, Charlotte Amalie* ☎ *340/777– 1189.*

FOODSTUFFS **Caribbean Chocolate.** Everything at this confectionery tastes as good as it smells. A wide assortment of Godiva chocolates shares space with Caribbean rum balls, tropical-flavor saltwater taffy, colorful jelly beans, homemade fudge, and Caribbean coffees. ✉ *Trompeter Gade, Charlotte Amalie* ☎ *340/774–6675.*

Cost-U-Less. This store sells everything from soup to nuts, but in giant sizes and case lots. The meat and seafood department, however, has smaller, family-size portions. ✉ *Rte. 38, 1 mi (1½ km) east of Charlotte Amalie and ¼ mi (½ km) west of Rte. 39 intersection, Estate Donoe* ☎ *340/ 777–3588.*

Food Center. Fresh produce, meats, and seafood, plus an on-site bakery and deli with hot and cold prepared foods, are the draw here, especially for those renting villas, condos, or charter boats in the East End area. ⊠ *Rte. 32, Estate Frydenhoj* ☎ *340/777–8806.*

Fruit Bowl. For fresh fruits and vegetables, this is the place to go. ⊠ *Rte. 38 and 313 intersection at the Wheatley Center, Charlotte Amalie* ☎ *340/774–8565.*

Gourmet Gallery. Visiting millionaires buy their caviar here. There's also an excellent and reasonably priced wine selection, as well as specialty ingredients for everything from tacos to curries to chow mein. A full-service deli offers imported meats, cheeses, and in-store prepared foods that are perfect for a gourmet picnic. ⊠ *Rte. 304 at Crown Bay Marina, Estate Contant* ☎ *340/776–8555* ⊠ *Rte. 30 at Havensight Mall, Charlotte Amalie* ☎ *340/774–4948.*

Marina Market. You won't find a better fresh-meat and seafood department anywhere on the island. ⊠ *Rte. 32 across from the Red Hook ferry, Red Hook* ☎ *340/779–2411.*

Plaza Extra. This large U.S.-style supermarket has everything you need from produce to meat, including fresh seafood, a fresh-foods deli, and a bakery. There's a bulk-size section and liquor department, too. ⊠ *Rte. 38 at Tutu Park Shopping Mall, Estate Tutu* ☎ *340/775–5646.*

Pueblo Supermarkets. These supermarkets carry stateside brands of most products —but at higher prices because of shipping costs to the islands. ⊠ *Rte. 38 at Four Winds Plaza, across from Tillett Gardens, Estate Tutu* ☎ *340/775–4655* ⊠ *Sub Base, 1 mi (1½ km) north of Havensight Mall, Estate Contant* ☎ *340/774–4200* ✉ *1 mi (1½ km) north of Havensight Mall, Estate Thomas* ☎ *340/774–2695.*

U.S. Virgin Islands Rum Cake Centre. The sales staff will tell you the 17th-century secrets behind these scrumptious rum cakes, available in several flavors. Samples are available of both cakes and rums, as are gift tins. ⊠ *Rte. 30 at Havensight Shopping Mall, Charlotte Amalie* ☎ *340/ 714–2936.*

HANDICRAFTS **Caribbean Marketplace.** This is a great place to buy handicrafts from the Caribbean and elsewhere. Also look for Sunny Caribee spices, soaps, coffee, and teas from Tortola, and coffee from Trinidad. ⊠ *Rte. 30 at Havensight Shopping Mall, Charlotte Amalie* ☎ *340/776–5400.*

Down Island Traders. These traders deal in hand-painted calabash bowls; finely printed Caribbean note cards; jams, jellies, spices, hot sauces, and herbs; teas made of lemongrass, passion fruit, and mango; coffee from Jamaica; and handicrafts from throughout the Caribbean. ⊠ *Waterfront Hwy. at Post Office Alley, Charlotte Amalie* ☎ *340/776–4641.*

Native Arts and Crafts Cooperative. More than 40 local artists—including schoolchildren, senior citizens, and people with disabilities—create the handcrafted items for sale here: African-style jewelry, quilts, calabash bowls, dolls, carved-wood figures, woven baskets, straw brooms, note cards, and cookbooks. ⊠ *Tolbod Gade, across from Emancipation Garden and next to visitor center, Charlotte Amalie* ☎ *340/777–1153.*

Tropical Memories. The emphasis here is on Virgin Islands artists. There are prints, pottery, gorgeous glass trays, carved mahogany bowls, and scented soaps. ⊠ *Royal Dane Mall, Charlotte Amalie* ☎ *340/776–7536.*

JEWELRY **Amsterdam Sauer.** Many fine one-of-a-kind designs are displayed at this jeweler's three locations. The Imperial Topaz Collection at the Main Street store is a stunner. ⊠ *1 Main St., Charlotte Amalie* ☎ *340/774–2222* ⊠ *Rte. 30 at Havensight Shopping Mall, Charlotte Amalie* ☎ *340/776– 3828* ⊠ *Ritz-Carlton Resort, Rte. 317, No. 6900, Estate Great Bay* ☎ *340/779–2308* ⊕ *www.amsterdamsauer.com.*

Blue Carib Gems. At family-owned and -run Blue Carib Gems, watch Alan O'Hara, Sr., polish Caribbean amber and larimar, agate, and other gems and mount them into gold and silver settings. ⊠ *2–3 Back St., Charlotte Amalie* ☎ *340/774–8525* ⊕ *www.bluecaribgems.com.*

Cardow Jewelry. A chain bar—with gold chains in several lengths, widths, sizes and styles—awaits you here, along with diamonds, emeralds, and other precious gems. You're guaranteed 40%–60% savings off U.S. retail prices or your money will be refunded within 30 days of purchase. ⊠ *33 Main St., Charlotte Amalie* ☎ *340/776–1140* ⊠ *Rte. 30 at Havensight Shopping Mall, Charlotte Amalie* ☎ *340/774–0530 or 340/774–5905* ⊠ *Rte. 315 at Marriott Frenchman's Reef Resort, Estate Bakkeroe* ☎ *340/774–0434* ⊕ *www.cardow.com.*

Colombian Emeralds. Well known in the Caribbean, this store offers set and unset emeralds as well as gems of every description. The watch boutique carries upscale Ebel, Tissot, and Jaeger LeCoultre brands. ⊠ *30 Main St., Charlotte Amalie* ☎ *340/777–5400* ⊠ *Waterfront at A. H. Riise Mall, Charlotte Amalie* ☎ *340/774–1033* ⊠ *Rte. 30 at Havensight Mall, Charlotte Amalie* ☎ *340/774–2442* ⊕ *www.dutyfree.com.*

Diamonds International. Choose a diamond, emerald, or tanzanite gem and a mounting, and you'll have your dream ring set in an hour. Famous for having the largest inventory of diamonds on the island, this shop welcomes trade-ins, has a U.S. service center, and offers free diamond earrings with every purchase. ⊠ *31 Main St., Charlotte Amalie* ☎ *340/774–3707* ⊠ *3 Drakes Passage, Charlotte Amalie* ☎ *340/775–2010* ⊠ *7AB Drakes Passage, Charlotte Amalie* ☎ *340/774–1516* ⊠ *Rte. 30 at Havensight Mall, Charlotte Amalie* ☎ *340/776–0040* ⊠ *Wyndham Sugar Bay Beach Club & Resort, Rte. 38, No. 6500, Estate Smith Bay* ☎ *340/777–7100* ⊕ *www.diusvi.vi.*

H. Stern Jewelers. The World Collection of jewels set in modern, fashionable designs and an exclusive sapphire watch have earned this Brazilian jeweler a stellar name. ⊠ *12 Main St., Charlotte Amalie* ☎ *340/776–1939* ⊠ *32AB Main St., Charlotte Amalie* ☎ *340/776–1146* ⊠ *Rte. 30 at Havensight Mall, Charlotte Amalie* ☎ *340/776–1223* ⊠ *Marriott Frenchman's Reef Resort, Estate Bakkeroe* ☎ *340/776–3550.*

Rolex Watches at A. H. Riise. As the Virgin Islands' official Rolex retailer, this shop offers one of the largest selections of these fine timepieces in the Caribbean. An After Sales Service Center assures that your Rolex keeps on ticking for your lifetime. ⊠ *37 Main St., at Riise's Alley, Charlotte Amalie* ☎ *340/776–2303* ⊠ *Rte. 30 at Havensight Mall, Charlotte Amalie* ☎ *340/776–4002.*

LEATHER GOODS **Coach Boutique at Little Switzerland.** Find a full line of fine leather handbags, belts, gloves, and more for women, plus briefcases and wallets for men. Accessories for both sexes include organizers, travel bags, and cellphone cases. ⊠ *5 Main Street, Charlotte Amalie* ☎ *340/776–2010.*

Purses and Things. This "house of handbags" has a wide selection of sizes and great prices (you can buy a five-in-one leather clutch for only $20). Bargains are equally good on eel-skin goods. ⊠ *International Plaza, Charlotte Amalie* ☎ *340/777–9717.*

Zora's. Fine leather sandals made to order are the specialty here. There's also a selection of made-only-in-the-Virgin-Islands backpacks, purses, and briefcases in durable, brightly colored canvas. ⊠ *Norre Gade across from Roosevelt Park, Charlotte Amalie* ☎ *340/774–2559.*

LINENS **Fabric in Motion.** Fine Italian linens share space with Liberty's of London silky cottons, colorful batiks, cotton prints, ribbons, and accessories at this small shop. ⊠ *Storetvaer Gade, Charlotte Amalie* ☎ *340/774–2006.*

Mr. Tablecloth. The friendly staff here will help you choose from the floor-to-ceiling selection of linens, from Tuscany lace tablecloths to Irish linen pillowcases. The prices will please. ⊠ *6–7 Main St., Charlotte Amalie* ☎ *340/774–4343.*

LIQUOR & TOBACCO

A. H. Riise Liquors. This Riise venture offers a large selection of tobacco (including imported cigars), as well as cordials, wines, and rare vintage Armagnacs, cognacs, ports, and Madeiras. It also stocks fruits in brandy and barware from England. Enjoy rum samples at the tasting bar. ⊠ *37 Main St., at Riise's Alley, Charlotte Amalie* ☎ *340/776–2303* ⊠ *Rte. 30 at Havensight Mall, Charlotte Amalie* ☎ *340/776–7713.*

Al Cohen's Discount Liquor. The wine selection at this warehouse-style store is very large. ⊠ *Rte. 30 across from Havensight Mall, Charlotte Amalie* ☎ *340/774–3690.*

Tobacco Discounters. Find a full line of discounted brand name cigarettes, cigars, and tobacco accessories. ⊠ *Port of $ale Mall, next to Havensight Mall* ☎ *340/774–2256.*

MUSIC

Modern Music. Shop for the latest stateside and Caribbean CD and cassette releases, plus oldies, classical, and New Age music. ⊠ *Rte. 30 across from Havensight Shopping Mall, Charlotte Amalie* ☎ *340/774–3100* ⊠ *Rte. 30 at Nisky Center, Charlotte Amalie* ☎ *340/777–8787.*

Parrot Fish Records and Tapes. A stock of standard stateside tapes and CDs, plus a good selection of Caribbean artists, including local groups, can be found here. Write them for a catalog of calypso, *soca* (up-tempo calypso), steel band, and reggae music. ⊠ *Back St., Charlotte Amalie* ☁ *Box 9206, St. Thomas, USVI 00801* ☎ *340/776–4514.*

PERFUME

Tropicana Perfume Shoppes. Tropicana has the largest selection of fragrances for men and women in all of the Virgin Islands, including those locally made by Gail Garrison from the essential oils of tropical fruits and flowers like mango and jasmine. ⊠ *2 Main St., Charlotte Amalie* ☎ *340/774–0010.*

SUNGLASSES

Davante. This designer eyewear store carries brands like Cartier, Dunhill, Giorgio Armani, and Christian Dior. ⊠ *Riise's Alley, Charlotte Amalie* ☎ *340/714–1220* ⊕ *www.davante.com.*

Fashion Eyewear. Take your pick from name-brand eyewear. A real plus here is prescription sunglasses, copied from your present eyewear, ready in a half hour for $99. ⊠ *International Plaza, Charlotte Amalie* ☎ *340/776–9075.*

TOYS

Quick Pics. Birds sing, dogs bark, and fish swim in this animated toyland that is part of a larger electronics and souvenir store. Adults have as much fun trying out the wares as do kids. ⊠ *Rte. 30 at Havensight Mall, Charlotte Amalie* ☎ *340/774–3500.*

Nightlife & the Arts

On any given night, especially in season, you'll find steel-pan orchestras, rock and roll, piano music, jazz, broken-bottle dancing (dancing atop broken glass), disco, and karaoke. Pick up a copy of the free, bright yellow *St. Thomas–St. John This Week* magazine when you arrive (it can be found at the airport, in stores, and in hotel lobbies); the back pages list who's playing where. The Friday edition of the *Daily News* carries complete listings for the upcoming weekend.

Nightlife

BARS

Agave Terrace. Island-style steel-pan bands are a treat that should not be missed. Pan music resonates after dinner here on Tuesdays and Thursdays. ⊠ *Rte. 38 at the Point Pleasant Resort, Estate Smith Bay* ☎ *340/775–4142.*

Bolongo Bay Beach Club & Villas. There's a Carnival Night complete with steel-pan music on Wednesdays. ⊠ *Rte. 30, No. 50, Estate Bolongo* ☎ *340/775–1800.*

Duffy's Love Shack. A live band and dancing under the stars are the big draws for locals and visitors alike. ⊠ *Red Hook Plaza parking lot, Red Hook* ☎ *340/779–2080.*

Epernay Bistro. This intimate nightspot has small tables for easy chatting, wine and champagne by the glass, and a spacious dance floor. Mix and mingle with island celebrities. The action runs from 4 PM until the wee hours Mondays through Saturdays. ⊠ *24-A Honduras, Frenchtown* ☎ *340/774–5348.*

Greenhouse Bar and Restaurant. Once this favorite eatery puts away the salt and pepper shakers at 10 PM, it becomes a rock-and-roll club with a DJ or live reggae bands raising the weary to their feet six nights a week. ⊠ *Waterfront Hwy. at Storetvaer Gade, Charlotte Amalie* ☎ *340/774–7998.*

Iggies Beach Bar. Sing along karaoke-style to the sounds of the surf or the latest hits at this beachside lounge. There are live bands on the weekends, and you can dance inside or kick up your heels under the stars. ⊠ *Rte. 30, No. 50, Estate Bolongo* ☎ *340/775–1800.*

Old Mill Entertainment Complex. In—you guessed it—an old mill, this is a rock-'til-you-drop late-night spot Thursday through Sunday. There's also a tamer piano bar and jazz club in the complex, as well as billiards and foosball tables. ⊠ *193 Contant, Charlotte Amalie* ☎ *340/774–7782.*

Ritz-Carlton, St. Thomas. On Monday nights, catch pan music at this resort's bar. ⊠ *Rte. 317, No. 6900, Estate Great Bay* ☎ *340/775–3333.*

The Arts

THEATER **Pistarkle Theater.** The air-conditioned theater with more than 100 seats, nestled in Tillett Gardens, is host to a dozen or more productions annually, plus a children's summer drama camp. ⊠ *Rte. 38, across from Tutu Park Shopping Mall, Estate Tutu* ☎ *340/775–7877.*

Reichhold Center for the Arts. This amphitheater has its more expensive seats covered by a roof. Schedules vary, so check the paper to see what's on when you're in town. Throughout the year there's an entertaining mix of local plays, dance exhibitions, and music of all types. ⊠ *Rte. 30, across from Brewers Beach, Estate Lindberg Bay* ☎ *340/693–1559.*

Exploring St. Thomas

St. Thomas is only 13 mi (21 km) long and less than 4 mi (6½ km) wide, but it's extremely hilly, and even an 8- or 10-mi (13- or 16-km) trip could take several hours. Don't let that discourage you, though; the mountain ridge that runs east to west through the middle and separates the island's Caribbean and Atlantic sides has spectacular vistas.

Charlotte Amalie

Look beyond the pricey shops, T-shirt vendors, and bustling crowds for a glimpse of the island's history. The city served as the capital of Denmark's outpost in the Caribbean until 1917, an aspect of the island often lost in the glitz of the shopping district.

Emancipation Gardens, right next to the fort, is a good place to start a walking tour. Tackle the hilly part of town first: head north up Government Hill to the historic buildings that house government offices and have incredible views. Several regal churches line the route that runs west back to the town proper and the old-time market. Virtually all the alleyways that intersect Main Street lead to eateries that serve frosty drinks, sandwiches and burgers, and West Indian fare. There are public rest rooms in this area, too. Allow an hour for a quick view of the sights, two hours if you plan to tour Government House.

A note about the street names: in deference to the island's heritage, the streets downtown are labeled by their Danish names. Locals will use both the Danish name and the English name (such as Dronningens Gade and Norre Gade for Main Street), but most people refer to things by their location ("a block toward the Waterfront off Main Street" or "next to the Little Switzerland Shop"). It's best to ask for directions by shop names or landmarks.

Numbers in the margin correspond to points of interest on the Charlotte Amalie map.

SIGHTS TO SEE

⑰ All Saints Anglican Church. Built in 1848 from stone quarried on the island, the church has thick, arched window frames lined with the yellow brick that came to the islands as ballast aboard ships. Merchants left the brick on the waterfront when they filled their boats with molasses, sugar, mahogany, and rum for the return voyage. The church was built in celebration of the end of slavery in the USVI. ⊠ *Domini Gade* ☎ *340/774–0217* ☯ *Mon.–Sat. 9–3.*

㉕ Cathedral of St. Peter and St. Paul. This building was consecrated as a parish church in 1848 and serves as the seat of the territory's Roman Catholic diocese. The ceiling and walls are covered with murals painted in 1899 by two Belgian artists, Father Leo Servais and Brother Ildephonsus. The San Juan–marble altar and side walls were added in the 1960s. ⊠ *Lower Main St.* ☎ *340/774–0201* ☯ *Mon.–Sat. 8–5.*

⑳ Danish Consulate Building. Built in 1830, this structure once housed the Danish Consulate. Today, it serves is the office of the territory's governor. This building is not open to the public. ✛ *Take stairs north at corner of Bjerge Gade and Crystal Gade to Denmark Hill.*

⑯ Dutch Reformed Church. This church has an austere loveliness that's amazing considering all it has been through. Founded in 1744, it has been rebuilt twice in the last 200 years following fires and hurricanes. The unembellished cream-color hall gives you a sense of peace—albeit monochromatically. The only other color is the forest green of the shutters and the carpet. Call ahead if you need to visit at a particular time; the doors are sometimes locked. ⊠ *Nye Gade and Crystal Gade* ☎ *340/776–8255* ☯ *Weekdays 9–5.*

❻ Educators Park. A peaceful place amid the town's hustle and bustle, the park has memorials to three famous Virgin Islanders: educator Edith Williams, J. Antonio Jarvis (a founder of the *Daily News*), and educator and author Rothschild Francis. The latter gave many speeches here. ⊠ *Main St., across from U.S. Post Office.*

㉖ Edward Wilmoth Blyden Marine Terminal. Locally called "Tortola Wharf," it's where you can catch the *Native Son* and other ferries to the BVI. The restaurant upstairs is a good place to watch the Charlotte Amalie harbor traffic and sip an iced tea. Next door is the ramp for the *Seaborne* seaplane, which offers commuter service to St. Croix, the BVI, and Puerto Rico. ⊠ *Waterfront Hwy.*

❷ Emancipation Garden. Built to honor the freeing of slaves in 1848, the garden was the site of a 150th anniversary celebration of emancipation. A bronze bust of a freed slave blowing a symbolic conch shell commemorates this anniversary. The gazebo here is used for official ceremonies. Two other monuments show the island's Danish-American

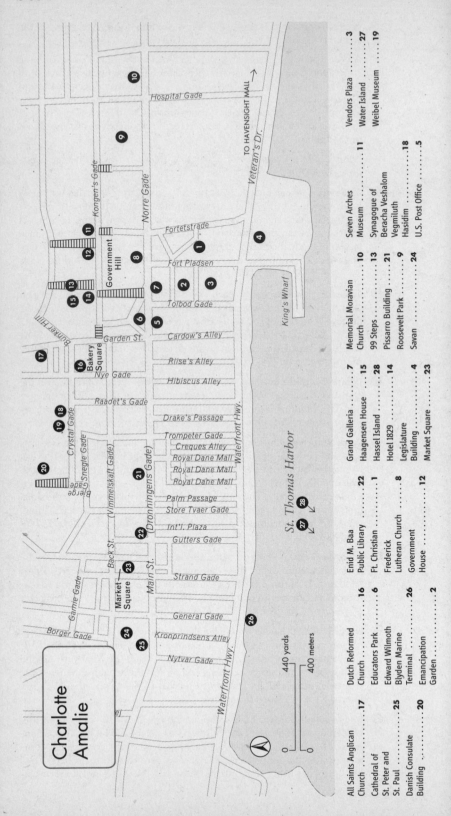

tie—a bust of Denmark's King Christian and a scaled-down model of the U.S. Liberty Bell. ⊠ *Between Tolbod Gade and Ft. Christian.*

㉒ Enid M. Baa Public Library. Like so many structures on the north side of Main Street, this large pink building is a typical 18th-century town house. Merchants built their houses (stores downstairs, living quarters above) across from the brick warehouses on the south side of the street. The library was once the home of merchant and landowner Baron von Bretton. It's the island's first recorded fireproof building, meaning it was built of ballast brick instead of wood. Its interior of high ceilings and cool stone floors is the perfect refuge from the afternoon sun. You can browse through historic papers or just sit in the breeze by an open window reading the paper. ⊠ *Main St.* ☎ *340/774–0630* ◷ *Weekdays 9–5, Sat. 10–3.*

① Ft. Christian. St. Thomas's oldest standing structure, this monument anchors the shopping district. It was built in 1672–80 and now has U.S. National Landmark status. The clock tower was added in the 19th century. This remarkable building has, over time, been used as a jail, governor's residence, town hall, courthouse, and church. Ft. Christian now houses **The Virgin Islands Museum,** where you can see exhibits on USVI history, natural history, and turn-of-the-20th-century furnishings. Local artists display their works monthly in the gallery. A gift shop sells local crafts, books, and other souvenirs. This is also the site of the Chamber of Commerce's Hospitality Lounge, where there are public rest rooms, brochures, and a place you can stash your luggage for some last-minute shopping on the way to the airport. ⊠ *Waterfront Hwy. just east of shopping district* ☎ *340/776–4566* ⊠ *Free* ◷ *Weekdays 8:30–4:30.*

⑧ Frederick Lutheran Church. This historic church has a massive mahogany altar, and its pews—each with its own door—were once rented to families of the congregation. Lutheranism is the state religion of Denmark, and when the territory was without a minister the governor—who had his own elevated pew—filled in. ⊠ *Norre Gade* ☎ *340/776–1315* ◷ *Mon.–Sat. 9–4.*

⑫ Government House. Built in 1867, this neoclassical white brick-and-wood structure houses the offices for the governor of the Virgin Islands. Inside, the staircases are of native mahogany, as are the plaques hand-lettered in gold with the names of the governors appointed and, since 1970, elected. Brochures detailing the history of the building are available, but you may have to ask for them. A deputy administrator can lead you on a guided tour; call ahead to schedule an appointment. ⊠ *Government Hill* ☎ *340/774–0001* ⊠ *Free* ◷ *Weekdays 8–5.*

⑦ Grand Galleria. This imposing building stands at the head of Main Street. Once the island's premier hotel, it has been converted into offices and shops. ⊠ *Tolbod Gade at Norre Gade* ☎ *340/774–7282* ◷ *Weekdays 8–5, Sat. 9–noon.*

⑮ Haagensen House. Behind Hotel 1829, this lovingly restored home was built in the early 1800s by Danish entrepreneur Hans Haagensen and is surrounded by an equally impressive cookhouse, outbuildings, and terraced gardens. A lower-level banquet hall now showcases an antique-print and photo gallery. Guided walking tours are available of Haagensen House itself or a combination tour that includes the circa-1860s Villa Notman, Hotel 1829, and lookout tower at Blackbeard's Castle. ⊠ *Government Hill* ☎ *340/774–5541* ⊠ *$5; $8 combination tour for 2 properties; $10 for all 4 properties* ◷ *Oct.–May, daily 9–4; May–Oct., by appointment only.*

㉘ Hassel Island. East of Water Island in Charlotte Amalie harbor, Hassel Island is part of the Virgin Islands National Park, as it has the ruins of a British military garrison (built during a brief British occupation of the USVI during the 1800s) and the remains of a marine railway (where ships were hoisted into drydock for repairs). There's a small ferry that runs from the Crown Bay Marina to the island; departure times are posted at Tickles Dockside Pub, and the fare is $5 or $10 round-trip.

⑭ Hotel 1829. As its name implies, it was built in 1829, albeit as a residence of a prominent merchant named Lavalette rather than as a hotel. The building's bright coral-color exterior walls are accented with fancy black wrought iron, and the interior is paneled in a dark wood, which makes it feel delightfully cool. From the terrace there's an exquisite view of the harbor framed by bright orange bougainvillea. You can combine a visit to this still-functioning hotel with a walking tour of Haagensen House, Villa Notman, and the lookout tower at Blackbeard's Castle just behind the hotel. ⊠ *Government Hill* ☎ *340/776–1829* ⬛ *$5; $8 combination tour for 2 properties; $10 for all 4 properties* ☉ *Tours, Mon.– Fri. 10–4.*

④ Legislature Building. Its pastoral-looking lime-green exterior conceals the vociferous political wrangling of the Virgin Islands Senate going on inside. Constructed originally by the Danish as a police barracks, the building was later used to billet U.S. Marines, and much later it housed a public school. You're welcome to sit in on sessions in the upstairs chambers. ⊠ *Waterfront Hwy., across from Ft. Christian* ☎ *340/774–0880* ☉ *Daily 8–5.*

㉓ Market Square. Formally called Rothschild Francis Square, this is a good place to find local produce. A cadre of old-timers sells mangoes and papayas, strange-looking root vegetables, and herbs; sidewalk vendors offer African fabrics and artifacts and tie-dyed cotton clothes at good prices. ⊠ *North side of Main St., at Strand Gade.*

⑩ Memorial Moravian Church. Built in 1884, it was named to commemorate the 150th anniversary of the Moravian Church in the Virgin Islands. ⊠ *17 Norre Gade* ☎ *340/776–0066* ☉ *Weekdays 8–5.*

☝ ⑬ 99 Steps. This staircase "street," built by the Danes in the 1700s, leads to the residential area above Charlotte Amalie and Blackbeard's Castle. The castle's tower, built in 1679, was once used by the notorious pirate Edward Teach. If you count the stairs as you go up, you'll discover, as have thousands before you, that there are more than 99. ✣ *Look for steps heading north from Government Hill.*

㉑ Pissarro Building. Housing several shops and an art gallery, this was the birthplace and childhood home of Camille Pissarro, who later moved to France and became an acclaimed Impressionist painter. The art gallery contains three original pages from Pissarro's sketchbook and two pastels by Pissarro's grandson, Claude. ⊠ *Main St., between Raadets Gade and Trompeter Gade.*

☝ ⑨ Roosevelt Park. You'll see members of the local legal community head to the nearby court buildings while you rest on a bench in this park—a good spot to people-watch. The small monument on the park's south side is dedicated to USVI war veterans. Kids enjoy the playground made of wood and tires. ⊠ *Norre Gade.*

㉔ Savan. A neighborhood of small streets and houses, it was first laid out in the 1700s as the residential area for a growing community of middle-class black artisans, clerks, and shopkeepers. There's a row of Rastafarian shops along the first block and restaurants that sell spicy vegetarian fare. It's best not to walk here at night and to exercise caution even in daylight. ⊠ *Turn north off lower Main St. onto General Gade.*

★ ⑪ **Seven Arches Museum.** This restored 18th-century home is a striking example of classic Danish–West Indian architecture. There seem to be arches everywhere—seven to be exact—all supporting a "welcoming arms" staircase that leads to the second floor and the flower-framed front doorway. The Danish kitchen is a highlight: it's housed in a separate building just off the main house, as were all cooking facilities in the early days (for fire prevention). Inside the house there are mahogany furnishings and gas lamps. ⊠ *Government Hill, 3 bldgs. east of Government House* ☎ *340/774–9295* ✉ *$5 suggested donation* ⊙ *Oct.–July, daily 10–4; Aug.–Sept., by appointment only.*

⑱ **Synagogue of Beracha Veshalom Vegmiluth Hasidim.** The synagogue's Hebrew name translates to the Congregation of Blessing, Peace, and Loving Deeds. The small building's white pillars contrast with rough stone walls, as does the rich mahogany of the pews and altar. The sand on the floor symbolizes the exodus from Egypt. Since the synagogue first opened its doors in 1833 it has held a weekly Sabbath service, making it the oldest synagogue building in continuous use under the American flag and the second-oldest (after the one on Curaçao) in the western hemisphere. An extensive renovation was completed in 2002. Guided ½ hour tours are offered weekdays beginning at 10:30 AM. Next door, the Weibel Museum showcases Jewish history on St. Thomas. ⊠ *15 Crystal Gade* ☎ *340/774–4312* ⊕ *new.onepaper.com/synagogue/* ⊙ *Mon.– Fri. 9–5.*

⑤ **U.S. Post Office.** While you buy your postcard stamps, contemplate the murals of waterfront scenes by *Saturday Evening Post* artist Stephen Dohanos. His art was commissioned as part of the Works Project Administration (WPA) in the 1930s. ⊠ *Tolbod Gade and Main St.*

③ **Vendors Plaza.** Here merchants sell everything from T-shirts to African attire to leather goods. Look for local art among the ever-changing selections at this busy market. ⊠ *West of Ft. Christian at the waterfront* ⊙ *Weekdays 8–6, weekends 9–1.*

㉗ **Water Island.** This island, once owned by the U.S. Department of the Interior and about ¼ mi (½ km) out in Charlotte Amalie Harbor, was once a peninsula of St. Thomas. A channel was cut through so that U.S. submarines could get to their base in a bay just to the west, known as Sub Base. Today, this is the fourth-largest U.S. Virgin Island. A ferry goes between Crown Bay Marina and the island several times daily, at a cost of $5 or $10 round-trip.

⑲ **Weibel Museum.** In this museum next to the synagogue, 300 years of Jewish history on St. Thomas are showcased. The small gift shop sells a commemorative silver coin celebrating the anniversary of the Hebrew congregation's establishment on the island in 1796. There are also tropically inspired items, like a shell seder plate and menorahs painted to resemble palm trees. ⊠ *15 Crystal Gade* ☎ *340/774–4312* ✉ *Free* ⊙ *Weekdays 9–4.*

Around the Island

To explore outside Charlotte Amalie you'll need to rent a car or hire a taxi. Your rental car should come with a good map; if not, pick up the pocket-sized "St. Thomas–St. John Road Map" at a tourist information center. Roads are marked with route numbers, but they're confusing and seem to switch numbers suddenly. If you stop to ask for directions, it's best to have your map in hand because locals probably know the road you're looking for by another name. Allow yourself a day to explore, especially if you want to stop for picture taking or to enjoy a light bite or refreshing swim. Most gas stations are on the island's more populated eastern end, so fill up before heading to the north side. And remember to drive on the left.

Although the eastern end has many major resorts and spectacular beaches, don't be surprised if a cow or a herd of goats crosses your path as you drive through the relatively flat, dry terrain. The north side of the island is more lush 'and hush—fewer houses and less traffic. Here there are roller-coaster routes (made all the more scary because the roads have no shoulders) and incredible vistas. Leave time in the afternoon for a swim at the beach. Pick up some sandwiches from delis in the Red Hook area for a picnic lunch, or enjoy a slice of pizza at Magens Bay. A day in the country will reveal the tropical pleasures that have enticed more than one visitor to become a resident.

Numbers in the margin correspond to points of interest on the St. Thomas map.

SIGHTS TO SEE   **Compass Point Marina.** It's fun to park your car and walk around this
30   marina. The boaters—many of whom have sailed here from points around the globe—are easy to engage in conversation. Turn south off Route 32 at the well-marked entrance road just east of Independent Boat Yard. ⊠ *Estate Frydenhoj.*

★ ⊙ **32**   **Coral World Marine Park.** Coral World has an offshore underwater observatory that houses the Predator Tank, one of the world's largest coral-reef tanks, and an aquarium with more than 20 portholes providing close-ups of Caribbean sea life. *Sea Trekkin'* lets you tour the reef outside the park at a depth of 15 ft under the sea, thanks to specialized high-tech headgear and a continuous air supply that's based on the surface. A guide leads the ½-hour tour and the narration is piped through a specialized microphone inside each trekker's helmet; the cost is $50 per person. The park also has several outdoor pools where you can touch starfish, pet a baby shark, feed stingrays, and view endangered sea turtles. In addition there's a mangrove lagoon and a nature trail full of lush tropical flora. Daily feedings and talks take place at most every exhibit. ⊠ *Coki Point, turn north off Rte. 38 at sign, Estate Frydendal* ☎ *340/ 775–1555* ⊕ *www.coralworldvi.com* ⊠ *$18* ⊙ *Daily 9–5.*

⊙ **34**   **Drake's Seat.** Sir Francis Drake was supposed to have kept watch over his fleet and looked for enemy ships from this vantage point. The panorama is especially breathtaking (and romantic) at dusk, and if you arrive late in the day you'll miss the hordes of day-trippers on taxi tours who stop here to take a picture and buy a T-shirt from one of the many vendors. ⊠ *Rte. 40, Estate Zufriedenheit.*

⊙ **35**   **Estate St. Peter Greathouse & Botanical Gardens.** This unusual spot is perched on a mountainside 1,000 ft above sea level, with views of more than 20 other islands and islets. You can wander through a gallery displaying local art, sip a complimentary rum or Virgin Punch while looking out at the view, or follow a nature trail that leads by nearly 200 varieties of trees and plants, including an orchid jungle. ⊠ *Rte. 40, Estate St. Peter* ☎ *340/774–4999* ⊕ *www.greathouse-mountaintop.com* ⊠ *$10* ⊙ *Mon.–Sat. 9–4:30.*

36   **Frenchtown.** Popular for its several bars and restaurants, Frenchtown is also the home of descendants of immigrants from St. Barthélemy (St. Barths). You can watch them pull up their brightly painted boats and display their equally colorful catch of the day along the waterfront. If you chat with them, you'll hear speech patterns slightly different from those of other St. Thomians. Get a feel for the residential district of Frenchtown by walking west to some of the town's winding streets, where tiny wooden houses have been passed down from generation to generation. ⊹ *Turn south off Waterfront Hwy. at the U.S. Post Office.*

★ ☾ ③③ **Mountain Top.** Stop here for a banana daiquiri and spectacular views from the observation deck more than 1,500 ft above sea level. There are also shops that sell everything from Caribbean art to nautical antiques, ship models, and T-shirts. Kids will like talking to the parrots—and hearing them answer back. ⊹ *Head north off Rte. 33; look for signs* ⊕ *www.greathouse-mountaintop.com.*

★ ☾ ㉙ **Paradise Point Tramway.** Fly skyward in a gondola to Paradise Point, an overlook with breathtaking views of Charlotte Amalie and the harbor. There are several shops, a bar, and a restaurant. A ¼-mi (½-km) hiking trail leads to spectacular views of St. Croix to the south. Wear sturdy shoes; the trail is steep and rocky. ⊠ *Rte. 30 across from Havensight Mall, Charlotte Amalie* ☎ *340/774–9809* ⊕ *www.paradisepointtramway. com* ⊠ *$15* ☉ *Daily 7:30–4:30.*

㉛ **Red Hook.** In this nautical center there are fishing and sailing charter boats, dive shops, and powerboat-rental agencies at the American Yacht Harbor marina. There are also several bars and restaurants, including Molly Molone's, Duffy's Love Shack, and Off the Hook. One grocery store and two delis offer picnic fixings—from sliced meats and cheeses to rotisserie-cooked chickens, prepared salads, and freshly baked breads.

ST. CROIX

Updated by
Lynda Lohr

St. Croix, the largest of the three USVI at 84 square mi (218 square km), lies 40 mi (65 km) south of St. Thomas. But unlike bustling St. Thomas, its harbor teeming with cruise ships and its shopping district crowded with bargain hunters, St. Croix has a slower pace and a more diverse economy, mixing tourism with light and heavy industry on rolling land that was once covered with waving carpets of sugarcane.

St. Croix's population has grown dramatically over the last 40 years, and its diversity reflects the island's varied history. The cultivation of sugarcane was more important here than on St. Thomas or St. John and continued as an economic force into the 1960s. After the end of slavery in 1848, the need for workers brought waves of immigrants from other Caribbean islands, particularly nearby Puerto Rico. St. Croix was divided into plantation estates, and the ruins of great houses and the more than 100 sugar mills that dot the land are evidence of an era when St. Croix was one of the greatest producers of sugar in the West Indies.

Tourism began and boomed in the 1960s, bringing both visitors and migrants from the mainland United States (whom locals refer to as Continentals). In the late 1960s and early 1970s industrial development brought St. Croix yet another wave of immigrants. This time they came mostly from Trinidad and St. Lucia to seek work at the Hess oil refinery or at the south shore aluminum-processing plants.

St. Croix is a study in contrasting beauty. The island isn't as hilly as St. Thomas or St. John. A lush rain forest envelops the northwest, the eastern end is dry, and palm-lined beaches with startlingly clear aquamarine water ring the island. The capital, Christiansted, is a restored Danish port on a coral-bound northeastern bay. The tin-roof 18th-century buildings in both Christiansted and Frederiksted, on the island's western end, are either pale yellow, pink, or ocher—resplendent with bright blazes of bougainvillea and hibiscus. The prosperous Danes built well (and more than once, as both towns were devastated by fire in the 19th century), using imported bricks or blocks cut from coral, fashioning covered sidewalks (galleries) and stately colonnades, and leaving an enduring cosmopolitan air as their legacy.

Where to Stay

From plush resorts to simple beachfront digs, St. Croix's accommodations are bound to suit every type of traveler. If you sleep in either the Christiansted or Frederiksted area, you'll be close to shopping, restaurants, and nightlife. Any of the island's other hotels will put you just steps from the beach. St. Croix has several small but special properties that offer personalized service. If you like all the comforts of home, you may prefer to stay in a condominium or villa. Room rates on St. Croix are competitive with those on other islands, and if you travel off-season, you'll find substantially reduced prices. Many properties offer honeymoon and dive packages that are also big money savers. Whether you stay in a hotel, a condominium, or a villa, you'll enjoy up-to-date amenities. Most properties have room televisions, but at some bed and breakfasts there might be only one in the common room.

Although a stay right in historic Christiansted may mean putting up with a little urban noise, you probably won't have trouble sleeping. Christiansted rolls up the sidewalks fairly early, and air-conditioners drown out any noise. Solitude is guaranteed at hotels and inns outside Christiansted and those on the outskirts of sleepy Frederiksted.

For approximate costs, *see* the dining and lodging price chart at the beginning of this chapter.

Hotels

CHRISTIANSTED

$–$$ ▣ **Hotel Caravelle.** The fetching, three-story Caravelle offers moderately priced in-town lodgings within walking distance of shops and restaurants. Rooms are tasteful and tropical, with white walls and floral-print bedspreads and curtains. Most rooms have some sort of ocean view; the best overlook the harbor. Staff members go out of their way to be helpful. The Rum Runners, a casual terrace eatery, serves local and Continental cuisine. ⊠ *44A Queen Cross St., 00820* ☎ *340/773–0687 or 800/524–0410* 🖷 *340/778–7004* ⊕ *www.hotelcaravelle.com* ➷ *43 rooms, 1 suite* ⌂ *Restaurant, refrigerators, cable TV, pool, gym, bar, Internet, meeting room, no-smoking rooms* ▤ *AE, D, DC, MC, V* �託 *EP.*

$–$$ ▣ **King's Alley Hotel.** In the center of Christiansted's hustle and bustle, this small hotel (part of the King's Alley shopping and restaurant complex) mixes convenience with charm. The 12 premium rooms in the section across the courtyard have mahogany four-poster beds, Mexican tile floors, and Indonesian print fabrics. French doors open onto balconies with a view of the waterfront and the shopping arcade. The 22 standard rooms in the older section are a tad less interesting but still attractive. ⊠ *57 King St.* 🖭 *Box 4120, 00822* ☎ *340/773–0103 or 800/843–3574* 🖷 *340/773–4431* ⊕ *www.kingsalley.com* ➷ *34 rooms* ⌂ *Some in-room data ports, cable TV, pool, dive shop, boating, fishing, meeting room* ▤ *AE, D, DC, MC, V* �託 *EP.*

$ ▣ **Breakfast Club.** This rambling guest house is within walking distance of downtown, but a taxi is a good idea if you're heading back late at night. Rooms of various sizes are clean, with colorful print spreads. Twin hammocks beckon, offering sea and town views. Guests like to gather at the bar, and owner Toby Chapin includes hearty breakfasts (featuring banana pancakes) in the room rates. ⊠ *18 Queen Cross St., 00820*

☎ *340/773–7383* 🖷 *340/773–8642* ⊕ *http://nav.to/thebreakfastclub*
📞 *7 rooms* ⚗ *Fans, some kitchens, some kitchenettes, hot tub; no a/c in some rooms, no room phones, no room TVs, no kids under 6* ⊟ *MC, V* ⦿| *BP.*

$ 🖼 **Pink Fancy Hotel.** Listed on the National Register of Historic Places, this venerable small hotel dates from 1780, but its amenities are definitely modern. The rooms are furnished with antiques, mahogany pieces, and oriental carpets, and lush gardens meander around the fenced-in compound. Both create a comfortable base for folks who like to get out and about. Guests gather poolside for breakfast and conversation. This hotel shines brightly in a neighborhood that's a bit on the run-down side, so take a taxi back after nighttime excursions. ⊠ *27 Prince St., 00820* ☎ *340/773–8460 or 800/524–2045* 🖷 *340/773–6448* ⊕ *www.pinkfancy. com* 📞 *13 rooms* ⚗ *Fans, in-room data ports, kitchenettes, cable TV with movies, no-smoking rooms* ⊟ *AE, MC, V* ⦿| *CP.*

OUTSIDE
CHRISTIANSTED
$–$$
🖼 **Villa Margarita.** Villa Margarita sits by the seaside near windswept Salt River, providing a quiet retreat that's just a 20-minute drive from Christiansted's shops and restaurants. The units vary in size, but come complete with kitchenettes, tropical furnishings, balconies, and spectacular sea views. While swimming directly offshore is a bit difficult because of shallow water, sandy beaches are just steps away. ⊠ *Off Route 80, Salt River* 🕭 *9024 Salt River, Christiansted 00820* ☎ *340-713-1930 or 866-274-8811* 🖷 *340719-3389* ⊕ *www.villamargarita.com* 📞 *3 units* ⚗ *Fans, kitchenettes, refrigerators, cable TV, pool, Internet; no room phones* ⊟ *V* ⦿| *CP.*

$
Fodor'sChoice
★
🖼 **Carringtons Inn.** This spacious B&B exudes style. Once the winter home of a well-off family, the inn has many nice touches. Each room is different, with a decorating theme that reflects its floral name. Wicker furniture, Asian carpets, and balconies in some rooms, colorful spreads, and sea or pool views are inviting touches. Hosts Claudia and Roger Carrington conjure up delicious breakfasts—rum-soaked French toast is a house specialty. As it is in a hillside suburban neighborhood, a stay here requires a rental car. ⊠ *4001 Estate Hermon Hill, Christiansted 00820* ☎ *340/713–0508 or 877/658–0508* 🖷 *340/719–0841* ⊕ *www. carringtonsinn.com* 📞 *5 rooms* ⚗ *Fans, some kitchenettes, refrigerators, pool, Internet; no room TVs, no smoking* ⊟ *AE, MC, V* ⦿| *BP.*

$ 🖼 **Innparadise.** A stay here is like a visit with your favorite relatives—if you're lucky enough to have kinfolk with a suburban-style home in St. Croix, that is. The rooms are squeaky clean, with tile floors or carpeting, colorful spreads, and fanciful names that reflect the island's plantation past. Some rooms share a bathroom. The common room features expansive views of the sea and suburban sprawl, comfy couches, a bar, and large dining room table, where a generous breakfast is offered each morning. A rental car is a necessity. ⊠ *1 Estate Golden Rock, Golden Rock* 🕭 *Box 428, Christiansted 00821* ☎ *340/713–9803 or 866/800–9803* 🖷 *340/713–8722* ⊕ *www.innparadisestcroix.com* 📞 *6 rooms* ⚗ *Fans, refrigerators, Internet; no room phones, no smoking* ⊟ *AE, MC, V* ⦿| *BP.*

EAST END
$$$–$$$$
🖼 **The Buccaneer.** On the grounds of an old 300-acre sugar plantation, this complex has it all: sandy beaches, swimming pools, golf, and many activities. A palm tree–lined main drive leads to the large, pink main building atop a hill; shops, restaurants, and guest quarters are scattered about rolling manicured lawns. Rooms have a Mediterranean feel, with tile floors, four-poster beds, massive wardrobes of pale wood, pastel fabrics, spacious marble baths, and local works of art. All rooms have such modern conveniences as hair dryers and irons. ⊠ *Rte. 82, Shoys* 🕭 *Box 25200, 00824* ☎ *340/712–2100 or 800/255–3881* 🖷 *340/712–2104*

St. Croix

TO
ST. THOMAS

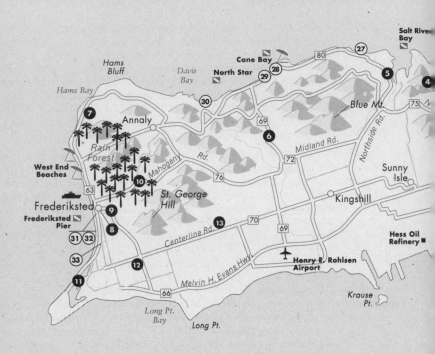

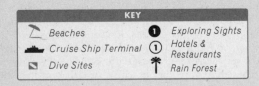

KEY
- 🔻 Beaches
- 🚢 Cruise Ship Terminal
- ◪ Dive Sites
- ❶ Exploring Sights
- ① Hotels & Restaurants
- 🌴 Rain Forest

Carib

Hotels ▼			Restaurants ▼
Breakfast Club 3	Hibiscus Beach Hotel 26	Sugar Beach 24	Blue Moon 32
The Buccaneer 16	Hotel Caravelle 2	Tamarind Reef Hotel 17	Breezez 23
Carambola Beach Resort 30	Innparadise 25	Villa Madeleine 20	Café Christine 12
Carringtons Inn 15	King's Alley Hotel 10	Villa Margarita 27	The Galleon 18
Chenay Bay Beach Resort 19	Pink Fancy Hotel 1	Waves at Cane Bay 28	Harvey's 4
Divi Carina Bay Resort 21	Sandcastle on the Beach 33		Indies 5
	Schooner Bay 13		Kendricks 9
			Morning Glory Coffee and Tea 14

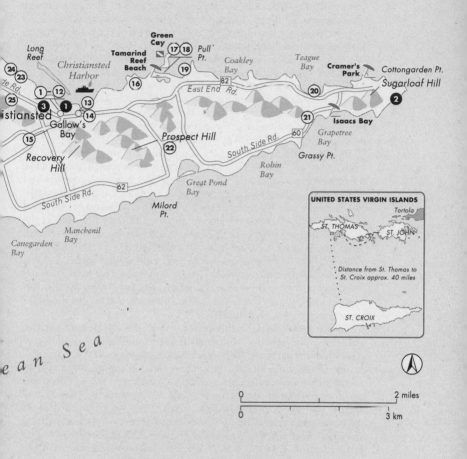

Buck Island

Buck Island Reef
National Monument

Long
Reef

Green
Cay

Tamarind
Reef
Beach

Christiansted
Harbor

24
23

25

1   12

3   1

15

Gallow's
Bay

Recovery
Hill

istiansted

17 18

16

19

13

14

22

Pull
Pt.

Coakley
Bay

82

East End   Rd.

Prospect Hill

South Side Rd.

62

South Side Rd.

Milord
Pt.

Manchenil
Bay

Canegarden
Bay

Great Pond
Bay

Teague
Bay

Cramer's
Park

Cottongarden Pt.

Sugarloaf Hill

2

20

21

Isaacs Bay

Grapetree
Bay

Grassy Pt.

Robin
Bay

60

e a n   S e a

UNITED STATES VIRGIN ISLANDS

Tortola

ST. THOMAS   ST. JOHN

Distance from St. Thomas to
St. Croix approx. 40 miles

ST. CROIX

0   2 miles

0   3 km

⊕ *www.thebuccaneer.com* 🛏 *138 rooms* ⚘ *4 restaurants, in-room safes, refrigerators, 18-hole golf course, 8 tennis courts, 2 pools, gym, spa, beach, snorkeling, hiking, bar, shops, children's programs (ages 4– 12), Internet, meeting rooms, no-smoking rooms* ⊟ *AE, D, DC, MC, V* ⊠ *BP.*

☙ **\$\$–\$\$\$\$** 🏨 **Chenay Bay Beach Resort.** The beachfront location and complimentary tennis and water-sports equipment (including kayaks) make this resort a real find—especially for families with active kids. Rooms are basic, with ceramic-tile floors, bright peach or yellow walls, rattan furnishings, and front porches. Gravel paths connect the terraced wood or stucco cottages with the shore, where there's a large L-shape pool, a protected beach, a picnic area, and a casual restaurant. The hotel offers a shuttle to grocery stores and shopping areas. ⊠ *Rte. 82, Green Cay* ⌖ *Box 24600, Christiansted 00824* ☎ *340/773–2918 or 800/548–4457* 🖷 *340/773–6665* ⊕ *www.chenaybay.com* 🛏 *50 rooms* ⚘ *Restaurant, picnic area, kitchenettes, cable TV, 2 tennis courts, pool, hot tub, outdoor hot tub, beach, snorkeling, boating, volleyball, bar, baby-sitting, children's programs (ages 4–12)* ⊟ *AE, MC, V* ⊠ *EP.*

\$\$\$ 🏨 **Divi Carina Bay Resort.** Opt for a ground-floor room at this oceanfront resort, and you're just steps from the water's edge. The rooms are fresh, with rattan and wicker furniture, white-tile floors, sapphire and teal spreads, and sea-tone accessories that complement the white walls. You're a long way from anywhere here, so if you're not content to just read a good book on your balcony or patio, hit the casino across the street, or lounge at the pool or beach, you'll need a car to get around. ⊠ *25 Rte. 60, Estate Turner Hole 00820* ☎ *340/773–9700 or 877/773–9700* 🖷 *340/773–6802* ⊕ *www.divicarina.com* 🛏 *128 rooms, 2 suites, 20 villas* ⚘ *2 restaurants, snack bar, fans, in-room data ports, in-room safes, microwaves, refrigerators, 2 tennis courts, pool, gym, hot tub, outdoor hot tub, beach, dock, snorkeling, billiards, 3 bars, casino, video game room* ⊟ *AE, D, DC, MC, V* ⊠ *EP.*

\$\$ 🏨 **Tamarind Reef Hotel.** At this casual, motel-like seaside spot you can sunbathe at the large pool and sandy beach or snorkel in the reef, which comes right to the shore (and which makes serious swimming here difficult). The spacious modern rooms have rattan furniture, tropical-print drapes and spreads, and either a terrace or a deck with views of the water and St. Croix's sister islands to the north. Many rooms have basic kitchenettes—handy for preparing light meals. There's a snack bar just off the beach and a restaurant at the adjacent Green Cay Marina. ⊠ *5001 Tamarind Reef, off Rte. 82, Annas Hope 00820* ☎ *340/773–4455 or 800/619–0014* 🖷 *340/773–3989* ⊕ *www.usvi.net/hotel/tamarind* 🛏 *46 rooms* ⚘ *Snack bar, in-room data ports, some kitchenettes, refrigerators, pool, snorkeling, meeting rooms, no-smoking rooms* ⊟ *AE, DC, MC, V* ⊠ *EP.*

OUTSIDE FREDERIKSTED
\$–\$\$ 🏨 **Sandcastle on the Beach.** Right on a gorgeous stretch of white beach, this resort caters mainly to gay men and lesbians. Most are couples, but singles also enjoy the house-party atmosphere. There are several categories of rooms; some put you steps from the water, and most have sea views. Rooms have a modern decor, with Mexican tile floors, tropical rattan furniture, and bright print spreads. ⊠ *127 Smithfield, Rte. 71, Frederiksted 00840* ☎ *340/772–1205 or 800/524–2018* 🖷 *340/772–1757* ⊕ *www.sandcastleonthebeach.com* 🛏 *6 rooms, 11 suites, 4 villas* ⚘ *Restaurant, fans, kitchenettes, cable TV, in-room VCRs, 2 pools, beach, snorkeling; no kids* ⊟ *AE, D, MC, V* ⊠ *CP.*

NORTH SHORE
\$\$\$ 🏨 **Carambola Beach Resort.** The 25 two-story red-roof villas are connected by lovely, lush walkways. Rooms are identical except for the view—ocean or garden—and have terra-cotta floors, ceramic lamps, mahogany ceil-

ings and furnishings, and rocking chairs and sofas. Each room has a patio and a huge bath (shower only). The beach is beautiful and the remote location peaceful, but maintenance at this luxury resort slipped during bankruptcy proceedings. New owners have things on the upswing, but it has a way to go to reach perfection. The resort provides a complimentary shuttle to the nearby Carambola Golf Club. ⊠ *Rte. 80, Davis Bay* ☐ *Box 3031, Kingshill 00851* ☎ *340/778–3800 or 888/503–8760* ☐ *340/778–1682* ☞ *150 rooms* ☖ *2 restaurants, snack bar, fans, cable TV, in-room VCRs, 4 tennis courts, pool, gym, beach, dive shop, snorkeling, library, meeting rooms* ☰ *AE, D, DC, MC, V* ⏍ *CP.*

$$ ⊞ **Hibiscus Beach Hotel.** Rooms here are in five pink two-story buildings—each named for a tropical flower. Most rooms have ocean views, but those in the Hibiscus Building are closest to the water. All have roomy balconies and are tastefully decorated with white-tile floors, white walls, pink-striped curtains, floral spreads, and fresh-cut hibiscus blossoms. Bathrooms are clean but nondescript—both the shower stalls and the vanity mirrors are on the small side. ⊠ *4131 Estate La Grande Princesse, off Rte. 752, La Grand Princesse 00820-4441* ☎ *340/773–4042 or 800/ 442–0121* ☐ *340/773–7668* ⊕ *www.1hibiscus.com* ☞ *37 rooms* ☖ *Restaurant, in-room data ports, in-room safes, minibars, cable TV, pool, beach, snorkeling* ☰ *AE, D, MC, V* ⏍ *CP.*

$–$$ ⊞ **Waves at Cane Bay.** Lapping waves lull you to sleep at this isolated inn. Although the beach here is rocky, Cane Bay Beach is next door, and the world-famous Cane Bay Reef is just 100 yards offshore (divers take note: this is a PADI resort). You can also sunbathe on a small patch of sand beside the very unusual pool: it's carved from the coral along the shore, and waves crash dramatically over its side, creating a foamy whirlpool on blustery days. Two peach and mint-green buildings house enormous, balconied guest rooms that are done in cream and soft pastel prints. ⊠ *Rte. 80, Cane Bay* ☐ *Box 1749, Kingshill 00851* ☎ *340/ 778–1805 or 800/545–0603* ☐ *340/778–4945* ⊕ *www.canebaystcroix. com* ☞ *12 rooms, 1 villa* ☖ *Restaurant, fans, in-room data ports, in-room safes, kitchenettes, cable TV, pool, dive shop, snorkeling, bar, Internet; no a/c in some rooms* ☰ *AE, MC, V* ⏍ *EP.*

Cottages & Condominiums

$–$$$$ ⊞ **Sugar Beach.** A stay here puts you on the beach at the north side of the island and five minutes from Christiansted. The apartments, which range from studios to four-bedroom units, are immaculate and breezy. Each has a full kitchen and a large patio or balcony with an ocean view; larger units have washers and dryers. Though the exteriors of these condos are ordinary beige stucco, the interiors are lovely (white with tropical furnishings). The pool occupies the ruins of a 250-year-old sugar mill. ⊠ *Rte. 752, Estate Golden Rock 00820* ☎ *340/773–5345 or 800/524–2049* ☐ *340/773–1359* ⊕ *www.sugarbeachstcroix.com* ☞ *46 apartments* ☖ *Fans, kitchens, cable TV, 2 tennis courts, pool, beach, meeting rooms* ☰ *AE, D, MC, V* ⏍ *EP.*

★ $$$ ⊞ **Villa Madeleine.** A West Indian plantation great house is the centerpiece of this exquisite resort complex. Richly upholstered furniture, Asian rugs, teal walls, and whimsically painted driftwood set the mood in the billiards room, the library, and the sitting room. Each villa has a full kitchen and a pool, but only bedrooms are air-conditioned. Villas are all done up in tropical motifs: rattan furniture with plush cushions, rocking chairs, and, in some, bamboo four-poster beds. Special touches include pink-marble showers and hand-painted floral wall borders. Enjoy fine dining on the terrace at the Villa Madeleine Restaurant. ⊠ *Off Rte. 82, Teague Bay* ☐ *52 King St., Christiansted 00820* ☎ *340/773–4850 or 800/237–1959* ☐ *340/773–8989* ⊕ *www.teaguebayproperties.com*

🛏 *43 villas* ♿ *Restaurant, fans, kitchens, cable TV, tennis court, 43 pools, billiards, bar, library, concierge, meeting room* ☐ *AE, MC, V* ⊙ *EP.*

$$ 🖼 **Schooner Bay.** This red-roof condo village climbs a hill above Gallows Bay. Each modern two- or three-bedroom apartment has a balcony, a washer and dryer, and lovely sea views. Rattan furnishings are set on beige-tile floors; floral-print fabrics add splashes of color. Three-bedroom units have spiral staircases. Sun worshipers might be disappointed that the nearest beach is east, at the Buccaneer, but those with a yen to get out and about will find the location ideal—adjacent to the busy Gallows Bay shopping center and within walking distance of Christiansted. ✉ *5002 Gallows Bay, Gallows Bay 00820* 📠 *340-713-9599* ⊕ *www. stcroixconnect.com* 🛏 *60 apartments* ♿ *Fans, kitchens, cable TV, in-room VCRs, tennis court, 2 pools* ☐ *AE, V* ⊙ *EP.*

Private Homes & Villas

Renting a house gives you the convenience of home as well as top-notch amenities. Many houses have pools, hot tubs, and deluxe furnishings. Most companies meet you at the airport, arrange for a rental car, and provide helpful information. **Caribbean Property Management** (📠 340/ 778–8782 or 800/496–7379 ⊕ www.enjoystcroix.com) has villas across the island. **The Collection** (📠 856/751–2413) specializes in villas east of Christiansted. **Island Villas** (📠 340/773–8821 or 800/626–4512 ⊕ www. stcroixislandvillas.com) rents villas across St. Croix. **Rent A Villa** (📠 800/ 533–6863 ⊕ www.rentavillavacations.com) specializes in villas on the island's east end. **Vacation St. Croix** (📠 340/778–0361 or 877/788–0361 ⊕ www.vacationstx.com) has villas island-wide.

Where to Eat

Seven flags have flown over St. Croix, and each has left its legacy in the island's cuisine. You can feast on Italian, French, Danish, and American dishes; there are even Chinese and Mexican restaurants in Christiansted. Fresh local seafood is plentiful and always good; wahoo, mahimahi, and conch are popular. Island chefs often add Caribbean twists to familiar dishes. For a true island experience, stop at a local restaurant for goat stew, curried chicken, or fried pork chops. Regardless of where you eat, your meal will be an informal affair. But be forewarned, prices are a lot higher than you'd pay on the mainland.

For approximate costs, *see* the dining and lodging price chart at the beginning of this chapter.

Christiansted

CARIBBEAN ✕ **Indies.** Tables covered with handmade floral-print cloths are scattered
★ **$$–$$$** through the historic courtyard of this wonderful restaurant. The menu of island-inspired dishes changes each day to take advantage of St. Croix's freshest bounties. Indulge in the mango-basil crab cakes with curry onion to start, then the wahoo with ginger-coconut dasheen and roasted-pineapple vinaigrette. Finish with a yam and pecan custard tart. Enjoy live jazz Thursday through Saturday evenings and Sunday afternoons. ✉ *55–56 Company St.* 📠 *340/692–9440* ☐ *AE, D, MC, V* ⊙ *Closed Mon.*

$–$$ ✕ **Harvey's.** The plain, even dowdy dining room has just 14 tables, and plastic floral tablecloths constitute the sole attempt at decor. But who cares? The food is delicious. Daily specials, such as mouthwatering goat stew and tender whelks in butter, served with big helpings of rice, fungi, and vegetables, are listed on the blackboard. Genial owner Sarah Harvey takes great pride in her kitchen, bustling out from behind the stove to chat and urge you to eat up. ✉ *11B Company St.* 📠 *340/773– 3433* ☐ *No credit cards* ⊙ *Closed Sun. No dinner.*

CONTEMPORARY
★ **$$-$$$$**

✕ **Restaurant Bacchus.** On the chic side, this restaurant is as famous for its wine list as it is for its food. Named after the god of wine, it sees to it that its cellars hold an impressive variety. The menu is interesting, with old favorites like oysters Rockefeller as well trendy dishes like sliced tomato, cucumber, and Vidalia onion salad with blue-cheese dressing. Entrées vary from savory wild mushroom strudel with spinach, garlic, and herbs in a creamy sauce to New York strip steak with a green-peppercorn and brandy sauce. For dessert you might try the rum-drenched sourdough-bread pudding. ✉ *Queen Cross St., off King St.* ☎ *340/692–9922* ▱ *AE, MC, V* ✆ *Closed Sun.–Mon. No lunch.*

★ **$$$**

✕ **Kendricks.** The chef at this open-air restaurant—a longtime favorite with locals—conjures up creative, tasty cuisine. Try the Alaskan king crab cakes with lemon black-pepper aioli to start, or the warm chipotle pepper with garlic and onion soup. Move on to the house specialty: pecan-crusted roast pork loin with ginger mayonnaise. ✉ *21–32 Company St.* ☎ *340/773–9199* ▱ *AE, MC, V* ✆ *Closed Sun. No lunch.*

★ **$$-$$$**

✕ **Savant.** Savant is one of those small but special spots that locals love. The cuisine is a fusion of Mexican, Thai, and Caribbean—a combination that works well. Everything from a veggie dish covered with Thai red-coconut curry sauce to enchiladas stuffed with chicken, beef, or seafood, to maple teriyaki pork tenderloin comes out of the tiny kitchen. Since it has only 10 candlelit tables placed cheek by jowl, diners call early for reservations. ✉ *4C Hospital St.* ☎ *340/713–8666* ▱ *AE, D, MC, V* ✆ *No lunch.*

CONTINENTAL
$$-$$$
Fodor'sChoice
★

✕ **Top Hat.** Owned by a delightful Danish couple, this restaurant has been serving international cuisine (with Danish specialties, of course) since 1970. Dishes include roast duck stuffed with apples and prunes, *frikadeller* (savory meatballs in a tangy cocktail sauce), conch beignets, and smoked eel. The signature dessert is a rum ice cream–filled chocolate windmill whose blades turn. ✉ *52 Company St.* ☎ *340/773–2346* ▱ *AE, D, DC, MC, V* ✆ *No lunch.*

ECLECTIC
$

✕ **Morning Glory Coffee and Tea.** Stop by this cozy spot in a popular shopping center for light fare. Lunch runs to wrap sandwiches filled with veggies, cheeses, and lunchmeats, turkey clubs, and panini (filled, pressed, and grilled to create a new twist on a grilled cheese–like favorite). For breakfast, the chef conjures up waffles, beignets, croissants, and eggs cooked any way. Smoothies are a house specialty. ✉ *Gallows Bay Marketplace* ☎ *340/773–6620* ▱ *No credit cards* ✆ *Closed Sun. No dinner.*

FRENCH
★ **$-$$**

✕ **Café Christine.** A favorite with the professionals who work in downtown Christiansted, Café Christine's presentation is as lovely as the food. The small menu changes daily, but look for dishes like a green salad with salmon and shrimp drizzled with a lovely vinaigrette dressing or a vegetarian plate with quiche, salad, and lentils. Desserts are perfection. If the pear pie topped with chocolate is on the menu, don't hesitate. This tiny restaurant has both air-conditioned indoor tables and an outside porch that overlooks historic buildings. ✉ *Apothecary Hall Courtyard, 4 Company St.* ☎ *340/713–1500* ▱ *No credit cards* ✆ *Closed weekends. No dinner.*

ITALIAN
$$-$$$

✕ **Tutto Bene.** Its yellow walls, brightly striped cushions, and painted trompe-l'oeil tables make Tutto Bene look more like a sophisticated Mexican cantina than an Italian cucina. One bite of the food, however, will clear up any confusion. Written on hanging mirrors is the daily menu, which includes such fare as grilled chicken and seasonal vegetables on a skewer and scallops with prosciutto, sage, and mozzarella. Desserts, including a decadent tiramisu, are on the menu as well. ⊠ *2 Company St.* ☎ *340/773–5229* ▱ *AE, MC, V.*

Outside Christiansted

ECLECTIC
$$–$$$
✕ **Breezez.** This aptly named restaurant sits poolside at Club St. Croix condominiums. Visitors and locals are drawn by its reasonable prices and good food. This is *the* place to be for Sunday brunch, where the menu includes lobster rolls, burgers, and blackened prime rib with Cajun seasonings and horseradish sauce. For dessert, try the flourless chocolate torte—a wedge of rich chocolate served with a river of chocolate sauce. ⊠ *Club St. Croix, 3220 Golden Rock, off Rte. 752, Golden Rock* ☎ *340/773–7077* ▱ *AE, D, MC, V.*

East End

CONTEMPORARY
$$$–$$$$
✕ **Villa Madeleine Restaurant.** The elegant restaurant at the Villa Madeleine resort serves such classics as roast whole rack of lamb seasoned with garlic and rosemary, as well as whole lobsters. The Sunday brunch is legendary, and the wine list equally extensive. Take Route 82 out of Christiansted, turn right at Reef Condominiums. ⊠ *19A Teague Bay, Teague Bay* ☎ *340/778–7377* ▱ *AE, MC, V* ☿ *No lunch.*

ECLECTIC
$$–$$$
✕ **The Galleon.** This dockside restaurant is popular with both locals and visitors. Start with the Caesar salad or escargots. Pasta lovers should sample the pasta primavera, a delightful dish made with fresh pasta, whatever vegetables the chef brings home, and olive oil and garlic or a cream sauce. The osso buco and rack of lamb are legendary. Take Route 82 out of Christiansted, turn left at the sign for Green Cay Marina. ⊠ *Annas Hope* ☎ *340/773–9949* ▱ *MC, V* ☿ *No lunch.*

$$–$$$
✕ **South Shore Cafe.** This casual bistro popular with locals for its good food sits near the Great Salt Pond on the island's south shore. The restaurant's menu includes dishes drawn from several different cuisines. Meat lovers and vegetarians can find common ground with a menu that runs from handmade pasta to prime rib. The selection isn't extensive, but the chef puts together a blackboard full of specials every day. ⊠ *Rte. 62 at Rte. 624, Sally's Fancy* ☎ *340/773–9311* ▱ *V* ☿ *Closed Mon.–Tues. No lunch.*

Frederiksted

ECLECTIC
$$–$$$$
✕ **Le St. Tropez.** A ceramic-tile bar and soft lighting set the mood at this pleasant Mediterranean bistro tucked into a courtyard off Frederiksted's main thoroughfare. Seated either inside or on the adjoining patio, you can enjoy such items as grilled meats in delicate French sauces. The menu changes daily, often taking advantage of local seafood. The fresh basil, tomato, and mozzarella salad is heavenly. ⊠ *227 King St.* ☎ *340/772–3000* ▱ *AE, MC, V* ☿ *Closed Sun. No lunch Sat.*

$$–$$$
✕ **Blue Moon.** This terrific little bistro, popular for its live jazz on Friday night, has a changing menu that draws on Asian, Cajun, and local flavors. Try the spicy gumbo with andouille sausage or crab cakes with a spicy aioli as an appetizer; shrimp scampi loaded with garlic and served over pasta as an entrée; and the Almond Joy sundae for dessert. ⊠ *17 Strand St.* ☎ *340/772–2222* ▱ *AE, MC, V* ☿ *Closed Mon.*

Cane Bay

ECLECTIC
$–$$
✕ **Off the Wall.** Divers fresh from a plunge at the north shore's popular Wall gather at this breezy spot right on the beach. If you want to sit a spell before you order, a hammock beckons. Burgers, fish sandwiches, quesadillas, and Philly steak sandwiches join pizza and hot dogs on the menu. The potato salad that comes with your sandwich is as good as you'd get at home. You might find blues and jazz Tuesday through Sunday nights. ⊠ *Rte. 80* ☎ *340/778–4771* ▱ *AE, MC, V.*

Beaches

★ **Buck Island.** A visit to this island beach, part of Buck Island Reef National Monument, is a must. The beach is beautiful, but its finest treasures are those you can see when you plop off the boat and adjust your mask, snorkel, and flippers. To get here, you'll have to charter a boat or go on an organized trip.

Cane Bay. The waters aren't always gentle at this breezy north shore beach, but there are seldom many people around, and the scuba diving and snorkeling are wondrous. You'll see elkhorn and brain corals, and less than 200 yards out is the drop-off called Cane Bay Wall.

Cramer's Park. This USVI territorial beach on the northeast coast (Route 82) is very popular with locals. It's a good spot for beach picnics and camping. Because of its isolation, though, it's not a good place to linger if you're traveling solo.

Isaacs Bay. This east-end beach is almost impossible to reach without a four-wheel-drive vehicle, but it's worth the effort. Here you can find secluded sands for sunbathing, calm waters for swimming, and a barrier reef for snorkeling. You can also get here via footpaths from Jack's Bay.

Tamarind Reef Beach. Small but attractive Tamarind Reef Beach is east of Christiansted. Both Green Cay and Buck Island seem smack in front of you—an arresting view. The snorkeling is good.

West End Beaches. There are several unnamed beaches along the coast road north of Frederiksted. Just pull over at whatever piece of powdery sand catches your fancy. The beach at the Rainbow Beach Club, a five-minute drive outside Frederiksted on Route 63, has a bar, a casual restaurant, water sports, and volleyball.

Sports & the Outdoors

BOAT TOURS Day sail to Buck Island aboard a charter boat. Most leave from the Christiansted waterfront or from Green Cay Marina. They stop for a snorkel at the island's eastern end before dropping anchor off a gorgeous sandy beach for a swim, a hike, and lunch. A full-day sail runs about $65 with lunch included on most trips. A half-day sail costs about $50. **Big Beard's Adventure Tours** (☎ 340/773–4482) takes you on a catamaran, the *Renegade* or the *Flyer,* from the Christiansted waterfront to Buck Island for snorkeling before dropping anchor at a private beach for a barbecue lunch. **Mile Mark Charters** (☎ 340/773–2628) departs from the Christiansted waterfront for half- and full-day trips on various boats. **Teroro Charters** (☎ 340/773–3161) trimaran *Teroro II* leaves Green Cay Marina for full- or half-day sails. Bring your own lunch.

FISHING In the past quarter century, some 20 world records—many for blue marlin—have been set in these waters. Sailfish, skipjack, bonito, tuna (allison, blackfin, and yellowfin), and wahoo are abundant. A charter runs about $100 an hour per person, with most boats going out for four-, six- or eight-hour trips. **Captain Peter's Sportfishing** (⊠ St. Croix Marina, Gallows Bay ☎ 340/773–1123) will take you fishing in his 27-ft *Louis G*. **Mile Mark Charters** (⊠ 59 King's Wharf, Christiansted ☎ 340/773–2628) will take you out on a 38-ft powerboat, the *Fantasy*.

GOLF St. Croix's courses welcome you with spectacular vistas and well-kept greens. Check with your hotel or the tourist board to determine when major celebrity tournaments will be held. There's often an opportunity to play with the pros. **The Buccaneer** (⊠ Rte. 82, Shoys ☎ 340/773–2100) has an 18-hole course that is conveniently close to Christiansted. The

★ spectacular 18-hole course at **Carambola Golf Club** (⊠ Rte. 80, Davis Bay ☎ 340/778–5638), in the northwest valley, was designed by Robert Trent

Jones, Sr. The **Reef Golf Course** (✉ Teague Bay ☎ 340/773–8844), in the northeastern part of the island, has 9 holes.

HIKING Although you can set off by yourself on a hike through a rain forest or along a shore, a guide will point out what's important and tell you why. The nonprofit **St. Croix Environmental Association** (✉ Arawak Bldg., Suite 3, Gallows Bay 00820 ☎ 340/773–1989) offers treks through several ecological treasures, including Estate Annaly, Estate Hermitage, Estate Punch, Salt River, and the northwest and northeast Scenic Ridge Road. The cost is $40 per person for a 3-hour hike.

HORSEBACK Well-kept roads and expert guides make horseback riding on St. Croix RIDING pleasurable. At Sprat Hall, just north of Frederiksted, Jill Hurd runs **Paul and Jill's Equestrian Stables** (✉ Rte. 58, Frederiksted ☎ 340/772–2880 or 340/772–2627) and will take you clip-clopping through the rain forest, across pastures, and to hilltops (explaining the flora, fauna, and ruins on the way). A 1½-hour ride costs $50.

KAYAKING **Caribbean Adventure Tours** (✉ Columbus Cove Marina, Rte. 80, Salt River ☎ 340/773–4599) takes you on trips through Salt River National Park and Ecological Preserve, one of the island's most pristine areas. A daytime ecotour runs $45, and a moonlight trip is $40.

SCUBA DIVING & At **Buck Island,** a short boat ride from Christiansted or Green Cay Ma-
SNORKELING rina, the reef is so nice that it's been named a national monument. You can dive right off the beach at **Cane Bay,** which has a spectacular dropoff. **Frederiksted Pier** is home to a colony of seahorses, creatures seldom seen in the waters off the Virgin Islands. At **Green Cay,** just outside Green Cay Marina in the east end, you can see colorful fish swimming around the reefs and rocks. Two exceptional north shore sites are **North Star** and **Salt River,** which you can reach only by boat. At Salt River you can float downward through a canyon filled with colorful fish and coral.

The island's dive shops take you out for one- or two-tank dives. Plan to pay about $50 for a one-tank dive and $70 for a two-tank dive, including equipment and an underwater tour. **Anchor Dive Center** (✉ Salt River Marina, Rte. 801, Salt River ☎ 340/778–1522 or 800/532–3483) takes divers to 35 sites, including the wall at Salt River Canyon and Buck Island Reef National Monument. It also offers PADI certification. **Cane Bay Dive Shop** (✉ Rte. 80, Cane Bay ☎ 340/773–9913 or 800/338–3843) takes you on boat and beach dives along the north shore. The famed Wall is just 150 yards from their shop. **Dive Experience** (✉ 40 Strand St., Christiansted ☎ 340/773–3307 or 800/235–9047) is a five-star PADI training facility that offers·everything from introductory dives to certification. It also runs trips to the north shore walls and reefs. **St. Croix Ultimate Bluewater Adventures** (✉ 14 Caravelle Arcade, Christiansted ☎ 340/773–5994 or 877/567–1367) is a PADI international outfit that will take you to your choice of over 20 sites. **Scuba Shack** (✉ Frederiksted Beach, Rte. 631, Frederiksted ☎ 340/772–3483) takes divers right off the beach near the Rainbow Beach Club or on boat trips to wrecks and reefs. **Scuba West** (✉ 330 Strand St., Frederiksted ☎ 340/772–3701 or 800/352–0107) operates out of Frederiksted. Although it runs trips to reefs and wrecks, its specialty is the seahorses that live around the Frederiksted Pier.

TENNIS The public courts in Frederiksted and out east at Cramer Park are in questionable shape. It's better to pay a fee and play at one of the hotel courts. Costs vary by resort, but count on paying at least $10 an hour. **The Buccaneer** (✉ Rte. 82, Shoys ☎ 340/773–2100) has eight courts (two lighted), plus a pro and a full tennis shop. **Carambola Beach Resort** (✉ Rte. 80, Davis Bay ☎ 340/778–3800) has four lighted courts. **Chenay**

Bay Beach Resort (⊠ Rte. 82, Green Cay ☎ 340/773–2918) has two courts (no lights). **Club St. Croix** (⊠ Rte. 752, Estate Golden Rock ☎ 340/773–4800) has three lighted courts.

WINDSURFING St. Croix's trade winds make windsurfing a breeze. Most hotels rent Windsurfers and other water-sports equipment to nonguests. **St. Croix Watersports** (⊠ Hotel on the Cay, Christiansted ☎ 340/773–7060) offers Windsurfer rentals, sales, and rides; parasailing; and water-sports equipment, such as Sea Doos and kayaks. Renting a Windsurfer runs about $25 an hour.

Shopping

Areas & Malls

Although the shopping on St. Croix isn't as varied or extensive as that on St. Thomas, the island does have several small stores with unusual merchandise. In Christiansted the best shopping areas are the **Pan Am Pavilion** and **Caravelle Arcade,** off Strand Street, **Kings Alley Walk,** and along **King** and **Company streets.** These streets give way to arcades filled with boutiques. **Gallows Bay** has a blossoming shopping area in a quiet neighborhood. Stores are often closed on Sunday.

The best shopping in Frederiksted is along **Strand Street** and in the side streets and alleyways that connect it with **King Street.** Most stores close Sunday except when a cruise ship is in port. One caveat: Frederiksted's bad boys have been known to cause some problems, so for safety's sake stick to populated areas of Strand and King streets.

Specialty Items

BOOKS **The Bookie.** This shop carries paperback novels, stationery, newspapers, and cards. Stop in for the latest gossip and to find out about upcoming events. ⊠ *1111 Strand St., Christiansted* ☎ *340/773–2592.*
Undercover Books. For Caribbean books or the latest good read, try this bookstore across from the post office in the Gallows Bay shopping area. ⊠ *5030 Anchor Way, Gallows Bay* ☎ *340/719–1567.*

CLOTHING **Coconut Vine.** Pop into this store at the start of your vacation, and you'll leave with enough comfy cotton or rayon batik men's and women's clothes to make you look like a local. Although the tropical designs and colors originated in Indonesia, they're perfect for the Caribbean. ⊠ *King's Alley, Christiansted* ☎ *340/773–1991.*
From the Gecko. Come here for the hippest clothes on St. Croix, from superb batik sarongs to hand-painted silk scarves. ⊠ *1233 Queen Cross St., Christiansted* ☎ *340/778–9433.*
The White House/Black Market. This contemporary store sells clothes in all-white, black, and natural colors. Look for exquisite lingerie, elegant evening wear, and unusual casual outfits. ⊠ *8B Kings Alley Walk, Christiansted* ☎ *340/773–9222.*

FOODSTUFFS If you've rented a condominium or a villa, you'll appreciate that St. Croix offers excellent shopping at its stateside-style supermarkets. Fresh vegetables, fruits, and meats arrive frequently. Try the open-air stands strung out along Route 70 for island produce.

Cost-U-Less. This warehouse-type store across from Sunshine Mall doesn't charge a membership fee. It's just outside Frederiksted, across from Kmart. ⊠ *Rte. 70, Hogensborg* ☎ *340/692–2220.*
Plaza Extra. Shop here for Middle Eastern foods in addition to the usual grocery-store items. ⊠ *United Shopping Plaza, Rte. 70, Sion Farm* ☎ *340/778–6240* ⊠ *Rte. 70, Mount Pleasant* ☎ *340/719–1870.*
Pueblo This stateside-style market has branches all over the island.

⊠ *Orange Grove Shopping Center, Rte. 75, Christiansted* ☎ *340/773–0118* ⊠ *Sunny Isle Shopping Center, Rte. 70, Sunny Isle* ☎ *340/778–5005* ⊠ *Villa La Reine Shopping Center, Rte. 75, La Reine* ☎ *340/778–1272.*

Schooner Bay Market. Although it's on the smallish side, Schooner Bay has good-quality deli items. ⊠ *Rte. 82, just outside of town, Mount Welcome* ☎ *340/773–3232.*

GIFTS **Gone Tropical.** Whether you're looking for inexpensive souvenirs of your trip or a special, singular gift, you'll probably find it here. On her travels about the world, owner Margo Meacham keeps her eye out for special delights for her shop—from tablecloths and napkins in bright Caribbean colors to carefully crafted metal birds. ⊠ *5 Company St., Christiansted* ☎ *340/773–4696.*

Island Webe. The coffees, jams, and spices—produced locally or elsewhere in the Caribbean—will tempt your taste buds. Small *mocko jumbie* dolls depict an African tradition transported to the islands during slave days (they represent the souls of the ancestors of African slaves). The fabric dolls wearing Caribbean costumes will delight kids of all ages. Turn the double dolls upside down to see a white face on one side and a black one on the other. ⊠ *210 Strand St., Frederiksted* ☎ *340/772–2555.*

Mitchell-Larsen Studio. Carefully crafted glass plates, sun-catchers, and more grace the shelves of this interesting store. All made on-site by two St. Croix glassmakers, the pieces are often whimsically adorned with tropical fish, flora, and fauna. ⊠ *58 Company St., Christiansted* ☎ *340/719–1000.*

Royal Poinciana. This attractive shop is filled with island seasonings and hot sauces, West Indian crafts, bath gels, and herbal teas. Shop here for tablecloths and paper goods in tropical brights. ⊠ *1111 Strand St., Christiansted* ☎ *340/773–9892.*

Soul of Africa. The African masks, wine glasses with African motifs, and aromatherapy candles will catch your eye. Elegant silk jackets, classy sandals, and batik bedspreads in unusual patterns also fill the shelves. ⊠ *Kings Alley, Christiansted* ☎ *340/773–3099.*

Tradewinds Shop. Whatever the wind blew in seems to land here. Glass sailboats glide across the shelves while metal fish sculptures swim nearby. Candles with tropical motifs, notecards, and costume jewelry jostle for space with Naot sandals. ⊠ *53 King St., Christiansted* ☎ *340/719–3920.*

HOUSEWARES **St. Croix Landmarks Museum Store.** If a mahogany armoire or cane-backed rocker catches your fancy, the staff will arrange to have it shipped to your mainland home at no charge from its mainland warehouse. Furniture aside, this store has one of the largest selections of local art along with Caribbean-inspired bric-a-brac in all price ranges. ⊠ *5A King St., Christiansted* ☎ *340/713–8102.*

Textiles with a Story. Asian rugs mingle with island-inspired batiks at this store that seems like it came straight out of an Arabian souk. Comfy pillows in varied motifs and colors invite you to rest. ⊠ *52 King St., Christiansted* ☎ *340/692–9867.*

JEWELRY **Crucian Gold.** This store carries the unique gold creations of St. Croix native Brian Bishop. His trademark piece is the Turk's Head ring (a knot of interwoven gold strands), but the chess sets with Caribbean motifs as the playing pieces are just lovely. ⊠ *59 King's Wharf, Christiansted* ☎ *340/773–5241.*

The Gold Shop. Specializing—of course—in gold jewelry, this store also carries diamonds, emeralds, rubies, and sapphires. Jewelers will create one-of-a-kind pieces to your design. ⊠ *1102 Strand St., Christiansted* ☎ *340/773–0365 or 800/416–9078.*

Karavan West Indies. The owner here designs her own jewelry and also sells an assortment of tchotchkes, including handmade Christmas ornaments. ⊠ *5030 Anchor Way, Gallows Bay* ☎ *340/773–9999.*

Sonya's. Sonya Hough invented the hook bracelet, popular among locals as well as visitors. With hurricanes hitting the island so frequently, she has added an interesting decoration to these bracelets: the swirling symbol used in weather forecasts to indicate these storms. ⊠ *1 Company St., Christiansted* ☎ *340/778–8605.*

LIQUOR & TOBACCO **Baci Duty Free Liquor and Tobacco.** A walk-in humidor with a good selection of Arturo Fuente, Partagas, and Macanudo cigars is the centerpiece of this store. It also carries sleek Danish-made watches and Lladro figurines. ⊠ *55 Company St., Christiansted* ☎ *340/773–5040.*

Cruzan Rum Distillery. A tour of the company's factory culminates in a tasting of its products, all sold here at bargain prices. ⊠ *West Airport Rd., Estate Diamond* ☎ *340/692–2280.*

Kmart. The two branches of this discount department store—a large one in the Sunshine Mall and a smaller one mid-island at Sunny Isle Shopping Center—carry a huge line of discounted, duty-free liquor. ⊠ *Sunshine Mall, Rte. 70, Frederiksted* ☎ *340/692–5848* ⊠ *Sunny Isle Shopping Center, Rte. 70, Sunny Isle* ☎ *340/719–9190.*

PERFUMES **Violette Boutique.** Perfumes, cosmetics, and skin-care products are the draws here. ⊠ *Caravelle Arcade, 38 Strand St., Christiansted* ☎ *340/773–2148.*

Nightlife & the Arts

The island's nightlife is ever-changing, and its arts scene is eclectic—ranging from Christmastime performances of the *Nutcracker* to whatever local group got organized enough to put on a show. Folk-art traditions, such as quadrille dancers, are making a comeback. To find out what's happening, pick up the local newspapers—*V.I. Daily News* and *St. Croix Avis*—which are available at newsstands. Christiansted has a lively and eminently casual club scene near the waterfront. Frederiksted has a couple of restaurants and clubs offering weekend entertainment.

Nightlife

Hotel on the Cay (⊠ Protestant Cay, Christiansted ☎ 340/773–2035) has a West Indian buffet on Tuesday nights in the winter season, when you can watch a broken-bottle dancer (a dancer who braves a carpet of broken bottles) and mocko jumbie characters. Easy jazz flows from the courtyard bar at **Indies** (⊠ 55–56 Company St., Christiansted ☎ 340/692–9440) Thursday, Friday, and Saturday evenings. The **2 Plus 2 Disco** (⊠ 17 La Grande Princesse, Christiansted ☎ 340/773–3710) spins a great mix of calypso, soul, disco, and reggae; there's live music on Saturdays.

Blue Moon (⊠ 17 Strand St., Frederiksted ☎ 340/772–2222), a waterfront restaurant, is the place to be for live jazz on Friday 9 PM–1 AM.

Outside Frederiksted, **Off the Wall** (⊠ Rte. 80, Cane Bay ☎ 340/778–4471) has blues or jazz Tuesday–Sunday from 6 PM to 9 PM.

The Arts

The **Whim Plantation Museum** (⊠ Rte. 70, Estate Whim ☎ 340/772–0598), which is just outside of Frederiksted, hosts classical music concerts during the winter season.

Exploring St. Croix

Though there are things to see and do in St. Croix's two towns, Christiansted and Frederiksted (both named after Danish kings), there are lots of interesting spots in between them and to the east of Christiansted. Just be sure you have a map in hand (pick one up at rental-car agencies, or stop by the tourist office for an excellent one that's free). Many secondary roads remain unmarked; if you get confused, ask for help.

Numbers in the margin correspond to points of interest on the St. Croix map.

Christiansted & the East

Christiansted is a historic Danish-style town that always served as St. Croix's commercial center. Your best bet is to see the historic sights in the morning, when it's still cool. This two-hour endeavor won't tax your walking shoes and will leave you with energy to poke around the town's eclectic shops. Break for lunch at an open-air restaurant before spending as much time as you like shopping.

An easy drive (roads are flat and well marked) to St. Croix's eastern end takes you through some choice real estate. Ruins of old sugar estates dot the landscape. You can make the entire loop on the road that circles the island in about an hour, a good way to end the day. If you want to spend a full day exploring, you'll find some nice beaches and easy walks with places to stop for lunch.

SIGHTS TO SEE
❶
Fodor's Choice
★

Christiansted. In the 1700s and 1800s this town was a trading center for sugar, rum, and molasses. Today there are law offices, tourist shops, and restaurants, but many of the buildings, which start at the harbor and go up into the gentle hillsides, still date from the 18th century. You can't get lost. All streets lead gently downhill to the water. Still, if you want some friendly advice, stop by the **Visitor Center** (✉ 53A Company St. ☎ 340/773–0495) weekdays between 8 and 5 for maps and brochures. Large, yellow **Ft. Christiansvaern** (✉ Hospital St. ☎ 340/773–1460 ⊕ www.nps.gov/chrii) dominates the waterfront. Because it's so easy to spot, it makes a good place from which to begin a walking tour. In 1749 the Danish built the fort to protect the harbor, but the structure was repeatedly damaged by hurricane-force winds and was partially rebuilt in 1771. It's now a national historic site, the best preserved of the few remaining Danish-built forts in the Virgin Islands, and houses the park's Visitor Center. The $3 admission includes admission to the Steeple Building. Hours are daily from 8 to 4:45. When you're tired of sightseeing, stop at **D. Hamilton Jackson Park** (✉ Between Ft. Christiansvaern and the Danish Customs House)—on the street side of Ft. Christiansvaern—for a rest. It's named for a famed labor leader, judge, and journalist who started the first newspaper not under the thumb of the Danish crown. Built in 1830 on foundations that date from 1734, the **Danish Customs House** (✉ King St. ☎ 340/773–1460 ⊕ www.nps.gov/chrii) near Ft. Christiansvaern originally served as both a customs house and a post office (second floor). In 1926 it became the Christiansted Library, and it has been a National Park office since 1972. It's open weekdays from 8 to 5. Constructed in 1856, the **Scale House** (✉ King St. ☎ 340/773–1460 ⊕ www.nps.gov/chrii) was once the spot where goods passing through the port were weighed and inspected. Park staff now sells a good selection of books about St. Croix history and its flora and fauna. The Scale House is open daily from 8 to 4:30. Built by the Danes in 1753, the **Steeple Building** (✉ Church St. ☎ 340/773–1460) was the first Danish Lutheran church on St. Croix. It's now a national park museum and contains exhibits that document the island's Indian inhabitants. It's worth the short walk from Ft. Christiansvaern to see the building's collection of archaeological artifacts, displays on plantation life, and exhibits on the architectural development of Christiansted, the early history of the church, and Alexander Hamilton, the first secretary of the U.S. Treasury, who grew up in St. Croix. Open daily from 9 to 4:30; the $3 admission includes admission to Ft. Christiansvaern. The **Post Office Building** (⊠ Church St.), built in 1749, was once the Danish West India & Guinea Company warehouse. It's closed for renovation, but it's worth a look from the outside. One of the town's most elegant structures, **Government House** (⊠ King St. ☎ 340/773–1404) was built as a home for a Danish merchant in 1747. Today it houses USVI government offices. If the building is open (hours are weekdays from 8 to 5), slip into the peaceful inner courtyard to admire the still pools and gardens. A sweeping staircase leads you to a second-story ballroom, still used for official government functions. Built in 1735 as a slave market, today **the market** (⊠ Company St.), housed in a wood and galvanized aluminum structure, is where farmers and others sell their goods every Wednesday and Saturday from 8 to 5. The **Buck Island Reef National Monument** (⊠ Buck Island, off the north shore of St. Croix ☎ 340/773– 1460 park headquarters ⊕ www.nps.gov/buis), off the northeast coast, has pristine beaches that are just right for sunbathing, but there's enough shade for those who don't want to fry. The snorkeling trail set in the reef allows close-up study of coral formations and tropical fish. It's suffered some in the spate of hurricanes that have hit the island since 1989, but scientists consider it to be on the mend. There's an easy hiking trail to the island's highest point, where you'll be rewarded for your efforts by spectacular views of the reef and St. John. Charter-boat trips leave daily from the Christiansted waterfront or from Green Cay Marina, about 2 mi (3 km) east of Christiansted. Check with your hotel for recommendations.

② **Point Udall.** This rocky promontory, the easternmost point in the United States, is about a half-hour's drive from Christiansted. A paved road takes you to an overlook with glorious views. More adventurous folks can hike down to the pristine beach below. On the way back, look for The Castle, an enormous mansion that can only be described as a cross between a Moorish mosque and the Taj Mahal. It was built by an extravagant recluse known only as the Contessa. ⊠ *Rte. 82, Et Stykkeland.*

Between Christiansted & Frederiksted

A drive through the countryside between these two towns will take you past ruins of old plantations, many bearing whimsical names (Morningstar, Solitude, Upper Love) bestowed by early owners. The traffic moves quickly—by island standards—on the main roads, but you can pause and poke around if you head down some side lanes. It's easy to find your way west, but driving from north to south requires good navigation. Don't leave your hotel without a map. Allow an entire day for this trip, so you'll have enough time for a swim at a north shore beach. Although you'll find lots of casual eateries on the main roads, pick up a picnic lunch if you plan to head off the beaten path.

SIGHTS TO SEE **Judith's Fancy.** In this upscale neighborhood are the ruins of an old great **④** house and tower of the same name, both remnants of a circa-1750 Danish sugar plantation. The "Judith" comes from the first name of a woman buried on the property. From the guard house at the neighborhood entrance, follow Hamilton Drive past some of St. Croix's loveliest homes. At the end of Hamilton Drive the road overlooks Salt River Bay, where Christopher Columbus anchored in 1493. On the way back, make a detour left off Hamilton Drive onto Caribe Road for a close look at the ruins. ⊹ *Turn north onto Rte. 751, off Rte. 75.*

③ **Little Princess Estate.** If the old plantation ruins decaying here and there around St. Croix intrigue you, a visit to this Nature Conservancy project will give you even more of a glimpse into the past. The staff has carved walking paths out of the bush that surrounds what's left of a 19th-century plantation. It's easy to stroll among well-labeled fruit trees and see the ruins of the windmill, the sugar and rum factory, and the laborers' village. This is the perfect place to reflect on St. Croix's agrarian past fueled with labor from African slaves. The property also has a community garden. ⚓ *Just off Rte. 75; turn north at the Five Corners traffic light* ☎ *340/773–5575* 💲 *Free* ⊘ *Tues. and Thurs. 3–5.*

❻ Mt. Eagle. This is St. Croix's highest peak (1,165 ft [356 m]). Leaving Cane Bay and passing North Star Beach, follow the coastal road that dips briefly into a forest, then turn left on Route 69. Just after you make the turn, the pavement is marked with the words THE BEAST and a set of giant paw prints. The hill you're about to climb is the famous Beast of the St. Croix Half Ironman Triathlon, an annual event during which participants must bike this intimidating slope. ✉ *Rte. 69.*

❺ Salt River Bay National Historical Park and Ecological Preserve. This joint national and local park commemorates the area where Christopher Columbus's men skirmished with the Carib Indians in 1493 on his second visit to the New World. The peninsula on the bay's east side is named for the event: Cabo de las Flechas (Cape of the Arrows). Although the park isn't developed, it has several sights with cultural significance. A ball court, used by the Caribs in religious ceremonies, was discovered at the spot where the taxis park. Take a short hike up the dirt road to the ruins of an old earthen fort for great views of Salt River Bay and the surrounding countryside. The area also encompasses a biodiverse coastal estuary with the largest remaining mangrove forest in the USVI, a submarine canyon, and several endangered species, including the hawksbill turtle and the roseate tern. ✉ *Rte. 75 to Rte. 80, Salt River* ☎ *340/773–1460* ⊕ *www.nps.gov/sari.*

Frederiksted & Environs

St. Croix's second-largest town, Frederiksted, was founded in 1751. A stroll around its historic sights will take you no more than an hour. Allow a little more time if you want to browse in the few small shops. The area just outside town has old plantations, some of which have been preserved as homes or historic structures that are open to the public.

SIGHTS TO SEE **Carl and Marie Lawaetz Museum.** For a trip back in time, tour this circa-❾ 1750 farm. Owned by the prominent Lawaetz family since 1899, just after Carl arrived from Denmark, the lovely two-story house is in a valley at La Grange. A Lawaetz family member shows you the four-poster mahogany bed Carl and Marie shared, the china Marie painted, the family portraits, and the fruit trees that fed the family for several generations. Initially a sugar plantation, it was subsequently used to raise cattle and produce. ✉ *Rte. 76, Mahogany Rd., Estate Little La Grange* ☎ *340/772–1539* ⊕ *www.stcroixlandmarks.com/lawaetz* 💲 *$6* ⊘ *Tues., Wed., Fri–Sun. 10–4.*

❼ Estate Mount Washington Plantation. Several years ago, while surveying the property, the owners discovered the ruins of a sugar plantation beneath the rain-forest brush. The grounds have since been cleared and opened to the public. You can take a self-guided walking tour of the mill, the rum factory, and other ruins, and there's an antiques shop in what were once the stables (watch for antiques shop sign). ✉ *Rte. 63, Mount Washington* ☎ *340/772–1026* ⊘ *Ruins open daily dawn–dusk; antiques shop open by appointment only.*

❽ Frederiksted. The town is noted less for its Danish than for its Victorian architecture, which dates from after the slave uprising and the great fire of 1878. One long cruise-ship pier juts into the sparkling sea. It's the perfect place to start a tour of this quaint city. The **Visitor Center** (⊠ Waterfront ☎ 340/772–0357), right on the pier, has brochures from numerous St. Croix businesses. You can stop in weekdays from 8 to 5 to view the exhibits on St. Croix. On July 3, 1848, 8,000 slaves marched on the red-brick **Ft. Frederik** (⊠ Waterfront ☎ 340/772–2021) to demand their freedom. Danish governor Peter von Scholten, fearing they would burn the town to the ground, stood up in his carriage parked in front of the fort and granted their wish. The fort, completed in 1760, houses a number of interesting historical exhibits as well as an art gallery and a display of police memorabilia. It's within earshot of the Visitor Center. Admission is free; hours are weekdays from 8 to 5. **St. Patrick's** Roman Catholic church (⊠ Prince St.), complete with three turrets, was built in 1843 of coral. Wander inside, and you'll see woodwork handcrafted by Frederiksted artisans. The churchyard is filled with 18th-century gravestones. **St. Paul's Anglican Church** (⊠ Prince St.), built circa 1812, is a mix of Georgian and Gothic Revival architecture. The bell tower of exposed sandstone was added later. The simple interior has gleaming woodwork and a tray ceiling (it looks like an upside-down tray) popular in Caribbean architecture. Built in 1839, **Apothecary Hall** (⊠ King Cross St.) is a good example of 19th-century architecture; its facade has both Gothic and Greek Revival elements. Stop at the Queen Street **market** for fresh fruits and vegetables (be sure to wash or peel this produce before eating it) sold each morning, just as they have been for more than 200 years.

⑩ St. Croix Leap. This workshop sits in the heart of the rain forest, about a 15-minute drive from Frederiksted. It sells mirrors, tables, bread boards, and mahogany jewelry boxes crafted by local artisans. ⊠ *Rte. 76, Brooks Hill* ☎ 340/772–0421 ⊘ *Weekdays 8–5, Sat. 10–4.*

⑬ St. George Village Botanical Gardens. At this 17-acre estate, lush, fragrant flora grows amid the ruins of a 19th-century sugarcane plantation village. There are miniature versions of each ecosystem on St. Croix, from a semiarid cactus grove to a verdant rain forest. ⊠ *Rte. 70, turn north at the sign, St. George* ☎ 340/692–2874 ⊕ *www.sgvbg.com* ☒ *$6* ⊘ *Tues.-Sat. 9–4.*

⑪ West End Salt Pond. A bird-watcher's delight, this salt pond attracts a large numbers of winged creatures, including flamingos. ⊠ *Veteran's Shore Dr., Hesselberg.*

★ ☚ ⑫ Whim Plantation Museum. The lovingly restored estate, with a windmill, cook house, and other buildings, will give you a sense of what life was like on St. Croix's sugar plantations in the 1800s. The oval-shape great house has high ceilings and antique furniture and utensils. Notice its fresh, airy atmosphere—the waterless stone moat around the great house was used not for defense but for gathering cooling air. If you have kids, the grounds are the perfect place for them to stretch their legs, perhaps while you browse in the museum gift shop. It's just outside of Frederiksted. ⊠ *Rte. 70, Estate Whim* ☎ 340/772–0598 ⊕ *www.stcroixlandmarks. com* ☒ *$6* ⊘ *Wed.–Mon. 10–4.*

ST. JOHN

Updated by Lynda Lohr

Beautiful and largely undisturbed St. John is 3 mi (5 km) east of St. Thomas across the Pillsbury Sound (a 20-minute ferry ride from Red Hook). In 1956 Laurance Rockefeller, who founded the Caneel Bay Resort, bought up much of St. John's 20 square mi (53 square km) to donate to the United States for a national park. The park now encompasses about two-thirds of the island. Because of this, the island comes close to realizing that travel-brochure dream of "an unspoiled tropical paradise." It's covered with vegetation, including a bay-tree forest that once supplied St. Thomas with the raw material for its fragrant bay rum. Along St. John's north shore, clean, gleaming white-sand beaches fringe bay after bay, each full of iridescent water perfect for swimming, fishing, snorkeling, diving, and underwater photography.

In 1675 Jorgen Iverson claimed the unsettled island for Denmark. The British residents of nearby Tortola, however, considered St. John theirs, and when a small party of Danes from St. Thomas moved onto the uninhabited island, the British "invited" them to leave (which they did). Despite this, in 1717 a group of Danish planters founded the first permanent settlement at Coral Bay. The question of who owned St. John wasn't settled until 1762, when Britain decided that maintaining good relations with Denmark was more important than keeping St. John.

By 1728 St. John had 87 plantations and a population of 123 whites and 677 blacks. By 1733 there were more than 1,000 slaves working more than 100 plantations. In that year the island was hit by a drought, hurricanes, and a plague of insects that destroyed the summer crops. Everyone felt the threat of famine, particularly the slaves, whose living and working conditions were already harsh. Sensing the growing desperation, the landowners enacted even more severe measures in a misguided attempt to keep control. On November 23 the slaves revolted. With great military prowess, they captured the fort at Coral Bay, took control of the island, and held on to it for six months. During this time nearly a quarter of the island's population—black and white—was killed. The rebellion was eventually put down by 100 Danish militia and 220 Creole troops brought in from Martinique. Slavery continued until 1848, when slaves in St. Croix marched on Frederiksted to demand their freedom from the Danish government. After emancipation, St. John fell into decline, with its inhabitants eking out a living on small farms. Life continued in much the same way until the national park was established in 1956 and tourism became an industry.

Today St. John may well be the most racially integrated of the three USVI. Its 5,000 residents, black and white, have a strong sense of community that seems rooted in a desire to protect the island's natural beauty. While the middle portion of the island remains undeveloped thanks to its status as a national park, the western end has boomed from the village of Cruz Bay into a small, sprawling town. On busy days it can suffer from traffic and parking woes. Coral Bay, at the eastern end of the island, is blossoming as the hillsides above it fill with homes and restaurants and shops appear at its shoreline. But, despite the growth, there are still many pockets of tranquillity. Here you can truly escape the pressures of modern life for a day, a week—perhaps, forever.

Where to Stay

St. John doesn't have many beachfront hotels, but that's a small price to pay for all the pristine sand. However, the island's two world-class resorts—Caneel Bay Resort and the Westin Resort, St. John—*are* on the beach. Sandy, white beaches string out along the north coast, which is popular with sunbathers and snorkelers and is where you'll find the Caneel Bay Resort and Cinnamon and Maho Bay campgrounds. Most villas are in the residential south shore area, a 15-minute drive from the north shore beaches. If you head east you'll come to the laid-back community of Coral Bay, where there are a few villas and cottages. A stay outside of Coral Bay will be peaceful and quiet.

If you're looking for West Indian village charm, there are a few inns in Cruz Bay. Just know that when bands play at any of the town's bars (some of which stay open till the wee hours), the noise can be a problem. Your choice of accommodations also includes condominiums and cottages near town; two campgrounds, both at the edges of beautiful beaches (bring bug repellent); ecoresorts; and luxurious villas, often with a pool or a hot tub (sometimes both), and a stunning view.

If your lodging comes with a fully equipped kitchen, you'll be happy to know that St. John's handful of grocery stores sells everything from the basics to sun-dried tomatoes and green chilies— though the prices will take your breath away. If you're on a budget, consider bringing some staples (pasta, canned goods, paper products) from home. Hotel rates throughout the island, though considered expensive by some, do include endless privacy and access to most water sports.

For approximate costs, *see* the dining and lodging price chart at the beginning of this chapter.

Hotels & Inns

$$$$ ☒ **Caneel Bay Resort.** Set on 170 lush peninsular acres—originally part
Fodor'sChoice of the Danish West India Company's Durloo Plantation—Caneel Bay
★ Resort mixes a good bit of peace and quiet into its luxurious air. You won't find crowds or glitz; your room won't have a TV, or even a phone (though management will loan you a cellular). Instead, you'll discover spacious, restful rooms that are open to the breezes and are tastefully decorated with tropical furnishings; seven beaches, each more gorgeous than the last; and an attentive staff that will fill your every need. ☒ *Rte. 20, Caneel Bay* ☎ *Box 720, Cruz Bay 00830* ☎ *340/776–6111 or 888/ 767–3966* ☎ *340/693–8280* ⊕ *www.caneelbay.com* ⇆ *166 rooms* ♨ *4 restaurants, fans, minibars, 11 tennis courts, beach, dive shop, dock, snorkeling, windsurfing, boating, billiards, children's programs (ages infant–12), meeting rooms; no room phones, no room TVs* ☐ *AE, DC, MC, V* ❙❍❙ *EP.*

$$$$ ☒ **Westin Resort, St. John.** Spread over 47 beachfront acres adjacent to Great Cruz Bay, the Westin Resort has lushly planted gardens, a white sandy beach that beckons sunbathers, comfortable rooms with tropical touches, and enough amenities to make stepping off the grounds unnecessary. You can keep very busy here with tennis and water sports or you can idle away a good portion of the day at the pool or beach. If you want to get out and about, though, taxi jaunts into Cruz Bay are a breeze. ☒ *Rte. 104, Great Cruz Bay* ☎ *Box 8310, Cruz Bay 00831* ☎ *340/693–8000 or 800/808–5020* ☎ *340/693–8888* ⊕ *www. thewestinstjohnresort.com* ⇆ *282 rooms* ♨ *3 restaurants, in-room data ports, in-room safes, minibars, refrigerators, cable TV, 6 tennis courts, pool, gym, outdoor hot tub, massage, beach, dive shop, snorkeling, windsurfing, boating, fishing, shops, children's programs (ages 3–12), meeting rooms, no-smoking rooms* ☐ *AE, D, DC, MC, V* ❙❍❙ *EP.*

$$ ☒ **Garden by the Sea Bed & Breakfast.** An easy walk from Cruz Bay, this cozy spot has rooms that reflect the sea and sky. White spreads and curtains provide pristine counterpoints. Enjoy views of a salt pond and the sea as you enjoy your piña colada French toast on the front porch. It's perfect for folks who enjoy peace and quiet—there are no phones or TVs in the rooms, but each room does have a small tabletop fountain. (If the gurgle of water over rocks annoys you, the fountain has an off switch.) ☒ *Enighed* ☎ *Box 1469, Cruz Bay 00831* ☎☎ *340/779–4731* ⊕ *www. gardenbythesea.com* ⇆ *3 rooms* ♨ *Fans, no-smoking rooms; no a/c, no room phones, no room TVs* ☐ *No credit cards* ❙❍❙ *BP.*

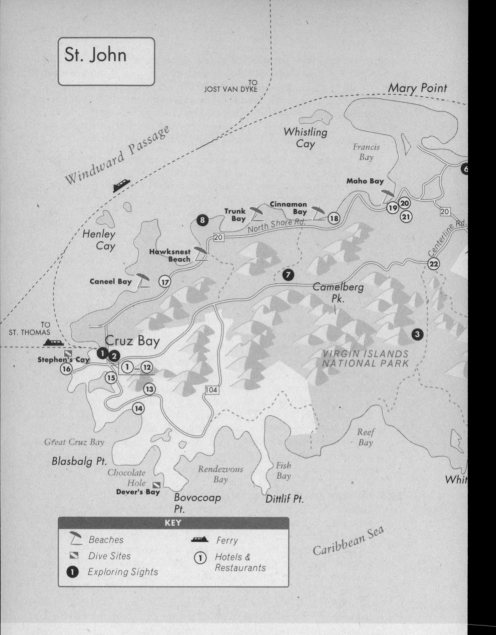

St. John

TO JOST VAN DYKE

Mary Point

Windward Passage

Whistling Cay

Francis Bay

Maho Bay

Henley Cay

Trunk Bay

Cinnamon Bay

North Shore Rd.

Hawksnest Beach

Caneel Bay

Camelberg Pk.

Centerline Rd.

TO ST. THOMAS

Cruz Bay

VIRGIN ISLANDS NATIONAL PARK

Stephen's Cay

104

Great Cruz Bay

Reef Bay

Blasbalg Pt.

Chocolate Hole

Rendezvous Bay

Fish Bay

Dever's Bay

Bovocoap Pt.

Dittlif Pt.

Caribbean Sea

Whit

KEY

- Beaches
- Dive Sites
- ① Exploring Sights
- Ferry
- ① Hotels & Restaurants

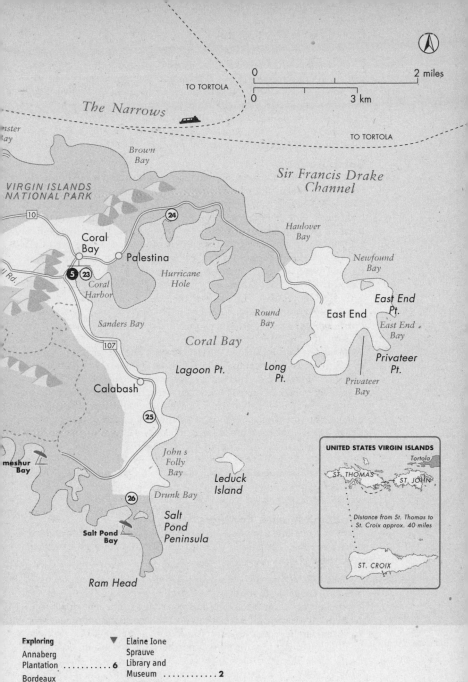

TO TORTOLA

0   2 miles

0   3 km

The Narrows

TO TORTOLA

Brown Bay

Sir Francis Drake Channel

VIRGIN ISLANDS NATIONAL PARK

Haulover Bay

10

Coral Bay

Palestina

Hurricane Hole

Newfound Bay

al Rd.

5   23

Coral Harbor

East End Pt.

East End

East End Bay

Sanders Bay

Round Bay

Coral Bay

Privateer Pt.

107

Lagoon Pt.

Long Pt.

Privateer Bay

Calabash

25

meshur Bay

Johns Folly Bay

Leduck Island

Drunk Bay

26

Salt Pond Peninsula

Salt Pond Bay

Ram Head

UNITED STATES VIRGIN ISLANDS

Tortola

ST. THOMAS   ST. JOHN

Distance from St. Thomas to
St. Croix approx. 40 miles

ST. CROIX

$–$$ 🏨 **St. John Inn.** Within walking distance of Cruz Bay's shops and restaurants, this inn offers not only a convenient location but also affordable accommodations with a touch of charm. You might find a four-poster bed or an antique-style armoire in rooms painted in lush hues. ✉ *Off Rte. 104, Cruz Bay* 📫 *Box 37, 00831* ☎ *340/693–8688 or 800/666–7688* 📠 *340/693–9900* 🌐 *www.stjohninn.com* 🛏 *13 units* 👍 *Fans, some kitchenettes, refrigerators, cable TV, pool* 💳 *AE, D, MC, V* 🍽 *EP.*

Campgrounds

🐤 $ ⛺ **Cinnamon Bay Campground.** Camping here puts you in Virgin Islands National Park, surrounded by trees and at the edge of lovely Cinnamon Bay Beach. Amenities are basic and include propane stoves and bed linens. Only the screened cottages have electric lights; tenters depend on propane lanterns. Bring your own tent and gear for the bare sites (a steal at $27 a night). The showers (on the cool side) and flush toilets, as well as a restaurant and a small store, are a short walk away. Hiking, water sports, and ranger-led evening programs are at your doorstep. ✉ *Rte. 20, Cinnamon Bay* 📫 *Box 720, Cruz Bay 00830-0720* ☎ *340/776–6330 or 800/539–9998* 📠 *340/776–6458* 🌐 *www.cinnamonbay.com* 🛏 *44 tents, 40 cottages, 26 bare sites* 👍 *Restaurant, beach, snorkeling, windsurfing, hiking; no a/c, no room phones, no room TVs* 💳 *AE, MC, V* 🍽 *EP.*

★ $ ⛺ **Maho Bay Camps.** Tucked into the greenery along the island's north shore, this seaside ecocamp is a lush hillside community of rustic structures. The tents (wooden platforms protected from the elements by canvas and screening) are linked by wooden stairs, ramps, and walkways—all of them elevated—so that you can trek around camp, down to the beach and to the coolish public showers without disturbing the terrain. The tents have some amenities like real beds and electricity, but ice-filled coolers keep your food from spoiling. ✉ *Maho Bay* 📫 *Box 310, Cruz Bay 00830* ☎ *340/776–6240 or 800/392–9004* 📠 *340/776–6504* 🌐 *www.mahobay.org* 🛏 *114 tent cottages* 👍 *Restaurant, beach, snorkeling, windsurfing, Internet, children's program (ages 10 and over); no a/c, no room phones, no room TVs* 💳 *D, MC, V* 🍽 *EP.*

Condominiums & Cottages

Many of the island's condos are just minutes from the hustle and bustle of Cruz Bay, but you'll find more condos and cottages around the island.

$$$–$$$$ 🏨 **Gallows Point Resort.** These soft-gray buildings are clustered on a peninsula a 10-minute walk south of the Cruz Bay ferry dock. The upper-level apartments have loft bedrooms and good views. The harborside villas get better trade winds, but they're also a tad noisier. Rooms have tropical rattan furniture and pastel tropical accents. The entranceway is bridged by Zozo's Ristorante, which serves northern Italian cuisine. ✉ *Gallows Point, Cruz Bay* 📫 *Box 58, 00831* ☎ *340/776–6434 or 800/323–7229* 📠 *340/776–6520* 🌐 *www.gallowspointresort.com* 🛏 *60 units* 👍 *Restaurant, fans, kitchens, cable TV, pool, beach, snorkeling; no a/c in some rooms* 💳 *AE, MC, V* 🍽 *EP.*

$$–$$$ 🏨 **Coconut Coast Villas.** Within walking distance of Cruz Bay's shops and restaurants, this small condominium complex—with studio and two- and three-bedroom units—sits so close to the water you'll fall asleep to the sound of waves. ✉ *Turner Bay* 📫 *Box 618, Cruz Bay 00831* ☎ *340/693–9100 or 800/858–7989* 📠 *340/779–4157* 🌐 *www.coconutcoast.com* 🛏 *9 units* 👍 *Fans, kitchens, cable TV, pool, beach* 💳 *MC, V* 🍽 *EP.*

$$–$$$ 🏨 **Concordia Studios and Eco-tents.** An ecofriendly resort in the Maho Bay Camps family, these studios and eco-tents sit hillside on 51 acres

near remote Salt Pond Bay. The spacious units are casually comfortable with tile floors and lovely sea views. They're made of recycled materials, and energy for all the appliances (even the ice makers) is wind- and solar-generated. Next door are five eco-tents, upscale camping structures made of environmentally friendly materials, equipped with solar power and composting toilets. Studios have kitchens; tents have kitchenettes. ⊠ *20–27 Estate Concordia, Concordia 00830* ☎ *340/693–5855 or 800/392–9004* 🖷 *340/693–5960* ⊕ *www.mahobay.org* ↴ *9 studios, 11 tents* ⟁ *Some kitchens, some kitchenettes, pool, beach, no-smoking rooms; no a/c, no room phones, no room TVs* ▭ *D, MC, V* ⦿ *EP.*

$$–$$$ ▣ **Estate Zootenvaal.** Set at the far reaches of the island, outside Coral Bay, this small complex provides modest cottages right at the water or across the street from the beach. It's a quiet spot perfect for people who like to sit in the chaise and read. ⊠ *Rte. 10, Hurricane Hole, Zootenvaal 00830* ☎ *340/776–6321* ⊕ *www.usviguide.com/zootenvaal* ↴ *3 units* ⟁ *Fans, kitchens, beach; no a/c, no room TVs* ▭ *No credit cards* ⦿ *EP.*

$$ ▣ **Harmony Studios.** The condominium-style units sit hillside at Maho Bay. They have the usual decks, sliding glass doors and great sea views, but the carpets are attractively made of recycled milk cartons, the pristine white walls of old newspapers, and the energy comes from the wind and the sun. Each unit has a laptop computer programmed to monitor energy consumption. Tile floors, undyed cotton linens, and South American handicrafts are in keeping with the ideals. ⊠ *Maho Bay* ⊚ *Box 310, Cruz Bay 00830* ☎ *340/776–6240 or 800/392–9004* 🖷 *340/776–6504* ⊕ *www.mahobay.org* ↴ *12 units* ⟁ *Restaurant, fans, kitchens, beach, snorkeling, windsurfing, Internet, children's program (ages 10 and up), no-smoking rooms; no a/c, no room phones, no room TVs* ▭*AE, D, MC, V* ⦿ *EP.*

$–$$ ▣ **Serendip.** This complex offers modest units on lush grounds with lovely views. You definitely need a rental car if you stay here, though; it's about 1 mi (1½ km) up a killer hill out of Cruz Bay. If air-conditioning is important to you, be sure to mention it when booking, as some units have only ceiling fans. ⊠ *Enighed* ⊚ *Box 273, Cruz Bay 00831* ☎ *340/776–6646 or 888/800–6445* ⊕ *www.serendipstjohn.com* ↴ *10 units* ⟁ *Fans, kitchens, cable TV; no a/c in some rooms* ▭ *MC, V* ⦿ *EP.*

Villas

Tucked here and there between Cruz Bay and Coral Bay are about 350 villas (prices range from $ to $$$$). With pools and/or hot tubs, full kitchens, and living areas, they provide a home away from home. They're perfect for couples and extended groups of families or friends. You'll need a car, since most are up in the hills (very few are at the beach). Villa managers usually pick you up at the dock, arrange for your rental car, and answer questions you have upon arrival as well as during your stay.

To rent a luxury villa, contact one of the following rental agents:

Caribbean Villas and Resorts (⊚ Box 458, Cruz Bay 00831 ☎ 340/776–6152 or 800/338–0987 🖷 340/779–4044 ⊕ www.caribbeanvilla.com) handles condo rentals for Cruz Views, Lavender Hill, and Gallow's Point Resort, as well as for private villas. **Catered To, Inc.** (⊚ 206 Marketplace, 5000 Estate Enighed, Cruz Bay 00830 ☎ 340/776–6641 🖷 340/693–8191 ⊕ www.cateredto.com) has luxury homes mainly in Great Cruz Bay and Chocolate Hole areas. **Destination St. John** (⊚ Box 8306, Cruz Bay 00831 ☎ 340/779–4647 or 800/562–1901 🖷 340/715–0073 ⊕ www.destinationstjohn.com) manages villas across the island. **Park Isle Villas** (⊚ Box 1263, Cruz Bay 00831 ☎ 340/693-8261 or 800/416–1205 🖷 340/693-8480 ⊕ www.parkislevillas.com) handles Battery

Hill and Villa Caribe condos. **Private Homes for Private Vacations** (⌁ Mamey Peak 00830 ☎☎ 340/776–6876 ⊕ www.privatehomesvi. com) has homes across the island. **Star Villas** (⌁ Box 599, Cruz Bay 00830 ☎ 340/776–6704 or 888/897–9759 ⊠ 340/776–6183 ⊕ www. starvillas.com) has cozy villas just outside Cruz Bay. **Vacation Homes** (⌁ Box 272, Cruz Bay 00831 ☎ 340/776–6094 ⊠ 340/693–8455) has luxury homes from outside Cruz Bay to mid-island. **Vacation Vistas** (⌁ Box 476, Cruz Bay 00831 ☎ 340/776–6462 ⊕ www.vacationvistas. com) manages villas mainly in the Chocolate Hole and Great Cruz Bay areas. **Windspree** (⌁ 7924 Emmaus, Cruz Bay 00830 ☎ 340/693–5423 ⊠ 340/693–5623 ⊕ www.windspree.com) handles villas mainly in the Coral Bay area.

Where to Eat

The cuisine on St. John seems to get better every year, with culinary school–trained chefs vying to see who can come up with the most imaginative dishes. There are restaurants to suit every taste and budget—from the elegant establishments at Caneel Bay Resort (where men may be required to wear a jacket at dinner) to the casual in-town eateries of Cruz Bay. For quick lunches, try the West Indian food stands in Cruz Bay Park and across from the post office. The cooks prepare fried chicken legs, pates (meat- and fish-filled pastries), and callaloo.

For approximate costs, *see* the dining and lodging price chart at the beginning of this chapter.

Bordeaux

CONTEMPORARY
★ $$$–$$$$

✕ **Chateau Bordeaux.** This rustic restaurant with a to-die-for view of Coral Bay is made elegant with lace tablecloths, candlelight, and stylish dinner presentations. You might start with chilled asparagus spears served with a julienne radish and mint salad and drizzled with a champagne-orange vinaigrette; then segue into seared mahimahi with couscous and asparagus or a grilled steak with potato au gratin and wilted spinach leaves. Save room for dessert—the fresh berry cups with Chambord and caramel are wonderful. ⊠ *Rte. 10, Bordeaux* ☎ *340/776–6611* ⊟ *AE, MC, V* ⊗ *No lunch.*

Coral Bay & Environs

AMERICAN
$
Fodor's Choice
★

✕ **Skinny Legs Bar and Restaurant.** Sailors who live aboard boats anchored just offshore and an eclectic coterie of residents gather for lunch and dinner at this funky spot. If owners Doug Sica and Moe Chabuz are around, take a gander at their gams; you'll see where the restaurant got its name. It's a great place for burgers, fish sandwiches, and watching whatever sports event is on the satellite TV. ⊠ *Rte. 10, Coral Bay* ☎ *340/779–4982* ⊟ *AE, D, MC, V.*

CARIBBEAN
★ $$–$$$

✕ **Miss Lucy's Restaurant.** Sitting seaside at remote Friis Bay, Miss Lucy's dishes up Caribbean food with a contemporary flair. Dishes like tender conch fritters, a spicy West Indian stew called callaloo, and fried fish make up most of the menu, but you'll also find a generous pot of seafood, sausage, and chicken paella on the menu. Sunday brunches are legendary, and if you're around on the full moon, stop by for the monthly full moon party. The handful of small tables near the water are the nicest, but if they're taken or the mosquitoes are bad, the indoor tables do nicely. ⊠ *Rte. 107, Friis Bay* ☎ *340/693–5244* ⊟ *AE, D, MC, V* ⊗ *Closed Mon. No dinner Sun.*

Cruz Bay

BARBECUE
$–$$

✕ **Uncle Joe's Barbecue.** Juicy ribs and tasty chicken legs dripping with the house barbecue sauce make for one of St. John's best dining deals.

An ear of corn on the cob, rice, and a generous scoop of macaroni salad or coleslaw round out the plate. This very casual spot crowds the edge of a busy sidewalk in the heart of Cruz Bay. Even though there are a few open-air tables for dining in, the ambience is more than a tad on the pedestrian side, so take-out is a better bet. ⊠ *North Shore Rd., across from post office* ☎ *340/693–8806* ▤ *No credit cards.*

CONTEMPORARY
$$$–$$$$

✕ **Stone Terrace Restaurant.** A delightful harbor view, soft lantern light, and white linen tablecloths provide the backdrop for chef Aaron Willis's imaginative cuisine. To standards like a roasted half duck, he adds a goat cheese–filled pumpkin crepe and cassava cake. He jazzes up the salad course with seared tuna sashimi perched on a spinach salad drizzled with a hoisin vinaigrette. The desserts change daily, but are always as intriguing as the other courses. ⊠ *Bay St.* ☎ *340/693–9370* ▤ *AE, D, MC, V* ⊗ *Closed Mon. No lunch.*

$$–$$$

✕ **Lime Inn.** Mainland transplants who call St. John home as well as visitors flock to this alfresco spot for the congenial hospitality and good food, including all-you-can-eat shrimp on Wednesday nights. There are shrimp and steak dishes and such specials as pistachio chicken breasts with plantains and Thai curry-cream sauce. Fresh lobster is the specialty every night. ⊠ *Lemon Tree Mall, King St.* ☎ *340/776–6425* ▤ *AE, MC, V* ⊗ *Closed Sun. No lunch Sat.*

$–$$$

✕ **Morgan's Mango.** A long flight of stairs leads you to this alfresco eatery, but good food makes it worth the climb. Although fish is the specialty—try the voodoo snapper topped with a many-fruit salsa—the chef also creates a vegetarian platter with black beans, fried plantains, salad, and even an ear of corn. ⊠ *North Shore Rd., across from V.I. National Park's Visitors Center* ☎ *340/693–8141* ▤ *AE, MC, V* ⊗ *No lunch.*

ECLECTIC
$$$–$$$$

✕ **Paradiso.** This popular spot is on the upper level of the island's largest shopping complex. The menu is a mix of everything, including pork tenderloin with a bourbon barbecue glaze; and an herb-grilled mahimahi. You can dine indoors in air-conditioned comfort or outdoors on a small terrace overlooking the street. ⊠ *Mongoose Junction shopping center, North Shore Rd.* ☎ *340/693–8899* ▤ *AE, MC, V.*

$–$$$$

✕ **Fish Trap.** The rooms and terraces here all open to the breezes and buzz with a mix of locals and visitors. Chef Aaron Willis, who also presides over the kitchen at Stone Terrace, conjures up such tasty appetizers as conch fritters and Fish Trap chowder (a creamy soup of snapper, white wine, paprika, and secret spices). The menu also includes an interesting pasta of the day, steak and chicken dishes, and hamburgers. ⊠ *Bay and Strand Sts., next to Our Lady of Mount Carmel Church* ☎ *340/693–9994* ▤ *AE, D, MC, V* ⊗ *Closed Mon. No lunch.*

$$

✕ **Pavillion Restaurant.** At the end of a long, partially paved road at Maho Bay Camps, this casual open-air restaurant is worth the drive. The menu changes daily, but there's always a handful of seafood, chicken, and vegetarian entrées. Give your order at the counter. While you wait for it to be cooked—the chef calls your name when it's done—help yourself to the salad bar, rolls, and iced tea included with your dinner. Arrive early to enjoy the spectacular sunset views. ⊠ *Maho Bay Camps, off Rte. 20* ☎ *340/776–6226* ▤ *AE, MC, V* ⊗ *No lunch.*

$

✕ **Sun Dog Cafe.** There's an unusual assortment of dishes at this charming restaurant, which is tucked into a courtyard in the upper reaches of the Mongoose Junction shopping center. Kudos to the white artichoke pizza with roasted garlic, artichoke hearts, mozzarella cheese, and capers. The Jamaican jerk chicken sub or the black-bean quesadilla are also good choices. ⊠ *Mongoose Junction shopping center, North Shore Rd.* ☎ *340/693–8340* ▤ *AE, MC, V* ⊗ *No dinner.*

ITALIAN   ✗ **Zozo's Ristorante.** Creative takes on old standards coupled with lovely
★ $$$ presentation are what draw the crowds to this restaurant. The monk
fish piccata is served over a warm pancetta and watercress salad with
vinaigrette dressing. The pastas are equally imaginative: the lobster
ravioli is stuffed with an herb ricotta and topped with pine nuts in a
tomato-cream sauce. It is located at Gallow's Point Resort, and the sun-
set views will take your breath away. ⊠ *Bay St.* ☎ *340/693–9200*
🖃 *AE, MC, V* ☺ *No lunch.*

$$–$$$ ✗ **Café Roma.** This casual second-floor restaurant in the heart of Cruz
Bay is *the* place for traditional Italian cuisine: lasagna, spaghetti and meat-
balls, and chicken piccata. There are also excellent pizzas. Mascarpone-
mango crepes are a dessert specialty. ⊠ *Vesta Gade* ☎ *340/776–6524*
🖃 *MC, V* ☺ *No lunch.*

$$–$$$ ✗ **Panini Beach Trattoria.** Taking its name from the pressed and grilled
Italian sandwich, available only at lunch, this cozy seaside bistro serves
delightful northern Italian fare. Lunch includes basics like pizza and soup
and salads, but at dinner the menu runs to fresh pasta and chicken dishes
cooked with herbs and spices. Save room for dessert. The chocolate panini
is heavenly. You can dine inside in air-conditioned comfort, although
the alfresco beachfront tables are the nicest bets. ⊠ *Wharfside Village
shopping center, Strand St.* ☎ *340/693–9119* 🖃 *AE, MC, V* ☺ *No
lunch weekends.*

PAN-ASIAN   ✗ **Asolare.** Contemporary Asian cuisine dominates the menu at this el-
★ $$$–$$$$ egant open-air eatery in an old St. John house. Come early and relax
over drinks while you enjoy the sunset over the harbor. Start with an
appetizer such as pork spring rolls served with sticky rice and a baby
greens salad. Entrées include such delights as beef fillet rolled in basil
and peppercorns, and sesame-sprinkled yellowfin tuna served with a
spinach, red onion, and smoked pepper–bacon salad. If you still have
room for dessert, try the chocolate pyramid, a luscious cake with home-
made ice cream melting in the middle. ⊠ *Rte. 20 on Caneel Hill* ☎ *340/
779–4747* 🖃 *AE, MC, V* ☺ *No lunch.*

Beaches

St. John is blessed with many beaches, and all of them fall into the good,
great, and don't-tell-anyone-else-about-this-place categories. Those
along the north shore are all within the national park. Some are more
developed than others—and many are crowded on weekends, holidays,
and in high season—but by and large they're still pristine. Beaches
along the south and eastern shores are quiet and isolated.

Caneel Bay. Caneel Bay is actually a catch-all name for seven white-sand
north shore beaches, six of which can be reached only by water if you
aren't a guest at the Caneel Bay Resort. (Access to beaches is a civil right
in the USVI, but access to land that leads to the beaches is not.) The
seventh, **Caneel Beach,** is open to the public and is easy to reach from
the main entrance of the resort; just ask for directions at the gatehouse.
Nonguests can also dine at three of the hotel's four restaurants and browse
in its gift shop.

Cinnamon Bay. This long, sandy beach faces beautiful cays and abuts the
national park campground. The facilities are open to the public and in-
clude cool showers, toilets, a commissary, and a restaurant. You can rent
water-sports equipment here—a good thing because there's excellent
snorkeling off the point to the right; look for the big angelfish and large
schools of purple triggerfish. Afternoons on Cinnamon Bay can be
windy, so arrive early to beat the gusts. The Cinnamon Bay hiking trail
begins across the road from the beach parking lot; ruins mark the trail-

head. There are actually two paths here: a level nature trail (signs along it identify the flora) that loops through the woods and passes an old Danish cemetery, and a steep trail that starts where the road bends past the ruins and heads straight up to Route 10.

Hawksnest Beach. Sea-grape trees line this narrow beach, and there are rest rooms, cooking grills, and a covered shed for picnicking. It's the closest beach to town, so it's often crowded.

Lameshur Bay. This nifty beach is toward the end of a very long, partially paved road on the southeast coast. It offers solitude, good snorkeling, and a chance to spy on some pelicans. The ruins of the old plantation are a five-minute walk down the road past the beach.

Maho Bay. This popular beach is below the Maho Bay Camps—a wonderful hillside enclave of tent cabins. The campground offers informal talks and slide and film presentations on nature, environmentally friendly living, and whatever else crosses the manager's mind. Another lovely strip of sand with the same name sits right along the North Shore Road.

Salt Pond Bay. If you're adventurous, this somewhat rocky beach on the scenic southeastern coast—next to Coral Bay and rugged Drunk Bay—is worth exploring. It's a short hike down a hill from the parking lot, and the only facilities are an outhouse and a few picnic tables scattered about. There are interesting tidal pools, and the snorkeling is good. Take special care to leave nothing valuable in your car; reports of thefts are common.

Fodor'sChoice
★ **Trunk Bay.** St. John's most-photographed beach is also the preferred spot for beginning snorkelers because of its underwater trail. (Cruise-ship passengers interested in snorkeling for a day come here, so if you're looking for seclusion, come early or later in the day.) Crowded or not, this stunning beach is sure to please. There are changing rooms, a snack bar, picnic tables, a gift shop, phones, lockers, and snorkeling-equipment rentals.

Sports & the Outdoors

BOATING &
SAILING
For a speedy trip to offshore cays and remote beaches, a powerboat is a necessity. It can cost you around $300 per day with gas and oil charges, depending on how far you're going. More leisurely day sails to islands not far offshore or longer sails to points east are also possibilities. If you're boatless, book with one of the island's agents. Most day sails include lunch, beverages, and at least one stop to snorkel. A full-day sail with lunch runs around $90 per person.

Adventures in Paradise (✉ Cruz Bay, across from the post office ☎ 340/779-4527) books fishing, sailing, and scuba trips on most of the island's charter boats. **Connections** (✉ Cruz Bay, a block up from the ferry dock and catercorner from Chase Manhattan Bank ☎ 340/776-6922) pairs you up with the sailboat that suits you. Have simple tastes? The smiling staff can help. If luxury is more your style, they can book that, too. **Ocean Runner** (✉ Cruz Bay, on the waterfront ☎ 340/693-8809) rents one- and two-engine boats for fast trips around the island's seas. **Proper Yachts** (✉ Caneel Bay ☎ 340/776-6256) books day sails and longer charters on its fleet of luxury yachts that depart from Caneel Bay Resort.

FISHING
Well-kept charter boats head out to the north and south drops or troll along the inshore reefs. The captains usually provide bait, drinks, and lunch, but you'll need to bring your own hat and sunscreen. Fishing charters run around $100 per hour per person. The **Charter Boat Center** (☎ 340/775-7990), in Red Hook on St. Thomas, also arranges fishing trips for folks on St. John. **Gone Ketchin'** (☎ 340/714-1175), in St. John, arranges trips with old salt Captain Griz. **St. John World Class Anglers**

(☎ 340/779–4281) offers light-tackle shore and offshore half- and full-day trips.

HIKING   Although it's fun to go hiking with a Virgin Islands National Park guide, don't be afraid to strike out on your own. To find a hike that suits your ability, stop by the park's Visitor Center in Cruz Bay and pick up the free trail guide; it details points of interest, dangers, trail lengths, and estimated hiking times. Although the park staff recommends pants to protect against thorns and insects, most people hike in shorts because pants are too hot. Wear sturdy shoes or hiking boots even if you're hiking to the beach. Don't forget to bring water and insect repellent.

Fodor'sChoice   The **Virgin Islands National Park** (☎ 340/776–6201 ⊕ www.nps.gov/
★   viis) maintains more than 20 trails on the north and south shores and offers guided hikes along popular routes. A full-day trip to Reef Bay is a must; it's an easy hike through lush and dry forest, past the ruins of an old plantation, and to a sugar factory adjacent to the beach. Take the public Vitran bus or a taxi to the trailhead, where you'll meet a ranger who'll serve as your guide. The park provides a boat ride back to Cruz Bay for $15 to save you the walk back up the mountain. The schedule changes from season to season; call for times and reservations, which are essential.

HORSEBACK   Clip-clop along the island's byways for a slower-pace tour of St. John.
RIDING   **Carolina Corral** (☎ 340/693–5778) offers horseback trips down quiet roads and scenic beaches. Rates start at $55 for a 1½-hour ride.

SCUBA DIVING &   Although just about every beach has nice snorkeling—Trunk Bay, Cin-
SNORKELING   namon Bay, and Waterlemon Cay at Leinster Bay get the most praise—you'll need a boat to head out to the more remote snorkeling locations and the best scuba spots. Sign on with any of the island's water-sports operators to get to spots farther from St. John. Their boats will take you to hot spots between St. John and St. Thomas, including the tunnels at **Thatch Cay,** the ledges at **Congo Cay,** and the wreck of the *General Rogers.* Dive off St. John at **Stephens Cay,** a short boat ride out of Cruz Bay, where fish swim around the reefs as you float downward. At **Devers Bay,** on St. John's south shore, fish dart about in colorful schools. Count on paying $65 for a one-tank dive and $80 for a two-tank dive. Rates include equipment and a tour.

Cruz Bay Watersports (☎ 340/776–6234) has two locations: in Cruz Bay and at the Westin Resort, St. John. Owners Marcus and Patty Johnston offer regular reef, wreck, and night dives and USVI and BVI snorkel tours. **Low Key Watersports** (☎ 340/693–8999 or 800/835–7718), at Wharfside Village, offers PADI certification and resort courses, one- and two-tank dives, and specialty courses.

SEA KAYAKING   Poke around crystal bays and explore undersea life from a sea kayak. **Arawak Expeditions** (☎ 340/693–8312 or 800/238–8687) has professional guides who use traditional and sit-on-top kayaks to ply coastal waters. Prices start at $40 for a half-day trip.

TENNIS   With hot weather the norm, tennis players take to the courts in the morning or late afternoon. The **public tennis courts,** near the fire station in Cruz Bay, are lighted until 10 PM and are available on a first-come, first-served basis. The **Westin Resort, St. John** (⊠ Rte. 104, Great Cruz Bay ☎ 340/693–8000), has six lighted tennis courts. Nonguests are welcome to play here for a fee of $15 an hour.

WINDSURFING   Steady breezes and expert instruction make learning to windsurf a snap. Try **Cinnamon Bay Campground** (⊠ Rte. 20, Cinnamon Bay ☎ 340/776–6330), where rentals are available for $25–$35 per hour. Lessons are available right at the waterfront; just look for the Windsurfers stacked up on the beach. The cost for a one-hour lesson starts at $70.

Shopping

Areas & Malls

Luxury goods and handicrafts can be found on St. John. Most shops carry a little of this and a bit of that, so it pays to poke around. The Cruz Bay shopping district runs from **Wharfside Village,** just around the corner from the ferry dock, through the streets of town to North Shore Road and **Mongoose Junction,** an inviting shopping center with stonework walls (its name is a holdover from a time when those furry island creatures gathered at a garbage bin that was here). Steps connect the two sections of the center, which has unusual upscale shops. Out on Route 104, stop in at **The Marketplace** to explore its handful of gift and crafts shops. At the island's other end, there are a few stores—selling clothes, jewelry, and artwork—here and there from the village of **Coral Bay** to the small complex at **Shipwreck Landing.**

Specialty Items

ART **Bajo el Sol.** A cooperative gallery, Bajo el Sol sells St. John local Aimee Trayser's expressionistic Caribbean scenes and Les Anderson's island scenes in oil and acrylics, as well as jewelry, sculptures, and ceramics by a handful of other artists. ⊠ *Mongoose Junction, North Shore Rd., Cruz Bay* ☎ *340/693–7070.*

Coconut Coast Studios. This waterside shop, a five-minute walk from Cruz Bay, showcases the work of Elaine Estern. She specializes in undersea scenes. ⊠ *Frank Bay, Cruz Bay* ☎ *340/776–6944.*

BOOKS **National Park Headquarters.** The headquarters sells several good histories of St. John, including *St. John Back Time,* by Ruth Hull Low and Rafael Lito Valls, and for linguists, Valls's *What a Pistarckle!*—an explanation of the colloquialisms that make up the local version of English (*pistarckle* is a Dutch Creole word that means "noise" or "din," which pretty much sums up the language here). ⊠ *The Creek, near Cruz Bay bulkhead and baseball field, Cruz Bay* ☎ *340/776–6201.*

CLOTHING **Big Planet Adventure Outfitters.** You knew when you arrived that some place on St. John would cater to the outdoor enthusiasts that hike up and down the island's trails. Well, this outdoor-clothing store is where you can find the popular Naot sandals and Reef footware, along with colorful and durable cotton clothing and accessories by Patagonia. The store also sells children's clothes. ⊠ *Mongoose Junction, North Shore Rd., Cruz Bay* ☎ *340/776–6638.*

Bougainvillea Boutique. If you want to look like you stepped out of the pages of the resort-wear spread in an upscale travel magazine, try this store. Owner Susan Stair carries *very* chic men's and women's resort wear, straw hats, leather handbags, and fine gifts. ⊠ *Mongoose Junction, North Shore Rd., Cruz Bay* ☎ *340/693–7190.*

The Clothing Studio. Several talented artists hand-paint original designs on clothing for all members of the family. This shop carries T-shirts, beach cover-ups, pants, shorts, and even bathing suits with beautiful hand-painted creations. ⊠ *Mongoose Junction, North Shore Rd., Cruz Bay* ☎ *340/776–6585.*

Jolly Dog. Stock up on the stuff you forgot to pack at this store. Sarongs in cotton and rayon, beach towels with tropical motifs, and hats and T-shirts sporting the Jolly Dog logo fill the shelves. ⊠ *Rte. 107, Shipwreck Landing, Sanders Bay* ☎ *340/693–5333.*

St. John Editions. Shop here for nifty cotton dresses that go from beach to dinner with a change of shoes and accessories. Owner Ann Soper also carries attractive straw hats and inexpensive jewelry. ✉ *North Shore Rd., Cruz Bay* ☎ *340/693–8444.*

FOODSTUFFS   If you're renting a villa, condo, or cottage and doing your own cooking, there are several good places to shop for food; just be aware that prices are much higher than those at home.

Marina Market. Although this market usually has the best prices, its selection is small. ✉ *Rte. 104, Cruz Bay* ☎ *340/779–4401.*

Starfish Market. The island's largest store usually has the best selection of meat, fish, and produce. ✉ *Marketplace Shopping Center, Rte. 104, Cruz Bay* ☎ *340/779–4949.*

Tropical Blend. You can get great take-out meals here in addition to its rather smallish selection of groceries. ✉ *Palm Plaza, Rte. 104, Cruz Bay* ☎ *340/714–7989.*

GIFTS   **Bamboula.** Owner Jo Sterling travels the Caribbean and the world to find unusual housewares, art, rugs, bedspreads, accessories, shoes, and men's and women's clothes for this multicultural boutique. ✉ *Mongoose Junction, North Shore Rd., Cruz Bay* ☎ *340/693–8699.*

The Canvas Factory. If you're a true shopper who needs an extra bag to carry all your treasures home, this store offers every kind of tote and carrier imaginable—from simple bags to suitcases with numerous zippered compartments—all made of canvas, naturally. It also sells great canvas hats. ✉ *Mongoose Junction, North Shore Rd., Cruz Bay* ☎ *340/ 776–6196.*

Donald Schnell Studio. In addition to pottery, this place sells unusual hand-blown glass, wind chimes, kaleidoscopes, fanciful water fountains, and more. Your purchases can be shipped worldwide. ✉ *Mongoose Junction, North Shore Rd., Cruz Bay* ☎ *340/776–6420.*

Fabric Mill. Shop here for soft toys, place mats, napkins, and batik wraps. Or take home a bolt of tropical brights from the upholstery-fabric selection. ✉ *Mongoose Junction, North Shore Rd., Cruz Bay* ☎ *340/ 776–6194.*

House of Dolls. Owner Esther Frett creates the most exquisite dolls at this tiny shop tucked away in Raintree Court. The ones dressed in gilded banana leaves make spectacular take-home gifts for that doll collector on your shopping list. Others come dressed in hand-crocheted and hand-sewn gowns of many styles and colors. ✉ *Raintree Court, Bay Street, Cruz Bay* ☎ *340/777–4100.*

Pink Papaya. This store is the home of longtime Virgin Islands resident M. L. Etre's well-known artwork, plus a huge collection of one-of-a-kind gifts, including bright tablecloths, unusual trays, dinnerware, and unique tropical jewelry. ✉ *Lemon Tree Mall, King St., Cruz Bay* ☎ *340/ 693–8535.*

Wicker, Wood and Shells. Shop the second floor of this store for lovely sculptures and other objets d'art, all with a tropical theme. On the first floor there's the island's best selection of greeting cards, notepaper, and other interesting gifts to tuck in your suitcase for friends back home. ✉ *Mongoose Junction, North Shore Rd., Cruz Bay* ☎ *340/776–6909.*

JEWELRY   **Blue Carib Gems.** This store sells custom-made jewelry, loose gemstones, and old coins as well as hand-crafted jewelry from local and other artists. ✉ *Wharfside Village, Strand St., Cruz Bay* ☎ *340/693–8299.*

Caravan Gallery. Owner Radha Speer travels the world to find much of the unusual jewelry she sells here. And the more you look, the more you see—folk art, tribal art, and masks for sale cover the walls and tables, making this a great place to browse. ✉ *Mongoose Junction, North Shore Rd., Cruz Bay* ☎ *340/779–4566.*

Colombian Emeralds. This branch of a St. Thomas store has high-quality emeralds and also sells rubies, diamonds, and other jewels in attractive yellow- and white-gold settings. ✉ *Mongoose Junction, North Shore Rd., Cruz Bay* ☎ *340/776–6007.*

Free Bird Creations. Head here for special handcrafted jewelry—earrings, bracelets, pendants, chains—as well as the good selection of water-resistant watches for your excursions to the beach. ✉ *Wharfside Village, King St., Cruz Bay* ☎ *340/693–8625.*

R&I Patton Goldsmiths. Rudy and Irene Patton design most of the lovely silver and gold jewelry in this shop. The rest comes from various jeweler friends of theirs. Sea fans (those large, lacy plants that sway with the ocean's currents) in filigreed silver, lapis set in gold, starfish and hibiscus pendants in silver or gold, and gold sand dollar–shape charms and earrings are tempting choices. ✉ *Mongoose Junction, North Shore Rd., Cruz Bay* ☎ *340/776–6548.*

Nightlife

St. John isn't the place to go for glitter and all-night partying. Still, after-hours Cruz Bay can be a lively little town in which to dine, drink, dance, chat, or flirt. Notices posted on the bulletin board outside the Connections telephone center—up the street from the ferry dock in Cruz Bay—or listings in the island's two small newspapers (the *St. John Times* and *Tradewinds*) will keep you apprised of special events, comedy nights, movies, and the like.

After a sunset drink at **Zozo's Ristorante** (✉ Gallows Point Resort ☎ 340/693–9200), up the hill from Cruz Bay, you can stroll here and there in town (much is clustered around the small waterfront park). Many of the young people from the U.S. mainland who live and work on St. John will be out sipping and socializing, too.

Duffy's Love Shack (✉ Veste Gade, Cruz Bay ☎ 340/776–6065) is the wild and crazy place to go. Loud music and drinks like the Shark Tank (rum and three tropical liqueurs) make this Cruz Bay's hottest late-night spot. There's calypso and reggae on Wednesday and Friday at **Fred's** (✉ King St., Cruz Bay ☎ 340/776–6363). The **Inn at Tamarind Court** (✉ Rte. 104, Cruz Bay ☎ 340/776–6378) serves up country rock on Friday. On the far side of the island, check out the action at **Skinny Legs Bar and Restaurant** (✉ Rte. 10, Coral Bay ☎ 340/779–4982). Young folks like to gather at **Woody's** (✉ Ferry Rd., Cruz Bay ☎ 340/779–4625). Its sidewalk tables provide a close-up view of Cruz Bay's action.

Exploring St. John

St. John is an easy place to explore. One road runs along the north shore, another across the center of the mountains. There are a few roads that branch off here and there, but it's hard to get lost. Pick up a map at the Visitor Center before you start out, and you'll have no problems. Few residents remember the route numbers, so have your map in hand if you stop to ask for directions. Bring along a swimsuit for stops at some of the most beautiful beaches in the world. You can spend all day or just a couple of hours exploring, but be advised that the roads are narrow and wind up and down steep hills, so don't expect to get anywhere in a hurry. There are lunch spots at Cinnamon Bay and in Coral Bay, or you can do what the locals do—picnic. The grocery stores in Cruz Bay sell Styrofoam coolers just for this purpose.

If you plan to do a lot of touring, renting a car will be cheaper and will give you much more freedom than relying on taxis, which are reluctant to go anywhere until they have a full load of passengers. Although you may be tempted by an open-air Suzuki or Jeep, a conventional car can get you just about everywhere on the paved roads, and you'll be able to lock up your valuables. You may be able to share a van or open-air vehicle (called a safari bus) with other passengers on a tour of scenic mountain trails, secret coves, and eerie bush-covered ruins.

Numbers in the margin correspond to points of interest on the St. John map.

Sights to See

★ ❻ **Annaberg Plantation.** In the 18th century, sugar plantations dotted the steep hills of the USVI. Slaves and free Danes and Dutchmen toiled to harvest the cane that was used to create sugar, molasses, and rum for export. Built in the 1780s, the partially restored plantation at Leinster Bay was once an important sugar mill. Though there are no official visiting hours, the National Park Service has regular tours, and some well-informed taxi drivers will show you around. Occasionally you may see a living-history demonstration—someone making johnnycake or weaving baskets. For information on tours and cultural events, contact the St. John National Park Service Visitors Center. ⊠ *Leinster Bay Rd., Annaberg* ☎ *340/776–6201* ⊕ *www.nps/gov/viis* ⊠ *$4 from 8 AM–4 PM; free after 4* ⊙ *Daily sunrise–sunset.*

★ ❹ **Bordeaux Mountain.** St. John's highest peak rises to 1,277 ft. Route 10 passes near enough to the top to offer breathtaking views. Drive nearly to the end of the dirt road for spectacular views at Picture Point and for the trailhead of the hike downhill to Lameshur. Get a trail map from the park service before you start. ⊠ *Rte. 10.*

❼ **Catherineberg Ruins.** At this fine example of an 18th-century sugar and rum factory, there's a storage vault beneath the windmill. Across the road, look for the round mill, which was later used to hold water. In the 1733 slave revolt, Catherineberg served as headquarters for the Amina warriors, a tribe of Africans captured into slavery. ⊠ *Rte. 10, Catherineberg.*

❺ **Coral Bay.** This laid-back community at the island's dry, eastern end is named for its shape rather than for its underwater life—the word *coral* comes from *krawl,* Dutch for "corral." It's a small, quiet, neighborhoody settlement—a place to get away from it all. You'll need a Jeep if you plan to stay at this end of the island, as some of the rental houses are up unpaved roads that wind around the mountain. If you come just for lunch, a regular car will be fine.

❶ **Cruz Bay.** St. John's main town may be compact (it consists of only several blocks), but it's definitely a hub: the ferries from St. Thomas and the BVI pull in here, and it's where you can get a taxi or rent a car to travel around the island. There are plenty of shops in which to browse, a number of watering holes where you can stop for a breather, many restaurants, and a grassy square with benches where you can sit back and take everything in. Look for the current edition of the handy, amusing "St. John Map" featuring Max the Mongoose. To pick up a handy guide to St. John's hiking trails, see various large maps of the island, and find out about current park service programs, including guided walks and cultural demonstrations, stop by the **V. I. National Park Visitors Center** (⊠ In an area known as the Creek, near Cruz Bay bulkhead and baseball field, Cruz Bay ☎ 340/776–6201 ⊕ www.nps.gov/viis). It's open daily from 8 to 4:30.

❷ **Elaine Ione Sprauve Library and Museum.** On the hill just above Cruz Bay is the Enighed Estate great house, built in 1757. *Enighed* is the Danish word for "concord" (unity or peace). The great house and its outbuildings (a sugar factory and horse-driven mill) were destroyed by fire and hurricanes, and the house sat in ruins until 1982. Today it houses a library and museum that contains a dusty collection of Indian pottery and colonial artifacts. ⊠ *Rte. 104, make a right past Texaco station, Cruz Bay* ☎ *340/776–6359* ☎ *Free* ⊘ *Weekdays 9–5.*

8 **Peace Hill.** It's worth stopping at this spot just past the Hawksnest Bay overlook for great views of St. John, St. Thomas, and the BVI. On the flat promontory is an old sugar mill. ⊠ *Off Rte. 20, Denis Bay.*

★ **9** **Reef Bay Trail.** Although this is one of the most interesting hikes on St. John, unless you're a rugged individualist who wants a physical challenge (and that describes a lot of people who stay on St. John), you'll probably get the most out of the trip if you join a hike led by a park service ranger, who can identify the trees and plants on the hike down, fill you in on the history of the Reef Bay Plantation, and tell you about the petroglyphs on the rocks at the bottom of the trail. A side trail takes you to the Reef Bay Plantation great house, a gutted, but mostly-intact structure that maintains vestiges of it former beauty. If you're without a car, take a taxi or the public Vitran bus from the Cruz Bay ferry dock to the trailhead on Route 10, where you'll meet a ranger for the hike downhill. A boat will take you to Cruz Bay, saving you the uphill return climb. ⊠ *Rte. 10, Reef Bay* ☎ *340/776–6201 Ext. 238 reservations* ⊕ *www.nps.gov/viis* ☎ *Free; return boat trip to Cruz Bay $15* ⊘ *Tours at 10 AM; days change seasonally.*

U.S. VIRGIN ISLANDS A TO Z

To research prices, get advice from other travelers, and book travel arrangements, visit www.fodors.com.

AIR TRAVEL
One advantage to visiting the USVI is the abundance of nonstop and connecting flights to St. Thomas and St. Croix that can have you at the beach in three to four hours from easternmost United States departures. Small island-hopper planes and a seaplane connect St. Thomas and St. Croix, and a ferry takes you from St. Thomas to St. John.

American Airlines is the territory's major carrier, with flights from Miami and New York. Continental flies from Newark. Delta flies from Atlanta. United flies from Chicago and Washington, D.C. US Airways flies from Philadelphia. American Eagle has frequent flights throughout the day from San Juan. Cape Air flies from San Juan to both St. Thomas and St. Croix. It has code-sharing arrangements with all major airlines, so your luggage can transfer seamlessly. Seaborne Airlines flies between St. Thomas and St. Croix.

🛪 **American Airlines** ☎ 340/774-6464 or 340/778-1140. **American Eagle** ☎ 340/776-2560 or 340/778-2000. **Cape Air** ☎ 800/352-0714 or 340/774-2204 ⊕ flycapeair.com. **Continental Airlines** ☎ 800/231-0856. **Delta Airlines** ☎ 340/777-4177 or 800/221-1212. **Seaborne Airlines** ☎ 340/773-6442 ⊕ www.seaborneairlines.com. **United Air Lines** ☎ 340/774-9190. **US Airways** ☎ 340/774-7885.

AIRPORTS
St. Thomas's Cyril E. King Airport sits at the western end of the island. There is no airport on St. John. St. Croix's Henry Rohlsen Airport sits outside Frederiksted, a 10-minute drive away. It takes about a half-hour to reach Christiansted from the airport.

Most hotels on St. Thomas don't have airport shuttles, but taxi vans at the airport are plentiful. From the airport, fees (set by the VI Taxi Commission) for two or more people sharing a cab are: $12 to the Ritz-Carlton, $9 to Renaissance Grand Beach Resort, $7.50 to Marriott Frenchman's Reef, and $5 to Bluebeard's Castle. Expect to be charged 50¢ per bag and to pay a higher fee if you're riding alone. During rush hour the trip to East End resorts can take up to 40 minutes, but a half hour is typical. Driving time from the airport to Charlotte Amalie is 15 minutes.

Getting from the airport to St. Croix hotels by taxi costs about $10–$20. You'll spend a half hour getting to the hotels in the Christiansted area, but those in the Frederiksted area are only about 10 minutes away. It takes about 45 minutes to get to the hotels on the East End.

Visitors to St. John fly into St. Thomas and take a taxi to either Charlotte Amalie or Red Hook, where they catch a ferry to Cruz Bay, St. John. The ferry from Charlotte Amalie makes the 45-minute trip several times a day and costs $7 a person. From Red Hook the ferry leaves on the hour; the 20-minute trip costs $3 a person.

🚹 **Cyril E. King Airport** ✉ St. Thomas ☎ 340/774-5100 ⊕ www.viport.com/aviation. html. **Henry Rohlsen Airport** ✉ St. Croix ☎ 340/778-0589 ⊕ www.viport.com/aviation.html.

BOAT & FERRY TRAVEL

Virtually every type of ship and major cruise line calls at St. Thomas; only a few call at St. Croix. Many ships that call at St. Thomas also call in St. John or offer an excursion to that island.

Ferries are a great way to travel around the islands; there's service between St. Thomas and St. John and their neighbors, the BVI. There's something special about spending a day on St. John and then joining your fellow passengers—a mix of tourists, local families, and construction workers on their way home—for a peaceful, sundown ride back to St. Thomas. Sometimes one of the St. John ferry services offers a special weekend trip to Fajardo, Puerto Rico. Such junkets depart from the waterfront in St. Thomas on a Friday evening and return to the same locale on Sunday afternoon.

FARES &
SCHEDULES
Ferries to Cruz Bay, St. John, leave St. Thomas from either the Charlotte Amalie waterfront west of the U.S. Coast Guard dock or from Red Hook. From Charlotte Amalie ferries depart at 9, 11, 1, 3, 4, and 5:30. To Charlotte Amalie from Cruz Bay, they leave at 7:15, 9:15, 11:15, 1:15, 2:15, and 3:45. The one-way fare for the 45-minute ride is $7 for adults, $3 for children. From Red Hook, ferries to Cruz Bay leave at 6:30 AM and 7:30 AM. Starting at 8 AM, they leave hourly until midnight. Returning from Cruz Bay, they leave hourly starting at 6 AM until 11 PM. The 15- to 20-minute ferry ride is $3 one-way for adults, $1 for children under 12.

Car ferries, called barges, run about every half-hour between Red Hook, St. Thomas, and Cruz Bay, St. John. The ride takes a half hour (one way) and costs $27 (round-trip). Plan to arrive 15 minutes before departure.

Reefer is the name of both of the brightly colored 26-passenger skiffs that run between the Charlotte Amalie waterfront and Marriott Frenchman's Reef hotel daily every hour from 9 to 4, returning from the Reef from 9:30 until 4:30. It's a good way to beat the traffic (and is about the same price as a taxi) to Morning Star Beach, which adjoins the Reef. And you get a great view of the harbor as you bob along in the shadow of the giant cruise ships anchored in the harbor. The captain of the *Reefer* may also be persuaded to drop you at Yacht Haven, but check first. The fare is $4 one-way, and the trip takes about 15 minutes.

There's daily service between either Charlotte Amalie or Red Hook, on St. Thomas, and West End or Road Town, Tortola, BVI, by either Smith's Ferry or Native Son, and to Virgin Gorda, BVI, by Smith's Ferry. The times and days the ferries run change, so it's best to call for schedules once you're in the islands. The fare is $22 one-way or $40 round-trip, and the trip from Charlotte Amalie takes 45 minutes to an hour to West End, up to 1½ hours to Road Town; from Red Hook the trip is only half an hour. The twice-weekly 2¼-hour trip from Charlotte Amalie to Virgin Gorda costs $28 one-way and $40 round-trip. There's also daily service between Cruz Bay, St. John, and West End, Tortola, aboard an Inter-Island Boat Service ferry. The half-hour one-way trip is $21. You'll need to present proof of citizenship upon entering the BVI; a passport is best, but a birth certificate with a raised seal in addition to a government-issued photo I.D. will suffice.

⚑ **Inter-Island Boat Service** ☎ 340/776-6597. **Native Son** ☎ 340/774-8685. *Reefer* ☎ 340/776-8500 Ext. 6814. **Smith's Ferry** ☎ 340/775-7292.

BUS TRAVEL

On St. Thomas, the island's 20 deluxe mainland-size buses make public transportation a very comfortable—though slow—way to get from east and west to Charlotte Amalie and back (service to the north is limited). Buses run about every 30 minutes from stops that are clearly marked with VITRAN signs. Fares are $1 between outlying areas and town and 75¢ in town.

Privately owned taxi vans crisscross St. Croix regularly, providing reliable service between Frederiksted and Christiansted along Route 70. This inexpensive ($1.50 one-way) mode of transportation is favored by locals, and though the many stops on the 20-mi (32-km) drive between the two main towns make the ride slow, it's never dull. The public Vitran buses aren't the quickest way to get around the island, but they're comfortable and affordable. The fare is $1 between Christiansted and Frederiksted or to places in between.

Modern Vitran buses on St. John run from the Cruz Bay ferry dock through Coral Bay to the far eastern end of the island at Salt Pond, making numerous stops in between. The fare is $1 to any point.

BUSINESS HOURS

BANKS Bank hours are generally Monday–Thursday 9–3 and Friday 9–5; a handful open Saturday (9–noon). Walk-up windows open at 8:30 on weekdays.

POST OFFICES Hours may vary slightly from branch to branch and island to island, but they are generally 7:30 or 8 to 4 or 5:30 weekdays and 7:30 or 8 to noon or 2:30 Saturday.

SHOPS On St. Thomas, stores on Main Street in Charlotte Amalie are open weekdays and Saturday 9–5. The hours of the shops in the Havensight Mall (next to the cruise-ships dock) are the same, though occasionally some stay open until 9 on Friday, depending on how many cruise ships are at the dock. You may also find some shops open on Sunday if a lot of cruise ships are in port. Hotel shops are usually open evenings, as well.

St. Croix shop hours are usually Monday–Saturday 9–5, but there are some shops in Christiansted open in the evening.

On St. John, store hours run from 9 or 10 to 5 or 6. Wharfside Village and Mongoose Junction shops in Cruz Bay are often open into the evening.

CAR RENTALS

Any U.S. driver's license is good for 90 days on the USVI, as are valid driver's licenses from other countries; the minimum age for drivers is 18, although many agencies won't rent to anyone under the age of 25. At the height of the winter season it may be tough to find a car, and occasionally all rental companies run out of cars at once; reserve well in advance to ensure you get the vehicle of your choice.

ST. THOMAS   Avis, Budget, and Hertz all have counters at the Cyril E. King Airport. Dependable Car Rental offers pickups and drop-offs at the airport and to and from major hotels. Other agencies, like Anchorage E-Z Car and Cowpet Rent-a-Car are located on the east end of the island, based at major hotels as well as at the Anchorage condominiums and villas. Discount has a location at Bluebeard's Castle hotel. Avis is at the Marriott Frenchman's Reef and Renaissance Grand Beach Resort; Budget has branches at the Sapphire Beach Resort & Marina and at the Havensight Mall, adjacent to the main cruise ship dock.

Anchorage E-Z Car ☎ 340/775-6255. **Avis** ☎ 340/774-1468 or 800/331-1084. **Budget** ☎ 340/776-5774 or 800/626-4516. **Cowpet Rent-a-Car** ☎ 340/775-7376. **Dependable Car Rental** ☎ 340/774-2253 or 800/522-3076. **Discount** ☎ 340/776-4858. **Hertz** ☎ 340/774-1879 or 800/654-3131.

ST. CROIX   Atlas is located outside Christiansted but provides pickups at hotels. Avis is located at the airport. Budget has branches at the airport and in the King Christian Hotel in Christiansted. Midwest is located outside Frederiksted, but picks up at hotels. Olympic and Thrifty are located outside Christiansted, but will pick up at hotels.

Atlas ☎ 340/773-2886 or 800/426-6009. **Avis** ☎ 340/778-9355 or 800/897-8448. **Budget** ☎ 340/778-9636 or 888/227-3359 ⊕ www.budgetstcroix.com. **Midwest** ☎ 340/772-0438 or 877/772-0438 ⊕ www.midwestautorental.com. **Olympic** ☎ 340/773-8000 or 888/878-4227. **Thrifty** ☎ 340/773-7200.

ST. JOHN   Best is just outside Cruz Bay near the public library, off Route 10. Cool Breeze is in Cruz Bay across from the Creek. Delbert Hill Taxi and Jeep Rental Service is in Cruz Bay around the corner from the ferry dock, across from Wharfside Village. Denzil Clyne is across from the Creek. O'Connor Jeep is in Cruz Bay at the Texaco Station. St. John Car Rental is across from Wharfside Village shopping center on Bay Street in Cruz Bay. Spencer's Jeep is across from the Creek in Cruz Bay. Sun and Sand is in Cruz Bay across from the Creek.

Best ☎ 340/693-8177. **Cool Breeze** ☎ 340/776-6588 ⊕ www.coolbreezecarrental.com. **Delbert Hill Taxi and Jeep Rental Service** ☎ 340/776-6637. **Denzil Clyne** ☎ 340/776-6715. **O'Connor Jeep** ☎ 340/776-6343. **St. John Car Rental** ☎ 340/776-6103 ⊕ www.raintree.com. **Spencer's Jeep** ☎ 340/693-8784 or 888/776-6628. **Sun and Sand Car Rental** ☎ 340/776-6374.

CAR TRAVEL

Even at a sedate speed of 20 mph, driving can be an adventure—for example, you may find yourself in a Jeep slogging behind a slow tourist-packed safari bus at a steep hairpin turn. Give a little beep at blind turns. Note that the general speed limit on these islands is only 25–35 mph, which will seem fast enough for you on most roads. If you don't think you'll need to lock up your valuables, a Jeep or open-air Suzuki with four-wheel drive will make it easier to navigate potholed dirt side roads and to get up slick hills when it rains. All main roads are paved.

GASOLINE   Gas is pricey on St. John and St. Thomas: about $2 per gallon. But on St. Croix, where the big Hess refinery is, the prices are much closer to what you might expect to pay stateside, about $1.25 per gallon.

ROAD CONDITIONS
In St. Thomas, traffic can get pretty bad, especially in Charlotte Amalie at rush hour (7–9 and 4:30–6). Cars often line up bumper to bumper along the waterfront. If you need to get from an east end resort to the airport during these times, find the alternate route (starting from the east end, Route 38 to 42 to 40 to 33) that goes up the mountain and then drops you back onto Veterans Highway. If you plan to explore by car, be sure to pick up the latest edition of "Road Map St. Thomas–St. John" that includes the route numbers *and* the names of the roads that are used by locals. It's available anywhere you find maps and guidebooks.

St. Croix, unlike St. Thomas and St. John, where narrow roads wind through hillsides, is relatively flat, and it even has a four-lane highway. The speed limit on the Melvin H. Evans Highway is 55 mph and ranges 35–40 mph elsewhere. Roads are often unmarked, so be patient—sometimes getting lost is half the fun.

In St. John, use caution. The terrain is very hilly, the roads are winding, and the blind curves numerous. You may suddenly come upon a huge safari bus careening around a corner or a couple of hikers strolling along the side of the road. Major roads are well paved, but once you get off a specific route, dirt roads filled with potholes are common. For such driving a four-wheel-drive vehicle is your best bet.

RULES OF THE ROAD
Driving is on the left side of the road (although your steering wheel will be on the left side of the car). The law requires *everyone* in a car to wear seat belts: many of the roads are narrow, and the islands are dotted with hills, so there's ample reason to put safety first.

ELECTRICITY

The USVI use the same current as the U.S. mainland—110 volts. European appliances will require adaptors. Since power fluctuations occasionally occur, bring a heavy-duty surge protector (available at hardware stores) if you plan to use your computer.

EMERGENCIES

⚠ Ambulance & Fire **Air Ambulance Network** ☎ 800/327-1966. **Ambulance and fire emergencies** ☎ 911. **Medical Air Services** ☎ 340/777-8580 or 800/643-9023.

⚠ Coast Guard **Marine Safety Detachment** ☎ 340/776-3497 in St. Thomas and St. John, 340/772-5557 in St. Croix. **Rescue Coordination Center** ☎ 787/289-2040 in San Juan, Puerto Rico

⚠ Hospital on St. Thomas **Roy L. Schneider Hospital & Community Health Center** ⊠ Sugar Estate, 1 mi [1½ km] east of Charlotte Amalie ☎ 340/776-8311.

⚠ Hospitals on St. Croix **Gov. Juan F. Luis Hospital and Health Center** ⊠ 6 Diamond Ruby, north of Sunny Isle Shopping Center on Rte. 79, Christiansted ☎ 340/778-6311. **Ingeborg Nesbitt Clinic** ⊠ 516 Strand St., Frederiksted ☎ 340/772-0260.

⚠ Hospital on St. John **Myrah Keating Smith Community Health Center** ⊠ Rte. 10, about 7 mins east of Cruz Bay, Susannaberg ☎ 340/693-8900.

⚠ Pharmacies on St. Thomas **Havensight Pharmacy** ⊠ Havensight Mall, Charlotte Amalie ☎ 340/776-1235. **Kmart Pharmacy** ⊠ Tutu Park Mall, Tutu ☎ 340/777-3854. **Sunrise Pharmacy** ⊠ Red Hook ☎ 340/775-6600 ⊠ Vitraco Park, near Havensight Mall ☎ 340/776-7292.

⚠ Pharmacies on St. Croix **D&D Apothecary Hall** ⊠ 501 Queen St., Frederiksted ☎ 340/772-1890. **Kmart Pharmacy** ⊠ Sunshine Mall, Cane Estate ☎ 340/692-2622. **People's Drug Store, Inc.** ⊠ Sunny Isle Shopping Center, Rte. 70, Christiansted ☎ 340/778-5537.

⚠ Pharmacy on St. John **Chelsea Drug Store** ⊠ The Marketplace Shopping Center, Rte. 104, Cruz Bay ☎ 340/776-4888.

⚠ Police **Police emergencies** ☎ 911.

⚠ Scuba-Diving Emergencies **Roy L. Schneider Hospital & Community Health Center** ⊠ Sugar Estate, 1 mi [1½ km] east of Charlotte Amalie ☎ 340/776-2686.

ETIQUETTE & BEHAVIOR

A smile and a "good day" greeting will start any encounter off on the right foot. Dress is casual throughout the islands, but cover up when you're sightseeing or shopping in town; bare chests and bathing suit tops are frowned upon.

FESTIVALS & SEASONAL EVENTS

ST. THOMAS January–April sees Classics in the Garden, a chamber music series at Tillett Gardens, where young musicians from all over the world perform. Tillett Gardens hosts annual Arts Alive festivals in November, March, and August. During Easter weekend, St. Thomas Yacht Club hosts the Rolex Cup Regatta, which is part of the three-race Caribbean Ocean Racing Triangle (CORT) that pulls in yachties and their pals from all over. Carnival is a weeklong major-league blowout of parades, parties, and island-wide events. The dates change from year to year, following the Easter calendar. Marlin mania begins in May and so do the sportfishing tournaments. There are also several locally sponsored fishing events throughout summer and fall.

The St. Thomas Gamefishing Club hosts its July Open Tournament over the Fourth of July weekend. There are categories for serious marlin anglers, just-for-fun fishermen, and even kids who want to try their luck from docks and rocks. The mid-July celebration of Bastille Day is marked by a mini-carnival in Frenchtown. During full moon in August, anglers compete for big-money prizes in the USVI Open/Atlantic Blue Marlin Tournament. September's Texas Society Chili Cook-Off is a party on Sapphire Beach—it includes country music performances, dancing, games, and, of course, chili tasting. In November the St. Thomas Agricultural Fair showcases fresh produce, home-grown herbs, and local dishes, such as callaloo, saltfish and dumplings, and fresh fish simmered with green banana, pumpkin, and potatolike *tannia*.

🛈 **Arts Alive Festival** ☎ 340/775-1405. **Carnival** ☎ 340/776-3112. **Classics in the Garden** ☎ 340/775-1405. **July Open Tournament** ☎ 340/775-9144. **Rolex Cup Regatta** ☎ 340/775-6320. **St. Thomas Agricultural Fair** ☎ 340/693-1080. **Texas Society Chili Cook-Off** ☎ 340/776-3595. **USVI Open/Atlantic Blue Marlin Tournament** ☎ 340/775-9500.

ST. CROIX The island celebrates Carnival with its Crucian Christmas Festival, which starts in late December. After weeks of beauty pageants, food fairs, and concerts, the festival wraps up with a parade in early January. In February and March the St. Croix Landmarks Society House Tours visit some of the island's most exclusive and historic homes and give you a chance to peek inside places you can usually view only from the road.

The St. Croix Half Ironman Triathlon attracts international-class athletes as well as amateurs every May for a 1-mi (2-km) swim, a 7-mi (12-km) run, and a 34-mi (55-km) bike ride; it includes a climb up the Beast on Route 69. Serious swimmers should join island residents in late October for the Coral Reef Swim. Participants swim about 5 mi (8 km) from Buck Island to Christiansted. The event also includes an awards dinner. The International Regatta sets sail in February at the St. Croix Yacht Club. Sailors converge on Teague Bay for three days of sailing and parties.

🛈 **Coral Reef Swim** ☎ 340/773-2100 Ext. 739. **International Regatta** ☎ 340/773-9531 ⊕ www.stcroixyc.org. **St. Croix Half Ironman Triathlon** ☎ 340/773-4470 ⊕ www.stcroixtriathlon.com. **St. Croix Landmarks Society House Tours** ☎ 340/772-0598 ⊕ stcroixlandmarks.org.

ST. JOHN The island dishes up its own version of Carnival with the July 4th celebration. Weeks of festivities—including beauty pageants and a food fair—culminate in a parade through the streets of Cruz Bay on July 4. On the two days after Thanksgiving an eclectic group of sailors takes to the waters of Coral Bay for the annual Coral Bay Thanksgiving Regatta. Some boats are "live-aboards," whose owners only pull up anchor for this one event; other boats belong to Sunday sailors; and a very few are owned by hotshot racers. If you'd like to crew, stop by Skinny Legs Bar and Restaurant.

🗹 **Coral Bay Thanksgiving Regatta** ☎ 340/779-4994.

HOLIDAYS

Public holidays, in addition to the U.S. federal holidays are: Three Kings Day (Jan. 6); Transfer Day (commemorates Denmark's 1917 sale of the territory to the United States, Mar. 31); Holy Thursday and Good Friday; Emancipation Day (when slavery was abolished in the Danish West Indies in 1848, July 3); Columbus Day and USVI–Puerto Rico Friendship Day (always on Columbus Day weekend); and Liberty Day (honoring David Hamilton Jackson, who secured freedom of the press and assembly from King Christian X of Denmark, Nov. 1).

Although the government closes down for 26 days a year, most of these holidays have no effect on shopping hours. Unless there's a cruise-ship arrival, expect most stores to close for Christmas and a few other holidays in the slower summer months.

LANGUAGE

English is the official language, though island residents often speak it with a lilting Creole accent, so you might not recognize certain words at first. If you have trouble understanding someone, ask them to speak slowly.

MAIL & SHIPPING

The main U.S. Post Office on St. Thomas is near the hospital, with branches in Charlotte Amalie, Frenchtown, Havensight, and Tutu Mall; there are post offices at Christiansted, Frederiksted, Gallows Bay, and Sunny Isle on St. Croix, and at Cruz Bay on St. John. The postal service offers Express Mail next-day service to major cities if you mail before noon; outlying areas may take two days. Letters to the United States are 37¢ and postcards are 23¢. Sending mail home to Canada you'll pay 46¢ for a letter and 40¢ for a postcard. To the United Kingdom and Australia, letters are 60¢, postcards 50¢.

On St. Thomas, Federal Express offers overnight service if you get your package to the office before 5 PM. Parcel Plus, across from Havensight Mall, also has express mail service. The Federal Express office on St. Croix is in Peter's Rest Commercial Center; try to drop off your packages before 5:30 PM. On St. John, Connections takes Federal Express packages or call for pick up.

🗹 **Connections** ⊠ On the unnamed street leading up from the ferry dock and across from Nazareth Lutheran Church, Cruz Bay, St. John ☎ 340/776-6922 or 340/774-3393 for pick up. **Federal Express** ⊠ Cyril E. King Airport, St. Thomas ☎ 340/777-4140 ⊕ www. fedex.com ⊠ Peter's Rest Commercial Center, Rte. 708, Peter's Rest, St. Croix ☎ 340/ 778-8180. **Parcel Plus** ⊠ across from Havensight Mall on Rte. 30, Charlotte Amalie, St. Thomas ☎ 340/776-9134.

MONEY MATTERS

Prices quoted in this chapter are in U.S. dollars.

BANKS & ATMS Each of the islands has several banks. On St. Thomas, First Bank is near Market Square. There are waterfront locations for both Banco Popular and V. I. Community Bank.

St. Croix has branches of Banco Popular in Orange Grove and Sunny Isle Shopping Centers. V. I. Community Bank is in Orange Grove Shopping Center and in downtown Christiansted. Scotia Bank has branches in Sunny Isle Frederiksted, Christiansted, and Sunshine Mall.

St. John's two banks are located near the ferry docks. First Bank is one block up from the ferry dock, and Scotia Bank is in a trailer just east of Chase.

Banco Popular ☎ 340/693-2777 ⊕ www.bancopopular.com. **First Bank** ☎ 340/776-9494 in St. Thomas, 340/775-7777 in St. John ⊕ www.firstbankpr.com. **Scotia Bank** ☎ 340/778-5350 in St. Croix, 340/776-6552 in St. John ⊕ www.scotiabank.com. **V. I. Community Bank** ☎ 340/773-4700.

CREDIT CARDS All major credit cards and traveler's checks are generally accepted. Some places will take Discover, though it's not as widely accepted as Visa, MasterCard, and American Express.

CURRENCY The American dollar is used throughout the territory, as well as in the neighboring BVI. If you need to exchange foreign currency, you'll need to go to the main branch of major banks.

PASSPORTS & VISAS

If you're a U.S. or Canadian citizen, you can prove citizenship with a current or expired (but not by more than five years) passport or with an original birth certificate (with a raised seal) along with a government-issued photo I.D. A valid passport, however, is best. Citizens of other countries need a passport.

SAFETY

Vacationers tend to assume that normal precautions aren't necessary in paradise. They are. Though there isn't quite as much crime here as in large U.S. mainland cities, it does exist. To be safe, stick to well-lit streets at night and use the same kind of street sense (don't wander the back alleys of Charlotte Amalie or Christiansted after five rum punches, for example) that you would in any unfamiliar territory. If you plan to carry things around, rent a car—not a jeep—and lock possessions in the trunk. Keep your rental car locked wherever you park. Don't leave cameras, purses, and other valuables lying on the beach while you snorkel for an hour (or even for a minute), whether you're on the deserted beaches of St. John or the more crowded Magens and Coki beaches on St. Thomas. St. Croix has several remote beaches outside Frederiksted and on the East End; it's best to visit them with a group rather than on your own.

SIGHTSEEING TOURS

AIR TOURS Air Center Helicopters, on the Charlotte Amalie waterfront (next to Tortola Wharf) on St. Thomas, has 30-minute island tours priced at $375 (for up to four passengers) per trip. You can also arrange longer flights that loop over to the neighboring BVI, as well as photography tours.

Air Center Helicopters ✉ Waterfront, Charlotte Amalie, St. Thomas ☎ 340/775-7335.

BOAT TOURS Caribbean Pelican Rides offers a unique land and sea tour of Charlotte Amalie aboard an amphibious British Alvis Stalward vessel. Tours depart from the Coast Guard dock opposite Vendors Plaza. The 55-minute excursions costs $55 for adults, $15 for children ages 12 and under.

St. Thomas's *Kon Tiki* party boat is a kick. Put your sophistication aside, climb on this big palm-thatch raft, and dip into bottomless barrels of rum punch along with a couple of hundred of your soon-to-be closest friends. Dance to the steel-drum band, sun on the roof (watch out: you'll fry), and join the limbo dancing on the way home from an afternoon of swimming and beachcombing at Honeymoon Beach on Water Island.

This popular 3½-hour afternoon excursion costs $29 for adults, $15 for children under 13 (although few come to this party).

⚑ **Caribbean Pelican Rides** ✉ Coast Guard Dock, opposite Vendor's Plaza, Charlotte Amalie, St. Thomas ☎ 340/774-7808. *Kon Tiki* ✉ Gregorie Channel East Dock, Frenchtown, St. Thomas ☎ 340/775-5055.

BUS & TAXI TOURS V. I. Taxi Association St. Thomas City-Island Tour gives a two-hour $45 tour for two people in an open-air safari bus or enclosed van; aimed at cruise-ship passengers, this tour includes stops at Drake's Seat and Mountain Top. For just a bit more money (about $45–$50 for two) you can hire a taxi and ask the driver to take the opposite route so you'll avoid the crowds. But do see Mountain Top: the view is wonderful.

Tropic Tours offers half-day shopping and sightseeing tours of St. Thomas by bus six days a week ($25 per person). The company also has a full-day ferry tour to St. John that includes snorkeling and lunch. The cost is $70 per person.

St. Croix Safari Tours offers van tours of St. Croix. They depart from Christiansted and last about five hours. Costs run from $25 per person plus admission fees to attractions. St. Croix Transit offers van tours of St. Croix. They depart from Carambola Beach Resort, last about three hours, and cost from $30 per person plus admission fees to attractions.

In St. John, taxi drivers provide tours of the island, making stops at various sites including Trunk Bay and Annaberg Plantation. Prices run around $15 a person. The taxi drivers congregate near the ferry in Cruz Bay. The dispatcher will find you a driver for your tour.

⚑ **St. Croix Safari Tours** ☎ 340/773-6700. **St. Croix Transit** ☎ 340/772-3333. **Tropic Tours** ☎ 340/774-1855 or 800/524-4334. **V. I. Taxi Association St. Thomas City-Island Tour** ☎ 340/774-4550.

WALKING TOURS The *St. Thomas–St. John Vacation Handbook,* available free at hotels and tourist centers, has an excellent self-guided walking tour of Charlotte Amalie on St. Thomas. The St. Thomas Historical Trust has published a self-guided tour of the historic district; it's available in book and souvenir shops for $1.95. A two-hour guided historic walking tour is available by reservation. It begins (at 9 AM) at the Emancipation Garden, covers all the in-town sights, and can be narrated in Spanish, Danish, German, and Japanese as well as in English. The cost is $35 per person; wear a hat and comfortable walking shoes.

Possible nature tours on St. Thomas include bird-watching, whale-watching, and waiting hidden on a beach while the magnificent hawksbill turtles come ashore to lay their eggs. Contact EAST (Environmental Association of St. Thomas–St. John).

St. Croix Heritage Tours leads walks through the historic towns of Christiansted and Frederiksted, detailing the history of the people and the buildings. Custom tours that cover the island are also available.

Along with providing trail maps and brochures about Virgin Islands National Park, the park service also gives several guided tours on- and offshore. Some are only offered during particular times of the year, and some require reservations. For more information, contact the V. I. National Park Visitors Center on St. John.

⚑ **EAST** (Environmental Association of St. Thomas–St. John) ✉ Box 12379, St. Thomas 00801 ☎ 340/776-1976. **St. Croix Heritage Tours** ✉ Box 7937, Sunny Isle 00823 ☎ 340/778-6997 ⊕ www.stcroixtours.com. **St. Thomas Historical Trust** ☎ 340/776-2726. **V. I. National Park Visitors Center** ✉ at area known as the Creek; across from Cruz Bay bulkhead and adjacent to ball field, Cruz Bay ☎ 340/776-6201 ⊕ www.nps.gov/viis.

TAXES & SERVICE CHARGES

TAXES There's no sales tax, but there is an 8% hotel-room tax in the USVI. The St. John Accommodations Council members ask that hotel and villa guests voluntarily pay a $1 a day surcharge to help fund school and community projects and other good works.

TAXIS

USVI taxis don't have meters, but you needn't worry about fare gouging if you check a list of standard rates to popular destinations (required by law to be carried by each driver and often posted in hotel and airport lobbies and printed in free tourist periodicals, such as *St. Thomas This Week* and *St. Croix This Week*) and settle on the fare before you start out. Fares are per person, not per destination, but drivers taking multiple fares (which often happens, especially from the airport) will charge you a lower rate than if you're in the cab alone.

ST. THOMAS On St. Thomas, taxi vans line up along Havensight and Crown Bay docks when a cruise ship pulls in. If you booked a shore tour, the operator will lead you to a designated vehicle. Otherwise, there are plenty of air-conditioned vans and open-air safari buses to take you to Charlotte Amalie or the beach. The cab fare from Havensight to Charlotte Amalie is $2.50 per person; you can, however, make the 1½-mi (2½-km) walk into town in about 30 minutes along the beautiful waterfront. From Crown Bay to town the taxi fare is $2.50 per person whether you travel solo or share; it's a 1-mi (1½-km) walk, but the route passes along a busy highway. Transportation from Havensight to Magens Bay for swimming is $6.50 per person ($4 if you share).

Additionally, taxis of all shapes and sizes are available at various ferry, shopping, resort, and airport areas, and they also respond to phone calls. There are taxi stands in Charlotte Amalie across from Emancipation Garden (in front of Little Switzerland, behind the post office) and along the waterfront. But you probably won't have to look for a stand, as taxis are plentiful and routinely cruise the streets. Walking down Main Street, you'll be asked "Back to ship?" often enough to make you never want to carry another shopping bag.

🚖 **East End Taxi** ☎ 340/775-6974. **Islander Taxi** ☎ 340/774-4077. **VI Taxi Association** ☎ 340/774-4550.

ST. CROIX Taxis, generally station wagons or minivans, are a phone call away from most hotels and are available in downtown Christiansted, at the Henry E. Rohlsen Airport, and at the Frederiksted pier during cruise-ship arrivals.

In Frederiksted all the shops are just a short walk away, and you can swim off the beach. Most ship passengers visit Christiansted on a tour; a taxi will cost $20 for one or two people.

🚖 **Antilles Taxi Service** ☎ 340/773-5020. **Cruzan Taxi and Tours** ☎ 340/773-6388. **St. Croix Taxi Association** ☎ 340/778-1088.

ST. JOHN Taxis meet ferries arriving in Cruz Bay. Most drivers use vans or open-air safari buses. You'll find them congregated at the dock and at hotel parking lots. You can also hail them anywhere on the road. You're likely to travel with other tourists en route to their destinations. It's very difficult to get taxis to respond to a phone call. If you need one to pick you up at your rental villa, ask the villa manager for suggestions on who to call or arrange a ride in advance.

Some cruise ships stop at St. John to let passengers disembark for a day. The main town of Cruz Bay is near the area where the ships drop off passengers. If you want to swim, the famous Trunk Bay is a $9 taxi ride (for two) from town.

TELEPHONES

On St. Thomas, AT&T has a state-of-the-art telecommunications center (it's across from the Havensight Mall) with 15 desk booths, fax and copy services, a video phone, and TDD equipment (for people with hearing impairments). Islander Services and East End Secretarial Services offer long-distance dialing, copying, and fax services. Parcel Plus in St. Thomas has three computers available for accessing e-mail; the cost is $5 per half hour. Express mail service, international calling, and phone cards are also available here. On St. John the place to go for phone or message needs is Connections.

AT&T ⊠ Across from Havensight Mall, Charlotte Amalie, St. Thomas ☎ 340/777-9201. **Connections** ⊠ Cruz Bay, St. John ☎ 340/776-6922 ⊠ Coral Bay, St. John ☎ 340/779-4994 ⊕ www.connectionsstjohn.com. **East End Secretarial Services** ⊠ Upstairs at Red Hook Plaza, Red Hook, St. Thomas ☎ 340/775-5262. **Islander Services** ⊠ 5302 Store Tvaer Gade, behind the Greenhouse Restaurant, Charlotte Amalie, St. Thomas ☎ 340/774-8128. **Parcel Plus** ⊠ Across from Havensight Mall, Charlotte Amalie, St. Thomas ☎ 340/776-9134.

COUNTRY & AREA CODES The area code for all of the USVI is 340. If you are calling from within the U.S., you need only dial 1 plus the area code and number. If you're calling from outside the United States, dial the U.S. country code 01.

INTERNATIONAL CALLS You can dial direct to and from the mainland United States, and to and from Australia, Canada, New Zealand, and the United Kingdom from most phones.

LOCAL CALLS Local calls from a public phone cost up to 35¢ for each five minutes. If you have a cell phone, you can dial 6611 for information about how to use it locally.

TIPPING

Many hotels add a 10% to 15% service charge to cover the room maid and other staff. However, some hotels may use part of that money to fund their operations, passing on only a portion of it to the staff. Check with your maid or bellhop to determine the hotel's policy. If you discover you need to tip, give bellhops and porters 50¢ to $1 per bag and maids $1 or $2 per day. Special errands or requests of hotel staff always require an additional tip. At restaurants bartenders and waiters expect a 10%–15% tip, but always check your tab to see whether service is included. Taxi drivers get a 15% tip.

VISITOR INFORMATION

Before You Leave USVI Government Tourist Office ⊕ www.usvitourism.vi ⊠ 245 Peachtree St., Center Ave. Marquis One Tower MB-05, Atlanta, GA 30303 ☎ 404/688-0906 ⊠ 500 N. Michigan Ave., Suite 2030, Chicago, IL 60611 ☎ 312/670-8784 ⊠ 3460 Wilshire Blvd., Suite 412, Los Angeles, CA 90010 ☎ 213/739-0138 ⊠ 2655 Le Jeune Rd., Suite 907, Coral Gables, FL 33134 ☎ 305/442-7200 ⊠ 1270 Ave. of the Americas, Room 2108, New York, NY 10020 ☎ 212/332-2222 ⊠ Hall of Streets, No. 298, 444 N. Capital St. NW, Washington, DC 20006 ☎ 202/624-3590 ⊠ 600 Washington St, Suite 1102, San Juan, Puerto Rico 00907 ☎ 787/722-0823 ⊠ 703 Evans Ave, Suite 106, Toronto, Ontario, Canada M9C 5E9 ☎ 416/622-7600 ⊠ Molasses House, Clove Hitch Quay, Plantation Wharf, York Place, London SW11 3TW, U.K. ☎ 020/7978-5262.

In the U.S. Virgin Islands St. Thomas–St. John Hotel & Tourism Association ⊕ www.sttstjhta.com ☎ 340/774-6835. **USVI Division of Tourism** ⌖ 78-123 Estate Contant, Charlotte Amalie, St. Thomas 00804 ☎ 340/774-8784 or 800/372-8784 ⊠ 53A Company St., Christiansted, St. Croix 00822 ☎ 340/773-0495 ⊠ Strand St., Frederiksted, St. Croix 00840 ☎ 340/772-0357 ⊠ Henry Samuel St. [next to the Post Office], Cruz Bay, St. John ☎ 340/776-6450. **Virgin Islands National Park** ⊕ www.nps.gov/viis ⊠ at the Creek, Cruz Bay, St. John 00831 ☎ 340/776-6201.

INDEX